Development Through Life

A HANDBOOK FOR CLINICIANS

EDITED BY

MICHAEL RUTTER

CBE, MD, FRCP, FRCPsych, FRS
Professor of Psychiatry and Honorary Director
MRC Child Psychiatry Unit
Institute of Psychiatry, London

AND

DALE F. HAY

PhD
Faculty of Social and Political Science
University of Cambridge

OXFORD

BLACKWELL SCIENTIFIC PUBLICATIONS

LONDON EDINBURGH BOSTON
MELBOURNE PARIS BERLIN VIENNA

© 1994 by
Blackwell Scientific Publications
Editorial Offices:
Osney Mead, Oxford OX2 0EL
25 John Street, London WClN 2BL
23 Ainslie Place, Edinburgh EH3 6AJ
238 Main Street, Cambridge
    Massachusetts 02142, USA
54 University Street, Carlton
    Victoria 3053, Australia

Other Editorial Offices:
Librairie Arnette SA
1, rue de Lille
75007 Paris
France

Blackwell Wissenschafts-Verlag GmbH
Düsseldorfer Str. 38
D-10707 Berlin
Germany

Blackwell MZV
Feldgasse 13
1238 Wien
Austria

First published 1994

Set by Setrite Typesetters, Hong Kong
Printed and bound in Great Britain
by The Bath Press, Bath, Avon

DISTRIBUTORS

Marston Book Services Ltd
PO Box 87
Oxford OX2 0DT
(*Orders*: Tel: 0865 791155
        Fax: 0865 791927
        Telex: 837515)

USA
Blackwell Scientific Publications, Inc.
238 Main Street
Cambridge, MA 02142
(*Orders*: Tel: 800 759-6102
        617 876-7000)

Canada
Times Mirror Professional Publishing Ltd
130 Flaska Drive
Markham, Ontario L6G 1B8
(*Orders*: Tel: 800 268-4178
        416 470-6739)

Australia
Blackwell Scientific Publications Pty Ltd
54 University Street
Carlton, Victoria 3053
(*Orders*: Tel: 03 347-5552)

A catalogue record for this title is available
from the British Library

ISBN 0-632-03693-1

Development through life : a handbook for clinicians/
    edited by Rutter Michael and Hay, Dale F.
        p.   cm.
    Includes bibliographical references and index.
    ISBN 0-632-03693-1
    1. Child development.   2. Developmental
psychology.   I.   Rutter, Michael.
II.   Hay, Dale F.
    [DNLM: 1. Child Development.   2. Life Change
Events — in infancy & childhood.   3. Mental
Disorders — in infancy & childhood.   4. Mental
Disorders — etiology.   WS 105 D48905 1994]
RJ131.D437 1994
155.4 — dc20
DNLM/DLC

Contents

Contributors

S. R. ASHER PhD, *Bureau of Educational Research, College of Education, University of Illinois at Urbana-Champaign, 230 Education Building, 1310 South Sixth Street, Champaign, IL 61820, USA*

J. G. BAKER-SENNETT PhD, *Department of Education, Faculty of Education, University of British Columbia, 2125 Main Hall, Vancouver, BC VST 1Z4, Canada*

P. B. BALTES PhD, *Max-Planck Institute for Human Development and Education, Lentzeallee 94, 14195 Berlin, Germany*

S. BARON-COHEN PhD, *Departments of Child and Adolescent Psychiatry and Psychology, Institute of Psychiatry, De Crespigny Park, London SE5 8AF, UK*

J. BELSKY PhD, *Department of Human Development and Family Studies, College of Health and Human Development, The Pennsylvania State University, S-110 Henderson Building, University Park, PA 16802, USA*

U. BRONFENBRENNER PhD, *Departments of Human Development and Family Studies and Psychology, Cornell University, Martha Van Rensselaer Hall, Ithaca, NY 14853-4401, USA*

J. BROOKS-GUNN PhD, *Center for the Study of Young Children and Families, Teachers College, Columbia University, New York, NY 10027, USA*

R. B. CAIRNS PhD, *Psychology Department, The University of North Carolina at Chapel Hill, CB No. 3270, Davie Hall, Chapel Hill, NC 27599-3270, USA*

J. CASSIDY PhD, *Department of Psychology, 514 Moore Building, The Pennsylvania State University, S-110 Henderson Building, University Park, PA 16802, USA*

J. CASTLE BSc, *MRC Child Psychiatry Unit, Institute of Psychiatry, De Crespigny Park, London SE5 8AF, UK*

S. J. CECI PhD, *Department of Human Development and Family Studies, Cornell University, Martha Van Rensselaer Hall, Ithaca, NY 14853-4401, USA*

J. DUNN PhD, *Center for the Study of Child and Adolescent Development, The Pennsylvania State University, S-211 Henderson Building, University Park, PA 16802, USA*

A. ENGFER PhD, *Universität Paderborn, Fachbereich 2, Psychologie, Warburger Strasse 100, D-33095 Paderborn, Germany*

C. A. ERDLEY PhD, *Department of Psychology, University of Maine, 5742 Little Hall, Orono, ME 04469-5742, USA*

S. W. GABRIEL PhD, *Bureau of Educational Research, College of Education, University of Illinois at Urbana-Champaign, 230 Education Building, 1310 South Sixth Street, Champaign, IL 61820, USA*

J. GARBER PhD, *Department of Psychology and Human Development, Peabody College, Box 512, Vanderbilt University, Nashville, TN 37203, USA*

R. GOODMAN MD, *Department of Child and Adolescent Psychiatry, Institute of Psychiatry, De Crespigny Park, London SE5 8AF, UK*

U. GOSWAMI PhD, *Department of Experimental Psychology, University of Cambridge, Downing Street, Cambridge CB2 3EB, UK*

D. F. HAY PhD, *Faculty of Social and Political Science, University of Cambridge, Free School Lane, Cambridge CB2 3QA, UK*

J. JEWETT BA, *MRC Child Psychiatry Unit, Institute of Psychiatry, De Crespigny Park, London SE5 8AF, UK*

A. B. KROLL PhD, *Psychology Department, The University of North Carolina at Chapel Hill, CB No. 3270, Davie Hall, Chapel Hill, NC 27599-3270, USA*

M. E. LACHMAN PhD, *Psychology Department, Brandeis University, Brown 125, Waltham, MA 02254-9110, USA*

R. LOEBER PhD, *Western Psychiatric Institute and Clinic, University of Pittsburgh Medical Center, 3811 O'Hara Street, Pittsburgh, PA 15213-2953, USA*

B. MAUGHAN PhD, *MRC Child Psychiatry Unit, Institute of Psychiatry, De Crespigny Park, London SE5 8AF, UK*

R. L. PAIKOFF PhD, *Institute for Juvenile Research (M/C 747), The University of Illinois at Chicago, 907 South Wolcott Avenue, Chicago, IL 60612, USA*

R. PLOMIN PhD, *Center for Development and Health Genetics, College of Health and Human Development, The Pennsylvania State University, S-211 Henderson Building, University Park, PA 16802, USA*

D. QUINTON PhD, *MRC Child Psychiatry Unit, Institute of Psychiatry, De Crespigny Park, London SE5 8AF, UK*

R. D. RENDE PhD, *Clinical and Genetic Epidemiology, New York State Psychiatric Institute, Columbia University College of Physicians and Surgeons, Unit 14, 722 West 168th Street, New York, NY 10032, USA*

M. RUTTER CBE, MD, FRCP, FRCPsych, FRS, *MRC Child Psychiatry Unit, Institute of Psychiatry, De Crespigny Park, London SE5 8AF; and Honorary Consultant Psychiatrist, Bethlem Royal and Maudsley Hospital, Denmark Hill, London SE5 8AZ, UK*

H. TAGER-FLUSBERG PhD, *Department of Psychology, University of Massachusetts, 100 Morrissey Boulevard, Boston, MA 02125-3393, USA*

E. A. TAYLOR MB, FRCP, *MRC Child Psychiatry Unit, Institute of Psychiatry, De Crespigny Park, London SE5 8AF, UK*

T. WALDEN PhD, *Department of Psychology and Human Development, Peabody College, Box 512, Vanderbilt University, Nashville, TN 37203, USA*

S. WALPER PhD, *Department of Psychology, University of Munich, Leopoldstrasse 13, D-8082 Munich, Germany*

D. WOLKE PhD, *Long-term Follow-up of Children at Biological Risk, Bavarian Longitudinal Study II, University of Munich Children's Hospital, Lindwurmstrasse 4, D-80337 Munich, Germany*

Preface

There are numerous reasons why clinicians need to have an understanding of developmental processes. However, perhaps four predominate. First, for many psychological and psychiatric disorders it is necessary to appreciate the patterns of continuity and discontinuity between variations within the normal range and overt disorder. Thus, it is crucial to consider whether the mechanisms involved in individual differences in mood are the same as, or different from, those that underlie severe depressive conditions requiring admission to hospital. Similar questions arise, for example, with respect to reading skills and dyslexia; intelligence and severe mental retardation; language and language disorders; patterns of drinking and alcoholism; disruptive behaviour and antisocial personality disorders; fearfulness and phobic disorders; and ageing and dementia. It is not, of course, that it would be sensible to presume parallels, or to expect a single answer. It is likely that some of those instances do represent continuity, with the disorders just the extreme of a continuum. In other cases, in spite of superficial similarities, the disorders will prove to be qualitatively distinct. In yet others, disorders may start out as extremes of normal variation, but the consequences of being extreme will bring secondary consequences that create a qualitative difference.

These issues are pervasive in medicine. Sometimes the so-called 'medical model' is portrayed by non-medics as if it deals only with categorically distinct disease states, but that constitutes a highly misleading, outdated, view of medicine. Most medical conditions have a multifactorial aetiology with the same complex patterns of continuity and discontinuity with normality. Thus, the same questions as those posed for psychological or psychiatric disorders arise with respect to normal variations in blood pressure and hypertension; convulsive threshold and epilepsy; cholesterol metabolism and atherosclerotic disease; and allergic liability and severe asthma, to mention but a few examples. Similarly, modern medicine has long been concerned with the role of living conditions, and of environmental circumstances more generally, in the pathogenesis of disease. Indeed it is clear that the improvements in living conditions that have taken place during this century constitute the main reason for the parallel reduction in infantile mortality and increase in life expectancy, rather than medical and surgical advances *per se*, although they have played some role.

The second reason why a developmental perspective is important in relation to clinical disorders is that there are major age differences in the manifestation of many types of psychopathology, and that an understanding of why that is so may throw light on the causal processes involved in the disorders. Thus, specific fears tend to become less frequent as children grow older, hyperkinetic disorders characteristically first become evident during the preschool years, depressive disorders increase in frequency during the teenage years, schizophrenia and anorexia nervosa both typically have an onset in late adolescence or early adult life, and delinquency reaches a peak in the mid-teens. The findings on these (and other) psychiatric disorders are discussed in detail in a companion volume focusing on psychopathology (Rutter *et al.*, 1994); this book considers the developmental trends from the starting point of normal development but with an explicit attention to the possible implications for abnormality.

Third, it is clear that many (but by no means all) of the psychiatric disorders of adult life have their roots in childhood. Thus, for example, although typically schizophrenia does not present in the form of psychosis until the late teens or early twenties, in about half the cases there have been attentional deficits, social difficulties and neurodevelopmental impairment in childhood. Antisocial personality disorders almost always arise on the basis of conduct problems in childhood (indeed that is a requirement in the American Diagnostic and Statistical Manual, DSM, criteria). Also, adverse parenting and family breakdown in early life increase the risk of depressive disorders in adult life. These three examples almost certainly exemplify rather different causal mechanisms and they have been chosen deliberately to make the point that a developmental perspective does *not* imply a focus on infantile trauma or maternal deprivation. Developmental considerations necessarily include neurobiological mechanisms as well as psychosocial risk factors.

Fourth, it is evident that there are variations with age in susceptibility, or patterns of response, to both brain injury (Goodman, Chapter 3) and certain types of psychosocial hazards (Belsky & Cassidy, Chapter 16). Again, an appreciation of the mechanisms involved is likely to be helpful in understanding some psychopathological processes.

These reasons, together with others, explain why most programmes of training in psychiatry, clinical psychology, social work, nursing, paediatrics and special education include a course on developmental issues. This book is primarily targeted at trainees and teachers in clinical disciplines who need to know about development, and trainees and teachers in developmental disciplines who are concerned with implications for psychopathology. One might ask why it is necessary to have produced this book for that purpose; after all there are several very good textbooks on child development, and a smaller number of texts covering lifespan development. However, excellent though they are, they provide a rather limited coverage of several aspects of development that are of crucial importance to clinicians. We have sought to highlight these features in this volume.

To begin with, there is a major focus in all chapters on the nature and origins of individual differences and on the developmental processes that may be involved in both normative progression and individuation. Thus the traditional topics of language development (Tager-Flusberg, Chapter 9), intellectual development (Ceci *et al.*, Chapters 10 and 11), attachment (Belsky & Cassidy, Chapter 16), emotional development (Walden & Garber, Chapter 17), aggression (Loeber & Hay, Chapter 19) and sexual development (Paikoff & Brooks-Gunn, Chapter 21) are all examined with respect to the mechanisms responsible for individual differences and for links to psychopathology. Furthermore, because of their clinical relevance, there are chapters that examine both normative processes and individual differences in reading and spelling (Goswami, Chapter 12), attention (Taylor, Chapter 8), sleeping and feeding (Wolke, Chapter 20) and theory of mind (Baron-Cohen, Chapter 13), topics less often given chapters of their own in textbooks on child development. Furthermore, the editors' own two chapters have examined individuality at a somewhat broader level of analysis by examining the developmental role of personal qualities such as temperament and facial appearance (Engfer *et al.*, Chapter 4) and the development of character (Hay *et al.*, Chapter 14). Each of these chapters involves an attempt to span normal and abnormal development.

Second, throughout the book, there has been an attempt to provide an integrated account of how multiple influences combine. Of course, all modern developmentalists accept the need to consider the effects of both nature and nurture, the interconnections between brain and mind, and the interplay between persons and their environments. Interactional and transactional models of one kind or another have become the order of the day. However, less attention has been paid to what these broad concepts mean in terms of actual mechanisms. Also, as critics have pointed out, by no means all psychopathology requires such models. There is a danger that the slogan of interaction precludes investigation of developmental processes because the term misleadingly seems to presuppose an explanation. Hence we have asked authors to review the evidence on many different sources of influence on normative progression and on individuation.

In addition, there are separate chapters dealing with some of the key specific influences and contexts of interaction in greater detail. Thus, we have included consideration of genetic influences (Rende & Plomin, Chapter 2), neurobiological forces (Goodman, Chapter 3), gender (Cairns & Kroll, Chapter 15), schooling (Maughan, Chapter 6), cultural and community influences (Quinton, Chapter 7), peer relations (Asher *et al.*, Chapter 18), as well as the family (Dunn, Chapter 5). With respect to the last of these, the focus is on siblings as much as parents. We have also considered the contribution individuals make to their own development (see especially Rende & Plomin, Chapter 2, and Engfer *et al.*, Chapter 4). Most of all, we have chosen authors who can tackle each of these topics in a way that seeks an integration across sources of influences and that focuses on mediating mechanisms. The need to consider developmental influences at many different levels of analysis is expressed by all authors, perhaps most explicitly in the two chapters by Ceci and his colleagues who, quite deliberately, seek to challenge some of the traditional notions of intelligence.

A third characteristic of the approach that we have adopted in this book is that we have sought to describe and explain development throughout the lifespan in the real sense of trying to link developmental mechanisms as they apply across life. Much writing on lifespan issues has mainly consisted of discussion of changes in later life periods with separate considerations of adolescence, early adulthood, mid-life and so forth. In this book we consider the ageing process in its own right (Lachman & Baltes, Chapter 22) as well as important transitions in adult life (Rutter, Chapter 1), but we have also attempted to consider development within each psychological domain in a manner that extends across different phases of life. Thus, for example, authors have focused on changes over the lifespan in sleeping and eating patterns (Wolke, Chapter 20), the rise in adolescence and fall in later adulthood of conduct disorder and criminality (Loeber & Hay, Chapter 19), and age-linked changes in sexual behaviour (Paikoff & Brooks-Gunn, Chapter 21). In choosing authors for all the chapters, we tried to select people who were not only expert in their field and able to synthesize concepts and findings in a manner that could provide a guide to likely future advances, but who were also willing and able to take on the challenge of this kind of lifespan perspective. Of course, they (and we) have necessarily been constrained by the considerable limitations of the available empirical data but we hope that the attempt to open up the topic in this fashion has been useful in dictating some of the directions that

developmental theory and research are likely to follow during the years to come. With the aim of providing a conceptual and organizational framework within which to consider lifespan development issues, the book starts with a discussion on continuities, transitions and turning points in development (Rutter, Chapter 1).

A fourth feature has been the deliberate aim of seeking integration across domains, an important characteristic of modern developmental research. Many traditional textbooks and handbooks have separate sections or volumes on social and cognitive development. However, during the last decade there has been a tremendous increase in the conceptualization and investigation of possible links between cognition and socialization. Such links are of several different kinds. They include the possibility that disorders such as autism and schizophrenia are based on cognitive deficits of some kind; the suggestion that certain normative progressions in social or emotional qualities (such as the development of morality or selective attachments or fears) depend on the acquisition of particular cognitive skills; and the hypothesis that some types of psychopathology, such as depression and conduct disorders, arise on the basis of biased attributions or social cognitions of some kind. Many chapters attempt such integration. For example, the cognitive deficits manifested in autism are described by Baron-Cohen and the determinants of depression are discussed by Walden and Garber. Social cognitive processes are also examined with respect to normative changes and individual differences in the realm of moral development (Hay *et al.*, Chapter 14) and aggression and conduct disorder (Loeber & Hay, Chapter 19). At the same time, social influences on intellectual development are noted by those authors discussing memory and intelligence (Chapters 10 and 11 by Ceci and his colleagues), reading and spelling (Goswami, Chapter 12) and educational attainment (Maughan, Chapter 6).

Because an understanding of developmental and interactional processes requires an interdisciplinary approach, and because advances derive from diverse sources, the authors span a range of disciplines including psychology, psychiatry, sociology, genetics and psycholinguistics. It is also no accident that one of the editors is a developmental psychologist and one a child psychiatrist and that the research of one has mainly focused on infancy whereas that of the other has entailed a prime interest in continuities and discontinuities from childhood into mid-life. We hope the result of this interdisciplinary effort is a portrayal of developmental processes that is both interesting and useful to a wide range of clinicians and developmentalists.

Michael Rutter

Dale F. Hay

REFERENCE

Rutter M., Taylor E. & Hersov L. (eds) (1994) *Child and Adolescent Psychiatry: Modern Approaches*, 3rd edn. Blackwell Scientific Publications, Oxford.

Acknowledgements

The preparation of this volume owes a great deal to the dedicated work of many people and we would like to thank all of those who have done so much to bring the book to completion. Most of all we owe a debt to the authors whose creative ideas were crucial in shaping the final product and who showed an admirable combination of patience and constructive thinking in response to our requests for re-shaping, modification and extension of their chapters in order better to fulfil the overall aims that we had set ourselves. Particular thanks are also due to Simon Baron-Cohen who served as special consultant during the initial planning of the book and provided responses to chapter outlines. His helpful suggestions were much appreciated. We are also deeply indebted to Ruth Timlett who played a crucial administrative role throughout, ensuring that the whole procedure ran to time so far as possible, liaising with authors, and undertaking careful checking of references. She was helped in some of these tasks by Joy Maxwell, Adele Summers, and Toyin Adigun-Saka. Our thanks also go to Jane Andrew for her speed and efficiency in translating the manuscripts into the printed page; to Susan Boobis for her skill and thoroughness in preparing the index; and to Mark Morris for his help in the checking of proofs.

1: Continuities, Transitions and Turning Points in Development

MICHAEL RUTTER

INTRODUCTION: CONCEPTS OF DEVELOPMENT

Most accounts of psychological development tend to take for granted that the concept of 'development' is self-evident and well understood. At first sight, that would seem a reasonable enough assumption. After all, it is clear that the concept applies to the process of growth from an immature to a mature organism. In the somatic arena, that might seem to work satisfactorily enough without further explanation in relation to, say, height or reproductive capacity. In both cases, there is a more or less straightforward progression through a series of phases, that occur in an invariant predetermined order, and which reach an end-point when that progression ceases. By implication, this is an entirely 'internal' organismic process. Accordingly, many developmental psychologists have extrapolated the concept to the psychological structures postulated to underlie language or intelligence or social relationships or morality. Again, the implication is that the changes involved in the process are intrinsic to the individual, and are universal and normative. According to this view, development would seem to involve a progressive increase in the level and complexity of 'structure' (and secondarily, therefore, of the functions they serve), up to the point when stabilization and therefore maturity is reached.

It needs to be appreciated that the term 'structure' is being used here in two somewhat different ways. First, there is the theoretical notion of qualitatively distinct cognitive skills, marked by discrete developmental stages, as suggested by Piaget and other stage theorists (Gelman & Baillargeon, 1983; Piaget, 1983; Demetriou, 1987). The hypothesis is that (in the context of, and through an interplay with, ordinary experiences) maturation brings with it the acquisition of various general capacities (or organized systems that provide the basis for particular cognitive operations) for which there is some inherent intraorganismic basis, not dependent on specific learning and which, once acquired, ordinarily persist. Thus, in the early months of life, no amount of teaching will bring about spoken language. However, once a certain point in development is reached, language is acquired under all ordinary environmental conditions. Thereafter, that capacity remains present without the need for specific environmental input.

This concept of basic cognitive structures is intuitively attractive and seems to make sense with features such as language (see Chapter 9), theory of mind (see Chapter 13), and the ability to feel shame or guilt (see Chapter 17). Moreover, the degree to which broadly similar cognitive progressions are evident across widely divergent cultures indicates that maturational influences are likely to play a key role (e.g. Kagan, 1981). Nevertheless, research findings show that most cognitive progressions do not emerge as a qualitative leap of an all-or-none nature that spans all cognitive domains. To an appreciable extent, skills are content-driven and context-specific (see Chapter 10). Moreover, resistance to unlearning is a feature of many overlearned skills (such as riding a bicycle) and does not seem to require the postulation of an underlying cognitive structure. As a consequence, the concept of psychological structures has proved frustratingly difficult both to operationalize and to put to the test, despite their having some face validity.

Second, the term refers to neural structures that are (at least potentially) observable through anatomical, neurochemical or other modes of investigation. Although there is still much to be learned about the details, a clear age-related progression

1

in brain development has been shown through research findings (see Chapter 3). The expectation is that psychological structures are based on neural structures but, in most cases, this (admittedly very reasonable) assumption is hypothesized, not demonstrated.

The contrasting term 'function' is more straightforward in that, in keeping with ordinary English usage, it refers simply to psychological performance in any domain — emotions, language, social relationships, and so on. Of course, function can also be used with the rather different meaning of 'fulfilling' and 'purpose' (see Hay, 1980) but that is not how it is used here!

Following this terminological digression, we need to return to the concept of psychological development. As noted, this often presupposes that it is based only on the acquisition of structurally based capacities of one sort or another. However, a review of the empirical evidence shows that the concept is a seriously misleading partial truth even with respect to somatic growth, and it is even more inadequate when applied to psychological development (Rutter, 1984, submitted; Rutter & Rutter, 1993). Seven main problems are evident.

First, the notion that development comprises a cumulative accretion in which each advance grows out of, and builds upon, the one preceding it with a steady unidirectional movement forward is mistaken (Kagan, 1984). Thus, brain development involves a phase of selective neuronal *loss* that serves to improve function through selectivity and not just more of the same (see Chapter 3). The same applies to psychological growth (Connolly & Prechtl, 1981). As children grow up, they lose many reflexes, skills and sensitivities that were established at an earlier age. This is not a case of the growth of some specific functions coming to an end in childhood, and being followed by an unusually early decline while growth in other domains continues. Rather, the situation is that the structures and the skills are lost because they have served their purpose and are no longer needed. The finding raises uncertainties about how to define both the endpoint of development and also the progression of the developmental process.

Second, it is obvious that the timing of developmental processes varies greatly across bodily systems (Tanner, 1989). Thus, it is common for the eruption of wisdom teeth to occur many years later than puberty and well after final height has been achieved. It might be thought that, regardless of this between-systems (and also marked interindividual) variation, all development can be regarded as coming to an end by about the later teens or early twenties, but even that generalization has its exceptions. For example, studies of neurotransmitters show that the levels of acetylcholine-esterase do not peak until the mid-forties (Court *et al.*, 1994). Does this mean that brain development is still continuing up to that age? The implication is that the end-point of developmental processes needs to be considered on a system by system, and even a subsystem by subsystem, basis, and that the reaching of 'maturity' may not occur until well into adult life. However, that leaves unresolved how to define 'maturity' (see below).

The third issue is that, although it may be desirable to consider development in organismic terms, somatic growth processes are much influenced by, indeed some are dependent upon (Greenough *et al.*, 1987), environmental input. For example, there is a mass of evidence that the growth of the visual system of the brain is crucially dependent upon visual experiences (Blakemore, 1991; see also Chapter 3). There are numerous other instances of the effects of experience on development; for example, the effects of exposure to pathogens on the immune system, and the effects of early diet on metabolic processes (Bock & Whelan, 1991). Similarly, animal studies have shown that the early experience of stress affects both the structure and function of the neuroendocrine system (Hennessy & Levine, 1979). The importance of these observations is that they raise queries about the role of experiences in adult life. If experiences influence development, does this mean that the concept of development must be extended into the adult years because some sorts of crucial experiences tend not to occur until then? Presumably so. For example, the structure and colour of the areola of the breast are permanently changed by pregnancy and this is so even if pregnancy does not occur until the age of 40. Is this developmental? It would seem reasonable to view it as such because it is normative. But, does this mean that the breasts of women who have not borne children are 'immature'? Perhaps, but the question raises queries about how maturity should be determined. One implication for social development of these findings is that if social growth is influenced by social experiences (which it is), and if key social experiences (such as marriage or child-rearing) tend not to occur until adult life, the concept of development must be extended into the adult years, as also suggested by the neurotransmitter findings noted above.

Fourth, there are complex interconnections between structure and function with respect to all bodily systems, but perhaps most problematic with respect to the links between brain development and the workings of the mind. Should the concept of development apply only to the former? That would seem absurdly limiting. To begin with, it is function that matters most in everyday life and to disregard it would seem perverse. Also, however, it may be presumed that there will always be some structural accompaniment of any lasting functional change. This is evident, for example, in the neural changes associated with the learning processes of imprinting (Horn, 1990). The point is an important one because there are many examples of functional gains that continue well into adult life. Thus, fluid intelligence goes on increasing up to middle life (see Chapter 22) and long-distance runners tend not to reach their peak until many years after physical growth (at least as indexed by height) has ceased. However, these examples refer back to the earlier point on experiential input, because the extent to which development continues is much affected by experiences (Rutter & Madge, 1976; see also Chapter 6 with respect to schooling influences). In that connection, it is relevant that similar considerations apply to physical and mental decline in the elderly (Baltes & Baltes, 1990; Rutter & Rutter, 1993). For example, the osteoporosis that was once thought to be an inevitable result of old age is now known to be much influenced by both exercise and sex hormones. It is this sort of finding that provides part of the underpinning of lifespan concepts of development and part of the reason why gerontologists, seemingly paradoxically, have come to appreciate the value of developmental notions in relation to the processes of ageing (see Chapter 22).

Fifth, it is necessary for concepts of development to encompass the process of individuation as well as

normative progression (Rutter & Rutter, 1993) — a need now accepted even by neo-Piagetians who had previously relegated individual differences to a residual category (Case & Edelstein, 1993). Thus, we need to consider why people differ in their levels of cognitive functioning, as well as the fact that cognitive skills increase with age during childhood (see Chapter 11). Similarly, it is necessary to ask why children vary in their social relationships or their value systems or their emotional patterns even though they went through broadly comparable phases in those psychological domains at roughly the same ages. It is crucial to appreciate that the forces that influence normative progression and those that determine individual differences are not necessarily synonymous (Rutter & Madge, 1976; Rutter, 1994a, b). For example, Kagan (1981) has argued that the reason why all children acquire moral values for the first time towards the end of the second year is because biologically based relevant cognitive skills are acquired at that age. He suggested (on the basis of persuasive circumstantial evidence) that children begin to appreciate the meaning of standards and of expectations because of intrinsic maturational processes rather than because of any particular training or experience. That is quite likely to be so, given ordinary expectable social experiences, but the *particular* standards acquired are probably influenced to a much greater extent by specific experiences (see Chapter 14).

The sixth issue is an extension of the fifth; namely that not only is it necessary to consider individual differences in level, we must also include within the concept of development, variations in the *content* and quality of functions (as implicit in the moral standards example above). Thus, there has been much developmental interest in the role of early imprinting on the nature of later sexual preferences (see Rutter, 1981 for an account of the basic evidence; but also Nash & Hay, 1993 for a discussion of the variations in those links); and of the effects of early social isolation on parenting behaviour in adult life (see Rutter, 1981 for a brief review of findings; also Chapter 16). The problem, however, is that if the content of behaviour, as well as its complexity, is to be included, how is developmental progression to be defined and what is to be taken as a measure or marker of having reached maturity? The question does not allow any simple answer.

Obviously, it would make no sense to view development as change of any kind, or even as change that seems to imply an advance. Thus, clearly it is an achievement to learn a second (or third) language in adult life but few developmentalists would regard it as a developmental gain. That is because the new language does not involve any change in the quality of functioning, and does not represent a new type of skill or capacity. The same applies to increases in self-esteem or the acquisition of new friendships. Reference to some form of lasting change helps but cannot be a criterion both because some lasting changes do not readily fit into developmental notions (e.g. the second language example) and because some developmental changes have no obvious long-term consequences (e.g. the phases of crawling or babbling). However, some degree of carry-forward (meaning implications for, or effects on, some later phase of development) would seem to be a requirement for a change to be considered developmental. Also, although the change may be strongly influenced by experiences, it would be expected that it involve some form of intraindividual alteration that is part of a universal, or at least usual, age-related progression.

The fuzzy concept, then, is of development as a systematic, organized, intraindividual change that is clearly associated with age-related progression, and which is carried forward in some way that has implications for a person's pattern or level of functioning at some later time (Rutter & Rutter, 1993).

The seventh issue is in some respects the most critical; that is whether the normative expectation should be for continuity or discontinuity, stabilization or change. Because the topic is so fundamental to developmental considerations, it needs to be considered at some length.

CONTINUITIES AND DISCONTINUITIES

It is necessary to begin by noting that the terms continuity and discontinuity, consistency and inconsistency, change and stability encompass a range of quite disparate concepts that need to be differentiated (Kagan, 1980; Rutter, 1987a; Rutter & Rutter, 1993). First, they may refer to alterations in the *level* of functioning over time. It is obvious, of course, that the process of development necessarily involves increases in level in so far as capacities or skills of any kind are concerned. Thus, cognitive skills increase markedly with age throughout childhood and adolescence. This change in level is so great that intelligence quotients (IQs) are specially designed to take into account, and hence to *remove*, changes in level (so that mental ages go up with increasing chronological age, whereas IQs do not). However, changes in levels of psychological function are by no means confined to skills. Thus, fears tend to decrease with age during early adolescence whereas depression increases (see Chapter 17), as does antisocial behaviour (see Chapter 19).

Second, these concepts may refer to *normative* consistency, meaning that people retain their *rank order* in the population. Thus, after the preschool years, there are substantial positive correlations over time in IQ, indicating that, on the whole, those who show superior levels of functioning tend to remain somewhat above average as they grow older, and vice versa. This is so despite marked changes in level (i.e. mental age) in the population as a whole.

Third, these concepts may refer to *ipsative* consistency, meaning a tendency to continue to show the same *pattern* over time. For example, someone may always exhibit a cognitive pattern of verbal skills being better than visuospatial ones even though their absolute level of both alters, and despite inconsistency in the relative degree to which they show either skill (i.e. despite low normative consistency).

Fourth, these concepts may refer to consistency over time in the *meaning* of a psychological feature. Thus, it is evident that close harmonious relationships are psychologically protective and their loss stressful throughout life (see Chapter 16). This is so in spite of considerable differences in the pattern of relationships over time and substantial changes in the ways in which closeness is manifest (thus, proximity-seeking at times of stress is an important index in infancy but confiding is so in later life). Also, there is limited consistency in quality across relationships or over time between, say, infancy and adolescence.

Fifth, these concepts may refer to the extent to which, despite changing surface manifestations, psychological features continue to reflect the same underlying psychological or neural *structure*. Thus, a liability to schizophrenia is reflected in attentional deficits, neurodevelopmental impairments and social abnormalities in childhood but recurrent psychotic episodes in adult life (see Rutter & Garmezy, 1983; Werry & Taylor, 1994). Similarly, a growing body of evidence suggests that attention and habituation qualities in infancy may index the same information-processing skills shown by problem-solving abilities in later childhood (see Chapter 8).

With these differences in mind, we need to consider which tendencies are ordinarily to be anticipated in the course of development, given an average expectable environment. Although it is accepted that there is bound to be a mixture of consistency and inconsistency and of continuity and discontinuity, there tends to be an assumption that with all concepts except the first, increasing stabilization is somehow expectable as a result of development and that it is only discontinuity and change that require special explanation. In other words, as children grow older, it is presumed that, because later skills and propensities derive out of earlier ones and because maturation tends to lead to better established psychological and neural structures, individuals become less likely to change over time in their relative position in the population, or in their pattern of functioning. Also, increasingly, behaviours are likely to show greater consistency in the extent to which they have the same meaning and reflect the same underlying structure. At first sight, that seems reasonable. After all, ordinarily (in the absence of disease processes), adults do not lose height or intelligence or language skills once they have been acquired; also the process of growth plateaus in early adult life. Once a structure has been gained, it tends to remain unless something unusual happens. In the same way, most psychological characteristics stabilize and show increasing consistency over time, however assessed, as children grow older, with consistency greatest in adult life (McCrae & Costa, 1990).

There are several sound reasons for supposing that a degree of stabilization is indeed the norm. Thus, on the whole genetic influences increase with age (at least during the phase of childhood) *and* the genetic correlations over time tend to be substantial (Plomin, 1986; Loehlin, 1992). The latter consideration means that the accumulation of genetic effects over time tends to pull in the same direction. This is an important matter because this is less strongly the case with environmental influences. The implication is that although environmental effects may be quite strong at any one point in time they do not have the same inevitable tendency to shape lasting characteristics (although for a range of different reasons they may do so in some circumstances — see below). However, it must also be added that genetic influences do not necessarily promote stabilization and continuity; they also programme change. This is most obviously so with respect to developmental transitions such as the menarche in girls or puberty in boys, both of which involve a quite strong genetic component (Meyer *et al.*, 1991; Pickles *et al.*, in press). But it also applies to changes over time in intellectual level (Matheny, 1990).

A second reason for expecting stabilization is that if influences (of whatever kind) serve to establish some kind of intrinsic 'structure' presumably that structure will ordinarily remain and go on shaping function. Three rather separate issues are pertinent here. First, what is meant by 'structure' and how good is the evidence that such entities exist? Second, are these postulated underlying structures, once established, self-perpetuating or is their maintenance dependent on some sort of input or use? Third, are their effects as evident on individual characteristics as on universal normative capacities? These seemingly straightforward questions do not allow entirely unambiguous answers (Rutter & Rutter, 1993).

Nevertheless, so far as universal normative capacities are concerned, there seems to be every reason to suppose that there is indeed some kind of underlying psychological (and presumably also neural) structure that does persist given any kind of ordinarily expectable experiences. Thus, this would seem to apply to features such as language (see Chapter 9) and theory of mind (see Chapter 13). It may also apply, perhaps somewhat less strongly, to the capacity to make enduring selective intense friendships and love relationships (see Chapter 16). Thus, this seems to be a general human proclivity but also one that, apparently, can be lastingly affected by an institutional upbringing in early childhood, the effects of which are not entirely reversed by positive experiences in adolescence

(Hodges & Tizard, 1989a, b; see also Chapter 16). In short, the hypothesis of important underlying structures that promote stabilization and continuity has some limited empirical support. However, it is much less obvious that they play an overwhelming role in individual differences in behavioural characteristics, it is not self-evident that they are impervious to later experiences, and it is likely that the 'structures' take more than one form.

Yet, despite these findings and considerations, there is reason to question the notion that increasing stabilization is the norm and requires no explanation. To begin with, if ordinarily expectable experiences stop, change can be quite dramatic. For example, this is obvious in the extraordinarily rapid and marked muscle wasting that occurs if, for any reason, a limb is immobilized in a plaster cast. Of course, with exercise the muscle bulk and strength return when the cast is removed (although the recovery period may extend over many months). But, the observation serves as a reminder that functions tend to be maintained through their use, and therefore that experiences play a role in the maintenance of stable functioning (this applies to most functions ranging from cognitive performance to sexuality — Rutter & Rutter, 1993). However, there are many different mechanisms that play a part in this maintenance process. Continuities tend to arise on the basis of indirect chain reactions of various kinds (Rutter, 1989). For example, some fears and phobias persist over astonishingly long time periods in spite of a lack of any obviously reinforcing or maintaining stress experiences (Rachman, 1977; Mineka, 1985). The available evidence suggests that this is *not* because once a fear is acquired it is very difficult to eliminate but rather because the extinguishing of a fear requires some form of contact or involvement that fails to bring about negative consequences, and which is associated with the development of feelings of self-efficacy. The main reason why fears persist is because people avoid contact with the fear stimulus and hence there is no opportunity for a non-harmful encounter to lead to a change of percept of the feared object. When, through desensitization, modelling or exposure, such opportunities are provided, successful rapid treatment is usual even with very long-standing specific phobias, provided that they are not part of a more general emotional disorder (O'Leary & Wilson, 1987; Herbert, 1994).

Accentuation principle

But there are also more positive reasons why individual propensities are stabilized as a result of new experiences. Thus, stressful or challenging experiences tend to emphasize and strengthen pre-existing characteristics — what Elder and Caspi (1990) have called the 'accentuation principle'. For example, the increase in delinquent activities associated with unemployment is most evident in young people already showing propensities of this kind (Farrington *et al.*, 1986); the increase in norm-breaking behaviour sometimes associated with early puberty in girls is particularly found in those girls exhibiting deviant behaviour (Caspi & Moffitt, 1991); negative life events are most likely to provoke depression in adults who showed more negative emotions before the events (Rodgers, 1990); the Depression in the 1930s had the greatest effect on men who had shown earlier emotional instability (Elder, 1984); and the experience of becoming a parent has been shown to accentuate psychological characteristics that were already present beforehand (Michaels & Goldberg, 1988; Cowan *et al.*, 1991). It is commonly supposed that major life experiences bring about change, but to a considerable extent the reverse is the case (Caspi & Moffitt, 1993). The presumption that they provoke change arises because of the good evidence that negative events carrying long-term psychological threat can provoke disorder in previously well individuals (Brown & Harris, 1978, 1989; Goodyer, 1990). That has indeed been demonstrated in numerous studies and there are good reasons for accepting a causal connection. Nevertheless, because such events have their biggest impact on the most vulnerable individuals, and because they tend to accentuate pre-existing characteristics, rather than give rise to entirely new behaviours, the overall developmental effect is to increase consistency, not to decrease it.

At first sight, that conclusion seems paradoxical but it is not, for reasons well articulated by Caspi and Moffitt (1993). When individuals are in situations that are characterized by novelty, uncertainty and unpredictability, but yet which require some sort of action or response, they necessarily must have recourse to their own inner resources in deciding how to negotiate the change. Those resources are likely to include both dispositional traits and habitual ways of thinking. Caspi and Moffitt (1993) noted the evidence that heritability tends to be higher for behaviours in unfamiliar or stressful circumstances or with strangers, than in familiar social contacts or with people whom they know well. In other words, genetically influenced individuality is most evident in novel situations rather than familiar ones. Also, aggressive boys' attributional biases tend to be most evident in ambiguous situations or in new encounters that lack familiar cues.

The finding that challenging situations are those most likely to reveal individual differences does not, of course, in itself explain why this should result in a lasting accentuation of the trait. However, the repeated elicitation of a particular style of behaviour is likely to strengthen it by virtue of habit strengthening. Also, probably it is at least as important that there is a general biological tendency to seek to restore predictability and that this is likely to mean that people will seek to assimilate the new experience by making sense of it and incorporating it in pre-existing cognitive schemata (a process that was central to Piaget's notions of developmental progress; Piaget, 1983). It would seem that such a process would tend to serve to accentuate and reinforce prior characteristics. The mechanisms involved are not well understood and little investigated but the limited empirical findings are rather consistent in showing that, whatever the explanation, stress or challenge situations do tend to have this accentuation effect.

Self-concepts

A second mechanism promoting stabilization derives from people's cognitive sets or self-concepts — two closely related concepts (Harter, 1983; Rutter, 1987b). Kagan (1984) has argued that most experiences have effects only through their cognitive transduction. In other words we think about what happens to us and it is those thought processes that matter. There is, of course, no doubt that human beings are thinking, feeling creatures and that we tend to build up ideas about ourselves, about other people, about our inter-

actions with them, and about our power to control what happens to us as a result of our experiences. Success and accomplishment are likely to be important, not so much because they make us feel happy at the time, but more because they tend to foster a positive self-image of ourselves as people who can control our lives and who are well regarded by our fellows.

What is less well established is the extent to which these self-concepts and social-cognitions regulate stabilization and persistence of behavioural characteristics. Attachment theorists have argued that they do — pointing out that the postulated 'internal working models' provide a basis for both continuity and change (i.e. as later experiences alter the cognitive set, or the model, so its effects on current relationships will alter; Bretherton & Waters, 1985; Bretherton, 1987; see also Chapter 16). Similarly, depression theorists have argued for the role of self-esteem, learned helplessness and similar concepts as the basis for the carry-forward of a propensity to depression (Brown & Harris, 1978, 1989; Segal & Dobson, 1992). Again, there is some supporting evidence but it has to be said that there is continuing uncertainty on the specific mediating role of the cognitive set. In much the same way, Dodge *et al.* (1990) have put forward evidence suggesting that self-cognition provides the mediating connection between the experience of physical abuse and the exhibition of aggressive behaviour (see also Chapter 19).

Continuities in the environment

A third feature fostering behavioural continuity and stabilization is continuity in environmental influences. Clarke and Clarke (1976) argued that this was the major factor because of the overriding influence on psychological functioning of the currently prevailing environmental circumstances. This postulate perhaps somewhat overemphasizes the power of contemporary over past experiences but, nevertheless, it is helpful in reminding us that any analysis of environmental effects must take into account continuities in environments. It is clear that, on the whole, children *do* tend to be exposed to broadly comparable environments as they grow up — whether the environments are assessed in terms of social status or quality of personal relation-

ships. Moreover, there is a limited amount of
evidence that continuity in psychological characteristics is in part determined by parallels in the
environmental continuities. Thus, when home
circumstances change markedly for the better or
worse this tends to have effects on children's own
psychological functioning (Rutter, 1971; Fogelman
& Goldstein, 1976; Richman *et al.*, 1982).

Shaping and selecting environments

However, it would be a seriously misleading over-
simplification to view continuities in environments
as some sort of given that is independent of the
actions of individuals; the reverse is the case (Scarr,
1992; Rutter & Rutter, 1993; Plomin, 1994; Rutter
et al., 1994a). It is clear that there are numerous
ways in which there is shaping and selecting of
environments (either through their own personal
actions or those of their families). For example,
there are the links that derive from opportunities
(or the lack of them). Thus, well-educated parents
are likely to be more affluent than average and
better able to choose good schools for their children
(both because they can afford to live in the right
areas and because they know what to look out for
as indicators of effective schools); attendance at
good schools is likely to foster better scholastic
attainments which, in turn, will make entry to
tertiary education more probable which, thereafter,
will aid the obtaining of a good job, a good income
and above average living conditions. The specific
environments change but the links between them
foster continuity because the overall effects of the
different environments tend to continue to be
advantageous or disadvantageous, in line with the
initial living circumstances.

Another way in which continuities in environmental risk (or the reverse) come about is through
people's own personal choice of their environments. For example, this is evident in the effects
of peer groups. Children choose the friends with
whom they associate but, nevertheless, the peer
group of which they are a part has effects on their
own behaviour (Quinton *et al.*, 1993; see also
Chapters 7 and 18). We know that this is so
because of the demonstration of effects stemming
from artificially constructed peer groups (e.g. Sherif
et al., 1961); from the effects on continuing delin-

quency stemming from whether or not a person is
part of a delinquent peer group (e.g. West, 1982;
Rowe & Gulley, 1992); from self-reports (e.g.
Sampson & Laub, 1993); from statistical modelling
of the effects of peer group on choice of marital
partner (Quinton *et al.*, 1993); and from the effects
of geographical moves (West, 1982).

One special sort of peer group is provided by
marital choice. Caspi and Herbener (1990) showed
that people who married someone of similar personality characteristics were more likely to show stability in their own personality features. Clausen
(1991) found that planful competence in adolescence tended to promote continuity in adaptive
functioning because people selected for themselves
appropriate social niches, including successful
marriages. Conversely, continuities in social *mal*-
adaptations in girls are promoted by early (teenage) impulsive, premature marriages to deviant men
from socially disadvantaged backgrounds (Quinton
& Rutter, 1988; Quinton *et al.*, 1993). Of course, it
would be quite wrong to see assortative mating as a
matter of choice. Sometimes it may be that but,
quite often, unsatisfactory marriages derive from a
lack of choice, from a lack of a pool of suitable
partners (because the peer group is so deviant), or
because people who themselves show undesirable
psychological characteristics are not much of a
'catch' in the marriage market and therefore get left
with few choices (see Chapter 4).

A further set of influences derives from the
reactions that individuals engender in other people.
It is clear that this does happen and that this is one
of the important ways in which individual characteristics influence psychological development (see
Chapter 4). One aspect of this process concerns
the effect of people's reputation (Hymel *et al.*, 1990;
see also Chapter 4). It is an important part of
human interpersonal functioning that we react
to people on the basis of our preconceptions or
prejudices about what they are like. This has
been shown for features as varied as gender (see
Chapter 15), ethnicity (see Chapter 7), social
standing and prior behaviour. In some instances
preconceptions have a basis in reality; thus behavioural stereotypes assume that people will go on
behaving in the same way that they have behaved
before. What is stereotypical about this presumption
is that most people are quite slow to recognize

when a change has taken place. As shown by several separate research strategies, each of which is able to separate the effects of reputation from current behaviour (see Chapter 4), there is a real and important effect of reputation that is independent of current behaviour. There is circumstantial evidence that this reputational effect promotes behavioural stability (we live up or down to what is expected of us), but the evidence on long-term sequelae is much less secure than that on immediate effects.

Yet another effect comes from the effects of people's behaviour in shaping their own environments. For example, Robins's (1966) classic follow-up study of patients from a child guidance clinic (and general population controls) showed that in adult life, antisocial boys had a greatly increased likelihood of being unemployed, without social support, having had multiple broken marriages, and of lacking intimate friendships — all features which are well known to be social stressors. Sampson and Laub (1993) found a closely similar pattern. Delinquents were much more likely than controls to drop out of school; were three times as likely to have unstable employment in adult life; were three to five times as likely to be divorced or separated; and, if married, were more than twice as likely to have a weak attachment to their spouse. Champion *et al.*'s (submitted) follow-up of a London sample of 10 year olds from the general population showed similar, if less dramatic, trends. Boys and girls with conduct problems at 10 had twice as many negative life events carrying long-term threats some 18 years later. This increased risk was especially the case for acute events associated with long-term difficulties, but did not apply to all mildly stressful events. Interestingly, the association between their own behaviours at age 10 and negative life events in adult life applied to events outside their own control as well as within it. It seems that the increased risks arose in part through their being part of a stressful family group as well as through the effects of their own behaviour.

As already noted, the extinguishing of fears is greatly facilitated by contact with the feared object in circumstances in which no harm results. A common feature of phobias is that they lead people to avoid whatever object or situation they fear; such avoidance is likely to perpetuate the fear.

All of these, and other, considerations serve as a powerful reminder that continuity and stabilization do not 'just happen'; they are brought about actively and passively by a variety of forces. The expectable norm is for neither continuity nor discontinuity, stabilization nor change, but rather for a complex mixture of each.

TRANSITIONS

Part of the argument against a cumulative accretion model of development (see above) is that many instances of developmental change are characterized by the emergence of a new psychological structure (and skill) that shows little connection with what has gone before, and which transforms developmental possibilities in such a dramatic fashion that it creates an essential transformation, or reorganization, of psychological functioning, and hence a developmental discontinuity (Kagan, 1984). This concept involves two rather separate propositions — on the degree to which there is radical change, and on the absence of continuity with what has gone before.

Intrinsic transitions

First, there is the suggestion that the new skill or structure involves a *qualitative* change or transformation that cannot be reduced to a quantitative increase in pre-existing capacities. This postulate has overwhelming empirical support as several rather different examples serve to illustrate. To begin with, there are maturational changes in neural functioning that are associated with qualitative shifts in important aspects of functioning. Not only does the part of the brain subserving some psychological functions change with age (Goldman-Rakic *et al.*, 1983; see also Chapter 3), but also the effects of sensory input alter. For example, in early life, infants from all manner of language backgrounds show similar skills in speech perception (Aslin *et al.*, 1983). However, in later childhood and adult life, people's ability to make phonetic discriminations is much influenced by the language they speak. It seems that, although initial perception skills are *not* dependent on particular experiences, the maintenance of the skills after the first few months is dependent, in part, on experience. A similar shift is evident in sound production. Thus, the vocalizations of deaf infants are closely similar to those of hearing infants in the first few months after birth, but become increasingly different thereafter, as auditory input is crucial for the phonetic sequences of the canonical babbling that emerges in the second half of the first year (Oller & Eilers, 1988).

Some types of sensitive period in development reflect transitions of this kind. Thus, it is well known that the establishment of binocular vision requires appropriate visual input in the first few years of life and, if that is not available, it will not ordinarily be possible to make up for that lack later (see Chapter 3). That is the reason that it is necessary to correct squints in early childhood. Less certainly, the development of verbal skills may also be influenced by auditory input during the period when language is acquired. It also appears that social development may be particularly influenced by the experience of attachment relationships during the preschool years (see Chapter 16). The mechanisms involved are not known, but it is possible that they reflect somewhat similar neural processes (see Chapter 3). The concept of fixed critical periods with irreversible consequences (derived from imprinting) rightly came under severe criticism and has been abandoned (Bateson, 1990), but the reality of sensitive periods in development is not in doubt.

There are numerous examples of transitions in which the acquisition of particular skills or capacities transforms functioning in ways that have wide-ranging, far-reaching implications. Thus, young infants (up to the age of, say, 4−6 months) do not react to separations from their parents in the same manner as do slightly older children (Rutter, 1979b). Probably as a consequence of that difference, hospital admissions tend to be much more distressing for 1−4-year-old children than for babies and young infants. It is likely that this age difference reflects the capacity for selective attachment relationships which develops during the middle of the first year of life (see Chapter 16). Babies are less likely to show adverse responses to separations because they have yet to develop selective relationships with strong attachment qualities. However, additionally it has been found that school-age children are also less likely to exhibit adverse reactions. Probably, that is because they have devel-

oped the cognitive skills to appreciate better what is happening and the capacity to maintain relationships during a separation.

It is even more obvious that the acquisition of language opens up new vistas in social communication and also in many other aspects of development, as is evident in what happens to children who fail to develop language for one reason or another (Howlin & Rutter, 1987; see also Chapter 9). Similarly, it is evident that the acquisition of an ability to understand other people's intentions and mental status, so-called 'theory of mind' skills, has important implications for socioemotional functioning (see Chapter 13). In comparable fashion, Kagan (1981) drew attention to the effects, around the age of 2 years, of children's developing capacity to make inferences about the causes of events and other people's expectations of their performance. He suggested that the accompanying self-awareness, recognition of standards, and ability to set goals, provided the necessary basis for a sense of morality, which was not possible before that age. Dunn (1988), too, indicated the significance of children becoming able to understand other people's feelings, goals, social rules and states of mind.

The physiological changes associated with puberty, equally dramatically, introduce radically new elements into a person's life. Moreover, they do so through several rather different mechanisms. The hormonal changes have a direct effect on sex drive and this plays a role in the initiation of sexual activity and the development of sexual love relationships (see Chapter 21). However, it is also the case that the acquisition of secondary sexual characteristics will, in addition, have effects through the changes they bring about in other people's perception of the adolescent. The achieving of reproductive fertility may result in pregnancy and a transition to parenthood, by which the arrival of offspring makes a further difference. Yet other effects stem from the major changes in physique that occur in association with puberty. Thus, many girls resent the fat acquisition that is a prominent feature of female puberty, and dieting becomes extremely prevalent in adolescent girls, whereas it is uncommon before this age period (Alsaker, in press; see also Chapter 20).

It is obvious, then, that the course of development

brings many examples of changes that involve radical qualitative alterations resulting in what may reasonably be regarded as transformations in psychological functions. However, the second proposition, that this involves total discontinuity with all that has occurred before, does not follow logically, and is open to serious question. Most of the transitions mentioned have striking, time-limited markers (first words, menarche, etc.), but most actually extend over quite lengthy time periods (e.g. puberty covers some 4–6 years). Moreover, most have some connection with prior skills. Thus, the emergence of 'theory of mind', or mind-reading skills, seems related to precursor skills such as joint attention (Baron-Cohen *et al.*, 1993; Frye, 1993; see also Chapter 13). Often, there is more continuity than is apparent in the dramatic appearance of a new skill. Nevertheless, that does not apply to all transitions; there are some new skills that have little or no connection with earlier ones, in spite of surface similarities. For example, although voluntary radial grasping replaces the primitive palmar grasp response, there is no consistent relationship between the emergence of the former and the loss of the latter (Connolly & Prechtl, 1981).

Reservations must be expressed, too, over the accompanying suggestion that the acquisition of new structures results in such a major reorganization that it, in effect, wipes out all that has gone before (Kagan, 1984). As Hinde (1983; Hinde & Bateson, 1985) pointed out, there are many examples of continuity across even the most major reorganizations. He indicated the finding that the learning of sensory preferences in the larval stage of insects may persist into adult life after metamorphosis. In humans, too, there are examples of behaviours that have been lost in early life but yet that re-emerge at a later age as a result of brain injury or changed environmental circumstances (Connolly & Prechtl, 1981).

It is clear that, in most ordinary circumstances, older children and adults cannot retrieve memories of experiences during the infancy period (Schachtel, 1947; Tulving, 1983), but that does not necessarily mean that they have left behind no residue. At least two distinctions must be drawn. First, there are important differences between the retention of episodic or autobiographical or sequential memories and the retention of semantic memories or knowledge. Young children lack the former (i.e. when older they tend not to remember particular incidents or happenings that occurred when they were very young) but they possess the latter (that is, knowledge acquired during the first few years can be shown to be still present many years later — e.g. as shown by the relearning of a language first used in early life but then not used for a long period). Second, there is a difference between the encoding (and therefore potential availability) of a memory and the ability consciously to recall it. It should be added that it is by no means clear that infantile amnesia represents a pure memory deficit; rather it could reflect the lack of a sense of self in the infancy period (Howe & Courage, 1993).

It may be concluded that there are very important radical psychological reorganizations in development associated with the acquisition of new skills and capacities, and that these introduce substantial elements of discontinuity. Nevertheless, it is going too far to assume that these involve no continuity with prior psychological structures or processes.

Role transitions

The transitions discussed so far have all involved some aspect of intrinsic psychological functioning but the concept has also been applied to chronological age periods and to social role changes. Levinson's (1978) concept of mid-life crises exemplifies the latter approach. He suggested that middle life is associated with a wide range of adaptations to altered life patterns (as with divorce, remarriage, job changes, blocked promotions and chronic illness); that this age period constitutes a time of reappraisal of what people have achieved and what they want to accomplish; and that it is necessary to experience tumult and turmoil to make the transition successfully. It is certainly clear that major adaptations are required in adult life for most people; it is also evident that self-questioning is part of coping with such adaptations (however, this is so at many age periods and not just in middle life). But, contrary to the mid-life crisis notion, the limited available evidence suggests that marked turmoil during transitions (in mid-life, adolescence or other age periods) tends to be disadvantageous rather than helpful with respect to later psychological functioning (e.g. Offer, 1969; Rutter, 1979a;

Vaillant, 1990; Wortman & Silver, 1990). There is a lack of sound supporting evidence for the concept of universal, age-defined transitions and, in view of the huge individual variation in the timing of the required major adaptations, this does not seem a promising way forward in the conceptualization of developmental processes.

A focus on social role changes seems more useful. During the period 1950–1970s, these tended to be viewed in terms of stages in a family cycle. There was an implicit assumption of a predictable script for a timetable beginning with a period before marriage, and proceeding to marriage without children, an active phase of parenting, the departure of children and the 'empty nest'. However, that concept has ceased to be tenable for three rather different reasons (Elder, 1991). First, there are far too many exceptions to this cycle for it to be useful. Thus, there has been a massive increase in many countries of the proportion of babies born outside marriage (Hess, 1994). In part this reflects teenage pregnancies, many of which arise outside a steady relationship (Furstenberg *et al.*, 1987; Hofferth & Hayes, 1987), but in part it reflects an increasing proportion of couples who decide to live together without getting married (Hess, 1994). Also, of course, the family cycle ignores the substantial minority of individuals who do not marry or, if married, do not have children. Second, it fails to take account of social role changes outside the family, such as those associated with work careers. Third, it ignores the large individual variation in what the roles mean and how they are causally linked with one another (Rindfuss *et al.*, 1987).

Accordingly, there has been a shift to the study of specific social role transitions as they actually impinge on individuals. This has given rise to a growing literature on an ever-widening range of normative and non-normative experiences such as puberty (e.g. Bancroft & Reinisch, 1990; Feldman & Elliot, 1990; Paikoff & Brooks-Gunn, 1991; Leffert & Petersen, 1994); marriage (Rutter & Rutter, 1993); teenage pregnancy (Furstenberg *et al.*, 1987; Hayes, 1987); army experience (Elder, 1986); parenthood (Michaels & Goldberg, 1988); infertility (Stanton & Dunkel-Schetter, 1991); divorce and remarriage (Hetherington & Clingempeel, 1992); grandparenthood (Smith, 1991);

unemployment and retirement (Warr, 1987); and bereavement (Raphael, 1984; Parkes, 1986).

The research findings show a complex mixture of commonalities and differences among these various social role transitions. However, the studies are consistent in indicating a large individual variation in both the meaning and effects of each transition. For each, the change of ascribed social role may make little difference to overall life patterns or result in a major alteration in social group, quality of relationships, responsibilities and leisure activities. Equally, when there is an alteration the net effect may be psychologically advantageous or disadvantageous. Because of this variation, Cowan *et al.* (1991) and others have argued that the term transition should be restricted to those changes of social role that result in an internal psychological reorganization of some kind. However, although such a convention would bring externally provoked transitions in line with internally mediated ones such as the acquisition of language or 'theory of mind', it has the serious drawback of assuming that, if there is a major change in life circumstances, the internal psychological consequences (if there are any) will necessarily involve change rather than stabilization (Rutter, submitted).

As already discussed, many types of life stress or challenge serve to *accentuate*, rather than alter, prior characteristics. Accordingly, the criterion of internal reorganization does not seem appropriate. Nevertheless, such an effect is of considerable interest and it is important to gain an understanding of how it comes about, how the effects are mediated, and what differentiates social role transitions that result in some sort of shift in life trajectory from those that do not. These shifts have come to be called 'turning points' in development. The term is perhaps somewhat unfortunate in implying a rather more dramatic effect than that actually found in most instances, but it is useful in highlighting the contrast with accentuation effects. However, both involve the same research need for investigative strategies that can provide rigorous tests for true psychological change and for testing causal hypotheses linking such change to specified characteristics of life transitions. As Caspi and Bem (1990) argued, the need is for studies of 'systematic' change and not just of absence of continuity.

TESTING FOR CHANGE

The concepts of change and stability, continuity and discontinuity, appear straightforward at first sight but, as discussed above, they have several quite different meanings. Most frequently, there has been a focus on the extent to which people tend to retain their rank order in the population. It is apparent that, after the first few years, this form of consistency is substantial for most characteristics, perhaps particularly so with respect to those associated with psychopathology (Rutter, 1989). Individuals who are most prone, or least prone, to exhibit disruptive behaviour (Earls, 1994; see also Chapter 19), or emotional disturbance (Harrington, 1994; Klein, 1994; see also Chapter 17) or cognitive impairment (Maughan & Yule, 1994; Scott, 1994; see also Chapter 11) tend to continue to be relatively extreme on these characteristics over lengthy periods of time in spite of (or because of — see above) major life changes.

Among several other concepts, there is the quite different issue of whether the *level* of some trait or characteristic alters over time. This concept is, of course, quite different from that of normative consistency and the two often give rise to quite different conclusions. Thus, cognitive skills increase markedly with age, but correlations over time (the index of normative consistency) remain quite high. Similarly, delinquent behaviour shows a marked drop in early adult life, but individuals' relative propensity to engage in delinquent activities remains fairly stable over this age period (see Chapter 19). In the same way, depressive disorders become much more frequent during adolescence but there is substantial consistency over time in the particular individuals who exhibit such disorders (see Chapter 17).

The concept of a 'turning point' (Pickles & Rutter, 1991; Sampson & Laub, 1993; Rutter, submitted) or 'intraindividual change' (Farrington, 1988) in life trajectory is based on an approach that is somewhat different yet again. Unlike the first two concepts, it refers to individuals, rather than the pattern in the population or sample as a whole. Indeed, it focuses on subgroups of individuals whose life course shows a shift in direction away from that expected (using overall population trends) on the basis of the behaviour shown up to the point of the shift. Thus, for example, the concept has been applied to the behavioural changes associated with an unusually early puberty, schooling experiences and marriage (see below). Of course, all population trends include substantial individual variation, so that shifts in trajectory in individual cases mean nothing unless consistent associations with the postulated causal factor can be demonstrated, and replicated. Obviously, shifts may involve changes in a positive or negative direction and may comprise either an intensification or a reduction in the behaviour in question. The importance of this approach lies in its attempt to delineate the mechanisms underlying both stability and change and, in so doing, to account for the marked individual variations found in developmental trends for virtually all psychological characteristics.

In order to test for intraindividual change in an adequate fashion, it is necessary to have longitudinal data with both measures at multiple time points of the behaviour to be studied and measures of the hypothesized causal influences whether they be 'internal' (such as with puberty or illness) or 'external' (in terms of some acute or chronic life experience). Thus, this combination of data has demonstrated that children's scholastic attainment shows a systematic association with the qualities of school attended (see Chapter 6); that people exhibit more delinquent behaviour and show more emotional disturbance when they become unemployed but that this change is reversed when they get paid work (Warr, 1987; Rutter, 1994b); and that severe head injuries often result in cognitive impairment and psychopathological disturbance (Rutter *et al.*, 1983), to mention but three examples. There are many ways in which longitudinal data can provide quite rigorous tests of causal hypotheses if there is a well-chosen selection of experiments of a nature that provides the necessary quasi-experimental contrasts; the notion that such testing can only be undertaken in the laboratory is quite mistaken (Rutter, 1994a, b), although obviously the control of variables that can be achieved in laboratory experiments is highly advantageous.

It might be assumed that the adjective 'intraindividual' is an unnecessary qualifier as that is what everyone means by developmental change. That may be so but, at least until very recently, most inferences about changes with age have been based on cross-sectional between-individual comparisons of children of different ages (de Ribaupierre, 1989), rather than within-individual comparisons of behavioural change over time. Moreover, most longitudinal studies have been analysed in ways that have failed to differentiate between alterations in the numbers of individuals showing some behaviour and changes over time in the level of that behaviour in individuals who show it (Farrington, 1986, 1988). The distinction is crucial.

Two particular methodological requirements warrant emphasis with respect to intraindividual change when considering longer term changes in developmental trajectory in non-experimental conditions. First, it is crucial to assess a sufficiently wide range of behaviours in order to avoid artefactual findings of turning point effects in the presence of heterotypic continuity (meaning that the behavioural manifestations of some underlying quality change with age). Thus, for a long time, the adult outcome of conduct disorder in childhood was considered only, or mainly, in terms of antisocial personality disorder (APD). Substantial continuity was found (Robins, 1978) but nevertheless most children with conduct problems did not show this adverse outcome. It appeared that the rate of 'escape' was considerable. Data from both retrospective (Robins, 1986) and longitudinal studies (Zoccolillo *et al.*, 1992) have shown, however, that conduct disorder leads to a wider range of psychopathology. APD is indeed the single most common outcome in men but it is less characteristic of females and it now appears that, although the form of the behaviour may change with age, the continuity is stronger than was appreciated hitherto. The question of *why* the continuity is as strong as it is remains and it cannot be assumed to be an inevitable feature (see below).

The finding of heterotypic continuity applies also to other psychological features in both normal and abnormal development. For example, it has been found that aspects of attention and habituation in infancy correlate with measures of verbal intelligence in later childhood (see Chapter 8); that language delay is associated with difficulties

in reading and spelling and with socioemotional deficits that may persist into adult life (Rutter & Mawhood, 1991; see also Chapter 9); and that schizophrenic psychoses are often preceded by neurodevelopmental impairment, attentional difficulties and sociobehavioural problems (Rutter & Garmezy, 1983). In each of these cases, it is necessary to note that the finding of continuity over time does not in itself indicate that the different behaviours reflect the same underlying trait; it could be that one creates a risk for the other.

Second, it is necessary to check that the measures of people's behaviour prior to the experience hypothesized to have brought about the change in behaviour provide an adequate reflection of the trait (i.e. underlying behavioural propensity) in question. In so far as people behave in ways that affect their experiences, weak measures of behaviour may result in an artefactual impression of change (because the supposed change may be nothing more than a reflection of unmeasured aspects of the trait being studied). The solution to this problem lies in the availability of multiple measures from different sources, together with the use of appropriate statistical techniques to tap the latent construct (Pickles & Rutter, 1991; Zoccolillo *et al.*, 1992; Sampson & Laub, 1993; Rutter, submitted).

These two methodological considerations have been emphasized because those longitudinal studies that have gone to some lengths to undertake the necessary methodological checks have shown the reality of intraindividual change in both positive and negative directions. For example, in their reanalysis of the Gluecks' delinquency data, Sampson and Laub (1993) showed that incarceration for delinquent acts in adolescence increased the likelihood of adult crime because it made it more difficult to achieve job security. Similarly, their findings showed that alcohol abuse increased the chances of adult criminality because it had adverse effects on marriage and employment. In both cases the factor bringing about the worse outcome (i.e. incarceration or alcohol abuse) was the result of the individual's own behaviour but, equally, the analyses showed that, nevertheless, the factor had an independent effect on outcome. The importance of findings such as these lies in the implication that interventions targeted on these factors might have beneficial effects on adult outcome even though they do not tackle the 'basic' underlying behavioural trait. Much the same implication for intervention probably applies to the finding that antisocial behaviour in childhood predisposes to later drug and alcohol abuse (Vaillant, 1983; Robins & McEvoy, 1990).

These examples underline the important point that the origin of a factor does not necessarily provide information about the mechanisms that mediate its effects (Rutter, 1986). Thus, personality and situational factors play a major role in people choosing to smoke cigarettes but the risk for lung cancer derives from carcinogenic tars that have nothing to do with the origins of smoking. Similarly, adoptee data suggest that, although genetic factors play an important role in the origins of APD, the strong association between this disorder and depressive symptomatology is environmentally mediated (Cadoret *et al.*, 1990). Causal mechanisms need to be analysed in causal chain terms rather than on the assumption of a misleading model of one 'basic' cause.

TURNING POINT EFFECTS

Up to this point, the main focus has been on the variety of mechanisms that may be involved in the perpetuation or accentuation of behaviours over time. However, depending on the specifics, much the same mechanisms may also bring about a degree of redirection in life trajectories or developmental pathways. If continuities are, to some extent, dependent on experiences that serve to prolong particular behaviours, it follows that the absence of such experiences or, more particularly, the presence of experiences having an opposite effect, may bring about change or discontinuity. Caspi and Moffitt (1993) argued that such experiences must be all-encompassing, contain a press for new ways of behaving, and provide clear information on how to behave adaptively. Their concept focused on adaptive shifts of direction and emphasized the characteristics of the immediate behavioural pressures at the time of the turning point. Rutter (submitted) included both adaptive and maladaptive changes and also included both internal and external stimuli. He argued, somewhat similarly, that the experiences involved in turning point effects

needed to involve some form of marked environmental or organismic discontinuity or changing quality *and* that the direction of change must be of a type that was likely to influence development onto a path that was different from that before the turning point. However, there was the further specification that the experiences needed to be of a kind that carried the potential for persistence of effects over time. It was suggested that such experiences were likely to fall into one of three broad categories: (i) those that shut down or open up opportunities (as, for example, with drop-out from schooling or persistence in education); (ii) those that involve a lasting change in the environment (as, for example, with geographical moves that entail a change of peer group, or events such as divorce or bereavement or parenthood, that lastingly change a person's most intimate social group through losses or additions); or (iii) those that have a lasting effect on a person's self-concept or views and expectations of other people. Thus, Dodge *et al.*'s (1990) longitudinal study suggested that cognitive mechanisms may play a role in the links between the experience of child abuse and the later behaviour of acting aggressively oneself. Similarly, it has been supposed that poor parenting creates a vulnerability to depression through effects on a person's cognitive/affective set as reflected in features such as perceived self-efficacy, learned helplessness and poor self-esteem (Brown *et al.*, 1990). This third mechanism is certainly plausible but it has to be said that we lack firm knowledge both on the sorts of experiences that have lasting effects on self-cognition, and also on the role of such cognitions in the carry-forward of the effects of such experiences to later age periods.

Sampson and Laub (1993) presented similar concepts of turning point effects but emphasized the relevance of experiences with respect to their effects on mechanisms that have been important in perpetuating behavioural consistency up to that point. The issues may be illustrated by taking several rather different examples of turning point effects.

Early menarche

Stattin and Magnusson (1990), in their analyses of the Stockholm longitudinal study, showed that girls who reached the menarche unusually early showed an increased tendency to engage in norm-breaking behaviour. Caspi and Moffitt (1991) found the same in the Dunedin longitudinal study but also demonstrated that the effect was most evident in girls clearly showing behavioural propensities of that type. Both investigations found that, although the stimulus was internal (the changes of puberty), the mediating mechanism was social. The increase in norm-breaking behaviour was found only in girls who formed part of an older peer group. The Dunedin study further demonstrated that the effect was found only in coeducational (not all-girls) schools (Caspi *et al.*, 1993), suggesting that the characteristics of the peer group may be important (with the effect perhaps requiring an adequate availability of deviant peer models). Interestingly, the Stockholm study showed that the increase in norm-breaking behaviour did not continue into adult life — presumably because the effect relied on age-related peer group pressures, which were likely to fade in importance with time. By contrast, however, the parallel increased tendency to drop out of schooling early did have persistent effects in terms of a lower percentage completing a college education. The probable explanation is that, once having dropped out of schooling, quite active steps were required to re-enter education. The persistence presumably lay in the (relative) shutting down of opportunities, rather than in the nature of the behavioural changes at the time of puberty.

Schooling

Research findings have been consistent in showing quite marked school effects on children's behaviour, attendance and educational achievements (see Chapter 6). The follow-up into early adult life by Gray *et al.* (1980), showed that these effects led on to differences in occupational level (not surprisingly in view of the importance placed on scholastic credentials in selecting people for jobs). However, there were no long-term effects of the quality of schooling that were independent of the immediate effects on behaviour and scholastic achievement. The lasting impact derived entirely from the chain effects deriving from the immediate behavioural change. This finding is fairly general to the effects of most sorts of life experience (Quinton *et al.*, 1993).

In much the same way, Quinton and Rutter (1988) found that for institution-reared girls, positive school experiences were associated with an increased tendency for them to exert planning in their marital and career choices (Rutter *et al.*, 1990, found the same for institution-reared boys). The same effect was not found in the general population comparison group. The increased tendency to exercise planning in important life choices was associated with better social functioning in adult life, but this long-term effect was almost entirely mediated through the consequences of a planning tendency that made it more likely that the individuals would make a harmonious marriage to a non-deviant spouse. Again, this was a persistence over time that was reliant on indirect chain effects (Rutter, 1989).

The contrast between the institutional and comparison groups with respect to the impact of school experiences brings out another feature of turning point effects — namely, that the experience must have an opportunity to make a difference. The group homes in which the institutional children were placed had a deliberate policy of dispersing the children across a range of schools; accordingly, there was a marked (and unusual) dysjunction between home and school experiences. Furthermore, the children tended to have a limited number of good experiences, so that a set of really positive school experiences was likely to make an important impact. By contrast, the comparison group children probably had more positive experiences at home so that a few more at school was less crucial for them. Also, because their families had some choice in their selection of schools, there was likely to be less of a dysjunction between home and school.

Geographical moves

In some countries, inner cities are associated with higher rates of psychopathology in young people (see Chapter 7). To a substantial extent, this seems to be a consequence of adverse effects of city life on family life and relationships (Rutter & Quinton, 1977), although peer group and school influences may also be operative. West (1982) showed, in his longitudinal study of inner London boys, that a move of home away from the metropolis was followed by a reduction in delinquent behaviour as evident in both self-reports and official crime records. This effect was not explicable in terms of the characteristics of the boys before the move; moreover, moves within London were not associated in the same way with any change in delinquency. A study by Buikhuisen and Hoekstra (1974) showed somewhat similar effects. The mediating factors remain obscure; they could stem from the change of peer group, from altered school influences, from a different social ethos, from a reduction of stresses for the family or from reduced crime opportunities. However, whatever the explanation, some sort of beneficial turning point effect had been brought about by this lasting change of environment.

Teenage pregnancy and marriage

Many studies have shown that teenage pregnancy also constitutes a time of decision or opportunity when life trajectories may be directed on to more adaptive or maladaptive paths (Rutter & Rutter, 1993). Studies of working-class London women (Brown & Harris, 1986, 1989), of girls reared in group homes (Quinton & Rutter, 1988), of black girls in Baltimore (Furstenberg *et al.*, 1987), and of other groups (Hayes, 1987; Hofferth & Hayes, 1987; Werner & Smith, 1992) have all shown that, in general, teenage motherhood tends to predispose to a negative trajectory (very little is known about the effects of teenage fatherhood). However, this comes about through several rather different mechanisms, each of which is open to a variety of influences.

Five key factors warrant emphasis. First, there is an increase in the school drop-out rate, which leads to a below-average level of educational attainment, which in turn predisposes to later low occupational status. But, this is not inevitable. In the Baltimore study, nearly half completed high school and a significant minority returned to school some years later, with a few going on to college. Second, marriage to the father of the child often means marriage to someone from a disadvantaged background in an unskilled job because, at that stage of their lives, these are the sorts of youths in the girls' social group. Third, teenage marriage carries a much increased risk of later marital discord and marital breakdown (Burgoyne *et al.*, 1987; Hayes, 1987; Hofferth & Hayes, 1987), a risk that is probably greater in marriages precipitated by pregnancy.

The effects on marriage tend to be the most persistent of all effects of teenage pregnancy. In the Baltimore study (Furstenberg *et al.*, 1987), the 17-year follow-up showed that only 16% had remained married to the father of the child, and two-thirds were without a marriage partner. Similarly, in the Kauai longitudinal study, although the overall social outcome at 32 years of age for teenage mothers was better than it had been at either 18 or 26, most marriages had not fared well (Werner & Smith, 1992). Two-fifths had already been divorced (mostly 'messily' so); nearly half were unmarried; and of those who were married, over half were not happy in their relationship. It has also been found that the effects of teenage marriage persist into the second marriage (Martin & Bumpass, 1989). The divorce rate following second marriages in the late twenties and thirties of women who were teenagers at the time of their first marriage is greater than that for other women. The mechanisms involved in this effect are not known and, in particular, it is not clear whether they derive from characteristics of women who make a teenage marriage or from the consequences of marriage at that age.

Associated with these first three factors, teenage motherhood carries with it a substantial short-term and long-term economic penalty. Almost a quarter of the Baltimore women were on welfare at the 17-year follow-up (about 70% had been on welfare at some time), a much higher proportion than in comparable women who had not become teenage mothers (Furstenberg *et al.*, 1987).

Finally, teenage mothers are more likely than older mothers to go on to have further unintended births during the next few years, although both the Baltimore and Kauai studies showed that this tendency did not persist into later years.

The findings from longitudinal studies are consistent in showing that teenage pregnancy does indeed constitute a negative turning point that is more than just a consequence of the girls' prior characteristics and circumstances. On the other hand, the teenage pregnancy has usually come about in part as a result of the girls' own behaviour (not just in having sex but in not using contraception and in not having an abortion). Moreover, the sequelae are quite varied and also influenced by the girls' own actions. Some teenage mothers go on to advance their education, find employment, go off welfare, establish their own household and regulate their fertility. Positive outcomes seem most likely if there are good economic and social resources (including parental support and good role models); if the girls show good personal competence and motivation with high educational aspirations; if there are appropriate societal interventions aimed at postponing further births and completing schooling; and if there are appropriate career decisions and the making of a stable marriage, the last being apparently most likely if marriage is postponed until after completing schooling (Furstenberg *et al.*, 1987).

Army experiences

A perhaps somewhat surprising example of a turning point effect is provided by army experiences, which in certain circumstances can constitute an adaptive influence for some youths from a disadvantaged background (Elder, 1986). The Californian longitudinal data showed that socially disadvantaged youths with a poor scholastic record and feelings of self-inadequacy were particularly likely to enter the armed forces at an early age. Compared with similar youths who did not enter the army, their outcome in adult life was superior in terms of psychological features, occupational level and marital stability. The results indicated that army service did not necessarily bring gains; the effects tended to be disadvantageous for those who entered the forces at a later age. Many of these later entrants had already married, started families and established a career. For them, joining the army was quite disruptive, with any benefits outweighed by disadvantages.

Elder (1986) suggested that the marked benefits for disadvantaged youths joining the army in their teens came about through four main pathways. One involved the situational imperatives of the army situation that promoted independence from the disadvantaged background, provided exposure to new ideas and models, and allowed a legitimate 'time-out' for those who had not yet made up their mind what they wanted to do with their lives. A second pathway concerned the educational benefits that came with army service. Most of the young men were thoroughly disenchanted with school, where they tended to be failing. The different ethos of adult education encouraged many to continue their schooling, with the consequence that they finished up with better qualifications than their peers who did not join the forces. The third avenue stemmed from the fact that early entry into the army tended to delay marriage and starting a family, thus avoiding the disadvantage of teenage marriage and also widening the choice of marriage partners. A fourth route reflected the importance of social ties (brought about by joint training and combat) as an aid in coping with stress. As with other potential turning point experiences, the effects depended greatly on what the experiences meant to the individuals in their circumstances at the time.

Work

For obvious reasons, the psychological effects of work are strongly dependent on the particular qualities, stresses and rewards of the specific job. Nevertheless, the involuntary loss of work through unemployment is psychologically damaging for most people (Warr, 1987). Sampson and Laub (1993), in their reanalysis of the Glueck's longitudinal data, also showed that chronic job instability made it much more likely that childhood delinquency would be followed by adult criminality. Conversely, those delinquents who managed to gain a regular job, and who were committed to it, were less likely to continue in crime. It was argued that the quality and strength of social bonds inherent in work played a key role in the persistence or non-persistence of antisocial behaviour, the effect being greater than that associated with stressful life events.

Harmonious marriage

The last example of a turning point is provided by marriage, an event that may be considered as one likely to constitute an important transition because it involves the acceptance of a lasting personal commitment to another person, together with the taking on of financial, and potentially family, responsibilities (Rutter & Rutter, 1993). Nevertheless, it is obvious that the transition means very different things to different people, the variation depending on attitudes, timing and circumstances.

For some, marriage will entail a major change in life pattern and social group, but for others the transition will involve very little alteration in their style of life. Moreover, it may be expected that the impact of marriage on people's psychological functioning will be determined, in large part, by the qualities of the relationship and by the characteristics and values of the marriage partner.

For these reasons, it is of limited value to consider marriage as a homogeneous experience. Nevertheless, it does seem that, on the whole, married men are physically and mentally healthier than single men as if marriage served as a sort of protective factor (Gove & Tudor, 1973; Gove, 1978; Kreitman, 1988; Bebbington *et al.*, 1991). Of course, in order to test for that postulated effect properly, it would be necessary to have longitudinal data on intraindividual behavioural change across the transition to marriage (in order to check that the married versus single difference was not just a consequence of the adverse characteristics of those who remain single). Few published data are available as yet but these suggest that at least part of the difference may reflect the factors involved in the selection into marriage (Kiernan, 1988). The finding that the loss of a spouse through death or divorce tends to be followed by some worsening in health or development of psychological disturbance indicates that the *loss* of a marriage partner is a serious stress event for most people. That is consistent with the suggestion that the failure to gain a partner could also be disadvantageous. However, in that connection, it is important to note the important differences in pattern between men and women. It is clear that divorce is a source of stress in both sexes but it appears that the loss of income and increased parental responsibilities impinge more on women; loss of support is a factor in both sexes but it is more likely to apply to men (Gerstel *et al.*, 1985).

However, the most striking sex difference concerns the married–single comparison, where the pattern for females tends to be the reverse of that for males (i.e. single women tend to be somewhat physically and mentally healthier than married women) (Gove, 1978; Briscoe, 1982; Bebbington *et al.*, 1991). It is clear that this does *not* mean that a close, confiding, harmonious relationship is less important for women; if anything, the reverse is the case (Brown & Harris, 1978; Brown *et al.*,

1990). Rather, the probable explanation is that many marriages do not provide such a relationship for women and that marriage has other consequences (such as housework/child-care responsibilities and career difficulties) that are not entirely positive (McRae & Brody, 1989). These findings underline the point made earlier that it is important to consider transitions in terms of their actual impact and meaning for individuals, rather than assume that they constitute the same experience for everyone.

Accordingly, it may be more useful to focus on some of the specifics of marriages, such as the extent to which there is a harmonious, supportive, committed relationship, and the personal qualities of the spouse. West's (1982) follow-up in inner London boys showed that marriage *per se* made little difference to whether or not delinquent young men persisted in their criminal behaviour. On the other hand, whether or not the wife, too, was criminal did make a difference. Men who married criminal wives tended to continue in crime, whereas if the wife was law-abiding and not part of the delinquent subculture, marriage was associated with a significant reduction in the man's antisocial activities. Quinton and Rutter (1988), in their follow-up of institutionalized girls, found that the adult outcome was markedly better for those who made harmonious marriages to non-deviant men. Much the same applied to institution-reared men (Rutter *et al.*, 1990, 1994b; Zoccolillo *et al.*, 1992). In this study, marital harmony and non-deviance of the spouse were so closely associated that it was not possible to separate the effects of the two. However, Sampson and Laub (1993), in their follow-up of delinquent males, found that the main effect stemmed from the quality of the marriage relationship, rather than the deviance or otherwise of the spouse. There are too few studies for firm conclusions but the Sampson and Laub (1993) conclusion that the benefits stem from strong social bonds is reasonable, particularly if these are in the context of commitment to community values.

In each of these studies the analyses were able to demonstrate that the protective effect of a harmonious marriage to a non-deviant spouse was a true one, the effect remaining after appropriate adjustments were made for the prior characteristics of the individuals. Equally, however, it was evident that the likelihood of landing up with such a marriage was to some extent predictable. Both a disturbed family background, or institutional rearing, and antisocial behaviour made it more probable there would be a discordant marriage to a deviant spouse. Conversely, positive school experience and a tendency to show planning increased the chances that the person would make a harmonious marriage.

The findings illustrate the vicious cycles by which risk features are perpetuated, and also the extent to which such cycles are dependent on multiple links in a chain each of which provides an opportunity for it to be broken, together with the major impact on functioning of the qualities of the marriage relationship.

CONCLUSION

Traditionally, development has sometimes been viewed as a cumulative accretion of skills, based on an internal organismic process, determined by biological maturation, and coming to an end with the cessation of physical growth. The evidence shows that this constitutes a rather misleading picture of what development is all about. Skills are lost as well as gained, the losses coming about because they have served their purpose and are no longer needed (a process closely paralleled by the phases of neuronal proliferation and selective loss in brain development). Moreover, growth processes are much influenced by environmental input, with some dependent on such input. Organismic change does not stop when adult height is reached; for reasons deriving from both genetic programming and the impact of life experiences, development continues well into the adult years. Furthermore, developmental processes involve individuation as well as normative progression, and it is necessary to consider how such individual differences arise and are maintained or attenuated. It is clear that the biological expectation is for a complex mixture of continuities and discontinuities, stabilization and change and that each requires explanation.

Contrary to what might be anticipated, stressful and challenging experiences serve to emphasize and strengthen pre-existing characteristics (the 'accentuation principle'), rather than alter them. Stabilization also derives from the role of self-concepts and social cognitions in maintaining consistent patterns of interpersonal interaction; from continuities in environmental influences and from the ways in which individuals shape and select their environment, as well as from genetic patterning.

However, there are also important forces, both internal and external, that serve to bring about change. Thus, maturation involves a number of radical qualitative transformations (such as with the acquisition of language or reproductive capacity) that carry the potential for a degree of redirection in life trajectory. Turning points may also stem from experiences that involve a marked environmental discontinuity and in which the direction of change is of a type likely to influence development onto a path or direction that is different from that operating before the experience. Such experiences usually involve the shutting down or opening up of continuities, or a lasting change in environment, or a lasting effect on people's self-concepts or views and expectations of other people. In many cases, indirect as well as direct, chain effects are implicated and it is common for the processes to operate over quite prolonged periods of time. The findings, together with the concepts to which they give rise, have important implications for the types of intervention most likely to influence either the maintenance of desired, or reduction in undesired, behaviour.

REFERENCES

Alsaker F. (in press) Timing of puberty and reactions to pubertal change. In Rutter M. (ed.) *Psychosocial Disturbances in Young People: Challenges for Prevention.* Cambridge University Press, Cambridge.

Aslin R.N., Pisoni D.B. & Jusczyk P.W. (1983) Auditory development and speech perception in infancy. In Haith M.M. & Campos J.J. (eds) *Infancy and Developmental Psychobiology*, Vol. 2, *Mussen's Handbook of Child Psychology*, 4th edn, pp. 573–688. Wiley, New York.

Baltes P.B. & Baltes M.M. (eds) (1990) *Successful Aging: Perspectives from the Behavioural Sciences.* Cambridge University Press, Cambridge.

Bancroft J. & Reinisch J.M. (eds) (1990) *Adolescence and Puberty.* Oxford University Press, New York.

Baron-Cohen S., Tager-Flusberg H. & Cohen D. (eds) (1993) *Understanding Other Minds: Perspectives from Autism.* Oxford University Press, Oxford.

Bateson P. (1990) Is imprinting such a special case?

Philosophical Transactions of the Royal Society of London **329**, 125–131.

Bebbington P.E., Tennant C. & Hurry J. (1991) Adversity in groups with an increased risk of minor affective disorder. *British Journal of Psychiatry* **158**, 33–40.

Blakemore C. (1991) Sensitive and vulnerable periods in the development of the visual system. In Bock G.R. & Whelan J. (eds) *The Childhood Environment and Adult Disease*, pp. 129–146. Ciba Foundation Symposium No. 156. Wiley, Chichester.

Bock G.R. & Whelan J. (eds) (1991) *The Childhood Environment and Adult Disease*. Ciba Foundation Symposium No. 156. Wiley, Chichester.

Bretherton I. (1987) New perspectives on attachment relations: Security communications, and internal working models. In Osofsky J. (ed.) *Handbook of Infant Development*, 2nd edn, pp. 1061–1100. Wiley, New York.

Bretherton I. & Waters E. (eds) (1985) Growing points of attachment theory and research. *Monographs of the Society for Research in Child Development* **50**, Serial No. 209.

Briscoe M. (1982) *Sex Differences in Psychological Well-Being.* Psychological Medicine Monograph Supplement 1. Cambridge University Press, Cambridge.

Brown G.W., Andrews B., Bifulco A. & Veiel H. (1990a) Self-esteem and depression. I. Measurement issues and prediction of onset. *Social Psychiatry and Psychiatric Epidemiology* **25**, 200–209.

Brown G.W., Bifulco A., Veiel H. & Andrews B. (1990b) Self-esteem and depression. II. Social correlates of self-esteem. *Social Psychiatry and Psychiatric Epidemiology* **25**, 225–234.

Brown G.W., Bifulco A., Veiel H. & Andrews B. (1990c) Self-esteem and depression. III. Aetiological issues. *Social Psychiatry and Psychiatric Epidemiology* **25**, 235–243.

Brown G.W., Bifulco A., Veiel H. & Andrews B. (1990d) Self-esteem and depression. IV. Effect on course and recovery. *Social Psychiatry and Psychiatric Epidemiology* **25**, 244–249.

Brown G.W. & Harris T.O. (1978) *Social Origins of Depression: A Study of Psychiatric Disorder in Women.* Tavistock, London.

Brown G.W. & Harris T.O. (1986) Stressor, vulnerability and depression: A question of replication. *Psychological Medicine* **16**, 739–744.

Brown G.W. & Harris T.O. (1989) *Life Events and Illness.* Guilford, New York.

Buikhuisen W. & Hoekstra H.A. (1974) Factors relating to recidivism. *British Journal of Criminology* **14**, 63–69.

Burgoyne J., Ormrod R. & Richards M. (1987) *Divorce Matters*. Penguin, Harmondsworth.

Cadoret R.J., Troughton E., Merchant L.M. & Whitters A. (1990) Early life psychosocial events and adult affective symptoms. In Robins L. & Rutter M. (eds) *Straight and Devious Pathways from Childhood to Adulthood*,

pp. 300–313. Cambridge University Press, Cambridge.

Case R. & Edelstein W. (eds) (1993) *The New Structuralism in Cognitive Development: Theory and Research on Individual Pathways*. Karger, Basel.

Caspi A. & Bem D.J. (1990) Personality continuity and change across the life course. In Pervin L. (ed.) *Handbook of Personality*, pp. 549–575. Guilford, New York.

Caspi A. & Herbener E.S. (1990) Continuity and change: Assortative marriage and the consistency of personality in adulthood. *Journal of Personality and Social Psychology* **58**, 250–258.

Caspi A., Lynam D., Moffitt T.E. & Silva P.A. (1993) Unraveling girls' delinquency: Biological, dispositional, and contextual contributions to adolescent misbehavior. *Developmental Psychology* **29**, 19–30.

Caspi A. & Moffitt T.E. (1991) Individual differences are accentuated during periods of social change: The sample case of girls at puberty. *Journal of Personality and Social Psychology* **61**, 157–168.

Caspi A. & Moffitt T.E. (1993) When do individual differences matter? A paradoxical theory of personality coherence. *Psychological Inquiry* **4**, 247–271.

Champion L., Goodall G.M. & Rutter M. Behaviour problems in childhood and stressors in early adult life: A twenty year follow-up of London school children. (Submitted)

Clarke A.M. & Clarke A.D.B. (1976) *Early Experiences: Myth and Evidence*. Open Books, London.

Clausen J.S. (1991) Adolescent competence and the shaping of the life course. *American Journal of Sociology* **96**, 805–842.

Connolly K.J. & Prechtl H.F.R. (eds) (1981) *Maturation and Development: Biological and Psychological Perspectives*. Clinics in Developmental Medicine No. 77/78. SIMP/ Heinemann, London; Lippincott, Philadelphia.

Court J.A., Perry E.K., Johnson M. *et al.* (1994) Regional patterns of cholinergic and glutamate activity in the developing and aging human brain. *Developmental Brain Research*. (In press)

Cowan C.P., Cowan P.H., Hemming G. & Miller N.B. (1991) Becoming a family: Marriage, parenting, and child development. In Cowan P.A. & Hetherington M. (eds) *Family Transitions*, pp. 79–109. Lawrence Erlbaum, Hillsdale, New Jersey.

de Ribaupierre A. (ed.) (1989) *Transition Mechanisms in Child Development*. Cambridge University Press, Cambridge.

Demetriou A. (1987) The neo-Piagetian theories of cognitive development: Toward an integration. *International Journal of Psychology* **22**(5/6).

Dodge K.A., Coie J.D., Pettit G.S. & Price J.M. (1990) Peer status and aggression in boys' groups: Developmental and contextual analyses. *Child Development* **61**, 1289–1309.

Dunn J. (1988) *The Beginnings of Social Understanding*. Basil Blackwell, Oxford.

Earls F. (1994) Oppositional-defiant and conduct disorders. In Rutter M., Taylor E. & Hersov L. (eds) *Child and Adolescent Psychiatry: Modern Approaches*, 3rd edn, pp. 308–329. Blackwell Scientific Publications, Oxford.

Elder Jr G.H. (1984) Families, kin, and the life course: A sociological perspective. In R.D. Parke (ed.) *Review of Child Development Research*, Vol. 7. *The Family*, pp. 80–136. University of Chicago Press, Chicago.

Elder Jr G.H. (ed.) (1986) Military times and turning points in men's lives. *Developmental Psychology* **22**, 233–245.

Elder Jr G.H. (1991) Lives and social change. In Heinz W.R. (ed.) *Theoretical Advances in Life Course Research V*. Deutscher Studien Verlag, Weinheim.

Elder Jr G.H. & Caspi A. (1990) Studying lives in a changing society: Sociological and personalogical explorations. In Rabin A.I., Zucker R.A., Frank S. & Emmons R.A. (eds) *Studying Persons and Lives*. Springer, New York.

Farrington D.P. (1986) Age and crime. In Tonry M. & Morris N. (eds) *Crime and Justice*, Vol. 7. Chicago University Press, Chicago.

Farrington D.P. (1988) Studying changes within individuals: The causes of offending. In Rutter M. (ed.) *Studies of Psychosocial Risk: The Power of Longitudinal Data*, pp. 158–183. Cambridge University Press, Cambridge.

Farrington D.P., Gallagher B., Morley L., St Ledger R.J. & West D.J. (1986) Unemployment, school leaving and crime. *British Journal of Criminology* **26**, 335–356.

Feldman S.S. & Elliot G.R. (eds) (1990) *At the Threshold: The Developing Adolescent*. Harvard University Press, Cambridge, Massachusetts.

Fogelman K.R. & Goldstein H. (1976) Social factors associated with changes in educational attainment between 7 and 11 years of age. *Educational Studies* **2**, 95–109.

Frye D. (1993) Causes and precursors of children's theories of mind. In Hay D.F. & Angold A. (eds) *Precursors and Causes in Development and Psychopathology*, pp. 145–168. Wiley, Chichester.

Furstenberg Jr F.F., Brooks-Gunn S. & Morgan S.P. (1987) *Adolescent Mothers in Later Life*. Cambridge University Press, Cambridge.

Gelman R. & Baillargeon R. (1983) A review of some Piagetian concepts. In Flavell J.H. & Markman E.M. (eds) *Cognitive Development*, Vol. 3, *Mussen's Handbook of Child Psychology*, 4th edn, pp. 167–230. Wiley, New York.

Gerstel N., Riessman C.K. & Rosenfield S. (1985) Explaining the symptomatology of separated and divorced women and men: The role of material conditions and social networks. *Social Forces* **64**, 84–101.

Goldman-Rakic P.S., Isseroff A., Schwartz M.L. & Bugbee N.M. (1983) The neurobiology of cognitive development. In Haith M.M. & Campos J.J. (eds) *Infancy and Developmental Psychobiology*, Vol. 2, *Mussen's Handbook of Child Psychology*, 4th edn, pp. 281–344. Wiley, New York.

Goodyer I. (1990) *Life Experiences, Development and Childhood Psychopathology*. Wiley, Chichester.

Gove W.B. (1978) Sex differences in mental illness among adult men and women: An evaluation of four questions raised regarding the evidence on the higher rates of women. *Social Science and Medicine* **12B**, 187–198.

Gove W.B. & Tudor J.F. (1973) Adult sex roles and mental illness. *American Journal of Sociology* **78**, 812–835.

Gray G., Smith A. & Rutter M. (1980) School attendance and the first year of employment. In Hersov L. & Berg I. (eds) *Out of School: Modern Perspectives in Truancy and School Refusal*, pp. 343–370. Wiley, Chichester.

Greenough W.T., Black J.E. & Wallace C.S. (1987) Experience and brain development. *Child Development* **58**, 539–559.

Harrington R. (1994) Affective disorders. In Rutter M., Taylor E. & Hersov L. (eds) *Child and Adolescent Psychiatry: Modern Approaches*, 3rd edn, pp. 330–350. Blackwell Scientific Publications, Oxford.

Harter S. (1983) Development perspectives on the self-system. In Hetherington E.M. (ed.) *Socialization, Personality and Social Development*, Vol. 4, *Mussen's Handbook of Child Psychology*, 4th edn, pp. 275–385. Wiley, New York.

Hay D.F. (1980) Multiple functions of proximity-seeking in infancy. *Child Development* **51**, 636–645.

Hayes C.D. (ed.) (1987) *Risking the Future: Adolescent Sexuality, Pregnancy, and Childbearing*, Vol. 1. National Academy Press, Washington, DC.

Hennessy J.W. & Levine S. (1979) Stress, arousal and the pituitary-adrenal system: A psychoendocrine hypothesis. In Sprague J.M. & Epstein A.N. (eds) *Progress in Psychobiology and Physiological Psychology*. Academic Press, New York.

Herbert M. (1994) Behavioural methods. In Rutter M., Taylor E. & Hersov L. (eds) *Child and Adolescent Psychiatry: Modern Approaches*, 3rd edn, pp. 858–879. Blackwell Scientific Publications, Oxford.

Hess L.E. (1994) Changing family patterns in Western Europe: Opportunity and risk factors for adolescent development. In Rutter M. & Smith D. (eds) *Psychosocial Disorders of Youth: Time Trends and Their Origins*. Wiley, Chichester. (In press)

Hetherington E.M. & Clingempeel W.G. (1992) Coping with marital transitions. *Monographs of the Society for Research in Child Development* **57**(2–3), Serial No. 227.

Hinde R.A. (1983) Ethology and child development. In Haith M.M. & Campos J.J. (eds) *Infancy and Developmental Psychobiology*, Vol. 2, *Mussen's Handbook of Child Psychology*, 4th edn, pp. 27–94. Wiley, New York.

Hinde R.A. & Bateson P. (1985) Discontinuities versus continuities in behavioural sciences. *Philosophical Transactions of the Royal Society of London* **329**, 217–227.

Hodges J. & Tizard B. (1989a) IQ and behavioural adjustments of ex-institutional adolescents. *Journal of Child Psychology and Psychiatry* **30**, 53–75.

Hodges J. & Tizard B. (1989b) Social and family relationships of ex-institutional adolescents. *Journal of Child Psychology and Psychiatry* **30**, 77−97.

Hofferth S.L. & Hayes C.D. (eds) (1987) *Risking the Future: Adolescent Sexuality, Pregnancy, and Childbearing*, Vol. 2, *Working Papers and Statistical Appendixes*. National Academy Press, Washington, DC.

Horn G. (1990) Neural bases of recognition memory investigated through an analysis of imprinting. *Philosophical Transactions of the Royal Society of London* **329**, 133−142.

Howe M.L. & Courage M.L. (1993) On resolving the enigma of infantile amnesia. *Psychological Bulletin* **113**, 305−326.

Howlin P. & Rutter M. (1987) The consequences of language delay for other aspects of development. In Yule W. & Rutter M. (eds) *Language Development and Disorders*, pp. 271−295. Blackwell Scientific Publications, Oxford.

Hymel S., Wagner E. & Butler L. (1990) Reputational bias: View from the peer group. In Asher S.R. & Coie J.D. (eds) *Peer Rejection in Childhood*, pp. 156−186. Cambridge University Press, Cambridge.

Kagan J. (1980) Perspectives on continuity. In Brim O. & Kagan J. (eds) *Constancy and Change in Human Development*. Harvard University Press, Cambridge, Massachusetts.

Kagan J. (1981) *The Second Year: The Emergence of Self-Awareness*. Harvard University Press, Cambridge, Massachusetts.

Kagan J. (1984) *The Nature of the Child*. Basic Books, New York.

Kiernan, K.E. (1988) Who remains celibate? *Journal of Behavioural Science* **20**, 253−263.

Klein R.G. (1994) Anxiety disorders: Developmental patterns of childhood fears and anxiety. In Rutter M., Taylor E. & Hersov L. (eds) *Child and Adolescent Psychiatry: Modern Approaches*, 3rd edn, pp. 351−374. Blackwell Scientific Publications, Oxford.

Kreitman N. (1988) Suicide, age and marital status. *Psychological Medicine* **8**, 711−715.

Leffert N. & Petersen A.C. (1994) Issues in adolescence. In Rutter M. & Smith D. (eds) *Psychosocial Disorders of Youth: Time Trends and their Origins*. Wiley, Chichester. (In press)

Levinson D.J. (1978) *The Seasons of a Man's Life*. Knopf, New York.

Loehlin J.C. (1992) *Genes and Environment in Personality Development*. Sage, Newbury Park, California.

McCrae R.R. & Costa Jr P.T. (1990) *Personality in Adulthood*. Guilford, New York.

McRae Jr J.A. & Brody C.J. (1989) The differential importance of marital experiences for the well-being of women and men: A research note. *Social Science Research* **18**, 237−248.

Martin T.C. & Bumpass L.L. (1989) Recent trends in marital disruption. *Demography*, **26**, 37−51.

Matheny Jr A.P. (1990) Developmental behaviour genetics: Contributions from the Louisville twin study. In Hahn M.E., Hewitt J.K., Henderson N.D. & Benno R. (eds) *Developmental Behavior Genetics: Neural Biometrical, and Evolutionary Approaches*, pp. 25−39. Oxford University Press, New York.

Maughan B. & Yule W. (1994) Reading and other learning difficulties. In Rutter M., Taylor E. & Hersov L. (eds) *Child and Adolescent Psychiatry: Modern Approaches*, 3rd edn, pp. 647−665. Blackwell Scientific Publications, Oxford.

Meyer J.M., Eaves L.J., Heath A.C. & Martin N.G. (1991) Estimating genetic influences on the age at menarche: A survival analysis approach. *American Journal of Medical Genetics* **39**, 148−154.

Michaels G.Y. & Goldberg W.A. (1988) *The Transition to Parenthood: Current Theory and Research*. Cambridge University Press, Cambridge.

Mineka S. (1985) Animal models of anxiety-based disorders: Their usefulness and limitations. In Tuma A. & Maser J. (eds) *Theoretical Foundations of Behavior Therapy*, pp. 81−111. Plenum, New York.

Nash A. & Hay D.F. (1993) Relationships in infancy as precursors and causes of later relationships and psychopathology. In Hay D.F. & Angold A. (eds) *Precursors and Causes in Development and Psychopathology*, pp. 199−232. Wiley, Chichester.

Offer D. (1969) *The Psychological World of the Teenager*. Basic Books, London.

O'Leary K.D. & Wilson F. (1987) *Behaviour Therapy: Application and Outcome*, 2nd edn. Prentice-Hall, Englewood Cliffs, New Jersey.

Oller D.K. & Eilers R.E. (1988) The role of audition in infant babbling. *Child Development* **59**, 441−449.

Paikoff R.L. & Brooks-Gunn J. (1991) Do parent−child relationships change during puberty? *Psychological Bulletin* **110**, 47−68.

Parkes C.M. (1986) *Bereavement: Studies of Grief in Adult Life*, 2nd edn. Tavistock Publications, London.

Piaget J. (1983) Piaget's theory. In W. Kessen (ed.) *History, Theory, and Methods*, Vol. 1, *Mussen's Handbook of Child Psychology*, 4th edn, pp. 103−129. Wiley, New York.

Pickles A., Crouchley R., Simonoff E. *et al.* (in press) Survival models for developmental genetic data: Age of onset of puberty and anti-social behavior in twins. *Genetic Epidemiology*.

Pickles A. & Rutter M. (1991) Statistical and conceptual models of 'turning points' in developmental processes. In Magnusson D., Bergman L.R., Rudinger G. & Törestadd B. (eds) *Problems and Methods in Longitudinal Research: Stability and Change*, pp. 133−165. Cambridge University Press, Cambridge.

Plomin R. (1986) *Development, Genetics and Psychology*. Lawrence Erlbaum, Hillsdale, New Jersey.

Plomin R. (1994) *Genetics and Experience*. Sage, Newbury Park, California.

Quinton D., Pickles A., Maughan B. & Rutter M. (1993)

Partners, peers and pathways: Assortative pairing and continuities in conduct disorder. *Development and Psychopathology* **5**, 763−783.

Quinton D. & Rutter M. (1988) *Parenting Breakdown: The Making and Breaking of Inter-Generational Links*. Avebury, Aldershot.

Rachman S. (1977) The conditioning theory of fear-acquisition: A critical examination. *Behaviour Research and Therapy* **15**, 375−388.

Raphael B. (1984) *The Anatomy of Bereavement: A Handbook for the Caring Professions*. Hutchinson, London.

Richman N., Stevenson J. & Graham P. (1982) *Pre-school to School: A Behavioural Study*. Academic Press, London.

Rindfuss R.R., Swicegood C.G. & Rosenfeld R.A. (1987) Disorder in the life course. *American Sociological Review* **52**, 785−801.

Robins L. (1966) *Deviant Children Grown Up*. Williams & Wilkins, Baltimore.

Robins L. (1978) Sturdy childhood predictors of adult antisocial behaviour: Replications from longitudinal studies. *Psychological Medicine* **8**, 611−622.

Robins L. (1986) The consequences of conduct disorder in girls. In Olweus D., Block J. & Radke-Yarrow M. (eds) *Development of Antisocial and Prosocial Behaviour: Research, Theories, and Issues*, pp. 385−414. Academic Press, Orlando.

Robins L.N. & McEvoy L. (1990) Conduct problems as predictors of substance abuse. In Robins L. & Rutter M. (eds) *Straight and Devious Pathways from Childhood to Adulthood*, pp. 182−205. Cambridge University Press, Cambridge.

Rodgers B. (1990) Influences of early-life and recent factors on affective disorder in women: An exploration of vulnerability models. In Robins L. & Rutter M. (eds) *Straight and Devious Pathways from Childhood to Adulthood*, pp. 314−328. Cambridge University Press, Cambridge.

Rowe D.C. & Gulley B.L. (1992) Sibling effects on substance use and delinquency. *Criminology* **30**, 217−233.

Rutter M. (1971) Parent−child separation: Psychological effects on the children. *Journal of Child Psychology and Psychiatry* **12**, 233−260.

Rutter M. (1979a) *Changing Youth in a Changing Society: Patterns of Adolescent Development and Disorder*. Nuffield Provincial Hospital Trust, London.

Rutter M. (1979b) Separation experiences: A new look at an old topic. *Journal of Pediatrics* **95**, 147−154.

Rutter M. (1981) *Maternal Deprivation Reassessed*, 2nd edn. Penguin, Harmondsworth.

Rutter M. (1984) Psychopathology and development: II. Childhood experiences and personality development. *Australian and New Zealand Journal of Psychiatry* **18**, 314−327.

Rutter M. (1986) Meyerian psychobiology, personality development and the role of life experience. *American Journal of Psychiatry* **143**, 1077−1087.

Rutter M. (1987a) Continuities and discontinuities

from infancy. In Osofsky J. (ed.) *Handbook of Infant Development*, 2nd edn, pp. 1256−1296. Wiley, New York.

Rutter M. (1987b) The role of cognition in child development and disorder. *British Journal of Medical Psychology* **60**, 1−16.

Rutter M. (1989) Pathways from childhood to adult life. *Journal of Child Psychology and Psychiatry* **30**, 23−51.

Rutter M. (1994a) Causal concepts and their testing. In Rutter M. & Smith D. (eds) *Psychosocial Disorders in Young People: Time Trends and their Origins*. Wiley, Chichester. (In press)

Rutter M. (1994b) Concepts of causation and implications for intervention. In Petersen A. & Mortimer J. (eds) *Youth Unemployment and Society*. Cambridge University Press, Cambridge.

Rutter M. Transitions and turning points in development. (Submitted)

Rutter M., Chadwick O. & Shaffer D. (1983) Head injuries. In Rutter M. (ed.) *Developmental Neuropsychology*, pp. 83−111. Guilford Press, New York.

Rutter M., Champion L., Quinton D., Maughan B. & Pickles A. (1994a) Origins of individual differences in environmental risk exposure. In Moen P., Elder G. & Luscher K. (eds) *Perspectives on the Ecology of Human Development*. Cornell University Press, Ithaca. (In press)

Rutter M. & Garmezy N. (1983) Developmental psychopathology. In Hetherington E.M. (ed.) *Socialization, Personality, and Social Development*, Vol. 4, *Mussen's Handbook of Child Psychology*, 4th edn, pp. 775−911. Wiley, New York.

Rutter M., Harrington R., Quinton D. & Pickles A. (1994b) Adult outcome of depressive and conduct disorders in childhood. In Ketterlinus R. & Lamb M. (eds) *Adolescent Problem Behaviours*. Lawrence Erlbaum, Hillsdale, New Jersey. (In press)

Rutter M. & Madge N. (1976) *Cycles of Disadvantage: A Review of Research*. Heinemann, London.

Rutter M. & Mawhood L. (1991) The long-term psychosocial sequelae of specific developmental disorders of speech and language. In Rutter M. & Casaer P. (eds) *Biological Risk Factors for Psychosocial Disorders*, pp. 233−259. Cambridge University Press, Cambridge.

Rutter M. & Quinton D. (1977) Psychiatric disorder − Ecological factors and concepts of causation. In McGurk H. (ed.) *Ecological Factors in Human Development*, pp. 173−187. North-Holland, Amsterdam.

Rutter M., Quinton D. & Hill J. (1990) Adult outcome of institution-reared children: Males and females compared. In Robins L. & Rutter M. (eds) *Straight and Devious Pathways from Childhood to Adulthood*, pp. 135−157. Cambridge University Press, Cambridge.

Rutter M. & Rutter M. (1993) *Developing Minds: Challenge and Continuity Across the Lifespan*. Penguin, Harmondsworth; Basic Books, New York.

Sampson R.J. & Laub J.H. (1993) *Crime in the Making:*

Pathways and Turning Points Through Life. Harvard University Press, Cambridge, Massachusetts.

Scarr S. (1992) Developmental theories for the 1990s: Development and individual differences. *Child Development* **63**, 1–19.

Schachtel E.G. (1947) On memory and childhood amnesia. *Psychiatry* **10**, 1–26.

Scott S. (1994) Mental retardation. In Rutter M., Taylor E. & Hersov L. (eds) *Child and Adolescent Psychiatry: Modern Approaches*, 3rd edn, pp. 616–646. Blackwell Scientific Publications, Oxford.

Segal Z.V. & Dobson K.S. (1992) Target article: Cognitive models of depression: Report from a consensus development conference (plus commentaries). *Psychological Inquiry* **3**, 219–282.

Sherif M., Harvey O.J., White B.J., Hood W.R. & Sherif C.W. (1961) *Intergroup Conflict and Cooperation: The Robbers' Cave Experiment*. University of Oklahoma Press, Norman, Oklahoma.

Smith P.K. (ed.) (1991) *The Psychology of Grandparenthood: An International Perspective*. Routledge, London.

Stanton A.L. & Dunkel-Schetter C. (eds) (1991) *Infertility: Perspectives From Stress and Coping Research*. Plenum, New York.

Stattin H. & Magnusson D. (1990) *Pubertal Maturation in Female Development*. Lawrence Erlbaum, Hillsdale, New Jersey.

Tanner J.M. (1989) *Foetus into Man: Physical Growth from Conception to Maturity*, 2nd edn. Castlemead Publications, Ware.

Tulving E. (1983) *Elements of Episodic Memory*. Oxford University Press, Oxford.

Vaillant G.E. (1983) *The Natural History of Alcoholism*. Harvard University Press, Cambridge, Massachusetts.

Vaillant G.E. (1990) Avoiding negative life outcomes: Evidence from a forty-five year study. In Baltes P.B. & Baltes M.M. (eds) *Successful Aging: Perspectives From The Behavioural Sciences*, pp. 332–358. Cambridge University Press, Cambridge.

Warr P. (1987) *Work, Unemployment and Mental Health*. Clarendon Press, Oxford.

Werner E.E. & Smith R.S. (1992) *Overcoming the Odds: High Risk Children from Birth to Adulthood*. Cornell University Press, Ithaca.

Werry J. & Taylor E. (1994) Schizophrenia and allied disorders. In Rutter M., Taylor E. & Hersov L. (eds) *Child and Adolescent Psychiatry: Modern Approaches*, 3rd edn, pp. 594–615. Blackwell Scientific Publications, Oxford.

West D. (1982) *Delinquency: Its Roots, Careers and Prospects*. Heinemann, London.

Wortman C.R. & Silver R.C. (1990) Successful mastery of bereavement and widowhood: A life-course perspective. In Baltes P.B. & Baltes M.M. (eds) *Successful Aging: Perspectives From the Behavioural Sciences*, pp. 225–264. Cambridge University Press, Cambridge.

Zoccolillo M., Pickles A., Quinton D. & Rutter M. (1992) The outcome of childhood conduct disorder: Implications for defining adult personality disorder and conduct disorder. *Psychological Medicine* **22**, 971–986.

2: Genetic Influences on Behavioural Development

RICHARD D. RENDE AND ROBERT PLOMIN

INTRODUCTION

The literature documenting genetic influence on human behaviour began in the 1920s and progressed slowly but steadily until the 1970s. As extreme environmentalism died, the pace of behavioural genetic research quickened. The pace continued to accelerate during the 1980s and promises to rocket as it becomes fuelled by the new genetics of molecular biology. Genetic influence has been documented for many fundamental domains of human development, especially cognitive abilities and personality, and for psychopathological conditions, especially schizophrenia and bipolar illness. Indeed, a challenge for research is to find behavioural domains that are not influenced to some degree by heredity.

At the outset, it should be noted that clinicians have no reason to fear or dislike genetic research. The concern often expressed by clinicians is that if a disorder is shown to be genetic there is nothing that can be done about it. To the contrary, finding genetic influence by no means implies that a disorder is immutable. As discussed later, genetic effects on psychopathology involve multiple-gene propensities rather than the hard-wired determinism of classical single-gene effects that operate as necessary and sufficient causes of a disorder, such as the gene for Huntington's disease that invariably leads to neural degeneration and death. Even in the case of single-gene disorders, cures are not necessarily related to causes. Rather than waiting in the hope that genetic engineering will one day correct defective DNA, a more feasible strategy is to devise rational treatment programmes based on knowledge of the genetic deficit, as in the classic example of low phenylalanine diets used to prevent children with phenylketonuria from becoming retarded.

Two other points are relevant to this issue. In the absence of single-gene effects that drastically disrupt development, the phrase *genetic influence* refers to genetic differences among individuals in a particular population at a particular time that contribute to variance in the population with that population's particular mix of genetic and environmental variance. Quantitative genetics describes 'what is' in a population but does not predict 'what could be' (and certainly does not prescribe 'what should be'). That is, finding substantial genetic influence for a particular trait implies that existing environmental variation does not importantly affect the trait, but by no means does it imply that novel environmental events not represented in the population's environmental variation could not have a major effect. For example, high heritability of tooth decay did not prevent the intervention of fluoridation of water from dramatically reducing tooth decay. In the same way, finding genetic influence for a psychiatric disorder does not proscribe prevention and intervention.

Understanding these points leads some clinicians to go to the other extreme to conclude that it makes no difference when faced with a suffering patient whether the disorder arose from genetic or environmental causes. It is the case that cures are not necessarily related to causes, and that quantitative genetic parameter estimates represent population averages, which means that their relevance to an individual case is only probabilistic. Nonetheless, it seems naive to ignore information about the origins of a psychiatric disorder, just as it would be naive for a physician not to care about the origins of an illness even if the acute treatment for the illness does not depend on its origins. Knowing the origins of a disorder is particularly useful in terms of prevention rather than acute intervention. For example, most clinicians would acknowledge that their approach to clients concerning alcohol abuse would differ depending on whether the disorder were highly heritable or not. If alcoholism or a subtype of alcoholism were highly heritable, an individual with a family history of alcoholism would be at considerable risk for alcohol abuse given our alcohol-diffused society. Ignoring family history and the warning signs of incipient alcohol abuse or treating an acute episode of alcohol abuse without regard to this larger issue would do a disservice to the patient. As a test on this point, consider whether your attitude towards treatment of alcohol abuse would be affected by the following information. Although alcoholism has come to be seen as a genetic disorder, new data and re-examination of older data question whether there is any genetic influence at all on alcoholism (e.g. McClearn & Plomin, in press).

Finally, it should be emphasized that behavioural genetic research provides the best available evidence for the importance of the environment. Genetic influence is often substantial but rarely accounts for more than half of the variance of behavioural dimensions and disorders. A decade ago, the important message from behavioural genetics was that, contrary to the environmentalism that dominated behavioural thinking, genetic influence was indeed an important source of variability among individuals. Now, however, the rush of the behavioural sciences away from environmentalism may be going too far, to a view that all behaviour is biologically determined. The message for the 1990s, based on the same behavioural genetic results, is that non-genetic factors are also important. Behavioural dimensions and disorders typically yield heritabilities substantially less than 100%, and usually less than 50%. Moreover, genetic research provides important insights into the mechanisms of environmental action. Two recent examples are the importance of environmental influences that are not shared by family members and genetic influence on widely used measures of the environment, topics discussed later in this chapter.

This chapter focuses on some specific themes that are especially important for the study of genetic influences on development and psychopathology. Our aim is not to summarize the major findings of human behavioural genetic research (see Plomin

et al., 1990a for an overview of the field; Vandenberg *et al.*, 1986 for an overview of psychiatric genetics; Rutter *et al.*, 1990b for a review of child psychiatric disorders; and Gottesman, 1991 for a review of schizophrenia research). Rather, we are interested in going beyond the basic nature–nurture question, which asks whether there is genetic influence. The chapter begins with an examination of the behavioural consequences of known genetic conditions as an introduction to the study of genetic influence on behaviour; then reviews the basic methods and designs used in quantitative genetic research, and provides a brief overview of major findings of behavioural genetic studies of psychopathology. Following this, four specific topics that go beyond the basic nature–nurture question will be considered: (i) the study of dimensions and disorders; (ii) multivariate genetic methods; (iii) longitudinal genetic analysis; and (iv) quantitative genetic approaches to the environment. A final section discusses a most important theme for future research: the merging of molecular and quantitative genetics.

BEHAVIOURAL CONSEQUENCES OF GENETIC CONDITIONS

Using maladaptation to reveal processes involved in development has been a tradition in the field of genetics. For example, examinations of inborn errors of metabolism led to the 'one-gene, one-enzyme' hypothesis that is the basic mechanism of normal gene action (Beadle & Tatum, 1941). Similarly, taking known genetic conditions and examining their behavioural consequences provides an important method for revealing genetic influence on behaviour (Rende & Plomin, 1990; Reiss & Freund, 1990).

Thousands of single-gene disorders have been compiled by McKusick (1990) and many of these display behavioural effects. Similarly, many chromosomal abnormalities are known that show pervasive behavioural consequences (Plomin *et al.*, 1990b). We will use as an example a genetic condition which has received much attention by researchers in the past few years: the fragile X syndrome. Fragile X refers to an observable break (or fragile site) in the structure of the X chromosome when cells are examined under specific culture conditions. It should be noted that the fragile X syndrome demonstrates a pattern of inheritance that is unusual for X-linked diseases (Hoffman, 1991). What is important from a clinical perspective is that although other fragile sites on other human chromosomes have been observed, specific clinical symptoms have been associated only with the fragile X site (Sutherland & Hecht, 1985).

Diverse phenotypic characteristics are associated with the fragile X syndrome. Fragile X is recognized as the second most frequent cause (surpassed only by Down's syndrome) of inherited mental retardation; it is found in 5–10% of retarded individuals (e.g. Turner *et al.*, 1986). Retardation is usually a consequence for males with the fragile X marker, whereas the consequences for females are more variable. In addition to general retardation, specific cognitive deficits have been reported. For example, deficits in visuospatial skills and sequential processing abilities have been noted, and speech characteristics may also be affected (see Reiss & Freund, 1990 for an overview). Additionally, it has been suggested that fragile X males also experience a decline in IQ throughout middle childhood (Lachiewicz *et al.*, 1987).

In addition to cognitive deficits, several other phenotypic characteristics associated with fragile X have been documented in recent years (Hagerman & Sobesky, 1989). For males, additional forms of disturbance include hyperactivity, attentional deficits and anxiety (Bregman *et al.*, 1988); females have been reported to show increased schizotypal and affective symptomatology (Reiss & Freund, 1990). Additionally, links between the fragile X marker and autistic behaviour have been suggested for males, including deficits in social interaction, stereotyped behaviour, atypical speech and language and abnormal non-verbal communication (Bregman *et al.*, 1988; Reiss & Freund, 1990).

How is the study of the fragile X condition important for our understanding of genetic influences on behavioural development? One consideration is that fragile X demonstrates that a single genetic factor can influence a vast array of behavioural domains, including cognition and language as well as psychopathological characteristics such as atypical personality and affective symptoms. Indeed, the diversity of domains affected reveals an important principle in genetics: behavioural consequences of localized genetic sites (such as the fragile site on the X chromosome) are not likely to be limited to a single circumscribed area of functioning. The specificity of gene action implied by the 'one-gene, one-enzyme' hypothesis does not imply 'one-gene, one-behaviour'. In genetics, this principle is referred to as pleiotropy, the manifold effects of genes.

Another consideration is that fragile X and other single-gene disorders hold out the promise of identifying the specific mechanisms by which genes have their diffuse effect on behaviour. For fragile X, the recent discovery of the genetic site of the fragile X mutation will intensify this search (Oberle *et al.*, 1991; Yu *et al.*, 1991). Knowing the molecular basis of the fragile X mutation may eventually reveal not only the specific gene product responsible for the mutation, but also the biological pathways that result in the behavioural symptoms associated with the fragile X site (Reiss & Freund, 1990). That is, in the future it may be possible to determine how this genetic condition affects neural development as well as to pinpoint specific areas in the brain that underlie the behavioural consequences of fragile X.

Although studying known genetic conditions represents an important method for assessing genetic influences on behaviour, research in psychopathology most often takes on a different task: to begin with a behavioural condition of interest (e.g. schizophrenia, depression, hyperactivity), and then to determine if genetics plays a role in the behaviour. If known single genes such as fragile X affect diverse behaviours (the principle of pleiotropy), it is likely that a specific behavioural characteristic is affected by multiple genes, each with small effect. For this reason, genetic strategies such as linkage that can only identify a gene if the gene is the necessary and sufficient cause of a disorder are not likely to be successful in genetic analyses of behaviour, a topic to which we return towards the end of the chapter. Moreover, substantial non-genetic influence is invariably important in the development of complex behavioural dimensions and disorders. Quantitative genetic strategies that consider multiple-gene influence as well as non-genetic influence provide a reasonable first step for documenting genetic influence on behaviour and, as we shall emphasize, for going beyond this basic nature–nurture issue.

QUANTITATIVE GENETICS

Human behavioural genetics began over a century ago with Darwin's cousin, Francis Galton. Reading Darwin's *On the Origin of Species*, Galton was inspired to devote the rest of his life to the investigation of the inheritance of human behaviour. At the turn of the century when Mendel's laws of inheritance were rediscovered, a bitter argument erupted between Mendelians and Galtonians. The Mendelians looked for discontinuous traits such as disorders and Mendelian segregation ratios that implicate the transmission of a single gene responsible for a disorder. The Galtonians, also called biometricians, at first argued that Mendel's laws were not applicable to complex traits because such traits are distributed continuously as dimensions. The resolution of the controversy, and the birth of quantitative genetics, came from the realization that a continuous distribution would emerge for a trait if several genes affect the trait.

Despite the resolution of the controversy, which was generally accepted before 1920, the two genetic approaches went their different ways. The Galtonians moved outwards from the gene towards the functioning of the whole organism, developed quantitative genetic strategies for animal and human research, and documented the important role of heritable genetic factors for complex traits including behavioural dimensions and disorders. The Mendelians moved inwards towards the gene at the cellular level, primarily using mutational analysis, and eventually developed the molecular genetic tools known as the new genetics.

An exciting prospect for the 1990s is that these two traditions will come back together as molecular genetic techniques are used to identify multiple specific genes that affect quantitative variation in complex phenotypes such as behavioural dimensions and disorders. This section begins with a brief overview of quantitative genetic theory and methods as applied to behaviour and then considers possibilities for harnessing the power of the new genetics to address quantitative genetic analyses of behaviour. Details concerning behavioural genetic methods are available in texts (e.g. Plomin *et al.*, 1990b) and in a recent discussion focused on child psychiatry (Rutter *et al.*, 1990a).

Quantitative genetic methods assess genetic influence even when many genes and substantial environmental variation affect a disorder or dimension. Applied behavioural genetics began thousands of years ago when animals were bred for their behaviour as much as for their morphology. The results of such artificial selection can be seen most dramatically in differences in behaviour as well as physique among dog breeds, differences that testify to the great range of genetic variability within a species and its effect on behaviour. Selection studies in the laboratory still provide the most convincing demonstrations of genetic influence on behaviour. For example, in one of the longest mammalian selection studies of behaviour, replicated high and low lines were selected for activity in a brightly lit open field, an aversive situation thought to assess emotional reactivity (DeFries *et al.*, 1978). After 30 generations of selection, a 30-fold difference exists between the activity of the high and low lines, with no overlap between them. It is noteworthy that such selection studies of behaviour typically yield steady divergence of selected lines fter many generations. These data provide the best available evidence that many genes affect behaviour. If only one or two major genes were responsible for genetic effects on behaviour, the relevant alleles would be sorted into the high and low lines in a few generations.

Other methods that have been used to demonstrate ubiquitous genetic influences on animal behaviour include family studies and studies of inbred strains. Family studies assess the *sine qua non* of transmissible genetic influence, resemblance between genetically related individuals. More so than in human studies, the family method suggests genetic sources of resemblance amongst family members because individuals are reared in the same laboratory conditions. Inbred strains are created by mating brother to sister for at least 20 generations. This severe inbreeding eliminates heterozygosity and results in animals that are virtually identical genetically. Behavioural differences between inbred strains reared under the same laboratory conditions can be ascribed to genetic differences. An especially powerful inbred strain method involves recombinant inbred (RI) strains which are multiple inbred strains derived from the same genetically segregating cross between two progenitor inbred strains (Bailey, 1971; Taylor, 1989).

Although RI strains were developed to identify and map single-gene effects, they are also valuable for identifying associations between behaviour and genes that account for relatively small amounts of variation in behaviour (Plomin *et al.*, 1991a).

For human behaviour, no quantitative genetic methods as powerful as selection or inbred strain studies exist. Human behavioural genetic research relies on family, adoption and twin designs. As in studies of non-human animals, family studies assess the extent of resemblance for genetically related individuals, although they cannot disentangle possible environmental sources of resemblance. That is the point of adoption studies. Genetically related individuals adopted apart provide evidence of the degree to which familial resemblance is due to hereditary resemblance. This is like a natural experiment in which family members share heredity but not environment. The flip side of the adoption design tests the influence of nature by studying the resemblance of genetically unrelated individuals living together in adoptive families. The concern with this experiment is that nature and nurture are not neatly cleaved if selective placement occurs in which children are placed with adoptive parents who resemble the birth parents. However, the extent of selective placement can be assessed empirically.

Twin studies are also like natural experiments in which the resemblance of identical twins, whose genetic identity can be expressed as genetic relatedness of 1.0, is compared to the resemblance of fraternal twins, first-degree relatives whose coefficient of genetic relatedness is 0.50. If heredity affects a behavioural trait, identical twins will resemble each other on the trait to a greater extent than will fraternal twins. The concern with the twin experiment is the possibility that identical twins experience more similar environments than fraternal twins and thus the greater similarity of identical twins as compared to fraternal twins may be mediated in part by environmental factors. This issue, referred to as the equal environments assumption of the twin method, is discussed in detail elsewhere (Plomin *et al.*, 1990b).

Genetic designs exist other than the classical adoption and twin designs. For example, a variant of the adoption design is the cross-fostering design in which adopted children are reared by parents

with the disorder under study. Variations of the classical twin design include the families-of-identical-twins design, cotwin control studies in which members of identical twin pairs are treated differently, and studies of discordant identical twin pairs. Combinations of designs are particularly important to triangulate on estimates of quantitative genetic parameters. For example, family and adoption designs can be combined by including non-adoptive or control families in which family members (siblings as well as parents and offspring) share both heredity and family environment in addition to adoptive families. Twin and adoption designs can be combined by studying twins reared apart as well as control twins reared together. Analysis of research employing such multiple groups is facilitated by model-fitting techniques which are discussed below.

Behavioural genetic methods can assess the statistical significance and the magnitude of the genetic effect. Heritability is a descriptive statistic that assigns an effect size to genetic influence. For example, the correlation for identical twins reared apart in uncorrelated environments directly estimates heritability. This correlation represents the proportion of variance that covaries for identical twins who share all their heredity but not their rearing environments. If hereditary influence were unimportant, their correlation would be low; their correlation would be high if heredity was primarily responsible for phenotypic variance. Although behavioural scientists reflexively square correlations to estimate variance — and this is appropriate to estimate the amount of variance in one trait that can be predicted by another trait — correlations for family members such as the correlation for identical twins reared apart represent components of variance and are not squared. Thus, a correlation of 0.40 for reared-apart identical twins implies that heritability is 40%. That is, genetic variance accounts for 40% of the observed variance in the population.

Model-fitting techniques are routinely used in behavioural genetic analyses to estimate heritability because they test a model, make assumptions explicit, analyse data from multiple groups simultaneously, provide standard errors of estimate, and make it possible to compare the fit of alternative models. Model-fitting essentially involves solving a series of simultaneous equations. For example, the twin method consists of two equations that express the observed correlations for identical and fraternal twins in terms of two unknowns that represent expected components of variance (1.0 G + E for identical twins and 0.5 G + E for fraternal twins). The solution to these two equations with two unknowns merely involves doubling the difference between the identical and fraternal twin correlations to estimate G; E is estimated as the residual twin similarity not explained by G. As data for other family groups are added, more equations are available which makes it possible to solve for more parameters and to compare alternative models. An excellent introduction to model-fitting that includes behavioural genetic model-fitting is available (Loehlin, 1987). Three recent behavioural genetics books include introductions to model-fitting in quantitative genetic analysis (Plomin *et al.*, 1988b, 1990b; Eaves *et al.*, 1989), and a special issue of the journal *Behavior Genetics* is devoted to LISREL model-fitting analyses of twin data (Boomsma *et al.*, 1989).

As mentioned at the outset of this chapter, quantitative genetics is limited to describing observed variation between individuals in a population and ascribing these phenotypic differences to genetic and environmental sources of variability. This focus on variance leads to several limitations. First, universal genetic and environmental factors may be critical for development but they cannot be detected by quantitative genetic methods unless these factors create observable differences between individuals. For example, genes are undoubtedly responsible for bipedalism and binocular vision but because these are essentially non-varying characteristics of the human species, quantitative genetics will not detect such universal genetic influences. Similarly, light, food and oxygen are essential for development but quantitative genetics can only assess the extent to which variation in such environmental factors creates variability among individuals. In terms of disease, if all individuals were exposed to a particular pathogen but only genetically susceptible individuals succumb to the disease, quantitative genetics would indicate the genetic variability responsible for expression of the disease but would not provide any clues that the ultimate cause of the disease is an environmental pathogen. Yet the disease would not occur if the pathogen were eradicated.

A second limitation of focusing on variance in a population is that variance describes average differences among individuals in the population. Moderate heritability in a population could mask total environmental aetiology for some individuals and total genetic aetiology for others. A related point is that genetic and environmental aetiologies that completely explain a disorder for a few individuals account for a negligible amount of variance in the population as a whole and could thus remain undetected if quantitative genetic analyses are restricted to total variation in the population. These issues have been put in extreme form in order to emphasize that the proportion of population variance explained should not be misinterpreted as a measure of strength of effect as it applies to individuals (Rutter, 1987).

Three complications of behavioural genetic analyses should also be mentioned. Although multiple genes can add up linearly in their effect on behaviour, it is likely that some genetic effects involve interactions among genes, that is, nonadditive rather than additive effects. Members of identical twins are identical genetically and thus resemble each other for all genetic effects, including higher order interactions among several genes. For this reason, genetic designs that involve identical twins assess all genetic variance, whether additive or non-additive. In contrast, first-degree relatives share half of the additive genetic variance but very little non-additive genetic variance. This distinction may be particularly important for psychiatric disorders which often suggest evidence for nonadditive genetic variance in that identical twins are much more than twice as similar as first-degree relatives such as fraternal twins.

Two other complications are assortative mating and genotype—environment interaction and correlation. The adage that opposites attract is not borne out by research — the saying that birds of a feather flock together is closer to the truth for behavioural dimensions and disorders. For couples, this resemblance is known as positive assortative mating. It increases additive genetic variance in the population, and it has implications for estimating heritability. For example, in the twin method, unless taken into account, assortative mating will lead to underestimates of heritability. Assortative mating increases the genetic resemblance among first-degree relatives beyond 0.50; however, it cannot increase the genetic resemblance of identical twins because they are identical genetically. Thus, assortative mating has the effect of lowering the difference between identical and fraternal twin correlations and decreasing heritability estimates for traits that show assortative mating. Genotype–environment correlation and interaction are effects at the interface of nature and nurture — they literally refer to the extent to which genetic and environmental effects correlate or interact. Although these concepts are important for conceptualizing transactions between genetic and environmental effects during development, their effect on quantitative genetic estimates is not easily assessed (Plomin *et al.*, 1977).

Despite these complications, quantitative genetic methods provide a powerful approach to the aetiological analysis of behavioural disorders and dimensions. Twin and adoption studies are especially needed in some areas of psychopathology. Family studies, which represent the only behavioural genetic research in some areas, are a reasonable starting point, but they are limited in several respects. An obvious limitation involves the interpretation of familial resemblance: when familial resemblance is observed, the resemblance could be due to nurture as well as to nature. Although, as discussed later, shared family environment does not appear to contribute importantly to the resemblance of family members in personality and psychopathology, the assumption cannot be made that a sparsely studied area of psychopathology will show no shared environmental influence. For this reason, twin and adoption studies are needed to determine the extent to which heredity underlies familial resemblance. A second limitation of family studies is less obvious. As mentioned earlier, studies of first-degree relatives are limited to detecting additive genetic variance, yet there is increasing evidence that genetic variance operates in part non-additively, at least for personality (Plomin *et al.*, 1990a). Identical twins, who are identical for all forms of genetic variance whether additive or non-additive, are needed to assess non-additive genetic variance.

Another issue especially relevant to develop-

mental psychopathology is that family studies often rely on parent–offspring rather than sibling comparisons. From the perspective of developmental behavioural genetics, the wide age gap between parents and offspring makes it unlikely that parent–offspring resemblance will be found if genetic influences on psychopathology differ in childhood and adulthood, an issue discussed later. For this reason, the twin design and sibling adoption design are to be recommended for quantitative genetic research in psychopathology.

A brief overview of the major findings of behavioural genetic research on psychopathology is now made. Following this overview, four sections will consider new developments in quantitative genetic analysis that push beyond the basic nature–nurture question concerning the relative magnitude of genetic and environmental influence. These sections are followed by a final section on the application of molecular genetic tools of the new genetics to quantitative genetic problems of behaviour.

BEHAVIOURAL GENETIC RESEARCH ON PSYCHOPATHOLOGY

What is the evidence for genetic and environmental influences on psychopathology? Although much more basic quantitative genetic research is needed to document genetic influence in developmental psychopathology, enough has been done to indicate that the results are likely to be similar to those in other behavioural domains such as cognition and personality. That is, we can expect to find some moderate genetic influence as well as evidence for the importance of the environment. In this section, an overview is presented of the main conclusions that can be drawn to date for many forms of psychopathology (see Vandenberg *et al.*, 1986 for an overview of psychiatric genetics; and Rutter *et al.*, 1990a, b, for a review of child psychiatric disorders).

Much interest surrounds possible genetic contributions to schizophrenia. Family, twin and adoption studies all converge on the conclusion that there is substantial genetic influence on schizophrenia (Gottesman, 1991). However, environmental influences are also recognized as an essential aetiological factor in the emergence of schizophrenia. For example, the average concordance rate for schizophrenia in identical twins is less than 50%. Thus, in a majority of cases, genetically identical individuals are discordant with respect to schizophrenia. Findings such as this highlight the recommendation that schizophrenia be considered as genetically influenced rather than genetically determined, and that both genetic and environmental influences should be considered in a comprehensive model for the development of this condition (Gottesman, 1991).

Research on affective disorders has involved distinctions between bipolar and unipolar disorders, as well as differentiations between severe, mild and dysthymic conditions (e.g. Rutter *et al.*, 1990b; Tsuang & Faraone, 1990). There is strong evidence from twin and adoption studies of genetic influence on bipolar disorder (Blehar *et al.*, 1988). More controversy surrounds the issue of genetic factors in unipolar disorders, especially given the phenotypic heterogeneity found with this condition or group of conditions. The emerging picture, however, includes genetic influence (Moldin *et al.*, 1991). It should be emphasized, however, that there are no twin or adoption studies of unipolar depression in childhood or adolescence; all the evidence to date for development before adulthood has come from family studies of children with depressed parents (Rutter *et al.*, 1990b).

A range of conclusions has been reached for other disorders seen in childhood and adolescence, as reviewed by Rutter *et al.* (1990b). For example, there is strong evidence for genetic influence on autism, reasonable evidence for Tourette's syndrome and related features such as tics and obsessive–compulsive behaviour, and little firm evidence for hyperactivity. In addition, although there is strong evidence for genetic effects on criminality and antisocial personality disorder in adults, the pattern of findings for conduct disorder and juvenile delinquency is less clear, as shared environmental factors appear to be especially important. The safest conclusion of course is that much more behavioural genetic research is needed in virtually all areas of developmental psychopathology.

DIMENSIONS AND DISORDERS

To date, the major application of behavioural genetic techniques has involved the examination of individual differences in quantitative, continuous dimensions of behaviour. For example, there is a wealth of information concerning genetic and environmental contributions to individual differences in normal dimensions such as personality and cognitive abilities. Behavioural genetic approaches to psychopathology, however, have used a different approach. Psychopathology has most often been assessed as a categorical disorder (e.g. a child is classified as having or not having autism) rather than as a dimension (e.g. a score on a continuous measure of symptoms characteristic of autism). A crucial question is whether the genetic and environmental influences on disorders also contribute to normal variations in the general population. That is, are there discrete aetiological factors specific to a disorder, or is there a continuum of risk factors that contribute to the aetiology of the disorder?

Geneticists have long recognized that disorders that are defined categorically may be due to a continuum of genetic and environmental risk factors. Specifically, it has been suggested that a hypothetical distribution of risk or 'liability' to categorical disorders may be assumed (Falconer, 1965). The normal distribution of liability may then have a 'threshold' which determines if an individual is diagnosed as having the disorder. Heritability estimates of this construct of liability can be calculated by transforming concordance rates for identical and fraternal twins (or adoptive and non-adoptive family members) into tetrachoric correlations (Smith, 1974).

The concept of liability is useful in research on diseases. For example, convulsive threshold is a dimension that underlies the diagnostic category of epilepsy. However, a difficulty with the liability approach is that it assumes that a normal distribution of risk factors underlies a disorder, rather than assessing the risk factors empirically. It has been suggested that there can be no presuppositions that the extremes do, or do not, involve the same aetiological mechanisms that operate in the normative range of functioning; hence there must be empirical tests for similarities and dissimilarities (Rutter, 1988). That is, the challenge is to translate the hypothesized liability into something measureable, such as a behavioural dimension representing degrees of a categorical disorder or processes related to a disorder (e.g. convulsive threshold in epilepsy).

Recently, DeFries and Fulker (1985, 1988) have developed a quantitative genetic method that assesses the extent to which dimensions are aetiologically related to disorders. This technique, which has been dubbed 'DF' analysis (Plomin & Rende, 1991), makes it possible to assess the extent to which the magnitude of genetic and environmental influences on extreme scores (on a quantitative measure) differ from the magnitude of aetiological influences on the entire range of individual differences. As such, the method represents a way of determining, in terms of aetiology, the extent to which extreme symptomatology (e.g. characteristic of a psychiatric disorder) reflects a qualitative or quantitative departure from the normal range of variation (Rende & Plomin, 1990; Plomin, 1991; Plomin *et al.*, 1991b).

The conceptual framework for DF analysis will be discussed with respect to the more straightforward case of siblings (rather than twins or adoptees). DF analysis introduces a new concept of familial resemblance (group familiality) which it contrasts with the traditional concept of individual familiality. The traditional concept of individual familiality is indexed by sibling resemblance for a quantitative trait. Specifically, the correlation between siblings indicates the extent to which individual differences on the trait of interest may be due to familial factors (i.e. genetic or environmental factors operating to produce similarities within families), and hence is termed 'individual familiality'.

A novel index of familial resemblance derived from DF analysis estimates familial factors involved in the expression of extreme scores on the trait (as in the case of clinical populations). This estimate — called 'group familiality' — is indexed by the regression towards the mean of sibling scores on the quantitative measure. As shown in Fig. 2.1, for a quantitative measure relevant to a particular disorder, diagnosed probands will fall towards the extreme of the distribution ($\bar{P}$ in Fig. 2.1). The mean of the siblings ($\bar{S}$ in Fig. 2.1) of the probands will regress to the unselected population mean to the extent that familial factors are unimportant in the aetiology of the disorder. In contrast, if familial factors are important, the mean of the siblings of the probands will be greater than the population mean.

The use of quantitative measures is important because they permit estimates of the magnitude of both types of indices of familial resemblance. As mentioned earlier, individual familiality is estimated by the correlation between siblings. In addition, the extent to which the mean difference between the siblings and the population approaches the mean difference between the probands and the population provides a quantitative estimate of the extent to which the mean difference between the probands and the population is due to familial factors. This quantitative estimate of group familiality (a/b in Fig. 2.1) may then be compared to the estimate of individual familiality. This comparison provides an empirical method for assessing whether the magnitude of familial influence on extreme scores differs from the magnitude of familial influence on the range of individual differences.

Twins or adoptees are needed to determine the extent to which familiality is due to heredity rather than environment shared by siblings. Group heritability (h_g^2) indicates the proportion of the difference between the probands and the unselected population that is due to genetic differences. It is based, for example, on the differential regression towards the mean for cotwins of MZ and DZ probands. That is, h^2 is zero if MZ and DZ cotwins regress to the population mean to the same extent. In contrast, h_g^2 is 1.0 if MZ cotwins do not regress towards the mean and if DZ cotwins regress half way back to the mean. Similar to individual familiality, individual heritability (h^2) is based on traditional estimates of heritability reviewed earlier, such as doubling the difference in correlations for MZ and DZ twins. In addition, estimates of both

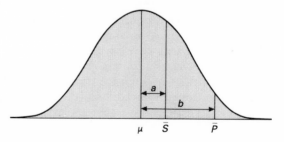

Fig. 2.1 Hypothetical distributions of behavioural variation of an unselected sample of siblings (mean = μ), diagnosed probands (mean = $\bar{P}$), and siblings of diagnosed probands (mean = $\bar{S}$). 'Group' familiality = a/b.

individual and group shared environment (c^2 and c_g^2, respectively) may also be determined in this approach. A multiple regression approach that estimates h^2, h_g^2, c^2 and c_g^2 is presented by DeFries and Fulker (1985, 1988).

It should be emphasized that the reliance on quantitative measures in DF analysis does not preclude the use of clinically diagnosed individuals. Rather, the inclusion of diagnosed individuals as probands strengthens the approach. The key, however, is to utilize quantitative measures that are relevant to the symptomatology of interest, so that links between the normal and abnormal may be addressed empirically (Rende & Plomin, 1990). Indeed, many behavioural disorders of interest — e.g. unipolar depression, hyperactivity, anxiety and conduct problems — clearly are present in varying degrees in the population, and the aetiological links or breaks between normative ranges of functioning and the extremes in these cases may be investigated directly.

The DF analysis was first applied to reading disability. Probands and twins were assessed using a continuous discriminant function score of reading-related tests (DeFries *et al.*, 1987a; DeFries & Gillis, 1990). Group heritability was found to be only about half the magnitude of individual heritability, suggesting that reading disability is aetiologically different from the continuous dimension of reading ability. A multivariate extension of the DF analysis suggested that phonological coding ability (e.g. speed and accuracy in pronouncing non-words such as 'ter' and 'tegwop') may be a key element in the genetics of reading disability (Olson *et al.*, 1991).

Recently, the authors have applied DF analysis to the study of depressive symptomatology in adolescence (Rende *et al.*, 1993). Data were collected from twins and siblings participating in the ongoing Nonshared Environment and Adolescent Development project (Reiss *et al.*, 1994). The sample consisted of 707 sibling pairs representing the following genetic relationships: MZ twins, DZ twins and non-twin full siblings in intact families; and full siblings, half siblings and biologically unrelated siblings in stepfamilies. Depressive symptomatology was assessed using the children's depression inventory (CDI; Kovacs, 1983); adolescent self-reports were obtained twice over a 1-month period.

An application of DF analysis to these data yielded the following results. There was moderate genetic influence on individual differences in depressive symptomatology, and no shared environmental influences. Moderate genetic influence also contributed to extreme scores on the CDI (i.e. adolescents who exceeded the suggested 'cut-off' score of 13 which is used to index risk for clinical depression). However, shared environmental influences were pronounced for the extremes (accounting for over 40% of the mean difference between probands and the population), and were significantly greater than the shared environmental effects on individual differences. These results were interpreted using a diathesis-stress model, in which a continuum of genetic risk and familial influences endemic to the extremes contribute to extreme depressive symptomatology in adolescence. It must be stressed, however, that the adolescents in this study were not assessed clinically, and research with clinical samples is necessary before firm conclusions can be drawn.

In summary, to date there is evidence that there are unique aetiological contributions to the extremes for both reading disability and depressive symptomatology. Future research employing the technique developed by DeFries and Fulker carries much promise for our understanding of both clinical disorders and variations within the general population.

MULTIVARIATE BEHAVIOURAL GENETICS: HETEROGENEITY AND COMORBIDITY

An important issue in psychiatric research is that the boundaries between clinical conditions are not always clear. Clinical heterogeneity — i.e. variations in the symptoms characteristic of a disorder — has been an issue for essentially all forms of psychopathology. For example, there have been many attempts to determine if there are distinct subtypes of schizophrenia, or merely variations in the symptoms characteristic of this disorder (e.g Goldstein & Tsuang, 1988; Tsuang *et al.*, 1990). Another concern is that some disorders that are treated as separate conditions often appear together in the same individual. The incidence of individuals receiving multiple psychiatric diagnoses — known as comorbidity — has also received much research attention in recent years. A good example is that depressed children and adolescents often are diagnosed as having comorbid conditions, especially anxiety disorders and conduct disorders (Kovacs & Gatsonis, 1989).

The crucial issue for behavioural genetic research is to assess the aetiological counterparts of comorbidity and heterogeneity. For example, if two clinical conditions tend to occur together, as do depression and anxiety, is there a common genetic aetiology that influences both types of symptoms? Conversely, if there is marked heterogeneity in the symptomatology characteristic of a syndrome, as is the case with schizophrenia (McGuffin *et al.*, 1987), is such variation due to aetiological (e.g. genetic) heterogeneity?

Behavioural genetic approaches to comorbidity and heterogeneity can be seen as specific examples of one of the major advances in quantitative genetics — multivariate analysis of the genetic and environmental aetiologies of covariance between traits (Plomin *et al.*, 1990a, b). The key concept is the genetic correlation: to what extent are genetic effects on a certain symptom or syndrome correlated with genetic effects on other symptoms or syndromes? A simple example will help to illustrate this concept. As mentioned above, depression and conduct disorder often occur together in children. If a suitable behavioural genetic design were chosen, e.g. a twin study, genetic and environmental influences on each syndrome could be estimated based on the difference in correlations for MZ and DZ twins. The two disorders can show the same degree of genetic influence but be affected by entirely different sets of genes. Alternatively, the two disorders can yield different heritabilities even though the same set of genes affects both — that is, one disorder might be more affected by the environment than the other. The genetic correlation is independent of the heritabilities of the two phenotypes. That is, both depression and conduct disorder might be moderately heritable but the genetic correlation between the disorders could be high, suggesting that the two disorders are genetically the same, or the genetic correlation can be low, implying that the two disorders are genetically distinct.

Multivariate genetic analysis represents the multivariate extension of traditional univariate quantitative genetic strategies. Its focus is on the covariance between phenotypes rather than the variance of each phenotype considered separately. Any quantitative genetic strategy that can be used to decompose the variance of a trait into genetic and environmental components can also be used to decompose the covariance between two traits. Rather than comparing MZ and DZ resemblance for a single trait X, the basis for multivariate genetic analysis is 'cross-twin' resemblance for one twin on trait X and the cotwin on trait Y. The phenotypic correlation between X and Y is assumed to be mediated genetically to the extent that MZ cross-twin resemblance exceeds DZ cross-twin resemblance. This genetic contribution to the phenotypic correlation can be shown to be the genetic correlation weighted by a function of the heritabilities of the two traits (Plomin & DeFries, 1979). Thus, even if the genetic correlation is high, the genetic contribution to the phenotypic correlation will be low if the heritability of one or both of the traits is low. A second type of question addressed by multivariate genetic analysis focuses on the genetic correlation itself. The genetic correlation indexes the extent to which genetic effects on one trait overlap with genetic effects on the other trait, independent of the heritabilities of the two traits. This is the essential question of genetic heterogeneity and comorbidity.

Research on heterogeneity has been dominated by 'splitters' who are interested in low genetic correlations within a syndrome in order to break down heterogeneity. However, there are also 'lumpers', especially in the developmental disorders, who look for high genetic correlations indicating that genetic influences spill over beyond the diagnosed disorders to other disorders or to a spectrum of less severe symptoms. Such an approach would also be an appropriate focus for comorbid conditions such as depression and conduct disorder.

Multivariate approaches to psychopathology have been receiving increasing attention in recent years (Plomin & Rende, 1991). For example, a number of family studies have indicated that the classical phenotypically derived subtypes of schizophrenia do not appear to breed true (Gershon *et al.*, 1988; Kendler & Tsuang, 1988; Kendler *et al.*, 1988; Squires-Wheeler *et al.*, 1988). In other words, familial cross-concordances for these subtypes are high, suggesting that these phenotypic subtypes are not distinct aetiologically. This body of work suggests that there may be a non-specific genetic contribution to schizophrenia which is expressed variably in different individuals, although there is still a great deal of interest in aetiological heterogeneity in schizophrenia (Schulz & Pato, 1989).

Recent research has also examined relations between comorbid conditions. For example, there is evidence for a common genetic component that influences both symptoms of depression and symptoms of anxiety (Kendler *et al.*, 1987); interestingly, environmental factors were largely responsible for differentiation of the syndromes. It should be noted that this study was conducted with a normative sample of individuals, and hence generalizations to clinically defined depression and anxiety must be made cautiously. Two other studies of depression did not find cross-familial links with comorbid conditions. First, although depression is associated with migraine across individuals, depression in probands is not related to migraine in first-degree relatives (Merikangas *et al.*, 1988). Second, panic disorder shows little cross-familiality with depression (Coryell *et al.*, 1988).

Most multivariate behavioural genetic research on psychopathology has focused on family studies. As discussed earlier in the context of univariate genetic analysis, multivariate family studies cannot separate genetic and environmental sources of covariance between disorders. For example, parents with psychopathology may induce or elicit disturbances in their children as a consequence of the environments that they provide, in addition to their transmission of genes that lead to a specific disorder. Two examples of such environmentally induced covariance follow (from Plomin *et al.*, 1991b).

First, genetic factors may operate to create environmental risks. For example, Huntington's disease (HD) is due to a dominant major gene but it appears that the increased rate of conduct disorder in HD families is a consequence of the family discord associated with the parental psychopathology rather than of the disease itself; by contrast, the raised incidence of depression probably represents an early manifestation of HD in that individual (Folstein *et al.*, 1983). In that case, the separation of direct and indirect (via induced environmental risk) genetic effects is facilitated by the fact that HD is entirely due to a single dominant gene. However, it is likely that similar indirect effects apply in the case

of psychopathological disorders in which genetic influences are polygenic and less predominant. For example, parental personality disorder (and other forms of psychopathology) may lead to family discord and disruption, with adverse consequences for the children dependent as much on the discord and disruption experienced as on any direct genetic vulnerability (Quinton & Rutter, 1988). Similarly, with respect to the manifold effects on offspring of parental depression, it is likely that a variety of different genetic and environmental mechanisms may be involved (Rutter, 1990). Thus, it is probable that the associated family discord may be more important in the increased risk for conduct disorders, whereas direct genetic effects may be more influential in the case of anxiety and depressive disorders in the offspring.

Second, genetic factors may lead to one form of psychopathological disorder that then predisposes to a second type of disorder through non-genetic mechanisms. For example, a recent adoption study suggests that antisocial problems in parents are associated with a markedly increased risk for affective disturbance in the offspring, perhaps because of the life stresses and adversities that they engendered (Cadoret *et al.*, 1990). There was no direct genetic path to affective symptomatology in the offspring.

Two directions for future research should be noted. First, as discussed earlier, twin and adoption studies are necessary to disentangle genetic and environmental contributions to behaviour, and such strategies will be especially useful using a multivariate approach. A second point made in the previous section on dimensions and disorders warrants repeating in this context: there is much to be gained by using quantitative measures of psychopathology in conjunction with diagnostic assessments. One advantage is that the multivariate quantitative genetic techniques are applicable to quantitative measures, and such techniques allow calculations of genetic correlations (Plomin *et al.*, 1990b). In addition, clinical phenotypes are not necessarily inherited as a diagnosed condition; rather specific domains of behaviour may be affected which do not fall within the confines of diagnostic criteria. For example, social and cognitive abnormalities are found in the relatives of autistic individuals, suggesting that genetic influence on autism may operate through these areas of functioning (Folstein & Rutter, 1988). The implication is that our definitions of the phenotype might be altered by such aetiological findings. That is, demonstrating that a disorder such as autism has a family history that includes dysfunction not clearly observed in the clinical phenotype might provide clues not only about the aetiology of the disorder but also about the way in which we conceptualize the disorder. Hence, recent approaches to autism have emphasized the broad range of social and cognitive dysfunction that might underlie this disorder.

A final consideration is the application of molecular genetic techniques to multivariate issues in psychopathology. There has been considerable excitement in the field of psychiatric genetics over the possibility that genetic heterogeneity will be pinpointed by molecular genetic studies — indeed, that a new psychiatric nosology will be established (Mullan & Murray, 1989; Pardes *et al.*, 1989; cf. Reiss *et al.*, 1991). To date, genetic heterogeneity has been a focal issue in molecular genetic research on schizophrenia, bipolar depression and Alzheimer's disease (Plomin & Rende, 1991). Although there are no clear findings to date, as mentioned later, molecular techniques may eventually help resolve issues of comorbidity and heterogeneity.

LONGITUDINAL GENETIC ANALYSIS

For many developmentalists, genetic influences are assumed to be static and unchanging, and these developmentalists are justifiably uneasy about such non-developmental phenomena. In research on the genetics of psychopathology, developmental change is rarely considered. However, quantitative genetic research describes sources of variance for a particular population at a particular occasion of measurement and a particular age that will change as genetic and environmental factors change. The new subdiscipline of developmental behavioural genetics focuses on genetic sources of change as well as continuity during behavioural development (Plomin, 1986a). Evidence to date, for example, suggests the finding that when heritability changes during development it increases. This finding is counterintuitive for developmentalists who make

the reasonable but wrong assumption that only environmental influences, not genetic ones, accumulate during development.

In addition to investigating age changes in heritability, quantitative genetic techniques developed during the past decade can address the issue of the genetic contribution to age-to-age change (Plomin & DeFries, 1981). The simplest way to approach age-to-age genetic change is to analyse a change score, asking directly whether genetic factors contribute to change from age to age (Plomin & Nesselroade, 1990). More generally, the concepts and analysis of age-to-age change are similar to the multivariate genetic approach described in the previous section (Plomin, 1986b). Instead of analysing the covariance between two traits, longitudinal analysis focuses on the covariance between a trait measured at different ages. The genetic correlation in this longitudinal analysis indicates the extent to which genetic effects at one age are correlated with genetic effects at another age; the extent to which the genetic correlation is less than 1.0 indicates that genetic factors contribute to developmental change.

For example, the heritability of a disorder or dimension might be high both in childhood and in adolescence, but if the genetic correlation from childhood to adolescence were low, the implication is that genes contribute to change not continuity. Age-to-age genetic change in this context refers to changes in the effects of genes on behavioural differences among individuals, not to changes in the transcription and translation of DNA. For example, a genetic correlation between two ages would be zero even though the same genes are transcribed at both ages if their gene products have different effects at the two ages. Conversely, the same genes need not be transcribed at two ages even if the genetic correlation between the two ages is 1.0. That is, the relevant genes at the second age might no longer be actively transcribed but their structural legacy (e.g. differences in neural networks) could produce a genetic correlation between the two ages.

As in the case of multivariate genetic analysis of genetic correlations, any behavioural genetic design that can estimate genetic and environmental components of the variance of a single trait can also be used to estimate genetic and environmental components of covariance across time if longitudinal data are available. Also similar to multivariate genetic analysis, the basis for estimating age-to-age genetic correlations, for example, for twin data, is the twin 'cross-correlation' across ages rather than the usual twin correlation at each age. In the case of IQ, genetic correlations from childhood to adulthood are surprisingly high (DeFries *et al.*, 1987b; Fulker *et al.*, 1988). Personality data, however, suggest more genetic change than continuity, especially during childhood (Plomin & Nesselroade, 1990). This suggests that age-to-age genetic change might be important in the development of disorders, especially in childhood. However, not a single longitudinal behavioural genetic study of psychopathology appears to have been reported in childhood or adolescence.

An obvious direction for research in psychiatric genetics is to extend behavioural genetic research designs longitudinally in order to take advantage of techniques to analyse genetic and environmental contributions to age-to-age genetic change and continuity. Combining multivariate and longitudinal genetic analyses is particularly powerful because continuity may be found in change. That is, genetic effects on a behaviour at one age might be more highly correlated with genetic effects on a different behaviour at a later age. In other words, changing patterns of behaviour over time may reflect genetic continuity in underlying traits. Combining multivariate and longitudinal genetic designs in this way can facilitate the search for such heterotypic continuity in which behaviour changes in form but still reflects the same underlying genetic processes. This multivariate perspective is also useful in conceptualizing the longitudinal association between risk factors and psychopathology.

QUANTITATIVE GENETICS AND THE ENVIRONMENT

The phrase *quantitative genetics* is something of a misnomer in that its theory and methods are useful for understanding the environment as well as genetics. A fundamental strength of behavioural genetic methods is the ability to assess both genetic and environmental provenances rather than assuming that either nature or nurture is omnipotent. As mentioned earlier, an increasingly important message from behavioural genetic research is that non-

genetic factors are at least as important as genetic factors for most behavioural dimensions and disorders. This is a message that needs to be heard now because there are signs that environmentalism is beginning to be replaced with an equally misguided biological determinism (Reiss *et al.*, 1991). It should be noted that in quantitative genetics, the word *environment* includes any non-hereditary influence, including biological factors (e.g. physical trauma, nutritional factors, and even DNA itself) in addition to the psychosocial environmental factors that are the focus of most environmental research on behavioural development.

In addition to providing the best available evidence for the importance of the environment, behavioural genetic research has led to two discoveries about environmental mechanisms that have far-reaching implications for understanding the influence of the environment in behavioural development: the importance of non-shared environment and genetic influence on measures of the environment.

Non-shared environment. One of the most surprising findings in human behavioural genetics involves the environment: environmental factors important to most domains of behavioural development are experienced differently by children in the same family. In the past, the reasonable assumption was usually made that resemblance among children in a family was caused by environmental factors shared by children growing up together. Instead, behavioural genetic research indicates that siblings resemble each other for genetic reasons — what runs in families is DNA, not experiences shared in the home. However, this same behavioural genetic research shows that, although experiences shared by siblings in a family have little effect, environmental factors are of great importance in development. Thus, these results have led to the conclusion that environmental influences that affect behavioural development involve experiences not shared by siblings. This conclusion is consistently supported by data from various behavioural genetic designs, such as the direct test of shared environment provided by the resemblance of adoptive siblings, pairs of genetically unrelated children adopted early in life into the same family. This category of environmental influence has been variously called non-shared, E_1, within-family, individual, unique or specific. A target article in *Behavioural and Brain Sciences* discussed the evidence for and the importance of non-shared environment; the article was followed by 32 commentaries and a response to the commentaries (Plomin & Daniels, 1987). An update on the evidence of the importance of non-shared environment is available that focuses on the possible exceptions to the rule, such as delinquent behaviour (Plomin *et al.*, 1994). Two books describe recent developments in research on non-shared environment (Dunn & Plomin, 1990; Hetherington *et al.*, 1994).

Non-geneticists sometimes find the conclusion that shared influences are unimportant difficult to accept because it seems obvious that environmentally mediated family influences must be important and, if siblings grow up in the same family, it would appear that the environmental effects must be shared. However, this represents a misunderstanding of what is meant by non-shared. The effects may stem from some general family feature (such as discord or deprivation) but the effects can be non-shared if they impinge differently on different siblings because, for example, siblings vary in age or temperament or parental expectation.

The example of family discord raises an additional point: most environmental factors probably involve a complex mixture of shared and non-shared effects. Family discord represents a shared factor to the extent that all children in a family are exposed to it and experience similar effects from it. However, it is possible that siblings may also have unique responses to the discord for various reasons such as differences in age or temperament. The challenge for researchers is to examine both the shared and non-shared impact of environmental influences, rather than categorizing environmental factors as either shared or non-shared. In this vein, it should be reiterated that shared environmental influence may be important for a few developmental domains. For example, as noted earlier, delinquent behaviour shows a strong shared environmental effect. In addition, it is possible that certain extreme environments overwhelm all children in a family (Rutter, 1991).

The conclusion that environmental factors operate primarily in a non-shared manner has important implications for clinicians and researchers. It suggests that instead of thinking about the environment on a family-by-family basis, we need to think on an individual-by-individual basis. The critical question is, why are children in the same family so different? The key to solving this puzzle is to study more than one child per family. The message is not that family experiences are unimportant but rather that environmental influences in behavioural development are specific to each child rather than general to an entire family. Only family systems researchers have previously emphasized the importance of differential experiences within the family (Minuchin, 1974; Minuchin, 1988).

Research on non-shared environment can be categorized into analyses of the magnitude of the non-shared environment component of variance, attempts to identify specific non-shared factors that are experienced differently by siblings in a family, and explorations of associations between non-shared factors and behaviour. Most is known about the first issue (Plomin *et al.*, 1994). Although research on the second issue has just begun, it seems clear that siblings growing up in the same family experience quite different family environments in terms of their parents' treatment, their interactions with their siblings, experiences beyond the family, and chance (Dunn & Plomin, 1990). Concerning the third direction for research, the few initial attempts to relate non-shared environmental factors to sibling differences in outcome are promising. As such associations are found, it becomes necessary to disentangle possible genetic sources of these associations. Because siblings differ genetically, associations between differences in their experience and behavioural outcomes may be due to their genetic differences rather than to their non-shared experiences. Identical twins provide a stringent test of differential experiences of siblings that cannot be due to genetic differences within sibling pairs (Baker & Daniels, 1990). A collaborative study addressing these issues is under way that involves a national sample of over 700 families of adolescent twins, full siblings, half-siblings and unrelated siblings visited in their homes for two 3-h visits with a focus on differential experiences of children growing up in the same family (Reiss *et al.*, 1994).

It is ironic that after decades of environmentalism, the limiting factor in this effort is the need for better measures of the environment. Especially scarce are environmental measures that are specific to a child rather than general to a family, measures of experience (the subjective, experienced environment) in contrast to measures of the objective environment, and measures that move beyond the passive model of the child as merely a receptacle for environmental influence to measures that can capture the child's active selection, modification, and creation of environments. These needs are great because researchers often apply measures designed to assess between-family effects to examine non-shared influences on children. Rather than assessing indirectly the way in which siblings may have different experiences within the family, we need to develop methods for capturing what each child experiences within the family as well as outside the family. Such advances in environmental assessment will contribute to our understanding of specific non-shared environmental influences, for example, by investigating observations of family interaction, differences in perceptions of the family environment, and ways in which children contribute to the creation of differential experiences. This research direction can also begin to elucidate the processes by which children in the same family experience different environments.

Genetic influence on environmental measures. Measures once assumed to assess the environment have been shown to be influenced by heredity (Plomin & Bergeman, 1991). For example, the first research on this topic was conducted by Rowe (1981, 1983) who demonstrated in two twin studies with different samples and different measures that adolescent identical twins are more similar in their self-reported perceptions of parental affection than are fraternal twins. It is interesting that, in the same studies, perceptions of parental control showed little genetic influence. These findings were replicated in analyses of adult twins rating their childhood rearing environment retrospectively 50 years later (Plomin *et al.*, 1988b), and genetic influence was also found for adults' ratings of the family in which they are now the parent (Plomin *et al.*, 1989). In the same study, life events, especially controllable life events (such as conflict with a spouse), yielded evidence for significant genetic influence (Plomin

et al., 1990c). Finally, genetic influence has also been suggested in comparisons between non-adoptive and adoptive siblings for videotaped observations of maternal behaviour and for a widely used observation/interview measure of the home environment (Plomin *et al.*, 1988a).

Especially important for research on psychopathology is the idea that genetic factors may influence how certain individuals actively create risk environments. That is, genetic factors undoubtedly play a role in the wide range of individual differences seen in exposure to risk environments (Rutter, 1991). For example, recent research on depression and life events suggests that a common familial factor predisposes individuals both to depression and to behaviour associated with stressful life events (e.g. McGuffin *et al.*, 1988); that this factor might be hereditary is a possibility suggested by the evidence for genetic influence on life events. The point then is that genetic influence may not merely be entangled in measures of the environment as an artefact of inadequate environmental assessment, but rather that genetics may play a role in how individuals create their own environmental influences, such as risk factors for psychopathology.

Research in the near future in this area will attempt to sort out environmental measures most and least influenced genetically. Research will also be aimed at identifying processes by which heredity affects measures of the environment. So far, the obvious candidates — for example, parental IQ and personality in the case of genetic influence on the family environment — do not seem to be the answer (Plomin & Bergeman, 1991). Continued research on the genetics of environmental measures is likely to enrich our understanding of the developmental interface between nature and nurture.

MOLECULAR GENETICS AND QUANTITATIVE GENETICS

During the past decade, advances in molecular genetics have led to the dawn of a new era for quantitative genetic research. The 'new genetics' involves techniques that make it possible to study DNA variation of any species directly, even for complexly determined characteristics such as psychopathology. McGuffin & Murray, 1991, provided an excellent overview of the new genetics and mental illness. It has been suggested that such complexly determined characteristics influenced by many genes as well as by environmental factors represent the new frontier for molecular genetics (Bodmer, 1986). The use of molecular genetic techniques in the service of quantitative genetic analyses of behavioural dimensions and disorders will revolutionize behavioural genetics as strategies are developed that can isolate DNA markers associated with small amounts of genetic variance (Plomin, 1990).

Quantitative genetic techniques do not assess genetic variation directly but rather through indirect means such as comparing MZ and DZ twins. This has been and will continue to be a source of great strength because quantitative genetics addresses the 'bottom line' of genetic influences on variability. That is, these methods assess the total impact of genetic variability of any kind, regardless of the complexity of its molecular source of variation. However, the advent of the new genetics has yielded many genetic markers that can be screened for their contribution, independently and jointly, to the variance of quantitative traits, even in the case of traits for which perhaps scores of genes each contribute small portions of variances in the population and for which environmental factors are important. Such multiple loci that affect quantitative traits have been called quantitative trait loci (QTL; Gelderman, 1975), although the notion of multiple-gene influence is just as relevant to qualitative traits such as psychiatric diagnoses.

As mentioned earlier, a fierce debate raged at the beginning of this century between Mendelians, who looked for single-gene effects and 3 : 1 phenotypic segregation ratios, and Galtonians or biometricians, who saw only continuous distributions. The debate was resolved with the recognition that continuous distribution rather than discontinuous Mendelian segregation ratios are expected if several genes affect a trait. The theory of quantitative genetics formalized by Fisher in 1918 assumed the presence of many genes with equal and additive effects. In 1941, Mather coined the word *polygenic* to refer to such multiple-gene influences. Although not intended by Mather, the word polygenic came to imply that so many genes were involved that each

had an infinitesimal and thus undetectable effect. Terms such as QTL attempt to rectify this misuse of the word polygenic by emphasizing a continuum of gene effect size and the possibility of detecting genes of intermediate effect size (McClearn *et al.*, 1991). Another term coming into use is *oligogenic* in which *oligo* refers to a few, although we prefer the more neutral term *multigenic* to distinguish multiple-gene approaches from monogenic approaches. Unlike the Fisherian version of quantitative genetics, these multiple-gene concepts do not assume equal and additive effects of genes and they all emphasize that several genes are likely to have detectable effect on complex dimensions and disorders.

The use of molecular techniques to clarify the inheritance of complex traits is not new, but the idea gains tremendous power from the thousands of genetic markers that are now available. Such analyses were previously limited to about 80 genetic markers expressed peripherally in blood, saliva or urine. Nearly 2000 DNA markers are now available that assess variability in DNA itself, not just DNA expressed as polypeptides in peripheral systems (Kidd *et al.*, 1989). Moreover, this is just the beginning: about 1 in 1000 nucleotide DNA bases differ for unrelated humans, which means that about 3 million of our 3 billion bases are variable.

Applications of molecular genetic techniques to the study of behaviour are unlikely to succeed if they need to assume that a major gene is largely responsible for genetic variation. This is the problem with linkage analyses of large family pedigrees which have failed to uncover replicable major gene effects for psychiatric disorders. Linkage is based on violations of Mendel's second law of independent assortment (i.e. two genes will be inherited independently) that occurs when a DNA marker and a gene for a disorder are close together on the same chromosome and thus transmitted within families as a unit rather than assorting independently. The mania following announcements during 1987 and 1988 of linkage for manic−depression and schizophrenia gave way to depression when the manic−depression report was withdrawn and the schizophrenia report could not be replicated. Problems with linkage studies such as ascertainment biases, diagnoses and significance levels are beginning to raise researchers' consciousness concerning the possibility of false positive results.

A linkage strategy that is likely to be more generalizable is the affected-sibling-pair or affected-relative method, developed first by Penrose (1935) and formalized by Haseman and Elston (1972; Weeks & Lange, 1988). This method involves sibling pairs in which both siblings are affected and it attempts to identify associations between genetic markers within such sibling pairs. The essence of the method is that linkage can be excluded if one affected sibling shows the marker but the other affected sibling does not. The results of the affected-sibling-pair method are likely to be more generalizable than linkage analyses of a single pedigree. Another important advantage is that, unlike the pedigree approach, the affected-sibling-pair method does not require a priori specification of the mode of inheritance of the disorder. A practical problem with the method is that sibling concordance is generally low for psychopathology and consequently it is difficult to find sibling pairs in which both siblings are affected. Another problem is that, like the pedigree approach to linkage, the affected-sibling-pair method will detect only relatively major gene effects, although the power of the method to detect QTL can be increased if very extreme cases are assessed (Fulker *et al.*, 1991).

More fundamentally, it is becoming increasingly recognized that major genes are unlikely to be found in the population for behavioural disorders. Exceptions to this rule may be found as in the case of positive evidence for linkage for hereditary breast–ovarian cancer in several families (Hall *et al.*, 1990), which is the first replicated linkage reported for a complex clinically heterogeneous disorder. Nonetheless, the shift towards recognition of multiple-gene influence is important in countering the naive assumption of earlier linkage studies in psychiatry that psychiatric disorders are like classical Mendelian disorders — dichotomous and due to a single gene that is necessary and sufficient to produce the disorder. Much current linkage research assumes that a major gene can be found in certain families, albeit not in the entire population. For this reason, linkage studies focus on a few very large pedigrees with many affected individuals in the hope of finding a major gene responsible for the disorder in a particular pedigree. From this perspective, multiple-gene influence is seen in the population because of the concatenation of different major genes in different families.

An alternative hypothesis is that major-gene effects will not be found for behaviour either in the population or in the family. Rather, for each individual, many genes may make small contributions towards variability and vulnerability. The genetic quest is to find, not *the* gene for a psychiatric disorder, but the *many* genes that increase susceptibility in a probabilistic rather than predetermined manner. One possibility is to employ allelic association strategies rather than linkage because sample sizes can be increased to provide sufficient power to detect associations that account for small amounts of variance among individuals in a population. Allelic association, usually called linkage disequilibrium, refers to covariation between allelic variation in a marker and phenotypic variation among individuals in a population (Edwards, 1991). The use of genetic markers to study associations with complex traits is not new; the first association between genetic markers and quantitative traits was found more than 60 years ago (Sax, 1923). For example, associations have been found for disease states and candidate genes such as HLA (Tiwari & Terasaki, 1985). For normal variation, the best example is serum cholesterol levels for which about a quarter of the genetic variance can be explained by associations with four apolipoprotein gene markers (Sing & Boerwinkle, 1987). For psychopathology, a blood marker (HLA A9) has been found that appears to be associated with paranoid schizophrenia (McGuffin & Sturt, 1986).

Instead of using random DNA markers to look painstakingly through the human genome for QTL, a more efficient initial strategy is to screen polymorphic candidate genes with known function, especially genes involved in neurological processes, for their individual and joint contributions to behaviour. For example, the apolipoprotein genes served as candidate genes in the search for QTL associations with serum cholesterol. Although allelic association studies using very large samples might begin to uncover some QTL associated with behavioural disorders, success in identifying all of the many genes responsible for genetic variance for a particular behaviour will depend on the development of new techniques. Given the pace of advances in this field, it many not be overly optimistic to expect such developments. For example, cDNA (DNA copied from messenger RNA) brain libraries have recently been used to identify and sequence parts of more than 200 new genes expressed in the brain but not in other organs, yielding unique identifiers called expressed sequence tag sites that make it possible for other investigators to use these new brain gene markers in their research (Adams et al., 1991).

What good is it if we find QTL associations with behaviour? Success in the QTL quest will revolutionize behavioural genetics. We can begin to replace our anonymous components of genetic variance estimated in twin and adoption studies with specific DNA variation measured directly in individuals. It will provide indisputable evidence of genetic influence on behaviour. It will transform quantitative genetic analyses of epistasis, pleiotropy, genetic correlations among variables from biology and behaviour, genotype−environment interaction and correlation, and age differences and age changes. We are especially interested in possible genetic links between normal and abnormal variation — that is, between dimensions and disorders. Genetic links between the normal and abnormal are suggested if QTL associated with dimensions of normal variation such as depression contribute as well to disorders such as diagnoses of clinical depression. For example, most apolipoprotein polymorphisms associated with normal variation in serum cholesterol levels are also associated with coronary heart disease (Breslow, 1988; Humphries, 1988). If such QTL links are found between the normal and abnormal, it suggests that the disorder represents the quantitative extreme of a normal dimension. As explained earlier in the section on dimensions and disorders, understanding the extent to which disorders are aetiologically part of the normal continuum of variability is critical to the goals of diagnosis, prediction, prevention and intervention of disorders.

In conclusion, the much overused phrase *paradigm shift* seems no exaggeration in relation to the impending merger of quantitative genetics and molecular genetics in the investigation of behavioural dimensions and disorders.

CONCLUSION

The goal of this chapter is to provide a selective overview of some important topics for behavioural genetic approaches to development and psychopathology. It is perhaps appropriate to conclude with a few comments concerning directions for future research, specifically highlighting some of the essential questions that can and should be addressed.

The most fundamental question of quantitative genetics, whether genetic influence is important, remains to be answered for many domains of psychopathology. Although there is accumulating evidence that diverse domains of psychopathology are influenced to some degree by genetics (Rutter et al., 1990b), many areas have only been the target of family studies and some areas have not been studied at all in terms of genetic strategies. Second, it matters whether the magnitude of genetic influence is slight or substantial, but only for a very few disorders have we sufficient information to gauge the strength of the genetic effect.

Even more pressing is the need to use new quantitative genetic strategies to go beyond these basic nature−nurture questions. Four such directions for research were discussed briefly: (i) the use of the DF approach to analyse aetiological relationship between the normal (dimensions) and abnormal (disorders); (ii) the application of multivariate genetic techniques to address issues of heterogeneity and comorbidity aetiologically; (iii) the use of longitudinal genetic analysis to address the provenances of change as well as continuity during development; and (iv) the incorporation of environmental measures in quantitative genetic studies in order to identify specific non-shared environmental influences and to assess genetic mediation of associations between environmental measures and pathological outcomes.

The final topic that was discussed in this chapter was the impending merger between quantitative genetics and molecular genetics. The implications of this topic for research are more conceptual than immediately applicable. However, as the whirlwind of molecular biology research looms closer to psychopathology, it adds to our sense of urgency to do the basic quantitative genetic research that will serve as the foundation for the application of the new genetics of molecular biology.

It is important to remember that quantitative genetics represents the beginning, not the end, of research. One of the next steps is to focus on the processes that are affected by genetics (Rutter *et al.*, 1990b) — that is, *what* is actually inherited? For example, if there is a genetic contribution to depression, genetic factors could operate on the regulation of moods, basic features of personality or cognitive tendencies such as attributional style. It must be emphasized that generating estimates of heritability and shared environmental influences does not indicate the processes through which these influences operate. Hence, a fundamental goal for the future will be to specify the underlying processes for different forms of psychopathology that are influenced by genetic and environmental factors.

A final consideration is to focus on mechanisms — *how* genetic and environmental influences transact during development. Clearly a hope for the future is that the ever-growing array of molecular genetic techniques will help to pinpoint not only the molecular basis for genetic influence on psychopathology, but also the biological pathways involved in maladaptive development. Such a goal was outlined earlier in the discussion of the fragile X syndrome, and it remains the ultimate challenge for all forms of psychopathology.

It should also be emphasized that molecular genetics cannot explain completely the emergence of most behavioural disorders. As reviewed earlier, quantitative genetic research yields solid evidence of the critical role of non-genetic influences and provides an important window on environmental processes. Thus, just as important as the future focus of genetic research on specific molecular mechanisms is the need to refine further our study of the environmental processes involved in the development of psychopathology. Indeed, an appropriate conclusion to this chapter is to emphasize the overarching goal for future research: to understand how both nature and nurture contribute to behavioural development and maladaptation.

ACKNOWLEDGEMENT

Preparation of this chapter was supported in part by grants from the US National Science Foundation (BNS 8806589), the National Institute of Mental Health (MH 43373 and 43899), the National Institute of Child Health and Human Development (HD 10333 and 18426), and the National Institute of Alcoholism and Alcohol Abuse (AA 08125).

REFERENCES

Adams M.D., Kelley J.M., Gocayne J.D. *et al.* (1991) Complementary DNA sequencing: Expressed sequence tags and human genome project. *Science* **252**, 1651−1656.

Bailey D.W. (1971) Recombinant-inbred strains, an aid to finding identity, linkage, and function of histocompatibility and other genes. *Transplantation* **11**, 325−327.

Baker L. & Daniels D. (1990) Nonshared environmental influences and personality differences in adult twins. *Journal of Personality and Social Psychology* **74**, 187−192.

Beadle G.W. & Tatum E.L. (1941) Experimental control of developmental reaction. *American Naturalist* **75**, 107−116.

Blehar M.C., Weissman M.M., Gershon E.S. & Hirschfeld R.M.A. (1988) Family and genetic studies of affective disorders. *Archives of General Psychiatry* **45**, 289−292.

Bodmer W.F. (1986) Human genetics: The molecular challenge. *Cold Spring Harbor Symposia on Quantitative Biology* **51**, 1−14.

Boomsma D.I., Martin N.G. & Neale M.C. (1989) Structural modeling in the analysis of twin data. *Behavior Genetics* **19**, 5−8.

Bregman J.D., Leckman J.F. & Ort S.I. (1988) Fragile X syndrome: genetic predisposition to psychopathology. *Journal of Autism and Developmental Disorders* **18**, 343−354.

Breslow J.L. (1988) Apolipoprotein genetic variation and human disease. *Physiological Review* **68**, 85−132

Cadoret R.J., Troughton E., Moreno L. & Whitters A. (1990) Early life psychosocial events and adult affective symptoms. In Robins L.N. & Rutter M. (eds) *Straight and Devious Pathways from Childhood to Adulthood*, pp. 300−313. Cambridge University Press, Cambridge.

Coryell W., Endicott J., Andreasen N.C., Keller M.B., Clayton P.J. & Hirschfeld R.M.A (1988) Depression and panic attacks: The significance of overlap as reflected in follow-up and family study data. *American Journal of Psychiatry* **145**, 293−300.

DeFries J.C. & Fulker D.W. (1985) Multiple regression analysis of twin data. *Behavior Genetics* **15**, 467−473.

DeFries J.C. & Fulker D.W. (1988) Multiple regression analysis of twin data: Etiology of deviant scores versus individual differences. *Acta Geneticae Medicae et Gemellologiae* **37**, 205−216.

DeFries J.C., Fulker D.W. & LaBuda M.C. (1987a) Evidence for a genetic aetiology in reading disability of twins. *Nature* **329**, 537−539.

DeFries J.C., Gervais M. & Thomas E.A. (1978) Response to 30 generations of selection for open-field activity in laboratory mice. *Behavior Genetics* **8**, 3–13.

DeFries J.C. & Gillis J.J. (1990) Etiology of reading deficits in learning disabilities: quantitative genetic analysis. In Obrzut J.E. & Hynd G.W. (eds) *Advances in the Neuropsychology of Learning Disabilities: Issues, Methods and Practice*, pp. 29–47. Academic Press, Florida.

DeFries J.C., Plomin R. & LaBuda M.C. (1987b) Genetic stability of cognitive development from childhood to adulthood. *Developmental Psychology* **23**, 4–12.

Dunn J.F. & Plomin R. (1990) *Separate Lives: Why Siblings are so Different*. Basic Books, New York.

Eaves L.J., Eysenck H.J. & Martin N. (1989) *Genes, Culture and Personality*. Academic Press, New York.

Edwards J.H. (1991) The formal problems of linkage. In McGuffin P. & Murray R. (eds) *The New Genetics of Mental Illness*, pp. 58–70. Butterworth-Heinemann, Oxford.

Falconer D.S. (1965) The inheritance of liability to certain diseases, estimated from the incidence among relatives. *Annals of Human Genetics* **29**, 51–76.

Fisher R.A. (1918) The correlation between relatives on the supposition of Mendelian inheritance. *Transactions of the Royal Society of Edinburgh* **52**, 399–433.

Folstein S.E., Franz M.L., Jensen B.A., Chase G.A. & Folstein M.F. (1983) Conduct disorder and affective disorder among the offspring of patients with Huntington's disease. *Psychological Medicine* **13**, 45–52.

Folstein S.E. & Rutter M.L. (1988) Autism: Familial aggregation and genetic implications. *Journal of Autism and Developmental Disorders* **18**, 3–30.

Fulker D.W., Cardon L.R., DeFries J.C., Kimberling W.J., Pennington B.F. & Smith S.D. (1991) Multiple regression analysis of sib-pair data on reading to detect quantitative trait loci. *Reading and Writing: An Interdisciplinary Journal* **3**, 299–313.

Fulker D.W., DeFries J.C. & Plomin R. (1988) Genetic influence on general mental ability increases between infancy and middle childhood. *Nature* **336**, 767–769.

Gelderman H. (1975) Investigations on inheritance of quantitative characters in animals by gene markers. I. Methods. *Theoretical and Applied Genetics* **46**, 319–330.

Gershon E.S., DeLisi L.E., Hamovit J., Nurnberger J.I., Maxwell M.E. & Schreiber J. (1988) A controlled family study of chronic psychoses. *Archives of General Psychiatry* **45**, 328–336.

Goldstein J.M. & Tsuang M.T. (1988) The process of subtyping schizophrenia: strategies in the search for homogeneity. In Tsuang M.T. & Simpson J.C. (eds) *Handbook of Schizophrenia*, Vol. 3, *Nosology, Epidemiology and Genetics*, pp. 63–83. Elsevier, New York.

Gottesman I.I. (1991) *Schizophrenia Genesis: The Origins of Madness*. W.H. Freeman, New York.

Hagerman R.J. & Sobesky W.E. (1989) Psychopathology in fragile-X syndrome. *American Journal of Orthopsychiatry* **59**, 142–152.

Hall J.M., Lee M.K., Newman B. *et al.* (1990) Linkage of early-onset familial breast cancer to chromosome 17q21. *Science* **250**, 1684–1689.

Haseman J.K. & Elston R.C. (1972) The investigation of linkage between a quantitative trait and a marker locus. *Behavior Genetics* **2**, 3–19.

Hetherington E.M., Reiss D. & Plomin R. (eds) (1994) *Separate Social Worlds of Siblings: Impact of Nonshared Environment on Development*. Lawrence Erlbaum, Hillsdale, New Jersey.

Hoffman M. (1991) Unraveling the genetics of fragile X syndrome. *Science* **252**, 1070.

Humphries S.E. (1988) DNA polymorphisms of the apolipoprotein genes: Their use in the investigation of the genetic component of the hyperlipidaemia and atherosclerosis. *Atherosclerosis* **72**, 89–108.

Kendler K.S., Gruenberg A.M. & Tsuang M.T. (1988) A family study of the subtypes of schizophrenia. *American Journal of Psychiatry* **145**, 57–62.

Kendler K.S., Heath A., Martin N.G. & Eaves L.J. (1987) Symptoms of anxiety and symptoms of depression: Same genes, different environments? *Archives of General Psychiatry* **44**, 451–457.

Kendler K.S. & Tsuang M.T. (1988) Outcome and familial psychopathology in schizophrenia. *Archives of General Psychiatry* **45**, 338–346.

Kidd K.K., Bowcock A.M., Schmidtke J. *et al.* (1989) Report of the DNA committee and catalogs of cloned and mapped genes and DNA polymorphisms. *Cytogenetics and Cell Genetics* **51**, 622–947.

Kovacs M. (1983) *Children's depression inventory: A self-rated depression scale for school-aged youngsters*. Unpublished ms, University of Pittsburgh.

Kovacs M. & Gatsonis C. (1989) Stability and change in childhood-onset depressive disorders: longitudinal course as a diagnostic validator. In Robins L.N. & Barrett J.E. (eds) *The Validity of Psychiatric Diagnosis*, pp. 57–73. Raven, New York.

Lachiewicz A., Gullian C., Spiridigliozzi G. & Aylsworth A. (1987) Declining IQs of young males with the fragile X syndrome. *American Journal of Mental Retardation* **92**, 272–278.

Loehlin J.C. (1987) *Latent Variable Models: An Introduction to Factor, Path, and Structural Analysis*. Lawrence Erlbaum, Hillsdale, New Jersey.

McClearn G.E. & Plomin R. (in press) Strategies for the search for genetic influences in alcohol-related phenotypes. In Begleiter H. & Kissin B. (eds) *Alcohol and Alcoholism*. Oxford University Press, Oxford.

McClearn G.E., Plomin R., Gora-Maslak G. & Crabbe J.C. (1991) The gene chase in behavioral science. *Psychological Science* **2**, 222–229.

McGuffin P., Farmer A. & Gottesman I.I. (1987) Is there really a split in schizophrenia? The genetic evidence. *British Journal of Psychiatry* **150**, 581–592.

McGuffin P., Katz R. & Bebbington P. (1988) The Camberwell Collaborative Depression Study. III. Depression and adversity in the relatives of depressed probands. *British Journal of Psychiatry* **152**, 775−782.

McGuffin P. & Murray R. (eds) (1991) *The New Genetics of Mental Illness*. Butterworth-Heinemann, Oxford.

McGuffin P. & Sturt E. (1986) Genetic markers in schizophrenia. *Human Heredity* **36**, 65−88.

McKusick V.A. (1990) *Mendelian Inheritance in Man*, 9th edn. Johns Hopkins University Press, Baltimore.

Mather K. (1941) Variation and selection of polygenic characters. *Journal of Genetics* **11**, 159−193.

Merikangas K.R., Risch N.J., Merikangas J.R., Weissman M.M. & Kidd K.K. (1988) Migraine and depression: association and familial transmission. *Journal of Psychiatry Research* **22**, 119−129.

Minuchin P. (1988) Relationships within the family: a systems perspective on development. In Hinde R.A. & Stevenson-Hinde J. (eds) *Relationships Within Families: Mutual Influences*, pp. 7−26. Oxford Science Publications, Oxford.

Minuchin S. (1974) *Families and Family Therapy*. Harvard University Press, Cambridge, Massachusetts.

Moldin S.O., Reich T. & Rice J.P. (1991) Current perspectives on the genetics of unipolar depression. *Behavior Genetics* **21**, 211−242.

Mullan M.J. & Murray R.M. (1989) The impact of molecular genetics on our understanding of the psychoses. *British Journal of Psychiatry* **154**, 591−595.

Oberle I., Rousseau F., Heitz D. *et al*. (1991) Instability of a 550-base pair DNA segment and abnormal methylation in fragile X syndrome. *Science* **252**, 1097−1102.

Olson R.K., Gillis J.J., Rack J.P. & Defries J.C. (1991) Confirmatory factor analysis of word recognition and process measures in the Colorado Reading Project. Special Issue: Genetic and neurological influences on reading disability. *Reading and Writing* **3**, 235−248.

Pardes H., Kaufmann C.A., Pincus H.A. & West A. (1989) Genetics and psychiatry: past discoveries, current dilemmas, and future directions. *American Journal of Psychiatry* **146**, 435−143.

Penrose L. (1935) The detection of autosomal linkage in data which consists of pairs of brothers and sisters of unspecified parentage. *Annals of Eugenics (London)* **6**, 133−138.

Plomin R. (1986a) *Development, Genetics, and Psychology*. Lawrence Erlbaum, Hillsdale, New Jersey.

Plomin R. (1986b) Multivariate analysis and developmental behavioral genetics: Developmental change as well as continuity. *Behavior Genetics* **16**, 25−43.

Plomin R. (1990) The role of inheritance in behavior. *Science* **248**, 183−188.

Plomin R. (1991) Genetic risk and psychosocial disorders: Links between the normal and abnormal. In Rutter M. & Casaer P. (eds) *Biological Risk Factors for Psychosocial Disorders*, pp. 101−138. Cambridge University Press, Cambridge.

Plomin R. & Bergeman C.S. (1991) The nature of nurture: Genetic influence on 'environmental' measures. *Behavioral and Brain Sciences* **14**, 373−386.

Plomin R., Chipuer H. & Loehlin J.C. (1990a) Behavioral genetics and personality. In Pervin L.A. (ed.) *Handbook of Personality Theory and Research*, pp. 225−243. Guilford, New York.

Plomin R., Chipuer H.M. & Neiderhiser J.M. (1994) Behavioral genetic evidence for the importance of non-shared environment. In Hetherington E.M., Reiss D. & Plomin R. (eds) *Separate Social Worlds of Siblings: Impact of Nonshared Environment on Development*, pp. 1−31. Lawrence Erlbaum, Hillsdale, New Jersey.

Plomin R. & Daniels D. (1987) Why are children in the same family so different from each other? *Behavioral and Brain Sciences* **10**, 1−16.

Plomin R. & DeFries J.C. (1979) Multivariate behavioral genetic analysis of twin data on scholastic abilities. *Behavior Genetics* **9**, 505−517.

Plomin R. & DeFries J.C. (1981) Multivariate behavioral genetics and development: Twin studies. In Gedda L., Parisi P. & Nance W.E. (eds) *Progress in Clinical and Biological Research, Twin Research 3*, Part B, *Intelligence, Personality, and Development*, Vol. 96B, pp. 25−33. Alan R. Liss, New York.

Plomin R., DeFries J.C. & Fulker D.W. (1988a) *Nature and Nurture in Infancy and Early Childhood*. Cambridge University Press, New York.

Plomin R., DeFries J.C. & Loehlin J.C. (1977) Genotype−environment interaction and correlation in the analysis of human behavior. *Psychological Bulletin* **84**, 309−322.

Plomin R., DeFries J.C. & McClearn G. (1990b) *Behavioral Genetics: A Primer*, 2nd edn. W.H. Freeman, New York.

Plomin R., Lichenstein P., Pedersen N.L., McClearn G.E. & Nesselroade J.R. (1990c) Genetic influence on life events. *Psychology and Aging* **5**, 25−30.

Plomin R., McClearn G.E., Gora-Maslak G. & Neiderhiser J.M. (1991a) Use of recombinant inbred strains to detect quantitative trait loci associated with behavior. *Behavior Genetics* **21**, 99−116.

Plomin R., McClearn G.E., Pedersen N.L., Nesselroade J.R. & Bergeman C.S. (1988b) Genetic influence on childhood family environment perceived retrospectively from the last half of the life span. *Developmental Psychology* **24**, 738−745.

Plomin R., McClearn G.E., Pedersen N.L., Nesselroade J.R. & Bergeman C.S. (1989) Genetic influence on adults' ratings of their current family environment. *Journal of Marriage and the Family* **51**, 791−803.

Plomin R. & Nesselroade J.R. (1990) Behavioral genetics and personality change. *Journal of Personality* **58**, 191−220.

Plomin R. & Rende R. (1991) Human behavioral genetics. *Annual Review of Psychology* **42**, 161−190.

Plomin R., Rende R.D. & Rutter M. (1991b) Quantitative genetics and developmental psychopathology. In Cicchetti D. & Tover S. (eds) *Rochester Symposium on Developmental Psychopathology*, Vol. 2, *Internalizing and Externalizing Expressions of Dysfunction*, pp. 155−202.

Lawrence Erlbaum, Hillsdale, New Jersey.

Quinton D. & Rutter M. (1988) *Parental Breakdown: The Making and Breaking of Intergenerational Links*. Gower, Aldershot.

Reiss A.L. & Freund L. (1990) Neuropsychiatric aspects of the fragile-X syndrome. *Brain Dysfunction* **3**, 9−22.

Reiss D., Hetherington E.M., Plomin R. *et al.* (1994) The separate worlds of teenage siblings: An introduction to the study of nonshared environment and adolescent development. In Hetherington E.M., Reiss D. & Plomin R. (eds) *Separate Social Worlds of Siblings: Impact of Nonshared Environment on Development*, pp. 63−109. Lawrence Erlbaum, Hillsdale, New Jersey.

Reiss D., Plomin R. & Hetherington E.M. (1991) Genetics and psychiatry: An unheralded window on the environment. *American Journal of Psychiatry* **148**, 283−291.

Rende R.D. & Plomin R. (1990) Quantitative genetics and developmental psychopathology: Contributions to understanding normal development. *Development and Psychopathology* **2**, 393−407.

Rende R.D., Plomin R., Reiss D. & Hetherington E.M. (1993) Genetic and environmental influences on depressive symptomatology in adolescence: Individual differences and extreme scores. *Journal of Child Psychology and Psychiatry* **34**, 1387−1398.

Rowe D.C. (1981) Environmental and genetic influences on dimensions of perceived parenting: A twin study. *Developmental Psychology* **17**, 203−208.

Rowe D.C. (1983) A biometrical analysis of perceptions of family environment: A study of twin and singleton sibling kinships. *Child Development* **54**, 416−423.

Rutter M. (1987) Continuities and discontinuities from infancy. In Osofsky J. (ed.) *Handbook of Infant Development*, 2nd edn, pp. 1256−1296. Wiley, New York.

Rutter M. (1988) Epidemiological approaches to developmental psychopathology. *Archives of General Psychiatry* **45**, 486−495.

Rutter M. (1990) Commentary: Some focus and process considerations are the effects of children of parental depression. *Developmental Psychology* **26**, 60−63.

Rutter M. (1991) Nature, nurture, and psychopathology: A new look at an old topic. *Development and Psychopathology* **3**, 125−136.

Rutter M., Bolton P., Harrington R., Le Couteur A., Macdonald H. & Simonoff E. (1990a) Genetic factors in child psychiatric disorders: I. A review of research strategies. *Journal of Child Psychology and Psychiatry* **31**, 3−37.

Rutter M., Macdonald H., Le Couteur A., Harrington R., Bolton P. & Bailey A. (1990b) Genetic factors in child psychiatric disorders: II. Empirical findings. *Journal of Child Psychology and Psychiatry* **31**, 39−82.

Sax K. (1923) The association of size differences with seed coat pattern and pigmentation in *Phaseolus vulgarus*. *Genetics* **8**, 552−560.

Schulz S.C. & Pato C.N. (1989) Advances in the genetics of schizophrenia: Editors' introduction. *Schizophrenia Bulletin* **15**, 361−364.

Sing C.F. & Boerwinkle E.A. (1987) Genetic architecture of inter-individual variability in apolipoprotein, lipoprotein and lipid phenotypes. In Bock G. & Collins G.M. (eds) *Molecular Approaches to Human Polygenic Disease*, pp. 99−122. Wiley, Chichester.

Smith C. (1974) Concordance in twins: Methods and interpretation. *American Journal of Human Genetics* **26**, 454−466.

Squires-Wheeler E., Skokol A.E., Friedman D. & Erlenmeyer-Kimling L. (1988) The specificity of DSM-III schizotypal personality traits. *Psychological Medicine* **18**, 757−765.

Sutherland G.R. & Hecht F. (1985) *Fragile Sites on Human Chromosomes*. Oxford University Press, New York.

Taylor B.A. (1989) Recombinant inbred strains. In Lyon M.F. & Searle A.G. (eds) *Genetic Variants and Strains of the Laboratory Mouse*, 2nd edn, pp. 773−789. Oxford University Press, Oxford.

Tiwari J. & Terasaki P.I. (1985) *HLA and Disease Associations*. Springer, New York.

Tsuang M.T. & Faraone S.V. (1990) *The Genetics of Mood Disorders*. Johns Hopkins University Press, Baltimore.

Tsuang M.T., Lyons M.L. & Faraone S.V. (1990) Heterogeneity of schizophrenia: Conceptual models and analytic strategies. *British Journal of Psychiatry* **156**, 17−26.

Turner G., Robinson H., Laing S. & Purvis-Smith S. (1986) Preventive screening for the fragile X syndrome. *New England Journal of Medicine* **315**, 607−609.

Vandenberg S.G., Singer S.M. & Pauls D.L. (1986) *The Heredity of Behavior Disorders in Adults and Children*. Plenum, New York.

Weeks D.E. & Lange K. (1988) The affected-pedigree-member method of linkage analysis. *American Journal of Human Genetics* **42**, 315−326.

Yu S., Pritchard M., Kremer E. *et al.* (1991) Fragile X genotype characterized by an unstable region of DNA. *Science* **252**, 1179−1181.

3: Brain Development

ROBERT GOODMAN

HOW TO BUILD A BRAIN*

Imagine that it is your task to design a human brain. The finished product has roughly 10^{14} connections and is capable of sophisticated cognitive processing guided both by phylogeny and ontogeny (i.e. reflecting both evolutionary and individual experience). Designing a product that worked would be hard enough, but you have the added burden of designing a product that is self-assembling. Unlike a computer, but like all other biological systems, the brain has to manufacture its own parts and assemble them into a functioning whole. The task is clearly extraordinarily complex. The main tools for the job are each individual's complement of roughly 10^5 genes, many of which are committed to functions that have nothing to do with brain development. How are you going to accomplish the task? In case you are stuck, here are a few hints to help you get started.

To begin with, you are allowed to devote a substantial proportion of the genome to the enterprise, with some 30 000 mammalian genes being expressed in the brain but not elsewhere (Sutcliffe et al., 1984). At the same time, however, the evol-

* This chapter should be accessible to all readers whether or not they have previously studied medicine or neuroscience. Although the main text assumes some basic knowledge of brain structure and function, additional explanatory notes are provided for newcomers to neuroscience. There is a glossary at the end of the chapter for various technical terms. Words that are included in this glossary are marked in italic on first appearance. In addition, Fig. 3.1 and its accompanying text on pp. 54–55 provide a brief introduction to brain structure and function, covering all the background material relevant to this chapter. Readers who do not have a foundation in neuroscience are advised to study the figures before reading the main text.

ution of the human brain has been remarkably rapid, suggesting that differences between the brains of humans and other primates must be based on a relatively limited number of genetic changes. How could changes in a small proportion of brain-specific genes result in a substantial increase in brain size and complexity? Genetically determined shifts in the timing rather than the sequence of developmental processes may have played a crucial role (cf. Gould, 1977). For example, if genetic changes resulted in just one extra round of cell division within a *precursor* population before that population became committed to the production of mature neurones, the result would be twice as many neurones. Thus the 10-fold increase in the size of the *cerebral cortex* in humans as compared with macaque monkeys could arise if the early phase of multiplication of precursor cells was prolonged by an average of just three or four extra rounds of cell division (Rakic, 1988). The evolutionary expansion of cortex has not been uniform, with *association areas* increasing much more rapidly than *primary motor and sensory cortex*. This suggests that genetic changes have resulted in disproportionate prolongation of the proliferation of some precursor populations, e.g. those generating the *prefrontal cortex*.

Generating 10^{14} *synapses* with fewer than 10^5 genes is clearly a daunting task. It is essential to remember, however, that the fine structure of the nervous system is very repetitious. The human cerebral *neocortex*, for instance, is made up of several hundred million *mini-columns*, each organized along fairly similar lines, though differing in external connections (Mountcastle, 1978; Rakic, 1988). The *cerebellar cortex* and many deep nuclei are similarly modular in structure. The number of modules clearly needs to be under genetic control, but the number of genes does not need to be proportionate to the number of modules. In principle, creating a million cerebral mini-columns may not require any more genes than creating 10 mini-columns, just as creating a million insulin molecules does not take any more genes than creating 10 molecules. This is a simplification, of course, since a cortex with a million rather than 10 mini-columns would probably need a more sophisticated genetic programme governing the way different mini-columns were connected both with one another and with extra-cortical structures. Despite this complicating factor, however, it is clear that the modular nature of neuronal organization does represent a major economy in the use of genetic information.

Scientists have long tried to explain the workings of the brain by drawing analogies with the most advanced technology of their time. It is not surprising, therefore, that analogies with computers are currently popular. Although these analogies can be illuminating, some major differences between brains and conventional electronic computers need to be emphasized. In an ordinary computer, a complex computation is broken down into a series of much simpler computations that are executed sequentially and extremely rapidly by a single powerful processor. The brain, by contrast, can be thought of as an assembly of vast numbers of slow and less powerful processors (whether these are conceived of as neuronal modules or as single neurones). Any one brain task simultaneously engages a multiplicity of processors acting in parallel with one another. Neural networks involve not just one set of parallel processors, but several such sets connected in series, with much divergence and convergence between sets. Electronic analogues of such networks can have remarkable brain-like properties, e.g. learning the rules of English pronunciation from examples only, with the system passing from a babbling stage to a stage when most new words can be pronounced correctly (Sejnowski & Rosenberg, 1987). Exciting though these analogues are, they do depend on types of error feedback that have no physiologically plausible equivalents (Crick, 1989a). Despite this reservation, studies of parallel computers may well contribute to our understanding of the brain (Nelson & Bower, 1990). The general principle that extremely powerful computers can be made from large numbers of

relatively modest processors harnessed in parallel is a useful insight. A process of brain development that generates repetitive modules that can operate in parallel clearly makes computing sense as well as representing an economical use of genes. Since the power of a parallel computer can be boosted by increasing the number of processors (Nelson & Bower, 1990), evolutionary changes in brain development that result in more neuronal modules operating in parallel can increase the brain's performance as well as its size. The modest correlation between intelligence and brain size can also be understood in these terms (Willerman *et al.*, 1991).

Parallel computers can be homogeneous, employing arrays of just one type of processor, or heterogeneous, employing several types of processor. The cerebral cortex can be thought of as a mixture of the two, with relative homogeneity within each cortical area, and with heterogeneity between cortical areas. Functionally, this regional heterogeneity presumably reflects specialization for different roles. Developmentally, the whole cortex is relatively uniform when it first forms; the subsequent emergence or accentuation of regional diversity provides a fascinating window on the interplay of predetermination and plasticity, as described later in this chapter.

Even if the highly repetitive structure of the nervous system makes the task of designing a self-assembling brain somewhat less daunting, the residual obstacles are still considerable. Molecular biologists can provide a detailed account of the deterministic and relatively direct manner in which genetic information is translated into a protein's linear sequence of amino acids. Developmental neurobiologists, by contrast, can only provide a rudimentary and very patchy account of the way genetic information is translated into intricate three-dimensional patterns of synaptic connections. As far as brain development is concerned, the relevant genes are best thought of as relatively simple instructions for generating the finished product rather than as detailed descriptions of the finished product. The potential power of simple instructions to generate complex products is well illustrated by origami, in which sequences of 'fold' and 'unfold' instructions generate shapes from sheets of paper that would take pages to describe. What are the developing brain's equivalent of 'fold' and 'unfold' instructions? Recent studies suggest a key role for genes coding for cell-surface glycoproteins, with the glycoproteins involved in cell adhesion playing an important part in regulating the proliferation, migration and differentiation of brain cells (e.g. Edelman, 1987, 1988). Thus the presence of complementary receptors and targets on the cell surfaces of two populations of neurones (X and Y) could provide the basis for a developmental 'instruction' that *axons* of type X neurones should preferentially form synapses with *dendrites* of type Y neurones. Relatively simple instructions of this sort may well underpin the brain's capacity for self-assembly. During the initial stages of vertebrate brain development, instructions based on cell recognition seem to generate a first approximation to the definitive pattern of neuronal interconnection — with the mature pattern of brain connections subsequently being established by a process of successive approximations, primarily involving subtractive fine-tuning and neuronal competition (Easter *et al.*, 1985).

Both additive and subtractive processes play an important part in brain development, as they do in the development of practically all biological systems (Glucksman, 1951). Additive (or progressive) processes can be likened to the production of a car, with a series of parts being added, each in the right place, until the finished model is ready to roll off the production line. By contrast, subtractive (or regressive) processes can be likened to the sculpting of a statue from a block of stone, with fragments of stone being chipped away until the finished statue remains. During brain development, additive processes determine the broad outline of brain organization and subtractive processes contribute to fine-tuning (Cowan *et al.*, 1984). The phases of additive and subtractive development overlap, but the subtractive phase starts later and continues longer. The role of additive and subtractive processes can be illustrated* by the findings of O'Leary

* Wherever possible, the concepts introduced in this chapter have been illustrated by specific examples, primarily to help readers who are already familiar with neuroscience. Since the specifics of the example are generally less central to the thrust of the chapter than the concept being illustrated, readers who are unfamiliar with neuroscience should not struggle to master the specifics once the underlying concept has been grasped.

and Stanfield (1985). In newborn rats, the *pyramidal* cells in layer V of the visual cortex contribute to the *corticospinal* tract — a projection that has no counterpart in adult life, and no apparent function. It seems that the additive process of axonal outgrowth is fairly crudely specified, with layer V pyramidal cells from all areas of cortex following a simple rule to project to a variety of *subcortical* structures, even if the resultant connections would serve no useful function. Over the course of postnatal development, the crude early pattern of subcortical projections is fine-tuned by subtractive processes, with axons originating in the visual cortex being selectively pruned so that layer V neurones no longer contribute to the corticospinal tract though they do continue to connect with the *pons* and *superior colliculus*. In this example, the pyramidal cell survives the pruning of its misconnected axon; in other instances, fine-tuning involves the death of misconnected neurones (Cowan *et al.*, 1984).

Competition between neurones and between their processes probably plays a key role in subtractive fine-tuning (Cowan *et al.*, 1984; Easter *et al.*, 1985). This competition, in the most general terms, is for some limited resource that is essential for survival. The limiting factor may, for example, be the availability of either synaptic space or trophic materials. A Darwinian struggle for survival — in which only the fittest neurones, axons and synapses survive — would clearly provide a powerful mechanism for improving on the level of synaptic specification produced by additive processes. Guillery (1988) draws a useful distinction between two broad types of competition. Type I competition, which involves a single population of neurones competing for some limited resource, may provide a useful mechanism for regulating the size of a neuronal population. If the additive processes that generate a particular neuronal population are fairly imprecise and cannot be relied upon to produce exactly the right number of neurones, it makes evolutionary sense to err on the side of overproduction if there is a mechanism for eliminating surplus or misconnected neurones. This sort of mechanism may be provided by competition for a limited supply of some trophic substance, such as a growth factor or *neurotransmitter* (Purves & Lichtman, 1985; Korsching, 1986; Lipton & Kater, 1989). Thus if type X neurones synapse on type Y neurones, and if there are initially more type

X neurones than can be supported by the limited supply of trophic factors released by type Y neurones, then surplus type X neurones will die off until a balance is reached. Competition between type X neurones will favour those neurones that have been particularly successful at making appropriate connections.

Whereas type I competition occurs between the members of a single population of neurones, type II competition occurs between the members of two or more different populations. In the visual cortex, for example, there is competition between *afferents* conveying information from the *contralateral* eye and the *ipsilateral* eye. At an early stage of development, most cells in the *striate* cortex can be driven by stimulation of either eye, reflecting the extensive intermingling of the two sorts of input. Subsequent competition between the two sorts of input results in axonal pruning that segregates the two sorts of input into alternating stripes of ipsilaterally and contralaterally driven cortex. In this and other instances of type II competition, the outcome is influenced by the spontaneous or environmentally driven activity of neurones — so that abolition of electrical activity interferes with the subtractive processes that normally result in fine-tuning (Dubin *et al.*, 1986; Stryker & Harris, 1986; Cline, 1991). As described later in this chapter, the relevant neural activity may occur after birth, reflecting the individual's postnatal experiences. Before birth, spontaneous neuronal activity also plays a key role in type II competition and subtractive fine-tuning (e.g. Sretavan *et al.*, 1988).

When statisticians are faced with a problem that is so complex that it cannot be solved by a one-off calculation, they often resort to a method of successive approximation: making a guess at the answer, trying out this approximate solution and noting its shortcomings, adjusting the solution to try to overcome the shortcomings, trying out the new solution, making further adjustments, and so on until the solution is adequate for the task in hand. The developing brain employs a similar strategy, using additive processes to generate a first approximation, and using error-driven subtractive processes to carry out the successive approximations. This additive then subtractive strategy permits the construction of a far more complex brain than could be constructed from additive processes alone — an advantage that evidently more than compensates for the wastefulness of creating large numbers of neurones, axons and synapses that are deliberately destroyed soon afterwards.

Creation followed by deliberate destruction also characterizes another aspect of brain development that has received little attention until recently, namely the existence of transient embryonic structures. These neuronal systems are created at one stage of development, serve their function, and are subsequently largely or entirely dismantled. One such system is the *subplate* zone, which lies beneath the cerebral cortex. Far from being an evolutionary vestige, as previously supposed, it appears to play a major role in the development of the cerebral cortex, being most prominent in species with a well developed cortex and reaching its maximum size in humans (Kostovic & Rakic, 1990).

In many everyday tasks, there is a trade-off between speed and accuracy. We can perform a task faster if we are prepared to tolerate more errors, and we can perform a task more accurately if we are prepared to take longer over it. Similar considerations may apply to brain development: faster development may result in a less precisely specified neuronal organization, and more precision may take longer to achieve. Slower development may have the added advantage of permitting more extensive fine-tuning of neuronal organization in the light of the individual's postnatal experiences. These considerations may help explain why human brain maturation is so slow, incurring the disadvantages of prolonged dependency in order to reap the advantages of greater precision and environmental openness. A conflict between speed and accuracy could potentially also account for instances in which two neurological systems subserve the same function, with one system being more important early in development, and with the other being more important thereafter — as may be the case for some aspects of vision and delayed-response (DR) learning (Goldman-Rakic *et al.*, 1983; Atkinson, 1984; Tresidder *et al.*, 1990). Perhaps a rapidly maturing but coarsely tuned neural system acts as a stop-gap until a slowly maturing but finely tuned system is ready to take over.

Since so many of the processes involved in brain development are probabilistic rather than deterministic, there is bound to be a fair degree of randomness in the organization of the final product. Although genes do not specify the architecture of synaptic connections as precisely as they specify the architecture of protein molecules, some degree of randomness in brain organization may have advantages as well as disadvantages. An individual's capacity to adapt to an enormous range of possible environments might well be jeopardized if the performance of the brain were too rigidly specified. Other open-ended biological processes — such as evolution by natural selection, or the development of a mature complement of B lymphocyte clones — involve a stochastic process that combines random variation with environmentally guided selection. An individual's immune system can respond to a wide range of antigens, including substances that the species has never previously encountered, because that individual's primary repertoire of antibody-bearing B lymphocytes is generated by a mixture of genetic determination and random variation — with different variants within this primary repertoire subsequently being eliminated or amplified in the light of the individual's experience. A comparable mixture of random variation and environmental selection probably contributes to the open-ended nature of brain function. Having been created by probabilistic and therefore partly random processes, synapses can subsequently be retained or disconnected according to their utility (Changeux & Danchin, 1976; Bear *et al.*, 1987; Edelman, 1987). At the level of the synapse, therefore, functional selection between randomly generated alternatives does seem to occur. Whether comparable mechanisms operate at more complex organizational levels within the nervous system remains controversial (see Edelman, 1987 and Crick, 1989b for opposing views on the likely importance of neuronal group selection).

STAGES OF BRAIN DEVELOPMENT

By the sixth week of gestation, the human embryo has a neural tube whose anterior portion is divided into three successive 'bulges' that give rise to the forebrain, midbrain and hindbrain (Nowakowski, 1987). (Throughout this chapter, timing in pregnancy is based on conventional obstetric dating from the last menstrual period — these dates can be converted into postconceptual ages by subtracting 2 weeks.) The precursors of the cerebral hemispheres are recognizable as out-pouchings of the forebrain bulge during the seventh week of pregnancy (Fig. 3.1a). Judging primarily from studies of the hindbrain, the parcellation of the developing nervous system into regions with distinctive fates is associated with the emergence of regional differences in the expression of transcription-regulating genes such as zinc-finger or *homeobox* genes (Lumsden, 1990; Wilkinson & Krumlauf, 1990). The involvement of related homeobox genes in the segmentation of species as different as the mouse and the fruit fly is a surprising and striking finding (Wilkinson & Krumlauf, 1990).

Although different parts of the nervous system develop at different rates and in somewhat different ways, the general sequence of events can be illustrated by focusing on the formation of the cerebral cortex. As described in the preceding section, brain development involves both additive and subtractive processes. For the sake of clarity, the additive stages of brain development are described before the subtractive stages even though there is actually considerable overlap in the timing of additive and subtractive processes.

Immature neurones are produced by the proliferation of precursor cells in *germinal* zones. In the case of the cerebral cortex, the precursor cells are situated in the *ventricular* and subventricular zones surrounding the lateral ventricles (Nowakowski & Rakic, 1981). The majority of neurones destined for the deeper cortical layers are generated in the ventricular zone, whereas the majority of neurones destined for the outer cortical layers are generated in the subventricular zone (Nowakowski & Rakic, 1981). In humans, the production of cortical neurones commences at about the eighth week of gestation and draws to a close around the eighteenth week of gestation (Rakic & Sidman, 1968; Dobbing & Sands, 1973; Sidman & Rakic, 1973; Rakic, 1978). In some other parts of the brain, neurogenesis continues substantially longer. In the cerebellum, the production of granule cells proceeds at a high rate during the first year after birth and then tails off in the second year (Raaf & Kernohan, 1944). Judging from studies of other primates, the production of *hippocampal* granule cells also extends into the early postnatal period (Eckenhoff & Rakic,

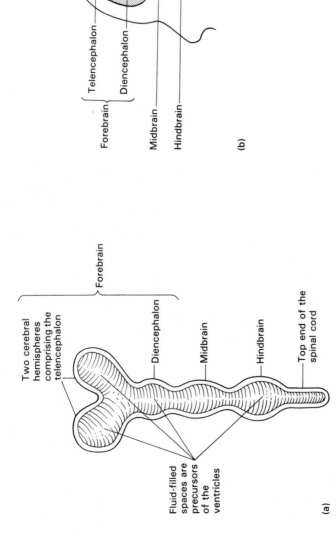

Fig. 3.1 An overview of brain structure and function. (a) The central nervous system is initially a simple tube. The brain begins as three successive bulges at the front end of this tube, giving rise to the forebrain, midbrain and hindbrain. The two cerebral hemispheres are outpouchings of the forebrain and the cerebellum is an outpouching of the hindbrain. The spaces within the tube and its out-pouchings are the precursors of the ventricular system, which is filled with cerebrospinal fluid (CSF). The inner surface of the wall of the tube and its out-pouchings is known as the ventricular surface. Early in development, many neurones are generated at or near the ventricular surface, subsequently migrating centrifugally from this germinal zone to take up their definitive positions. (b) Shows a schematic cross-section through the head showing the main structures of the brain. The cerebral hemispheres account for about two-thirds of the brain's mass and roughly three-quarters of the brain's synapses. Surprisingly, most of the brain's neurones are in the relatively small cerebellum — though most of these cerebellar neurones are small inter-neurones with relatively few synapses.

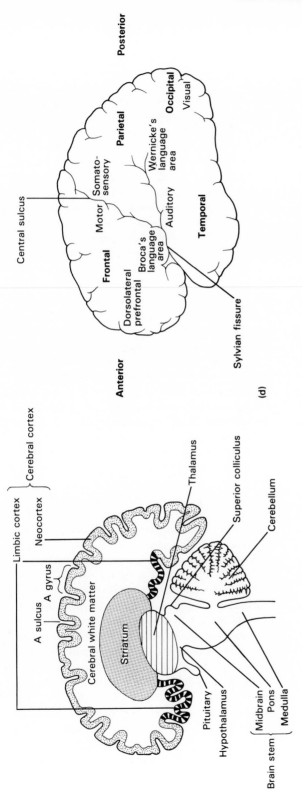

Fig. 3.1 (*Continued*) (c) Shows a more detailed though equally schematic cross-section of the brain. Within each cerebral hemisphere, neuronal cell bodies are concentrated either in the cortex, which is the corrugated surface of the hemisphere, or in deep nuclei such as the striatum or amygdala. The white matter that separates the cortex from the deep nuclei contains several sorts of fibre tracts: (i) descending tracts, e.g. from the visual cortex to the superior colliculus, or from the motor cortex to the spinal cord; (ii) ascending tracts, e.g. from the thalamus to the cortex; (iii) association tracts within the same hemisphere, e.g. from the frontal lobe to the parietal lobe on the same side; and (iv) commissural tracts that cross from the cortex of one hemisphere to the cortex of the opposite hemisphere, mostly through the corpus callosum. Most of the inputs to the cerebral cortex (e.g. from sense organs or cerebellum) are channelled through the thalamus. The striatum and cerebellum are primarily involved in motor control. The limbic cortex (including the hippocampal formation) and the amygdala are particularly important for short-term memory, motivation and affect. The hypothalamus and brain stem play key roles in regulating somatic function via the endocrine and autonomic nervous systems. Various brain stem nuclei are the source of ascending tracts (releasing noradrenaline, dopamine or serotonin) that modulate cerebral function and influence arousal and attention. (d) Shows a lateral view of a cerebral hemisphere showing the conventional division into four lobes: occipital, parietal, temporal and frontal. Visual input from the optic nerves is relayed through the lateral geniculate portion of the thalamus into the striate cortex at the pole of the occipital lobe. The rest of the occipital lobe is devoted to further processing of this visual information. The primary cortical targets for somatosensory and auditory input are in the parietal and temporal lobes respectively. Much of the temperoparietal region is association cortex that receives indirect input from multiple sensory modalities. While the occipital, parietal and temporal lobes are dominated by perceptual processing, the role of the frontal lobe is more closely related to action. The posterior portion of the frontal lobe is primarily involved in the relatively direct control of movement. The anterior portion of the frontal lobe (also known as the 'prefrontal' portion) is more concerned with 'higher functions', e.g. the dorsolateral portion of the prefrontal cortex is particularly concerned with delayed responses. Wernicke's and Broca's areas are the two classical language-related cortical areas. Wernicke's area is near the primary auditory cortex and is particularly involved in processing language input while Broca's area is near the portion of the motor cortex that controls speech muscles and is particularly involved in speech output.

1988). Whereas some neuronal production occurs in adult life in rats, neurogenesis is entirely restricted to the developmental period in primates (Rakic, 1985).

Since neurones are produced some distance from their final destination, they have to migrate from their site of origin to their site of functioning — a process reviewed by Nowakowski (1987), Rakic (1988) and Hatten (1990). The migration of newly formed neurones from the germinal zones to the cortex is guided by radial *glial* fibres that span the cerebral wall from the inner ventricular surface to the outer cortical surface. In a process that Hatten (1990) graphically describes as riding the glial monorail, a newly formed neurone attaches itself to the ventricular end of a radial fibre, migrates along the fibre rather like an amoeba, and finally detaches itself at the cortical end of the fibre. Cell-surface proteins, such as astrotactin, appear to play a crucial role in neurone—glia binding and loco-motion. Many of the earliest arrivals in the cortex contribute to the subplate zone. Later arrivals migrate through the subplate zone to form the various layers of the definitive cortex. The cortex is formed inside out, with each new wave of arrivals migrating through the layers formed by previous arrivals. Thus the neurones that make up the deepest layer of the definitive cortex (layer VI) arrive first; layer V neurones arrive later and have to migrate through layer VI to reach their destination; layer IV neurones arrive later still and have to migrate through both layer VI and layer V; and so on. The adaptive value of this inside—out development is unclear since mice with the reeler mutation function fairly normally even though their cortex forms the other way round, with layer VI being superficial to layer V, and so on (Caviness & Rakic, 1978; Nowakowski, 1987).

The neurones that migrate successively up a single radial glial fibre stack on top of one another, thereby generating an embryonic mini-column. Though Rakic (1988) originally proposed that each mini-column arose from a few related precursor cells, more recent evidence suggests that the descendants of a single precursor cell contribute to several mini-columns (which may be adjacent or widely dispersed) and that single columns are commonly descended from more than one clone of precursor cells (Walsh & Cepko, 1992). Whether mini-columns form the modular processors of the functioning cerebral cortex has yet to be resolved (Mountcastle, 1978; Swindale, 1990).

Each mini-column contains a wide variety of neuronal types, such as layer III pyramidal cells projecting to other cortical areas, layer VI pyramidal cells projecting to the *thalamus*, and layer IV granule cells with purely local axonal connections. Each neurone's destiny, in terms of the type of neurone it will differentiate into, is partly determined during the last cell cycle of the precursor cell that generates the neurone (McConnell, 1991). The commitment of the newly formed neurone to a particular fate may be evident before it has even completed its migration. For example, Schwartz *et al.* (1991) have demonstrated in monkeys that some layer III neurones that contribute to the *corpus callosum* send their axons to the contralateral hemisphere even before their cell bodies have migrated into the ipsilateral cortex. Although studies of this sort suggest that the differentiation of a newly produced neurone is broadly determined from the outset, the finer details of neuronal connectivity remain open to modification for much longer, as described elsewhere in this chapter.

The growth of an axon from its site of origin to a distant target is an extraordinary developmental accomplishment. The growth cone at the tip of the developing axon must not only navigate the complex path to its appropriate destination, but it must also recognize when it has arrived at that destination and then stop growing and form synaptic connections. Cell-surface recognition probably plays a key role in these processes, with various specific glycoproteins on the surface of the axonal growth cone interacting with complementary proteins in the extracellular matrix or on the surface of other cells (Trisler & Collins, 1987; Hankin & Lund, 1991). Some of these cell-surface glycoproteins, both in vertebrates and in insects, are members of the immunoglobulin superfamily (Edelman, 1988; Harrelson & Goodman, 1988). Over short distances, axonal growth may also be guided by concentration gradients of soluble substances released by the axon's target (Hankin & Lund, 1991; Tessier-Lavigne & Placzek, 1991). Navigating to the correct destination is likely to be a particularly complex task for those axons that pioneer a route; the axons that follow have the simpler task of recognizing the pioneer axons and growing along them. There is increasing evidence that the subcortical, *callosal* and *intrahemispheric* projections from the cerebral cortex are first established by pioneer neurones from the transient subplate zone (McConnell *et al.*, 1989; Blakemore, 1991). These pioneer fibres probably act as guides for the axons that subsequently grow out from the permanent layers of the cerebral cortex. Most subplate neurones are eliminated after the definitive projections are established, perhaps in much the same way that scaffolding can be removed once a building has been completed.

The subplate zone probably plays another key role too, acting as a 'waiting' compartment for axons growing into the cortex from the *brain stem*, the thalamus, the contralateral cortex and distant regions of the ipsilateral cortex (Kostovic & Rakic, 1990). At an early stage of development, while the definitive cortex is still forming, incoming afferents accumulate in the subplate zone. Transient synaptic connections between 'waiting' afferents and subplate neurones may permit different sorts of afferents to interact, and possibly compete, with one another even at this early stage. Later in development, the waiting axons resume their growth into the cortex, forming synaptic connections in one or more layers of the definitive cortex.

In primates, the general pattern of axonal interconnection is established before birth (Schwartz & Goldman-Rakic, 1990), but the growth of dendrites and axonal terminals continues after birth, with an accompanying increase in the number of synapses. In the human prefrontal cortex, for example, there are marked postnatal increases in both dendritic length (Schade & van Groenigen, 1961) and synaptic density (Huttenlocher, 1979). Regional differences in rates of dendritic development generally parallel regional differences in rates of functional maturation (Parmelee & Sigman, 1983). Regional differences in the rate of *myelination* provide another index of functional maturity. Myelination starts before birth but continues well into childhood (and even into adulthood in some brain regions), with myelination generally proceeding most slowly in those regions, such as the prefrontal cortex, that take longest to reach functional maturity (Yakovlev & Lecours, 1967).

If brain development just involved the sorts of additive processes described up to this point, the result would be a first approximation to normal brain structure. Subtractive fine-tuning, involving the selective elimination of neurones, axons and synapses, plays an essential role in establishing the brain's definitive pattern of neuronal and synaptic organization (see Cowan *et al.*, 1984 for a review). In most neuronal systems, a substantial proportion of the original neurones are eliminated in the course of development, with this selective cell death occurring during a well-defined period that is characteristic of each neuronal population. Roughly half of the original neurones are eliminated in many neuronal systems, though the proportion lost is lower in the cerebral cortex (Finlay & Slattery, 1983). Selective cell death probably serves several purposes, including the elimination of surplus or misconnected neurones, and the removal of transient neural structures that have outlived their usefulness. Local variations in the rate of cell death in the cerebral cortex may contribute to the emergence of regional and hemispheric specialization (Finlay & Slattery, 1983; Galaburda *et al.*, 1987). Variations between individuals in the pattern or extent of selective cell loss may also be relevant. For example, the sexually dimorphic nucleus of the human *hypothalamus* is substantially larger in men that in women — a difference that reflects greater neuronal death in females rather than greater neuronal production in males (Swaab & Hofman, 1988). The loss of cells from the sexually dimorphic nucleus occurs during middle childhood; this late loss is exceptional, with most selective neuronal death taking place earlier in development (Cowan *et al.*, 1984).

Since axons can have multiple *collaterals*, a single neurone can project to multiple targets. Selective elimination of some of these collaterals can increase the specificity of a neurone's connections. In the primary *somatosensory* cortex of the rhesus monkey, for example, many cortico-cortical projection neurones have at least two collaterals early in fetal life, one of which projects within the same hemisphere, while the other projects across the corpus callosum to the contralateral hemisphere; many of these neurones lose their contralateral projections later in fetal life, thereby becoming purely ipsilateral projection fibres (Chalupa & Killackey, 1989). In humans, the peak period for axonal loss from the corpus callosum probably extends from the seventh month of pregnancy into the second postnatal month at least, with sex differences in the form and size of the corpus callosum first appearing at this time (Clarke *et al.*, 1989). As discussed earlier in this chapter, the pruning of axonal collaterals can be influenced by competition between axons, and by a neurone's spontaneous or environmentally driven electrical activity.

During the early stages of brain development, synapses increase in number. This trend is reversed later in development, with the number of synapses decreasing as subtractive processes such as axonal pruning outpace additive processes such as axonal growth. In the human prefrontal cortex, for example, synaptic density reaches its peak in the second year of life and then declines throughout childhood and adolescence before stabilizing in adulthood at about two-thirds of the peak value (Huttenlocher, 1979). Although the number of synapses stabilizes in adulthood, this probably reflects a dynamic balance between synaptic creation and removal rather than a frozen state in which no synaptic turnover occurs (Greenough *et al.*, 1987). In addition to this physical turnover of synapses, some synapses can be turned off and on without being removed and recreated — see Wall (1977) for a discussion of latent synapses.

Different brain regions go through the various stages of brain development at different rates. For example, the proliferative and migratory phases progress more slowly in the cerebellar cortex than in the cerebral cortex (Sidman & Rakic, 1973). It seems likely that different regions of the cerebral cortex also mature at different rates (although Rakic *et al.*, 1986 have presented some contrary evidence). In humans, for example, four lines of evidence suggest that the maturation of the prefrontal cortex proceeds more slowly than the maturation of the primary visual cortex. Thus, the visual cortex leads in dendritic growth (Schade & van Groenigen, 1961; Takashima *et al.*, 1980), in intracortical myelination (Yacovlev & Lecours, 1967), in the time of attainment of peak synaptic density (Huttenlocher, 1979; Huttenlocher *et al.*, 1982), and in the postnatal upsurge in cortical metabolic rate (Chugani *et al.*, 1987).

FAULTS AT DIFFERENT STAGES OF BRAIN DEVELOPMENT

Gross errors in brain development result in obvious pathology and recognizable neurological disorders. Thus failure of the neural tube to close at its anterior end results in *anencephaly*, while marked abnormalities in proliferation and migration are probably responsible for cortical malformations such as *lissencephaly* and *polymicrogyria* (Nowakowski, 1987; Rakic, 1988). Abnormalities in proliferation and migration may also mediate the effects of prenatal exposure to alcohol or X-rays on mental development (Otake & Schull, 1984; Miller, 1986).

It is tempting to suppose that some abnormalities in brain development usually present with specific psychiatric or educational problems rather than with frank neurological problems. Subtle or localized abnormalities of neuronal migration and connection could potentially contribute to a wide range of behavioural and learning problems. This supposition is supported by neuropathological studies suggesting that migration defects may be relevant to schizophrenia and dyslexia (Galaburda *et al.*, 1985; Jones & Murray, 1991; Mednick *et al.*, 1991). Migration abnormalities, and associated misconnections, can be secondary to environmental insults to the developing brain or to defects in genes that affect brain development (or to some combination of the two). Genetically determined migration disorders have been extensively studied in mice (Caviness & Rakic, 1978; Nowakowski, 1987); some of these disorders result in widespread disruption of normal brain architecture, while other disorders result in abnormalities that are patchily distributed or restricted to a single brain region (Nowakowski, 1984; Sherman *et al.*, 1985). By analogy, genes that affect the pattern of neuronal migration in the developing human brain could potentially result in the sorts of localized defects reported in schizophrenia or dyslexia. Environmental insults during the migratory phase of brain development could have similar effects, potentially explaining the possible association between prenatal exposure to influenza around the middle of pregnancy (when neuronal migration is still in progress) and subsequent schizophrenia (Mednick *et al.*, 1988; Sham *et al.*, 1992). If schizophrenia is due, in some cases at least, to neuronal abnormalities that are present before birth, why do psychotic symptoms not emerge until many years later? The answer is not known. One possibility is that the lesion lies in a late-maturing part of the brain that does not come 'on line' until adolescence or adulthood. Alternatively, the lesion may lie dormant until unmasked either by progressive myelination or by the selective pruning of synapses and axonal collaterals — processes that continue into adolescence or adulthood.

Since the production and migration of neurones continues for longer in the cerebellum and hippocampus than in the cerebral neocortex, environmental insults that affect the developing brain late in pregnancy and early in infancy may have their greatest impact on cerebellar and hippocampal development. In rats, this sort of selective damage has been linked to hyperactivity and learning deficits (Altman, 1987).

Even when neuronal migration proceeds normally, so that brain architecture is grossly intact, abnormalities in axonal growth could still result in misconnections. For example, axons may navigate to, and form synapses with, inappropriate targets because of genetically determined abnormalities in some of the membrane proteins involved in cell-surface recognition. Environmental insults that damage the developing brain may also result in anomalous connections, i.e. neuronal connections that are either absent or inconspicuous in a normal brain (Devor, 1975; Schneider, 1979). There is limited circumstantial evidence that misconnections may be relevant to psychiatric disorders (Goodman, 1989).

Abnormalities in subtractive processes could also have psychiatric and educational consequences. For example, if the selective pruning of axons and synapses is slow and incomplete, the result will be a diffusely overconnected brain that may be functionally immature in a number of respects (Goodman, 1991a). Speculatively, diffuse overconnection or misconnection could result in an unfavourable signal : noise ratio, reflected in poor performance on tasks involving attention, learning, problem-solving and coordination (Goodman, 1989, 1991a).

SPECIALIZATION OF THE CEREBRAL CORTEX: REGIONAL AND LATERAL VARIATION

Although all areas of the cerebral neocortex share a similar basic structure, there are marked regional variations on this basic theme. Indeed, the cerebral cortex can be thought of as a patchwork of different cytoarchitectural areas, with each area having distinctive cellular, connectional and functional characteristics. Distinctive features of the striate cortex, for example, include a particularly well-developed layer IV, a *retinotopic* input from the lateral geniculate portion of the thalamus, and a primary role in visual perception. How do regional variations in cortical structure and function come into being? Current evidence suggests a complex interplay of predetermination and plasticity (Rakic, 1988; O'Leary, 1989). To some extent, the cortical patchwork probably reflects a corresponding mosaicism in the precursor cell lineages that gave rise to the cortex. For example, the precursor cell lineages that generate the striate cortex may be committed from the start to a particularly long proliferative period, thereby accounting for the particularly large number of neurones in each of the striate cortex's mini-columns (Rakic, 1988). Another feature of the striate cortex, namely its lack of callosal connections, also seems to date back to a very early stage of development in primates (but not in other species) (Dehay *et al.*, 1988).

If predetermination were the whole story, the fate of each cortical region would be fixed from the start. In fact, evidence from a variety of species suggests considerable cortical plasticity early on in development (O'Leary, 1989). For example, if visual information is diverted at an early stage of development into a cortical region that would normally subserve hearing or touch, that region of cortex comes to have many of the properties of ordinary visual cortex (Sur *et al.*, 1990). Similarly, if an immature portion of cortex is transplanted from one site to another, the axons that grow out from that portion of cortex form permanent connections that are appropriate to the recipient site rather than to the donor site (O'Leary & Stanfield, 1989). Although these studies were conducted on rodents and carnivores, primate studies also demonstrate that cortical fate can be partly respecified, provided that the experimental intervention occurs well before birth (Goldman-Rakic *et al.*, 1983; Rakic *et al.*, 1991). While these studies demonstrate considerable plasticity within the neocortex, transplants between *limbic* cortex and neocortex appear to be more resistant to respecification, suggesting that the distinction between limbic cortex and neocortex arises earlier in development than distinctions within different neocortical regions (Barbe & Levitt, 1991).

Of late, lateralization studies have rather dominated neuropyschological research, even though the division of labour between the two cerebral hemispheres is less striking than the division of labour within each hemisphere. The appeal of lateralization studies can be attributed to several factors, including the attraction of a simple dichotomy, the abiding public interest in 'left brain, right brain' issues, and the easy availability of techniques, such as tachistoscopic viewing and dichotic listening, that can be used to examine lateral specialization. Differences between the two hemispheres in adulthood have been reviewed extensively (Bradshaw & Nettleton, 1983; Springer & Deutsch, 1989). Four general features of adult lateralization are worth summarizing, particularly since they seem to apply to childhood lateralization too (Goodman, 1987). First, both hemispheres are specialized, and it is inaccurate to think of one hemisphere as being dominant in all respects. In a typical right-handed adult, for example, speech depends primarily on the left hemisphere, while face recognition depends primarily on the right hemisphere. Second, a major skill may involve component subskills that are lateralized in opposite directions. In the case of communication skill, for example, the left hemisphere specializes in speech— sound production and syntax, while the right hemisphere specializes in communication through tone of voice, facial expression and gesture. Third, lateral specialization is more often a matter of degree than an all-or-nothing phenomenon. Thus although the left hemisphere is specialized in syntax, the right hemisphere does have some linguistic capability even in this domain. Finally, the degree of lateralization varies between skills and between individuals.

Contrary to the traditional view that the two hemispheres are functionally equivalent at birth and only become asymmetrically specialized as childhood progresses, there is now a wealth of evidence that differences between the two hemispheres are already present early on in development (Molfese & Segalowitz, 1988). Anatomically, hemispheric asymmetry dates back to prenatal life. For example, the planum temporale, which is a language-related region of cerebral cortex within *Wernicke's area*, is already generally larger on the left than on the right side by 29 weeks of gestation (Wada *et al.*, 1975). Studies of normal infants and children have revealed functional asymmetries at all stages of development. Cortical evoked responses suggest that the two hemispheres are differentially activated by a range of speech and non-speech sounds, even in premature babies (Molfese & Betz, 1988). Judging from dichotic listening tests, there is a left-hemisphere advantage for speech sounds from the preschool years onwards, and there may be a corresponding right-hemisphere advantage for non-verbal sounds (Hiscock, 1988). Similar findings emerge from concurrent-task studies. In the elegant study of Piazza (1977), for instance, 3−5-year-old children were asked to tap either their left or right index finger as fast as possible while either humming or reciting a rhyme. In all age groups, right-sided tapping was more impaired by concurrent speech than by humming, presumably because language was lateralized to the left hemisphere and two left-hemisphere tasks (movement of the right side of the body and speech) were interfering with one another. Conversely, left-sided tapping was more impaired by concurrent humming. Studies of children with early brain injuries provide additional evidence for early lateralization. Thus Woods and Teuber (1978) found that from the time language first develops, acquired childhood *aphasia* is far more likely to result from left-hemisphere than from right-hemisphere lesions. Although, as discussed later in the chapter, language recovery is better after left-sided brain damage acquired in childhood than after comparable left-sided damage acquired in adulthood, this childhood advantage should be attributed to the developing brain being better at respecialization after injury — and not to the developing brain being unspecialized prior to injury, as used to be taught.

HANDEDNESS

The nature and degree of hemispheric specialization varies between individuals. Since handedness is the most visible marker of hemispheric asymmetry, a great deal of speculation and research has focused on individuals who are not right-handed. Non-right-handedness is a term that encompasses definite left-handedness, mixed but stable handedness (in which hand preference varies between tasks but is consistent over time for any one task), and ambiguous handedness (in which hand preference is inconsistent between tasks and from one occasion to another). Much has been written about the possible origins and consequences of non-right-handedness. The key concepts and findings in this controversial area are well reviewed in Bishop's (1990) thoughtful monograph. In order to make sense of the literature on non-right-handedness and developmental disorders, it is helpful to distinguish between pathological non-right-handedness, which is relatively rare, and ordinary non-right-handedness, which is common. Pathological non-right-handedness arises when left-sided or diffuse brain abnormalities convert someone who would otherwise have developed into a right-hander into a non-right-hander instead. The high rate of non-right-handedness in mental handicap and autism may not reflect any specific link between handedness and mental development, but may simply reflect the fact that pathological non-right-handedness and abnormal mental development are both consequences of a variety of underlying brain disorders. Alternatively, markedly delayed brain maturation could account for the particularly high rate of ambiguous handedness in mental handicap and autism, with inconsistent hand preference being an immature rather than a pathological state.

Genes and chance are probably the key determinants of ordinary non-right-handedness. The most widely accepted genetic model is Annett's (1985) 'right shift' theory, which postulates a single gene locus with two alleles that can be represented as rs+ and rs−. In the common homozygote (rs++), language and handedness are typically strongly lateralized to the left hemisphere. In the heterozygote (rs+−), handedness and language are usually moderately lateralized to the left hemisphere. In the rarer homozygote (rs−−), the degree of lateralization is typically weaker still, and the direction of lateralization is random — with handedness and language lateralizing independently of one another, and with each being equally likely to lateralize to the left or right hemisphere. The existence of a balanced polymorphism for left- and right-handedness suggests a heterozygote advantage (as in the case of the sickle-cell polymorphism). In keeping with that supposition, there is some evidence that individuals with moderate right-handedness (many of whom are rs+−) have fewer reading problems than either left-handed individuals (mostly rs−−) or strongly right-handed individuals (mostly rs++) (Annett & Manning, 1990).

THE IMPACT OF EXPERIENCE: SENSITIVE PERIODS, ENVIRONMENTAL ENRICHMENT AND LEARNING

A computer is hard wired — its electronic circuitry is not rewired by the information it processes. A brain, by contrast, is only firm wired — its synaptic circuitry can, within limits, be modified by the information it processes. As described earlier, the initial stages of brain development generate a first approximation to the definitive pattern of neuronal connections, with subsequent fine-tuning being partly driven by neuronal activity. Spontaneous neuronal activity plays an important part in pre-natal fine-tuning. Neuronal activity driven by the individual's experiences is important after birth (and may conceivably play some part before birth too).

When an individual's experiences affect the fine-tuning of neuronal connections, and when that effect is largely or entirely restricted to one phase of postnatal development, that phase is referred to as a sensitive period (or critical period). The effect of monocular deprivation on monkeys provides one of the clearest instances of a sensitive period (Wiesel, 1982; Greenough *et al.*, 1987; Blakemore, 1991). Closure of one eye for a few weeks in infancy leaves that eye permanently *amblyopic*, i.e. once the eye is reopened, the individual is only able to make limited use of visual information from that eye. Monocular deprivation in adulthood does not result in amblyopia. The neural basis of the amblyopia induced by early monocular deprivation has been extensively investigated. In the primary visual cortex of a normal juvenile or adult monkey, the number of neurones driven mainly or exclusively by the left eye approximately equals the number of neurones driven mainly or exclusively by the right eye. Monocular deprivation in adulthood does not permanently alter this left–right balance. By contrast, monocular deprivation in infancy results in the great majority of cells being driven exclusively or mainly by the eye that remains open. Major changes can be induced by relatively brief periods of monocular deprivation in early infancy. During later infancy, comparable changes can only be induced by more prolonged periods of monocular deprivation. The changes in neuronal organization induced by early monocular deprivation are permanent if the eye remains closed throughout the sensitive period, but these changes can be reversed, at least partially, if the eye is opened again before the end of the sensitive period. In cats, cortical plasticity can be artificially restored after the end of the sensitive period by local cortical perfusion with noradrenaline (Kasamatsu *et al.*, 1979).

The cortical reorganization induced by early monocular deprivation is primarily mediated by changes in subtractive rather than additive processes (Wiesel, 1982). The *geniculostriate* axons that carry information from the closed eye to the cortex are more heavily pruned than normal, while the axons from the open eye are less heavily pruned than normal (and may sprout extra collaterals too). Ascending *noradrenergic* and *cholinergic* inputs to the cortex, arising from the locus coeruleus in the brain stem and from the basal forebrain respectively, modulate cortical plasticity to monocular deprivation (Bear & Singer, 1986). Experience-dependent modifications in the visual cortex probably occur primarily at excitatory axospinous synapses, where axon terminals that release the neurotransmitter glutamate meet dendritic spines (Bear *et al.*, 1987). The plasticity of these axospinous synapses appears to be governed by calcium ion flow into the dendritic spine, regulated by the NMDA (*N*-methyl-D-aspartate) type of postsynaptic glutamate receptor (Kleinschmidt *et al.*, 1987). Cyclic adenosine monophosphate (cAMP) mediated changes in the phosphorylation of cytoskeletal proteins also appear to play an important role in corti-

cal plasticity during the sensitive period (Aoki & Siekevitz, 1988).

There is no single phase of development during which all aspects of postnatal brain development are particularly responsive to the nature of an individual's experiences. Some brain systems do not have a sensitive period at all, i.e. environmental factors have a fairly similar impact (or lack of impact) on the neuronal organization of these systems at all stages of development. Even when there is a sensitive period, its timing varies between different brain systems, and between different functions of the same system (Harwerth *et al.*, 1986).

Are sensitive periods relevant to human brain development? The evidence is strongest for vision and hearing, and much weaker for 'higher functions'. Early monocular deprivation is liable to induce amblyopia (Birch & Stager, 1988; Vaegan & Taylor, 1979). There are also indications of a sensitive period in the development of auditory discrimination (Werker & Tees, 1984). Thus at the age of 6 months, infants from English-speaking families can recognize phonetic distinctions that are important in Hindi but not in English. By the end of their first year, however, these infants are no longer able to recognize phonetic distinctions that are unimportant in their native language. It seems likely that infants are born with the neural pathways to make many phonetic discriminations, but that those pathways that are not reinforced (because the relevant contrasts are unimportant in the infant's native language) are selectively eliminated by about 12 months.

It is uncertain whether sensitive periods are relevant to any aspect of human development other than perception. Early psychosocial deprivation can have lasting effects, both in humans and in other primates, but it does not follow that these lasting effects are necessarily due to irreversible changes in neuronal organization. The point can be illustrated by considering the effect on subsequent social development when an infant is deprived of normal attachment experiences. Children who grow up in an institution for the first few years of their lives are more likely, as teenagers, to have difficulties in their peer relationships even if they have lived for over a decade in a loving adoptive family (Hodges & Tizard, 1989). Rhesus monkeys reared in abnormal environments are also more liable to enduring problems with relationships (Suomi, 1991). It is easy to speculate that early social deprivation leads to a sort of 'social amblyopia' due to permanent changes in the neuronal substrate of social competence. There are, however, many alternative non-neurological explanations for the continuities between early social deprivation and later social difficulties (Rutter, 1989). For example, early deprivation may leave the individual without the social skills needed to establish normal relationships later in childhood, thereby cutting the individual off from precisely the sorts of experiences needed to redress the early deficits (Suomi, 1991).

At present, speculations about 'social amblyopia' are hard to subject to empirical scrutiny. If the neural substrate of social relatedness were known, it might be possible to examine the impact of early deprivation on the relevant brain systems fairly directly, e.g. by neuropathological studies in experimental animals, and perhaps by functional brain imaging studies in humans. For as long as the neural substrate is a 'black box', however, the possibility that early social deprivation has a lasting impact on neuronal organization can only be tested indirectly. One approach is to examine whether the effects of early deprivation can be reversed if the individual's circumstances subsequently change for the better. Lack of reversibility makes it more plausible that the effects of deprivation are mediated by permanent changes in brain structure. Conversely, full reversibility makes it less plausible that the brain has been permanently rewired by the early deprivation. However, neither the presence nor absence of reversibility is conclusive. The apparent absence of reversibility may simply reflect an inadequate rehabilitation programme. In rhesus monkeys, for example, early social isolation results in behavioural deficits that persist even when the monkeys are subsequently given extensive experience with socially normal age-mates. This apparent irreversibility probably reflects a behavioural vicious cycle — with social deficits standing in the way of the sorts of peer contacts that would redress the deficits — rather than a permanent change in brain structure. This vicious cycle can be broken by exposing the isolation-reared monkeys to much younger monkeys — the young 'therapist' monkeys interact with the isolation-reared monkeys despite their oddities, resulting in considerable social gains for

the latter (Suomi, 1991). Just as apparent irreversibility is not hard evidence for a sensitive period in brain development, so the presence of reversibility does not totally rule out a sensitive period. As described earlier, English-speaking infants who are not exposed to Hindi lose the ability to make phonetic discriminations that are present in Hindi but not in English. Despite this persuasive evidence for a sensitive period, it is obviously the case that children and adults can learn to speak Hindi (and make the relevant phonetic discriminations) even if they have not been exposed to Hindi during infancy. Though some sensitive period effects are irreversible, others can be at least partially reversed with enough remedial input. Furthermore, behavioural reversibility may reflect substitution rather than restitution, with persisting deprivation-induced deficits in one neurological system being masked by the compensatory activity of another intact neurological system.

In conclusion, the existence of a sensitive period for the neural substrate of social relatedness is possible but unproven — and is difficult to subject to empirical scrutiny. Much the same applies to language (Goodman, 1987), intelligence and attention (Goodman, 1991a). In the case of language, for example, mild fluctuant deafness in early childhood probably results in some degree of persisting language impairment long after the hearing loss has resolved (Chalmers *et al.*, 1989) — a partial irreversibility that provides suggestive but not conclusive evidence for a sensitive period for language acquisition.

Studies of sensitive periods in brain development have primarily focused on the effects of specific types of environmental restriction, e.g. monocular deprivation, or exposure to a visual environment containing horizontal but not vertical lines. Brain structure and function can also be affected by environmental enrichment, as reviewed by Greenough *et al.* (1987) and Diamond (1988). If rats who have been reared in social groups and given plenty of opportunities for play and exploration are compared with rats who have been reared alone in ordinary laboratory cages, the 'enriched' rats not only perform substantially better on a wide range of behavioural tasks, but they also have larger brains and up to 25% more synapses per neurone. Whereas sensitive period effects occur at specific developmental stages, environmental enrichment can have an effect at any age. Even in adulthood, transferring a rat from an ordinary laboratory cage to an enriched environment results in substantial increases in cortical weight and dendritic arborization. The effects of environmental enrichment are probably mediated by the formation of new synapses as a result of environmentally driven neuronal activity. Since visual deprivation — which increases the relevance of auditory stimuli without altering the individual's exposure to auditory input — leads to an increase in the size and synaptic density of the auditory cortex in rodents (Gyllensten *et al.*, 1965; Ryugo *et al.*, 1975), the salience of an experience may be as relevant as its richness or intensity.

An individual's lifelong capacity for learning may depend on reversible alterations in synaptic circuitry. The selective elimination and creation of synapses may be important, involving mechanisms that are similar or identical to those responsible for sensitive periods and the effects of environmental enrichment (Singer, 1986; Greenough *et al.*, 1987). In addition, synapses may be functionally inactivated and reactivated without being physically destroyed and recreated (Wall, 1977). What sort of mechanism for modifying synapses could result in learning? Some variant on Hebb's (1949) rule is still the most likely explanation. Hebb postulated that a synapse is strengthened whenever a *presynaptic* impulse occurs at approximately the same moment as the firing of the *postsynaptic* cell — and conversely that the synapse is weakened whenever a presynaptic impulse does not approximately coincide with postsynaptic firing. If the presynaptic cell is activated by some particular stimulus, and if the postsynaptic cell is involved in some particular response, the synapses between the two cells will be strengthened if the stimulus and response are correlated, and will be weakened if the stimulus and response are uncorrelated. Two proposed modifications of Hebb's original rule are worth noting. First, even if the postsynaptic cell does not fire, a synapse may be strengthened if that synapse is active at about the same time as neighbouring synapses — resulting in depolarization of that portion of the dendritic tree (Edelman, 1987). Second, synapses may only be 'Hebb modifiable' when the individual is suitably aroused, attentive

or motivated — a form of modulation that may be mediated by noradrenergic and cholinergic systems (Singer, 1986).

Postsynaptic NMDA receptors seem to provide a suitable molecular basis for Hebb's rule, permitting calcium ions to flow into the postsynaptic cell when two conditions are met: (i) the postsynaptic membrane is depolarized; and (ii) the receptor is activated by glutamate released by a presynaptic impulse (Bear *et al.*, 1987; Cotman & Iversen, 1987). Since NMDA receptors are also involved in the *excitotoxicity* that contributes to some forms of brain injury in early life, there is growing interest in the role of NMDA blockers in limiting excitotoxicity — with a corresponding concern that even the short-term use of these blockers in early life could have lasting adverse effects on learning and experience-driven fine-tuning (Hattori & Wasterlain, 1990). In the wake of the molecular characterization of the NMDA receptor (Moriyoshi *et al.*, 1991), the development of novel agonists and antagonists is likely to accelerate.

CORRELATING NEUROLOGICAL AND PSYCHOLOGICAL DEVELOPMENT

Links between cognitive and neurological development are well illustrated by primate studies of the association between delayed-response (DR) learning and the dorsolateral prefrontal cortex (DLPC) (Goldman-Rakic *et al.*, 1983; Diamond, 1989). In a typical DR task, a monkey observes food being hidden in one of two food-wells, after which both wells are hidden by a screen for between 1 and 10 seconds. DR learning is judged by the monkey's ability to remember, after delays of various durations, which well contains the food. The DR task is equivalent to Piaget's (1954) 'A, not B' object permanence test for human infants (Diamond, 1989). In adult monkeys, the dependence of DR learning on the DLPC has been demonstrated using a variety of techniques, including lesioning, reversible inactivation by cooling, and single unit recording. In infant monkeys, by contrast, DR learning is not linked to the DLPC. Although infant monkeys perform relatively poorly on DR tasks, this low level of performance is not further impaired if the DLPC is lesioned or temporarily inactivated by cooling. On both DR and 'A, not B' tests, 2-month-old monkeys and 8-month-old humans perform at the same level as adult monkeys with DLPC lesions. It seems likely that the improvements in DR performance from late infancy onwards reflect the maturation of the DLPC. It is probably no coincidence, therefore, that the emergence of object permanence in the second half of the human infant's first year occurs at about the same time as the upsurge in the metabolic rate of the prefrontal cortex (Chugani *et al.*, 1987). In this instance, linked neurological and psychological processes do appear to follow parallel time courses.

In other instances, however, neurological processes and their psychological sequelae may have a more complex temporal relationship. For example, brain lesions acquired at one stage in development may have no overt psychological consequences until some while later. Thus although lesioning the DLPC in an infant monkey results in no deficit in DR performance initially (because DR performance does not normally depend on the DLPC at this early stage), a permanent deficit in DR learning emerges later in development as the monkey matures to a stage when the DLPC would normally come 'on line' (Goldman-Rakic *et al.*, 1983). As mentioned earlier, this sort of 'sleeper' effect could account for the emergence of schizophrenic symptoms many years after a neurodevelopmental insult. As suggested elsewhere (Goodman, 1991a), a similar effect could account for the minority of autistic children who develop relatively normally as infants and lose previously acquired skills in social interaction, communication and play during their second year. Although it is possible that this regression reflects brain abnormalities that begin or worsen during the second year, it is also possible that the regression reflects a shift in neural substrate. Imagine, for example, that social interest and awareness depend primarily on one neural system (S1) in infancy and on a different system (S2) thereafter. If so, a congenital fault in S2 will have little or no impact during infancy, but will result in a loss of social interest and awareness during the transitional phase in the second year when S1 fades out and S2 should take over. (According to this model, most autistic children have deficits in both S1 and S2, resulting in marked abnormalities in social interest and awareness from early infancy onwards.)

The resolution of a psychological abnormality over the course of development could reflect a shift in neural substrate rather than the resolution of the underlying neurobiological abnormality. For instance, language delay and subsequent catch-up could arise from a permanent fault in a neuronal system that is essential for language in the early toddler years but not thereafter.

IMPLICATIONS OF THE ROLE OF CHANCE IN BRAIN DEVELOPMENT

Although much of this chapter describes developmental processes common to all individuals, the study of brain development is also relevant to the differences between individuals. It is widely assumed that if two individuals differ in intelligence, personality or some other psychological construct, then those differences must ultimately arise either from genetic differences between the two individuals, or from differences in the environments that they have been exposed to. A consideration of the probabilistic nature of brain development suggests that this may not be the whole story.

As described in the introduction to this chapter, an individual's genes determine the broad outlines of brain development but do not specify the precise architecture of every synaptic connection. The role of non-genetic factors is evident, for example, in the water flea, *Daphnia magna*, where it is possible to study equivalent neurones in different animals since the number of neurones is small and the arrangement of neurones is predictable. As water fleas reproduce by parthenogenesis, it is easy to study genetically identical individuals. As shown in Fig. 3.2, Levinthal *et al.* (1976) demonstrated marked differences in the pattern of dendritic branching of homologous neurones of isogenic water fleas. Comparable variability in the dendritic branching of homologous neurones has also been demonstrated in isogenic vertebrates (Levinthal *et al.*, 1976). These differences in dendritic development could potentially reflect the unique experiences of each individual, but it is just as plausible that the exact pattern of dendritic branching is affected by truly random factors such as the Brownian movement of intracellular particles.

If the mechanisms that translate genetic instruc-

Left   Right

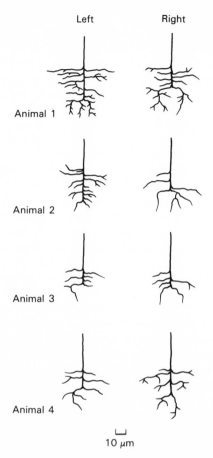

Animal 1

Animal 2

Animal 3

Animal 4

10 μm

Fig. 3.2 Schematic representation of the branching patterns of dendrites from the homologous neurones on the left and right sides of the optic ganglion neuropil in four genetically identical water fleas. The order, position and relative lengths of all the branches have been maintained, but angular distortions were introduced in order to avoid overlapping. The differences between the four individuals demonstrate that dendritic branching is not completely genetically determined (adapted with permission from Levinthal *et al.*, 1976).

tions into neuronal organization reflect chance as well as necessity, the brains of genetically identical individuals will develop somewhat differently from one another even if those individuals grow up in environments that are, to all intents and purposes, identical. If 'environment' is used in its everyday sense to refer to those aspects of the external world that surround and impinge on an individual, the term would not encompass randomness that arises

from within. Perhaps the current duo of genes and environment needs to be expanded into a trio of genes, environment and epigenetic randomness (Goodman, 1991b). This is not to say that the role of chance in development is restricted to epigenetic randomness. On the contrary, chance clearly plays a part in the reshuffling of genes between generations, as well as in freak accidents, fortuitous meetings and many other environmental contingencies. It seems likely, however, that this genetic and environmental randomness is compounded by an additional level of randomness that is inherent in the developmental process itself — a phenomenon that could be termed 'aleatory epigenesis' (from aleatory: dependent on the throw of a die; hence, dependent on uncertain contingencies).

If all individual differences in the psychological domain are ascribed to the trio of genes, environment and aleatory epigenesis, what room does this leave for the relevance of internal states? When two people behave differently in the same circumstances, it is often appropriate to ascribe that behavioural difference to an underlying difference in inner state, e.g. to differences in the individuals' beliefs, value systems or internal working models of the world. We cannot reasonably ignore inner states if we want to know about the processes that mediate individual differences in behaviour. We must enquire further, however, if our focus is on the ultimate origins of individual differences. Why, for instance, should two individuals have different working models of the world? To what extent does it reflect genetic differences? To what extent does it reflect differences in early or more recent environment? And to what extent does it reflect the randomness inherent in brain development?

Two lines of evidence suggest that aleatory epigenesis could be relevant to individual differences in human brain development. First, as described earlier, studies of handedness suggest that chance plays a major role in the development of the brain's pattern of lateral specialization (Annett, 1985). Second, chance is important in other aspects of human development, including the *Lyonization* of X chromosomes in females (Lyon, 1961; Vandenberg *et al.*, 1962), the specification of antibody idiotypes (Alt *et al.*, 1987), and the occurrence of *situs inversus* in individuals with *Kartagener's syndrome* (Afzelius, 1976). In each of these instances, chance rather than non-shared environment can account for discordance between monozygotic twins (e.g. Revesz *et al.*, 1972; Burn *et al.*, 1986).

If epigenetic randomness does significantly influence the course of brain and behavioural development, and the case is admittedly unproven, then some of the conclusions of behavioural geneticists about the role of the environment will need to be revised. Schizophrenia provides a convenient illustration. Most schizophrenic identical twins do not have an affected cotwin (Gottesman & Shields, 1982). This finding clearly demonstrates that genetic predisposition is not the whole story. Despite many assertions to the contrary, however, it does not *prove* that environmental factors are necessarily important (assuming that 'environmental' is used in its everyday sense and not simply as a synonym for 'non-genetic'). Discordance for schizophrenia may reflect the effect of non-shared environment, e.g. differential exposure of the two twins to expressed emotion or perinatal anoxia. It is equally plausible, however, that the discordance reflects the operation of chance in brain development. The possible interaction of genes and epigenetic randomness can be visualized in terms of a landscape in which different developmental paths skirt a schizophrenic abyss. Individuals with a normal genotype follow a path that is so far from the abyss that minor deviations from the path (due to random 'wobble') carry no risk. By contrast, individuals with a high genetic risk for schizophrenia follow a path that comes so close to the edge of the abyss that random wobble influences who falls over the edge and who escapes. This is not to argue that environmental factors, such as prenatal infections, play no part in the aetiology of schizophrenia. The point is that a role for environmental factors needs to be demonstrated directly and not simply inferred from the fact that heritability is less than 100%. This point is clearly relevant not just to schizophrenia but to any disorder or category.

A similar issue arises for dimensional measures, such as intelligence, emotionality and sociability. According to conventional teaching, if the differences between monozygotic twins who have grown up together are larger than can be accounted for by measurement error alone, non-shared environ-

mental factors *must* be responsible. This is not necessarily so. Quantitative differences between identical twins may arise not from differential exposure to specific environmental factors, but from random differences in the way genetic instructions were translated into synaptic connections in the course of each twin's brain development. Once again, the importance of environmental factors needs to be demonstrated directly — inference from genetic data is not enough.

Finally, it is worth noting that although the hypothesis that chance plays an important part in brain development is plausible enough to warrant testing, it may well be impossible to demonstrate unequivocally that aleatory epigenesis does make a significant contribution to individual differences. Imagine, for example, that you are interested in individual differences in the psychological characteristics of rats. You choose an inbred strain to eliminate genetic causes for the individual differences. You find that marked individual differences persist even when the rats are raised in as uniform an environment as possible. It is never possible to eliminate all environmental variation, but systematic manipulation of all recognized sources of environmental variation (such as *in utero* position) persuades you that these factors are not powerful enough to account for the residual differences between individuals. Can you unequivocally attribute the residual individual variability to the operation of epigenetic randomness? Unfortunately not. The residual variability could still be due to some source of environmental variability that you have neither considered nor measured. Since you can only estimate the role of chance by observing how much individual variability persists after allowing for all known genetic and environmental sources of this variability, any unknown source of variability will masquerade as chance.

DEVELOPMENT AFTER BRAIN DAMAGE

What effect does brain damage in early life have on the subsequent course of neurological and psychological development? Many studies of experimental animals have examined the consequences of specific lesions acquired at different points in the lifespan — for reviews see Finger and Stein (1982) and Kolb and Whishaw (1989). The lessons drawn from these studies may well be relevant to children whose brains are damaged — by a stroke or a head injury, for example — after a period of normal development. It is less clear how far the lessons also apply to children whose brains develop abnormally from the outset, as may be the case for many children with cerebral palsy or severe mental retardation.

Brain damage at any stage of life can be followed by a striking degree of recovery. Although the age at which damage occurs does influence outcome, it is not simply a matter of the young brain being generally more resilient or less resilient. As detailed below, the outcome of early damage is better in some respects but worse in others. In much the same way, the young brain is neither more vulnerable nor less vulnerable to all insults — it is more vulnerable to some insults, such as some infections (Levin, 1991), and less vulnerable to others, such as anoxia (Duffy *et al.*, 1975).

The relationship between the age at which brain damage is sustained and the degree of subsequent recovery is a complex one, being affected by the choice of outcome measure and also by whether the damage involves just one cerebral hemisphere or both. When a skill is normally strongly lateralized, that skill may develop remarkably normally if just one hemisphere is damaged in early life, even if the damaged hemisphere would normally have mediated the skill. For example, language development is usually remarkably good after early unilateral damage, even if the damage is on the left side (Goodman, 1987; Bishop, 1988). Although the left hemisphere usually plays a key role in language, an individual whose left hemisphere has been extensively damaged prenatally or during infancy can still acquire language that is normal or nearly normal (Smith & Sugar, 1975; Dennis & Whitaker, 1977; Woods & Carey, 1979; Vargha-Khadem *et al.*, 1985). When the left hemisphere is damaged in somewhat older children, persistent language deficits are more likely, though these too may be relatively subtle (Woods & Carey, 1979). After puberty, the capacity for left-to-right transfer is still present in some individuals (Kinsbourne, 1971), but is generally less dramatic than after earlier brain damage. It would seem, then, that as brain development progresses, the right hemisphere

becomes less able to take over a skill that is normally lateralized to the left hemisphere. Conversely, the left hemisphere becomes progressively less able to take over right-hemisphere functions such as visuospatial reasoning (Woods, 1980). This progressive restriction in the capacity for contralateral transfer used to be attributed to an age-related increase in hemispheric asymmetry. As described above, however, hemispheric asymmetry is prominent from infancy onwards. Consequently, the developing brain's greater potential for contralateral transfer seems to be related to a greater capacity for respecialization after injury, and not to the absence of specialization prior to injury.

When cortical damage is unilateral, the function of the damaged cortex can potentially be taken over by the homologous cortex on the intact side. This 'mirror image' shift is clearly impossible if damage is bilaterally symmetrical. Recovery from bilateral damage necessarily depends on intra-hemispheric shifts. If prefrontal cortex is damaged bilaterally, for example, full recovery will depend on prefrontal functions being taken over by other cortical regions. Judging from primate experiments (Goldman-Rakic *et al.*, 1983), this is most likely to occur if the damage is prenatal. When a monkey's dorso-lateral prefrontal cortex (DLPC) is bilaterally destroyed before birth, the monkey is unimpaired on delayed-response (DR) tasks even when it has matured to the point when DR performance normally depends on the DLPC (see above). The role of the DLPC would appear to have been taken over by the remaining cortex. By contrast, if a monkey's DLPC is bilaterally destroyed during infancy, a permanent impairment on DR tasks becomes evident once the monkey reaches the age when the DLPC normally comes 'on line'. In this instance, bilateral damage early in postnatal life does not have a markedly better outcome than comparable damage in later life. If much the same applies to humans, recovery from bilaterally symmetrical brain damage (caused, for example, by severe closed head injury) may be roughly as poor after childhood injury as after adult injury. The persistence of 'frontal lobe' symptoms, such as social disinhibition, after severe closed head injuries in childhood supports this gloomy prediction (Brown *et al.*, 1981).

Even in those instances when early damage does seem to result in better long-term recovery, this advantage may only apply to some specific skills. Kolb and Whishaw (1981) demonstrated an interesting dissociation in their study of rats whose frontal cortex was bilaterally lesioned either at 1 week of age or in adulthood. Compared with adult-lesioned rats, early-lesioned rats were much less impaired on tests of learned behaviours, but were equally impaired on tests of species-typical behaviours. A similar effect in humans could account for instances in which an individual with early-acquired brain damage performs relatively well on neuropsychological tests and yet has subtle but important impairments in social competence (Kolb, 1989).

New techniques for imaging brain function are promising tools for investigating the relocation of brain functions after early or late damage. Approaches that have been successfully applied to the localization of function in normal individuals can potentially be applied to individuals who have sustained particular types of brain damage at different stages of development. For example, Petersen *et al.* (1988) have used positron emission tomography (PET) images obtained at rest and in the course of various language tasks to investigate the cerebral localization of language processing in normal volunteers. There is no reason why the same sort of technique cannot be used to investigate language localization in individuals who have sustained extensive damage to their left hemisphere, whether prenatally, during childhood or during adulthood. Is the better language recovery after early damage linked to differences in the degree or type of relocalization? Are unusual patterns of relocalization associated with a particularly high risk of learning difficulties or psychiatric problems? Though exposure to radiation makes PET an unsuitable tool for investigating children, this does not rule out studies of adults whose brain lesions were acquired prenatally or during childhood. Furthermore, new techniques that allow magnetic resonance imaging (MRI) to generate functional as well as structural images should be applicable to children (Belliveau *et al.*, 1991).

Though the prognosis for specific skills is sometimes better when brain damage occurs early rather than late, the prognosis for overall intellectual and scholastic ability may be worse when damage occurs early (Rutter, 1984). In children with unilateral brain damage, impaired long-term development of intelligence and memory is particularly likely if there is associated epilepsy (Vargha-Khadem *et al.*, 1992). It is tempting to attribute diminished cognitive 'power' to the effect of crowding too many functions into too little remaining brain, or to a disruptive effect of seizures on the subtractive developmental processes that fine-tune the brain. These suppositions may turn out to be well founded, but it is worth noting that there are well-authenticated instances of excellent intellectual and academic outcome after extensive early brain loss accompanied by severe and frequent seizures (Smith & Sugar, 1975). In addition to the possible roles of overcrowding and epilepsy, four additional factors might contribute to the link between early damage and diminished 'power'. First, the brain insults that produce localized damage in early life may commonly result in diffuse generalized damage as well. Second, studies of rats have demonstrated that early focal lesions sometimes result in widespread cortical thinning due to restricted dendritic growth, though the mechanism of this effect is unknown (Kolb & Whishaw, 1989). Third, if brain injury disrupts new learning more than it disrupts the retention of previously acquired skills (Hebb, 1942), this effect will inevitably be more handicapping to the individual whose brain damage occurred early in life. Finally, the neuronal reorganization induced by early brain damage may sometimes be maladaptive (see below), generating widespread misconnections that could potentially interfere with a wide range of brain activities by transmitting irrelevant information ('noise') between neurones that should not be connected.

To summarize so far, the degree of recovery from brain damage is influenced by a complex interaction of three factors: (i) the age at which the damage was sustained; (ii) whether the damage was unilateral or bilateral; and (iii) whether the outcome is judged by specific skills or general abilities. Other factors may also be relevant. When brain damage occurs gradually, as a result of a slowly expanding lesion or a succession of small injuries, the degree of recovery is generally greater than when the same amount of damage occurs suddenly (Finger & Stein, 1982). Individual differences may be important too. For example, right-handed individuals with left-handed relatives seem to recover better from aphasic strokes than do right-handed individuals without left-handed relatives (Subirana, 1958; Zangwill, 1960). In terms of the genetic model described above, this could be accounted for by improved recovery in individuals with an rs+− rather than an rs++ genotype. Finally, the degree of recovery may be affected by whether a region of the brain is totally or partially destroyed. Although common sense suggests that total destruction will be more devastating than partial destruction, there are hints that recovery from early damage is sometimes worse after partial rather than total destruction (Carlson, 1984), perhaps because the surviving but dysfunctional portion interferes with successful reorganization.

At the neuronal level, a variety of processes may contribute to the brain's capacity to recover from injury. The sort of synaptic plasticity that is involved in ordinary learning (see above) is also likely to contribute to the capacity of the surviving parts of the brain to take on roles that substitute for lost abilities. For example, if a right-handed individual has a stroke affecting the right hand, that individual may recover the ability to write by learning to use the left hand instead — a substitution that presumably involves the kind of 'ordinary' synaptic remodelling involved in other sorts of learning as well.

Recovery from brain damage may also involve more profound changes in brain organization that recreate some or all of the missing neuronal circuitry. For example, if the occipital cortex of cats is bilaterally lesioned shortly after birth, there is remarkably little long-term visual impairment because the neuronal circuitry of an adjacent cortical region (the lateral suprasylvian cortex) is reorganized to resemble that of the lost visual cortex — a reorganization that does not occur after similar ablations in adulthood (Spear, 1979).

What sorts of processes reconstitute neuronal circuits that have been lost? Dead neurones cannot be replaced after the end of the normal proliferative period, but surviving neurones can form new connections after brain damage, particularly when that damage occurs early in life (Finger & Stein, 1982). When an axon is transected by brain injury the distal portion dies, as may the proximal portion and cell body (Bray *et al.*, 1987). If the proximal portion of the axon does survive, however, it may sprout

growth cones and regenerate new terminals. This regenerative sprouting can result in the formation of appropriate new connections close to the site of injury (Kromer *et al.*, 1981). One of the main reasons that axons do not regenerate over long distances in the central nervous system is that there are potent membrane-bound inhibitors of axonal growth on *oligodendrocytes* and the *myelin* they produce (Schwab, 1990). Since these inhibitors are not present in the peripheral nervous system, segments of peripheral nerves that have been transplanted into the central nervous system can act as conduits for long-range axonal regeneration in experimental animals (Bray *et al.*, 1987). Besides stimulating regenerative sprouting, brain injury can also stimulate collateral sprouting: when the injury destroys some of the axons innervating an area, the remaining axons produce side-branches (collateral sprouts) that reoccupy the vacated synaptic sites. Although regenerative and collateral sprouting can occur after injury at any age, they seem to occur more readily after early damage (Lynch *et al.*, 1973; Fawcett, 1992).

The neuronal response to brain injury differs with age in two other ways as well. First, if the brain is injured at a very early stage, before the developing axons have reached their normal destination, some of the growing axons are rerouted to alternative destinations instead (Schneider, 1979; Sur *et al.*, 1988). Second, if the brain is damaged before or during the stage of selective axonal pruning, the accidental losses of some axonal collaterals can potentially be counterbalanced by a reduction in the normal losses of other axonal collaterals (Janowsky & Finlay, 1986). As a result of these age-related differences, early brain damage elicits more regeneration and remodelling, and the young brain is said to show greater neuroplasticity.

Age-related changes in neuroplasticity may account for some of the constraints on recovery that were reviewed earlier in this section. Recovery from symmetrical damage to both hemispheres requires an intrahemispheric shift in function, and it is likely that this shift depends on the sort of major modification of neuronal circuitry that can only be brought about by axonal rerouting and substantial changes in the pattern of axonal pruning. In primates, as discussed in an earlier section of this chapter, axons have generally reached their targets before birth, and the bulk of axonal pruning occurs around the time of birth. Consequently, major modifications in neuronal circuitry may no longer be possible if the injury occurs after the prenatal or neonatal period. Although this may seriously limit recovery from postnatally acquired bilateral damage, different considerations seem to apply to recovery from unilateral damage. Shifting a function from a damaged area of one hemisphere to the corresponding area on the other side may not require major neuronal reorganization. Perhaps the normal direction of asymmetry can be reversed by relatively minor changes in the fine-tuning processes that continue throughout childhood. This would explain why the capacity for left-to-right and right-to-left transfer progressively diminishes throughout childhood as the phase of selective axonal pruning moves towards completion.

The greater neuroplasticity of the young brain is sometimes beneficial, but it is not invariably so. Schneider's (1979) classical study illustrates the point. If the superior colliculus of a hamster is lesioned at birth, redirected growth of the optic tract leads to the formation of anomalous connections, i.e. neuronal connections that are either absent or inconspicuous in the brain of a normal hamster. In some instances, these anomalous connections result in the sparing of visually elicited turning responses that are lost after comparable lesions in adulthood. In other instances, however, the anomalous connections lead to maladaptive turning responses, e.g. persistently turning the wrong way as a result of anomalous retinal projections to the wrong side of the brain. In humans too, it seems plausible that the greater neuroplasticity of the young brain is a mixed blessing (Goodman, 1989). On the one hand, greater neuroplasticity may enhance some aspects of functional recovery. On the other hand, greater neuroplasticity may sometimes result in more harm than good because of the maladaptive consequences of widespread new misconnections. Perhaps advances in developmental neurobiology will eventually lead to therapeutic interventions that promote the formation of adaptive new connections after brain injury while inhibiting the formation of maladaptive misconnections.

GLOSSARY

Afferents are nerve fibres conveying incoming information.

Amblyopia means dimness of vision, often affecting just one eye. The amblyopia that follows closure of one eye in early development is due not to a defect in the eye itself but to the subsequent inability of the brain to make full use of information from that eye.

Anencephaly refers to the congenital absence of most of the brain and skull vault.

Aphasia is the loss of ability to use language, e.g. as a result of a stroke affecting the left cerebral hemisphere.

Association areas are regions of the cerebral cortex that are not devoted to just one sensory or motor system but play a more complex integrative role.

An *axon* is the neurone's output channel. It is a thin filament that transmits electrical impulses from the cell body of a neuron to its terminal synapses. Some axons are very short while others extend for up to a metre. Rapidly conducting axons are wrapped in a sheath of myelin insulation.

The *brain stem* (Fig. 3.1c) is the stalk of the brain to which the forebrain and cerebellum are attached.

Callosal projection fibres are the axons that pass from one cerebral hemisphere to the other through the corpus callosum.

The *cerebellum* (Fig. 3.1b & c) is attached to the posterior aspect of the brain stem. It is primarily involved in the control of movement.

The *cerebral hemispheres* account for over half of the brain's mass, lying to the left and the right side of the midline above the brain stem. Each hemisphere derives from one of the telencephalic outpouchings of the forebrain (Fig. 3.1a). The cerebral cortex makes up the outer surface of each hemisphere.

Cholinergic nerves use acetylcholine as their neurotransmitter.

Collaterals are side-branches of the main axon. Because of its collaterals, the axon of one neurone can innervate several different targets (which are sometimes widely separated).

Contralateral: relating to the opposite side of the body. Thus the left eye is contralateral to the right cerebral hemisphere.

The *corpus callosum* is the main structure conveying nerve fibres from one cerebral hemisphere to the other.

The *cortex* is a multilayered sheet of neurones at the surface of the brain. The cerebral cortex is on the outside of the cerebral hemispheres. The cerebellar cortex is on the outside of the cerebellum.

The *corticospinal* tract consists of the axons that run from the cerebral cortex to the spinal cord.

Dendrites are the filaments of a neurone that form its input. Most axons synapse on dendrites (though some synapse onto the cell body directly or onto other axons).

Excitotoxicity refers to the neuronal damage and death that

occurs when excessive amounts of excitatory neurotransmitters (such as glutamate) are released, e.g. in the
wake of a prolonged epileptic fit or a marked reduction
in the brain's blood supply.

The *geniculostriate* tract consists of axons that run from the
lateral geniculate body (a portion of the thalamus) to
the striate cortex. The tract relays visual information
transmitted from the retina to the lateral geniculate
body.

Germinal zones are regions of the developing brain that
contain the multiplying precursor cells that generate
neurones and glia.

Glia are a heterogeneous group of non-neuronal cells in
the nervous system that perform a variety of functions,
e.g. radial glia act as guide wires for neuronal migration
early on in brain development.

The *hippocampus* is a portion of the limbic system that is
located in the temporal lobe and that is particularly
important for short-term memory.

Homeobox genes all contain a conserved sequence,
the homeobox, that codes for approximately 60 amino
acids. This portion of the polypeptide product of a
homeobox gene is a helix—loop—helix structure that
mediates sequence-specific binding to DNA and contributes to the regulation of gene transcription.

The *hypothalamus* (Fig. 3.1c) forms the base of the diencephalon and plays an important part in the regulation
of the endocrine and autonomic nervous systems.

Intrahemispheric: within the same cerebral hemisphere.

Ipsilateral: relating to the same side of the body. Thus the
left eye is ipsilateral to the left cerebral hemisphere.

Kartagener's syndrome arises from an inherited defect in
cilia that results in bronchial and sinus problems. Half
of the individuals with the genetic disorder have *situs
solitus* (i.e. normal visceral asymmetry, e.g. heart on the
left, liver on the right) and the other half have *situs
inversus* (heart on the right, liver on the left, etc.). In the
absence of functioning cilia, chance alone appears to
determine whether the individual develops *situs solitus*
or *inversus*.

The *limbic cortex* consists of various evolutionarily ancient
regions of cortex on the medial surface of the cerebral
hemispheres. Acting in concert with subcortical limbic
structures, such as the amygdala, the limbic cortex
is important for motivation, affect and short-term
memory.

Lissencephaly refers to a group of brain malformations
characterized by a relative or total absence of convolutions on the cerebral surface.

Lyonization refers to the inactivation of one of the two X
chromosomes in the somatic cells of a female. Whether
it is the maternally or paternally derived X chromosome
that is inactivated in any one cell line appears to depend
on chance alone.

A *mini-column* is a stack of neurones in the cerebral cortex,
including cells from each cortical layer. The cortex can

be thought of as a mosaic of mini-columns.

Myelin is the insulating wrapping of axons and is produced
by glial cells: by oligodendrocytes in the central nervous
system and by Schwann cells in the peripheral nervous
system.

Myelination is the formation of the myelin sheath. Myelination proceeds at different rates in different portions of
the nervous system.

Neocortex is the most recently evolved portion of the
cerebral cortex. It is much more extensive than the
limbic cortex and includes all the areas of motor, sensory
and association cortex shown in Fig. 3.1d.

Neurotransmitters are the chemical messengers at synapses.
They are released when electrical impulses arrive at
axonal terminals. After diffusing across the synaptic
space, they activate receptors on the dendritic surface.

Noradrenergic nerves use noradrenaline as their neurotransmitter.

Oligodendrocytes are the type of glia that produce myelin in
the central nervous system.

Polymicrogyria refers to a group of brain malformations in
which the convolutions of the cerebral surface are too
crowded, too narrow, and abnormal in pattern.

The *pons* (Fig. 3.1c) is part of the hindbrain.

Postsynaptic means 'downstream' of a synapse, i.e. on the
output (usually dendritic) side.

Precursor cells are the ancestors of neurones. Unlike
neurones, precursor cells can proliferate, generating
immature neurones or more precursor cells, or both.

Prefrontal cortex (Fig. 3.1d) is the surface of the anterior
portion of the frontal lobe. It is important for various
'higher functions', including delayed-response learning.

Presynaptic means 'upstream' of a synapse, i.e. on the
input (axonal) side.

Primary motor and sensory cortex are those regions of the
cerebral cortex most immediately concerned with
outgoing motor commands and incoming perceptual
information. The primary motor, visual, auditory and
somatosensory areas are shown in Fig. 3.1d.

Pyramidal neurones are so called because of the pyramidal
shape of their cell bodies. Pyramidal neurones in various
layers of the cerebral cortex give rise to the axons that
relay messages from the cortex to subcortical structures
or to other cortical regions.

Retinotopic refers to an arrangement of visual information
that is topologically equivalent to that of the retina, e.g.
visual information from adjacent portions of the retina
is relayed to adjacent portions of the retinotopically
organized striate cortex.

Somatosensory refers to somatic senses such as touch and
the perception of bodily position.

The *striate* cortex is the primary visual cortex situated at
the posterior pole of the occipital lobe (Fig. 3.1d).

Subcortical refers to all structures other than cortex. Thus
projections from the cerebral cortex to the thalamus,
pons and spinal cord (and numerous other structures)

are all termed subcortical projections.

The *subplate* lies beneath the cerebral cortex. It arises early in development and probably plays an important part in the development and differentiation of the overlying cortex.

The *superior colliculus* (Fig. 3.1c) is a part of the midbrain primarily concerned with visual localization and eye movement.

A *synapse* is a junction between an axon terminal and another neuronal structure — commonly a dendrite. When an electrical impulse arrives at the axon terminal, neurotransmitter is released into the narrow synaptic space, stimulating or suppressing electrical activity 'downstream'.

The *thalamus* (Fig. 3.1d) is the largest structure in the diencephalon and acts as a relay station for most of the information passing into the cerebral hemispheres.

The *ventricles* are spaces within the brain filled with cerebrospinal fluid (CSF). Early in development, many neurones are generated in parts of the brain that are adjacent to the ventricles, i.e. at or near the ventricular surface.

Wernicke's area (Fig. 3.1d) is a portion of the temporal cortex involved in language processing.

REFERENCES

Afzelius B.A. (1976) A human syndrome caused by immotile cilia. *Science* **193**, 317–319.

Alt F.W., Blackwell K. & Yancopoulos G.D. (1987) Development of the primary antibody repertoire. *Science* **238**, 1079–1087.

Altman J. (1987) Morphological and behavioral markers of environmentally induced retardation of brain development: an animal model. *Environmental Health Perspectives* **74**, 153–168.

Annett M. (1985) *Left, Right, Hand and Brain: The Right Shift Theory*. Lawrence Erlbaum, London.

Annett M. & Manning M. (1990) Reading and a balanced polymorphism for laterality and ability. *Journal of Child Psychology and Psychiatry* **31**, 511–529.

Aoki C. & Siekevitz P. (1988) Plasticity in brain development. *Scientific American* **259**, 34–42.

Atkinson J. (1984) Human visual development over the first 6 months of life: A review and hypothesis. *Human Neurobiology* **3**, 61–74.

Barbe M.F. & Levitt P. (1991) The early commitment of fetal neurons to the limbic cortex. *Journal of Neuroscience* **11**, 519–533.

Bear M.F., Cooper L.N. & Ebner F.F. (1987) A physiological basis for a theory of synapse modification. *Science* **237**, 42–48.

Bear M.F. & Singer W. (1986) Acetylcholine, noradrenaline and the extrathalamic modulation of visual cortical plasticity. *Nature* **320**, 172–176.

Belliveau J.W., Kennedy D.N., McKinstry R.C. *et al.* (1991) Functional mapping of the human visual cortex by magnetic resonance imaging. *Science* **254**, 716–719.

Birch E.E. & Stager D.R. (1988) Prevalence of good visual acuity following surgery for congenital unilateral cataract. *Archives of Ophthalmology* **106**, 40–43.

Bishop D. (1988) Language development after focal brain damage. In Bishop D. & Mogford K. (eds) *Language Development in Exceptional Circumstances*, pp. 203–220. Churchill Livingstone, Edinburgh.

Bishop D.V.M. (1990) *Handedness and Developmental Disorder*. Clinics in Developmental Medicine, No. 110. MacKeith Press/Blackwell Scientific Publications, Oxford.

Blakemore C. (1991) Sensitive and vulnerable periods in the development of the visual system. In Bock G.R. & Whelan J. (eds) *The Childhood Environment and Adult Disease*, pp. 129–154. Ciba Foundation Symposium, No. 156. Wiley, Chichester.

Bradshaw J.L. & Nettleton N.C. (1983) *Human Cerebral Asymmetry*. Prentice-Hall, New Jersey.

Bray G.M., Villegas-Perez M.P., Vidal-Sanz M. & Aguayo A.J. (1987) The use of peripheral nerve grafts to enhance neuronal survival, promote growth and permit terminal reconnection in the central nervous system of adult rats. *Journal of Experimental Biology* **132**, 5–19.

Brown G., Chadwick O., Schaffer D., Rutter M. & Traub M. (1981) A prospective study of children with head injuries: III. Psychiatric sequelae. *Psychological Medicine* **11**, 63–78.

Burn J., Povey S., Boyd Y. *et al.* (1986) Duchenne muscular dystrophy in one of monozygotic twin girls. *Journal of Medical Genetics* **23**, 494–500.

Carlson M. (1984) Development of tactile discrimination capacity in *Macaca mulatta*. III. Effects of total removal of primary sensory cortex (SmI) in infants and juveniles. *Developmental Brain Research* **16**, 103–117.

Caviness V.S. & Rakic P. (1978) Mechanisms of cortical development: A view from mutations in mice. *Annual Review of Neuroscience* **1**, 297–326.

Chalmers D., Stewart I., Silva P. & Mulvena A. (1989) *Otitis Media with Effusion in Children: The Dunedin Study*. Clinics in Developmental Medicine, No. 108. MacKeith Press/Blackwell Scientific Publications, Oxford.

Chalupa L.M. & Killackey H.P. (1989) Process elimination underlies ontogenetic change in the distribution of callosal projection neurons in the postcentral gyrus of the fetal rhesus monkey. *Proceedings of the National Academy of Sciences of the United States of America* **86**, 1076–1079.

Changeux J-P. & Danchin A. (1976) Selective stabilisation of developing synapses as a mechanism for the specification of neuronal networks. *Nature* **264**, 705–712.

Chugani H.T., Phelps M.E. & Mazziotta J.C. (1987) Positron emission tomography study of human brain functional development. *Annals of Neurology* **22**, 487–497.

Clarke S., Kraftsik R., van der Loos H. & Innocenti G.M. (1989) Forms and measures of adult and developing human corpus callosum: Is there sexual dimorphism? *Journal of Comparative Neurology* **280**, 213−230.

Cline H.T. (1991) Activity dependent plasticity in the visual systems of frogs and fish. *Trends in Neurosciences* **14**, 104−111.

Cotman C.W. & Iversen L.L. (1987) Excitatory amino acids in the brain − Focus on NMDA receptors. *Trends in Neurosciences* **10**, 263−265.

Cowan W.M., Fawcett J.W., O'Leary D.D.M. & Stanfield B.B. (1984) Regressive events in neurogenesis. *Science* **225**, 1258−1265.

Crick F. (1989a) The recent excitement about neural networks. *Nature* **337**, 129−132.

Crick F. (1989b) Neural Edelmanism. *Trends in Neurosciences* **12**, 240−248.

Dehay C., Kennedy H., Bullier J. & Berland M. (1988) Absence of interhemispheric connections of area 17 during development in the monkey. *Nature* **331**, 348−350.

Dennis M. & Whitaker H.A. (1977) Hemispheric equipotentiality and language acquisition. In Segalowitz S.J. & Gruber F.A. (eds) *Language Development and Neurological Theory*, pp. 93−106. Academic Press, New York.

Devor M. (1975) Neuroplasticity in the sparing or deterioration of function after early olfactory tract lesions. *Science* **190**, 998−999.

Diamond A. (1989) Differences between adult and infant cognition: Is the crucial variable presence or absence of language? In Weiskrantz L. (ed.) *Thought Without Language*, pp. 337−370. Oxford University Press, Oxford.

Diamond M.C. (1988) *Enriching Heredity*. Free Press, New York.

Dobbing J. & Sands J. (1973) Quantitative growth and development of human brain. *Archives of Disease in Childhood* **48**, 757−767.

Dubin M.W., Stark L.A. & Archer S.M. (1986) A role for action-potential activity in the development of neuronal connections in the kitten retinogeniculate pathway. *Journal of Neuroscience* **6**, 1021−1036.

Duffy T.E., Kohle S.J. & Vannucci R.C. (1975) Carbohydrate and energy metabolism in perinatal rat brain: Relation to survival in anoxia. *Journal of Neurochemistry* **24**, 271−276.

Easter S.S., Purves Jr D., Rakic P. & Spitzer N.C. (1985) The changing view of neural specificity. *Science* **230**, 507−511.

Eckenhoff M.F. & Rakic P. (1988) Nature and fate of proliferative cells in the hippocampal dentate gyrus during the life span of the rhesus monkey. *Journal of Neuroscience* **8**, 2729−2747.

Edelman G.M. (1987) *Neural Darwinism*. Oxford University Press, Oxford.

Edelman G.M. (1988) Morphoregulatory molecules. *Biochemistry* **27**, 3533−3543.

Fawcett J.W. (1992) Intrinsic neuronal determinants of regeneration. *Trends in Neurosciences* **15**, 5−8.

Finger S. & Stein D.G. (1982) *Brain Damage and Recovery: Research and Clinical Perspectives*. Academic Press, New York.

Finlay B.L. & Slattery M. (1983) Local differences in the amount of early cell death in neocortex predict local specializations. *Science* **219**, 1349−1351.

Galaburda A.M., Corsiglia J., Rosen G.D. & Sherman G.F. (1987) Planum temporale asymmetry, reappraisal since Geschwind and Levitsky. *Neuropsychologia* **25**, 853−868.

Galaburda A.M., Sherman G.F., Rosen G.D., Aboitz F. & Geschwind N. (1985) Developmental dyslexia: Four consecutive patients with cortical anomalies. *Annals of Neurology* **18**, 222−233.

Glucksman A. (1951) Cell death in normal vertebrate ontogeny. *Biological Reviews* **26**, 59−86.

Goldman-Rakic P.S., Isseroff A., Schwartz M.L. & Bugbee N.M. (1983) The neurobiology of cognitive development. In Haith M.M. & Campos J.J. (eds) *Mussen's Handbook of Child Psychology*, 4th edn, Vol. II, *Infancy and Developmental Psychobiology*, pp. 281−344. Wiley, New York.

Goodman R. (1987) The developmental neurobiology of language. In Yule W. & Rutter M. (eds) *Language Development and Disorders*, pp. 129−145. Clinics in Developmental Medicine, No. 101/102. MacKeith Press/Blackwell Scientific Publications, Oxford.

Goodman R. (1989) Neuronal misconnections and psychiatric disorder: Is there a link? *British Journal of Psychiatry* **154**, 292−299.

Goodman R. (1991a) Developmental disorders and structural brain development. In Rutter M. & Casaer P. (eds) *Biological Risk Factors for Psychosocial Development*, pp. 20−50. Cambridge University Press, Cambridge.

Goodman R. (1991b) Growing together and growing apart: The non-genetic forces on children in the same family. In McGuffin P. & Murray R. (eds) *The New Genetics of Mental Illness*, pp. 212−224. Butterworth-Heinemann, Oxford.

Gottesman I.I. & Shields J. (1982) *Schizophrenia: The Epigenetic Puzzle*. Cambridge University Press, Cambridge.

Gould S.J. (1977) *Ontogeny and Phylogeny*. Harvard University Press, Cambridge, Massachusetts.

Greenough W.T., Black J.E. & Wallace C.S. (1987) Experience and brain development. *Child Development* **58**, 539−559.

Guillery R.W. (1988) Competition in the development of the visual pathways. In Parnavelas J.G., Stern C.D. & Stirling R.V. (eds) *The Making of the Nervous System*, pp. 356−379. Oxford University Press, New York.

Gyllensten L., Malmfors T. & Norrlin M-L. (1965) Growth alteration in the auditory cortex of visually deprived mice. *Journal of Comparative Neurology* **126**, 463−470.

Hankin M. & Lund R. (1991) How do retinal axons find their targets in the developing brain? *Trends in Neuro-*

sciences **14**, 224–228.

Harrelson A.L. & Goodman C.S. (1988) Growth cone guidance in insects: Fasciclin II is a member of immunoglobulin superfamily. *Science* **242**, 700–708.

Harwerth R.S., Smith E.L., Duncan G.C., Crawford M.L.J. & von Noorden G.K. (1986) Multiple sensitive periods in the development of the primate visual system. *Science* **232**, 235–238.

Hatten M.E. (1990) Riding the glial monorail: a common mechanism for glial-guided neuronal migration in different regions of the developing mammalian brain. *Trends in Neurosciences* **13**, 179–184.

Hattori H. & Wasterlain C.G. (1990) Excitatory amino acids in the developing brain: ontogeny, plasticity, and excitotoxicity. *Pediatric Neurology* **6**, 219–228.

Hebb D.O. (1942) The effect of early and late brain injury upon test scores, and the nature of normal adult intelligence. *Proceedings of the American Philosophical Society* **85**, 275–292.

Hebb D.O. (1949) *The Organization of Behavior: A Neuro-Psychological Theory.* Wiley, New York.

Hiscock M. (1988) Behavioural asymmetries in normal children. In Molfese D.L. & Segalowitz S.J. (eds) *Brain Lateralization in Children: Developmental Implications*, pp. 85–171. Guilford, New York.

Hodges J. & Tizard B. (1989) Social and family relationships of ex-institutional adolescents. *Journal of Child Psychology and Psychiatry* **30**, 77–97.

Huttenlocher P.R. (1979) Synaptic density in human frontal cortex — Developmental changes and effects of aging. *Brain Research* **163**, 195–205.

Huttenlocher P.R., de Courten C., Garey L.J. & van der Loos H. (1982) Synaptogenesis in human visual cortex — Evidence for synapse elimination during normal development. *Neuroscience Letters* **33**, 247–252.

Janowsky J.S. & Finlay B.L. (1986) The outcome of perinatal brain damage: The role of normal neuronal loss and axonal retraction. *Developmental Medicine and Child Neurology* **28**, 375–389.

Jones P. & Murray R.M. (1991) The genetics of schizophrenia is the genetics of neurodevelopment. *British Journal of Psychiatry* **158**, 615–623.

Kasamatsu T., Pettigrew J.D. & Ary M. (1979) Restoration of visual cortical plasticity by local microperfusion of norepinephrine. *Journal of Comparative Neurology* **185**, 163–181.

Kinsbourne M. (1971) The minor cerebral hemisphere as a source of aphasic speech. *Archives of Neurology* **25**, 302–306.

Kleinschmidt A., Bear M.F. & Singer W. (1987) Blockade of 'NMDA' receptors disrupts experience-dependent plasticity of kitten striate cortex. *Science* **238**, 355–358.

Kolb B. (1989) Brain development, plasticity, and behavior. *American Psychologist* **44**, 1203–1212.

Kolb B. & Whishaw I.Q. (1981) Neonatal frontal lesions in the rat: Sparing of learned but not species-typical behavior in the presence of reduced brain weight and cortical thickness. *Journal of Comparative and Physiological Psychology* **95**, 863–879.

Kolb B. & Whishaw I.Q. (1989) Plasticity in the neocortex: Mechanisms underlying recovery from early brain damage. *Progress in Neurobiology* **32**, 235–276.

Korsching S. (1986) The role of nerve growth factor in the CNS. *Trends in Neurosciences* **9**, 570–573.

Kostovic I. & Rakic P. (1990) Developmental history of the transient subplate zone in the visual and somatosensory cortex of the macaque monkey and human brain. *Journal of Comparative Neurology* **297**, 441–470.

Kromer L.F., Bjorklund A. & Stenevi U. (1981) Innervation of embryonic implants by regenerating axons of cholinergic septal neurones in the adult rat. *Brain Research* **210**, 153–171.

Levin M. (1991) Infections of the nervous system. In Brett E.M. (ed.) *Paediatric Neurology*, 2nd edn, pp. 603–665. Churchill Livingstone, Edinburgh.

Levinthal F., Macagno E. & Levinthal C. (1976) Anatomy and development of identified cells in isogenic organisms. *Cold Spring Harbor Symposia on Quantitative Biology* **40**, 321–333.

Lipton S.A. & Kater S.B. (1989) Neurotransmitter regulation of neuronal outgrowth, plasticity and survival. *Trends in Neurosciences* **12**, 265–270.

Lumsden A. (1990) The cellular basis of segmentation in the developing hindbrain. *Trends in Neurosciences* **13**, 329–335.

Lynch G., Stanfield B. & Cotman C.W. (1973) Developmental differences in post-lesion axonal growth in hippocampus. *Brain Research* **59**, 155–168.

Lyon M. (1961) Gene action in the X-chromosome of the mouse (*Mus musculus* L.) *Nature* **190**, 372–373.

McConnell S.K. (1991) The generation of neuronal diversity in the central nervous system. *Annual Review of Neuroscience* **14**, 269–300.

McConnell S.K., Ghosh A. & Shatz C.J. (1989) Subplate neurons pioneer the first axon pathway from the cerebral cortex. *Science* **245**, 978–982.

Mednick S.A., Cannon T.D., Barr C.E. & Lyon M. (eds) (1991) *Fetal Neural Development and Adult Schizophrenia.* Cambridge University Press, Cambridge.

Mednick S.A., Machon R., Huttunen M.O. & Bonett D. (1988) Adult schizophrenia following prenatal exposure to an influenza epidemic. *Archives of General Psychiatry* **45**, 189–192.

Miller M. (1986) Effects of alcohol on the generation and migration of cerebral cortical neurons. *Science* **233**, 1308–1311.

Molfese D.L. & Betz J.C. (1988) Electrophysiological indices of the early development of lateralization for language and cognition, and their implications for predicting later development. In Molfese D.L. & Segalowitz S.J. (eds) *Brain Lateralization in Children: Developmental Implications*, pp. 171–191. Guilford, New York.

Molfese D.L. & Segalowitz S.J. (1988) *Brain Lateralization in Children: Developmental Implications.* Guilford,

New York.

Moriyoshi K., Masu M., Ishii T., Shigemoto R., Mizuno N. & Nakanishi S. (1991) Molecular cloning and characterization of the rat NMDA receptor. *Nature* **354**, 31–37.

Mountcastle V.B. (1978) An organizing principle for cerebral function: The unit module and the distributed system. In Edelman G.M. & Mountcastle V.B. (eds) *The Mindful Brain: Cortical Organization and the Group-Selective Theory of Higher Brain Function*, pp. 7–50. MIT Press, Cambridge, Massachusetts.

Nelson M.E. & Bower J.M. (1990) Brain maps and parallel computers. *Trends in Neurosciences* **13**, 403–408.

Nowakowski R.S. (1984) The mode of inheritance of a defect in lamination in the hippocampus of *BALB/c* mice. *Journal of Neurogenetics* **1**, 249–258.

Nowakowski R.S. (1987) Basic concepts of CNS development. *Child Development* **58**, 568–595.

Nowakowski R.S. & Rakic P. (1981) The site of origin and route and rate of migration of neurons to the hippocampal region of the rhesus monkey. *Journal of Comparative Neurology* **196**, 129–154.

O'Leary D.D.M. (1989) Do cortical areas emerge from a protocortex? *Trends in Neurosciences* **12**, 400–406.

O'Leary D.D.M. & Stanfield B.B. (1985) Occipital cortical neurons with transient pyramidal tract axons extend and maintain collaterals to subcortical but not intracortical targets. *Brain Research* **336**, 326–333.

O'Leary D.D.M. & Stanfield B.B. (1989) Selective elimination of axons extended by developing cortical neurons is dependent on regional locale: Experiments utilizing fetal cortical transplants. *Journal of Neuroscience* **9**, 2230–2246.

Otake M. & Schull W.J. (1984) *In utero* exposure to A-bomb radiation and mental retardation; a reassessment. *British Journal of Radiology* **57**, 409–414.

Parmelee J.R. & Sigman M.D. (1983) Perinatal brain development and behaviour. In Haith M.M. & Campos J.J. (eds) *Mussen's Handbook of Child Psychology*, 4th edn. Vol. II, *Infancy and Developmental Psychobiology*, pp. 95–155. Wiley, New York.

Piaget J. (1954) *The Construction of Reality in the Child*. Basic Books, New York.

Piazza D.M. (1977) Cerebral lateralization in young children as measured by dichotic listening and finger-tapping tasks. *Neuropsychologia* **15**, 417–425.

Petersen S.E., Fox P.T., Posner M.I., Mintun M. & Raichle M.E. (1988) Positron emission tomographic studies of the cortical anatomy of single-word processing. *Nature* **331**, 585–589.

Purves D. & Lichtman J.W. (1985) *Principles of Neural Development*. Sinauer, Sunderland, Massachusetts.

Raaf J. & Kernohan J.W. (1944) A study of the external granular layer in the cerebellum. *American Journal of Anatomy* **75**, 151–172.

Rakic P. (1978) Neuronal migration and contact guidance in the primate telencephalon. *Postgraduate Medical Journal* **54**(Suppl. 1), 25–40.

Rakic P. (1985) Limits of neurogenesis in primates. *Science* **227**, 1054–1055.

Rakic P. (1988) Specification of cerebral cortical areas. *Science* **241**, 170–176.

Rakic P., Bourgeois J-P., Eckenhoff F., Zecevic N. & Goldman-Rakic P.S. (1986) Concurrent overproduction of synapses in diverse regions of the primate cerebral cortex. *Science* **232**, 232–235.

Rakic P. & Sidman M.D. (1968) Supravital DNA synthesis in the developing human and mouse brain. *Journal of Neuropathology and Experimental Neurology* **27**, 246–276.

Rakic P., Suner I. & Williams R.W. (1991) A novel cytoarchitectonic area induced experimentally within the primate visual cortex. *Proceedings of the National Academy of Sciences of the United States of America* **88**, 2083–2087.

Revesz T., Schuler D., Goldschmidt B. & Elodi S. (1972) Christmas disease in one of a pair of monozygotic twin girls, possibly the effect of Lyonization. *Journal of Medical Genetics* **9**, 396–400.

Rutter M. (1984) Issues and prospects in developmental neuropsychiatry. In Rutter M. (ed.) *Developmental Neuropsychiatry*, pp. 577–598. Churchill Livingstone, Edinburgh.

Rutter M. (1989) Pathways from childhood to adult life. *Journal of Child Psychology and Psychiatry* **30**, 23–51.

Ryugo D.K., Ryugo R., Globus A. & Killackey H.P. (1975) Increased spine density in auditory cortex following visual or somatic deafferentation. *Brain Research* **90**, 143–146.

Schade J.P. & van Groenigen W.B. (1961) Structural organization of the human cerebral cortex. I. Maturation of the middle frontal gyrus. *Acta Anatomica* **47**, 74–111.

Schneider G.E. (1979) Is it really better to have your brain lesion early? A revision of the 'Kennard Principle'. *Neuropsychologia* **17**, 557–583.

Schwab M.E. (1990) Myelin-associated inhibitors of neurite growth. *Experimental Neurology* **109**, 2–5.

Schwartz M.L. & Goldman-Rakic P.S. (1990) Prenatal specification of callosal connections in rhesus monkey. *Journal of Comparative Neurology* **307**, 144–162.

Schwartz M.L., Rakic P. & Goldman-Rakic P.S. (1991) Early phenotype expression of cortical neurons: Evidence that a subclass of migrating neurons have callosal axons. *Proceedings of the National Academy of Sciences of the United States of America* **88**, 1354–1358.

Sejnowski T.J. & Rosenberg C.R. (1987) Parallel networks that learn to pronounce English text. *Complex Systems* **1**, 145–168.

Sham P.C., O'Callaghan E., Takei N., Murray G.K., Hare E.H. & Murray R.M. (1992) Schizophrenia following pre-natal exposure to influenza epidemics between 1939 and 1960. *British Journal of Psychiatry* **160**, 461–466.

Sherman G.F., Galaburda A.M. & Geschwind N. (1985)

Cortical anomalies in brains of New Zealand mice: A neuropathologic model of dyslexia? *Proceedings of the National Academy of Sciences of the United States of America* **82**, 8072–8074.

Sidman R.L. & Rakic P. (1973) Neuronal migration with special reference to developing human brains: a review. *Brain Research* **62**, 1–35.

Singer W. (1986) The brain as a self-organizing system. *European Archives of Psychiatry and Neurological Sciences* **236**, 4–9.

Smith A. & Sugar O. (1975) Development of above normal language and intelligence 21 years after left hemispherectomy. *Neurology* **25**, 813–818.

Spear P.D. (1979) Behavioural and neurophysiological consequences of visual cortex damage: Mechanisms of recovery. In Sprague J.M. & Epstein A.N. (eds) *Progress in Psychobiology and Physiological Psychology*, Vol. 8, pp. 45–90. Academic Press, New York.

Springer S.P. & Deutsch G. (1989) *Left Brain, Right Brain*, 3rd edn. W.H. Freeman, San Francisco.

Sretavan D.W., Shatz C.J. & Stryker M.P. (1988) Modification of retinal ganglion cell axon morphology by prenatal infusion of tetrodotoxin. *Nature* **336**, 468–471.

Stryker M.P. & Harris W.A. (1986) Binocular impulse blockade prevents the formation of ocular dominance columns in cat visual cortex. *Journal of Neuroscience* **6**, 2117–2133.

Subirana A. (1958) The prognosis in aphasia in relation to cerebral dominance and handedness. *Brain* **81**, 415–425.

Suomi S.J. (1991) Early stress and adult emotional reactivity in rhesus monkeys. In Bock G.R. & Whelan J. (eds) *The Childhood Environment and Adult Disease*, pp. 171–188. Ciba Foundation Symposium, No. 156. Wiley, Chichester.

Sur M., Garraghty P.E. & Roe A.W. (1988) Experimentally induced visual projections into auditory thalamus and cortex. *Science* **242**, 1437–1441.

Sur M., Pallas S.L. & Roe A.W. (1990) Cross-modal plasticity in cortical development: Differentiation and specification of sensory neocortex. *Trends in Neurosciences* **13**, 227–233.

Sutcliffe J.G., Milner R.J., Gottesfeld J.M. & Reynolds W. (1984) Control of neuronal gene expression. *Science* **225**, 1308–1315.

Swaab D.F. & Hofman M.A. (1988) Sexual differentiation of the human hypothalamus: ontogeny of the sexually dimorphic nucleus of the preoptic area. *Developmental Brain Research* **44**, 314–318.

Swindale N.V. (1990) Is the cerebral cortex modular? *Trends in Neurosciences* **13**, 487–492.

Takashima S., Kashima S., Chan F., Becker L.E. & Armstrong D.L. (1980) Morphology of the developing visual cortex of the human infant: A quantitative and qualitative Golgi study. *Journal of Neuropathology and Experimental Neurology* **39**, 487–501.

Tessier-Lavigne M. & Placzek M. (1991) Target attraction: are developing axons guided by chemotropism? *Trends in Neurosciences* **14**, 303–310.

Tresidder J., Fielder A. & Nicholson J. (1990) Delayed visual maturation: Ophthalmic and neurodevelopmental aspects. *Developmental Medicine and Child Neurology* **32**, 872–881.

Trisler D. & Collins F. (1987) Corresponding spatial gradients of TOP molecules in the developing retina and optic tectum. *Science* **237**, 1208–1209.

Vaegan & Taylor D. (1979) Critical period for deprivation amblyopia in children. *Transactions of the Ophthalmological Society of the United Kingdom* **99**, 432–439.

Vandenberg S.G., McKusick V.A. & McKusick A.B. (1962) Twin data in support of the Lyon hypothesis. *Nature* **194**, 505–506.

Vargha-Khadem F., Isaacs E., van der Werf S., Robb S. & Wilson J. (1992) Development of intelligence and memory in children with hemiplegic cerebral palsy: The deleterious consequences of early seizures. *Brain* **115**, 315–329.

Vargha-Khadem F., O'Gorman A.M. & Watters G.V. (1985) Aphasia and handedness in relation to hemispheric side, age at injury and severity of cerebral lesion during childhood. *Brain* **108**, 677–696.

Wada J.A., Clarke R. & Hamm A. (1975) Cerebral hemispheric asymmetry in humans: Cortical speech zones in 100 adult and 100 infant brains. *Archives of Neurology* **32**, 239–246.

Wall P.D. (1977) The presence of ineffective synapses and the circumstances which unmask them. *Philosophical Transactions of the Royal Society of London, Series B* **278**, 361–372.

Walsh C. & Cepko C.L. (1992) Widespread dispersion of neuronal clones across functional regions of the cerebral cortex. *Science* **255**, 434–440.

Werker J.F. & Tees R.C. (1984) Cross-language speech perception: evidence for perceptual reorganization during the first year of life. *Infant Behavior and Development* **7**, 49–63.

Wiesel T.N. (1982) Postnatal development of the visual cortex and the influence of environment. *Science* **299**, 583–591.

Wilkinson D.G. & Krumlauf R. (1990) Molecular approaches to the segmentation of the hindbrain. *Trends in Neurosciences* **13**, 335–339.

Willerman L., Schultz R., Rutledge J.N. & Bigler E.D. (1991) *In vivo* brain size and intelligence. *Intelligence* **15**, 223–228.

Woods B.T. (1980) The restricted effects of right-hemisphere lesions after age one: Weschler test data. *Neuropsychologia* **18**, 65–70.

Woods B.T. & Carey S. (1979) Language deficits after apparent clinical recovery from childhood aphasia. *Annals of Neurology* **6**, 405–409.

Woods B.T. & Teuber H.L. (1978) Changing patterns of

childhood aphasia. *Annals of Neurology* **3**, 273−280.
Yakovlev P.I. & Lecours A-R. (1967) The myelogenetic cycles of regional maturation of the brain. In Mirkowski A. (ed.) *Regional Development of the Brain in Early Life*, pp. 3−70. Blackwell Scientific Publications, Oxford.
Zangwill O.L. (1960) *Cerebral Dominance and its Relation to Psychological Function*. Oliver & Boyd, Edinburgh.

4: Individual Characteristics as a Force in Development

ANETTE ENGFER, SABINE WALPER AND MICHAEL RUTTER

INTRODUCTION

More than 10 years have passed since the publication of the book *Individuals as Producers of their Development* (Lerner & Busch-Rossnagel, 1981). The topic of this chapter is phrased less deterministically, referring not to individuals as producers of their fate, but rather to individual characteristics with respect to their impact on development. The idea that individuals actively 'produce' their own development replaced previous theories that either emphasized the 'mechanistic' role of environmental input in development, or focused on the 'organismic' maturation or unfolding of psychological structures according to a predetermined order (Reese & Overton, 1970). Within this new model, individuals were seen as active contributors to their development, instead of being more or less passive recipients of external or internal forces. There is no doubt that the model was correct in drawing attention to the fact that even very young children are active agents in responding to their experiences. However, it carried the danger of replacing the simplistic view that individual troubles were all to be blamed on society, by the equally misleading implications that individuals were the source of their own misfortunes (and implicitly, therefore to blame if things went wrong) (Meacham, 1981).

A focus on the active individual does not mean that external influences on development should be ignored. Rather, it raises questions on whether, how, under which conditions and to what extent individual characteristics affect life-course patterns and developmental outcomes. These are empirical issues that have to be dealt with differentially for men and women, for different characteristics, for different stages of the life-cycle, and for contextual conditions of development. Much of the research on individual differences has been concerned with their impact on here-and-now interactions in particular situations. These are important, but so far as possible, we shall be concerned with the possible developmental implications — meaning a degree of carry-forward to later age periods (see Rutter & Rutter, 1993 for a discussion of the difficult issue of differentiating between developmental and non-developmental changes in psychological functioning).

If individual characteristics are considered as a force in development, four basic issues require some discussion. First, since such characteristics are the starting point constructs, it is necessary to consider which ones might be relevant. Traditionally, there has been a tendency to focus on temperamental variables thought to be related to dimensions of adult personality. These are discussed but, in addition, attention will be paid to differences in other socially relevant characteristics such as attractiveness, body build, age, gender and facial disfigurement. This broadening of individuality has been necessary because evidence suggests that these other characteristics have a psychological impact, too.

Second, in conceptualizations of individuality there has been a major interest in the ways in which personality is constructed. Commonly, the main focus is on basic personality dimensions, the so-called 'big five' (Digman, 1990; John, 1990; Loehlin, 1992; see below). This chapter indicates the relatively little that is known about developmental processes in relation to those facets of personality. However, their relation to broader concepts of personality functioning is briefly discussed (Rutter, 1987b).

Third, there will be some discussion of the various ways in which interindividual differences in one domain are related to other aspects of development and to psychopathology. One way of looking at these issues is to consider individual characteristics as independent variables determining the life-course of individuals. Temperament research is a good example here. Starting with the description of behavioural characteristics on which infants and young children differ, one can study the way in which these characteristics are maintained, modified or replaced by other characteristics over the course of their development, and investigate their role as risk factors for psychopathology (Maziade, 1989; Rutter, 1989c; Thomas & Chess, 1989; Prior, 1992).

Fourth, individual characteristics may also be viewed as dependent variables in the study of development as evident in the literature on socialization. Although the topic of this chapter implies a different perspective, the malleability of given characteristics needs to be taken account of in order to identify the processes and experiences through which individual characteristics derive their 'causal' force. For example, depressed mothers interact with their infants in a manner that may lead to a 'depressed' behavioural style in their children. In one study, this depressed interactional style of infants was found to generalize to interactions with other non-depressed adults who in turn were negatively affected by it (Field, 1992). Girls who have been exposed to prolonged and very serious sexual abuse by family members apparently sometimes develop behavioural characteristics (such as a generalized helplessness, sexualization of behaviour) that may perhaps facilitate subsequent rape or sexual abuse by other perpetrators (Russell, 1986; Drajer, 1990; Smith & Bentovim, 1994). Also, of course, genetic factors play a vital role in shaping individual characteristics (Loehlin, 1992). Consequently, individual characteristics may function both as dependent and independent variables in the study of developmental processes.

Interindividual differences in development appear as one of the core issues in psychology, not only for researchers trying to predict developmental outcomes, but also for clinicians who need to know when, with whom and in which way to intervene to prevent problematic development. However, the study of interindividual differences in development is hampered by several difficulties. Scientific disci-plines usually work in isolation and rarely include multiple perspectives. Investigations of interindividual differences scarcely ever refer to developmental processes and to the contexts within which they emerge, and developmental psychology has just begun to describe interindividual differences in outcomes (see, however, Hoffman, 1991 for a discussion of how the interplay between persons and their environments may lead siblings to differ from each other). The same holds true for psychopathology. Here issues of diagnostic classification, epidemiology and treatment prevail, and only recently has the rather new field of developmental psychopathology incorporated developmental perspectives into the study of child and adolescent disorders (Rutter, 1988, 1989b, 1993; Cicchetti, 1989; Lewis & Miller, 1990; Robins & Rutter, 1990).

Another problem encountered concerns the fact that characteristics that have been found to have a profound impact on short-term social interactions are rarely studied longitudinally. This is especially true for characteristics such as attractiveness, body build, obesity, speech abnormalities or facial disfigurement. For some of these characteristics (such as attractiveness and facial disfigurement) there exist numerous experimental studies that demonstrate their effect on social interactions (Bull & Rumsey, 1988). However, real-life studies are scarce, and the impact of attractiveness on the life course has rarely been studied (Elder, 1969; Elder et al., 1985).

Furthermore, we are uncertain on the extent to which findings of experimental studies can be generalized to processes involved in development. Whereas in experimental studies, subjects (usually college students) react to the stimulus characteristics of targets unknown to them, developmental processes mainly take place in relationships between people knowing each other very well, and their characteristics are part of, determine, and will be influenced by the nature of their relationship (Hinde, 1979).

Experiments try to simulate developmental processes by using different age groups and by varying the age of targets and judges or interaction partners independently of one another. In real life, however, people grow older together and share a history of their relationships. Inevitably that affects the meaning and functions of characteristics considerably. For instance, the well-known effect of the 'what is beautiful is good' stereotype operating in superficial contacts may be reversed into the notion of 'what is good is beautiful' for people involved in satisfying intimate relationships (Bull & Rumsey, 1988).

A final reason why experiments may be unsuited to model developmental processes is the fact that subjects are rarely allowed to choose their own environments and the experimentally predetermined options of responses restrict their natural range of behaviour (Buss & Plomin, 1984). Consequently, some of the findings presented in this chapter should be viewed with caution, just because they stem from experimental studies of interactions that occur at one moment of time in a controlled situation. In many instances, too, we cannot refer to substantiated empirical findings but have to speculate instead about the way in which individual characteristics might be related to lifespan development.

In discussing the role of individual characteristics as a force in lifespan development, the authors first address the ways in which temperamental features of childhood are thought to be related to personality as it is shown in adult life. Here the authors will also refer to biologically rooted predispositions having direct behavioural implications for individual reactions to social situations. Then the authors will point to major dimensions or properties of individual characteristics that render them more or less salient and powerful in their potential impact on individual development. Finally, the authors describe processes or mechanisms involved in the interplay between individual characteristics and contextual conditions, arguing that the impact of individual characteristics on development is mainly mediated by the interpretation and reaction of the social environment. However, intrinsic qualities of characteristics are also important. This will be our first point.

DIRECT BEHAVIOURAL IMPLICATIONS AND THE ROUTES TO ADULT PERSONALITY: THE CASE OF TEMPERAMENT

Intrinsic qualities of characteristics have been crucial in the concept of temperamental traits as personal, stylistic attributes that reflect biologically rooted behavioural predispositions (Kohnstamm *et al.*, 1989). Thus, many personality theorists have chosen their behavioural typologies on the basis of the supposed neurobiological origins of particular behavioural dimensions (Rothbart, 1989). This has led some to argue for temperamental constructs that combine behavioural and physiological features, as with Kagan *et al.*'s (1987) concept of 'behavioural inhibition'. Behavioural inhibition refers to physiological arousal and fearful withdrawal as response to stressful or challenging situations and has been shown to be important, in both humans and monkeys. Similarly, Quay's (1965) concept of 'sensation-seeking' is considered a temperamental attribute with strong implications for how people will behave in social situations. It describes an intolerance for routine and boredom, an inability to delay gratification and a tendency to seek out thrilling or exciting experiences — perhaps as a consequence of diminished reactivity to ordinary stresses, challenges and stimulation. It is easy to see how such a tendency might predispose to delinquency. There is no doubt that both children and adults can be characterized in terms of attributes that have fairly direct behavioural implications for how they themselves will respond to social situations. It is an empirical matter, however, to determine whether this constitutes the main mechanism for effects on development or risks for psychopathology, an issue to which this chapter will return.

If one tries to connect features of childhood temperament with adult personality the core question is: how are simple, non-motivational, non-cognitive, behavioural characteristics such as activity level or behavioural inhibition transformed into the patterning that each person, as a thinking being, develops to deal with the traits he or she is endowed with, the social contexts encountered or the experiences received (Rutter, 1987b)? Personality functioning includes a set of cognitions about ourselves, our relationships, and our interactions with the environment (Rutter, 1987a), all of which serve to make up the so-called 'self-system' incorporating self-esteem, self-efficacy and social problem-solving skills (Harter, 1983), and it is these cognitions that the authors consider to be crucial.

Four main points need to be made at the outset.

First, at *all* ages, the concept of temperament is an abstraction or latent construct, rather than anything that can be observed directly (Rutter, 1987b, 1989c). There is good reason to accept the reality of biologically based individual differences in behavioural style but, even in infancy, observed behaviour will be affected by babies' cognitive processing of their environment and by situation-specifities. Second, neither are temperamental influences confined to childhood nor are they simply replaced by personality with increasing age. There is every reason to suppose that biological dispositions operate in adult life, as they do in childhood. It may well be that as cognitive skills increase with age, so motivational components come more to the fore, but it is only a matter of degree. Third, it is a mistake to suppose that innate characteristics are best seen in pure culture in the neonatal period, being progressively modified by the environment as children grow older. Genetic effects may take time to operate and empirical findings indicate that the heritability of most characteristics is quite *low* in infancy, and increases over the course of the childhood years (Plomin, 1986). Fourth, although the research literature on adult personality traits tends to be rather separate from that on the 'self-system', it is obvious that the two are interwoven.

The data on consistency over time for temperamental dimensions in childhood are rather contradictory and difficult to interpret (Prior, 1992). However, the few longer term longitudinal studies show that temperamental variables in the first couple of years of life have a near-zero correlation with supposedly comparable measures in adolescence (Thomas & Chess, 1977; Torgersen, 1989), but more consistency (with correlations mainly in the 0.3–0.5 range) between the early school years and the teenage period. However, consistency for extreme temperamental characteristics may be somewhat greater than that for the same characteristics in the middle of the range. Findings by Kagan *et al.* (1989) suggest that is so for behavioural inhibition.

Less is known about continuities between childhood and adult life. Adult personality theorists have been much concerned with establishing a general taxonomy of personality traits and it seems that a consensus has been achieved on what have come to be called the 'big five' characteristics of: (i) surgency/extraversion (including features such as sociability, impulsivity, activity and self-assertion); (ii) agreeableness/friendliness (including like-ability, warmth and trust); (iii) conscientiousness/will to achieve (including organization, planfulness and reliability); (iv) emotional stability versus neuroticism (comprising anxiety, moodiness, worrying, etc.); and (v) culture/openness to experience (including curiosity, ingenuity and intellectual qualities) (Digman, 1990; John, 1990; Loehlin, 1992). The basis for this consensus is that these broad dimensions have been reasonably consistently identified in a range of different studies involving quite varied samples (John, 1990), show moderate heritability in the range of 22–46% (Loehlin, 1992), and that the traits show substantial stability over time during adult life (MacCrae & Costa, 1990). However, it has to be added that there is some inconsistency in the precise qualities included in each trait by different personality theorists (Digman, 1990; John, 1990; Loehlin, 1992).

There is no doubt that the 'big five' traits summarize reasonably well individual features that appear socially meaningful in the ways that we all characterize what is distinctive about other people. Some interest has therefore been directed to the study of how these traits arise and what predictive effects they have (for psychopathology, social interactions, responses to stress or other significant outcomes). The results of research on these two issues are decidedly disappointing and we remain somewhat sceptical about how much has been learned regarding personality development from the use of questionnaire measures of personality dimensions. Nevertheless, some important implications do derive from the findings.

There is considerable uncertainty on whether the questionnaire measures of temperament/ personality used at different ages are comparable with one another. However, if a degree of comparability can be assumed, it appears that there is a negligible genetic component in the neonatal period, only a small genetic effect in the first year and then an increasing genetic contribution over the years of childhood (Loehlin, 1992). This contradicts the commonly held view that biogenetic influences are gradually replaced by socialization and other environmental influences. Instead it seems that one's genetic endowment becomes more and more powerful in shaping personality development just as if genetically driven experiences need to accumulate over time. Similarly, as dizygotic (DZ) twins (which share no more genes than siblings do) grow older, they tend to become less alike (McCartney *et al.*, 1990). The implication is that shared environmental influences (i.e. those that impinge equally on all children in the same family) become less important as children grow older, and non-shared influences (those that impinge differently on different children) become more important.

Although personality theorists tend to view the key dimensions as in some way intrinsic and biologically determined, it is striking that the adult studies show only a moderate genetic component, with additive genes accounting for about a third of the variance, and another sixth being due to either non-additive genetic effects or special environmental resemblance for monozygotic (MZ) twins (Loehlin, 1992). In the study of mechanisms influencing personality development quantitative genetic analyses are potentially helpful, although their fruits so far are modest.

Various mechanisms in the development of personality characteristics need to be considered. One issue concerns the possibility that genetic effects shape environmental experiences (Scarr & McCartney, 1983; Scarr, 1992). These effects may be 'passive'; for example, intellectual parents may pass on to their children genes predisposing to high IQ and also provide them with experiences that are conducive to the same outcome. There is evidence that this mechanism does operate with respect to IQ but its effect appears negligible in the case of temperamental/personality dimensions (Loehlin, 1992). Alternatively, the effects may be 'reactive' (so that, for example, an easily upset child may be specially protected by parents or teachers or become the butt of extra teasing by peers), or 'active' (so that, for instance, a particularly sociable child is likely to seek more social encounters than a withdrawn, inhibited child). Evidence on the strength of these three effects is rudimentary in the extreme. However, it is important to appreciate that individuals may have a strong effect on other people, or a strong tendency to select environments, without that effect being genetically determined (see below).

A further mechanism — and a special case

in point — concerns possible contrast or de-identification effects (Schacter & Stone, 1985; Goodman, 1991) — the tendency for siblings to accentuate their differences in order to assert their individuality. Thus, one may become the leader and the other the follower, one the naughty and one the good one, and so on. Twin analyses (showing very low or even negative DZ correlations) suggest that this tendency may apply to self-concepts more than to purely behavioural attributes (Loehlin, 1992). It also seems that the effect may be greater in others' perceptions of temperament than in behaviour as assessed directly (Mebert, 1991). The occasional (but only occasional) finding that MZ twins reared apart are more similar on some personality measures than those reared together, suggests that the contrast effect may sometimes apply to other features (Plomin, 1986; Loehlin, 1992).

However, the measurement of this effect in the population as a whole is extremely difficult because, if some twins strive to accentuate their differences and yet others try to make themselves more alike, these tendencies will counterbalance one another in any overall analysis, giving the misleading impression that neither are operative (Goodman, 1991). Clearly, there is a need to study such de-identification and assimilation processes directly and not just infer their effects from multivariate analyses. Almost no research of this kind has been undertaken to date.

In view of what has been noted about the likely role of cognitive processing in the shaping of personality, it ought to be possible to draw attention to a literature on the topic, but there is a paucity of research that deals directly with these issues. There clearly is substantial overlap between measures such as neuroticism that supposedly reflect a behavioural predisposition and those, such as low self-esteem or learned helplessness, that purport to tap cognitive sets (Teasdale & Dent, 1987; Hammen, 1990), but little is known on the developmental processes involved in their interplay.

So far, the case of childhood temperament and adult personality provided the background for addressing some major issues in the study of developmental mechanisms and outcomes as they may be triggered by individual characteristics. Our main focus was on factors residing within the individual: on the role of genetic determination, behavioural channelling and cognitive mediation. The next section will go beyond personality and turn to other characteristics, asking which features may render them more or less relevant for individual development. Possible social processes involved are given particular attention. Finally, a more systematic view is provided on how individual characteristics may become a force in development.

THE NATURE OF CHARACTERISTICS

The extent to which characteristics can affect development will partly depend on their nature and on the way in which they are evaluated by the individuals themselves or by their social environment. Therefore, in the next section we will try to define some dimensions along which characteristics may be classified.

'Visibility'

Characteristics differ depending on how visible or noticeable they are in various kinds of social encounters and different situations. Differences in visibility tend to make characteristics more or less salient and relevant for forming expectations, planning actions and interpreting reactions, not only for those who respond to their social partners' characteristics but also for the subjects themselves. Characteristics of high visibility are sex, age, race, body build, hair colour, weight, attractiveness or the converse (i.e. unattractiveness), disfigurement, facial deformity, etc. Visibility may be enhanced by extremes of these characteristics within a given population. Intermediate differences in age, attractiveness, weight may go unnoticed, but their extremes catch the attention of the observer. Therefore, visibility will also depend on variance of characteristics in the reference group used for comparison. The extraordinary beauty of a girl will be more visible if compared with her usual class-mates than with other girls at a beauty contest.

Characteristics of intermediate visibility include those that are only revealed under certain situational conditions or in certain settings: shyness or behavioural inhibition may be observable only if individuals are confronted with (social) novelty (Kagan *et al.*, 1987; Asendorpf, 1990b). High giftedness may easily be discerned in school or other achievement-related settings, much less so when we meet a person in the street. For highly gifted students, the comparison with ordinary class-mates may bolster their academic self-confidence at the expense of 'feeling different' with corresponding attempts to camouflage their special abilities. In programmes including similarly gifted students, the visibility of their special talents is reduced and they feel more at ease socially (Coleman & Cross, 1988).

Characteristics of low visibility include those that may not be visible at all to outside observers or to individuals themselves (unless they are physiologists), but which nevertheless have observable behavioural correlates. The complex associations between hormones and behaviour (Bancroft & Reinisch, 1990) or patterns of cognitive abilities (Jacklin *et al.*, 1988) are instances of this kind. Another example is provided by the association between minor congenital anomalies and hyperactive behaviour, and other types of psychopathology (Steg & Rapoport, 1975; Waldrop *et al.*, 1978; Deutsch *et al.*, 1990). These can be well identified by trained researchers, whereas they go unnoticed by most other people.

The finding that some characteristics of low visibility may have substantial behavioural correlates indicates that by no means all effects of individual characteristics derive from other people's responses to them. Nevertheless, visibility does seem to be a salient feature. Why should it be an important dimension of characteristics? Visible characteristics are particularly powerful in initial or superficial contacts as they channel attention and elicit social stereotypes even before social interactions have taken place. They determine if others will interact at all with persons showing these characteristics, and will influence the quality of the interaction. Finally, the visibility of characteristics will determine the extent to which the individuals themselves feel 'different', and, depending on the social desirability of these characteristics, will feel at ease or anxious about their own social competence and the reactions they experience from others.

Physical attractiveness is a good example, here. Marked attractiveness is known to trigger the social stereotype of 'what is beautiful is good' (Eagly *et al.*, 1991), particularly so far as ascribed social competencies are concerned. However, this attribution probably mainly applies at the extremes, with less effect from variations within the middle of the range; also, although people *perceive* physically attractive people more positively, attractive individuals show rather smaller differences in measured traits (Feingold, 1992). Perceiving persons as attractive determines the sympathy felt for them and the inclination to date these persons (Walster *et al.*, 1966). Men's dating choices are especially susceptible to this effect, whereas for women superiority of age and social status in men seem more crucial (Green *et al.*, 1984).

Visibility and salience of characteristics may also be linked to certain stages in the life course. Although attractiveness influences social interactions throughout life, its social significance is particularly pronounced in the time span between adolescence and early adulthood, that is in the phase of beginning heterosexual relationships and mating. Elder (1969) showed that physically attractive girls from the working class were able to marry 'upwards', as it were, trading in their beauty for the higher social status of their husbands. Similarly, Belsky *et al.* (1989) found that women with problematic child-rearing histories tended to end up in poorer marriages unless they were attractive. Presumably their attractiveness was one way to break with their unhappy past because it raised their chances of getting married to a better mate. Attractiveness may decrease in relevance in older age, when other characteristics such as physical and emotional well-being may take over.

Physical appearance determines responses by the social environment as well as expectations and behaviour of the individuals themselves. It has been observed that obese women not only expect their partners to be less interested in them, but actually behave in ways causing uneasiness and making them less liked even when their weight was not visible to their social partners because they were talking on the phone (Miller *et al.*, 1990). Consequently, the knowledge of being obese (as a very visible characteristic) affected these women's expectations about the (unfortunate) course of their social interaction and the way in which they behaved, thereby validating their negative expectations in terms of a self-fulfilling prophecy.

Likewise, the visibility of child disability seems to be the critical variable determining whether or not it results in a social and psychological handicap (Busch-Rossnagel, 1981). For instance, adolescents with the invisible handicap of congenital heart disease had higher vocational aspirations, post high-school career plans, work values and a better self-image than youngsters with a highly visible handicap, e.g. facial burns (Goldberg, 1974). Consequently, the visible handicap without physical limitations had a more deleterious effect than the invisible disability with severe limitations, and this may be particularly true during adolescence when physique and appearance become increasingly salient.

There may be discrepancies between the social stereotypes or expectations elicited by visible characteristics and the behavioural intentions, motivations, and preferences the individuals themselves may feel. If highly salient aspects of one's self-concept are involved, a threatening mismatch between social and personal identity may be experienced. Such a mismatch or discrepancy exists in individuals whose physical sex-linked characteristics do not correspond with their psychological gender preference, as is the case in individuals seeking gender-reassignment surgery (Abramowitz, 1986; Kockott & Fahrner, 1988; Kuiper & Cohen-Kettenis, 1988). Surgery appears to be one means of resolving this discrepancy. However, the fear that characteristics of the original sex (such as beard growth, deep voice, strong body build) may still be visible and reveal transsexualism is a matter of continuous concern in men who have changed into women (Eicher *et al.*, 1991).

The concept of visibility seems to imply that visible characteristics are 'real'. However, the concepts into which the visible characteristics are cast are person-made and a matter of definition. This is most obvious in concepts of low visibility such as unrecognized diseases or hormone levels functioning as constructs 'explaining' observable behavioural correlates. But it applies just as well to highly visible characteristics since the definitions of what constitutes attractiveness or obesity depend on the frame of reference used. Scientific definitions usually refer to the distribution of characteristics given in a certain population and identify extreme groups in terms of deviations from population means. However, as in the case of attractiveness, the full range of attractiveness is scarcely known and, in the main, comparative judgements of higher or lower degrees of attractiveness (usually by means of matched comparisons) are possible. In the case of weight, even the scientifically defined norms of average or ideal weight undergo constant revisions (Rodin *et al.*, 1984). Lay conceptions of characteristics are even more vague, in flux, and dependent on the range of individual experience, anchor points used for comparisons, personal inferences, etc.

On the other hand, there seems to be a socially mediated consensus about the content and salience of certain characteristics. For instance interrater correlations for judgements about facial attractiveness are about 0.50 in different studies and show intermediate retest correlations in the magnitude of 0.40 across a time span of 5 years (Maruyama & Miller, 1981). Even for more setting-specific characteristics such as shyness we found correlations in the magnitude of 0.50 between parents' and observers' ratings of child shyness (Engfer, 1993). Presumably, the effect of characteristics on interactions depends partly on the extent to which they are socially defined and evaluated with corresponding rules or role prescriptions about appropriate ways of responding. Lack of clear role prescriptions and contradictory notions about appropriate ways of responding may partly account for the insecurity felt by many people when interacting with disabled or facially disfigured patients (Bull & Rumsey, 1988; Goldson, 1992).

These findings underscore the notion that social consensus concerning the definition and, thus, the perception of individual characteristics partly determines the way in which these characteristics channel development. Since highly standardized attributes elicit recurrently similar experiences in social interactions they are likely to influence developmental outcomes more consistently than characteristics for which this consensus is lacking or more vague. The same holds true for the evaluation of individual attributes, which is dealt with next.

Social desirability of characteristics

Another important dimension along which individual characteristics can be classified is the extent to which they are considered as socially desirable. Attractiveness is one of the characteristics being

highly valued in past and present society. High-giftedness had and still has a more ambiguous reputation as indicated by sayings such as 'early ripe, early rot', and by the myths about 'genius and insanity' despite the empirical evidence that high-giftedness is generally associated with good psycho-social adjustment (Janos & Robinson, 1985; Rost, 1993). Other characteristics that are generally evaluated positively are personality characteristics such as emotional stability and empathy, whereas ill-temperedness, explosiveness, lack of self-control are usually considered as undesirable. However, many characteristics show differential desirability depending on their association with gender role stereotypes. Activity, strength, assertiveness are characteristics usually associated with masculinity, whereas tenderness, nurturance, sensitivity are typically ascribed to women (Hinde, 1984).

Moreover there exist social norms concerning the 'match' of characteristics in couples. Although there is empirical evidence that couples tend to be somewhat similar in attractiveness, intelligence and social class (an effect attributed to assortative mating) there is likewise the social norm of husband superiority concerning height, age and social status (James, 1989). This may be one reason why extremely tall girls experience their height as particularly distressing at the life stage of dating and mating, since it reduces their options of eligible partners (Degenhardt & Kollmann, 1986); presumably, the same may apply to men who, relative to population means, are of short stature.

Norms for social desirability vary between cultures and subcultures. For example, physical strength, independence and non-submission to authority have been found to be particularly pronounced norms among male working-class youth, and acting according to these norms strongly supports the perpetuation of class-related differences. Dropping out of school and looking for 'masculine' jobs, involving hard physical labour, precludes the chances for higher academic achievement and socioeconomic upward mobility (Willis, 1977).

The social desirability of characteristics depends on age and associated expectations or developmental tasks to be mastered successfully. This is particularly notable in the characteristics perceived as 'easy' or 'difficult' in young children. In the early phase of infancy, frequent crying and lack of soothability are found to be particularly distressing (Van den Boom, 1988, 1989). During the second year, restlessness, moodiness and high activity are perceived as being difficult by mothers. The more mothers expect their children to behave independently and cooperatively, the more they resent them remaining dependent on them in a clingy way, displaying temper tantrums and aggressive non-compliance beyond the age of 4 (Engfer, 1992).

Another example of age-related changes in the desirability of characteristics comes from studies on ageing. Here it seems most functional for the well-being of men and women if they follow a certain cross-over in sex role characteristics with women becoming more assertive and autonomous and men becoming more socially oriented (Deutsch *et al.*, 1986; Fooken, 1992).

It is important to note that the characteristics viewed as socially desirable or undesirable may have little or nothing to do with the behaviour of the individuals themselves. Thus, racial discrimination has been shown experimentally to operate at the level of written or telephoned applications for jobs or housing, even before the people are interviewed personally (e.g. Daniel, 1968).

Why and in which way can the social desirability of characteristics affect development? Socially desirable characteristics are more rewarded by the social environment. Individuals displaying these characteristics experience more positive feedback for what they do and how they are, and receive a favourable reputation within social groups. This affects not only the way in which others behave towards them, but also the way in which they feel about themselves and the options they have over the life-course. For example, there is a small amount of evidence suggesting that people may behave in ways that fit stereotypes set by their assigned names (Jahoda, 1954; Bagley & Evan-Wong, 1970). Similarly, a match between personal characteristics and age-dependent social expectations may partly account for the greater stability of personality characteristics indicative of social and cognitive competence as observed in German (Asendorpf & van Aken, 1991) and American (Ozer & Gjerde, 1989) studies.

Conversely, individuals displaying undesirable characteristics experience more criticism and attempts from others to change or control their behaviour. This is most evident in the highly aversive behavioural characteristics of aggressive children that may provoke punishment or even abusive forms of discipline. As Patterson and co-workers have shown, these parental attempts to change the aggressive non-compliance of their children may fail, and parents and children can become trapped in progressively escalating cycles of conflict and coercion (Patterson, 1982). Consequently, even undesirable characteristics can be maintained in ongoing interactions by the reactions they provoke from other people, a mechanism referred to as 'interactional continuity' by Caspi *et al.* (1987).

So far, we have focused on the ways in which socially desirable or undesirable characteristics may be linked to the social environment in a general sense. According to this view individuals with desirable characteristics usually fare better than individuals with undesirable ones. This perspective neglects the fact, however, that individuals are frequently embedded in relationships where highly desirable characteristics evoke envy, jealousy or misgivings in other individuals competing for social resources.

If one child in a family is labelled as highly gifted and thereby enjoys parental pride and special attention, the siblings may suffer from feelings of inferiority induced by direct comparisons (especially if the gifted child exceeds an older brother or sister) or by the inequity of social attention they experience. Cornell (1983) found that siblings of highly gifted children suffer from poorer personality adjustment due to the family 'idealization' of the gifted child, which he considered to be the counterpart to family 'scapegoating' of problem children. In a similar vein, the uneven attractiveness of children and corresponding social attention they invite may be a source of sibling rivalry, particularly between sisters. Conversely, the need or lack of prestigious characteristics can also trigger nurturance or protection from others. Thus, it was found that child disability or chronic illness may evoke particular parental protectiveness (Busch-Rossnagel, 1981; Goldson, 1992). Occasionally, unattractive individuals receive more lenient ratings than attractive ones (Barden, 1990), as if the lack of attractiveness evokes pity or the judges overcompensate in their attempt not to be biased by attractiveness, especially if they think that beauty is something beyond personal control.

Controllability of characteristics

Another important dimension along which characteristics can be classified is the degree to which they are perceived as being within personal control. Characteristics that are generally considered as being beyond personal control are body height, eye colour and race, and this holds true in spite of attempts to limit tall stature in girls by hormonal treatment (Degenhardt & Kollmann, 1986), to change race-linked facial characteristics by cosmetic surgery or to wear coloured contact lenses for decorative reasons. Sex is usually not subject to personal control and few individuals seek sex-reassignment surgery. Characteristics that are believed to be intermediate in personal control are physical appearance, school performance and personality characteristics such as shyness or irritability. Characteristics that are considered to be more or less completely within personal control are the goals individuals set for themselves, the decisions they make and the interests they pursue in their leisure time, the people they choose to be with — despite the fact that the options available are not only dependent on biographical factors in individuals themselves, but also on situational and historical constraints.

Why is the aspect of personal control important? First, for the individuals themselves the perceived degree of personal control motivates activities intended to achieve higher congruence between the real and the ideal of these characteristics. Many women equate physical attractiveness and femininity with thinness, and this culturally transmitted ideal of the slim body contributes to the high percentage of women of all ages being on diets much of the time (Rodin *et al.*, 1984), also this may partly account for the higher prevalence of anorexia in girls than in boys (Whitaker *et al.*, 1989; Lask & Bryant-Waugh, 1992). In a similar vein, cosmetic advertisement conveys successfully the somewhat illusionary notion that beauty can be bought, and increasing numbers of individuals dye their hair, use cosmetics or have cosmetic surgery (Graham & Kligman, 1985).

Second, to the extent that characteristics are believed to be within personal control, individuals are assigned personal responsibility for these characteristics by the social environment and this, in turn, can influence causal attributions and evaluative emotions (feelings of guilt, shame or pride) in the individuals themselves. If low-achieving boys are blamed for not trying hard enough, this is meant to induce feelings of guilt, but at the same time it conveys the notion that they are capable of more. Conversely, if girls receive the supportive 'never mind, you did your best' response to failure, their attempt to do their best is acknowledged, but their basic capability is questioned (Dweck & Elliot, 1983). According to Eccles (1985), these gender-specific attributions for success and failure are internalized so that gifted girls tend to ascribe their maths success mainly to effort, skill and diligence, whereas boys claim their natural talent as the cause. This sex-linked attributional style may partly account for the reluctance of gifted girls to enrol in advanced maths courses. As their success seems to depend on continuous effort, they fear the increasing expenditure of time and effort to keep up their level of success, whereas for boys their 'talent' guarantees continuing success with little or no increment in their effort.

Consequently, ascribed personal control and social desirability partly determine the social pressure for the maintenance or change of characteristics. These expectations for personal control grow with age as children acquire skills, knowledge of social rules, learn to delay gratification, and to cope with environmental demands. Nobody would expect a 2 year old to sit still for 2 hours, but school-children are required to do this, otherwise they are considered as immature or 'hyperactive'. However, there may be a discrepancy between what is ascribed and the self-perceived controllability of characteristics. Obese people feel the subtle moral blame conveyed to them for their inability to control their weight. This social pressure and associated feelings of guilt or shame presumably drive individuals into therapies from which they hope to receive help in breaking bad habits and changing things they feel unable to change themselves such as alcohol or drug addiction, problems with weight control, lack of assertiveness or irritability, etc.

Patterns of characteristics matter more than isolated traits

Although isolated behavioural traits may be important in some circumstances, most effects derive from patterns of characteristics and not just single features (Magnusson & Bergman, 1990). Thus, in the field of temperament research, there has been a particular focus on the constellation of traits labelled 'difficultness'. The concept is open to a variety of objections (Bates, 1980), including the fact that its definition seems to lie in the eye of the beholder. Nevertheless, it has proved an important risk predictor (Garrison & Earls, 1987; Maziade, 1989).

Similarly, it is likely to make a difference if beauty is paired with good naturedness or with wickedness, with prudence or with foolishness. The developmental outcome depends on the configuration of characteristics within the individual. Block's (1971) findings neatly underscore this notion. Whereas in ego-resilient boys, intelligence was paired with very good social adaptation, this was not the case in the type of boys he described as 'unsettled undercontrollers'. For them, intelligence was associated with rebelliousness, egotism and ruthlessness leading to downward mobility. In a similar vein, presumably due to peer rejection, the developmental prognosis seems to be particularly poor for children exhibiting a syndrome of both social withdrawal and aggression (Ledingham & Schwartzman, 1984; Asendorpf, 1990a; Mayr, 1992).

There are different ways in which relations between characteristics can function. First, certain characteristics have an overriding influence on almost every other domain of life and self-evaluation. This is particularly apparent in crippled (Kleck & Strenta, 1985) or extremely small (Skuse, 1987) individuals; and in patients suffering from facial disfigurement (Bull & Rumsey, 1988) or from serious speech handicaps. Even within the more average range of characteristics individuals may ascribe an unrealistically high salience to certain aspects of their appearance or to particular attributes. Anorexic individuals are pathologically preoccupied with their desire to be thin; some people define themselves almost exclusively by their professional success.

Second, characteristics can overlap and/or be associated with attributes that are evaluated similarly in positive or negative ways. For instance, highly gifted students are generally good at school, and in spite of gender-related preferences for different subjects (Eccles, 1985), they surpass their classmates in almost all courses. At the same time they seem to enjoy a fairly good reputation with peers, at least as far as their academic competence is concerned (Eccles *et al.*, 1989), and show good psychosocial adjustment (Janos & Robinson, 1985; Rost, 1993). Therefore it looks as if for gifted students good things go together. Similar effects have been observed for attractive individuals or for mothers who not only relate sensitively to their infants but also have husbands who are very content with their marital relationship (Engfer, 1988).

Therefore, if certain characteristics interlink to form a cluster, then changes in one of them should also affect the others. Youth, beauty and femininity seem to make up such a cluster of correlated attributes — if youth fades, beauty and femininity also should be affected. Indeed, this has been shown to be the case. Masculinity on the other hand, being more linked to competence, strength, success and activity, does not show this age-dependent decline, at least not between young and middle adulthood (Deutsch *et al.*, 1986).

Third, characteristics may work in a compensatory fashion. Folk wisdom tells us that girls can compensate for their lack of beauty by intellectual achievement, and among the different developmental outcomes described by Block (1971) the type of 'lonely independent' seems to fit this picture. In one study, men who appeared resilient in spite of environmental adversity and who managed to achieve career and job success in young adulthood, nevertheless often had to pay a price for it by delaying their commitments to marriage and by exhibiting serious stress-related health problems (Werner, 1989).

Another compensatory way in which characteristics can be related is the replacement of one attribute by another over the course of development. As mentioned above, over the life course women 'replace' their feminine attributes by characteristics traditionally thought to be more masculine by becoming more assertive and independent and by giving up some of their former social orientation (Fooken, 1992). In a similar vein, older people can compensate for their decline in short-term memory by use of special memorizing strategies (Baltes & Baltes, 1990).

INDIVIDUAL CHARACTERISTICS AND DEVELOPMENTAL OUTCOMES: THE ROLE OF CONTEXTUAL CONDITIONS

If we think of individual characteristics as a force in normal and abnormal development, we need to describe the processes and mechanisms through which interindividual differences are related to developmental outcome and pay attention to ways in which these effects may be moderated by contextual conditions. In this description of dimensions relevant for the classification of characteristics, the authors referred to some processes linking characteristics to the social environment. The following section delineates more systematically the interplay between individual characteristics and contextual conditions in developmental processes.

Direct effects

The most straightforward way in which interindividual differences are related to developmental outcomes is that individual behavioural characteristics in childhood or adolescence lead more or less directly to psychopathology at a later age that represents an accentuation or distortion of those same characteristics. There are two main candidates for this direct route: (i) behavioural inhibition leading to anxiety disorders; and (ii) temperamental difficulties leading to conduct disorder. In both cases, however, the empirical evidence is quite limited (Prior, 1992).

The main data on behavioural inhibition derive from the follow-up from 21 months to 7.5 years of a non-clinical sample of very inhibited and very uninhibited children undertaken by Kagan and co-workers (Hirshfeld *et al.*, 1992). Two main points warrant emphasis. First, only half the inhibited children continued to show this characteristic over this period of time and the association with anxiety disorders was evident only in this 'stable inhibited' subsample. Second, this subsample was also characterized by having parents who exhibited anxiety

disorders in childhood and/or adulthood. Because the study involved quite a small group of children, 75 in all, it was not possible to separate the child effects from the parent effects. It may well be that behavioural inhibition serves as a direct risk factor for anxiety disorders but, until further studies have been undertaken, the notion must remain as a plausible hypothesis and not a fact.

There are rather more data (although still few) demonstrating an association between temperamental difficultness in early childhood (but *not* in infancy) and the later development of disruptive behaviour disorders of various kinds (Maziade, 1989; Prior, 1992). It is clear that the link in this case is with a different psychopathological outcome from that seen with behavioural inhibition. However, it is evident from all studies that temperament mainly predicts disorder when it is combined with other risk factors such as family discord or adversity. There may be some direct effects but it seems that on their own temperamental features are not strong predictors of disorder.

Aggressiveness is another characteristic that, at least in males, shows quite high consistency over time (Olweus, 1979) and that is associated with psychopathology. The issue is discussed further in Chapter 19 but we note here that it is rather uncertain whether aggressiveness should be considered as a temperamental attribute. The predictive effects mainly come from an extreme group showing other negative features (such as hyperactivity and poor peer relationships) in addition (Loeber, 1990; Magnusson & Bergman, 1990; McColloch & Gilbert, 1991), and again the behavioural features tend to predict most strongly in conjunction with adverse family features (Robins, 1991).

Given the great variety of possible mediating influences, indirect links between characteristics and developmental outcomes are difficult to rule out. Direct effects of characteristics on developmental outcomes appear particularly obvious in characteristics related to skills or competencies that can be acquired over the life course. This is not only evident in the longitudinal stability of IQ scores (Conley, 1984). It is even more apparent in the life course of highly gifted men whose academic accomplishments were followed by professional careers in prestigious high-income jobs (Terman & Oden, 1959; Eccles, 1985). However, even in this domain a recent path-analytic evaluation of the Terman data revealed that the occupational achievement of these gifted men in later mid-life was only partly accounted for by their intellectual competencies. The strongest predictor of occupational achievement in mid-life was their educational attainment which in turn was best explained by their parents' education influencing both their intellectual skills and their educational attainments (Tomlinson-Keasey & Little, 1990). Thus, even for characteristics suggesting a very direct influence on lifespan development, the impact of environmental conditions enhancing or inhibiting developmental outcomes needs to be considered: indirect effects mediated by environmental conditions or — as in this case — effects of 'third variables' affecting individual characteristics as well as their supposed outcome are as likely as direct effects of characteristics on development.

Individuals selectively attend to and interpret their environment

Individuals differ in the way they attend to and interpret their social environment as well as their own behaviour and experiences. An example of selective attention concerning self-related information is provided by individual differences in public and private self-consciousness. With public self-consciousness the emphasis is on socially relevant aspects of self, such as one's public image, whereas private self-consciousness refers to the awareness and reflection of feelings and somatic states. Although this distinction is somewhat controversial, nonetheless it seems useful in certain respects (Scheier & Carver, 1982). High private self-consciousness can be advantageous because it helps to prepare for appropriate adaptive actions: people who attend to their psychological and somatic states may cope better with stressful life events (Mullen & Suls, 1982).

At the same time, however, states of increased public self-awareness (Duval & Wicklund, 1972) and even more so stable states of elevated self-consciousness, seem to undermine the prevailing self-serving bias which tends to ignore negative self-related feedback. The more people focus on public aspects of self the more they are affected by evaluative, especially negative, feedback (Ickes

et al., 1973; Fenigstein, 1979). In line with these experimental findings, adolescents concerned about the way they are seen by significant others are particularly vulnerable to the negative impact of family discord and lack of support (Silbereisen *et al.*, 1990). This anxious preoccupation with socio-evaluative concerns is presumably one of the main factors increasing shy inhibition in children whose attempts to initiate social interactions have failed repeatedly (Asendorpf, 1990b).

In this latter case it seems to be the relevance selectively ascribed to certain experiences, rather than actual perceptual differences, that shapes the impact of sociocontextual conditions. Systematic biases in discounting specific self-related information have also proven relevant for children's self-esteem. While children with high self-esteem tend to see negative self-related information as less relevant than positive information, children with low self-esteem seem to assign similar importance to negative as well as to positive feedback (Harter, 1986).

How differential interpretations of a given situation influence performance and psychosocial development is well exemplified by causal attributions. Reactive depression has been explained as 'learned helplessness' which is based on cognitive biases in explaining positive and negative events. The risk of depression tends to be increased if failures are overgeneralized and attributed to stable internal factors (but success attributed to unstable external and specific factors such as 'good luck' — Peterson & Seligman, 1984; Sweeney *et al.*, 1986).

Although this 'depressive' attributional style seems to be somewhat more realistic than its reverse (Alloy & Abramson, 1988), an optimistic bias in favour of one's own capabilities is psychologically more healthy as well as more efficient. In a study with fifth and sixth graders, children's overestimation of their academic skills predicted higher achievement 2 years later, while the more realistic perception of competencies led to average level achievement (Helmke, 1992). In a similar vein, subjective well-being and 'objectively' assessed health status were found to be concurrently unrelated in ageing people. However, subjective well-being significantly predicted longevity and objective health status 10 years later, whereas subjective illness was found to forecast impaired health status and early death (Lehr, 1987).

Another example of distorted interpretations of social cues is provided by the tendency of aggressive boys to infer hostile intentions in others when circumstances are ambiguous (Dodge, 1980). Similarly, maltreated children are prone to misinterpret the behaviour of others as provocative and this biased style of processing social information may be one of the main mechanisms by which the original *experience* of harm transforms into an exhibition of aggressive behaviour (Dodge *et al.*, 1990).

Experimental research supports the notion that social perception and self-presentation often serve to confirm given expectations. These processes also seem to operate in the perception of social support. The subjective evaluation of social relations as more or less supportive was found to be crucial in research on stress and coping. Cross-sectional studies suggest that perceived social support buffers stress better than more objective indicators of social integration (Cohen & Wills, 1985; Kessler & McLeod, 1985; Schwarzer & Leppin, 1989). Interestingly, however, longitudinal research controlling for personality differences in the perception of support reveals a different picture (Bolger & Eckenrode, 1991). Perceived support contributes little to the attenuation of stress, because both the subjective evaluation of social relationships and the experience of stress are largely influenced by personality characteristics such as neuroticism and extraversion. According to Bolger and Eckenrode (1991), social interactions can nevertheless function as buffers to stress, but it is not so much the intentionally activated support that matters in coping with major life events. Instead, emotional comfort, encouragement and distraction seem to be gained from the experience of companionship, and these are subjectively unrelated to stress and coping.

Interindividual differences in reactivity

Partly as a consequence of differences in the perception, evaluation and interpretation of a given situation, but also due to differences in psychophysiological functioning, individuals differ in their reactivity to stress and challenge. The concept of differential reactivity is central to several conceptions of infant temperament (Fox & Stifter, 1989; Higley & Suomi, 1989; Kagan *et al.*, 1989; Rothbart,

1989; Strelau, 1989) and, as already noted, it is used to explain differences in adaptive behaviour and later personality. Specifically, it describes the fact that infants have different thresholds of response to stimuli, and/or differ in the intensity, the timing and variability of psychophysiological reactions. Kagan *et al.* (1987) found a number of physiological measures on which highly inhibited children differed from uninhibited ones: they had higher heart rates, stronger cardiac acceleration over the course of a testing battery, larger mean pupil size, less variability in the pitch of verbal utterances and higher average cortisol levels. These differences between inhibited and uninhibited children were found to be fairly stable between 3.5 and 7.5 years of age. All these physiological correlates of behavioural inhibition point to higher levels of autonomic arousal in children showing behavioural inhibition.

However, as with all psychophysiological correlates of behaviour, it is difficult to infer the quality of emotions from physiological indices alone, since some indices of higher arousal (i.e. cortisol level, vagal tone) can be associated with positive or negative states and among negative states it may be anxiety (as suggested by inhibited behaviour) or anger leading to higher levels of arousal. The latter may be exemplified by the finding that child-abusing parents showed increased, rigidly stable, levels of heart rate in response to videotapes depicting babies in various states of happiness, distress or neutral emotional expression. By contrast, non-abusing parents showed a variable pattern of heart rate acceleration (as response to tapes of crying infants) and deceleration (seeing babies in a neutral or happy state). Maltreating parents' heart rates accelerated quickly on viewing a crying baby and rigidly remained on that level in spite of the changing emotional content of the videotapes (Disbrow *et al.*, 1977; Frodi & Lamb, 1980). Although these findings neatly support interindividual differences in reactivity, it is questionable whether this atypical style of psychophysiological responding played a causative role in the behavioural expression of anger, such as in abusive parenting. Therefore, even if interindividual differences in reactivity are found, their role in explaining observable behaviour often remains ambiguous (Gunnar & Mangelsdorf, 1989).

A further issue in the use of physiological reactivity as an explanatory construct is that its meaning may change with age. Thus, Fox and Stifter's (1989) findings suggest that a low-level response to stimuli may be a precursor to inhibited social behaviour during the toddler years, although Kagan *et al.* (1987) found high physiological reactivity to accompany behavioural inhibition later.

If the concept of reactivity is not limited to psychophysiological reactions, but used to refer to behavioural and emotional correlates as well, infant moodiness and lack of adaptability were found to precede shyness as observed at 33 months, but only in boys (Engfer, 1993). Furthermore, children who, as infants, were moody and had problems in the establishment of sleeping and feeding routines were affected adversely by abrupt changes in their social environment. If they had to change class in their last year of preschool, they showed a marked increase in shyness which was exacerbated by their impaired verbal ability to express themselves. Similar findings about the special vulnerability of inhibited children to changes in extrafamilial social environments were reported by Asendorpf (1992) and Broberg (1993).

Apart from research on temperament, evidence for the mechanisms that explain increased reactivity is rarely provided. For example, stronger reactions to stress have been ascribed to personality characteristics such as neuroticism (Bolger & Schilling, 1991) and emotional instability (Liker & Elder, 1983) in adults. Most often, responsivity served as a hypothetical construct used to explain differences in the intensity of reactions, but the processes accounting for these differences were not independently assessed. As a rare exception, one study showed that differences in coping with a critical life event relate to personality (in this case: neuroticism) as well as to level of stress reaction (anxiety) providing the mediating link between both (Bolger, 1990). Here it is important to note that these individual approaches to stressful situations do not seem to be mere epiphenomena of individual differences. Rather they should be viewed as explanatory links in a chain of recursive processes in personality development.

It may seem difficult to distinguish differences in the perception of situations from differences in reaction, because coping with stressful conditions entails redefinitions of the situation like denial or disengagement. However, such distinctions are possible. For example, people high in neuroticism are more likely to be negatively affected by interpersonal conflict, but they are no more likely than their partners to see a given episode as conflict (Bolger & Schilling, 1991).

A special case of intensified emotional or behavioural responses to daily hassles and stressful life events is described as 'accentuation' (see Chapter 1). Pre-established dispositions or response styles are activated if changes in life conditions require non-routine adaptations and emotional coping. These examples of accentuation may involve negative traits becoming more visible and pronounced as stress increases. The stronger impact of financial loss on the emotional stability of men who were already less stable before they were hit by the financial crisis is a case in point (Liker & Elder, 1983).

On the whole, major life events do not function as turning points in personality development but rather emphasize individual styles of behaviour and psychosocial functioning (Caspi *et al.*, 1987, 1988; Caspi & Moffitt, 1991). According to Caspi and Moffitt (1991), early puberty seems to create stress in girls and thus contributes to an increase in problem behaviour, particularly in girls who already had a history of behaviour problems in childhood. If situational demands are ambiguous and ill-defined, it becomes more likely that previously established behavioural patterns are activated to structure the situation according to the accustomed behavioural repertoire of individuals.

However, an accentuation of previously established, problematic characteristics does not always occur. In a study of children's adaptation to a stepfather, it was the formerly 'easy' boys who caused more trouble in the initial phase of family formation, whereas 'difficult' boys did not seem to change (Hetherington, 1991). In the long run, however, the easy boys developed a good relationship with their stepfathers, whereas the difficult boys remained hard to handle. Therefore, it looks as if children's initial resistance to stepparents and concomitant behaviour problems constitute a normative phase in stepfamily formation.

Selective exposure to environment

Selective exposure to environment can be conceived in several ways. Broadly speaking it describes the fact that there is a systematic link between characteristics of individuals and the environments they are exposed to. These links may involve a number of different processes: passive exposure and active selection of and *by* environments, including sequential and progressive chaining of environments, and other more specific mechanisms such as matching or contrast effects. These will be discussed in a separate section.

Passive exposure to environment can be conceived in at least three ways. First, according to certain individual characteristics such as gender or age, the passages through certain environments are institutionalized. In most Western European societies only men (not women) are drafted to the military service if they reach a certain age. Also the age range of school entrance and of retirement from work is regulated by laws. Second, within given societies, there may be normative ways in which individuals enter or leave certain environments. In Germany, most children are taken care of within their families until they are able to enter kindergarten. Subsequently, children pass through different educational environments according to their age and ability. Third, passive exposure to environments may occur because individual characteristics determine their membership in certain groups: in general, children grow up in families whose members are genetically similar to them. Children are members of classrooms whose composition is usually beyond their own control although these may have been selected by others (parents, teachers) to match their special talents, ethnic background or gender.

Selective exposure in this passive normative way can be exemplified by age-graded differences in family dependence. During times of family stress, younger children are often more vulnerable to conflict and friction than adolescents. Since their mobility is limited, they cannot escape as easily by leaving the situation, hence they are more exposed to parental conflict. During the Depression in the 1930s, this was found to be particularly true for young boys, whereas adolescent boys were able to leave the situation and to affiliate with peers or other adults (Elder *et al.*, 1985). In contrast, due to greater parental control and gender-specific division of labour, adolescent girls were largely tied to the household and thus exposed to their fathers' increased irritability and explosiveness.

Children with chronic illnesses or major disabilities spend part of their lives in hospitals or institutional environments — in this case, their diseases or disorders determine their long-term social and physical environments, mainly because parents or other responsible agents select these environments for them (Busch-Rossnagel, 1981; Goldson, 1992).

Selective exposure to environments may not only happen in this more 'passive' way. Instead, individuals actively select their environments: the people they associate with as friends and partners, and the educational, occupational or leisure activities they choose according to their interests, capabilities and personal needs. Probably, this active role of individuals in this purposeful, deliberate choice of their environments becomes increasingly important with age (Scarr, 1992).

The active selection of environments is closely linked to the way in which individuals selectively attend to and evaluate situations. One's evaluation of a situation as dangerous, challenging or enjoyable influences the decision between approach and avoidance which, in turn, restricts or opens the range of possible experiences. Such decisions for or against situations, places, educational or professional opportunities, people to associate with, tend to accumulate and — just as institutionalized career patterns — create 'cumulative continuity' over the life-course (Caspi *et al.*, 1987, 1988).

This cumulative continuity is very evident in the life-course of highly gifted men. Being born to intelligent, well-educated parents (Tomlinson-Keasey & Little, 1990), and residing in affluent neighbourhoods (Terman & Oden, 1947; Rost & Albrecht, 1985), they not only had the cognitive capabilities to master school requirements successfully, but also received the financial support necessary for completing their academic career with advanced degrees (Eccles, 1985). These in turn were the prerequisites for their professional careers in prestigious, high-income jobs (Terman & Oden, 1959). Their homogamous mating choices of cognitively capable and well-educated women were another aspect or consequence of their self-selected social environments, since their chance to meet such women was presumably enhanced by going to prestigious universities or by affiliating with people of similar social backgrounds. Consequently, in harmony with age-graded developmental tasks and stages in their academic development their educational, professional and social accomplishments progressively accumulated over the life-course and added up towards a successful career.

Here it seems worthy of note that cumulative continuity produced a different, less coherent pattern in the life-course of highly gifted women. According to Eccles (1985) they were much less likely to receive financial support for obtaining college or advanced degrees in spite of their excellent school grades being equivalent or even superior to their male counterparts. Consequently, fewer of them were in full employment and working in traditionally female fields (education, social work, administration, etc.) and their income level was far below that of gifted men. The majority of these gifted women chose to get married and to have children in their early twenties, less than half of them trying to combine family work with employment. In retrospect, housewives and women combining family and income work were much less content with the course of their lives than the small group of professional women who did not get married, remained childless and pursued their careers (Sears & Barbee, 1977).

Cumulative continuity not only operates over the life-course of individuals with characteristics such as giftedness, that are positively evaluated in Western achievement-oriented societies. It may also account for the way in which less desirable temperamental characteristics affect the life-course patterns of shy or highly irritable individuals. Here it describes the fact that individuals progressively select themselves into social environments allowing for the continuation of their accustomed behavioural style. Shy men may avoid situations requiring the display of assertiveness and consequently are delayed in their transitions to marriage, parenthood and stable careers where they have to master new tasks and negotiate new demands (Caspi *et al.*, 1988). Due to their late entrance into stable careers their chances for higher professional achievements were restricted and less stable employment patterns followed. There were no direct effects of childhood shyness on occupational success and stability; instead, the professional disadvantages of formerly shy men were the consequence of their delayed entrance into a career.

The principle of cumulative continuity is likewise applicable to the life-course of highly irritable individuals. Compared with emotionally stable men, explosive men were more likely to experience downward mobility in occupational status, to receive lower military ranks, to lead an erratic work-life and to get divorced (Caspi *et al.*, 1987). This sequence of deteriorating life conditions was mainly triggered by their lower academic accomplishments.

Thus, dispositional characteristics can guide the selection and construction of social environments, but at the same time environments exclude individuals whose characteristics do not match environmental demands. The selection by environments operates in schools, at work, in social networks, presumably also in families when women decide to divorce their alcoholic or violent husbands. Individuals who are expelled from school, lose their jobs or are deserted by their spouse are subsequently forced to make choices about new environments fitting their needs. Therefore, both principles (namely active selection of environments and exclusion from or selection by environments) operate contemporaneously or in succession, and partly account for the progressive deterioration of life-chances experienced by some individuals with undesirable characteristics. However, these chains of effects can be interrupted and discontinuous developmental paths are likely under certain conditions (Rutter, 1989b; Robins & Rutter, 1990).

Matching

There is a general tendency for people to associate with others who resemble themselves in some key characteristics. This matching in social relationships, such as choice of friends, playmates and marital partners, provides a potentially influential selective exposure to social environments. Such exposure is likely to predispose to stabilization of behaviour both because it leads to continuities in environments and because it validates the person's own behaviour. However, in some circumstances, it may also contribute to the development of new characteristics and similarities by socialization processes within relationships or groups (Hartup, 1992).

This process is illustrated by the emergence of sex segregation and the development of gender roles in childhood. According to Archer (1992), the initial slight tendency for girls and boys to differ in activity levels and interactional styles makes it easier for boys to dominate girls. Consequently, the first step in sex segregation is initiated by girls retreating from unrewarding interactions with boys. This is the reverse of what is found later on when avoidance of feminine activities is most pronounced in boys. Gender differences are then more or less rigidly stabilized by the establishment of gender group boundaries. However, the status superiority of the male gender role makes some girls try to gain access to the world of boys, whereas boys are teased, ridiculed or shunned by other boys if they display feminine behaviour or associate with girls. Conversely, boys respond positively to male typical behaviour in other boys and are selectively influenced by reinforcements given by same sex peers (Fagot, 1985). These group processes of socialization may partly account for the greater rigidity of male sex role development during childhood.

During adolescence, youngsters with multiple problems of academic failure and antisocial behaviour are likely to experience rejection by non-deviant class-mates and peers. If they then associate with groups of peers who steal, vandalize and use drugs, their own repertoire of antisocial behaviour may tend to expand and increase in frequency. It has not been easy to disentangle 'selection' and 'socialization' effects, i.e. the extent to which peers are chosen to match one's interests and the extent to which the chosen peer group actually influences a person's own behaviour; presumably both processes are at work. The findings by Kandel (1986) on friendship formation and dissolution as related to substance use, minor delinquency, political attitudes and educational aspirations underscore this point. Similarities were higher between adolescents who became friends within a few months than between those who dissolved their friendship, similarities increased from newly formed to stable friendships, and were lowest prior to and after friendship dissolution. This pattern was most pronounced for marijuana use and weakest for educational aspirations, the latter being much more influenced by parents than peers. It seems that the relative impact of different 'sources' of influence and the processes involved differ according to the behaviour or attitudes considered as well as to the stage of their development (Kandel, 1986; Kandel & Andrews, 1987). Of course, the strength and other qualities of the relationship matter, too. Rowe

and Gulley (1992) showed that the tendency for siblings to share delinquent activities was a function of the closeness of their relationship and their sharing of friends.

Two studies in Sweden and New Zealand indicate the importance of differential access to peer groups which may model and reinforce problem behaviour. According to their findings, early maturing girls tended to engage in increased norm-breaking behaviour because, due to their early puberty, they became part of an older peer group in which this behaviour was more prevalent (Stattin & Magnusson, 1990; Caspi *et al.*, 1993). The New Zealand study also revealed accentuation processes since this effect of early puberty mainly applied to girls who had already shown a tendency to engage in disapproved behaviour prior to puberty and who attended a coeducational school. This provides a nice example of the interplay between personal characteristics and social environment. It seems that children's own behaviour serves to influence the choice of peer groups but thereafter their own behaviour may be facilitated and intensified as a consequence of peer group pressure, modelling and reinforcement — including the learning of new antisocial acts (Emler *et al.*, 1987; Cairns *et al.*, 1988).

It should not be assumed, however, that everyone shows the same tendency to associate with others like themselves. Kandel *et al.* (1990) showed that, to a significant extent, individual differences in homophily were relatively stable over time.

A degree of matching also seems to operate in mate selection; that is, spouses tend to show similarities in age, socioeconomic status, intelligence, height, attractiveness and attitudes (although there is very little matching on personality characteristics — Loehlin, 1992). This matching of characteristics in marital partners is not necessarily a matter of deliberate choice and cannot solely be attributed to the fact that similarity increases interpersonal attraction (Mikula & Stroebe, 1991). First, the characteristics of spouses will be influenced by the pool of potential partners in a person's social group. Quinton and Rutter's (1988) follow-up of institution-reared girls showed that there was a strong tendency for them to marry a deviant man from a similarly disadvantaged background. This was especially so for those who married in their teens when their social group was largely made up of similar people (Pickles & Rutter, 1991). The likelihood of landing up with a deviant spouse was also greater when there was a lack of planning; the matching arose from a failure to choose and not from deliberate selection. For disadvantaged youths, postponement of marriage is likely to increase the heterogeneity of the pool of potential partners and, in some circumstances, this may be advantageous (Elder, 1986). Second, the choice of spouse is likely to reflect a person's 'value' in the marriage market in which competition is affected by calculations of the balance between one's own resources in status and attractiveness and the costs of rejection by somebody far superior in these characteristics. People may choose to marry someone of roughly similar intelligence because this increases the likelihood of shared interests. However, it is less likely that someone who is particularly unattractive will deliberately seek a partner who lacks attractive qualities. 'Choice' is affected by one's own power to attract other people.

Spouse characteristics may affect development in a variety of different ways. Thus, similarity between partners may serve to perpetuate the characteristics on which they match just because the matching validates and reinforces them. For example, Caspi & Herbener (1990) found greater psychological consistency over time for individuals whose spouses were similar to themselves in characteristics. Also however, just as compatibility in interests and attitudes may be the outcome of satisfying relationships so also they may contribute to the maintenance of relationships. Marital breakdown is more likely when marriage has been to a deviant spouse (Quinton & Rutter, 1988).

The dyadic adjustment of married couples may depend on a compensatory match in specific role-appropriate attitudes as well as similarity in attitudes and behaviour. In a German study on marital adjustment, problems arose if wives surpassed their husbands in their emphasis on occupational success and self-assertiveness, whereas positive effects on dyadic adjustment were noted if husbands emphasized these domains more than their wives (Brandstädter *et al.*, 1989). A similar effect of gender role appropriate matching was observed in the marital adjustment of Terman's highly gifted individuals (Sears, 1979): wives' participation in the labour force and their own income had a negative impact on their husbands' satisfaction with family life and raised the probability of marital dissolution, whereas the income of men had the opposite effect of stabilizing the marital relationship.

Contrast effect

Whereas, in the process of matching, people select themselves into the company of others being similar to themselves, contrasting occurs when people living in close relationships become increasingly different instead of similar. The reasons for this contrast effect are not yet clear. Is it the enactment of complementary roles where one may take the role of the leader and the other the role of the follower or — such as in young marital relationships — one (usually the woman) striving for closeness and intimacy while the other (usually the man) seeking independence and undisturbed solitude? Or are such differences due to role ascription, e.g. by parents who may accentuate their children's individuality? Even MZ twins may experience contrasting treatment in infancy due to differences in birth weight and maturity with the smaller and weaker twin eliciting more parental care and protectiveness.

Contrast effects are also noticeable in marriages where one partner suffers from depression. Although in general a supportive marital relationship functions as a buffer against depression, depressed patients may stretch the coping abilities of their spouses too far and their relationship deteriorates by feedback loops leading to contrasting roles: initially wives of depressed men react by being reassuring and protective. In the long run, however, they will become more dominant and mother-like while their depressed husbands become more dependent and child-like. Due to this development, depressed husbands feel their self-esteem to be threatened and start to reject the emotional support they need so badly (Hinchliffe, 1977, cited from Hinde, 1979).

Characteristics are part of and determined by relationships

The above described contrast effects illustrated the general principle that people's characteristics are part of and influenced by relationships (Hinde & Stevenson-Hinde, 1988). For example, Dunn's (1988) studies of the effects on family interactions of the birth of a second child revealed that most first-borns showed some emotional disturbance; that this, in turn, adversely affected their relationship with their mothers; that girls who before the birth of the second child had enjoyed a particularly close relationship with their mother were more likely to show a negative reaction to the newly arrived sibling; and that a particularly affectionate relationship between mothers and the second-born also tended to be associated with negative sibling–sibling relationships. Thus the 'dethroned' sibling clearly displayed symptoms of sibling rivalry affecting negatively their relationships both with their mothers and their later-born sibling.

Concerning the interplay between characteristics in the mother–child relationship and qualities of the marital relationship, Engfer (1988) found that mothers in conflict-laden marital relationships sometimes sought comfort in their children and became anxiously overprotective of them. On the other hand, child difficultness tended to have a detrimental effect on the marital relationship, but only if mothers responded to the difficult behaviour with irritability and depression.

Reciprocal effects in relationships may also account for the fact that in the study by Caspi and Elder (1988) women with a history of irritable temperament displayed an explosive style of marital interaction and parenting only if married to a submissive husband. Although the chances were high that they ended up with a husband not being able to assert himself, because they married socially 'downwards', this pattern was interrupted if they happened to get married to a husband who was able to counteract their irritability. When this was the case the women tended to be particularly well controlled in their social behaviour (Caspi & Elder, 1988).

Effects on others

Ever since Bell's (1968) seminal paper suggesting a reinterpretation of the direction of effects in studies of socialization, and his book a decade later (Bell & Harper, 1977), it has become clear that children's behaviour (and other characteristics) are likely to affect other people. However, systematic attempts to test the reality and strength of these effects have been slower to appear. Bell and Chapman (1986) summarized the five main research strategies that have been used, together with their key findings. The strategies are: (i) confederate participant; (ii) altered behaviour; (iii) altered perception; (iv) sample selection; and (v) longitudinal design methods. Brunk and Henggeler's (1984) study provides an example of the first kind. They trained 10-year-old child confederates to exhibit oppositional or socially withdrawn behaviour while playing a board game with a range of different mothers. The findings showed that mothers behaved quite differently in the new conditions and, perhaps surprisingly, that they did so even in response to neutral behaviours. Thus, it seemed that, even over the course of some minutes, the adults tended to react in terms of their anticipations of the meaning of child behaviours, and not just the actual behaviours. Reputations are quickly formed!

The use of stimulant medication with children showing the hyperkinetic syndrome illustrates the 'altered behaviour' research strategy. Both Barkley and Cunningham (1979) and Schachar *et al.* (1987) found that the mothers of drug responders altered their style of interaction with their children as compared with their behaviour when the children were on a placebo. Because the mothers did not know whether the children were on an active drug or placebo, the changed parental behaviour must have been a response to shifts in the child's behaviour and not just a function of parental expectations.

The 'baby X' experiments illustrate the 'altered perception' strategy (e.g. Smith & Lloyd, 1978; Condry & Ross, 1985). In these studies, toddlers aged about a year or so are dressed in snowsuits (or some equivalent clothing) that are unisex in design so that you cannot tell who is a boy or who is a girl. The children are then given names that indicate gender, the names coinciding with their own gender half the time, and half the time not. The children are then looked after by adults who play with them and whose behaviour is observed and coded. In this way, it is possible to differentiate between the effects of adult expectations (i.e. according to whether they *think* the toddler is male or female) and of actual child behaviour (i.e. whether the child is in fact male or female). Both have been found to be influential.

The sample selection strategy is best exemplified by a design probably first used by Gardner (1977) with autistic children, and later employed by Anderson *et al.* (1986) with conduct-disordered boys. In brief, mothers of normal and of deviant children are observed interacting with their own child, someone else's normal child and someone else's deviant child. By these means, it is possible to separate the effects of the maternal style, of the child being their's or someone else's, and of the child being normal or deviant. Both studies showed a substantial effect of child deviance on maternal behaviour.

Longitudinal investigations provide a less rigorous testing of the direction of causal relations, but carry the advantage of studying effects over time in real-life settings. Martin's (1981) investigation following children from 10 to 42 months provides a good exemplar of this approach. He found that demanding behaviour in infancy was followed by a tendency for mothers to back away, which in turn was associated with an increased tendency for the boys' non-compliant behaviour to persist. This well exemplifies two-way effects that served to create a vicious cycle.

Against these convincing studies demonstrating substantial child effects on adult behaviour must be set a variety of investigations of infant temperament in which only a few, small, child effects were evident (Bates, 1987). The chief difference is that the former (with the exception of the 'baby X' studies) were largely concerned with relatively extreme behaviours in older children whereas the latter were concerned with variations within the normal range of behaviour in infancy. It may be concluded that relatively extreme child behaviours clearly do have effects on other people but that such effects are probably rather minor in the middle of the range of behavioural variation. It is necessary, therefore, to consider the possible longer term developmental implications.

Stabilizing or intensifying effects

Linking individual characteristics to developmental outcomes, responses of the social environment are important in several ways. A person's characteristics may elicit responses from other people that stabilize or even intensify their attributes. Thus, the behaviour of highly aggressive boys is maintained or increased by the angry punishment they receive from their parents (Patterson, 1982). Dodge's (1980) findings indicate that aggressive behaviour may also be maintained by the reputations held by aggressive children. Peers tend to attribute hostile intentions to them, are more ready to retaliate to their aggressive behaviour and refuse to trust them. All these tendencies contribute to the continuation and escalation of aggressive exchanges between aggressive boys and their peers.

Much the same effects of reputation and expectation are evident in children's responses to popular and unpopular children (Hymel *et al.*, 1990). Of course, ordinarily, reputations have been formed initially on the basis of actual behaviour. However, other children's responses are influenced by reputation based on past behaviour as well as by current behaviour. This has been demonstrated through four main types of design, each of which separates reputation from behaviour. First, interpersonal interactions have been compared between groups of peers who have not met before (i.e. there are no reputations in that group), and those who know one another (i.e. they bring their reputations with them). Second, responses to the *same* behaviours have been compared according to the reputations of the children. Third, responses have been studied in analogue situations when subjects have been given false information about children's reputations. Fourth, responses have been observed in relation to reputations that are independent of the subject's own behaviour (because they derive from social group, ethnicity, etc.). The results of such studies indicate that reputations *do* have effects on how children are treated by their peers. The same probably applies to teachers' interactions with children at school (see Chapter 6).

These vicious cycles, by which a person's initial behaviour sets up expectations that serve to perpetuate the behaviour, may be interrupted if problematic children leave their accustomed social environment. Hetherington *et al.* (1982) reported that young boys profited from a school change subsequent to their parents' divorce. Although one might expect that this accumulation of changes would increase stress and thus exacerbate their suffering from parental separation, the contrary was the case. When boys displayed increased behaviour problems due to family disruption, these problems tended to be maintained by exchanges with their accustomed peers, and were correspondingly reduced if they entered a different peer group. However, the timing of such changes appears to be crucial for beneficial outcomes. Instead of creating a chance for a 'new beginning', too many concurrent changes may function as accumulated stressors and make outcomes worse because they leave no 'arena of comfort' (Simmons *et al.*, 1987).

The stabilization of negative characteristics in social interaction is not restricted to aggressive behaviour, but has also been observed for depression. Depressed persons tend to show an interactional style that is very contagious and frustrating for people living with, or emotionally close to, them (Gotlieb & Hooley, 1988). Consequently, their marital relationships suffer and, in the long run, friends who formerly were close and willing to offer support either withdraw or begin to respond with frustration and anger. These interpersonal conflicts with friends and intimates may then, in turn, exacerbate the state of depression (Hokansen & Rubert, 1991).

Protective effects

Certain desirable characteristics may serve to protect individuals from negative responses that would otherwise occur. Girls' attractiveness functioned this way when fathers under the stress of economic deprivation showed a highly irritable, explosive style of parenting. Attractive girls were found to be relatively protected from this explosive and exploitative style of paternal behaviour (Elder *et al.*, 1985). Similarly, Rutter (1978) and co-workers found that temperamentally easy children were less likely than those with difficult characteristics to be the target of parental hostility or criticism when the parents suffered from some form of mental disorder. According to Buck (1991), charismatic political leaders can get away with transgressions that would not be tolerated in others. Due to their expressive style of talking and acting, they involve the emotions of others and do not lose their persuasive appeal despite their making major factual errors, showing lack of knowledge or violating

social norms. This so-called 'Teflon factor' (nothing negative seems to stick) was used to explain the steady popularity of President Reagan even during times when his political decisions provoked a lot of public criticism.

Destabilizing effects

Social responses may also destabilize characteristics and, thus, lead to differences in developmental outcome for initially similar characteristics. This can be illustrated by several examples which — not surprisingly — relate to undesirable characteristics and show that specific strategies are needed to modify them. If parents are taught alternative and more consistent ways of dealing with their children's aggressiveness, these behaviour problems can sometimes be modified (Patterson, 1982). In the intensive longitudinal study by van den Boom (1988, 1989), highly irritable infants generally caused their mothers to withdraw from them within the first weeks and months after birth and this maternal unresponsiveness was subsequently linked to insecure attachment in their children. However, a small group of mothers was able to respond very sensitively to their irritable babies, thereby decreasing infant crying between the fourth and fifth month. Furthermore, mothers taught to soothe their irritable babies effectively, subsequently had more sociable, alert and securely attached babies. Thus, the initially rather distressing behaviour of their babies could be replaced by mutually satisfying playful interactions.

In a similar vein, Suomi (1991) reported that the vulnerability of highly reactive young monkeys to subsequent anxiety, social isolation and low status could be ameliorated if they were reared by exceptionally good, high status (monkey) mothers, whereas their vulnerability tended to persist if they were reared by their 'normal' mothers.

These examples show that some aversive or problematic characteristics of children cannot easily be modified by caretakers providing a normal range of emotional and educational reactions. Only exceptionally competent parents or parents receiving professional support may be able to cope with and/or modify these characteristics. The same may apply to people who permanently live in intimate and obviously very stressful relationships with depressed patients. Although it is difficult to know which factors enable some of them to endure or even to improve the miserable condition of their depressed mates, it seems likely that many of them eventually give up and shift the responsibility for care to therapeutic facilities (Hokansen & Rubert, 1991).

However, under certain environmental conditions, characteristics that would normally provoke anger or withdrawal by caretakers, can even have advantageous consequences. This may be illustrated by two examples: Infants exhibiting behavioural correlates of 'difficult' temperament (i.e. frequent crying and negative emotionality) were found to survive more easily under conditions of famine in Africa, presumably because due to their crying and demanding behaviour they received more attention and food (De Vries, 1984). Similarly, Schaffer (1966) found that, for infants raised in a poor institution, high activity tended to protect from developmental retardation. In both cases, it is likely that the extreme temperamental features had benefits just because they created a 'press' for more adult attention.

This discussion of child effects on other people has concentrated on the effects of negative child behaviours, because that has been the focus of most research. However, it is important to note that positive behaviours may also have an impact on others. Thus, Werner and Smith (1992), in their long-term follow-up of children on Kauai, found a significant link between an 'easy' infant temperament and more positive reactions from mothers and other caregivers at age 2. In middle childhood, too, such children tended to have a wider network of caring adults. Less directly, too, the route through social support extended to an effect on adult outcomes.

The role of time

Time is another condition that may affect the meaning of characteristics and the mechanisms by which they relate to environment. Time in terms of age is the core dimension in developmental research as maturation, the acquisition of skills, the emergence and content of characteristics are described according to the age when they occur (Rutter, 1989a). Thus, characteristics that are supposedly

the 'same' can have different meanings and functions according to the age at which they are observed. Hareven (1982) introduced two other conceptions of time being useful for the present discussion. Her conception of 'social time' refers to socially defined timetables at which normative transitions (such as school entrance, starting a family, retirement) occur within a given society. 'Historical time' refers to political and historical events (such as world wars, times of economic recession, etc.) affecting the lives of different cohorts in different ways. According to these distinctions, time can affect the meaning and functions of characteristics in several ways.

First, apparently similar characteristics have different meanings at different ages. Thus, in one study, the observed shyness of 33-month-old girls was preceded and followed by characteristics indicative of adaptability, alertness, social and cognitive competence. However, girls' shyness as observed at 6 years of age had a different, far more negative, meaning; it was found to be related to aggressiveness, moodiness, immaturity and lack of social competence as perceived by parents and preschool teachers (Engfer, 1993).

Second, age and associated developmental tasks may lead to heterotypic manifestations of underlying characteristics. Thus, Asendorpf and van Aken (1991) found that children exhibiting a fairly consistent pattern of socially desirable characteristics from age 4 to 10 shifted from emotional stability and good peer relations in preschool to intellectual capacities and skills in later childhood. Thus, the temporal consistency of personality involved the fit between the age-dependent developmental tasks and specific competencies in mastering them. Loeber (1990) described comparable 'chains' of heterotypic and age-dependent manifestations of problem behaviour for the developmental antecedents of hyperactivity and antisocial aggressiveness.

Third, individuals may be 'on' or 'off' socially provided timetables and being 'off' these timetables can be caused by certain characteristics and/or lead to life circumstances subsequently affecting characteristics. That individual characteristics contribute to being 'off time' is exemplified by the finding that shy men enter major life-course transitions such as marriage, parenting, the establishing of a professional career at a point in time which, compared to the life-course of their age-mates, appears to be delayed (Caspi *et al.*, 1988). A similar delay in the timing of major transitions was observed in young adults after operation for cleft palate facial disfigurement (Barden, 1990). Likewise, the achievement-oriented girls of the Oakland growth study (Elder & MacInnis, 1983; see below) and the resilient men studied by Werner (1989) postponed marriage and parenting presumably for the sake of completing their academic and professional careers.

The second notion that being 'off time' induces life circumstances subsequently affecting individual characteristics may be exemplified by early maturation in girls. As already noted, early maturation in girls was found to a have a number of negative consequences (such as alcohol consumption, smoking of hashish) only if they associated with older peers (Magnusson *et al.*, 1986). While these different forms of norm-breaking behaviour were found to be transient and to wash out with time, this was not the case with their educational careers. Compared with later maturing girls, early maturers were more likely to drop out of school and much less likely to finish tertiary education.

Last but not least, the meaning and the social relevance of individual characteristics may change across cohorts due to changing norms. In the Oakland cohort, the family- and mate-centredness of girls born in 1920/1921 was associated with early and smooth transitions into marriage and child-bearing. Conversely, in those times, girls' career orientation appeared as 'less feminine' and caused atypical peer-relationships in school and a delay in the transition to marriage and parenthood (Elder & MacInnis, 1983). Nowadays, the formerly 'less feminine' orientation has become more the rule than the exception, and at least in educated women late child-bearing is very common and socially accepted (Gloger-Tippelt, 1988).

In a similar vein, the above-reported finding about the relative discontent of highly gifted women who chose to have children instead of pursuing a career (Sears & Barbee, 1977) may be less likely in present days. Due to the availability of birth control methods, women can postpone child-bearing and limit the number of their children. Maternal employment has become much more common and accepted over the last decades and in certain European countries (such as Sweden) women find public assistance for child care such as extended maternal leave with guaranteed employment and good child care facilities even for children of a very young age. Under such improved conditions their chances to achieve both child-bearing and a professional career may be greatly enhanced.

CONCLUSION

How people's life-course is affected by their individual characteristics is a question that does not give rise to an easy answer. According to popular views, 'postmodern societies' provide a broader range of life options and, hence, increased demands for self-determination. Thus, it is tempting to emphasize the intentional and voluntary side of individual development: how people actively try to promote their own development by selecting relevant developmental tasks, by defining and redefining goals, by searching for appropriate strategies, and by reassessing or modifying them. Theory and research findings support such active pursuits of developmental pathways (Deci & Ryan, 1986; Bussey & Bandura, 1992). On the other hand, the unintended and sometimes even unnoticed influences emanating from one's emotionality, social skills, looks, gender, age, name or race should not be underestimated.

This chapter started with the case of temperament to exemplify how intrinsic qualities of individual characteristics have rather direct implications for people's behaviour. Linking childhood temperament to adult personality, we addressed some common misunderstandings about the role of biological versus cognitive factors and about the timing and impact of genetic influences. Genetic determination seems to become increasingly important over the lifespan, at least in part due to the cumulative effect of others' reactions evoked by one's behaviour and to the active selection of environments. However, the strength of these effects may be attenuated (or enforced) by subjective definitions of one's individuality — contrast or de-identification effects occasionally observed in twins are a good example here. Unfortunately, the cognitive processes involved in personality development have received very little attention in research so far.

Some individual differences make a difference,

others do not. We suggest that the extent to which characteristics can affect development is influenced by factors such as their visibility, social desirability, controllability and their configuration with other characteristics. This classification is far from complete and other dimensions are likely to be operative. Nevertheless, these aspects are supposed to be particularly relevant because *social mediation*, i.e. others' reactions to one's characteristics, often plays a role. In social interaction, the visibility of personal features and their normative evaluation determine which characteristics may become salient and how others react to them — reinforcing or preventing continuity. Of course, the salience and evaluation of characteristics matters not only on the side of the observer, but also for the individuals themselves, influencing their expectations and behavioural strategies. Hence, it may often be these individually enacted modes of *self-presentation* provoking certain reactions by others rather than the given characteristics as such. Finally, perceived controllability is supposed to matter particularly for *self-regulatory attempts*, providing the prerequisite for individual efforts to change or stabilize one's characteristics. Again, however, social mediation is involved, since ascribed control implies responsibility and thus contributes to social pressure for change if negative characteristics are concerned.

The emphasis here on patterns of characteristics being more important than isolated traits underscores the general point that the social meaning of specific features depends on their context. Depending on their embeddedness in other characteristics individual features may override, compensate or accentuate each other. Thus, a person-centred approach is often more fruitful than generalized accounts of how certain characteristics influence development.

The last part of this chapter outlines more specific processes through which individual characteristics exert their influence on development. First, apparent direct effects leading from childhood characteristics to outcomes in later life were addressed. The empirical evidence for these effects was moderate, at best, and often limited to individuals exhibiting extremes of characteristics such as behavioural inhibition or aggressiveness. Furthermore, apparent direct effects were sometimes found to be mediated by variables linking

individual characteristics to their developmental outcomes. Therefore, with research progressing, some findings presently still viewed as evidence for direct effects may come to be reinterpreted as indirect effects when the relevant causal mechanisms are identified.

Then we discussed six mechanisms linking individual characteristics to contextual conditions. First, people differ in how they attend to and interpret their environment. Two aspects are relevant here: (i) the sensitivity to given circumstances; and (ii) the evaluative emotional bias in one's perception of the context. These subjective 'definitions of the situation' channel emotional responses and behavioural tendencies.

Second, people differ in the way they react to given demands, both in terms of strategies employed and in terms of the intensity of their reaction. Recent coping research provides some insight into such personal styles of dealing with situational pressure. Just like the perceptual biases mentioned above, such personality-driven coping styles are mostly in line with given characteristics like one's emotionality and thus lead to an accentuation of individual dispositions.

Third, individuals may selectively be exposed to certain environments, be it due to their own choice or due to 'admission rules' of the given context. Selective exposure creates differences in experiences which in turn influence developmental processes and outcomes. These mechanisms of active or passive selection into certain environments presumably contribute to the cumulative continuity of individual characteristics. A predictable 'career' of individual dispositions being manifested across the lifespan appears particularly likely if strongly institutionalized or normatively determined selection rules operate. Such selection processes have received very little attention so far. Instead, they are neglected or even prevented by experimental studies in personality research where subjects are randomly assigned to treatments. Thus, the ecological validity of their findings is questionable.

Fourth, as a special case of selective exposure, the matching between one's characteristics and those of significant others was discussed. Although it seems feasible to consider various processes under the general heading of 'matching' between personal and contextual conditions, we reserved this term for the selection of relevant social partners such as peers and spouses. Available options are quite important here, and initial disadvantage due to one's physical, psychological and social characteristics apparently requires deliberate efforts to prevent a negative social career. However, matching is not only a matter of choice, but also a matter of mutual adjustment, be it in terms of similarity, contrast or complementarity. Contrast effects, the fifth mechanism considered here, reminds us that personality development not only results from differential treatment but also from the differential enactment of social roles in close relationships.

Finally, moving from the personal to the interpersonal level of relevant processes, others' reactions to one's characteristics were considered. Three kinds of influence were mentioned: first, certain attributes (and sometimes just their reputation) may evoke reactions which stabilize or intensify these attributes. Unfortunately, this pertains to positive as well as negative characteristics. If social evaluation is important here, one is led to assume that neutral characteristics are less likely to be stabilized than positive ones which are deliberately reinforced. Despite the fact that negative characteristics are usually rejected and responded to in negative ways, some of them seem to stabilize if they evoke vicious cycles of escalating social conflicts. Second, one's characteristics may also prevent certain kinds of negative treatment which otherwise would be expected due to others' lack of social competence or due to one's own deficiencies. Finally, characteristics may be destabilized by others' reactions. The latter case, however, seems rather difficult for negative social behaviour and requires special efforts.

Selective exposure, selective attention and differential reactions by self and others are probably often linked, and several of these processes may be triggered by one's personal endowments. Which individual characteristics are likely to contribute to which processes under what conditions, still remains to be answered. A more comprehensive theory about the relationship between individual characteristics, situational demands and developmental transitions is required. Some of the findings reported here suggest that within a range of attributes extreme types are more likely to evoke

stabilizing responses and that unstructured situations with high demands for problem solving are particularly likely to evoke and accentuate pre-existing individual differences instead of inducing fundamental personality change.

Individual characteristics are likely to have different effects for different sociocultural subgroups, for men and women, and at different points in historical time. Obviously, the meaning and functional value of attributes often change with the social context. Gender is a case in point, moderating the consequences of, for example, high giftedness at least in previous generations. Such differential effects are particularly revealing since they allow researchers to study more specific processes involved. For example, the lack of clear-cut career patterns among highly gifted women and the higher satisfaction of those few who did lead a career-oriented life suggest to what extent situational restrictions were operating: women's (but not men's) individual potential for a professional career was blocked by given *options*. If, on the other hand, marriage was delayed only among shy men but not among shy women, another kind of mismatch between individual and situational characteristics is implied: here the gender-specific *situational demands* calling for men's initiative in courtship put shy men at a disadvantage whereas the socially restrained behaviour of shy women was well in line with former norms of the feminine role.

REFERENCES

Abramowitz S.I. (1986) Psychosocial outcomes of sex reassignment surgery. *Journal of Consulting and Clinical Psychology* **54**, 183–189.

Alloy L.B. & Abramson L.Y. (1988) Depressive realism: Four theoretical perspectives. In Alloy L.B. (ed.) *Cognitive Processes in Depression. Treatment Research, Theory*, pp. 223–265. Guilford, New York.

Anderson K.E., Lytton H. & Romney D.M. (1986) Mothers' interactions with normal and conduct-disordered boys: who affects whom? *Developmental Psychology* **22**, 604–609.

Archer J. (1992) Childhood gender roles: Social context and organisation. In McGurk H. (ed.) *Childhood Social Development: Contemporary Perspectives*, pp. 31–61. Lawrence Erlbaum, Hillsdale, New Jersey.

Asendorpf J.B. (1990a) Beyond social withdrawal: Shyness, unsociability, and peer avoidance. *Human Development* **33**, 250–259.

Asendorpf J.B. (1990b) Development of inhibition during childhood: Evidence for situational specificity and a two-factor model. *Developmental Psychology* **26**, 721–730.

Asendorpf J.B. (1992) Beyond stability: Predicting interindividual differences in intraindividual change. *European Journal of Personality* **6**, 103–117.

Asendorpf J.B. & van Aken M.A.G. (1991) Correlates of temporal consistency of personality patterns in childhood. *Journal of Personality* **59**, 689–703.

Bagley C. & Evan-Wong L. (1970) Psychiatric disorder and adult and peer group rejection of the child's name. *Journal of Child Psychology and Psychiatry* **11**, 19–27.

Baltes P.B. & Baltes M.M. (eds) (1990) *Successful Ageing: Perspectives from the Behavioural Sciences.* Cambridge University Press, Cambridge.

Bancroft J. & Reinisch J.M. (eds) (1990) *Adolescence and Puberty. The Kinsey Institute Series.* Oxford University Press, Oxford.

Barden R.C. (1990) The effects of craniofacial deformity, chronic illness, and physical handicaps on patient and family adjustment. Research and clinical perspectives. In Lahey B.B. & Kazdin A.E. (eds) *Advances in Clinical Child Psychology*, Vol. 13, pp. 343–375. Plenum, New York.

Barkley R.A. & Cunningham C.E. (1979) The effects of methylphenidate on the mother–child interactions of hyperactive children. *Archives of General Psychiatry* **36**, 201–208.

Bates J.E. (1980) The concept of difficult temperament. *Merrill-Palmer Quarterly* **26**, 299–319.

Bates J.E. (1987) Temperament in infancy. In Osofsky J.D. (ed.) *Handbook of Infant Development*, pp. 1101–1149. Wiley, New York.

Bell R.Q. (1968) A reinterpretation of the direction of effects in studies of socialization. *Psychological Review* **75**, 81–95.

Bell R.Q. & Chapman M. (1986) Child effects in studies using experimental or brief longitudinal approaches to socialization. *Developmental Psychology* **22**, 595–603.

Bell R.Q. & Harper L.V. (1977) *Child Effects on Adults.* Lawrence Erlbaum, Hillsdale, New Jersey.

Belsky J., Youngblade L. & Pensky E. (1989) Childrearing history, marital quality, and maternal affect: Intergenerational transmission in a low-risk sample. *Development and Psychopathology* **1**, 291–304.

Block J. (1971) *Lives Through Time.* Bancroft Books, Berkeley, California.

Bolger N. (1990) Coping as a personality process: A prospective study. *Journal of Personality and Social Psychology* **59**, 525–537.

Bolger N. & Eckenrode J. (1991) Social relationships, personality, and anxiety during a major stressful event. *Journal of Personality and Social Psychology* **61**, 440–449.

Bolger N. & Schilling E.A. (1991) Personality and the problems of everyday life: The role of neuroticism in exposure and reactivity to daily stressors. *Journal of Personality* **59**, 355–386.

Brandtstädter J., Baltes-Götz B. & Heil F.E. (1989) Entwicklung von Partnerschaften: Analysen zur Partnerschaftsqualität bei Ehepaaren im mittleren Erwachsenenalter (Development of relationships: Quality of partnership in middle-aged couples). *Zeitschrift für Entwicklungspsychologie und Pädagogische Psychologie* **22**, 183–206.

Broberg A.G. (1993) Inhibition and children's experiences of out-of-home care. In Rubin K.H. & Asendorpf J.B. (eds) *Shyness, Inhibition, and Social Withdrawal*, pp. 151–176. Lawrence Erlbaum, Hillsdale, New Jersey.

Brunk M.A. & Henggeler S.Q. (1984) Child influences on adult controls: An experimental investigation. *Developmental Psychology* **20**, 1074–1081.

Buck R. (1991) Temperament, social skills, and the communication of emotion. A developmental–interactionist view. In Gilbert D.G. & Connolly J.J. (eds) *Personality, Social Skills, and Psychopathology: An Individual Differences Approach*, pp. 86–105. Plenum, New York.

Bull R. & Rumsey N. (1988) *The Social Psychology of Facial Appearance.* Springer, New York.

Busch-Rossnagel N.A. (1981) Where is the handicap in disability? The contextual impact of physical disability. In Lerner R.M. & Busch-Rossnagel N.A. (eds) *Individuals as Producers of Their Development: A Life-span Perspective*, pp. 281–312. Academic Press, New York.

Buss A.H. & Plomin R. (1984) *Temperament: Early Developing Personality Traits.* Lawrence Erlbaum, Hillsdale, New Jersey.

Bussey K. & Bandura A. (1992) Self-regulatory mechanisms governing gender development. *Child Development* **63**, 1236–1250.

Cairns R.B., Cairns B.D., Neckerman H.J., Gest S.D. & Gariépy J.L. (1988) Social networks and aggressive behavior: Peer support or peer rejection? *Developmental Psychology* **24**, 815–823.

Caspi A. & Elder Jr G.H. (1988) Emergent family patterns: The intergenerational construction of problem behaviour and relationships. In Hinde R.A. & Stevenson-Hinde J. (eds) *Relationships Within Families: Mutual Influences*, pp. 218–240. Clarendon Press, Oxford.

Caspi A., Elder Jr G.H. & Bem D.J. (1987) Moving against the world: Life course patterns of explosive children. *Developmental Psychology* **23**, 308–313.

Caspi A., Elder Jr G.H. & Bem D.J. (1988) Moving away from the world: Life course patterns of shy children. *Developmental Psychology* **24**, 824–831.

Caspi A. & Herbener E.S. (1990) Continuity and change: Assortative marriage and the consistency of personality in adulthood. *Journal of Personality and Social Psychology* **58**, 250–258.

Caspi A., Lynam D., Moffitt T.E. & Silva P.A. (1993) Unraveling girls' delinquency: Biological, dispositional and contextual contributions to adolescent misbehavior. *Developmental Psychology* **29**, 19–30.

Caspi A. & Moffitt T.E. (1991) Individual differences are accentuated during periods of social change: The sample case of girls at puberty. *Journal of Personality and Social Psychology* **61**, 157–168.

Cicchetti D. (1989) Developmental psychopathology: Some thoughts on its evolution (editorial). *Development and Psychopathology* **1**, 1–4.

Cohen S. & Wills T.A. (1985) Stress, social support, and the buffering hypothesis. *Psychological Bulletin* **98**, 310–357.

Coleman L.J. & Cross T.L. (1988) Is being gifted a social handicap? *Journal for the Education of the Gifted* **11**, 41–56.

Condry J.C. & Ross D.F. (1985) Sex and aggression: The influence of gender label on the perception of aggression in children. *Child Development* **56**, 225–233.

Conley J.J. (1984) The hierarchy of consistency: A review and model of longitudinal findings on adult individual differences in intelligence, personality and self-opinion. *Personality and Individual Differences* **5**, 11–25.

Cornell D.G. (1983) Gifted children: The impact of positive labeling on the family system. *American Journal of Orthopsychiatry* **53**, 322–335.

Daniel W.W. (1968) *Racial Discrimination in England.* Penguin, Harmondsworth.

Deci E.L. & Ryan R.M. (1986). The dynamics of self-determination in personality and development. In R. Schwarzer (ed.) *Self-related Cognitions in Anxiety and Motivation*, pp. 171–194. Lawrence Erlbaum, Hillsdale, New Jersey.

Degenhardt A. & Kollmann F. (1986) *Abschlussbericht über das Forschungsprojekt: Psychische Korrelate und Wechselwirkungen der hormonellen Wachstumsbremsung (Final report about the research project: Psychological correlates and interaction effects in the hormonal control of growth).* Unpublished research report, Frankfurt University, Germany.

Deutsch C.K., Matthysse S., Swanson J.M. & Farkas L.G. (1990) Genetic latent structure analysis of dysmorphology in attention deficit disorder. *Journal of American Academy of Child and Adolescent Psychiatry* **29**, 189–194.

Deutsch F.M., Zalenski C.M. & Clark M.E. (1986) Is there a double standard of aging? *Journal of Applied Social Psychology* **16**, 771–785.

DeVries M.W. (1984) Temperament and infant mortality among the Masai in East Africa. *American Journal of Psychiatry* **141**, 1189–1194.

Digman J.M. (1990) Personality structure: Emergence of the five-factor model. *Annual Review of Psychology* **41**, 417–440.

Disbrow M.A., Doerr H. & Caulfield C. (1977) Measuring the components of parents' potential for child abuse and neglect. *Child Abuse and Neglect* **1**, 279–296.

Dodge K.A. (1980) Social cognition and children's aggressive behavior. *Child Development* **51**, 1386–1399.

Dodge K.A., Bates J.E. & Pettit G.S. (1990) Mechanisms in the cycle of violence. *Science* **250**, 1678–1683.

Drajer N. (1990) Die Rolle von sexuellem Missbrauch und körperlicher Misshandlung in der Ätiologie psychischer Störungen bei Frauen (The role of sexual and physical abuse in the etiology of women's mental disorders. The Dutch survey on sexual abuse of girls by family members). In Martinius J. & Frank R. (eds) *Kindesmisshandlung, Vernachlässigung und Sexueller Missbrauch (Child Abuse, Neglect and Sexual Abuse)*, pp. 128–142. Huber, Bern.

Dunn J. (1988) Connections between relationships: Implications of research on mothers and siblings. In Hinde R.A. & Stevenson-Hinde J. (eds) *Relationships Within Families: Mutual Influences*, pp. 168–180. Clarendon Press, Oxford.

Duval S. & Wicklund R.A. (1972) *A Theory of Objective Self-Awareness.* Academic Press, New York.

Dweck C.S. & Elliot E.S. (1983) Achievement motivation. In Hetherington E.M. (ed.) *Socialization, Personality and Social Development*, Vol. 4, *Mussen's Handbook of Child Psychology*, 4th edn, pp. 643–692. Wiley, New York.

Eagly A.H., Ashmore R.D., Makhijani M.G. & Longo L.C. (1991) What is beautiful is good, but...: A meta-analytic review of research on the physical attractiveness stereotype. *Psychological Bulletin* **110**, 109–128.

Eccles A.L., Bauman E. & Rotenberg K. (1989) Peer acceptance and self-esteem in gifted children. *Journal of Social Behavior and Personality* **4**, 401–409.

Eccles J.S. (1985) Why doesn't Jane run? Sex differences in educational and occupational patterns. In Horowitz F.D. & O'Brien M. (eds) *The Gifted and Talented. Developmental Perspectives*, pp. 251–295. American Psychological Association, Washington, DC.

Eicher W., Schmitt B. & Bergner C.M. (1991) Transformationsoperation bei Mann-zu-Frau-Transsexuellen. Darstellung der Methode und Nachuntersuchung von 50 Operierten (Male-to-female sex reassignment surgery. Method and follow-up findings of 50 patients). *Zeitschrift für Sexualforschung* **4**, 119–132.

Elder Jr G.H. (1969) Appearance and education in marriage mobility. *American Sociological Review* **34**, 519–533.

Elder Jr G.H. (1986) Military times and turning points in men's lives. *Developmental Psychology* **22**, 233–245.

Elder Jr G.H. & MacInnis D.J. (1983) Achievement imagery in women's lives from adolescence to adulthood. *Journal of Personality and Social Psychology* **45**, 394–404.

Elder Jr G.H., van Nguyen T. & Caspi A. (1985) Linking family hardship to children's lives. *Child Development* **56**, 361–375.

Emler N., Reicher S. & Ross A. (1987) The social context of delinquent conduct. *Journal of Child Psychology and Psychiatry* **28**, 99–109.

Engfer A. (1988) The interrelatedness of marriage and the mother–child relationship. In Hinde R.A. & Stevenson-

Hinde J. (eds) *Relationships Within Families: Mutual Influences*, pp. 104—118. Clarendon Press, Oxford.

Engfer A. (1992) Difficult temperament and child abuse. Notes on the validity of the child-effect model. Relacoes parentais (Special Issue: Parent—Child Relationships). *Analise Psicologica* **10**, 51—61.

Engfer A. (1993) Antecedents and consequences of shyness in boys and girls: A 6-year longitudinal study. In Rubin K. & Asendorpf J.B. (eds) *Shyness, Inhibition and Social Withdrawal*, pp. 49—79. Lawrence Erlbaum, Hillsdale, New Jersey.

Fagot B.I. (1985) Beyond the reinforcement principle: Another step towards understanding sex role development. *Developmental Psychology* **21**, 1097—1104.

Feingold A. (1992) Good-looking people are not what we think. *Psychological Bulletin* **111**, 304—341.

Fenigstein A. (1979) Self-consciousness, self-attention, and social interaction. *Journal of Personality and Social Psychology* **37**, 75—86.

Field T. (1992) Infants of depressed mothers. *Development and Psychopathology* **4**, 49—66.

Fooken I. (1992) Gesund älter werden. Streben Sie nach einem androgynen Lebensstil (Healthy ageing: Strive for an androgeneous life-style). *Sexualmedizin* **14**, 29—31.

Fox N.A. & Stifter C.A. (1989) Biological and behavioral differences in infant reactivity and regulation. In Kohnstamm G.A., Bates J.E. & Rothbart M.K. (eds) *Temperament in Childhood*, pp. 169—183. Wiley, New York.

Frodi A.M. & Lamb M.E. (1980) Child abusers' responses to infant smiles and cries. *Child Development* **51**, 238—241.

Gardner J. (1977) *Three aspects of childhood autism: Mother—child interactions, autonomic responsivity, and cognitive functioning.* Unpublished PhD thesis, University of Leicester, Leicester.

Garrison W. & Earls F. (1987) *Temperament and Child Psychopathology.* Sage, Newbury Park, California.

Gloger-Tippelt G. (1988) *Schwangerschaft und Erste Geburt. Psychologische Veränderungen der Eltern (Pregnancy and First Birth. Psychological Changes in Parents).* Kohlhammer, Stuttgart.

Goldberg R.T. (1974) Adjustment of children with invisible and visible handicaps. Congenital heart disease and facial burns. *Journal of Counseling Psychology* **21**, 428—432.

Goldson E. (1992) The behavioral aspects of chronic illness. In Greydanus D.E. & Wolraich M.L. (eds) *Behavioral Pediatrics*, pp. 204—216. Springer, Heidelberg.

Goodman R. (1991) Growing together and growing apart: The non-genetic forces on children in the same family. In McGuffin P. & Murray R. *The New Genetics of Mental Illness*, pp. 212—224. Butterworth-Heinemann, Oxford.

Gotlieb I. & Hooley J.M. (1988) Depression and marital distress: Current status and future directions. In Duck S. (ed.) *Handbook of Personal Relationships*, pp. 543—570. Wiley, Chichester.

Graham J.A. & Kligman A.M. (eds) (1985) *The Psychology of Cosmetic Treatments.* Praeger, New York.

Green S.K., Buchanan D.R. & Heuer S.K. (1984) Winners, losers, and choosers. A field investigation of dating initiation. *Personality and Social Psychology Bulletin* **10**, 502—511.

Gunnar M.R. & Mangelsdorf S. (1989) The dynamics of temperament—physiology relations: A comment on biological processes in temperament. In Kohnstamm G.A., Bates J.E. & Rothbart M.K. (eds) *Temperament in Childhood*, pp. 145—152. Wiley, New York.

Hammen C. (1990) Cognitive approaches to depression in children: Current findings and new directions. In Lahey B.B. & Kazdin A.E. (eds) *Advances in Clinical Child Psychology*, Vol. 13, pp. 139—173. Plenum, New York.

Hareven T.K. (1982) The life course and aging in historical perspective. In Hareven T.K. & Adams K.J. (eds) *Aging and Life Course Transitions: An Interdisciplinary Perspective*, pp. 1—26. Guilford, New York.

Harter S. (1983) Developmental perspectives on self-system. In Hetherington E.M. (ed.) *Socialization, Personality and Social Development*. Vol. 4, *Mussen's Handbook of Child Psychology*, 4th edn, pp. 275—385. Wiley, New York.

Harter S. (1986) Processes underlying the construction, maintenance and enhancement of the self concept in children. In Suls J. & Greenwald A. (eds) *Psychological Perspectives on the Self*, Vol. 3, pp. 137—181. Lawrence Erlbaum, Hillsdale, New Jersey.

Hartup W.H. (1992) Friendships and their developmental significance. In McGurk H. (ed.) *Childhood Social Development: Contemporary Perspectives*, pp. 175—205. Lawrence Erlbaum, Hillsdale, New Jersey.

Helmke A. (1992) *Selbstvertrauen und Schulische Leistungen (Self-confidence and School Achievement)*. Hogrefe, Göttingen.

Hetherington E.M. (1991) The role of individual differences and family relationships in children's coping with divorce and remarriage. In Cowan P.A. & Hetherington E.M. (eds) *Family Transitions*, pp. 165—194. Lawrence Erlbaum, Hillsdale, New Jersey.

Hetherington E.M., Cox M.J. & Cox R. (1982) Effects of divorce on parents and children. In Lamb M.E. (ed.) *Nontraditional Families*, pp. 233—288. Lawrence Erlbaum, Hillsdale, New Jersey.

Higley J.D. & Suomi S.J. (1989) Biological and behavioral differences in infant reactivity and regulation. In Kohnstamm G.A., Bates J.E. & Rothbart M.K. (eds) *Temperament in Childhood*, pp. 153—168. Wiley, New York.

Hinde R.A. (1979) *Towards Understanding Relationships.* Academic Press, New York.

Hinde R.A. (1984) Why do sexes behave differently in

close relationships? *Journal of Social and Personal Relationships* **1**, 471−501.

Hinde R.A. & Stevenson-Hinde J. (eds) (1988) *Relationships Within Families: Mutual Influences*. Clarendon Press, Oxford.

Hirshfeld D.R., Rosenbaum J.F., Biederman J. *et al.* (1992) Stable behavioral inhibition and its association with anxiety disorder. *Journal of the American Academy of Child and Adolescent Psychiatry* **31**, 103−111.

Hoffman L.W. (1991) The influence of the family environment on personality: Accounting for sibling differences. *Psychological Bulletin* **110**, 187−203.

Hokansen J.E. & Rubert M.P. (1991) Interpersonal factors in depression. In Gilbert D.G. & Connolly J.J. (eds) *Personality, Social Skills, and Psychopathology: An Individual Differences Approach*, pp. 157−184. Plenum, New York.

Hymel S., Wagner E. & Butler L. (1990) Reputational bias: view from the peer group. In Asher S.R. & Coie J.D. (eds) *Peer Rejection in Childhood*, pp. 156−186. Cambridge University Press, Cambridge.

Ickes W.J., Wicklund R.A. & Ferris C.B. (1973) Objective self awareness and self esteem. *Journal of Experimental Social Psychology* **9**, 202−219.

Jacklin C.N., Wilcox K.T. & Maccoby E.E. (1988) Neonatal sex steroid hormones and intellectual abilities of six year old boys and girls. *Developmental Psychobiology* **21**, 567−574.

Jahoda G. (1954) A note on Ashanti names and their relationship to personality. *British Journal of Psychology* **45**, 192−195.

James W.H. (1989) The norm for perceived husband superiority: A cause of human assortative marriage. *Social Biology* **36**, 271−278.

Janos P.M. & Robinson N.M. (1985) Psychosocial development in intellectually gifted children. In Horowitz F.D. & O'Brien M. (eds) *The Gifted and Talented. Developmental Perspectives*, pp. 149−195. American Psychological Association, Washington, DC.

John O.P. (1990) The 'big five' factor taxonomy of personality descriptors. In Pervin L.A. (ed.) *Handbook of Personality: Theory and Research*, pp. 66− 100. Guilford, New York.

Kagan J., Reznick J.S. & Snidman N. (1987) Physiology and psychology of behavioral inhibition. *Child Development*, **55**, 2212−2225.

Kagan J., Reznick J.S. & Snidman N. (1989) Issues in the study of temperament. In Kohnstamm G.A., Bates J.E. & Rothbart M.K. (eds) *Temperament in Childhood*, pp. 133−144. Wiley, New York.

Kandel D. (1986) Processes of peer influence in adolescence. In Silbereisen R.K., Eyferth K. & Rudinger G. (eds) *Development as Action in Context*, pp. 203−227. Springer, Heidelberg.

Kandel D.B. & Andrews K. (1987) Processes of adolescent socialization by parents and peers. *International Journal of the Addictions* **22**, 319−342.

Kandel D., Davies M. & Baydar N. (1990) The creation of interpersonal contexts: Homophily in dyadic relationships in adolescence and young adulthood. In Robins L. & Rutter M. (eds) *Straight and Devious Pathways from Childhood to Adulthood*, pp. 221−241. Cambridge University Press, Cambridge.

Kessler R.C. & McLeod J.D. (1985) Social support and mental health in community samples. In Cohen S. & Syme S.L. (eds) *Social Support and Health*, pp. 219−240. Academic Press, San Diego, California.

Kleck R.E. & Strenta A.C. (1985) Physical deviance and the perception of social outcomes. In Graham J.A. & Kligman A.M. (eds) *The Psychology of Cosmetic Treatments*, pp. 161−182. Praeger, New York.

Kockott G. & Fahrner E.M. (1988) Male-to-female and female-to-male transsexuals: A comparison. *Archives of Sexual Behavior* **17**, 539−546.

Kohnstamm G.A., Bates J.E. & Rothbart M.K. (eds) (1989) *Temperament in Childhood*. Wiley, New York.

Kuiper B. & Cohen-Kettenis P. (1988) Sex reassignment surgery: A study of 141 Dutch transsexuals. *Archives of Sexual Behavior* **17**, 439−457.

Lask B. & Bryant-Waugh R. (1992) Early-onset anorexia nervosa and related eating disorders. *Journal of Child Psychology and Psychiatry* **33**, 281−300.

Ledingham J.E. & Schwartzman A.E. (1984) A 3-year follow-up of aggressive and withdrawn behavior in childhood: Preliminary findings. *Journal of Abnormal Child Psychology* **12**, 157−168.

Lehr U. (1987) *Zur Situation der älterwerdenden Frau. Bestandsaufnahme und Perspektiven bis zum Jahre 2000 (Situation of the Aging Woman. Review and Perspectives up to the Year 2000)*. Beck, München.

Lerner R.M. & Busch-Rossnagel N.A. (eds) (1981) *Individuals as Producers of Their Development: A Life-span Perspective*. Academic Press, New York.

Lewis M. & Miller S.M. (eds) (1990) *Handbook of Developmental Psychopathology*. Plenum Press, New York.

Liker J.K. & Elder Jr G.H. (1983) Economic hardship and marital relations in the 1930s. *American Sociological Review* **48**, 343−359.

Loeber R. (1990) Development and risk factors of juvenile antisocial behaviour and delinquency. *Clinical Psychology Review* **10**, 1−41.

Loehlin J.C. (1992) *Genes and Environment in Personality Development*. Sage, Newbury Park, California.

McCartney K., Harris M.J. & Bernieri F. (1990) Growing up and growing apart: A developmental meta-analysis of twin studies. *Psychological Bulletin* **107**, 226−237.

McColloch M.A. & Gilbert B.O. (1991) Development and maintenance of aggressive behavioral patterns. In Gilbert D.G. & Connolly J.J. (eds) *Personality, Social Skills, and Psychopathology: An Individual Differences Approach*, pp. 185−210. Plenum, New York.

MacCrae R.R. & Costa P.T. (1990) *Personality in Adulthood*. Guilford, New York.

Magnusson D. & Bergman L.R. (1990) A pattern approach to the study of pathways from childhood to adulthood. In Robins L.N. & Rutter M. (eds) *Straight and Devious Pathways from Childhood to Adulthood*, pp. 101–115. Cambridge University Press, Cambridge.

Magnusson D., Stattin H. & Allen V.L. (1986) Differential maturation among girls and its relations to social adjustment. A longitudinal perspective. In Baltes P.B., Featherman D.I. & Lerner R.M. (eds) *Life-span Development and Behavior*, Vol. 7, pp. 113–134. Lawrence Erlbaum, Hillsdale, New Jersey.

Martin J.A. (1981) A longitudinal study of the consequences of early mother-infant interaction: A microanalytic approach. *Monographs of the Society for Research in Child Development* **46**(3), Serial No. 190.

Maruyama G. & Miller N. (1981) Physical attractiveness and personality. *Progress in Experimental Personality Research* **10**, 203–280.

Mayr T. (1992) Die soziale Stellung schüchterngehemmter Kinder in der Kindergartengruppe (The peer status of shy-inhibited children in the kindergarten-group). *Zeitschrift für Entwicklungspsychologie und Pädagogische Psychologie* **24**, 249–265.

Maziade M. (1989) Should adverse temperament matter to the clinician? An empirically based answer. In Kohnstamm G.A., Bates J.E. & Rothbart M.K. (eds) *Temperament in Childhood*, pp. 421–435. Wiley, New York.

Meacham J.A. (1981) Political values, conceptual models, and research. In Lerner R.M. & Busch-Rossnagel N.A. (eds) *Individuals as Producers of Their Development: A Lifespan Perspective*, pp. 447–474. Academic Press, New York.

Mebert C.J. (1991) Dimensions of subjectivity in parents' ratings of infant temperament. *Child Development* **62**, 352–361.

Mikula G. & Stroebe W. (1991) Theorien und Determinanten der zwischenmenschlichen Anziehung (Theories and determinants of interpersonal attraction). In Amelang M., Ahrens H.J. & Bierhoff H.W. (eds) *Attraktion und Liebe. Formen und Grundlagen Partnerschaftlicher Beziehungen (Attraction and Love. Forms and Bases of Close Relationships)*, pp. 61–104. Hogrefe, Göttingen.

Miller C.T., Rothblum E.D., Barbour L., Brand P.A. & Felicio D. (1990) Social interactions of obese and non-obese women. *Journal of Personality* **58**, 365–380.

Mullen B. & Suls J. (1982) 'Know thyself': Stressful life changes and the ameliorative effects of private self-consciousness. *Journal of Experimental Social Psychology* **18**, 43–55.

Olweus D. (1979) Stability of aggressive reaction patterns in males: A review. *Psychological Bulletin* **86**, 852–875.

Ozer D.J. & Gjerde P.F. (1989) Patterns of personality consistency and change from childhood through adolescence. *Journal of Personality* **57**, 483–507.

Patterson G.R. (1982) *Coercive Family Process*. Castalia, Eugene, Oregon.

Peterson C. & Seligman M.E.P. (1984) Causal explanations as a risk factor for depression: Theory and evidence. *Psychological Review* **91**, 347–374.

Pickles A. & Rutter M. (1991) Statistical and conceptual models of 'turning points' in developmental processes. In Magnusson D., Bergman L.R., Rudinger G. & Törestad B. (eds) *Problems and Methods in Longitudinal Research, Stability and Change*, pp. 133–165. Cambridge University Press, Cambridge.

Plomin R. (1986) *Development, Genetics and Psychology*. Lawrence Erlbaum, Hillsdale, New Jersey.

Prior M. (1992) Childhood temperament. *Journal of Child Psychology and Psychiatry and Allied Disciplines* **33**, 249–279.

Quay H.C. (1965) Psychopathic personality as pathological stimulation-seeking. *American Journal of Psychiatry* **122**, 180–183.

Quinton D. & Rutter M. (1988) *Parental Breakdown: The Making and Breaking of Intergenerational Links*. Gower, Aldershot.

Reese H.W. & Overton W.F. (1970) Models of development and theories of development. In Goulet L.R. & Baltes P.B. (eds) *Life-span Developmental Psychology: Research and Theory*, pp. 115–145. Academic Press, New York.

Robins L.N. (1991) Conduct disorder. *Journal of Child Psychology and Psychiatry, Annual Research Review* **32**, 193–199.

Robins L.N. & Rutter M. (eds) (1990) *Straight and Devious Pathways From Childhood to Adulthood*. Cambridge University Press, Cambridge.

Rodin J., Silberstein L. & Striegel-Moore R. (1984) Women and weight: A normative discontent. *Nebraska Symposium on Motivation* **32**, 267–307.

Rost D. (1993) *Die Lebensumwelten Hochbegabter Kinder (The Environments of Highly Gifted Children)*. Hogrefe, Göttingen.

Rost D.H. & Albrecht H.T. (1985) Expensive homes; clever children? *School Psychology International* **6**, 5–12.

Rothbart M.K. (1989) Temperament in childhood: A framework. In Kohnstamm G.A., Bates J.E. & Rothbart M.K. (eds) *Temperament in Childhood*, pp. 59–73. Wiley, New York.

Rowe D.C. & Gully B.L. (1992) Sibling effects on substance use and delinquency. *Criminology* **30**, 217–233.

Russell D.E.H. (1986) *The Secret Trauma. Incest in the Lives of Girls and Women*. Basic Books, New York.

Rutter M. (1978) Family, area and school influences in the genesis of conduct disorders. In Hersov L., Berger M. & Shaffer D. (eds) *Aggression and Antisocial Behaviour in Childhood and Adolescence*, pp. 95–113. Journal of Child Psychology and Psychiatry Book Series, No. 1. Pergamon, Oxford.

Rutter M. (1987a) The role of cognition in child development and disorder. *British Journal of Medical Psychology* **60**, 1–16.

Rutter M. (1987b) Temperament, personality and personality disorder. *British Journal of Psychiatry* **150**, 443–458.

Rutter M. (1988) Epidemiological approaches to developmental psychopathology. *Archives of General Psychiatry* **45**, 486–500.

Rutter M. (1989a) Age as an ambiguous variable in developmental research: Some epidemiological considerations from developmental psychopathology. *International Journal of Behavioral Development* **12**, 1–34.

Rutter M. (1989b) Pathways from childhood to adult life. *Journal of Child Psychology and Psychiatry* **30**, 23–51.

Rutter M. (1989c) Temperament: Conceptual issues and clinical implications. In Kohnstamm G.A., Bates J.E. & Rothbart M.K. (eds) *Temperament in Childhood*, pp. 463–479. Wiley, New York.

Rutter M. (1993) Developmental psychopathology as a research perspective. In Magnusson D. & Casaer P. (eds) *Longitudinal Research on Individual Development: Present Status and Future Perspectives*, pp. 127–152. Cambridge University Press, Cambridge.

Rutter M. & Rutter M. (1993) *Developing Minds: Challenge and Continuity across the Lifespan*. Penguin, Harmondsworth; Basic Books, New York.

Scarr S. (1992) Developmental theories for the 1990s: Development and individual differences. *Child Development* **63**, 1–19.

Scarr S. & McCartney K. (1983) How people make their own environments: A theory of genotype–environment effects. *Child Development* **54**, 424–435.

Schachar R., Taylor E., Wieselberg M.B., Thorley G. & Rutter M. (1987) Changes in family function and relationships in children who respond to methylphenidate. *Journal of the American Academy of Child and Adolescent Psychiatry* **26**, 728–732.

Schacter F.F. & Stone R.K. (1985) Difficult sibling, easy sibling: Temperament and the within-family environment. *Child Development* **56**, 1335–1344.

Schaffer H.R. (1966) Activity level as a constitutional determinant of infantile reaction to deprivation. *Child Development* **37**, 595–602.

Scheier M.F. & Carver C.S. (1982) Two sides of the self: One for you and one for me. In Suls J. (ed.) *Psychological Perspectives on the Self*, Vol. 1, pp. 123–157. Lawrence Erlbaum, Hillsdale, New Jersey.

Schwarzer R. & Leppin A. (1989) *Socialer Rückhalt und Gesundheit. Eine Meta-Analyse (Social Support and Health. A Meta-Analysis)*. Hogrefe, Göttingen.

Sears P.S. (1979) The Terman Genetic Studies of Genius, 1922–1972. *The 78th Yearbook of the National Society for the Study of Education* **78**, 75–96.

Sears P.S. & Barbee A.H. (1977) Career and life satisfaction among Terman's gifted women. In Stanley J.C., George W.C. & Solano C.H. (eds) *The Gifted and the Creative: A Fifty-Year Perspective*, pp. 28–66. Johns Hopkins University Press, Baltimore.

Silbereisen R.K., Walper S. & Albrecht H. (1990) Family income loss and economic hardship: Antecedents of adolescents' problem behaviour. In McLoyd V.C. & Flanagan C.A. (eds) *Economic Stress: Effects on Family Life and Child Development. New Directions for Child Development*, No. 46, pp. 27–46. Jossey-Bass, San Francisco.

Simmons R., Burgeson R., Carlton-Ford S. & Blyth D.A. (1987) The impact of cumulative change in early adolescence. *Child Development* **58**, 1220–1234.

Skuse D. (1987) Annotation. The psychological consequences of being small. *Journal of Child Psychology and Psychiatry* **28**, 641–650.

Smith C. & Lloyd B. (1978) Maternal behavior and the perceived sex of infant: revisited. *Child Development* **49**, 1263–1266.

Smith M. & Bentovim A. (1994) Sexual abuse. In Rutter M., Taylor E. & Hersov L. (eds) *Child and Adolescent Psychiatry: Modern Approaches*, 3rd edn, pp. 230–251. Blackwell Scientific Publications, Oxford.

Stattin H. & Magnusson D. (1990) *Pubertal Maturation in Female Development*. Lawrence Erlbaum, Hillsdale, New Jersey.

Steg J.P. & Rapoport J. (1975) Minor physical anomalies in normal, neurotic, learning disabled, and severely disturbed children. *Journal of Autism and Childhood Schizophrenia* **5**, 299–307.

Strelau J. (1989) The regulative theory of temperament as a result of East–West influences. In Kohnstamm G.A., Bates J.E. & Rothbart M.K. (eds) *Temperament in Childhood*, pp. 35–48. Wiley, New York.

Suomi S.J. (1991) Early stress and adult emotional reactivity in rhesus monkeys. In Bock G.R. & Whelan J. (eds) *The Childhood Environment and Adult Disease*, pp. 171–183. Ciba Foundation Symposium No. 156. Wiley, Chichester.

Sweeny P.B., Anderson K. & Bailey S. (1986) Attributional style in depression. A meta-analytic review. *Journal of Personality and Social Psychology* **50**, 974–991.

Teasdale J.D. & Dent J. (1987) Cognitive vulnerability to depression: An investigation of two hypotheses. *British Journal of Clinical Psychology* **26**, 113–126.

Terman L.M. & Oden M.H. (1947) *The Gifted Child Grows Up. Twenty-Five Years' Follow-Up of a Superior Group*. Stanford University Press, Stanford, California.

Terman L.M. & Oden M.H. (1959) *The Gifted Child at Mid-Life. Thirty-Five Years' Follow-Up of a Superior Group*. Stanford University Press, Stanford, California.

Thomas A. & Chess S. (1977) *Temperament and Development*. Brunner/Mazel, New York.

Thomas A. & Chess S. (1989) Temperament and personality. In Kohnstamm G.A., Bates J.E. & Rothbart M.K. (eds) *Temperament in Childhood*, pp. 249–261. Wiley, New York.

Tomlinson-Keasey C. & Little T.D. (1990) Predicting

educational attainment, occupational achievement, intellectual skill, and personal adjustment among gifted men and women. *Journal of Educational Psychology* **82**, 442–455.

Torgersen A.M. (1989) Genetic and environmental influences on temperamental development: Longitudinal study of twins from infancy to adolescence. In Doxiadis S. (ed.) *Early Influences Shaping the Individual*, pp. 269–281. Plenum, New York.

Van den Boom D. (1988) *Neonatal irritability and the development of attachment. Observation and intervention.* Doctoral dissertation, University of Leiden, The Netherlands.

Van den Boom D. (1989) Neonatal irritability and the development of attachment. In Kohnstamm G.A., Bates J.E. & Rothbart M.K. (eds) *Temperament in Childhood*, pp. 299–318. Wiley, New York.

Waldrop M.F., Bell R.Q., McLaughin B. & Halverson C.R. (1978) Newborn minor physical anomalies predict short attention span, peer aggression and impulsivity at age 3. *Science* **199**, 563–565.

Walster E., Aronson E., Abrahams D. & Rottman L. (1966) The importance of physical attractiveness in dating behavior. *Journal of Personality and Social Psychology* **4**, 508–516.

Werner E.E. (1989) High-risk children in young adulthood: A longitudinal study from birth to 32 years. *American Journal of Orthopsychiatry* **59**, 72–81.

Werner E.E. & Smith S. (1992) *Overcoming the Odds. High Risk Children From Birth to Adulthood.* Cornell University Press, Ithaca.

Whitaker A., Davies M., Shafer D. *et al.* (1989) The struggle to be thin: A survey of anorexic and bulimic symptoms in a non-referred adolescent population. *Psychological Medicine* **19**, 143–163.

Willis P. (1977) *Learning to Labour.* Saxon House, Westmead.

5: Family Influences

JUDY DUNN

INTRODUCTION

The influence of experiences within the family on children's development is the focus of research by developmental and clinical psychologists, by child psychiatrists, sociologists and family therapists, each with their different goals, distinctive theoretical perspectives, and empirical approaches. Some examine the family as a system, stressing that its influence as a unit is more than the sum of its parts, others focus on particular dyadic relationships within the family and their links with other dyadic relationships, or on individuals' interactions within different family dyads. The level of description and analysis in these studies varies greatly, from a focus on the fine-grain analysis of family discourse to epidemiological approaches employing nationally representative samples. In the past 15 years increasing attention has been paid to family relationships *other* than that of mother and child, such as children's relationships with their fathers (Lewis & O'Brien, 1987; Belsky & Rovine, 1988), grandparents (Tinsley & Parke, 1984) and siblings (Boer & Dunn, 1992). There is increasing interest in the links between these different relationships (Hinde & Stevenson-Hinde, 1988), in triads of family members, in families as systems of interrelated individuals (e.g. Cooper *et al.*, 1984), and in patterns of family interaction over generations (e.g. Caspi & Elder, 1988). There is also increasing attention to differences in family interaction within different cultural groups (Bornstein, 1991).

In the face of this range of different research approaches, any review of family influences on individual development must inevitably be very selective, and can encompass only a small section of current research and ideas. However, a number of themes stand out in the recent work on families

that illustrate how these diverse approaches each illustrate key developmental principles; this chapter is organized around these themes.

The first two themes are concerned with the nature of family units and family relationships. The first concerns the variety of familial arrangements in which children grow up, and their changing nature. Large-scale demographic and sociological research has given us a new appreciation of how 'the family' as a norm has changed, while more fine-grain research has demonstrated how family processes may be shaped by particular cultural, political and economic settings.

The second theme concerns the nature of the relations among relationships within families — how we conceptualize the family and the connections between family members through which family influence may be mediated.

The third theme concerns the links between differences in these characteristics of families and family relationships and the individual adjustment and well-being of children, with the focus on stressors and disruptions to families. Here the recent research brings together a variety of approaches, demographic, historical and the more detailed analyses of family process.

The fourth theme concerns new perspectives on the significance of differences in children's experiences within the same family, developed from recent research in developmental behavioural genetics and developmental psychology.

In this selection of themes, the large literature on parenting *per se* will not be discussed in detail; rather the framework is one in which parents are considered as family members. For recent research and reviews on parenting the reader is referred to Bornstein (1991), Pillemer and McCartney (1991) and Maccoby and Martin (1983). For a useful discussion of the complexity of the issues involved in understanding family influences on children's development, see Wachs (1992). In terms of child outcome, the focus here will be chiefly upon children's personality and adjustment; the literature on parenting influences on IQ and moral development will not be discussed, although links with family configuration will be briefly considered.

WHAT IS A FAMILY?

Trends in family structure

Much of the theoretical writing on family influence was until relatively recently based on the presumption that the family unit consisted of two parents and their children (e.g. Hinde, 1980). Yet there have been notable changes in the last decade in the variety of familial arrangements within which children develop, both within and between different cultural groups (for comparative studies of European countries see Boh *et al.*, 1989; for the USA see Zill, 1991). Most striking have been the increases in the number of single-parent families, of stepparents, stepsiblings and half-siblings in families, of parental separation and divorce, and of teenage and unmarried parents.

The figures on single-parent families, for example, show that within the USA, nearly one child in four is currently growing up in a single-parent family; the proportion of single-parent families varies considerably in different European and Asian countries, ranging, for instance, from 6% in Japan to 14% in the UK and 17% in Sweden, in 1988 (Children's Well-Being, International Population Reports Series, 1990). The changes that began to be evident in the 1960s have continued, dramatically, into the 1980s and 1990s. Thus in 1988, 13.5 million children in the USA were living with their mothers only, an 80% increase over the number that were doing so in 1970, while 2 million lived with their fathers only, more than double the number in 1970 (Zill, 1991). The increase in single-parent families has occurred in all ethnic groups in the USA, but black and Hispanic children are most likely to be living in single-parent families. As many as 51% of black children and 27% of Hispanic lived with their mothers only, in 1988. A considerable proportion of these children were born to unmarried mothers, however these mothers were by no means always teenagers: two out of three unmarried mothers' births in 1986 were to women over 20 (Zill, 1991).

Disruption and change in the family 'unit' is also very common. The number of children who experience the separation and divorce of their parents is, for example, high. There has been an increasing trend in many industrialized countries towards cohabitation after the ending of a marriage, with rising rates of cohabitation and increase in births outside marriage (see, for example, Norton & Moorman, 1987; Richards, 1987).

Two important features of family life that are associated with the increased frequency of single parenthood and divorce are the stress of poverty, and the presence of stepparents and stepsiblings. Children living in single-parent families and with their divorced mothers are especially likely to be living in poverty (Garfinkel & McLanahan, 1986; Glendinning & Millar, 1988). This means that specifying how far the higher incidence of disturbance in children from these families is related to the family changes *per se*, rather than the accompanying effects of poverty, is a real problem; family stressors frequently occur in multiple combinations.

The increase in separation and remarriage of parents means that the family world of many children includes stepparents, stepsiblings and half-siblings. A recent attempt at classifying children's family composition at the time of referral to a psychiatric clinic included, for example, 26 different kinds of siblings, when step, biological, fostered, and adopted siblings were included, as well as birth position (Treffers *et al.*, 1990).

Non-familial care and parental employment

Two other changes in family arrangements have dramatically affected young children's experiences in the last two decades. The first is the growth in the proportion of children whose mothers are employed in the labour force. For children under 6, this proportion has increased in the USA from 29% in 1970 to 61% in 1988. The most striking growth has been in the number of women with children under 2 years who are employed: about 60% of the married mothers with under-2s in the USA are now in the labour force; the figure is lower in Britain but is rapidly rising (Brannen & Moss, 1988).

What these figures mean is a huge change in the pattern of daily family life for young children. With the difficulties in finding adequate affordable child care, many parents with young children have to resort to shift work, with mother and father rarely at home together (Martin & Roberts, 1984; Presser, 1988); mothers are especially likely to work night shifts. Once children reach school age, many are 'latch-key' children, returning from school to a home without parents (Hayes *et al.*, 1990).

In summary, the data from epidemiological and demographic studies show that the nature of family life is, for a considerable proportion of children, very far from the presumed two-parent, mother-at-home norm — the norm that has until recently been the focus of much of the detailed research on family influence. What is more, a high proportion of children experience disruption and change in the structure of their families, with separation of parents, the acquisition of stepparents, stepsiblings and half-siblings. In considering the influence of the network of relationships that comprise a child's family we have, then, to be aware of (i) how varied the network of family relationships can be; (ii) how such relationships are affected by the wider social network and cultural group to which the family belongs; and (iii) how family networks are changing historically, and how likely they are to change during a child's own lifetime.

Before turning to a discussion of the relation of the experience of family change and stress to children's outcome, and of the correlates of family structure (in the third and fourth sections below), some principles concerning the nature of the influence of family relationships will be considered.

RELATIONS AMONG RELATIONSHIPS WITHIN THE FAMILY

One set of approaches to the study of family influence focuses on the family as a unit; here the functioning of the family is seen as different from the sum of its parts, derived from the properties of the 'subsystems' of relationships within the family (spousal, parent–child, sibling–child) rather than from the characteristics of the individuals in the

family. Examples of such a focus on the family unit include, for instance, the characterization of the response of families to life events in terms of *family style* (Minuchin, 1974) or *family world view* (Ferreira, 1963; Watzlawick, 1984) within a family systems framework. Olson and Lavee (1989), for example, type families in terms of dimensions of family cohesion, flexibility and well-being. Other researchers group families as 'distressed' versus 'non-distressed' or 'enmeshed' versus 'disengaged' (Hoffman, 1975), and subsequently analyse possible associations with children's outcome. Characterizing the family as a unit in this way does not, it must be noted, allow us to address the fact that different family members have different perspectives on their family, and view their relationships within it differently from one another (Powers, 1989).

In contrast to research that focuses on the family unit as a whole, other studies focus on dyadic relationships, such as marital or parent–child relationships. The importance of integrating data across these different levels of family unit, dyadic relationships and individuals is increasingly widely recognized (Hinde, 1987; Hinde & Stevenson-Hinde, 1988), and the following principles from recent research on relationships within families — much of which crosses these different levels of complexity of description — stand out as particularly relevant for clinicians.

Relationships involve mutual influence

First, the individuals within a dyadic relationship influence one another: thus, earlier views of children as shaped by their parents' child-rearing behaviour in a passive fashion have been revised, in the face of evidence that, from birth onwards, the individual characteristics of babies influence their parents' behaviour (Bell, 1968; see also Chapter 4). Reciprocal influences are evident within each family dyad: parents are influenced by children, children by parents, husband by wife, wife by husband, siblings by each other, grandparents by their grandchildren and vice versa (Tinsley & Parke, 1984) and so on. The quality of children's attachment to their parents is related, for instance, both to the individual characteristics of the child *and* to the sensitivity and responsiveness of the parent (see Chapter 16). And children's aggressive behaviour and hostility to their siblings, for instance, is correlated with their siblings' earlier negative behaviour towards them (Dunn, 1992).

Relationships within the family affect one another

Second, not only do children have relationships with each member of their families, including grandparents and siblings, but within the network of relationships in the family, each relationship is affected by the other family relationships. The ideas of family systems theorists have been especially important in articulating this notion for clinical work. Their focus has been upon the patterns of mutual influence in family relationships that are developed and maintained over time; particular attention is paid to how different subsystems within the family (for example, the spouse subsystem, the parent−child subsystem, the sibling subsystem) are linked. The emphasis on the family as both a changing and a self-regulating, homeostatic system has also usefully focused attention, for instance, on the significance of transitions − both normative and non-normative − in family relationships.

Empirical studies are now documenting in detail the patterns of association between different relationships within the family. Of particular relevance for clinicians is the evidence for associations between the quality of the marital relationship and the relationship each parent has with the child. For example the quality of mother−child relationships has been found in a number of studies to be less adequate in families in which there is marital conflict or lack of support from the spouse (e.g. Christensen & Margolin, 1988; Easterbrooks & Emde, 1988; Engfer, 1988; Quinton & Rutter, 1988; Rutter, 1988). It should be noted that in families who are not under social or psychological stress, the links between marital and parent−child relationships are not as clear-cut as those from studies of distressed families, and that it may be important to move away from global indices towards more precise and specific measures of marital quality (McHale *et al.*, 1991).

There is also evidence that *differences* between mother−child and father−child relationships are linked both to the quality of marital relationships and to child outcome (McHale *et al.*, 1991). Christensen and Margolin (1988), for instance, report associations between weak marital alliances, highly discrepant mother−child and father−child relationships, the spread of conflict between marital and parent−child dyads, and the development of problem behaviour in children − results that are consistent with the predictions of family systems theorists. Such findings amplify the earlier evidence for associations between married couples' agreement regarding child-rearing and children's outcome in terms of self-esteem, and school adjustment, for instance from Block's studies (Block *et al.*, 1981; Vaughn *et al.*, 1988; see also Johnson *et al.*, 1991).

Complex associations are also found between the quality of parent−child and sibling−child relationships. The idea that parent−child relationships play a crucial role in shaping sibling relationships has a long history from Freud onwards. Some evidence supports this view, showing that children with secure attachment relationships with their parents were most likely to develop non-antagonistic relationships with their siblings (Teti & Ablard, 1989), and that positive parental care is linked to positive sibling relationships in middle childhood (Boer, 1990). However, it cannot be assumed that attachment status played a causal role in these links, as other factors such as the children's temperaments may be implicated. And a substantial percentage of sibling dyads in fact differ in their attachment status (Ward *et al.*, 1988) − a finding that is difficult to reconcile with predictions from attachment theory that, since a mother's relationship with her children is influenced by her own childhood experiences, consistency in her parental behaviour and thus in her various children's security of attachment would be expected.

Studies of the associations between parent−child and sibling relationships illustrate a further general point concerning relations among relationships. This is that *relative differences* in parents' relations with their different children show associations with the quality of the children's relationships, and with their developmental outcome. There is a striking consensus in the research findings that differential treatment by parents of their different children is associated with more conflict between the siblings (Bryant & Crockenberg, 1980; Brody & Stoneman,

1987; Brody *et al.*, 1987; Stocker *et al.*, 1989; Boer, 1990). Similar findings are reported for siblings with disabilities (McHale & Gamble, 1989), in siblings of cancer patients (Cairns *et al.*, 1979) and for siblings after divorce (Hetherington, 1988).

Processes linking relationships

While evidence for statistical associations between these different family relationships is rapidly accumulating, the nature, direction and mechanisms of these connections is by no means clear. One possibility, for instance, is that the personality or self-esteem of an individual is affected by a particular relationship, and this effect on the individual constrains or influences the nature of the other relationships she or he forms in the future (Caspi & Elder, 1988). Another possibility is that the individual incorporates a 'model' of relationships from his or her experiences within the early parent–child relationship, and this model then influences later relationships (e.g. Bretherton, 1985; see also Chapter 16). Thus the connections between good marital and parent–child relationships might be due to some personal attribute of the parent which colours both relationships; a second possibility is that a good spousal relationship enhances a mother's well-being and self-esteem, and this makes her feel confident and happy in her relationship with her child. Other possibilities are that spousal support involves instrumental help, or that the spouse provides a model for parenting. It is important to distinguish the *protection* from stress that a good spousal relationship can provide from the *stress* that a poor spousal relationship may add to the burdens of a parent (Rutter, 1988).

The evidence for associations between parent–child and sibling–child relationships makes clear another principle that is key to understanding relationships within families: that many different processes are probably implicated in such connections (Dunn, 1988b). There is evidence for processes that range from, for example, general emotional reactions engendered by changes in one relationship which then affect other relationships (as when first-born children react with general emotional disturbance to the birth of a sibling), to more focused connections — alliances and hostilities — between particular relationships. One study reports, for

instance, that in families in which first-born girls enjoyed an especially close relationship with their mothers, a hostile relationship developed between the siblings. In contrast, in families in which a detached or conflictual relationship existed between parent and child, the siblings developed close relationships — suggesting that a need for affection can sometimes be met within the sibling relationship for children whose relationships with their parents are distant or difficult (see also Bank & Kahn, 1982).

There is also evidence that suggests more cognitive mechanisms, involving 'attributional style' and the interpretation of others' behaviour and motives, may link relationships. For example, a number of different lines of evidence indicate that communication between mother and child is systematically related to differences in the quality of relationship that develops between young siblings (Dunn, 1988b; Howe & Ross, 1990).

The lesson from these findings is that we should not assume that the mechanisms that link family relationships are simple or few; which of these various processes are emphasized will depend on the theoretical background, and on the measures and methods chosen to employ in research. The relative importance of these different kinds of processes may well vary with the developmental stage of the child, with the particular relationship in question, and indeed with the particular personalities of the individuals concerned.

Relationships and the social world beyond the family

Each individual, each dyadic relationship, and the pattern of relationships within the family are all affected by the social world outside the family (Hinde, 1987). The levels and processes through which the influences of the external world are felt are very diverse, and connections between extrafamilial factors and family relationships and child outcome have been documented in a variety of research approaches, which have highlighted the following principles.

First, the relation of economic and social stress to psychiatric disorder in adults and to disturbance in children has been widely documented, and it is generally assumed that patterns of parent–child interaction are implicated: that the quality of parenting is influenced by life events, daily hassles and by social support (Crnic & Greenberg, 1990; Quinton & Rutter, 1988). Second, patterns of parent–child and of grandparent–child interaction differ within different cultural and social class groups (Newson & Newson, 1978; Tinsley & Parke, 1984; Bornstein, 1991). Differences in expectations about children, in what is valued and striven for, in the social rules emphasized and in disciplinary practices, in involvement in education and didactic style are found in families from different social groups. More generally, the cultural world in which children grow up impacts on children surprisingly early, through familial interactions (Dunn & Brown, 1991; see also Chapter 7). Studies of different cultural groups within the same country show that the significance of particular experiences — such as separation from parents — can be strikingly different for children growing up in these different groups (Hackett *et al.*, 1991).

Third, socially supportive relationships outside the family are associated with positive parent–child relationships within the family (e.g. Crockenberg, 1981; Seitz *et al.*, 1985). Fourth, women's employment and work experiences outside the family are related to their relationships with their children (Crouter, 1994); however, to trace the effects on children of women's roles outside the family we need to attend also to the joint effects of work experiences of both mothers and fathers (Alvarez, 1985). Changes in these work experiences are also important: if parents are made redundant, sacked or demoted, family tensions can increase, and parents are likely to become less responsive to their children's needs (Flanagan, 1990). Social class differences in children's educational opportunities both within and outside the family are exacerbated by changes in parents' work situations. Longitudinal research has now documented a distressing pattern by which income loss leads to lower family integration, and subsequent loss of self-esteem in adolescents, which then leads to increased proneness for transgression (Silbereisen *et al.*, 1990). The complexity of the different pathways by which maternal work experiences can affect child outcome is currently being explored in a number of studies. Menaghan and Parcel (1991), for instance, argued that maternal working conditions affect women's

well-being and thus the quality of their maternal behaviour, but also the quality of the housing and material stimulation they can provide for their children, and the quality and stability of the extra-familial child care arrangements that they are able to make for their children.

Fifth, children's relationships within their family are linked to the quality of their peer relations and friendships outside the family. A fast-growing body of research is exploring the concurrent and over-time associations between children's family and peer relationships (Ladd, 1991; Parke & Ladd, 1992). As with the connections between family relationships, the mechanisms linking family and peer relationships are not clear, and a variety of processes appear to be implicated. Most attention has been paid to parent–child and peer relationships: here warm and close parent–child relationships are generally found to be associated with good peer relations; connections between children's relationships with siblings and with peers have also been examined in a few studies, and here the links are less clear — indeed there is some evidence for 'compensatory' links in which poor sibling relationships are associated with close friendships (Stocker & Dunn, 1990).

Changes over time

As children develop new capabilities and new understanding, their relationships with other family members change (Dunn, 1988a); moreover, the normative transitions in their lives — such as starting school — which for many children are accompanied by emotional disturbance, can also have reverberating effects on family relationships (Dunn, 1988c). In addition, transitions in the lives of other family members can also have consequences for children's experiences within the family, as the research on changes in parents' work experience illustrates. The general point of significance is that changes in family structure, or changes in any one family member, can affect other relationships within the family. Thus the marital relationship can change following the birth of a baby (Belsky & Isabella, 1985; Belsky & Rovine, 1990), the relationship between mother and first-born changes with the birth of a second child (Dunn & Kendrick, 1982), and mother–child relationships change when a stepparent joins the family (Hetherington, 1988).

Within a family systems perspective, changes in families' well-being and stress have been traced across the life-cycle. The satisfaction of family members with the marriage, the family and their quality of life is reported to be highest at the first stage of family development (that is, before children are born), and after all children have left home (Olson & Lavee, 1989), while both strains *and* satisfactions are high during the period when the children in the family are young. Family strains are reported to be highest and satisfactions lowest when the children are adolescent.

STRESS AND CHANGE IN FAMILIES

The question of how far such changes in families, or differences in family structure, are related to children's outcome is of particular importance to clinicians. Before considering the evidence on how structure and change in families affect children, the problems in establishing cause−effect relations with children's outcome should be noted.

Cause−effect relations?

It is very difficult in many cases to draw conclusions about causal relations between family experiences and children's outcome, and their direction. For many associations, models in which particular family experiences are seen as influencing outcome are now thought to be far too simple — the exception rather than the rule. The notable individual differences between children from birth onwards which affect parents' behaviour (see Chapter 4), the evidence for genetic transmission (see Chapter 2), the active role children have in selecting their own environments, the mutual influences within and between relationships, the self-regulating properties of these relationships, and the complex patterns linking factors outside the family to relationships within, all militate against simple cause−effect relations from parent behaviour to child outcome.

In some instances, however, it is clear that the family variable under consideration could not have been caused by the child's behaviour — such as parental death or the birth of a sibling. In other instances, the timing of the factors is relevant, as for example in the case of links between parental childhood experiences such as institutionalization and later difficulties in parent-child relationships (Quinton & Rutter, 1988). In other cases, the evidence strongly suggests — but does not establish — a causal link. For instance, studies of conduct disorder in boys show a link between family discord, poor parental discipline and monitoring, and child conduct disorder (Rutter, 1985a). Now in these families it is common for several sons to show the problem behaviour, although there is not a major genetic contribution to its incidence. The most likely explanation for the link, then, is that there is a general effect of the family discord and lack of discipline on all of the brothers, and this effect stems from the parents' problems.

In the following section the evidence on the case of divorce and stepparenting is considered, to illustrate some of the developmental and methodological principles involved.

Divorce, discord and parental separation

Although the focus here will chiefly be upon disruptions to family structure, it should be noted at the outset that children in two-parent families with much parental discord can have as many or more problems as those whose parents have separated (e.g. Rutter, 1971; Emery, 1982; Mechanic & Hansell, 1989). Moreover, children whose families do not conform to the traditional mother−father pattern can in fact do very well. Thus Kellam *et al.* (1977) reported that the children in a low-income sample who came from families headed by a mother and a grandmother did as well on measures of well-being as children from mother−father homes — and much better than those from single-mother homes.

The separation of parents can involve a wide range of varying experiences for children (for reviews of the research see Burgoyne *et al.,* 1987; Emery, 1988; Hetherington & Arasteh, 1988). It may or may not involve a long period of conflict between parents — including violence — and a series of absences by one parent, before the final separation. After the parent (commonly the father) has left, there may be little contact between the parent who has left and the child (Seltzer, 1991). The separation is frequently accompanied by major changes in the financial circumstances of the family, by disorganization and uncertainty about financial resources; often there is also a house move, change of school, loss of friends for the child and strained relations or severing of contact with relatives. The parent with whom the child lives may be under considerable stress and in poor mental health. There may also be a new partner in a stepparenting role with the child. These changes, each potentially stressful, may be short term or may be drawn out over several years.

The variability of these experiences means that a simple dichotomy into children who have experienced 'divorce' and those from 'intact' families does not allow the researcher to examine with any precision the key processes influencing children's adjustment. Adding to the complexity is the evidence that the changes in children's family situations are far from static. A 10-year longitudinal study of 1265 children in New Zealand, for example, showed that significant numbers of separated parents remarried or were reconciled, but that such reconciliations were frequently not permanent (Fergusson *et al.*, 1984, 1985; for comparable figures for the USA see Wallerstein, 1985, and for England and Wales see Leete, 1979). There are also a number of social correlates of parental separation and divorce, which need to be taken into account when comparing children from divorced and intact families (for review see White, 1990). For example, higher frequencies of divorce are associated with early marriages, prenuptial conception, closely spaced conceptions and four or more children. There are also correlations with social class but much of the variance with social class is accounted for by demographic factors (Murphy, 1985). The extent of parents' social networks also varies with the divorce rate, and it has been argued that this is key to divorce rates (Shelton, 1987).

To understand the significance of these experiences for children's development and adjustment, one would, ideally, need to have information on the children from the point at which parents first began to experience difficulties in their relationships, through the period of separation and over the ensuing years. Unfortunately many studies are based on unrepresentative samples, do not include information on the predivorce period, and have only short-term follow-up information. Neverthe-less, some general points on child outcome emerge with consistency from studies in the USA and Britain (for reviews see Wallerstein & Kelly, 1980; Cherlin, 1981; Hetherington *et al.*, 1982; Emery, 1988; Hetherington & Arasteh, 1988).

First, children typically show signs of disturbance, such as anger, depression and anxiety, during the year following the divorce. However, there are marked individual differences in their reactions, some of which are related to their age at the time of family disruption, some related to gender. Among preschool children, boys have been reported to be more likely to show aggressive acting out, and lack of self-control, though both sexes show greater fantasy aggression and attention seeking, and less sharing and helping in group situations (Hetherington *et al.*, 1979, 1982). Their behaviour tended to lead to negative behaviour from adult teachers and peers.

Second, some findings indicate that poor maternal control and family disorganization contributed to the disturbance in preschool-aged children, with continuing parental conflict after divorce being associated with high levels of problem behaviour in children; a small proportion of young children are reported to become clinically depressed (Wallerstein & Kelly, 1980). School-aged children are reported to become very sad, and in some cases depressed, following their parents' divorce, with boys being particularly affected in some studies, but not all (Wallerstein & Kelly, 1980; Zaslow, 1987; Allison & Furstenberg, 1989). Older school-aged children, who have a greater range of ways of coping, appear to be better able to deal with the situation; somatic symptoms and a decline in school performance are however reported (Hess & Camara, 1979; Elliott & Richards, 1991).

Third, there is evidence from prospective studies in both Britain and the USA that there were differences in the behaviour of children from divorced and non-divorced families *long before parental separation* took place (Block *et al.*, 1986; Cherlin *et al.*, 1991; Elliott & Richards, 1991). Thus in the Blocks' study in California, boys from families that later divorced were significantly 'undercontrolled' up to 11 years before the dissolution of their parents' marriage. Elliott and Richards, using the data from the British National Child Development Study, a longitudinal follow-up study of all the children born in 1 week in Britain in 1958, found that the children whose parents had separated when the children were between 7 and 16 had higher scores on disruptive, unhappy and worried behaviour, and poorer reading and mathematics attainment *before* their parents' divorce. Cherlin *et al.* examined both the British data and a similar data set from the USA National Survey of Children, and showed that the apparent effect of separation or divorce was sharply reduced when the incidence of behaviour problems, children's achievement and family difficulties present at an earlier time point were taken into account. It appears that the predivorce differences may be attributable to the direct or indirect effect of higher parental conflict, and/or to differences in the parent–child relationships in these families, and the findings draw attention to the importance of understanding the processes that occur in troubled intact families, as well as to the stress of parental separation.

Fourth, longitudinal studies indicate that there may be effects of divorce that persist into adulthood. Research in the UK and in the USA indicates that a wide range of effects are linked to childhood experience of divorce: a higher probability of depression, poorer marital relationships, higher divorce rates and lower SES (socioeconomic status) and income (Amato & Keith, 1991; Richards, 1991). Richards noted that in the British data, these findings indicate that parental divorce is associated with downward social mobility for children. The data from the 1958 national survey suggest, for instance, that the chances of going to a university were halved for children whose parents divorced. This association with educational consequences illustrates how little is known of the processes by which effects persist into adulthood. The drop in income following divorce, parental stress and preoccupation with problems, and children's own social and emotional problems may all have contributed to the differences in educational achievement. Difficulties between parent and child may also have encouraged children to become involved in social relationships outside the home that did not foster educational attainment.

Stepparent and single-parent families

Close to half of today's children in the USA will spend some time in a single-parent family, and about a quarter will have lived with a stepparent by the time that they are 16 (Zill, 1988). The effects on children's well-being and adjustment of these experiences are summarized in recent reviews (Ferri, 1984; Coleman & Ganong, 1990). Generally, a significant minority of children in both single-parent families and stepfamilies are found to have serious persistent problems. For example, in Zill's (1988) analysis of 1300 children living with a stepparent, drawn from the 15 416 children in a national survey in the USA, differences between the children in stepparent and in biological-parent families were particularly evident in behavioural and emotional adjustment, and the frequencies of problems were similar to those among children in single-parent families. Children in stepparent families had fewer learning problems and were in better physical health than those in single-parent families, but these differences were probably attributable to the higher educational level of the stepparent families.

In general, the children of more educated parents and stepparents showed fewer behavioural and learning problems, and the income level of the families was also related to behavioural problem frequencies, with lower levels associated — though weakly — with more problems. A notable feature of stepfamilies, as compared with single-parent families, concerns half-siblings and stepsiblings. The presence of half-siblings and stepsiblings in the household is associated with more behaviour problems, and generally with more distant stepparent–stepchild relationships. Interestingly, the age and sex of the stepsiblings did not in Zill's study relate strongly to the incidence of problems, in contrast to other studies, in which boys were more clearly affected by the presence of stepsiblings (e.g. Hetherington, 1988). There was also only weak support for the idea that family disruption early in the children's lives would be linked to a higher incidence of problems. The financial well-being of stepfamilies is greater than that of single-parent families; however there was not strong evidence that within the stepparent group this difference translated directly to better functioning of the children. There is some evidence that stepparent–stepchild relationships get worse over time (Coleman & Ganong, 1990), and that in spite of the widely held belief to the contrary, the quality of these relationships does not improve with the birth of a child from the remarriage.

Mother–stepfather families differ from father–stepmother families in a number of significant ways, in terms of the patterns of stepparent–stepchild relationships that develop, and of child outcome. Living with stepmothers has been reported to be associated with more problems than living with stepfathers (Zill, 1988). It appears that it is more difficult to supplement or substitute for a child's mother than for a father, perhaps because the tie with fathers who have left home is less strong than ties to mothers. In families in which the biological mother was dead, the father–stepmother families appeared to be relatively free from problems.

Three general points stand out from the studies of stepfamilies. First, there is evidence that stepfather–stepdaughter relationships are more problematic than stepfather-stepson relationships (Santrock *et al.*, 1982; Brand *et al.*, 1988; Hetherington, 1988). Second, the relation of marital satisfaction to the quality of parent–child relationships differs — at least in some studies — in non-divorced and remarried families. Marital satisfaction in stepparent families was related to increased family conflict and behavioural problems in the children, especially in families with stepdaughters. In Hetherington's study, for instance, although both stepsons and stepdaughters did eventually adapt to the remarriage of their mothers, the daughters continued to have more problems in adjustment than girls in non-divorced families, or in families in which the divorced mother did not remarry.

Third, the associations between children's problems and parenting style differed in the non-divorced and stepfamilies in Hetherington's study. While in both non-divorced and single-parent families an authoritative pattern of parenting (Baumrind, 1971) was related to fewer behaviour problems in the children, in stepparent families, authoritative control attempts by stepfathers were associated with rejection of the stepfather, and with more behaviour problems in the children. It appears that some of the principles learned from the study of non-divorced families do not necessarily apply to step-families.

General principles illustrated by research on divorce and stepparenting

The research on divorce and stepparenting illustrates a number of general principles relating to family experience and child outcome, which will next be summarized; the parallels with the consequences of other family stresses will be noted.

Individual differences in response to family change and stress are marked. There are notable differences in children's responses to parental separation and stepparenting, obscured in comparisons of the mean differences between divorced, remarried and intact families. Much of this variance remains to be explained. However, the age of children and their gender are linked to these differences, though there is inconsistency in findings on both gender and age effects (Zaslow, 1987; Emery, 1988; Allison & Furstenberg, 1989), and children's personality and family relationships before the family change are also important. Individual differences in children's responses to other family stresses are marked, too; studies of the response of children to the birth of a sibling, to the stress of starting school, and to economic hardships that impact on the family illustrate this same point (Dunn, 1988c; Flanagan, 1990).

Children's relationships with family members other than the mother are important. A significant role in children's outcome following divorce is played by their relationships with other family members. Thus a good relationship with siblings can be a support for children in disrupted or divorcing families (Jenkins & Smith, 1990); grandparents can also be a support (Tinsley & Parke, 1984). Similarly, relationships with fathers and grandparents are important in mitigating the stress on first-born children following the birth of a sibling (Dunn & Kendrick, 1982).

The impact of apparently acute events may be mediated through long-term changes in family relationships. Many stressful changes in children's families, such as the loss or illness of a parent, or parental separation or divorce, are accompanied by long-term changes in parent–child relationships. After divorce the behaviour of both the parent who has custody and the parent who does not changes (Hetherington *et al.*, 1976). And two studies of attempted suicide have shown that the link between early loss of parent and suicidal ideation is closely associated with the occurrence of major and long-standing loss of family organization (Adam, 1982). It appears probable that the differences in children's outcome following divorce and bereavement are linked to the differences in the ways in which family interaction patterns are affected.

The relationships between other family members are also important. The quality of the relationships between other family members is also linked to the incidence of disturbance in children following family change. Thus following divorce, differential treatment of the siblings within a family is associated with extreme conflict between the siblings (Hetherington, 1988); parallel patterns are found following the birth of a sibling (Dunn, 1988c). As already noted, the quality of the marital relationship is linked to children's outcome, but in different ways for non-divorced parents and for stepparents.

Relationships outside the family are important. Children's outcome following family change is associated with the quality of their relationships outside the family, though the direction of the connection is not clear — indeed the links are likely to be bidirectional. Thus, children from recently divorced families are more isolated at school and have problems in their peer relationships (Richards, 1991). Close friendships can, however, provide support for children experiencing family disruption even as preschoolers; friendship appears to buffer children from the impact of a sibling's birth (Kramer, 1990), while there can also be increases in difficulties with peer relations following a sibling birth.

Finally, family stressors frequently occur in multiple combinations. Studies of family experiences following economic hardship make the same point noted for the combination of stresses following divorce (Menaghan & Parcel, 1991). The relations between economic strain, parental adjustment and behaviour, and child health, well-being and behaviour problems are reviewed by McLoyd (1989), Targ and Perrucci (1990) and Voydanoff (1990).

Family relationships and protective processes

Family relationships not only act as the mediators of stressful impact on children, but can also function to protect children from the effects of stressful experiences. Several aspects of family life have been identified as possibly protective, including the cohesion and warmth of the family (Garmezy, 1983), the nature of parental supervision and monitoring, the presence of one good relationship with a parent, a good marital relationship and a close sibling relationship. Evidence for the protective role of a good relationship with one parent was found, for example, in a longitudinal study of children with mentally ill parents, in which the psychiatric risk to the child associated with family discord was reduced if he or she had one close relationship with a parent (Rutter, 1990). It is not clear what processes were involved here: as Rutter pointed out, it could be that with one harmonious relationship in the family, the overall level of discord is reduced. Another possibility is that the parent with whom the child had a good relationship made sure that the child was not exposed to the parental fights; alternatively — or in addition — it is possible that the good parent–child relationship increased the child's self-esteem, and it was this self-confidence that protected the child from the impact of the family discord.

The protective effects of good marital relationships have been documented in several studies. For example, in a study of women who were reared in institutions, it was found that those who had supportive spouses were more likely to function well as parents (Quinton & Rutter, 1988; see also Brown & Harris, 1978; Campbell *et al.*, 1983). Again, the mechanism through which the protective effect operates is not clear. Similarly, a protective effect of a good relationship with siblings in families with high marital discord has been described, but the precise process by which the effect is exerted remains unclear (Jenkins *et al.*, 1989).

A study by Masten *et al.* (1988) that attempts to separate out which of a number of different family processes act to protect children from stress illustrates a number of general points concerning protective processes. First, the results indicate that the same factor may act as a protective factor with regard to one outcome criterion, but as a 'vulnerability' factor in relation to other outcome measures. Second, processes of vulnerability and protection appeared to differ for girls and for boys. Indeed, boys appeared to be less protected by family factors than were girls. Third, the parenting qualities that were protective were themselves related to children's social response style, and the authors point out that differences in children's social style may themselves contribute to the differences in parenting that appear to be protective.

CORRELATES OF FAMILY STRUCTURE

Sibship size and birth order

Research on the significance of family size and birth order for children's personality, adjustment and cognitive development is complicated by the fact that birth order and sibship size are related to social class differences (large family size being associated with lower social class), to ethnicity and religious affiliations, to single-parent versus dual-parent families (with greater representation of only and first-born children in single-parent families), and to urban versus rural background. There are also historical trends towards smaller families among some social groups but not others, which affect the representation of different birth positions in cohorts from different time periods. A comprehensive discussion of these methodological issues, and the evidence on birth order and sibship size, was provided by Ernst and Angst (1983), and their general conclusions remain well supported.

In terms of patterns of parent—child relationships, for example, when social class is controlled, increasing sibship size is found to be associated — very weakly — with poorer parent—child relationships, and less parental interest in school progress. It is generally assumed that with larger families, parental attention and responsiveness is diminished, but there is little direct study of how a child's social relationships are affected by family size (see below for some research findings on twins).

In terms of child outcome, the findings are clearest for juvenile delinquency and antisocial problems: both are more frequent among children from large families (Rutter *et al.*, 1970; Ernst &

Angst, 1983). In a national sample of 7-year-old British children, those from large sibships were less well adjusted at school, when sex and social class were controlled for (Davie *et al.*, 1972), and over the next 9 years those children in the sample who had more than three siblings were very much more likely to become or remain deviant (Ghodsian *et al.*, 1980). However the widely held belief that children with several siblings are more likely to be sociable is not supported by research (Blake *et al.*, 1991). Similarly the view that only children have more problems and are less well adjusted than children with siblings is not upheld by meta-analysis of the various studies available, once the social and economic background of single-parent families is taken into account (Polit & Falbo, 1987).

A number of field studies report overrepresentation of first and middle children among children with neurotic symptoms, though others report conflicting findings. Ernst and Angst (1983) concluded that the evidence for problems among first and middle children is not likely to reflect some special resilience of last-born children, but rather is to be explained by a higher proportion of single-parent families among the first-born children. Their overall conclusion is that small sibship size may be related to neurosis not because of parental overattention or anxiety, but because broken homes are over-represented among such families; in any case, sibship size explains only a very small amount of the variance when other background variables are controlled. Among children referred to psychiatric clinics, first-borns are overrepresented; however, studies that include control groups indicate that this is due to the greater use of medical services by middle-class families, rather than to higher risk of psychiatric illness among first-born children.

In contrast to the possible disadvantage of being first-born for socioemotional development, eldest children may be at a slight advantage over later-born children in terms of their scholastic achievement and verbal IQ (Rutter, 1985b). Recent research suggests, however, that it is the number of siblings in a family, rather than birth order, that shows the clearest relation to cognitive development (Blake, 1989). Blake's large-scale research indicates that children with but one or two siblings have significantly more education and greater verbal ability than those from large families (an association that holds for all SES groups), though no relations are found with non-verbal cognitive abilities. The effects of birth order, family size and sibling spacing on cognitive development have been explored in a number of studies following Zajonc *et al.*'s (1979) 'confluence model', which examines the variation in intellectual development related family configuration variables, with an attempt to describe how the family intellectual environment changes with the arrival of subsequent siblings. This model has been strongly and effectively criticized on methodological and other grounds (Galbraith, 1982a, b; Rodger, 1984; see, however, Berbaum & Moreland, 1985).

It also remains unclear *how* family size and configuration affect children's cognitive development — that is, what family processes are involved in the differences in intellectual achievement attributed to children from families of different size. It is usually suggested that differences in parental attention are implicated: 'the more children, the more parental resources are divided ... and hence, the lower the quality of output' (Blake, 1981). A number of correlational studies have suggested that there are links between differences in parental discipline, teaching styles, support, as well as verbal interaction that are correlated with intellectual development (Maccoby & Martin, 1983), but how these are related to family configuration is not clear. And — especially significant — it is also unclear how far these variables affect children's intellectual development *independently* of parental IQ, education and SES. A recent attempt to answer the question of what family interaction variables mediate the impact of family configuration on intellectual development reports that the family interaction variables studied only accounted for a very small percentage of the variance (Widlak & Perrucci, 1988). Parental encouragement emerged as the most significant component of the interaction indices studied. Children from small families are also reported to spend more time engaged in intellectual and cultural pursuits (Blake, 1989) — but again the matter of how far these variables are independent of parental education and SES remains unclear.

In general, the issue of how family configuration influences cognitive development raises a number of considerations not given prominence in the discussion of family influences on development so far, which will be briefly summarized in the following section.

Family correlates of cognitive development

The first issue concerns the confound between genetic and environmental influences which is encountered in most studies of family influence, whether the research is correlational studies of parenting measures and children's IQ as outcome, or assessments of disadvantaged children (see Chapter 2 for strategies to tease apart genetic and environmental influences).

The second issue concerns the question of whether the nature of family influence changes with the developmental stage of the child. This issue has been more extensively studied for intellectual development than for socioemotional development or adjustment, though the results remain controversial and inconsistent. Wachs and Gruen (1982) argued that parental conversation and responsiveness are more important in the second and later preschool years than in the early months of infancy, while Bradley and Caldwell (1984) argued that after 7 years, maternal responsiveness is less important but that parental encouragement is still salient. The picture is made more complex by the finding that the genetic contribution to cognitive development apparently increases with age (Plomin & Neiderhiser, 1992), and thus demonstrations of increasing family influence on cognitive ability with age could reflect increasing *genetic* importance in individual differences in cognitive abilities, rather than increasing family environmental influences *per se* (Plomin & Bergeman, 1991).

A third issue is that the nature and developmental patterns of family influence may differ for different aspects of cognitive development and scholastic achievement — for example, the verbal and non-verbal aspects (see Blake, 1989 for evidence on sibship size and verbal but not non-verbal cognitive abilities). Little is known about this matter. The impact of different family members may well vary for different aspects of cognitive development. For instance, it appears likely that siblings exert some influence on aspects of social cognition, as opposed to verbal abilities: a recent study reports that interaction between siblings makes a significant contribution to assessments of social understanding that is independent of the contribution of mother–child verbal interaction (Dunn *et al.*, 1991).

A fourth issue is that the aspects of family change and stress which were discussed above in relation to children's emotional adjustment appear to have rather less marked effects on children's intellectual development; however, again more research is needed into the different aspects of cognitive ability and achievement. As noted above, motivation for scholastic work and adjustment to school may be affected by such stresses, and thus school achievement and years of education in turn may be affected.

Finally, it should be noted that in much of the current theoretical and empirical work on cognitive development that focuses on *normative* developmental patterns, rather than on individual differences, there is a new attention to the significance of social context in both revealing and fostering cognitive development. Vygotsky's (1978) general proposal that development takes place in the context of social interaction is now being explored in a number of empirical studies of cognitive development: Rogoff's (1990) studies of children as 'apprentices in learning' is one recent example. A second is the detailed study of the development of children's causal reasoning in different social contexts, such as arguments with family members (Scholnick & Wing, 1991). The significance of this research for clinicians' interest in individual development remains largely unexplored, as yet (see, however, Dunn *et al.*, 1991).

Twins

The family experiences of children growing up with a twin, or triplets, obviously differ in a number of ways from those of singleton children. First, bringing up twins, triplets or quads involves considerable stress for parents, and is extremely exhausting. And the stress does not end with infancy: a recent national cohort study, for instance, reported that mothers of 5-year-old twins showed higher levels of maternal emotional distress than mothers of singletons (Thorpe *et al.*, 1991). Second, children who grow up with a twin are likely to interact less with their parents — as individuals — than do singleton children, and this is particularly marked for conver-

sational exchanges. Mothers talk less to each twin, and in simpler language than do mothers of singletons (Conway *et al.*, 1980). It is perhaps not surprising, then, that a number of studies report that twins are behind on language development (for review, see Rutter & Redshaw, 1991) — though there is considerable individual variation. Twins also show deficits in verbal IQ and reading, and these deficits are still detectable at adolescence. It is possible that these language problems are linked to pre- and perinatal factors as well as to the differences in family interaction patterns, though in general such obstetric and perinatal factors are not thought to contribute strongly to the language delay.

Given the evidence for language delay, the stress under which parents of twins labour, and the links between language delay and behaviour problems within the general population, we might well expect twins to show a higher frequency of behaviour problems than singletons. The evidence, reviewed by Rutter and Redshaw (1991), shows however that there are only marginal, non-significant differences in rates of referral and in measures of socioemotional development. In terms of psychopathology, that is, twins do not differ from singletons, in spite of the differences in their family experiences.

NON-SHARED FAMILY INFLUENCES

A new perspective on the nature of the processes influencing children's development within the family has recently emerged from an unlikely source, the field of behavioural genetics. The starting point for this research was the evidence that siblings growing up in the same family are quite different from one another in personality and psychopathology, even though they share 50% of their segregating genes and what is usually assumed to be the 'same' family environment (Scarr & Grajek, 1982; Plomin & Daniels, 1987). The geneticists' analyses of the similarity and differences between identical and fraternal twins, and adoptive and biological siblings, have established that about a third of the variance on personality measures is due to genetic differences between individuals (Plomin & Daniels, 1987; Plomin *et al.*, 1990). Heritability of this magnitude *completely accounts* for the similarity between siblings — which implies that environmental influences that make the siblings similar to one another are negligible. Rather, the evidence from this research shows that growing up together within the same family does not make siblings similar, but different from one another.

A direct test of this idea is provided by studies of unrelated children growing up within the same family. Any similarity between adopted siblings must be due to their common experiences within the same family. The results of studies of adopted siblings show that the siblings hardly resemble each other at all: the average correlation between them on personality measures, for example, is 0.05. That is, the shared experiences of growing up in the same family account for only about 5% of the variance in personality. Studies of identical twins also provide direct assessments of environmental influences on children's development, because any differences between the twins must be due to non-genetic factors. For many measures of psychopathology, the discordance between identical twins is relatively high (Kendler & Robinette, 1983; Plomin & Daniels, 1987; Plomin *et al.*, 1994); as the individuals are identical genetically, there can be no hereditary explanation for these differences. That is, the differences result from their experiences, including their experiences growing up within the same family (but see Chapter 3 for a discussion of what 'experiences' might include). There is evidence for some shared family environment effects on conduct disorders, aggression, and delinquency, but not for other aspects of personality and psychopathology (Plomin *et al.*, 1990; see also Chapter 2).

The challenge these findings present to family researchers is to explain how growing up within the same family makes children so different from one another. The factors that have been the focus of so much family research — such as the quality of the marital relationship, the mental health of the mother and the support she gets from others, the economic background and cultural world to which the family belongs — are apparently shared by siblings. Yet they develop to be so unlike each other. What, then, are the experiences within the family that influence the siblings' development? The geneticists' work has shown that the experiences that are important must be those that are specific to each sibling — and not shared. Many clinicians who

work within a family-systems or family-therapy framework are, of course, sensitive to the different lives that children can lead within the same family and, as noted above, family systems theorists have emphasized the importance of differential experiences within the family (Minuchin, 1985, 1988). However, until recently there has been little systematic research that focuses on more than one child within a family and examines the differences in their experiences. In the last few years some progress has been made towards specifying the processes of influence within the family that make siblings so different, and these will be briefly summarized (for a detailed discussion of the evidence, see Dunn & Plomin, 1990).

Differences in parent—child relationships and child outcome

One obvious candidate for salient differential experiences within the family is the parent—child relationship. Evidence from interviews with both parents and children (e.g. Koch, 1960), and from direct observation shows that parents often have rather different relationships with their different children, and children are aware of and sensitive to such differences. From a very early age children are extremely responsive to what is happening between other family members, and interaction between their parents and siblings is especially salient to them (Kendrick & Dunn, 1982; Dunn, 1988a; Dunn & Shatz, 1989). The question of how far such differences are related to the differences in children's outcome is currently under investigation, and the initial studies indicate that differential parental treatment relates to sibling differences in adjustment and delinquency (Daniels *et al.*, 1985; Daniels, 1986) and to individual emotional adjustment (Dunn *et al.*, 1990). The direction of causal influence is, of course, open to question here.

Differences within sibling relationships

A second possible source of differences in family experiences is the sibling relationship. A consistent picture is emerging from studies that investigate how each child within a dyadic sibling relationship experiences that relationship: there are considerable differences in the siblings' perceptions of the relationship and in their experiences within it — frequently greater than the differences the children report in their relations with their parents (e.g. Daniels *et al.*, 1985; Anderson, 1989; Stocker & McHale, 1992). The first studies of the relation of such differences to children's outcome indicate there are links to children's adjustment. Current research is investigating both the possible genetic contribution to such differences, and the issue of the direction of cause–effect relations.

Another less direct form of sibling influence is also under investigation — the impact of growing up with a child who is different from oneself. There is evidence that, surprisingly early in development, children are conscious of the differences between themselves and their siblings, and that they compare themselves with these siblings — moreover family discourse concerning such social comparisons is related to the children's self-esteem 3 years later (Brown & Dunn, 1990).

Other sources of differential experience

There are many other sources of differential experience for siblings, especially when they begin school and become part of a wider social world beyond the family. One potentially powerful source that acts within the family is the impact of life events. Stressful events that impact on the family and are apparently shared by all family members have been reported to have very different effects on siblings (Beardsall & Dunn, 1992). Thus the impact of maternal illness, or paternal unemployment, house moves or financial problems was found to be different for siblings within the same family; moreover, the impact of these events was related to the later self-esteem of the siblings, which differed markedly for the siblings.

In summary, the central issue in the research on non-shared family experiences is this: that to understand the processes that lead to the development of individual differences, we need to move away from approaches that focus on general family variables, such as the 'enmeshed' or 'distressed' family, and which employ family-by-family comparisons, towards a finer grained focus on the microenvironments of each child within the family. To understand, for instance, how having a depressed mother affects children, we need to focus on two children

within the family and explain why one is affected and the other not. As yet, most of the detailed empirical work on differential experiences has focused on normal rather than distressed families, and it is possible that in cases where, for instance, parents are extremely disturbed, the effects of that disturbance overwhelm all the children and have similar effects on all siblings. However, the evidence is accumulating that even under stress each family is experienced differently by the different children who are its members (e.g. Powers, 1989), and it is the differences in their experiences that need to be examined.

CONCLUSION

This chapter has examined four themes in recent research on families, in what was inevitably a selective review of a very extensive field: the diversity and changing nature of family units, the relations between family relationships, the associations between stress and change in families and children's outcome, and the significance of non-shared family experiences. In conclusion, three notes of caution must be sounded, concerning issues that deserve greater attention — and that should be the focus of future research.

First, we have made progress in appreciating the variety and complexity of possible processes of influence within family relationships: we have moved away from a simple notion of mothering as the key to later adjustment, and from the idea of the family as a monolithic unit. However, while empirical research has demonstrated a rich array of associations, we remain ignorant concerning the mechanisms underlying many of these connections. The issue of what mechanisms underlie continuities and discontinuities over time and over generations (see Chapter 1) remains intractable — and of central importance to both developmental theory and clinical practice. What is needed now is research that elucidates which processes are important at which stage of children's development, for which individuals.

Second, it is important to recognize that processes of influence may well be different in families that are under stress or disrupted, and in those that are not distressed; they may differ too in families from different social class and subcultural groups. The range of families studied to date remains limited.

Third, the challenge of explaining why children growing up in the same family develop so differently highlights how important it is to focus our attention on differences within as well as between families, if we are to make progress in understanding developmental influences.

REFERENCES

Adam K.S. (1982) Loss, suicide, and attachment. In Murray-Parkes C. & Stevenson-Hinde J. (eds) *The Place of Attachment in Human Behavior*, pp. 269–294. Basic Books, New York.

Allison P.D. & Furstenberg F.F. (1989) How marital dissolution affects children: Variations by age and sex. *Developmental Psychology* **25**, 540–549.

Alvarez W.F. (1985) The meaning of maternal employment for mothers and their perceptions of their three-year-old children. *Child Development* **56**, 350–360.

Amato P.R. & Keith B. (1991) Parental divorce and adult well-being: A meta-analysis. *Journal of Marriage and the Family* **53**, 43–58.

Anderson S.L. (1989) *Differential within-family experiences as predictors of adolescent personality and attachment style differences*. Honors thesis, Department of Psychology, Harvard University.

Bank S. & Kahn M.D. (1982) *The Sibling Bond*. Basic Books, New York.

Baumrind D. (1971) Current patterns of parental authority. *Developmental Psychology Monographs* **4**.

Beardsall L. & Dunn J. (1992) Adversities in childhood: Siblings' experiences, and their relations to self-esteem. *Journal of Child Psychology and Psychiatry* **33**, 349–359.

Bell R.Q. (1968) A reinterpretation of the direction of effects in studies of socialization. *Psychological Review* **75**, 81–95.

Belsky J. & Isabella R.A. (1985) Marital and parent–child relationships in family of origin and marital change following the birth of an infant. *Child Development* **56**, 342–349.

Belsky J. & Rovine M. (1988) Nonmaternal care in the first year of life and the security of infant–parent attachment. *Child Development* **59**, 157–167.

Belsky J. & Rovine M. (1990) Patterns of marital change across the transition to parenthood: Pregnancy to three years postpartum. *Journal of Marriage and the Family* **52**, 5–19.

Berbaum M.L. & Moreland R.L. (1985) Intellectual development within transracial adoptive families: Retesting the confluence model. *Child Development* **56**, 207–216.

Blake J. (1981) Family size and the quality of children. *Demography* **18**, 421–442.

Blake J. (1989) *Family Size and Achievement*. University of California Press, Berkeley.

Blake J., Richardson B. & Bhattacharya J. (1991) Number of siblings and sociability. *Journal of Marriage and the Family* **53**, 271–283.

Block J.H., Block J. & Gjerde P.F. (1986) The personality of children prior to divorce: A prospective study. *Child Development* **57**, 827–840.

Block J.H., Block J. & Morrison A. (1981) Parental agreement-disagreement on child-rearing orientations and gender-related correlates in children. *Child Development* **52**, 965–974.

Boer F. (1990) *Sibling Relationships in Middle Childhood*. DSWO University of Leiden Press, Leiden.

Boer F. & Dunn J. (1992) *Sibling Relationships in Childhood: Developmental and Clinical Implications*. Lawrence Erlbaum, Hillsdale, New Jersey.

Boh K., Bak M., Clason C. *et al.* (1989) *Changing Patterns of European Family Life*. Routledge, London.

Bornstein M.H. (1991) *Cultural Approaches to Parenting*. Lawrence Erlbaum, Hillsdale, New Jersey.

Bradley R.H. & Caldwell B.M. (1984) The relation of infants' home environment to achievement test performance in first grade: A follow-up study. *Child Development* **55**, 803–809.

Brand E., Clingempeel W.G. & Bowen-Woodward K. (1988) Family relationships and children's psychological adjustment in stepmother and stepfather families. In Hetherington E.M. & Arasteh J.D. (eds) *Impact of Divorce, Single Parenting, and Stepparenting on Children*. Lawrence Erlbaum, Hillsdale, New Jersey.

Brannen J. & Moss P. (1988) *New Mothers at Work*. Unwin Hyman, London.

Bretherton I. (1985) Attachment theory: Retrospect and prospect. In Bretherton I. & Waters E. (eds) Growing points of attachment theory and research. *Monographs of the Society for Research in Child Development* **50**, Serial No. 209, 3–35.

Brody G.H. & Stoneman Z. (1987) Sibling conflict: Contribution of the siblings themselves, the parent–sibling relationship, and the broader family system. *Journal of Children in Contemporary Society* **19**, 39–53.

Brody G.H., Stoneman Z. & Burke M. (1987) Child temperaments, maternal differential behavior, and sibling relationships. *Developmental Psychology* **23**, 354–362.

Brown G.W. & Harris T.O (1978) *Social Origins of Depression: A Study of Psychiatric Disorders in Women*. Tavistock Publications, London.

Brown J. & Dunn J. (1990) *Evaluative discourse within the family and children's later self-esteem*. Presentation at the International Conference on Infancy Studies, Montreal, April.

Bryant B.K. & Crockenberg S.B. (1980) Correlates and dimensions of prosocial behavior: A study of female siblings with their mothers. *Child Development* **51**, 529–544.

Burgoyne J., Ormrod R. & Richards M.P.M. (1987) *Divorce Matters*. Penguin, London.

Cairns N., Clark G., Smith S. & Lansky S. (1979) Adaptation of siblings to childhood malignancy. *Journal of Pediatrics* **95**, 484–487.

Campbell EA., Cope S.J. & Teasdale J.D. (1983) Social factors and affective disorder: An investigation of Brown and Harris's model. *British Journal of Psychiatry* **143**, 548–553.

Caspi A. & Elder G.H. (1988) Emergent family patterns: The intergenerational construction of problem behavior and relationships. In Hinde R.A. & Stevenson-Hinde J. (eds) *Relationships Within Families: Mutual Influences*, pp. 218–240. Clarendon Press, Oxford.

Cherlin A.J. (1981) *Marriage, Divorce, Remarriage*. Harvard University Press, Cambridge, Massachusetts.

Cherlin A.J., Furstenberg F.F., Chase-Lansdale P.L. *et al.* (1991) Longitudinal studies of the effects of divorce on children in Great Britain and the United States. *Science* **252**, 1386–1389.

Children's Well-Being: An International Comparison (1990) International Population Reports Series No. 80. US Department of Commerce, Bureau of the Census, Washington.

Christensen A. & Margolin G. (1988) Conflict and alliance in distressed and non-distressed families. In Hinde R.A. & Stevenson-Hinde J. (eds) *Relationships within Families: Mutual Influences*, pp. 263–282. Clarendon Press, Oxford.

Coleman M. & Ganong L.H. (1990) Remarriage and stepfamily research in the 1980s: Increased interest in an old family form. *Journal of Marriage and the Family* **52**, 925–940.

Conway D., Lytton H. & Pysh F. (1980) Twin–singleton language differences. *Canadian Journal of Behavioral Science* **12**, 264–271.

Cooper C.R., Grotevant H.D., Moore M.S. & Condon S.M. (1984) Predicting adolescent role-taking and identity exploration from family communication patterns: A comparison of one- and two-child families. In Falbo T. (ed.) *The Single-Child Family*, pp. 263–282. Guilford, New York.

Crnic K.A. & Greenberg M.T. (1990) Mild parenting stresses with young children. *Child Development* **61**, 1628–1637.

Crockenberg S.B. (1981) Infant irritability, mother responsiveness, and social support influences on the security of mother–infant attachment. *Child Development* **52**, 857–865.

Crouter A.C. (1994) Processes linking families and work: Implications for behavior and development in both settings. In Parke R. & Kellam S. (eds) *Advances in Family Research*, Vol. 4. Lawrence Erlbaum, Hillsdale, New Jersey. (In press)

Daniels D. (1986) Differential experiences of siblings in the same family as predictors of adolescent sibling personality differences. *Journal of Personality and Social Psychology* **51**, 339–346.

Daniels D., Dunn J., Furstenberg F.F. & Plomin R. (1985) Environmental differences within the family and adjustment differences within pairs of siblings. *Child Development* **56**, 764–774.

Davie R., Butler N. & Goldstein H. (1972) *From Birth to Seven*. Longman, London.

Dunn J. (1988a) *The Beginnings of Social Understanding*. Harvard University Press, Cambridge, Massachusetts; Basil Blackwell, Oxford.

Dunn J. (1988b) Connections between relationships: Implications of research on mothers and siblings. In Hinde R.A. & Stevenson-Hinde J. (eds) *Relationships Within Families: Mutual Influences*, pp. 168–180. Clarendon Press, Oxford.

Dunn J. (1988c) Normative life events as risk factors. In Rutter M. (ed.) *Studies of Psychosocial Risk*, pp. 227–244. Cambridge University Press, Cambridge.

Dunn J. (1992) Sisters and brothers: Current issues in developmental research. In Boer F. & Dunn J. (eds) *Children's Sibling Relationships: Clinical and Developmental Issues*, pp. 1–17. Lawrence Erlbaum, Hillsdale, New Jersey.

Dunn J. & Brown J.R. (1991) Becoming American or English? Talking about the social world in England and the United States. In Bornstein M. (ed.) *Cultural Approaches to Parenting*, pp. 155–172. Lawrence Erlbaum, Hillsdale, New Jersey.

Dunn J., Brown J., Slomkowski C., Tesla C. & Youngblade L. (1991) Young children's understanding of other people's feelings and beliefs: Individual differences and their antecedents. *Child Development* **62**, 1352–1366.

Dunn J. & Kendrick C. (1982) *Siblings: Love, Envy and Understanding*. Harvard University Press, Cambridge, Massachusetts.

Dunn J. & Plomin R. (1990) *Separate Lives: Why Siblings are So Different*. Basic Books, New York.

Dunn J. & Shatz M. (1989) Becoming a conversationalist despite (or because of) having an elder sibling. *Child Development* **60**, 399–410.

Dunn J., Stocker C. & Plomin R. (1990) Nonshared experiences within the family: Correlates of behavior problems in middle childhood. *Development and Psychopathology* **2**, 113–126.

Easterbrooks M.A. & Emde R.N. (1988) Marital and parent–child relationships: The role of affect in the family system. In Hinde R.A. & Stevenson-Hinde J. (eds) *Relationships Within Families: Mutual Influences*, pp. 83–103. Clarendon Press, Oxford.

Elder G.H., Nguyen T.A. & Caspi A. (1985) Linking family hardship to children's lives. *Child Development* **56**, 361–375.

Elliott B.J. & Richards M.P.M (1991) Children and divorce: Educational performance and behaviour before and after parental separation. *International Journal of Law and the Family* **5**, 258–276.

Emery R.E. (1982) Interpersonal conflict and the children

of discord and divorce. *Psychological Bulletin* **92**, 310–330.

Emery R.E. (1988) *Marriage, Divorce, and Children's Adjustment*. Sage, Newbury Park, California.

Engfer A. (1988) The interrelatedness of marriage and the mother–child relationship. In Hinde R.A. & Stevenson-Hinde J. (eds) *Relationships Within Families: Mutual Influences*, pp. 104–118. Clarendon Press, Oxford.

Ernst C. & Angst J. (1983) *Birth Order: Its Influence on Personality*. Springer, Berlin.

Fergusson D.M., Horwood L.J. & Dimond M.E. (1985) A survival analysis of childhood family history. *Journal of Marriage and the Family* **47**, 287–295.

Fergusson D.M., Horwood L.J. & Shannon F.T. (1984) A proportional hazards model of family breakdown. *Journal of Marriage and the Family* **46**, 539–549.

Ferreira A. (1963) Family myths and homeostasis. *Archives of General Psychiatry* **9**, 457–428.

Ferri E. (1984) *Stepchildren*. National Children's Bureau, Windsor.

Flanagan C.A. (1990) Families and schools in hard times. In McLoyd V.C. & Flanagan C.A. (eds) *Economic Stress: Effects on Family Life and Child Development*, pp. 7–26. Jossey-Bass, San Francisco.

Furstenberg F.F. (1976) Premarital pregnancy and marital instability. *Journal of Social Issues* **32**, 67–86.

Furstenberg F.F. (1985) Sociological ventures in child development. *Child Development* **56**, 281–288.

Galbraith R.C. (1982a) Just one look was all it took: Reply to Berbaum, Markus and Zajonc. *Developmental Psychology* **18**, 181–191.

Galbraith R.C. (1982b) Sibling spacing and intellectual development: A closer look at the confluence models. *Developmental Psychology* **18**, 151–173.

Ganong L.H. & Coleman M. (1988) Do mutual children cement bonds in stepfamilies? *Journal of Marriage and the Family* **50**, 687–698.

Garfinkel I. & McLanahan S.S. (1986) *Single Mothers and Their Children*. The Urban Institute Press, Washington, DC.

Garmezy N. (1983) Stressors of childhood. In Garmezy N. & Rutter M. (eds) *Stress, Coping, and Development in Children*, pp. 43–84. McGraw-Hill, New York.

Ghodsian M., Fogelman K. & Lambert L. (1980) Changes in behaviour ratings in a national sample of children. *British Journal of Social and Clinical Psychology* **19**, 247–256.

Glendinning C. & Millar J. (1988) *Women and Poverty in Britain*. Wheatsheaf, Brighton.

Hackett L., Hackett R. & Taylor D.C. (1991) Psychological disturbance and its associations in the children of the Gujerati community. *Journal of Child Psychology and Psychiatry* **32**, 851–856.

Hayes C.D., Palmer J.L. & Zaslow M.J. (eds) (1990) *Who Cares for America's Children?* National Academy Press, Washington, DC.

Hess R.D. & Camara K.A. (1979) Post-divorce family relationships as mediating factors in the consequences of divorce for children. *Journal of Social Issues* **35**, 79–96.

Hetherington E.M. (1988) Parents, children, and siblings: Six years after divorce. In Hinde R.A. & Stevenson-Hinde J. (eds) *Relationships Within Families: Mutual Influences*, pp. 311–331. Clarendon Press, Oxford.

Hetherington E.M. & Arasteh J.D. (1988) *Impact of Divorce, Single Parenting and Stepparenting on Children*. Lawrence Erlbaum, Hillsdale, New Jersey.

Hetherington E.M., Cox M. & Cox R. (1976) Divorced fathers. *Family Coordinator* **25**, 417–428.

Hetherington E.M., Cox M. & Cox R. (1979) Play and social interaction in children following divorce. *Journal of Social Issues* **35**, 26–49.

Hetherington E.M., Cox M. & Cox R. (1982) Effects of divorce on parents and children. In Lamb M.E. (ed.) *Non-traditional Families: Parenting and Child Development*, pp. 233–288. Lawrence Erlbaum, Hillsdale, New Jersey.

Hinde R.A. (1980) Family influences. In Rutter M. (ed.) *Scientific Foundations of Developmental Psychiatry*, pp. 47–66. Heinemann, London.

Hinde R.A. (1987) *Individuals, Relationships, and Culture: Links between Ethology and the Social Sciences*. Cambridge University Press, Cambridge.

Hinde R.A. & Stevenson-Hinde J. (eds) (1988) *Relationships Within Families: Mutual Influences*. Clarendon Press, Oxford.

Hoffman M.L. (1975) Moral internalization, parental power, and the nature of parent–child interaction. *Developmental Psychology* **11**, 228–239.

Howe N. & Ross H.S. (1990) Socialization, perspective-taking, and the sibling relationship. *Developmental Psychology* **26**, 160–165.

Jenkins J.M. & Smith M.A. (1990) Factors protecting children living in disharmonious homes: Maternal reports. *Journal of the American Academy of Child and Adolescent Psychiatry* **29**, 60–69.

Jenkins J.M., Smith M.A. & Graham P.J. (1989) Coping with parental quarrels. *Journal of the American Academy of Child and Adolescent Psychiatry* **28**, 182–189.

Johnson B.M., Schulman S. & Collins W.A. (1991) Systemic patterns of parenting as reported by adolescents: Developmental differences and implications for psychosocial outcomes. *Journal of Adolescent Research* **6**(2), 235–252.

Kellam S.G., Ensminger M.E. & Turner J. (1977) Family structure and the mental health of children. *Archives of General Psychiatry* **34**, 1012–1022.

Kendler K.S. & Robinette C.D. (1988) Schizophrenia in the National Academy of Sciences — National Research Council Twin Registry: A 16-year update. *American Journal of Psychiatry* **140**, 1551–1563.

Kendrick C. & Dunn J. (1982) Protest or pleasure? The response of firstborn children to interactions between their mothers and infant siblings. *Journal of Child Psychology and Psychiatry* **23**, 117−129.

Koch H.L. (1960) The relation of certain formal attributes of siblings to attitudes held toward each other and toward their parents. *Monographs of the Society for Research in Child Development* **25**(4).

Kramer L. (1990) *Becoming a sibling: With a little help from my friends*. Paper presented at the 7th International Conference on Sibling Studies, Montreal, April.

Ladd G.W. (ed.) (1991) Special issue on family−peer relationships. *Journal of Social and Personal Relationships* **8**, 307−314.

Leete R. (1979) *Changing Patterns of Family Formation and Dissolution in England and Wales 1964−1976*. OPCS/ HMSO, London.

Lewis C. & O'Brien M. (1987) *Reassessing Fatherhood*. Sage, London.

Maccoby E.E. & Martin J.A. (1983) Socialization in the context of the family: Parent−child interaction. In Hetherington E.M. (ed.) *Socialization, Personality, and Social Development*, Vol. 4, *Mussen's Handbook of Child Psychology*, 4th edn, pp. 1−101. Wiley, New York.

McHale S.M., Freitag M.K., Crouter A.C. & Bartko W.T. (1991) Connections between dimensions of marital quality and school-age children's adjustment. *Journal of Applied Developmental Psychology* **12**, 1−17.

McHale S.M. & Gamble W.C. (1989) Sibling relationships and adjustment of children with disabled brothers and sisters. *Developmental Psychology* **25**, 421−429.

McLoyd V.C. (1989) Socialization and development in a changing economy. *American Psychologist* **44**, 293−302.

Martin J. & Roberts C. (1984) *Women and Employment: A Lifetime Perspective*. HMSO, London.

Masten A.S., Garmezy N., Tellegen A., Pellegrini D.S., Larkin K. & Larsen A. (1988) Competence and stress in school children: The moderating effects of individual and family qualities. *Journal of Child Psychology and Psychiatry* **29**, 745−764.

Mechanic D. & Hansell S. (1989) Divorce, family conflict, and adolescents' well-being. *Journal of Health and Social Behavior* **30**, 105−116.

Menaghan E.G. & Parcel T.L. (1991) Transitions in work and family arrangements: Mothers' employment conditions, children's experiences, and child outcomes. In Pillemer K. & McCartney K. (eds) *Parent−Child Relations Throughout Life*, pp. 112−251. Lawrence Erlbaum, Hillsdale, New Jersey.

Minuchin P. (1985) Families and individual development: Provocations from the field of family therapy. *Child Development* **56**, 298−302.

Minuchin P. (1988) Relationships within the family: A systems perspective on development. In Hinde R.A. & Stevenson-Hinde J. (eds) *Relationships Within Families: Mutual Influences*, pp. 7−26. Clarendon Press, Oxford.

Minuchin S. (1974) *Families and Family Therapy*. Harvard University Press, Cambridge, Massachusetts.

Murphy M.J. (1985) Demographic and socioeconomic influences on recent British marital breakdown patterns. *Population Studies* **39**, 441−460.

Newson J. & Newson E. (1978) *Seven Years Old in the Home Environment*. Penguin, Harmondsworth.

Norton A.J. & Moorman J.E. (1987) Current trends in marriage and divorce among American women. *Journal of Marriage and the Family* **49**, 3−14.

Olson D.H. & Lavee Y. (1989) Family systems and family stress: A family life cycle perspective. In Kreppner K. & Lerner R.M. (eds) *Family Systems and Life-span Development*, pp. 165−195. Lawrence Erlbaum, Hillsdale, New Jersey.

Parke R.D. & Ladd G.W. (eds) (1992) *Family-Peer Relationships: Modes of Linkage*. Lawrence Erlbaum, Hillsdale, New Jersey.

Pillemer K. & McCartney K. (1991) *Parent−Child Relations Throughout Life*. Lawrence Erlbaum, Hillsdale, New Jersey.

Plomin R. & Bergeman C.S. (1991) The nature of nurture: Genetic influence on 'environmental' measures. *Behavioral and Brain Sciences* **14**, 373−427.

Plomin R., Chipuer H.M. & Neiderhiser J.M. (1994) Behavioral genetic evidence for the importance of nonshared environment. In Hetherington E.M., Reiss D. & Plomin R. (eds). *Nonshared Environment*, pp. 1−31. Lawrence Erlbaum, Hillsdale, New Jersey.

Plomin R. & Daniels D. (1987) Why are children in the same family so different from one another? *Behavioral and Brain Sciences* **10**, 1−16.

Plomin R., DeFries J.C. & McClearn G.E. (1990) *Behavioral Genetics: A Primer*, 2nd edn. W.H. Freeman, New York.

Plomin R. & Neiderhiser J.M. (1992) Quantitative genetics, molecular genetics, and intelligence. *Intelligence* **15**, 369−387.

Plomin R., Nitz K. & Rowe D.C. (1990) Behavioral genetics and aggressive behavior in childhood. In Lewis M. & Miller S.M. (eds) *Handbook of Developmental Psychopathology*, pp. 119−133. Plenum, New York.

Polit D.F. & Falbo T. (1987) Only children and personality development: A quantitative review. *Journal of Marriage and the Family* **49**, 309−325.

Powers S.I. (1989) Family systems throughout the lifespan: Interactive constellations of development, meaning, and behavior. In Kreppner K. & Lerner R.M. (eds) *Family Systems and Life-span Development*, pp. 271−287. Lawrence Erlbaum, Hillsdale, New Jersey.

Presser H.B. (1988) Shift work and child care among young dual earner American parents. *Journal of Marriage and the Family* **50**, 3−14.

Quinton D. & Rutter M. (1988) *Parenting Breakdown: The Making and Breaking of Intergenerational Links*. Avebury, Aldershot.

Richards M.P.M. (1987) Children, parents, and families: Developmental psychology and the re-ordering of relationships at divorce. *International Journal of Law and the Family* **1**, 295–317.

Richards M.P.M. (1991) *Children and parents after divorce*. Paper presented at the Seventh World Conference of the International Society on Family law, Opatija, Yugoslavia.

Rodger J.L. (1984) Confluence effects: Not here, not now! *Developmental Psychology* **20**, 321–331.

Rogoff B. (1990) *Apprenticeship in Thinking: Cognitive Development in Social Context*. Oxford University Press, Oxford.

Rutter M. (1971) Parent–child separation: Psychological effects on the children. *Journal of Child Psychology and Psychiatry* **12**, 233–260.

Rutter M. (1985a) Family and school influences on behavioral development. *Journal of Child Psychology and Psychiatry* **26**, 349–368.

Rutter M. (1985b) Family and school influences on cognitive development. *Journal of Child Psychology and Psychiatry* **26**, 683–704.

Rutter M. (1988) Functions and consequences of relationships: Some psychopathological considerations. In Hinde R.A. & Stevenson-Hinde J. (eds) *Relationships Within Families: Mutual Influences*, pp. 332–353. Clarendon Press, Oxford.

Rutter M. (1990) Psychosocial resilience and protective mechanisms. In Rolf J., Masten A.S., Cichetti D., Nuechterlein K.H. & Weintraub S. (eds) *Risk and Protective Factors in the Development of Psychopathology*, pp. 181–214. Cambridge University Press, Cambridge.

Rutter M. & Redshaw J. (1991) Growing up as a twin: Twin–singleton differences in psychological development. *Journal of Child Psychology and Psychiatry* **32**, 885–895.

Rutter M., Tizard J. & Whitmore K. (1970) *Education, Health and Behaviour*. Longman, London.

Rutter M., Yule B., Quinton D., Rowlands O., Yule W. & Berger M. (1975) Attainment and adjustment in two geographical areas. *British Journal of Psychiatry* **126**, 520–533.

Santrock J., Warshak R., Lindberg C. & Meadows L. (1982) Children and parents' observed social behavior in stepfather families. *Child Development* **53**, 472–480.

Scarr S. & Grajek S. (1982) Similarities and differences among siblings. In Lamb M.E. & Sutton-Smith B. (eds) *Sibling Relationships: Their Nature and Significance Across the Lifespan*, pp. 357–381. Lawrence Erlbaum, Hillsdale, New Jersey.

Scholnick E.K. & Wing C.S. (1991) Speaking deductively: Preschoolers' use of *if* in conversation and in conditional inference. *Developmental Psychology* **27**, 249–258.

Schwarz J.C., Barton-Henry M.L. & Prnizsky T. (1985) Assessing child-rearing behaviors: A comparison of ratings made by mother, father, child and sibling on the CRPBI. *Child Development* **56**, 462–479.

Seitz V., Rosenbaum L.K. & Apfel N.H. (1985) Effects of family support intervention: A ten year follow up. *Child Development* **56**, 376–391.

Seltzer J.A. (1991) Relationship between fathers and children who live apart: The father's role after separation. *Journal of Marriage and the Family* **53**, 79–102.

Shelton B.A. (1987) Variations in divorce rates by community size: A test of the social integration explanation. *Journal of Marriage and the Family* **49**, 827–832.

Silbereisen R.K., Walper S. & Albrecht H.T. (1990) Family income loss and economic hardship: Antecedents of adolescents' problem behavior. In McLoyd V.C. & Flanagan C.A. (eds) *Economic Stress: Effects on Family Life and Child Development*, pp. 27–47. Jossey-Bass, San Francisco.

Stocker C.M. & Dunn J. (1990) Sibling relationships in childhood: Links with friendships and peer relationships. *British Journal of Developmental Psychology* **8**, 227–244.

Stocker C.M., Dunn J. & Plomin R. (1989) Sibling relationships: Links with child temperament, maternal behavior, and family structure. *Child Development* **60**, 715–727.

Stocker C.M. & McHale S.M. (1992) The nature and family correlates of preadolescents' perceptions of their sibling relationships. *Journal of Social and Personal Relationships* **9**, 179–195.

Targ D. & Perrucci C. (1990) Plant closings, unemployment, and families. *Marriage and Family Review* **15**, 131–145.

Teti D.M. & Ablard K.E. (1989) Security of attachment and infant–sibling relationships: A laboratory study. *Child Development* **60**, 1519–1528.

Thorpe K., Golding J., MacGillivray I. & Greenwood R. (1991) Depression in mothers of twins. *British Medical Journal* **302**, 875–878.

Tinsley B.R. & Parke R.D. (1984) Grandparents and support and socialization agents. In Lewis M. (ed.) *Beyond the Dyad*, pp. 161–194. Plenum, New York.

Treffers P.D.A., Goedhart A.W., Waltz J.W. & Kouldijs E. (1990) The systematic collection of patient data in a center for child and adolescent psychiatry. *British Journal of Psychiatry* **157**, 744–748.

Vaughn B., Block J.H. & Block J. (1988) Parental agreement on child rearing during early childhood and the psychological characteristics of adolescents. *Child Development* **59**, 1020–1033.

Voydanoff P. (1990) Economic distress and family relations: A review of the eighties. *Journal of Marriage and the Family* **52**, 1099–1115.

Vygotsky L.S. (1978) *Mind in Society: The Development of Higher Psychological Processes*. Harvard University Press, Cambridge, Massachusetts.

Wachs T.D. (1992) *The Nature of Nurture*. Sage, Newbury Park, California.

Wachs T.D. & Gruen G.E. (1982) *Early Experience and Human Development*. Plenum, New York.

Wallerstein J.S. (1985) Children of divorce — emerging

trends. *Psychiatric Clinics of North America* **8**, 837–855.

Wallerstein J.S. (1991) The long-term effects of divorce on children: A review. *Journal of American Academy of Child and Adolescent Psychiatry* **30**, 349–360.

Wallerstein J.S. & Kelly J.B. (1980) *Surviving the Break Up: How Children and Parents Cope with Divorce.* Basic Books, New York.

Ward M.J., Vaughn B.E. & Robb M.D. (1988) Social-emotional adaptation and infant–mother attachment in siblings: Role of the mother in cross-sibling consistency. *Child Development* **69**, 643–651.

Watzlawick P. (1984) *The Invented Reality.* Norton, New York.

White L.K. (1990) Determinants of divorce: A review of research in the eighties. *Journal of Marriage and the Family* **52**, 904–912.

Widlak P.A. & Perrucci C.C. (1988) Family configuration, family interaction, and intellectual attainment. *Journal of Marriage and the Family* **50**, 33–44.

Zajonc R.B., Markus H. & Markus G.B. (1979) The birth order puzzle. *Journal of Personality and Social Psychology* **37**, 1325–1341.

Zaslow M.J. (1987) *Sex differences in children's response to parental divorce.* Paper presented at the Symposium on Sex Differences in Children's Response to Psychosocial stress, Woods Hole, Massachusetts.

Zill N. (1988) Behavior, achievement and health problems among children in stepfamilies: Findings from a national survey of child health. In Hetherington E.M. & Arasteh J.D. (eds) *Impact of Divorce, Single Parenting, and Stepparenting on Children*, pp. 325–368. Lawrence Erlbaum, Hillsdale, New Jersey.

Zill N. (1991) US children and their families: Current conditions and recent trends, 1989. Summary of the report of the Select Committee on Child, Youth and Families, US House of Representatives. *Society for Research in Child Development Newsletter*, Winter 1991.

6: School Influences

BARBARA MAUGHAN

INTRODUCTION

Next to the family, the school is the major agent of socialization for children in most societies; much of a child's time is spent in school, and many public hopes and concerns centre on its effects. We expect schools to foster children's cognitive growth, but also to contribute in shaping many other aspects of their development — attitudes and values, social and emotional maturity, views of self and relationships with others. For the child, entering school means entering a new social world, with its own particular demands and expectations. For some, that world will be stimulating and self-enhancing, meshing easily with the values of their homes, and providing expanded opportunities to develop skills and competencies. For others, the fit between home and school, or between the child's capacities and the demands of schooling, will be less close. And for a small group, school life will form the backdrop for more serious difficulties, compounding existing vulnerabilities, or perhaps contributing to new ones.

School constitutes one of the major contexts of childhood, and its potential to affect development has long been recognized. Bronfenbrenner and Crouter (1983), tracing the evolution of environmental models in developmental research, found that the first study meeting their criteria — published in 1870 — was one demonstrating the benefits of attending kindergarten. But much the greater volume of developmental research, and the more sophisticated models of environmental influences, have of course centred on the family. Despite the massive array of research on schooling, surprisingly little has taken a specifically developmental focus. Entwisle and Stevenson (1987), introducing a special issue of *Child Development* devoted to school influences, confirmed this view: '... curiously,

research on schools and on development has evolved along separate paths in such a way as to ignore natural overlaps' (p. 1149). At times, these divergences have been wider, with serious claims that schooling exerted little independent influence on development even in the cognitive domain (e.g. Jencks *et al.*, 1972), and that home and family were by far the more important determinants of attainments and later life-chances. More recently, evidence from many different sources has modified that view: although family influences are indeed likely to be more powerful overall, school experiences clearly play a moderating role in many aspects of development, and may be especially significant for some. For developmentalist and clinician alike, any comprehensive account of the forces shaping children's progress must include the school.

VARIETIES OF SCHOOL EXPERIENCE

Like all other aspects of children's experience, schooling takes many forms. The pattern of children's lives at school varies widely in different cultures and communities, reflecting not only differing educational philosophies, but also wider social and political values. Schools and school systems differ markedly, for example, in their approaches to ability grouping, in emphases on cooperation or competition, behavioural expectations, and their focus on academic or more widely defined concerns. Within any system, the pattern of school life then changes systematically with age, expanding in scope and complexity as children develop. The protected world of the nursery, centring on relationships with one teacher and a small group of peers, gives way to increasingly more differential activities and relationships as time goes on. The child's social field expands to take in first the classroom as a social unit, and later the school as a whole. Alongside teachers, peers grow in salience as sources of friendships, status and social comparisons. And at each stage, the demands and challenges of schooling intersect with children's own developing capacities, and the stresses and supports in their lives outside, to form particular configurations of effects.

Research on schooling mirrors these changing concerns, emphasizing different developmental outcomes at each stage of children's school careers. Different theoretical perspectives then highlight the many facets of the school experience that might go to affect development. At the most detailed level of analysis, ethnographers and others have described the distinctive features of classroom interaction, and the characteristic activities, styles of behaviour and modes of discourse that are the hallmarks of classroom life (Weinstein, 1991). Schooling makes quite particular demands on children, and offers them relationships, activities and expectations that differ sometimes quite markedly from those they experience at home. Ecological psychologists point to the importance of the physical environment, and its effects in shaping and organizing behaviour. Variations in school and class size, contrasts between open and more traditional classrooms, and even differences in classroom seating patterns, have all been found to affect children's behaviour and learning (Gump, 1987). At yet another level of analysis, sociologists have assessed the implications of schooling for later life-chances, and examined the impact of the many organizational variants in school life — streaming or tracking by ability, integration or segregation of social and ethnic groups, instruction in coeducational or single-sex settings. Sociologists and social psychologists alike have studied the social 'climate' that develops in schools, shaped by and shaping the behaviour of individual participants (Moos, 1980). And educationalists have studied the instructional components of schooling — curriculum content, teaching styles and classroom management techniques.

Against this varied background, this chapter must inevitably be selective. Excellent recent reviews and commentaries cover developments in a number of specific areas: associations between children's progress and measures of many different aspects of classroom life, including perceived classroom climate (Fraser, 1989b; MacAulay, 1990), the social context of the classroom (Weinstein, 1991), teacher strategies for managing and organizing classes (Doyle, 1986), instructional styles (Brophy & Good, 1986), class size (Kulik & Kulik, 1989), and the physical layout of the classroom (Gump, 1987). Rutter (1983), Purkey and Smith (1983), Reynolds (1992) and Mortimore (in press) all provided syntheses of findings at the school level. Minuchin and Shapiro (1983) focused specifically on school effects on social development, and Howlin (1994) discussed special educational provision.

This chapter concentrates on selected topics, chosen to highlight issues of particular developmental and clinical concern, and to illustrate something of the range of current research on schooling. It begins with some general questions: what exactly is meant by school influences; how have investigators attempted to test them; and are the effects simply unidirectional, or do children also have an impact on their teachers and schools? It then turns to look at examples of school influences in three particular domains of children's functioning: (i) cognitive development; (ii) self-esteem; and (iii) the role that school experiences may play in the genesis of behavioural and emotional problems. In each of these areas, schooling is just one of the influences shaping children's growth, and its impact will cumulate over time. Besides these ongoing processes, school life also poses some more particular demands and challenges. Among them, the key transition points in children's school careers — starting and changing schools and, in the teens, moving from the world of the classroom to the world of work — are attracting increasing attention. In the light of the more general interest in life events in children's development (Goodyer, 1990), later sections explore the impact of these specifically school-based, normative 'transitions'. Finally, the discussion turns to the longer term effects of schooling, and how far influences may extend beyond the years of formal education.

ASSESSING SCHOOL INFLUENCES: SOME CONCEPTUAL AND METHODOLOGICAL ISSUES

Models of school effects, and ways to test them

One of the main problems in isolating the effects of schooling is, as Entwisle and Alexander (1992) have succinctly put it, that children live at home and go to school at the same time. By the time they start school, children's abilities and aptitudes vary widely, shaped by both biological and social factors. Throughout childhood, these individual differences almost certainly play a larger part in explaining variations in cognitive and other skills than do experiences at school. The last 20 years have seen major debates in the research and policy literature on how far schooling does in fact exert independent effects on development, or whether it serves primarily to reinforce and reproduce pre-existing variations.

These debates have arisen most often in studies of cognitive development, and reflect differing conceptions of the effects that schooling — or indeed any other environmental influence — might show on development. Two models in particular emerge in the literature. One stems most clearly from studies of the persisting links between educational and social disadvantage (Mortimore & Blackstone, 1982). Individual differences in attainment continue to be one of the most potent predictors of social position, and so of social inequality (e.g. Douglas *et al.*, 1968; Fogelman *et al.*, 1978). For many years, educationalists and policy-makers alike looked to schooling as a central tool in reducing those inequalities. During the 1960s and 1970s, liberal optimism on these issues seemed quashed: the Head Start programmes in the USA, designed to promote IQ gains in socially disadvantaged groups, seemed only to have short-term effects, and large-scale surveys suggested that family and social background were by far the most important determinants of achievement on a wider scale. To many commentators, schooling had been tested, and found wanting: 'schools appear to have little effect on any measurable attribute of those who attend them . . . equalizing the quality of high schools would reduce cognitive inequality by one per cent or less' (Jencks

et al., 1972). As we shall see, although there are some recent challenges to this conclusion, it has in general withstood the test of time. Schooling does little to reduce individual differences in achievement, and we should not, except perhaps at the margins, expect that it can 'compensate' for society.

But there are, of course, other possible models of school effects. Many educationalists in particular would conceive of their task in quite a different light: not to reduce individual differences, but to maximize the varying potentials of all the children in their care. On this view, individual differences in abilities, aptitudes and temperament are accepted as given, and schooling, like other environmental influences, seen as a force that might raise (or lower) levels of functioning across the board. Schools and teachers, like families, will vary in the ways they approach these tasks, and the success with which they achieve them. Some aspects of the school experience, like some aspects of experiences in families, may act as stressors for children, while others may act to protect them. From this perspective, the aim is to trace how schooling may add to, complement, or interact with other influences from children's everyday lives outside. It is these possibilities for school influences — often discussed in the educational literature in terms of the 'value added' by schooling — that will primarily concern us here.

Methodologically, particular approaches are needed to test for effects of this kind. Controlled experiments would be the ideal solution, with children randomly allocated to different types of school experience. These are of course rarely possible during the years of compulsory schooling, though there have been important experiments in the preschool years, and some more limited interventions at later points. In the main, the literature on schooling depends on 'quasi-experiments' (Cook & Campbell, 1979; Rutter, 1994), that capitalize on naturally occurring variations in children's school experiences to highlight effects. In the social sciences, natural experiments of this kind are often crucial in testing the effects of experiential and environmental factors. They depend on investigators pinpointing telling contrasts in individuals' existing experiences, and taking these as their experimental paradigms. As we shall see throughout this chapter, many studies of schooling have been highly imaginative in this respect. In many instances it would be hard to find more elegant contrasts than those already part of the fabric of children's experience. If we want, for example, to isolate the short-term effects of schooling on some particular aspect of development, how better to do it than to study children during term time, when they are in school, then look at the same groups in the long school holidays? If we want to assess the outcomes of different curricula, different teaching styles or different approaches to ability grouping, existing examples of all the variants we need will usually be close at hand. In some instances individuals act as their own controls in contrasts of this kind, and in others they will be 'allocated' to different school experiences in ways that are in effect random. Where this is not the case, relevant aspects of children's backgrounds need to be taken into account by matching, statistical controls or by the use of longitudinal data (Maughan, 1988). These are not simple requirements, but they are critical to a proper estimation of school effects. Studies of intact groups, such as schools or classrooms, also raise other, more complex, methodological problems. Early studies were unable to deal with these explicitly, but important statistical advances, applied to educational data in the last 10 years or so, allow for more appropriate modelling of the nested, 'multilevel' structure of child, class and school level effects (Raudenbush & Bryk, 1986; Goldstein, 1987; Cheung *et al.*, 1990). Comparative studies of 'school effectiveness' have become much more sophisticated in all these methodological areas in recent years.

Reciprocal influences

One final general point concerns reciprocal influences. This chapter focuses primarily on school influences on children. In studies of families, however, reciprocal effects are now widely recognized as important. Children influence parents — and so in some senses act to create their own family environments — quite as much as parents influence children (see Chapter 4). In the literature on schooling, reciprocal effects of this kind have been less widely studied, but equally certainly exist. Just as children form a critical part of the family constellation, affecting the relationships between other family members, so too they constitute an import-

ant dimension of the schools they attend, affecting both teachers and peers alike.

Peer influences are central channels for school effects in a number of arenas, and figure prominently throughout this chapter. Equally clearly, children have an impact on their teachers. We know that teachers value particular temperamental characteristics in pupils (Lerner *et al.*, 1985), and most interact more with those they perceive as having positive temperamental profiles (Keogh & Burstein, 1988). They also quickly develop expectations of children's abilities, and these in turn have modest but still educationally significant effects on subsequent attainment (Brophy, 1983). In part, these effects seem to reflect differential treatment. Teachers respond in particular ways to children for whom they hold high expectations: they pay them more attention, teach them more, with more difficult material, and give them more opportunities to perform (Jussim, 1986; Blatchford *et al.*, 1989). They also give them clearer and more favourable feedback in the classroom, and offer them more emotional support. Over time, a complex interplay of processes can be detected here, children's characteristics affecting teacher expectations, and these in turn affecting many of the teacher behaviours that seem central in promoting both intellectual performance and positive self-evaluations.

Child characteristics also affect teachers' approaches to behaviour management. Eder (1982), for example, has described how interruptions were much more quickly reprimanded in high-ability than low-ability groups, so that cumulatively, over the course of a year, the classroom atmosphere became increasingly more disrupted in lower ability classes. At a much wider level of analysis, Ouston and Maughan (1991) have characterized staff in some schools with high levels of truancy or disruptive behaviour as showing the institutional equivalent of learned helplessness, retreating from active attempts to manage difficult situations when problems extended beyond a critical level. These examples could easily be multiplied. Although this chapter focuses on school effects on children, these are just one strand in a much more complex nexus of transactional effects. As we turn to consider school influences in particular domains of children's development, these more subtle possibilities for reciprocal influence need to be borne in mind throughout.

COGNITIVE DEVELOPMENT

School effects on IQ and general intellectual skills

Enhancing children's cognitive development is clearly one of the central aims of schooling. Most research in this area has centred on subject-based attainments, but there is also important evidence that schooling has an impact on more general intellectual skills. Variations in the amounts of schooling that children receive, and indeed whether they attend school at all, both have clear effects on cognitive development. Reviews of the range of studies in this vein (Rutter & Madge, 1976; Ceci, 1991) suggest quite substantial effects of school attendance on performance on standard IQ tests, amounting to a decrement of between 0.25 and 6 IQ points for each year of schooling missed.

Particular types of investigation highlight more detailed aspects of this picture. Cross-cultural studies, for example, suggest that 'schooled' children, in cultures where schooling is not generally available, show clear advantages in particular cognitive domains (Rogoff, 1981). Schooling appears to benefit modes of thinking, categorizing and remembering that are relatively disembedded from personal experience. It stresses analytic approaches, and methods of reasoning and learning separated out from practical applications, where information is considered on its own grounds (Rogoff, 1991). Studies of US and European children who have received very limited schooling because of isolated living environments, extended school closures, and for other reasons, point in a similar direction.

These findings are illuminating, but they are of course vulnerable to selection effects: children who receive different amounts of schooling in these rather unusual circumstances may also differ in other important ways. If similar effects emerged for children in the same school system, this would be a more powerful test. As it happens, school enrolment policies provide an ideal natural experiment of just this kind. Because children are usually placed in age groups by birth date, the youngest and oldest children in adjacent grades differ by only days in chronological age, but by 1 full year's exposure to schooling. In one large-scale study, Cahan and Cohen (1989) found clear differences between grade levels: on 10 out of 12 tests, 1 year of schooling equalled or exceeded the effect of 1 year of chronological age. School effects were most marked on tests tapping more crystallized skills (vocabulary sentence completion, and so forth), but were also apparent on what are assumed to be more fluid aspects of intelligence.

Finally, controlled evaluations of some Head Start and other preschool programmes have confirmed that quite wide-ranging benefits accrue, in the short term at least, from providing disadvantaged children with early 'compensatory' education (Zigler & Valentine, 1979; McKey *et al.*, 1985; Lee *et al.*, 1988). Reviewing studies published up to the early 1980s, Clarke-Stewart and Fein (1983) found that many showed differences in the order of 10 IQ points between programme children and controls. Programme children were advanced in both verbal and non-verbal skills; on tests of arithmetic or knowledge of the physical world, that reflect direct teaching, but also on measures such as digit span and perspective-taking, much less likely to do so; and in skills such as eye—hand coordination, that might be enhanced by exposure to materials, as well as those more obviously derived from interaction with adults and peers. In the severely disadvantaged groups included in these studies, control children often showed a decline in scores over the preschool period. This decline was clearly halted for programme participants, and in some instances they appeared to have made real gains in scores.

In part, all these findings almost certainly reflect an element of 'test-wiseness' on the part of longer schooled children, and the acquisition of specific knowledge that is useful in taking IQ tests. But that seems unlikely to be the whole explanation. Instead, exposure to formal education seems to have some direct effects on particular modes of cognizing. How do they come about? Does schooling offer qualitatively different experiences from those available at home, or does its impact rest on providing more of the same sorts of good experiences available to children outside?

As yet, we only have tentative answers to these questions. On balance, however, commentators on both the cross-cultural and early childhood findings argue for some qualitative differences between home and school. Clarke-Stewart and Fein (1983) discussed many possibilities here, but highlighted in particular the different interactional styles of teachers and mothers in the early childhood years. Observations of the same young children at home and at school suggest that verbal interactions with mothers and nursery teachers can be equally cognitively demanding — and indeed that children often respond in much more elaborated ways at home — but that home and school conversations do often have a somewhat different focus (Tizard *et al.*, 1982). Teachers' questions tend to be more oriented towards explanations and classifications of activities or materials, while mothers' questions focus more strongly on understanding people and their behaviour. Talk at home tends to be more inductive; talk with adults at school, though often apparently less interesting to children, may nevertheless be of a more deductive kind that would equip them to do well on standardized tests of intelligence.

These differences seem likely to be amplified as time goes on. Although 'higher order' questions, encouraging children to think in more abstract ways, only ever account for a small proportion of teacher–child interactions in the classroom, they nevertheless increase in higher grades. Specific teaching on memory and other strategies again probably only occupies very limited amounts of classroom time, but may nevertheless be sensitively targeted by teachers, and phased to mesh with children's developing capacities and needs (Moely *et al.*, 1992). Other aspects of direct instruction may also be important. Many children, for example, first meet certain classes of constructs, such as hypotheticals, at school, and are exposed there to a formal, descriptive and disembedded form of language less likely to be used at home. And the full pattern of school life of course includes much more than direct instruction alone. Schooling also places particular value on behaviours and attitudes that support learning: attending to others, monitoring one's own performance, and focusing on learning and remembering as ends in themselves. These non-cognitive emphases, reinforced across a range of school activities, may play a critical role in mediating effects (Ceci, 1991).

Findings from the cross-cultural literature point in a similar direction. Schools confront children with activity settings that are different in both their cognitive and behavioural demands from those that they meet in the rest of their everyday lives (Laboratory of Comparative Human Cognition, 1986). In the language of these investigators, schooling represents a particular form of cultural practice, involving a recurrent, goal-directed sequence of activities that leads eventually, through cumulated experience, to particular types of expertise (Scribner & Cole, 1981). It may be this coherence in the focus of the school experience, quite as much as specific aspects of teaching, that contributes to its rather particular effects.

School effects on attainment

These suggestions are fleshed out in investigations of subject-based attainments. Studies of 'summer learning' — or, as it has perhaps more appropriately been termed, 'summer setback' (Entwisle & Alexander, 1992) — have consistently found that children make slower progress during the long school holidays than in term time (Heyns, 1978, 1987). Summer skill declines are especially marked in particular areas. Vocabulary and language seem relatively unaffected, but progress falls off more strongly in areas requiring specific factual information, or, like spelling and mathematics, depending on repeated practice. In addition, summer setbacks are greatest in socially disadvantaged groups. Indeed, one recent US study has shown that poor African-American and white children made comparable mathematics progress with their more advantaged peers during term time in the early grades, but systematically lost ground each summer (Entwisle & Alexander, 1992). If replicated, these findings are of major significance. As the authors argued, annual assessments of children's progress inevitably conflate school and 'summer' learning, and may well disguise the real extent of school effects. At least in the early grades, schools may do more to equalize opportunity than had been appreciated: 'Contrary to the idea that "schools make no difference" ... our data indicate that schools are most beneficial for those that need them most' (Entwisle & Alexander, 1992, p. 83).

Studies of the impact of different curricula, teaching styles and school characteristics add to this picture, showing consistent differences in 'effectiveness' between teachers, schools and school systems. In all cases the size of the effects has been modest, but still non-trivial. Precise estimates inevitably vary: taking differences between schools as an example, school effects have been found to account for between 5 and 10% of variance in attainments at the secondary level (Gray *et al.*, 1990), and up to 20% or more among younger children (Mortimore *et al.*, 1988). Initial attainments and home background account for the majority of the explained variance in measures taken at any particular point in time. When the focus is on *progress* in particular subject areas, school effects are often stronger than home background influences (Mortimore *et al.*, 1988).

There are a number of important provisos to bear in mind here. First, many 'school effects' studies have found marked outliers: most ordinary schools probably do not vary greatly in their impact, but some clearly are outstandingly successful, and others correspondingly poor. Second, the range of differences documented to date inevitably reflects the historical and social conditions when the studies were undertaken — in this case, the US, UK and continental European educational systems of the late 1960s to the 1980s. The moves towards more decentralized control of education now taking place in many Western societies, together with other developments in educational policies, may well increase the importance of school-related effects in future decades (Reynolds & Packer, 1992). And finally, if we are mainly concerned with *levels* of attainment rather than proportions of individual variance explained, we need to examine the findings in a rather different way. From this perspective, the central question is how children with similar background characteristics might fare in different school settings. Purkey and Smith (1983) concluded that, on average, the attainments of similar children attending schools in the top and bottom 20% of the effectiveness range could be expected to differ by two-thirds of a standard deviation — approximately one grade level in the US context. Gray *et al.* (1990), using English data, and focusing on the interquartile range of school scores, estimated differences of approaching one O level equivalent pass — a grade achieved by perhaps the most able 20% of children in the UK. Though modest, such

variations are by no means negligible, and might be of considerable importance for the future life-chances of individual pupils.

Many of the more detailed questions these findings provoke are still being clarified. Most studies, for example, have suggested that 'effective' schools are of equal benefit to boys and girls, children from different social class or ethnic backgrounds, and those of differing abilities (Rutter *et al.*, 1979; Mortimore *et al.*, 1988; Smith & Tomlinson, 1989). Some recent findings have however challenged that view (Nuttall *et al.*, 1989), and pointed to possible interactions between school and pupil characteristics. There have been debates on the stability of school differences from year to year (Bosker & Scheerens, 1989), and it is still difficult to answer quite basic questions such as the relative importance of school effects for children of different ages. To date, the findings suggest that younger children may be more sensitive to school influences in the cognitive domain, but we need much more evidence to be certain of this.

School and classroom effects

Comparative studies of this kind have been undertaken at many different 'levels' of educational provision, from international comparisons of children's progress in widely differing educational systems (Husen, 1967; Stevenson & Lee, 1990) to the large literature on teacher effectiveness in individual classrooms. We thus have evidence for teacher effects, school effects and broader school system variations. For both practical and theoretical reasons, it is important to know at which 'level' the most potent influences lie: are effective schools simply the sum of effective teachers, or do significant influences emanate from the institutional level as well? Answers to these questions might begin to point to processes of influence for the child, as well as guiding efforts to improve schools.

Investigators have only recently begun to address these questions empirically. Scheerens *et al.*, (1989), using data from the Second International Mathematics Study, found interesting cross-national differences. In some countries, variations in maths achievement were almost entirely accounted for at the classroom level, while in others — including the USA and Scotland (English data were not included in the data set) — relatively large classroom effects were combined with moderate school-level differences. Results from the Inner London Education Authority (ILEA) Junior School Study (Mortimore *et al.*, 1988) suggest that English findings might fall in this second category. Although classroom factors accounted for the majority of the schooling effects in maths and English progress, some school-level variation also entered into the equation. It seems that we need to look to both institutional and classroom factors to understand 'school' effects.

Three main types of factors have been examined here: (i) relatively 'given' features of schools and classrooms, such as size, physical plant, resource levels and administrative status; (ii) more 'controllable' factors, in the shape of school and teacher policy and practice; and (iii) effects that might stem more directly from the composition of the peer group. The well-developed tradition of research on teacher effectiveness offers a quite coherent pattern of findings at the classroom level (Brophy & Good, 1986), while studies of schools are still in many ways at a more exploratory stage. Even so, some fairly consistent conclusions have emerged.

Summarizing very briefly, it seems the quality and quantity of instruction, along with psychosocial aspects of the school and classroom environment, are in general more important for attainment than resource factors *per se*. Once again, we must enter an historical caveat here: much of the existing school differences work has been undertaken while schools were quite generously resourced, and conclusions might well differ under different economic conditions.

Focusing first on instructional techniques, a range of findings suggest that children learn most efficiently when teachers first structure new information, relating it to what is already known, then provide feedback on their performance on the new materials (Brophy & Good, 1986). Higher order questioning, and a judicious focus on specific modes of learning and remembering, are also associated with increased gains. In addition, one of the strongest and most consistent predictors of children's achievement is 'academically engaged time': effective teachers take an active instructional role, pace their curriculum coverage briskly, and engage their pupils for the maximum feasible time in direct, learning-related activities (Brophy & Good, 1986).

Instructional techniques are not, however, the only important features. The ways that teachers manage children's behaviour in the classroom, and the more general 'tenor' of classroom life, also show consistent links with patterns of attainment (Doyle, 1986). Creating an atmosphere conducive to learning, and engendering attitudes, motivations and behaviours that support it, seem critical elements in effective teaching (Fraser, 1989b; MacAulay, 1990). Effective teachers organize their classes so that activities run smoothly, transitions are brief and orderly, and rules and procedures are established in advance, pre-empting disruptions as far as possible. Many of these 'non-cognitive' aspects of classroom life seem as important for attainment as those more immediately associated with instruction alone.

Findings at the school level show many parallels here (for reviews see Purkey & Smith, 1983; Rutter, 1983; Reynolds, 1992). In general, academically effective schools have been characterized by purposeful leadership; an emphasis on the quality of instruction; a pleasant but orderly and work-oriented environment; effective classroom management; stimulating teaching; appropriate levels of praise and reinforcement; and, for older children in particular, opportunities for them to be involved in, and take responsibility for, their lives at school. Rutter *et al.* (1979) argued that these different elements combined together to create an overall school ethos, a psychosocial environment more or less conducive to learning, and characteristic of the school as a whole.

The third set of factors associated with differential effectiveness also seem to have their roots in social and group processes. Rutter *et al.* (1979) found that the balance in the composition of a school's intake — the proportions of more and less able pupils, or those from socially disadvantaged backgrounds, for example — showed cumulative links with children's outcomes, over and above those attributable to individual background factors. In this inner-city study, ability composition seemed most important: both behavioural and academic outcomes were depressed in schools with large proportions of less able pupils, and more positive for those with more balanced intakes. A number of other studies have reported similar effects (Willms,

1985), though not all reports have been consistent (Gray *et al.*, 1990).

These findings seem likely to reflect peer processes, with differing peer cultures, more and less supportive of school values, developing in schools with different intake patterns. The development of antischool subcultures has been well-documented in the sociological literature for many years (Hargreaves, 1967), and shown to have cumulatively negative effects. Large proportions of less able pupils, less likely to gain success or satisfaction in school-related activities, may contribute to a culture that amplifies individual lack of involvement in schooling. In a rather different way, intake balance may more directly affect styles of teaching and behaviour management in different schools. Comparisons between academically selective and non-selective schools (Maughan & Rutter, 1987), for example, have suggested that particular styles of teaching and curriculum coverage may be feasible with relatively homogeneous pupil groups, but difficult if not impossible to implement in other contexts.

These findings bring us back to the question of reciprocal effects of children on their schools. School and classroom climate are clearly important influences on patterns of attainment. To an extent, however, they reflect pupil characteristics. Are these the most important determining factors? A range of evidence suggests that, although they contribute, they are only one of the elements mediating effects. Maughan *et al.* (1980), for example, found that measures of school environment showed much stronger links with children's later outcomes than with their characteristics at intake. In a rather different way, more effective schools are often marked by particular organizational characteristics — consistency and consensus among staff, teacher involvement in decision-making, and some degree of parental involvement — that are relatively unlikely to be affected by pupil intakes. Perhaps most important, longitudinal and intervention studies are beginning to demonstrate that children's outcomes can be improved in response to planned changes in school policy and practice. Especially in North America, findings from school effectiveness research have been translated into many programmes of planned change in schools. To date, much of this work has been concerned with the important question of how best to bring about change in the complex organizational climate of the school (Louis & Miles, 1990; Mortimore, in press). Some positive results on pupil outcomes have, however, already been documented (Hawkins & Lishner, 1987; Lezotte, 1989). Although it is difficult to achieve, change at the organizational level clearly can have implications for pupils' progress.

Case studies of naturalistic change point in a similar direction. Maughan *et al.* (1990) and Ouston and Maughan (1991) studied the effects of the appointment of new headteachers in inner-city schools facing severe difficulties. Over a 5-year period, there were marked gains in both academic attainments and pupil attendance at some schools, even though intakes remained largely unchanged. Retrospective accounts from staff suggested that these improvements reflected the phased introduction of many of the characteristics identified in the earlier literature: purposeful leadership, clear expectations for teachers and pupils alike, an atmosphere that was both pleasant and constructive, and active involvement at both staff and student levels.

Drawing together these various findings, it seems that schooling complements and expands the learning opportunities open to children in their homes and families, adding dimensions that may be especially critical for some. Schools and teachers differ in the success with which they promote children's attainments. Academically effective schools place a strong emphasis not only on teaching and learning, but also on the organizational and social processes that support it. This picture sorts well with what we know about learning at the individual level. Walberg (1986), Fraser *et al.* (1987) and Fraser (1989a) in meta-analyses of the vast literature on children's learning, highlight the importance of supportive attitudes, behaviours and motivations, as well as exposure to effective teaching. Fostering a commitment to education, and providing children with the skills they need to progress in particular areas, are crucial accompaniments to direct instruction for many pupils.

This chapter turns now to evidence of school effects on one central element in this motivational complex: children's perceptions of themselves as learners, their self-evaluations and self-esteem.

SELF-ESTEEM

William James's (1890) famous formula

self-esteem = success/pretensions

highlights the interplay between affect and performance which, despite numerous definitional problems, lies at the heart of most concepts of self-esteem. In the academic sphere, it was assumed for many years that the 'causal order' of the links ran from self-esteem to achievement: in part at least, under-achievement resulted from low self-esteem. One main impetus for the desegregation movement of the 1960s was based on this reasoning. Desegregating schools would enhance the self-perceptions of minority children, and this in turn would act to raise their achievement levels (e.g. Coleman *et al.*, 1966). Many affective curricula, and other programmes designed to improve children's self-views, stem from a similar rationale.

More recent findings have modified that view in a number of ways. First, we now know that there are important developmental changes in how children perceive and evaluate their performance in a range of arenas (Harter, 1983). For young children, self-descriptions, like their descriptions of others, are largely expressed in terms of specific attributes and behaviours. Their awareness of regularities in behaviour, linked to more abstract concepts such as traits, only begins to emerge at the age of seven or eight. This is also the stage when the ability to use social comparisons begins to develop (Ruble, 1983). Before this, children's self-perceptions are largely self-comparative, and often 'inaccurate' when compared with more objective measures of performance. One study of London 7 year olds, for example, found that most children rated themselves 'better than' others in maths and reading at this stage (Tizard *et al.*, 1988).

From about 8 onwards, academic self-perceptions show growing links with external referents. A follow-up of the London children showed generally much more 'accurate' self-ratings by age 11 (Blatchford, 1992), and US data have documented increasing correlations between perceived academic competence and attainments between grades 3 and 6 (Harter, 1982). These and other studies have also shown that self-esteem is not a unitary concept (Harter, 1983). From the age of about 8 or 9,

children make clear distinctions between perceptions of their academic, physical and social competence, as well as having a more global sense of self-worth. Minton (1979) found that different sources of information were used in making judgements in these different domains: peer feedback and personal attributes, for example, were most important for social acceptance, while speed, effort and 'authority evaluations' — what parents and teachers tell the child — figured most centrally in judgements of cognitive competence. And perhaps most important, more detailed investigations have suggested that the causal ordering of the links between self-esteem and attainment are different from those first assumed. There is now considerable evidence (Harter, 1983; Dweck, 1986; Chapman *et al.*, 1990) for a more complex sequence of effects, with self-esteem following from (rather than contributing directly to) achievement, but in its turn playing a crucial role in mediating future motivation and achievement-related behaviours.

School experiences may contribute to these processes in a number of ways. Most evidence to date relates to perceived competence in the academic sphere. Here, objective markers such as test scores, grades and class positions clearly play an important role, and, as we have seen, seem to become increasingly salient with age. Teacher behaviours and expectations also contribute to children's self-evaluations. Classroom life often has an apparently negative tenor, with reprimands being used far more frequently than praise. Many writers have questioned the implications of these trends for children's self-perceptions. Mortimore *et al.* (1988), in one of the few school effects studies examining children's self-concepts, found that high levels of critical control in the classroom showed strong negative links with 10 year olds' views of themselves at school.

More subtle processes involving teacher expectations and peer comparisons also seem important, and developmental studies suggest that both increase in significance with age. Weinstein *et al.* (1987), for example, found that fifth graders were more aware of teacher expectations than younger children, and that their self-perceptions were more congruent with those of their teachers. The role of peer comparisons has been most tellingly illustrated in relation to learning-disabled (LD) groups. Renick and Harter (1989) highlighted the key importance of the reference group children use in making self-evaluations. LD students rated their cognitive competence significantly higher when comparing themselves with LD peers than with their non-disabled class-mates. In addition, their views of their competence decreased markedly by comparison with normal peers between grades 3–4 and 7–8, but showed no such developmental changes when compared with other LD students. If self-esteem is indeed critical to motivation, these findings are of major importance not only for specifically LD groups, but for the much larger group of children who are low or underachievers in school.

The role of school context more generally has been graphically illustrated in studies of the transition from elementary to junior high school (Simmons & Blyth, 1987). The move from a familiar, usually relatively small school environment to the much larger world of the high school, with its greater emphasis on evaluation and social comparisons, seems especially damaging to self-esteem. Students' self-evaluations show marked drops after the transition, as do correlations between self-esteem and measured attainment. Apparently more minor changes may also have a similar impact. Mortimore *et al.* (1988), for example, found that a change of teacher in the previous year was negatively associated with the self-views of 10 year olds. Change in the school setting seems particularly likely to disrupt the basis for children's self-assessments.

Gender and ethnic group differences in the content of children's self-evaluations, and in the links between attainments and self-esteem, are further important themes in the self-concept literature. Entwisle *et al.* (1987), for example, found that although girls did as well as boys in maths in the first grade, maths performance only played a part in the self-definitions of boys, and did not affect the way that girls construed themselves as learners. Cross-cultural comparisons (Lummis & Stevenson, 1990) have demonstrated a consistent pattern of gender differences in beliefs about maths and reading achievement from the first grade onwards, shared by children and their mothers. In the USA, China and Japan, mothers and children all tended to believe that boys were better at maths, and girls at reading. Even these widespread stereotypes, however, do not necessarily ensure that girls will hold positive academic self-perceptions. One especially striking feature of the London follow-up of 7–11 year olds was that while boys' self-assessments generally became more realistic over this period, and black girls' self-evaluations at 11 mirrored their very positive performance, white girls seemed consistently to underestimate their ability in reading (Blatchford, 1992). Much earlier research has suggested that able girls in particular are likely to show more shaky achievement expectations, a greater tendency to attribute failure to lack of ability, and a lower preference for novel or challenging tasks than either their equally able male counterparts, or less able girls (Dweck, 1986). The implications of these differing motivational patterns for later achievement are clearly worrying. It is encouraging that black girls in more recent studies do not seem to be prey to these vulnerabilities, but equally important that we gain a clearer idea of how they arise, and how they might be remedied.

To date, we know very little about the ways that school experiences may reinforce these particular processes. What is clear, however, is that experiences of success and failure at school may have quite long-term implications, not simply limited to the academic domain. As shown in later sections, low self-esteem has frequently been implicated in the links between poor attainment and delinquency, and positive self-views seen as one of the most beneficial legacies of some preschool programmes. For some especially vulnerable groups of children, schooling may be one of the few arenas offering opportunities for success. Quinton and Rutter (1988), for example, traced the long-term effects of schooling for a group of women raised in children's homes. Positive experiences at school — mainly in terms of opportunities to gain personal satisfaction, rather then achievement *per se* — showed links with a more constructive attitude towards planning later life-choices which, in its turn, predicted better general adult functioning. No similar effects were found for a comparison group raised in their own families. For the institution-reared girls, opportunities to gain self-esteem, and a sense of personal control, may have been limited in other aspects of their lives, so that school experiences took on an increased significance. Although these interpretations are largely speculative, we should not underestimate the 'protective' effects that positive experiences at school may have for the self-perceptions of especially vulnerable groups.

BEHAVIOURAL AND EMOTIONAL PROBLEMS

To date, little systematic attention has been given to the role of school experiences in the genesis of most behavioural or emotional problems. But although the evidence is scattered, it is clear that many aspects of children's behaviour are sensitive to school experiences, and that different school environments are associated with different patterns of behavioural development. Three rather separate channels for school-related influences can be identified here. First, echoing studies of attainment, there is evidence that variations in school and classroom climate are associated with a range of behavioural indicators, from on-task behaviour in the classroom to delinquency, psychiatric symptomatology and alcohol use. Second, individual characteristics may render particular groups of children vulnerable to behaviour problems in the school setting. And finally, there are the normative demands and challenges of school life that affect all children, and may be especially problematic for some.

School climate and organization

Although 'school effectiveness' research has concentrated most heavily on academic outcomes, one of the first English studies in fact highlighted school differences on behavioural indicators. Power *et al.* (1972) found marked differences between inner-city secondary schools in rates of delinquency and referral to child guidance clinics. Power's data were cross-sectional. More recent work, with longitudinal measures to take account of intake variations, has confirmed a similar picture. Schools differ in rates of delinquency, non-attendance and classroom behaviour problems (Rutter *et al.*, 1979), and in rates of exclusion for severely disruptive behaviour (Galloway *et al.*, 1985). Using a somewhat different design, Kasen *et al.* (1990) found that school climate measures were also associated with changes in rates of psychopathology.

The ILEA Junior School Study has provided perhaps the most sophisticated analyses of behaviour measures to date. There, school differences in levels of teacher-rated behaviour problems were less marked than for measures of attainment, but still both statistically and substantively significant, accounting for approaching 10% of explained variance (Mortimore *et al.*, 1988). In addition, school effectiveness on non-cognitive outcomes seemed to represent a separate dimension from academic effectiveness: the primary schools that were effective in promoting children's learning were not necessarily those with the most positive profiles on measures of behaviour, attitudes or self-esteem. Finally, where classroom-based factors were the most important correlates of academic achievement, non-cognitive indicators (though often less well explained) seemed to owe more to school-wide effects.

Rutter (1985b) has argued that the environmental factors that show the strongest links with behavioural functioning are likely to be different from those that affect children's cognitive development. Family correlates of conduct problems and delinquency, for example, have consistently centred on discordant relationships, lack of supervision and monitoring, and models of deviant behaviour (Rutter, 1985a). Findings from school studies suggest a number of parallels here. Kasen *et al.* (1990), for example, found that student reports of higher levels of 'conflict' in the school setting (indexed by items such as teachers often shouting at pupils) were associated with increases in attention deficits, oppositional behaviours and conduct problems over a 2-year period, while a strong academic focus showed negative associations with both externalizing behaviours and alcohol use. Rutter *et al.* (1979) also found that academic emphasis, both classroom-based and school-wide, together with constructive classroom management strategies and consistent but not oversevere sanctions, were associated with better in-school behaviour. And Nicol *et al.* (1985), in a detailed longitudinal study of children eventually suspended from school, described an escalating spiral of child behaviours and teacher responses strongly reminiscent of the coercive family processes documented by Patterson (1982). The school environment factors associated with disruptive behaviours may thus have much in common with patterns found in families. We know much less as yet about the aspects of school climate that may show links with anxiety or depression (Kasen *et al.*, 1990).

Contextual effects associated with the peer group have emerged as especially important in the behavioural domain. As early as the first grade, different classroom groupings are associated with the development of both shy and aggressive behaviours (Werthamer-Larsson *et al.*, 1991). Peer context effects have been explored most fully, however, in late childhood and adolescence, in relation to delinquency. Involvement with antisocial peers is one of the strongest predictors of adolescent deviance, and the school is clearly one context where such involvements might arise. Empirically, Rutter *et al.* (1979) found that school differences in boys' delinquency related strongly to the academic balance in school intakes. Over and above the well-established links between low ability and offending at the individual level, risks were elevated further in schools admitting high proportions of less-able pupils. Several classical delinquency theories are consistent with these observations. Hawkins and Lishner (1987), for example, draw on a range of models to suggest that although earlier problem behaviour, and possibly learning difficulties, may have direct effects on delinquency and drop-out, indirect pathways can also be traced through school effects. Poor academic performance is likely to contribute to weak attachment to school and its values; this in turn increases chances of association with delinquent peers; these, in conjunction with earlier influences, provide the more proximal links with offending.

Recent evidence suggests that processes of this kind may be set in train well before the peak years for offending. Dishion *et al.* (1991), for example, found that academic failure at age 10 was a significant predictor of later involvement with antisocial peers, and Lynam *et al.* (1993) have shown that the IQ–delinquency relationship was mediated by school achievement for black but not white youths in the early teens. As these authors argued, commitment to schooling and the more conventional values it supports may be especially important when other social bonds are lacking. In the US context of this study, informal social controls were likely to be weak in the poor neighbourhoods where black youths were growing up. For them, low achievement and lack of commitment to schooling became

correspondingly more important vulnerability factors.

School context also affects adolescent behaviour problems and delinquency in girls. In this case, contextual effects appear to vary with both individual dispositional characteristics and biological maturity. A number of studies have demonstrated that early maturing girls are at increased risk of norm violations and conduct problems in their teens (Stattin & Magnusson, 1990; Caspi & Moffitt, 1991). These risks are heightened for girls with pre-existing behaviour problems, and seem mediated through social processes: early maturers associate with older peers, and so may be differentially exposed to models of behaviour that are relatively 'precocious' for their own age. Caspi *et al.* (1993) have recently examined the role of schooling in this process. Familiarity with delinquent peers played an important part in both the initiation and maintenance of girls' delinquent behaviours. These trends were especially highlighted in mixed (coeducational) schools, where peer support for delinquency was presumably more widespread. Once again, biological maturation seemed important in potentiating these effects. Early maturing girls in mixed schools were at increased risk of norm-violations from age 13, but for 'on time' maturers, rates of delinquent behaviours only began to differ between mixed and single-sex schools in the mid-teens. School context only came into play as girls reached particular stages in their own development.

More complex models of this kind have only recently begun to be explored in studies of schooling. They create important bridges between the more global approach of much earlier school effects research — where school context was implicitly assumed to carry the same meaning for all children — and the detailed accounts of ethnographers, which have for many years highlighted the varying impact of school and classroom context for different individuals. Individual characteristics, the supports available to children, and the stresses in their lives outside, will all have an important bearing on the impact and meaning of their experiences at school. In some instances, they may act to select children into particular subsystems within the school that amplify existing difficulties. Nicol *et al.* (1985), for example, showed how suspended children inhabited a very particular personal world at school from the outset, marked by negative evaluations and rejection by their peers. Person−environment correlations of this kind have been widely documented in other contexts (Scarr, 1992). We are only just beginning to chart the intricacies of these processes during schooling; these few examples, however, are enough to suggest that they will be an important area for future investigation.

Individual vulnerabilities

One further implication of these findings is that some children may be especially vulnerable to behaviour problems during schooling. Underachievers are clearly one such at-risk group. Both clinical and epidemiological studies have repeatedly demonstrated strong links between behavioural and emotional problems and poor school achievement (Hinshaw, 1992). These seem most marked in middle childhood (Rutter *et al.*, 1970), but low achievement may still be associated with some increased risk of disorder in the mid-teens (McGee *et al.*, 1992).

These associations almost certainly reflect shared early risk factors at the individual level (Hinshaw, 1992). In addition, school experiences may well exacerbate these links. The value placed on achievement in the school setting almost inevitably means that underachievers will be faced with particular problems at school. Negative evaluations from teachers, as well as social comparison with peers, are likely to add to frustrations experienced at the individual level, and may find expression in a variety of behaviour problems. There is evidence, for example, that disruptive behaviours increase among poor readers over the early years of schooling (McGee *et al.*, 1988), when children are becoming increasingly conscious of their academic limitations. Self-esteem seems especially sensitive to variations in reading skill at this stage (Chapman *et al.*, 1990), and may be an important link in this chain. Others have argued for longer term links between underachievement and depression (Kellam *et al.*, 1983), and, as we have seen, lack of opportunities for success in the school setting, together with reduced attachment to school values, have been proposed as important mediators in the underachievement−delinquency connection

(Farnworth *et al.*, 1985; Hawkins & Lishner, 1987).

Difficulties in peer relationships constitute a second set of problems likely to create special vulnerabilities at school. Peer rejection in childhood carries well-known risks for a range of negative outcomes, both behavioural and emotional (Kupersmidt *et al.*, 1990). Early problems in peer relations are associated with difficulties from the time children start school. Ladd (1990), for example, found that early peer rejection was a precursor to less favourable school perceptions, higher levels of school avoidance and poorer attainments over the first year. These findings in normative samples have strong echoes in more clinically oriented studies. School problems occur at high rates in many clinical populations; early peer rejection at school, clearly documented, for example, among aggressive and hyperactive children (Pope *et al.*, 1989) may well play an important part in compounding their difficulties. Rubin *et al.* (1990) have proposed two different developmental pathways that may be involved here, varying with the temperamental characteristics of the child, but each implicating school experiences. The first focuses on hostile, aggressive preschoolers, who establish negative peer relationships at an early stage. Teachers are likely to perceive such children as impulsive and problematic, adding a negative school reputation to existing peer problems. As each of these tendencies becomes more entrenched, the child will increasingly perceive school as a negative milieu. Peer rejection and isolation from the peer group are likely to increase in middle childhood, reinforcing tendencies to disruptive behaviour disorders and drop-out from school.

The second model focuses on the anxious, inhibited child, likely to withdraw from peer contacts in the early years of schooling. As social comparisons become possible in middle childhood, such children will become increasingly aware of their own failures. Negative self-regard and social anxiety may now be added to the picture, contributing to further withdrawal and isolation from the peer group. In this instance, long-term outcomes are likely to involve loneliness and the possibility of depression or other emotional symptoms.

As yet, these models have still to be tested empirically. Bullying and victimization have already been studied extensively (Besag, 1989). Olweus (1991,

1993), in an important series of investigations, has examined many aspects of bully–victim problems, their management and long-term implications. Large-scale surveys in Norwegian schools have indicated that bullying occurs on quite an extensive scale: 16–18% of second graders reported some bullying, and though rates declined with age, around 5% of junior high school students still reported being bullied at least occasionally. Interestingly, boys were more likely to be both perpetrators and victims. Problems were as marked in country as in city schools, and usually involved intimidation of younger children by their older peers. The majority of reported incidents took place in school, but teachers seemed to show little awareness of the problem, and children only rarely discussed it with their parents. Intervention programmes, widely implemented and evaluated in the Norwegian studies, have been important in showing that rates of bullying can be significantly reduced (Olweus, 1993).

More detailed studies showed that bullying is by no means a random phenomenon. Many children were persistently victimized over extended periods of their schooling, and both bullies and victims had recognizable characteristics. The typical bully showed an aggressive personality pattern (expressed in relations with teachers and parents as well as with peers), combined, for boys at least, with physical strength. Victims, by contrast, tended to be more anxious and insecure than other children, were often socially isolated at school, and, again especially among boys, physically weak. Interviews with parents suggested that many of these characteristics had been evident from an early age; these children's individual characteristics clearly contributed to their low social status, which constituted a special vulnerability at school.

A small-scale follow-up of one group of systematically victimized boys is especially revealing here (Olweus, 1993). Even some years after leaving school, ex-victims still showed some effects of their earlier experiences, with low scores on measures of self-esteem and depressive symptomatology. Extended exposure to bullying clearly had some long-term effects. In general, however, the later findings indicated a much more positive picture. Free in their twenties to select their own social environments, ex-victims no longer reported being harassed by others in their adult lives, and their levels of anxiety and other internalizing symptoms, elevated during schooling, had normalized. As Olweus argued, these findings suggest that although individual characteristics had played a part in these boys' experiences of bullying at school, the stability of their low social status was as much a function of environmental as personal continuities. To a considerable extent, the subjective difficulties they had experienced during schooling seemed situationally determined.

Normative school-related experiences

Finally, we consider the effects of school-related experiences that may impinge on much wider groups of children. School life inevitably brings with it a series of particular demands and challenges. Some, such as starting and changing school, may constitute quite major events, affecting many aspects of children's functioning. They are discussed in more detail in the next section. Others, such as taking regular tests or completing homework assignments, may still be sources of some more minor stress.

Taking tests, getting bad marks, and not completing homework on time, figure regularly in check-lists of children's fears, or situations that cause them distress. Self-reports on inventories of this kind show few sex differences on individual school-related items, though girls generally have higher scores on composite measures of distress. Age trends in relation to school events are more marked: in one recent study, for example, fears of failure or criticism loaded heavily on school-related items among 7–12 year olds, but were overtaken by difficulties in relationships with parents and peers among teenagers (Gullone & King, 1992). Although in most instances fears of this kind will not be severe, they do show associations with clinically significant symptoms. Distress over poor academic and physical competence, for example, was present in a third of 15 years olds with disorder involving anxiety with or without other types of problems in one recent study, by contrast with only 13% of those without disorder (McGee & Stanton, 1992). Parent reports of anxious and depressive behaviours showed similar links. These findings cannot, of course, clarify the direction of the influences involved, but certainly suggest that school-related stressors would repay attention as possible antecedents of disorder in adolescence.

Among these various school-related fears, test anxiety has received perhaps the most detailed attention (Wigfield & Eccles, 1990). Anxiety scores increase systematically over the early school years, and also show increasing correlations with performance: when children start school, links between anxiety and test performance are negligible, but they increase considerably into the middle school years (Willig *et al.*, 1983). Children's developing skills in processing evaluative information, from peers as well as teachers, seem likely to be important here. Changes in test procedures (in particular the relaxation of time constraints) have been shown to result in improved performance for anxious children (Wigfield & Eccles, 1990). It is less clear how far improved performance reduces anxiety.

For many teenagers, school-leaving examinations may be the most major tests they ever take. Cairns *et al.* (1991) have argued that these examinations have a considerable impact on teenagers' general psychological well-being. A number of studies have shown that self-ratings of psychological distress fall markedly between the final year of schooling and the first 1 or 2 years in the job market (Banks & Jackson, 1982). This might reflect a general increase in feelings of well-being with age, or might signal some more rather specific factors. Cairns *et al.* (1991) obtained General Health Questionnaire scores for large groups of teenagers shortly before public examinations, and again some 18 months later. The results suggested both developmental and environmental effects: psychological well-being did seem to show a slight general improvement as young people entered their late teens, but there were also effects that seemed more specifically linked with the approach of the public examinations. It is unknown what proportions of teenagers experience clinically significant problems at this stage; what does seem clear, however, is that this particular phase of school life is more than usually distressing for many young people.

STAGES AND TRANSITIONS IN SCHOOLING

Transition points in children's school careers are attracting increasing interest as we learn more about the impact of life events on development in childhood (Goodyer, 1990). Starting and changing schools are likely to be events of quite major significance for children, when they must adapt to a range of new demands and expectations, negotiate new roles, form new relationships with adults and peers and incorporate new dimensions in their self-evaluations. Hughes *et al.* (1979) have described some of the adaptations required as children first start school, and Elizur (1986) has documented links between parental coping strategies and children's early school adjustment. Ladd (1990) and Ladd and Price (1987) have focused in detail on the rôle of peer relations at school entry. Starting school with a known group of preschool peers facilitated children's early school adjustment, and showed links with more positive attitudes to school. Making new friends in the first year was associated with gains in school performance, while early peer rejection, as we have seen, was associated with poorer attainments.

Alexander and Entwisle (1988) have undertaken a detailed study of influences on cognitive development during the first 2 years of school. Particular groups of children seemed to face special difficulties in adapting to, or benefitting from, their new environments. In the US context of this study, black pupils made less progress than their white peers during the first year in school, although their scores at school entry had been broadly comparable. Achievement patterns were relatively fluid at the start, but quickly stabilized; as this happened, so the black children's early losses persisted into their second year achievements. A not dissimilar picture has emerged from comparisons of the reading progress of middle class and socially disadvantaged English children over the early months of schooling (Raz & Bryant, 1990). Again, the groups entered school with essentially similar prereading skills, but the disadvantaged children showed much slower subsequent progress in reading. As yet, the reasons for these differences are unclear. They may reflect a range of processes: slower adaptation to the social expectations of classroom life, which in turn impedes learning; a greater disparity between the values of home and school; or possibly lesser involvement on the part of parents at a point when home–school links may be specially important (Stevenson & Baker, 1987). Whatever their origins, these findings point to the vulnerability of particular groups of children at what may be an especially influential stage in their school careers, when both their own and others' views of themselves as learners are being crystallized, and when the cumulative nature of learning is perhaps especially important.

School transitions are also likely to affect behavioural adjustment. Some studies have found that as many as 10% of children show some noticeable disturbance when they start school (Beardsall & Dunn, 1992), and rather higher proportions are rated by teachers as showing adjustment problems after transfer to secondary school (Inner London Education Authority, 1987). We must be cautious, however, in interpreting quite what these findings mean. Young children's own ratings of the 'upsettingness' of starting school show wide variations (Rende & Plomin, 1991). Non-normative school changes may be more unsettling; in one recent study, for example, 15 year olds rated a change of school as little less distressing than parental separation or arguments (McGee & Stanton, 1991). To date, most of our other evidence on the behavioural effects of school transitions comes from studies that have assessed rates of problems only after a change. Longitudinal studies of other disruptions in children's lives suggest that although many children do indeed show disturbed behaviour after divorce (Cherlin *et al.*, 1991) or reception into care (St Claire & Osborn, 1987), these same children had often already been troubled well before these particular 'events'. This may also be the case with some school transitions. Investigators have only recently begun to examine school entry from a longitudinal perspective (Hay, 1988). Davies (1992) found that parents' ratings of children's hostility and anxiety were actually lower 3 months after school entry than shortly before, and that some teacher ratings reflected similar trends. We clearly need more longitudinal evidence to clarify this intriguing picture.

Some disruptions in the expected patterns of children's school careers are generated within the educational process itself. In the USA in particular, low-achieving children, or those seen to be less mature than their peers, are often retained in grade, repeating one or more years of schooling until they achieve expected grade levels. This practice, designed to enhance children's opportunities for development, in fact seems to carry many negative effects. As early as the second grade, retained children make less academic progress than their 'promoted' peers (Alexander & Entwisle, 1988), and effects seem to cumulate over time. In a follow-up to age 17, Spivack and Marcus (1989) have shown how retention and special class placement in the early grades were associated with decreasing academic performance and independence across the school careers of boys, and with increasing delinquency, antisocial behaviour and negative attitudes in girls. These effects remained even after earlier attainments and adjustment had been taken into account. Early school placement decisions, and their cumulative impact over time, appeared to have had marked effects on these young people's subsequent development.

Later school transitions may be of no less import. Hirsch and Rapkin (1987) documented a marked decline in students' perceptions of the quality of school life following the transition from elementary to junior high school. As we have seen, self-esteem also seems especially vulnerable at this point (Simmons & Blyth, 1987). For many young people, the institutional move to junior high school occurs at the same time as important personal developmental changes, with the onset of puberty, beginning dating, and so forth. The cumulative impact of these transitions can be considerable, with marked effects on self-esteem for girls, and on grade point averages and participation in extracurricular activities for young people of both sexes (Simmons *et al.*, 1987). The pattern of effects may be quite complex. Peterson *et al.* (1991), for example, found that the transition to junior high school was among the important factors affecting reactions to puberty: early maturers, who reached puberty before the transition, expressed more depressed affect than their peers, and these trends persisted some 4 years later. Caspi *et al.* (1993), examining the effects of early puberty on behaviour problems in girls, found higher rates of difficulties for early developers in mixed, but not single-sex, schools. Here once again we see how particular types of school setting can intersect with the effects of a biological transition, to show effects on behavioural development.

Although global self-esteem scores appear to recover after the junior high school transition, declines in self-concept in more specific areas (achievement in maths or English, for example) may not, and lower ability pupils may be especially at risk of developing negative views in specific subject areas (Wigfield *et al.*, 1991). Felner and Adnan (1988) have reported positive effects of an intervention programme designed to maintain peer networks across the transition, and increase the supports provided by homeroom teachers. Four years later, school drop-out rates, known to be strongly associated with poor school performance and a range of other difficulties (Cairns *et al.*, 1989), were only half as high in the experimental as in a control group. Steps to minimize the disruptiveness of school transitions may thus be of particular value to potentially vulnerable groups.

LONG-TERM EFFECTS

Leaving school poses further challenges, discussed in detail in the lifespan development literature (Hogan & Astone, 1986; Kerckhoff, 1990). In the context of the present discussion, however, the transition from school to work and other adult roles is perhaps of greatest interest for the light it can cast on the persistence of school effects. The findings discussed to this point suggest that children's functioning shows at least short-term responses to school experiences. But it is also important to know how far effects persist beyond the end of schooling: do school experiences show any continuing impact on later modes of functioning, or are the effects essentially situation-specific?

Many of the outcomes of schooling — formal qualifications, for example, and patterns of school-leaving — have a clear impact on later life-chances. There is a massive literature documenting associations between educational attainments and later occupational status, and many studies have pointed to the deleterious effects of school drop-out (Steinberg *et al.*, 1984) and truancy (Berg, 1992). In each case, however, these school-related markers may be no more than indicators of troubled or talented individuals, so that individual character-istics, rather than school experiences, might account for later effects. In practice, quite complex patterns of relationships may be involved.

Taking the example of truancy, US data have shown independent effects on later employment records and income levels, and also on such diverse outcomes as marital stability, crime and even mor-tality rates, when a range of earlier factors were taken into account (Robins & Ratcliffe, 1980). But truants and drop-outs are also likely to have poorer educational qualifications, and it may be these, at least in employment-related areas, that are of prime importance. Here, evidence is somewhat con-flicting. Gray *et al.* (1980) found few effects of poor school attendance on a range of employment measures in the first year after leaving school once qualifications had been taken into account. Hibbert *et al.* (1990), examining employment outcomes at 23, did, however, find independent effects of truancy, and data on older samples have suggested that these may become if anything more pro-nounced with age (Cherry, 1976). Although longi-tudinal data on other behavioural indicators are still limited, it seems clear that some aspects of school behaviours do have an important bearing on later life-chances.

How are these long-term effects mediated? In some instances school experiences may show con-tinuing effects on individual dispositions or coping styles. As we have seen, persistent bullying at school seemed to cast some long-term shadows of this kind (Olweus, 1993). In most cases, a more plausible model seems to be one of indirect effects. Pedersen *et al.* (1978), for example, traced exceptionally posi-tive effects of one first-grade teacher on her pupils' outcomes through to adulthood. In that study, direct effects were evident in the children's grade levels and initiative during first and second grades, but after this point the effects were all indirect, building on the benefits accrued in their first years of schooling. Rutter (1989) in a more general dis-cussion of pathways to adulthood, suggested that many aspects of development are best seen as a series of interlinked steps, where outcomes at any one point are often primarily of importance in raising or lowering chances of successful adaptation at the next. Many of the findings on school influ-ences seem most consonant with an analysis of this kind.

Long-term follow-ups of the preschool pro-grammes provide perhaps the best-articulated examples here to date. In many early studies, initial improvements in IQ scores faded after 3 or 4 years in the ordinary school system. Early evaluations concluded that although the programmes had provided some short-term benefits, they had failed to produce the long-term 'inoculations' against disadvantage that were initially desired. In some cases, however, evaluators continued to track participants' progress through their schooling, and into adolescence and early adulthood (Lazar & Darlington, 1982; Berrueta-Clement *et al.*, 1984). These longer term studies revealed a consistent pattern of results: although IQ gains did indeed diminish, other, more 'real-world', measures of school progress suggested persisting effects.

In general, children enrolled in the programmes had been at marked risk of failure in the school system. By contrast with controls, however, they were only half as likely to be referred for special education, and rather less likely to be retained in grade. The children's mothers were more satisfied with their progress, and the children themselves had stronger achievement motivation later in their schooling. In adolescence, broader effects were apparent: programme participants more often completed high school, were more likely to have found employment, and, in some studies, showed lower rates of delinquency, teenage pregnancy and reliance on welfare benefits. Although their academic attainments were still modest in absolute terms, they seemed more likely than their peers to have engaged in what some writers described as the 'school success flow'.

Berrueta-Clement *et al.* (1984), reporting in detail on results from the Perry Preschool Program, have proposed a transactional, incremental model for these effects that both echoes and develops many of the themes raised in earlier sections. It suggests that the experimental children's progress reflected a series of interlinked developments over time, each in turn raising or lowering the probability of positive developments at the immediately succeeding stage. The analogy of a relay race, where position at each of a series of handovers may be the most critical factor, has been widely used here. The effects of the preschool experience on the initial transition into kindergarten seemed the first of these crucial 'hand-overs'. In addition to boosting IQ scores, preschool may have conveyed many other benefits: prior experience of classroom procedures, knowledge of how to approach schoolwork, and, equally important, experience of some success in preschool that could contribute to children's own beliefs that they could achieve in school.

Success in the initial transition to kindergarten, supported by more positive attitudes on the part of parents, may have contributed to positive teacher expectations, which in turn were seen as playing a crucial role at later stages. Although achieving better than anticipated, these highly disadvantaged children still faced major difficulties in learning. Their lower rates of special education placement and retention in grade suggest that teachers saw them as capable of achieving within regular classrooms; given the damaging consequences of some special placement decisions, these attitudes in themselves may have played a central part in maintaining positive trajectories at later stages in their school careers, and amplifying earlier effects (Woodhead, 1985). Finally, the children's attitudes to schooling, to their own abilities, and to their capacities to achieve through this route, may have provided a further essential platform for building on earlier gains. To return to the analogy of the relay race: the overall impact of the programme seemed to depend less on boosting children's long-term 'stamina' in achievement terms than on supports for a series of much shorter term developments, each of which provided building blocks for the next.

CONCLUSION

Developmental theories are paying increasing attention to social context. As Richards and Light (1986) have argued, '... social context is, at a variety of levels, intrinsic to the developmental process itself; rather than the icing on the cake it is as much a part of its structure as the flour or eggs that may be used to make it' (p. 1). This chapter gives many pointers to the role of school experiences in this mixture. Perhaps predictably, the picture is clearest in relation to cognitive growth. Simple variations in the extent of schooling affect performance on IQ tests, and variations in the nature of that schooling then contribute to progress in more specific curriculum areas. These effects, like those of other environmental influences, cumulate over time. Some phases of school life may be especially important here: a hesitant start may have long-term effects on learning trajectories, and later changes in the pattern of school life, as much as stressors in the family or the demands of individual growth, can cause perturbations in the flow.

School influences, however, are by no means limited to the cognitive domain. As shown here, variations in school experience show links with many other aspects of development, more and less directly related to success in learning. Factors as varied as the child's view of his or her own competencies on the one hand, or likelihood of engaging in delinquency on the other, have each been shown to be sensitive to experiences at school. In some areas, investigators have already begun to map in intervening steps in these processes, providing more developmentally oriented accounts that highlight the complex interplay between individual, family, school and wider structural influences on development. In most cases, however, the intervening steps are still largely a *terra incognita*, where speculations are only gradually beginning to be put to the test.

The school effects work, deliberately focused at the institutional level, makes no direct claims to illuminate individual processes, but nevertheless provides pointers that mesh well with other knowledge. We know that children's learning depends not only on their cognitive abilities, but on attitudes and motivations to learning, and behaviours and strategies that support its acquisition. To maximize children's potential, it follows that schools should attend as carefully to these supportive functions as to the quality of their teaching *per se*. 'Process-product' findings at both the classroom and school levels reflect these conclusions: effective teachers are characterized as much by their approaches to classroom management as by their instructional style, and effective schools are those that use the full range of institutional supports and encouragements at their disposal to bind their pupils into the learning process. For many children, especially those with limited or ineffective supports for learning in their homes and families, school influences may be as important for their impact on attitudes to learning, and views of the self as a learner, as for processes of direct instruction.

Peer contacts also play a central role in children's school experience. Evidence for this role has emerged at many points: familiar peers ease the passage into schooling; lack of acceptance or more overt rejection by peers can influence many other aspects of progress in the ensuing years; and later still, deviant peer groups, arising in part as a response to problems in school, may in their turn contribute to the initiation or continuance of difficulties outside.

The examples cited in this chapter point to both positive and negative effects of school life on children's development. Though modest by comparison with family influences, they are by no means trivial. They warrant attention for their implications for children we meet in clinical or educational settings today, and for the potential they offer for change in the future. Unlike families, schools are instruments of public policy; where we are often constrained in our efforts to intervene in children's home situations, social institutions are, at least potentially, more open to change. To date, action-research in the school setting has had a chequered history (Maughan & Rutter, 1985; Hawkins & Lishner, 1987), but has shown some positive effects. Expanding our understanding of school influences holds out the promise that we can increase those effects and, in so doing, benefit the lives of many children.

REFERENCES

Alexander K.L. & Entwisle D.R. (1988) Achievement in the first two years of school: Patterns and processes. *Monographs of the Society for Research in Child Development* **55**(2), Serial No. 218.

Banks M.H. & Jackson P.R. (1982) Unemployment and the risk of minor psychiatric disorder in young people: Cross-sectional and longitudinal evidence. *Psychological Medicine* **12**, 789−798.

Beardsall L. & Dunn J. (1992) Adversities in childhood: Siblings' experiences, and their relations to self-esteem. *Journal of Child Psychology and Psychiatry* **33**, 349−359.

Berg I. (1992) Absence from school and mental health. *British Journal of Psychiatry* **161**, 154−166.

Berrueta-Clement J.R., Schweinart L.J., Barnett W.S., Epstein S.S. & Weikart D.P. (1984) *Changed Lives: The Effects of the Perry Pre-school Program on Youths Through Age 19*. High Scope, Ypsilanti, Michigan.

Besag V.E. (1989) *Bullies and Victims in Schools*. Open University Press, Milton Keynes.

Blatchford P. (1992) Academic self assessment at 7 and 11 years: Its accuracy and association with ethnic group and sex. *British Journal of Educational Psychology* **62**, 35−44.

Blatchford P., Burke J., Farquhar C., Plewis I. & Tizard B. (1989) Teacher expectations in infant school: Associations with attainment and progress, curriculum coverage and classroom interaction. *British Journal of Educational Psychology* **59**, 19−30.

Bosker R.J. & Scheerens J. (1989) Issues in the interpretation of the results of school effectiveness research. *International Journal of Educational Research* **13**, 741−751.

Bronfenbrenner U. & Crouter A.C. (1983) The evolution of environmental models in developmental research. In Kessen W. (ed.) *History, Theory and Methods*, Vol. 1, *Mussen's Handbook of Child Psychology*, 4th edn, pp. 357−414. Wiley, New York.

Brophy J.E. (1983) Research on the self-fulfilling prophecy and teacher expectations. *Journal of Educational Psychology* **75**, 631−661.

Brophy J.E. & Good T.L. (1986) Teacher behavior and student achievement. In Wittrock M.C. (ed.) *Handbook of Research on Teaching*, pp. 328−375. Macmillan, London.

Cahan S. & Cohen N. (1989) Age versus schooling effects on intelligence development. *Child Development* **60**, 1239−1249.

Cairns E., McWhirter L., Barry R. & Duffy U. (1991) The development of psychological well-being in adolescence. *Journal of Child Psychology and Psychiatry* **32**, 635−643.

Cairns R.B., Cairns B.D. & Neckerman H.J. (1989) Early school dropout: Configurations and determinants. *Child Development* **60**, 1437−1452.

Caspi A., Lynam D., Moffitt T.E. & Silva P.A. (1993) Unraveling girls' delinquency: Biological, dispositional, and contextual contributions to adolescent misbehavior. *Developmental Psychology* **29**, 19−30.

Caspi A. & Moffitt T.E. (1991) Individual differences are accentuated during periods of social change: The sample case of girls at puberty. *Journal of Personality and Social Psychology* **61**, 157−168.

Ceci S. (1991) How much does schooling influence general intelligence and its cognitive components? A reassessment of the evidence. *Developmental Psychology* **27**, 703−722.

Chapman J.W., Lambourne R. & Silva P.A. (1990) Some antecedents of academic self-concept: A longitudinal study. *British Journal of Educational Psychology* **60**, 142−152.

Cherlin A.J., Furstenberg F.F., Chase-Lansdale P.L. *et al.* (1991) Longitudinal studies of the effects of divorce on children in Great Britain and the United States. *Science* **252**, 1386−1389.

Cherry N. (1976) Persistent job-changing − Is it a problem? *Journal of Occupational Psychology* **49**, 203−221.

Cheung K.C., Keeves J.P., Sellin N. & Tsoi S.C. (1990) The analysis of multilevel data in educational research: Studies of problems and their solutions. *International Journal of Educational Research* **14**, 215−319.

Clarke-Stewart K.A. & Fein G.G. (1983) Early childhood programs. In Haith M.M. & Campos J.J. (eds) *Infancy and Developmental Psychobiology*, Vol. 2, *Mussen's Handbook of Child Psychology*, 4th edn, pp. 919−999. Wiley, New York.

Coleman J.S., Campbell E.Q., Hobson C.J. *et al.* (1966) *Equality of Educational Opportunity*. US Government Printing Office, Washington.

Cook T.D. & Campbell D.T. (1979) *Quasi-Experimentation: Design and Analysis Issues for Field Settings*. Rand-McNally, Chicago, Illinois.

Davies L.C. (1992) *A longitudinal study of the life event of starting school*. Paper presented at the Fifth European Conference on Developmental Psychology, Seville.

Dishion T.J., Patterson G.R., Stoolmiller M. & Skinner M.L. (1991) Family, school, and behavioral antecedents to early adolescent involvement with antisocial peers. *Developmental Psychology* **27**, 172−180.

Douglas J.W.B., Ross J.M. & Simpson H.R. (1968) *All our Future: A Longitudinal Study of Secondary School Education*. Davies, London.

Doyle W. (1986) Classroom organization and management. In Wittrock M.C. (ed.) *Handbook of Research on Teaching*, pp. 392−432. Macmillan, London.

Dweck C.S. (1986) Motivational processes affecting learning. *American Psychologist* **41**, 1040−1048.

Eder D. (1982) Differences in communicative styles across ability groups. In Wilkinson L.C. (ed.) *Communicating in the Classroom*, pp. 245−265. Academic Press, New York.

Elizur J. (1986) The stress of school entry: Parental coping behaviours and children's adjustment to school. *Journal of Child Psychology and Psychiatry* **27**, 625−638.

Entwisle D.R. & Alexander K.L. (1992) Summer setback: Race, poverty, school composition, and mathematics achievement in the first two years of school. *American Sociological Review* **57**, 72−84.

Entwisle D.R., Alexander K.L., Pallas A.M. & Cadigan D. (1987) The emergent academic self-image of first-graders: Its response to social structure. *Child Development* **58**, 1190−1206.

Entwisle D.R. & Stevenson H.W. (1987) Schools and development. *Child Development* **58**, 1149−1150.

Farnworth M., Schweinhart L.J. & Berrueta-Clement J.R. (1985) Preschool intervention, school success and delinquency in a high-risk sample of youth. *American Educational Research Journal* **22**, 445−464.

Felner R.D. & Adnan A.M. (1988) The school transitional environment project: An ecological intervention and evaluation. In Price R.H., Cowen E.L., Lorion R.P., Serrano-Garcia I. & Ramon-McKay J. (eds) *Fourteen Ounces of Prevention: A Casebook for Practitioners*, pp. 111−122. American Psychological Association, Washington.

Fogelman K., Goldstein H., Essen J. & Ghodsian, M. (1978) Patterns of attainment. *Educational Studies* **4**, 121−130.

Fraser B.J. (1989a) Instructional effectiveness: Processes on the micro level. In Creemers B., Peters T. & Reynolds

D. (eds) *School Effectiveness and School Improvement: Proceedings of the Second International Congress, Rotterdam, 1989*, pp. 23–37. Swets & Zeitlinger, Amsterdam.

Fraser B.J. (1989b) Twenty years of classroom climate work: Progress and prospect. *Journal of Curriculum Studies* **21**, 307–327.

Fraser B.J., Walberg H.J., Welch W.W. & Hattie J.A. (1987) Synthesis of educational research. *International Journal of Educational Research* **11**, 145–252.

Galloway D., Martin R. & Wicox B. (1985) Persistent absence from school and exclusion from school: The predictive power of school and community variables. *British Educational Research Journal* **11**, 51–61.

Goldstein H. (1987) *Multilevel Models in Educational and Social Research*. Oxford University Press, Oxford.

Goodyer I.M. (1990) *Life Experiences, Development and Childhood Psychopathology*. Wiley, Chichester.

Gray G., Smith A. & Rutter M. (1980) School attendance and the first year of employment. In Hersov L. & Berg I. (eds) *Out of School: Modern Perspectives in Truancy and School Refusal*, pp. 343–370. Wiley, Chichester.

Gray J., Jesson D. & Sime N. (1990) Estimating differences in the examination performance of secondary schools in six LEAs: A multi-level approach to school effectiveness. *Oxford Review of Education* **16**, 137–158.

Gullone E. & King N.J. (1992) Psychometric evaluation of a revised fear survey for children and adolescents. *Journal of Child Psychology and Psychiatry* **33**, 987–998.

Gump G.V. (1987) School and classroom environments. In Stokols D. & Altman I. (eds) *Handbook of Environmental Psychology*. Macmillan, New York.

Hargreaves D. (1967) *Social Relations in the Secondary School*. Routledge & Kegan Paul, London.

Harter S. (1982) The perceived competence scale for children. *Child Development* **53**, 87–97.

Harter S. (1983) Developmental perspectives on the self-system. In Hetherington E.M. (ed.) *Socialization, Personality and Social Development*, Vol. 4, *Mussen's Handbook of Child Psychology*, 4th edn, pp. 275–385. Wiley, New York.

Hawkins J.D. & Lishner D.M. (1987) Schooling and delinquency. In Johnson E.H. (ed.) *Handbook on Crime and Delinquency Prevention*, pp. 179–221. Greenwood Press, New York.

Hay D. (1988) Studying the impact of ordinary life: A developmental model, research plan and words of caution. In Rutter M. (ed.) *Studies of Psychosocial Risk: The Power of Longitudinal Data*, pp. 245–254. Cambridge University Press, Cambridge.

Heyns B. (1978) *Summer Learning and the Effects of Schooling*. Academic Press, New York.

Heyns B. (1987) Schooling and cognitive development: Is there a season for learning? *Child Development* **58**, 1151–1160.

Hibbert A., Fogelman K. & Manor O. (1990) Occupational outcomes of truancy. *British Journal of Educational Psychology* **60**, 23–36.

Hinshaw S.P. (1992) Externalizing behavior problems and academic underachievement in childhood and adolescence: Causal relationships and underlying mechanisms. *Psychological Bulletin* **111**, 127–155.

Hirsch B.J. & Rapkin B.D. (1987) The transition to junior high school: A longitudinal study of self-esteem, psychological symptomatology, school life, and social support. *Child Development* **58**, 1235–1243.

Hogan D.P. & Astone N.M. (1986) The transition to adulthood. *American Review of Sociology* **12**, 109–130.

Howlin P. (1994) Special educational treatment. In Rutter M., Taylor E. & Hersov L. (eds) *Child and Adolescent Psychiatry: Modern Approaches*, 3rd edn, pp. 1071–1088. Blackwell Scientific Publications, Oxford.

Hughes M., Pinkerton G. & Plewis I. (1979) Children's difficulties on starting infant school. *Journal of Child Psychology and Psychiatry* **20**, 187–196.

Husen T. (1967) *International Study of Achievement in Mathematics: A Comparison of Twelve Countries*. Wiley, New York.

Inner London Education Authority (1987) *Secondary Transfer Project Bulletin 16: Pupils' Adjustment to Secondary School*. RS 1073/86. ILEA, London.

James W. (1890) *Psychology*. Fawcett, New York.

Jencks C., Smith A., Acland H. *et al.* (1972) *Inequality: A Reassessment of the Effect of Family and Schooling in America*. Basic Books, New York.

Jussim L. (1986) Self-fulfilling prophecies: A theoretical and integrative review. *Psychological Review* **93**, 429–445.

Kasen S., Johnson J. & Cohen P. (1990) The impact of school emotional climate on student psychopathology. *Journal of Abnormal Child Psychology* **18**, 165–177.

Kellam S.G., Brown C.H., Rubin B.R. & Ensminger M.E. (1983) Paths leading to teenage psychiatric symptoms and substance use: Developmental epidemiological studies in Woodlawn. In Guze S.B., Earls F.J. & Barratt J.E. (eds) *Childhood Psychopathology and Development*, pp. 17–51. Raven, New York.

Keogh B.K. & Burstein N.D. (1988) Relationship of temperament to preschoolers' interaction with peers and teachers. *Exceptional Children* **54**, 69–74.

Kerckhoff A.C. (1990) *Getting Started: Transition to Adulthood in Great Britain*. Westview, Boulder, Colorado.

Kulik J.A. & Kulik C.L.C. (1989) Meta-analysis in education. *International Journal of Educational Research* **13**, 309–318.

Kupersmidt J.B., Coie J.D. & Dodge K.A. (1990) The role of poor peer relationships in the development of disorder. In Asher S.R. & Coie J.D. (eds) *Peer Rejection in Childhood*, pp. 274–305. Cambridge University Press, Cambridge.

Laboratory of Comparative Human Cognition (1986) Contributions of cross-cultural research to educational practice. *American Psychologist* **41**, 1049–1058.

Ladd G.W. (1990) Having friends, keeping friends, making friends, and being liked by peers in the classroom: Predictors of children's early school adjustment? *Child Development* **61**, 1081–1100.

Ladd G.W. & Price J.M. (1987) Predicting children's social and school adjustment following the transition from preschool to kindergarten. *Child Development* **55**, 1168–1189.

Lazar I. & Darlington R. (1982) Lasting effects of early education: A report from the Consortium for Longitudinal Studies. *Monographs of the Society for Research in Child Development* **47**, Serial No. 195.

Lee V.E., Brooks-Gunn J. & Schnur E. (1988) Does Head Start work? A 1-year follow-up comparison of disadvantaged children attending Head Start, no preschool, and other preschool programs. *Developmental Psychology* **24**, 210–222.

Lerner J.V., Lerner R.M. & Zabski S. (1985) Temperament and elementary school children's actual and rated academic performance: A test of a 'goodness of fit' model. *Journal of Child Psychology and Psychiatry* **26**, 125–136.

Lezotte L.W. (1989) School improvement based on the effective schools research. *International Journal of Educational Research* **13**, 815–825.

Louis K.S. & Miles M.B. (1990) *Improving Urban High Schools: What Works and Why*. Teachers College Press, New York.

Lummis M. & Stevenson H.W. (1990) Gender differences in beliefs and achievement: A cross-cultural study. *Developmental Psychology* **26**, 254–263.

Lynam D., Moffitt T. & Stouthamer-Loeber M. (1993) Explaining the relation between IQ and delinquency: Class, race, test motivation, school failure or self-control? *Journal of Abnormal Psychology* **102**, 187–196.

MacAulay D.J. (1990) Classroom environment: A literature review. *Educational Psychology* **10**, 239–253.

McGee R., Feehan M., Williams S. & Anderson J. (1992) DSM-III disorders from age 11 to age 15 years. *Journal of the American Academy of Child and Adolescent Psychiatry* **31**, 50–59.

McGee R., Share D., Moffitt T.E., Williams S. & Silva P.A. (1988) Reading disability, behaviour problems and juvenile delinquency. In Saklofske D. & Eysenck S. (eds) *Individual Differences in Children and Adolescents: International Research Perspectives*, pp. 158–172. Hodder & Stoughton, New York.

McGee R. & Stanton W.R. (1992) Sources of distress among New Zealand adolescents. *Journal of Child Psychology and Psychiatry* **33**, 999–1010.

McKey R.H., Condelli L., Granson H., Barrett B., McConkey C. & Plantz M. (1985) *The Impact of Head Start on Children, Families and Communities. Final Report of the Head Start Evaluation, Synthesis and Utilization Project*. CSR Inc., Washington, DC.

Maughan B. (1988) School experiences as risk/protective factors. In Rutter M. (ed.) *Studies of Psychosocial Risk: The Power of Longitudinal Data*, pp. 200–220. Cambridge University Press, Cambridge.

Maughan B., Mortimore P., Ouston J. & Rutter M. (1980) Fifteen thousand hours: A reply to Heath and Clifford. *Oxford Review of Education* **6**, 289–303.

Maughan B., Ouston J., Pickles A. & Rutter M. (1990) Can schools change? I. Outcomes at six London secondary schools. *School Effectiveness and School Improvement* **1**, 188–210.

Maughan B. & Rutter M. (1985) Education: Improving practice through increasing understanding. In Rapoport R.N. (ed.) *Children, Youth and Families: The Action–Research Relationship*, pp. 26–49. Cambridge University Press, Cambridge.

Maughan B. & Rutter M. (1987) Pupil progress in selective and non-selective schools. *School Organization* **7**, 50–68.

Minton B. (1979) *Dimensions of information underlying children's judgements of their competence*. Unpublished Master's thesis, University of Denver (cited in Harter, 1983).

Minuchin P.P. & Shapiro E.K. (1983) The school as a context for social development. In Hetherington E.M. (ed.) *Socialization, Personality and Social Development*, Vol. 4, *Mussen's Handbook of Child Psychology*, 4th edn, pp. 197–274. Wiley, New York.

Moely B.E., Hart S.S., Leal L. *et al.* (1992) The teacher's role in facilitating memory and study strategy development in the elementary school classroom. *Child Development* **63**, 653–672.

Moos R.H. (1980) *Evaluating Educational Environments: Procedures, Measures, Findings and Policy Implications*. Jossey-Bass, San Francisco.

Mortimore J. & Blackstone T. (1982) *Disadvantage and Education*. Heinemann, London.

Mortimore P. (in press) The positive effects of schooling. In Rutter M. (ed.) *Psychosocial Disturbances in Young People: Challenges for Prevention*. Cambridge University Press, Cambridge.

Mortimore P., Sammons P., Stoll L., Lewis D. & Ecob R. (1988) *School Matters*. Open Books, London.

Nicol A.R., Wilcox C. & Hibbert K. (1985) What sort of children are suspended from school and what can we do for them? In Nichol A.R. (ed.) *Longitudinal Studies in Child Psychology and Psychiatry*, pp. 33–49. Wiley, Chichester.

Nuttall D., Goldstein H., Prosser R. & Rasbash J. (1989) Differential school effectiveness. *International Journal of Educational Research* **13**, 769–776.

Olweus D. (1991) Bully/victim problems among schoolchildren: Basic facts and effects of a school based intervention programme. In Peplar D.J. & Rubin K.H. (eds) *The Development and Treatment of Childhood Aggression*, pp. 441–448. Lawrence Erlbaum, Hillsdale, New Jersey.

Olweus D. (1993) Victimization by peers: Antecedents and long-term outcomes. In Rubin K.H. & Asendorf J.B. (eds) *Social Withdrawal, Inhibition and Shyness in*

Childhood. Lawrence Erlbaum, Hillsdale, New Jersey.

Ouston J. & Maughan B. (1991) Can schools change? II: Practice in six London secondary schools. *School Effectiveness and School Improvement* **2**, 3–13.

Patterson G.R. (1982) *Coercive Family Process.* Castalia, Eugene, Oregon.

Pedersen E., Faucher T.A. & Eaton W.W. (1978) A new perspective on the effects of first grade teachers on children's subsequent adult status. *Harvard Educational Review* **48**, 1–31.

Peterson A.C., Sarigiani P.A. & Kennedy R.E. (1991) Adolescent depression: Why more girls? *Journal of Youth and Adolescence* **20**, 247–271.

Pope A.W., Bierman K.L. & Mumma, G.H. (1989) Relations between hyperactive and aggressive behavior and peer relations at three elementary grade levels. *Journal of Abnormal Child Psychology* **17**, 253–267.

Power M.J., Benn R.T. & Morris J.N. (1972) Neighbourhood, school and juveniles before the Courts. *British Journal of Criminology* **12**, 111–132.

Purkey S.C. & Smith M.S. (1983) Effective schools: A review. *Elementary School Journal* **83**, 427–452.

Quinton D. & Rutter M. (1988) *Parenting Breakdown: The Making and Breaking of Inter-generational Links.* Avebury, Aldershot.

Raudenbush S. & Bryk A. (1986) A hierarchical model for studying school effects. *Sociology of Education* **59**, 1–17.

Raz I.S. & Bryant P. (1990) Social background, phonological awareness and children's reading. *British Journal of Developmental Psychology* **8**, 209–225.

Rende R.D. & Plomin R. (1991) Child and parent perceptions of the upsettingness of major life events. *Journal of Child Psychology and Psychiatry* **32**, 627–633.

Renick M.J. & Harter S. (1989) Impact of social comparisons on the developing self-perceptions of learning disabled students. *Journal of Educational Psychology* **81**, 631–638.

Reynolds D. (1992) Research on school effectiveness and school improvement: An updated review of the British literature. In Reynolds D. & Cuttance P. (eds) *School Effectiveness: Research, Policy and Practice*, pp. 1–24. Cassell, London.

Reynolds D. & Packer A. (1992) School effectiveness and school improvement in the 1990s. In Reynolds D. & Cuttance P. (eds) *School Effectiveness: Research, Policy and Practice*, pp. 171–187. Cassell, London.

Richards M.P.M. & Light P. (1986) *Children of Social Worlds.* Polity Press, Cambridge.

Robins L. & Ratcliff R. (1980) The long-term outcomes of truancy. In Hersov L. & Berg I. (eds) *Out of School*, pp. 65–83. Wiley, Chichester.

Rogoff B. (1981) Schooling and the development of cognitive skills. In Triandis H.C. & Heron A. (eds) *Handbook of Cross-cultural Psychology*, Vol. 4, pp. 233–294. Allyn & Bacon, Boston.

Rogoff B. (1991) *Apprenticeship in Thinking: Cognitive Development in Social Context.* Oxford University Press, New York.

Rubin K.H., LeMare L.J. & Lollis S. (1990) Social withdrawal in childhood: Developmental pathways to rejection. In Asher S.R. & Coie J.D. (eds) *Peer Rejection in Childhood*, pp. 217–249. Cambridge University Press, Cambridge.

Ruble D.N. (1983) The development of social comparison processes and their role in achievement-related socialization. In Higgins E.T., Ruble D.N. & Hartup W.W. (eds) *Social Cognition and Social Development*, pp. 134–157. Cambridge University Press, Cambridge.

Rutter M. (1983) School effects on pupil progress: Research findings and policy implications. *Child Development* **54**, 1–29.

Rutter M. (1985a) Family and school influences on behavioural development. *Journal of Child Psychology and Psychiatry* **26**, 349–368.

Rutter M. (1985b) Family and school influences on cognitive development. *Journal of Child Psychology and Psychiatry* **26**, 683–704.

Rutter M. (1989) Pathways from childhood to adult life. *Journal of Child Psychology and Psychiatry* **30**, 23–51.

Rutter M. (1994) Causal concepts and their testing. In Rutter M. & Smith D. (eds) *Psychosocial Disorders in Young People: Time Trends and their Origins.* Wiley, Chichester. (In press)

Rutter M. & Madge N. (1976) *Cycles of Disadvantage.* Heinemann, London.

Rutter M., Maughan B., Mortimore P. & Ouston J. (1979) *Fifteen Thousand Hours: Secondary Schools and their Effects on Children.* Open Books, London.

Rutter M., Tizard J. & Whitmore K. (1970) *Education, Health and Behaviour.* Longman, London.

St Claire L. & Osborn A.F. (1987) The ability and behaviour of children who have been 'in care' or separated from their parents. *Early Child Development and Care* **28**, 187–353.

Scarr S. (1992) Developmental theories for the 1990s: Development and individual differences. *Child Development* **63**, 1–19.

Scheerens J., Vermeulen C.J.A.J. & Pelgrum W.J. (1989) Generalizability of instructional and school effectiveness indicators across nations. *International Journal of Educational Research* **13**, 789–799.

Scribner S. & Cole M. (1981) *The Psychology of Literacy.* Harvard University Press, Cambridge, Massachusetts.

Simmons R.G. & Blyth D.A. (1987) *Moving into Adolescence: The Impact of Pubertal Change and School Context.* de Gruyter, Hawthorne, New York.

Simmons R.G., Burgeson R., Carlton-Ford S. & Blyth D.A. (1987) The impact of cumulative change in early adolescence. *Child Development* **58**, 1220–1234.

Smith D. & Tomlinson S. (1989) *The School Effect: A Study of Multi-racial Comprehensives.* Policy Studies Institute, London.

Spivack G. & Marcus J. (1989) *Long term effects of retention in grade and special class placement among inner city school children*. Unpublished ms, Hahnemann University, Philadelphia, Prevention Intervention Research Center, Department of Mental Health Sciences.

Stattin H. & Magnusson D. (1990) *Pubertal Maturation and Female Development*. Lawrence Erlbaum, Hillsdale, New Jersey.

Steinberg L., Blinde P.L. & Chan K.S. (1984) Dropping out among language minority youth. *Review of Educational Research* **54**, 113−132.

Stevenson D.L. & Baker D.P. (1987) The family−school relation and the child's school performance. *Child Development* **58**, 1348−1357.

Stevenson H.W. & Lee S. (1990) Contexts of achievement. *Monographs of the Society for Research in Child Development* **55**(1−2), Serial No. 221.

Tizard B., Blatchford P., Burke J., Farquhar C. & Plewis I. (1988) *Young Children at School in the Inner City*. Lawrence Erlbaum, Hove, Sussex.

Tizard J., Schofield W.N. & Hewison J. (1982) Collaboration between teachers and parents in assisting children's reading. *British Journal of Educational Psychology* **52**, 1−15.

Walberg H.J. (1986) Synthesis of research on teaching. In Wittrock M.C. (ed.) *Handbook of Research on Teaching*, 3rd edn, pp. 214−229. American Educational Research Association, Washington, DC.

Weinstein C.S. (1991) The classroom as a social context for learning. *Annual Review of Psychology* **42**, 493−525.

Weinstein R.S., Marshal H.H., Sharp L. & Botkin M. (1987) Pygmalion and the student: Age and classroom differences in children's awareness of teacher expectations. *Child Development* **58**, 1079−1093.

Werthamer-Larsson L., Kellam S.G. & Wheeler L. (1991) Effect of classroom environment on shy behavior, aggressive behavior and concentration problems. *American Journal of Community Psychology* **19**, 585−602.

Wigfield A. & Eccles J.S. (1990) Test anxiety in the school setting. In Lewis M. & Miller S.M. (eds) *Handbook of Developmental Psychopathology*, pp. 237−250. Plenum, New York.

Wigfield A., Eccles J.S., MacIver D., Reuman D.A. & Midgley C. (1991) Transitions during early adolescence: Changes in children's domain-specific self-perceptions and general self-esteem across the transition to junior high school. *Developmental Psychology* **27**, 552−565.

Willig A., Harnisch D.L., Hill K.T. & Maehr M.L. (1983) Sociocultural and educational correlates of success−failure experiences and evaluation anxiety in the school setting for Black, Hispanic and Anglo children. *American Educational Research Journal* **20**, 385−410.

Willms J.D. (1985) The balance thesis: Contextual effects of ability on pupils' O grade examination results. *Oxford Review of Education* **11**, 33−41.

Woodhead M. (1985) Pre-school education has long-term effects: But can they be generalized? *Oxford Review of Education* **11**, 133−155.

Zigler E.F. & Valentine J. (eds) (1979) *Project Head Start: A Legacy of the War on Poverty*. Free Press, New York.

7: Cultural and Community Influences

DAVID QUINTON

INTRODUCTION

Human beings are social animals, their lives are lived in social groups constituted in various ways, their needs are met through social activities and social cooperation, and their normal development depends on stable, nurturing and predictable social relationships. Of all the social animals humans have developed a remarkable capacity to modify forms of social organization to allow the exploitation of a very wide range of environmental conditions. This adaptability has developed with, and depends on, the capacity for *culture*: the ability to represent in symbolic form relationships between humans and between them and the non-human world, and thus to allow great flexibility in social structures and to promote their persistence over time through beliefs, sanctioned behaviours and symbols of group membership and identity. The capacity for symbolic representations has, of course, also led to the unique capacity to accumulate knowledge and transmit it to succeeding generations.

Most definitions of culture include the beliefs, conventional or approved behaviours and symbolic representations that are *shared* by a group of people, have some persistence over time, and are transmitted to new members of a society or institution. However, these broad cultural features are not static and, in addition, within all societies individuals will belong to more than one social grouping constituted with respect to age, sex, kinship, social status, ethnicity, etc., often with competing interests. Indeed, it is clear from studies such as the robbers' cave experiment that even transitory or *ad hoc* groupings rapidly negotiate or develop rules of membership and behaviour and status structures (Sherif *et al.*, 1961), represent their distinctness through visible symbols and private codes and maintain their boundaries by rules or ceremonies of admission and departure. In industrial societies individuals are simultaneously members of a number of groups and during their development must negotiate transitions between groups, settings and statuses (Bronfenbrenner, 1979). All these groups, including families, have cultural features special to themselves as well as ones they share in common with wider groupings. Moreover in industrial societies, unlike traditional ones, a much higher proportion of statuses and roles are *achieved* rather than *ascribed*. In consequence, there is greater potential for the expression of individual differences and thus for a proliferation of cultural representations of these. Our social identities are made up of assemblages of these symbols and our social worlds are defined via the ways we use them for incorporation and exclusion. The construction of early adult identity during adolescence is very striking for its use of cultural elements to assist differentiation from the sphere of family and parents via music and fashion.

However, the role of cultural symbols for defining the self through both incorporation and exclusion has an impact on the way in which we think about cultural and community influences on development. This is because it is easier to perceive the cultural features of an out-group as a distinct construction than to see these features in our own social circle, for whom our own defining elements can be 'the way the world is'. A consequence has been a tendency to study culture in terms of overall aggregate-level similarities and consistencies and to pay less attention to within-culture variations. This is important when we try to answer the question of how cultural or community factors have an impact on individual development or contribute to the development of individual differences. A second problem arises because many of the terms we use to discuss these broad social and cultural influences are themselves included amongst the labels we use for purposes of cultural inclusion and exclusion, for example, in sentences such as: 'the Catholic community and the Protestant community in Northern Ireland are part of the whole community'.

It can be concluded, from the above, that terms such as 'culture', 'community' and 'neighbourhood' are used to refer to at least three rather different kinds of influence. First, there is the characteristic of a culture or community as a *setting* that provides the opportunity for individual activities and the context for social control by other persons, whether known to the individual or not. Second, the culture or community can refer to the *group or network* of people with whom the individual interacts and who he or she thinks of as part of 'my neighbourhood'. Finally, the culture or community may consist in the *idea* of that culture, group or neighbourhood, against which the individual judges or plans his or her actions and judges the actions of others (a 'reference group'). Human societies vary very greatly in the extent to which these meanings overlap. In some traditional small-scale societies the three components of 'culture' or community may be essentially the same thing. In Western industrialized societies all three can be, and often are, different. For this reason cultural influences in modern society are often harder to pin down because the impact of one aspect of culture may depend on the characteristics of another. For example, the impact of the local built environment may depend sharply on the level of individual resources or the importance of the network on the need for social support.

Given this, in what ways might cultural and community influences have an impact on development? In the first place, cultures help to determine the *developmental objective*, that is the kinds of behaviour and patterns of values appropriate to well-functioning child and adult members of the society. Cultures also importantly set the norms for the appropriate ages for and approved method of transition between major life-stages (Caspi *et al.*, 1990) as well as the appropriate institutional forms in which development takes place. A possible consequence of this is that the impact of a particular form, such as an atypical family structure, or of the abnormal timing of a transition, such as early pregnancy, may depend more on the atypicality than on the form or the timing itself. Of course, the lack of agreement between cultural norms and social behaviours may arise through social change as well as through 'deviant' actions by individuals.

There is good evidence that the influence of wider social factors on development within Western societies is mediated first through their impact on family relationships and the family's ability to provide adequate material care and stimulation (Rutter & Quinton, 1977), and second through the effectiveness of the family's monitoring and control of the child's life outside the home, at school or with friends (Rutter & Giller, 1983). The impact of family, school and peer relationships are the subject of other chapters in this volume (Chapters 5, 6 and 18). This chapter is concerned with the impacts of wider sociocultural influences. These will be discussed first as they operate within industrial societies, but second, comparisons with traditional and non-industrial societies will be used to highlight issues concerned with cultural forms, definitions of normality and abnormality and the impacts of different forms of rearing environment.

SOCIOCULTURAL INFLUENCES ON DEVELOPMENT IN INDUSTRIAL SOCIETIES

It is common in public debate to blame a decline in the quality of parenting in industrial societies for the rise in conduct, drug and other problems: this decline being linked to changes in family forms, especially the increase in single-parent households. In this argument, a contrast with parenting in traditional societies is sometimes used as evidence that current problems arise through a departure from the 'natural' form of the family, as seen in the nuclear conjugal form. Earlier in this century this argument was couched in terms of the 'isolation' of the urban nuclear family, rather than single-parent households (Wirth, 1938), but the direction of the argument was the same. In such a debate it is easy for scientific evidence to be diverted to support normative beliefs or political ideas, and for the requirements for normal development to be confused with the forms through which those requirements are satisfied. However, it is important to point out that the intact Western conjugal family is itself an unusual form (Werner, 1984) and that its child-rearing patterns differ in a number of ways from the pattern in most traditional cultures. For example, mothers in Western societies spend a much higher proportion of their time alone with their infants than in the company of other mothers (Whiting & Whiting, 1975; Sostek *et al.*, 1981; Richman *et al.*, 1988) and have far smaller families. The Western nuclear family carries a wide range of functions, from a near exclusive responsibility for child-rearing, to the emotional cosupport of each partner for the other, as well as an ideology of economic independence that limits the level of reciprocity between families and kin (Young & Wilmott, 1973).

These differences have certain consequences: parenting behaviour is less visible, and thus less open to intervention or support and less available to serve as a model; in combination with smaller families, lack of visibility also reduces the opportunity for children and young adults to learn parenting skills; and greater isolation and anonymity decreases the likelihood of a community of adults exercising informal social control on older children outside the home. In addition, industrialized cultures make large developmental demands in terms of skills; demands that need considerable resources to satisfy them, the coordination of which is linked to the form of the family that the culture considers to be the 'proper' type. Any variation from this form carries an increased risk that one or other function will not be adequately performed and thus that some developmental requirements will not be met. On the other hand, there is no evidence that any particular family form now common in Western society is intrinsically unable to provide an adequate or 'expectable' environment for development (Hartmann, 1958; Scarr, 1992).

The relationship between new and traditional Western family forms and the meeting of developmental needs is important since the world is being transformed through the economic pressures associated with capitalism, with an increase in the pressures on families. These transformations are particularly apparent in the very rapid rise in urbanization, the associated migration into towns and cities, the development of Western forms of social stratification, and the attendant marginalization of the economically unsuccessful. In addition, modern communications provide a very rapid dissemination of new ideas and images and thus are an engine for culture change, generally beyond the control of parents. It is therefore necessary to consider the developmental impacts of these large social processes as they translate themselves into the environments through which children are being raised.

Social class and social stratification

The term 'social class' is sometimes narrowly defined, following Marxian analyses, to refer to a person's social status with respect to the ownership and control of the means of production (Runciman, 1990), and the term 'social stratification' to refer to a person's socioeconomic status (SES) as indexed by occupational ranking, sometimes with educational level also taken into account. The ranking of status according to occupation is justified by surveys of attributed status ranks in a number of countries (Trieman, 1977). However, ranking by occupational status is often also referred to as 'social class': the choice between the two terms relating to whether it is believed that the society has a class structure or not. Some authors have attempted to index social class and social stratification separately, but the indices produced have been shown to be highly correlated, not only in Western countries but also in ones in the former Eastern bloc and in Japan (Kohn *et al.*, 1990). For most purposes, therefore, it is reasonable to treat the terms 'social class' and 'social stratification' as interchangeable.

Class and culture

Comparisons between social classes have shown consistent differences in parenting behaviours at the aggregate level, with particular attention having been focused on parent—child communications, because of the relationship between this and language development and academic attainment. It is clear that broad social class differences in language use persist and show a similar pattern cross-nationally, with middle-class mothers being less directive in their speech and responding more with extension and elaboration to child-initiated conversation. These differences do not appear to be related to beliefs about language development and are smallest within the context of play or reading but are much greater outside of this (Hoff-Ginsberg, 1991). However, it is also clear that studies generally show very wide variations of behaviour *within* social classes on a wide range of parenting behaviours from disciplinary techniques (Newson & Newson, 1968, 1976) to kinds of play and language use, so that the idea that the differences in communication patterns reflect cultural values or norms cannot be sustained. This is clear from Field and Widmayer's (1981) comparison in a deprived area of Miami of Cuban, South American and Puerto Rican immigrants and black American families of similar social status. There were marked differences between the groups in both the frequency and length of mother–child communications, with the Cuban immigrants highest, followed by the South Americans, then the Puerto Ricans and finally the black Americans. These differences related to the length of time the groups had been in the USA, but this did not explain the cultural variations.

The consistency in aggregate social class differences cross-nationally is impressive, nevertheless. For example, parents' responses to tape recordings of children's behaviour have been reported as more similar by class than by nationality, in a study comparing Americans, English, English and French Canadians, Belgians, French, Italians, Japanese and Portuguese (Lambert *et al.*, 1979).

The reason for these differences is not clear. As discussed above, these seem not to be explained by normative values. Further, social mobility also means that individuals are frequently not of the same social class as their parents. The question arises, therefore, whether the parenting differences are a consequence of some broader features of the social structure. Kohn and co-workers have continued to develop the idea of a *direct* relationship between class position and individual and parenting values, with those whose work either allows more self-direction or requires more conformity espousing similar values in child-rearing (Kohn & Schooler, 1983). A social class ranking of American, Polish and Japanese samples of men showed significant correlations between class position and such values, but the relationship was stronger with the degree of autonomy in work rather than with class position as such (Kohn *et al.*, 1990). It is unclear whether this association is due to selection processes through which the kind of occupation is determined by prior values, but it seems implausible that the degree of a man's autonomy in work should affect the way in which a mother talks to her children.

The culture of poverty and the underclass

The consequences of macrosocial economic changes in recent years have focused attention on the development of the 'underclass': a group characterized as poor, jobless, uneducated, frequently single parents and chronically supported through welfare payments (Smith, 1992). The underclass is feared to be self-perpetuating through a culture of dependency and an antipathy to mainstream values as indicated through drugs, crime and high-school drop-out, and alienation from the work ethic. Although many of these features have increased recently, more striking is the change in their concentration within geographical areas. Thus, although the proportion of the US population in poverty increased only slightly between 1970 and 1980, the number of poor neighbourhoods increased by 75% (Mincy *et al.*, 1990).

The idea of a self-perpetuating 'culture of poverty' has a long pedigree (Lewis, 1968), but the evidence is against the idea that there is a self-perpetuating culture of this kind. For example, in Britain unemployed adults who are or have recently been in receipt of income support show few differences from employed adults in family or parenting values. More importantly, they show no sign of chronic welfare dependence or lack of desire to get paid work (Heath, 1992). Studies of neighbourhoods (discussed below) show little evidence of a common perception of the neighbourhood or set of neighbourhood values and no evidence that criminal or other activities are accepted as culturally normal. Thus intergenerational patterns of continuity in the features of the 'culture of the underclass' seem more likely to arise through the impact of these features on intellectual and social development, and therefore on the potential for escape, than on cultural values. Childhood hardships show continuity into adult ones (i) depending on secular changes in the general level of opportunity in adulthood; and (ii) through the effects of hardship on development via its effects on the parenting environment (Elder, 1974; Quinton & Rutter, 1988). For example, Long and Vaillant (1984) followed a group of non-delinquent boys from childhood to age 47. For this group, the extent of family problems or welfare dependency in childhood was not related to occupational status, antisocial behavior or global mental health in adult life. On the other hand, the continuities to the reproduction of adverse parenting environments are substantial when the childhood experiences lead to conduct disorders (Zoccolillo *et al.*, 1992).

Social class and abnormal development

Social class differences have been reported for many aspects of development and disorder, but more frequently for physical ill-health (Townsend & Davidson, 1982) and educational delays (Mortimore & Blackstone, 1982) than for psychiatric disorders, with the exception of official delinquency (West, 1985), although such class differences have been reported in Puerto Rico for oppositional disorders, depression and emotional disorders (Bird *et al.*, 1988). Usually these differences do not show a steady class gradient, but rather a substantial increase in problems for children from families headed by a parent with an unskilled manual occupation. Social class differences on emotional or behavioural problems, apart from persistent delinquency, have generally been weak when occupational status is used as an index, but stronger when the index reflects multiple disadvantage (Offord *et al.*, 1989).

The finding of a class gradient is a starting point for investigation, not an explanation of the phenomenon. As the above studies suggest, social class is a 'block-booked' variable: class position can be variably correlated with a whole range of advantages or disadvantages that may be the proximal cause of variations in development. Of course, the accumulation of such disadvantages is itself a sociocultural process, as are the judgements of professionals and administrators on the behaviour of the disadvantaged.

There is little evidence that the genesis of the most substantial social class difference, that of antisocial problems, is primarily cultural: a protest by the dispossessed against the blocking of their aspirations to goods and resources, or an alternative,

culturally sanctioned route to these (Merton, 1957). First, it is clear that members of the delinquents' own communities view their behaviours as undesirable (Kornhauser, 1978); second, it is clear that juvenile crimes are not particularly utilitarian (West, 1985); and third, that the delinquents' own rationalizations of their behaviour do not include this class-conflict element (Matza, 1964). On the other hand there is some evidence of the effect of unsatisfied aspirations on self-reported delinquency when a high orientation towards success is associated with school failure (Hurrelman & Engel, 1992).

Neighbourhood and community influences

A great deal of the attention on neighbourhood and community effects on development has focused on high-problem urban areas in contrast with rural or small town communities. The statistics on the rise of urban/metropolitan living are striking. At the beginning of the nineteenth century less than 3% of the world's population lived in urban areas but by 1980 this had risen to 43% and is predicted to increase further to over 50% — some 3.2 thousand million people — by the year 2000, of whom about three-fifths will be in the Third World, mostly living in megalopoles of over 5 million people (Queloz, 1991). This process has led to the development of large, very poor, high-density areas (favelas, barrios, bidonvilles, etc.) which may occupy up to 80% of a city (Harpham *et al.*, 1988). In these areas mothers carry nearly all the parenting burden in conditions of gross poverty and anxiety, and develop strategies that may have longer term developmental consequences. For example, mothers have been reported to employ a strategy of non-attachment to newborn infants and a complete indifference to early infant death, in the face of very high infant mortality (Scheper-Hughes, 1990). These rapidly developing Third World cities also have substantial numbers of street-children, a pattern similar to that in the development of London in the nineteenth century.

The developmental consequences of these extreme environments are not known. Current knowledge on the developmental consequences of city living comes entirely from studies in developed nations, but even there the topic is remarkably under-researched. The available evidence comes from studies of the relationships between features of the built environment and various social problems, and from the comparative study of differences in psychosocial problems between geographical or administrative areas. Two kinds of comparison have been undertaken: the first involving epidemiological comparisons between rural and urban areas to see whether and why rates of disorder are higher in cities; and the second using intra-urban comparisons of districts or census tracts to examine the association between indicators of area disadvantage, such as poverty or single-parent households and levels of delinquency, school drop-out, teenage pregnancy and other indicators of 'social pathology'. Unfortunately, these traditions have not yet come together. The rural—urban comparisons have used epidemiological methods, and are thus able to ask whether child disorders are primarily mediated through the family or whether there are additional area influences, but have been unable to examine area factors because of small sample sizes. The intra-urban area comparisons have the advantage of large samples and measures of area characteristics but no means of linking these to individual pathology or family life.

Rural—urban comparisons

Rural—urban comparisons have led to three main conclusions: (i) that where there are differences the urban areas are much more likely to show higher rates of disorder; (ii) that variations in findings make it clear that there is no inevitable urban effect underlying these differences; and (iii) that the differences are primarily the result of the greater concentration of family problems in the city and the direct effect of these on development. Lavik (1977) found a marked increase in school and behaviour problems in adolescents in Oslo compared with a rural area, and Vikan (1985) showed rural/small town differences in Norway. Similarly, Rutter *et al.* (1975a) found an increase in emotional and conduct problems in 10-year-old children in an inner London borough compared with the Isle of Wight, an area of small towns. The inner-city rates were twice those for the rural area; the difference applied as much to emotional as to conduct problems and to girls as well as boys, and was particularly marked for chronic child disorders of early onset (Rutter, 1979). Cederblad (1988) showed similar

rural—urban differences in non-European societies in a comparison of Sweden, the Sudan and Nigeria. City children in all three cultures had somewhat higher rates of disorder than rural children, according to psychiatrists' ratings. However, rural—urban differences were not replicated in studies in Denmark (Kastrup, 1977), nor in Japan (Matsuura *et al.*, 1989), and one study has reported differences that run in the opposite direction. Shen *et al.* (1985) used a four-item teachers' screening questionnaire in the Beijing province in China and found the lowest rates of disorder in the urban areas, higher rates in the suburbs and highest rates in impoverished mountain communities.

In the Isle of Wight/inner London comparative study the associations between city living and higher levels of children's problems were convincingly shown to be due to the greater overlap of adverse family factors in the urban area. In both geographical areas the family factors associated with childhood disorders were the same and once the two areas were equated statistically for the occurrence of these risk factors, there was little area difference left to explain (Rutter & Quinton, 1977). These family factors were especially associated with chronic disorders of early onset, which showed the greatest area difference, an association replicated in Mannheim (Blanz *et al.*, 1991).

This account of area differences in terms of family influences does not explain how the concentration of family problems arises, nor whether neighbourhood and cultural factors are influential in this. Further, the influence of family factors appears to apply mostly to disorders of early onset and it is therefore important to consider whether aspects of urban environment and culture beyond the family contribute to problems first appearing in adolescence.

Intra-urban comparisons

The variations between rates of children's emotional or behavioural problems apparent in the rural—urban comparisons have equally been shown for areas within cities. These data usually rely on official statistics, such as census data, and explanations of differences have relied on ecological correlations, that is, an association between indicators of individual and social adversity (Rutter &

Giller, 1983). Such data are often interpreted as showing causal connections between area indicators such as housing characteristics, and deviance or disorder, but problems inevitably arise in drawing conclusions from indicators that may not relate to the same individuals — the so-called 'ecological fallacy' (Robinson, 1950; Rutter, 1994). Problems also arise in the use of official statistics because these may be influenced by local area differences in the referral, recording, processing or visibility of deviance or disorder.

Intra-urban comparisons have identified areas high in such problems as delinquency or teenage pregnancy (Mincy *et al.*, 1990). These areas often show impressive temporal stability (Wallis & Maliphant, 1967), although area stability has been shown to be limited to relatively short periods (Buisik & Webb, 1982). A general conclusion about these areas is that they are more similar in their concurrent rates of family and social problems than in their environmental characteristics. They may be older city slums or new housing estates and variations may occur at borough, ward, enumeration district or even street level (Quinton, 1988).

Community influences

Although these differences are often discussed in terms of 'community' or 'neighbourhood' differences, it is important to note that the areas are always defined either with respect to administrative boundaries or on the basis of the clustering of problems arrived at through statistical techniques. Community effects are presumed on the basis of contiguity, not on measures of area attachment or identification from the inhabitants themselves. Indeed, there is little evidence that local areas are conceived in this way by those who live there. Even in the classic accounts of stable working-class areas, it is apparent that attachments are to family and friends and not to some notion of the community (Young & Wilmott, 1957; Gans, 1962). It is only when some outside threat or interest promotes temporary coalitions that the notion of community cohesiveness may be used as a basis for inclusion or exclusion and therefore as a basis for action. Rieder (1985) has shown how, in the Canarsie district of New York, the resident Jewish and Italian communities reacted to the influx of blacks first through

ad hoc fighting between teenage boys that later became organized and condoned on a community basis to encompass the bombing of houses occupied by blacks and a high school race riot.

Of course, the community does not have to be constantly in consciousness for it to exist or to have influence. As with personal social support, the importance on a day-to-day basis may be as much in the presumption of something that could be activated as of something that is felt to be always impinging on life. For this reason, the local community will be more important on an individual basis depending on the need for its resources or the need to protect oneself against it, and this may vary with life-cycle or other needs. But the implication of this also is that the community is defined by the individual as much as the individual by the community. For this reason, except in isolated areas, communities cannot be mapped on to geographical or administrative boundaries.

It has been pointed out that there have been no systematic intra-urban area comparative studies that allow the direct influences of family factors and the indirect influences of area characteristics to be separated out. Nevertheless, a number of theories have been proposed to explain the associations between measures of area characteristics and deviant development or social problems. The first explanations, deriving from the first ecological studies by Shaw and McKay (1942) in Chicago, suggested that the problems arose from a *lack* of community, that is that the social indicators were indexing community disorganization and that the associated decay in social control allowed crime and delinquency to flourish: a theory of *opportunity*. An alternative to this explanation is the idea that the social pathology arises from the resentment bred by relative deprivation: a *cultural* theory. Both these explanations are plausible for antisocial acts but less so for school drop-out or teenage pregnancy. A related idea is that of an additional area influence arising through *contagion*, that is, through disadvantaged or deviant neighbours being a bad influence. Most of the tests of these ideas have involved examination of the association between mean levels of income or other area indicators with rates of problems such as school drop-out or teenage pregnancy. The associations found have generally been modest (Mayer & Jencks, 1989) and have not supported theories either of contagion or of relative deprivation. Crane (1991) has argued that marked effects occur only when some important factor is at a critical level of incidence, and has shown marked changes in the level of school drop-out and teenage child-bearing when the proportion of professional inhabitants in an area becomes very low.

A number of studies support the idea of the effects of community organization and informal social control on levels of delinquency. In a reanalysis of data from the British crime survey, Sampson and Groves (1989) showed a strong connection between unsupervised teenage peer groups and rates of robbery and violence by strangers. Conversely, the density of local friendship networks was associated with lower robbery rates. However, it can be difficult to separate the effects of community organization from the effects of population turnover, especially the in-migration of ethnically distinct groups. Crime levels, gang activity and homicide are highest in such areas (Reiss, 1986), but, as is apparent from the Canarsie study, these problems can sometimes be associated with heightened community activity, as well as disorganization.

How does the accumulation of family problems in particular areas come about? Two obvious possibilities are either that the physical characteristics of the areas themselves affect family life or that the differential distribution of problems is the result of complex population movements.

Features of the built environment

Although city life is often contrasted unfavourably with life in rural areas, there seems little evidence of a straightforward connection between environmental characteristics and family problems. Today's problem areas may well be yesterday's fashionable suburbs, and yesterday's inner-city ghettos today's chic neighbourhoods. None of the most visible and frequently canvassed aspects of the urban environment have been shown to relate directly to family problems. Population density appears on its own to contribute little (Freedman, 1975); where associations occur, they seem to arise because of the overlap with household crowding (Booth, 1976), and the crowding itself with poverty and large families (Dye, 1975). It is unclear which is the most important variable, but poverty seems to be the

likely candidate. Where crowding occurs it is likely that cultural mediation is important, both in terms of affecting the perception of crowding (Rapoport, 1975) and the means of handling crowded conditions. As yet, the contributions of crowding, density and absolute numbers have not been resolved (Freedman, 1975), partly because the impact of these features is markedly affected by cultural factors. For example, Chinese families living in Hong Kong appear to manage without ill-effect in levels of crowding that would cause serious stress in Western societies (Mitchell, 1971; Anderson, 1972).

No systematic relationships have been found between housing type and parental and child disorders independent of their associations with other family difficulties. This lack of connection seems partly due to the fact that the impact of housing may depend critically on family history, circumstances and life-cycle stage (Freeman, 1984a), so that effects may occur in small subsamples of the population only. Quinton and Rutter have shown how adverse family experiences in childhood are linked both to a vulnerability to psychosocial problems in adulthood and independently to a higher probability of housing disadvantage. In a comparison of families with children in local authority care and families in the same geographical area, poor housing appeared to have some impact on parenting but the effects were more marked in the families with children in care. These families appeared to be more vulnerable to such influences because of their own very adverse childhoods (Quinton & Rutter, 1984b). Similar effects were found in a related study of women reared in children's homes (Quinton & Rutter, 1988). However, such vulnerable groups are a relatively small part of the population as a whole and for this reason associations are often difficult to detect (Quinton, 1985).

Housing estates

In the 1970s, Newman developed the idea of a link between levels of deviance in an area and the physical characteristics of buildings, especially the extent to which design features limited individuals' abilities to protect or defend themselves or their property — the idea of 'defensible space' (Newman, 1973). Coleman (1985, 1991) has continued work in this tradition, demonstrating impressive associations between the number of adverse design features (such as the presence of overhead walkways or the number of interconnected exits or entrances) and increased levels of burglary, theft, assault and other residential crime. The interpretation of these associations is that poor design increases the opportunities afforded to those disposed to criminality, rather than turning the law-abiding to it. The data on some features such as overhead walkways are so strong as to make it unlikely that the effects would disappear if the extent of family problems on the estates were taken into account, although it is less clear why the number of walkways should relate as strongly to motor vehicle crime as it does to burglary and theft. Nevertheless, these findings are in tune with data that suggest that the physical environment has an impact on urban deviancy rates in both children and adults because of increased difficulties in supervision and increased opportunity for theft and vandalism. Earlier studies showed that parents in crowded conditions were, not unnaturally, more likely to encourage their children to play outside and were less likely to have superviseable play space (Jephcott & Carter, 1954; Mitchell, 1971). Problems in supervision have been linked to delinquency (Loeber & Stouthamer-Loeber, 1986; Wilson, 1980), but it is also true that families who show poorer supervision also show a range of other pathogenic features (Wilson & Herbert, 1978).

Self-report studies show petty theft and vandalism to be very common amongst urban teenagers. It is also clear that urban environments provide greater temptation both as regards the range of targets for theft and vandalism and greater anonymity for the commission of offences (Rutter & Giller, 1983). A number of studies have convincingly shown an effect on the level of delinquency of measures designed to make crime more difficult (Clarke, 1992). For example, the introduction of compulsory steering locks on cars in Germany (Rutter, 1979) or greater directed supervision (but not community surveillance), such as the use of doorkeepers in apartment blocks (Waller & Okihiro, 1978). Coleman (1991) has proposed that specific design features as well as more general urban opportunities for crime not only increase the levels of transitory teenage crime but also breed more persistent criminals through their effects on community integration. There are, as yet, no data to test this proposition but it is clear that to do so will require a careful control for family characteristics.

Migration and area differences

The processes through which population movements might affect the differential distribution of family problems have been discussed in terms of *social drift* (the tendency for people with particular characteristics to move into a particular area) and *social residue* (the tendency for people with particular characteristics to be left behind when the better adjusted members of the population move out). Existing data suggest that both processes operate and that they also apply to movement into and out of rural areas (Freeman, 1984b). However, very little is known about the characteristics of parents or potential parents who in-migrate, either at times of urban development or at times of urban decline. Two studies have shown contrasting findings for young adults in-migrating during rapid urbanization. Barquero *et al.* (1982) have shown a marked increase in neuroses in a rapidly developing Spanish urban population compared with its 'feeder' rural villages and isolated farms. On the other hand, young women in-migrants into urban areas in Taiwan had lower rates of minor psychiatric morbidity (Cheng, 1989). Even during a time of urban decline the available evidence suggests that in-migrating families are not noticeably more deviant than the existing population. In the inner London/Isle of Wight study rates of disorder in parents and children moving into London were no greater than among families born and bred in the inner city, nor were in-migrants overrepresented amongst those with children in care (Quinton & Rutter, 1984a). The importance of measuring individual characteristics prior to any migration in or out was shown in Osborn's (1980) comparison of delinquency rates amongst London residents and out-migrants. The behaviour of the out-migrants after they had left London showed lower delinquent activity. This might have led to the conclusion of differential out-migration, but in fact the two groups did not differ on their behaviour when they both lived in the London area.

Intracity migration may explain the geographical

concentration of families with problems. Such families have very few material resources and also move house more frequently (Quinton & Rutter, 1984a). The accumulation of financial problems channels them through both public and private housing routes into the more environmentally deprived areas and may result in the areas retaining their low status. The impact of public housing policies in this process has been shown in Bottoms and Wiles's (1986) study of housing allocation. A policy that involved the differential placement of single mothers and families with young children on particular estates was associated with higher delinquency rates, especially when population movement through the estate was also high. This led to low community control over young males and high rates of vandalism, theft and burglary.

Migration across cultures

There is evidence that the level of neighbourhood problems, especially in crime and gang violence, is especially high when neighbourhoods are experiencing the rapid in-migration of ethnically different groups (Reiss, in press). It is therefore necessary to discuss the consequences of this kind of migration. There is no doubt that migration is, itself, an unsettling experience because of major disturbances in the sense of identity and self-efficacy (Berry *et al.*, 1992). Cross-cultural migrants are especially subject to these problems, as well as to stresses associated with dislocation of family and friendship ties, and to poor housing and occupational restrictions due to prejudice. For the second generation, further stresses arise through conflicts between parental cultural beliefs and the children's desire to acculturate and become more like the young people in the new culture.

First-generation populations of cross-cultural migrants as diverse as Norwegians in the USA and West Indians in Britain have been consistently shown to have higher rates of psychiatric disorders, especially schizophrenia (Leff, 1988). On the other hand, migrating populations do not appear to have higher rates of affective disorders, despite the stresses associated with migration, although it is not known whether this is a consequence of the different ways of expressing distress or of culturally protective factors.

There are very few studies of the children of migrants. Comparisons of Greek and Turkish migrant workers with indigenous children in Germany suggest substantial cultural differences (Steinhausen *et al.*, 1990), with overall rates of disorder on a symptom checklist lowest for the Greek children (16%) and highest for the Turkish (34%). Much of this overall variation appeared due to large differences in the rated frequency of problems such as hyperactivity or enuresis, rather than emotional or conduct disorders. The overall differences were largely explained by disturbances in parental behaviour, marriage and health rather than features such as the size of the originating community or current living conditions.

It is not known whether these family differences arise because some cultures have family forms that are more vulnerable to cultural change than others. Moreover, family patterns that are initially protective during cultural change may generate problems for succeeding generations by their cohesiveness. For example, families migrating to the UK from India and Pakistan bring family forms with low marital breakdown rates and high cultural values for family maintenance (Ballard, 1982). These, together with language differences, provide a cultural coherence and family stability that is protective in the face of migration stresses. On the other hand, this first-generation coherence may provide more problems for the second generation. Recent studies have suggested low rates of disturbance in younger children in these communities (Hackett *et al.*, 1991) although the family correlates of disturbance are very similar (Newth & Corbett, 1993). As the children reach adolescence the family strengths may become strains through conflicts between the children's ties to their families and their desire to adopt the lifestyles of their peers. These strains may underlie some of the increases in psychological problems in Asian girls. For example, in this group self-harm has increased rapidly (Soni Raleigh *et al.*, 1990; Handy *et al.*, 1991) as have eating disorders (Mumford & Whitehouse, 1988; Mumford *et al.*, 1991). These problems are not associated with open rebellion against the traditional culture but rather with a commitment to it. The disorders may, therefore, be related to a conflict between a desire to hold to the existing culture and the pressure for change. Raised rates of bulimia have also been reported for Greek girls in Germany in comparison with girls in Greece, another culture that appears initially protective for migrating families (Fichter *et al.*, 1988).

Differences in rates of children's problems in migrating families should not be taken to mean that the migrant group's problems necessarily have the same origins or the same meaning. For example, in an early study of the children of Afro-Caribbean parentage in London in the early 1970s, Rutter *et al.* (1975b, c) confirmed impressions of a somewhat elevated level of behaviour problems at school. However, the children showed fewer such problems at home than did white children and the family correlates of the problems were different. For the white children, behaviour problems were strongly related to parental discord and marital disruption, but this was not true for the Afro-Caribbean children. For them, although the classroom misbehaviour was patterned in the same way as misbehaviour in the indigenous group, its correlates were different, suggesting that it was much more a reaction to the school experience.

In other circumstances apparent differences in rates of problems may not reflect real differences between groups. For example, black youngsters are over-represented in official delinquency statistics in both the USA and the UK, but this excess is not generally repeated in epidemiological studies of conduct disorder (Robins, 1991). This suggests that labelling and differential police practice are implicated in the difference in the official statistics since there is evidence that black delinquents are more likely than whites to be prosecuted for the same level of offence (Landau, 1981; Tuck & Southgate, 1981). On the other hand these differences in the identification and processing of offences do not fully explain the excess of adult criminal behaviour amongst African-Americans or British males of Afro-Caribbean origin, where the excess over white males varies between 2.6 and 5 to 1, depending on the source of information (Smith, 1994). The smaller differences are found in epidemiological studies and the larger in official crime statistics, but the differences remain substantial. In both the USA and the UK individuals from the Chinese or Asian communities have lower rates of criminality than whites. Since the rates in first-generation British Afro-Caribbeans were also lower than in the

white population, the increase seems likely to be a consequence of the particular circumstances and family patterns in this community and not a direct consequence of migration.

The effects of television

TV is the major source of cultural information for children and young people and is very rapidly bringing the images of the Western world to radically different societies. TV provides a remarkable diversity of symbols, images, models and stereotypes for human activity; an input that it is difficult or impossible for adults to control. Although other media are involved in the production and manipulation of cultural images, TV dominates. In Western industrial countries it has been estimated that by the age of 18 young people will have spent more time watching TV than doing any other single thing but sleep (Liebert & Sprafkin, 1988). Watching TV peaks at about 4 hours a day during early adolescence, and then declines. TV watching has reduced the amount of time spent in active leisure pursuits and in reading (Robinson, 1972). Adults have been particularly concerned about the possible adverse impacts of TV on aggressive behaviour (Comstock & Strasburger, 1990), sexuality (Brown *et al.*, 1990), the creation or perpetuation of cultural stereotypes (Signorelli, 1990), education (Corteen & Williams, 1986) and the exploitation of the young by commercial forces. Of these concerns, the effects on increasing aggression and violence are by far the most systematically studied, although there is an increasing number of studies of effects on sexuality as well (Peterson *et al.*, 1991).

Television and violence

Since Bandura first focused research attention on the issue (Bandura, 1963), there has been a large number of experimental studies examining the connections between watching aggressive actions on TV and subsequent behaviour and attitudes. It is clear from these studies that subsequent behaviour is affected in the expected direction in the short term, whether in younger children's play or in 'real life' tasks such as the administration of electric shocks by older subjects using the 'aggression machine' (e.g. Hartmann, 1969). In the latter case the level of subsequent aggression seems influenced by the perceived justification of the aggression shown in the film (Berkowitz, 1965).

Further work has attempted to deal with the nature of the connection, the direction of the effects and their persistence. It seems clear that in children short-term play effects are predominantly through copying of the actions seen (Bandura *et al.*, 1961). Using older subjects, Tannenbaum (1971) tested whether the effects were specifically modelling ones or were related to general arousal, and achieved rather comparable effects on subsequent aggression with erotic as with aggressive material. Clearly, modelling and arousal mechanisms are not incompatible and, indeed, actions following the former may depend on the latter, but effects following arousal alone may be more related to individual differences in aggressive tendencies. Such individual effects have been shown in studies of institutionalized delinquents in America and Belgium using naturalistic observational methods (Parke *et al.*, 1977). Baseline measures of aggressiveness were taken and the boys randomly assigned to a week of watching movies with high or low aggressive content, followed by subsequent naturalistic observation. There were marked increases in aggressive behaviour for the aggressive film groups, especially in boys initially high on aggression.

Although it seems unlikely that watching TV violence will, on its own, cause children to develop serious problems with aggressive behaviour, there is evidence of a cumulative increase in general levels of aggressive behaviour, net of initial individual differences in aggression (Singer *et al.*, 1984). In a 3-year prospective study in the USA and Finland, Huesmann *et al.* (1984) studied 978 children from first to fifth grade using an overlapping cohort design. The extent of TV violence viewed initially was related to an increase in aggression in subsequent years, as measured by peer nominations. The boys most affected were those who identified most readily with violent characters, whereas amongst the girls it was those who preferred masculine activities. In an earlier 10-year follow-up study of children in the third grade, also using peer nominations, Lefkowitz *et al.* (1972) showed a significant relationship between the amount of TV violence watched and aggressive behaviour at age 19, but not vice versa. In a follow-up of this group to age 30, very strong associations were found between the amount of exposure to TV violence at age 8 and the seriousness of adult criminal acts (Huesmann, 1986).

All of the studies so far discussed have attempted to assess the effects of TV violence on individual behaviour. A more general cultural issue is the extent to which the routine portrayal of violence alters cultural expectations concerning the acceptable level of violence as a means of solving problems. There is evidence that the portrayal of violence changes perceptions of the dangerousness of the real environment (Bryant *et al.*, 1981) regardless of individual disposition to anxiety; that it influences children's views of what children their age *would* do, but not what they *should* do (Thomas & Drabman, 1977); and that it changes adults' perceptions of themselves as willing to use aggression, but not of measured levels of aggression (Atkin, 1983): but does TV violence affect the general level of violence in the community?

An answer to this question requires a comparison between communities with and without TV but otherwise socially and demographically similar, and a study of the consequences of the introduction of TV. This design has been achieved by Joy *et al.* (1986) in a study of three Canadian communities: one without TV, one with only one Canadian channel and one with three major US networks. These were called Notel, Unitel and Multitel by the researchers. Measures were taken from direct observations and teachers' ratings prior to and 2 years after the introduction of TV into Notel. There was a significant increase of aggression in children in this community. This applied to those initially low and high on aggression, but the increase was not related to the amount of TV watched. There was no change in levels of aggression in the communities that already had TV.

In summary, there is consistent evidence of an association between watching violence on TV and antisocial behaviour and attitudes and physical aggression. The association is similar for boys and girls up to about age 10, but subsequently strengthens for boys and markedly weakens for girls (Hearold, 1986). The repeated presentation of violence on TV affects expected levels of violence in the community, as well as views of the acceptability of aggression as part of assertiveness; and appears initially to increase the general level of aggressiveness in children's behaviour. In this way acceptable as well as expected levels may alter, thus producing a change in culture. However, the extent to which TV violence can be held responsible for antisocial behaviour or conduct problems is unclear. It seems most likely that TV provides models and justifications for violent behaviour for those in pathogenic environments, and may thus contribute to the perpetuation of deviance. It seems improbable that TV violence is a major contributor to the development of persistent conduct problems.

Television and sexuality

The effects of TV on sexual behaviour have been much less researched, despite the very high level of adult concern. The presentation of sex has been shown to be slanted towards fantasy rather than reality. Thus, sex is portrayed as the province of the young; unmarried couples are shown as engaging in sex four to eight times more frequently than married ones; the role of sex in expressing affection in long-standing intimate relationships is seldom presented and precautions against pregnancy and disease are seldom discussed (Brown *et al.*, 1990). It seems likely that the presentation of more explicit sexual activity, as well as of homosexual relationships or 'atypical' family forms, has followed social changes rather than promoted them. However, this presentation also serves to change expectations about what activity will occur, and may eventually alter normative beliefs. It is not clear how seriously teenagers take these portrayals. There is evidence that they rate TV after friends, parents and school courses as a source of information on sex, although they also tend to take the portrayal of sex on TV as realistic (Louis Harris *et al.*, 1986). Peterson *et al.* (1991) have examined the association between the extent of viewing TV with a sexual content and the early initiation of sexual intercourse. They found no consistent association between the two variables, but not surprisingly the viewing of sexual material was a trigger for the activity if the circumstances were propitious.

It seems likely that family and peer influences will be more powerful in determining the initiation of sexual activity, although TV may have some effect on the age at which peer pressures begin to operate. On the other hand, TV may have an effect on attitudes. For example, the viewing of even non-aggressive pornographic films has been shown to reduce older male adolescents' views of the seriousness of rape and the extent to which women mean 'no' when they turn down sexual advances (Zillerman & Bryant, 1982). It is not known whether this change reflects a change in attitude or an increased willingness to reveal concealed views. Nor is it known whether these attitudes last or relate to subsequent behaviour.

Television and gender identity

There is ample evidence that the presentation of men and women on TV predominantly promotes cultural stereotypes (Signorelli, 1990). Women are generally under-represented in both prime-time and children's programmes, they are much less often portrayed as working than is actually the case, and in the great majority of portrayals those that are working are unmarried. Their nurturant or 'romantic interest' role is emphasized. Boys and girls appear to prefer programmes centred on adults of the same sex as themselves, but there is evidence that they can pick up 'counter-stereotypical' attitudes from same sex models, although there is also evidence of selective attention to information depending on sex role preferences. Studies covering ages from three through to adolescence have shown that children who watch more TV are more likely to move in attitude towards the stereotypes, although this effect is most apparent in boys. For boys who watch little TV stereotyping declines with age, but this is not the case for those who watch a great deal. These studies of individual children's viewing behaviour are supported by Joy *et al.*'s (1986) comparison of communities with and without TV, which showed a convergence in stereotyping with the introduction of TV.

DEVELOPMENT IN CROSS-CULTURAL PERSPECTIVE

The preponderance of data from Western societies in the study of development raises the issue of whether the associations found in these data reflect universal developmental principles or cultural specificities.

There is little dispute that humans share the same basic capacities and that the biological requirements for normal development are the same regardless of culture (Hinde, 1991). On the other hand, even such basic non-verbal responses as the 'eyebrow flash' are used to carry subtly different meanings across cultures (Eibl-Eibesfeldt, 1972). The extraordinary variation in human social patterns may be viewed as a laboratory of natural experiments in which propositions about the requirements for normal development or the risk factors for deviance or disorder may be tested: for example whether attachment patterns have the same form and the same implications in different cultures; or whether family forms and the quality of parental relationships carry similar risks everywhere.

However, the use of cross-cultural material to investigate developmental processes is not without controversy. Objections have primarily focused on the transferring of ideas of 'normality' or 'deviance' or 'disorder' from one culture to another (Kleinman, 1987), such a transfer being seen variously as: a process of labelling or social control; a medicalization of distress (Obeyesekere, 1985); or as an enterprise that lacks meaning, because a particular behaviour is only interpretable when its unique cultural context is taken into account (Rosaldo, 1984). Such objections have also been raised concerning the use of categories of normality and deviance *within* the same culture, notably in the study of social class differences in normal and deviant development (Mays, 1972), or ethnic differences in rates of psychiatric disorders (Burke, 1984), although here the effect appears to operate through the impact of ethnic stereotypes on the type of disorder rated rather than on the threshold for disorder (Lewis *et al.*, 1990). Labelling, the medicalization of distress and the failure to take context properly into account commonly occur, but this is not a reason for rejecting cross-cultural comparisons, rather a reminder that these issues need to be considered in the interpretation of cross-cultural material.

In summary, caution is necessary in the use of cross-cultural material because of the ways in which cultural factors modify the meaning of observations. The problem of meaning can be summarized under five questions: (i) is the behaviour patterned in the same way (do the same sorts of behaviours go together); (ii) is it culturally interpreted in the same way (is it 'normal' or 'deviant'); (iii) does it have the same correlates cross-culturally; (iv) is its course

or outcome the same (do cultural factors modify the outcome); and (v) do the associated personal experiences vary with culture (do they mean the same thing to individuals in different cultures)? Issues surrounding the normative interpretation of behaviours and the associated personal experience have been especially taken up in medical anthropology (Kleinman, 1987; Littlewood, 1990), although often not using a comparative methodology (Kleinman & Good, 1985). Data on cross-cultural differences in patterning and correlates of developmental problems have begun to appear for both psychiatric disorders and cognitive development. The caveats detailed above become especially focused around issues of measurement, where both the translation of instruments and the question of thresholds present conceptual and empirical problems.

Methodological issues

Translation of instruments

The cross-cultural study of developmental problems has almost always involved the translation and adaptation of Western measuring instruments such as standardized psychiatric interviews or cognitive tests. The translation of interviews is usually made by members of the 'target' culture who have been educated in a Western tradition and are conversant with Western psychological/psychiatric concepts. The forward translation tries to find words or phrases in the target culture that tap the concept of emotion or behaviour behind the items in the original, and the success of this is checked for consistency with the original instrument via translation back into the originating language (back-translation).

It is now recognized that simply to translate instruments in this way is not satisfactory (Fegert, 1989), because the universality of symptom patterns cannot be presumed, and because the ways in which distress is expressed may vary from culture to culture. Therefore, recent approaches to translation often involve the addition of culture specific items to instruments, based on the clinical experience of professionals from the culture. An alternative approach has been to construct scales *de novo* on the basis of Western concepts and to see how the structure then compares with the general pattern of findings in the Western literature (Lambert *et al.*, 1989b).

The most common form of validation has been to examine factor structures. Factor analyses using both straight and modified versions of established measures have generally shown similar factor structures to those found in the originating culture (Elton *et al.*, 1988), or a patterning of symptomatology that appears translatable into Western disorder categories. The finding of a similar and coherent factor structure can be taken as strong evidence for the cross-cultural usefulness of a scale, since there is no reason to suppose that the scale itself will generate such a structure if this does not exist within the behaviour or beliefs of those within the culture. In general, studies using Western instruments and categories show a broad level of consistent patterning of symptomatology cross-culturally, but with the addition of certain culturally specific features. On the other hand, such instruments may fail to detect or may misinterpret reactions that are not part of a Western repertoire (the so-called 'culture-specific disorders', Favazza, 1985).

Threshold problems

Regardless of whether satisfactory instrument or concept translation can be achieved, a major problem remains with regard to thresholds for disorder. These problems are likely to be most acute for standard interviews or questionnaires rather than clinical interviews and may partly explain the remarkable cross-cultural variation in rates of adult affective disorder (estimates have varied from 0.8 to 89.0 per thousand; Leff, 1988). Threshold problems may also affect the very wide frequencies of individual symptoms checked on questionnaire measures such as the Rutter A and B scales. For example, overactivity in boys varies from 4% in Ethiopia to 38% in China, and anxiety in girls from 0.1% in the Sudan to 39% in Britain (Ekblad, 1990). Matsuura *et al.* (1989) have used the Rutter B scale to examine rates of rural/urban differences in Japan and found very low rates of disorder, using the normal scale cut-offs, with only 3% of children rated as showing disorder, of whom the great majority (93%) showed antisocial or mixed

problems. That threshold differences are a problem is shown in a direct observation study of hyperactivity (Sonuga-Barke *et al.*, 1993), where teachers and Asian parents rated Asian, but not indigenous, children as showing deviant levels of activity that were not confirmed by direct observation. The same group has reported similar differences on parental reports in Hong Kong.

Culture and development

Cognitive development

The issues surrounding translatability of instruments and interpretation of differences in the level of performance apply to the measurement of both normal and abnormal development, even when the measurement involves non-verbal tasks, because test materials or the testing experience may not be equally familiar. It seems plausible to assume that the greater the difference in cultural circumstances and priorities the more likely it will be to find capacities that are highly developed in one culture and not in another, and that cross-cultural differences may increase with age, as capacities become more shaped by culture (Super, 1980; Shweder, 1985), although this has not been formally tested through cross-cultural comparisons of children and adults. Certainly young children in very different cultures are able to do Western cognitive tests including Piagetian tasks (Bentley, 1987), the Bayley mental scale (Sigman *et al.*, 1988) or tests of belief—desire reasoning (Avis & Harris, 1991), whereas adults may not. For example, traditionally educated men on the Polynesian island of Pulawat failed a straightforward Piagetian task of the multiplication of classes (Gladwin, 1970). Highly specialized abilities have been reported. For example, Blurton-Jones and Konner (1976) documented the very advanced (but specialized) ability of the !Kung hunter—gatherers of the Kalahari to assemble facts about animal behaviour and to discriminate fact from hearsay and interpretation. Ten and 11-year-old street vendors in north-east Brazil have been shown to develop individual and highly sophisticated ways of representing large numerical values and performing arithmetic operations and ratio comparisons (Saxe, 1988; see also Chapter 10).

The very sizeable influence of culture on educational attainment within societies with similar academic objectives has been shown in a careful series of comparisons between the USA, China and Japan (Stevenson *et al.*, 1987, 1990; Stigler & Perry, 1990). First grade children in Chicago performed significantly worse than either the Japanese or Chinese children on all aspects of mathematics measured, regardless of the ethnic background of the American children. There was no catch-up by grade 11 (Stevenson *et al.*, 1993) and in a repeat study 10 years later the cultural differences at age 5 were, if anything, greater. These differences were related to marked differences between the cultures in classroom organization, with the USA being most informal and with children more frequently off task; the Chinese most didactic; and the Japanese both on task *and* with high interaction between teacher and children and between the children themselves. Within the USA both Asian-American and Anglo-American children scored higher than African-Americans or Spanish-Americans in grade 1, but by grade 5 a substantial gap had also developed between the Asian-American and the Anglo-American children.

There were revealing differences in parental and child attitudes across cultures. American children rated mathematics an easy subject and themselves as above average, irrespective of level of attainment, whilst Chinese children thought mathematics difficult, even when they were succeeding. The American parents were more likely to think their children were doing well or that, where problems did exist, that these were not serious. Even where the norms for achievement are similar, cultural differences appear markedly to affect performance. For example, Hamilton *et al.* (1990) have shown that although academic striving in children is associated with norms stressing achievement in both the USA and Japan, higher Japanese attainment was associated with a greater stress on social rewards for achievement — a response in line with the more communal and less individualistic orientation of Japanese culture.

Culture and child disorder

Unless the problems of threshold are addressed, cross-cultural comparison of rates of disorders will be uninformative, although study of the cross-cultural correlates of behaviours is still possible. Weisz *et al.* (1987a, b, 1989) have made an interesting attack on the problems of threshold and cultural correlates and meanings in studies of the epidemiology of childhood disorders in the USA and Thailand. In these studies parents in both cultures were asked to rate the seriousness of emotional/behavioural difficulties from vignettes of children's behaviour. In *both* cultures, undercontrolled behaviours were seen as more problematic, but the Thai parents' threshold for rating behaviours as problematic was higher. Strikingly, parents in the two cultures were not more likely to rate as 'normal' behaviours more in accord with general cultural preferences for behaviour. Buddhist culture in Thailand emphasizes self-control and resignation but, nevertheless, Thai children were more frequently rated as showing *overcontrolled* problems and children in the individualistic American culture undercontrolled ones.

These data have been paralleled in a comparison of Jamaican and American clinic referrals (Lambert *et al.*, 1989a) where the cultural background presents a similar contrast to the Thai—American comparison, with Afro-British culture also discouraging child aggression. In this case also overcontrolled problems were significantly more common in the Jamaican referrals. In these examples cultural preferences for particular types of behaviour appeared to lead to an increase in problems related to this preference, an increase that remained even when culturally adjusted thresholds were used. It seems likely that this effect stemmed from parenting practices designed to inculcate the behaviour, but studies of this have yet to be done.

Culture and developmental processes

Cross-cultural comparisons based on differences on standard Western measures of development or disorder provide one way into the study of cultural influences. An alternative approach is to take social factors or parenting practices that are strongly correlated with particular developmental outcomes in the West and to see whether they carry the same meaning in other cultures. This approach is potentially valuable because it provides the opportunity better to understand how a particular environmental indicator relates to the underlying developmental process. For example, the developmental outcome from some 'risk' may be broadly similar cross-culturally but may have different consequences, either because of the way in which it is viewed within the culture or because of the ways in which it is subsequently modified by other cultural features. Alternatively, the outcome may be very different because the risk indicator carries a very different cultural meaning, and does not have the same developmental implications.

It is clear from the anthropological accounts collected in the Human Relations Area Files (HRAF) that children are socialized via a remarkably diverse range of parental practices (Murdock *et al.*, 1982) that should have clear developmental implications. Thus infants' physical movements may be virtually unrestricted or highly limited by being bound for much of the time to a cradle board; the child may be carried nearly all the time by an adult or only picked up in emergencies; parental reactions to crying may vary from indifference or punitiveness to a highly tolerant and nurturant response; weaning may begin below the age of 6 months and be severely applied or be delayed until after the age of 2 or later; and the early development of motor skills may be punished or strongly encouraged.

Aggregate level studies

Data from the HRAF show that values emphasized in child-rearing are related to the means of subsistence and the complexity of political structure (Barry *et al.*, 1976). For example, hunter—gatherer societies, where people live in small mobile groups or bands, in which cooperation is at a premium and the minimization of tension important, show an absence of competitive play and games (Schwartzman, 1978) and an absence of domestic violence (Levinson, 1989). Increasing levels of social complexity are associated with increasing levels of attention-seeking and competitiveness in children (Whiting & Whiting, 1975), and more use of physical punishment (Levinson, 1989).

Analyses of HRAF have uncovered plausible developmental connections. Bacon *et al.* (1963), for example, reported a relationship between suspiciousness and distrust in adulthood and socialization methods that involved strongly dependent

early child—mother relationships and an abrupt and punitive transition to independence. Equally intriguing are the cultures where there is a close mother—child relationship and low father salience in infancy. Where this pattern is associated with pronounced male—female status differences in adulthood the transition of boys to adult status tends to be marked by harsh male initiation rites or a culture of 'machismo'. Where the childhood pattern is associated with matrilocal residence and less difference in adult male—female status, the institution of the 'couvade' — in which men mimic the pregnancy and childbirth behaviours of their wives — may occur (Werner, 1979; Segall *et al.*, 1990).

The interpretation of such associations was dominated in earlier years by the *culture and personality* school, which attempted to link individual psychological development to the form and content of particular cultures as a whole. This approach developed from within a psychoanalytic tradition with one line of research attempting to test the universality of developmental processes, such as the Oedipus complex (Roheim, 1950), and another developing the idea that the expressive aspects of culture were a kind of projective system that dramatized subconscious tensions and contradictions arising from socialization practices (Benedict, 1934, 1949). There is an inevitable circularity in these ideas and Geertz (1973) has plausibly argued that the expressive aspects of culture dramatize and contain tensions inherent in the social system rather than within the individual.

There is a limit to the usefulness of these aggregate-level analyses because they are based on descriptions of modal cultural patterns and do not relate individual developmental experiences to outcome. Because of this it is not possible to know to what extent the 'outcomes' simply reflect a cultural style rather than an impact of experiences on individual functioning. In addition, these analyses have, in the past, assumed much greater within-culture consistency than exists. It is clear from a number of analyses that within-culture variation on a whole range of parenting behaviours can be as great, if not greater, than cross-cultural variation. For example, Minturn and Lambert (1964), in an analysis of data from the Six Cultures Study, showed that this was especially true for responsibility training and the proportion of their time that mothers cared for their babies, but also for the amount of aggression tolerated by the mother towards herself and the child's peers. A general conclusion would be that cultural differences will be greater for parenting techniques — such as how a baby is carried — and less in features depending on the quality of individual relationships. There is evidence, too, that relationships can be affected in similar ways by similar conditions, despite the fact that they may be otherwise embedded in very different cultural contexts. For example, the more people there are in the household the less exclusive the mother–infant attachment (Werner, 1979); the greater maternal indulgence; and the greater the discouragement of peer aggression (but the greater that aggression). The presence of another adult in the household to support the mother has a clear effect across cultures on the amount of warmth the child receives (Rohner, 1986).

Risk factors in cross-cultural perspective

It has been argued that individual behaviours or cultural factors that would constitute developmental risks in Western society may not have the same implications universally, because their cultural meaning or correlates may be different. Examples of four different kinds of 'risks' can be given: (i) parent–child interaction; (ii) multiple parenting and fostering; (iii) the child's attachment classification; and (iv) parental marital discord or disruption.

Parent–child interaction. The consequences of parental behaviours and their outcome according to cultural context can be illustrated by the well-documented case of the Guisii of Kenya. In this culture mother–child mutual gaze is much lower than observed in Western samples (Dixon *et al.*, 1981). This behaviour is related to a cultural complex in which a quiet child is desired, because it is believed that demonstrations of joy or pleasure in one's own fortune are likely to attract envy and witchcraft (LeVine, 1990). Gaze avoidance serves to dampen affect and helps to produce child behaviours that fit with the cultural requirements and protect the child against imputed harm. This style of parenting had predictable developmental conse-

quences. Guisii children were generally more passive than Western children, initiated interactions with adults less, and engaged in less sociodramatic play. These consequences appeared not to affect goal-striving, self-esteem or social adaptation in adult life, as they might in the West, because the traditional culture emphasized the dangers of personal accomplishment. But these behaviours become increasingly problematic as the culture accommodates to modern pressures. Guisii adults who are successful in education or employment exaggerate the power of neighbours' jealousy and disavow their own striving. Guisii children are more worried about striving or showing skills or abilities at school, because of the danger of being noticed. In this culture a consistent effect of parent–child interaction of development can be seen, with consequences that were normally adapted to the traditional culture but which are problematic as the requirements for a well-adapted adult change.

Multiple and substitute care-taking. Multiple and substitute care-taking provide examples of situations in which the meaning of the risk indicator varies with culture. In the West multiple mothering in early infancy is often associated with abnormal psychosocial development. Indeed, the strength of this association has led to the proposal that continuous care and contact by a single caretaker is the biologically based species prototypical form of early child-rearing (Blurton-Jones, 1972). This is a form of mothering that occurs in some hunter–gatherer societies and is thus seen as the form most similar to that of our early ancestors (Konner, 1977), and, by extension, the model of child-rearing to which we are biologically most adapted.

However, Tronick *et al.* (1987) have provided a very well-documented observational example of a hunter–gatherer society in which continuous care by one parent does not occur, but which nevertheless raises highly socialized and cooperative adults. Amongst the Efe of Zaire there is a belief that an infant will come to harm if it is first held by its mother. Instead, most female members of a group attend the birth and the newborn infant is passed amongst the group and suckled by them, whether or not they are lactating. The first contact with the mother is usually several hours postpartum and feeding continues to be shared between the mother and others. At 18 weeks infants were observed to spend on average 60% of the time in physical contact with other women, transferring between them over eight times an hour on average. Any woman comforted a fretting infant by suckling. In this culture the infant's basic needs for nurturance and security were provided communally, although the amount of transfer between women was affected by the child's temperament and birth weight, fussy and low birth weight infants spending more time with their mothers.

In this case the parenting pattern was part of a different child-rearing ecology compared with the West, where multiple caretaking often reflects a *failure* in the child-care system. For the Efe the group of caretakers was stable and the mother part of the group. Interestingly Efe children were observed to be precociously sociable, but it seems unlikely that this resembles the 'indiscriminate friendliness' observed in institutionalized children in the West (Wolkind, 1974). Rather, it may indicate the successful inculcation of the high level of sociability that is necessary for social stability in this society.

In similar fashion the fostering of children is usually associated with parenting breakdown in the West. This is not necessarily the case in other cultures, where the transfer of children between households in kin-fostering or adoption arrangements is very common (Goody, 1970). In Pulau Langkawi, Malaysia, such transfers were used to avoid divorce amongst childless couples; to correct an imbalance in the sex ratio of children within a household; or to balance the rights of both sets of grandparents in the grandchildren (Carsten, 1991). Amongst the Gonja in Northern Ghana patrilineal kin are entitled to request the movement of children at the age of 7 or 8. Goody estimated that up to half of the children moved households in this way and were brought up in the second household for the rest of their childhoods. There is some evidence that in earlier years West African migrants to Britain mistakenly saw fostering arrangements as a way of advancing their children, totally mistaking the meaning of the practice in the host culture.

These traditional kin-fostering patterns have seldom been investigated with respect to possible impacts on development, although in the fostering arrangements described by Goody, comparisons in adulthood between fostered and non-fostered children revealed no differences in success in the political system or the stability of marriages.

Attachment. In the case of attachment, the quality of the parent–child relationship, as coded from the Ainsworth 'strange situation' (Ainsworth, 1977), has been shown to be predictive of later psychosocial problems (Erikson *et al.*, 1985; see also Chapter 16). However, a number of studies have now been conducted in a range of cultures including American middle-class and disadvantaged families, Western European countries, Israeli kibbutzim and Japan. Although the modal pattern in all cultures — not surprisingly — is secure attachment, substantial cross-cultural differences have been found for the other classifications. Thus, avoidant behaviours have been found to be more common in Western Europe than in the USA and resistant patterns more common in Japan and Israel (Bretherton, 1985). Despite queries about the comparability of samples, it seems likely that these differences reflect true cultural differences in children's and mothers' responses to the 'strange situation'. However, it is unclear whether the same responses are associated with a similar 'internal working model' in children of different cultures, or whether they have the same developmental implications. One problem is that the samples used in all studies are neither epidemiological nor large, so the estimates of the size of cultural differences may be subject to considerable error. Second, a meta-analysis of 32 studies has suggested that intracultural variation in attachment behaviours is larger than cross-cultural variation (IJzendoorn & Kroonenberg, 1988) so that explanations of the differences largely in terms of cultural differences may be premature. Nevertheless, this analysis substantiated the general pattern of cross-cultural variations and these therefore warrant attention. In the Japanese case, the higher proportion of resistant children has been linked to marked differences in parenting practices, with Japanese mothers' emphasis on physical proximity with their babies (Miyake *et al.*, 1985). This is associated with fewer separations for the child from the mother, a pattern likely to increase the strangeness of the 'strange situation' for the children. Thus the meaning of the test response for Japanese and American children may be different. If this is so the predictions to later behaviour should also be different, but such data have not yet been reported. A different outcome might also arise if the cultural meaning and mediation of the child's behaviour were also different, even if the experiential antecedents of the children's responses were similar cross-culturally.

Marital discord and disruption. Similar issues arise with respect to experiential as to behavioural risks. The association between marital discord and disruption provides an example of this. In Western cultures the association between the experience of parental discord and divorce and behavioural problems in children, especially boys, is well documented (Emery, 1982). Experimental studies of children's responses to adult arguments show that such behaviours are very distressing to children (Cummings *et al.*, 1988) and it seems unlikely that cultural practices or beliefs would obliterate this response. On the other hand, the connection between the termination of marriage and the prior occurrence of discord is more variable cross-culturally, as is the extent of paternal involvement in child-rearing. It seems likely that children's disturbances following marital separation will depend on the strength of these links. Amongst the Nez Perces of Idaho a high rate of marital breakdown was traditionally balanced by a system of discipline that was largely located in the community rather than the family. Only when the external system of control began to decline did marital breakdown become associated with delinquent behaviour (Ackerman, 1971). Whether this was due to a more general collapse of the traditional culture or whether there were behavioural consequences of the marital break that were contained by the traditional culture but became apparent when the system of control broke down, is not known.

CONCLUSION

Any survey of sociocultural influences on development is inevitably both wide ranging and partial. On the other hand, a number of general issues and conclusions stand out. First, cross-cultural differences in development need to be examined in terms of the *meaning* of the particular developmental feature or outcome within a particular culture. An outcome deviant or problematic in one culture may not be so in another; it may have a different meaning because its correlates or antecedents are different; or it may have different long-term implications because of the way in which it dovetails with cultural requirements. On the other hand, it seems clear that many features of parent–child relationships have similar outcomes in widely different cultural settings and that within-culture variation on these features can be as great, if not greater, than cross-cultural variations. Second, because these developmental consistencies can be identified, the argument that cross-cultural studies of development are essentially flawed through ethnocentric bias is clearly wrong. This is true for both normal and abnormal development. However it is approached, there is an impressive consistency in the broad patterning of symptoms and related behaviours cross-culturally, together with interesting and instructive differences both in details of patterning and of threshold. Third, it is clear that scientific progress requires a continuing attempt to go beyond surface indicators or risks to the processes leading to particular outcomes, and a vigilance against simple interpretation of risks, or conclusions about the cultural meaning of outcomes. Lastly, with regard to disorders in childhood, the evidence across-cultures that sociocultural influences are primarily mediated by their relation to and effects on the child's close family relationships is very persuasive, although this will not necessarily remain the case for adolescent problems as the pace of urbanization increases and the complexities of post-industrial cultures develop. Comparative cross-cultural studies will remain a difficult and challenging, but essential, element in our understanding of development.

REFERENCES

Ackerman L.A. (1971) Marital instability and juvenile delinquency amongst the Nez Perces. *American Anthropologist* **73**, 595–603.

Ainsworth M.D.S. (1977) Attachment theory and its utility in cross-cultural research. In Liederman P.H., Tulkin S.R. & Rosenfeld A. (eds) *Culture and Infancy: Variations in the Human Experience*, pp. 49–67. Academic Press, New York.

Anderson Jr E.N. (1972) Some Chinese methods of dealing with crowding. *Urban Anthropology* **1**, 141–150.

Atkin C. (1983) Effects of realistic TV violence vs fictional violence on aggression. *Journalism Quarterly* **60**, 615−621.

Avis J. & Harris P. (1991) Belief−desire reasoning among Baka children: Evidence for a universal conception of mind. *Child Development* **62**, 460−469.

Bacon M.K., Child I.L. & Barry H.I. (1963) A cross-cultural study of correlates of crime. *Journal of Abnormal Social Psychology* **66**, 291−300.

Ballard R. (1982) South Asian Families. In Rapoport R., Rapoport R.N. & Fogarty M.P. (eds) *Families in Britain*, pp. 179−204. Routledge & Kegan Paul, London.

Bandura A. (1963) What TV violence can do to your child. *Look* 22 Oct., 46−52.

Bandura A., Ross D. & Ross S.A. (1961) Transmission of aggression through imitation of aggressive models. *Journal of Abnormal Social Psychology* **63**, 575−582.

Barquero J.L.V., Munoz P. & Jauregui V.M. (1982) The influence of the process of urbanization on the prevalence of neurosis. *Acta Psychiatrica Scandinavica* **65**, 161−170.

Barry H.I., Josephson L., Lauer E. & Marshall C. (1976) Traits inculcated in childhood: Cross-cultural codes 5. *Ethnology* **15**, 83−114.

Benedict R.F. (1934) *Patterns of Culture*. Houghton-Mifflin, Boston.

Benedict R.F. (1949) Child rearing in certain European countries. *American Journal of Orthopsychiatry* **19**, 342−350.

Bentley A.M. (1987) Swazi children's understanding of time concepts: A Piagetian study. *Journal of Genetic Psychology* **148**, 443−452.

Berkowitz L. (1965) Some aspects of observed aggression. *Journal of Personality and Social Psychology* **2**, 359−369.

Berry J.W., Poortinga Y.H., Segall M.H. & Dasen P. (1992) *Cross-cultural Psychology: Research and Applications*. Cambridge University Press, Cambridge.

Bird H.R., Canino G., Rubio-Stipec M. *et al.* (1988) Estimates of the prevalence of childhood maladjustment in a community survey in Puerto Rico. *Archives of General Psychiatry* **45**, 1120−1126.

Blanz B., Schmidt M.H. & Esser G. (1991) Family adversities and child psychiatric disorders. *Journal of Child Psychology and Psychiatry* **32**, 939−950.

Blurton-Jones N. (1972) Comparative aspects of mother−child contact. In Blurton-Jones N. (ed) *Ethological Studies of Child Behavior*, pp. 315−328. Cambridge University Press, New York.

Blurton-Jones N. & Konner M.J. (1976) !Kung knowledge of animal behavior. In Lee R.B. & DeVore I. (eds) *Kalahari Hunter Gatherers*, pp. 325−348. Harvard University Press, Cambridge, Massachusetts.

Booth A. (1976) *Urban Crowding and its Consequences*. Praeger, New York.

Bottoms A.E. & Wiles P. (1986) Housing tenure and residential community crime careers in Britain. In Reiss Jr A.E. & Tonry M. (eds) *Communities in Crime*, pp. 101−162. University of Chicago Press, Chicago.

Bretherton I. (1985) Attachment theory: Retrospect and prospect. In Bretherton I. & Waters E. (eds) Growing points of attachment theory and research. *Monographs of the Society for Research in Child Development* **50**, Serial No. 209, 3−35.

Bronfenbrenner U. (1979) *The Ecology of Human Development: Experiments by Nature and Design*. Harvard University Press, Cambridge, Massachusetts.

Brown J.D., Childers K.W. & Waszak C.S. (1990) Television and adolescent sexuality. *Journal of Adolescent Health Care* **11**, 62−70.

Bryant J., Carveth R.A. & Brown D. (1981) Television viewing and anxiety: An experimental examination. *Journal of Communication* **31**, 106−119.

Buisik Jr R.J. & Webb J. (1982) Community change and patterns of delinquency. *American Journal of Sociology* **88**, 24−42.

Burke A. (1984) Racism and psychological disturbance among West Indians in Britain. *International Journal of Social Psychiatry* **30**, 50−68.

Carsten J. (1991) Children in-between: Fostering and the process of kinship on Pulau Langkawi, Malaysia. *Man* **26**, 425−443.

Caspi A., Elder Jr G.H. & Herbener E.S. (1990) Childhood personality and the prediction of life-course patterns. In Robins L. & Rutter M. (eds) *Straight and Devious Pathways from Childhood to Adulthood*, pp. 13−35. Cambridge University Press, Cambridge.

Cederblad M. (1988) Behavioural disorders in children from different cultures. *Acta Psychiatrica Scandinavica* **344**(Suppl.), 85−92.

Cheng T.A. (1989) Urbanization and minor psychiatric morbidity — A community study in Taiwan. *Social Psychiatry and Psychiatric Epidemiology* **24**, 309−316.

Clarke R.V. (ed.) (1992) *Situational Crime Prevention: Successful Case Studies*. Harrow & Heston, New York.

Coleman A. (1985) *Utopia on Trial*. Hilary Shipman, London.

Coleman A. (1991) The contribution of architecture to the prevention of deviance. In Parry-Jones W.L. & Queloz N. (eds) *Mental Health and Deviance in Inner Cities*, pp. 91−100. World Health Organization, Geneva.

Comstock G. & Strasburger V. (1990) Deceptive appearances: Television, violence and aggressive behavior. *Journal of Adolescent Health Care* **11**, 31−44.

Corteen R.S. & Williams T.M. (1986) Television and reading skills. In Williams T.M. (ed.) *The Impact of Television: A Natural Experiment in Three Communities*, pp. 39−84. Academic Press, Orlando, Florida.

Crane J. (1991) The epidemic theory of ghettos and neighborhood effects on dropout and teenage child-bearing. *American Journal of Sociology* **96**, 1226−1259.

Cummings J.S., Pelligrini D.S., Notarius C.I. & Cummings E.M. (1988) Children's response to angry adult behavior as a function of marital distress and history of inter-parental hostility. *Child Development* **60**, 1035−1043.

Dixon S., Tronick E., Keefer C. & Brazelton T.B. (1981) Mother−infant interaction amongst the Guisii of Kenya. In Field T.M., Sostek A.M., Vietze P. & Liederman P.H. (eds) *Culture and Early Interactions*, pp. 149−165. Lawrence Erlbaum, Hillsdale, New Jersey.

Dye T.R. (1975) Population density and social pathology. *Urban Affairs Quarterly* **11**, 265−275.

Eibl-Eibesfeldt I. (1972) Similarities and differences between cultures in expressive movements. In Hinde R.A. (ed.) *Nonverbal Communication*, pp. 297−312. Cambridge University Press, Cambridge.

Ekblad S. (1990) The children's behaviour questionnaire for completion by parents and teachers in a Chinese sample. *Journal of Child Psychology and Psychiatry* **31**, 775−791.

Elder Jr G.H. (1974) *Children of the Great Depression*. University of Chicago Press, Chicago.

Elton M., Patton G., Weyerer S., Diallina M. & Fichter M. (1988) A comparative investigation of the principal component structure of the 28 item version of the General Health Questionnaire (GHQ): 15-year-old schoolgirls in England, Greece, Turkey and West Germany. *Acta Psychiatrica Scandinavica* **77**, 124−132.

Emery R. (1982) Marital turmoil: Interparental conflict and the children of discord and divorce. *Psychological Bulletin* **92**, 310−330.

Erikson M.F., Sroufe A.L. & Egeland B. (1985) The relationship between quality of attachment and behavior problems in pre-school in a high-risk sample. In Bretherton I. & Waters E. (eds) Growing points of attachment theory and research. *Monographs of the Society for Research in Child Development* **50**, Serial No. 209, 147−166.

Favazza A.R. (1985) Anthropology and psychiatry. In Kaplan H.I. & Sadock B.J. (eds) *Comprehensive Textbook of Psychiatry*, pp. 247−294. Williams & Wilkins, Baltimore.

Fegert J.M. (1989) Bias factors in the translation of questionnaires and classification systems in international comparative child and adolescent psychiatric research. *Acta Paedopsychiatrica* **52**, 279−286.

Fichter M.M., Elton M., Sourdi L., Weyerer S. & Koptagelilal G. (1988) Anorexia nervosa in Greek and Turkish adolescents. *European Archives of Psychiatric and Neurological Sciences* **237**, 200−208.

Field T.M. & Widmayer S.M. (1981) Mother−infant interactions among lower SES Black, Cuban, Puerto Rican and South American Migrants. In Field T.M., Sostek A.M., Vietze P. & Liederman P.H. (eds) *Culture and Early Interactions*, pp. 41−62. Lawrence Erlbaum, Hillsdale, New Jersey.

Freedman J.L. (1975) *Crowding and Behavior*. W.H. Freeman, San Francisco.

Freeman H.L. (1984a) Housing. In Freeman H.L. (ed.) *Mental Health and the Environment*, pp. 197−225. Churchill Livingstone, London.

Freeman H.L. (1984b) The scientific background. In Freeman H.L. (ed.) *Mental Health and the Environment*, pp. 23−70. Churchill Livingstone, London.

Gans H.J. (1962) *The Urban Villagers: Group and Class in the Life of Italian-Americans*. Free Press, New York.

Geertz C. (1973) *The Interpretation of Cultures*. Basic Books, New York.

Gladwin T. (1970) *East is a Big Bird*. Harvard University Press, Cambridge, Massachusetts.

Goody E. (1970) Kinship fostering in the Gonja: Deprivation or advantage? In Mayer P. (eds) *Socialization: The Approach from Social Anthropology*, pp. 51−74. Tavistock, London.

Hackett L., Hackett R. & Taylor D.C. (1991) Psychological disturbance and its associations in the children of the Gujarati community. *Journal of Child Psychology and Psychiatry* **32**, 851−856.

Hamilton V.L., Blumenfeld P.C., Akoh H. & Miura K. (1990) Credit and blame among American and Japanese children: Normative, cultural, and individual differences. *Journal of Personality and Social Psychology* **59**, 442−451.

Handy S., Chithiramohan R.N., Ballard C.G. & Silveira W.R. (1991) Ethnic differences in adolescent self poisoning: A comparison of Asian and Caucasian groups. *Journal of Adolescence* **14**, 157−162.

Harpham T., Lusty T. & Vaughan J.P. (eds) (1988) *In the Shadow of the City*. Oxford University Press, Oxford.

Hartmann D.P. (1969) Influence of symbolically modelled instrumental aggression and pain cues on aggressive behavior. *Journal of Personality and Social Psychology* **11**, 280−288.

Hartmann H. (1958) *Ego Psychology and the Problem of Adaptation*. International Universities Press, New York.

Hearold S. (1986) A synthesis of 1043 effects of television on social behavior. In Comstock G. (ed.) *Public Communication and Behavior*, Vol. I, pp. 65−133. Academic Press, New York.

Heath A. (1992) The attitudes of the underclass. In Smith D.J. (ed.) *Understanding the Underclass*, pp. 32−47. Policy Studies Institute, London.

Hinde R.A. (1991) A biologist looks at anthropology. *Man* **26**, 583−608.

Hoff-Ginsberg E. (1991) Mother−child conversation in different social classes and communicative settings. *Child Development* **62**, 782−796.

Huesmann L.R. (1986) Psychological processes promoting the relation between exposure to media violence and aggressive behavior by the viewer. *Journal of Social Issues* **42**, 125−139.

Huesmann L.R., Lagerspetz K. & Eron L.D. (1984) Intervening variables in the TV violence−aggression relation: Evidence from two countries. *Developmental Psychology* **20**, 746−775.

Hurrelman K. & Engel U. (1992) Delinquency as a symptom of adolescents' orientation towards status and success. *Journal of Youth and Adolescence* **21**, 119–138.

IJzendoorn M. & Kroonenberg P. (1988) Cross-cultural patterns of attachment: A meta-analysis of the strange situation. *Child Development* **59**, 147–156.

Jephcott A.P. & Carter M.P. (1954) *The Social Background and Delinquency*. University of Nottingham, Nottingham.

Joy L.A., Kimball M.M. & Zabrack M.L. (1986) Television and children's aggressive behavior. In Williams T.M. (ed.) *The Impact of Television: A Natural Experiment in Three Communities*, pp. 303–360. Academic Press, Orlando, Florida.

Kastrup M. (1977) Urban–rural differences in six-year-olds. In Graham P.J. (ed.) *Epidemiological Approaches in Child Psychiatry*, pp. 181–194. Academic Press, London.

Kleinman A. (1987) Anthropology and psychiatry: The role of culture in cross-cultural research on illness. *British Journal of Psychiatry* **151**, 447–454.

Kleinman A. & Good B. (eds) (1985) *Culture and Depression: Studies in the Anthropology and Cross-cultural Psychiatry of Affect and Disorder*. University of California Press, Berkeley.

Kohn M., Naoi A., Schoenbach C., Schooler C. & Slomoczynski K.M. (1990) Position in the class structure and psychological functioning in the United States, Japan, and Poland. *American Journal of Sociology* **95**, 964–1008.

Kohn M.L. & Schooler C. (1983) *Work and Personality: An Enquiry into the Impact of Social Stratification*. Ablex, Norwood, New Jersey.

Konner M. (1977) Infancy among the Kalahari Desert San. In Liederman P.H., Tulkin S.R. & Rosenfeld A. (eds) *Culture and Infancy*, pp. 287–328. Academic Press, New York.

Kornhauser R.R. (1978) *Social Sources of Delinquency: An Appraisal of Analytic Methods*. University of Chicago Press, Chicago.

Lambert M.C., Weisz J.R. & Knight F. (1989a) Over- and under-controlled clinic referral problems in Jamaican clinic-referred children: Teacher reports for ages 6–17. *Journal of Abnormal Child Psychology* **17**, 553–562.

Lambert M.C., Weisz J.R. & Thesiger C. (1989b) Principal components analyses of behaviour problems in Jamaican clinic-referred children: Teacher reports for ages 6–17. *Journal of Abnormal Child Psychology* **17**, 553–562.

Lambert W.E., Hamers J. & Frasure-Smith N. (1979) *Child Rearing Values*. Praeger, New York.

Landau S.F. (1981) Juveniles and the police. *British Journal of Criminology* **21**, 27–46.

Lavik N.J. (1977) Urban–rural differences in rates of disorder: A comparative psychiatric population study of Norwegian adolescents. In Graham P.J. (ed.) *Epidemiological Approaches in Child Psychiatry*, pp. 223–251. Academic Press, London.

Leff J. (1988) *Psychiatry Around the Globe: a Transcultural View*. Gaskell, London.

Lefkowitz M.M., Eron L.D., Walder L.O. & Huesmann L.R. (1972) Television violence and child aggression: A follow-up study. In Comstock G.A. & Rubinstein E.A. (eds) *Television and Social Behavior*, Vol. III. *Television and Adolescent Aggressiveness*, pp. 35–135. US Government Printing Office, Washington, DC.

LeVine R.A. (1990) Infant environments in psychoanalysis: A cross-cultural view. In Stigler J.W., Shweder R.A. & Herdt G. (eds) *Cultural Psychology: Essays on Comparative Human Development*, pp. 454–474. Cambridge University Press, Cambridge.

Levinson D. (1989) *Family Violence in Cross-Cultural Perspective*. Sage, Newbury Park, California.

Lewis G., Croft-Jeffreys C. & David A. (1990) Are British psychiatrists racist? *British Journal of Psychiatry* **157**, 410–415.

Lewis O. (1968) The culture of poverty. In Moynihan D.P. (ed.) *On Understanding Poverty: Perspectives from the Social Sciences*, pp. 187–200. Basic Books, New York.

Liebert R.M. & Sprafkin J. (1988) *The Early Window: Effects of Television on Children and Youth*, 3rd edn. Pergamon, New York.

Littlewood R. (1990) From categories to contexts — A decade of the new cross-cultural psychiatry. *British Journal of Psychiatry* **156**, 308–327.

Loeber R. & Stouthamer-Loeber M. (1986) Family factors as correlates and predictors of juvenile conduct problems and delinquency. In Tonry M. & Morris N. (eds) *Crime and Justice: An Annual Review of Research*, pp. 29–149. University of Chicago Press, Chicago.

Long J.V. & Vaillant G.E. (1984) Natural history of male psychological health. XI: Escape from the underclass. *American Journal of Psychiatry* **141**, 341–346.

Louis Harris and Associates (1986) *American Teens Speak: Sex, Myths, TV and Birth Control*. Planned Parenthood Federation of America, New York.

Matsuura M., Okubo Y., Kato M. *et al.* (1989) An epidemiological investigation of emotional and behavioural problems in primary school children in Japan. The report of the first phase of a WHO collaborative study in the Western Pacific Region. *Social Psychiatry and Psychiatric Epidemiology* **24**, 17–22.

Matza D. (1964) *Delinquency and Drift*. Wiley, New York.

Mayer S.E. & Jencks C. (1989) Growing up in poor neighborhoods: How much does it matter? *Science* **243**, 1441–1445.

Mays J.B. (ed.) (1972) *Juvenile Delinquency, the Family and the Social Group: A Reader*. Longman, London.

Merton R.K. (1957) *Social Theory and Social Structure*. Free Press, New York.

Mincy R.B., Sawhill I.V. & Wolf D.A. (1990) The underclass: Definition and measurement. *Science* **248**, 450–453.

Minturn L. & Lambert W.W. (1964) *Mothers of Six Cultures:*

Antecedents of Child-rearing. Wiley, New York.

Mitchell R.E. (1971) Some social implications of high density housing. *American Sociological Review* **36**, 18−29.

Miyake K., Shen S.-J. & Campos J.J. (1985) Infant temperament, mother's mode of interaction and attachment in Japan: An interim report. In Bretherton I. & Waters E. (eds) Growing points of attachment theory and research. *Monographs of the Society for Research in Child Development* **50**, Serial No. 209, 276−297.

Mortimore J. & Blackstone T. (1982) *Disadvantage and Education*. Heinemann, London.

Mumford D.B. & Whitehouse A.M. (1988) Increased prevalence of bulimia nervosa among Asian schoolgirls. *British Medical Journal* **297**, 718.

Mumford D.B., Whitehouse A.M. & Platts M. (1991) Sociocultural correlates of eating disorders among Asian schoolgirls in Bradford. *British Journal of Psychiatry* **158**, 222−228.

Murdock G.P., Ford C.S., Simmons L.W. & Whiting J.M.W. (1982) *Outline of Cultural Materials*, 5th edn. HRAF, New Haven, Connecticut.

Newman O. (1973) *Defensible Space*. Architectural Press, London.

Newson J. & Newson E. (1968) *Four Years Old in an Urban Community*. Allen & Unwin, London.

Newson J. & Newson E. (1976) *Seven Years Old in the Home Environment*. Allen & Unwin, London.

Newth S.J. & Corbett J. (1993) Behaviour and emotional problems in three-year-old children of Asian parentage. *Journal of Child Psychology and Psychiatry* **34**, 333−352.

Obeyesekere G. (1985) Depression, Bhuddism, and the work of culture in Sri Lanka. In Kleinman A. & Good B. (eds) *Culture and Depression: Studies of the Anthropology and Cross-cultural Psychiatry of Affect and Disorder*, pp. 134−152. University of California Press, Berkeley.

Offord D.M., Boyle M.H. & Racine Y. (1989) Ontario Child Health Study: Correlates of disorder. *Journal of the American Academy of Child and Adolescent Psychiatry* **28**, 856−860.

Osborn S.G. (1980) Moving home, leaving London and delinquent trends. *British Journal of Criminology* **20**, 54−61.

Parke R.D., Berkowitz L., Leyens J.P., West S.G. & Sebastian R.J. (1977) Some effects of violent and non-violent movies on the behavior of juvenile delinquents. In Berkowitz L. (ed.) *Advances in Social Psychology*, Vol. 10, pp. 135−172. Academic Press, New York.

Peterson J.L., Moore K.A. & Furstenberg F.F. (1991) Television viewing and early initiation of sexual intercourse − Is there a link? *Journal of Homosexuality* **21**, 93−138.

Queloz N. (1991) Urban process and its role in strengthening social disadvantages, inequalities and exclusion. In Parry-Jones W.L. & Queloz N. (eds) *Mental Health and Deviance in Inner Cities*, pp. 31−36. World Health Organization, Geneva.

Quinton D. (1985) The measurement of intergenerational change: A view from developmental psychology. In *Measuring Socio-demographic Change*, pp. 26−38. Office of Population Censuses and Statistics, London.

Quinton D. (1988) Urbanism and child mental health. *Journal of Child Psychology and Psychiatry* **29**, 11−20.

Quinton D. & Rutter M. (1984a) Parents with children in care. I: Current circumstances and parenting skills. *Journal of Child Psychology and Psychiatry* **25**, 211−229.

Quinton D. & Rutter M. (1984b) Parents with children in care. II: Intergenerational continuities. *Journal of Child Psychology and Psychiatry* **25**, 231−250.

Quinton D. & Rutter M. (1988) *Parenting Breakdown: The Making and Breaking of Intergenerational Links*. Avebury, Aldershot.

Rapoport A. (1975) Towards a redefinition of density. *Environment and Behavior* **7**, 133−158.

Reiss A.J. (in press) Community influences on adolescent behavior. In Rutter M. (ed.) *Psychosocial Disturbances in Young People: Challenges for Prevention*. Cambridge University Press, Cambridge.

Reiss Jr A.J. (1986) Why are communities important in undestanding crime? In Reiss Jr A.J. & Tonry M. (eds) *Communities and Crime*, pp. 1−33. University of Chicago Press, Chicago.

Richman A.L., LeVine R.A., New R.G., Horrigan G.A., Welles-Nystrom B. & LeVine S.E. (1988) Maternal behaviour to infants in five cultures. In LeVine R.A., Miller P.M. & West M.M. (eds) *Parental Behaviour in Diverse Cultures*, pp. 81−96. Jossey-Bass, San Francisco.

Rieder J. (1985) *Canarsie: The Jews and Italians of Brooklyn against Liberalism*. Harvard University Press, Cambridge, Massachusetts.

Robins L.N. (1991) Conduct disorder. *Journal of Child Psychology and Psychiatry (Annual Research Review)* **32**, 193−212.

Robinson J.P. (1972) Television's impact on everyday life: Some cross-national evidence. In Rubinstein E.A., Comstock G.A. & Murray J.P. (eds) *Television and Social Behavior*, Vol. IV. *Television in Day-to-day Life: Patterns of Use*, pp. 410−431. US Government Printing Office, Washington, DC.

Robinson W.S. (1950) Ecological correlations and the behavior of individuals. *American Sociological Review* **15**, 351−357.

Roheim G. (1950) *Psychoanalysis and Anthropology, Culture, Personality and the Unconscious*. International Universities Press, New York.

Rohner R. (1986) *The Warmth Dimension: Foundations of Parental Acceptance−Rejection Theory*. Sage, Newbury Park, California.

Rosaldo M. (1984) Toward an anthropology of self and feeling. In Shweder R.A. & LeVine R.A. (eds) *Culture Theory: Essays on Mind, Self and Emotion*, pp. 137−157. Cambridge University Press, Cambridge.

Runciman W.G. (1990) How many classes are there in

contemporary British society? *Sociology* **24**, 377–396.

Rutter M. (1979) *Changing Youth in a Changing Society*. The Nuffield Provincial Hospitals Trust, London.

Rutter M. (1994) Causal concepts and their testing. In Rutter M. & Smith D.J. (eds) *Psychosocial Disorders in Young People: Time Trends and their Origins*. Wiley, Chichester. (In press)

Rutter M., Cox A., Tupling C., Berger M. & Yule W. (1975a) Attainment and adjustment in two geographical areas. I: The prevalence of psychiatric disorder. *British Journal of Psychiatry* **126**, 493–509.

Rutter M. & Giller H. (1983) *Juvenile Delinquency: Trends and Perspectives*. Penguin, Harmondsworth.

Rutter M., Maughan B., Mortimore P., Ouston J. & Smith A. (1979) *Fifteen Thousand Hours: Secondary Schools and their Effects on Children*. Open Books, London.

Rutter M. & Quinton D. (1977) Psychiatric disorder — Ecological factors and concepts of causation. In McGurk H. (ed.) *Ecological Factors in Human Development*, pp. 173–187. North-Holland, Amsterdam.

Rutter M., Yule B., Morton J. & Bagley C. (1975b) Children of West Indian migrants. III: Home circumstances and family patterns. *Journal of Child Psychology and Psychiatry* **16**, 105–123.

Rutter M., Yule B., Quinton D., Rowlands O. & Yule W. (1975c) Attainment and adjustment in two geographical areas. III: Some factors accounting for area differences. *British Journal of Psychiatry* **126**, 520–533.

Sampson R. & Groves W. (1989) Community structure and crime — Testing social-disorganization theory. *American Journal of Sociology* **94**, 774–802.

Saxe G.B. (1988) The mathematics of child street vendors. *Child Development* **59**, 1415–1425.

Scarr S. (1992) Developmental theories for the 1990s: Development and individual differences. *Child Development* **63**, 1–19.

Scheper-Hughes N. (1990) Mother love and child death in north-east Brazil. In Stigler J.W., Shweder R.A. & Herdt G. (eds) *Cultural Psychology: Essays on Comparative Human Development*, pp. 542–565. Cambridge University Press, Cambridge.

Schwartzman H.B. (1978) *Transformations: The Anthropology of Children's Play*. Plenum, New York.

Segall M.H., Dasen P.R., Berry J.W. & Poortinga Y.H. (1990) *Human Behaviour in Global Perspective: An Introduction to Cross-cultural Psychology*. Pergamon, New York.

Shaw C.R. & McKay H.D. (1942) *Juvenile Delinquency in Urban Areas: A Study of Delinquents in Relation to Differential Characteristics of Local Communities in American Cities*. University of Chicago Press, Chicago.

Shen Y.-C., Wong Y.F. & Yang X.L. (1985) An epidemiological investigation of minimal brain dysfunction in six elementary schools in Beijing. *Journal of Child Psychology and Psychiatry* **26**, 777–788.

Sherif M., Harvey O., Hoyt B., Hood W. & Sherif C. (1961) *Intergroup Conflict and Cooperation: The Robbers' Cave Experiment*. University of Oklahoma Book Exchange, Norman.

Shweder R.A. (1985) Menstrual pollution, soul loss, and the comparative study of emotions. In Kleinman A. & Good B. (eds) *Culture and Depression: Studies in the Anthropology and Cross-cultural Psychiatry of Affect and Disorder*, pp. 182–215. University of California Press, Berkeley.

Sigman M., Neumann C., Carter C., Cattle J., D'Souza S. & Bwibo N. (1988) Home interactions and the development of Embu toddlers in Kenya. *Child Development* **59**, 1251–1261.

Signorelli N. (1990) Children, television and gender roles. *Journal of Adolescent Health Care* **11**, 50–58.

Singer J.L., Singer D.G. & Rapaczynski W. (1984) Family patterns and television viewing as predictors of children's beliefs and aggression. *Journal of Communication* **34**, 73–89.

Smith D.J. (ed.) (1992) *Understanding the Underclass*. Policy Studies Institute, London.

Smith D.J. (1994) Youth crime and conduct disorder: Sociocultural patterns and time trends. In Rutter M. & Smith D.J. (eds) *Psychosocial Disorders in Young People: Time Trends and their Origins*. Wiley, Chichester. (In press)

Soni Raleigh V., Bulusu L. & Balaraian R. (1990) Suicide among immigrants from the Indian sub-continent. *British Journal of Psychiatry* **156**, 46–50.

Sonuga-Barke E., Minocha K., Taylor E. & Sandberg S. (1993) Inter-ethnic bias in teachers' ratings of childhood hyperactivity. *British Journal of Developmental Psychology* **11**, 187–200.

Sostek A.M., Vietze P., Zaslow M., Kreiss L., Van der Waals C. & Rubenstein D. (1981) Social context in caregiver–infant interactions: A film study in Fais and the United States. In Field T.M., Sostek A.M., Vietze P. & Liederman P.H. (eds) *Culture and Early Interactions*, pp. 21–37. Lawrence Erlbaum, Hillsdale, New Jersey.

Steinhausen H.C., Edinsel E., Fegert J.M., Gobel D., Reister E. & Rentz A. (1990) Child psychiatric disorder and family dysfunction in migrant workers and military families. *European Archives of Psychiatry and Neurological Sciences* **239**, 257–262.

Stevenson H.W., Chen C. & Lee S.Y. (1993) Mathematics achievement in Chinese, Japanese, and American children: 10 years later. *Science* **259**, 53–58.

Stevenson H.W., Lucker G.W., Shin-Ying L. & Stigler J.W. (1987) Poor readers in three cultures. In Super M. (ed.) *The Role of Culture in Developmental Disorder*, pp. 153–177. Academic Press, San Diego, California.

Stevenson J.W., Lee S.Y., Chen C.S. *et al.* (1990) Mathematics achievement of children in China and the United States. *Child Development* **61**, 1053–1066.

Stigler J.W. & Perry M. (1990) Mathematics learning in Japanese, Chinese and American classrooms. In Stigler J.W., Shweder R.A. & Herdt G. (eds) *Cultural Psychology:*

Essays on Comparative Human Development, pp. 328–353. Cambridge University Press, Cambridge.

Super C.M. (1980) Cognitive development: looking across at growing up. In Super C.M. & Harkness S. (eds) *Anthropological Perspectives on Child Development*, pp. 59–69. Jossey-Bass, San Francisco.

Tannenbaum P.H. (1971) *Emotional Arousal as a Mediator of Communication Effects*. US Government Printing Office, Washington, DC.

Thomas M.H. & Drabman R.S. (1977) *Effects of television violence on expectations of others' aggression*. Paper presented at the Annual Convention of the American Psychological Association.

Townsend P. & Davidson N. (1982) *Inequalities in Health*. Penguin, Harmondsworth.

Trieman D.J. (1977) *Occupational Prestige in Comparative Perspective*. Academic Press, New York.

Tronick E.Z., Morelli G.A. & Winn S. (1987) Multiple caretaking of Efe (pygmy) infants. *American Anthropologist* **89**, 96–106.

Tuck M. & Southgate P. (1981) *Ethnic Minorities, Crime and Policing*. Her Majesty's Stationery Office, London.

Vikan S. (1985) Psychiatric epidemiology in a sample of 1510 ten-year-old children I: Prevalence. *Journal of Child Psychology and Psychiatry* **26**, 55–76.

Waller L. & Okihiro N. (1978) *Burglary: The Victim and the Public*. University of Toronto Press, Toronto.

Wallis C.P. & Maliphant R. (1967) Delinquency areas in the county of London: Ecological factors. *British Journal of Criminology* **7**, 250–284.

Weisz J.R., Suwanlert S., Chaivasit W. & Walter B.R. (1987a) Over- and undercontrolled referral problems among children and adolescents from Thailand and the United States: The wat and wai of cultural differences. *Journal of Consulting and Clinical Psychology* **55**, 719–726.

Weisz J.R., Suwanlert S., Chaivasit W., Weiss B., Achenbach T.M. & Trevathan D. (1989) Epidemiology of behavioral and emotional problems among Thai and American children: Teacher reports for ages 6–11. *Journal of Child Psychology and Psychiatry* **30**, 471–484.

Weisz J.R., Suwanlert S., Chaivasit W., Weiss B., Achenbach T.M. & Walter B.R. (1987b) Epidemiology of behavioural and emotional problems among Thai and American children: Parent reports for ages 6–11. *Journal of the American Academy of Child and Adolescent Psychiatry* **26**, 890–897.

Werner E.E. (1979) *Cross-cultural Child Development: A View from the Planet Earth*. Brooks/Cole, Monterey, California.

Werner E.E. (1984) *Child Care: Kith, Kin and Hired Hands*. University Park Press, Baltimore, Maryland.

West D.J. (1985) Delinquency. In Rutter M. & Hersov L. (eds) *Child and Adolescent Psychiatry: Modern Approaches*, pp. 414–423. Blackwell Scientific Publications, Oxford.

Whiting J.B.B. & Whiting J.M.W. (1975) *Children of Six Cultures: A Psycho-cultural Study*. Harvard University Press, Cambridge, Massachusetts.

Wilson H. (1980) Parental supervision: A neglected aspect of delinquency. *British Journal of Criminology* **20**, 203–235.

Wilson H. & Herbert G.W. (1978) *Parents and Children in the Inner City*. Routledge & Kegan Paul, London.

Wirth L. (1938) Urbanism as a way of life. *American Journal of Sociology* **44**, 1–24.

Wolkind S.N. (1974) The components of 'affectionless psychopathy' in institutionalized children. *Journal of Child Psychology and Psychiatry* **15**, 215–220.

Young M. & Wilmott P. (1957) *Family and Kinship in East London*. Routledge & Kegan Paul, London.

Young M. & Wilmott P. (1973) *The Symmetrical Family: A Study of Work and Leisure in the London Region*. Routledge & Kegan Paul, London.

Zillerman D. & Bryant J. (1982) Pornography, sexual callousness, and the trivialization of rape. *Journal of Communication* **32**, 10–21.

Zoccolillo M., Pickles A., Quinton D. & Rutter M. (1992) The outcome of childhood conduct disorder: Implications for defining adult personality disorder and conduct disorder. *Psychological Medicine* **22**, 971–986.

8: Development and Psychopathology of Attention

ERIC A. TAYLOR

INTRODUCTION

Impairment of attention is an idea often used in psychopathology. Clinicians employ it to explain why some patients, whose intellect is normal, are nevertheless impaired in working and learning. More fundamentally, several theories have suggested that a breakdown in the ability to concentrate can cause psychiatric disorders such as schizophrenia. In childhood, an attention deficit is considered by many psychiatrists to be a disorder in itself, to be the cause of hyperactivity, and to have profound effects on personality development (American Psychiatric Association, 1987).

'Attention' comprises many functions (Taylor, 1980). The main concepts behind the word refer to a set of active processes, through which people choose some stimuli and not others for further processing, and regulate their own responsiveness to stimuli. 'Attention' is needed when there is too much information to be able to cope with it all; it is achieved when the information is sampled in an orderly and efficient way.

This chapter will distinguish the main processes involved in attending, and will describe for each the tests that are used most frequently, the way that they describe development, and what is known of the reasons for developmental change. The relationships with other lines of development (such as intellectual and emotional) then need to be considered to appreciate the complex factors determining individual differences. The analysis of attentional impairment in psychopathology can then draw upon developmental concepts. First, some crucial distinctions must be made: between attending as an observed behaviour, a test score and an inferred psychological process; between overt and covert attention; controlled and automatic processing; and between several types of attention that can be involved in the controlled processing of information.

Behaviours, processes and tests

Attention is, first, a description of behaviour. People orient themselves to some stimuli rather than others, so observation can describe the way in which they are sampling information from different parts of their environment. Eye movements are a sensitive indicator of how people explore their world.

Behaviour, however, is not a direct reflection of how well stimuli are being processed by the brain. A child, for example, might stare fixedly at a teacher yet take in nothing of what the teacher is saying. A worker may be concentrating very effectively on a simple task but still be able to look around and talk of other things. In assessment of a child it is important not to be taken in by appearances. The theoretical constructs of attention have to be inferred from a wide range of information.

Psychological tests of performance are often used as the basis for inferring what processes of attention are going on. However, the inference needs to be cautious and circumstantial. A test may have high face validity of measuring something believed to be attention; but it will nearly always be affected by many other processes as well. Motivation to perform, compliance with the task and ability to carry it out will all play strong parts. Since so much has to be controlled, experimental ingenuity is needed in research, and cautious judgement in clinical work. The distinction between *overt* and *covert* processes of attention follows: overt attention is inferred from behaviour, from the way the organism directs its sense organs; while covert attention is inferred from test performance, and the effects of manipulating experimental variables, once overt attention has been excluded as an explanation. It is an empirical question whether the same processes account for both overt and covert concentration.

Information processing

Covert information processing has been divided into two types: controlled and automatic (Shiffrin & Schneider, 1977). The controlled mode is needed when people are dealing with an unfamiliar task: effort is needed, a large amount of processing capacity has to be used, and it is hard to do anything else at the same time. By contrast, a familiar task is dealt with in a more automatic way, large amounts of information are dealt with rapidly and it may well be possible to do several things simultaneously.

Controlled processing requires the various processes of attention, but is not the same thing as attention. For one thing, attending is involved during automatic processing, because people must still be selective and sustained in what they are doing and yet at the same time maintain a readiness to recognize unfamiliar circumstances and respond quickly. For another, controlled processing requires much more than self-organization for the task. Perception, decision-making and motor skill are all involved.

Many theoretical accounts of controlled information processing follow Sternberg (1966) in supposing several stages in strict succession. For example, Sanders (1980) considered the reaction to a stimulus in six stages: (i) stimulus preprocessing; (ii) feature extraction; (iii) identification; (iv) response choice; (v) response programming; and (vi) motor adjustment. Each stage is supposed to deal with one signal at a time and is independent of all the others. The times taken for each step add together to yield the reaction time. No one stage can be identified with 'attention'; all of them have a complex relationship with processes of attending. Attending is needed before a stimulus is admitted to processing; information processing has to take place to guide attention. Indeed, much of the selection and organization of responsiveness to stimuli should be thought of as a very high-level executive function and involves the operation of a supervisory system modulating lower-level programmes (Norman & Shallice, 1986).

Types of attention process

Even though high-level executive functions are probably involved in decisions about where to allocate resources, still there may be simple processes that form the elements. Information processing in different situations will require irrelevant information to be ignored, focused attention to be sustained, processing resources to be deployed intensely, and impulsive responses to be inhibited. It is an empirical question whether the course of development brings increased efficiency of these elementary processes, or whether the developmental changes are primarily those of more skilful coordination of the elements. Accordingly this chapter will consider psychopathology and developmental trends, not only in the behaviour of attention but also in the elementary processes of selective attention, sustained attention, intensity and inhibitory control.

DEVELOPMENT OF OVERT ATTENTION

Orienting behaviour is spontaneous in newborn children. They direct their gaze selectively to particular aspects of the environment. Their visual fixations can be observed and recorded; the length of time for which they inspect a stimulus can be measured; their physiological reactions to a stimulus can be described without any need to condition a response.

These orienting behaviours are the material on which the study of infant attention is based. They are relatively easy to record and they occur naturally, so they have also been powerful tools with which to study perception and learning. Indeed, they have usually been employed by researchers to study processes other than attention, and interest in the processes of attention themselves has been lacking. This has the useful result, for our purposes, of emphasizing that many processes other than those of attention can determine orienting behaviours.

The time for which a baby looks, for example at a new toy, can be thought of as determined by many interacting factors. Some of these will be organismic. Children may vary in their processing speed, and therefore in the time for which they need to look in order to extract information; they may have individual preferences in what they look at; their memory for whether they have seen the toy before may vary, as may their experience with it (although in an experimental setting this last would be controlled). Their abilities to perceive the object and to sustain a gaze, and their motivation to do so, also help to determine the final measure of orienting behaviour. The stimulus itself may also affect the extent to which it is attended: different things appeal at different ages, at different times and to different people. Stimulus properties will interact not only with the traits of the children but also with their state. Neonates vary greatly in their alertness, often irregularly so, and it has been easy for experiments to neglect this. Habituation experiments lasting for 15 min or more are regularly reported, even though it is unusual for an alert period in a neonate to last for longer than 10 min on end.

The first 3 months

Even in the neonatal period, the visual examination of the world is planned. There has been a great deal of laboratory research about the direction of eye gaze over various kinds of picture. A monograph by Haith (1980) gives a fine summary of a large literature. In brief, newborn children scan the world in a controlled and systematic fashion even when a patternless visual field has been encountered. Under these circumstances, they scan with relatively broad, jerky sweeps of the eyes. However, if there is a simple edge of high contrast to be seen, then it is selectively fixated; and there appear finer eye movements that systematically cross the edge, backwards and forwards. Simple edges such as these are more salient to the neonate than are more complex contours making up patterns. In this sense, attention is being captured by qualities of the stimuli. Even so, the active contribution of neonates is emphasized by Haith's conclusion that the above rules, by which they scan, subserve a basic purpose of keeping the firing rate of visual cortical neurones at a high level.

The novelty of the stimulus may also play a role in capturing the attention of the neonate. There has been some controversy over this. Earlier work was in agreement that neonates preferred familiar to novel stimuli, and would look for longer at them and direct gaze preferentially towards them (Greenberg *et al.*, 1970; Wetherford & Cohen, 1973).

More recent work has produced an even stronger agreement that children of less than 3 months of age show a selective attention to novel stimuli (shown particularly clearly by Friedman, 1972, 1975; Slater *et al.*, 1982). State changes may have produced some of the disagreement: most modern experiments use an infant control procedure in which a stimulus is presented only when a child is ready and the length of presentation is determined by the child's fixation. It is therefore clear that a preference for novelty is within the repertoire of the newborn child. What is less clear is the extent to which such a preference governs the usual activity of the child. The point is of some importance because of the implications for cognitive development considered below.

Habituation experiments can also be thought of as an index of response to novelty. They consist of a series of presentations of identical stimuli over a fairly short time period, when the length of gaze and physiological indices of response both tend to wane, and to recover when a new stimulus is subsequently given. Many factors affect this, including memory; but one result of repetition is to reduce the novelty of the stimulus. Habituation can indeed be evoked during the neonatal period: indeed, it can be detected in the last trimester of gestation, when it distinguishes between normal fetuses and those with Down's syndrome (Hepper & Shahiddullah, 1992).

3–12 months

Visual preferences during later infancy have also been studied extensively, and are reviewed by Olson and Sharman (1983). After the age of 3 months, there are much longer periods of alert attentiveness and perceptual sensitivity has matured to the point where much more complex differentiation of stimuli is possible. Many more aspects of stimuli come to attract the infant's gaze, including greater complexity of stimuli, curved rather than straight lines, irregular rather than regular patterns and symmetry rather than asymmetry. All these have been suggested to reflect an underlying tendency of the child to prefer an optimal level of contour density; and for the preferred level to become steadily denser as the infant approaches the end of the first year of life (Karmel & Maisel, 1975). The result is a much more elaborated pattern of attention to the visual world, and, of course, one that allows much more information to be obtained from it.

Complex stimuli can be processed as a whole even in the neonatal period (Slater *et al.*, 1991); but during the later part of the first year of life it becomes possible to discriminate changes in a compound stimulus that is embedded inside another (Milewski, 1978). Prior to that age, discriminations that can be made when the figure is not embedded within another, are lost when it is. The advance can be seen as one of increasing flexibility of attention.

The increasing preference for more complex patterns is parallelled by a general decrease in the average time for which a given stimulus holds the attention. The shorter periods of looking imply, of course, that more things are inspected in a given time. Visual attention is becoming more active and varied.

However, under some circumstances the length of looking at a stimulus is increasing during this time. When stimuli are discrepant from what is expected, then children look for longer (Kagan, 1970). This effect can be found even in the neonatal period (Weiss *et al.*, 1988). Thereafter, the preferential regard for discrepancy increases through the first year. Furthermore, the available means of exploring are increasing dramatically as the motor abilities of children mature. Visual exploration is supplemented by, and coordinated with, manual exploration that can alter the outside world and so create the opportunity of much richer understanding.

1–5 years

The preschool years are marked by an increasing range and flexibility of attention; increasingly, a child's exploration is guided by knowledge about the world. Kagan's (1970) classic experiment on discrepancy used clay masks that resembled faces as the stimuli. At the age of 6 months a distorted mask was looked at for longer than one closely resembling a face: it was discrepant from what, by then, a face was expected to look like. At the age of 12 months, distorted and regular masks were looked at for equal periods of time: the concept of 'face' was so well established that even a distorted mask could be readily assimilated as such. However, by the age of 18 months, children once again began to gaze for longer periods at a distorted than at a regular mask. They could form more ideas about it — had it been broken? who had changed it? — and their increasing knowledge about the world made the distorted mask more interesting.

Increasing knowledge about the world also implies that more stimuli carry meaning. Stimuli that have previously been rewarded come to evoke longer gazes than do novel stimuli (Grabbe & Campione, 1969). Toys become more interesting: Ruff and Lawson (1990) have provided descriptions of age changes from 1 to 5 years in the way children orient themselves to a standard set of toys. They distinguished between casual attention, simply looking at the toys; and focused attention, in which the child's facial expression was intent upon them. As the children grew older, their focused attention increased with time but their casual attention did not. Focused attention virtually always started after a period of casual attention, as would be expected if a first exploration of the toy raised a set of ideas about it and, therefore, the full deployment of active and focused orientation. The relationship between focused orientation and cognitive ability is close. The reasons for longer focused attention may simply be that an older child finds more to do with the toys. If so, this type of attention is an index of other abilities rather than a key ability in itself. It is possible that longer attention could be evoked from younger children with more developmentally appropriate stimuli.

The increasingly active and planned deployment of orienting behaviour is shown during early school years as an increasingly effective system for exploring the environment. Perceptual exploration, on the basis of preferential regard to that which is salient and novel, gradually gives way to more active and organized search (Wright & Vlietstra, 1975).

The child's increasing knowledge about the world may play a part in the development of search skills. One may suppose that the meaning of stimuli does not reside only in the reinforcement history of individual stimuli. Rather, children must develop some understanding about what classes of stimuli are likely to be relevant in different circumstances. A 'theory of relevance' may implicitly be formed, and help to guide the way children orient themselves. However, we do not yet know about the relative importance of this metacognitive understanding and the simple processes involved in the ability to select and sustain, in directing the developmental changes in exploring the world.

There is at present no systematic information about the way that overt attention develops in later childhood and adolescence. It is very likely that it does develop — on the face of it, adults apply themselves to frustrating tasks for longer periods than do adolescents. For the moment, this awaits study. Scientific work on attention in older age groups has focused on the aspects of covert attention that are considered below — largely because they allow for testing the subtler distinctions between ways of attending that are appropriate to adult life.

In summary, children are born with a capacity for prolonged direction of attention to important aspects of the environment — initially to relatively simple (but still very informative) features such as edge and novelty; and increasingly orient themselves towards complexity and meaningfulness in the stimulus array. This normative course is only the beginning of what needs to be known about development to understand pathology. The nature of individual differences and their determinants will now need a good deal more enquiry.

Individual differences

There is a good deal of variation between infants in the length of time for which they fixate visual stimuli. These differences show a significant stability over the first year of life, and they predict cognitive ability (Bornstein & Sigman, 1986). Short-looking infants at 3 months typically perform better than long-looking ones when they are cognitively tested in later childhood. This might be because they are processing information more quickly, or because they show a superior attention to the detailed features of the stimuli. Colombo *et al.* (1991) gave children at 4 months of age a set of discrimination tasks that required either global processing or the processing of detailed features: short-lookers' performance in discrimination was superior on the global task, and especially superior to that of long-lookers when there was less time available. It is therefore probable that inspection time in infancy is a measure of the speed (and efficiency) of processing visual stimuli.

There are also stable individual differences in visual preferences (see below). There is stability over the first year in the extent to which infants prefer novelty (Colombo *et al.*, 1988). The infants with the best cognitive performance are also those with the strongest tendency to prefer a novel to a familiar stimulus (Berg & Sternberg, 1985). This is related to performance on tests of habituation, for a high preference for novelty is associated with a large difference between the reaction to novel and familiar stimuli and therefore with rapid habituation. Individual differences in habituation have quite frequently been studied. The time taken for visual attention to reduce to a pre-established criterion, such as 50% of the original attention to the first presentation of the stimulus, has been taken to index a trait of the child such as the ability to process information. This evidently assumes that the individual differences are stable over time, though the point has been little studied. Over periods of a couple of weeks there is a moderate stability, but long-term stability is low (Bornstein & Benasich, 1986). Pecheux and Lecuyer (1989) reported a longitudinal study of visual habituation from 3 to 8 months of age: the stability of a measure of habituation speed fell with increasing time between measures, and was zero after a 5-month interval.

However, in spite of this low stability, habituation speed does predict later development. Several researchers have now reported a significant correlation between speed of habituation in the first few months and subsequent performance on tests of language and intelligence (Lewis & Brooks-Gunn, 1981; Bornstein & Sigman, 1986). A quantitative meta-analytic review by McCall and Carriger (1993) has confirmed that infant habituation, like recognition memory, predicts later IQ quite strongly, and does so more powerfully than standardized infant tests of general development. The association is stronger when the predicting assessments are made between 2 and 8 months of age than when they are made either earlier or later.

It is probable that the high predictiveness and low stability of habituation measures signify that the determinants of habituation speed are changing as children mature. There is, over the first year of life, a general decrease in total looking time and this affects habituation measures (Pecheux &

Lecuyer, 1989). However, as already noted, looking time at *relevant* stimuli increases during later childhood. Individual differences over this period also have developmental significance. Ruff *et al.* (1990) have found a significant correlation between observational measures of inattention at 1 year, and behaviour and a parental rating of hyperactivity at the age of 3.5 years.

These measures of infants' orientation constitute an increasingly effective means for assessing their information processing. Rose *et al.* (1992) have reviewed the predictive value of tests and contributed their own data on the relationships between information processing at 7 months of age and the cognitive outcome at age 6. Visual memory at 7 months predicts several measures at age 6: not only performance IQ but also verbal IQ, language skills and reading proficiency. By contrast, visual memory at 12 months was a much weaker predictor, a finding in keeping with the conclusion above that such a test is an index of different psychological processes at different ages and can therefore show low stability yet high predictive validity.

The measures may go deeper than simply the empirical prediction of individual differences in later childhood. The work by Rose *et al.* suggests that, even after allowing for verbal and performance IQ, there was a continuity in specific ability. Visual memory at 7 months was correlated specifically with visual sequential memory at 6 years. The processes themselves, and not just IQ, may be indexed by measures in infancy.

Measures such as visual preference and habituation constitute the strongest way of predicting later cognitive development during infancy, and they are well established as research tools. There are many clinical purposes for which it would be most helpful to have measures of individual differences in cognition during infancy. For example, large numbers of children are known to be at risk from birth because of stressors such as fetal exposure to toxins, birth prematurity or neonatal hypoxia. If the specifically vulnerable babies could be identified, then efficient preventive interventions could become feasible. A simple test of visual preference for novel stimuli has been developed by Fagan and Shepherd (1987) and widely used as a test of infant intelligence. Its value as a diagnostic tool has been contested, both for the rather weak data on which the standardization was based and for its

high misclassification rate, with about 40% of infants being wrongly characterized as low or high risk (Benasich & Bejar, 1992). The state of the infant is crucial, so that several testing occasions may be necessary to obtain the score of an individual child. The instability of the tests, referred to above, means that a test such as the Fagan may only be applicable within a very narrow age range. Many of the measurement problems still have to be conquered, but it is clear that individual differences can be quite strongly predictive and that measures of infant attention capture something important about cognitive development.

The reasons for these individual differences will need a good deal more research. It is often assumed that they are of constitutional origin because they appear so early; but the contribution of different causes has been little examined and a genetic strategy (e.g. comparing monozygotic and dizygotic twin concordances) should have a good deal to offer. Emde *et al.* (1992) have, for example, reported assessments on 200 pairs of twins, assessed in the laboratory and at home at 14 months. Several temperamental and cognitive traits showed significant heritability, but the results for attention were not very clear: parental ratings of persistence showed a significant heritability (monozygotic twin correlations 0.38, dizygotic 0.04); while an observational measure of task orientation did not show a genetic contribution (monozygotic twin correlations 0.15, dizygotic 0.22). Environmental influences, such as the level of stimulation given by an adult, are capable of influencing attention (Parrinello & Ruff, 1988). Tamis-LeMonda and Bornstein (1989) predicted language ability and pretend play at 13 months with child and parent measures, taken for the same children at the age of 5 months. Both habituation speed at 5 months, and the extent to which mothers encouraged attention at 5 months, had independent effects upon later language and play. Presumably, therefore, the effects of attentional changes cannot all be attributed to the interpersonal environment.

Psychopathology

Several of the individual differences considered above might, at their extreme, be important in psychopathology. If focused attention remained unduly short, then the resulting behaviour would be obvious to teachers and parents as a 'short attention span'. A failure to develop independence from the salience of stimuli could be identified with distractible behaviour; lack of system in scanning could give rise to impulsiveness; impaired development of flexibility and organization in search skills would be expected to lead to problems in complex learning and perhaps to perseveration. It would therefore be worthwhile to invest a good deal more experimental effort into analysing these overt patterns of scanning the world in psychopathologically defined groups.

COVERT SELECTIVE ATTENTION

Many situations require that only one stimulus is responded to when many stimuli are present. Children in a classroom may be expected thoroughly to understand their teacher's voice and to ignore all the sounds of a noisy class which also reach their ears. If they fail to do this, they will be regarded as distractible. One way of achieving this selection would be to process all the stimuli received, and then to choose the most relevant from amongst them. A more efficient strategy would be to exclude irrelevant information from being processed at all.

The core measures of selective attention are tests in which performance is worsened when irrelevant information is added. The additional irrelevant information could worsen performance because it calls forth a response incompatible with the main test, or because it uses up processing capacity, leaving insufficient for the main task. The details of the tasks will therefore be crucial. If the main test is very simple, then it can be done with little load on the central processors, leaving plenty of spare capacity to cope with additional information. If the main test is familiar then it can be solved by automatic processing and again there need be little interference from extra information. If the distractor is simple or familiar then it may neither make much call upon central processing, nor have much likelihood of evoking an incompatible response.

Development of selectiveness

There has been much argument and confusion about whether selectiveness develops at all. In many tests, the addition of irrelevant information has no effect on test performance, even in children (Doleys,

1976). Even within a single experiment, irrelevant stimuli can improve performance at one time and worsen it at another (Belmont & Ellis, 1968). White (1966) found that irrelevant variation in visual stimuli actually improved learning in children over the age of 5 (though, to be sure, it impaired performance before that age).

Such experiments are cautionary: they emphasize that, even early in development, attention is not passively dependent upon the amount of stimuli present. However, they can say nothing about the development of selectiveness, since they have evidently failed to stress the abilities involved in selective attention.

There are also experiments in which the presence of irrelevant information worsens performance (Pick *et al.*, 1975). Visual search tests have shown this distracting effect, and a more marked effect in younger children (Gibson & Yonas, 1966; Day, 1978). Speeded classification tests have also shown a developmental trend, in which the usual tendency for older children to perform better is even more marked when the irrelevant information is present (Strutt *et al.*, 1975; von Wright & Nurmi, 1979). Both visual search and speeded classification tests share the characteristic that all information has to be examined systematically: this may help to make children look at all the information presented even if some of it has been designated as 'irrelevant' by experimenters.

Another clue about the nature of distraction comes from studies that have varied the stimuli systematically. Enns and Girgus (1985) used a speeded classification test in which complex visual stimuli required a rapid response. There were also irrelevant aspects of the stimuli that could either be close in space to the relevant ones or else more widely separated. Performance on the central test was better if the irrelevant information was more widely separated. This was not a matter only of visual perception, for performance was worse with more widely separated stimuli when the central test required all the information to be used. The distracting effect of more closely spaced information was disproportionately greater in 8 year olds than 10 year olds and in 10 year olds compared with university students.

Some of the confusion about selectiveness in childhood can now be resolved. The presence of irrelevant information does not necessarily worsen performance on laboratory tests. Even young children are highly selective when it is clear to them what is relevant. Distractibility tends to appear when it is harder to distinguish the relevant from the irrelevant. Tests that show distractibility also show an age trend, from the age of 4 to adulthood, for a progressive reduction in the effects of distraction. People become harder to distract.

By the time of adulthood, the ability to ignore whole classes of stimuli is well established. It may even be too firmly ingrained, at the expense of good observation and noticing the implications of apparently incidental information. Many of the jobs in industrial society require the operator of a machine to attend to different sorts of information at different times and, therefore, to focus particularly on a few stimuli out of many presented. Much modern research stemmed from Broadbent's (1958) theories, emphasizing that the adult human has a strictly limited capacity for processing information. Selective attention protects the core processor by limiting the amount of information from the senses that is presented for processing. Stimuli, if they are easily discriminable on the basis of their physical properties, can be ignored by filtering through only those which belong to a physical class previously chosen as relevant. Later work (Deutsch & Deutsch, 1963; Triesman, 1969) showed that this ignoring was not total. The theory was therefore amended (Broadbent, 1971) to allow both for 'filtering', in which some stimuli are attenuated on the basis of physical properties, and for 'pigeon-holing', in which the surviving stimuli are assigned to different categories on the basis of decisions about the probabilities and relative importance of the categories.

An alternative way of thinking about adult selectiveness emphasizes the later stages of information processing (Norman, 1968; Keele, 1973). One can ignore the filter and suppose instead that a very large amount of information is perceived and presented to the central processor. The limiting stage comes when sensory information is matched to information in memory and a response selected: distractibility is then the consequence of failing to inhibit irrelevant responses.

These theoretical emphases on the early or the late stages of information processing are not exclusive alternatives. Both can operate in different circumstances: selectiveness is a property of all levels of information processing.

Why are younger children less selective?

The increased resistance to distractibility with age might be accounted for in several ways. Older children might orient themselves better, and look away from a task less often; or have a more effective filter; or be better at inhibiting responses to irrelevant stimuli; or make a sharper distinction between what is relevant and what is not; or they might have a greater capacity to process information and therefore be better able to cope with distractors.

The first possibility to consider is that *overt behaviour* accounts for the whole of the resistance to distractors in laboratory experiments.

Many experiments do not allow this distinction to be made, but some do. For example, Enns and Brodeur (1989) measured children's performance, on a speeded classification test, as a function of how a warning signal was presented. The time between the warning and the target was only 200 ms — too short for eye movements to be made. Nevertheless, the warning made a difference. If it was not in the same place as the target, then reaction times were considerably longer than they were when the warning was a valid indicator of where the target would appear. There is, in other words, a covert orientation towards place as well as an overt one. Furthermore, misleading information made more of a difference to children at age 6 than to older children or to adults. Age brings a greater ability to ignore misleading information which is partly due to covert processes of attention. High level cognitive processes also contribute to the maturing ability to ignore irrelevant information. The predictive value of a warning signal makes little difference to the performance of 6 and 8 year olds, but it improves the performance of adults (Enns & Brodeur, 1989). Adults can work out when a warning signal is relevant and use its information to guide their attention.

Rather similarly, Pick *et al.* (1972) investigated schoolchildren's ability to select relevant material in a visual display, as a function of whether they were given distractions before or after the visual display. Older children were better at using the previous instructions and their performance on the selective attention test correspondingly went up.

It therefore appears as if some, at least, of the developing ability to select out relevant information comes as a result of an increasing understanding about what is relevant. This does not imply that simpler processes of attention have been excluded — just that they are unlikely to be the full story.

Filtering processes may be involved as well. Experiments suggest that several developing abilities contribute to the increasing resistance to distraction. A speeded classification test was again the basic measure of performance for an experiment in which the details of distracting stimuli were manipulated (Enns & Akhtar, 1989). Young children were less good than older children at focusing on a specific stimulus: their attention set and the presence of a distractor both influenced their performance strongly, while other factors — such as response competition, that would have affected response organization — had an effect on adults but not on children. The poor performance of young children was therefore a function of strategy used and early stages of processing; it could not be ascribed entirely to the late stages of deciding on a response. The higher level processes involved in forming an attention set were not the whole story, for the simple presence of another stimulus had an effect: a filtering mechanism is working better as children get older.

What is the filtering mechanism? Several metaphors can be applied from technology — the variable-width filter that can tune to one wavelength and exclude others; the spotlight that can expand its range at the expense of the intensity at any one part; the zoom lens that can include a wider or a smaller field. They all imply that distractors are excluded from processing at an early stage. If this is true, then the more selective attention of an older child is obtained at a cost. Some of the increasing ability to respond accurately to a relevant stimulus will entail a decreasing accuracy of response to stimuli that are not relevant to a task in progress.

Incidental learning offers a powerful way of examining this. Hagen and Hale (1973) tested the ability of children of different ages to recall the positions in which they had seen picture cards of animals. They were instructed beforehand in the task, and were presumed to be concentrating on it. In addition, at the end of the experiment, they were asked to recall features of the cards on which they had not been asked to concentrate. On the main task there was a clear trend for accuracy of recall to increase with age, as expected. The inci-

dental learning task, however, showed no such improvement with age. There had been increased selectiveness in the older children. After the age of about 12 years, performance on the incidental task actually declined. Siegel and Stevenson (1966) also found a curvilinear relation between age and incidental learning, which at first improved and then declined, again at about 10–12 years. Filtering becomes more exclusive through adolescence into adult life.

SUSTAINING ATTENTION

One of the fundamental properties of an information processing system is that it must continue to work for long enough to do its job. When children play, they are sustaining their orientation on a task chosen by themselves; when they study at school, then they often have to maintain an activity to which their teacher has directed them; as they grow older then they are expected to work with perseverance even when their tasks are difficult and frustrating.

Several tests are intended to give operational measures of what is involved in sustaining attention.

Maintaining readiness is tested by the improvement in performance and reaction time, in response to a stimulus, that appears when a warning signal is given. If the time interval between the warning and the stimulus is too short, then full readiness is not reached: the maximum usually comes with a warning period of about 500 milliseconds (Posner & Boies, 1971). If the time interval is too long, then readiness can no longer be maintained. The experimental manipulation of the length of the warning period is then a way of testing how well attention is sustained. By the age of about 7 years, readiness is maintained for several seconds; but the full developmental course is not yet described.

Vigilance has been examined by investigators focusing on the maintenance, not of readiness, but of accuracy of performance over longer periods of time (typically from a few minutes to a few hours). At their simplest, such tests just require a prolonged and repetitive task such as the coding subtest of the WISC, on which performance improves with age (Cohen, 1959). However, these self-paced tasks are not very good indices of vigilance, because brief lapses of attention can be made up for by rapid work between times, and because the subjects' ability at the test may be a stronger determinant of performance than their persistence. A person who is responding to a continuous source of information does not lock inflexibly on to it. Rather, attention to it is punctuated by frequent brief switches to the rest of the world (Broadbent, 1958). These result in lapses of attention. One therefore requires a test of vigilance that is paced by the experimenter, and in which stimuli occur unpredictably.

By far the commonest test to be used is the continuous performance test (CPT). It was introduced by Rosvold *et al.* (1956) and researchers in psychopathology have used it very widely. Indeed in many parts of the world it is used for the clinical diagnosis of attention deficit and to monitor the effects of treatment. Developmental norms have been provided by Levy (1980) and it is clear that average scores improve with age through the early school years (Klee & Garfinkel, 1983). There are many forms of the CPT. In the commonest, letters are presented visually on a screen. Each presentation lasts for about 0.5 s; a new stimulus appears about every 2 s. The stimuli appear very regularly, and most do not require a response. One particular letter is the target, and every time it appears the subject must press a button. Target stimuli usually make up about 10% of the stimuli presented.

Apparently minor differences in stimulus presentation can make fundamental differences to the theoretical processes being measured. In some versions of the CPT, a letter (e.g. 'X') is the target and requires a response whenever it appears (the 'X' presentation). In others, it is only a target if preceded by another letter, say 'A' (the 'A−X' type of test). In others again, it is only a target if it occurs twice in succession (the 'X−X' type of test). The 'A−X' and 'X−X' types are ways of making the test harder so that it discriminates better. But they also convert it into a warning-signal paradigm of sustained attention — and rather different abilities are therefore being tested.

Indeed, it is often not at all clear just what psychological abilities are determining performance. Many processes are involved. For instance, the ability to read letters quickly is essential for many forms of the test and reading disability can directly cause a poor score. Even with non-verbal stimuli, the ability to discriminate and classify shapes will contribute to the score. In an attempt to avoid this, some versions of the test continuously adjust the level of test difficulty according to the performance of the child. The intention is laudable — to standardize the difficulty and therefore the load on information-processing capacity. Unfortunately, difficulty is nearly always increased by raising the speed of presentation of stimuli. A faster rate may be more arousing and will entail a shorter warning period; it may actually make the test easier to attend to.

Movements of the eyes away from the screen, a lack of inhibitory motor control, and reduced readiness for the next stimulus can also lead to poor scores. For all these reasons, the CPT must be seen as a complex performance measure of low specificity, and a poor score does not automatically imply an impairment of vigilance. Much research is still needed before we have a developmental account of how the span of attention increases with age.

INTENSITY OF ATTENTION

Another aspect of the way people organize themselves is their general responsiveness to the environment. Berlyne (1970) identified this as the 'intensive' aspect of attention, and in many ways it is close to lay theories. When a pupil is told to pay attention, the meaning is often that more resources need to be put into the task in hand, and more effort needs to be exerted. Some of this can be thought of as resources switched from other activities — the process already considered as selective attention. Some of this idea of paying attention is persisting at a task — as reviewed under sustained attention. But there is still more in the idea — the notion that there is a pool of unused resource that can be summoned up when the task requires it.

There have been difficulties in making a rigorous description of this process. Indeed, no single test score can be seen as an index of intensity. It is hard to distinguish ability at a test from engagement upon it — and impossible when the only measure is the score of how well one has done at the test. One therefore needs to take non-cognitive measures of effort such as muscular tension, or neurophysiological changes, or the facial appearance of hard work.

The most widely used physiological measure is the averaged evoked potential (AEP). This technique records the electroencephalogram (EEG) responses to a sequence of identical stimuli, and averages them to remove unrelated noise. The result is a summary description of the changes that have a constant temporal relationship with the stimulus. The late components of the resulting waveform are partly determined by the psychological meaningfulness of the stimuli. For example, a positive wave is generated at about 300 ms after a stimulus (P300), when the stimulus is discrepant from what would have been expected.

Developmental changes can be seen in physiological reactions to stimuli. During the first 3 months of life the orienting reflex becomes more complex and intense, both in the autonomic, nervous response to stimuli (Graham & Jackson, 1970); and in the EEG response (Ellingson, 1967). By the age of 5 months a P300 component can be elicited in the AEP and during later childhood it becomes larger and its latency falls (McIsaac & Polich, 1992). There is a trend in later childhood for the autonomic nervous system responses to become larger; and children with generalized developmental delays resemble younger children in having smaller responses (Luria, 1961).

Pribram and McGuinness (1975) proposed a theory of the neurological mechanisms controlling responsiveness. They distinguished three systems of control. 'Activation' was the tonic readiness of an animal to respond, and depended on the activity of dorsal thalamus and basal ganglia. A 'phasic', short-term response to stimulation was under the control of circuits centring on the amygdala. These two kinds of control of responsiveness were themselves coordinated by a third system of 'effort', determined by circuits focusing on the hippocampus.

This idea, of different energy pools, can also be developed as a psychological theory of how they might determine cognitive performance. Kahnemann (1973) differentiated these ways of controlling responsiveness, and therefore performance, according to the effect of experimental manipulations. Noise and incentive, for example, have separate effects and are supposed to alter different energy pools. A methodology can therefore be used in which experimental variables such as noise and incentive are tested for the presence of separately additive or interactive effects. These approaches have not yet yielded developmental formulations. They are, however, likely to become important in psychopathology because several pathological conditions, notably hyperactivity, are characterized both by cognitive changes and by autonomic physiological changes.

Inhibitory control

One aspect of attending successfully is being able to suppress immediate but wrong responses, and correspondingly to take enough time over processing information to do it successfully. It might seem that this would be easier to measure than the other processes considered above. A simple trade-off of accuracy against response time can be detected in reaction time experiments. However, this straightforward notion has not been implicated in psychopathology (Sergeant, 1981) and — perhaps for that reason — has received little developmental attention. Another fairly simple 'stop' test was applied to children by Schachar and Logan (1990b). This set up a situation in which children respond to a light; unless the light has been preceded by a 'stop' signal, in which case their task is to make no response. The independent variable, manipulated by the experimenter, is the time between the 'stop' signal and the response. No developmental trend was found on this test: second-grade children were as capable as young adults of inhibiting the expected response.

The most widely used test of inhibitory control is considerably more complex: the matching familiar figures test (MFF) (Kagan *et al.*, 1964). A difficult task is given to the child, in which a target picture must be matched to an identical one presented in an array of subtly different pictures. The time taken to do this successfully is usually quite long — in excess of 10 seconds — because the target needs to be compared closely with all the other pictures. A response that is both rapid and inaccurate is classed as 'impulsive'.

On this test there are indeed developmental changes. From the age of 7–8 years upwards children become both slower and more accurate in their responses (Cairns & Cammock, 1978). They have not just increased in ability to match (or they would become quicker as well as more accurate), but have responded in a more reflective manner. This distinction, between reflectiveness and impulsiveness, is usually expressed in terms of individual differences in cognitive style, and indeed there is some stability in individual differences; but the evidence from children at different ages suggests that one should also recognize it as a developmental function.

Why should there be a developmental trend on this test and not on the other more rigorous measures of inhibitory control? The time scale of response to this test is very much longer than that of a typical reaction time experiment. It represents the amount of time that a person is willing to give to a lengthy test, and also reflects how much evidence a person needs to collect before they conclude that a match has been made. These overlap greatly with the lines of development considered already as search and sustained attention: indeed, children who were impulsive on this test were also low scorers on a CPT (Zelniker *et al.*, 1972) and unsystematic scanners of pictures (Ault *et al.*, 1972). The decision-making involved in the test makes it necessary carefully to consider questions of motivation and incentive.

What are the rewards involved, and how might motivation alter with age? The ability to delay gratification is not complete, even in adult life. Other things being equal, people will prefer an immediate reward to a delayed one. Nevertheless, adults will choose a large delayed reward in preference to a small immediate one. Indeed, the capacity to do so is often thought of as distinguishing the mature citizen from the immature child or the psychopath. Mischel (1974) described how, with increasing age, children become more and more likely to choose a large delayed reward rather than an immediate gratification.

The age changes could be a function of the strategy chosen rather than a developing ability to inhibit the need for gratification. The importance of the strategy chosen, rather than the basic ability, is emphasized by studies of modifying performance on tests of impulsiveness. In early studies on the MFF, Kagan *et al.* (1966) found it possible to train children to go more slowly; but by itself this did not lead them to make fewer errors. Several later studies, however, found it possible to teach a strategy of self-control in problem-solving that both reduced errors on the MFF and led children to spend longer on thinking before acting (Meichenbaum & Goodman, 1971; Camp *et al.*, 1974; Egeland, 1974). This modification of cognitive tempo does not necessarily lead to better learning or conduct outside the laboratory (Gittelman *et al.*, 1989). But the modifiability of impulsiveness underlines the point

that it is under situational control and not a fixed property of the child's level of development.

ONE PROCESS OR MANY

Several different lines of development have now been distinguished: they clearly affect each other and must work in a coordinated way. It is not clear, however, that they are all part of a unitary faculty of attention.

The issue has been looked at in various ways. Individual differences in one type of attention can be correlated with others. Thus, Richards (1987) found that infants whose looking is accompanied by sustained heart deceleration (the *intensive* aspect of attention) are less distractible than other infants (the *selective* aspect). In a more generalized way, a whole set of tests can be compared, and factor analyses of the resulting matrix of intercorrelations can be carried out. In the adult psychopathology literature, this has often yielded very low intercorrelations between tests: they do not measure the same thing (Spring, 1980). In more representative adults, a factor-analytic approach by Wittenborn (1943) was interpreted as supporting a dimension of attention with loadings from several tests, but this is not a replicated or accepted finding (Moray, 1969). Factor analyses in disturbed children have found a factor with loadings from several tests requiring sustained effort and the control of impulsiveness (Douglas, 1972; Taylor, 1986). Whether this is truly a factor of attention is another matter. Pelham (1979) found little relationship between different attention tests. It seems that, while some tests have something in common, we do not know what it is. Some motivational quality of engaging in tests, or a general ability in test performance, could account for what the different tests have in common. Simple correlations between different tests are unlikely to give a definitive answer about the processes involved.

Another approach would be to see whether different kinds of attention loading compete for the same processing capacity. If, for example, the effects of adding irrelevant stimuli to a test are quite independent from the effects of making a warning interval longer on the same test, then one could conclude that sustaining attention and resisting distraction do not share the same mechanism.

Akhtar and Enns (1989) took a similar approach.

They found that covert orienting towards a stimulus (without eye movements) and resisting distraction were not independent. Children's performance on a test was worsened by a misleading cue, and worsened by incompatible distracting stimuli; both together were much worse than the sum of the two taken separately. Covert orienting and filtering therefore share resources. By contrast, overt orienting (visual search) was independent of resistance to distraction in another experiment with children (Enns & Cameron, 1987). This is a somewhat surprising finding in view of the suggestion from psychopathology that the same parts of the brain are used for overt and covert orienting (see section on neurological disorders below).

For the present, it is not possible to be clear that there is any unitary process of attention. What is clear is that distinct lines of attention development can be distinguished, and that in some circumstances they influence each other. A developmental understanding of psychopathology will therefore need to go beyond findings of poor performance in one disorder or another to analyse which elementary processes are impaired and/or the different strategies with which they are being employed.

ATTENTION IN LATER LIFE

In later life, a decline in performance on tests of effortful information processing has often been noted. Welford's research programme has documented a range of such changes (Welford, 1980). Reaction time on simple tests increases — by about 20% when people in the seventh decade of life are compared with those in the third (Birren *et al.*, 1980). There is an even greater increase with age in choice reaction time — which tends to disappear on tests that subjects have practised intensively (Rabbitt, 1980).

A good deal of this slowing may well be simply that — a reflection of slower neuronal processes rather than of worse self-organization. The role of the various processes of attention identified above is not at all clear. Poor attention has often been invoked as an explanation of the changes in memory seen during ageing (Craik & Byrd, 1982). However, in this sense 'attention' is being used in a rather vague and global sense, and is invoked *post hoc* as an explanation rather than tested directly. The failure to grasp instructions may well be a very important

aspect of cognitive changes in ageing and emphasizes that a high level of functioning may be needed to explain changes in attention (Rabbitt, 1979).

RELATIONSHIP WITH OTHER LINES OF DEVELOPMENT

Intelligence and learning

There is not much doubt about the presence of an association between attending and intelligence. Attending as a behaviour is related to intelligence: children selected from epidemiological surveys on the basis of teachers' ratings of poor concentration have a mean IQ one standard deviation below that of children who are not behaviourally deviant (Taylor *et al.*, 1991). Scores on some tests intended to measure attention correlate with IQ (Taylor, 1986), but the correlations are usually small.

To understand the relationship between the processes of attention and intelligence is much more difficult. Neither 'attention' nor 'intelligence' are unitary constructs, but shorthand summary terms for domains of mental function. The two domains overlap considerably. Many of the tests, whose results are combined to yield an IQ score, can plausibly be seen as measures of attention. For example, factor analysis of the Wechsler test battery yields, as well as the familiar 'verbal' and 'performance' factors, a third dimension of 'freedom from distractibility' (Cohen, 1959). It has high loadings from the subtests of arithmetic, digit span and coding. Whether these are in fact specifically affected by sustained or selective attention is not certain — in fact, it would be useful to analyse the way children solve these tests to see how far they can be interpreted as indices of attending. Nevertheless, the illustration makes the point that attention is one of the functions assessed by intellectual testing.

Individually administered IQ tests are not necessarily very sensitive to changes of attention. The psychologist structures the situation, gives clear instructions, controls the setting and often shows the child what is relevant. All these can be expected to reduce the load on attention and make it less probable that poor attention will limit performance. This is a common-sense argument, not a demonstrated fact; but it suggests that impaired attention will give rise to worse learning in real life than would be predicted by IQ scores.

Intelligence and attention may have complex relationships. Intelligence can be expected to affect attending through a better metacognitive understanding about where one should orient in different circumstances — one of the determinants of selective attention considered above. Attention might also affect intelligence; to demonstrate the process would require longitudinal evidence that attention is not just a correlate of intelligence in cross-sectional studies, but also a predictor of the development of problem-solving abilities later. The firmest evidence here comes from work on infants' visual inspection times as predictors of later mental development. Measures of infant habituation are unrelated to concurrent measures of psychological development, which are of necessity based on simple sensorimotor function; they do predict intellectual performance in later childhood, when tasks can be given that measure more cognitive abilities (Berg & Sternberg, 1985).

This prediction, from longer periods looking at a novel stimulus to later psychological development, implies that visual attention to novelty is an integral component of intellectual development. One possibility is that a preference for novelty spurs on intellectual development. According to this idea, infants' attention shapes the complexity of the world they experience. If they prefer novel stimuli, then they are experiencing more interesting stimulation and more information that contradicts their expectations; consequently, perhaps, they develop more complex cognitive structures. Another possibility is that intelligence in later life should be seen as one kind of response to novelty: intellectual grasp of familiar material reflects primarily what one has learned, so the powers of understanding are only really tested when they are needed for something outside previous experience. According to this view, the infant inspecting a novel stimulus and the child solving a novel problem are at different points along the same line of development. It should be illuminating to study the interaction between infants' orientation to novelty and the complexity of their psychological environment. Genetic analyses (for instance in designs where monozygotic and dizygotic twins are followed longitudinally) should be useful in clarifying the relationships between attention and the other components of cognitive development. Neuroimaging studies of brain function have already shown an ability to distinguish between different sorts of cognitive processes (Paulesu *et al.*, 1993; Raichle, 1993); they are likely to help in the analysis of attentional processes also.

Social and emotional development

The influence of other people on cognitive and neurological functioning is an outstanding challenge to developmental science. First, attention may be an influence upon the way other people react to children, and therefore upon the children's development. It is possible that inattentiveness is unpleasant for parents and that distractibility may be misread as a lack of emotional engagement. Good evidence has been hard to come by because of the lack of really adequate measures of parental reaction, together with the frequency of comorbidity between attention deficit and conduct disorder, and uncertainty about the direction of causality. An epidemiological survey of children with attention deficit and hyperactivity suggested that parent–child relationships were less satisfactory, and parents were more critical, than was the case for normal controls (Taylor *et al.*, 1991). However, it was the component of hyperactivity rather than of inattentiveness in behaviour that generated the association; attention deficit on its own was not associated with adversity in relationships.

When hyperactive children are treated with stimulant medication, they become less inattentive and more focused in their behaviour; and expressed criticism by parents falls (Schachar *et al.*, 1987). This indicates that one reason for an association between inattentive behaviour and family adversity is likely to be the direct result of the behaviour upon other family members.

Other routes are probable. For example, there is an association between being brought up in a residential children's home and being inattentive that probably reflects the results of institutionalization. This is not likely to reflect material disadvantage. Rather, the experience of changing caretakers and the lack of opportunity for stable attachments seem to be at the heart of the experience. Children who have grown up in this way are particularly likely to be inattentive in their classrooms, even after they have been adopted into a family home and their other psychological problems have improved (Tizard & Hodges, 1978; Roy, 1983).

Similarly, it is possible but unproven that adversity in close personal relationships causes impaired attention, and that this accounts for the association between hyperactivity and marital discord (Brandon, 1971), hostile parent–child relationships (Battle & Lacey, 1972; Tallmadge & Barkley, 1983), parents who sought a termination of the pregnancy (Matejccek *et al.*, 1985) and discordant family life (Gillberg *et al.*, 1983). Taylor *et al.* (1991) reported that adverse family relationships were associated with the persistence of hyperactive disorder over time: their developmental role may be the maintenance rather than the initiation of disorder.

The social environment might also be understimulating, or be so chaotic that children have little opportunity to acquire the skills of selection and persistence. This route is suggested by the finding that impaired attention without hyperactivity is associated with low socioeconomic status and poor housecraft during early childhood (Taylor *et al.*, 1991). However, genetic and longitudinal studies will be needed to tell us the processes that account for the links between the family environment and the development of attention.

PSYCHOPATHOLOGY

Several principles from the study of development now need to be born in mind when thinking about disorders. First, several processes are involved in attending. It is unusual for a test directly to chart an underlying ability; rather, tests give the resultants of several types of attention. Second, these processes are all candidates for impairment in psychopathology. To ask whether 'attention is impaired' is a vague question; rather, one must consider the various ways in which attention may be altered. Third, the course of development of each ability is affected by several factors, which may vary at different ages. Both psychosocial and biological factors are involved. Fourth, the details of experiments and the context of observation make a substantial difference to attending. It follows that the assessment of psychopathology needs to consider the situation as well as changes in the individual.

Schizophrenia

Changes in 'attention tests'

Attention changes in schizophrenia are important for several reasons. First, they are common: very many studies have found changes in psychological and physiological tests (reviewed by Holzman, 1987). More than this, they offer some promise of explaining many of the most characteristic features of schizophrenic pathology. The abnormal thoughts of affected people can be conceived, loosely, as a failure to filter out irrelevant associations and half-formed thoughts from consciousness. 'Loosely', because it is not at all clear in any rigorous sense that normal people do in fact generate such associations and thoughts that need to be screened out, nor that they would experience anything approaching thought disorder if such filtering failed. Nevertheless, subjective accounts of people with schizophrenia have described sensations of being overwhelmed by experiences and of seeing huge significance in trivial events.

Most investigations have of course been cross-sectional case control comparisons. There are many findings of altered information processing from decades of study. For example, the CPT is performed poorly by nearly half of patients with schizophrenia — even after the acute episode is over (Wohlberg & Kornetsky, 1973). Reaction time has long been known to be prolonged in schizophrenia and used as an index of impaired set (Rodnick & Shakow, 1940). Irrelevant, distracting information impairs performance on simple tests of memory in schizophrenia (Lawson *et al.*, 1964). The amplitude of the P300 component of the evoked potential is reduced (Baribeau-Brown *et al.*, 1983).

Developmental perspectives

A developmental perspective would take the issues considerably further. It raises in strong form questions such as whether the information-processing deficits result from changes in any of the developmental lines of attention noted above; the time course of the deficits and whether they parallel clinical changes; whether they are a deviant form of information processing or an incomplete development, and whether they are similar to alterations of attention encountered in other developmental contexts; how the deficits are affected by the interaction of genes and experience; and how they relate to the different components of the clinical syndrome of schizophrenia.

The clearest line of development to be involved is that of *selective attention*. The CPT impairment is not the result of poor vigilance, for it is not a function of the length of time for which the test is given. Rather, it depends upon the load that is placed on the early stages of information processing. Perceptual sensitivity, as assessed from signal-to-noise discrimination, is the measure that is impaired; populations at risk for schizophrenia show a deficit when the perceptual difficulty is increased by presenting a very blurred image to be detected (Neuchterlein, 1983). Rather similarly a 'span of apprehension' task showed a difference between people with schizophrenia and normal controls (Asarnow & MacCrimmon, 1981). Superficially this is a memory task, requiring recognition of very briefly presented letters. However, the deficit only appears when irrelevant letters are presented at the same time, and is worse when there is more irrelevant information.

The interpretation of these findings in terms of a selective attention breakdown is not certain. They could also (like many of the developmental experiments supposed to be about selective attention) result from a reduction of the capacity to process information. However, a failure of selective attention has also been implicated in analyses of the problems people with schizophrenia (and depression) have in memory for dichotic listening (Hemsley & Zawada, 1976). Their difficulty came especially in distinguishing between relevant and irrelevant digits, read out loud by different voices.

The developmental studies of selective attention reviewed above indicated that resistance to distraction could be seen in part as a relatively mechanical 'filtering' process, but also that higher level decisions about what is relevant had to be included in the account. Research on what is treated as irrelevant in different circumstances therefore deserves a good deal more emphasis. One simple, related experimental paradigm is that of *latent inhibition*. A stimulus, X, is consistently paired with a signal for some other task (T); and then itself becomes a signal for a new task. Under these circumstances, stimulus X is less well processed: the new task based upon it is learned less efficiently and reaction time is longer. One can argue that the person originally learned that X was irrelevant during the course of task T, and so does not pay much attention to it. People with acute schizophrenia show less of this inhibition of responsiveness to X. Their reactions to X in the new task are actually faster than those of controls (Baruch et al., 1988). This is not to be explained by filter breakdown and increased incidental learning, for then people with schizophrenia would have to have learned more about X during the initial task — including that it is irrelevant. Rather it implies that schizophrenia is associated with a diminished ability to form or use knowledge about the previous importance of stimuli. It should be useful to apply developmental analyses to this kind of test; and to apply to schizophrenia the experimental manipulations of instructions, and the relevance of precues, that have been helpful in developmental research.

Developmental course

The longitudinal course of attention deficit in schizophrenia has received some study. It is clear, for instance, that poor test performance is relatively stable over periods of a few months after a first schizophrenic illness (Asarnow & MacCrimmon, 1981; Harvey et al., 1990). This does not by itself mean that we are dealing with a trait problem — concentration may take months to recover after an acute schizophrenic episode even when recovery is eventually complete. But longer term evidence comes from the findings of the New York High Risk Project (Erlenmeyer-Kimling & Cornblatt, 1987). They found, like others, that children, who were at risk because they had a schizophrenic illness, had deficits on a range of 'attention tests' (CPT, span of apprehension and digit span). The study was able to follow the children to their early adult life, by which time a few had undergone psychiatric hospitalization. Their breakdown could be predicted from childhood status by their score on these attention tests.

It is tempting to conclude that the impairment of attention is in itself the risk factor for schizophrenia. This, however, would go too far. For one thing, many children in the general population (around

5%) will show comparable impairment of attention and it is not at all clear that they are also at risk. If it is only a risk in those with a schizophrenic inheritance, then perhaps it is an indirect marker rather than a specific vulnerability. Another query arises from a report by the same study that those who later broke down had also had a lower IQ in childhood (Erlenmeyer-Kimling *et al.*, 1984). Perhaps the risk factor was not specifically a failure of selective attention, but a more general cognitive problem.

A better understanding of developmental course will also need information about the relationship between disturbances of attention and different types of symptomatology. Schizophrenia is not a homogeneous syndrome, and several of the disturbances of attention described above are also encountered in mania and depression. Evidence has appeared that poor performance on the CPT and span of apprehension tasks is correlated with the severity of the 'negative' symptoms of mental impoverishment, not with the 'positive' symptoms of bizarre thinking (Neuchterlein *et al.*, 1986). There is also some evidence that direct tests of distractibility may be linked to positive rather than negative symptoms (Harvey *et al.*, 1990), so further analyses of the selective attention deficit will be required.

In summary, present understanding suggests that some of the information-processing deficit in schizophrenia is due to an alteration of the development of selective attention that antedates the symptoms of illness. Impaired attention could be a marker of the schizophrenia genotype that impairs social information processing, so that stress and social avoidance are both indirect consequences. Developmental research should have a good deal to contribute to clarifying the ways in which the genotype is expressed. Fruitful next steps include the further analysis of the nature of the problem in adults; the comparison of attention in people at high risk for schizophrenia with those who show other patterns of attention deficit; and the identification and follow-up of children in the general population with impairments of selective attention.

Brain damage

We have seen that attention considered developmentally is not a single process. Correspondingly,

no single relevant locus is likely to be responsible and no unitary brain syndrome of attention deficit is to be expected. There could, however, be several different psychological mechanisms through which localized brain injury might disrupt attention.

One of the clearest pathways is that through which parietal lobe lesions lead to sensory neglect. Neglect can be seen as an extreme of impairment of the 'intensive' aspect of attention considered above; in which stimuli — though obviously present and salient in the external world — elicit no response and no awareness. For example, visual information may be ignored, in the field contralateral to a lesion, even though peripheral pathways are intact. Such phenomena, like many of the intensive aspects of attention, are hard to distinguish from failures of perception. A closely similar problem is that of extinction, in which, for example, stimuli contralateral to a lesion can be seen when presented on their own but not when ipsilateral stimuli are present at the same time.

Neuropsychological analyses of shifting visuospatial attention, carried out by Posner *et al.* (1984), have suggested specific correlates of neurological lesions. For example, parietal lobe lesions can produce a deficit in the operation of 'disengaging'. The experiments 'cue' attention by informing subjects where a target will be presented: the time needed to respond is less when attention has previously been focused on the right place. The key observation in parietal lesions was that a cue summoning attention to the side of the lesion produced a massive increase in time taken to detect targets in the opposite field; the interpretation was that they could not disengage from an ipsilateral cue (Posner *et al.*, 1984).

By contrast, the same research group found a different kind of deficit in people suffering from progressive supranuclear palsy (Posner *et al.*, 1982). This disease, affecting the control of eye movements, also impairs covert visual attention (measured when stimuli are presented so quickly that the eyes do not have a chance to move). Patients showed longer reaction times when they had to shift attention, but this applied whether there was a cue or not. The interpretation was that their deficit lay, not in disengaging but in moving the focus of their attention. The experiment makes it likely that the same brain structures involved in shifting overt attention via eye movements are involved in inner processes of attention as well.

Dementia

Dementia includes, virtually by definition, a diminution in information-processing resources. Tasks requiring effortful, controlled processing are particularly sensitive and show abnormalities in the early stages of dementia of Alzheimer's type (Jorm, 1986).

Analysis of the reasons for impairment in information processing still leaves some doubt about whether attention is specifically affected. Dementia brings with it a slowing of reaction time; but the slowing is apparent in simple reaction tests as well as in choice discrimination (Hart & Semple, 1990). A generally slower speed of functioning is implicated rather than a change in attending. Hart and Semple (1990) reported briefly an attempt to analyse the problem further, by varying the time between a response and the onset of the next stimulus. Patients with dementia reacted more quickly when the stimuli came at predictable times, rather than being irregularly spaced; they did particularly badly when stimuli were both irregular and crowding hard on the heels of the previous response. One implication from this could be that they were relying heavily upon the improvement of performance that comes when one is adequately prepared; so presumably they were still able to deploy attention successfully.

Investigation of sustaining preparedness after a warning stimulus would be well worth carrying out. Sustained attention has been studied — mostly with the CPT. Patients with dementia scored poorly on this test by comparison with normal age-matched controls and patients suffering from functional psychiatric disorders (Alexander, 1973). One has to say that the finding of test impairment may well be correct, but the evidence of poor attention as the cause of it remains lacking.

Selective attention has been studied with the Stroop test (Hart & Semple, 1990). In its original form, this test requires subjects to name the colour of the ink in which words are printed, when the words are themselves names of colours. This is a confusing task because of the interference between similar types of input, and it must measure an effortful form of information processing. Whether impairment in performance is due chiefly to ineffec-

tive stimulus selection is another matter entirely — competition for response selection or generalized slowing of information processing could have the same result. Hart found that patients with dementia were impaired in their speed and accuracy on this test; and disproportionately impaired when the stimuli were at their most confusing. A poor performance on an embedded figures test in dementia was found by Capitani *et al.* (1988) and construed as a selective attention deficit. This sort of test certainly requires a figure to be picked out from a confusing background — but, since the picture has to be analysed before one can tell what is relevant and what is not, the finding is perhaps evidence of a problem in spatial perception rather than selective attention.

The intensive aspects of attention in dementia have been investigated using the P300 component of the auditory AEP (Blackwood & Christie, 1986; Blackwood *et al.*, 1987). The amplitude is decreased and the latency increased; and as dementia progresses the changes become more marked (St Clair *et al.*, 1988).

The control of attending has been stressed by Baddeley's (1988) analysis of the changes in memory that are seen in senile dementia of Alzheimer type. In some experiments, for example, patients with dementia can remember experimental material well when the interval between items allows them to rehearse; but forget particularly quickly when a second task is presented in the interval so that rehearsal is suppressed. The interpretation is that new learning may be impaired chiefly by the resource demands of carrying out two tasks simultaneously. Clearly, more research would be needed to determine whether this is truly a matter of attention, for it might result from a restriction of the capacity for effortful processing rather than from altered strategies about how to deploy those resources. Baddeley's analysis emphasizes the interdependence of different types of impairment of mental performance.

The difficulties in the analysis of dementia parallel those encountered in the study of intellectual retardation. The problem is to understand the significance of changes in tests of attention when all cognitive tests are to some extent impaired. Experimental analyses of the reasons for deteriorating performance, along the lines of those used to describe increasing abilities during development, should be illuminating.

Hyperactivity

Theories about the psychopathology of hyperactivity have suggested that the fundamental defect is an inability to concentrate. The view has been so influential that it is sometimes forgotten that it is merely a theory and that empirical evidence is required. The American Psychiatric Association's (1987) third edition of its diagnostic and statistical manual, DSM-III, and its revisions into DSM-III-R and DSM-IV have all named the condition 'attention deficit disorder' and the power of the phrase is so great that it can seduce the unwary into supposing that there is indeed a deficit of attention.

The evidence is strong that children with 'attention deficit disorder' (ADDH) get poor scores when they perform on tests that are supposed to measure attention. These tests include the CPT (Ross & Ross, 1976; Whalen & Henker, 1976; Hoy *et al.*, 1978; Rosenthal & Allen, 1978; Loiselle *et al.*, 1980), the matching familiar figures test (Messer, 1976; Fuhrman & Kendall, 1986), visual memory tests where there is a high demand upon information-processing resources (Sprague & Sleator, 1977; Douglas, 1983), repetitive reaction time tests and speeded classification tests (Sykes *et al.*, 1973), the allocation of processing capacity in line with changing task demands (Sergeant & Scholten, 1985), and the maintenance of readiness to respond in reaction time tests with varying delays after a preparatory signal (Sonuga-Barke & Taylor, 1992).

In the face of so much evidence, how can there be a doubt about whether there is a disturbance of attention? The uncertainty comes because of questions over the specificity of these findings to hyperactivity, the direction of causality in the link between behaviour and cognition, the nature of changes over time, and the nature of the psychological processes that are in fact being tapped by these tests.

Specificity of findings

The first of these doubts — the specificity of impairment — has partly been allayed by recent research. True, several reviewers have argued that the impairment of test scores is a non-specific accompaniment of many types of disturbance in behaviour and learning, not just of hyperactivity (e.g. Prior & Sanson, 1986; McGee & Share, 1988). It is now clearer that this does not apply to all forms of disturbance. Conduct disorder has been thought to be associated with poor scores on a variety of neuro-psychological tests; but this is not so when adequate allowance is made for the frequency with which conduct disorder and hyperactivity are present together. Recent studies have shown that poor test performance is relatively specific to the behaviours of hyperactivity rather than conduct disorder (Schachar, 1991). Hyperactivity in population-based samples is correlated with reduced scores; non-hyperactive conduct disorder is not; the association is clearest at severe degrees of hyperactivity (McGee *et al.*, 1984; Sergeant, 1989; Szatmari *et al.*, 1989; Taylor *et al.*, 1991). Furthermore, reduced scores are associated with one component of hyperactivity — inattention — rather than restlessness, fidgeting and impulsiveness (Lahey *et al.*, 1987; Taylor *et al.*, 1991).

It may still be the case that other forms of behavioural psychopathology are associated with poor scores on tests of 'attention'. It would be desirable to make a systematic examination of the behaviours that are associated with low scores. The specificity of impairment needs a good deal more research, but it has passed the simple hurdle of differentiating between hyperactivity and conduct disorder. This differentiation does also make it less likely that mere disinclination to be involved with the tests is the reason for poor scores — since a motivational factor such as this would plausibly be considered to characterize antisocial conduct disorder as much as or more than it would hyperactivity.

What is the nature of the attention deficit?

The next issue is that of the type of psychological disturbance that is in fact indexed by the tests. Earlier parts of this chapter indicated that these 'attention' tests could be influenced by many factors other than attention. The ability to perform well on tests can be seen as a rather general ability, indexed by the IQ.

IQ may account for some of the difference between hyperactive and control groups. The reduction in scores is found in a wide variety of tests and indeed the IQ is reduced in hyperactive children in most of these studies. However, some abnormalities are still to be found even after IQ has been controlled for by analysis of covariance.

Impairment can also be seen in a number of tests that are not particularly intended to assess attention — such as short-term memory (the digit span test, Taylor *et al.*, 1991), speed of response (serial and choice reaction time tests, Sykes *et al.*, 1973), new learning (paired associate learning tests, Swanson & Kinsbourne, 1976) — and even tachisto-copically presented tests that were originally designed to avoid effects of attention (McIntyre *et al.*, 1978).

Controlled information processing is therefore likely to be impaired in hyperactivity. However, the subtractive analysis of different stages of information processing has not indicated anything that looks much like an attention deficit. Attempts to implicate encoding, search and decision stages of processing information (Sergeant & Scholten, 1985) and over-all attentional capacity (Schachar & Logan, 1990a) have been unsuccessful. There is some evidence of abnormalities at the later stages of response selection and enaction — as witnessed, for example, by a disproportionate effect on hyperactive children of making the response incompatible with the stimulus (van der Meere & Sergeant, 1988).

An impairment of response stages of information processing could still be compatible with a specific disability in one of the elementary processes of attention whose development was considered above.

Sustained attention failure is suggested by the poor scores on the CPT, but not supported when the experimental variable is the time in which the test must be done. For example, the deficit is mani-fest in tests lasting a few seconds just as it is in those lasting for 10 min or more (Taylor *et al.*, 1991) and is much the same in tests lasting for several hours (van der Meere & Sergeant, 1986). The problem is therefore unlikely to be one of sustaining attention over time.

Selective attention failure is often suggested, if only because it seems self-evident that distractibility is a part of hyperactivity. However, this too gets little support from the experimental literature based upon psychopathological groups. While hyper-

activity may well be associated with distractibility in the behavioural sense that one changes activities often, this is not the same as the disruptive effect of irrelevant information that is sought by the exper-imentalist. The addition of irrelevant information to test stimuli does not worsen performance dis-proportionately in children with hyperactivity (Douglas & Peters, 1979; Sergeant & Scholten, 1985). Some have suggested that the deficit lies in an excessive breadth of attention, so that perform-ance on incidental tests should be improved to the same extent as performance on a central test is reduced. The evidence is contradictory here. One investigation did find a shift of attention from what is centrally relevant to what is peripheral (Ceci & Tishman, 1984); but the majority of studies investi-gating this possibility have not found it (Douglas & Peters, 1979; Taylor *et al.*, 1991).

Intensity of attention has been studied with psychophysiological measures in children diagnosed as showing hyperactivity or ADDH. A number of studies have found that such children — while showing no changes in their basal activation — have a reduced phasic response of the autonomic nervous system to stimuli that have novelty or signal value (reviewed by Taylor, 1986). The P300 component of the auditory evoked response to stimuli requiring a response is also reduced (Loiselle *et al.*, 1980).

However, we cannot proceed from these findings to infer an impairment in the intensity of attention in hyperactivity. Unlike the scores on attention tests, these measures have not yet been shown to be specific to hyperactivity. Indeed, some evidence suggests that they are not; Conners (1975) reported that reduced amplitude of the skin conductance response did characterize a hyperactive group, but did not correlate with levels of hyperactivity within that group, but rather with neuromuscular incoor-dination. The orienting response is smaller in chil-dren with intellectual retardation (Luria, 1963) and specific learning disorders (Sroufe *et al.*, 1973; Cousins, 1976); these conditions are often comorbid with hyperactivity.

Inhibitory control has a much stronger claim to being a process that is impaired in hyperactivity. The best-known way of testing the idea of impul-siveness is through Kagan's matching familiar figures test (cited above). In conditions of uncer-tainty, impulsive children make rapid and inaccurate responses; in the theory, they are inaccurate because they are too rapid. The analysis applies well in some epidemiological research. Not only are hyperactive children unduly quick in their response, but accuracy falls as they take less time to do it (Fuhrman & Kendall, 1986; Taylor *et al.*, 1991). In clinical research, the analysis has not always worked very well. In some studies, especially of pervasive hyperactivity where there is likely to be a high rate of developmental disorders, children with hyperactivity have proved to be less accurate but no faster in their responses than clinically referred controls (Sandberg *et al.*, 1978; Firestone & Martin, 1979). The likely reason for this comes from the high rate of other developmental disabilities in these series. Such children are likely to have slower reactions because their processing time takes longer. Many studies have shown that they have slow reactions in conventional information-processing experiments (Sergeant, 1989). Their responses may therefore be premature, even when they take the same amount of time as ordinary children. Their usual tendency is still to take less time in inspecting new material than most children do; when this is prevented by the experimenter's controlling the amount of time that they spend looking at a visual test then their performance is no worse than anybody else's (Sonuga-Barke *et al.*, 1992a).

Schachar and Logan (1990b) have directly tested the idea that children with hyperactivity are less able to inhibit a response than others, and found that the prediction holds for children with the serious problem of hyperkinetic disorder (not for those with ADDH). Rapport *et al.* (1986) tied this more closely to the obtaining of reward with the finding that children with hyperactivity were more likely to respond for a small immediate reward than for a large delayed one. More recently still, investigators have made a systematic examination of the effects of delay and size of incentive on children's choices (Sonuga-Barke *et al.*, 1992b). In one sense, this confirmed the impulsiveness of children with pervasive hyperactivity: under some circumstances they were indeed maladaptive in responding too quickly and not waiting for a reward. But the research also showed that, when the total amount of time they had to wait was controlled, they were no more impulsive than ordinary children. The difficulty should not be seen as a fixed impairment

of inhibitory control but as a change in the decision-making about when to inhibit.

The result of this impulsiveness is that children choose to take less time over tasks they are given. If the task needs more time to be completed accurately, then their accuracy will suffer. If this is so, then their performance should increase to normal levels when the time taken is controlled experimentally, and indeed in one experiment involving new learning this has proved to be the case (Sonuga-Barke *et al.*, 1992a, c).

Such a formulation is of course rather different from the traditional explanations of hyperactivity, and more study will be needed to test its predictions. It is not yet clear whether all the impairments in attention tests that have been noted above can be accounted for by cognitive impulsiveness. They cannot all be accounted for, of course, in the sense that children are often slow in their reactions, etc., but it is possible that all the deficits that are specifically attributable to hyperactivity may be explicable on this basis.

Direction of causality

The above analysis of the nature of attention deficit opens up the possibility of complex relationships between constitution and environment (see section on relationships with other lines of development). A 'traditional' theory conceives the effect of developmental abnormality of the brain as impairing the powers of concentration and thereby leading to disorders of behaviour and learning. This is one possibility, but it has not been demonstrated. It is also possible, for instance, that qualities of the caretaking relationship in the early years of life determine the style of the child's approach to the world in which brief inspection and avoidance of delay are the norm; it could also be that this style of impulsive exploration leads to the child living in a less socially responsive world as well as a less stimulating one.

There may also be complex relationships between impairment of attention and learning disabilities. Pennington *et al.* (1993) have recently described a comparison between reading disability and attention deficit suggesting that the two disorders have different associated patterns of neuropsychological deficits and that the coexistence of both problems can be seen as the secondary elaboration of attention deficit symptoms in children at risk for reading impairment. The full pathways involved are not yet clear, but the general issue is that the relationship between attention deficit and other psychological problems is likely to be more complex than that between a disease and its complications. Developmental understanding will be needed.

CONCLUSION

Research so far has established useful tests of some of the processes involved in attention. Usually these processes have to be inferred — often from manipulating the experimental details of tests. No single test score can be taken as an index of attention. Nevertheless, the analyses have taken the study of attention beyond the point where one could only say that impairment of information processing was a common association of many types of psychopathology. Different lines of development can be distinguished; and there is some evidence that disorders have characteristic patterns of impairment. The selective attention deficit of schizophrenia, the impaired shifting of attention in parietal damage, and the reduced inhibitory control in hyperactivity can all be distinguished from non-specific problems in processing information.

The beginnings of research on the determinants of these associations have indicated considerable complexity. Several lines of research have been suggested in this chapter. There are some basic problems, including the question of how far there is similarity of different lines of development, and whether overt and covert measures are indeed tapping the same psychological functions. The later development of overt attention and the nature of continuities across childhood are in pressing need of exploration. The understanding of the relation between attention and intellectual development will need conceptual advances. Nevertheless, basic knowledge should now be enough to sustain an approach to fuller analysis of the nature of the impairments to be found in neurological and psychiatric disorders. The genetic and cultural determinants of individual variations in attention processes can now be studied; and the contribution from the psychological environment is important enough to justify the development of satisfactory methods of assessing the subtleties of personal interactions that are likely to be involved.

The general need is for a developmental psychopathology of this area rather than a quasimedical paradigm leading chiefly to simple case — control comparisons. There will need to be both more longitudinal study and an extending of the perspective farther back into earlier childhood. Developmental studies are being enriched by the need to examine functions whose importance has been indicated by the study of disorders; psychopathology by the distinctions and analyses that have been brought in from the study of development.

REFERENCES

Akhtar N. & Enns J.T. (1989) Relations between covert orienting and filtering in the development of visual attention. *Journal of Experimental Child Psychology* **48**, 315–334.

Alexander D.A. (1973) Attention dysfunction in senile dementia. *Psychological Reports* **32**, 229–230.

American Psychiatric Association (1987) *Diagnostic and Statistical Manual of Mental Disorders*, 3rd edn. American Psychiatric Association, Washington, DC.

Asarnow R.F. & MacCrimmon D.J. (1981) Span of apprehension deficits during postpsychotic stages of schizophrenia: A replication and extension. *Archives of General Psychiatry* **38**, 1006–1011.

Ault R.L., Crawford D.E. & Jeffrey W.E. (1972) Visual scanning strategies of reflective, impulsive, fast-accurate and slow-inaccurate children in the Matching Familiar Figures test. *Child Development* **43**, 1412–1417.

Baddeley A. (1988) *Working Memory*. Oxford Psychology Series, No. 11. Clarendon Press, Oxford.

Baribeau-Brown J., Picton T.W. & Gosselin J.Y. (1983) Schizophrenia: A neurophysiological evaluation of abnormal information processing. *Science* **219**, 874–876.

Baruch I., Hemsley D.R. & Gray J.A. (1988) Differential performance of acute and chronic schizophrenics in a latent inhibition task. *Journal of Nervous and Mental Disease* **176**, 598–606.

Battle E.S. & Lacey B. (1972) A context for hyperactivity in children over time. *Child Development* **43**, 757–773.

Belmont J.M. & Ellis N.R. (1968) Effects of extraneous stimulation upon discrimination learning in normals and retardates. *American Journal of Mental Deficiency* **72**, 525–532.

Benasich A.A. & Bejar I.I. (1992) The Fagan test of infant intelligence: A critical review. *Journal of Applied Developmental Psychology* **13**, 153–171.

Berg C.A. & Sternberg R.J. (1985) Response to novelty: Continuity versus discontinuity in the developmental course of intelligence. In Reese H.W. (ed.) *Advances in*

Child Development and Behaviour, Vol. 19, pp. 2—42. Academic Press, Orlando.

Berlyne D.E. (1970) Attention as a problem in behaviour theory. In Mostofsky D.I. (ed.) *Attention: Contemporary Theory and Analysis*, pp. 25—49. Appleton-Century-Crofts, New York.

Birren J.E., Woods A.M. & Williams M.V. (1980). Behavioral slowing with age: Causes, organization and consequences. In Poon L.W. (ed.) *Ageing in the 1980s — Psychological Issues*, pp. 293—308. American Psychological Association, Washington, DC.

Blackwood D.H.R. & Christie J.E. (1986) The effects of physostigmine on memory and auditory P300 in Alzheimer-type dementia. *Biological Psychiatry* **21**, 557—560.

Blackwood D.H.R., St Clair D.M., Blackburn I.M. & Tyrer G. (1987) Cognitive brain potentials in Alzheimer's dementia and Korsakoff amnesic syndrome. *Psychological Medicine* **17**, 349—358.

Bornstein M.H. & Benasich A.A. (1986) Infant habituation: Assessments of short-term reliability and individual differences at 5 months. *Child Development* **57**, 87—99.

Bornstein M.H. & Sigman M.D. (1986) Continuity in mental development from infancy. *Child Development* **57**, 251—274.

Brandon S. (1971) Overactivity in childhood. *Journal of Psychosomatic Research* **15**, 411—415.

Broadbent D.E. (1958) *Perception and Communication*. Pergamon, London.

Broadbent D.E. (1971) *Decision and Stress*. Academic Press, London.

Cairns E. & Cammock T. (1978) Development of a more reliable version of the matching familiar figures test. *Developmental Psychology* **14**, 555—560.

Camp B.W., Blom G.E., Herbert F. & van Doorninck W.J. (1974) 'Think aloud': A program for developing self-control in young aggressive boys. *Journal of Abnormal Child Psychology* **5**, 157—169.

Capitani E., Della Sala S., Lucchelli F., Soave P. & Spinnler H. (1988) Gottschaldt's hidden figure test: Sensitivity of perceptual attention to ageing and dementia. *Journal of Gerontology* **43**, 157—163.

Ceci S.J. & Tishman J. (1984) Hyperactivity and incidental memory: Evidence for attentional diffusion. *Child Development* **55**, 2192—2203.

Cohen J. (1959) The factorial structure of the WISC at ages 7.6, 10.6 and 13.6. *Journal of Consulting Psychology* **23**, 285—299.

Colombo J., Mitchell D.W., Coldren J.T. & Freeeseman L.J. (1991) Individual differences in infant visual attention: Are short lookers faster processors or feature processors? *Child Development* **62**, 1247—1257.

Colombo J., Mitchell D.W. & Horowitz F.D. (1988) Infant visual attention in the paired-comparison paradigm: Test—retest and attention—performance relations. *Child Development* **59**, 1198—1210.

Conners C.K. (1975). Minimal brain dysfunction and psychopathology in children. In Davids A (ed.) *Child Personality and Psychopathology*. Current Topics, Vol. 2. Wiley, New York.

Cousins L. (1976) Individual differences in the orienting reflex and children's discrimination learning. *Psychophysiology* **13**, 479—487.

Craik F.I.M. & Byrd M. (1982) Aging and cognitive deficits: The role of attentional resources. In Craik F.I.M. & Trehub S. (eds) *Aging and Cognitive Processes*, pp. 191—211. Plenum, New York.

Day M.C. (1978) Visual search by children: The effect of background variation and the use of visual cues. *Journal of Experimental Child Psychology* **25**, 1—16.

Deutsch J.A. & Deutsch D. (1963) Attention: Some theoretical considerations. *Psychological Review* **70**, 80—90.

Doleys D.M. (1976) Distractibility and distracting stimuli: Inconsistent and contradictory results. *Psychological Record* **26**, 279—287.

Douglas V.I. (1972) Stop, look and listen: The problem of sustained attention and impulse control in hyperactive and normal children. *Canadian Journal of Behavioral Science* **4**, 259—281.

Douglas V.I. (1983) Attentional and cognitive problems. In Rutter M. (ed.) *Developmental Neuropsychiatry*, pp. 280—329. Guilford, New York.

Douglas V.I. & Peters K.G. (1979) Toward a clearer definition of the attentional deficit of hyperactive children. In Hale G.A. & Lewis M. (eds) *Attention and the Development of Cognitive Skills*, pp. 173—247. Plenum, New York.

Egeland B. (1974) Training impulsive children in the use of more efficient scanning techniques. *Child Development* **45**, 165—171.

Ellingson R.J. (1967) Study of brain electrical activity in infants. In Lipsitt L.P. & Spiker G.C. (eds) *Advances in Child Development and Behaviour*, Vol. 2. Academic Press, New York.

Emde R.N., Plomin R., Robinson J. *et al.* (1992) Temperament, emotion and cognition at fourteen months: The MacArthur longitudinal twin study. *Child Development* **63**, 1437—1455.

Enns J.J. & Akhtar N. (1989) A developmental study of filtering in visual attention. *Child Development* **60**, 118—119.

Enns J.T. & Brodeur D.A. (1989) A developmental study of covert orienting to peripheral visual cues. *Journal of Experimental Child Psychology* **48**, 171—189.

Enns J.T. & Cameron S. (1987) Selective attention in young children: The relations between visual search, filtering, and priming. *Journal of Experimental Child Psychology* **44**, 38—63.

Enns J.T. & Girgus J.S. (1985) Developmental changes in selective and integrative visual attention. *Journal of Experimental Child Psychology* **40**, 319—337.

Erlenmeyer-Kimling L. & Cornblatt B. (1987) The New York High Risk Project: A follow up report. *Schizophrenia*

Bulletin **13**, 451−461.

Erlenmeyer-Kimling L., Kestenbaum C.J., Bird H. & Hilldoff U. (1984) Assessment of the New York High Risk Project subjects in sample A who are now clinically deviant. In Watt N.F., Anthony E.J., Wynne L.C. & Rolf J.E. (eds) *Children at Risk for Schizophrenia: A Longitudinal Perspective*, pp. 227−239. Cambridge University Press, New York.

Fagan J.F. & Shepherd P.A. (1987) *Fagan Test of Infant Intelligence: Training Manual*. Infantest Corporation, Cleveland, Ohio.

Firestone P. & Martin J.E. (1979) An analysis of the hyperactive syndrome: A comparison of hyperactive, behavior problem, asthmatic and normal children. *Journal of Abnormal Child Psychology* **7**, 261−273.

Friedman S. (1972) Habituation and recovery of visual response in the alert human newborn. *Journal of Experimental Child Psychology* **13**, 339−349.

Friedman S. (1975) Infant habituation: Process, problems and possibilities. In N. Ellis (ed.) *Aberrant Development in Infancy*. Lawrence Erlbaum, Hillsdale, New Jersey.

Fuhrman M.J. & Kendall P.C. (1986) Cognitive tempo and behavioural adjustment in children. *Cognitive Therapy and Research* **10**, 45−50.

Gibson E.J. & Yonas A. (1966) A developmental study of visual search behaviour. *Perception and Psychophysics* **1**, 169−171.

Gillberg C., Carlstrom G. & Rasmussen P. (1983) Hyperkinetic disorders in children with perceptual, motor and attentional deficits. *Journal of Child Psychology and Psychiatry* **24**, 233−246.

Gittelman Klein R. & Abikoff H. (1989) The role of psychostimulants and psychosocial treatments in hyperkinesis. In Sagvolden T. & Archer T. (eds) *Attention Deficit Disorder: Clinical and Basic Research*, pp. 167−180. Lawrence Erlbaum, Hillsdale, New Jersey.

Grabbe W. & Campione J.C. (1969) A novelty interpretation of the Moss-Harlow effect in pre-school children. *Child Development* **40**, 1077−1084.

Graham F.K. & Jackson J.C. (1970) Arousal systems and infant heart rate responses. In Reese H.W. and Lipsitt L.P. (eds) *Advances in Child Development and Behaviour*, Vol. 5. Academic Press, New York.

Greenberg D.J., Uzgiris I.C. & Hunt J.M. (1970) Attentional preference and experience III: Visual familiarity and looking time. *Journal of Genetic Psychology* **117**, 123−135.

Hagen J.W. & Hale G.A. (1973) The development of attention in children. In Pick A.D. (ed.) *Minnesota Symposia on Child Psychology*, Vol. 7. University of Minnesota Press, Minneapolis.

Haith M.M. (1980) *Rules that Babies Look By: The Organization of Newborn Visual Activity*. Lawrence Erlbaum, Hillsdale, New Jersey.

Hart S. & Semple J.M. (1990) *Neuropsychology and the Dementias*. Taylor & Francis, London.

Harvey P.D., Docherty N.M., Serper M.R. & Rasmussen M. (1990) Cognitive deficits and thought disorder: II. An 8-month follow-up study. *Schizophrenia Bulletin* **16**, 147−156.

Hemsley D.R. & Zawada S.L. (1976) Filtering and the cognitive deficits in schizophrenia. *British Journal of Psychiatry* **128**, 456−461.

Hepper P.G. & Shahidullah S. (1992) Habituation in normal and Down's syndrome fetuses. *Quarterly Journal of Experimental Psychology* **44**, 305−317.

Holzman P.S. (1987) Recent studies of psychophysiology in schizophrenia. *Schizophrenia Bulletin* **13**, 49−75.

Hoy E., Weiss G., Minde K. & Cohen N. (1978) The hyperactive child at adolescence: Cognitive, emotional, and social functioning. *Journal of Abnormal Child Psychology* **6**, 311−324.

Jorm A.F. (1986) Controlled and automatic information processing in senile dementia; A review. *Psychological Medicine* **16**, 77−88.

Kagan J. (1970) The determinants of attention in the infant. *American Scientist* **38**, 298−306.

Kagan J., Pearson L. & Welch L. (1966) Modifiability of an impulsive tempo. *Journal of Educational Psychology* **57**, 359−365.

Kagan J., Rasman B.L., Day D., Albert J. & Phillips W. (1964) Information processing in the child: Significance of analytic and reflective attitudes. *Psychological Monographs* **78**(1), Series No. 578.

Kahnemann D. (1973) *Attention and Effort*. Prentice-Hall, Englewood Cliffs, New Jersey.

Karmel B.Z. & Maizel E.B. (1975) A neuronal activity model for infant visual attention. In Cohen L.B. & Salapatek B. (eds) *Infant Perception: From Sensation to Cognition*, Vol. 1. Academic Press, New York.

Keele S.W. (1973) *Attention and Human Performance*. Goodyear, Pacific Palisades, California.

Klee S.H. & Garfinkel B.D. (1983) The computerized continuous performance task: A new measure of inattention. *Journal of Abnormal Child Psychology* **11**, 487−496.

Lahey B.B., Schaughency E.A., Hynd G.W., Carlson C.L. & Nieves W. (1987) Attention deficit disorder with and without hyperactivity: Comparison of behavioural characteristics of clinic-referred children. *Journal of the American Academy of Child and Adolescent Psychiatry* **26**, 718−723.

Lawson J.S., McGhie A. & Chapman J. (1964) Perception of speech in schizophrenia. *British Journal of Psychiatry* **110**, 375−380.

Levy F. (1980) The development of sustained attention (vigilance) and inhibition in children: Some normative data. *Journal of Child Psychology and Psychiatry* **21**, 77−84.

Lewis M. & Brooks-Gunn J. (1981) Visual attention at three months as a predictor of cognitive functioning at two years of age. *Intelligence* **5**, 131−140.

Loiselle D.L., Stamm J.S., Maitinsky S. & Whipple S.C.

(1980) Evoked potential and behavioural signs of attentive dysfunctions in hyperactive boys. *Psychophysiology* **17**, 193−201.

Luria A.R. (1961) *The Role of Speech in the Regulation of Normal and Abnormal Behavior*. Liverlight, New York.

Luria A.R. (1963) *The Mentally Retarded Child*. Pergamon, London.

McCall R.B. & Carriger M.S. (1993) A meta-analysis of infant habituation and recognition memory performance as predictors of later IQ. *Child Development* **64**, 57−79.

McGee R. & Share D.L. (1988) Attention deficit disorder−hyperactivity and academic failure: Which comes first and what should be treated? *Journal of the American Academy of Child and Adolescent Psychiatry* **27**, 318−325.

McGee R., Williams S. & Silva P.A. (1984) Behavioral and developmental characteristics of aggressive, hyperactive and aggressive-hyperactive boys. *Journal of the American Academy of Child and Adolescent Psychiatry* **23**, 270−279.

McIntyre C.W., Blackwell S.L. & Denton C.L. (1978) Effect of noise distractibility on the span of apprehension of hyperactive boys. *Journal of Abnormal Child Psychology* **6**, 483−492.

McIsaac H. & Polich J. (1992) Comparison of infant and adult P300 from auditory stimuli. *Journal of Experimental Child Psychology* **53**, 115−128.

Matejccek Z., Dytrych Z. & Schuller V. (1985) Follow-up study of children born to women denied abortion. In Porter R. & O'Connor M. (eds) *Abortion: Medical Progress and Social Implications*. Ciba Foundation Symposium, No. 115. Pitman, London.

Meichenbaum D. & Goodman J. (1971) Training impulsive children to talk to themselves: A means of developing self-control. *Journal of Abnormal Psychology* **77**, 115−126.

Messer S. (1976) Reflection-impulsivity: A review. *Psychology Bulletin* **83**, 1026−1052.

Milewski A.E. (1978) Young infants' visual processing of internal and adjacent shapes. *Infant Behaviour and Development* **1**, 359−371.

Mischel W. (1974) Processes in delay of gratification. In Berkowitz L. (ed.) *Advances in Experimental Child Psychology*, pp. 249−292. Academic Press, New York.

Moray N. (1969) *Attention: Selective Processes in Vision and Hearing*. Hutchinson Educational, London.

Neuchterlein K.H. (1983) Signal detection in vigilance tasks and behavioral attributes among offspring of schizophrenic mothers and among hyperactive children. *Journal of Abnormal Psychology* **92**, 4−28.

Neuchterlein K.H., Edell W.S., Norris M. & Dawson M.E. (1986) Attention vulnerability indicators, thought disorder, and negative symptoms. *Schizophrenia Bulletin* **12**, 408−426.

Norman D.A. (1968) Toward a theory of memory and attention. *Psychological Review* **75**, 522−536.

Norman D.A. & Shallice T. (1986) Attention to action: Willed and automatic control of behaviour. In Davidson R.J., Schwartz G.E. & Shapiro D. (eds) *Consciousness and Self Regulation*, Vol. 4. Plenum, New York.

Olson G.M. & Sherman T. (1983) Attention, learning and memory in infants. In Haith M.M. & Campos J.J. (eds) *Infancy and Developmental Psychobiology*, Vol. 2, *Mussen's Handbook of Child Psychology*, 4th edn, pp. 1001−1080. Wiley, New York.

Parrinello R.M. & Ruff H.A. (1988) The influence of adult intervention on infants' level of attention. *Child Development* **59**, 1125−1135.

Paulesu E., Frith C.D. & Frackowiak R.S.J. (1993) The neural correlates of the verbal component of working memory. *Nature* **362**, 342−345.

Pecheux M.G. & Lecuyer R. (1989) A longitudinal study of visual habituation between 3, 5 and 8 months of age. *British Journal of Developmental Psychology* **7**, 159−169.

Pelham W.E. (1979) Selective attention tests in poor readers: Dichotic listening, speeded classification, and auditory and visual and incidental learning tasks. *Child Development* **50**, 1050−1061.

Pennington B.F., Groisser D. & Welsh M.C. (1993) Contrasting cognitive deficits in attention deficit hyperactivity disorder versus reading disability. *Developmental Psychology* **29**, 511−523.

Pick A.D., Christy M.D. & Frankel G.W. (1972) A developmental study of visual selective attention. *Journal of Experimental Child Psychology* **14**, 165−175.

Pick A.D., Frankel D.G. & Hess V.L. (1975) Children's attention: The development of selectivity. In Hetherington E.M. (ed.) *Review of Child Development Research*, Vol. 5. University of Chicago Press, Chicago.

Posner M. & Boies J. (1971) Components of attention. *Psychological Review* **78**, 391−408.

Posner M.I., Cohen Y. & Rafal R.D. (1982) Neural systems control of spatial orienting. *Philosophical Transactions of the Royal Society of London (Biology)* **298**, 187−198.

Posner M.I., Walker J.A., Friedrich F.J. & Rafal R.D. (1984) Effects of parietal injury on covert orienting of attention. *Journal of Neuroscience* **4**, 1863−1874.

Pribram K.H. & McGuinness D. (1975) Arousal, activation and effort in the control of attention. *Psychological Review* **82**, 116−149.

Prior M. & Sanson A. (1986) Attention deficit disorder with hyperactivity: A critique. *Journal of Child Psychology and Psychiatry* **27**, 307−319.

Rabbitt P.M.A. (1979) Some experiments and a model for changes in attentional selectivity with old age. In Hoffmeister F. & Muller C. (eds) *Brain Function in Old Age: Evaluation of Changes and Disorders*, pp. 82−94. Springer, Berlin.

Rabbitt P.M.A. (1980) A fresh look at changes in reaction times in old age. In Stein D.G. (ed.) *The Psychobiology of Aging: Problems and Perspectives*, pp. 425−442, Elsevier, Amsterdam.

Raichle M.E. (1993) The scratchpad of the mind. *Nature* **363**, 583−584.

Rapport M.D., Tucker S.B., DuPaul G.J., Merlo M. &

Stoner G. (1986) Hyperactivity and frustration: The influence of control over and size of rewards in delaying gratification. *Journal of Abnormal Child Psychology* **14**, 191−204.

Richards J.E. (1987) Heart rate responses and heart rate rhythms, and infant visual sustained attention. In Ackles P.K., Jennings J.R. & Coles M.G.H. (eds) *Advances in Psychophysiology*, Vol. 3, pp. 189−221. JAI Press, Greenwich, Connecticut.

Rodnick E.H. & Shakow D. (1940) Set in the schizophrenic as measured by a composite reaction time index. *American Journal of Psychiatry* **97**, 214−225.

Rose A.S., Feldman J.F. & Wallace I.F. (1992) Infant information processing in relation to six-year cognitive outcomes. *Child Development* **63**, 1126−1141.

Rosenthal R.H. & Allen T.W. (1978) An examination of attention, arousal and learning dysfunctions of hyperkinetic children. *Psychological Bulletin* **85**, 689−715.

Ross D.M. & Ross S.A. (1976) *Hyperactivity: Research, Theory and Action*, Wiley, New York.

Rosvold H.E., Mirsky A.F., Sarason I., Bransome E.D. & Beck L.H. (1956) A continuous performance test of brain damage. *Journal of Consulting Psychology* **20**, 343−352.

Roy P. (1983) *Is continuity enough? Substitute care and socialisation*. Paper presented at the Spring Scientific Meeting, Child and Adolescent Specialist Section, Royal College of Psychiatrists, London, March.

Ruff H.A. & Lawson K.R. (1990) Development of sustained, focused attention in young children during free play. *Developmental Psychology* **26**, 85−93.

Ruff H.A., Lawson K.R., Parrinello R. & Weissberg R. (1990) Long-term stability of individual differences in sustained attention in the early years. *Child Development* **61**, 60−75.

St Clair D.M., Blackburn I.M., Blackwood D.H.R. & Tyrer G. (1988) Measuring the course of Alzheimer's disease: A longitudinal study of neuropsychological function and changes in P3 event-related potential. *British Journal of Psychiatry* **152**, 48−54.

Sandberg S., Rutter M. & Taylor E. (1978) Hyperkinetic disorder in psychiatric clinic attenders. *Developmental Medicine and Child Neurology* **20**, 279−299.

Sanders A.F. (1980) Stage analysis of reaction processes. In Stelmach G.E. & Regin J. (eds) *Tutorials in Motor Behavior*. North-Holland, Amsterdam.

Schachar R. (1991) Childhood hyperactivity. *Journal of Child Psychology and Psychiatry* **32**, 155−192.

Schachar R. & Logan G.D. (1990a) Are hyperactive children deficient in attentional capacity? *Journal of Abnormal Child Psychology* **18**, 493−513.

Schachar R. & Logan G.D. (1990b) Impulsivity and inhibitory control in development and psychopathology. *Developmental Psychology* **26**, 1−11.

Schachar R., Taylor E., Wieselberg M., Thorley G. & Rutter M. (1987) Changes in family function and relationships in children who respond to methylphenidate. *Journal of the American Academy of Child and Adolescent Psychiatry* **26**, 728−732.

Sergeant J.A. (1981) *Attentional Studies in Hyperactivity*. University of Groningen, Groningen.

Sergeant J.A. (1989) Attention deficit from an information processing perspective. In Bloomingdale L.M. & Sergeant J. (eds) *Attention Deficit Disorder − Criteria, Cognition, Intervention*, pp. 65−81. Pergamon, New York.

Sergeant J.A. & Scholten C.A. (1985) On data limitations in hyperactivity. *Journal of Child Psychology and Psychiatry* **26**, 111−124.

Shiffrin R.M. & Schneider W. (1977) Controlled and automatic human information processing: II. Perceptual learning, automatic attending, and a general theory. *Psychological Review* **84**, 127−190.

Siegel A.W. & Stevenson H.W. (1966) Incidental learning: A developmental study. *Child Development* **37**, 811−818.

Slater A., Mattock A., Brown E., Burnham D. & Young A. (1991) Visual processing of stimulus compounds in newborn infants. *Perception* **20**, 29−33.

Slater A., Morison V. & Rose D. (1982) Visual memory at birth. *British Journal of Psychology* **73**, 519−525.

Sonuga-Barke E.J.S., Taylor E. & Heptinstall E. (1992a) Hyperactivity and delay aversion: II. The effects of self versus externally imposed stimulus presentation periods on memory. *Journal of Child Psychology and Psychiatry* **33**, 399−410.

Sonuga-Barke E.J.S. & Taylor E. (1992) The effect of delay on hyperactive and non-hyperactive children's response times: Research note. *Journal of Child Psychology and Psychiatry* **33**, 1091−1096.

Sonuga-Barke E.J.S., Taylor E., Sembi S. & Smith J. (1992b) Hyperactivity and delay aversion: I. The effect of delay on choice. *Journal of Child Psychology and Psychiatry* **33**, 387−398.

Sprague R.L. & Sleator E.K. (1977) Methylphenidate in hyperkinetic children: Differences in dose effects on learning and social behaviour. *Science* **198**, 1274−1276.

Spring B.J. (1980) Shift of attention in schizophrenia, siblings of schizophrenic, and depressed patients. *Journal of Nervous and Mental Disease* **168**, 133−140.

Sroufe L.A., Sonies B., West W., & Wright F. (1973) Anticipatory heart rate deceleration and reaction time in children with and without referral for learning disability. *Child Development* **44**, 267−273.

Sternberg S. (1966) High speed scanning in human memory. *Science* **153**, 652−654.

Strutt G., Anderson D.R. & Well A.D. (1975) A developmental study of the effects of irrelevant information on speeded classification. *Journal of Experimental Child Psychology* **20**, 127−135.

Swanson J. & Kinsbourne M. (1976) Stimulant related state-dependent learning in hyperactive children. *Science* **192**, 1354−1356.

Sykes D.H., Douglas V.I. & Morgenstern G. (1973) Sustained attention in hyperactive children. *Journal of Child Psychology and Psychiatry* **14**, 213−220.

Szatmari P., Offord D.R. & Boyle M.H. (1989) Ontario Child Health Study: Prevalence of attention deficit disorder with hyperactivity. *Journal of Child Psychology and Psychiatry* **30**, 219−230.

Tallmadge J. & Barkley R.A. (1983) The interactions of hyperactive and normal boys with their fathers and mothers. *Journal of Abnormal Child Psychology* **11**, 565−579.

Tamis-LeMonda C.S. & Bornstein M.H. (1989) Habituation and maternal encouragement of attention in infancy as predictors of toddler language, play and representational competence. *Child Development* **60**, 738−751.

Taylor E. (1980) Development of attention. In Rutter M. (ed.) *Scientific Foundations of Developmental Psychiatry*, pp. 185−197. Heinemann, London.

Taylor E. (1986) Attention deficit. In Taylor E. (ed.) *The Overactive Child*, pp. 73−106. MacKeith Press/Blackwell Scientific Publications, Oxford.

Taylor E., Sandberg S., Thorley G. & Giles S. (1991) *The Epidemiology of Childhood Hyperactivity*. Maudsley Monographs, No. 33. Oxford University Press, Oxford.

Tizard B. & Hodges J. (1978) The effect of early institutional rearing on the development of eight year old children. *Journal of Child Psychology and Psychiatry* **19**, 99−118.

Treisman A.M. (1969) Strategies and models of selective attention. *Psychological Review* **76**, 282−299.

van der Meere J. & Sergeant J. (1986) Acquisition of attention skills in pervasively hyperactive children. *Journal of Child Psychology and Psychiatry* **29**, 301−310.

van der Meere J. & Sergeant J. (1988) Focused attention in pervasively hyperactive children. *Journal of Abnormal Child Psychology* **16**, 627−639.

von Wright J. & Nurmi L. (1979) Effects of white noise and irrelevant information on speeded classification: A developmental study. *Acta Psychologia* **43**, 157−166.

Weiss M.J., Zelazo P.R. & Swain I.U. (1988) Newborn response to auditory stimulus discrepancy. *Child Development* **59**, 1530−1541.

Welford A.T. (1980) Relationship between reaction time and fatigue, stress, age and sex. In Welford A.T. (ed.) *Reaction Times*, pp. 321−354. Academic Press, New York.

Wetherford M.J. & Cohen L.B. (1973) Developmental changes in infant visual preferences for novelty and familiarity. *Child Development* **44**, 416−424.

Whalen C.K. & Henker B. (1976) Psychostimulants and children: A review and analysis. *Psychological Bulletin* **83**, 1113−1130.

White S.H. (1966) Age differences in reaction to stimulus variation. In Harvey O.J. (ed.) *Experience, Structure and Adaptability*. Springer, New York.

Wittenborn J. (1943) Factorial equations for tests of attention. *Psychometrika* **8**, 19−35.

Wohlberg G.W. & Kornetsky C. (1973) Sustained attention in remitted schizophrenia. *Archives of General Psychiatry* **28**, 533−537.

Wright J.C. & Vlietstra A.G. (1975) The development of selective attention: From perceptual exploration to logical search. In Reese H.W. (ed.) *Advances in Child Development and Behaviour*, Vol. 10. Academic Press, New York.

Zelniker T., Jeffrey W.E., Ault R. & Parsons J. (1972) Analysis and modification of search strategies of impulsive and reflective children on the matching familiar figures test. *Child Development* **43**, 321−335.

9: Language Development

HELEN TAGER-FLUSBERG

INTRODUCTION

By the time they reach their first birthday children begin to produce their first words; before their second birthday they have begun combining words to form simple sentences; by 3 years of age they have sizeable vocabularies and they use a range of grammatical rules; and when they enter school their language is almost indistinguishable from those of the adults around them. In just a few short years children have acquired the most remarkable and complex of human achievements which not only opens up an unlimited channel for communication, it also transforms their social and cultural worlds (Bruner, 1986).

How do children accomplish this unique achievement in so short a time? Given such limited exposure to language input, and the apparent lack of explicit teaching of language forms, how does the child develop abstract linguistic knowledge and the capacity for infinite expression? Is language connected to or embedded within other cognitive systems or is it an autonomous aspect of the mind? These questions are at the core of research on language acquisition in both normal and clinical populations. As shown in later sections, studies of both typical and atypical children have followed parallel tracks and together they have shaped our theoretical understanding of the nature and significance of language acquisition.

Over the past three decades the study of language acquisition has grown rapidly out of two related fields: linguistics and developmental psychology. Linguistic theory has informed our understanding of the system that children acquire (cf. Chomsky, 1965, 1980), while developmental psychology has provided the broader perspective, which allows us to view language development in relation to the child's changing conceptual, social and emotional knowledge. Language is a complex computational system or representational code with three major structural components: (i) phonology (the speech sound system); (ii) semantics (meaning as expressed in words and sentences); and (iii) syntax (the grammatical rule system for creating sentences). In addition to acquiring these formal aspects of the linguistic code, children must learn how to use language competently, which includes acquiring the full range of language functions, the ability to select according to pragmatic rules the means for communicating in a contextually appropriate way, and to develop skills in the full range of discourses available through language. Each of these aspects of language involves complex abstract rule systems for the child to unravel simultaneously without benefit of formal instruction.

Although there is still much to learn about how children come to internalize this knowledge and become competent users of the language in their community, based on research on the acquisition of English and many other languages, there is growing acceptance of the idea that language acquisition is multiply determined by the complex interaction of biological, cognitive and social aspects of maturation (e.g. Slobin, 1985). On this view children construct language for themselves making use of innate language-specific capacities and other conceptual developments that interact with specific experiences in the physical and social environment. In the normally developing child these multiple determinants of language function in close connection with one another leading to the development of an integrated linguistic system that is used with ease in all contexts. When one or more of these crucial factors are disrupted, it has a profound impact on the course of language development. For

212

example, sensory impairments will leave a child unable to process crucial information from the environment: the deaf or hearing-impaired child cannot process incoming acoustic information and therefore can hardly construct a spoken linguistic system at all; visually impaired children will have restricted information available about the external physical and social world that also leaves an indelible mark on their developing language. Children with severe cognitive deficits show particular patterns of language impairment; while other children show specific difficulty in acquiring language without problems in other aspects of cognitive or social development. In autism, where the primary deficit is in acquiring social cognitive knowledge, there is yet another distinct pattern of language deficit and language development.

The different patterns of language in developmentally disordered populations, which are detailed in later sections of this chapter, suggest that any disruption to the crucial determinants of language, either within the child or within the environment, leads to asynchronies in development among the different domains of language, which may be the hallmark of all language disorders (Tager-Flusberg, 1988). Yet despite these asynchronies in language development research on a variety of language impaired populations suggests that within each domain of language, such as syntax, or phonology, the course of development follows a relatively fixed pathway. In the remainder of this chapter these points will be illustrated by describing the acquisition of language abilities in both normally developing children and some clinical populations.

THE COURSE OF DEVELOPMENT

Consider the task faced by all infants. They are surrounded by talk, action, multiple sounds, stimulation from the physical world and especially from the social world. From all this stimulation of their perceptual systems, infants must distinguish speech sounds from other kinds of acoustic signals; they then need to parse the stream of speech sounds into units of words, phrases and sentences; the social and cognitive significance of these units must be recognized and have meaning attached; rules for combining basic units of language must be derived; and then they must work out how to use all this

knowledge to create new meanings in order to communicate with other people. This description makes clear the fact that language development begins well before children utter their first word.

Prelinguistic development

Infants come into the world prepared to acquire language. At birth they are able to distinguish speech from other sounds (Morse, 1972), and indeed to perceive and discriminate speech sounds as well as adults (Aslin *et al.*, 1983; Eimas *et al.*, 1987). From the start these sophisticated speech perceptual abilities are closely tied to the infant's social experience. Studies of newborns have shown that they distinguish their own mothers' voices from those of other mothers which is most likely related to prenatal exposure to the acoustic properties of the mothers' voices (DeCasper & Fifer, 1980). In the visual domain, newborns also show a preference for human faces (Gore *et al.*, 1975; Bushnell *et al.*, 1989), and can even imitate facial expressions (Meltzoff & Moore, 1977). Thus from the beginning, the social niche for language is clearly established.

These newborn preferences for human language and non-verbal interaction lead to rapid changes over the first few months of life. Mothers and their infants begin to interact in a finely tuned way with one another. They synchronize their patterns of eye gaze, movements, facial expressions of affect and vocalizations (Jaffe *et al.*, 1973; Condon & Sanders, 1974) in ways that resemble turn-taking patterns in conversations (Trevarthen, 1974, 1979). At 3 or 4 months of age, there is a marked increase in the amount of vocal turn-taking during these rich interactions that reinforces the analogy between these prelinguistic social events and genuine conversational dialogue.

During this period the infant's vocal abilities are also changing. Initially, because of anatomical limitations, newborns produce mostly cries and occasional gurgling or other vegetative noises. By 2 months, infants begin cooing, which involves sounds that are predominantly vowel-like combined with a few back consonants such as k or g. At first, coos involve single sounds, but these give way to strings of cooing sounds that are referred to as vocal play (Stark, 1986), reflecting changes in the infant's articulatory structure and nervous system. Vocal play may be a transitional stage before the onset of babbling at about 5 months. Babbling, which consists of consonant–vowel combinations that are repeated in a stereotyped fashion, again marks advances in the infant's control over articulatory mechanisms. Unlike earlier vocalizations, babbling in its initial phases is not used for social interactive purposes; however by the time infants reach around 9 months of age their babbling increases in complexity, becoming more syllabic in structure, the repertoire of babbled consonants expands, and it is also used more within a social and communicative context.

One question that has been addressed in research on babbling is whether there is a connection between the sounds that an infant selects to produce and those in the target language in the infant's environment. A second question concerns the relationship between babbling and the onset of language. Both Jakobson (1968) and Lenneberg (1967) claimed that babbling was not related to the particular language to which an infant is exposed, and that there is no relationship or continuity between babbling and early words. However, recent research casts doubt on both these claims and suggests instead that there are important developmental patterns in babbling, reflecting the influence of the environment. For example, De Boysson-Bardies *et al.* (1981, 1984) found that at least in the later stages of babbling the sounds produced by infants, and especially the intonation contours of their babbling sequences, did closely resemble the input language. There is also growing evidence to suggest that there is important continuity between prelinguistic babbling and the first words produced by infants. Not only do those stages overlap, but there is also considerable overlap in sounds incorporated in babbles and early words (Oller *et al.*, 1976). Finally, research on the development of babbling in deaf infants suggests that the auditory feedback that infants receive from their own, as well as others' sounds is crucial in shaping the course of development (Stoel-Gammon & Otomo, 1986; Oller & Eilers, 1988). Thus, recent studies have shown that deaf infants begin babbling later than hearing infants; they use fewer syllables which are less likely to occur as repeated syllable sequences (Oller & Eilers, 1988). Even the sounds themselves

are somewhat different presumably because deaf infants lack auditory feedback from their own sounds and have no access to the speech sounds in their environment.

The development of vocal production in infancy is largely determined by the maturation of underlying language-specific biological structures in the articulatory mechanisms and central nervous system, coupled with environmental feedback. Towards the end of the first year of life, vocalizations as well as other non-vocal behaviours again become integrated into social interaction as infants' developing social cognitive capacities lead to the onset of intentional communication. At this point infants becomes capable of coordinating their attention to objects or events with other people through eye gaze patterns (joint attention), gestures and vocalizations. This developmental achievement is generally viewed as a critical step not only in language acquisition, but also in social and cognitive developments (Bates *et al.*, 1975; Bruner, 1975a; Trevarthen & Hubley, 1978). Infants at this stage are able to communicate to others a variety of meanings (Bates *et al.*, 1975) including protodeclaratives, which involves pointing or other gestures to draw another person's attention to an object of interest (for example, an airplane in the sky or a dog barking in the street), and protoimperatives, meaning a gesture or vocalization to express a request or demand for an object (for example, pointing to a tin for a biscuit or to a high shelf for a toy that cannot be reached). From a Piagetian perspective, these communicative achievements are part of the infant's sensorimotor developments, especially the capacity for means–end, or goal-directed behaviour, and developing object permanence (Bates *et al.*, 1979). More recently, some have argued that these sociocognitive achievements reflect the initial manifestation of a developing theory of mind (e.g. Baron-Cohen, 1989; Leslie & Happe, 1989; Gomez, 1990), and may be part of a distinct, highly specialized neural system (Leslie & Frith, 1990; Leslie & Roth, 1993).

The picture to emerge from this survey of prelinguistic developments suggests that the foundations of language may lie in two distinct yet crucial biologically based systems: one which is dedicated to language-specific functions, and a second which is dedicated to the development of an understanding of minds (Locke, 1992). These developmental systems that are crucial to the development of language and communication are also dependent on stimulation from the social and linguistic environment. Normal development of language depends on the smooth integration of these distinct mechanisms with one another.

Phonological development

Although children spend time in the prelinguistic period practising and refining their speech sound repertoire, the ability to coordinate the pronunciation of phonemes in linguistic contexts, that is in words that carry meaning, is a task that many children take several years to master. Phonological errors are made by most children especially in the early stages of language development. An adequate theory of phonological development must account for how the child comes to develop the abstract rules that underlie speech sound production, as well as to provide an explanation for the particular kinds of systematic errors that are typically made.

The classic theoretical positions in this area were proposed by nativists and behaviourists. Jakobson (1968) argued that phonological development was determined by the maturation of the underlying perceptual, motor and central nervous systems. This view emphasized the invariant and universal order of acquiring phonemic contrasts. The behaviourist view, presented by Mowrer (1954) and more recently Olmsted (1971), emphasized the environmental influences on phonological development. On this view the infant is likely to imitate highly frequent speech sounds; feedback in the form of reinforcement and correction gradually helps to shape the phonological repertoire of the young child. Neither of these positions is able to account for the fact that phonological development is not always in a smooth forward direction; on the contrary many children show regressions in development and there is enormous individual variation (e.g. Menn, 1971).

The current approach that dominates theory and research in phonological development emphasizes the rule-governed nature of the child's developing system. In an effort to explain individual differences and the systematic error patterns that have been identified, children are viewed as taking an active or strategic problem-solving approach to the task of acquiring the adult system of phonological rules (Vihman, 1976; Macken & Ferguson, 1982; Menn, 1983). A child hears a word pronounced by an adult in a particular way, and must then translate that perception into a sequence of articulatory movements that will produce a matching sound. Between the perceptual input and the motor output the child builds an internal representation of the target sound pattern which then must be transformed into a motor output command before the articulatory system can operate. These abstract cognitive representations bridge the input/output system and are the source of a child's systematic errors.

One set of examples that illustrate the importance of the role of representations in the child's developing phonological system was offered by Smith (1973) from observations of his own son. At about the age of 2, Smith's son would say 'puggle' instead of puddle, while at the same time he pronounced the word puzzle as 'puddle'. These examples are systematic in that for the first pair (puddle—puggle) one phonetic feature — place of articulation — has been changed. Similarly for the second pair (puzzle—puddle) another phonetic feature has been changed — manner of articulation. Presumably these errors enter at the point where the internal representation of the perceived target is transformed into a motor output command. Interestingly, such systematic errors are rare in the child's earliest word productions, suggesting that first words are learned and produced as whole units. Errors become more frequent as the child begins to seek regularities and formulates a rule system for speech sound production at the point when their vocabulary increases rapidly and they begin combining words into sentences.

The previous examples illustrate one type of rule governed error process: substitution, in which one phonetic feature is substituted for another. Other types of processes that guide children's word productions include assimilation, in which one sound is changed to become more like another (e.g. making consonants that precede vowels voiced as in calling a pen, 'ben'), and deletion, in which one or more sounds are completely omitted (e.g. consonant cluster reductions as in 'pill' for spill).

Menn (1989) argued that children discover these kinds of rules and processes through trial and error.

Much less attention has been given to the development of non-segmental phonology which includes the use of stress, intonation and other prosodic features. Crystal (1975, 1986) argued that prosody plays a central role in speech, interacting with syntax, semantics and pragmatics, and in fact can only be interpreted in relation to these other aspects of language. Prosody is used to mark grammatical distinctions (for example an ambiguous question such as 'When did John believe that Mary stole the money?' — when he saw her with it, or when she was alone in the room — may be disambiguated with the appropriate placement of a pause), to convey nuances of meaning, and it is critical for expressing or interpreting between types of direct and indirect speech acts (to distinguish jokes, ironic statements or sarcasm) and for marking other pragmatic functions (for example, rising intonation on a statement such as 'The book is good', will convey a question). It is also intimately linked to the communication of affect and attitude (Frick, 1985).

Once language begins to develop, children use clearly determined prosodic 'envelopes' (Bruner, 1975b; Dore, 1975) and by the end of the second year children use prosody to convey various pragmatic functions (for example statements end with falling intonation, while questions end with rising intonation), as well as social and affective information (Furrow, 1984). Specific control over tone patterns, and variations in pitch and timing continue developing throughout the preschool period (Weeks, 1971; Allen, 1983), and it is not until puberty that children have full mastery over rhythm and stress patterns that are important for syntactic and semantic interpretation (Atkinson-King, 1973; Allen & Hawkins, 1980; Myers & Myers, 1983). Thus far then, research suggests that social, affective, and pragmatic aspects of prosody are acquired relatively early. In contrast, those components of intonation that interact with other parts of the linquistic system develop more gradually. Despite these general conclusions that we can draw from the current literature, there is still much to be learned about the child's developing speech sound system.

Development of word meaning

One of the most striking features of children's developing lexicons, or vocabularies, is the speed and effortlessness with which toddlers and preschoolers learn on average six to 10 new words each day (Templin, 1957). With little information to guide them and perhaps only a single exposure, children are able to induce an approximation to the adult's full meaning of lexical terms they acquire. Research on the development of words and word meaning suggest three major influencing factors. First, there is the role of conceptual development which facilitates the mapping between words and meaning (Tomasello & Farrar, 1984; Gopnik & Meltzoff, 1987). Acquisition patterns are also guided by the input addressed to children. Parental naming practices, for example, are related to the kinds of words acquired by children (Adams & Bullock, 1986), and it has also been suggested that children are able to use syntactic information to figure out not only the category of word they are learning, but also aspects of its meaning (Gleitman, 1990). Finally, children may bring to the task of word learning a set of principles which help constrain the potential meanings of new words that they hear (Clark, 1988; Markman, 1989).

Lexical development can be divided into three periods (de Villiers & de Villiers, 1992). The first period covers the acquisition of the initial 50 words or so, during which children are learning what words do (Nelson, 1985). At this stage, some words appear to be tied to particular contexts and serve primarily social or pragmatic purposes. A word may be equivalent to a child's holistic representation of an event. The child's vocabulary at this stage is dominated by names for objects, especially in Western middle-class children, including animals, people, toys and familiar household things. There will also be some social words (e.g. hi, bye), modifiers (e.g. more, wet) and relational terms which express success, failure, recurrence, direction, and so forth (Nelson, 1973). Studies by Gopnik and Meltzoff (1986, 1987) demonstrate how specific conceptual developments at this stage are closely related to the acquisition of particular words. For example, in one study they found that infants were able to succeed on tests of object permanence within a few weeks of acquiring words such as 'gone' which encode the concept (Gopnik & Meltzoff, 1986). In some children the words were acquired before the concept, in others the reverse was found. This suggests that while conceptual development can influence semantic development (as suggested by Piaget, 1952, 1962), it is also the case that semantic development can influence conceptual change (as proposed by Whorf, 1956). Thus the relationship between language and conceptual development, or more generally between language and thought, is highly complex with each system placing constraints on the other, and both dependent on the social environment for their elaboration in development (Byrnes & Gelman, 1991).

By the middle of the second year, there is a marked increase in the rate at which children acquire new words. This new period is called the naming explosion, and may be punctuated by many requests from children for adults to label things in the world around them (Bloom, 1973; Dromi, 1987; but see also Goldfield & Reznick, 1990). Objects tend to be named at the so-called basic object level (Rosch *et al.*, 1976), for example dog, or car, rather than at the subordinate (e.g. dalmatian; Mercedes) or superordinate (e.g. animal; vehicle) levels. Objects within the same category at the basic object level tend to share perceptual and functional features, and they do not overlap with related semantic categories. Thus this level may be the most useful for children for both functional and cognitive reasons (Mervis & Crisafi, 1982). Parents also have been found to name objects for children at the basic object level and this too might explain why this is the preferred level for children's early words (Adams & Bullock, 1986).

Once a new word is learned it is now quickly generalized to new contexts. Much of the focus of research on word meanings has focused on the extension of a word. At this stage, children will sometimes overextend the meaning of a word broadening the use of a term beyond its semantic boundaries. Typical examples include calling all women 'Mummy' or using 'ball' to name any round object. Overextension errors may be made on the basis of functional (Nelson, 1974) or, more frequently, perceptual similarity (Clark, 1973), or may involve an associative complex of features

(Bowerman, 1978). Another kind of extension error that is not so easily noticed is when the child underextends the use of a word. Barrett (1986) cited an example from his son who only used the word duck to refer to his toy ducks but not to real ones! Underextension errors tend to be noted at earlier stages of lexical development while overextension errors are more typical of this period, after the naming explosion. Occasionally, children may hypothesize a completely incorrect meaning for a word and thus appear to have invented a new word. Clark and Clark (1977) cited an example of a young boy who interpreted the phrase 'on purpose' to mean 'you're looking at me', after his mother rebuked him for not wiping his feet yet again by saying 'You did that on purpose'. These kinds of mismatches in meaning usually disappear quickly after corrective feedback is provided.

The most widely accepted view of what guides the acquisition of word meanings is the prototype theory, which argues that children represent the meanings of words in the form of prototypical exemplars (Anglin, 1977; Bowerman, 1978; Greenberg & Kuczaj, 1982). The initial representation may be of a particular referent to which new examples are compared. Later this semantic representation becomes more abstract and may be composed of a composite image or set of features for a prototype. This theory can explain both underextension and overextension errors, by reference to the defining features of the prototype representations; however, it is a theory of lexical development that is most usefully applied to the child's acquisition of names for concrete objects.

By the time children reach their third birthday, they begin to develop a more organized lexicon, in which the meaning relations among groups of words are discovered (Anglin, 1977). For example, at this time children begin to learn words from a semantic domain, such as kinship terms (Haviland & Clark, 1974), and they are able to organize the words according to their similarities and differences on dimensions of meanings. For nouns labelling concrete objects, children begin to organize taxonomies, now also learning words at the superordinate and subordinate levels and understanding the hierarchical relations among terms like dachshund, dog and animal. Semantic developments at this stage will often lead to reorganizational processes as these kinds of relationships among words are realized by the child (Bowerman, 1982).

During the preschool years as the child's vocabulary is rapidly expanding and becoming more organized, children are able to acquire new words after only a single exposure (Carey & Bartlett, 1978; Dockrell & Campbell, 1986; Rice, 1990). Carey (1978) termed this process 'fast mapping' of at least a partial meaning for new lexical terms. A number of researchers have argued that what makes this kind of fast mapping possible is a set of internal constraints that guides the child's hypotheses about the possible meanings of words (Markman, 1989). Clark (1983, 1990) has proposed a very general kind of constraint, called the principle of contrast, which states that every two words in a language contrast in meaning. This principle operates in conjunction with the principle of conventionality, which states that there are conventional words that children expect to be used to express particular meanings so that if a speaker does not use the conventional word, then the child assumes that the new word must have a somewhat different meaning. A stronger version of the principle of contrast was proposed by Markman (1989), called the mutual exclusivity constraint. This constraint leads the child to assume that each object only has a single name, and that a name can only refer to one category of objects. When children hear a new word, then, they will look around for a referent for which they do not currently have a label. This explains why young children are reluctant to accept superordinate labels for individual objects (Macnamara, 1982). Other constraints proposed by Markman include the whole-object constraint, which states that new words refer to whole objects rather than parts of objects (if however the child already knows the name of the object then the word might be considered as labelling a part or property of the object); and the taxonomic constraint, which states that words refer to categories of objects.

While some view these kinds of constraints as innate principles that are specific to lexical development (Markman, 1989), others view them as more general biases that may be an aspect of broader pragmatic (Clark, 1990) or cognitive

processes (Flavell, 1989) and that may in fact develop during the course of development as the child gains experience with words. Although there are still disagreements about how to characterize constraints on the child's hypotheses about the meanings of new words they encounter (Nelson, 1988), most researchers accept that children do need to use these kinds of heuristics to help them with the rapid mapping of words on to underlying meaning representations.

Much of the research on semantic development has focused on the acquisition of nouns. Verbs, on the other hand, pose a different kind of problem as there is often not enough information in the context to help the child distinguish between related verbs such as 'look' and 'see'. Gleitman and co-workers (Landau & Gleitman, 1985; Gleitman, 1990) argued that children also need to use syntactic information to help them work out the meanings of verbs. The particular kinds of information that children can use include the number and kind of arguments that occur with the verb. Thus transitive verbs take object arguments while intransitive verbs do not. This kind of information is useful in helping the child interpret verb meaning (Naigles, 1990). Syntactic bootstrapping, as Gleitman called this process, is also useful for helping the child distinguish mass nouns (e.g. spaghetti) from count nouns (e.g. a potato), or common nouns from proper names, and very young children have been shown to be able to use this information when they hear new words in ambiguous contexts (Katz *et al.*, 1974). As children's language progresses and they begin acquiring knowledge about the syntactic frames in which words occur, they begin to integrate syntactic and semantic information in this way. This process underscores the interrelationships that drive both semantic and syntactic development, which may not be as separable in acquisition as researchers assume.

Development of syntax and morphology

Before the end of the second year, soon after the naming explosion, children reach the next important milestone in language development: they begin to combine words together to form their first sentences. This is a crucial turning point because even the simplest two-word utterances show evidence of early grammatical development. The child's task in acquiring the grammar of his or her native language is complex: the child must be able to (i) segment the stream of language into morphemes (the minimal unit of language that carries meaning), phrases and sentences; (ii) discover the major word classes such as noun, verb and determiner, and map the appropriate lexical terms into these word classes; (iii) learn how to encode grammatically tense, aspect, plurality, gender, and so forth; (iv) acquire the major phrase structure rules for organizing basic phrasal units like noun phrase and verb phrase, as well as for organizing basic sentence structures for declaratives, questions and negation; and (v) work out the syntactic rules for complex sentences involving coordinating and embedding multiple clauses.

Research on these issues grew out of Chomsky's seminal work on transformational grammar (Chomsky, 1957, 1965, 1980), initially focusing on the acquisition of English grammar, but more recently important cross-linguistic studies have complemented our knowledge about how the child acquires the abstract rules of grammar. Studies suggest that children make use of semantic and pragmatic, as well as syntactic and morphological, information in developing the underlying grammatical knowledge that allows them to produce and comprehend the full range of unlimited and novel sentences in their native language.

One of the obvious ways that children's sentences change over time is that they gradually grow longer. This fact is the basis for one of the most widely used measures of grammatical development: the mean length of utterance (MLU), which is the average length of a child's utterances as measured in morphemes (Brown, 1973). The assumption underlying this measure is that each newly acquired element of grammatical knowledge adds length to the child's utterances. Longitudinal and cross-sectional studies confirm that MLU increases gradually over time, and that it is a better predictor of the child's language level than chronological age. Nevertheless it is only valid as a measure of development up to an average sentence length of four morphemes, and it may not be useful without significant modifications as a measure for languages other than English (Dromi & Berman, 1982).

When children begin to combine words to form simple sentences most are limited in length to two words, although a few may be as long as three or four words. These early sentences are often unique and creative, composed primarily of nouns, verbs and modifiers. In English, function words (such as coordinations, prepositions or articles) and grammatical morphemes (such as tense markings or plural endings on nouns) are typically omitted, making the child's productive speech sound telegraphic; however, this is less true for children learning other languages such as Italian (Hyams, 1989) or Hebrew (Levy, 1988) which are rich in inflectional morphology and less reliant than English on word order to express the basic grammatical relationships in a sentence.

Cross-linguistic studies of children at this stage have shown that there is a universal small set of meanings or semantic relations that are expressed (Brown, 1973). These include talk about objects: they point them out and name them (demonstrative) and they talk about where the objects are (location), what they are like (attribution), who owns them (possessive), and who is doing things to them (agent—object). They also talk about actions carried out by people (agent—action), on objects (agent—object), and oriented towards certain locations (action—location). Objects, people and actions and their interrelationships form the basis for this universal set of semantic relations that preoccupy the toddler during the early stages of language development.

Initial studies of utterances produced in the two-word stage found that children used highly consistent word order (Bloom, 1970; Brown, 1973). In part, this was because the focus at the time was on the acquisition of English which is very reliant on word order rules for marking the grammatical relations in a sentence. However, it is now acknowledged that there is variation among children learning different languages in their reliance on word order. Braine (1976) noted that even for English-speaking children their early two-word combinations had more limited scope than Brown (1973) had suggested, with word order rules being applied to specific formulae or lexical terms rather than to broad linguistic categories. However, other evidence by Bloom (1990) found that children very rapidly move from a semantically based word order rule (e.g. rules for ordering nominals and attributes) to one based on syntactic categories such as noun phrases, nouns and adjectives. And evidence from children's comprehension of simple sentences at this stage indicates that they are able to use word order to identify the correct event that maps onto a sentence such as 'Big Bird is tickling Cookie Monster' (Golinkoff *et al.*, 1987).

Pinker (1984, 1987) argued that children at the earliest stages of grammatical development use semantic information to provide the key bootstrap into the linguistic system. Thus, the child can use the correspondence between things and names to map onto the linguistic category of nouns. Names for physical attributes or changes of state are expressed as predicates or verbs. Because all sentence subjects at this stage are essentially semantic agents, children use this semantic–syntactic correspondence to begin to work out the abstract syntactic relations for more complex sentences that require the grammatical category of subject, but that do not entail semantic agents (e.g. experiencer or instrumental).

As children's sentences grow longer than two words, a number of substantive changes are reflected in their language. One is that children begin combining two or more basic semantic relations to yield progressively more complex sentences in content, as the child expands and elaborates the semantic relationships expressed within a single sentence (Brown, 1973). Another change is the gradual appearance of noun and verb inflections and some functional terms, generally referred to as grammatical morphology.

The most complete study on the acquisition of English morphology was conducted by Brown (1973). Following earlier work by Cazden (1968), Brown investigated the development of 14 grammatical morphemes including prepositions (in, on), articles, (a, the), noun inflections marking plural (-s) and possessive ('s), verb inflections marking progressive aspect (-ing), third person present tense, both regular and irregular (-s, has), regular and irregular past tense (-ed, had), the verb 'to be', as a main verb and auxiliary when it can be contracted (e.g. 'It's red; I'm walking'), and when it cannot. In a longitudinal study of three children Brown charted the proportion of obligatory contexts for each of these morphemes that were filled with the correct morpheme. He found that the process was a gradual one, but that the order in which these 14 morphemes was acquired was remarkably similar across the children. This invariant order of acquisition was confirmed in a cross-sectional study of a larger group of children (de Villiers & de Villiers, 1973). This order of acquisition could not be accounted for by the frequency of these morphemes in the input; rather it was linguistic complexity, either semantic or syntactic, that was best able to explain the order.

One striking error that children make during the acquisition of grammatical morphology is the overgeneralization of regular forms to irregular examples. For example the plural ending -s may be overgeneralized to nouns such as mans or mouses; and the past tense may be overgeneralized to verbs such as falled or goed. These errors may not be that frequent; however, they persist well into the school years and are quite resistant to feedback or correction. They are taken as evidence that the child is indeed acquiring a rule-governed linguistic system, rather than learning these inflections on a word by word basis. Overgeneralization errors have been noted in the acquisition of languages other than English (Slobin, 1985). However, the slow piecemeal fashion in which English morphology is acquired does not hold for languages that have a richer inflectional system. For example Hyams (1986) reports the very rapid, complete and early acquisition of some aspects of verb morphology in Italian.

Thus far, we have focused on the child's use of simple declarative sentences. Children must also acquire the use and comprehension of other sentence modalities including negation, questions, and passive voice sentences. Although even at the one-word stage children do express negation (No!), fully formed sentential negation is not acquired until much later. Klima and Bellugi (1966) identified three stages in the acquisition of negation in English. During the first stage, the negative marker is placed outside the sentence, usually preceding it (e.g. 'No go park'; 'No Daddy do it'). At the next stage, the negative marker is internal to the sentence next to the verb but there is no productive inclusion of the obligatory auxiliary verb (e.g. 'I no like that', 'Mommy not push me'). Finally, the child's negative sentences are fully formed, with the productive use of the auxiliary verb system (e.g. 'I can't see you'; 'I don't need that').

Negation can be used to express different meanings including rejection (e.g. 'No want that') and existence (e.g. 'No car here'), which appear very early in children's speech, and denial (e.g. 'That's not my ball') which is a later meaning to be acquired. This order for the semantic aspects of negation is found not only for English (Bloom, 1970) but also for other languages including Japanese (McNeill & McNeill, 1968) and Tamil (Vaidyanathan, 1991). Studies of comprehension of negation find that children are sensitive to the pragmatic contexts in which a sentence is presented. Thus, sentences expressing plausible denials are more easily understood by young children than those expressing implausible denials (de Villiers & Tager-Flusberg, 1974). Taken together, these studies suggest that the development of negation is influenced by grammatical, semantic as well as pragmatic factors.

A similar complex of interactions influence the acquisition of questions. English allows several different kinds of questions including the use of rising intonation on a declarative sentence (e.g. 'We're going shopping now?'), yes−no questions with inverted subject and auxiliary verb (e.g. 'Do you have a pencil?'), wh-questions that involve wh-movement and inversion (e.g. 'What are you doing?' 'Why is John crying?'), and tag questions involving either lexical tags (e.g. 'We will go now, okay?') or grammatical tags (e.g. 'We will go now, won't we?'). Initially, most children's questions involve rising intonation, and perhaps one or two formulaic wh-questions (e.g. 'What's that?'). Gradually, as the child acquires the auxiliary verb system children come to form appropriately inverted wh-questions and yes−no questions (Erreich, 1984). Some recent research (de Villiers, 1991) suggests children acquire the inversion rule for wh-questions separately for each wh-word (e.g. what, where, how, why), and that these developments are closely linked in time to the child's use of the particular wh-word as a complement (e.g. 'You know what he wants'; 'John found out why Mary left').

Parallel to the acquisition of negation, studies have found that there is a systematic order in which different wh-questions are acquired: what, where and who are early to appear, while when, how, which and why develop later (Ervin-Tripp, 1970; Tyack & Ingram, 1977). This order may reflect the semantic complexity of the concepts encoded by these wh-words (Ervin-Tripp, 1970), or the syntactic complexity of the phrase that is replaced by the wh-word (Bloom *et al.*, 1982). Pragmatic contexts also influence the comprehension of questions. Thus Winzemer (1980) found that children made more errors when asked questions such as 'Where is the girl eating?' than they did when asked 'What is the girl eating?'

Children use questions to express a range of functions. Most questions asked in the early stages of development seek information (such as the names for things or the locations of objects), or facilitate conversation by asking for clarification or expressing agreement. Some children appear to ask endless questions simply to maintain conversation and interaction with others. Older children begin asking questions to direct the behaviour of others, especially to gain attention (James & Seebach, 1982). Typically, there are strong form−function relationships in the children's questions (Vaidyanathan, 1988; Clancy, 1989) that may reflect the input addressed to the child (Shatz, 1982). In particular, studies have found that wh-questions are primarily used to seek information while yes−no questions are used for conversational and directive purposes. Thus, as for negation, the development of questions is determined by linguistic complexity which interacts with semantic and pragmatic factors. Moreover, the use of different kinds of questions for different functions underscores the significance of the social context in which language forms develop.

Studies on the acquisition of passive sentences in English (e.g. 'The lamp was broken by the boy') has also found that syntactic factors interact with semantic and pragmatic factors to influence the course of development in both comprehension and production (Bever, 1970; Horgan, 1978; Maratsos *et al.*, 1979; Pinker *et al.*, 1987). Because it is a very rare construction in everyday speech, English-speaking children acquire full mastery over the passive construction relatively late, generally not before the age of 5. In contrast, studies of the development of some non-Indo-European languages have found that children learning these languages in fact acquire the passive construction very much earlier than children learning languages like English (Suzman, 1987; Pye, 1988; Demuth, 1990). For example Demuth's study of children acquiring Sesotho, a language spoken in southern Africa, found that these children began using the passive in everyday conversation by the time they were 2 years old, and it was quite frequent by the time they were 4. Demuth (1990) suggested that this is because in Sesotho, where subjects always mark the topic of a sentence, the passive is a very basic and quite frequent construction since most verbs can be passivized. She argued that the typology of a language, and the importance of the passive to a particular language, will influence the timing of its development.

Later grammatical developments involve the child creating more complex sentences that include more than one verb. This is initially accomplished in conjoined sentences (e.g. 'John went to school and Mary stayed at home') and sentences involving infinitival (e.g. 'Billy wanted to buy a new book'), or propositional complement constructions (e.g. 'Chris knows that John has a new bike'). By the time children are about 3 or 4 they begin using embedded relative clauses (e.g. 'Susie picked out the elephant that had a very long trunk'). Again, we find that the acquisition of these aspects of the grammar involve a complex interaction of syntactic, semantic and pragmatic factors. This can be illustrated by the research that has been conducted on the acquisition of coordinations.

The earliest form used to conjoin sentences is 'and' which appears before the child reaches the age of 3. Initially, it is used to conjoin noun phrases such as 'carrots and peas' but soon it is used in more complete sentences. There are two grammatical forms of coordinated sentences: phrasals (e.g. 'Joe and Jim went bike riding') and sententials (e.g. 'Joe went bike riding and Jim went bike riding'). These two forms appear simultaneously in children's spontaneous speech (Bloom *et al.*, 1980), and they are equally well understood (Tager-Flusberg *et al.*, 1982), suggesting that they develop independently. These studies suggest that children are sensitive to the differences in meaning expressed in phrasal and sentential coordinations. Phrasal coordinations suggest events that involve the same referents, and which occur at the same time and place (Jeremy, 1978); while sentential coordinations suggest events involving different referents and which occur at different times or places. From the beginning, children appear to be sensitive to these semantic differences that are encoded in distinct grammatical forms. The study by Bloom *et al.* (1980) also found that children gradually move from simply expressing additive meanings in conjoined sentences, to then expressing temporal (e.g. 'Joey is going home and take his sweater off') and causal relationships (e.g. 'She put a plaster on her shoe and maked it feel better').

We can summarize the course of grammatical developments during the preschool years and beyond in the following way. Generally, within a language there is an invariant order in which grammatical constructions are acquired that generally reflects a complicated set of factors including the complexity of the rules that underlie the construction, as well as the importance of the construction and the obligatory nature of its use. By and large, grammatical development does not reflect the frequency of particular constructions within the input addressed to the child. Development of the use of a particular construction tends to be quite gradual, but there are clear exceptions to this. At first a construction may be used with only one or two fixed lexical items; it then may be used in a semantically restricted way; finally the use of a particular construction will be generalized across all contexts. Grammatical development, which depends on language-specific biological mechanisms, interacts at all stages with relevant semantic and pragmatic factors, though these are not necessarily involved in determining the sequence of development.

Pragmatic development

Over the past decade or so there has been increased interest in investigating how children acquire the ability to use language to fulfill a range of functions and in a variety of communicative contexts (Bates, 1976). This newer emphasis reflects the notion that to become a competent speaker requires not only knowledge of the structural forms and meanings of a language, but also the ability to communicate using those forms in a competent, flexible and appropriate manner. Some researchers have argued that language forms develop to serve new communicative functions, not vice versa (e.g. Bates & MacWhinney, 1982). This aspect of language development is closely tied to the child's developing social knowledge and social relationships, and even in prelinguistic communication there is an attempt to meet functional goals.

What are the communicative functions expressed in children's speech? This approach to the child's language is based on the theory of speech acts proposed by Austin (1962) and Searle (1969), among others, and has been very influential in child language research. These philosophers argued that many utterances do not simply make an assertion, but they also operate as performatives — that is they perform an act (e.g. promise, refuse). Each utterance has three components: (i) the illocutionary intent, or goal of the speaker; (ii) the locutionary act, or the actual form of the utterance; and (iii) the perlocutionary effect, the influence on the listener. In this way we can account for the many different utterances that can be used, both direct and indirect, literal or metaphorical, to convey the same message. Thus one of the questions that derives from this approach to language is how children come to use and interpret indirect and non-literal uses of language.

A number of researchers have focused on identifying and classifying the functions of early language, investigating the development of illocutionary intent and its relation to locutionary acts, and several coding systems have been developed. Halliday (1975), for example, noted seven different functions (or speech acts) that children below the age of 2 use. These include instrumental, regulatory, personal, interactional, informative, heuristic and imaginative. By the time children are 3, new functions emerge. Dore *et al.* (1978) included in their set of functions for children at this stage descriptions, assertions, regulative, performative and conversational devices. At this point, too, children are able to express each of these functions using a variety of different syntactic forms.

Garvey (1975) has focused in her research on when children begin to use indirect requests. Although 2 year olds use terms such as want or need as a way of asking for something (e.g. 'I need new ball'), genuine indirect requests do not emerge until around the age of 3 (e.g. 'Where is the truck?') By 4 children can use polite forms including modal verbs to make their request (e.g. 'Would you give me a cookie?'), but hints or oblique indirect requests are not used until the early school years. Shatz (1974) tested 2 year olds' comprehension of different kinds of requests, and found that they did not discriminate between requests for action and requests for information. Some evidence suggests that 3 year olds do respond appropriately to indirect requests (Reeder, 1980), but this work has been criticized for not including true indirect requests (Ervin-Tripp, 1977). Other studies indicate that throughout the early school years children gradually become able to understand more and more oblique levels of indirect speech acts (Leonard *et al.*, 1978).

A number of studies have focused on children's developing awareness of the perlocutionary effect of their utterances, and the ability to modify locutionary acts to take into account their listeners' knowledge. Maratsos (1973) found that 5 year olds knew when to use definite and indefinite articles (the, a/an), depending on the listener's presuppositional knowledge about an object. However, children below the age of 7 or 8 do not perform well on referential communication tasks, in which they are required to describe a scene or unusual object that is hidden from the listener's view (Krauss & Glucksberg, 1977). Using more naturalistic data, such as spontaneous speech, other studies have found that even 4 year olds do change the way they speak, using simpler sentences for example, if they are talking to 2 year olds, which shows some awareness of the distinct needs of a very young conversational partner (Shatz & Gelman, 1973).

Communicative competence also entails knowing how to engage in conversations in appropriate and informative ways. A number of studies have focused on the development of conversational abilities, especially the ability to take turns and maintain the topic of conversation. From the earliest stages children are able to take turns in conversation, following their mother's utterance with their own (Garvey, 1975; Bloom *et al.*, 1976) usually, though not always, in a semantically related way. This ability to maintain topic increases during the preschool years and the child is now able to respond to its mother by expanding on the information in her utterances. This ability to add new information correlates highly with the child's developing linguistic skills, as measured by MLU (Bloom *et al.*, 1976), and leads to the ability to maintain a topic over longer chains of conversational turns.

The social uses of language provide the interactive, communicative framework within which children acquire knowledge of the linguistic structures available in their native language so that they can express more fully the ideas that are generated by their developing cognitive and social systems.

INDIVIDUAL DIFFERENCES

Thus far we have considered language development from the perspective of typical patterns of development. During the early years of research in the field, the focus was exclusively on describing such universal aspects of language acquisition without considering whether there are individual differences in the patterns and processes among normally developing children. More recently, some of the variation among children acquiring language has been appreciated; variation that may reflect stylistic or environmental influences on language development or variations that come from learning more than one language. In this section we briefly discuss these aspects of individual variation in the experience of language acquisition in order to provide a taste of the richness and diversity that exists in this critical aspect of human experience.

Stylistic differences

Nelson (1973) was the first to investigate in detail individual differences in the earliest stages of language development. Her study focused on the initial lexicons of 18 children. She found that some children, whom she labelled referential, acquired larger vocabularies which included many nominals, and other content words, and which were used one at a time. At the other end of the continuum were children Nelson called expressive, who had fewer nominals, more social expressions, smaller vocabularies and who used some unanalysed phrases or routines. In a related study Bloom *et al.* (1975) also identified two clusters of children among the six

whom they were following in a longitudinal study. At the early stages of language development these children were identified as either nominal, because they used lots of content words, or pronominal, because they used more pronouns, relational terms, and were more likely to imitate the speech of their mothers.

Peters (1977) argued that these two different groups of children are acquiring language in fundamentally different ways. The referential or nominal children are what she called analytic: they break down the stream of language they hear into minimal units of sounds and words, and focus on analysing and building up the rules systems of their language. In contrast, the expressive or pronominal children have a different cognitive style, called gestalt: these children rely more heavily on whole phrases, routines and imitations which are stored without initial analysis. Only later are these broader holistic representations analysed into smaller units from which abstract rules are derived.

Peters suggested that these individual differences may reflect functional differences: gestalt children are more interested in language to serve social needs, whereas the analytic child is interested in the cognitive challenge of breaking into the linguistic code. Others (Bloom & Lahey, 1978; Tager-Flusberg & Calkins, 1990) suggested that these individual differences are not different approaches to acquiring language; rather they reflect different styles for communicating. Nelson (1981) emphasized the role of the environment in promoting these differences among children, including birth order (later-born children are more likely to be expressive), and educational status (the referential child is more likely to come from homes where parents have a higher level of education); while Lieven (1978) suggested that children's communicative and language styles are a clear reflection of their mothers' styles.

The most complete study of individual differences in language development was conducted by Bates *et al.* (1988) who followed a group of about 30 children from the age of 10 months to 28 months. They proposed that there are different mechanisms involved in acquiring language: a comprehension mechanism, a rote production mechanism and a mechanism for analysed production. All three, which they argued are dissociable, are necessary aspects of the language acquisition process and perhaps the best way to characterize individual differences is in the relative reliance that particular children have on one or other of these fundamental mechanisms. This study of individual differences suggested that the comprehension and production of language depend on somewhat independent modules and perhaps underlying brain mechanisms in normally developing children. This has important implications for the kinds of impairments that can be found in children with language disorders. At the individual child level the only factor that predicted stylistic variation was temperament: more sociable children tended to rely more on rote production. Bates *et al.* also pointed to the role of context in influencing stylistic differences: thus the same child in different contexts may use different approaches to language and communication.

Bilingual language development

It had previously been believed that there are major disadvantages for the young child learning two languages (Hakuta, 1986), with concerns that progress in one or both languages may be seriously delayed. Recent research suggests that this may not be the case for many children. Several factors influence the course of the development of bilingual language competence including the age of the child, the contexts in which the child is exposed to the two languages, and the way in which the languages are acquired. However, in general, research suggests that the rate and manner of development appear to be the same whether a child is monolingual or bilingual (Padilla & Lindholm, 1976; Doyle *et al.*, 1978), with growth in the length of the child's utterances from single words to longer sentences, and the gradual development of grammatical morphology and more complex aspects of syntactic structure.

One important distinction that is made is between simultaneous and sequential acquisition before the age of about 3 (McLaughlin, 1982). Children who acquire two languages at the same time at a young age show few differences compared to monolingual children even in rate of development (Padilla & Liebman, 1975; Dulay *et al.*, 1978). Not even the degree of dissimilarity between the two languages affects the rate of development in simultaneous

bilinguals. There are three phases in the acquisition of two languages simultaneously. At first the child has two independent lexicons (Swain, 1972; Vihman, 1985), and the two vocabularies rarely overlap (Prinz & Prinz, 1979). Even when there is overlap the child may not treat the words as equals (cf. the mutual exclusivity constraint), and they may be mixed together by the child indiscriminately. The optimal way for a child to learn two languages is for the contexts in which they are used to be kept distinct for the child (Genesee, 1989). For example, this can be accomplished if one parent uses one language consistently, while the other parent uses the second language; alternatively, in the home one language may be used while in day care or nursery school the second language is used (Redlinger & Park, 1980). At the initial stage mixing is less likely if the languages are kept functionally separate; though some mixing may occur because the child who wants to say something in one language may only know the words or grammatical expressions that serve those functions in the second language. This may be a form of overextension.

Although initially the two phonological systems may not be fully separated, by the age of 2 bilingual children have made the appropriate differentiation (Albert & Obler, 1978; Dulay *et al.*, 1978). During the second developmental phase the child may apply the same syntactic rules to the two independent lexicons. While at this point bilingual children can translate words from one language into the second language, they are not so flexible with syntactic and morphological rule systems. This may be because of the substantive differences in linguistic difficulty of the particular grammatical structures in the two languages (Slobin, 1973).

In the final phase of development the child has developed the lexical, phonological and syntactic knowledge of both languages with almost no interference or mixing between the two (Lindholm & Padilla, 1978). Children who acquire two languages in this way seem to have a dual processing system (Altenberg & Cairns, 1983) and the two languages are represented independently in the brain (Albert & Obler, 1978).

Successive acquisition of two languages leads to greater variation in the process and degree of success. It is harder to attain complete fluency in two languages if the second is not learned before late adolescence or early adulthood. However, younger children can become fluent in two languages depending to a large extent on the child's attitude towards the culture of the second language, and the degree of identification with its native users. Successive learners will initially be heavily reliant on rote unanalysed phrases, if they are learning in naturalistic rather than academic settings (Fillmore, 1979), thus relying more on an expressive style. There is generally less interference or mixing between the languages during the development of the second language than is found among simultaneous bilinguals (Dulay *et al.*, 1978), but the second language still follows the same developmental pathway as first language acquisition across all domains of language.

Children who acquire a second language have many advantages. They have access to more than one culture and social group, and may even develop an earlier awareness about language forms (metalinguistic awareness) which may serve the child's developing literacy skills, and certainly does not compromise their intellectual achievements as was originally believed (Hakuta, 1986). In general the research on bilingualism indicates that children have an amazing capacity to learn and use more than one language, and there are fewer differences in the process of acquiring two languages either simultaneously or successively than one might have predicted.

Language environments

One of the most important kinds of variation that can be identified is the language environment to which children are exposed. There has been a considerable amount of research that has addressed the question of whether variation in the environment and language input leads to individual differences in language acquisition (Puckering & Rutter, 1987).

At one extreme are children raised in almost complete isolation in severely deprived conditions. The most well-known case was that of Genie (Curtiss, 1977), who had been isolated from about the age of 18 months until she was finally removed from her abusive family when she was 13 years old. Genie was essentially mute when she was found, but after extensive therapy in the context of a normal family environment she gained considerable

language abilities in both comprehension and production. Nevertheless, Genie never reached full mastery in language, especially in the areas of pragmatic functioning and more complex aspects of syntax and morphology. Other examples of children raised in very deprived circumstances with grossly deficient language have also been documented. Skuse (1984) reviewed nine such cases (including Genie) who ranged in age from 2 to 13. Six of these children gained language skills that were almost age appropriate after being placed in a more normal environment; the three who remained severely language impaired also suffered from organic impairments. These cases indicate that severe deprivation and abuse lead to extreme delays in language development, yet once the children are placed in a better environment they are able to make substantial recovery (Puckering & Rutter, 1987).

Over the past 20 years there has also been considerable research focusing on whether variation in the input provided within the range of normal environments has an influence on language acquisition. Parents and other adults across almost all cultures employ a special register when they speak to young language-learning children, which is sometimes called 'motherese'. Features of motherese include higher pitch, exaggerated intonation, simplified pronunciation of words, more basic level vocabulary, shorter sentences and few errors (Snow & Ferguson, 1977). Mothers may use these and other features to a greater or lesser extent and studies have investigated whether the use of motherese indeed influences the course of language acquisition. By and large this body of work indicates that motherese serves the primary purpose of increasing intelligibility to the child but does not really influence the child's mastery of language. Only one aspect of mothers' speech may affect the rate of language development: the degree to which their utterances are semantically contingent with their children's speech. Thus mothers who respond in a topically related way to their children's utterances may have children who acquire language somewhat faster (Cross, 1977). This influence may be more related to the higher degree of social interaction between these mother−child dyads, rather than to any particular dimensions of the language input (Puckering & Rutter, 1987).

DISORDERS OF LANGUAGE DEVELOPMENT

What happens when a child has special difficulties in acquiring language? Problems in acquiring language are common in many clinical groups, and each group may exhibit a distinct pattern of delay and deficit that reflects the core nature of the clinical syndrome (Tager-Flusberg, 1988). In this section we consider three examples of language disorders that illustrate a number of important theoretical issues that have motivated research in this area.

Mental retardation

Definitions of mental retardation that focus on levels of intellectual or adaptive functioning include problems in language development and language functioning (Grossman, 1977). One of the central questions that has guided the study of language development in this population is whether language delays are closely tied to delays in other areas of cognitive functioning. The most widely studied mentally retarded children are those with Down's syndrome, probably because they are easily identified and it is one of the most common forms of mental retardation. There are indications, however, that different subgroups of mentally retarded individuals may actually show distinct patterns of language development. For example, in Down's syndrome children language seems to lag somewhat behind cognitive development for reasons that are not well understood (Miller *et al.*, 1981; Fowler, 1988). In contrast, in William's syndrome, a rare metabolic disorder that results in distinctive physical characteristics and neurodevelopmental impairment, language skills are quite superior and significantly higher than would be predicted from overall IQ levels (Bellugi *et al.*, 1988; Reilly *et al.*, 1990). Although these broad asynchronies between language and cognition are not well understood they do suggest differences in the spared and impaired biological and psychological mechanisms in various groups of mentally retarded populations.

Given this diversity among different subgroups it is not easy to provide an overall picture of language functioning in mentally retarded children, especially as many studies do not provide a detailed enough description of their subjects. Nevertheless, based primarily on studies of Down's syndrome or non-specified mental retardation we can discuss the general course of language development in this population. Overall, it is clear that language development follows the same general pathway in mentally retarded children, though the rate of development is significantly slower, and may be related to the child's IQ level (Rondal, 1987). Moreover, children with mental retardation, especially in the moderate or severe range, may never reach the normal adult level of competence. There is some indication that development of language, at least in the areas of syntax and morphology, in Down's syndrome reaches a plateau at about the age of 7 or 8 (Fowler, 1988), which may reflect underlying maturational processes in the brain. Fowler did, however, find that her Down's syndrome subjects showed a new growth spurt during the adolescent years as reflected in growth in MLU. Her findings support other research which finds that language can continue to develop in Down's syndrome adolescents (Seagoe, 1965; Rondal, 1988).

Although some researchers (e.g. Lackner, 1968) have argued that mentally retarded children's grammars are normal in all respects except for rate of development, other studies have found that the constructions used by mentally retarded children are significantly less complex, contain more errors, and are lower in the frequency of use of some constructions than those used by mental age matched non-retarded controls (Naremore & Dever, 1975; Ryan, 1975; Kamhi & Johnston, 1982). In contrast, it is generally found that mentally retarded children's lexical knowledge may outstrip their grammatical abilities (Fowler, 1984; Rondal, 1987).

Recent research on the language abilities of mentally retarded children has focused on their acquisition of communicative competence. In a recent review of this body of work Abbeduto and Rosenberg (1987) concluded that while there are some aspects of communicative competence that are not specifically impaired in mentally retarded children relative to their non-verbal cognitive level, including turn-taking abilities, and the development of the use and interpretation of speech acts, other aspects of communicative competence, especially those aspects of communicative competence that involve taking into account a listener's needs and knowledge are somewhat more impaired. This shows up not only in conversation but also in more complex forms of narrative discourse (e.g. Hemphill *et al.*, 1991). Abbeduto and Rosenberg argued that communicative competence involves a diverse set of skills, some of which are more closely tied to specific language abilities, while others require the child to integrate its linguistic abilities with other aspects of cognitive and social knowledge. These latter more integrative and complex aspects of communicative competence are relatively more impaired in mentally retarded individuals.

Specific language disorders

Specific language impairment (SLI) is defined primarily on exclusionary criteria (Leonard, 1987). Children are classified as SLI if they are significantly delayed in acquiring language in the absence of hearing impairment, mental retardation, emotional disorder, autism or frank neurological abnormalities (American Psychiatric Association, 1987). SLI forms a very varied population of children, and over the years many different terms have been used to label them (Leonard, 1982; Bishop, 1992). Some children with SLI have good comprehension abilities but difficulties with productive or expressive language while others have significant deficits in both comprehension and production. More recently a new subgroup of SLI has been identified, called semantic—pragmatic disorder (Rapin & Allen, 1983). Characteristics of semantic—pragmatic disorder include fluent speech with adequate articulation, verbosity, comprehension deficits coupled with more literal interpretation of utterances, perseveration, semantic paraphasias, lack of semantic specificity, and deficits in turn-taking and topic maintenance (Bishop & Rosenbloom, 1987). Analyses of the conversations produced by children with semantic—pragmatic disorder suggest that they have a different profile of impairments compared to other children with SLI (Adams & Bishop, 1989). Specifically, their conversations included many inappropriate utterances defined as providing the listener with either too much or too little information, suggesting some underlying cognitive problems (Bishop & Adams, 1989).

In general children with SLI begin as 2 year olds with significant delays in developing language. Many children identified with language delay at 2 go on to be classified as SLI, though some may outgrow their early problems and catch up with other preschoolers (Rescorla & Schwartz, 1990). Children with SLI appear to have many articulatory problems and make large numbers of phonological errors. Nevertheless these children exhibit the same kinds of error patterns that are found among normally developing children. It has also been found that children with SLI may have special problems acquiring the grammatical morphology of their language (e.g. Gopnik, 1990), especially certain functional categories (cf. Rice, 1991) though these claims are currently in dispute (Leonard, 1987). Overall, because of the extreme heterogeneity of this population it is very hard to identify characteristic profiles of language functioning and language development in children who are identified as SLI.

Children with SLI may never fully catch up with the normal population. Instead, these children continue to show some language related problems during the school years and they are at high risk for learning disabilities and academic failure once they reach school and begin learning to read (Aram *et al.*, 1984; Silva *et al.*, 1987; Bishop & Adams, 1990). These children also encounter a number of social difficulties with their peers and may have other kinds of adjustment problems that stem from difficulties with conversational skills (Rice *et al.*, 1991).

A number of clinical and epidemiological studies have addressed the issue of long-term consequences of early language delay. Despite some serious methodological problems with many of these studies (Rutter & Mawhood, 1991), the findings from these studies suggest that there is wide variation in the outcome of individuals with SLI. Bishop & Edmundson (1987) found that those children with a pure phonological disorder had the best prognosis, while children with more global impairments in language development had the poorest outcome. A recent study by Rutter and co-workers (cited in Rutter & Mawhood, 1991) documents the lives of adults who had been diagnosed with severe childhood developmental language disorders, in a unique long-term follow-up study. A significant proportion of their sample continued to experience substantial problems in developing social relationships as adults and difficulties in coping with the demands of a work environment.

There have been a number of different theoretical explanations for the causes of SLI. On the one hand, Leonard (1987) argued that SLI does not have a specific cause. It simply represents the low end of normal variation in language abilities that one would expect to find in any population. This perspective views SLI as analogous to non-organic mental retardation which represents the low end of the continuum for cognitive abilities. Indeed these may well be overlapping populations. Other researchers argue that SLI does have a specific cause, but there are different views about the nature of the underlying causes of SLI.

Early work suggested that the communicative environment of children with SLI contributed to their problems. Either their mothers were not providing appropriate input and sufficient amounts of stimulation (e.g. Wulbert *et al.*, 1975), or the children have less need to talk perhaps because others talk for them and their needs are met without language (Wellen & Broen, 1982). Based on a critical review of the literature, Lederberg (1980) concluded that parents were not responsible for their children's problems in acquiring language; on the contrary they seem as sensitive to their children's needs as non-SLI parents. A similar conclusion was reached by Leonard (1987) in his more recent review.

Another explanation for SLI was proposed by Tallal and Piercy (1973, 1974). They found that children with SLI were specifically impaired in their ability to process rapidly changing acoustic stimuli. While their findings have been replicated by others it is not clear how this deficit in basic auditory processing can explain the full range of language problems that are characteristic of SLI children. Leonard (1987) suggested that rather than viewing these processing deficits as the underlying cause of SLI, they may be the result of it. The tasks used by Tallal and Piercy require the child to process and make judgements about the similarity or differences between stimuli they hear. This kind of metalinguistic skill may be the result of an underlying problem with language.

A third theory of SLI argues that it is part of a more general problem in acquiring symbolic skills. While several studies have found that children with SLI show some impairments in their symbolic play (Williams, 1978) and in their imagery abilities (Johnston & Ramstad, 1983), these children generally show higher levels of play and imagery than language-matched control groups. Thus this does not provide a complete explanation for the kinds of difficulties in language acquisition that define the SLI population.

Perhaps the most integrative and comprehensive hypothesis about the nature of SLI is suggested by Bishop (1992) in her recent critical analysis of the relevant literature. Bishop suggested children with SLI have subtle auditory perceptual problems which may reflect a more fundamentally slowed rate of information processing. This information processing deficit leads to impairments in tasks that require integrating rapidly presented information. This will especially impair auditory processing which leads to problems in phonology and syntax; it also accounts for some of the non-linguistic impairments that are found in children with SLI.

Clearly there is still much to be learned about the underlying causes, and the development of language, in children with SLI, although there has been recent progress on the possible genetic factors that may contribute to the syndrome of SLI (Gopnik, 1990).

Autism

One of the defining characteristics of autism is difficulty in the acquisition of language. Both delays in the age of onset and deviant patterns of development are generally found among children with this pervasive developmental disorder (American Psychiatric Association, 1987; Paul, 1987; Tager-Flusberg, 1989). About half of the population never really acquires functional language, and many more are characterized as echolalic, simply parroting the speech of others. Nevertheless, about 20 or 30% of autistic children do acquire functional language, and those who begin acquiring language before 5 have the best prognosis (Rutter *et al.*, 1967).

Recent work has attempted to tie the nature of the autistic child's language impairment with other aspects of the syndrome. Autism is defined as a social and affective disorder that is associated with behavioural deficits and paucity of imagination (Wing & Attwood, 1987). The social cognitive deficits of autistic children are generally considered primary (Rutter, 1983) and one current influential theory is that autistic children are specifically impaired in their acquisition of a theory of mind. This impairment, which may be related to particular biological mechanisms, is viewed as the underlying problem that may explain many of the behavioural characteristics of the syndrome (Baron-Cohen *et al.*, 1985, 1993; see also Chapter 13).

In an earlier section language development was characterized as dependent on two distinct mechanisms: one is specific to language, the other is specific to a theory of mind. On this view, some of the language deficits of even verbal and high-functioning autistic children may be explained by the autistic child's impaired theory of mind (Tager-Flusberg, 1993). The patterns of language ability and impairment in autistic children are briefly reviewed here from this perspective.

Even at the prelinguistic stage, autistic children are specifically impaired in using protodeclarative gestures and vocalizations (Curcio, 1978; Wetherby, 1986) that are more related to a theory of mind than protoimperatives, which pose no special problems for autistic children. Once autistic children begin to talk, they continue to use fewer declarative utterances that are not just responses to adult questions (Ball, 1978). And even beyond the one-word stage autistic children are less likely to provide new information to their mothers or to be informative in their communications (Tager-Flusberg & Anderson, 1991). Thus overall, their patterns of communicative abilities fit with the view that they fail to conceive of language as essentially a means for communicating to others what they may not currently know.

In contrast, autistic children do not appear to show particular deficits in acquiring structural aspects of language, which are less dependent on theory of mind abilities. Thus autistic children are not different from mentally retarded or normal control subjects in their acquisition of a phonological system (Bartolucci *et al.*, 1976), the development of semantic knowledge (Tager-Flusberg, 1985, 1986), or in acquiring the grammar of the native language (Tager-Flusberg, 1989; Tager-Flusberg

et al., 1990). There is even some evidence to suggest that the processes underlying developments in these domains of language are similar to those found in normal children (Tager-Flusberg & Calkins, 1990).

It is in the area of pragmatics that autistic children show the most severe difficulties (Paul, 1987). This is not surprising given the close relationship between pragmatic and social abilities, and a number of studies have identified a striking dissociation between the autistic child's grammatical knowledge and communicative competence (Mermelstein, 1983; Tager-Flusberg & Anderson, 1991), which underscores the view that the language deficits of autistic children are tied to their problems in theory of mind, not to damage to any language-specific mechanisms (cf. Churchill, 1972).

Nevertheless, the enormous range of language abilities that is found among autistic children still requires further investigation. There are also some aspects of the language in autistic individuals that go beyond a theory of mind interpretation. For example, autistic individuals often misuse words and phrases producing idiosyncratic terms and neologisms (Volden & Lord, 1991) or metaphorical language, as Kanner (1946) described it. Rutter (1987) suggested that these abnormal uses of words may be functionally similar to the kinds of early word meaning errors made by young normally developing children. It is their persistence in autistic children that defines them as abnormal and they may reflect the fact that autistic children are not sensitive to the corrective feedback provided by their parents because of their social impairments. Despite the advances made in our current understanding of underlying deficits in this population, there is still much to be learned about why many autistic children never acquire language at all.

CONCLUSION

Language acquisition is probably the most significant accomplishment that almost all people achieve with ease during a brief window of developmental opportunity. While there is some variation in our experiences in acquiring language, and some children show special difficulty in this domain, nevertheless it is the essential similarities across individuals and across languages in the patterns and processes involved in language development that are most striking. This is particularly true when each area of language is viewed independently but we have also shown that it may be less true for children with language impairments who show different kinds of asynchronies or dissociations between structural and functional aspects of language and communication.

Once language is acquired, a child's social, cultural and cognitive worlds are transformed by the ability to translate one's experience into words and to interpret and incorporate the experience of others. These influences and interrelationships between language, cognitive and social development have special implications for children with disorders of language development. There is a profound impact of language delay, resulting from specific language impairment, hearing impairment, mental retardation, or other disorders on the child's learning processes, literacy, cognitive functioning, play and peer relationships (Howlin & Rutter, 1987). Children with delayed or impaired language are also much more likely to experience behavioural and emotional problems, which persist into adulthood (Silva, 1987; Rutter & Mawhood, 1991). Thus language is a formal symbolic and communication system that is deeply connected to the individual's socioemotional and cognitive functioning. Its development is profoundly influenced by these factors and, in turn, language comes to influence socialization and intellectual life. It is these interactive aspects of language and other domains in the developing child that must be further studied in order to provide a unified and enriched perspective on the world of children.

ACKNOWLEDGEMENT

Support for the preparation of this chapter was provided by a grant from the National Institute on Deafness and Other Communication Disorders (RO1 DC 01234). I am especially grateful to Dale Hay and Michael Rutter for their comments and suggestions.

REFERENCES

Abbeduto L. & Rosenberg S. (1987) Linguistic communication and mental retardation. In Rosenberg S. (ed.) *Advances in Applied Psycholinguistics*, Vol. 1. *Disorders of First Language Development*, pp. 76–125. Cambridge University Press, New York.

Adams C. & Bishop D.V.M. (1989) Conversational characteristics of children with semantic–pragmatic disorder. I. Exchange structure, turn-taking, repairs and cohesion. *British Journal of Disorders of Communication* **24**, 211–239.

Adams A. & Bullock D. (1986) Apprenticeship in word use: social convergence processes in learning categorically related nouns. In Kuczaj S. & Barrett M. (eds) *The Development of Word Meaning*, pp. 155–197. Springer, New York.

Albert M. & Obler L. (1978) *The Bilingual Brain*. Academic Press, New York.

Allen G. (1983) Linguistic experience modifies lexical stress perception. *Journal of Child Language* **10**, 535–549.

Allen G.D. & Hawkins S. (1980) Phonological rhythm: Definition and development. In Yeni-Komshian G.H., Kavanaugh J.F. & Ferguson C.A. (eds) *Child Phonology*, Vol. I, *Production*. Academic Press, New York.

Altenberg E. & Cairns H. (1983) The effects of phonotactic constraints on lexical processing in bilingual and monolingual subjects. *Journal of Verbal Learning and Verbal Behavior* **22**, 174–178.

American Psychiatric Association (1987) *Diagnostic and Statistical Manual*, 3rd edn. American Psychiatric Association, Washington, DC.

Anglin J. (1977) *Word, Object and Conceptual Development*. Norton, New York.

Aram D., Ekelman B. & Nation J. (1984) Preschoolers with language disorders 10 years later. *Journal of Speech and Hearing Research* **27**, 232–244.

Aslin R.N., Pisoni D.B. & Jusczyk P.W. (1983) Auditory development and speech development in infancy. In Haith M.M. & Campos J.J. (eds) *Handbook of Child Psychology*, Vol. 2, *Infancy and Developmental Psychobiology*, pp. 573–688. Wiley, New York.

Atkinson-King K. (1973) Children's acquisition of phonological stress contrasts. *UCLA Working Papers in Phonetics*, No. 25, University of California, Los Angeles.

Austin J.L. (1962) *How to do Things with Words*. Oxford University Press, Oxford.

Ball J. (1978) *A pragmatic analysis of autistic children's language with respect to aphasic and normal language development*. Unpublished doctoral dissertation, Melbourne University.

Baron-Cohen S. (1989) Joint attention deficits in autism: Towards a cognitive analysis. *Development and Psychopathology* **1**, 185–189.

Baron-Cohen S., Leslie A. & Frith U. (1985) Does the autistic child have a 'theory of mind'? *Cognition* **21**, 37–46.

Baron-Cohen S., Tager-Flusberg H. & Cohen D.J. (eds) (1993) *Understanding Other Minds: Perspectives from Autism*. Oxford University Press, Oxford.

Barrett M. (1986) Early semantic representations and early word-usage. In Kuczaj S. & Barrett M. (eds) *The Development of Word Meaning*, pp. 39–68. Springer, New York.

Bartolucci G., Pierce S.J., Streiner D. & Eppel P.T. (1976) Phonological investigation of verbal autistic and mentally retarded subjects. *Journal of Autism and Childhood Schizophrenia* **6**, 303–316.

Bates E. (1976) *Language and Context*. Academic Press, New York.

Bates E., Benigni L., Bretherton I., Camaioni L. & Volterra V. (1979) From gestures to the first word: on cognition and social prerequisites. In Lewis M. & Rosenblum L. (eds) *Interaction, Conversation, and the Development of Language*, pp. 247–307. Wiley, New York.

Bates E., Bretherton I. & Snyder L. (1988) *From First Words to Grammar: Individual Differences and Dissociable Mechanisms*. Cambridge University Press, Cambridge.

Bates E., Camaioni L. & Volterra V. (1975) The acquisition of performatives prior to speech. *Merrill-Palmer Quarterly* **21**, 205–224.

Bates E. & MacWhinney B. (1982) Functionalist approaches to grammar. In Gleitman L. & Wanner E. (eds) *Language Acquisition: The State of the Art*, pp. 173–218. Cambridge University Press, Cambridge.

Bellugi U., Marks S., Bihrle A. & Sabo H. (1988) Dissociation between language and cognitive functions in Williams syndrome. In Bishop D.V.M. & Mogford K. (eds) *Language Development in Exceptional Circumstances*, pp. 168–192. Churchill Livingstone, Edinburgh.

Bever T. (1970) The cognitive basis for linguistic structures. In Hayes J. (ed.) *Cognition and the Development of Language*, pp. 279–362. Wiley, New York.

Bishop D.V.M. (1992) The underlying nature of specific language impairment. *Journal of Child Psychology and Psychiatry* **33**, 3–66.

Bishop D.V.M. & Adams C. (1989) Conversational characteristics of children with semantic–pragmatic disorder. II. What features lead to a judgement of inappropriacy? *British Journal of Disorders of Communication* **24**, 241–263.

Bishop D.V.M. & Adams C. (1990) A prospective study of the relationship between specific language impairment, phonological disorders, and reading retardation. *Journal of Child Psychology and Psychiatry* **31**, 1027–1050.

Bishop D.V.M. & Edmundson A. (1987) Language-impaired 4-year-olds: Distinguishing transient from persistent impairment. *Journal of Speech and Hearing Disorders* **52**, 156–173.

Bishop D.V.M. & Rosenbloom L. (1987) Childhood language disorders: classification and overview. In Yule W. & Rutter M. (eds) *Language Development and Disorders*, pp. 16–41. MacKeith Press, London.

Bloom L. (1970) *Language Development: Form and Function in Emerging Grammars*. MIT Press, Cambridge, Massachusetts.

Bloom L. (1973) *One Word at a Time: The Use of Single Word Utterances Before Syntax*. Mouton, The Hague.

Bloom L. & Lahey M. (1978) *Language Development and Language Disorders*. Wiley, New York.

Bloom L., Lahey M., Hood L., Lifter K. & Feiss K. (1980) Complex sentences: acquisition of syntactic connectives and the semantic relations they encode. *Journal of Child Language* **7**, 235–262.

Bloom L., Lightbown P. & Hood L. (1975) Structure and variation in child language. *Monographs of the Society for Research in Child Development* **40**, Serial No. 160.

Bloom L., Rocissano L. & Hood L. (1976) Adult–child discourse: Developmental interaction between information processing and linguistic knowledge. *Cognitive Psychology* **8**, 521–552.

Bloom L., Wootten J., Merkin S. & Hood L. (1982) Wh-questions: Linguistic factors that contribute to the sequence of acquisition. *Child Development* **53**, 1084–1092.

Bloom P. (1990) Syntactic distinctions in child language. *Journal of Child Language* **17**, 343–355.

Bowerman M. (1978) The acquisition of word meaning: An investigation in some current conflicts. In Waterson N. & Snow C. (eds) *The Development of Communication*, pp. 263–287. Wiley, New York.

Bowerman M. (1982) Reorganizational processes in lexical and syntactic development. In Gleitman L. & Wanner E. (eds) *Language Acquisition: The State of the Art*, pp 319–346. Cambridge University Press, Cambridge.

Braine M. (1976) Children's first word combinations. *Monographs of the Society for Research in Child Development* **41**, Serial No. 164.

Brown R. (1973) *A First Language*. Harvard University Press, Cambridge, Massachusetts.

Bruner J. (1975a) From communication to language: A psychological perspective. *Cognition* **3**, 255–287.

Bruner J. (1975b) The ontogenesis of speech acts. *Journal of Child Language* **2**, 1–19.

Bruner J. (1986) *Actual Minds, Possible Worlds*. Harvard University Press, Cambridge, Massachusetts.

Bushnell I., Sai F. & Mullin J.T. (1989) Neonatal recognition of the mother's face. *British Journal of Developmental Psychology* **7**, 3–15.

Byrnes J.P. & Gelman S.A. (1991) Perspectives on thought and language: traditional and contemporary views. In Gelman S.A. & Byrnes J.P. (eds) *Perspectives on Language and Thought: Interrelations in Development*, pp. 3–27. Cambridge University Press, Cambridge, Massachusetts.

Carey S. (1978) The child as word learner. In Halle M., Bresnan J. & Miller G. (eds) *Linguistic Theory and Psychological Reality*, pp. 264–293. MIT Press, Cambridge, Massachusetts.

Carey S. & Bartlett E. (1978) Acquiring a single new word. *Papers and Reports on Child Language Development* **15**, 17–29.

Cazden C.B. (1968) The acquisition of noun and verb inflections. *Child Development* **39**, 433−448.

Chomsky N. (1957) *Syntactic Structures*. Mouton, The Hague.

Chomsky N. (1965) *Aspects of the Theory of Syntax*. MIT Press, Cambridge, Massachusetts.

Chomsky N. (1980) *Rules and Representations*. Columbia University Press, New York.

Churchill D. (1972) The relation of infantile autism and early childhood schizophrenia to developmental language disorders of childhood. *Journal of Autism and Childhood Schizophrenia* **2**, 182−197.

Clancy P. (1989) Form and function in the acquisition of Korean wh-questions. *Journal of Child Language* **16**, 323−347.

Clark E.V. (1973) What's in a word? On the child's acquisition of semantics in his first language. In Moore T.E. (ed.) *Cognitive Development and the Acquisition of Language*. Academic Press, New York.

Clark E.V. (1983) Meanings and concepts. In Flavell J.H. & Markman E.M. (eds) *Cognitive Development*, Vol. 3, *Handbook of Child Psychology*, pp. 787−840. Wiley, New York.

Clark E.V. (1988) On the logic of contrast. *Journal of Child Language* **15**, 317−335.

Clark E.V. (1990) On the pragmatics of contrast. *Journal of Child Language* **17**, 417−431.

Clark H. & Clark E.V. (1977) *Psychology and Language*. Harcourt Brace, New York.

Condon W. & Sanders L. (1974) Neonate movement is synchronized with adult speech: Interactional participation and language acquisition. *Science* **183**, 99−101.

Cross T. (1977) Mothers' speech adjustment: The contribution of selected child listener variables. In Snow C.E. & Ferguson C.A. (eds) *Talking to Children: Language Input and Acquisition*, pp. 151−188. Cambridge University Press, Cambridge, Massachusetts.

Crystal D. (1975) *The English Tone of Voice*. Edward Arnold, London.

Crystal D. (1986) Prosodic development. In Fletcher P. & Garman M. (eds) *Language Acquisition*, 2nd edn, pp. 174−197. Cambridge University Press, Cambridge, Massachusetts.

Curcio F. (1978) Sensorimotor functioning and communication in mute autistic children. *Journal of Autism and Childhood Schizophrenia* **8**, 281−292.

Curtiss S. (1977) *Genie: A Psycholinguistic Study of a Modern Day 'Wild Child'*. Academic Press, London.

De Boysson-Bardies B., Sagart L. & Bacri N. (1981) Phonetic analysis of late babbling: A case study of a French child. *Journal of Child Language* **8**, 511−524.

De Boysson-Bardies B., Sagart L. & Durand C. (1984) Discernible differences in the babbling of infants according to target language. *Journal of Child Language* **11**, 1−15.

DeCasper A.J. & Fifer W.P. (1980) Of human bonding: Newborns prefer their mothers' voices. *Science* **208**, 1174−1176.

Demuth K. (1990) Subject, topic and Sesotho passive. *Journal of Child Language* **17**, 67−84.

de Villiers J. (1991) *Why Questions*. University of Massachusetts Occasional Papers: Papers in the Acquisition of wh-, University of Massachusetts, Amherst.

de Villiers J. & Tager-Flusberg H. (1974) Some facts one simply cannot deny. *Journal of Child Language* **2**, 279−286.

de Villiers J.G. & de Villiers P.A. (1973) A cross-sectional study of the acquisition of grammatical morphemes in child speech. *Journal of Psycholinguistic Research* **2**, 267−278.

de Villiers P.A. & de Villiers J.G. (1992) Language development. In Bornstein M. & Lamb M. (eds) *Developmental Psychology: An Advanced Textbook*. Lawrence Erlbaum, Hillsdale, New Jersey.

Dockrell J. & Campbell R. (1986) Lexical acquisition strategies in the preschool child. In Kuczaj S. & Barrett M. (eds) *The Development of Word Meaning*, pp. 121−154. Springer, New York.

Dore J. (1975) Holophrases, speech acts, and language universals. *Journal of Child Language* **2**, 21−40.

Dore J., Gearhart M. & Newman D. (1978) The structure of nursery school conversation. In Nelson K.E. (ed.) *Children's Language*, Vol. 1. Gardner Press, New York.

Doyle A., Champagne M. & Segalowitz N. (1978) Some issues in the assessment of linguistic consequences of early bilingualism. In Paradis M. (ed.) *Aspects of Bilingualism*. Hornbeam Press, Columbia, South Carolina.

Dromi E. (1987) *Early Lexical Development*. Cambridge University Press, New York.

Dromi E. & Berman R. (1982) A morphemic measure of early language development from modern Hebrew. *Journal of Child Language* **9**, 403−424.

Dulay H., Hernandez-Chavez E. & Burt M. (1978) The process of becoming bilingual. In Singh S. & Lynch J. (eds) *Diagnostic Procedures in Hearing, Language, and Speech*, pp. 73−92. University Park Press, Baltimore.

Eimas P., Miller J. & Jusczyk P.W. (1987) On infant speech perception and the acquisition of language. In Harnad S. (ed.) *Categorical Perception: The Groundwork of Cognition*, pp. 161−195. Cambridge University Press, Cambridge, Massachusetts.

Erreich A. (1984) Learning how to ask: Patterns of inversion in yes/no and wh-questions. *Journal of Child Language* **11**, 579−592.

Ervin-Tripp S. (1970) Discourse agreement: How children answer questions. In Hayes J. (ed.) *Cognition and the Development of Language*, pp. 79−108. Wiley, New York.

Ervin-Tripp S. (1977) 'Wait for me roller skate!' In Ervin-Tripp S. & Mitchell-Kernan C. (eds) *Child Discourse*, pp. 165−188. New York, Academic.

Fillmore L.W. (1979) Individual differences in second

language acquisition. In Fillmore C.J., Kempler D. & Wang W. S-Y. (eds) *Individual Differences in Language Ability and Language Behavior*, pp. 203−228. Academic Press, New York.

Fisher C., Gleitman H. & Gleitman L. (1991) On the semantic content of subcategorization forms. *Cognitive Psychology* **23**, 331−392.

Flavell J. (1989) The development of children's knowledge about the mind: From cognitive connections to mental representations. In Astington J., Harris P. & Olson D. (eds) *Developing Theories of Mind*, pp. 244−267. Cambridge University Press, New York.

Fowler A. (1984) *Language acquisition in Down's syndrome children: production and comprehension*. Unpublished doctoral dissertation, University of Pennsylvania.

Fowler A. (1988) Determinants of the rate of language growth in children with Down syndrome. In Nadel L. (ed.) *The Psychobiology of Down Syndrome*, pp. 217−245. MIT Press, Cambridge, Massachusetts.

Frick R.W. (1985) Communicating emotion: The role of prosodic features. *Psychological Bulletin* **97**, 412−429.

Furrow D. (1984) Young children's use of prosody. *Journal of Child Language* **11**, 203−213.

Garvey C. (1975) Requests and responses in children's speech. *Journal of Child Language* **2**, 41−63.

Genesee F. (1989) Early bilingual development: One language or two? *Journal of Child Language* **16**, 161−179.

Gleitman L. (1990) The structural sources of verb meanings. *Language Acquisition* **1**, 3−55.

Goldfield B. & Reznick J. (1990) Early lexical acquisitions: Rate, content, and the vocabulary spurt. *Journal of Child Language* **17**, 171−183.

Golinkoff R., Hirsh-Pasek K., Cauley K. & Gordon L. (1987) The eyes have it: Lexical and syntactic comprehension in a new paradigm. *Journal of Child Language* **14**, 23−45.

Gomez J.C. (1990) The emergence of intentional communication as a problem-solving strategy in the gorilla. In Parker S. & Gibson K. (eds) *Language and Intelligence in Monkeys and Apes: Comparative Developmental Perspectives*, pp. 333−355. Cambridge University Press, New York.

Gopnik M. (1990) Feature blindness: A case study. *Language Acquisition* **1**, 139−164.

Gopnik A. & Meltzoff A. (1986) Relations between semantic and cognitive development in the one-word stage: The specificity hypothesis. *Child Development* **57**, 1040−1053.

Gopnik A. & Meltzoff A. (1987) The development of categorization in the second year and its relation to other cognitive and linguistic developments. *Child Development* **58**, 1523−1531.

Gore C.C., Sarty M. & Wu P. (1975) Visual following and pattern discrimination of face-like stimuli by newborn infants. *Pediatrics* **56**, 544−549.

Greenberg J. & Kuczaj S. (1982) Towards a theory of substantive word-meaning acquisition. In Kuczaj S. (ed.) *Language Development*, Vol. 1, *Syntax and Semantics*, pp. 275−311. Lawrence Erlbaum, Hillsdale, New Jersey.

Grossman H. (1977) *Manual on Terminology and Classification in Mental Retardation*. American Association of Mental Deficiency, Washington, DC.

Hakuta K. (1986) *The Mirror of Language*. Basic Books, New York.

Halliday M.A.K. (1975) *Learning How to Mean: Explorations in the Development of Language*. Edward Arnold, London.

Haviland S. & Clark E.V. (1974) 'This man's father is my father's son': A study of the acquisition of English kin terms. *Journal of Child Language* **1**, 23−47.

Hemphill L., Picardi N. & Tager-Flusberg H. (1991) Narrative as an index of communicative competence in mildly mentally retarded children. *Applied Psycholinguistics* **12**, 263−279.

Horgan D. (1978) The development of the full passive. *Journal of Child Language* **5**, 63−80.

Howlin P. & Rutter M. (1987) The consequences of language delay for other aspects of development. In Yule W. & Rutter M. (eds) *Language Development and Disorders*, pp. 271−294. MacKeith Press, London.

Hyams N. (1986) *Language Acquisition and the Theory of Parameters*. Reidel, Dordrecht.

Hyams N. (1989) The null subject parameter in language acquisition. In Jaeggli O. & Safir K. (eds) *The Null Subject Parameter*, pp. 36−62. Kluwer, Dordrecht.

Jaffe J., Stern D. & Perry J. (1973) Conversational coupling of gaze behavior in prelinguistic human development. *Journal of Psycholinguistic Research* **2**, 321−329.

Jakobson R. (1968) *Child Language, Aphasia, and Phonological Universals*. Mouton, The Hague.

James S. & Seebach M. (1982) The pragmatic function of children's questions. *Journal of Speech and Hearing Research* **25**, 2−11.

Jeremy R.J. (1978) Use of coordinate sentences with the conjunction 'and' for describing temporal and locative relations between events. *Journal of Psycholinguistic Research* **7**, 135−150.

Johnston J. & Ramstad V. (1983) Cognitive development in preadolescent language impaired children. *British Journal of Disorders of Communication* **18**, 49−55.

Kamhi A. & Johnston J. (1982) Towards an understanding of retarded children's linguistic deficiencies. *Journal of Speech and Hearing Research* **25**, 435−445.

Kanner L. (1946) Irrelevant and metaphorical language. *American Journal of Psychiatry* **103**, 242−246.

Katz N., Baker E. & Macnamara J. (1974) What's in a name? A study of how children learn common and proper names. *Child Development* **45**, 469−473.

Klima E. & Bellugi U. (1966) Syntactic regularities in the speech of children. In Lyons J. & Wales R.J. *Psycholinguistic Papers*, pp. 183−208. Edinburgh University Press, Edinburgh.

Krauss R.M. & Glucksberg S. (1977) Social and non-social speech. *Scientific American* **236**, 100–105.

Lackner J. (1968) A developmental study of language behavior in retarded children. *Neuropsychologia* **6**, 301–320.

Landau B. & Gleitman L. (1985) *Language and Experience: Evidence from the Blind Child*. Harvard University Press, Cambridge, Massachusetts.

Lederberg A. (1980) The language environment of children with language delays. *Journal of Pediatric Psychology* **5**, 141–159.

Lenneberg E.H. (1967) *Biological Foundations of Language*. Wiley, New York.

Leonard L. (1982) Phonological deficits in children with developmental language impairment. *Brain and Language* **16**, 73–86.

Leonard L. (1987) Is specific language impairment a useful construct? In Rosenberg S. (ed.) *Advances in Applied Psycholinguistics*, Vol. I, *Disorders of First Language Development*, pp. 1–39. Cambridge University Press, Cambridge, Massachusetts.

Leonard L., Wilcox J., Fulmer K. & Davis A. (1978) Understanding indirect requests: An investigation of children's comprehension of pragmatic meanings. *Journal of Speech and Hearing Research* **21**, 528–537.

Leslie A. & Frith U. (1990) Prospects for a cognitive neuropsychology of autism: Hobson's choice. *Psychological Review* **97**, 122–131.

Leslie A. & Happe F. (1989) Autism and ostensive communication: The relevance of metarepresentation. *Development and Psychopathology* **1**, 205–212.

Leslie A. & Roth D. (1993) What autism teaches us about metarepresentation. In Baron-Cohen S., Tager-Flusberg H. & Cohen D.J. (eds) *Understanding Other Minds: Perspectives from Autism*, pp. 83–111. Oxford University Press, Oxford.

Levy Y. (1988) On the early learning of formal grammatical systems: Evidence from studies of the acquisition of gender and countability. *Journal of Child Language* **15**, 179–188.

Lieven E. (1978) Conversations between mothers and young children: Individual differences and their possible implications for the study of language learning. In Waterson N. & Snow C. (eds) *The Development of Communication*, pp. 173–187. Wiley, New York.

Lindholm K. & Padilla A. (1978) Language mixing in bilingual children. *Journal of Child Language* **5**, 327–335.

Locke J.L. (1992) Neural specializations for language: A developmental perspective. *Seminars in the Neurosciences* **4**, 425–431.

Macken M. & Ferguson C.A. (1982) Cognitive aspects of phonological development: Model, evidence, and issues. In Nelson K.E. (ed.) *Children's Language*, Vol. 4, pp. 131–149. Gardner Press, New York.

McLaughlin B. (1982) *Second Language Acquisition in Childhood*. Lawrence Erlbaum, Hillsdale, New Jersey.

Macnamara J. (1982) *Names for Things: A Study of Human Learning*. MIT Press, Cambridge, Massachusetts.

McNeill D. & McNeill N.B. (1968) What does a child mean when he says 'no'? In Zales E.M. (ed.) *Language and Language Behavior*, pp. 62–84. Appleton-Century-Crofts, New York.

Maratsos M. (1973) Preschoolers' use of definite and indefinite articles. *Child Development* **44**, 697–700.

Maratsos M., Kuczaj S.A., Fox D.M. & Chalkley M.A. (1979) Some empirical studies in the acquisition of transformational relations: Passives, negatives, and the past tense. In Collins W.A. (ed.) *Children's Language and Communication*, pp. 1–45. Lawrence Erlbaum, Hillsdale, New Jersey.

Markman E. (1989) *Categorization and Naming in Children*. MIT Press, Cambridge, Massachusetts.

Meltzoff A. & Moore M. (1977) Imitation of facial and manual gestures by human neonates. *Science* **198**, 75–78.

Menn L. (1971) Phonotactic rules in beginning speech. *Lingua* **26**, 225–251.

Menn L. (1983) Development of articulatory, phonetic and phonological capabilities. In Butterworth B. (ed.) *Language Production*, Vol. II, pp. 3–50. Academic Press, New York.

Menn L. (1989) Phonological development: learning sounds and sound patterns. In Gleason J.B. (ed.) *The Development of Language*, 2nd edn, pp. 59–100. Merrill, Columbus, Ohio.

Mermelstein R. (1983) *The relation between syntactic and pragmatic development in autistic, retarded, and normal children*. Paper presented at the Eighth Annual Boston University Conference on Language Development.

Mervis C. & Crisafi M. (1982) Order of acquisition of subordinate-, basic-, and superordinate-level categories. *Child Development* **53**, 258–266.

Miller J., Chapman R. & McKenzie H. (1981) *Individual differences in the language acquisition of mentally retarded children*. Paper presented at the Society for Research in Child Development, Boston, Massachusetts.

Morse P. (1972) The discrimination of speech and non-speech stimuli in early infancy. *Journal of Experimental Child Psychology* **14**, 477–492.

Mowrer O. (1954) A psychologist looks at language. *American Psychologist* **9**, 660–694.

Myers F. & Myers R. (1983) Perception of stress contrasts in semantic and nonsemantic contexts by children. *Journal of Psycholinguistic Research* **12**, 327–338.

Naremore R. & Dever R. (1975) Language performance of educable mentally retarded and normal children at five age levels. *Journal of Speech and Hearing Research* **18**, 82–92.

Naigles L. (1990) Children use syntax to learn verb meanings. *Journal of Child Language* **17**, 357–374.

Nelson K. (1973) Structure and strategy in learning

to talk. *Monographs of the Society for Research in Child Development* **38**, Serial No. 149.

Nelson K. (1974) Concept, word, and sentence: Interrelations in acquisition and development. *Psychological Review* **81**, 267–285.

Nelson K. (1981) Individual differences in language development: Implications for development and language. *Developmental Psychology* **17**, 170–187.

Nelson K. (1985) *Making Sense: The Acquisition of Shared Meaning.* Academic Press, New York.

Nelson K. (1988) Constraints on word learning? *Cognitive Development* **3**, 221–246.

Oller D.K. & Eilers R. (1988). The role of audition in infant babbling. *Child Development* **59**, 441–449.

Oller D., Wieman L., Doyle W. & Ross C. (1976) Infant babbling and speech. *Journal of Child Language* **3**, 1–12.

Olmsted D. (1971) *Out of the Mouth of Babes.* Mouton, The Hague.

Padilla A. & Leibman E. (1975) Language acquisition in the bilingual child. *Bilingual Review* **2**, 34–55.

Padilla A. & Lindholm K. (1976) Acquisition of bilingualism: A descriptive analysis of the linguistic structures of Spanish/English speaking children. In Keller G. (ed.) *Bilingualism in the Bicentennial and Beyond*, pp. 97–142. Bilingual Review Press, New York.

Paul R. (1987) Communication. In Cohen D.J. & Donnellan A.M. (eds) *Handbook of Austism and Pervasive Developmental Disorders*, pp. 61–84. Wiley, New York.

Peters A.M. (1977) Language learning strategies: Does the whole equal the sum of the parts? *Language* **53**, 560–573.

Piaget J. (1952) *The Origins of Intelligence in Children.* International University Press, New York.

Piaget J. (1962) *Play, Dreams, and Imitation in Childhood.* Norton, New York.

Pinker S. (1984) *Language Learnability and Language Development.* Harvard University Press, Cambridge, Massachusetts.

Pinker S. (1987) Constraint satisfaction networks as implementations of nativist theories of language acquisition. In MacWhinney B. (ed.) *Mechanisms of Language Learning*, pp. 399–441. Lawrence Erlbaum, Hillsdale, New Jersey.

Pinker S., Lebeaux D. & Frost L. (1987) Productivity and constraints in the acquisition of the passive. *Cognition* **26**, 195–267.

Prinz P. & Prinz E. (1979) Simultaneous acquisition of ASL and spoken English. *Sign Language Studies* **25**, 283–296.

Puckering C. & Rutter M. (1987) Environmental influences on language development. In Yule W. & Rutter M. (eds) *Language Development and Disorders*, pp. 103–128. MacKeith Press, London.

Pye C. (1988) *Precocious passives (and antipassives) in Quiche Mayan.* Paper presented at the Child Language Research Forum, Stanford, California.

Rapin I. & Allen D. (1983) Developmental language disorders: Nosologic considerations. In Kirk U. (ed.) *Neuropsychology of Language, Reading, and Spelling*, pp. 155–184. Academic Press, New York.

Redlinger W. & Park T. (1980) Language mixing in young bilinguals. *Journal of Child Language* **7**, 337–352.

Reeder K. (1980) The emergence of illocutionary skills. *Journal of Child Language* **7**, 13–28.

Reilly J., Klima E.S. & Bellugi U. (1990) Once more with feeling: Affect and language in atypical populations. *Development and Psychopathology* **2**, 367–391.

Rescorla L. & Schwartz E. (1990) Outcome of specific expressive language delay. *Applied Psycholinguistics* **11**, 393–407.

Rice M. (1990) Preschoolers' QUIL: Quick incidental learning of words. In Conti-Ramsden G. & Snow C.E. (eds) *Children's Language*, Vol. 7, pp. 171–195. Lawrence Erlbaum, Hillsdale, New Jersey.

Rice M. (1991) *Morphological deficits of specific language impairment: A matter of missing functional categories.* Paper presented at the Sixteenth Annual Boston University Conference on Language Development.

Rice M., Sell M.A. & Hadley P.A. (1991) Social interactions of speech and language impaired children. *Journal of Speech and Hearing Research* **34**, 1299–1307.

Rondal J. (1987) Language development and mental retardation. In Yule W. & Rutter M. (eds) *Language Development and Disorders*, pp. 248–261. MacKeith Press, London.

Rondal J. (1988) Language development in Down's syndrome: A life-span perspective. *International Journal of Behavioral Development* **11**, 21–36.

Rosch E., Mervis C., Gray W.D., Johnson D.M. & Boyes-Braem P. (1976) Basic objects in natural categories. *Cognitive Psychology* **8**, 382–439.

Rutter M. (1983) Cognitive deficits in the pathogenesis of autism. *Journal of Child Psychology and Psychiatry* **24**, 513–533.

Rutter M. (1987) The 'what' and 'how' of language development: a note on some outstanding issues and questions. In Yule W. & Rutter M. (eds) *Language Development and Disorders*, pp. 159–170. MacKeith Press, London.

Rutter M., Greenfeld D. & Lockyer L. (1967) A five to fifteen year follow up of infantile psychosis: II. Social and behavioural outcome. *British Journal of Psychiatry* **113**, 1183–1199.

Rutter M. & Mawhood L. (1991) The long-term psychosocial sequelae of specific developmental disorders of speech and language. In Rutter M. & Casaer P. (eds) *Biological Risk Factors for Psychosocial Disorders*, pp. 233–259. Cambridge University Press, Cambridge.

Ryan J. (1975) Mental subnormality and language development. In Lenneberg E. & Lenneberg E. (eds) *Foundations of Language Development.* Vol. 2, pp. 269–278. Academic Press, New York.

Seagoe M.W. (1965) Verbal development in a mongoloid. *Exceptional Children* **31**, 269–275.

Searle J.R. (1969) *Speech Acts*. Cambridge University Press, London.

Shatz M. (1974) *The comprehension of indirect directives: Can two-year-olds shut the door?* Paper presented at Linguistic Society of America.

Shatz M. (1982) On mechanisms of language acquisition: Can features of the communicative environment account for development? In Gleitman L. & Wanner E. (eds) *Language Acquisition: The State of the Art*, pp. 102–127. Cambridge University Press, New York.

Shatz M. & Gelman R. (1973) The development of communication skills: Modifications in the speech of young children as a function of the listener. *Monographs of the Society for Research in Child Development* **38**, Serial No. 152.

Silva P.A. (1987) Epidemiology, longitudinal course, and some associated factors: An update. In Yule W. & Rutter M. (eds) *Language Development and Disorders*, pp. 1–15. MacKeith Press, London.

Silva P., Williams S. & McGee R. (1987) A longitudinal study of children with development language delay at age three: Later intelligence, reading, and behavior problems. *Developmental Medicine and Child Neurology* **29**, 630–640.

Skuse D. (1984) Extreme deprivation in early childhood: II. Theoretical issues and a comparative review. *Journal of Child Psychology and Psychiatry* **25**, 543–572.

Slobin D.I. (1973) Cognitive prerequisites for the development of grammar. In Ferguson C.A. & Slobin D.I. (eds) *Studies of Child Language Development*, pp. 175–208. Holt, Rinehart & Winston, New York.

Slobin D.I. (ed.) (1985) *A Cross-linguistic Study of Language Acquisition*. Lawrence Erlbaum, Hillsdale, New Jersey.

Smith N. (1973) *The Acquisition of Phonology: A Case Study*. Cambridge University Press, Cambridge.

Snow C.E. & Ferguson C.A. (eds) (1977) *Talking to Children: Language Input and Acquisition*. Cambridge University Press, New York.

Stark R. (1986) Prespeech segmental feature development. In Fletcher P. & Garman M. (eds) *Language Acquisition*, 2nd edn, pp. 149–173. Cambridge University Press, New York.

Stoel-Gammon C. & Otomo K. (1986) Babbling development of hearing-impaired and normally hearing subjects. *Journal of Speech and Hearing Disorders* **51**, 33–41.

Suzman A. (1987) Passives and prototypes in Zulu children's speech. *African Studies* **46**, 241–254.

Swain M. (1972) *Bilingualism as a first language*. Unpublished doctoral dissertation, University of California, Irvine.

Tager-Flusberg H. (1985) The conceptual basis for referential word meaning in children with autism. *Child Development* **56**, 1167–1178.

Tager-Flusberg H. (1986) Constraints on the representation of word meaning: Evidence from autistic and mentally retarded children. In Kuczaj S. & Barrett M. (eds) *The Development of Word Meaning*, pp. 139–166. Springer, New York.

Tager-Flusberg H. (1988) On the nature of a language acquisition disorder: The example of autism. In Kessel F. (ed.) *The Development of Language and Language Researchers: Essays Presented to Roger Brown*, pp. 249–267. Lawrence Erlbaum, Hillsdale, New Jersey.

Tager-Flusberg H. (1989) A psycholinguistic perspective on language development in the autistic child. In Dawson G. (ed.) *Autism: Nature, Diagnosis, and Treatment*, pp. 92–115. Guilford, New York.

Tager-Flusberg H. (1993) What language reveals about the understanding of minds in children with autism. In Baron-Cohen S., Tager-Flusberg H. & Cohen D.J. (eds) *Understanding Other Minds: Perspectives from Autism*, pp. 138–157. Oxford University Press, Oxford.

Tager-Flusberg H. & Anderson M. (1991) The development of contingent discourse ability in autistic children. *Journal of Child Psychology and Psychiatry* **32**, 1123–1134.

Tager-Flusberg H. & Calkins S. (1990) Does imitation facilitate the acquisition of grammar? Evidence from autistic, Down syndrome and normal children. *Journal of Child Language* **17**, 591–606.

Tager-Flusberg H., Calkins S., Nolin T., Baumberger T., Anderson M. & Chadwick-Dias A. (1990) A longitudinal study of language acquisition in autistic and Down syndrome children. *Journal of Autism and Developmental Disorders* **20**, 1–20.

Tager-Flusberg H., de Villiers J. & Hakuta K. (1982) The development of sentence coordination. In Kuczaj S. (ed.) *Language Development*, Vol. I, *Syntax and Semantics*, pp. 201–245. Lawrence Erlbaum, Hillsdale, New Jersey.

Tallal P. & Piercy M. (1973) Defects of non-verbal auditory perception in children with developmental aphasia. *Nature* **241**, 468–469.

Tallal P. & Piercy M. (1974) Developmental aphasia: Rate of auditory processing and selective impairment of consonant perception. *Neuropsychologia* **12**, 83–93.

Templin M. (1957) *Certain Language Skills in Children*. University of Minnesota Press, Minneapolis.

Tomasello M. & Farrar M.J. (1984) Cognitive bases of lexical development: Object permanence and relational words. *Journal of Child Language* **11**, 477–493.

Trevarthen C. (1974) Prespeech in communication of infants with adults. *Journal of Child Language* **1**, 335–337.

Trevarthen C. (1979) Communication and cooperation in early infancy: A description of primary intersubjectivity. In Bullowa M. (ed.) *Before Speech*, pp. 321–349. Cambridge University Press, New York.

Trevarthen C. & Hubley P. (1978) Secondary intersubjectivity: Confidence, confiding, and acts of meaning in the first year. In Lock A. (ed.) *Action, Gesture, and*

Symbol: The Emergence of Language, pp. 183–230. Academic Press, New York.

Tyack D. & Ingram D. (1977) Children's production and comprehension of questions. *Journal of Child Language* **4**, 211–224.

Vaidyanathan R. (1988) Development of forms and functions of interrogatives in children: A longitudinal study in Tamil. *Journal of Child Language* **15**, 533–549.

Vaidyanathan R. (1991) Development of forms and functions of negation in the early stages of language acquisition: A study of Tamil. *Journal of Child Language* **18**, 51–66.

Vihman M. (1976) From prespeech to speech: On early phonology. *Papers and Reports on Child Language Development* **12**, 36–48.

Vihman M. (1985) Language differentiation by the bilingual infant. *Journal of Child Language* **12**, 297–324.

Volden J. & Lord C. (1991) Neologism and idiosyncratic language in autistic speakers. *Journal of Autism and Developmental Disorders* **21**, 109–130.

Weeks T. (1971) Speech registers in young children. *Child Development* **42**, 1119–1131.

Wellen C. & Broen P. (1982) The interruption of young children's responses by older siblings. *Journal of Speech and Hearing Disorders* **47**, 204–210.

Wetherby A.M. (1986) Ontogeny of communication functions in autism. *Journal of Austism and Developmental Disorders* **16**, 295–316.

Whorf B.L. (1956) *Language, Thought and Reality*. MIT Press, Cambridge, Massachusetts.

Williams R. (1978) *Play behavior of language-handicapped and normal-speaking preschool children*. Paper presented at the American Speech-Language-Hearing Association, San Francisco, California.

Wing L. & Atwood A. (1987) Syndromes of autism and atypical development. In Cohen D.J. & Donnellan A.M. (eds) *Handbook of Autism and Pervasive Developmental Disorders*, pp. 3–19. Wiley, New York.

Winzemer J. (1980) *A lexical expectation model for children's comprehension of wh-questions*. Paper presented at the Fifth Annual Boston University Conference on Language Development.

Wulbert M., Inglis S., Kriegsman E. & Mills B. (1975) Language delay and associated mother–child interactions. *Developmental Psychology* **11**, 61–70.

10: Cognition In and Out of Context: a Tale of Two Paradigms

STEPHEN J. CECI, URIE BRONFENBRENNER AND
JACQUELINE G. BAKER-SENNETT

INTRODUCTION

The history of twentieth century cognitive psychology is, in many respects, the history of two paradigms. On the one hand, there is a group of cognitive scientists who can today trace the origin of their work to the earliest psychological research on memory and perception, originating with the German psychologist, Hermann Ebbinghaus (1885) in the 1880s. These early explorers, with only a few exceptions, viewed the study of human cognition as a form of 'pure' science, rooted in the same kind of universal principles as classical physics. Their pursuit of knowledge about human cognition resulted in research on thinking and reasoning disembedded from the everyday contexts in which people developed. Such study nevertheless proved valuable in two ways. First, it generated information applicable to and valued in the contexts in which the research was conducted. Second, it provided the foundation for the development of a contrasting approach.

The adherents of the second paradigm studied cognition embedded in the content and context of prior knowledge and experience. This tradition, originating with Bartlett (1932) in the 1930s, emphasized the importance of studying cognition in its substantive and social context. For almost two decades this new theoretical paradigm remained unrecognized and its scientific power overlooked. It was not until the late 1960s that it experienced a rebirth in the work of Ulric Neisser (1967). Since that time, the key role of context in cognitive development has received increasing attention in both theory and empirical work.

This chapter traces the evolution of both of these theoretical trajectories and, ultimately, argues for the integration of the two approaches in a more coherent and complementary theoretical framework. More specifically, we propose that everyday cognition reflects the operation of contextual elicitors and moderators that significantly influence the form, power and direction of cognitive functioning and development.

Investigators in this sphere have used the term context in two different senses. It was first applied to the psychological framework persons bring with them to a mental task. Each individual, it is argued, perceives and understands phenomena by means of structured representations; that is, a phenomenon is assimilated into a pre-existing framework, or else a framework must be created or altered to accomodate what is being experienced. The more one knows about a specific domain (e.g. chess) and the more integrated one's knowledge in this domain is, the more elaborate the cognitive structure will be. This is an example of a mental context: as will be seen, the manner in which individuals represent phenomena in a domain exerts a powerful influence on their problem-solving ability in that domain.

More recently, the term context has also been used to refer to an aspect of the environment that is external to the organism (Bronfenbrenner, 1979). It is in this sense that we speak of the physical and social setting that influences cognition. Later, examples of this phenomenon will be described. At this point, however, we call attention to what the two senses of the concept have in common; namely, both involve, and take into account, the framework, mental and environmental, in which cognition takes place. It is through interaction with persons and objects that individuals develop presentations of mental and environmental contexts that either invite or dissuade interaction (i.e. a motivational dynamic). Moreover, through experience mental representations become increasingly elaborated and integrated so that the individual makes more differentiated distinctions and classifications that aid cognition.

A BRIEF HISTORY OF THE STUDY OF COGNITION

One hundred years ago, Ebbinghaus created 2300 meaningless consonant–vowel–consonant syllables that possessed no semantic relationship with adjacent syllables in the list (e.g. 'nin', 'dalt'). These became known as nonsense syllables. Ebbinghaus served as his own subject, as he attempted to memorize these syllables repeatedly. He then plotted retention curves revealed by his analysis. In so doing, Ebbinghaus was able to provide estimates of the learning that resulted when the same meaningless stimuli were represented at a later time. Thus began what was to become a systematic study of human memory out of context. Ebbinghaus introduced to the field of psychology a number of concepts such as 'savings', 'retention curves' and, of course, the nonsense syllable itself (Ebbinghaus, 1885).

This approach to the study of memory was to have an enormous influence on the practices and values of cognitive psychologists for the next century. Although Ebbinghaus recognized that the use of highly artificial conditions in his study of memory might differ in important ways from the way individuals remember in everyday contexts, he felt that his procedures allowed him to obtain estimates of basic processing parameters uncontaminated by individual differences in pre-existing knowledge about the stimuli. Ebbinghaus argued that had he used everyday memory tasks, such as recalling shopping lists or addresses, there might have been some individuals who had greater familiarity with such materials than others, and this would have obscured the assessment of their 'true' memory ability. Instead, Ebbinghaus opted to purge the study of memory of all context in the hope that doing so would permit him to access the underlying memory system. In the preface to his classic volume, Ebbinghaus wrote that the study of everyday memory would eventually need to move outside of the laboratory, and to use meaningful contexts, but his words seem not to have been heard by most of those who succeeded him.

Most memory researchers, however, continued along the path charted by Ebbinghaus, focusing on the study of memory out of context. These researchers conducted thousands of studies of the basic processing parameters of various aspects of memory, and did so by using highly artificial conditions and stimuli. The 1960s were the heyday for this type of research, when investigators diligently and creatively probed the memory system and quantified its various operations. A tradition sprang up, called 'verbal learning', in which the dominant paradigm was the acquisition of word lists and the generation of verbal associations. Like Ebbinghaus before them, these researchers took great care to control all aspects of the stimuli they used, including the association value, concreteness, frequency of appearance in written and spoken language, etc. The assumption was that it was necessary to slavishly sanitize the material to be remembered, so that no extraneous variable (such as concreteness or meaningfulness) could be invoked to account for the findings. Researchers were in search of universal principles, not stimulus-specific findings. And they found many — or so they thought.

Around the turn of this century, a group of investigators began to challenge the view that cognition could be adequately studied out of context (e.g. Henderson, 1903; Whipple, 1915). This view was most fully and systematically set forth by the Cambridge psychologist, Sir Frederick Bartlett (1932). It is of interest that Bartlett, and a few others like him who chose not to follow the path that Ebbinghaus had traced, had little influence on their contemporaries. In Britain, Bartlett was largely ignored by his colleagues and students, though today it is acknowledged that he anticipated a major and important line of research that arguably was more influential than that begun by Ebbinghaus. Certainly today, a large number of memory researchers are following the Bartlettian tradition of studying memory in mental context (e.g. see edited volumes by Rogoff & Lave, 1984; Gruneberg *et al.*, 1989; Fivush & Hudson, 1990; Doris, 1991; Winograd & Neisser, 1992; Light & Butterworth, 1994).

What are the hallmarks of Bartlett's approach? First, he departed from the mechanical view of human memory. In its place, he proposed that memory was a dynamic process in which one's prior beliefs, values, experience, and knowledge were used to make sense of incoming stimuli. He referred to this process as 'effort after meaning', by which he meant that human beings attempt to make sense of what they confront in a memory task, deploying their beliefs and knowledge of the world in the process. Bartlett showed that, even when verbatim recall is poor, the gist of what was studied may be easily retained, particularly if the subject tries to 'make sense' of it.

For example, Bartlett's subjects were given stories about anomalous events and later asked to recall them. The most famous of these, *The War of the Ghosts*, described two young Indians who while canoeing meet a war party of other Indians, who invite them to join in a raid. One of the young Indians in the canoe declines, but his companion joins, and is injured in an encounter. He is taken back to his home where, after surviving the night, he dies at sunrise. In the course of the story a number of unusual things occur that had little meaning for Bartlett's Cambridge University subjects. Indeed, these events were completely incomprehensible to Western minds because they hinted at ghosts and unfamiliar symbolism.

Bartlett discovered that his subjects, when they attempted to recall *The War of the Ghosts*, reconstructed the plot to make it fit with their own beliefs. Through findings such as these, Bartlett challenged the entire tradition of Ebbinghaus by asserting that memory was not merely a mechanical input/output (encoding/retrieval) system but a highly dynamic process that distorted what was presented to make it fit with one's pre-existing belief and knowledge. Thus, memory could not be separated from the rest of cognitive and social experience. To evaluate it independently from the other processes was akin to evaluating a smile independently of the face on which it appears. For Bartlett, it made little sense to strip memory tasks of context because such tasks were inevitably imbued with meaning for subjects.

The cognitive revolution

By the late 1960s the so-called 'cognitive revolution' was just getting under way in psychology, and Bartlett was rediscovered. A new generation of cognitivists departed from the mechanical view of Ebbinghaus in favour of an approach similar to

Bartlett's. This shift is reflected in the introduction of such concepts as 'schema', 'scripts' and 'semantic representations' to explain the manner in which one's past knowledge influenced present cognition. The term *schema*, which was first introduced to psychologists by Bartlett (who borrowed it from the neurologist Sir Henry Head), refers to a structured body of facts about a concept that organizes information about that concept in an orderly representation (e.g. one has a schema for baseball, wild animals, and so on). A related term, *script*, refers to temporally ordered information about a habitual event (e.g. what normally happens in a given setting or situation such as at a restaurant, a doctors's office or an exercise class). Scripts lead us to expect the order in which events occur — first, second, and so on. When stories are presented that violate their script, subjects commonly reorder the sequence of events to fit the script. Scripts can be changed, but it usually requires repeated violations of a pre-existing script for this to happen.

By invoking concepts like schema and script, cognitivists were stepping outside of Ebbinghaus' acontextual tradition; they were promulgating a view that embedded cognition in a larger framework including not only a set of encoding, storage and retrieval processes, but also what the organism knew and felt about what was being processed.

Broadening the Ebbinghaus tradition. There were two primary stimuli for retaining but expanding the classical model of cognition. First, findings began to appear that were difficult to reconcile with the psychological principles that had been derived from the exclusive study of memory out of context. For example, there was nothing in the verbal learning literature that would have led to the prediction of a learning curve like the one Bahrick (1984) found for older adults' retention of Spanish 40 years after they studied it in high school; namely, he demonstrated that older adults retained more Spanish than would have been expected on the basis of classical forgetting curves, and their forgetting levelled off within the first few years following high school. Neither of these findings would have been predicted from research conducted within the Ebbinghaus tradition. Similarly, nothing in the verbal learning literature to led to the expectation that recency effects would be as enduring as

Baddeley and Hitch (1977) observed them to be when they studied rugby players' recall of teams they had played during the past season. Prior to their work, recency effects were not thought to endure beyond a few seconds. Rugby players' memories of the last few teams they played in a past season, however, lasted far longer than would have been thought possible from the perspective of classical cognitive theory and research. In sum, when researchers ventured outside of the laboratory and examined cognition in everyday contexts, they made discoveries that were difficult to reconcile with principles that had been constructed exclusively on the basis of laboratory studies of cognitive behaviours that had no real-world analogue.

A second stimulus for the departure from the Ebbinghaus tradition was of a different sort. It was a person named Ulric Neisser. Neisser is often credited with starting the cognitive revolution by reintroducing Bartlett to cognitive psychologists in his influential book *Cognitive Psychology* (1967). Later, Neisser (1982) enjoined cognitive psychologists to study the types of cognition that occurred in everyday contexts. He authored several books that reported on studies of real-world types of remembering, such as that produced by a defendant in the American Watergate scandal in 1974 (*John Dean's memory*), and, more recently, children's recollections of the space shuttle disaster in 1987 (*Challenger*). Neisser urged psychologists not to build laboratory models of memory processes that had no real-world analogues, because to do so might result in elegant descriptions of behaviours that had little relevance in the real world. Note that he did not argue against laboratory studies of cognition, but only against those laboratory studies that had no real-world analogue.

In making this entreaty, Neisser (1978) lamented psychology's 'thundering silence' on questions of interest and importance in our everyday lives, e.g. remembering appointments. He asked why it is that we may forget what we had for breakfast today yet remember our way around our home town after a 30-year absence. He pointed to the fact that the truly interesting issues (such as why early childhood is a period of near complete mnemonic inaccessibility for adults) are avoided by those working out of the Ebbinghaus tradition, while the problems that are studied merely reaffirm our preconceived theories. He could not point to a single finding in the field that his Aunt Martha would have judged interesting and important. Such strong entreaty did not pass unnoticed or unrebutted by those favouring the Ebbinghaus tradition. For example, Banaji and Crowder (1989) argued forcefully that the study of cognition in everyday settings was ill-wrought because it could not result in generalization beyond the specific context. In addition, they pointed out that many studies of everyday cognition could be criticized on similar grounds.

Why have some cognitivists disdained context?

The reason for traditionally giving context short-shrift is not difficult to find; taking physics as their theoretical model, psychologists have generally preferred universal explanations of cognition, as opposed to those that are situationally bound (Weisz, 1978); that is, they hoped to show that a process operates unchanged across the idiosyncrasies and vicissitudes of context. Consistent with this long-held view, Weisz (1978) asserted that the ultimate goal of science is to find universal principles that 'can be shown to hold across physical and cultural setting, time, or cohort' (p. 2). Many others have similarly argued that scientific methods can only succeed if the 'operations of invariant mechanisms can be shown' (Banaji & Crowder, 1989, p. 1188).

But in their search for universal cognitive mechanisms, laboratory researchers have misconstrued an important function of all developmental sciences. A distinctive property of species *Homo sapiens* is its ability to adapt to its environment, to respond differentially to different contexts. This insight led Bronfenbrenner (1979) to decry the search for context-invariant mechanisms as illusory.

> One can question whether establishing transcontextual validity is ... the ultimate goal of science ... Given the ecologically interactive character of behavior and development in humans, processes that are invariant across contexts are likely to be few in number and fairly close to the physiological level. What behavioral scientists should be seeking, therefore, are not primarily these

universals but rather the laws of invariance at the next higher level — principles that describe how processes are mediated by the general properties of settings and of more remote aspects of the ecological environment. (p. 128)

Current cognitive research: a semi-reconciliation

By the late 1960s, psychologists in both traditions were beginning to borrow from each other. On the one hand, those who followed Neisser, in the line begun by Bartlett, started utilizing paradigms from the Ebbinghaus tradition. On the other hand, adherents of the classical view maintained their study of cognition in highly restricted laboratory contexts, but often with the addition of some socially meaningful variables (e.g. reading text on a computer screen that describes some personally meaningful event). Today, followers of the Ebbinghaus line continue to search for universal principles by decomposing basic cognitive processes into their micro components, and by manipulating variables thought to influence the efficiency of each component. Rarely, however, do they sanitize their tasks of all context the way that Ebbinghaus once did.

Factors continuing from the Ebbinghaus Tradition

In what follows we provide a synopsis of the Bartlettian and Ebbinghaus legacies as continued by today's cognitive psychologists. As will be seen, it is sometimes difficult to characterize research as either totally in or out of context, because many contemporary studies combine Bartlettian paradigms with Ebbinghaus' mechanical orientation and search for universal principles. Nowhere is this more apparent than in the area called 'information processing'.

The most basic distinction among information processing researchers is that between two types of long-term memory, semantic and episodic memory, a distinction made popular by Tulving (1983). This is the distinction between remembering information about conceptual knowledge and language, such as fruits or animals, or the rules of arithmetic, such as recalling what 2×6 equals. This type of information is called semantic knowledge, and it is context-free. In contrast, episodic memory refers to the recollection that a particular fruit or animal was on a list that we were asked to recall, or that we were sitting in a specific chair when we last recalled how much 2×6 was. Thus, episodic memory is autobiographical in the sense that recollection conveys information about its specific temporal and spatial occurrence. We recall where and when we last saw an item or performed a computation, whereas the semantic knowledge about the item or computation is independent of its last occurrence. Episodic memory is constantly changing, whereas semantic memory changes much more slowly. Semantic and episodic memories differ in their susceptibility to forgetting and interference (Klatzky, 1980). From Ebbinghaus to the present, the study of memory has primarily been the study of episodic memory. Only during the past decade has the study of semantic memory taken on greater importance, as clinical studies of various pathologies have suggested that semantic deficits are of interest.

Another basic information processing distinction is that of short-term versus long-term memory (Baddeley, 1988). Basically, this is the distinction between the neurological site of information we are currently thinking of (i.e. the seat of consciousness) and information not currently in consciousness. Short-term memory refers to the former. It is also labelled 'working memory', 'primary memory' and 'immediate memory', all to suggest its role in ongoing cognitions. The capacity of short-term memory is tightly restricted. For example, verbal material such as a word or label is lost from it in less than 30 seconds unless it is refreshed through rehearsal. Only about seven items can be held in short-term memory simultaneously. Additional items can enter only if currently stored items are lost. In contrast, long-term memory is the repository of all semantic and procedural knowledge we possess. It is thought to be limitless in storage space, though this is still open to debate. Many cognitive tasks require an interplay between the contents of long-term and short-term memory, as when we need to retrieve semantic rules from long-term storage and deploy them consciously to solve some current problem. Numerous experiments have shown dissociations between short-term and long-term memory, and various clinical syndromes are localizable at one or the other.

Researchers in this domain undertake analyses of the various operations that individuals employ to transform a sensory event into a meaningful act (e.g. the recognition of a visual array as a familiar face). Today, the primary variables that have been studied by this group are the following: strategies, knowledge and metacognition. Aspects of Bartlett's constructivism are often incorporated into these studies, particularly the latter's emphasis on 'effort after meaning', and the role of knowledge in remembering.

Three factors have been used to describe the development of the information processing, strategies, knowledge and metacognitive insights (Brown, 1975). These three factors have been the subject of intensive research by developmentalists attempting to devise universal theories of how children remember. For the most part, these studies follow the Ebbinghaus tradition of seeking to discover trans-contextual processes. Correspondingly, their findings are more effective in accounting for cognitive processes in the laboratory than in settings of everyday life.

Strategies. The essence of strategic cognitive behaviour is its planful and goal-oriented character (Kail, 1990). Numerous strategies have been researched, but the two that have received the most attention are rehearsal and organization. In rehearsal, items to be recalled are mentally repeated. Rehearsal refers to an entire class of behaviours that range from simply repeating items without any transformation of them, to transforming them in the process of repetition (e.g. converting a list of numbers such as 1−1−1−9−5−0 to a birthdate such as 1 January 1950, then repeating it covertly).

Strategies develop in different ways, depending on their complexity. Rehearsal of several items together does not appear before the age of 7, and often not until much later. Flexible rehearsal (e.g. repeating only those items that were forgotten on prior retrieval attempts) does not occur before the age of 12 or 13. For example, when given the chance to restudy a list of items, children younger than 7 will not give preferential rehearsal to those items they previously failed to recall. In general,

the literature on strategies characterizes the young child as far more passive than older children and adults; older children spontaneously engage in strategies, and the use of strategies can be directly linked to their superior memory and problem solving ability.

Organizational strategies refer to a group of behaviours that involve the use of some conceptual basis to link items that share a common attribute. Thus, if one were presented a list of words to recall, it would behove him or her to try to group those words together that share some feature. For example, all of the words that refer to animals may be linked together, as well as all of those referring to fruits, transports, and so on. Organizing a list of words in this way facilitates retention.

But the ability to organize is intimately tied to the amount and type of knowledge an individual possesses. It does little good to encourage children to organize a list if they have no appreciation of the attributes that the items on the list share. This is especially critical when the child being tested is from a culturally different background. And sometimes even if the shared attributes are known by the child being tested, he or she does not perceive their commonality during the act of remembering. For instance, suppose you are presented three animals at a time and are later asked to recall them. The first three animals are: dog, cow, pig; the next three are: cat, horse, sparrow; the next three are: chicken, squirrel, deer; and the final three are: lion, zebra, rhinoceros. When such three-word lists are presented to subjects, the first three are usually recalled perfectly. But as one attempts to recall more, recall suffers greatly. The reason it suffers is that efficacy of the retrieval cue (in this example, the cue 'animal') becomes overloaded with exemplars, and retroactive interference builds up, wherein the earlier items inhibit the recall of the later ones. This is referred to as the cue-overload effect, and it is a robust finding. By the time one gets to the final three items on the list, recall is very poor. But if the subject realizes that the last three items share a new common attribute (they are all 'exotic' animals), then this allows the use of a new retrieval cue (exotic or African), with the result being that they will recall all three final items perfectly. Normally, people possess such knowledge but they fail to perceive its relevance when they are trying to recall. It is an example of the interplay between strategies and knowledge.

Knowledge. The amount and type of knowledge people possess about a particular domain (e.g. sports, cooking, science) influences the extent and content of what they remember, as well as how well they solve problems, in that domain. For example, it has been shown (Means & Voss, 1985; Walker, 1987; Coltheart & Walsh, 1988) that if a house tour is presented in a house-buying context it will instantiate different knowledge structures among professional burglars than prospective home-buyers, and significantly different memory performance will result (Logie & Wright, 1988). Similarly, depending on whether the material is presented as part of a baseball game, a bird-watching exercise, or a Star Wars game, it can have dramatically different consequences because it will activate different bodies of knowledge that can be used to draw different inferences and create different expectations (Means & Voss, 1985; Walker, 1987; Coltheart & Walsh, 1988). These kinds of 'knowledge effects' have been the grist for a decade of research on adult expertise. If the problem-solving task requires the use of a well-structured domain of knowledge, then performance is enhanced. Ten-year-old chess experts can recall board positions of games better than can graduate students who are not chess experts (Chi, 1978), even though their memory for non-chess material is inferior to that of the graduate students.

As can be seen from the above investigations, modern studies are not as devoid of context as Ebbinghaus' classic studies were. Specifically, the representation of knowledge can be viewed as a context that differentiates the efficiency of memory and problem-solving ability. Tasks that are couched in rich knowledge contexts are easier to solve. Yet, this research has as its aim the discovery of trans-contextual principles that are insensitive to properties of settings, personal beliefs and values. In contrast, the work reported below involves context in an even more prominent role.

Factors continuing from the Bartlettian tradition

Unlike the research in the Ebbinghaus tradition, contemporary research deriving from Bartlett's work can not be described in terms of specific variables or processes. Instead, it tends to focus on the entire psychological system, rather than only isolated parts of it. For example, it is common for modern researchers in the Bartlettian tradition to use stimuli that produce strong emotional responses in their subjects (such as memories for past accidents, love affairs, deaths of parents, etc.); to investigate the role of personal beliefs in the reconstruction of one's past (e.g. one's belief in their political stability); or to study the cognitive, social and cultural factors that influence deceit. In short, contemporary Bartlettian research grapples with the interaction of multiple psychological systems, some social, some cognitive and some biological. A brief description is provided of some of these lines of research so the reader can judge how they differ from the studies in the Ebbinghaus mode. Following this brief description, we review some of our own work that attempts to make explicit connections between the Ebbinghaus and Bartlettian traditions.

Autobiographical memory. One of the most important areas of everyday cognitive research concerns the ability to recollect personally experienced, emotionally salient events, so-called autobiographical memories. Some researchers believe that autobiographical recall is a highly constructive process, with subjects' current personal beliefs guiding their recollections of past behaviours and beliefs. Personal beliefs form a powerful filter through which autobiographical information is reconstructed, as Ross (1989) has shown in his work. By analysing longitudinal data in which individuals were asked for their opinions about personal experiences, he was able to demonstrate that their current recollections were shaped by a web of beliefs they held about the stability of feelings. Thus, events such as one's past medical problems, prior political beliefs and former romantic relationships appear to be recollected according to one's current attitudes and beliefs, and not strictly in terms of the historical events themselves. For example, a middle-aged woman's memory of the pain associated with her menstrual cycle when she was young turned out to be a function of her implicit theory of consistency over time, and her current state of menstrual pain, rather than her actual experiences with menstruation when she was young. To take another example, we tend to believe that we are politically consistent, with the result that our recollection of our past electoral preferences is guided by our current political philosophy (Ross, 1989). Work in the autobiographical tradition is a direct descendant of Bartlett's idea of a schema, but here it is a personal schema that directs one's recollections. Our personal schema contains information about what kind of person we see ourselves as, including our values, expectations and beliefs.

Autobiographical recall often involves emotionally salient events such as assassinations of political figures, airline crashes and romantic experiences. It is because of this emotional salience that some researchers claim these types of memories cannot be adequately understood in the same manner that out-of-context memorizing can. Currently, there is also debate as to whether high levels of emotionality at the time of an experience render the subsequent memory of the experience more or less accessible, resistant to suggestions or constructive (see Winograd & Neisser, 1992, for a variety of research and opinions on the role of affect in memory).

Lying. Lying can be defined as the deliberate production of a response that one believes to be incorrect for the purpose of misleading another into believing that it is correct. According to this definition, it is not necessary for one to infer the contents of the listener's mind (cf. Chandler, 1989). False productions to achieve some goal without trying to mislead another may happen when, for example, a child makes a false statement merely because of a desire to appear 'good' to the listener, independent of any idea of the listener's stance on this issue. In order to lie successfully according to the definition above, however, one needs at least a rudimentary 'model of mind', that is, to have some appreciation of how another will interpret what one says (Flanagan, 1993).

One might think that sophisticated forms of deception are beyond the grasp of very young chil-

dren, since more traditional research seems to indicate they are unable to assume an alternate reality and modify their own stance accordingly. But this conclusion is not supported by investigators who have moved beyond the laboratory into ecologically interactive contexts that are imbued with meaningful motives for young children.

A variety of psychological and social factors have been shown to influence the accuracy of children's statements, such as threats, inducements and various 'demand characteristics'. Any of these can take a toll on the accuracy of children's reports. If children are fearful about certain disclosures (e.g. disclosing to an interviewer that they saw their parent break a toy that the parent had been told not to touch), then this can lead to their 'keeping secrets' (Bottoms *et al.*, 1990; Peters, 1990; Bussey, 1993). Similarly, the possibility of gaining material rewards, avoiding embarrassment, and conforming to a stereotype all can lead to inaccurate reports (Ceci & Bruck, 1993). Finally, children's definition of what it means to lie is also capable of producing distortions in their reports. If they are told by their mothers that they should mislead a police officer when they are interviewed, 29% of preschoolers readily do this (Haugaard *et al.*, 1991), apparently because their own understanding of what it means to lie is incompatible with the idea that their loved ones lie. Thus, if their mothers told them this is what happened, then it must have happened, because their mothers are not liars.

Evidence of the sophistication of very young children's lies comes from research that attempts to insert a strong social context into the experiment and embed the assessment in the child's everyday ecology. Ceci and Leichtman (1992) showed that children as young as 30 months old frequently misled interviewers about events that they believed the interviewers did not observe. They did this to gain material rewards, avoid punishments and protect loved ones. When interviewed by a different person who did observe the events, the children shifted their reports to be consistent with the observer's knowledge. Below, we provide a brief description of one part of their study, showing how children differentiate their statements in accordance with their assumptions about their listener's beliefs.

Soon after a child's arrival at a nursery playroom

with a parent or baby-sitter, a confederate who assumed the role of a nursery schoolteacher instructed 3 year olds and their parents or sitters not to play with a particularly attractive mechanical toy. After the confederate left the room, the parent/sitter touched and pretended to break the forbidden toy, remarking, 'Gee, I didn't mean to break it. I hope I don't get into trouble'. Several minutes following this episode, the parent/sitter also committed other violations of several norms, including borrowing two small toys (stating 'these will not be missed'). Following these behaviours, the parent/sitter excused herself from the playroom to do some chores and promised to return shortly. While she was out of the room the confederate teacher returned and questioned the child in the parent's or sitter's absence. During this interrogation the child was asked whether he or she knew who had broken the toy and who had taken the small toys. Following the questioning, the confederate teacher left the room. Approximately 45 min later, when the parent/sitter returned, they asked the children whether the teacher had returned during her absence and, if so, whether the child had told the teacher who had broken the toy and who had taken the two small toys.

Interestingly, two-thirds of the children told the confederate teacher they did not know who broke the toy, or that it was someone other than their parent/sitter. But when their parent/sitter returned, these same children usually reported that they had told the teacher the truth (i.e. that it was their mother or babysitter who had touched the taboo toy and broken it)! In other words, it seems as though these 3 year olds believe that the teacher does not know who broke the toy, so they mislead her by claiming they do not know; they also believe that the parent does not know what they told the teacher, but assume that the parent would want them to tell her the truth, so they also lie to the parent/sitter by claiming to have told the teacher the truth. This suggests that even fairly young children possess some 'theory of mind', but it may not be exhibited unless the context is one that represents for them an important environmental challenge, such as protecting a loved one while simultaneously appearing to meet the loved one's standards of honesty.

Infantile amnesia. Experiences during the first 2 years of life are seemingly inaccessible to older children and adults, a condition known as infantile amnesia (Pillemer & White, 1989). The study of infantile amnesia is a meeting ground for researchers from both the Ebbinghaus and Bartlettian traditions. According to the findings of these researchers, the ability to recall our past is not without boundaries. The inability of older individuals to remember events that occurred before the age of 4 or 5 presents somewhat of a parodox for developmentalists because we take it as an article of faith that early experiences influence later behaviour and bad experiences during early childhood may even be associated with later forms of psychopathology such as depression. Thus, while it is agreed that the environment during early development is important, documenting children's ability to process consciously and retain experiences from their environment has proven to be quite difficult.

Numerous studies, employing research designs out of the Ebbinghaus tradition (both prospective and retrospective), have demonstrated the almost total occlusion of early experience from later efforts to recall them (see Howe & Courage, 1993 for review). According to these studies, memory is absent for this early period and context would not seem to matter much. But this view has been challenged by others who offer evidence that the context of early experience influences whether it will be recollected accurately; that is, some early contexts are more supportive of later recall than are others.

For example, Usher and Neisser (1993) have shown that the ability to recollect an early childhood experience depends on the nature of the experience (e.g. its emotional salience) and the degree of its rehearsal. These investigators found that adults could recollect births of their younger siblings that occurred when they themselves were as young as 24 months old. And these same adults could recall details of moving to a different home when they were as young as 36 months. In contrast, deaths of grandparents could not be recalled if they occurred prior to when the adult was 48 months old, probably because these are not highly publicized events in most families and there is little adult-provided rehearsal. (Since the child is so young, they lack the linguistic ability to rehearse it, so they are dependent on their family members for discussing it.) In short, according to contextualists, infantile amnesia is a variable phenomenon between the ages of 24 and 48 months, rather than demarcated by a crisp cut-off point around 36 months, as once thought by researchers working out of the Ebbinghaus tradition. The context of the early experience matters.

Eyewitness testimony of children. Increasingly, children are making forays into North American and British courtrooms to offer their uncorroborated testimony about events they witnessed. The most common context for their testimony is that of alleged sexual abuse. Sexual molestation of children is a crime that, by its very nature, is private. Because there are seldom witnesses to sexual abuse, other than the victim and perpetrator, and because medical evidence is too elliptical, courts have come to rely on the child's testimony with increasing frequency. Researchers working out of the Bartlettian tradition have designed scores of studies of children's testimonial accuracy by examining the influence of personal beliefs, motives and emotional arousal upon what is recalled. A typical context for such research is to assess children's recall of details for a genital examination that occurred at the doctor's office.

Recently, we have reviewed the scientific and legal literature on children's testimonial competence (Ceci & Bruck, 1993). It is an area fraught with contradictory findings. Some studies depict the young child witness as hopelessly vulnerable to confusions between reality and fantasy, susceptible to leading questions and erroneous suggestions by an interrogator, and eager to please adult authority figures. In contrast, other studies characterize young child witnesses as resistant to suggestions, and able to distinguish between fantasy and reality, at least when the context was an autobiographical event that involved their own bodies and in which they were a participant as opposed to a bystander.

Probably the most prudent conclusion to be drawn from this large and contradictory literature is that children's memory in everyday contexts is uneven. It depends on a host of factors that have to do with the prevalent motivations, the manner of questioning and the degree of the child's participation. The bulk of the evidence demonstrates that

there are reliable age differences in suggestibility, with younger children falling prey to leading questions more than older children and adults. If an interviewer uses leading questions (e.g. 'Did the woman's glasses break in the struggle?' when she was not wearing glasses), preschool children are disproportionately more likely to later claim that she was wearing glasses than are older children and adults. This does not mean that young child witnesses cannot provide the courts with forensically valuable testimony — they most certainly can. But it does mean that there is a need to take into consideration the motives of those who have had access to the child prior to the testimony, and the type of questioning that was used.

The major dispute that remains unresolved, to date, is whether leading questions alter a child's memory for the original event or whether they merely prompt the child to acquiesce to their impressions of an interviewer's wishes. Approximately 90% of the studies that have examined preschoolers' reports of witnessed events (16 out of 18) have found youngsters to be susceptible to an interviewer's suggestions. But there is a debate raging over whether this is because they incorporated the interviewer's suggestions into their memory, or merely that they trusted and/or wanted to please the interviewer and set aside their own memories in favour of his or hers (for review, see Ceci & Bruck, 1993; Zaragoza *et al.*, 1992).

Interviewing. The final aspect of everyday cognition that we shall discuss concerns the manner in which information is obtained. The focus here is on the interview format, as this is the single most common vehicle used in everyday settings to elicit reports of memories. It is also the method that poses the most serious problems.

An interview is a form of conversation in which one party tries directly and indirectly to obtain a complete and accurate account from the other party. To be successful, participants must have an understanding of a broad set of conversational rules that bind questions and answers. Interviews can be especially important when the witness is a child. Unfortunately, many of the techniques used by law enforcement professionals and social workers run the risk of tainting the reports of children (Ceci & Bruck, 1993).

The study of both infantile amnesia and of interviewing not only raise a set of interesting theoretical questions that memory developmentalists have not resolved, but they also pose some thorny practical problems. For example, in *Moran vs the Commonwealth of Massachusetts*, the defendants, William Moran, a Harvard professor, and his wife, were accused by their two grandchildren of molesting them when the youngest grandchild was around 20 months old. The youngest grandchild recollected the alleged abuse for the first time when she was nearly 4 years old, following a therapy session of her mother's, which she attended. (The mother had herself allegedly been abused by her parents as a child and was in therapy as a survivor of childhood incest.) The question at bar in this case was whether the child's 'memory' of abuse was accurate; is it possible for a 4 year old to recollect what happened to her when she was 20 months old, or were the powerful adult suggestions contained in therapy instrumental in planting a false memory? We shall never knew the answer to this question, but one thing is certain: studies of infantile amnesia, lying and 'theory of mind' frequently find their way into courts. It makes little difference to juries, unfortunately, whether the research is described by the researcher, complete with the appropriate caveats and qualifications about external validity, or by someone who has only heard about the work second or third hand. Researchers must exercise great care in how they describe their results to minimize the chance that material gets misused by those involved in the adversarial process.

ISOMORPHS IN DIFFERENT SETTINGS

As evidenced in a number of studies previously cited, cognitive processes are affected not only by the mental context in which they are interpreted, but the mental contexts themselves are also influenced by the objective environment in which the cognition takes place. Studies of problem-solving in everyday settings are particularly instructive in demonstrating a high degree of variation in levels of cognitive functioning as a function of changes in mental and physical contexts. When the same task is couched in two different contexts, often the subject will succeed in only of them.

This phenomenon is not confined to those who are developmentally immature. Indeed, variation by context is the rule, not the exception, and it occurs across social classes, IQ scores and levels of formal education (Ceci & Roazzi, 1993). Because some readers may question this interpretation, some systematic empirical and anecdotal evidence is provided in its support. To introduce the nature of the phenomenon, we begin with the latter.

Anecdotal evidence for context-specificity. Suppose that you are told that you tested positive for some very rare virus, one that infects only 1% of the population. And further suppose that the test that diagnosed you with this virus is 90% accurate and therefore has a 10% false positive rate: in other words, if 100 individuals are tested, half of whom actually do have the virus, then the test will correctly detect 45 of the 50 who are infected, and it will claim to have detected the virus in 10%, or five persons, who are not actually infected. Armed with this knowledge, what are the odds that you actually have this virus merely because you tested positive?

Most college students give the odds as 9 in 10. The same is true even for graduate students and professionals with advanced skills in mathematics. Yet, this answer is wrong. The actual odds are only about 8%.

The reason that university students and even qualified professionals fail in estimating the odds is not for lack of knowledge but because, for them, the problem is stated out of context. For example, if the same problem is given to engineers who deal with quality control issues, but stated in quality control terms (e.g. the chance of detecting a flaw in a product coming off the production line), most of them quickly produce an approximation of the correct answer.

The above anecdotal evidence illustrates the context-specific nature of everyday cognition. Cognitive processes do not operate with uniform efficiency across all situations. In some situations they are deployed far more effectively than in others. The implication of this anecdotal evidence is that even well-educated people tend to be a lot less 'general' in their reasoning than we might assume. In fact, people tend to be a lot less general on virtually every aspect of intelligence that has been studied so far (Ceci, 1990).

University professors are no exception to the claim that people are context-bound in their everyday reasoning. The following riddle has, in one version or another, baffled academics for years, even quantitatively sophisticated ones: you are presented three boxes and told that one of them has a $5 bill hidden inside. If you guess which box it is, you can keep the $5. But after you make your selection, one of the two remaining boxes is opened, but it is always one that does not contain the $5. So, you are left with two unopened boxes, the one which you originally selected and the other one. Now if you are asked whether you want to stick with your original choice before these last two boxes are opened, or whether you wish to switch to the remaining unopened box, what should you do? Many stubbornly refuse to believe that the best solution is to switch. Piatteli-Palmarini (1991) has reported that even distinguished mathematicians and Nobel prize physicists argue that it does not matter if you switch or stick because the odds of being correct if you stick or switch when you have just two boxes left is always the same. They become enraged when told otherwise.

But when viewed properly, the correct strategy is always to switch because the odds after one box is opened alters the odds that the remaining unopened box is correct from $1:3$ to $2:3$. As Piatteli-Palmarini (1991) explains,

> The box you have initially chosen had, and will forever have, a $\frac{1}{3}$ probability of containing the banknote. The other two boxes taken together will have a $\frac{2}{3}$ probability. But once I remove a box that is empty, the other one now has a $\frac{2}{3}$ probability all by itself. Therefore, you must always switch. By switching you raise the odds from $\frac{1}{3}$ to $\frac{2}{3}$ ... Given that Nobel laureates draw their guns and resist this conclusion, it will be useful to add another way of seeing why you must always switch. If you happen to have chosen the right box, then after one of the remaining empty boxes is opened you are certainly penalized by switching ... If you happen to have chosen an empty box, then you are certainly rewarded by switching ... How often will you happen to choose the right box? One time out of three. How often will you happen to choose an empty box? Two times out of

> three. Therefore switching is the correct strategy. It pays two times out of three. Sticking with the initial choice is a bad strategy. It pays only one time out of three. (p. 34)

In research with adult and child gamblers, in both the USA and Brazil, we have been impressed at how many of them 'see' the correct solution to the three-box problem immediately, almost before their name can be entered on the coding sheet. Why is it that these gamblers, many of whom have no formal schooling beyond fourth grade, can frequently solve this problem while distinguished mathematicians and physicists sometimes cannot? The answer is the same one for the virus problem: people are often far better at solving problems that represent important and familiar environmental challenges than they are at solving the identically structured problems when they seem disconnected from their everyday experiences — it is in the former contexts that they acquired the skill in question, and often the skill cannot be deployed outside these contexts. Some forms of gambling require exactly this type of thinking; thus these individuals realize by analogy that it is better to switch. However, if this problem is presented in a different context, these same gamblers do not see the solution as readily. In sum, everyday cognition is far less uniform in its functioning than we might expect from an analysis of school-based problem solving. Cognitive processes are acquired in specific contexts and seem to be yoked to them for their successful activation. When subjects who can solve school-based problems are presented isomorphs that are not couched in the language of the school, they frequently cannot solve them.

A similar conclusion was reached by Detterman (1992), following an analysis of the transfer literature. Detterman claimed that the only transfer experiments that have resulted in significant (non-specific) transfer are those that 'rigged' the conditions to obtain transfer by making the basis of transfer explicit. In other words, he argued that people will deploy a cognitive process that they used in one context to another context only when they are explicitly made aware of the isomorphism between the two contexts. So, if they are told that the same strategy they used in one context will also work in another, individuals are fully capable of transferring it to the new context. But very few actually use cognitive skills transcontextually on their own. Detterman (1992) claimed that university professors, a group that hopes to make at least one significant non-trivial transfer in their career, also do not transfer, but stay within their narrow sphere of specialization:

> If a professor can apply what he has learned to one new situation he will have earned his keep. The truth is that most professors pass their entire careers without a single, important novel insight. Novel insights as cases of transfer are probably rarer than volcanic eruptions and large earthquakes. (Detterman, 1992, p. 3)

From anecdote to experimentation. One might object to the evidence presented so far on the grounds that it lacks scientific rigour and contains unrepresentative samples. However, similar conclusions emerge from systematic empirical studies, as documented below.

We have conducted a series of studies into the importance of the physical and social context on children's everyday cognition, employing a dual-context paradigm. In this work, school-aged children are asked to perform some task in two or more environments. The motivation behind the use of two contexts is that some settings are postulated to result in more effective forms of cognition than others because they elicit different strategies or activate different knowledge structures that allow for more efficient processing. For instance, if a task is perceived as a video game it may recruit strategies that children have acquired specifically to conquer video game challenges that might not be recruited if the same task is perceived differently. A complete description of our procedures and findings is beyond the scope of this chapter (see Ceci & Bronfenbrenner, 1985; Ceci *et al.*, 1988; Ceci, 1990 for details). What is relevant here is the integration of the Ebbinghaus and Bartlettian approaches that can provide valuable insights into the nature of cognitive development. In our work we have combined a componential approach that is favoured by those in the Ebbinghaus tradition, while simultaneously studying the power of contextual factors to alter this analysis.

Capturing butterflies. In one experiment, 10 year olds were asked to guess which direction a geometric shape that appeared in the centre of a computer screen would migrate. The shape (circle, square or triangle) always appeared in the centre of the screen but it would migrate to some other location. Children were instructed to point to the location on the screen where they thought the shape would migrate. They were not informed of the algorithm that we had written to determine where the shape would migrate. For example, an algorithm might simply specify the following: (i) shape indicates left/right directionality (e.g. if it is a square it will move rightward; if it is a circle it will move leftward; if it is a triangle it will remain unchanged); (ii) colour indicates up/down directionality (e.g. if the shape's colour is dark it will move upward; if light it will move downward); and (iii) size indicates distance (e.g. if the shape is large it will go a short distance; and small shapes will go a long distance). Such an algorithm would be an example of an additive type of reasoning wherein one needs only to add the various features to determine where a specific shape will migrate on the screen. A large, dark circle, for instance, should move upward, leftward and a short distance from the centre.

Ten year olds are not very proficient at working out such rules on their own. Even after 750 trials they still seem to be confused about where the shape will migrate. As can be seen in Fig. 10.1, they are slightly above chance after 750 trials, but this is accomplished entirely by having memorized a few specific combinations of features, and not by having solved the underlying rule. They may have learned, for example, that a large, dark circle migrates to a certain spot on the screen, but they have no understanding of the values associated with colour, shape or size, and that this is why they move. It is important to understand that these 10 year olds are doing exactly what university students do on similar tasks. In fact, the 'decision science' literature is full of examples of how university students behave in similar laboratory reasoning contexts (Klayman, 1984).

When we made a slight alteration to the task, children's performance dramatically improved. We replaced the three shapes (square, circle and triangle) with animals (birds, bees and butterflies) and we added sound effects, thus making the context resemble a video game. The algorithm was

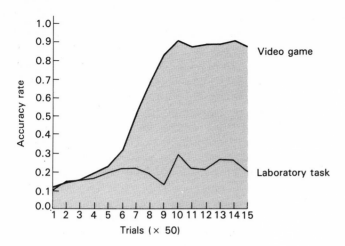

Fig. 10.1 Children's mean proportion of accurate estimates of a moving object in game versus laboratory contexts (simple main effects algorithm).

unchanged; the only difference was one of surface transformation. We substituted the laboratory context of predicting geometric shapes with a new context, a video game context, and asked children to place a cursor that looked like a butterfly net at the spot on the screen where they thought the bird, bee or butterfly would migrate. In other words, they were challenged to capture the animals in the net. As can be seen in Fig. 10.1, this contextual change resulted in nearly perfect performance after about 300 trials. This same experiment has been done with a variety of algorithms, including complex sine functions, and the result has been the same: children solve the same algorithm in the video game context far better than they solve it in the disembedded laboratory context. (Parenthetically, it is of interest to note that the decision science literature would lead to the expectation that neither children nor adults could internalize these algorithms. However, any parent who accompanies their 10 year old to the video arcade at the local mall knows this to be untrue. To do well on some of those games requires the appreciation of algorithms more complex than the ones that we have written.)

Next, we gave 10 year olds problems in the video game context first; then, after they had solved them, switched to disembedded geometric shapes, presented in a laboratory setting. We did this to find out if they would then transfer the knowledge gained in the former to the latter. The answer seems to be that they will, but only if the laboratory context is presented within a few hours of solving the video game context, and only if the testing room is unchanged, and the same computer and mouse are used. Thus, the 'generality' of their reasoning is still tightly bounded. Similar boundaries have been observed in the adult everyday cognitive literature whenever transfer between contexts is found (Nisbett *et al.*, 1988; Schooler, 1989).

Baking cupcakes and charging batteries. In another set of studies, we asked 10- and 14-year-old children either to charge a motorcycle battery or bake cupcakes for exactly 30 min (Ceci & Bronfenbrenner, 1985). While they waited to remove the battery cables or the cupcakes from the oven, the children were allowed to play a video game that was positioned in such a manner that each time they checked the clock to see if the 30 min had elapsed, the experimenter could record it. Some children were asked to charge the battery or bake the cupcakes in their homes and others were asked to do so in a university laboratory.

The children who performed these tasks in their homes exhibited a U-shaped pattern of clock-checking during the 30 min waiting period. They checked the clocks a lot during the first 10 min; then they hardly looked at the clock again until the waning minutes, when they would look incessantly at the clock. In contrast, the children who performed these tasks in the laboratory exhibited a completely different pattern of clock-checking, one that was ascending and linear over the 30-min period. These two patterns of clock-checking reflect different cognitive strategies and different efficiencies.

The U-shaped pattern of clock-checking indicates that the children who charged the battery or baked the cupcakes in their homes deployed an early calibration strategy. They checked the clock every few minutes during the early part of the period in order to confirm their estimation that a few minutes had elapsed, no more and no less. Once they received multiple confirmations of their subjective assessment of the passage of time, they were free to immerse themselves in the video game without concern for watching the clock. Their mental clocks had been 'set' by these early clock checks and they now were on 'auto-pilot' until the final minutes. Support for this interpretation was obtained in a follow-up study in which the clocks were programmed to run faster or slower than real time and the children were able to recover similar U-shaped patterns unless the clocks ran 50% or more faster or slower than real time. In other words, children as young as 10 years old spontaneously calibrated their mental clocks and this is reflected in the U-shaped pattern of clock-checking.

What is so strategic about a U-shaped pattern of clock-checking? There are two useful purposes that this pattern serves. First, it results in the same level of punctuality that was seen in children who performed the task in a laboratory setting, but with one-third fewer clock-checks. So, this strategy is more economical in terms of energy expended. Second, the U-shaped pattern allowed the children to immerse themselves in the video game once they calibrated their mental clocks. This meant that they were able to invest all of their conscious resources in improving their scores in the game instead of worrying about the time. Thus, a coefficient representing the U-shaped quadratic was associated with superior video game performance.

In summary, the home setting allowed children to engage in a relaxed, yet strategic form of time-monitoring that had significant advantages. If one had only observed these children in the laboratory setting, there would be far less evidence that they possessed such a strategy. It was only on the female sex-typed task (baking cupcakes) that any evidence was found for the use of this strategy in the laboratory context. It was on this task that the older boys displayed the U-shaped strategy in the laboratory that was seen only in the home for the male sex-typed task. The reason for this departure seems to be that teenage boys did not regard the baking task as serious, thus they were more relaxed in the way they monitored the passage of time — even when they were in the laboratory setting. In contrast, older girls did not behave in the more relaxed manner in the laboratory when the task was male sex-typed, thus demonstrating the contextual subtleties of cognitive development.

Racetracks and stock markets. In a case study of two men who were known to employ a certain form of reasoning at the racetrack, we asked them to solve a stock market prediction task that was isomorphic in structure to the one they routinely used at the racetrack (Ceci & Ruiz, 1991, 1992). The type of reasoning these men use at the racetrack requires a specific multiplicative interaction term to predict outcomes, and it is the use of this specific interaction term that is the basis of their success at the racetrack (see Ceci & Liker, 1986a, b for validation of this term). Yet, when they were given the opportunity to deploy this same interaction term in the stock market simulation (that was similarly structured to the racetrack problem), they failed to do so. As can be seen in Fig. 10.2, even after 611 trials they were still only slightly better than chance, and the man with the high IQ was no better than the man with the low IQ at transferring his knowledge.

After 611 trials both men were given a hint: they were told that predicting the price-earning ratio at the stock market is similar to predicting odds at the racetrack. This hint resulted in immediate transfer of their racing knowledge to perfect performance in the stock market context. In short, these gamblers behaved just like the graduate students who fail to solve the virus infection example until they are told that it is important to consider base rates. When given such hints, many graduate students immediately realize that Bayes' theorem can be applied; similarly, these gamblers realized that a form of reasoning deployed elsewhere can be applied here — but only after the instructions make the transferrability salient! Detterman (1992) notes that context-boundedness is the rule, not the exception, in transfer studies, even when the transfer task is highly similar to the original task:

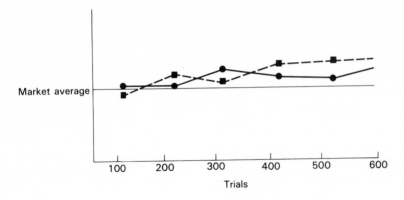

Market average

100   200   300   400   500   600

Trials

Fig. 10.2 Probability of predicting whether a stock will exceed the market average. 'Rule' reference information that the task was analogous to the racetrack task (+), and subsequently altering the weightings (−) without warning. ■, low IQ; ●, high IQ.

What is truly amazing about all of these studies is not that they don't really produce transfer across contexts. What is amazing is the extent of similarity it is possible to have between problems without subjects realizing that the situations are identical and require the same process. (Detterman, 1992, p. 14)

The cross-cultural literature is replete with similar examples of context-specificity (see Ceci & Roazzi, 1994 for review). With only a few exceptions, it is clear that schooled individuals solve problems better when the problems are couched in the language of schooling, while unschooled individuals solve the same problems better when they are couched in the language of their jobs. For example, isomorphs that require proportional reasoning were solved better by Brazilian street vendors who had little or no schooling than by schooled individuals when the problems involved selling–purchasing operations; on the other hand, the reverse was true when the same problems were couched in the language of the mathematics texts used in Brazilian schools (Roazzi & Bryant, 1994; Schliemann & Carraher, 1994). Similarly, Piagetian assessments of logical operations like conservation and class inclusion are tightly bound to the context in which the material is presented. Roazzi and Bryant (1994) have reviewed evidence showing poor children solve conservation of liquid problems better when the instructions make explicit that a quantitative judgement is being requested (e.g. if children are shown two unequal glasses of lemonade and asked: 'Would you charge the same amount of money for the two glasses of lemonade, or does one

contain more than the other?') than when the instructions merely suggest that a perceptual judgement is being requested ('Do the two glasses look alike?'). Lest one imagine that schooling makes children impervious to the influence of context, these same researchers showed that schooled children do worse than unschooled children when the context used to present the problems involves a vendor–purchaser relation, a context that is familiar to the unschooled street vendors but not to the middle-class school-children in Brazil.

As one example of the power of context, consider the following results from a study by Schliemann and Nunes (1990). Groups of fisherman were asked to calculate prices and quantities having to do with catching, processing and selling fish — all of which are activities that matter to them, and with which they are quite familiar. One such problem stated that another fisherman is selling fish at a rate of 75 cruzados for 5 kg. They were asked to calculate how much that fisherman was earning per kilogram. Between 70 and 95% of the fishermen obtained the correct answers to such problems, and there was no correlation between years of formal education (ranging from 0 to 9) and accuracy.

A slightly more difficult type of proportionality problem is worded as follows: 'In the south there is a type of shrimp that yields 3 kg of shelled (i.e. deveined) shrimp for each 15 kg you catch. Now if a customer wants 9 kg of shelled shrimp, how much would you have to catch?'. On such problems the accuracy rate is around 60%; again, there is no correlation between accuracy and years of formal schooling. Of interest is that even those subjects who attended school long enough to learn the Brazilian method of computing scalar proportions did not use it. The national Brazilian method for teaching public school children scalar proportions, the so-called 'rule of 3', states that you multiply the missing term (x) by the cross-multiplication process. For example,

$$a/b = c/x$$

is solved in Brazilian schools as follows:

$$a \times x = b \times c; \text{ thus } x = (b \times c)/a.$$

To see how even those subjects who had been schooled do not use the knowledge they were taught in school, consider the following problem in which the desired number of kilograms of shelled shrimp is neither a multiple nor a divider of the number given in the problem, making it a harder problem to calculate using a scalar solution (i.e. adding or multiplying) than with the rule of 3 that they were taught. For example, 'How much fish for a customer who wanted 2 kg of processed fish when 18 kg of unprocessed fish yielded 3 kg of processed fish?' One of Schliemann and Nunes' (1990) subjects, a ninth-grade educated fisherman, who had learned the rule of 3 before he quit school, answered as follows:

> ... one and a half kilos (processed) would be 9 (unprocessed), it has to be 9, because half of 18 is 9 and half of 3 is one and a half. And a half kilo (processed) is 3 kilos (unprocessed). Then it'd be 9 plus 3 is 12 (unprocessed), the 12 kilos would give the 2 kilos (processed). (Schliemann & Nunes, 1990, p. 263)

Even though this subject had been exposed to proportion algorithms as part of his formal education, he preferred not to use it. Perhaps he did not even know that it was applicable in such a context. One cannot be sure. But it does drive home the risk in presuming that school-taught knowledge is the basis for solving problems in non-schooled contexts, or that schooling frees individuals from the constraints imposed by context.

Problem isomorphs. The context-specific reasoning examples that we have been describing are special instances of what are called 'problem isomorphs'. An isomorph is an analogue of the same problem but couched in different terminology or in a differ-

ent context. For example, the famous problem about missionaries and cannibals, wherein a single missionary cannot be left alone with more than one cannibal, can be converted into an analogous problem about wives and jealous husbands, in which a wife cannot be left alone with more than one man unless her own husband is present (Gholson *et al.*, 1988). The general finding in the cognitive literature is that cross-task generalization between a problem and its isomorph is usually low: knowing how well individuals can solve one problem is of little help in predicting how well they will solve the same problem in another context even when it is isomorphic to it.

Perhaps the best known case of a failure to transfer in isomorphic reasoning is that of Johnson-Laird and Wason's card task (Johnson-Laird & Wason, 1972; Johnson-Laird, 1983). In this task subjects are asked to decide whether a rule is true. For example, the proposed rule might be: 'If a card has a vowel on one side, it will have an even number on its other side'. Then subjects, who are university students, are shown the following four cards:

A, B, 2, 5

and asked to turn over only those cards that are critical to verifying the rule. In this example, the best decision is to turn over the 5 and A, as these allow one to disconfirm the rule with the minimum number of card turns. Although university students have great difficulty with this problem, they do much better when the isomorph is framed in the context of a travel game in which one must decide whether to turn over cards that have a picture of a type of transportation or the name of a town on them; or to decide whether a traveller can disembark from a plane that lands in a country that has cholera or diptheria (Kunda & Nisbett, 1986; Nisbett *et al.*, 1988). From a cognitive perspective, there is nothing in these latter two travel isomorphs to make them easier than the number−letter task. Their underlying structure is identical to the one involving the numbers and letters. And yet, performance on them is vastly different from performance on the task in its more abstract and less familiar form (Johnson-Laird, 1983; Nisbett *et al.*, 1988).

Such findings as these have led researchers of

transfer to become pessimistic about the generaliz-ability of cognitive operations. For instance, Schooler (1989) concluded his review of the cog-nitive training literature by noting that transfer from one subject or domain to another was quite limited:

> The question for which we do have some empirical answers has to do with how generalizable cognitive training is from one subject area to another. As of now, the answer is not very much. (Schooler, 1989, p. 11).

CONCLUSION: THE DOMAIN-SPECIFICITY OF EVERYDAY COGNITION

The tradition begun by Ebbinghaus looked upon context as noise, to be gotten rid of by slavishly sanitizing experiments of meaning, prior experi-ence, personal values and motivation. Whenever it proved impossible to purge context from an exper-iment, researchers opted to control for contextual factors such as meaningfulness and motivation through statistical partialling. The idea that context should be studied in its own right rather than be 'partialled out' of the experiment seems to have appealed to few of the early cognitive researchers (Yuille & Wells, 1991). Beginning with Bartlett, however, a countertradition cropped up that viewed context as an integral part of cognition. These researchers showed that many theoretically interesting and practically important real-world cognitions could not be explained on the basis of the Ebbinghaus tradition. Today, the descendants of Ebbinghaus and Bartlett are increasingly likely to cross-fertilize their research with each other's para-digms and insights. But critical differences remain, and recent writers have railed against the methods and assumptions of each other's tradition (see Banaji & Crowder, 1989 for an argument against studies of everyday cognition, and Ceci & Bronfenbrenner, 1991 for a reply).

Contemporary cognitive psychology seems to be on a converging course. The search for invariances that characterized the Ebbinghaus tradition for so much of the past century is yielding to an acknowl-edgement of the power of context to mediate cog-nition. Winograd (1992) has argued that the merger of the Ebbinghaus and Bartlettian traditions is slowly unfolding and can be seen in the types of researches that adherents of both traditions are carrying out. The search for invariances still con-tinues, but the focus of attention has moved to the next higher level of analysis — principles that describe how processes are mediated by the general features of proximal settings as well as the distal aspects of the environment at the level of class, culture and belief systems (Bronfenbrenner, 1989, in press).

One of the implications of this chapter is that there are aspects of both paradigms that need to be integrated to achieve the most appropriate assess-ment of an individual's cognitive powers both in terms of present status and developmental poten-tial. The focus of the Ebbinghaus tradition on cog-nition out of context is only part of the story; in the final analysis it is, of course, 'cognitive process' that does the job. But, as we have shown, context differentiates the effectiveness of a process. Thus, both Bartlett's and Ebbinghaus' paradigms must be wed to yield an optimally effective approach to cognitive assessment. Assessments made out of con-text, or solely in laboratory settings, are apt to lead to misjudgements of the individual's competence, underestimating capabilities in some contexts and overestimating them in others. Everyday cog-nitive behaviour is more diverse than what can be measured in the ecologically reduced settings of the laboratory or the testing office. Because of this, one often observes low cross-task correlations on the same problem when it is presented in differing contexts. In view of the ecologically interactive character of everyday cognitive behaviour (influ-encing and being influenced by the environment), processes that are invariant across contexts are few in number and fairly close to the physiological level. Behavioural scientists should be seeking, therefore, not universals but rather the laws of invariance at the next higher level — principles that describe how cognitive processes are mediated by the general properties both of settings and of persons (Bronfenbrenner, 1979).

Thus, there has been an evolution in our knowl-edge about the cognitive complexity of organisms and their environments. The knowledge produced by the followers of Ebbinghaus' tradition can be wed to the observations of discoveries following Bartlett's lead, with the progressive result producing an even more powerful cognitive science.

ACKNOWLEDGEMENT

Preparation of this chapter was supported by grants from the National Institutes of Health, DHHS Nos 5RO1HD22839 and KO4HD00801, and a Senior Fullbright-Hayes award to the first author.

REFERENCES

Baddeley A. (1988) *Working Memory*. Oxford Psychology Series, No. 11. Clarendon Press, Oxford.

Baddeley A. & Hitch G. (1977) Recency re-examined. In Dornic S. (ed.) *Attention and Performance*, Vol. VI, pp. 647–667. Lawrence Erlbaum, Hillsdale, New Jersey.

Bahrick H. (1984) Semantic memory content in permastore: Fifty years of memory for Spanish learned in school. *Journal of Experimental Psychology: General* **113**, 1–29.

Banaji M. & Crowder R. (1989) The bankruptcy of everyday memory. *American Psychologist* **44**, 1185–1193.

Bartlett F.C. (1932) *Remembering*. Cambridge University Press, Cambridge.

Bottoms B., Goodman G., Schwartz-Kenney B., Sachsenmaier T. & Thomas S. (1990) *Keeping secrets: Implications for children's testimony*. Paper presented at the Biennial Meeting of the American Psychology and Law Society, Williamsburg, March.

Bronfenbrenner U. (1979) *The Ecology of Human Development*. Harvard University Press, Cambridge, Massachusetts.

Bronfenbrenner U. (1989) Ecological systems theory. *Annals of Child Development Research* **6**, 185–246.

Bronfenbrenner U (in press) The ecology of cognitive development: Research models and fugitive findings. In Wozniak R.H. & Fischer K. (eds) *Specific Environments: Thinking in Context*. Lawrence Erlbaum, Hillsdale, New Jersey.

Brown A.L. (1975) The development of memory: Knowing, knowing about knowing, and knowing how to know. In Reese H.W. (ed.) *Advances in Child Development and Behavior*, Vol. 10, pp. 103–152. Academic Press, New York.

Bussey K. (1993) Children's lying and truthfulness: Implications for children's testimony. In Ceci S.J., Leichtman M.D. & Putnick M.E. (eds) *Cognitive and Social Factors in Early Deception*, pp. 89–110. Lawrence Erlbaum, Hillsdale, New Jersey.

Ceci S.J. (1990) *On Intelligence ... More or Less: A Bioecological Treatise on Intellectual Development*. Prentice Hall, New Jersey.

Ceci S.J. & Bronfenbrenner U. (1985) Don't forget to take the cupcakes out of the oven: Strategic time-monitoring, prospective memory, and context. *Child Development* **56**, 175–190.

Ceci S.J. & Bronfenbrenner U. (1991) On the demise of everyday memory: Rumors of my death are much exaggerated. *American Psychologist* **46**, 27–31.

Ceci S.J., Bronfenbrenner U. & Baker J.G. (1988) Memory in context: The case of prospective remembering. In Weinert F. & Perlmutter M. (eds) *Memory Development: Universal Changes and Individual Differences*, pp. 243–256. Lawrence Erlbaum, Hillsdale, New Jersey.

Ceci S.J. & Bruck M. (1993) The suggestibility of children's testimony: An historical review and synthesis. *Psychological Bulletin*, **113**, 403–439.

Ceci S.J. & Leichtman M. (1992) Memory cognition and learning. In Segalowitz S.J. & Rapin I. (eds) *Handbook of Neuropsychology*, pp. 223–240. Elsevier, Amsterdam.

Ceci S.J. & Liker J. (1986a) Academic and nonacademic intelligence: An experimental separation. In Sternberg R.J. & Wagner R. (eds) *Practical Intelligence: Origins of Competence in the Everyday World*, pp. 119–142. Cambridge University Press, New York.

Ceci S.J. & Liker J. (1986b) A day at the races: A study of IQ, expertise, and cognitive complexity. *Journal of Experimental Psychology: General* **115**, 255–266.

Ceci S.J & Roazzi A. (1994) The effects of context on cognition: Postcards from Brazil. In Sternberg R.J. & Wagner R. (eds) *Mind in Context*, pp. 74–101. Cambridge University Press, Cambridge.

Ceci S.J. & Ruiz A. (1991) Cognitive complexity and generality: A case study. In Hoffman R. (ed.) *The Psychology of Expertise*, pp. 41–55. Springer, New York.

Ceci S.J. & Ruiz A. (1992) Transfer, abstractness, and intelligence. In Detterman D. & Sternberg R.J. (eds) *Transfer on Trial: Intelligence, Cognition, and Instruction*, pp. 136–157. Ablex, Norwood, New Jersey.

Chandler M. (1989) Doubt and developing theories of mind. In Astington J., Harris P.L. & Olson D.R. (eds) *Developing Theories of Mind*, pp. 387–413. Cambridge University Press, New York.

Chi M.T.H. (1978) Knowledge structures and memory development. In Siegler R.S. (ed.) *Children's Thinking: What Develops?*, pp. 73–96. Lawrence Erlbaum, Hillsdale, New Jersey.

Coltheart V. & Walsh P. (1988) Expert knowledge and semantic memory. In Gruneberg M., Morris P. & Sykes P. (eds) *Practical Aspects of Memory*, Vol. 12. Wiley, London.

Detterman D. (1992) The case for the prosecution: transfer as an epiphenomenon. In Detterman D. & Sternberg R. (eds) *Transfer on Trial: Intelligence, Cognition, and Instruction*, pp. 3–36. Ablex, Norwood, New Jersey.

Dias M.G. & Harris P.L. (1988) The effect of make-believe

play on deductive reasoning. *British Journal of Developmental Psychology* **6**, 207–221.

Doris J.L. (ed.) (1991) *The Suggestibility of Children's Recollections: Implications for their Testimony.* American Psychological Association, Washington, DC.

Ebbinghaus H. (1885) Über das Gedächtnis (On thinking) (translated by Ruger & Bussenius, *Memory*, 1913). Teacher's College Press, New York.

Fivush R. & Hudson J. (eds) (1990) *Knowing and Remembering in Young Children.* Cambridge University Press, New York.

Flanagan O. (1993) Other minds, obligations, and honesty. In Ceci S.J., DeSimone M. & Putnick M.E. (eds) *Cognitive and Social Factors in Early Deception.* Lawrence Erlbaum, Hillsdale, New Jersey.

Gholson B., Eymard L., Long D., Morgan D. & Leeming F. (1988) Problem solving, recall, isomorphic transfer, non-isomorphic transfer among third grade and fourth grade children. *Cognitive Development* **3**, 37–53.

Gruneberg M.M., Morris P. & Sykes P. (eds) (1989) *Practical Aspects of Memory.* Academic Press, London.

Haugaard J., Repucci N.D., Laird J. & Nauful T. (1991) Children's definitions of the truth and their competency to testify. *Law and Human Behavior* **15**, 253–272.

Henderson E.N. (1903) *Psychological Monographs*, Vol. 5, No. 23.

Howe M.L. & Courage M. (1993) Infantile amnesia: A reconsideration. *Psychological Bulletin* **113**, 305–326.

Johnson-Laird P.N. (1983) *Mental Models.* Harvard University Press, Cambridge, Massachusetts.

Johnson-Laird P.N. & Wason P.C. (1972) A theoretical analysis of insight into a reasoning task. In Johnson-Laird P.N. & Wason P.C. (eds) *Thinking: Readings in Cognitive Science.* Cambridge University Press, Cambridge.

Kail R.V. (1990) *Memory Development in Children*, 3rd edn. Freeman, San Francisco.

Klatzky R. (1980) *Human Memory.* W.H. Freeman, San Francisco, California.

Klayman J. (1984) *Learning from feedback in probabilistic environments.* Unpublished manuscript, University of Chicago Graduate School of Management, Chicago.

Kunda Z. & Nisbett R.E. (1986) The psychometrics of everyday life. *Cognitive Psychology* **18**, 195–224.

Leshowitz B. (1989) It is time we did something about scientific illiteracy. *American Psychologist* **44**, 1159–1160.

Light P. & Butterworth G. (eds) (1994) *Context and Cognition: Ways of Learning and Knowing.* Harvester-Wheatsheaf, Hemel Hempstead.

Logie R. & Wright R. (1988) Specialized knowledge and recognition memory performance in residential burglars. In Gruneberg M.M., Morris P. & Sykes P. (eds) *Practical Aspects of Memory*, Vol. 2. Wiley, London.

Means M. & Voss J. (1985) Star Wars: A developmental study of expert novice knowledge structures. *Memory and Language* **24**, 746–757.

Neisser U. (1967) *Cognitive Psychology.* Appleton-Century-Crofts, New York.

Neisser U. (1978) Memory: What are the important questions? In Gruneberg M.M., Morris P. & Sykes P. (eds) *Practical Aspects Of Memory*, pp. 3–24. Academic Press, London.

Neisser U. (1982) John Dean's memory. In U. Neisser (ed.) *Memory Observed.* W.H. Freeman, San Francisco.

Nisbeth R.E., Fong G., Lehman D. & Cheng P. (1988) *Teaching reasoning.* Unpublished manuscript, University of Michigan, Ann Arbor.

Peters D.P. (1990) *Confrontational stress and lying.* Paper presented at the Biennial Meeting of the American Psychology and Law Society. Williamsburg, March.

Peters D.P. (1991) The influence of stress and arousal on the child witness. In Doris J.L. (ed.) *The Suggestibility of Children's Recollections*, pp. 60–76. American Psychological Association, Washington, DC.

Piattelli-Palmarini M. (1991) Probability: Neither rational nor capricious. *Bostonia* (March/April), 28–35.

Pillemer D. & White S. (1989) Childhood events recalled by children and adults. In Reese H.W. (ed.) *Advances in Child Development and Behavior*, Vol. 21, pp. 297–340. Academic Press, Florida.

Roàzzi A. & Bryant P. (1994) Social class, context, and cognitive development. In Light P. & Butterworth G. (eds) *Context and Cognition: Ways of Learning and Knowing.* Harvester-Wheatsheaf, Hemel Hempstead.

Rogoff B. & Lave J. (eds) (1984) *Cognition in a Social Context.* Harvard University Press, Cambridge, Massachusetts.

Ross M. (1989) Relation of implicit theories to the construction of personal histories. *Psychological Review* **96**, 341–357.

Schliemann A.D. & Carraher D.W. (1994) Proportional reasoning in and out of school. In Light P. & Butterworth G. (eds) *Context and Cognition: Ways of Learning and Knowing.* Harvester-Wheatsheaf, Hemel Hempstead.

Schliemann A.D. & Nunes T. (1990) A situated schema for proportionality reasoning. *British Journal of Developmental Psychology* **8**, 259–268.

Schooler C. (1989) Social structural effects and experimental situations: Mutual lessons of cognitive and social science. In Schaie K.W. & Schooler C. (eds) *Social Structure and Aging: Psychological Processes.* Lawrence Erlbaum, Hillsdale, New Jersey.

Tulving E. (1983) *Elements of Episodic Memory.* Oxford Psychology Series, No. 2. Clarendon Press/Oxford University Press, Oxford.

Usher J. & Neisser U. (1993) Childhood amnesia in the recall of four target events. *Journal of Experimental Psychology: General* **122**, 155–165.

Walker C.H. (1987) Relative importance of domain knowledge and overall aptitude or acquisition of domain related information. *Cognition and Instruction* **4**, 25–42.

Weisz J. (1978) Transcontextual validity in developmental

research. *Child Development* **49**, 1−12.

Whipple G.M. (1915) *Manual of Mental and Physical Tests,* Vol. 2, pp. 9−42.

Winograd E. (1992) Memory in the laboratory and every-day memory: The case for both. In Puckett J.M. & Reese H.W. (eds) *Life-span Developmental Psychology: Mechanisms of Everyday Cognition.* Lawrence Erlbaum, Hillsdale, New Jersey.

Winograd E. & Neisser U. (1992) *Affect and Accuracy in Recall: The Problems of Flashbulb Memories.* Cambridge University Press, New York.

Yuille J. & Wells G. (1991) Concerns about the application of research findings: The issue of ecological validity. In Doris J. (ed.) *The Suggestibility of Children's Recollections: Implications for Their Testimony,* pp. 118−128. American Psychological Association, Washington, DC.

Zaragoza M.S., Dahlgren D. & Muench J. (1992) The role of memory impairment in children's suggestibility. In Howe M.L., Brainerd C.J. & Reyna V.F. (eds) *The Development of Long-term Retention,* pp. 184−216. Springer, New York.

11: Psychometric and Everyday Intelligence: Synonyms, Antonyms and Anonyms

STEPHEN J. CECI, JACQUELINE G. BAKER-SENNETT AND
URIE BRONFENBRENNER

INTRODUCTION

This chapter presents the concept of intelligence by first describing how historically major groups of researchers have each conceptualized intelligence and then by showing how these conceptualizations of intelligence relate to other domains of behavioural and psychological functioning (e.g. school, work, creativity and social interactions). Special emphasis is placed on the three key constructs important in the validation of psychometric intelligence, namely its presumed singularity, biological basis and transcontextual stability. Various measures of psychometric intelligence, although possessing good predictive validity in some school and work settings, should not be equated with a general measure of native intelligence that purports to index intellectual functioning across the board. That is, cognitive potentials in diverse intellectual spheres are not capable of being captured by a single static psychometric instrument. The caveat is critical because the context in which intellectual skills are developed and deployed is a potent determinant of their efficiency; the same skill operates with differential effectiveness as a function of its physical, social and mental context.

The second part of this chapter is focused on the development of intellectual abilities, skills and processes. Here, special attention is paid to factors that influence intellectual development, such as abstraction and creativity. Finally, the differing claims that intelligence is primarily effected by either endogenous or exogenous factors are reviewed. We argue that views of intellectual development that emphasize either the environment or biology as prepotent are not in accord with the full corpus of developmental research. Additionally, we suggest that the traditional 'interactionist' view of intellectual development is poorly articulated and, as a result of its lack of clarity, has no compelling defence against strong biological or environmental 'main effects' arguments. We conclude with a presentation of the bioecological view of intelligence that was recently developed to incorporate both biological and environmental explanations of intellectual development.

CONCEPTUAL AND DEFINITIONAL ISSUES

Historical backdrop

Throughout history, a debate has raged over the definition and philosophical nature of intelligence (for a historical review see Sternberg *et al.*, 1981; Sternberg & Detterman, 1986; Sternberg, 1990). Today, researchers are no closer to a consensus on the definition and nature of intelligence than they were in 1921 when the *Journal of Educational Psychology* convened a symposium to address this issue and discovered that there were nearly as many conceptions of intelligence as there were participants in the symposium. We do know, however, that there is some continuity between researchers' visions of intelligence in 1921 and current conceptualizations of intelligence (Sternberg & Detterman, 1986, $r = 0.50$). When modern researchers convened a few years ago to discuss the nature of intelligence, they described more than two dozen attributes of intelligence that included one's ability to learn, speed of processing, adaptation, elementary processes (e.g. perception, sensation and attention), and higher level components of cognition (e.g. abstract reasoning, problem-solving and decision-making).

Despite some lack of consensus regarding the

nature of intelligence, research on this construct has prevailed throughout the twentieth century. The history of research on intelligence reflects the range of definitional attributes suggested at the 1921 and 1986 symposia. Some of the earliest scientific research on intelligence was conducted in London by Sir Francis Galton, a cousin of Charles Darwin. Galton's view of intelligence was decidedly hereditarian in his belief that it ran along family lines (Galton, 1869, 1892). Galton believed that intelligence among adults could be assessed by measuring very basic sensory and information-processing mechanisms, such as reacting to illumination changes and detecting pressure changes on the surface of the skin (Galton, 1883; Cattell, 1890). For Galton, the inferiority of so-called morons, imbeciles and idiots could be traced to their sluggish sensory and perceptual processing:

> The discriminative facility of idiots is curiously low; they hardly distinguish between heat and cold, and their sense of pain is so obtuse that some of the more idiotic seem hardly to know what it is. In their dull lives, such pain as can be excited in them may literally be accepted with a welcome suprise. (Galton, 1883, p. 28)

For 7 years Galton operated an anthropometric laboratory in South Kensington, London, and tested patrons' 'intelligence'. Galton expected to find that those from the upper walks of society (jurists, scientists, writers and their offspring) would exhibit faster perceptual reactions, and exhibit more sensitive sensory discriminations, than those from the common classes. For example, Galton blindfolded patrons and asked them judge the weights of finely graded gun cartridges that were filled with various layers of shot and cotton wadding. He predicted that those individuals who possessed the finest discriminative sensitivity to slight changes in the weight of the cartridges would come from the upper strata of society.

James McKean Cattell visited Galton on his return to the USA from Germany and was greatly impressed by the latter's approach to quantifying intelligence. Cattell set up a laboratory at Columbia University in America and used many of Galton's tests, as well as nearly 40 new ones that resembled Galton's. One of Cattell's students, Clark Wissler, found that the tests were not highly correlated with each other, and they did not predict Columbia

University students' academic performance (Wissler, 1901). Considering Galton's data as well as the findings of Wissler, researchers concluded that there was no convincing evidence that intelligence, as measured by sensory and perceptual processing skills, differentiated eminent individuals and their offspring from the rest of society (see Eysenck, 1986 for a brief history of this position), nor did it predict achievement at school. Parenthetically, it should be noted that in the latter quarter of this century, researchers have revisited Galton's approach, using new sensory and perceptual tests that are more reliable than the ones Cattell and Galton employed, and selected on the basis of theoretical considerations not known when Galton was alive. Contemporary research shows these tests are correlated with each other, and they predict many types of academic performance (Detterman *et al.*, in press), though the magnitudes of the correlations are almost always modest, at best (Vernon, 1987).

Following the failure to demonstrate a link between simple tests and complex behaviour, subsequent researchers abandoned measurement of individual differences in basic sensory and perceptual skills. Instead, they followed the lead of the French psychologist, Alfred Binet, and began assessing performance of school children on more global types of intelligence tests, comprised of subtests such as vocabulary, arithmetic and spatial reasoning (Binet & Simon, 1916). At the core of these tests was the notion of complex mental judgement, as opposed to Galton's simple sensory discriminations.

Those familiar with the history of intelligence testing are aware of the great success that Binet's test and its successors have enjoyed. Thousands of validity studies now have documented the reliability and predictive value of this genre of mental tests. IQ tests (as measured by the Stanford–Binet and Wechsler intelligence tests) predict a range of real-world successes, but their most significant success is in predicting school performance. This ought not to surprise anyone, however, because Binet developed his test by asking teachers in Parisian schools to list the types of problems that poor learners found to be the most difficult. The fact that items selected by Binet to discriminate between good and poor learners could do so is to be expected; so can items on virtually all achievement tests. However, to call the former items measures of intelligence implies that the underlying ability needed to answer them is something that we have an independent measure of, namely *intelligence*. The potential circularity is evident: school failure is both 'explained' as a lack of intelligence and is itself the basis for the definition of a lack of intelligence. The extra step in inference is logically unnecessary, as school failure is the only touchstone. This gets at the heart of one of the conceptual issues that has mired the field; namely, the presumed independence of different cognitive ability measurements. These complaints are addressed later.

The singularity versus modularity of mind

A fundamental question that one can ask about intelligence is whether it represents a singular, general ability or resource or whether it involves a variety of statistically independent abilities or resources. Notwithstanding the conceptual quagmire in which the notion of intelligence became embedded (due to the lack of agreement among researchers on its definition), the practical usefulness of IQ tests was acknowledged by all. A single score could predict a child's future school learning with better success than any other psychological test devised. Although Binet's test and its successors are avowedly eclectic, containing tasks that index many different kinds of cognition (verbal fluency, spatial reasoning, short-term memory, etc.), most researchers argued that these varied types of cognition are saturated with what came to be called general intelligence, or '*g*'. And herein lies the heart of an acrimonious debate among researchers. One camp of researchers claims that the intellect is comprised of a variety of qualitatively different and statistically independent cognitions (Thompson, 1948; Thurstone & Thurstone, 1962; Gardner, 1983; Keating, 1984; Keating *et al.*, 1985; Ceci, 1990a) while the other camp holds that these seemingly independent cognitions are themselves underpinned by general intelligence, or *g* (Spearman, 1904; Vernon, 1969; Jensen, 1982; Hunter, 1983; Thorndike, 1985; Gottfredson, 1986). Due to space limitations, we shall not delve into this debate here, but we can provide a concrete example of its manifestation.

Suppose a child is administered a battery of cognitive tests (vocabulary, memory, spatial reasoning, etc.) and found to produce performances on each that is moderately intercorrelated with the others; that is, the child who does best on vocabulary tends to do best on the other tests as well (e.g. the correlation between vocabulary performance and performance on other tasks ranges between 0.5 and 0.8). Through principal component analysis it is possible to assess the maximum linear variance among the test correlations that can be accounted for. The first principal component from such analyses is often taken as a surrogate for *g* or general intelligence.* Historically, it has been assumed that this singular underlying resource pool (*g*) subserves all of the diverse cognitive skills required by vocabulary, spatial reasoning, memory,

---

* The traditional way of assessing *g* was devised by Charles Spearman, a distinguished British statistician and early proponent of the notion of general intelligence. Spearman observed that scores on cognitive tests are positively intercorrelated, with a high score on one test tending to be associated with a high score on others. When Spearman arranged a matrix of correlations so that the first column represented the test that had the highest total correlation with the sum of the other tests, and the second column represented the next highest total correlation, and so on, he noticed that a hierarchy existed wherein the ratio of correlations in any two columns remained fairly constant as one moved down the columns. Spearman explained this constant ratio of correlations as the result of all correlations in the matrix being produced by the correlations between individuals' tests and an inferred third factor, he termed '*g*'. The test at the top of the column was viewed as the most *g*-loaded. Thus, the correlations between all tests are the result of their individual correlations with *g*. In principal component analysis, the first principal component is a measure of the interrelatedness among a battery of cognitive tests or tasks. Technically, it reflects the maximum amount of linear variance that can be accounted for, independent of rotation. Thus, *g*-loaded tests are those that are highly saturated with the first principal component and tend to be thought of as good indices of 'general intelligence'. The full scale scores on the most common IQ tests correlate very highly with both Spearman's *g* and first principal components, which themselves usually correlate in excess of 0.8. Both of these measures of general intelligence have heritability coefficients that range between 0.45 and 0.8, depending on the sample, the test battery, and the specific statistical assumptions used, such as how one chooses to 'factor' (e.g. Plomin *et al.*, 1988).

and so on (Spearman, 1904, 1927). Those with a cognitive bent view this single resource as 'attention' or internal awareness (Sternberg, 1985), while others with a more physiological bent view it as the signal : noise ratio in the transmission of information in the central nervous system, and still others view it as blood glucose levels or event-related potentials in the cortex during listening (Eysenck, 1986, 1988; Lehrl & Fischer, 1988).

Whatever one's view, a large first principal component is seen as a singular and common resource that some individuals possess more of than do other individuals. It is important to note that this view of *g* does not deny that special talents coexist with a singular intellectual resource. Every researcher that supports the singularity of mind view also acknowledges that many independent types of abilities also exist, arranged in a hierarchical model in which they are subsumed under this common or general intellectual resource, *g*. Thus, in theory, it is possible to be so well endowed with a special ability that it can compensate for a deficit in *g*, at least when performing in the specific area where the talent is well endowed. Individuals such as savants with specialized skills despite exceptionally low IQ scores are the paradigmatic example, but many less extreme examples can be found. Alternatively, it is possible to possess such a high level of *g* that it can compensate for a lower endowment of specific abilities. This perspective is reflected in the employment screening literature. That is, industrial–organizational pyschologists have argued that the single best predictor of occupational success is a measure of general intelligence as opposed to a specific talent that might seem related to a particular job (Hunter & Hunter, 1984; Gottfredson, 1986).

The assessment of intelligence

A variety of means exist for assessing general intelligence, the most common of which is the familiar IQ test (e.g. Stanford–Binet and Wechsler intelligence tests) and its surrogates like the scholastic aptitude tests (SATs) and a host of employment screening instruments (e.g. the general aptitude test battery), and various military qualification tests (e.g. the armed forces vocational aptitude battery — ASVAB). All of these, and many others like them, have as their goal the assessment of an individual's

general intellectual status, and most of these yield comparable results as far as a measure of general intelligence is concerned. Ordinarily, measures of general intelligence or *g*, whether they are called IQ tests, SATs, employment screening instruments, ASVAB tests, or something else, intercorrelate 0.65 and higher (Ceci, 1990a). Often such tests can be analysed into similar factor structures with similar *g*-loadings that possess similar demographic correlations (e.g. racial, social class and ethnic differences on one test will also be found on the others).

In addition to IQ-type tests, there are tests that have as their focus the assessment of the degree to which one engages in specific types of cognition. For instance, tests of 'fluid' intelligence were devised to measure one's ability to solve abstract problems (e.g. matrices, missing number series and verbal or symbolic syllogisms). Such tests are touted as measures of 'culture-reduced' fluid reasoning because of the test-marker's presumption that schooling and the home environment are relatively unimportant for their successful completion. This claim is made because the materials (but not the process itself) used on such tests are either ones that all examinees are familiar with (e.g. familiar numbers or elementary words: 'Fill in the missing number: 2, 5, 11, 23, — , 95') or because the materials used on them are equally unfamiliar to all examinees, regardless of their social origins or school attainments (e.g. use of nonsense words to solve syllogisms: 'No Gox box when wearing purple sox. Jox is a Gox wearing purple sox. Therefore: does Jox box?'). Unlike tests of 'crystallized' abilities which measure the amount of cultural knowledge that a child has gleaned from his or her environment (e.g. Zeus : Artemis; Diana : ?), tests of fluid abilities are thought to be unrelated to cultural experiences beyond some very minimal level of schooling. For example, Horn (1978) argued that so-called fluid intelligence, indexed by such tasks as figural oddities, number series and matrices, is acquired 'incidentally' and independently of schooling (see also Jensen, 1980; Gordon, 1987; Eysenck, 1988 for similar views).

If not due to schooling and acculturation, then what are differences on such tests attributed to? Researchers claim that individual differences on tests of fluid abilities primarily reflect physiological differences:

A relatively large proportion of the reliable variance in fluid intelligence (defined as abstract problem solving) reflects a pattern of physiological influences and a relatively small proportion of this variance reflects acculturation. (Horn, 1978, p. 247)

The view that schooling and cultural experiences have no causal impact on the development of IQ dates back to the earliest days of psychometric research when there was an explicit belief that IQ was impervious to the types of environmental interventions encountered in British and American schools. Cyril Burt, one of the seminal psychometric researchers in the UK, espoused this position in a number of public speeches he gave:

By intelligence the psychologist understands inborn, all-around intellectual ability . . .

inherited, not due to teaching or training . . .

uninfluenced by industry or zeal. (Quoted in Carroll, 1982, p. 90)

Lest one imagine that Burt stood alone in his view of the immutability of IQ through schooling, many of his contemporaries expressed similar doubts as to the effectiveness of schools to alter the preordained unfolding of IQ (see Ceci, 1991 for a comprehensive review of this position). Today, many psychometric researchers continue to claim that scores on certain types of IQ tests are not susceptible to change as a function of schooling experiences. For example, the developers of a well-known test that supposedly provides a culture-free measure of intelligence (the Raven's progressive matrices) assert that 'a person's total score provides an index of his intellectual capacity whatever his educational level' (Raven *et al.*, 1975, p. 1).

Other tests have as their focus the extent to which an individual engages in 'cognitive complexity' during the attempt to solve some problem presented to him or her. Cognitive complexity is best viewed as the tendency of a person to think about problems in a multiplicity of ways, integrating the various pieces of information into a cohesive unit. Cognitive complexity has been claimed to be a better predictor of successful business managers' performance than traditional IQ scores, and has been shown to be a superior predictor of naval commanders' leadership skills than measures of *g* (Streufert, 1986).

Predictive validity of IQ

Throughout the years there have been calls for the abandonment of IQ tests. However, there are those researchers and practitioners who steadfastly insist on their use because of their utility for making educational and career placement decisions and clinical diagnoses. IQ tests and their surrogates have been validated repeatedly in a variety of employment, clinical and academic settings. In addition to their well-documented prediction of school grades ($r = 0.55$, on average, Anastasi, 1968; Matarazzo, 1970), IQ scores predict occupational success, criminality proneness and life satisfaction ratings — both before and after social class is controlled (for review of the predictive validity literature see Ceci, 1990a, 1991). IQ scores have been reported to have impressive validity coefficients for predicting everything from mental health to marital dissolution rates and job performance (Gordon, 1976, 1980, 1987; Hunter, 1983, 1986; Gottfredson, 1986; Barrett & Depinet, 1991). For example, IQ scores have been shown to predict postal workers' speed and accuracy of sorting mail by zip code, military recruits' ability to steer a Bradley tank through an obstacle course, mechanics' ability to repair engines, and many other real-world endeavours (Hunter & Schmidt, 1982; Hunter *et al.*, 1984).

Hunter and Hunter (1984) estimated that if the city of Philadelphia were to choose entry level police officers randomly, instead of using its cognitive battery to select them, it would lose approximately $170 million over a 10-year period because of lost efficiency (additional police officers would need to be hired to do the work performed by the present force). Similarly, the US Department of Labor has estimated that the use of IQ scores to place workers in jobs would result in large increases in productivity and save the national economy upwards of $178.2 billion (Hunter & Schmidt, 1982). Estimates such as these have prompted meta-analysts to remark that there is no substitute for IQ scores to screen workers:

General cognitive ability not only predicts job performance moderately well, but it also predicts performance better than does any other single worker attribute. It also predicts performance equally well for blacks, Hispanics, and whites . . . and performance in training and on the job is linearly related to performance on ... general intelligence. On the average, increasingly higher intelligence levels are associated with increasingly better job performance ... It appears likely then that more extensive training or experience in relevant jobs skills can temporarily render less intelligent workers equally productive as more intelligent but less experienced workers, but that the latter will outperform the former within at least a few years, if not much sooner, depending on the complexity of the job ... There is no evidence that less *g*-loaded traits (e.g. motivation) compensate substantially for differences in intelligence, on the average. (Gottfredson, 1986, p. 395)

Data from approximately 750 studies on the general aptitude test battery (GATB) showed that the test validly predicted job performance for many different occupations (Hartigan & Wigdor, 1989) ... meta-analysis demonstrated that in entry-level positions, cognitive ability predicted job performance with an average validity of 0.53. This study also showed an average correlation of 0.45 between intellectual ability and job proficiency. Other studies using a number of different measures of job proficiency have found similar relationships to cognitive ability ... Cognitive ability is the best predictor of performance in most employment situations (Arvey, 1986; Hunter, 1986), and this relationship remains stable over extended periods of time (Austin & Hanisch, 1990). Thorndike (1985) concluded that cognitive *g* is the best predictor of job success. (Barrett & Depinet, 1991, pp. 1015−1016)

As compelling as the predictive validity studies appear on first glance, they are not without contest. For instance, some researchers have argued that the correlations between IQ and success in school and in work give the misleading impression that the causal route by which the prediction is accomplished is a cognitive one. In other words, there is a presumption that IQ scores are related to subsequent school and work performance because these latter endeavours require the same cognitive resources that are indexed by IQ tests. But such a view fails to distinguish between description and explanation. There are a host of alternative causal paths that have been shown to mediate the link between IQ and future success, and these are not cognitive or biological in any direct sense. For instance, in a recent set of analyses, Henderson and Ceci (1992) have suggested that the correlation between IQ and occupational success may be an artefact of the social origins of the workers' families, rather than a direct pathway from the workers' cognitive efficiency to job success. They found that when the families' social origins were taken into account in a structural model that allowed for the assessment of direct and indirect effects, there was no net effect of IQ on predicting how much an individual earned 10−15 years after high school. Low IQ individuals who were born into high-status homes were earning more than high IQ individuals who had been born into low-status homes.

FACTORS THAT INFLUENCE INTELLECTUAL DEVELOPMENT

Cognitive correlates and components

As just seen, the psychometric approach to studying intelligence has centered on an analysis of inter-correlations among cognitive test scores. When psychometric researchers have studied the inter-correlations among various types of cognition (spatial, verbal, quantitative, memory) across a wide age range, they have found that the pattern of intercorrelations changes, thus revealing the dynamic nature of intellectual development. For example, factor analyses have shown that some types of general and specific factors are more (or less) important at different ages, though in general intercorrelations between different IQ subtests tend to decrease with age (Sternberg, 1988). For the most part, however, the developmental nature of intelligence has not been at the forefront of psychometricians' research.

Instead of following a psychometric approach, many developmentalists have taken a quite differ-ent approach to the question of intelligence (Case, 1985; Kail & Pellegrino, 1985). Instead of focusing on off-the-rack tests of intelligence, develop-mentalists have emphasized the internal psycho-logical processes that underpin cognitive test performances, such as the nature of the mental representation (i.e. how much knowledge one has about the problem in question and how this knowledge is structured or represented in memory), changes in processing efficiency and the use of control strategies, and the social context in which cognitive structures and processes are formulated and given meaning. For example, Sternberg (1985) has provided a model of the interactive roles of information processing, context and biology in producing intellectual performance. His focus is on specific routes that lead to cognitive outcomes as opposed to a single manifestation of general intelligence, namely *g*. This is not to say that Sternberg's theory denies the prediction of cross-task correlations that is made by hierarchical *g*-based theories; he does not. But for him the basis of the correlations in performance across diverse cognitive tests involves the individual's competence at assessing his or her introspective state, and planning, revising and monitoring ongoing cognitions. This is referred to as 'metaknowledge' and for Sternberg it is the presence or absence of such metaknowledge that is responsible for cross-task correlations because virtually every complex task requires some of this knowledge. This is quite a different level of discourse from the researchers who maintain that the basis for these same correlations is a singular biological resource pool that is involved in all tasks, i.e. *g*.

It is possible to account for individual differences on mental tests by doing a componential analysis of the tests and determining the ingredients that separate high-scoring persons from low-scoring ones. Such analyses have been the 'bread-and-butter' of the so-called cognitive correlates camp (e.g. Hunt, 1985). They have determined, for example, that university students who score in the top quartile on *g*-loaded tests are faster at retrieving lexical information from memory (e.g. recognizing the names of letters and familiar words that are visually presented) than are their peers who score in the bottom quartile on such tests, despite the fact that both groups are highly familiar with the lexical information that is presented. Many such studies have been done and there is a compendium of components that have been found to discriminate among groups who differ on measures of general intelligence. It is not possible to describe this work in any detail here (see Hunt, 1985; Sternberg, 1985; Vernon, 1987).

Perhaps the most central aspect of the componential approach is that dealing with the nature of the mental representation. Two individuals that both can recognize a stimulus may represent it in memory differently, and it is this representational difference that is correlated with performance on tasks that involve that stimulus (Ceci, 1990a, b). For example, a child who represents the digit nine only in terms of its ordinal properties (less than 10, greater than eight) and its odd/even property will take longer to encode this digit than will a child who represents it in terms of added dimensions such as cardinality, non-primeness, root property, etc. Generally, it has been shown that the degree of elaboration in the mental representation is tied to how efficiently one can operate on the contents of memory. When low IQ persons possess mental representations that are more elaborate than those of a high IQ person, they often outperform the latter on some complex problem-solving task. For instance, when a low IQ racetrack gambler possesses a more elaborate and complex representation of horse racing than does a high IQ gambler, he will invariably exhibit more efficient problem-solving than the latter (Ceci & Liker, 1986), and children with lower IQs who are highly knowledgeable about soccer outperform their higher IQ peers on reading comprehension, inferential and memory tasks that involve learning new information in the domain of soccer. There is a growing body of evidence illustrating that complex performance on reading, memory and inferential reasoning tasks is predicted by individual differences in subjects' representation of knowledge at least as much, if not more so, than it is by differences in IQ scores (Means & Voss, 1985; Walker, 1987; Bjorklund & Muir, 1988).

Cognitive structures

An important tradition in developmental psychology has viewed intellectual development from a 'structuralist' perspective. Unlike the psychometric and cognitive processing traditions that view the child's intelligence as becoming quantitatively more sophisticated with age and experience, the structuralist perspective views the emerging intellect as an indivisible whole that unfolds over time into qualitatively different structures. Each new stage of development represents a qualitatively distinct structure from that which came before it; each new structure permits a new way of thinking. Thus, in contrast to purely quantitative increments in cognitive ability, structuralists posit a more differentiated structure with development.

The most influential structuralist was Jean Piaget (Piaget, 1952, 1970, 1972). Although Piaget worked for a brief time as a young man with Binet in the latter's efforts to develop the first intelligence test, this was not Piaget's preferred way of pursuing intellectual development. He reported being far less interested in children's answers to IQ test questions than he was in their reasoning about why they gave these answers. This was because in Piaget's view the justifications of their answers held the key to children's level of development.

Piaget's theory of intellectual development posits four major stages with many substages: sensorimotor, preoperational, concrete and formal operations. The first stage, known as the sensorimotor stage, is characterized as a period during the first 18 months of life during which time the organism builds representations about the world by acting on it physically. In subsequent stages of development cognitive structures not only become more sophisticated, but they are reorganized in an ontogenetically evolving fashion. Eventually, around the age of 12, according to Piaget, children achieve the highest level of Piagetian development, formal operations. It is only now that the child can reason in an abstract and scientific fashion.

Over the years Piaget's theory of intellectual development has been criticized on many grounds. Critics have condemned Piaget on the basis of the content and cultural appropriateness of his tasks, his methods of questioning and inferring responses from children, and even with regard to the usefulness of his theory in accounting for developmental data (for critiques see Siegel & Brainerd, 1978; Brown & Desforges, 1979; Beilin, 1980). In his search for universal principles, Piaget exposed his theory to attacks from information-processing researchers who rejected what they perceived as grand overarching theories in favour of more 'local theorettes'. While Piaget and his followers have been criticized on a number of grounds, the core complaint is that Piagetians do not provide a persuasive explanation of the problem of 'horizon-

tal decalage'. This term refers to the frequent finding that children will often be able to solve a problem in one domain years earlier than they can solve a similar problem in a different domain. For instance, a child's ability to recognize that a clay ball, when reshaped into a pancake, retains its amount seems to be structurally similar to a child's ability to recognize that a tall thin glass of lemonade when poured into a short wide glass retains the same amount. Both tasks require the ability to decenter (i.e. to avoid focusing on a single dimension such as height or width) and both require the ability to 'reverse' operations mentally (i.e. to reverse in one's mind the pouring of the lemonade from the short wide glass back into the tall thin glass). Yet, children can often solve conservation of mass years before they solve conservation of liquid. Many such horizontal decalages have been discovered and this has led to a call for a more contextualized, less universalistic, approach to explaining intellectual development. Elsewhere, one of us has provided a detailed account of many of the arguments against Piagetian assumptions, and shown that poor street children with little or no formal schooling can solve classical Piagetian problems if the instructions are altered slightly to make the object clear. Such research calls into question the main structural assumptions of intellectual development that are based on these tasks (Ceci & Roazi, 1994).

Abstractness, generality and transfer

Abstract thinking has been viewed as the *sine qua non* of intelligence for most of the twentieth century, by both researchers and laypersons alike (e.g. Terman, 1921; Cattell, 1971; Sternberg *et al.*, 1981). In fact, Jensen (1969), commenting on the difficulty of defining intelligence verbally, asserted, 'If we must define it in words, it is probably best thought of as a capacity for abstract reasoning and problem solving' (p. 19). Moreover, in the child development literature, abstract thinking has been viewed as the pinnacle of intellectual development (Vygotsky, 1962; Piaget, 1976; Case, 1985). By abstractness is meant the detection and/or reliance on principles or rules that underlie problems; abstract individuals solve problems by inferring the deep structure rather than by retrieving memorized solutions. Thus, abstraction allows one to generalize from the solution at hand to cases in other domains that, while superficially dissimilar, are governed by similar underlying principles (Pikas, 1966).

Abstractness figures into discussions of intelligence because of the presumed role that it plays in 'transfer'. An exploration of the relationship between transfer and intelligence necessitates that we say something about the role of abstractness, because both intelligence and transfer are alleged by many to require the abstraction of a hidden structure (i.e. the education of underlying principles). Consistent with this claim, Das (1987) remarked:

> I have suggested that transfer . . . depends on the education of a principle. More intelligent children are apt to observe that apparently different tasks may require the same processing; less intelligent children are less likely to notice this. Therefore, the extent of transfer must depend on intelligence to some degree. The relation between IQ and transfer is supported by more than one author in this book. I have a hunch that there is an IQ threshold (70–75) below which the education of an underlying process does not occur.

Das's claim about the role of IQ in transfer is interesting and important, but it warrants scrutiny. This claim presupposes that IQ scores reflect the degree to which individuals can be abstract enough to educe underlying structure — a characteristic of an intelligent person. Further, it suggests that the child who does not generalize fails to do so because of a lack of abstractness.

When children do not generalize, the assumption is made that they do not solve problems in terms of underlying rules or principles. According to this line of reasoning, instances of complex behaviour among individuals who possess low IQs are the result of their focus on the contents of a single highly, but delimited, elaborated domain of knowledge (e.g. chess, work, sports, gambling, love). Focusing on a single domain allows such individuals to accrue elaborate information which is often sufficient to solve even very complex problems in that domain. Accordingly, it is alleged that low IQ individuals do not solve complex problems from the vantage point of having abstracted an underlying rule or principle, but rather simply because they have learned a great deal of highly specific

material that is tied to highly specific solutions. They cannot transfer their skill to related problems in domains that are not well known to them, and therefore their complex behaviour is not thought to be 'intelligent'. Incidentally, this line of reasoning places the cart before the horse; after all, performance measures should serve as validators of IQ scores — not the reverse!

The preceding argument begs the question of abstractness in two ways. First, it presupposes that high IQ individuals are complex across different domains — something that bears challenge since it has not adequately been demonstrated that they regularly do so in non-academic or verbal domains. Ceci and Ruiz (1992) have shown that men who are complex at racetrack gambling are not equivalently complex at a task that involves similar types of reasoning to that exhibited at the racetrack, but couched in a stock market game. Their abstractness is not consistent across domains. And second, the argument assumes that even if high IQ persons were found to function on a complex level in a variety of domains, it is because of their greater invocation of abstract rules as opposed to their greater possession of elaborate but highly specific information in a variety of domains. Above, we cited a number of studies that show that complex reasoning, memory and comprehension were a result of the degree of elaboration of one's mental representation, rather than their IQ (e.g. Schneider *et al.*, 1989).

As if the above difficulties were not sufficiently problematic to abandon the notion of abstractness, there are two remaining problems that are even more serious. First, the idea that low IQ persons who perform complex tasks do so via non-abstract routes is highly questionable. Suppose, for example, that a person can perform the following problem rapidly and accurately: he is given the names of 7 months and asked to consider which month differs from the other 6. There are numerous ways for them to differ, of course, for example, in their number of days, number of full weeks, seasons of the year in which they occur, days of the week on which they begin, etc. Suppose that this individual is not allowed to visually inspect a calendar and is required to perform this task solely from memory. Would you assume that it requires abstractness to be able to arrive quickly at the correct answer (provided that we have identified 7 months, among which there is only one defining characteristic that separates 6 of them from the seventh)? This task is similar to tasks that appear on major IQ tests that ask for underlying similarities, such as 'In what way are scissors and a copper pan alike?' Thus, it is assumed by many that the solution process of this type of IQ problem requires abstractness, even though Howe and Smith (1988) reported that an idiot savant with an IQ in the mentally retarded range could answer it rapidly and accurately without looking at a calendar.

> Next, he was read aloud a list of seven months falling in particular years, as follows: January, 1971, September, 1972; June, 1973; July, 1974; August, 1975; February, 1971; October, 1976. All of these months except one start on a Friday. However, he was not told this, but was simply asked, 'Which one is the odd one out?' With little hesitation he gave the correct answer (February, 1971), and when asked why he chose that month he said that he did so because, unlike the others, it began on a Monday. Note that the question he was asked provided no hint of the kind of difference that is to be sought. (p. 380)

The second serious problem with the concept of abstractness is that it is virtually impossible to find a single definition of it that different individuals are willing to accept (Ceci, 1990a). Ceci and Nightingale (1992) asked 40 eminent scholars from science, mathematics, philosophy, linguistics and social science to judge how abstract one's thought process needed to be in order to solve certain problems. These individuals were nominated by their peers as among the most brilliant and important scholars in their fields, and the list included 18 Nobel prize winners as well as winners of a host of other prestigious honours. Unbeknown to these eminent persons was the fact that the problems they were given were selected from a major IQ test and were chosen because they are associated either with the largest or smallest racial and social class differences. Jensen (1980) and others have claimed that such differences are due to genetic differences in the ability to engage in abstract reasoning. If correct, then these eminent scholars ought to agree that the problems that result in the largest racial differences (favouring whites) require more abstract thought

processes. In a nutshell, Ceci and Nightingale found that there was no consensus among the scholars as to which problems were the most or least abstract. Even within a single field of scholarship (e.g. mathematics, philosophy), eminent individuals did not agree as to which items were abstract, and the overall correlation between ratings of abstractness and the magnitude of racial differences was negligible and insignificant. Thus, it is methodologically disagreeable to speak about a concept that cannot be reliably defined, and no matter how real or important abstractness might be, we have no basis for claiming that it is a source of individual or developmental differences until we can agree on exactly what it is.

Creative and intellectual processes

In this chapter we have discussed both historical and contemporary notions of intelligence and intellectual development. Our definitions of intelligence and the tasks employed to investigate this construct have focused on individuals' ability to arrive at correct responses to predetermined questions in a timely and parsimonious fashion. One might infer, from our discussion, that intelligence does not involve the ability to create new and unusual ideas and products. If anything, from our description of the psychometric tradition, it is easy to conclude that creative attempts at problem solutions are discouraged. In fact, this is the case. Because correct responses to items on IQ tests are determined according to age-appropriate responses, children who provide novel responses are penalized on these tests.

Even though many researchers interested in intelligence have avoided discussions of creativity, a few have attempted to examine the relationship between creativity and intelligence and to incorporate creativity into a definition of intelligence. One approach has suggested that if we can understand the 'cognitive lives' and intellectual precursors of creative genius we may begin to understand everyday forms of intelligence *and* creativity (Cox & Terman, 1926; Hadamard, 1945; Roe, 1952; Arnheim, 1962; Gruber, 1974; John-Steiner, 1985). Following this belief, the earliest explorations of the relationship between creativity and intelligence were derived from case study investigations. In one seminal investigation, Cox and Terman collected information on the childhood attainments of 300 creative 'geniuses' ranging from politicians to musicians to criminals (Cox & Terman, 1926). Each individual's childhood performance was then compared with performances of average children of a corresponding age. For example, John Stuart Mill's intelligence quotient was estimated at 170/190. The following excerpt provides an indication as to how both a cognitive profile and an intelligence quotient were derived:

> At 5 the precocious lad maintained an animated conversation with Lady Spencer on the comparative merits of Marlborough and Wellington. This alone indicates a level of development of which the IQ index reaches or exceeds 200. At 6½ the child was able to use intelligently such words as 'government', 'conquest', 'defeat', 'expulsion', 'reign', 'opposed', and to write such expressions as 'the country had not been entered by any foreign invader', ... Both the words and the expressions are typical of somewhat more than an average 12-year-old vocabulary. Before he reached the age of 7 young Mill evidenced the ability adequately to handle historical material and to prepare 'erudite and critical notes', a performance which indicates an IQ near 200 thus corroborating the vocabulary rating. (Cox & Terman, 1926, pp. 158–159)

Cox was not the only investigator to obtain detailed information about the intellectual development of creative achievers. As early as 1869 Galton's study, *Hereditary Genius*, attempted to assess the heritability of creativity. More recently, Gruber (1974) chronicled the intellectual and creative life of Charles Darwin, and Holton (1978) has examined the creative life of Einstein and others. Using a somewhat different approach, a small group of investigators have examined the cognitive steps and intellectual processes that result in a creative product. As examples, Margolis (1987) analysed the creative processes related to discoveries by Copernicus. Perkins (1977) has detailed the evolution of poetic works from inception to completion. And both Weisberg (1986) and Arnheim (1962) have analysed the evolution of Picasso's masterpiece *Guernica*.

Much of the case study research aimed at understanding intelligent and creative problem solving ground to a halt in the middle of this century. As already mentioned, at that time there was a need and a market for the development of a variety of aptitude tests aimed at assessing a range of human abilities. Following the academic and commercial success of intelligence tests, psychometricians proceeded to devise more 'objective' ways of assessing creativity (Torrance, 1966; Guilford, 1967).

Many psychometricians have argued that creativity can be measured by the assessment of three primary abilities: fluency, flexibility and originality. While the possession of these three abilities does not guarantee that an individual will behave in a creative manner, it is believed that a high level of ability in each of these areas will increase the likelihood that an individual will behave creatively, and low levels of ability in each of these areas preclude the development of creativity. In brief, fluency refers to the ability to come up with a large number of ideas or problem solutions. Flexibility involves one's tendency to represent a number of different types of ideas, to shift from one approach to another, and to use a variety of strategies. Finally originality is typically viewed as the ability to produce ideas that are away from the obvious and commonplace (Guilford, 1959; Torrance, 1966). In order to assess these abilities, creativity 'tests' are comprised of tasks that require children to generate new and unusual uses for tools or objects, to think of unusual questions, and/or to draw innovative pictures.

Once creativity tests were developed it was suggested that the construct of creativity (divergent production) would best be understood and validated in relation to 'intelligence' (e.g. convergent abilities). During the past 20 years much of the ensuing research has focused on the psychometric differentiation of the constructs of convergent and divergent thinking (Getzel & Jackson, 1962; Wallach & Kogan, 1965; Wallach, 1971). Nearly all of these investigations were based on correlational techniques and most found the simple correlation between measures of creativity and intelligence to be quite low (Hammer, 1961; Getzel & Jackson, 1962; Torrance, 1962; Flescher, 1963; Cicirelli, 1965; Butcher, 1968; MacKinnon, 1968; Wade, 1968; Smith, 1971; Schubert, 1973; Welsh, 1975;

Persaud & Stimpson, 1983). Additionally, it was concluded that the magnitude of the relationship between intelligence and creativity does not vary significantly with age. In one investigation Persaud and Stimpson (1983) assessed students in fourth, seventh and tenth grades on Guilford's circles game and Cattell's culture fair intelligence scale. The investigators reported correlations ranging from low negative to low positive.

The absence of significant correlations has implied that intelligence and creativity are fairly independent rather than overlapping constructs. Yet, some investigators have argued otherwise. Yamamoto (1965) as well as Anastasi and Schaefer (1971) found correlations between the two constructs to be quite high and concluded 'Both terms will undoubtedly survive as independent concepts because they provide convenient shortcuts in designating complex behaviour domains of considerable practical importance. But neither corresponds to a precisely defined or distinct entity'.

One reason for the discrepancy between investigations supporting the absence of a relationship between creativity and intelligence and those suggesting that the two constructs are related can be attributed to the measures of creativity and intelligence used to assess these two constructs. We have already outlined the controversy surrounding the use of intelligence tests. Not surprisingly, many of the same complaints have been lodged against the use of 'creativity' tests (Perkins, 1988).

Most recently, researchers have moved away from the use of psychometric instruments to understand the relationship between creativity and intelligence. They have turned their focus to an examination of the cognitive, social and cultural processes that underpin both of these constructs (Csikszentmihalyi, 1988; Sternberg, 1988; Baker-Sennett *et al.*, 1994); and have suggested that creativity often involves being the first person to arrive at a novel idea or discovery. If we trace the discovery process we find that creative solutions can be accounted for by the ways that individuals approach problems. Those individuals who require little information before attempting to solve problems (regardless of whether their initial hunches are correct or not) and who avoid perseverating on a single incorrect response arrive at discoveries in a more timely and efficient manner.

Additionally, these same individuals tend to perform significantly better than others on traditional tests of insight. Looking at this problem developmentally Baker-Sennett and Ceci found that as children get older they not only tend to require more information before attempting problem solutions, but they also tend to perseverate on incorrect responses longer than younger children. This research begins to illuminate the integral relationship betwen processes traditionally associated with intelligent and creative problem-solving.

Baker-Sennett *et al.* (1994) make a similar argument but use a very different approach to argue that creativity is an integral aspect of all intellectually demanding tasks involving future-oriented activities, such as problem-solving and planning. In an investigation of children's collaborative planning processes they conclude that the symbiotic nature of intelligence and creativity is not typically considered because researchers have elected to focus on intellectual and creative products as opposed to the cognitive and sociocultural processes of which these two constructs are comprised. While the research continues, it is likely that this shift away from a reliance on psychometric tools and the move towards a vision of the creative nature of problem-solving processes will enhance our future understanding of intellectual development.

The bioecology of intellectual development

Traditionally, it has been claimed that psychometric tests are an adequate index of an individual's intellectual ability, and that such tests measure a singular, pervasive ability called general intelligence (*g*) that permeates virtually all intellectual endeavours. The evidence for this view is the manifold positive correlations among diverse mental test scores (vocabulary, spatial reasoning, maths, reading comprehension) that was mentioned earlier in this chapter. It is difficult to imagine how an individual's performance on such seemingly different tests could be related if not because each of them are saturated with *g*. Moreover, construct validation research has attempted to show that measures of general intelligence are more potent predictors of a range of behaviours (job success, school grades, training scores) than are measures of specific cognitive abilities, motivation, or background experience (e.g. Hunter & Schmidt, 1982; Hunter *et al.*, 1984; Gottfredson, 1986; Barrett & Depinet, 1991). And, finally, it has been argued that measures of general intelligence (*g*) derived from psychometric tests are related to theoretical constructs such as heritability, cranial blood flow, evoked potential recordings and information-processing efficiency. Taken together, this evidence has persuaded many to view scores on psychometric tests as reflections of a singular, biologically determined resource pool that permeates virtually all intellectual feats. This is not to deny the role that environment plays in such performance, of course, but it does emphasize the relative ascendancy of biology, with reports of high heritabilities now being the norm (Plomin *et al.*, 1988).

In this chapter we have tried to suggest that there is ample evidence to permit alternate views about psychometric performance that do not require the assumptions above. For example, we have suggested that cognitive test performance can be due to the elaborateness of the underlying mental representation as opposed to the ability to be abstract, and we have proposed that traditional measures of intellectual functioning are highly domain-specific and do not predict complex performance in non-academic domains such as gambling, stock market analysis or the comprehension of sporting events (e.g. Ceci & Liker, 1986; Walker, 1987; Schneider *et al.*, 1989; Ceci & Ruiz, 1992). It is not that traditional assumptions about generality, singularity and abstractness are decidedly incorrect. Rather, it is that the evidentiary basis for them is open to criticism and/or different interpretations. There is a growing trend to view both psychometric test performance and intellectual development as the result of a concatenation of factors — some cognitive, some social, some biological — that argue against the assumptions of singularity, heredity and pervasiveness we have discussed in this chapter (e.g. Sternberg, 1985, 1990).

FOUR VIEWS OF INTELLECTUAL DEVELOPMENT

Logically, it is possible to discuss four views of intelligence, but because of space constraints we shall provide only a caricature of each here. All of

them acknowledge the importance of both biology and ecology in the development of intelligence, but they differ in the relative contributions they assign to each, the manner in which they interact, and, most profoundly, in their assumptions about what intelligence is and how it is to be assessed.

The environmentalist view

Adherents of this view claim that most of the differences observed among individuals on IQ tests can be traced to differences in their ecologies. Proponents, like Howard Gardner, tend to come from the professional education community, where the emphasis on environmentalism fits in well with their interventionist mandate. Notwithstanding Jensen's (1969) claim that acknowledging a high heritability (h^2) for intelligence was compatible with effective educational programming, educators have been notably reluctant to endorse hereditarian views. Some environmentalists assert that *if* biology is an important source of individual differences in IQ, then the evidence that has been presented thus far has not made the case (e.g. Kamin, 1974). For example, environmentalists have argued that observed racial differences in IQ cannot be explained in terms of biologically related ethnic and racial differences in the size of *g* (Isham & Kamin, in press).

Environmentalists tend to focus their argument on means instead of correlations, thus emphasizing the large increments in IQ that are associated with interventions and training, and ignoring the equally large correlations between the IQs of the biological parents and their adopted-away offspring whom they did not rear. For example, a seminal adoption study (Skodak & Skeels, 1949), followed children who had been born to mothers with an average IQ of only 85, but were reared by upper middle-class families. It was found that, at adolescence, these adopted children had IQs that were on average 22 points higher than their biological mothers' IQs (107). Similarly dramatic intervention effects have been reported by others (e.g. Schiff *et al.*, 1982). This brief description of the environmentalist position is, of course, woefully inadequate to capture the diversity within the environmental ranks. Some environmentalists assume that even if biology is important, it is the ecology that determines how it will be manifested. It becomes a matter of judgement where one draws the line between such views and ones that will be described below, especially the interactionist position, but it is fair to say that the environmentalist position today is more likely to acknowledge the role of biology than was true of its adherents a few decades ago.

The biological view

Adherents of this view assert that even though the environment is important, biology is relatively more important in shaping an individual's test performance. The main evidence for this claim comes from the high heritability scores obtained in five large adoption studies in North America and Scandinavia, as well as the numerous behaviour genetic analyses of the similarity of IQs among collaterals (cousins, aunts, uncles). Not only is it now a consensus among behaviour geneticists that h^2 accounts for somewhere between 0.5 and 0.8 (i.e. 50–80% of the variation in test scores being uniquely biologically determined), but even some former ardent environmentalists now seem to agree with such estimates (e.g. Jencks & Crouse, 1982; Zigler, 1988). For example, Jencks and his colleagues believe that h^2 is around 0.45, while Zigler (1988) states that, 'until we have more evidence, our best estimate of (h^2) is probably at least 0.5' (p. 7). These estimates represent the lower end of a range that goes upwards of the figure with which Jensen (1969) shocked the social science community with 26 years ago. In short, the central tendency among social scientists today is decidedly more biological than it was 25 years ago, and may be more hereditarian than at any time this century. In summarizing the new evidence that has led to this shift in beliefs about the relative ascendancy of biology, Plomin (1985) commented:

> The convergence of evidence in the area of IQ is impressive ... the data converge on the conclusion, remarkable as it seems, that fully half of the variance in IQ scores is due to genetic differences among individuals ...
> There is no finding in the behavioral sciences that begins to approach the magnitude of this result. (p. 304)

Since writing this, Plomin and co-workers have reported heritability estimates for specific groups of individuals that range in excess of 0.80 (Pedersen *et al.*, 1992), and the psychometrist Carroll (1992) has echoed the claim that at least 50% of the variance in cognitive ability (and probably more) is genetic in origin. If these claims are correct, then one can ask how much an interaction with ecology can influence development, as at least half, and possibly upwards of 80%, of the variation in intelligence test scores appears to be accounted for solely by genetic variation. We shall return to this issue below when we discuss one particular type of interactionist perspective called the bioecological approach.

The biological view is distinguishable from the old nature–nurture (interactionist) views in that it assumes that although the environment is an important contributor to individual and developmental differences, it exerts its influence as a result of genetically determined forces, through gene-environment correlations. The environment, it is alleged, is 'genetically-loaded' (Plomin & Bergeman, 1991), and does not interact with genes in the calculation of h^2 (heritability analyses must assume an absence of interaction with genetic action, lest the additive assumption of the statistical model be violated).

An example of what biologically oriented researchers mean when they claim that environmental effects are mediated by genetic influences can be seen in the work of Scarr (1992). She has reanalysed studies that purported to show large environmental influences on children's IQs, and argued that the true cause of variation in these children's IQs was not putative differences in the child's proximal environment (e.g. in parental disciplinary styles) but rather variations in their mothers' IQs, a presumed marker for genetics. For instance, Scarr (1989) showed that the relationship between maternal disciplinary style and a child's IQ could be completely accounted for by the fact that mothers who employed positive types of discipline had higher Wechsler adult intelligence scale vocabulary scores. Thus, what appeared to be an environmental influence (type of discipline) was really a result of gene-environment correlation. In her presidential address at the Society for Research in Child Development, Scarr (1992) asserted that as long as some minimum (i.e. non-abusive) environmental context is provided, variations in children's intelligence will be unrelated to variations in their environment, because behaviour is the result of genetically driven processes that wind their way to their destination independent of the environments that families provide. In her words:

> Being reared within one family, rather than another, within the range of families sampled makes few differences in children's personality and intellectual development. These data suggest that environments most parents provide for their children have few differential effects on the offspring (p. 5) ... The important point here is that variations among environments that support normal human development are not very important as determinants of variations in childrens' outcomes (p. 6) ... for children whose development is on a predictable but undesirable trajectory and whose parents are providing a supportive environment, interventions have only temporary and limited effects. Should we be surprised? Feeding a well-nourished but short child more and more will not give him the stature of a basketball player. Feeding a below-average intellect more and more information will not make her brilliant ... The child with a below-average intellect ... may gain some specific skills and helpful knowledge of how to behave in specific situations, but (her) enduring intellectual and personality characteristics will not be fundamentally changed. (Scarr, 1992, pp. 16−17)

The interactionist view

This view emphasizes the ecologically dependent nature of intellectual development. 'Biology proposes, ecology disposes' might be the rallying cry for its adherents. Like Waddington's well-known canalization hypothesis, interactionists view biology as a set of genetically constrained cognitive potentials that are twisted and reformed as they unfold over the bumpy landscape of experience. Evidence consistent with this view includes differences in mean IQ scores that result when genetically similar individuals are reared in different ecologies, as well as different variances among children who are genetically different but are reared in the same

environment. Bronfenbrenner's (1974) reanalysis of the then known twin data is in accord with this claim. Interactionists search for the nexus between a genotypic propensity and an environmental condition in order to understand why individuals develop differently.

Despite its reasonableness, the traditional interactionist view is not well articulated in the domain of intellectual development. It does not, for example, address many of the most important issues raised by the biological camp (e.g. singularity versus multiplicity of intelligence, or whether very high h^2 estimates imply that there is little room left over for the environment to make a difference).

The interactionist view was developed primarily to account for social behaviours, and therefore it is not surprising to find that it does not go very far in the domain of intellectual development before it runs head-on into the problems on three levels. First, proponents of the biological view claim that proximal environmental influences on intellectual growth (e.g. the effect of parental disciplinary style on an offspring's IQ) are actually mediated by distal genetic forces, and therefore that they exert little influence independent of that exerted by the genes themselves (Plomin & Bergeman, 1991; Scarr, 1992). Second, most psychometric researchers claim that there is but one biological propensity, not many, and therefore the continuity of mental development (e.g. stable IQ scores over long periods of development, infant short-term memory efficiency predicting age 7 IQ scores) reflects a simpler and more deterministic unfolding than the diversity of environments of these individuals might lead one to assume. Third, there are many findings that would seem hard to explain in terms of the traditional interactionist perspective, such as why university students who score high on g-based tests like IQ are faster at recognizing letters of the alphabet than are their university peers who have somewhat lower scores on g-based tests (e.g. Hunt, 1985). It is hard to imagine how environment could matter at all in such cases since all subjects are highly familiar with the stimuli, yet the higher IQ subjects are faster at 'seeing' them. Speed of processing is claimed by biological proponents to result from more efficient signal : noise ratios in the nervous system, thus leading to different patterns of electrical activation even during resting states of high and low IQ persons (e.g. Eysenck, 1982, 1986; Hendrickson & Hendrickson, 1982; Schafer, 1987; Weiss, 1990). Recently, Jensen (in press) reviewed the evidence favouring the view that a singular biological resource pool (central nerve conductance velocity and oscillation) underpins a large portion of the individual differences in intelligence. To date, interactionist proponents have not attempted to address this evidence.

The bioecological view

Recently, Ceci (1990a) and Bronfenbrenner and Ceci (1993) have developed an interactionist view of intellectual development that attempts to accommodate and integrate the full body of biological and environmental research findings into a cognitive and developmental account. This view, known as the bioecological view, differs from existing perspectives on intellectual development in the assumptions it makes about the nature of intelligence as well as its developmental course and contextual sensitivity. As will be seen, the bioecological view extends and qualifies the traditional behaviour genetic model in several important ways. Because this view is the progeny of two of the authors of this chapter, we shall delve into it in somewhat greater detail.

To begin with, the bioecological view, like other interactionist views, acknowledges the role of biology in virtually every important aspect of human functioning, from physical to psychological characteristics. It is hard to imagine the development of a single characteristic that would not be influenced to some degree by biology. Having said this, the bioecological perspective differs from other interactionist views (even though it adopts an interactionist perspective, too) in three respects. But before describing these divergences from the biological view, we shall briefly describe the main tenets of the bioecological view, specifically, its developmental nature, its insistence on a multiplicity of cognitive resources, and its assertion that intellectual performance is highly sensitive to context (including mental context) and motivation.

According to the bioecological view, the data of intellectual development necessitate a three-pronged framework for their explication. First, the evidence from cognitive and psychometric analyses favours a view of intelligence as a modular (or multiple resource system), rather than the singular resource pool which is endorsed by the vast majority of psychometric researchers. Therefore, it should be possible to find discordances among various types of intellectual performance, over and above the magnitude that might be expected from traditional hierarchical models of intelligence that posit general intelligence at the top of a flow model that subsumes under it 'family' and 'specific' factors (see Chapters 6 and 7 of Ceci, 1990a for the evidence in favour of this assertion). The importance of this claim gets at the heart of an acrimonious debate over the nature and malleability of intellectual functioning. If all forms of intellectual behaviour are controlled by the magnitude of a single resource pool in the central nervous system, this implies that assessing a single resource (indexed by any g-saturated test, such as IQ) will suffice to predict an applicant's job success in virtually all types of occupations. Moreover, it carries an additional implication: intervention efforts should be based on enhancing the efficiency of a singular intelligence rather than strengthening certain types of intelligence to offset weaknesses in others. It is beyond the scope of this chapter to delve into these issues (for an extended discussion see Ceci, 1990).

Second, like all interactionist perspectives, the bioecological view asserts that from the very beginning of life there exists interaction between biological potentials and environmental forces, such that two individuals who are born with equivalent biological resources for a variety of intelligences may end up with disparate cognitive profiles by adolescence. In order to understand how individuals could begin life possessing comparable intellectual potentials but differ in the level of intelligence they subsequently manifest, the bioecological view posits an interplay between various biologically influenced cognitive potentials, such as the capacity to store, scan and retrieve information, and the ecological contexts that are relevant for each of their unfolding. At each point in development, an interaction between biology and ecology results in changes that may themselves produce other changes until a full cascading of effects is set in motion. The exact mechanism that is posited to translate genotypes into phenotypes is called 'proximal processes'; these are reciprocal interactions between the developing organism and consistent persons, objects and symbols in the near environment that foster progressively more complex forms of interaction (e.g. for an infant a proximal process might be an activity between a caregiver and infant that serves to maintain the infant's attention). Bronfenbrenner and Ceci (1993) have suggested that the size of h^2 changes substantially in response to changes in the level of proximal processes in the child's environment. Far higher as well as far lower h^2s than heretofore have been reported in the behaviour genetic literature are to be found in settings that contain either very low or very high levels of proximal processes. This may be why Bronfenbrenner (1974) was able to show that identical twins reared apart resembled each other very highly (h^2s approaching 0.8) when they were both reared in similar ecologies (mining, agricultural, manufacturing), but differed markedly when they were reared in very different ecologies, the h^2s in the latter case falling to 0.28.

The bioecological view suggests that environmental influences are specific to each type of cognitive resource or potential, both in the timing of its onset and the rate of its unfolding. Thus, the timing of events, both in one's personal and historical development, may have profound implications for some facets of behaviour, but little, if any, for others, as demonstrated in the lifecourse literature (e.g. Elder *et al.*, 1991). Whether a genetically influenced disposition creates difficulties or is used to one's advantage depends on the personal and historical niche that the proband occupies, a case in point being the influence of exposure to economic adversity on intellectual and economic outcomes as a function of how old the child was at the time of exposure (e.g. Caspi *et al.*, 1987).

Unlike biological and environmental theories of intelligence, the bioecological framework is inherently developmental. It posits the existence of periods of development when specific cognitive 'muscles' may be differentially sensitive to the environment. Although biology and ecology are interwoven into an indivisible whole, their relationship is continually changing, and with each change a new set of possibilities is set in motion until soon even small changes produce cascading effects. Hence, developmental change is not always or even usually linear, but rather is synergistic and non-

additive. A small environmental influence on a protein-fixing gene may initially result in only tiny changes, but over time the chain of events may produce a magnification of effects on other processes. In addition, certain epochs in development can be thought of as sensitive periods during which a unique disposition exists for a specific cognitive muscle to crystallize in response to its interaction with the environment. During such periods, neurones within specific compartments rapidly 'overarborize' (spreading their tentacle-like synaptic connections to other neurones). Even though some of the arboreal connections laid down during these periods of brain spurts will not be used at that time, they can be recruited to enable future behaviours to occur, provided they are not 'pruned' because of atrophy or disuse. Siegler (1989) concluded that 'the timing of the sensitive period seems to be a function of both when synaptic overproduction occurs and when the organism receives relevant experience' (p. 358). It appears that while some neural processes are more fully under maturational control, others are responsive to the environment, and synapses are formed in response to learning that may vary widely among humans. Similar contextual roles have been found for the social environments of various animals' cognitive skills, too (Smith & Spear, 1978; Lickliter & Hellewell, 1992).

So, the bioecological framework is predicated on various brain compartments, comprised of specific types of neurones, growing at different times, and at different rates in response to the growing organism's ecology (see also Chapter 3). Both human and animal research indicates quite unequivocally that experience accounts for some of the specificity in nervous system developments that are themselves at least partly heritable.

Finally, the bioecological view incorporates motivation and context as key ingredients in its explanation of empirical findings. Briefly, an individual must not merely be endowed with some biological potential for a given cognitive resource, or even be exposed to an environment that is facilitative for its elicitation; the individual must also be motivated to benefit from exposure to such an environment. Men in Ceci and Liker's (1986) study who demonstrated highly complex forms of reasoning at the racetrack did not exhibit the same degee of complex reasoning in other domains. Had they been exposed to environments that were conducive to, say, science or philosophy, and motivated to take advantage of such environments, they would have undoubtedly acquired the ability to think as complexly in those domains as they did at the racetrack, given the isomorphism that was built-in between the type of reasoning needed to handicap a race and to reason scientifically in that experiment.

Having described the bioecological view of intellectual development briefly, it now can be constrasted with the biological, environmental and psychometric views of intelligence on three grounds.

First, as already alluded to, the bioecological view claims that the evidence in favour of the generality and singularity of intelligence is open to alternative interpretations. Recall that generality refers to the fact that performances tend to be correlated across seemingly diverse cognitive tasks, and the explanation given for this is that intelligence, or *g*, is a singular entity that flows into all cognitive behaviours, hence leading to generality of performance. It has been asserted that it 'has proved impossible to devise a mental test that is not *g*-loaded to some degree' (Jensen, 1992, p. 275), and it is this general factor that correlates with neurophysiological variables, the efficiency of information-processing measures, educational attainment, job success, etc. (Jensen, 1982; Schmidt & Ones, 1992). When cognitive test batteries are diversified and administered in varying contexts, however, measures derived from them to reflect generality are reduced; the tendency of performance on one test to be correlated with the performance on the others is significantly reduced.

Furthermore, even when generality across tests *is* observed, this occurs disproportionately as a result of persons with very low IQs behaving generally. That is, over most of the IQ range there is a substantially greater differentiation of cognitive abilities (i.e. lower *g*) than there is among persons with IQs below 85 (Detterman & Daniel, 1989; Detterman & Persanyi, 1990; Deary & Pagliari, 1991; Detterman, 1991). The first person to recognize that *g* was smaller among persons with average or above average cognitive ability than among persons with low cognitive ability was Spearman himself (Deary & Pagliari, 1991). This means that the concept of 'general intelligence', that has been at the core of twentieth century thinking about intelligence, is possibly a misnomer; the individuals who behave most generally are those with low IQs. If true, then what is 'general' is not intelligence but the lack thereof, namely stupidity (Detterman, 1991).*

Another reason why factor analytic studies of mental test performance yields a large measure of general intelligence (in addition to the fact that they are disproportionately influenced by the lack of cognitive differentiation among individuals with very low IQs), is because they rely on tasks that involve the operation of many independent cognitive abilities that interact with each other for successful performance (e.g. Detterman, 1986; Detterman *et al.*, in press). Put succinctly, the evidence from various analyses suggests that there may not be a singular intellectual ability that pervades all cognitive test performances, but a host of statistically and logically independent skills. Accordingly, measures of general intelligence, such as IQ tests, may reflect the operation of diverse cognitive skills in a single context that leads to shared variance and, ultimately, to what appears on the surface to be a singular form of intelligence. Because IQ tests and other *g*-saturated measures are comprised of a multitude of cognitive skills, performance on them is related to a wide range of cognitive performances. But this may have little to do with a single skill. All complex tasks are heterogeneous, requiring for their successful completion the workings of many independent cognitive components, structures, and processes. Factor analysts have only rarely sought to separate such diverse components (usually by altering the order in which regression analyses are run to see whether the variance associated with

---

* The idea that *g* might be distributed in a non-linear manner, more among low IQ persons than high IQ persons, also suggests that it could be the case that h^2 estimates are higher among low IQ persons. As tantalizing as this possibility is, the available evidence is mixed (see Cherny *et al.*, 1992 for review of five studies that have examined the possibility of differential h^2 estimates as a function of level of IQ). Independent of this issue, however, the finding that *g* is non-linearly distributed across IQ *is* well-documented and has important implications for the meaning of general intelligence and its screening and remediation value.

one is absorbed by another when it is entered earlier), but when this is done, the evidence in favour of generality is often diminished (Detterman, 1986), and the evidence in favour of a multiplicity of cognitive abilities that are independent of g is compelling to some (e.g. Horn, 1989). So, the bio-ecological view proposes multiple cognitive abilities that are, at best, only imperfectly gauged by tests of general intelligence. This point is useful to understand because it helps explain how psychometric assessments can possess good predictive validity despite being conceived of as measures of general intelligence.

Second, like other interactionist views of development, the bioecological view argues that the efficiency of cognitive processes depends on aspects of the context. According to Ceci (1990a), context is not an adjunct to cognition, but a constituent of it. Unlike traditional cognitive science, which has assumed that context is merely a background for cognition (see Chapter 10), the bioecological view regards context as an inextricable aspect of cognitive efficiency. As discussed elsewhere in this volume, context is defined broadly to include not only external features of the near and far environment and their motivational properties, but internal features of the organism's mental representation, such as the manner in which a stimulus or problem is represented in memory. Thus, speed in recognizing letters and numerals can be shown to depend on how those stimuli are represented in memory, with more elaborate representations leading to faster recognition rates (Ceci, 1990a). This explains why the same cognitive ability, no matter how basic or microlevel it is, operates inconsistently across diverse contexts (Ceci, 1990b). The same individuals who are slow at recognizing a stimulus in one domain, may recognize it in another domain more quickly if its representation in the latter domain is more elaborate. In short, cognition-in-context research has shown that context, including the mental representation or mental context of a task, determines the efficiency of cognition.

The bioecological view assumes that the nature of what is inherited may be non-intellective, yet highly important for subsequent intellectual development. For example, a child may inherit various types of temperament, physical traits (e.g. skin colour, facial shape), and 'instigative characteristics'

(e.g. reward-seeking) that may influence later learning and development. While these traits are themselves influenced by gene systems, and can be shown to exert direct as well as indirect effects on subsequent IQ performance and school success, they are not intellectual in nature. They can account for heritabilities and continuities in mental development without claiming that they do so as a consequence of the inheritance of a central nervous system with a determinate signal : noise ratio that limits processing capacity. Accounts of rate-limiting cognitive functioning that are based on electro-encephalographic power spectral density measures (e.g. Weiss, 1990), blood glucose levels in the brain, central nerve conductance velocity and oscillation (Jensen, in press), and heritability analyses (e.g. Pedersen *et al.*, 1992), cannot distinguish between cognitive and non-cognitive bases of performance. This is not to deny the importance of genes in intellectual performance, but is merely a caution that not all that is genetic and leads to intellectual differences is intellectual in nature.

Finally, the bioecological view departs from traditional behaviour genetic models regarding the nature and meaning of h^2. It states that h^2 reflects the proportion of 'actualized' genetic potential, leaving unknown and unknowable the amount of unactualized genetic potential (Bronfenbrenner & Ceci, 1993). If there are insufficient proximal processes in one's life, then h^2s will reflect only that portion of one's potential that has been brought to fruition. Measures of heritability are extremely sensitive to secular trends, generally dropping during times of economic scarcity and climbing during times of plenty (see Bronfenbrenner & Ceci, 1993). This is consistent with the view that the ecology brings to fruition differing levels of genetic potential, and h^2s will fluctuate by a magnitude of 3 in conjunction with economic fluctuations. So, if genes provide the fuel for intellectual development, then proximal processes are the engines, and context is the rudder. In regard to our earlier question about the meaning of a heritability estimate as high 0.8, this would *not* imply that only 20% of the variation among individuals' IQ scores can possibly be influenced by the environment, because the size of h^2 tells us nothing about the size of unactualized potential.

In sum, current research on intelligence and

intellectual development points in a direction that emphasizes the role of context in the formation and assessment of an individual's manifold cognitive potentials. Although traditional measures of general intelligence possess good predictive validity in school, job and training situations, they do not achieve this prediction through a convincing set of demonstrations that the basis for the predictions is cognitive in nature, or that it is a singular resource pool that underpins a significant portion of the prediction, or that the size of heritability estimates reflect the amount of variation due to purely genetic processes. Thus, prediction and explanation can be fundamentally disjunctive enterprises in science. The bioecological view of intellectual development aims to fulfil the promissory note of the inter-actionist perspective, taking full cognizance of the biological and cognitive findings that have been reported throughout this century. It does this by importing Bronfenbrenner's (1979, in press) process × person × context × time approach into the domain of intellectual development. Individuals (i.e. the 'person' or biological variable) who demonstrate a superior level of a specific cognitive processing ability (i.e. the 'process' variable) in one domain than in another (i.e. the context variable), are assumed to have the neuroarchitecture necessary to make this process operate at equally high levels of efficiency in all domains, but only if the ecology of development (including the timing of personally and historically important developments) resulted in similar mental representations or motivations in all domains. While it is premature to assess the adequacy of this process × person × context × time view of intellectual development, the short-comings of the other three views appear to be already in sight.

ACKNOWLEDGEMENT

Preparation of this chapter was supported by grants from the National Institutes of Health, DHHS Nos 5R01HD22839 and KO4HD00801.

REFERENCES

Anastasi A. (1968) *Psychological Testing*, 3rd edn. Macmillan, New York.

Anastasi A. & Schaefer C.E. (1971) Note on the concepts of creativity and intelligence. *Journal of Creative Behavior* **5**, 113–116.

Arnheim R. (1962) *Picasso's 'Guernica': The Genesis of a Painting*. University of California Press, Berkeley.

Arvey R. (1986) General ability in employment: A discussion. *Journal of Occupational Behavior* **29**, 415–420.

Austin J. & Hanisch K. (1990) Occupational attainment as a function of abilities and interests. *Journal of Applied Psychology* **75**, 77–86.

Baker-Sennett J., Matusov E. & Rogoff B. (1994) Social processes of creativity and planning. In Light P. & Butterworth G. (eds) *Context and Cognition: Ways of Learning and Knowing*, pp. 161–187. Harvester-Wheatsheaf, Hemel Hempstead.

Barrett G.V. & Depinet R.L. (1991) A reconsideration of testing for competence rather than for intelligence. *American Psychologist* **46**, 1012–1024.

Beilin H. (1980) Piaget's theory: Refinement, revision, or rejection? In Kluwe R.H. & Spada H. (eds) *Developmental Models of Thinking*, pp. 245–261. Academic Press, New York.

Binet A. & Simon T. (1916) *The Development of Intelligence in Children* (translated by E.S. Kite). Williams & Wilkins, Baltimore, Maryland.

Bjorklund D.F. & Muir J.E. (1988) Children's development of free recall memory: Remembering on their own. In Vasta R. (ed.) *Annals of Child Development*, Vol. 5, pp. 79–123. JAI Press, Greenwich, Connecticut.

Bronfenbrenner U. (1974) Nature with nurture: A reinterpretation of the evidence. In Montague A. (ed.) *Race and IQ*. Oxford University Press, New York.

Bronfenbrenner U. (1979) *The Ecology of Human Development*. Harvard University Press, Cambridge, Massachusetts.

Bronfenbrenner U. (in press) The ecology of cognitive development. In Wozniak R. & Fischer K.W. (eds) *Development in Context: Acting and Thinking in Specific Environments*. Lawrence Erlbaum, Hillsdale, New Jersey.

Bronfenbrenner U. & Ceci S.J. (1993) Heredity, environment, and the question 'how'? A first approximation. In Plomin R. & McClearn G. (eds) *Nature, Nurture, and Psychology*, pp. 313–324. American Psychological Association, Washington, DC.

Brown G. & Desforges C. (1979) *Piaget's Theory: A Psychological Critique*. Routledge & Kegan Paul, Boston.

Burt C. (1932) BBC Radio interview; quoted in Carroll, 1982. The measurement of intelligence. In Sternberg R.J. (ed.) *Handbook of Human Intelligence*, pp. 29–120. Cambridge University Press, New York.

Butcher H.J. (1968) *Human Intelligence*. Methuen, London.

Carroll J.B. (1992) Cognitive abilities: The state of the art. *Psychological Science* **3**, 266–270.

Case R. (1985) *Intellectual Development: Birth to Adulthood*. Academic Press, Florida.

Caspi A., Elder G. & Bem D. (1987) Moving against the world: Life course patterns in explosion. *Developmental*

Psychology **23**, 308–313.

Cattell J.M. (1890) Mental tests and measurements. *Mind* **15**, 373–380.

Cattell R.B. (1971) *Abilities: Their Structure, Growth, and Action.* Houghton-Mifflin, Boston.

Ceci S.J. (1990a) *On Intelligence . . . More or Less: A Bioecological Treatise on Intellectual Development.* Prentice Hall, New Jersey.

Ceci S.J. (1990b) The relationship between microlevel and macrolevel processing: Some arguments against reductionism. *Intelligence* **14**, 1–9.

Ceci S.J. (1991) How much does schooling influence intellectual and cognitive development? A reassessment of the evidence. *Developmental Psychology* **27**, 703–722.

Ceci S.J. & Liker J. (1986) A day at the races: A study of IQ, expertise, and cognitive complexity. *Journal of Experimental Psychology: General* **115**, 255–266.

Ceci S.J. & Nightingale N.N. (1992) *Abstractness, intelligence, and race.* Unpublished ms, Cornell University, Ithaca, New York.

Ceci S.J. & Roazi A. (1994) Cognition in context: Postcards from Brazil. In Sternberg R.J. & Wagner R.K. (eds) *Intellectual Development*, pp. 74–107. Cambridge University Press, New York.

Ceci S.J. & Ruiz A. (1992) The role of general ability in cognitive complexity: A case study. In Hoffman R. (ed.) *The Psychology of Expertise*, pp. 218–232. Springer, New York.

Cherny S.S., Cardon L.R., Fulker D.W. & DeFries J.C. (1992) Differential heritability across levels of cognitive ability. *Behavior Genetics* **22**, 153–162.

Cicirelli V.G. (1965) Form of the relationship between creativity, I.Q. and academic achievement. *Journal of Educational Psychology* **56**, 303–308.

Cox C.M. & Terman L. (1926) *Genetic Studies of Genius*, Vol. II. *The Early Mental Traits of Three Hundred Geniuses.* Stanford University Press, Stanford, California.

Csikszentmihalyi M. (1988) Society, culture, and person: A systems view of creativity. In Sternberg R.J. (ed.) *The Nature of Creativity*, pp. 325–339. Cambridge University Press, Cambridge.

Das J.P. (1987) Foreword. In Lidz C.S. (ed.) *Dynamic Assessment*, pp. vii–xi. Guilford, New York.

Deary I.J. & Pagliari C. (1991) The strength of *g* at different levels of ability: Have Detterman and Daniel rediscovered Spearman's 'Law of Diminishing Returns'? *Intelligence* **15**, 247–250.

Detterman D.K. (1986) Human intelligence is a complex system of separate processes. In Sternberg R.J. & Detterman D. (eds) *What is Intelligence?* pp. 57–61. Ablex, Norwood, New Jersey.

Detterman D.K. (1991) Reply to Dear and Pagliari: Is *g* intelligence or stupidity? *Intelligence* **15**, 251–255.

Detterman D.K. & Daniel M.H. (1989) Correlations of mental tests with each other and with cognitive vari-

ables are highest for low IQ groups. *Intelligence* **13**, 349–359.

Detterman D.K., Mayer J.D., Caruso D.R., Legree P.J., Conners F.A. & Taylor R. (in press) The assessment of basic cognitive abilities in relationship to cognitive deficits. *American Journal on Mental Retardation.*

Detterman D.K. & Persanyi M. (1990) *Mental tests correlate highest in low IQ groups: Evidence from KABC.* Paper presented at the Annual Meeting of the American Educational Research Association, Boston, April.

Elder G., Hastings T. & Pavalko E. (1991) *Adult pathways to greater distinction and disappointment.* Paper presented at the Life-History Research Society Meeting, Montreal, June.

Eysenck H.J. (ed.) (1982) *A Model for Intelligence.* Springer, New York.

Eysenck H.J. (1986) Toward a new model of intelligence. *Personality and Individual Differences* **7**, 731–736.

Eysenck H.J. (1988) The biological basis of intelligence. In Irvine S.H. & Berry J.W. (eds) *Human Abilities in Cultural Context*, pp. 87–104. Cambridge University Press, New York.

Flescher I. (1963) Anxiety and achievement of intellectually gifted and creatively gifted children. *Journal of Psychology* **56**, 251–268.

Galton F. (1869) *Hereditary Genius: An Inquiry into its Laws and Consequences.* Macmillan, New York.

Galton F. (1883) *Enquiry into Human Faculty and its Development.* Macmillan, London.

Galton F. (1892) *Hereditary Genius: An Enquiry into its Laws and Consequences.* Macmillan, London.

Gardner H. (1983) *Frames of Mind: A Theory of Multiple Intelligence.* Basic Books, New York.

Getzel J.W. & Jackson P.W. (1962) *Creativity and Intelligence.* Wiley, New York.

Gordon R.A. (1976) Prevalence: The rare datum in delinquency measurement and its implication for a theory of delinquency. In Klein M. (ed.) *The Juvenile Justice System*, pp. 201–284. Sage, Beverly Hills.

Gordon R.A. (1980) Labelling theory, mental retardation, and public policy: Larry P. and other developments since 1974. In Gove W.R. (ed.) *The Labelling of Deviance: Evaluating a Perspective*, pp. 175–224. Sage, Beverly Hills, California.

Gordon R.A. (1987) SES versus race in the race–IQ–delinquency mode. *International Journal of Sociology* **7**, 30–96.

Gottfredson L.S. (1986) Societal consequences of the *g* factor in employment. *Journal of Vocational Behavior* **29**, 379–410.

Gruber H.E. (1974) *Darwin on Man: A Psychological Study of Scientific Creativity. Together with Darwin's Early and Unpublished Notebooks.* Dutton, New York.

Guilford J.P. (1959) Traits of creativity. In Anderson H.H. (ed.) *Creativity and its Cultivation*, pp. 142–161. Harper & Row, New York.

Guilford J.P. (1967) *The Nature of Human Intelligence.* McGraw-Hill, New York.

Hadamard J. (1945) *The Psychology of Invention in the Mathematical Field.* Princeton University Press, Princeton, New York.

Hammer E.F. (1961) *Creativity.* Random House, New York.

Hartigan J.A. & Wigdor A.K. (eds) (1989) *Fairness in Employment Testing.* National Academy Press, Washington, DC.

Henderson C.R. & Ceci S.J. (1992) Is it better to be born rich or smart? A bioecological analysis. In Billingsley K.R., Brown H.U. & Derohanes E. (eds) *Scientific Excellence in Supercomputing: The 1990 IBM Supercomputing Competition Winners*, pp. 705–751. University of Georgia Press, Athens, Georgia.

Hendrickson A.E. & Hendrickson D.E (1982) The psychophysiology of intelligence. In Eysenck H.J. (ed.) *A Model for Intelligence*, pp. 151–228. Springer, New York.

Holton G. (1978) *Scientific Imagination: Case Studies.* Cambridge University Press, Cambridge.

Horn J.L. (1978) Human ability systems. In Baltes P. (ed.) *Life-span Development and Behavior*, Vol. 1, pp. 211–256. Academic Press, New York.

Horn J.L. (1989) Models of intelligence. In Linn R. (ed.) *Intelligence: Measurement, Theory and Public Policy*, pp. 29–73. University of Illinois Press, Urbana, Illinois.

Howe M.J.A. & Smith J. (1988) Calendar calculating in 'idiot savants': How do they do it? *British Journal of Psychology* **79**, 371–386.

Hunt E. (1985) Verbal ability. In Sternberg R.J. (ed.) *Human Abilities: An Information Processing Approach*, pp. 31–58. W.H. Freeman, San Francisco, California.

Hunter J. (1983) *The Dimensionality of the General Aptitude Test Battery and the Dominance of General Factors over Specific Factors in the Prediction of Job Performance in the US Employment Service.* Uses Test Research Report, No. 44. US Dept of Labor, Employment, and Training Administration, Division of Counselling and Test Development, Washington, DC.

Hunter J. (1986) Cognitive ability, cognitive aptitudes, job knowledge, and job performance. *Journal of Vocational Behavior* **29**, 340–363.

Hunter J. & Hunter R.F. (1984) Validity and utility of alternative predictors of job performance. *Psychological Bulletin* **96**, 72–98.

Hunter J. & Schmidt F. (1982) Fitting people to jobs: The impact of personnel selection on national productivity. In Dunnette M. & Fleishman E. (eds) *Human Performance and Productivity*, Vol. 1, pp. 233–284. Lawrence Erlbaum, Hillsdale, New Jersey.

Hunter J., Schmidt F. & Rauschenberger J. (1984) Methodological, statistical, and ethical issues in the study of bias in psychological tests. In Reynolds C.R. & Brown R.T. (eds) *Perspectives on bias in mental testing*, pp. 41–97. Plenum, New York.

Isham W.P. & Kamin L.J. (in press) Blackness, deafness, IQ, and *g*. *Intelligence.*

Jencks C. & Crouse J. (1982) Aptitude versus achievement: Should we replace the SAT? In Schrader W. (ed.) *New Directions for Testing and Measurement, Guidance, and Program Evaluation*, No. 13, pp. 251–261. Jossey Bass, San Francisco, California.

Jensen A.R. (1969) How much can we boost IQ and scholastic achievement? *Harvard Educational Review* **39**, 1–123.

Jensen A.R. (1980) *Bias in Mental Testing.* Free Press, New York.

Jensen A.R. (1982) The chronometry of intelligence. In Sternberg R.J. (ed.) *Advances in the Psychology of Human Intelligence*, pp. 225–310. Lawrence Erlbaum, Hillsdale, New Jersey.

Jensen A.R. (1992) Commentary: Vehicles of *g*. *Psychological Science* **3**, 275–278.

Jensen A.R. (in press) Central conductance velocity and oscillation. *Current Directions.*

John-Steiner V. (1985) *Notebooks of the Mind: Explorations of Thinking.* Harper & Row, New York.

Kail R. & Pellegrino J. (1985) *Human Intelligence: Perspective and Prospects.* W.H. Freeman, New York.

Kamin L.J. (1974) *The Science and Politics of IQ.* Lawrence Erlbaum, Hillsdale, New Jersey.

Keating D. (1984) The emperor's new clothes: The 'new look' in intelligence research. In Sternberg R.J. (ed.) *Advances in the Psychology of Human Intelligence*, Vol. 2, pp. 104–129. Lawrence Erlbaum, Hillsdale, New Jersey.

Keating D., List J. & Merriman W. (1985) Cognitive processing and cognitive ability: A multivariate validity investigation. *Intelligence* **9**, 149–170.

Lehrl S. & Fischer B. (1988) The basic parameters of human information processing: Their role in the determination of intelligence. *Personality and Individual Differences* **9**, 883–896.

Lickliter R. & Hellewell T.B. (1992) Contextual determinants of auditory learning in Bobwhite quail embryos and hatchlings. *Developmental Psychobiology* **17**, 17–31.

MacKinnon D.W. (1968) Selecting students with creative potential. In Heist P. (ed.) *The Creative College Student: the Unmet Challenge.* Jossey Bass, San Francisco, California.

Margolis H. (1987) *Patterns, Thinking, and Cognition. A Theory of Judgement.* University of Chicago Press, Chicago.

Matarazzo J.D. (1970) *Wechsler's Measurement and Appraisal of Adult Intelligence*, 5th edn. Williams & Wilkins, Baltimore, Maryland.

Means M. & Voss J. (1985) Star Wars: A developmental study of expert and novice knowledge structures. *Memory and Language* **24**, 746–757.

Muir J. & Bjorklund D.F. (1989) Developmental and individual differences in children's memory strategies: The role of knowledge. In Schneider W. & Weinert F. (eds) *Interactions among Aptitudes, Strategies, and Knowledge in Cognitive Performance*, pp. 99–114. Springer, New

York.

Pedersen N.L., Plomin R., Nesselroade J. & McClearn G.E. (1992) A quantitative genetic analysis of cognitive abilities during the second half of the life span. *Psychological Science* **3**, 346–353.

Perkins D.N. (1977) A better word: Studies of poetry editing. In Perkins D. & Leondar B. (eds) *The Arts and Cognition*. Johns Hopkins University Press, Baltimore, Maryland.

Perkins D.N. (1988) The possibility of invention. In Sternberg R.J. (ed.) *The Nature of Creativity*, pp. 362–385. Cambridge University Press, Cambridge.

Persaud G. & Stimpson A. (1983) Creative thinking and nonverbal IQ among three grades of school children. *Journal of Creative Behavior* **20**, 142.

Piaget J. (1952) *The Origins of Intelligence in Children*. International Universities Press, New York.

Piaget J. (1970) Piaget's theory. In Mussen P.H. (ed.) *Carmichael's Manual of Child Psychology*, Vol. 1, 3rd edn, pp. 703–732. Wiley, New York.

Piaget J. (1972) *The Psychology of Intelligence*. Littlefield, Adams, New Jersey.

Piaget J. (1976) Problems in equilibration. In Appel M. & Oldberg L. (eds) *Topics in Cognitive Development*, Vol. 1. Plenum, New York.

Pikas A. (1966) *Abstraction and Concept Formation*. Harvard University Press, Cambridge, Massachusetts.

Plomin R. (1985) Behavioral genetics. In Detterman D. (ed.) *Current Topics in Human Intelligence*, Vol. 1. Ablex, Norwood, New Jersey.

Plomin R. & Bergeman C.S. (1991) The nature of nurture: Genetic influence on 'environmental' measures. *Behavioral and Brain Sciences* **14**, 373–427.

Plomin R., Defries J. & Fulker D.W. (1988) *Nature and Nurture During Infancy and Early Childhood*. Cambridge University Press, New York.

Raven J.C., Court J. & Raven J. (1975) *Manual for Raven's Progressive Matrices and Vocabulary Scales*. Lewis, London.

Roe A. (1952) A psychologist examines sixty-four eminent scientists. *Scientific American* **187**, 21–25.

Scarr S. (1989) Protecting general intelligence: Constructs and consequences for interventions. In Linn R.L. (ed.) *Intelligence*, pp. 74–115. University of Illinois Press, Chicago.

Scarr S. (1992) Developmental theories for the 1990s: Development and individual differences. *Child Development* **63**, 1–19.

Schafer E.W.P. (1987) Neural adaptability: A biological determinant of *g*-factor intelligence. *Behavioral and Brain Sciences* **10**, 240–241.

Schiff M., Duyme M., Dumaret A. & Tomkiewitz S. (1982) How much can we boost scholastic achievement and IQ scores? A direct answer from a French adoption study. *Cognition* **12**, 165–196.

Schmidt F.L. & Ones D. (1992) Personnel selection. *Annual Review of Psychology* **43**, 627–670.

Schneider W., Körkel J. & Weinert F.E. (1989) Expert knowledge and general abilities and text processing. In Schneider W. & Weinert F.E. (eds) *Interactions Among Aptitudes, Strategies, and Knowledge in Cognitive Performance*, pp. 235–251. Springer, New York.

Schubert D.S. (1973) Intelligence as necessary but not sufficient for creativity. *Journal of Genetic Psychology* **1222**, 45–47.

Siegel L.S. & Brainerd C.J. (1978) *Alternatives to Piaget: Critical Essays on the Theory*. Academic Press, New York.

Siegler R.S. (1989) Mechanisms of cognitive development. *Annual Reviews of Psychology* **40**, 353–379.

Skodak M. & Skeels H. (1949) A follow-up study of 100 adopted children. *Journal of Genetic Psychology* **75**, 85–125.

Smith G.J. & Spear N.E. (1978) Effects of home environment on withholding behaviors and conditioning in infant and neonatal rats. *Science* **202**, 327–329.

Smith I.L. (1971) IQ, creativity, and achievement: interaction and threshold. *Multivariate Behavioral Research* **6**, 51–62.

Spearman C. (1904) General intelligence objectively determined and measured. *American Journal of Psychology* **15**, 206–221.

Spearman C. (1927) *The Abilities of Man*. Macmillan, New York.

Sternberg R.J. (1985) *Beyond IQ: A Triarchic Theory of Intelligence*. Cambridge University Press, New York.

Sternberg R.J. (1988) Intellectual development: Psychometric and information processing approaches. In Bornstein M.H. & Lamb M. (eds) *Developmental Psychology: An Advanced Textbook*, 2nd edn, pp. 216–243. Lawrence Erlbaum, Hillsdale, New Jersey.

Sternberg R.J. (1989) A three-facet model of creativity. In Sternberg R.J. (ed.) *The Nature of Creativity*, pp. 125–147. Cambridge University Press, Cambridge.

Sternberg R.J. (1990) *Metaphors of Mind: Conceptions of the Nature of Intelligence*. Cambridge University Press, New York.

Sternberg R.J., Conway B., Ketron J. & Bernstein M. (1981) People's conceptions of intelligence. *Journal of Personality and Social Psychology* **41**, 37–55.

Sternberg R.J. & Detterman D.K. (1986) *What is intelligence? Contemporary Viewpoints on its Nature and Definition*. Ablex, Norwood, New Jersey.

Streufert S. (1986) Individual differences in risk taking. *Journal of Applied Social Psychology* **16**, 482–497.

Terman L.M. (1921) Contribution to intelligence and its measurement symposium. *Journal of Educational Psychology* **12**, 127–133.

Thomson G.H. (1948) *The Factorial Analysis of Human Ability*, 3rd edn. Houghton-Mifflin, Boston.

Thorndike R. (1985) The role of general ability in prediction. *Journal of Occupational Behavior* **29**, 332–339.

Thurstone L.L. & Thurstone J. (1962) *Test of Primary Mental Abilities*. Chicago Science Research Association,

Chicago.

Torrance E.P. (1962) *Guiding Creative Talent*. Prentice-Hall, New Jersey.

Torrance E.P. (1966) *Torrance Tests of Creative Thinking*. Personnel Press, New Jersey.

Vernon P.A. (1987) *Speed of Information Processing and Intelligence*. Ablex, Norwood, New Jersey.

Vernon P.E. (1969) *Intelligence and Cultural Environment*. Methuen, London.

Vygotsky L. (1962) *Thought and Language*. MIT Press, Cambridge, Massachusetts.

Wade S. (1968) Differences between intelligence and creativity. Some speculation on the role of environment. *Journal of Creative Behavior* **2**, 97–102.

Walker C.H. (1987) Relative importance of domain knowledge and overall aptitude on acquisition of domain-related information. *Cognition and Instruction* **4**, 25–42.

Wallach M.A. (1971) *The Intelligence/Creativity Distinction*. General Learning Press, New Jersey.

Wallach M.A. & Kogan N. (1965) *Modes of Thinking in Young Children*. Holt Rhinehart, New York.

Weisberg R.W. (1986) *Creativity, Genius and Other Myths*. W.H. Freeman, New York.

Weiss V. (1990) From short term memory capacity toward the EEG resonance code. *Personality and Individual Differences* **10**, 501–508.

Welsh G.S. (1975) *Creativity and Intelligence: A Personality Approach*. Institute for Research in Social Science, University of North Carolina at Chapel Hill, North Carolina.

Wissler C. (1901) The correlation of mental and physical tests. *Psychological Review Monograph* **3**(6)(Suppl.).

Yamamoto K. (1965) Effects of restriction of range and test unreliability on correlations between measures of intelligence and creative thinking. *British Journal of Educational Psychology* **35**, 300–305.

Zigler E. (1988) The IQ pendulum. *Readings* **21**, 4–9.

12: Development of Reading and Spelling Skills

USHA GOSWAMI

INTRODUCTION

One of the most interesting features of learning to read and to spell is that the same set of skills seems to influence the development of these abilities across the lifespan. Whether you begin learning to read and to write as a child at school, or as an adult taking special classes, the most important skills that you will need are phonological ones. The ability to analyse the sounds in words governs the development of reading and spelling in childhood, and also the degree to which most adult illiterates will benefit from special instruction. Deficiencies in phonological skills cause the difficulties experienced by most dyslexic children, and by most dyslexic adults. The idea that differences in phonological skills are at the root of differences in reading and spelling skills has been firmly established (Bryant & Bradley, 1985; Lundberg *et al.*, 1988; Goswami & Bryant, 1990; Snowling & Thomson, 1991).

The question of how individual differences in phonological ability arise is less easily answered. Psychologists have collected a lot of evidence that shows that phonological skills are crucial for the development of reading and spelling, but they have had less success in working out why differences in these skills occur. Genetic factors certainly seem implicated in differences between individuals, and so do early experiences with language, which may or may not be related to social class. Intelligence will also play a role in how well a child learns to read, as there is a strong relationship between a child's IQ and a child's reading ability (an overall association of between 0.5 and 0.6). However, children with high IQs can still be poor readers if they have deficient phonological skills.

Factors that do not seem to be especially implicated in the development of reading and spelling skills are general problem-solving abilities, or general differences in attention or motivation. This is not to say that differences in attention and motivation will not *result* from early experiences of failure in trying to learn to read and to write: this is frequently the case, and these differences will then play their own role in the effectiveness of remediation. That is one of the reasons that the research reported here has concentrated on the *precursors* of reading development, reading difficulty and reading delay. The aim is to try and identify children likely to experience problems *before* they are put off reading and writing by repeated experiences of failure, and in consequence lose the desire to learn.

It is also interesting that phonological factors are implicated in the development of reading and spelling skills in all the cultures that have so far been studied, irrespective of their different orthographies. Even China and Japan, which use logographic and syllabic scripts respectively, have their share of dyslexic children and adults. Words in Chinese are represented by single characters (logographs) that are unrelated to sound. Words in Japanese are represented by a combination of the Chinese characters (*Kanji*), and symbols representing individual syllables (*Kana*). Most European countries represent words by alphabetic symbols that are related to subsyllabic units of sound called *phonemes*, but in spite of this variation in representational level, phonological factors seem to be related to reading development in all of these countries. It is often pointed out that the alphabet was only invented once, by the Phoenicians (Gelb, 1963), which implies that the *idea* of representing the sounds of language by symbols is not a particularly natural one.

Given the 'unnaturalness' of reading and writing,

we should perhaps not be surprised that a large number of children have difficulties in learning to read and to spell, with between 2 and 4% actually likely to be identified as dyslexic in terms of having a reading level that is much worse than would be expected from their IQ (Miles, 1991b). Similarly, the large number of adult illiterates may partly reflect the 'unnaturalness' of written language. What can we do to help the development of reading and spelling across the lifespan? To answer this question, we must begin with the precursors of reading. There is a great deal of evidence that phonological skills are at the root of reading and spelling development, but we need to be careful about which kinds of phonological skills are being measured.

PHONOLOGICAL AWARENESS AND THE DEVELOPMENT OF READING AND SPELLING

Levels of phonological awareness

Phonological awareness was described earlier as the ability to analyse the sounds in words. However, there are many sounds in most words. There is the sound of the word itself, which conveys meaning, and which reflects the level at which children first analyse spoken language as they learn to speak, and to understand what is said to them. To learn to read and write in most scripts, however, it is important to *ignore* meaning, and instead to listen to the sounds within the word itself.

A word like 'jigsaw' can be broken down into two *syllables*, 'jig' and 'saw', which bear no relation to the meaning of the complete word 'jigsaw'. Each syllable can be broken down into individual phonemes, which are the smallest units of sound that change a word's meaning. The phonemes in 'jig' are $|j|$, $|i|$ and $|g|$, but phonemes can also be represented by more than one alphabetic letter, such as 'sh', 'ch' and 'ck'. Finally, there is another phonological level distinguished by linguists, the *intrasyllabic* level, at which syllables are divided into subunits that are usually greater than phonemes, the *onset* and the *rime*. The onset of a syllable corresponds to the first consonant(s), and the rime corresponds to the vowel sound and the terminal consonant(s). The onset of 'jig' corresponds to the 'j-' (also a phoneme), and that of 'tree' to the 'tr-' (two phonemes). The rime of 'jig' corresponds to '-ig' (two phonemes), and that of 'tree' to '-ee' (one phoneme). Onsets and rimes seem to be particularly important for children who are learning to read.

A number of different tasks have been devised to measure phonological awareness in children and in adults. These include deleting sounds in words (e.g. jam — am, snail — sail); tapping a dowel to indicate the number of syllables in a word like 'valentine' (3), or the number of phonemes in a word like 'dog' (also 3); spotting which words sound different at the beginning (bun, bud, bus, *rug*), in the middle (lot, pot, *hat*, cot), or at the end (pin, win, *sit*, fin) in an oddity task; and substituting sounds in different words in a 'spoonerism' task (saying Dob Bylan for Bob Dylan).

These tasks, which were originally thought of as measuring a single skill, in fact measure phonological awareness at all of the different levels described above. The deletion task includes both phoneme and onset components, the tapping task measures both syllabic and phonemic awareness, and the oddity task involves phonemes, onsets and rimes. In spite of this diversity, a relatively straightforward picture of children's phonological skills has emerged from research using these different tasks. Children seem to be able to analyse words into syllables, onsets and rimes prior to learning to read. After beginning to learn to read, and particularly as a consequence of learning to spell, children (and adults) become able to analyse words at the phonemic level (see Goswami & Bryant, 1990 for a more detailed description of this sequence).

Precursors and products of reading and spelling

So some levels of phonological awareness are precursors of reading, and others are products of learning to read and to spell. Rhyming is an example of a phonological analysis skill that seems to be a precursor rather than a product of reading. One of the most useful tasks for predicting a child's reading development is that child's performance on the oddity task described above, and particularly on the subtests that measure rhyme. Bradley and Bryant

(1983) gave 368 children the oddity task before they could read, when they were 4 and 5 years old. They then followed their progress in reading and spelling for a period of 4 years. When the children were 8 and 9, they measured their reading and spelling levels. The children's performance on the rhyming oddity tasks turned out to be highly predictive of their reading and spelling progress, but not of their progress in other academic skills such as mathematics. Their performance on the alliteration task (bun, bud, bus, *rug*) was also a strong predictor of reading, but was weakly predictive of mathematical achievement as well. So it was rhyming that had a special connection with reading.

A large-scale study in Sweden found similar results. Lundberg *et al.* (1980) gave a large group of Swedish children different phonological tasks before they learned to read, when they were 6 and 7 years old. The tests included a test of rhyme production. Lundberg *et al.* then measured the children's reading and spelling progress after 2 years. They found that the children's performance in the rhyme production task significantly predicted their reading and spelling levels 2 years later. The fact that children in Sweden begin school when they are much older than English children (at around 7 years of age) did not affect the relationship between rhyming and reading. A special connection between rhyming ability and later reading skill has also been found in longitudinal studies by Ellis and Large (1987), and by Bryant *et al.* (1989).

However, once children have been in school for some time, the special relationship between rhyming skill and reading progress wanes. When children are taught to read, they begin learning about phonemes, as these are usually represented by alphabetic letters. Partly as a consequence of this, their phonological analysis skills seem to move on to a new level. Stanovich *et al.* (1984) studied 6-year-old children in America, who had been learning to read for a year, and did not find a predictive relationship between the children's rhyming skills and reading measured a year later. In this study, the predictive relationships were between *phonemic* analysis skills (tasks such as phoneme deletion) and reading. In the studies mentioned above, Lundberg *et al.* also found a relationship between a measure of phoneme detection and later reading progress, and Bryant

et al. (1989) demonstrated a relationship between early rhyming skill and later phoneme deletion. So phonological awareness continues to be related to reading development while children are being taught to read, but the level of awareness that shows the strongest connections with reading may differ depending on the stage of reading development that has been reached.

Other research confirms the view that different levels of phonological awareness develop as a consequence of learning to read. Liberman *et al.* (1974) showed that prior to learning to read, when they were 5 years old, American children could tap out the number of syllables in a word like 'valentine', but not the number of phonemes in a word like 'dog'. Once they began to learn to read, however, their phonemic tapping skills improved tremendously. Exactly the same pattern of results was found in Italian children, who were unable to perform the phoneme tapping task at preschool, but who showed large gains on the task once they began to be taught to read in first grade (Cossu *et al.*, 1987). These children were 7 and 8 years old when they began to learn to read. So it is not age *per se* that governs phonological development. Learning to read itself seems to change children's phonological abilities. Early phonological skills govern the development of reading, but reading in turn will affect the development of phonological skills.

Research with adults

Other evidence that syllables, onsets and rimes are the important precursors of reading comes from research conducted with illiterate adults. If reading level rather than age affects the ability to analyse words into phonemes, then even adults should have difficulty in phonemic tasks if they have never learned to read. It is only once they have been taught to read that they should develop phonemic skills. So illiterate adults should find phonological tasks involving onsets, rimes and syllables much easier than phonological tasks involving phonemes.

Some elegant research conducted in Portugal suggests that this is indeed the case. Morais *et al.* (1979) asked a group of illiterate Portuguese adults to perform two simple phonemic tasks, adding a sound to a word ('alhaco' — 'palhaco'), and deleting a sound from a word ('purso' — 'urso'). They found that the illiterate adults had much more difficulty with these tasks than a comparable group of adults who had learned to read through an illiteracy programme. However, later research demonstrated that if the phonological tasks were syllabic ones, then the disadvantage of the illiterate group was much smaller (Morais *et al.*, 1986). So it is reading development rather than age *per se* that seems to control the development of phonemic awareness.

A final piece of evidence that phonemic awareness develops as a consequence of being taught to read comes from a study of adults carried out in China. Read *et al.* (1986) compared two groups of Chinese adults, a *'pinyin'* group who had learned to read an alphabetic version of written Chinese (called *'pinyin'*), and a *'non-pinyin'* group who had learned to read the traditional Chinese *Kanji* characters, which are logographic. The beauty of this study was that both groups of adults had learned to read, but only one group (the *pinyin* group) had learned to read alphabetically. So if phonemic awareness is a product of learning to read an *alphabetic* script, then only the *pinyin* group should be successful in phonological awareness tasks requiring phonemic analysis. Read *et al.* found that the *pinyin* group were much better at adding and deleting phonemes from words than the non-*pinyin* group. So not only does the ability to read affect the development of phonemic awareness, but the kind of reading experience that one has is important as well.

The fact that children and adults only become able to recognize phonemes after they have begun to learn to read may at first sight seem surprising. After all, alphabetic scripts work at the phonemic level, as most alphabetic letters represent phonemes rather than onsets, rimes or syllables. The letters in the simple word 'dog' each represent a separate phoneme, and if children know the phonemes represented by the 'd', 'o' and 'g', in 'dog', then they can 'decode' it as dog even if they have never encountered it before. Quite how an awareness of syllables, onsets and rimes will help a child to learn to read is not immediately apparent.

Before turning to a discussion of how these precursors may operate in the development of reading, however, we need to think about how the precursors themselves may develop. As individual differences in the ability to recognize syllables, onsets and rimes seem to govern the development of reading and spelling, we need to ask why people differ in their ability to analyse words at these phonological levels.

THE DEVELOPMENT OF PHONOLOGICAL SKILLS

For reasons that are not yet well understood, children seem to find the categorization of words into onsets and rimes a very natural one. Much early language play involves the repetition of sounds at the beginnings of words, or the invention of (sometimes nonsense) strings of words that rhyme. For example, a Russian study of children's language games found many examples of invented poems based on rhymes. Two-and-a-half year old Tania produced a poem about her buckwheat cereal (*Kasha*) that ran as follows:

> Ilk-silk-tilk
> I eat Kasha with milk
>
> Ilks-silks-tilks
> I eat Kashas with milks.
>
> (Chukovsky, 1963)

Two to 3 years of age seems to be a particularly fertile time for rhyming, but alliteration is found too, and much early babbling is alliterative (consisting of strings of onsets such as ba-ba-ba-ba-ba or da-da-da-da). Rhyming and alliteration continue to form the basis of many games that older children play in the street and in the playground (Opie & Opie, 1987), and both children and adults seem to derive a great deal of pleasure from rhyming (think of advertising jingles, pop songs and poetry).

Any categorization of words by rhyme necessarily involves recognition of rimes, and the use of alliteration involves the use of onsets. Treiman (1983, 1985) has shown that both children and adults find it easier to learn novel word games that are based on onset and rime units than word games based on other parts of the syllable. The naturalness of the onset–rime level of phonological analysis has so far only been documented in English-speaking cultures, however.

Phonological skills and early language

The spontaneous manipulation of onsets and

rimes in early language play suggests a hypothesis about the early development of phonological skills. As children differ in the amount of linguistic stimulation that they receive, such differences in early linguistic experiences may result in individual differences in children's knowledge of units such as syllables, onsets and rimes. MacLean *et al.* (1987) decided to study this idea by looking at individual differences in children's experiences with these early linguistic routines. They measured children's knowledge of nursery rhymes when they were 3 years old, and then looked at their phonological analysis skills 15 months later. The 3 year olds were asked to say as much as they could of common nursery rhymes like 'Twinkle Twinkle Little Star' and 'Humpty Dumpty'. Phonological awareness was measured by the alliteration and rhyme oddity tests, which were administered at the beginning and at the end of the study.

MacLean *et al.* found that the children's nursery rhyme knowledge was significantly related to their performance on the oddity test when they were 4 years old. This relationship held even after the effects of performance on a simplified version of the oddity task at age 3 was removed, to control for initial phonological ability. Thus nursery rhyme performance predicted the development of phonological skills in a very specific way (age, intelligence and mother's educational level were also controlled in these analyses). Nursery rhyme knowledge was also related to the rudiments of reading. MacLean *et al.* showed the 4 year olds some simple words like 'car', 'dog' and 'boy', and found a strong connection between nursery rhyme knowledge at 3 years and knowledge of one or more of these simple words 15 months later. Therefore, early language routines play a role in later phonological development, and are also linked to the development of reading.

The link between early linguistic ability and reading was recently confirmed by Scarborough (1990) in a prospective study of children who later developed reading disabilities. Although the existence of linguistic impairments in reading disabled children has frequently been reported (see Kamhi & Catts, 1989 for a recent review), most of the data have come from older children who are already at school. Scarborough began studying her sample of 52 children when they were 30 months old. She gave them a variety of tests of early language skill, including vocabulary recognition, naming vocabulary, natural language production and speech discrimination, and then followed their reading progress when they began school.

Scarborough found that the children who later became disabled readers differed significantly from the other children on some language measures when they were 2 year olds, but not on others. Differences were found for syntactic complexity and pronunciation accuracy, but not for early vocabulary development or receptive language ability. The children who developed reading difficulties used simpler syntax and made more consonant errors at 30 months than those who did not, but did not have speech discrimination disabilities or vocabulary deficits (although vocabulary deficits did begin to emerge when the children were 42 months old). The specificity of the linguistic impairments that Scarborough found is important. These seem to be the aspects of language that require phonological processing, as verbal short-term memory (a phonologically based system) is involved in syntactic production, and consonant substitutions (e.g. 'b' for 'd') are also phonologically based. As it is the phonological aspects of linguistic development that are the precursors of reading difficulties, a primary phonological problem may be at the root of *both* linguistic and reading difficulties. A primary phonological impairment would explain why clinically a progression can often be observed from language difficulties to reading difficulties and then to spelling difficulties.

Social class effects: the home and the school

This study by MacLean *et al.* had a second aim, which was to examine social class effects in phonological development. As middle-class parents are popularly supposed to provide a richer linguistic environment for their offspring than working-class parents, taking more time to play language games with them and to sing nursery rhymes, another obvious hypothesis is that middle-class children should have superior phonological skills to working-class children. This early class difference in phonological skills might in turn give middle-class children an advantage when they begin school and start learning to read. Indeed, when they began the study, the researchers expected to find a difference between middle-class and working-class children in their phonological skills. Their results, however, suggested that there was no such simple relationship.

MacLean *et al.* used three measures of social class in their analyses: mother's educational level, father's educational level, and the social class groups I to V used by the Registrar General. They also measured phonological skills half-way through the study, by administering the oddity tasks (which were given three times in all). The only social class differences that they found in phonological abilities were fleeting ones. For example, social class affected performance in the alliteration oddity task at the beginning of the study, but not performance on any of the rhyming oddity tasks or the nursery rhyme task, and no longer affected alliteration performance by the second testing session. Parents' educational level showed an effect in the first rhyming and alliteration measures, but did not differentiate the children for nursery rhyme knowledge at any point in the study, even when age and IQ were controlled, and had lost its effect on the rhyming and alliteration measures by the second testing session. Thus, the only effects of social class occurred at the beginning of the study: there was no evidence that family background had a lasting effect on phonological development.

This finding suggests that individual differences in phonological sensitivity do not result from experiences in the home. Scarborough (1990) reached a similar conclusion in her study. She found that the family environment of the children in her sample who later became reading disabled did not differ notably from that of the children who did not. Instead, the main environmental effects on phonological development seem to take place once a child reaches school. In a study of social class and phonological awareness conducted by Raz and Bryant (1990), it was found that socially disadvantaged children only fell behind middle-class children in phonological awareness after school entry.

Raz and Bryant studied four groups of children, a younger and an older group of children from middle-class homes, and a younger and an older group of children from seriously disadvantaged backgrounds (social classes IV and V). The children in these groups were aged 4 years (younger pre-school group) and 5 years (older school group) at the beginning of the study, and had the same initial IQ levels. All the children were followed for a period of 18 months.

Raz and Bryant's main measure of phonological awareness was the rhyme oddity task, although they included a measure of initial phoneme recognition as well. They found that the younger children from the two social groups did not differ in their performance in the two phonological tasks, but that the older children did. In the older age group, the middle-class children were better at the phonological tasks than the disadvantaged children. This turned out to be because the middle-class children's performance improved in the phonological tasks with increasing age. The disadvantaged children's performance in these tasks showed no such improvement. Raz and Bryant tentatively concluded that it was experiences at school rather than experiences at home that lead to social class differences in phonological awareness.

This idea was supported by their analyses of the effects of home environment on phonological skills. They measured a number of home environment factors that might be related to phonological development, such as how often the parents played language games with their children, the level of story reading in the home, and the variety of books in the home. Although there was a significant social class difference in all of the measures of home environment, especially in the number of books owned by the children, most of these differences turned out not to affect the children's phonological scores on the rhyme oddity task. The one exception was the measure of the variety of books available to the children. Children with more books had higher levels of phonological awareness.

Accordingly, in general, it may be experiences at school rather than experiences at home that cause social class differences in phonological awareness. The phonological skills of middle-class children develop further when they begin going to school. The phonological skills of disadvantaged children do not. This in turn must affect their reading development. The finding that it is not early experiences in the home that lead to individual differences in phonological ability is a surprising and important one.

Quite what happens when these children begin school is unfortunately not yet clear. However, evidence from children who later develop conduct disorders suggests that it is the period between the ages of 5 and 7 years that may be crucial. This is, of course, the time at which most children are first taught to read, and there is a well-documented relationship between reading failure and attention deficit disorder (ADD), with some reports suggesting that reading failure precedes many cases of problem behaviour (e.g. McGee *et al.*, 1988).

Recently, Moffit (1990) has reported further on a cohort of New Zealand children who have been followed since birth in a multidisciplinary health and development study, and who are now adolescent. Moffit showed that ADD and reading failure were not necessarily linked. Boys who had ADD but were non-delinquent, or who were delinquent but not ADD, did not show significant deficits in reading development compared to controls. However, boys who were *both* ADD and delinquent showed clear reading impairments, and moreover the most striking exacerbation of their antisocial behaviour compared to their peers had occurred between the ages of 5 and 7. Moffit suggests that the temporal co-occurrence of school entry, reading failure and increased antisocial behaviour is not accidental. The later delinquency of these boys may have arisen partly from the problems that they experienced in learning to read. Unfortunately, no information on the phonological skills of these children at school entry is available. However, Moffit suggested that a focus on helping the early reading development of such children could provide an important preventive intervention in the onset of conduct disorders.

HOW PHONOLOGICAL SKILLS HELP READING AND SPELLING DEVELOPMENT

Having considered the somewhat scarce data on the origins of the phonological skills that are the precursors of reading, let us turn to the role of these precursors themselves. Why should syllables, onsets and rimes be the important level of phonological analysis prior to learning to read? As mentioned

earlier, it would be plausible to expect that the important skills for early reading should be phonemic ones, as phonemic skills enable children to work out new words on a letter-by-letter basis. Yet phonemic awareness seems to be a *consequence* of learning to read and to spell rather than a causal factor in initially acquiring literacy.

Analogies in reading

One explanation for the relationship between onsets and rimes and early reading could be that it is easier to learn the alphabetic principle — the principle that sounds in words are consistently represented by certain alphabetic letters — through a knowledge of onsets and rimes than through a knowledge of phonemes. Many written words in English are highly ambiguous at the phonemic level, but are actually quite consistent at the onset — rime level.

For example, consider the spelling patterns of words like 'light', 'beak' and 'time'. A child who attempts to sound out these words letter by letter and then to read the words by blending the sounds into a pronunciation will have a difficult job. For each of these words, the resulting sequence of sounds will bear little similarity to the target word: for example, 'light' would become something like 'lig-hut'. However, at the rime level an irregular word like 'light' becomes quite predictable. At this level, an entire group of words shares the same alphabetic representation of the rime (light, fight, night, might, tight, etc.). So a child who begins analysing printed words into onsets and rimes might actually have an easier time in starting to learn to read than a child who is taught to analyse words into phonemes.

Research supports the idea that onsets and rimes, and particularly rimes, are important units for beginning readers. Children who are taught to read a word like 'beak' will go on to read new words like 'peak' and 'weak', words that they were previously unable to read, by analogy to 'beak'. They seem to do so by making connections between the spelling patterns and sounds of the *rimes* of these words, as control words like 'bead' and 'beat' do not show similar levels of improvement (Goswami, 1986, 1988b), and neither do words in which the rimes are spelled differently (learning to read 'head' does not really help in decoding 'said', Goswami, 1990b). Children who are better at rime tasks, such as the oddity rhyme task, will make more rime analogies than children who are poor at rhyming (Goswami, 1990a, Goswami & Mead, 1992), showing that there is a direct link between these phonological analysis skills and the use of letter sequences in reading. Finally, children will also make analogies between onsets in words, such as the 'tr-' in 'trim' and 'trap' (Goswami, 1991).

The use of analogies in early reading thus provides one path by which a child's knowledge of onsets and rimes can help in the development of reading. As onsets and rimes in words reflect spelling at a more consistent level than the phoneme, children who begin with these larger subunits of the syllable may be making a more natural link between their early phonological skills and the process of reading. As reading itself develops, children's phonological analyses will become more fine grained, and phonemic awareness will develop. The fact that many onsets are single phonemes (e.g. the 'b' in 'beak' and 'bat') probably helps in this process.

Phonemes in spelling

However, the factor that seems to play the biggest role in the development of phonemic awareness is the growth of spelling skills. Although onsets and rimes also play a role in early spelling (Goswami, 1988a; Treiman, 1993), it is the experience of having to generate sequences of letters that represent words when writing that really seems to promote children's phonemic abilities. Spelling development in its turn thus feeds into the development of reading, by helping to stimulate new levels of phonological awareness (e.g. Cataldo & Ellis, 1988).

To think about how this process might work, imagine that you are a child trying to generate a spelling pattern for a word like 'cheese'. The simplest strategy is to try and work out the individual sounds in the word 'cheese', and then to represent them by alphabet letters. Analyses of children's early misspellings suggest that this is exactly what they do (e.g. Read, 1986; Treiman, 1993). The variety of misspellings of the word 'cheese' documented by Treiman included *tese*, *cez*, *jes* and *tz*, all of which show a reasonable

awareness of the word's phonemic structure. Sometimes children represent a whole rhyme by a single letter, as in *cr* for 'car' and *hn* for 'hen', but frequently their misspellings show a more detailed analysis of the sounds in words.

This is not to say that spelling errors never reflect phonological misanalyses, of course. Some spelling errors do show phonological errors, and these are especially likely to occur with longer words, where whole syllables may be omitted (such as *bottsris* for 'brontosaurus', and *jogjm* for 'Jungle Jim'). However, many spelling errors arise from an insufficient knowledge of the orthography rather than from phonological mistakes. Children often make errors based on 'letter name' spellings, using the name of a letter to represent its sound, as in the misspellings *bik* for 'bike' and *tim* for 'time'. These children have analysed the phonemes in these words perfectly, but have not learned to use a final 'e' to lengthen the vowel. Other spelling errors can arise because children's phonological judgements will sometimes differ from those of adults. For example, Read found that young children consistently used *chr* to represent the sound that adults represent by 'tr-', as in the misspellings *aschray* for 'ashtray', *chrac* for 'truck', and *chribls* for 'troubles'. He also found that children hear preconsonantal nasals like 'n' and 'm' as part of the vowel, resulting in misspellings like *ad* for 'and', and *bopy* for 'bumpy'.

Such errors, which are really a matter of learning the conventional means of representing sounds in English spelling, normally drop out with increasing experience of the orthography (partly gained through reading). The misspellings of young children are interesting because they show us how busily the children are analysing the constituent sounds of the words that they are learning to spell (see Goswami, 1992 for a recent review). This effortful activity then feeds back into reading, as children apply their developing phonemic knowledge to decoding new words as well as to writing them.

Developmental models of reading and spelling

The developmental interactions between reading and spelling skills have been neatly captured in an influential model of reading and spelling development proposed by Frith (1985). She argued that the same three stages of development occurred in both reading and spelling. These were (i) a logographic stage; (ii) an alphabetic stage; and (iii) an orthographic stage. In the *logographic* stage, children were said to read words without any analysis of the alphabetic letters, as though they were reading Chinese *Kanji* characters. Spelling was largely absent. In the *alphabetic* stage, children read in a letter-by-letter fashion, using grapheme–phoneme correspondences, and spelled that way too. Finally, in the *orthographic* stage, children became able to use larger sequences of letters as units in reading and writing. The operation of this stage was somewhat unclear, however, as Frith has defined it as being both non-phonological and non-visual.

The most interesting part of Frith's theory for our purposes concerns the links that she proposes between the development of reading and spelling skills. In her model, it is the onset of alphabetic spelling skills that promotes the use of alphabetic skills in reading — in other words, phonemic awareness in reading develops as a consequence of spelling experience. This proposal fits the developmental data on early reading and spelling very well (e.g. Ellis, 1991). The actual stages in Frith's model have been the source of some dispute, however. For example, children learning to read in some languages, such as German, do not seem to pass through a logographic stage at all (Wimmer & Hummer, 1990), and not all English children do either (Stuart & Coltheart, 1988). Read and Treiman's work has shown that the logographic stage does not really apply to spelling, as even the earliest spelling attempts of young children have an alphabetic basis. Finally, orthographic strategies, such as the use of letter sequences in analogies, are used from the beginning of learning to read (e.g. Goswami, 1986).

An alternative approach is to think about reading and spelling development in terms of causal connections rather than in terms of separate stages. We took this approach in our causal model of reading development (Goswami & Bryant, 1990). In our model, we do not identify separate developmental stages. Instead, we argue that three causal factors can be distinguished in thinking about reading and spelling development. These three factors are shown in Fig. 12.1. The first causal factor

concerns the way in which preschool phonological skills affect reading. As discussed above, it is the awareness of syllables, onsets and rimes (reflected in rhyming and alliteration skills) that are the precursors of early reading, and not the awareness of phonemes. The second causal factor captures the way in which learning to read in itself seems to promote an awareness of phonemes in words. Finally, the third causal factor concerns the interaction between reading and spelling, first proposed by Frith. Children's use of phonemic strategies when they spell will come to affect the strategies that they use when they read, and children's reading experiences will feed into their spelling. For example, reading experience should help children to learn the conventionally correct alphabetic letters for representing sounds in words: a child who knows how to read the word 'school' should recognize that the phonologically correct misspelling *skool* is an error. Spelling experience will help with the development of phonemic analysis.

This causal model is based on the empirical findings discussed in the first two parts of this chapter concerning the relationships between

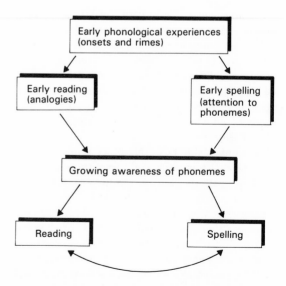

Fig. 12.1 A causal developmental model of reading development (from Goswami & Bryant, 1990).

phonological skills and reading and spelling development. It also predicts that early phonological difficulties will lead to difficulties in learning to read and to spell. The research findings that will be covered in the next two parts of this chapter are consistent with this prediction. Research has shown that children who have phonological problems have difficulties in learning to read and to spell, and also that training children's phonological skills can promote the reading and spelling development of both normal children and of children with reading difficulties.

DEVELOPMENTAL DELAY IN READING AND SPELLING

Methodological issues

Which comparisons do we make?

Before discussing research on children who are having difficulties in learning to read and to spell, there are some methodological issues to consider. The dyslexia literature is dogged by contradictory and confusing data, and at least part of the problem lies in designing a study that will actually tell one something about the causes of reading delay. A particular controversy concerns the use of *chronological age match* designs and *reading level match* designs, and the debate about what the possible combinations of results in the two designs can actually show about the causes of the children's difficulties.

Many early studies of dyslexia relied on a design that matched backward readers with children reading normally who were the same age: the chronological age match design. The logic was that the children who were behind their peers in reading would differ from them on certain tests, and many such differences were found. For example, studies using this design found differences between good and poor readers in short-term memory skills, in word naming speed, and in phonological tasks. The problem was that this design made it impossible to tell whether these differences were the cause of the children's reading delay, or a consequence of that delay. As reading level varied between the two groups being studied, the difficulties that the backward readers

experienced with the phonological tasks could have been caused by their poor reading level.

A better design is to compare backward readers to a control group matched on reading level: the reading level match design. In this case, reading skills no longer vary between the two groups being compared, and the normally reading children are much younger than their dyslexic counterparts. If differences are still found between these two groups in a task such as a phonological one, then there is a stronger case for thinking that the phonological deficit is part of the cause of the reading problem rather than a result of it.

However, the best design of all is to use *both* of these groups as controls when studying children who are backward readers and spellers. If backward readers are just as good on a particular test as older children who have superior reading skills (the group matched on chronological age), then the skill measured by this test is unlikely to be concerned with their poor reading. For example, Vellutino (1979) has shown that backward readers are as good at remembering visual patterns as better readers of the same age. This result implies that visual memory is not implicated in the problems of the backward readers. On the other hand, if backward readers do not differ from their reading level controls on a particular test, then interpretation is less straightforward. The backward readers may genuinely have no deficit in the skill measured by the test, or they may have a deficit that they are able to mask (either as their memories and other cognitive skills that will affect test performance are superior to that of their younger controls, or because they have received extensive remediation that affects performance on this particular test). Alternatively, the negative result could reflect regression to the mean, which will operate in opposite directions for the skilled and the less-skilled groups.

Although debate about methodology is still very lively (Bryant & Goswami, 1990; Clark, 1990; Francis, 1990; Gathercole, 1990; Hulme & Snowling, 1990; Maughan & Rutter, 1990; Pumfrey, 1990; Yule, 1990), there is general agreement on one point. The most striking result in studies of backward readers is when dyslexic children turn out to be significantly *worse* at something than their reading level controls, who are much younger than they are, and who consequently have a lower mental age. In such cases, longitudinal and training designs should be used to examine whether this factor plays a causal role in the difficulties of the backward group.

Quantitative versus qualitative differences

The controversy over the appropriate comparison group to use in studies of reading delay has also led to a second methodological debate, which is whether the deficits found in backward readers reflect a qualitative difference from the normal population, or a quantitative one. Early research suggested that the differences between dyslexic children and normal readers might be qualitative, as there seemed to be an excess of children scoring poorly in reading compared to the number that might be expected on the basis of the normal distribution (Yule *et al.*, 1974). However, more recently it has been suggested that this apparent 'hump' at the bottom of the normal distribution was a test artefact, and that the prevalence of dyslexia in the population is in line with the 2–4% that would be expected via normal variation (Rodgers, 1983; van der Wissel & Zegers, 1985; Miles, 1991b).

The issue is an important one, because of its implications for aetiology and remediation. If dyslexic children are qualitatively different from normal readers, then they may be suffering from a special problem that does not affect the normal course of reading development. If dyslexic children are quantitatively different from normal readers, then the same factors should affect both their reading progress and normal reading development. The dyslexic children will simply progress much more slowly. Of course, a lag that is initially quite small may become a serious deficit in time via the interdependence of reading, spelling and phonological development. Stanovich (1986) has called this phenomenon the 'Matthew' effect in reading, where the 'rich' get 'richer' in terms of reading skills, and the 'poor' get 'poorer'. So a developmental lag may well end up looking like a qualitative difference.

Unfortunately, it is impossible to distinguish between qualitative and quantitative explanations of reading failure on the basis of the reading level and chronological age match designs discussed above. A positive result in a reading level match study is not evidence for a qualitative difference between backward and normal readers, and a negative result in a reading level match study is not evidence for a quantitative difference (Bryant & Goswami, 1986; Goswami & Bryant, 1989). One possible way of differentiating between qualitative and quantitative differences is to perform multiple regression analyses of twin data. By comparing the concordance rates of reading difficulties in identical (monozygotic) and fraternal (dizygotic) twins and then applying multiple regression models, DeFries and Fulker (1985) have argued that it is possible to work out whether the deviant scores of probands represent the lower tail of a normal distribution or arise from a qualitatively different causal variable. To date, their results are consistent with a quantitative description of dyslexia, although the differences that they find between the probands and their cotwins are of a sufficient magnitude to make further sampling desirable (De Fries, 1991).

More recently, Stanovich (1991) has shown that when dyslexic children (unexpectedly poor readers given their IQs) are compared with 'garden variety' poor readers (children reading poorly in line with their poor IQs), the two groups are virtually indistinguishable in terms of their cognitive profiles. There do not seem to be clear differences in the cognitive correlates of individual differences in reading achievement between poor readers with high IQs and poor readers with low IQs. This finding calls into question the very notion of defining dyslexia in relation to IQ (a discrepancy measure). Instead, it seems that poor readers are bad at the same things (namely phonological tasks), irrespective of their IQ level (Siegal, 1988). Although this approach to defining dyslexia is still controversial, it does suggest that reading disability should be considered quantitatively rather than qualitatively. Serious disorders of reading (and probably also of spelling) constitute no more than the extremes of the normal distribution, a conclusion that in no way undermines their seriousness for the children concerned.

Heterogeneity of dyslexia

The final methodological issue to consider before turning to the experimental evidence is whether all dyslexic children are the same. In other words, do all children experience reading delay for the same reasons, or are there multiple causal factors in dyslexia? Traditionally, it has been suggested that there are at least two types of dyslexic child, those with primarily visual problems and those whose problems are primarily auditory in nature. An influential model of this type was proposed by Boder (1973), who argued that 'dysphonetic' dyslexic children made primarily sound-based errors, like writing 'rember' or 'werber' for 'remember', whereas 'dyseidetic' dyslexic children made primarily visually based errors, like reading 'laugh' as 'log'. In her sample, 63% of the children were classified as dysphonetic, 9% were dyseidetic, and most of the remaining children were classified as a mixture of the two.

More recent surveys have tended to question the purity of a visual dyslexic category (Miles, 1991a). Many of the apparently visual errors noted in dyslexia, such as reversing words ('was' for 'saw'), turn out to be characteristic of normal readers who are reading at the same level as the dyslexic children, and Vellutino (as noted earlier) found no evidence for a visual deficit in dyslexia (Vellutino, 1979). Even in Boder's original data, the number of children who were supposed to have primarily visual problems was small. The issue of heterogeneity is also important for teaching, as one needs to decide whether to attempt different kinds of remediation for different kinds of dyslexia. As the existence of different types of dyslexia is being increasingly questioned, the message would seem to be that one does not. This chapter returns to the issue of remediation later. First, let us consider the empirical evidence on the development of reading difficulties.

Phonological skills and reading delay

If we return to the causal developmental model of reading and spelling discussed in the last section, then one very clear prediction emerges concerning reading delay. It is that children with reading difficulties should have phonological difficulties. There are at least three kinds of experimental evidence that are consistent with this prediction. The first kind comes from research studies that have used a reading level design to investigate the problems experienced by backward readers. The second

comes from studies of the heritability of reading difficulties, and the third comes from studies that have followed dyslexic children into adulthood.

Studies using the reading level design

If we limit our discussion of empirical studies of backward readers to those rather few studies that have used the reading level design, then a very coherent pattern of results emerges. The tests that consistently differentiate backward readers from children who are reading normally are those that require phonological skills. Backward readers usually have phonological problems.

One example of such a study was carried out by Bradley and Bryant (1983). They gave the oddity task to 10 year olds who were reading at the 7-year-old level, and compared their performance to that of a group of normally reading 7 year olds. The backward readers made significantly more errors than the younger normal readers on all the versions of the oddity task, and were also poor at a task of rhyme production. Rhyming deficits in backward readers were also found in a reading level match study by Holligan and Johnston (1988). So backward readers have difficulties in tasks based on onsets and rimes.

The phonological problems of backward readers are not restricted to the onset–rime level, however. Backward readers also perform more poorly than younger reading level controls on tests of nonsense word reading, even though they perform as well as these controls in reading lists of real words. Reading a nonsense word like 'dake' or 'molsmit' is a phonological task, because the word is an unfamiliar one, and so cannot be recognized visually as a complete unit. A pronunciation must be derived either by working out the letter–sound correspondences (grapheme–phoneme correspondences) in the word, or by using an analogy to a real word (for example, 'dake' is analogous to 'cake'). There is evidence that both analogies and grapheme–phoneme correspondences are used by children when they read nonsense words (Treiman et al., 1990). As a number of studies have shown that dyslexic children find nonsense word reading tasks very difficult (Snowling, 1980; Baddeley et al., 1982; Frith & Snowling, 1983; Olson, 1985), this suggests that the phonological difficulties of backward readers extend beyond the onset—rime level.

Genetic data

Recently, a number of investigators have studied dyslexia in twins, in order to try and assess whether dyslexia is genetically carried and therefore heritable. As noted above, the use of twin studies also provides another way of looking at the qualitative/quantitative issue. The genetic argument is at one level very simple. It is that monozygotic twins, who share all of their genes, should show a higher concordance for reading difficulties than dizygotic twins, who share on average only half of their genes. A number of studies have found concordance rates ranging from 33 to 100% for monozygotic twins, and from 29 to 54% for dizygotic twins (see DeFries, 1991 for a review). However, the most reliable estimate of concordance is probably provided by the Colorado twin study, which has used a much larger sample of twins than earlier studies, and has also employed more rigorous methods for defining reading disability. In the Colorado twin study, the concordance rate for monozygotic twins was 70%, compared to 48% for dizygotic twins. This suggests a strong heritable component in reading difficulties.

The nature of this heritable component has been examined in an interesting way by Olson *et al.* (1990), who have studied different subcomponents of the reading skills of the twins in the Colorado sample. Olson *et al.* were particularly interested in comparing the phonological coding and orthographic coding skills of these children. Phonological coding was measured by the ability to read nonsense words like 'calch', and orthographic coding by the ability to recognize the real word in word/nonsense word pairs like 'sleep'/'sleap'. The former measure was intended to provide an index of phonological skill, and the latter of visual lexical access. Olson *et al.* found that the heritability of phonological skills and of orthographic skills differed. The heritability of word recognition and phonological coding was relatively high and significant, whereas that of orthographic coding was relatively low and non-significant. Stevenson (1991) has recently found similar results in a twin study based on a London sample.

Moreover, Olson's group has recently shown that the reading ability of the probands (the reading disabled children) is highly predictive of the phonological abilities of their cotwins (who are not reading disabled) (reported in DeFries, 1991). In a model predicting the cotwins' phonological or orthographic scores from the word recognition scores of their probands, the relationship between word recognition and phonological coding was 0.81 ± 0.14, compared to 0.27 ± 0.18 for word recognition and orthographic coding. So the reading abilities of one twin are highly predictive of the phonological abilities of the other. This is strong evidence that it is heritable differences in phonological coding that underlie the genetic aetiology of reading disability. Other statistical approaches such as factor analysis have also suggested that it is heritable variation in phonological skills that explains the genetic transmission of reading disability (Gillis *et al.*, 1991).

Persistence into adulthood

Finally, there is evidence that phonological problems persist into adulthood, as would be expected if a primary phonological deficit continues to hamper the development of reading throughout the lifespan. Bruck (1990) studied a group of adults who had been diagnosed as dyslexic when they were children, and gave them a number of different tests. These included tests of syllable and phoneme counting, and phoneme deletion. She found that the adults performed more poorly on the phonological tests than a group of (child) reading level controls, even on the syllable task. Although these adults were on average 13 years older than their child controls, their phonological skills were significantly poorer. In the more difficult tasks, such as phoneme counting, the performance of the dyslexic adults was actually worse than that of children with poorer reading and spelling levels. So for these adults, the acquisition of some reading and spelling skills had not particularly improved their phonological skills.

Similar evidence for the persistence of phonological problems comes from a study of adult dyslexics carried out by Pennington *et al.* (1990). They studied two groups of adult dyslexics, a 'familial' group who were recruited from families with a history of dyslexia, and a 'clinic' group who were recruited from a reading disability treatment centre. Each group was matched to reading level and chronological age controls, and all groups were then given a number of different tests, including two tests of phonological skill. The phonological tests required the accurate recognition and production of stimuli in a 'pig Latin' task (e.g. 'draw' — raw-day'). Pennington *et al.* found that the dyslexic adults were impaired on the phonological tasks compared to controls, but were not impaired on other language processing tasks such as phoneme perception and lexical retrieval (naming). The authors concluded that problems in phoneme awareness met all the criteria for a primary underlying deficit — those of universality, persistence and causal precedence.

Finally, a study of high-achieving adult dyslexics by Watson and Brown (1992) showed that even in this special group, the subjects' problems were still primarily phonological. These adult dyslexics were all pursuing higher education courses, and might have been supposed to have developed efficient and possibly idiosyncratic visually based compensatory strategies for reading. However, Watson and Brown found that in a word-naming task, these adults showed the same effects of orthographic neighbourhood size (the number of words sharing a similar spelling pattern) as reading level controls and skilled adult readers. This finding implies that the dyslexic adults were not using qualitatively different strategies from their controls in reading words aloud, even though they read aloud very slowly. Watson and Brown's data provide further support for the hypothesis that reading difficulties constitute a developmental delay rather than a qualitative deficit.

Phonological skills and spelling delay

Not surprisingly, phonological difficulties also seem to be at the root of spelling difficulties. As spelling development is connected to reading development, studies of backward spellers almost by definition involve studying children who are also backward readers. The use of a spelling level match is therefore problematic: if backward spellers are matched for their spelling skills with normal children, then they will not be matched for reading. Even so, this is a better experimental design than using a chrono-

logical age match. Most such studies show that children with spelling difficulties show clear signs of a phonological deficit.

One study that used a spelling level match was carried out in Australia. Rohl and Tunmer (1988) compared three groups of children who were spelling at the 8-year-old level. One group were precocious spellers, who were spelling a year ahead of their age norms, one group were normal 8 year olds, and one group were backward spellers, who were aged around 10 years. The phonological task used was the Liberman *et al.* tapping task. Rohl and Tunmer found that for longer words, the backward spellers were much worse at phoneme tapping than the other groups, even though they could spell as many words as the younger children. In another spelling match study, Bruck and Treiman (1990) used a sound deletion task to compare backward spellers with normal children spelling at the same level, and found a selective deficit in the backward spellers. So there is evidence for a special phonological difficulty in children who are backward in spelling.

Although the exact sequence of cause and effect cannot be clearly distinguished in these studies (since the poor spellers were also poor readers, the phonological problems of the poor spellers could have initially caused them to experience reading delay, which in turn caused a spelling delay), it is at least clear that phonological difficulties are common in children with spelling difficulties. However, there is a way to try and control for differences in reading, and that is to use a design pioneered by Frith (1980), in which poor spellers who are good readers are compared with poor spellers who are poor readers, and also with good spellers who are good readers.

Perin (1983) used this design. She asked some 14 and 15 year olds who fell into these three groups to perform two phonological tasks. The tasks that she chose were the spoonerism task mentioned earlier, and a task of phoneme counting. Perin found that it was the children's spelling levels rather than their reading levels that determined their performance on the phonological tasks. The poor spellers were worse at the phonological tasks than the good spellers, irrespective of their reading levels. Phonological deficits in poor spellers using this design have also been found by Bruck and Waters (1988).

So a phonological deficit seems to have a direct effect on spelling delay as well as an indirect effect on spelling via reading. Further support for the idea that phonological skills are particularly important for spelling comes from studies that have trained children in phonological skills. These studies suggest that while phonological training benefits reading development, it causes especially great benefits to spelling.

HELPING CHILDREN TO READ AND SPELL MORE EFFICIENTLY

The research discussed so far has distinguished the important causal factors in reading and spelling development and delay. The final part of this chapter discusses ways of helping children who are experiencing difficulties in acquiring these skills. The causal−developmental model of reading and spelling makes a clear prediction here as well. It is that training children's phonological skills should help with the development of reading and spelling. Establishing such a link by conducting training studies is particularly important for remediation. In fact, the outcome of training studies does indeed suggest that one way to help children who have reading difficulties is to work on improving their phonological skills.

Training phonological skills

An important training study in this respect was conducted by Bradley and Bryant (1983). They took a group of 65 children who had performed poorly on the oddity task, and divided them into four groups. One group was trained on sound categorization using pictures: for example, this group might learn to categorize pictures of a cat, a rat and a bat together. This was the phonological training group. Another group also received this phonological training, but in addition were shown how to write the picture names using plastic letters. This group learned about the connections between shared sounds in words and reading and spelling. For example, a word like 'cat' could be changed into the word 'rat' by changing the first plastic letter, so that the spelling pattern of the rime — the common sound — remained the same. A third (control) group also learned to categorize pictures, but this time the pictures had to be sorted by semantic category. For example, if the category was 'animals you see in the farmyard', then the cat, the rat and a pig would go together. A final group provided an unseen control.

Training lasted for a period of 2 years, and the children's reading and spelling skills were tested after the training was over. Although the groups had initially been matched on IQ, age and phonological ability, and could not read at the beginning of the study, their progress in reading and spelling was very different. Both the phonological training group and the group who had received the plastic letters were ahead of the two control groups in reading and spelling. The plastic letters group was particularly far ahead, being 12 months ahead in reading and a startling 23 months ahead in spelling compared to the unseen control group — virtually 1 and 2 years respectively. In the stricter comparison with the semantic categorization group, who were equated for extra time with the teacher, these children were still 8 months ahead in reading and 17 months ahead in spelling. So here is strong evidence that training in phonological skills will help children's reading and spelling development, especially when such training involves the use of plastic letters.

Other long-term training studies have since confirmed Bradley and Bryant's results, using a variety of phonological tasks, and training children at both the onset−rime and the phonemic level (Lundberg *et al.*, 1988; Cunningham, 1990). The study by Lundberg *et al.*, which was carried out in Denmark, also replicated the finding that phonological training effects were even more marked for spelling (Cunningham's study only examined reading). As the Scandanavian training programme was purely oral, without the use of letters, even greater benefits may have been found if alphabetic instruction had supplemented the phonological training. Nevertheless, phonological training is clearly beneficial to reading and spelling development, with or without additional training about letters.

Accordingly, one way to set about trying to help children with reading difficulties is to concentrate on developing their phonological skills. Bryant and Bradley's (1985) findings suggest that children with reading and spelling difficulties should benefit from phonological instruction, and especially from combining this instruction with alphabetic letters. Some possible approaches to such instruction are outlined in their book. Another message from these training studies is that every child will benefit from phonological instruction. Thus, it might be worth giving every child extra phonological experiences when they arrive in school.

Methods of remediation in the classroom

What about teaching methods once the child is a bit older, and is still experiencing difficulties with print? Although the empirical findings are somewhat unclear, there is a general consensus that the continued teaching of backward readers should focus on their phonological weakness, rather than on developing alternative methods of reading that may rely more on other processes such as visual memorization (Cooke, 1991). Given the finding that even highly skilled adult dyslexics approach reading in the same way as young normal children (discussed earlier), and the robust performance of phonics-based reading programmes compared to other teaching methods (Chall, 1967, 1983), this approach of teaching to the deficit would seem to be the right one.

The reason that it is difficult to comment on exactly which aspects of phonics-based training programmes are most useful is that studies with backward groups have tended to use unseen controls (Wallach & Wallach, 1976; Williams, 1980), and to use a combination of instruction about phonology and alphabetic letters at both the onset–rime and the phonemic level, making any more fine-grained advice about how to proceed premature. More recently, however, some remedial programmes have concentrated specifically on linking onset–rime units and sequences of letters, and have shown marked success (Gaskins *et al.*, 1986; White & Cunningham, 1990). Furthermore, work from Lovett's group in Toronto has suggested that both instruction about decoding *and* instruction about oral language skills are important in remediation (Lovett *et al.*, 1989), while the necessity of giving older children and adults the ability to take charge of their own learning has been stressed by many authors (Klein, 1991; Sonday, 1991). There is also a widespread acceptance that multisensory approaches to learning about phonics are the most

effective ones (see Snowling and Thomson, 1991 for a recent selection of reviews).

The effectiveness of multisensory approaches to learning have been most clearly demonstrated in studies of the spelling of backward readers, however. Although it is usually assumed that improving a child's reading skills will also improve that child's spelling skills (an assumption that seems to be largely correct), to particularly remediate spelling a multisensory teaching method seems to be the best approach (Gillingham & Stillman, 1956; Bradley, 1981). The idea is to teach children with learning difficulties by using all the sensory channels involved in written language learning — vision, hearing, touch and movement.

For example, Thomson (1991) has recently compared the multisensory simultaneous oral spelling technique for teaching spelling with a visual inspection method, in which children learn to write words by studying their visual appearance, covering them up, saying the letters in them and then checking them visually again. In the simultaneous oral spelling method, the children listen to the sound of the word first, repeat it, spell it orally letter by letter, write it down letter by letter saying each letter as it is written, and finally read aloud the word that has been written. Thomson compared the effects of these two teaching methods on the spelling performance of a group of dyslexic children and a group of normal children matched for spelling age. He found that although the normal controls were helped by both methods, the dyslexic children were only helped by the simultaneous oral spelling technique. The dyslexic children were not helped by an emphasis on visual memorization, even though they could spell as many words on a standardized test as their younger controls. Backward spellers are only helped by methods that involve all the sensory components of the writing task, and the same may be true of backward readers as well.

CONCLUSION

This chapter uses a certain perspective about how reading and spelling develop, but it is a perspective that has a lot of evidence to support it. Much of the research into the development of reading and spelling skills conducted over the last decade has led to a rather consistent set of results. This research has shown that it is specifically phonological skills that occupy a central role in the developmental course of normal reading and spelling, and in delays in reading and spelling development. Reading and spelling skills are thus an example of a type of development that is fairly domain-specific. Domain-general skills, such as memory, attention and motivation, do not play a special role in the development of reading and spelling, although deficits in these areas will certainly affect the acquisition of written language skills (as they will affect all intellectual skills).

The evidence for a special developmental role for phonological awareness has come from a number of sources. Phonological skills measured before a child goes to school or begins to be taught to read are the best predictors that we have of that child's reading and spelling progress years later. Children who fail to read and to spell normally turn out to have deficits in their phonological skills, deficits that persist into adulthood, and that seem to be inherited. If children are trained in phonological skills, then their reading and spelling progress is improved, and this is especially true if that training includes information about how sounds are related to alphabetic letters. Finally, evidence that phonological skills are important in reading and spelling has been found across cultures, and in a variety of different orthographies. Age itself does not seem to be the pacesetter for reading acquisition, and neither (in the first instance) does social class or home environment. Instead, it is the level of a child's or an adult's phonological skills that determines their progress in reading and spelling, and that continues to do so across the lifespan.

REFERENCES

Baddeley A.D., Ellis N.C., Miles T.R. & Lewis V.J. (1982) Developmental and acquired dyslexia: A comparison. *Cognition* **11**, 185−199.

Boder E. (1973) Developmental dyslexia: A diagnostic approach based on three atypical reading−spelling patterns. *Developmental Medicine and Child Neurology* **15**, 663−687.

Bradley L. (1981) The organisation of motor patterns for spelling: An effective remedial strategy for backward readers. *Developmental Medicine and Child Neurology* **23**, 83−91.

Bradley L. & Bryant P.E. (1983) Categorising sounds and learning to read: A causal connection. *Nature* **310**, 419−421.

Bruck M. (1990) Word recognition skills of adults with childhood diagnoses of dyslexia. *Developmental Psychology* **26**, 439−454.

Bruck M. & Treiman R. (1990) Phonological awareness and spelling in normal children and dyslexics: The case of initial consonant clusters. *Journal of Experimental Child Psychology* **50**, 156−178.

Bruck M. & Waters G. (1988) An analysis of the spelling errors of children who differ in their reading and spelling skills. *Applied Psycholinguistics* **9**, 77−92.

Bryant P.E. & Bradley L. (1985) *Children's Reading Problems*. Basil Blackwell, Oxford.

Bryant P.E., Bradley L., MacLean M. & Crossland J. (1989) Nursery rhymes, phonological skills, and reading. *Journal of Child Language* **16**, 407−428.

Bryant P.E. & Goswami U. (1986) The strengths and weaknesses of the reading level design. *Psychological Bulletin* **100**, 101−103.

Bryant P.E. & Goswami U. (1990) Comparisons between backward and normal readers: A risky business. Open dialogue − Backward and normal readers: Peer review. *BPS Education Section Review* **14**(2), 3−10.

Cataldo S. & Ellis N.C. (1988) Interactions in the development of spelling, reading and phonological skills. *Journal of Research in Reading* **11**(2), 86−109.

Chall J.S. (1967) *Learning to Read: The Great Debate*. McGraw-Hill, New York.

Chall J.S. (1983) *Stages of Reading Development*. McGraw-Hill, New York.

Chukovsky K. (1963) *From Two to Five*. University of California Press, Berkeley.

Clark M.M. (1990) Open dialogue − Backward and normal readers. Peer review. *BPS Education Section Review* **14**(2), 10−12.

Cooke A. (1991) The dyslexic child's transfer of learning from the individual lesson to work in the classroom. In Snowling M. & Thomson M. (eds) *Dyslexia: Integrating Theory and Practice*, pp. 302−308. Whurr, London.

Cossu G., Shankweiler D., Liberman I.Y., Tola G. & Katz L. (1987) *Awareness of Phonological Segments and Reading Ability in Italian Children*. Haskins Labs Status Report on Speech Research, No. SR-91, New Haven, Connecticut.

Cunningham A.E. (1990) Implicit vs. explicit instruction in phonemic awareness. *Journal of Experimental Child Psychology*, **50**, 429−444.

DeFries J.C. (1991) Genetics and dyslexia: An overview. In Snowling M. & Thomson M. (eds) *Dyslexia: Integrating Theory and Practice*, pp. 3−20. Whurr, London.

DeFries J.D. & Fulker D.W. (1985) Multiple regression analyses of twin data. *Behaviour Genetics* **15**, 467−473.

Ellis N. (1991) Spelling and sound in learning to read. In Snowling M. & Thomson M. (eds) *Dyslexia: Integrating Theory and Practice*, pp. 80−94. Whurr, London.

Ellis N.C. & Large B. (1987) The development of reading:

As you seek, so shall ye find. *British Journal of Psychology* **78**, 1–28.

Francis H. (1990) Open dialogue — Backward and normal readers. Peer review. *BPS Education Section Review* **14**(2), 12–14.

Frith U. (1980) Unexpected spelling problems. In Frith U. (ed.) *Cognitive Processes in Spelling*, pp. 495–515. Academic Press, London.

Frith U. (1985) Beneath the surface of developmental dyslexia. In Patterson K., Coltheart M. & Marshall J. (eds) *Surface Dyslexia*, pp. 301–330. Academic Press, Cambridge.

Frith U. & Snowling M. (1983) Reading for meaning and reading for sound in autistic and dyslexic children. *British Journal of Developmental Psychology* **1**, 329–342.

Gaskins I.W., Downer M.A. & Gaskins R.W. (1986) *Introduction to the Benchmark School Word Identification/Vocabulary Development Program*. Benchmark Press, Media, Pennsylvania.

Gathercole S.E. (1990) Open dialogue — Backward and normal readers. Peer review. *BPS Education Section Review* **14**(2), 14–16.

Gelb I.J. (1963) *A Study of Writing*. University of Chicago Press, Chicago.

Gillingham A.M. & Stillman B.U. (1956) *Remedial Training for Children with Specific Disability in Reading, Spelling and Penmanship*, 5th edn. Sackett & Wilhelms, New York.

Gillis J.J., DeFries J.C., Olson R.K. & Rack J.P. (1991) Confirmatory factor analysis of reading and mathematics performance measures in the Colorado Reading Project. *Behaviour Genetics* **21**(6), 572–573.

Goswami U. (1986) Children's use of analogy in learning to read: A developmental study. *Journal of Experimental Child Psychology* **42**, 73–83.

Goswami U. (1988a) Children's use of analogy in learning to spell. *British Journal of Developmental Psychology* **6**, 21–33.

Goswami U. (1988b) Orthographic analogies and reading development. *Quarterly Journal of Experimental Psychology* **40A**, 239–268.

Goswami U. (1990a) Phonological priming and orthographic analogies in reading. *Journal of Experimental Child Psychology* **49**, 323–340.

Goswami U. (1990b) A special link between rhyming skills and the use of orthographic analogies by beginning readers. *Journal of Child Psychology and Psychiatry* **31**, 301–311.

Goswami U. (1991) Learning about spelling sequences: The role of onsets and rimes in analogies in reading. *Child Development* **62**, 1110–1123.

Goswami U. (1992) Annotation: Phonological factors in spelling development. *Journal of Child Psychology and Psychiatry* **33**, 967–975.

Goswami U. & Bryant P.E. (1989) The interpretation of studies using the reading level design. *Journal of Reading Behaviour* **21**(4), 413–424.

Goswami U. & Bryant P.E. (1990) *Phonological Skills and Learning to Read*. Lawrence Erlbaum, Hillsdale, New Jersey.

Goswami U. & Mead F. (1992) Onset and rime awareness and analogies in reading. *Reading Research Quarterly* **27**(2), 152–162.

Holligan C. & Johnston R.S. (1988) The use of phonological information by good and poor readers in memory and reading tasks. *Memory and Cognition* **16**, 522–532.

Hulme C. & Snowling M. (1990) Connections, only connections! *BPS Education Section Review* **14**(2), 16–18.

Kamhi A.G. & Catts H.W. (1989) *Reading Disabilities: A Developmental Language Perspective*. Little, Brown & Co., Boston, Massachusetts.

Klein C. (1991) Setting up a learning programme for adult dyslexics. In Snowling M. & Thomson M. (eds) *Dyslexia: Integrating Theory and Practice*, pp. 293–301. Whurr, London.

Liberman I.Y., Shankweiler D., Fischer F.W. & Carter B. (1974) Explicit syllable and phoneme segmentation in the young child. *Journal of Experimental Child Psychology* **18**, 201–212.

Lovett M.W., Ransby M.J., Hardwick N., Johns M.S. & Donaldson S.A. (1989) Can dyslexia be treated? Treatment-specific and generalised treatment effects in dyslexic children's response to remediation. *Brain and Language* **37**, 90–121.

Lundberg I., Frost J. & Petersen O. (1988) Effects of an extensive programme for stimulating phonological awareness in pre-school children. *Reading Research Quarterly* **23**, 163–284.

Lundberg I., Olofsson A. & Wall S. (1980) Reading and spelling skills in the first school years predicted from phonemic awareness skills in kindergarten. *Scandinavian Journal of Psychology* **21**, 159–173.

McGee R., Share D., Moffit T.E., Williams S. & Silva P.A. (1988) Reading disability, behaviour problems and juvenile delinquency. In Saklofske D. & Eysenck S. (eds) *Individual Differences in Children and Adolescents: International Research Perspectives*, pp. 158–172. Hodder & Stoughton, New York.

MacLean M., Bryant P.E. & Bradley L. (1987) Rhymes, nursery rhymes and reading in early childhood. *Merrill-Palmer Quarterly* **33**, 255–282.

Maughan B. & Rutter M. (1990) Open dialogue — Backward and normal readers. Peer review. *BPS Education Section Review* **14**(2), 19–21.

Miles E. (1991a) Visual dyslexia/auditory dyslexia: Is this a valuable distinction to make? In Snowling M. & Thomson M. (eds) *Dyslexia: Integrating Theory and Practice*, pp. 195–203. Whurr, London.

Miles T.R. (1991b) On determining the prevalence of dyslexia. In Snowling M. & Thomson M. (eds) *Dyslexia: Integrating Theory and Practice*, pp. 144–153. Whurr, London.

Moffit T.E. (1990) Juvenile delinquency and attention deficit disorder: Boys' developmental trajectories from age 3 to age 15. *Child Development* **61**, 893–910.

Morais J., Bertelson P., Cary L. & Alegria J. (1986) Literacy training and speech segmentation. *Cognition* **24**, 45−64.

Morais J., Cary L., Alegria J. & Bertelson P. (1979) Does awareness of speech as a sequence of phones arise spontaneously? *Cognition* **7**, 323−331.

Olson R.K. (1985) Disabled reading processes and cognitive profiles. In Gray D. & Kavanagh J. (eds) *Biobehavioural Measures of Dyslexia*, pp. 215−244. York Press, Parkton, Maryland.

Olson R., Wise B., Connors F. & Rack J. (1990) Organisation, heritability, and remediation of component word recognition and language skills in disabled readers. In Carr T.H. & Levy B.A. (eds) *Reading and Its Development: Component Skills Approaches*, pp. 261−322. Academic Press, San Diego, California.

Opie I. & Opie P. (1987) *The Lore and Language of Schoolchildren*. Oxford University Press, Oxford.

Pennington B.F., Van Orden G.C., Smith S.D., Green P.A. & Haith M.M. (1990) Phonological processing skills and deficits in adult dyslexics. *Child Development* **61**, 1753−1778.

Perin D. (1983) Phonemic segmentation and spelling. *British Journal of Psychology* **74**, 129−144.

Pumfrey P. (1990) Open dialogue — Backward and normal readers. Peer review. *BPS Education Section Review* **14**(2), 21−24.

Raz I.S. & Bryant P.E. (1990) Social background, phonological awareness, and children's reading. *British Journal of Developmental Psychology* **8**, 209−226.

Read C. (1986) *Children's Creative Spelling*. Routledge & Kegan Paul, London.

Read C., Zhang Y., Nie H. & Ding B. (1986) The ability to manipulate speech sounds depends on knowing alphabetic spelling. *Cognition* **24**, 31−44.

Rodgers B. (1983) The identification and prevalence of specific reading retardation. *British Journal of Educational Psychology* **53**, 369−373.

Rohl E.M. & Tunmer W. (1988) Phonemic segmentation skill and spelling acquisition. *Applied Psycholinguistics* **9**, 335−350.

Scarborough H.S. (1990) Very early language deficits in dyslexic children. *Child Development* **61**, 1728−1743.

Siegal L.S. (1988) Evidence that IQ scores are irrelevant to the definition and analysis of reading disability. *Canadian Journal of Psychology* **42**, 201−215.

Snowling M.J. (1980) The development of grapheme—phoneme correspondence in normal and dyslexic readers. *Journal of Experimental Child Psychology* **29**, 294−305.

Snowling M. & Thomson M. (eds) (1991) *Dyslexia: Integrating Theory and Practice*. Whurr, London.

Sonday A.W. (1991) The road to reading: Basic skills to college allowances. In Snowling M. & Thomson M. (eds) *Dyslexia: Integrating Theory and Practice*, pp. 283−292. Whurr, London.

Stanovich K.E. (1986) Matthew effects in reading: Some consequences of individual differences in the acquisition of literacy. *Reading Research Quarterly* **21**, 360−407.

Stanovich K.E. (1991) The theoretical and practical consequences of discrepancy definitions of dyslexia. In Snowling M. & Thomson M. (eds) *Dyslexia: Integrating Theory and Practice*, pp. 125−143. Whurr, London.

Stanovich K.E., Cunningham A.E. & Cramer B.R. (1984) Assessing phonological awareness in kindergarten: Issues of task comparability. *Journal of Experimental Child Psychology* **38**, 175−190.

Stevenson J. (1991) Which aspects of processing text mediate genetic effects? *Reading and Writing: An Interdisciplinary Journal* **4**, 57−77.

Stuart M. & Coltheart M. (1988) Does reading develop in a sequence of stages? *Cognition* **30**, 139−181.

Thomson M. (1991) The teaching of spelling using techniques of simultaneous oral spelling and visual inspection. In Snowling M. & Thomson M. (eds) *Dyslexia: Integrating Theory and Practice*, pp. 244−250. Whurr, London.

Treiman R. (1983) The structure of spoken syllables: Evidence from novel word games. *Cognition* **15**, 49−74.

Treiman R. (1985) Phonemic awareness and spelling: Children's judgements do not always agree with adults'. *Journal of Experimental Child Psychology* **39**, 182−201.

Treiman R. (1993) *Beginning to Spell: A Study of First-grade Children*. Oxford University Press, New York.

Treiman R., Goswami U. & Bruck M. (1990) Not all nonwords are alike: Implications for reading development and theory. *Memory and Cognition* **18**, 559−567.

van der Wissel A. & Zegers F.E. (1985) Reading retardation revisited. *British Journal of Developmental Psychology* **3**, 3−9.

Vellutino F.R. (1979) *Dyslexia*. MIT Press, Cambridge, Massachusetts.

Wallach M.A. & Wallach L. (1976) *Teaching All Children to Read*. University of Chicago Press, Chicago.

Watson F.L. & Brown G.D.A. (1992) Single word reading in college dyslexics. *Applied Cognitive Psychology* **6**(3), 263−272.

White T.G. & Cunningham P.M. (1990) *Teaching disadvantaged students to decode by analogy*. Paper presented at the annual meeting of the American Educational Research Association, Boston, Massachusetts, April.

Williams J. (1980) Teaching decoding with an emphasis on phoneme analysis and phoneme blending. *Journal of Educational Psychology* **72**, 1−15.

Wimmer H. & Hummer P. (1990) How German-speaking first graders read and spell: Doubts on the importance of the logographic stage. *Applied Psycholinguistics* **11**, 349−368.

Yule W. (1990) Open dialogue — Backward and normal readers. Peer review. *BPS Education Section Review* **14**(2), 24−25.

Yule W., Rutter M., Berger M. & Thompson J. (1974) Over- and under-achievement in reading: Distribution in the general population. *British Journal of Educational Psychology* **44**, 1−12.

13: Development of a Theory of Mind: Where would we be without the Intentional Stance?

SIMON BARON-COHEN

INTRODUCTION

This chapter focuses on one topic within social cognition: 'theory of mind'. This term (coined by Premack & Woodruff, 1978) refers to the conceptual knowledge children and adults possess about the mind (its function and its contents: mental states such as beliefs, desires, intentions, etc.), and the use to which they put this knowledge in making sense of the social world. Hence its place within the larger domain of social cognition. Social cognition encompasses the full range of cognitive processes and mechanisms involved in understanding the social world (Sherrod & Lamb, 1981): person perception, perspective taking, the self-concept, imitation, moral reasoning, emotion comprehension, even communication development. In focusing this chapter on the development of a theory of mind, these other topics will not be covered here. Many of them are covered elsewhere in this volume (see Chapters 14, 17 and 19), and in addition, good reviews of the broader field of social cognition also exist (Shantz, 1983; Cicchetti & Beeghly, 1990). Before turning to the question of why the development of a theory of mind is of special interest, let us briefly consider the basic question of the nature of social cognition.

THE NATURE OF SOCIAL COGNITION

Why is it useful to separate social from non-social cognition? Why separate perception and knowledge about people from perception and knowledge about objects in general? One reason is that the stimuli to be processed are qualitatively different in the social and non-social worlds. People are self-propelling, they respond to non-physical causal events (such as beliefs), and they can reciprocate. In contrast, inanimate objects only move when acted upon by physical-causal events (Gelman & Spelke, 1981). One reason, then, for isolating social cognition as a separate domain of study, is to investigate if the cognitive system uses qualitatively different information-processing mechanisms for understanding social and non-social stimuli.

A second, related reason for studying social cognition in its own right is to investigate how social cognition has evolved independently of non-social cognition. That these two forms of cognition are dissociable is not contentious. For example, a homing pigeon's ability to navigate its way across enormous distances in the physical world matches (or even outstrips) the equivalent ability in a human adult. However, the homing pigeon's ability to recognize simple deception in the social world appears even less developed than that of a human child. Explaining the evolution of social cognition is a major task that has hardly begun (Jolly, 1966; Humphrey, 1984; Byrne & Whiten, 1988).

A third, related reason for studying social cognition comes from the finding that some fundamental cognitive processes that operate in both social and non-social cognition sometimes operate with less effort in the social than the non-social domain, perhaps reflecting the types of problems they were first evolved to solve. Thus, Cheney and Seyfarth (1990) argue that monkeys solve transitive inference problems (e.g. If $A > B$, and $B > C$, then what is A to C?) whenever they understand social dominance relationships (which they do all the time); yet they have considerable difficulty in solving these logical tasks in the non-social domain. Cosmides (1989) also demonstrated that for adult humans, logical reasoning (e.g. on the Wason selection task; Wason, 1983) is more accurate in the social than in the non-social domain (but see also Chapter 10).

It is clear, then, that social and non-social cognition can function independently, yet may interact in important ways. They may have their own domain-specific, purpose-built information-processing mechanisms, and also use some general processing mechanisms. With these broader issues in mind, let us turn to the question of why theory of mind is of special interest.

Why focus on theory of mind?

A number of reasons guided the selection of this topic. First, it is one of the most exciting growth areas in the field of social cognition, as the number of new books and dedicated conference symposia in recent years testifies (Astington *et al.*, 1988; Harris, 1989; Wellman, 1990; Butterworth *et al.*, 1991; Frye & Moore, 1991; Perner, 1991; Whiten, 1991; Baron-Cohen *et al.*, 1993b; Davies & Stone, 1994; Mitchell & Lewis, 1994).

Second, theory of mind is not just another aspect of development to document. Rather, it seems to be a central mechanism that underlies many other domains of development, such as social development, communication, symbolic development and self-reflection (Baron-Cohen, 1988).

Third, theory of mind seems to be one of the major explanatory theories children (and adults) use in making sense of the world. The other important one, of course, is a theory of physical causality, but it is clear that young children use their theory of mind not only to make sense of the behaviour of people (e.g. 'Mummy is looking under the bed because she *thinks* I'm hiding there; she doesn't *know* I'm in the wardrobe!'), but also of animals (e.g. 'The cat *wants* to chase the mouse, but the mouse *wants* to escape'). They even use it to make sense of the behaviour of inanimate systems, when they have no other way of understanding them (Inagaki & Hatano, 1991). For example, children might reason: 'The clouds have gone dark because they *want* to *pretend* it's night'.

Finally, recent evidence suggests that theory of mind, like other cognitive abilities such as language and memory, is vulnerable to impairment. The major clinical syndromes relevant to impairment in theory of mind are autism, schizophrenia, person-

ality disorder and conduct disorder. Such cases of psychopathology may shed light on what happens to children and adults when the normal facility to employ a theory of mind is lost, in different ways. However, before considering the pathological, let us start by mapping out the normal development of this ability.*

DEVELOPING A THEORY OF MIND: A REVIEW OF THE CHANGES IN CHILDHOOD

One starting point has been to ask if infants understand that actions are caused by mental states. Whilst infants can distinguish animate movement from inanimate movement (Gelman & Spelke, 1981) — they are sensitive to the difference between internal and external causation of movement — it is still unresolved whether they recognize the internal causes of animate movement as mental states (Premack, 1990; Wellman, 1990). By the time toddlers start to talk, however, it is clear that they talk about actions in terms of mental states. From as early as 18–30 months, normal children refer to a range of mental states: desires, beliefs, thoughts, dreams, pretence, etc. (Shatz *et al.*, 1983; Wellman, 1990). This suggests that at the very least they have what Bretherton *et al.* (1981) call an 'implicit' theory of mind. Other evidence for an implicit theory of mind can be seen in the changes Kagan (1982) described in the second year of life: appreciation of other people's expectations and standards. Studies with slightly older children have focused on obtaining evidence for an explicit theory of mind. This is reviewed next.

---

* A note on terminology: in this chapter, the term 'theory of mind' will be used, since it has now acquired considerable short-hand value within developmental psychology. Later in the chapter the question of whether it is appropriate or misleading to think of this ability as a *theory* the child possesses will be discussed. The reader should be aware that a range of other terms are also used in the literature to refer to the same cognitive function. These include: mentalizing (Morton, 1989), folk psychology (Dennett, 1978b), mind-reading (Whiten, 1991) and role-taking (Flavell *et al.*, 1978). For present purposes, these should be taken as coterminous with the phrase 'theory of mind'.

Understanding beliefs

Perhaps the first study of an explicit theory of mind was by Premack and Woodruff (1978), who investigated if a chimpanzee could understand another's mental states. Their tests included, for example, showing the subject a short film, and then freezing the film at a crucial point in the action sequence, and inviting the subject to choose between several outcomes in still photographs. In the discussion that followed their article, several commentators raised the criticism that such tasks need not necessarily require any reasoning about mental states for their solution (Dennett, 1978a). Instead, they proposed that the 'acid test' of when an organism was judging another's mental state arose in situations of false belief, in which the subject is exposed to current reality but another person is only exposed to partial (or wrong) information about reality. Under such conditions it is possible to separate unambiguously the subjects' judgements about their own mental state (their true belief) from ones based on their awareness of another person's different mental state (a false belief). Thus, if the subject knows the money is in the old china vase, but that Burglar Bill thinks it's in the desk drawer, if asked where Burglar Bill will look for the money, the subject should judge that he will look in the wrong place — the desk drawer.

Within developmental psychology* Wimmer and Perner (1983) employed a false belief test, and showed that not until around 4 years of age do children pass such a test. An adaptation of their test (Baron-Cohen *et al.*, 1985) is illustrated in Fig. 13.1. As can be seen, the test involves appreciating that, since Sally was absent when her marble was moved from its original location, she won't know it was moved, and therefore must still believe it is in its original location. On the belief question ('Where will Sally look for her marble?') 85% of 4-year-old children passed. Since in this and in the Wimmer and Perner study all subjects passed a memory control question ('Where was the marble in the beginning?') and a reality control question ('Where

is the marble really?'), as well as a naming question ('Which doll is Sally?'), failure on the belief question by young 3 year olds was unlikely to have been due to such factors as inattention, memory or language overload, or lack of motivation. The large numbers of replications of Wimmer and Perner's (1983) result have essentially confirmed the finding that false beliefs are not well understood until 4 years of age (Perner *et al.*, 1987; Gopnik & Astington, 1988). Nevertheless, in recent years, the finding that 4 years old is a turning point in understanding false beliefs has been challenged by a number of investigators. Thus, whereas Wimmer and Perner (1983) argued that the false belief data indicated the presence of a cognitive deficit in younger children, later studies (Wellman, 1990; Freeman *et al.*, 1991; Siegal & Beattie, 1991; Zaitchik, 1991) suggest that when alternative experimental methods are employed, normal children younger than 4 years of age show evidence of understanding false belief. It still remains controversial as to when there is a genuine cognitive limitation on young children's understanding of other people's beliefs.

Understanding desires and intentions

So much for tests of understanding beliefs. What about understanding the mental state of desire? Desire is often thought to be the other key mental state, next to belief, in our folk psychology (Dennett, 1978b). With beliefs and desires, all kinds of behaviour become interpretable. For example, in watching a movie and trying to understand why the protagonist tiptoes into his empty flat, we might refer to his belief that there is someone in the flat, and his desire to get in unnoticed. Several studies show that for normal children, desire is understood earlier than belief — in fact, desire is clearly understood by normal 2 year olds (Wellman, 1990). Indeed, the 'terrible twos' have been interpreted as evidence of this age group's growing awareness of the frustrating difference between their own and their parent's desires (Wellman, 1990).

A mental state closely related to desire is intention. These are distinguishable, as Astington and Lee (1991) and Phillips (1993) make clear: it is possible to desire something and yet to have no intention of fulfilling that desire. (You might desire to go to the new play at the local theatre, but have

---

* Research into children's developing theory of mind has its roots in cognitive psychology (e.g. Piaget's work) and social psychology (e.g. attribution theory), as well as in philosophy of mind (see Perner & Wilde-Astington, 1991).

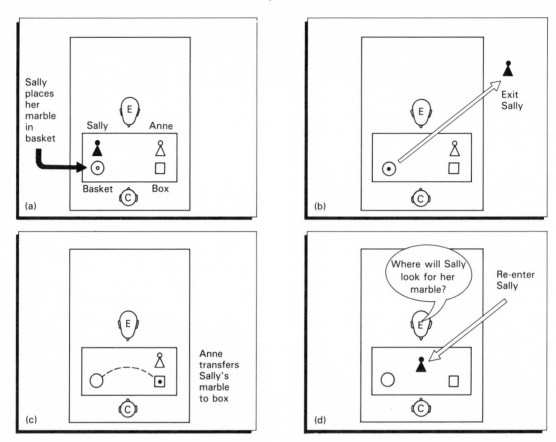

Fig. 13.1 A false belief test adapted from Baron-Cohen *et al.* (1985): (a) Sally places her marble in the basket and then (b) leaves the room. (c) Anne transfers the marble to the box. (d) When Sally comes back into the room the examiner (E) asks the child where Sally will look for the marble. See text for further details. C = child.

no intention of actually going to see it.) However, intention is related to desire in that one way of fulfilling one's desires is to formulate an intention — a plan of action — to fulfil them. Desires are of course sometimes fulfilled fortuitously (e.g. a friend might phone up unexpectedly and announce that they have tickets for you to go to the play), but the principal means for fulfilling desires is via intentional actions. When do young children grasp the concept of intention?

A large part of the literature on children's understanding of morality centres on their appreciation of the distinction between intentional and accidental acts, and children's judgements of responsibility and blame (Piaget, 1929; see also Chapter 14). However, understanding intention can and has been studied separately from moral development.

Some early studies in this area, by King (1971), Berndt and Berndt (1975) and Smith (1978), found a significant change around 4 years of age in the ability to distinguish acts 'done on purpose' from accidental acts. Children younger than this were reported to err on the side of assuming that everything was intentional, and this echoes Piaget's (1929) findings.

More recent studies by Astington and Lee (1991) have extended this work by investigating young children's ability to distinguish outcomes that appear the same, but that differ in the crucial respect of the actor's intention. Thus, in one of her stories, a girl intends to feed her bread to the birds, and then she does so, whilst in another story, a girl accidentally drops some breadcrumbs. The birds end up being fed just the same. In such a test, the child is asked, 'Which girl meant to feed the birds?' These findings are broadly similar to the earlier studies, in finding chance performance before 3 years old.

Understanding pretence

Another important mental state that has been well studied is that of pretence. Children begin to produce pretend play from as early as 10–18 months of age (Bates, 1979). Experiments with verbal children also show that as soon as they can answer questions, they also seem to understand that pretence is distinct from reality (Wellman, 1990). This is clearly a complex achievement. In terms of the acquisition of different mental state concepts, understanding pretence may predate understanding desire (Baron-Cohen, 1991a; Gopnik & Slaughter, 1991), although longitudinal data on this are needed.

Pretence was for a long time studied as part of symbolic development (Piaget, 1962; McCune-Nicholich, 1981). In an important article rethinking the nature of pretence, Leslie (1987) put forward a theory that focused on children's understanding of pretence as a mental state. He argued that the logical properties of pretence (namely, suspension of normal truth conditions) resembled the logical properties of other mental states (such as belief), and on these grounds it might be that children's understanding of pretence reflected an important stage in the origins of a theory of mind.

Part of Leslie's claim also centred on the sort of cognitive architecture that would be needed to support not only comprehension of pretence, but comprehension of all mental states. His suggestion was that a capacity for metarepresentation would be minimally required. He defined this as the ability to represent an agent's mental attitude to a proposition. This capacity, he maintains, ensures that the object's pretend identity is represented separately from its real identity. (For details of the component parts of this system see Leslie, 1987, 1991; Leslie & Roth, 1993; and for counter-arguments, see Perner, 1988, 1991, 1993). The implication is that pretence might mark not only a developmental stage in the acquisition of a theory of mind, but a qualitative change in the sort of representational mechanisms available to cognition.

Understanding perception

What about children's ability to understand perception and visual perspectives? Piaget and Inhelder's (1956) 'three-mountains task' broke new ground in suggesting that children between 4 and 6 years old were unable to select a picture that showed how a view would appear to different people at different locations. Such children, Piaget and Inhelder reported, tended to attribute their own spatial perspective to other people — an error that became the hallmark of Piaget's concept of 'childhood egocentrism'.*

Flavell *et al.* (1978) challenged this view by employing far simpler experimental techniques. They distinguished between two levels of visual perspective-taking. The first they called level 1 — the ability to infer what another person can see. This appears to be present even by 2 years old (Lempers *et al.*, 1977; Flavell *et al.*, 1978, 1981). Thus, 2 year olds can put things out of or bring things into sight, when requested to do so. Level 2 visual perspective taking is the ability to infer how the object appears to another person. This seems to take longer to develop. In fact it is not until 3–4 years of age that children reliably pass level 2 tasks. For example, when shown a picture of a turtle which appears either right-side up or upside-down (depending on which side of the table it is viewed from), young 3 year olds fail to identify correctly which of these two perspectives the experimenter would have (Flavell *et al.*, 1981).

A related achievement in the development of a theory of mind is in children's understanding of the principle that 'seeing-leads-to-knowing'. Pratt and Bryant (1990) for example showed that 3 year olds are easily able to indicate which of two people will know what is in a container, if one of them has looked into the container whilst the other has simply touched it. Such an ability demonstrates that even at this young age, children are aware of the role of informational access in the formation of knowledge.

Before moving on to consider the importance of

---

* Light and Nix (1983) showed however that even the notion that children are biased to select their own view is not correct: rather, children are biased to select a 'good' view.

a theory of mind, it is worth noting that there has been relatively little work looking at later normal development of this ability. Perner and Wimmer (1985) studied slightly older children for the ability to attribute beliefs about beliefs to others (so-called second-order belief attribution), and found this appears for the first time at around 6 years of age. Leekam (1991) reported on related developments in the use and comprehension of figurative speech such as irony and sarcasm. Tests that tap adult levels of functioning in theory of mind are still needed. Equally, reliability and validity studies are needed in this area. Often, the tests used are 'one-shot' assessments, with no test−retest reliability, or attempt to correlate scores on tests with other aspects of the child's behaviour. The possibility of artefacts should nevertheless be considered against the impressive number of successful replications of results by independent research groups in this field.

THE IMPORTANCE OF A THEORY OF MIND: WHAT DO WE USE IT FOR?

Making sense of social behaviour

At this stage, it is worth pausing to reflect on why children are acquiring this extraordinarily rich body of knowledge: what are the benefits to the child in developing a theory of mind? Dennett (1978b) was perhaps one of the first to put forward the case for the necessary role of a theory of mind in understanding the human world. His strong thesis, entitled the intentional stance theory, claimed that attributing mental states to a complex system (such as a human) was by far the easiest way of understanding it. By understanding, he meant coming up with explanations of its behaviour, and predicting what it would do next. He called this ability adopting the intentional stance, though others after him used the term theory of mind, precisely because the child (and later, the adult), seemed to use this ability in theory-like ways: for explanation and prediction. Dennett's choice of the term intentional stance refers to our ability to attribute the full set of intentional states (beliefs, desires, intentions, imaginings, hopes, memories, fears, promises, deceptions, etc.) and not just the specific mental state of intention.

The alternatives, Dennett argued, to adopting the intentional stance, are either to attempt to understand systems in terms of their physical make-up (adopting the physical stance), or their functional design (the design stance). We adopt the physical stance to understand systems whose physical make-up we are aware of, such as the human body. For example, we might reason that the skin bleeds when it is cut because blood vessels have been severed. In this instance, the physical stance takes the form of a 'folk biology'. It is equally clear we possess a 'folk physics' to make sense of other phenomena in the physical world (see Chapter 10). Attempting to understand human behaviour in terms of physical entities is of course not possible, given the state of our knowledge: we would need to know about millions of different brain states that give rise to different behaviours in order to understand human behaviour in physical terms. A theory of mind (or the intentional stance) is an infinitely simpler and more powerful solution than the physical stance.

We adopt the design stance when we are ignorant about the physical make-up of a system (the physical stance is therefore not available to us), but wish to understand the system in terms of the functions of its observable parts. Thus, when making sense of my computer, I need know nothing about silicon chips or other physical details, to predict its behaviour. Instead, I can refer to some of its design features, such as the delete key (whose function is to rub out what I have just typed), the escape key (whose function is to clear the screen) and so on.

The design stance works well when we wish to explain a system with observable and operational parts (such as alarm clocks, televisions, thermostats, etc.), though note that a theory of mind would work just as well. Indeed, many people reason about their computer in very mentalistic ways. They might say 'My computer is displaying this command because it *thinks* I have finished', etc. However, the design stance seems just as useful in these cases, e.g. 'My computer isn't working because it is not plugged in', etc. Adopting the design stance towards understanding people would not however get one very far, since people have very few external operational parts for which one could work out a functional or design description. Furthermore, few if any of these would be at all useful in predicting moment by moment changes in the person's behaviour.

Dennett (1978b) and Fodor (1987) therefore concluded that the solution evolution has come up with to enable us to understand and predict our own and other people's behaviour — or the behaviour of any complex system — is the intentional stance, or what has become better known as a theory of mind. It is a simple to use and powerful theory, which is exactly what we need when we are in the thick of a social situation. For example, imagine an insurance salesman is standing at your front door, waiting for you to sign a piece of paper. You need to reason quickly about his behaviour, and what he is likely to do next. Making inferences about his desires, intentions and motives allows you to do this. In place of this modern example can easily be substituted an equivalent example from our likely evolutionary past. Imagine you are an early hominid. Another early hominid offers to groom you and your mate. You need to reason quickly about whether you should let him approach or not. Again, making inferences about whether his motives are purely altruistic, or whether he might be deceitful, is a reasoning strategy that can be applied in time to react to possible social threat. Whilst the necessary testing remains to be done, our intuition suggests that our theory of mind reasoning is both extremely quick and automatic.

A theory of mind also goes under the name of 'folk psychology', and this may be a better term for it. This gets away from the notion that children acquire this knowledge in similar ways to how scientists develop theories. There is a case for arguing that children are theorists in much of their knowledge acquisition (Carey, 1985; Keil, 1988) and in the acquisition of their theory of mind in particular* (Wellman, 1990; Perner, 1991; Gopnik & Wellman, 1992), but the attractive benefit of talking about this ability in terms of folk psychology is that it reminds us that it is simply our everyday way of understanding people. We all use it all the time, as Dennett (1979, pp. 8–9) pointed out:

> We use folk psychology all the time, to explain and predict each other's behaviour; we attribute beliefs and desires to each other with confidence — and quite unselfconsciously — and spend a substantial portion of our waking lives formulating the world — not excluding

ourselves — in these terms . . . Every time we venture out on the highway, for example, we stake our lives on the reliability of our general expectations about the perceptual beliefs, normal desires and decision proclivities of the other motorists. We find . . . that it is a theory of great generative power and efficiency. For instance, watching a film with a highly original and unstereotyped plot, we see the hero smile at the villain and we all swiftly and effortlessly arrive at the same complex theoretical diagnosis: 'Aha!' we conclude (but perhaps not consciously), 'He wants her to think he doesn't know she intends to defraud her brother!'

Making sense of communication

A second function of a theory of mind is to understand communication. Perhaps the clearest case for this was put by Grice (1975), a philosopher of language. He argued that aside from decoding the referent of each word (its semantics), and the syntax of speech, the key thing that we do when we search for meaning in what someone has said, is to imagine what their communicative intention might be. Thus, when the cop shouts 'Drop it!', the robber is not left in some state of acute doubt over the ambiguity of the term 'it'. Rather, the robber makes a rapid assumption that the cop intended to use the word 'it' to refer to the gun in the robber's hand, and furthermore intended the robber to recognize his intention to use the word in this way. Clearly, in decoding figurative speech (such as irony, sarcasm, metaphor or humour), a theory of mind is also essential, since in such cases the speaker does

---

* The reader should be alerted to a current controversy in this field over whether, in the normal case, we have to develop a theory about the mind in order to use a folk psychology, or whether we instead have privileged access to our own mental states and then, by pretending to be in the other person's situation, run a mental simulation of what we would think and feel in their place. The former theory is known as the 'theory theory', whilst the latter is known as the simulation theory. A good source for further reading about this debate is the special issue of *Mind and Language* on this topic (Vol. 7(1 + 2), 1992). As things stand at present, it can be argued that the data from developmental psychology fit both theories equally well. Critical experiments enabling these two theories to be tested against each other remain to be done.

not intend their utterance to be taken literally (Baron-Cohen, 1988; Happe, 1993).

This analysis of language in terms of complex communicative intentions makes clear that in decoding speech we are doing a lot more than simply working through the semantics of the spoken words. We are going beyond the perceptual input, to hypothesize about the speaker's mental state. Grice did not limit this analysis to speech, but argued that exactly the same process was used in non-verbal communication. Thus, when I gesture towards the doorway with an outstretched arm and with the palm of my hand open, you immediately assume that I mean (i.e. intend you to understand) that you should go through the doorway. This way of thinking about meaning can be seen in the theories developed by the Speech Act School (Austin, 1962; Searle, 1979) and in more recent work, such as relevance theory (Sperber & Wilson, 1986).

The other way in which a theory of mind is held to play an essential part in successful communication is in the speaker monitoring his or her listener's informational needs: that is, in judging what the listener already knows or does not know, and what information must still be supplied in order that the listener can understand the communicative intention. Furthermore, for communication to succeed, the speaker needs to be monitoring if their message has been understood as they intended it to be, or if rephrasing is required to clarify ambiguity. Once again, dialogue understood in this way becomes much more than simply the production of speech: it is revealed as intrinsically linked to the use of a theory of mind.

Other applications of a theory of mind

The importance of a theory of mind to social understanding and communication has been emphasized because these are arguably the most important of its functions. However, there are several other functions of this crucial ability. Let us explore just a few here.

First, there is deception. Deception, of course, is all about making someone believe that something is true when it is actually false. Clearly, this is a sophisticated use of a theory of mind, and some

have argued that the benefits of being able to deceive might have been an important evolutionary pressure in the development of a theory of mind (Byrne & Whiten, 1988). This is known as the Machiavellian intelligence hypothesis. Normal children begin to engage in very convincing deception soon after they understand the notion of false belief (Sodian *et al.*, 1991), around 4 years of age. Older children, and adults, show the ability for more sophisticated deception, such as 'double-bluff' — evidence that their theory of mind continues to develop in later childhood and during the teens (Happe, 1993).

Second, there is empathy. A theory of mind naturally confers on the user an ability to infer what someone else is thinking, and how someone might be interpreting events. Empathy is often thought of in a rather restricted sense, as simply about appreciating another person's emotional state. Whilst this is part of empathy, it cannot be all of it. Appreciating a person's emotional state can to some extent be read off their facial emotional expressions, but understanding why they feel the way they do often requires appreciating what they are thinking. Harris (1989) has shown that children of 3 years of age can understand another person's emotional state as caused by external situations, but by around 5 years old they are adept at understanding a person's emotions in terms of what they thought was likely to happen (e.g. 'Jane is happy because she *thinks* she's won the race'), irrespective of whether their thought coincides with reality.

A third spin-off of a theory of mind is that it allows for self-consciousness or self-reflection. As soon as a child (or indeed any organism or system) can attribute mental states to itself, it can begin to reflect on its own mind. Thus, 4 year olds succeed at distinguishing appearance from reality and recognizing the fallibility of their beliefs ('I thought it was an x, but maybe I was wrong'; Flavell *et al.*, 1986), and about the causes of their own behaviour ('I looked for my ball under the car because I *thought* that's where it was'), as well as the source of their knowledge ('I *know* it's Kate's birthday because my mother told me'). Clearly, this transforms their thoughts from a focus on the here and now to a focus on their own subjectivity. An added advantage of this is that they can rehearse possible solutions to problems in their own mind, before trying them out in real action ('Let's *imagine* I did x; would that work?', etc.).

A fourth application of a theory of mind is in teaching, or attempting to change a person's mind through persuasion, etc. The realization that other people's thoughts and beliefs are shaped by the information to which they are exposed allows for the possibility of informing others, in order to change what they know. Thus, there are good accounts of 4 year olds teaching their younger siblings in different ways, and older children simplifying the information in recognition of the limited knowledge of the younger child (see Chapter 11). The same phenomenon has been documented in the ways in which older children talk to younger ones (Shatz & Gelman, 1973; Sachs & Devin, 1976). In terms of the species, it is clear that human beings use their theory of mind to inform and persuade in all sorts of ways (advertising, politics, education, etc.), but finding even simple, convincing instances of teaching in other species is quite rare (Cheyney & Seyfarth, 1990). This latter point leads us next to consider a theory of mind from the vantage point of comparative psychology.

THE EVOLUTION AND ORIGINS OF A THEORY OF MIND: EVIDENCE FROM PRIMATOLOGY AND INFANCY

Because of the discovery of specific neuropsychological deficits in theory of mind (see below), it seems plausible that a theory of mind has a specific neural basis, with its own brain system. This theory of its biological basis has been one important reason leading primatologists to investigate theory of mind in non-human primates, in order to trace a possible evolutionary development of this ability. We have already mentioned the likely value a theory of mind would confer on an individual's fitness, and the Machiavellian intelligence hypothesis of how such an ability might have evolved (by natural selection) if it arose in the gene pool. Whiten's (1993) review of the evolution of a theory of mind concluded that non-human primates show little if any convincing evidence of understanding mental states like knowledge and belief, though they do understand the 'simpler' mental states of percep-

tion, and possibly desire. There thus seems to be a quantum leap between the highest ability in the apes and monkeys, and that found in 3–4-year-old humans.

The precise ontogenesis of a theory of mind in the first years of life in the human case is still controversial. One theory holds that the earliest manifestation of understanding mental states is in joint-attention behaviour (Baron-Cohen, 1989c, d, 1991c, 1993). Another theory holds that infant's sensitivity to emotional states in others is the key precursor to understanding cognitive mental states such as thoughts, beliefs, knowledge and intentions (Hobson, 1990, 1993). A final theory holds that imitation is the mechanism that allows infants to appreciate the similarity between themselves and others, and thus to extend their subjective awareness of internal states to their existence in others (Gopnik & Meltzoff, 1993). Testing these causal claims is part of the current research agenda.

ABNORMALITIES IN THE COMPREHENSION OF MENTAL STATES

Autism

There is a sizeable body of work documenting deficits in understanding mental states in children with autism (Baron-Cohen et al., 1993b). For example, on tests of false belief comprehension, children with autism make more errors than both normal and mentally handicapped children of a younger mental age (Baron-Cohen et al., 1985, 1986; Leslie & Frith, 1988; Baron-Cohen, 1989a, b; Perner et al., 1989; Reed & Peterson, 1990; Leekam & Perner, 1991). This deficit does not seem to be due to a general difficulty in representing representations, as children with autism can understand non-mental representations (such as photographs and drawings) as representations (Leekam & Perner, 1991; Charman & Baron-Cohen, 1992; Leslie & Thaiss, 1992). The difficulty they have on false belief tests appears to relate to the symptoms these children show in social and communicative development (Baron-Cohen, 1988; Happe, 1993; Siddons et al., in press).

Whilst most children with autism fail tests of

belief understanding, a minority of them do pass. This subgroup ranges from 20 to 35% in different samples. But when these subjects are given a more taxing test of belief understanding (comprising understanding second-order, nested beliefs, or beliefs about beliefs, e.g. of the form 'Anne thinks Sally thinks x') — these being well within the comprehension of normal 6–7-year-old children (Perner & Wimmer, 1985) — even these teenagers with autism fail outright (Baron-Cohen, 1989b; Ozonoff *et al.*, 1991). It appears that, whilst most children with autism do not understand beliefs even at the level of normal 3–4-year-old children, some do; but these show impaired understanding of beliefs at the level of normal 6–7-year-old children. Clearly, something is going wrong in the development of the concept of belief in children with autism. This has been discussed in terms of specific developmental deviance and delay in autism (Baron-Cohen, 1989b, 1991a, 1992a).

This inability to understand others' beliefs reveals itself most dramatically on tests of deception in autism (Sodian & Frith, 1992). As discussed earlier, since deception entails belief manipulation, this is consistent with their difficulties in belief comprehension. Thus, in the penny hiding game (Gratch, 1964), a simple test of deception, children with autism fail to hide the clues that enable the guesser to infer the whereabouts of the penny (Oswald & Ollendick, 1989; Baron-Cohen, 1992b). For example, they omit to close the empty hand, or they hide the penny in full view of the guesser, or they show the guesser where the penny is, before the guesser has guessed. In contrast, subjects with mental handicap and normal 3-year-old children make far fewer errors of this sort.

What of their understanding of other mental states? When children with autism are asked how a story character will feel when given something they either want or do not want, no impairments are found, relative to a mental-age matched control group without autism (Baron-Cohen, 1991b; Tan & Harris, 1991). Understanding desire at this simple level thus seems to be within their ability. However, in studies of pretence in autism (Ungerer & Sigman, 1981; Baron-Cohen, 1987), children with autism seem to produce significantly less spontaneous pretend play than mentally handicapped control groups. On tests of understanding perception,

children with autism have been tested at both levels of visual perspective taking (Hobson, 1984; Leslie & Frith, 1988; Baron-Cohen, 1989d, 1991a; Reed & Peterson, 1990; Tan & Harris, 1991), and appear to show no deficits.

One key set of mental states that has been a major focus of some studies (Hobson, 1993) is emotion. In his early studies, Hobson (1986a, b) found that subjects with autism performed significantly worse than control groups on emotion expression matching tasks. In later studies, these differences were not found when groups were matched on verbal mental age (Hobson *et al.*, 1988a, b, 1989; Braverman *et al.*, 1989; Tantam *et al.*, 1989; Ozonoff *et al.*, 1990; Prior *et al.*, 1990). Furthermore, since emotion recognition deficits are also found in a range of other clinical disorders, such as schizophrenia (Cutting, 1981; Novic *et al.*, 1984), mental handicap (Gray *et al.*, 1983), abused children (Camras *et al.*, 1983), deaf children (Odom *et al.*, 1973) and prosopagnosia (Kurucz *et al.*, 1979; De Kosky *et al.*, 1980), the status of this deficit as an explanation is called into question.

Some studies have focused not on emotion recognition, but emotion prediction. The aim in these studies is to establish how much children with autism understand about the causes of emotion — how a person will feel, given a set of circumstances. As mentioned earlier, Harris *et al.* (1989) showed that normal 3–4-year-old children understand that emotion can be caused by situations (e.g. nice situations make you feel happy, nasty ones make you feel sad) and desires (e.g. fulfilled desires make you feel happy, unfulfilled ones make you feel sad). They also showed that by 4–6 years old, normal children understand that beliefs can affect emotion (e.g. if you think you're getting what you want, you'll feel happy, and if you think you're not, you'll feel sad — irrespective of what you're actually getting).

Baron-Cohen (1991b) found that subjects with autism were easily able to judge a story character's emotion when this was caused by a situation, and were as good as a group with mental handicap at predicting the character's emotion given her desire. However, they were significantly worse at predicting the character's emotion given her belief, than either normal 5-year-old children or subjects with mental handicap. The implication is that 'simple' emotions may be within the understanding of people with autism, whilst 'cognitive' or belief-based emotions (Wellman, 1990) may pose considerable difficulty for them. This has also been found in a more fine-grain analysis of emotion-recognition tasks in these terms (Baron-Cohen *et al.*, 1993a).

The picture emerging from these studies is that not all mental states pose difficulties for children with autism: perception, simple emotion and desire do not, but pretence, knowledge and belief do. Explaining why this specific pattern of intact and impaired comprehension is found is currently the focus of debate (Baron-Cohen *et al.*, 1993). However, the claim that these deficits are specific to autism appears less controversial, and relies on experimental evidence from other clinical groups. Thus, other childhood clinical populations tend to pass false belief tests. These populations include children with Down's syndrome (Baron-Cohen *et al.*, 1985), Williams' syndrome (Karmiloff-Smith, 1993), mental handicap of unknown aetiology (Baron-Cohen, 1989a), language-impairment (Leslie & Frith, 1988), conduct disorder (Siddons *et al.*, in press), deafness (Sellars & Leslie, 1990), and children with callosal agenesis (Temple & Vilarroya, 1990). Further clinical populations remain to be tested, but the deficit does seem to be autism-specific. That most disorders leave the development of a theory of mind relatively intact is some confirmation for the view that a theory of mind is so important that it has been innately built in to the human mind, and is a universal. Avis and Harris (1991) provide some cross-cultural data in support of this view.

Other clinical groups

Whilst autism seems to reflect the most severe disruption to the normal acquisition of a theory of mind — these children often not even arriving at the fundamental stage of appreciating that such mental states as beliefs even exist — there are other disorders in which children do reach this basic level, but show difficulties in the accurate use of a theory of mind. Thus, in schizophrenia some have argued that symptoms of paranoia (Baron-Cohen, 1989e) are an expression of inaccurate attribution of beliefs to others (e.g. consider the paranoid delusion 'The man on the television *knows* what I am thinking', etc.). Frith and Frith (1991) have suggested that there may be a link between autism and schizophrenia in terms of the same mechanism (theory of mind) becoming impaired at very different times in development, with radically different outcomes. In autism, the abnormality would be in infancy or prenatally, whilst in schizophrenia the impairment in theory of mind may only be 'switched on' (genetically?) in adolescence or later. Such a theoretical comparison remains to be empirically tested.

Aggressive behaviour in children with conduct disorder has also been associated with inaccurate attribution of intentions to others ('You *deliberately* bumped into me', etc.; Dodge, 1980). Such distortions in accurate identification of intentions may in part be a product of the child's learning history. For example, Dodge *et al.* (1990) found that distorted perception of others' intentions was more likely in children who had experienced physical abuse, and appeared to mediate between the experience of abuse and the risk of later aggressive behaviour.

A third disorder in which it has been hypothesized that abnormal theory of mind development may occur is narcissistic personality disorder (Fonagy, 1989). In these patients, it is argued — on the basis of clinical rather than experimental studies — that the striking lack of empathy such individuals show may reflect not a lack of awareness that other people have minds, but a psychological defence against confronting the contents of other people's minds.

Finally, patients with semantic–pragmatic disorder (Bishop, 1989) are thought to have particular difficulties in accurately identifying a speaker's communicative intent, and taking into account a listener's informational needs — what they need to know for an utterance to be understood. Whilst these subjects may well overlap considerably with autism (Baron-Cohen, 1988; Lister-Brook & Bowler, 1992) it is possible that the two conditions are also distinguishable. Future work is needed to establish the extent to which they are separable disorders, and to what extent deficits in theory of mind use differ between them.

CONCLUSION

The impressive ability of even very young normal children to use a theory of mind, apparently effortlessly, and the serious consequences of its impairment in autism, suggest the existence of specialized cognitive mechanisms for understanding mental states. The studies from autism have been enriched by and in turn have challenged models of the normal development of a theory of mind (Baron-Cohen, 1990, 1991a, 1993). A theory of mind is a strong candidate for a modular mechanism in the brain (Leslie, 1991; Baron-Cohen, 1992a; Leslie & Roth, 1993). It is assumed to be biological in origin first because autism has a biological basis (Rutter, 1983), and second because it appears to be universal (Avis & Harris, 1991).

In attempting to speculate about likely developments in this field, in the next decade, four fruitful areas seem worth identifying. First, using current neuroimaging techniques, if a theory of mind does indeed depend on a localizable, discrete neural mechanism (or set of neural mechanisms), the use of theory of mind tasks as cognitive activation during brain imaging might bring us closer to an understanding of the links between brain and cognition. Second, if the traditional laboratory methods for studying infants (habituation, perceptual preference, etc.) are applied to the investigation of early theory of mind knowledge in the first year of life, we may need to revise our ideas of how a theory of mind develops, and how we should characterize the 'initial state' of the infant. Third, it will be important for progress in understanding normal processes in the development and employment of a theory of mind to continue to inform our understanding of disorders (such as autism). Finally, and related to this last point, it is both likely and desirable that such cross-fertilization between developmental psychology and psychopathology will not only lead to greater understanding of processes and mechanisms, but also to new advances in the application of such knowledge: in the fields of early diagnosis, and intervention. Such cross-fertilization is already taking place (Baron-Cohen *et al.*, 1992; Baron-Cohen & Howlin, 1993).

In closing, it is worth restating the vital role that theory of mind plays in development. It is likely that this piece of cognitive machinery has captured the centre stage of developmental psychology precisely because of its importance to human development. As mentioned earlier, Leslie (1987; Leslie & Roth, 1993) has argued that underlying a theory of mind is a mechanism for representing mental representations, and traces the importance of this through the lifespan, from its emergence in the pretend games of the toddler, through to the use of the imagination all through life. The bald implication is: no theory of mind, no art. Similarly, no theory of mind, no culture or society, at least not as we understand the term as applied to the human case. Hence Fodor's (1987, p. 133) claim that 'There is, so far as I know, no human group that doesn't explain behaviour by imputing beliefs and desires to the behaviour. (And if an anthropologist claimed to have found such a group, I wouldn't believe him.)'. In autism, one theory holds, we see the cruel consequence of a lack of theory of mind: an inability to join the group.

ACKNOWLEDGEMENT

This chapter was written whilst the author was supported by grants from the Mental Health Foundation, and the Medical Research Council. Parts of this work appeared in a separate chapter by the author (Baron-Cohen, in press).

REFERENCES

Astington J., Harris P. & Olson D. (1988) *Developing Theories of Mind*. Cambridge University Press, New York.

Astington J. & Lee E. (1991) *What do children know about intentional causation*? Paper presented at the Society for Research in Child Development Conference, Seattle, Washington.

Austin J. (1962) *How to do Things with Words*. Basil Blackwell, Oxford.

Avis J. & Harris P. (1991) Belief—desire reasoning among Baka children: Evidence for a universal conception of mind. *Child Development* **62**, 460—467.

Baron-Cohen S. (1987) Autism and symbolic play. *British Journal of Developmental Psychology* **5**, 139—148.

Baron-Cohen S. (1988) Social and pragmatic deficits in autism: Cognitive or affective? *Journal of Autism and Developmental Disorders* **18**, 379—402.

Baron-Cohen S. (1989a) Are autistic children behaviourists? An examination of their mental—physical and appearance—reality distinctions. *Journal of Autism and Developmental Disorders* **19**, 579—600.

Baron-Cohen S. (1989b) The autistic child's theory of mind: A case of specific developmental delay. *Journal of Child Psychology and Psychiatry* **30**, 285−298.

Baron-Cohen S. (1989c) Joint attention deficits in autism: Towards a cognitive analysis. *Development and Psychopathology* **1**, 185−189.

Baron-Cohen S. (1989d) Perceptual role-taking and protodeclarative pointing in autism. *British Journal of Developmental Psychology* **7**, 113−127.

Baron-Cohen S. (1989e) Thinking about thinking: How does it develop? Critical notice. *Journal of Child Psychology and Psychiatry* **30**, 931−933.

Baron-Cohen S. (1990) Autism: A specific cognitive disorder of 'mind-blindness'. *International Review of Psychiatry* **2**, 79−88.

Baron-Cohen S. (1991a) The development of a theory of mind in autism: Deviance and delay? *Psychiatric Clinics of North America* **14**, 33−51.

Baron-Cohen S. (1991b) Do people with autism understand what causes emotion? *Child Development* **62**, 385−395.

Baron-Cohen S. (1991c) Precursors to a theory of mind: Understanding attention in others. In Whiten A. (ed.) *Natural Theories of Mind*, pp. 233−252. Basil Blackwell, Oxford.

Baron-Cohen S. (1992a) On modularity and development in autism: A reply to Burack. *Journal of Child Psychology and Psychiatry* **33**, 623−629.

Baron-Cohen S. (1992b) Out of sight or out of mind? Another look at deception in autism. *Journal of Child Psychology and Psychiatry* **33**, 1141−1155.

Baron-Cohen S. (1993) From attention−goal psychology to belief−desire psychology: The development of a theory of mind, and its dysfunction. In Baron-Cohen, S., Tager-Flusberg H. & Cohen D.J. (eds) *Understanding Other Minds: Perspectives from Autism*, pp. 59−82. Oxford University Press, Oxford.

Baron-Cohen S. (in press) Theory of mind and face-processing: How do they interact in development and psychopathology? In Cicchetti D. & Cohen D. (eds) *Manual of Developmental Psychopathology*. Wiley, Chichester.

Baron-Cohen S., Allen J. & Gillberg C. (1992) Can autism be detected at 18 months? The needle, the haystack, and the CHAT. *British Journal of Psychiatry* **161**, 839−843.

Baron-Cohen S. & Howlin P. (1993) The theory of mind deficit in autism: Some questions for teaching and diagnosis. In Baron-Cohen S., Tager-Flusberg H. & Cohen D.J. (eds) *Understanding Other Minds: Perspectives from Autism*, pp. 466−480. Oxford University Press, Oxford.

Baron-Cohen S., Leslie A.M. & Frith U. (1985) Does the autistic child have a 'theory of mind'? *Cognition* **21**, 37−46.

Baron-Cohen S., Leslie A.M. & Frith U. (1986) Mechanical, behavioural and intentional understanding of picture stories in autistic children. *British Journal of Developmental Psychology* **4**, 113−125.

Baron-Cohen S., Spitz A. & Cross P. (1993a) Can children with autism recognize surprise? *Cognition and Emotion* **7**, 507−516.

Baron-Cohen S., Tager-Flusberg H. & Cohen D.J. (eds) (1993b) *Understanding Other Minds: Perspectives from Autism*. Oxford University Press, Oxford.

Bates E. (ed.) (1979) *The Emergence of Symbols: Cognition and Communication in Infancy*. Academic Press, New York.

Berndt T. & Berndt E. (1975) Children's use of motives and intentionality in person perception and moral judgement. *Child Development* **46**, 904−912.

Bishop D. (1989) Autism, Asperger's syndrome, and semantic−pragmatic disorder: Where are the boundaries? *British Journal of Disorders of Communication* **24**, 107−122.

Braverman M., Fein D., Lucci D. & Waterhouse L. (1989) Affect comprehension in children with pervasive developmental disorders. *Journal of Autism and Developmental Disorders* **19**, 301−316.

Bretherton I., McNew S. & Beeghly-Smith M. (1981) Early person knowledge as expressed in gestural and verbal communication: When do infants acquire a 'theory of mind'? In Lamb M. & Sharrod L. (eds) *Infant Social Cognition*, pp. 333−374. Lawrence Erlbaum, Hillsdale, New Jersey.

Butterworth G., Harris P., Leslie A. & Wellman H. (1991) *Perspectives on the Child's Theory of Mind*. Oxford University Press/British Psychological Society, Oxford.

Byrne R. & Whiten A. (eds) (1988) *Machiavellian Intelligence: Social Expertise and the Evolution of Intellect in Monkeys, Apes, and Humans*. Oxford University Press, Oxford.

Camras L.A., Grow G. & Ribordy S.C. (1983) Recognition of emotional expression by abused children. *Journal of Child Psychology and Psychiatry* **12**, 325−328.

Carey S. (1985) *Conceptual Change in Childhood*. MIT Press/Bradford Books, Boston.

Charman T. & Baron-Cohen S. (1992) Research note: Understanding beliefs and drawings: A further test of the metarepresentation theory of autism. *Journal of Child Psychology and Psychiatry* **33**, 1105−1112.

Cheyney D. & Seyfarth R. (1990) *How Monkeys see the World*. University of Chicago Press, Chicago.

Cicchetti D. & Beeghly M. (1990) *The Self in Transition*. University of Chicago Press, Chicago.

Cosmides L. (1989) The logic of social exchange: Has natural selection shaped how humans reason? Studies with the Wason selection task. *Cognition* **31**, 187−276.

Cutting J. (1981) Judgement of emotional expression in schizophrenics. *British Journal of Psychiatry* **139**, 1−6.

Davies M. & Stone M. (eds) (1994) *The Theory-Theory and the Simulation Theory*. Basil Blackwell, Oxford.

De Kosky S., Heilman K., Bowers M. & Valenstein E. (1980) Recognition and discrimination of emotional faces and pictures. *Brain and Language* **9**, 206−214.

Dennett D. (1978a) Beliefs about beliefs. *Behaviour and Brain Sciences* **4**, 568−570.

Dennett D. (1978b) *Brainstorms: Philosophical Essays on Mind and Psychology*. Harvester, Brighton.

Dennett D. (1979) *Three kinds of intentional psychology*. Paper presented to the International Conference on Knowledge and Representation, Netherlands Institute for Advanced Study, Wassenaar, The Hague.

Dodge K. (1980) Social cognition and children's aggressive behaviour. *Child Development* **51**, 162−170.

Dodge K., Bates J. & Pettit S. (1990) Mechanisms in the cycle of violence. *Science* **250**, 1678−1683.

Flavell J.H., Everett B., Croft K. & Flavell E. (1981) Young children's knowledge about visual perception: Further evidence for the level 1−level 2 distinction. *Developmental Psychology* **17**, 99−103.

Flavell J.H., Green E. & Flavell E.R. (1986) Development of knowledge about the appearance−reality distinction. *Monographs of the Society for Research in Child Development* **51**.

Flavell J., Shipstead S. & Croft K. (1978) Young children's knowledge about visual perception: Hiding objects from others. *Child Development* **49**, 1208−1211.

Fodor J.A. (1987) *Psychosemantics: The Problem of Meaning in the Philosophy of Mind*. MIT Press, Cambridge, Massachusetts.

Fonagy P. (1989) On tolerating mental states: Theory of mind in borderline personality. *Bulletin of the Anna Freud Centre* **12**, 91−115.

Freeman N., Lewis C. & Doherty M. (1991) Preschoolers' grasp of desire for knowledge in false-belief prediction: Practical intelligence and verbal report. *British Journal of Developmental Psychology* **9**, 139−158.

Frith C. & Frith U. (1991) Elective affinities in schizophrenia and childhood autism. In Bebbington P. (ed.) *Social Psychiatry: Theory, Method, and Practice*, pp. 65−88. Rutgers, New Brunswick.

Frye D. & Moore C. (1991) *Children's Theories of Mind*. Lawrence Erlbaum, Hillsdale, New Jersey.

Gelman R. & Spelke E. (1981) The development of thoughts about animate and inanimate objects: Implications for research on social cognition. In Flavell J. & Ross L. (eds) *Social Cognitive Development*, pp. 43−66. Cambridge University Press, Cambridge.

Gopnik A. & Astington J. (1988) Children's understanding of representational change and its relation to the understanding of false belief and the appearance−reality distinction. *Child Development* **59**, 26−37.

Gopnik A. & Meltzoff A. (1993) The role of imitation in understanding persons and developing a theory of mind. In Baron-Cohen S., Tager-Flusberg H. & Cohen D.J. (eds) *Understanding Other Minds: Perspectives from Autism*, pp. 335−366. Oxford University Press, Oxford.

Gopnik A. & Slaughter V. (1991) Young children's understanding of changes in their mental states. *Child Development* **62**, 98−110.

Gopnik A. & Wellman H. (1992) Why the child's theory of mind really is a theory. *Mind and Language* **7**, 145−171.

Gratch G. (1964) Response alternation in children: A developmental study of orientations to uncertainty. *Vita Humana* **7**, 49−60.

Gray J.M., Frazer W.L. & Leudar I. (1983) Recognition of emotion from facial expression in mental handicap. *British Journal of Psychiatry* **142**, 566−571.

Grice H.P. (1975) Logic and conversation. In Cole R. & Morgan J. (eds) *Syntax and Semantics: Speech Acts*, pp. 41−58. Academic Press, New York.

Happe F. (1993) Communicative competence and theory of mind in autism: A test of relevance theory. *Cognition* **48**, 101−119.

Harris P. (1989) *Children and Emotion*. Basil Blackwell, Oxford.

Harris P., Johnson C.N., Hutton D., Andrews G. & Cooke T. (1989) Young children's theory of mind and emotion. *Cognition and Emotion* **3**, 379−400.

Hobson R.P. (1984) Early childhood autism and the question of egocentrism. *Journal of Autism and Developmental Disorders* **14**, 85−104.

Hobson R.P. (1986a) The autistic child's appraisal of expressions of emotion. *Journal of Child Psychology and Psychiatry* **27**, 321−342.

Hobson R.P. (1986b) The autistic child's appraisal of expressions of emotion: A further study. *Journal of Child Psychology and Psychiatry* **27**, 671−680.

Hobson R.P. (1990) On acquiring knowledge about people and the capacity to pretend: Response to Leslie (1987). *Psychological Review* **97**, 114−121.

Hobson R.P. (1993) Understanding persons: The role of affect. In Baron-Cohen S., Tager-Flusberg H. & Cohen D.J. (eds) *Understanding Other Minds: Perspectives from Autism*, pp. 204−227. Oxford University Press, Oxford.

Hobson R.P., Ouston J. & Lee A. (1988a) What's in a face? The case of autism. *British Journal of Psychology* **79**, 441−453.

Hobson R.P., Ouston J. & Lee A. (1988b) Emotion recognition in autism: Coordinating faces and voices. *Psychological Medicine* **18**, 911−923.

Hobson R.P., Ouston J. & Lee T. (1989) Naming emotion in faces and voices: Abilities and disabilities in autism and mental retardation. *British Journal of Developmental Psychology* **7**, 237−250.

Humphrey N. (1984) The social function of the intellect. In Humphrey N. (ed.) *Consciousness Regained*, pp. 14−28. Oxford University Press, Oxford.

Inagaki K. & Hatano G. (1991) Constrained person analogy in young children's biological inference. *Cognitive Development* **6**, 219−231.

Jolly A. (1966) Lemur social behaviour and primate intelligence. *Science* **153**, 501−506.

Kagan J. (1982) The emergence of self. *Journal of Child Psychology and Psychiatry* **23**, 363−381.

Kanner L. (1943) Autistic disturbance of affective contact. *Nervous Child* **2**, 217−250.

Karmiloff-Smith A. (1992) *Beyond Modularity*. MIT Press/Bradford Books, Boston.

Keil F. (1988) *Concepts, Kinds, and Cognitive Development*. MIT Press/Bradford Books, Boston.

King M. (1971) The development of some intention concepts in children. *Child Development* **42**, 1145−1152.

Kurucz J., Feldmar G. & Werner W. (1979) Prosopo-affective agnosia associated with chronic organic brain syndrome. *Journal of the American Geriatrics Society* **27**, 91−95.

Leekam S. (1991) Jokes and lies: Children's understanding of intentional falsehood. In Whiten A. (ed.) *Natural Theories of Mind*, pp. 159−174. Basil Blackwell, Oxford.

Leekam S. & Perner J. (1991) Does the autistic child have a metarepresentational deficit? *Cognition* **40**, 203−218.

Lempers J., Flavell E. & Flavell J. (1977) The development in very young children of tacit knowledge concerning visual perception. *Genetic Psychology Monographs* **95**, 3−53.

Leslie A.M. (1987) Pretence and representation: The origins of 'Theory of Mind'. *Psychological Review* **94**, 412−426.

Leslie A.M. (1991) The theory of mind impairment in autism: Evidence for a modular mechanism of development? In Whiten A. (ed.) *Natural Theories of Mind*, pp. 63−78. Basil Blackwell, Oxford.

Leslie A.M. & Frith U. (1988) Autistic children's understanding of seeing, knowing, and believing. *British Journal of Developmental Psychology* **6**, 315−324.

Leslie A.M. & Roth D. (1993) What autism teaches us about metarepresentation. In Baron-Cohen S., Tager-Flusberg H. & Cohen D.J. (eds) *Understanding Other Minds: Perspectives from Autism*, pp. 83−111. Oxford University Press, Oxford.

Leslie A.M. & Thaiss L. (1992) Domain specificity in conceptual development: Evidence from autism. *Cognition* **43**, 225−251.

Light P. & Nix C. (1983) Own view versus good view: A perspective taking task. *Child Development* **54**, 480−483.

Lister-Brook S. & Bowler D. (1992) Autism by another name? Semantic and pragmatic impairments in children. *Journal of Autism and Developmental Disorders* **22**, 61−82.

McCune-Nicholich L. (1981) Towards symbolic functioning: Structure of early use of pretend games and potential parallels with language. *Child Development* **52**, 785−797.

Mitchell P. & Lewis C. (1994) *Origins of an Understanding of Mind*. Cambridge University Press, Cambridge.

Morton J. (1989) The origins of autism. *New Scientist* **1694**, 44−47.

Novic J., Luchins D.J. & Perline R. (1984) Facial affect recognition in schizophrenia: Is there a differential deficit? *British Journal of Psychiatry* **144**, 533−537.

Odom P.B., Blanton R.L. & Laukhuf C. (1973) Facial expressions and interpretations of emotion-arousing situations in deaf and hearing children. *Journal of Abnormal Child Psychology* **1**, 139−151.

Oswald D.P. & Ollendick T. (1989) Role taking and social competence in autism and mental retardation. *Journal of Autism and Developmental Disorders* **19**, 119−128.

Ozonoff S., Pennington B. & Rogers S. (1990) Are there emotion perception deficits in young autistic children? *Journal of Child Psychology and Psychiatry* **31**, 343−363.

Ozonoff S., Pennington B. & Rogers S. (1991) Executive function deficits in high-functioning autistic children: Relationship to theory of mind. *Journal of Child Psychology and Psychiatry* **32**, 1081−1106.

Perner J. (1988) Developing semantics for theories of mind: From propositional attitudes to mental representations. In Astington J., Harris P. & Olson D. (eds) *Developing Theories of Mind*, pp. 141−172. Cambridge University Press, Cambridge.

Perner J. (1991) *Understanding the Representational Mind*. MIT Press/Bradford Books, Boston.

Perner J. (1993) The theory of mind deficit in autism: Rethinking the metarepresentation theory. In Baron-Cohen S., Tager-Flusberg H. & Cohen D.J. (eds) *Understanding Other Minds: Perspectives from Autism*, pp. 112−137. Oxford University Press, Oxford.

Perner J., Frith U., Leslie A.M. & Leekam S. (1989) Exploration of the autistic child's theory of mind: Knowledge, belief, and communication. *Child Development* **60**, 689−700.

Perner J., Leekam S. & Wimmer H. (1987) Three year olds' difficulty with false belief: The case for a conceptual deficit. *British Journal of Developmental Psychology* **5**, 125−137.

Perner J., Astington J., Beilin H. & Pufall P. (eds) (1992) The child's understanding of mental representation. In *Piaget's theory: Prospects and Possibilities*, pp. 141−160. Hillsdale, New Jersey.

Perner J. & Wimmer H. (1985) 'John *thinks* that Mary *thinks* that . . .' Attribution of second-order beliefs by 5−10 year old children. *Journal of Experimental Child Psychology* **39**, 437−471.

Phillips W. (1993) *Understanding desires and intentions by children with autism*. Unpublished PhD thesis, Institute of Psychiatry, University of London.

Piaget J. (1929) *The Child's Conception of the World*. Harcourt Brace, New York.

Piaget J. & Inhelder B. (1956) *The Child's Conception of Space*. Routledge & Kegan Paul, London.

Piaget J. (1962) *Dreams, Play and Imitation in Childhood*. Routledge & Kegan Paul, London.

Pratt C. & Bryant P. (1990) Young children understand that looking leads to knowing (so long as they are looking into a single barrel). *Child Development* **61**,

973–982.

Premack D. (1990) The infant's theory of self-propelled objects. *Cognition* **36**, 1–16.

Premack D. & Woodruff G. (1978) Does the chimpanzee have a 'theory of mind'? *Behaviour and Brain Sciences* **4**, 515–526.

Prior M., Dahlstrom B. & Squires T. (1990) Autistic children's knowledge of thinking and feeling states in other people. *Journal of Child Psychology and Psychiatry* **31**, 587–602.

Reed T. & Petersen C. (1990) A comparative study of autistic subjects' performance at two levels of visual and cognitive perspective taking. *Journal of Autism and Developmental Disorders* **20**, 555–568.

Rutter M. (1983) Cognitive deficits in the pathogenesis of autism. *Journal of Child Psychology and Psychiatry* **24**, 513–531.

Sachs J. & Devin J. (1976) Young children's use of age-appropriate speech styles in social interaction and role-playing. *Journal of Child Language* **3**, 81–89.

Searle J. (1965) What is a speech act? In Black M. (ed.) *Philosophy in America*, pp. 221–239. Allen & Unwin, London.

Searle J. (1979) What is an intentional state? *Mind* **88**, 74–92.

Sellars L. & Leslie A. (1990) *The deaf child's theory of mind.* Unpublished ms, Cognitive Development Unit, London.

Shantz C. (1983) Social cognition. In Mussen P. (ed.) *Handbook of Child Psychology*, Vol. 3, *Cognitive Development*, pp. 495–555. Wiley, New York.

Shatz M. & Gelman R. (1973) The development of communicative skills: Modifications in speech of young children as a function of the listener. *Monographs of the Society for Research in Child Development* **38**.

Shatz M., Wellman H. & Silber S. (1983) The acquisition of mental verbs: A systematic investigation of the first reference to mental states. *Cognition* **14**, 301–321.

Sherrod L. & Lamb M. (1981) Infant social cognition: an introduction. In Lamb M. & Sherrod L. (eds) *Infant Social Cognition: Empirical and Theoretical Considerations*, pp. 1–10. Lawrence Erlbaum, Hillsdale, New Jersey.

Siddons F., Happe F., Whyte R. & Frith U. (1994) Theory of mind in everyday life: An interview-based study with autistic, retarded, and disturbed children. Unpublished ms, MRC, Cognitive Development Unit, London.

Siegal M. & Beattie K. (1991) Where to look first for

children's knowledge of false beliefs. *Cognition* **38**, 1–12.

Smith M. (1978) Cognizing the behavioral stream: the recognition of intentional action. *Child Development* **49**, 736–748.

Sodian B. & Frith U. (1992) Deception and sabotage in autistic, retarded, and normal children. *Journal of Child Psychology and Psychiatry* **33**, 591–605.

Sodian B., Taylor C., Harris P. & Perner J. (1991) Early deception and the child's theory of mind: False trails and genuine markers. *Child Development* **62**, 468–483.

Sperber D. & Wilson D. (1986) *Relevance: Communication and Cognition.* Basil Blackwell, Oxford.

Tan J. & Harris P. (1991) Autistic children understand seeing and wanting. *Development and Psychopathology* **3**, 163–174.

Tantam D., Monaghan L., Nicholson H. & Stirling J. (1989) Autistic children's ability to interpret faces: A research note. *Journal of Child Psychology and Psychiatry* **30**, 623–630.

Temple C. & Vilarroya O. (1990) Perceptual and cognitive perspective-taking in two siblings with callosal agenesis. *British Journal of Developmental Psychology* **8**, 3–8.

Ungerer J. & Sigman M. (1981) Symbolic play and language comprehension in autistic children. *Journal of Abnormal Child Psychology* **9**, 149–165.

Wason P. (1983) Realism and rationality in the selection task. In Evans J. StB.T. (ed.) *Thinking and Reasoning: Psychological Approaches*, pp. 44–78. Routledge & Kegan Paul, London.

Wellman H. (1990) *The Child's Theory of Mind.* MIT Press/Bradford Books, Boston.

Whiten A. (ed.) (1991) *Natural Theories of Mind.* Basil Blackwell, Oxford.

Whiten A. (1993) Evolving a theory of mind: The nature of non-verbal mentalism in other primates. In Baron-Cohen S., Tager-Flusberg H. & Cohen D.J. (eds) *Understanding Other Minds: Perspectives from Autism*, pp. 367–396. Oxford University Press, Oxford.

Wimmer H. & Perner J. (1983) Beliefs about beliefs: Representation and constraining function of wrong beliefs in young children's understanding of deception. *Cognition* **13**, 103–128.

Zaitchik D. (1991) Is only seeing really believing? Sources of the true belief in the false belief task. *Cognitive Development* **6**, 91–103.

14: Character Development

DALE F. HAY, JENNIFER CASTLE AND JESSICA JEWETT

INTRODUCTION

. . . Character is a slow and gradual growth through action in relation to the circumstances of life; it cannot be fashioned suddenly and through reflection only . . . It was a pregnant saying, that the history of a man is his character; to which one might add that whosoever would transform a character must undo a life history. (Henry Maudsley, 1897, p. 292)

Amongst those children presenting the greatest challenges to parents, teachers and clinicians are those who are dishonest or cruel, who violate social norms or appear to be amoral. These attributes may join with overt aggression to create entrenched conduct problems or promote delinquent behaviour (see Chapter 19), but, even at less worrisome levels, they pose considerable problems for children's social relationships. To understand why some children are dishonest or cruel, it is important to examine how most children develop a cooperative, empathic approach to the social world and acquire the values of their societies. The old-fashioned name for this developmental process is 'character development'. We have adopted it for several reasons.

Use of the term 'character development' underscores the fact that there are meaningful individual differences in social sensitivities and values, even within the normal range of acceptable social behaviour. The fact that well-intentioned, moral individuals of 'good character' adhere to different moral principles contributes to the confusing nature of many of the great moral debates of our time, such as capital punishment, pacifism and the right to choose abortion, as well as many everyday life decisions (choice of state-supported or private education for one's children, use of private medicine, choice of disciplinary practices, and the like).

Furthermore, the term 'character development' connotes a general approach to social life that spans many different topics, including prosocial behaviour and altruism, self-regulation and social control, acquisition of social conventions and moral values, honesty and integrity, and so forth. And, finally, character is neither a purely behavioural nor a purely cognitive term. To quote an earlier writer on the topic:

> Morality concerns itself with conformity to existing standards of a given time or place. Character does not necessarily imply such conformity . . . This does not mean, of course, that character is not related to morality. It means that character is a more dynamic and more inclusive concept. In character development much more attention is given to volitional factors and to individual creativeness in the realm of goals to be achieved . . . If we add to morality the ability to reconstruct one's values and the volitional powers sufficient to direct conduct progressively toward such evolving values, then we have character as we shall think of it in this chapter. (Jones, 1946)

Throughout the chapter character is defined as an individual's general responsiveness to the dilemmas and responsibilities of social life, based on any number of sensitivities, skills, conventions and values. As we shall see, character is actively constructed, modified, and reflected upon throughout the lifespan. We now review normative trends in character development before examining factors responsible for individual differences in character.

DIMENSIONS OF CHARACTER DEVELOPMENT THROUGHOUT THE LIFESPAN

Before trying to explain differences in character

amongst individuals, it is important to examine how valued social behaviours develop for children in general. Character formation entails a synthesis of affect, behaviour and cognition; behavioural choices are informed by a person's feelings and beliefs, but past choices also serve to consolidate character. Here we highlight some of the dimensions of character that undergo development during the lifespan. These include (i) sensitivity to the emotions and needs of others; (ii) provision of care to the young and others in need; (iii) cooperative versus competitive orientations towards the use of common resources; (iv) helping others to meet their goals, through active helping or more passive compliance and obedience; (v) social problem-solving skill that permits the successful resolution of conflict with others; (vi) the development of standards for truth-telling and trustworthiness; and (vii) awareness of and adherence to social conventions and moral norms. Furthermore, character development is inextricably bound up with (viii) the development of a sense of self; it involves self-regulation, self-evaluation and self-reflection. In this section we note the general developmental course of each dimension, particularly with respect to the earliest manifestations in infancy and early childhood.

Social sensitivity: empathic and sympathetic responses to other people

Children take their places in their societies when they become aware of other people as beings with perceptions, feelings and beliefs different from as well as similar to their own. It takes some time before children are accurate in their inferences about other people's desires and beliefs (see Chapter 13); however, it seems likely that the process rests on a much earlier interest in and responsiveness to the behaviours of others, particularly their expressions of emotion.

People may respond to their distressed companions in a variety of ways: with wonder, disinterest, repugnance or pity, to name but a few possibilities. The extent to which individuals try to alleviate the distress of others long has been of concern to philosophers of ethics (Hume, 1957; Kant, 1959). The labels applied to persons' responses to their companions' distress seem to depend on the nature and intensity of the distress. The motivational basis of such actions has been ascribed to sympathy or empathy (Hume, 1957; Aronfreed, 1968; Hoffman, 1975); to a sense of duty or social responsibility (e.g. Kant, 1959; Berkowitz, 1972); or to the establishment of reciprocity (Gouldner, 1960), as well as to pure self-interest. In recent years, much attention has been given to empathy as a phenomenon in its own right and as an explanation of overtly helpful or cooperative actions.

Empathy has been defined in two basic ways: (i) the cognitive ability to identify the emotions of others on the basis of facial expressions and situational cues (Burns & Cavey, 1957; Borke, 1971) and (ii) the affective tendency to respond to another person's emotional behaviour with a parallel emotional reaction (Feshbach & Roe, 1968; Hoffman & Levine, 1976). Whether a response is described as empathic or rather as a precursor to genuine empathy will therefore depend on which definition we choose to adopt. It is not clear whether the emotional reaction accompanies the cognitive inference, nor whether vicarious emotional reactions actually limit individuals' abilities to alleviate other persons' distress (Miller & Eisenberg, 1988).

Whichever definition is used, it is clear that even very young infants notice the emotions of others. For example, infants are reported to cry when other infants are crying (Darwin, 1877; Simner, 1971); the longer one infant fusses or cries, the more likely another is to cry as well (Hay *et al.*, 1981). Facial expressions are salient cues by which we identify the expression of felt emotions; even newborns imitate the emotional expressions of others (Field *et al.*, 1982). Darwin (1872) first carried out cross-cultural studies of infants' recognition and use of facial expressions and found a general similarity across nations, suggesting to him that there was an innate and universal basis for emotional expression in the form of a direct, unlearned link between particular emotional states and particular facial expressions. However, infants' discrimination of distinct expressions does not necessarily imply that they perceive the link to particular felt emotions; although imitating correctly, they may simply be responding to the variant stimulus properties of different expressions. More convincing evidence of their understanding of the emotional meaning of different facial expressions is provided by Haviland and Lelwica (1987), who found that, from 10 weeks, babies react differently and appropriately to different emotions their mothers express in face-to-face play. In contrast to Darwin's proposition of an innate process, however, infants' abilities to express and perceive emotion are affected by their experiences. Abused children and their mothers pose less recognizable emotional expressions, and the abused children are less accurate than other children in recognizing facial expressions of emotion (Camras *et al.*, 1988). By the end of the first year infants start 'checking' with adult caregivers in uncertain circumstances, using emotional cues in order to assist their own assessments of ambiguous situations. This behaviour is called 'social referencing' (see Chapter 17). Parents' encouraging smiles or anxious frowns influence children's approach or avoidance in such situations (Camras, 1980; Klinnert *et al.*, 1983; Boccia & Campos, 1989). Here the parents' expressions of emotion are not taking the form of direct communication with their children, but rather an emotional stance towards some object or event in the immediate environment. The children's use of these expressions to regulate their own behaviour implies that they are moving beyond a purely perceptual discrimination or imitative response to the expressions of others.

Theories of empathy focus on individuals' responses to the overt or inferred distress of other persons, as indexed by facial expressions but by other channels as well. Toddlers' reactions to distress move beyond the earlier tendency to cry in tandem with other infants (Simner, 1971; Hay *et al.*, 1981). Over the second year of life, children faced with the distress of a companion are less likely to show signs of distress themselves and more likely to try to intervene to alleviate the problem (Murphy, 1937; Freud & Burlingham, 1944). For example, a 15-month-old boy brought his own teddy bear to a crying friend; when that did not help, he brought the friend's security blanket from the next room (Hoffman, 1975). The emergence of prosocial initiatives such as these seems to imply that the child is beginning to identify the conditions that will terminate an emotional state in another person, i.e. is beginning to appreciate how emotions fit into a causal sequence.

In the second year of life, as children begin to try to help their distressed companions, so they are acquiring an emotional language in which they can articulate the distress of others (Stern, 1924; Church, 1966) as well as their own inner experience. Thus, increased verbal fluency and the growth of representational thought promote prosocial development in the second and third years of life. At this point the child not only looks at situational cues and salient causal events to explain distress, but may also infer possible psychological reasons for the emotional state. Furthermore, the growing capacity for representation means that the children are better able to take on the perspectives of other persons, setting aside what they know to be the case in a given situation and imagining the situation from another person's point of view. Here the more cognitive form of empathy — as opposed to vicarious emotional reaction to the distress of others — begins to become evident in children's behaviour.

Age-related changes in empathic behaviour are thus closely associated with underlying changes in children's cognitive abilities. When children are still very young, their inferences concerning others' emotional experiences in subtle role-taking situations are much less robust than those of older children. However, simple psychological inferences may still be quite adequate in many situations; the experimental tasks that tap children's understanding of the minds of others in confusing situations (e.g. where a story character has a false belief) address the issue of competence, rather than performance in ordinary situations where the children's perspectives often match those of their companions. Furthermore, when another person's emotions are clearly expressed, children's own vicarious responding will be shown more frequently (Pearl, 1985), suggesting that the two forms of empathy — cognitive inferences and vicarious emotional reactions — are somewhat intertwined.

It is by no means clear whether either form of empathy promotes prosocial responding. Although delinquent adolescents, who by and large do not respond to others in helpful, empathic manners, have been shown to be deficient in role-taking abilities (Chandler, 1973), and young children who have been trained to take on the perspectives of others are more likely to comfort their distressed siblings (Stewart & Marvin, 1984), role-taking ability does not lead inexorably to sympathetic responding. An interview and observational study of 3−4-year-old children showed that preschoolers know perfectly well when a classmate is in distress and how to help, but do not often show such behaviour in the classroom; in the course of the interviews, the children noted that adult caregivers are the persons responsible for alleviating their classmates' distress (Caplan & Hay, 1989).

These children's deference to adult authority figures resembles the 'diffusion of responsibility' phenomenon noted by social psychologists who have observed adult bystanders' tendencies to respond to the distress of others (Latane & Darley, 1970). North American research on bystander intervention was stimulated by a well-known case in which a number of apartment dwellers watched a young woman, Kitty Genovese, being murdered without intervening, even at the level of phoning the police (for a review see Staub, 1978). Subsequent experimental studies in which individuals were observed in simulated emergencies (as when, whilst they were filling out questionnaires, smoke began billowing into the experimental testing room or when a confederate simulated a heart attack on a crowded underground train) showed that the tendency to respond to such emergencies depended not only on situational cues and characteristics of the victim, but also on whether there had been an implicit permission to abandon the given task. For example, school-aged children helped a distressed peer in an adjoining room only if they had already been given permission to go out of the room for another reason — to sharpen their pencils, if need be (Staub, 1979). In general, it seems that adults and children alike make decisions to respond to the distress of others or not on the basis of a host of factors; there is little evidence that there is a general linear increase in comforting others with age.

Nurturance and care for others

The experimental literature on bystander intervention typically focuses on the tendency for adults and children to respond to the distress of strangers. The picture is somewhat different when we consider comfort and sympathy in the context of close personal relationships, particularly those between infants and older persons. Young humans are altricial mammals who require a lot of care. There appear to be species-characteristic perceptual biases and actions that make it likely they will receive such care.

Species-characteristic responses to the young

In his early theoretical writings, Bowlby (1958) described the way in which the infant's emotional expressions serve as signals to caregivers (see Chapter 16). He noted both the preselected species-specific nature of these early communicative gestures and the species-characteristic responses they provoke from adults. Furthermore, he proposed that such signals as crying and smiling (what he referred to as 'component instinctual responses') serve not only to alert the adult to the infant's immediate needs, but also to promote proximity to protective figures. In this view, both adult and infant are predisposed to act in a manner that will ultimately enhance the survival of the species. Bowlby's initial statements on this were couched in the language of group selection, the evolutionary perspective dominant at the time; in his final writings, he attempted to reinterpret his ideas with respect to more current cost−benefit arguments at the individual level of analysis (Bowlby, 1982). This has implications for the interpretation of adults' responses to the young, because such responsiveness would no longer be limited to the biological parent and would no longer be mediated by concern for the group as a whole (Nash, 1988). Rather, it seems highly likely that infants are biased towards social relationships in general — not just the special ones with their parents — and adults in general are biased to respond positively to babies (Nash & Hay, 1993). Whilst some writers have stressed an aversive stimulation model to account for caregivers' responses to infants' cries (see, for example, Moss & Robson, 1968), the evidence supports a view that positive attention and caring responses are evoked almost automatically by infants' naturally occurring behaviour.

Mothers often attest to a wide range of facial expressions in their very young babies and to some extent these claims have received research support. For example, Izard *et al.*, in their detailed observations of neonates, reliably identified a number of expressions, including disgust, distress and a rudimentary smile, that serve to attract the attention of caregivers and foster closeness to them (Izard *et al.*, 1980). These sensitive interactions help lay the foundation for close emotional ties between infant and caregivers (see Chapter 16). Furthermore, infants' appearance (their round shape, large eyes, and so on) are thought by some authors to evoke interest and affection (Lorenz, 1943; but see Power *et al.*, 1982).

Care-giving activities

Giving care to the young involves a number of different activities, such as feeding, grooming, settling to sleep, and so on. These actions are salient to young children themselves, who show in their play with dolls and toy animals that they know a great deal about how to care for babies (Rheingold & Emery, 1986). However, successful care-giving involves more than behavioural routines: parents and others must make inferences as to when it is appropriate to offer care, based on situational cues and perceptions of the nature and degree of the child's needs. Thus care-giving is a cognitive as well as a psychological process. It is necessary to respond promptly to infants' signals, but, as children grow older, parents' desire to train their children to be more independent and to understand that all their requests will not be answered favourably means that care-giving reactions are more variable; furthermore, the needs of an older child must be pitted against the needs of a younger sibling, and so a degree of conflict comes into care-giving interactions when infants become toddlers. Sociobiological theorists have discussed this in terms of the limited investment parents can make in any one of their offspring (Trivers, 1971). At this point in development, in many circumstances, the older children themselves are expected to take on caregiving roles (Whiting, 1983).

In many families in Britain today, it is fairly common for older children to play some part in caring for their younger siblings. Indeed, secondary school teachers report occasions where teenage children, usually daughters of working parents unable to afford alternative care arrangements, are kept away from school in order to look after their younger siblings when ill. However, at least in

modern Western societies, the central role of siblings as caregivers has declined in parallel with the decrease in family size that has occurred this century.

By extending the concept of nurturance to encompass a range of prosocial caring actions, the origins of such behaviour have been traced to early in the second year of life. One study of older and younger siblings (Dunn *et al.*, 1981) found that one-quarter of 2−4-year-olds frequently comforted a distressed younger sibling; one-third occasionally did so; and a further third rarely did so. Dunn and her colleagues reported that by the age of 14−16 months, some of the younger siblings attempted to comfort their parents and older brothers and sisters when they believed they were upset.

Most accounts of sibling care-giving in later childhood derive from ethnographic studies. For economic and social reasons, the older siblings in many non-Western societies are assigned a major role in caring for their younger brothers and sisters. Edwards (1986) has discussed the opportunities such nurturing experiences extend to older siblings, both in terms of learning the concepts of negotiation and responsibility and in influencing the actions of others. She claimed that children learn social conventions and moral rules regarding reciprocity through the process of caring for other children.

As mentioned earlier, sibling care-giving tends to be the province of girls rather than boys, at least in later childhood. Pelletier-Stiefel *et al.* (1986), reviewing a number of studies of sibling care giving, reported that even between the ages of 3 and 6 years girls are delegated more nurturing tasks than boys are, and such care-giving activities may result in girls becoming more generally nurturant, even beyond the particular care-giving roles assigned to them.

Sharing, cooperation and standards of fairness

Sharing

Human societies need to regulate the use of common resources, according to particular rules. The nature of the rules depend on the society — for example, not every society adopts the rule of primogeniture to regulate the transmission of property from one generation to the next — land divisions in France versus England reflects this fact. The children of different cultures differ in the extent to which they advocate and strive for cooperative use of common resources.

Experimental and observational studies of Western children have also noted that the rules whereby children share resources change with age. A basic impulse to share what one sees and finds in the world with other persons emerges around 8 months of life, when infants first begin offering bits of food and other items to their parents and siblings (Rheingold *et al.*, 1976). This early form of sharing is extremely common in the second year of life. In a series of eight experimental studies, 100% of the 18 month olds tested showed or gave toys and other items to their parents (Rheingold *et al.*, 1976). The behaviour is so common that its absence is noteworthy; it has been observed that young autistic children do not show or offer objects to their companions (Sigman & Mundy, 1993). Furthermore, 18–36-month-old children who do not share at all in the course of a 45-min interaction with familiar peers are independently rated by their mothers as more likely to show problematic behaviour in other situations (Hay *et al.*, in press).

The tendency to share with others does not seem to be a simple operant or imitative response. Maternal reinforcement exaggerates the playfulness of the behaviour, but does not increase its frequency (Rheingold, 1973). At 12 months of age, the frequency of the behaviour is enhanced by requests, and by an adult's beginning a game of give-and-take, but not by modelling alone (Hay & Murray, 1982). On the other hand, the development of early sharing parallels the development of vocabulary; it emerges just before the development of the first words and declines in frequency at about the time children become fluent conversationalists. Cross-sectional analyses have indicated that spontaneous sharing occurs at relatively similar rates across the second year of life, but appears to decline thereafter; sharing in response to requests declines over the second year (Hay *et al.*, 1991). Longitudinal analyses corroborate the trend for a decline over the second and third years, but indicate that it is only in the third year that sharing with peers becomes a stable characteristic of individuals (Hay *et al.*, in press).

As children grow older, they become aware of the fact that it is not always practical to share with others, and a general prosocial impulse seems to be supplanted by more pragmatic reasoning. For example, 24-month-old children are less likely than 12 month olds to share in response to a peer's requests, but are more likely than the younger children to share when resolving a dispute (Caplan *et al.*, 1991; Hay *et al.*, 1991). The second and third years of life reveal increased concern with issues of fairness and justice, and toddlers developing language begin to justify their actions to parents and siblings (Dunn, 1988). Preschool children note that they would rather share a toy than a sweet with another child, and they would rather share with a friend than with an acquaintance (Liu & Hay, 1986). These claims can be evaluated with respect to an experimental study in which children had the opportunity to share food they liked and food they disliked with friends and acquaintances; in all cases the focal child had many more pieces of food to eat than did the peer (Birch & Billman, 1986). The distinction between friend and acquaintance seemed more important than that between liked and disliked food, particularly for girls. There was no overall tendency to share disliked food more than preferred food, whereas there was an overall greater likelihood of sharing food with a friend than with an acquaintance. However, boys shared reliably more often with their friends than with their acquaintances only with respect to preferred food; though they shared non-preferred food with their acquaintances as often as with their friends, the authors noted that 'we came to refer to most of these incidents as being "dumping" rather than "sharing"' (p. 394). Thus, with increasing age, sharing seems to become less of a universally friendly impulse and more of a rational decision that reflects informed self-interest.

Birch and Billman (1986) noted that there was very little spontaneous sharing of food in their study; most of the food that was shared was offered to a recipient who had asked for it. This underscores the point that elicited and spontaneous sharing are not necessarily measures of a common construct. Amongst toddlers, spontaneous sharing remains more or less stable over the second year of life, while sharing in response to a peer's request or demand declines (Hay *et al.*, 1991). Amongst preschoolers, spontaneous sharing and sharing in response to requests are not reliably correlated (Eisenberg-Berg & Lennon, 1980).

Most studies of primary school-aged children report a more or less linear increase in sharing over the primary school years (Underwood *et al.*, 1977; Froming *et al.*, 1983). Many such studies focus on elicited sharing that involves a certain level of self-sacrifice, rather than the mutual spontaneous use of common resources in the course of ordinary interaction. Thus the focus has often been on children's tendencies to make charitable donations of prizes they have recently won, sometimes to familiar class-mates (Handlon & Gross, 1959) but rather more often to amorphous groups of needy individuals, such as 'poor children'. Usually, the poor children are not themselves present, and the child is expected to place coins or tokens in a charity box. Occasionally, a degree of verisimilitude is present, as in one study of American children, conducted during Halloween week (a time when American children are exhorted to collect money for UNICEF and other charities), when, in a follow-up assessment, the children were given the opportunity to donate money for 'Trick or treat for the poor' (Wilson *et al.*, 1990). Support for the notion of a linear increase in sharing over the primary school years is primarily provided by cross-sectional studies; however, a longitudinal analysis of a sub-sample in one study confirmed the trend (Froming *et al.*, 1983).

It seems likely that charitable donations, in adults and children alike, are influenced by different sets of factors from those that regulate the mutual use of resources with familiar companions. Social desirability is obviously one such factor. Some investigators contend that the increase in generosity observed over the primary school years is best interpreted as an increase in responsiveness to the demand characteristics of the experimental situation. For example, in a cross-sectional study of children between the ages of 6 and 10 years, where sharing decisions were made in a full-scale voting booth, the older children only donated more often than the younger ones when the experimenter was watching and exhorting them to share (Zarbatany *et al.*, 1985). At the same time, one should not take evidence of social desirability affecting children's decisions simply as a methodological problem; it

may reflect exactly what is developing over the period of childhood. In many cases, children seem to have acquired a strong, general tendency to donate to charity when given the opportunity to do so. In some studies, after pilot testing, experimenters are obliged to introduce extreme sanctions for and constraints on sharing in response to opportunity and need, in order to eliminate ceiling effects (Peterson, 1980; Mills & Grusec, 1989).

Cooperation

Throughout the early childhood years, children become better able to coordinate their activities, as well as sharing resources; indeed, sharing resources may be seen as one particular form of cooperation. Deutsch (1949) set forth a theoretical distinction between competition and cooperation, using the spatial language characteristic of Lewinian social psychology; he noted that interdependence amongst individuals was a hallmark of competition as much as cooperation, but distinguished between *promotively interdependent and contriently interdependent goals*:

> In a *co-operative social situation* the goals for the individual or sub-units in the situation under consideration have the following characteristic: the goal regions for each of the individuals or subunits in the situation are defined so that a goal region can be entered (to some degree) by any given individual or sub-unit only if all the individuals or sub-units under consideration can also enter their respective goal-regions (to some degree) . . . In a *competitive social situation* the goals for the individuals or sub-units in the situation under consideration have the following characteristic: the goal-regions for each of the individuals or sub-units in the situation are defined so that if a goal region is to be entered by any individual or sub-unit (or by any given portion of the individuals or sub-units under consideration) the other individuals or sub-units will, to some degree, be unable to reach their respective goals in the social situation under consideration. (p. 132)

Thus Deutsch defined cooperation and competition in terms of social situations, rather than individual characteristics. He also noted that 'there are prob-

ably very few, if any real-life situations which ...
are "purely" cooperative or competitive'. What the
individual must do, therefore, is strike a balance
between promotively interdependent and contriently interdependent goals.

An example of such a dilemma is provided by a
study of 9- and 13-year-old children who were
placed in a situation where they were rewarded
for competing, but had the opportunity to share;
because they were tested with friends, it can be
assumed that the 'promotively interdependent' goal
of maintaining the friendship was being pitted
against the situational goal of winning a prize
(Berndt *et al.*, 1986). The children were expected to
colour geometric designs, and were told that they
would need a special artist's template to do so
neatly. Only one such template was available, and
thus some degree of sharing was required if both
children were to have a chance at getting a prize. At
the same time, there was a penalty for each child's
slowing down his or her own rate of completion of
the task. In response to this dilemma, most children
shared, but the 9 year olds shared a bit less than the
13 year olds did.

The conventional games played by children similarly call for a combination of pursuit of one's own
goals with attention to the goals of others. Six year
olds tested in three game situations (a basketball
game, a handheld computer space game, and a
game involving tossing a beanbag) were observed
to adopt one of five primary orientations to the
situation: (i) competition, which involved pursuit
of one's own goals at the expense of another's;
(ii) accommodation, which entailed neglect of one's
own concerns in favour of another's; (iii) avoidance of the dilemma and the game simultaneously;
(iv) collaboration, which entailed trying to work
with the peer to find a solution that was jointly
satisfying; and (v) compromise, in which some
expedient, though only partially satisfying, solution
was attempted (Putallaz & Sheppard, 1990). The
children attempted either to collaborate or to seek a
partially satisfying compromise at very high rates
(64% of the orientations scored fell into these two
categories).

The capacity for cooperation may well derive
from the individual's earliest attempts to coordinate
his or her actions with another's, namely, the contingent interactions that occur between parents and

their very young infants. Some investigators have
queried whether mother and infant are really influencing each other's behaviour (Messer & Vietze,
1988); it is possible that the illusion of reciprocity is
created by periodic cycles in mother's and infant's
behaviour. However, careful time series analyses of
video records of mothers and infants in face-to-face
interaction provide evidence for clear mutual influence, beyond any cyclicity that is observed (Cohn
& Tronick, 1988). As infants grow older, their coordinated interactions with adults move beyond
simple exchanges of glances and vocal imitation;
they use gestures in conventional ways, gradually
taking on a more active role in the interactions
(Gustafson *et al.*, 1979).

Cooperative games with adults other than the
parents can be seen towards the end of the first
year of life (Ross & Goldman, 1977), and increase
in frequency during the next year (Hay, 1979).
Coordinated interactions with peers emerge and
grow in frequency during the second and third
years of life (Eckerman *et al.*, 1975, 1989; Howes,
1988). The attainment of conversational competence over the second and third years of life is
itself a measure of young children's growing abilities
to cooperate (Dorval & Eckerman, 1984). Cooperation continues to be an important dimension of
peer relations in the preschool years. In natural
groups of preschoolers, reciprocity of action can be
identified, beyond what would be predicted from
individual differences amongst the actors (see Ross
et al.'s, 1988, analysis of Bott's, 1934, observational
data).

All of the studies in this line of research make the
implicit assumption that harmonious relations with
one's companions are, in Deutsch's (1949) words, a
'promotively interdependent goal'. What happens
when such a goal is set through external means, as
in the demands of an experimental situation? Are
very young children able to work together to meet
such goals? Toddlers between the ages of 12 and 30
months of age, tested in pairs with a child of the
same age, were confronted with a problem to solve
together (Brownell & Corriger, 1990). The goal was
to gain access to a set of toy animals encased in
plastic; to retrieve them, one toddler had to hold
down a lever whilst the other child had to go
around to the other side of the apparatus to retrieve
the animals. Neither child could solve the problem

alone, and general gregariousness would work against solution — joining the partner on the same side of the apparatus meant that the animals could not be retrieved. Children of 12−15 months could not solve the problem, and 18−21 month olds only seemed to solve it by accident; they could not repeat their technique on a second occasion. However, children over the age of 24 months were indeed able to work together effectively on the problem. Their ability to do so was reliably associated with their ability to understand agency in pretend play; thus the ability to cooperate seems related to overall levels of cognitive development.

Helping others with their tasks and complying with their requests

As we have seen, even quite young children can coordinate their actions and work together to pursue mutual goals. In toddlerhood, they are also asked on innumerable occasions to adapt their behaviour with respect to other person's goals, i.e. to comply with the requests of others. Compliance with an adult's requests is an item on normative tests of development such as the Bayley scales; it is also a standard way of assessing a child's receptive vocabulary and hearing. At the same time, very young children may spontaneously offer to help other people perform various tasks. An everyday example of this is children's participation in household work, including tidying up their own play-things; the latter is often used as an experimental test of compliance in laboratory assessments (Howes & Olenick, 1986; Schneider-Rosen & Wenz-Gross, 1990).

Anecdotal reports suggest that, as early as the second year of life, children spontaneously try to help their parents with the housework (Church, 1966). These observations were corroborated by a systematic study of 18-, 24- and 30-month-old children in a laboratory furnished to look like a house, with a number of tasks undone — laundry to be folded, groceries to be stacked on shelves, and so on (Rheingold, 1982). The parents were instructed to start completing these tasks, at a slow pace, and to talk about what they were doing, but not explicitly to ask for the children's help. All the children spontaneously helped their parents at least once, and most helped a good deal, entering into the tasks swiftly and cheerfully. The older children were more likely than the younger ones to announce their intentions and when they thought the task had been completed. Almost all the children also helped an unfamiliar person clear a table and put groceries away.

A similar cross-sectional study of children at the same ages examined children's tendencies to clean up a playroom on their mothers' or fathers' request (Schneider-Rosen & Wenz-Gross, 1990). No age differences on this task were observed, and neither parent was complied with more often than the other. Age differences were observed on other tasks administered within the same protocol; for example, 30 month olds were reliably more likely than younger children to respond to a request to play independently, and 24 month olds were reliably less likely than either younger or older children to stop playing independently and look at a book with the parent instead. These data suggest that compliance with adults' requests may be task-specific, and, indeed, even spontaneous helping is more likely to occur on some tasks than others (Rheingold, 1982).

With age, children also become able to articulate why they do or do not comply with other persons' requests in different situations. Preschoolers were observed over a period of 10−18 weeks, during which their responses to requests made by adult caregivers and classmates were charted (Eisenberg et al., 1985). If the child complied with the request, the experimenter who was present in the classroom inquired why he or she had done so. Compliance occurred at high rates: in general, children refused to comply with 11% of the adults' requests and 25% of those made by other children. Their reasons for complying, however, differed for adult and peer requests; the children were more likely to invoke issues about authority and possible punishment when justifying their compliance with adults' requests, whereas they were more likely to talk about others' needs and friendship relations when complying with peers. In general, it seems that young children do on the whole respond positively to others' requests, and that what may develop over time is an ability to reason why not to respond favourably in a given instance. Milgram's (1974) classic experiments on obedience indicate that the tendency to comply with quite unreasonable requests is still strong in adulthood.

Social problem-solving and conflict resolution

Around the time that human infants begin to share spontaneously with other people, they also begin to express anger and protest about the actions of other people (Stenberg & Campos, 1983); in other words, they begin to engage in conflict with their companions. Conflict may be defined as the incompatibility in the behaviours and desires of two or more persons; operationally, conflict is in progress when one person objects to something that has been done by another (Hay & Ross, 1982). It seems that the capacity for conflict emerges between 6 and 12 months of age; 6 month-old infants do not object to such things as being rolled upon or having a toy seized by a peer, but 12 month olds do (Hay *et al.*, 1983; Caplan *et al.*, 1991). One year olds and two year olds engage in conflict at about the same rate, but 2 year olds, unsurprisingly, are more likely to use words to further their objectives and are more likely to attempt to resolve their disputes with peers in prosocial ways (Caplan *et al.*, 1991).

An analysis of children's attempts to resolve conflict reveals prosocial development in action. Younger toddlers are more likely simply to crawl or walk away from disputes; older children are more likely than younger ones to share with the peer (Caplan *et al.*, 1991). By the end of the preschool years, children have clear notions about the rights and wrongs in conflict with peers. They are more likely to blame the initial aggressor than an individual who was aggressing in retaliation or self-defence (Berndt, 1977; Ferguson & Rule, 1988), although a substantial minority of children say that a child who refuses to share a toy is at fault if a conflict then ensues (Hay *et al.*, 1992; Sheather, 1992). By the beginning of the primary school years, at a point at which these general norms regulating peer conflict are in place, a child's failure to resolve social dilemmas constructively is linked to rejection by peers and overall poorer prognosis for social and psychological adjustment (see Chapter 18).

Conflict of course occurs in the family circle as well as on playgrounds and in classrooms. Children enter into and must learn how to resolve conflicts with their parents and siblings, as well as with their peers (Dunn & Munn, 1986). For example, Vuchinich *et al.* (1988), sampling from 52 families

from five different American states, charted routine verbal conflicts that occurred whilst the families were eating their evening meal (American parents regularly eat dinner with their children, who in this study ranged from 3 to 22 years of age). Of particular interest was the extent to which family members entered into ongoing disputes; daughters were generally more likely to attempt to resolve other family members' conflicts than were fathers, mothers or sons. The only exception to this was conflict that began between the parents; sons were slightly more likely to intervene in those conflicts than were daughters. The effectiveness of these attempts to resolve other persons' conflicts was not great; conflicts were about equally likely to end in a stand-off or a compromise, regardless of whether another family member had intervened.

These findings, which pertain to normal levels of family conflict, underscore the point that children are routinely exposed to outbursts of anger and argument (Cummings *et al.*, 1981); severe levels of conflict between parents have adverse effects on children, especially boys (Emery, 1988; Grych & Fincham, 1990). In contrast, investigators of children's conflicts with peers have been at pains to point out the potentially constructive function of conflict and its distinction from aggression (Hay, 1984; Shantz, 1987); it seems likely that children's social problem-solving abilities are similarly honed in the less intense forms of family conflict, and that differences between girls and boys in their approaches to conflict with peers (Hay *et al.*, 1992) may arise partly as a function of these socializing experiences in family arguments.

Honesty and dishonesty

Very young children seem almost incapable of not telling the truth, although that may depend on the circumstances in which they are asked to lie (see Chapter 13; Dunn, 1988). Contemporary work on childhood deception and judgements about lying stems from Piaget's theory of cognitive development. In Piagetian theory, very young children are seen as being unable to separate their internal wishes from external reality. Thus, although they may often utter 'untruths' they seem unable to lie in the adult sense of the word. Furthermore, they assess actions without regard to intention, judging deliberate deceptions equivalent to unintended misstatements. According to Piaget, 'since he takes rules literally and thinks of good only in terms of obedience, the child will first evaluate acts not in accordance with the motive that has prompted them but in terms of their exact conformity with established rules' (Piaget, 1972, p. 107). In this scheme, it is not until the ages of 10 or 11 that the child classifies only intended misstatements as lies.

However, more recent studies suggest modifications to the Piagetian view. One such study by Lickona (1976) showed that USA first-grade school children (6 year olds), unlike the children studied by Piaget, judged a plausible intentional deception worse than an implausible but not malicious exaggeration. Lickona contended that the children's judgements of intentionality were affected by the interaction between the structural nature of their thinking and the situation in question. Another investigation by Wimmer *et al.* (1985) drew attention to young children's understanding of 'to lie', noting that their subjective moral thinking about lying is in advance of their definition of 'to lie'.

The ability to deceive another person intentionally seems to emerge in tandem with other abilities to understand other persons' thoughts and beliefs, probably between the third and fourth birthdays (see Chapter 13). The notion is that children cannot intentionally manipulate the beliefs of others until they themselves can understand a person can have false beliefs. Certainly, by the age of 5, children have been shown to employ deceptive acts in order to create false beliefs (Gordon & Flavell, 1977). In a study of younger children's ability to deceive in a puppet game, 70% of 2.5 year olds, 85% of 3 year olds and 85% of 4 year olds employed at least one deceptive strategy (Chandler *et al.*, 1989). Other reports suggest that intentional deception can occur as early as 2 years of age (Mazzoni, 1992), and that very young girls (who are in general more cognitively precocious) show more verbal deception than do boys (Lewis *et al.*, 1989). These cognitive requirements of lying have been emphasized by theory of mind researchers, who have pointed to the emergence of a capacity for deception in the great apes. This distinction between the great apes and lower primates is also found with respect to other theory of mind tasks and assessments of self-consciousness.

The most systematic analysis of deception and dishonesty in childhood remains the classic 'character education inquiry' by Hartshorne and May (1930), who administered a number of tests designed to measure deception to nearly 11 000 schoolchildren, primarily between 10 and 13 years of age. Various puzzles given to the children afforded the opportunity to fake a successful solution — for example, the 'puzzle peg' consisted of a circular board with holes and a set of pegs in all but the centre hole; the problem required the child to 'jump' pegs over each other until all but one are off the board, and the remaining peg is in the centre hole. The child could cheat on the task completely by simply removing all the pegs and sticking a single peg in the centre of the board; a more sophisticated deception would be to remove some of the pegs to make the problem easier. Other tests administered to the children included verbal or arithmetic problems from Thorndike's intelligence batteries, active races and games, and naturalistic opportunities to steal money. In general, the tendency to cheat or steal increased with age; however, Hartshorne and May believed this was due to an increase with age in the ability to cheat on these particular tasks, not an increase in the overall motivation to do so. Cheating varied somewhat in the different school populations studied, but the highest levels observed rarely exceeded the 50% level, at certain ages, in certain schools. Systematic gender differences were not observed. In general, what Hartshorne and May concluded was that 'honesty or dishonesty is not a unified character trait in children of the ages studied, but a series of specific responses to specific situations' (p. 243). We shall return to this point regarding the coherence of character across contexts and domains.

At this point we must note that, in the course of character formation, in most societies, children must become familiar with the set of rules that regulate deviations from strict honesty. The complex contingencies for lying and truth-telling in different circumstances must be quite confusing for young children. Censure for those who fail to tell the truth is noted at all levels, from the children's playground taunt of 'Liar, liar, your tongue's on fire', through charges of contempt of court where a witness fails to tell the truth whilst under oath, to instances, as in the Profumo case, where a government minister resigned because he had been shown to have lied to

Parliament. Yet Burton (1976, p. 173), playfully updating the Old Testament commandment, commented as follows: 'It is wrong to lie in most circumstances; but sometimes it is neither right nor wrong, and under some conditions it would be immoral not to lie'. If an outright lie can exceptionally be classed as moral, how are less clear-cut untruths to be regarded — for example, children's wish fulfilments, exaggerations and 'sharpened' accounts of events deliberately designed to amuse an audience of friends? Moreover, inasmuch as the accomplished liar is vilified, is the person who habitually tells the truth, irrespective of convention and people's feelings or sensibilities, inversely held in high regard? In many circumstances, honest children must learn to inhibit their honesty in the interest of tact and consideration. The ways in which they do so deserve further investigation.

Moral choices

Hartshorne and May's emphasis on the domain specificity of dishonest actions stands in contrast to more general theories of moral development, which emphasize the coherence of an approach to moral dilemmas at a given age or stage. In many ways, these differing approaches resemble the two general approaches to cognitive development outlined by Ceci *et al.* (Chapter 10). Here we examine the theories that have interpreted children's and adults' moral choices with respect to discontinuities from one developmental stage to the next.

Moral choices represent a dimension of character development to account for which formal developmental theories have been proposed. Much contemporary work on the development of moral reasoning stems from or is a reaction against Piaget's (1972) and Kohlberg's (1964) influential writings on the subject. Piaget's stated concern was with the moral judgement of the child, rather than with behaviour or feelings about morality. Believing that morality consists of a system or rules, he developed his theory through conversations with schoolchildren, in the course of which he and his workers probed the children's attitudes, both to the rules of social games and to adults' moral rules.

According to Piaget, the young child progresses through four major stages in early game play. The first of these, which he termed 'the motor rule', describes a phase where the child plays individually, showing no concern for prescribed rules, imposing instead his or her own schemata on the objects of play. In the second stage, 'egocentrism', emerging generally between the ages of 2 and 5, the child displays behaviour intermediate between individual and socialized play: in Piaget's (1972, p. 27) words, the child 'plays in an individualistic manner with material that is social. Such is egocentrism'. Rules are used in a minimal sense only, in that children at this stage playing together employ totally different 'rules', each enjoying individual games and trying to win in purely personal terms.

The third stage, that of 'incipient cooperation', is marked by the child's attempts — not fully realized — to follow the official rules of the game. It is only at the fourth stage, around the ages of 11 or 12, that children consistently apply general rules and take interest in the formal operation of game play. Thus, Piaget traced a continuum of development along which the child travels: from play for its own sake to playing to win; from minimal to maximal rule application; and from heteronomy to autonomy, where finally 'the rule of the game appears to the child no longer as an external law, sacred in so far as it has been laid down by adults, but as the outcome of a free decision and worthy of respect in the measure that it has enlisted mutual consent' (p. 57). Subsequent research focusing on the relationship between moral judgement and communicative egocentrism has suggested that the underlying factor common to both measures may be the child's increasing ability to decentre (Rubin & Schneider, 1973).

Piaget believed that the conformity of young children was based on consequences of action and derives from respect for the rules of older children and adults. As the child develops, moving towards the cognitive stage of formal operations, and he or she is supervised less by adults and the family circle, a change occurs in the nature of this respect and, consequently, in the conception of rules. Through the processes of reasoning and progressive cooperation, the child begins to base judgments on perceived intentions, moving the norms of reciprocity and consistency, where 'cooperation' replaces 'constraint', and 'autonomy' overrides 'conformity'. This shift is further reflected in the child's emerging sense of fairness and retribution. Piaget described the young child's belief in so-called immanent justice, that is, the conviction 'that the physical universe functions like a policeman' (p. 256). Recounting to children a story in which a boy falls into a river after having stolen apples from an orchard, Piaget found that 86% of 6 year olds thought the child would not have fallen, had he not earlier stolen the fruit, whilst by the ages of 11–12 years only 34% of children used such reasoning. Furthermore, 57% of mentally backward 13–14 year olds affirmed similar acceptance of automatic punishment, providing support for a view of declining belief in immanent justice with increasing cognitive competence. However, close enquiry with even quite young children indicates that the children come up with causal mechanisms that mediate the punishment; on further questioning, they might say, for example, that the reason the boy fell into the river was because the apples in his pocket were weighing him down (Karniol, 1980). Thus their responses may betray a faith in the principle that crimes will be found out and punished, but not a complete ignorance of physical causality.

Whilst questioning certain substantive aspects of Piaget's thinking, Kohlberg acknowledged and built on many aspects of his theory. Kohlberg emphasized the influences of rational cognition on the development of morality, and extended the range of study into adolescence. Through a series of interviews about hypothetical moral dilemmas with children and teenagers, Kohlberg identified six stages, within three general levels of moral development.

The first level in Kohlberg's theory was termed 'preconventional morality', and comprised two stages. In the first stage, the young child sees morality as an external entity and is concerned only with the personal consequences of moral actions. At stage 2, although the child is still seen to operate at a preconventional level, there is recognition that different people might hold different views. The child's perspective is broadened to take on the notion of concrete exchange, albeit chiefly from a viewpoint of self-interest.

The second overall level in Kohlberg's account is termed 'conventional morality'. Stage 3 is usually reached by adolescence. It is characterized by the desire to attain and maintain harmony in relationships, to be 'good', and to seek the approval of others. In stage 4, the concept of morality opens out to societal concerns, rather than the confines of family and close associates. The young person is oriented towards obeying laws and performing duties, and the notion of just reward becomes salient.

The third level is called 'postconventional morality'. Individuals at the fifth stage of reasoning believe that laws are, generally speaking, social contracts that should be recognized in the interests of democracy. However, it is acknowledged that there may occasionally be conflict between moral justice and the law, and that in such cases there must be democratic means to change the law. In his last writings, Kohlberg tended to regard stage 6 solely as a 'theoretical' stage, one that demonstrates commitment to broad ethical ideals and individual rights over and above the demands of law and contract. It is clear that the existence of stage 6 reasoning is not easy to demonstrate empirically (Colby *et al.*, 1983).

Kohlberg's cognitive–rational approach emphasized the way in which an individual's moral development is brought about by moral reasoning, rather than through maturational processes or social influence *per se*. He proposed an hierarchical scheme in which moral thought proceeds through a series of invariant stages of increasing complexity. As each stage is seen to provide a more integrated and clearly differentiated framework than the one it succeeds, it is implicit in Kohlberg's theory that an individual operating at a given stage of reasoning would be capable of understanding the preceding, qualitatively different, stages, but would regard them as inferior modes of reasoning. In this view, much development in the capacity for moral reasoning occurs over the transition to adolescence; it is interesting that at least some of Hartshorne and May's (1930) findings found dishonesty to be similarly increasing over the same period of development.

More recent research has focused on early periods in development. There is evidence that, contrary to Piaget's description of heteronomy in rule evaluation, even preschool children can differentiate moral issues from issues about social conventions (Smetana, 1981, 1985), although investigations of this distinction need to be culturally based. The same behaviours classified within one culture as mere conventions may be regarded in other cultures as intrinsically wrong (Nisan, 1987).

Self-control and self-monitoring

Much of what we might consider integral to character development is not action but the control and inhibition of action and reaction. In his discussion of adult constraint and moral realism, Piaget described how external social controls are internalized by the child into self-control systems. From believing that 'right is to obey the will of the adult' (p. 193), the child graduates to generalizing the adult rule in an original way and, ultimately, to the stage where, through a process of reciprocity, the child genuinely wishes to behave towards others as he or she would wish others to behave towards him or her. In this way young children come to inhibit socially undesirable impulses and to adopt the prevailing standards of their family and milieu.

Similar conceptualizations are found in the psychoanalytic tradition, which views this process in terms of the child's developing ego and, subsequently, superego. The first generation of social learning theorists operationalized these concepts, emphasizing the child's behavioural identification with parental standards (Sears *et al.*, 1965), but subsequent formulations have stressed the situation-specific nature of self-control and the effects that punishment and modelling exert on its development. Bandura (1977), in particular, has argued for the need to understand the processes involved in regulating self-imposed gratification as well as resistance to temptation. Other theorists have commented on the role of inner speech in mediating self-control (Luria, 1961; Vygotsky, 1962), and of the child's introjection of the values of significant others in order to gain approval (Ausubel & Sullivan, 1970).

Empirical research makes clear that very early in life children learn to control their impulses and to regulate their emotions and behaviours. Self-control is often assessed by procedures that ask that child to refrain from touching an attractive toy or from eating or playing with food or toys given as rewards; in other procedures, they may simply be asked to sit still or to play on their own. To the extent that these elements in the situation are drawn to the children's attention through instruc-

tions, these tasks resemble those used to measure helping and compliance. Generally, compliance tasks ask children to do something in particular and delay of gratification or other forms of self-control tasks ask children to refrain from doing something they would normally do. Occasionally the requirements for the child in such tasks represent ordinary dilemmas for parents and children, such as refraining from touching items on shelves in a supermarket (Holden, 1983), or from touching decorative items on a display shelf in another person's home (Kuczynski & Kochanska, 1990).

The ability to regulate one's behaviour seems to increase considerably over the toddler years. For example, Vaughan *et al.* (1984) found a linear increase with age between 18 and 30 months in children's ability to delay gratification on a number of different tasks, including one where they were asked not to touch an attractive telephone and one where they were asked to refrain from eating raisins or opening a brightly wrapped package. Even the 18 month olds, however, were able to refrain from touching the forbidden items for some period of time. In this sample, delay of gratification was not reliably related to compliance with specific requests, when the effect of age was taken into consideration. It appeared that individual differences in self-control and compliant behaviour only began to consolidate after 30 months of age. During the second and third years of life children's emerging competence in understanding the mental states of others seems to be a major factor in their control of aggression and inhibition of undesirable impulses. Dunn (1988) described how this ability to 'mind read' is first apparent in emotion-laden contexts, where, for example, children are intensely involved or where their self-interest is under threat.

Investigators of older children in delay of gratification paradigms have examined the strategies children use to get through their waiting times (Meichenbaum & Goodman, 1971), as well as the ways in which caregivers make waiting and self-control easier for children. Early socializing experiences appear to equip some children with better self-control strategies. Evidence of this was found in a naturalistic study of mothers pushing their trolleys around a supermarket with their toddlers in the little seats (Holden, 1983); an audio recorder, cleverly concealed in a cereal packet in a nearby trolley pushed by the investigator, recorded mothers' efforts to control their toddlers' behaviour. Some mothers responded to trouble when it arose but others avoided conflict by distracting the child, most commonly by talking about the shopping trip (which was a stable strategy used by particular mothers on successive occasions) or, less frequently, distracting it with food or other objects. The more mothers acted in advance to avoid trouble, the less likely it was that there would be 'power-relation bouts' between mother and child. Mothers also tried to steer their trolleys down the centre of the supermarket aisles rather than drawing close to the shelves, bypassed particularly attractive aisles, and whipped around the supermarket as rapidly as possible. We shall return to these socialization techniques later.

Children's developing awareness of adult standards for behaviour has been explored by Kagan (1981). He noted that parents' initial attempts to socialize their 1 and 2 year olds are directed towards eliminating undesired behaviour through punishment and reward, mainly because they feel children at that stage are not mature enough to learn prosocial values through other techniques. Kagan commented on a number of phenomena emerging during the second year of life that serve to prepare the ground for children's acquisition of standards. For example, towards the end of the second year, children start to show concern with occurrences that appear to contravene normative adult standards, such as broken toys or missing buttons, and their speech first begins to reveal an awareness of standards. Even playful violations of standards may be somewhat upsetting. For example, when 18 month olds watch adult models demonstrate unconventional uses of familiar objects (such as putting a hat on someone's foot as if it were a shoe), some children appear to object to this violation of usual procedure, though many find the violation amusing; how positively the unconventional model is received predicts the children's own likelihood of imitation (Hay *et al.*, 1985). In Kagan's view, 1 year olds' sensitivity to adult standards, together with the developing cognitive ability to evaluate actions as good or bad through prior experience of parental approval or displeasure, operates as a major force in promoting the adoption of parental standards. Thus, in his view, children are motivated by a desire both to gain affection and to avoid punishment, and parental socialization practices provide them with a secure framework that reduces uncertainty in their worlds.

As children progress through the preschool years, they begin more fully to recognize that the behaviour of older children, adults, and, in particular, parents, is characterized by certain 'grown-up' standards. Kagan described how children strive to adopt these values because they believe they are appropriate and, consequently, the motivation for so doing shifts gradually away from the extrinsic goals of avoidance of punishment and desire for social reward. Although the capacity for self-regulation seems to increase dramatically over the period of early childhood, self-control issues remain important ones for both children and parents in the years to come. In particular, preadolescents' and adolescents' experimentation with precocious sexuality and the use of alcohol and prescribed substances may well be studied under the rubric of delay of gratification, with the delay in this case measured in years rather than minutes. It would seem that both biological maturity, in the case of early puberty, and social context, such as sibling models or enrolment in coeducational versus same-sex schools, make it more or less difficult for adolescents to delay such gratifications (Caspi *et al.*, 1993). Those adolescents who come to these experiences particularly early, however, often have had a history of other forms of behavioural problems (see Chapter 19).

Summary

In general, the capacity for prosocial behaviour of various sorts seems to emerge around the first birthday and to consolidate over the course of the next 2 years. Reflection on one's actions and understanding of social norms governing prosocial behaviour develop over the preschool years, although sophisticated forms of moral reasoning are not typically shown until adolescence. The extent to which there are linear increases in the occurrence of such actions over the childhood years seems to depend on the situation in which children are tested and the way in which the behaviour in question is being measured. There is some evidence that, over the first years of life, these behaviours change from being a general impulse of the young of the species to a stable trait of individuals. For example, a short-term cohort longitudinal study of sharing found that the frequency of offering items to a peer was not stable over a 6-month period for children who were 18 and 24 months old at the first assessment, but was so for children who were 30 months old when first studied (Hay *et al.*, in press). Vaughan *et al.* (1984) similarly proposed that the second birthday was a point at which there was cognitive reorganization that fostered the development of self-control, at which point consistency across tasks became apparent. These observations are both congruent with a general claim that individuality consolidates in the second and third years of life (Bronson, 1985). At this point, it becomes important to examine coherence of individual differences across the various dimensions of character we have been discussing.

THE COHERENCE OF CHARACTER: CONTINUITIES AND DISCORDANCE ACROSS DIMENSIONS

To what extent is character a valid construct, showing both convergent and discriminant validity? In other words, to what extent do the various dimensions we have been considering correlate with each other, and fail to correlate with theoretically distinct constructs? Hartshorne and May (1930) argued forcefully for the situational specificity of various measures of character, and indeed there is evidence that aspects of character such as sociability do not necessarily correlate with measures of overt prosocial action (Stanhope *et al.*, 1987; Stevenson, 1992). At the same time, during the flowering of prosocial behaviour in very early childhood, the tendency to share objects does appear to be correlated with the tendency to engage in cooperative games (Hay, 1979). By and large, those investigators interested in the coherence of character across domains have focused on three issues: associations between moral judgement and prosocial action; associations between empathy and prosocial action; and the paradoxical relationship between empathy, prosocial behaviour and aggression. The latter is of course an issue of discriminant validity — most theories of character development would posit some important distinctions between prosocial and antisocial behaviour.

Moral reasoning and prosocial action

The relationship between moral reasoning abilities and prosocial action has been much debated. Whilst Piaget's and Kohlberg's theories of moral development have taken as their remit moral reasoning, Blasi (1980) argued that studies should take moral *action* as their final criterion. In general, the relationship between judgement and action in the moral realm seems to be a rather weak one. A review of Kohlberg's approach by Kurtines and Greif (1974) described one study of activism—nonactivism, as defined by participation in a free speech movement sit-in, with a sample of male college students and peace corps volunteers (Haan *et al.*, 1968). It was found that 75% of individuals judged as stage 6 types were activists, as were 41% of those at stage 5, 6% of those at stage 4, 18% of those at stage 3, and 60% of those at stage 2. Although the authors attribute the ostensibly similar performances of stage 2 and stage 6 males to different underlying mechanisms, that is that stage 2 individuals were motivated by individual rights in conflict and stage 6 individuals were more concerned with civil liberties, Kurtines and Greif emphasized that the behavioural similarity of males at such widely differing stages of moral reasoning throws doubt upon the predictive validity of the Kohlbergian scheme.

Blasi (1980), addressing the connection between moral tendencies and behaviour, reviewed 12 studies: six yielded a significant relationship between moral cognition and behaviour, three reported a negative relationship, and three found mixed results. He argued that a complete theory of morality must be able to clarify the relationship between executive and cognitive functioning and, in particular, to explain why such connections might conceivably break down. A promising line of enquiry into this problem was presented by Thoma *et al.* (1991), who sought to discover additional variables that might link moral judgement in producing actions. They identified one such variable, the use of justice-based moral reasoning, that appears to affect action, the correlation between moral cognition scores and behaviour intensifying as justice-based judgements increase.

Empathy and prosocial action

Predictions about the association between empathy and prosocial action are by no means clear. Empathic concern might motivate an individual to help or nurture others; yet vicarious emotional reactions might inhibit or interfere with effective prosocial interventions. As we have seen, the mere cognitive ability to identify another person's distress accurately may facilitate prosocial behaviour (Stewart & Marvin, 1984), but need not do so (Caplan & Hay, 1989).

Prosocial behaviour and aggression

The relationship between prosocial behaviour and aggression is a complex one, which appears to differ in different periods of development. Although some have argued that prosocial behaviour and aggression are opposite poles of a single dimension (Eron & Huesmann, 1986), observational studies of preschool children (Green, 1933; Murphy, 1937) noted that the two tendencies tended to go together in early childhood — more sociable children tended to sympathize and cooperate with, but also aggress against their class-mates. In later childhood, mothers' reports of their twins' antisocial and prosocial tendencies are negatively, though modestly, correlated, but only aggression is positively related to sociability (Stevenson, 1992). Whether or not the association between prosocial behaviour, aggression, and basic sociability disentangles over the life course requires longitudinal analysis.

Miller and Eisenberg (1988) have examined the relationship between empathy and aggression, conducting a meta-analysis of studies in which both constructs have been measured. Such an analysis is complicated by the fact that different sorts of measurement strategies have been used with respect to both constructs with different populations of subjects. In general, a low to moderate negative correlation was found between empathy and aggression; stronger associations were found with questionnaire measures of empathy than with measures of facial expression, experimental induction of empathy, or picture/story methods.

In general, those studies that have looked for associations across dimensions of character development have found some positive relationships, as well as some differentiation from antisocial behav-

iour, but also divergence across domains and situational specificity. Proper, theoretically guided construct validation studies across a variety of measurement strategies have yet to be done.

DEVELOPMENTAL INFLUENCES ON INDIVIDUAL DIFFERENCES IN CHARACTER DEVELOPMENT

So far we have been focusing on normative trends in the realm of character and on the extent to which the construct itself has coherence. We now turn to the important question of the determinants of individual differences in this domain. The following section considers a variety of influences that create and maintain differences amongst individuals in the dimensions of character described above. These include biological propensities, socializing influences and individual dispositions that carry children forward along particular developmental trajectories.

Biological influences

With the change in evolutionary thinking that occurred between the 1960s and the 1970s, and the resulting emphasis on costs and benefits to individuals, rather than group selection, evolutionary biologists had to confront the problem of altruism (Campbell, 1983). If selection operates on individuals, not groups, on what basis is altruistic behaviour selected for? In some species, the question is relatively straightforward; in the social insects, altruists are morphologically distinct from other individuals. Things become more complicated for species where altruism is a more quantitative trait — where individuals may all possess the ability to help and nurture others, but may do so to a greater or lesser extent. Here theories of kin selection and reciprocal altruism have been proposed to account for the benefits that accrue to altruistic or cooperative individuals (Trivers, 1971). Kin selection accounts note that, to the extent that altruists are more likely to help their relatives, the relatives are more likely to survive; by fact of being relatives, they are more likely to possess the altruistic trait as well, and so it continues to appear in the population. In addition, to the extent that the golden rule applies in most populations, altruists might expect to be helped in turn by those individuals the altruists have helped; in that case, the altruists themselves are more likely to survive and so the altruist trait is more likely to be passed down to subsequent generations. These arguments of course depend somewhat on organisms' abilities to recognize their kin and those from whom they have received help in the past.

Recently, investigators of human altruism have begun to explore evidence for the heritability of the various dimensions of affect, cognition and behaviour described above. Comparisons of MZ and DZ adult twin pairs have shown significant heritabilities for empathy and other forms of prosocial behaviour (Mathews *et al.*, 1981; Rushton *et al.*, 1986). It is not completely clear at which point in development the heritable component of character stabilizes. Stevenson (1992) observed 160 MZ and 213 DZ twin pairs whose prosocial and antisocial behaviour and sociable temperament had been rated by parents. Overall mean scores on these dimensions did not differ as a function of zygosity. The prosocial index revealed a higher degree of influence for genetic constitution than for environmental influences; the reverse was true for antisocial behaviour, which showed a higher degree of influence for the environment than for genetic constitution (see Chapter 19). Sociable temperament showed the highest heritability of the three traits, with no effect of environment common to both members of the twin pair.

The extent to which children's empathic responding in particular is heritable has been investigated by Zahn-Waxler *et al.* (1992). This research extends Stevenson's in going beyond parental reports (which might be more similar for MZ than DZ twins for a number of reasons) and measuring differences between the two sets of twins in the second year of life, when prosocial behaviour is being shown at a high rate in the population in general. 94 MZ and 90 same-sex DZ twin pairs were observed at home and tested in the laboratory, at 14 and 20 months of age; simulations of distress were used to reveal the children's empathic responses, which were recorded by observers who were blind to the other twin's response. Objectively measured empathic concern, as well as maternal reports of prosocial patterns, showed significant heritability at both ages.

The social environment

Child-rearing practices. Behavioural genetics studies indicate that, although there may be a heritable basis to character, there is considerable room for manoeuvre with respect to social influences accruing over the course of development. The development of character has long been ascribed to particular sorts of upbringings, and philosophers have long debated how best to produce children of good character. Some, such as Aristotle (*Nichomachean Ethics*, translated by Thomson, 1955), have advocated formal character training to be the responsibility of the state. Others, such as Rousseau (1979), have warned against too much interference by unthinking parents. Nonetheless, even a *laissez-faire* theorist like Rousseau cautions parents against giving in to every whim of the child and therefore encouraging 'tyranny'.

Empirical studies of the role of family socialization in character development have stressed impulse control — obeying the parents' strictures and refraining from aggression — and overt prosocial actions such as sharing with peers. However, there is evidence of long-term influence of child-rearing practices on more generalized and internalized empathic concern in adulthood. Koestner *et al.* (1990) administered a self-report measure of empathic concern, derived from the adjective checklist, to a subsample of 75 31 year olds who had been studied as children in the well-known child-rearing research of Sears *et al.* (1957). Mothers had been interviewed about their child-rearing practices and those of their spouses when the children were five years of age. The mother's tolerance for dependent behaviour at 5 years and the father's involvement in child care significantly predicted self-reported empathic concern at 31 years of age; the mother's inhibition of the child's aggression and her satisfaction with the maternal role were marginally predictive of the adult offspring's empathic concern as well. These links between child-rearing practices and adult concern were somewhat qualified by the child's sex. The mother's inhibition of aggression and maternal strictness were significantly predictive of empathic concern for women but not for men. By and large, mothers' and teachers' contemporaneous ratings of the children's behaviour did not predict empathic concern in adulthood; however, 5 year olds who had been rated as being disobedient at home were less likely to show empathic concern at the age of 31 years. In general, at this point in adulthood, empathy seemed consolidated into a personality pattern that emphasized personal relationships and pro-social values and de-emphasized self-direction, achievement and power.

Moral reasoning is also likely to be affected by child-rearing practices. Eisenberg *et al.* (1983) presented evidence of the effect of socialization practices on moral judgement, reporting that children who were not overprotected and who were encouraged to take part in active decision-making tended to operate at high levels of moral reasoning. They hypothesized that the children's functioning was enhanced by increased opportunities to exercise reasoning and perspective taking. Similarly, an exploratory study by Walker and Taylor (1991) suggested that children's moral development could be predicted by a supportive parental discussion style, combined with the presentation of higher level moral reasoning.

It should be noted that child-rearing practices may operate to inhibit prosocial responding on some occasions, while promoting it on others. Caplan (1993) has noted that there are a number of inhibitory influences on prosocial behaviour, and that adult caregivers do little to encourage children's prosocial responding, outside of the context of pretence; caregivers tend to advocate sharing when the cost for the child is relatively low (Peterson & Reaven, 1984). The situational specificity of pro-social behaviour noted by many investigators may itself be a direct product of socialization.

Social learning processes. The correlational studies of family socialization variables are supplemented by a large experimental literature, in which various socialization processes are simulated in laboratory paradigms. These studies have indicated that pro-social behaviours can be facilitated by modelling, strengthened by reinforcement, and exhorted by verbal instruction (for reviews see Bryan & London, 1970; Radke-Yarrow *et al.*, 1983).

Particular concern has been given to the things children might learn from filmed and televised models; under some circumstances prosocial tele-vision programmes facilitate prosocial action (Friedrich & Stein, 1973), but there is continued worry about the disinhibiting effects of televised violence (Stein & Friedrich, 1972; see also Chapter 7). Advances in moving image technology have been paralleled by concerns over new threats to character development. In the 1930s, investigators were testing the effects of films and comic books on children's moral behaviour (for a review see Jones, 1946); in the 1980s and 1990s, investigators have been examining deleterious effects of playing competitive video games and constructive effects of playing prosocial ones (Chambers & Ascione, 1987).

Much research on children's reactions to televised material focuses on the imitation of aggressive content, particularly that which dominates the cartoons that very young children prefer (Murray, 1973; Hapkiewicz, 1979); in one American survey in the 1970s, 98% of cartoons were found to be aggressive in content (Gerbner, 1972). On exposure to violent, as opposed to non-violent, cartoons, children become more overtly aggressive towards their peers (Steuer *et al.*, 1971). It thus becomes of much interest to determine whether the reverse holds as well — can televised material stimulate children's sharing, helping and cooperation? Televised models can modify children's behaviour in a prosocial direction. For example, in one study, children viewed different segments from an episode of the commercial programme *Lassie* (Sprafkin *et al.*, 1975). In the prosocial condition, the video contained a specific prosocial example, an act of helping, which was omitted in the control condition. The children's own willingness to engage in helpful behaviour was increased if they had viewed the prosocial segment. Insofar as *Lassie* is generally prosocial in content, it is of interest to note that the effects on children's own behaviour were mediated by specific modelling cues, not the overall positive tone of the programme.

Many studies of the effects of television on children's behaviour have been criticized on the grounds that these effects would not hold beyond the experimental situations in which they were assessed. Studies of naturalistic viewing generally confirm those found in the laboratory (Friedrich & Stein, 1973), although they identify particular factors that mediate the effects of television on prosocial behaviour, including the children's intelligence, socioeconomic background and initial propensity to aggression. Long-term longitudinal studies of viewing habits generally corroborate the findings from short-term experiments (see Chapter 7).

In the last decade video games have become very popular, and it has been proposed that they may be even more effective vehicles of social learning than television alone, in that video games simultaneously provide opportunities for modelling, reinforcement and rehearsal; Barton (1981) found that the combination of these social learning mechanisms was more effective in changing children's behaviour than any single treatment alone. Chambers and Ascione (1987) investigated the effect of playing video games under circumstances that manipulated the opportunities for modelling, reinforcement and rehearsal. Children played either aggressive or prosocial games, either on their own or socially (competitively or cooperatively, depending on the aggressive or prosocial content and aims of the game). The children's subsequent sharing and helpful actions were assessed. Experience with prosocial games did not prove effective in promoting prosocial behaviour, but experience with aggressive games tended to suppress it; the rather weak effects in this study deserve replication.

An interesting dimension of the literature on the social learning of prosocial behaviour is the extent to which particular learning processes have limited or paradoxical effects. For example, praise must be directed to individuals, not to their actions (Mills & Grusec, 1989), if the children in question are going to carry on being helpful. Modelling and reinforcement processes are not always effective in encouraging sharing and regulating conflict (Hay & Murray, 1982; Hay & Ross, 1982). This may be partly due to the fact that even very young children are affected by the verbal content of their experiences, as well as the physical actions they see modelled and reinforced (Hay *et al.*, 1985).

Close personal relationships

It has been proposed that the attachment relationship between infant and parent is an arena in which prosocial development may flourish (Waters *et al.*, 1986). Security of attachment is indeed associated with various measures of competence with

parents and peers (see Chapter 16), and so it seems likely to be a major influence on the development of character. For example, infants judged at 12–18 months of age to be securely attached to their mothers were found 6–9 months later to be more obedient and cooperative, and to exhibit more self-control, in comparison with an anxiously attached sample of infants (Londerville & Main, 1981). Interestingly, however, one attempt to test the relationship between attachment security and the positive versus negative qualities of peer relations found that a child's attachment classification appeared to affect a peer's behaviour more than the child's own: secure children tested with secure peers showed positive behaviour, but showed more negative behaviour when tested with insecure peers (Jacobson & Wille, 1986).

Sibling relationships also provide an arena in which character develops; sibling conflict in particular seems to provide opportunities for children to solve social problems in different sorts of ways and to develop justifications for their own behaviour (see Dunn, 1988). A particularly interesting type of sibling relationship is that which exists between twins, and zygosity appears to affect whether prosocial behaviour extends beyond the twin relationship. Amongst MZ twins, high rates of prosocial behaviour with the twin are negatively associated with prosocial responding to other persons; in contrast, amongst DZ twins, prosocial behaviour directed to the twin generalizes to other recipients (Zahn-Waxler *et al.*, 1994). The relationship between identical siblings thus seems to be an especially exclusive one.

Peer groups

As children grow older, their positive social behaviour becomes more closely linked to their particular peer relationships (Birch & Billman, 1986). At the same time, it is important to note that friendships can tolerate a certain degree of conflict and competition (e.g. Hartup *et al.*, 1988). For example, 9-year-old boys are more likely to compete and less likely to share with friends than with acquaintances; the reverse holds for 13-year-old boys (Berndt *et al.*, 1986).

As children spend years with their peers in classrooms and other settings, they take on various stable roles in peer society (see Chapter 18). Negative reputations are partially derived from high rates of aggression, low rates of prosocial behaviour and difficulties in solving social problems; however, the stable reputations appear to have their own causal status, so that rejected children become less and less likely to approach situations in a positive way (Dodge & Frame, 1982). As children approach adolescence, the role of peer relationships becomes important in a different sort of way. Close personal relationships with delinquent peers may encourage antisocial behaviour directed to other individuals.

Cultural influences

Values as well as actions differ markedly from society to society (see Chapter 7), and so we may expect to see clear influences of cultural background on character development. This issue has been of particular concern to those investigators who wish to differentiate moral from conventional values (Smetana, 1981, 1985; Sugarman, 1987). Simpson (1974), noting the apparent absence of higher stage moral reasoning in certain cultures, contended that Kohlberg's model reflected a somewhat parochial view of morality, failing to acknowledge the values and strategies of people of non-Western cultures. A number of researchers have reported cross-cultural differences in moral reasoning consistent with societal demands and values (Fuchs *et al.*, 1986; Tietjen, 1986). For example, one study of kibbutz and Israeli city children found differences in reasoning that reflected the children's social environments, the kibbutz children advocating reciprocity and the city children using more hedonistic and pragmatic reasoning (Eisenberg *et al.*, 1990).

Cross-cultural comparisons have shown that the same behaviours may be classified within one culture as mere conventions but in others as intrinsically, morally, wrong. For example, Nisan (1987) questioned the working definition offered by Western researchers, namely, that evaluations of moral norms rest on the principle of welfare, whereas evaluations of social conventions depend on consensual agreement. He found that judgements of morals and conventions made by traditional Arab village children were consistently different from those made by modern, secular urban and kibbutz Jewish children. The Arab children tended to base their judgements on the norms existing in their culture, and their tendency to do so increased with age. In contrast, the non-traditional Jewish children's moral evaluations were less influenced by existing norms than by criteria of justice and welfare.

CHARACTER AND INDIVIDUALITY

Character clearly is influenced by heritable propensities and social factors operating at various levels of analysis; differences in character flower, however, in the context of other important differences amongst individuals which come to have causal force in their own right. Here we consider four important differences among individuals that appear to shape character: temperament, gender, self-evaluations and psychiatric disorder.

Temperament

Jones (1946) was at pains to make certain distinctions between character and morality; similarly he thought it necessary to distinguish between character and temperament: 'Whether a person is good-tempered, sanguine, phlegmatic, melancholic, or choleric is certainly of interest to anyone rating him for practical purposes of living or working with him, and no claim can be made that such characteristics have no relation to character. Strictly speaking, however, the readiness and capacity of an individual for such relatively prevailing affective experiences are not central to the problem of his character ... character concerns itself more with the volitional powers of the individual and the directions or goals of his striving' (pp. 707–708). Even when more modern conceptualizations of temperament are considered (for a review see Chapter 4), this distinction seems to have merit. Nonetheless, it is of interest to enquire how temperamental characteristics might provide particular children with particular social experiences that shape their characters in particular ways.

The influence of temperament on social behaviour has primarily been examined with respect to two main domains, attachment and aggression (see Chapters 16 and 19). The contribution of temperament to the security of attachment relationships is a matter of intense debate; the status of difficult temperament as a precursor to conduct problems is similarly open to argument (Moffitt, 1993). What is somewhat neglected, however, is the question of how temperamental differences might influence children's prosocial tendencies. That is, children who are judged to have difficult temperaments may be more likely to show aggression; are they similarly *less* likely to engage in sharing or cooperation? For example, 1- and 2-year-old children who declined to share objects with familiar peers were independently judged by their mothers to be more possessive, selfish and aggressive (Hay *et al.*, in press).

Because character development is multifaceted, it seems likely that different temperamental features might contribute to different sorts of prosocial activities. For example, the rhythmicity of certain infants noted by Thomas *et al.* (1968) might make for smooth, patterned interactions with caregivers in which the capacity for cooperative exchange soon emerges. Sociability (Buss & Plomin, 1975) might promote certain sorts of positive interactions with caregivers and peers, but might militate against other prosocial actions and judgements that require some distancing from social convention. For example, London's (1970) classic account of Gentiles who rescued Jews during the Holocaust identified three general features of the rescuers. First, they had been socialized by prosocial parents, who modelled and advocated altruistic behaviour. Second, they tended to be risk-takers, for whom the rescue attempts were somewhat attractive, not daunting. And, third, they tended to be somewhat at odds with their own social milieu, so that they were less likely to conform to and collaborate with the Nazi regime. In other words, they might have shown some signs of unsociable, difficult temperament that actually facilitated prosocial action in these extreme circumstances.

Gender

Across cultures, gender would seem to be a major organizing principle for the development of character, although differences in prosocial propensities may be more in the eye of the beholder or in self-reflection than in overt behaviour (see Chapter 15). Although the traditional rhyme would have it that, in contrast to boys, small girls are composed of 'sugar and spice and everything nice', gender dif-

ferences in early appearing prosocial behaviours are not striking, or are seen at the level of the gender composition of the group, not the gender of individuals (Caplan *et al.*, 1991; Hay *et al.*, 1991). Gender-constrained approaches to social relationships appear to emerge in the preschool years and consolidate over the years of middle childhood. By adulthood, women and men are seen by many observers to be fundamentally different in character.

An influential contemporary perspective on the relationship between gender and character was set forth by C. Gilligan (1977), who argued that women in general live by an ethic of care whereas men live by an ethic of justice. Gilligan's formulation was proposed to account for findings from the Kohlberg tradition of studies of moral judgement, in which female respondents would tend to score as less advanced in moral reasoning than men. In the Kohlberg coding scheme, an emphasis on the importance of personal relationships, as opposed to more abstract principles of justice, puts one at a lower point on a presumably linear scale. It should be noted that not all investigators find consistent evidence of a gender difference in response to Kohlberg-type moral dilemmas (Snarey *et al.*, 1985; Smetana *et al.*, 1991). However, there is evidence that adult women and men, in their roles as parents, take differing approaches to real-world ethical conflicts. When intervening in conflicts between young siblings, mothers tend to stress the importance of caring relationships, whereas fathers tend to stress issues of justice, to girls and boys alike (H. Ross, personal communication). These findings suggest that a child's eventual adoption of one or the other general approach to moral issues may be bound up with the complex set of processes involved in identification with the parent of the same sex — an old-fashioned topic that would still appear to have considerable relevance to character development. The relationship of maternal and paternal child-rearing practices to the development of character and conscience is still worthy of systematic attention.

The emerging sense of self

A critical strand in the formation of character may be the child's gradual adoption of the role of caregiver, as opposed to receiver of care, which may progress at least partly along gender-differentiated lines. But another strand is certainly the acquisition of adult standards of conduct, as discussed by Kagan (1989). An important contributor to character development, then, is the individual's own emerging conception of self and the extent to which he or she meets expectations set by parents and other authority figures and adopted and elaborated on by oneself. It is here that character development again moves beyond behavioural acquisition and cognitive development and is much influenced by the moral emotions of shame and guilt.

The subjective experiences of guilt and shame are powerful regulators of human behaviour. J. Gilligan (1976) argued that the capacity for shame emerged developmentally before the capacity for guilt, and that whereas the former is concerned with the avoidance of public censure and humiliation, the latter is fuelled by internalized conscience and feelings of culpability. Other theorists have queried this traditional distinction between guilt and shame, preferring conceptualizations based on the self (Lewis, 1971; Nathanson, 1987) or on attributions (Weiner, 1985). A study of children's conceptions of guilt and shame showed that 10–12-year-old children can understand the adaptive implications of the two emotions, and experience shame as impinging on self-worth, whilst 7–9 year olds tend to see both shame and guilt in terms of the judgement of others (Ferguson *et al.*, 1991). Although shame and guilt have certain features in common (Tangney, 1990), the two emotions often occur independently, children being capable of experiencing shame in response to the moral reproof of others even though they may not feel they have committed a wrongdoing and thus feel no guilt: Ausubel (1955) cited the example of a child shamed to be caught lying, even though he did not believe lying to be wrong. However, once young children have developed an awareness of agency and sense the responsibility of their actions towards other people, they become capable of experiencing guilt on those occasions when they fail to live up to an ideal self image.

Earlier in the chapter, in discussing children's reactions to others' distress, it was noted that toddlers often attempt to alleviate the plight of others. Such examples of sympathetic responding can occur in situations where the child feels no culpability for the other person's distress. In circumstances where young children do perceive themselves to be responsible for the distress of others, they may experience feelings of guilt; furthermore, as noted by Hoffman (1976), with increasing cognitive competence, children begin to experience guilt when they believe they should have helped but failed so to do. Attributions of intentionality also become more salient with age. Piaget (1962), discussing objective responsibility, noted: 'It is very easy to notice — especially in very young children, under 6–7 years of age — how frequently the sense of guilt on the occasion of clumsiness is proportional to the extent of the material disaster instead of remaining subordinate to the intentions in question' (p. 132). In similar vein, Graham *et al.* (1984) found that 6–7 year olds reported feeling guilty even for accidental outcomes, whilst older children most often reported guilt feelings for intentional misdemeanours.

The emergence of shame and guilt clearly is associated with children's adherence to standards of conduct set by adults and adopted for themselves. Kagan argued that, having adopted certain values, children experience discomfort if their behaviour deviates from those values, such dissonance being expressed as guilt. Shame, on the other hand, is felt when children violate standards set for them by others, rather than those they themselves have adopted. Kagan believed that some irrational fears and ritualistic behaviours exhibited by 5 and 6 year olds result from defence against excessively intense feelings of shame and guilt. At the same time, an optimal level of guilt seems to be a powerful facilitator for prosocial behaviour. A study of pre-schoolers to sixth-grade children, which related motivation for helping to a number of attributional variables, including guilt, empathy and altruism, indicated that attributions for guilt were most strongly and consistently related to helping across all the sample's age range (Chapman *et al.*, 1987). Given the prominence of guilt in promoting positive attitudes, it is interesting to note that children who are given prior encouragement to empathize with a victim show more extreme guilt than those not so encouraged (Thompson & Hoffman, 1980).

The emerging sense of self, of course, comprises positive as well as negative reflections on one's actions, which presumably contribute to prosocial action. Positive affect in general promotes prosocial behaviour (Moore *et al.*, 1973); it seems likely that more general feelings of well-being promote a general tendency to relate harmoniously with others, and thus a positive sense of self would be fundamentally intertwined with character development. What is perhaps more interesting, however, is not generosity and consideration in easy circumstances, but prosocial responding when one is under pressure or threatened or experiencing financial or social adversity. One possibility that deserves increased attention is the role of another form of self-reflection, a sense of humour, in such adverse circumstances. In other words, individuals' differential abilities to see the funny side of themselves and their various predicaments on the face of it would seem to be an important component of character. The developmental course of this feature of character is by no means clear; studies of children's understanding of humour have primarily focused on comprehension and generation of particular sorts of jokes and riddles at different ages; for example, children have considerable difficulty appreciating absurd humour (such as that embodied in 'elephant jokes') until they approach the preadolescent period (Prentice & Fathman, 1975; McGhee, 1976). This development in many ways parallels children's growing understanding of ambiguous language, such as sarcasm and the use of metaphors (Dent & Rosenberg, 1990). Acquiring the ability to be amused by the absurd in one's own circumstances may be a relatively late development, but one that fundamentally affects character. Links between humour and positive relations with peers and teachers can be demonstrated, even when basic intellectual ability is controlled for (Masten, 1986).

Character and psychopathology

Throughout the history of attempts to diagnose psychopathology, theorists have confronted the thorny distinction between 'poor character' and 'mental illness'. For example, Maudsley (1897) speculated that 'There is a borderland between crime and insanity, near one boundary of which we meet with something of madness but more of sin, and near the other boundary something of sin but more of madness' (p. 36). He argued further that: 'As there are persons who cannot distinguish certain colours, having what is called colour-blindness, and

others who, having no ear for music, cannot distinguish one tune from the other, so there are some few who are congenitally deprived of moral sense. Associated with this defect is frequently more or less intellectual deficiency, but not always; it sometimes happens that there is a remarkably acute intellect with no trace of moral feeling' (pp. 62–63). The spirit of Maudsley's enquiries lives on in contemporary attempts to find congenital precursors to conduct problems and personality disorder (Moffitt, 1993; see Chapter 19). Furthermore, there have been a number of attempts to relate conduct problems or delinquent acts to deficiencies in the basic social cognitive skills that contribute to character formation. It has been observed, for example, that delinquents may be deficient in role-taking or moral reasoning abilities (Chandler & Moran, 1990). Here however, the multifaceted nature of character development raises complex issues for the analysis of delinquency and personality disorder. Delinquents, for example, may take an amoral stance with respect to the society at large, yet show high levels of cooperative endeavour within their own set of activities.

On the other side of the coin, there are some theorists who fear an excess of prosocial sensitivity might lead to an increased risk for psychopathology. These formulations are very closely tied up with the renewed interest in the development of shame and guilt and in the notion of gender-specific pathways to psychopathology. The claim is made that, when excessive or inappropriate, guilt can be dysfunctional, perhaps contributing to patterns of depression in later childhood (Zahn-Waxler et al., 1990). There is evidence that young children experience very strong, stable feelings of responsibility (Cummings et al., 1986), and that these feelings may become further exaggerated through their difficulties in attributing intent and differentiating self from other. Zahn-Waxler et al. (1991) have proposed a theoretical model to account for the transmission of depression from mothers to daughters in which prosocial sensitivity and guilt serve as mediating links. In their view, the experience of being cared for by a depressed mother has differential effects on girls and boys; boys may respond, as they do to other forms of social adversity, with aggression and other oppositional problems, whereas girls may be more likely to attempt to nurture and care for the depressed mother. Because the care they can offer is by its very nature limited and probably ineffective in lifting the mother's depression, these caring daughters may experience elevated feelings of guilt, leaving them vulnerable themselves to eventual depression.

Some components of this model are confirmed by research on the impact of maternal depression on young children; in particular, an interaction between the child's gender and the mother's psychiatric status is often observed, with the daughters of depressed women seeming particularly competent on standardized assessments and in the judgements of blind observers and the sons particularly vulnerable to problems (Hay *et al.*, 1992a; Murray, 1992). Such findings would imply that the sons are more likely than the daughters to show generally disorganized behaviour, and thus would be less likely to offer a source of support for the mother. Nonetheless, it is not completely clear that the daughters of depressed women are more *prosocial* than their male counterparts. In an interview study, using puppet characters, 5-year-old children were asked to recommend tactics for dealing with a conflict between peers and to evaluate certain actions made by the puppet antagonists (Hay *et al.*, 1992b). From their responses, two composite measures of 'aggressive' and 'socialized' approaches to the dilemma were generated. The two composite measures were negatively associated, but not polar opposites.

Analysis of the aggressive profile scores yielded the familiar interaction between gender and maternal diagnosis: sons of depressed women were especially likely to recommend aggressive tactics for the resolution of peer conflict, whereas daughters of depressed women were especially unlikely to do so. This measure was highly correlated with actual behaviour with familiar peers in a free play setting. In contrast, however, the socialized profile was unaffected by the mother's history of depression; girls in general were more likely to recommend socialized tactics than boys were, although the gender difference was only reliable for children of mothers who had not been depressed. This means that the sons of depressed women were advocating *both* aggressive and prosocial approaches to social dilemmas; the daughters were certainly not more prosocial than other girls, and not reliably more

prosocial than the sons of depressed women.

Despite the lack of clarity of findings to date, however, the role of prosocial activities in the development of psychopathology deserves attention. Furthermore, the extent to which children take on different roles in social situations, as caregivers, as conflict mediators, as recipients of care, as refusers of care (e.g. girls who refuse food, as described in Chapter 20), may clarify certain developmental pathways in the emergence of different forms of psychopathology. One domain of enquiry that remains of interest is that of passivity and dependency in social contexts. Developmental research on dependency received a fatal blow with the publication of an influential book on attachment and dependency in the 1970s (Gewirtz, 1972), in which a consensus was reached that attachment did not imply dependency and was therefore no bad thing. What was unfortunately thrown out with the bath water in this case, however, was an analysis of the ontogeny of dependency and its contributions to non-aggressive forms of personality disorder. This lack of attention to an important social phenomenon deserves redress.

CONCLUSION

In this chapter, we have resurrected the term 'character development' in order to provide an organizing framework for a diverse body of empirical findings and theoretical speculations. It is our hope that the framework offered here translates into a set of clear propositions for future research. At the same time, however, we too have been guilty of perpetuating the most fundamental schism in this field: We have concentrated attention almost solely on the more positive sides of character development, leaving much of the rest to the chapter that focuses on aggression (see Chapter 19). Although this division of responsibility is convenient and accurately reflects current thinking in the field, in the long run it cannot help but obscure the truth about human development. One's character is presumably a mix of prosocial and antisocial proclivities, and life requires the suitable regulation of opposing tendencies in one or the other direction. In this volume, Cairns and Kroll (Chapter 15) argue strongly for a 'holistic' approach to the study of gender, in which variables of interest are not segregated one from the other. A similar argument must be set forth with respect to the study of character, which by its very nature cannot permit the fragmentation of persons into orthogonal variables.

REFERENCES

Alloway T., Kramer L. & Pliner P. (eds) *Advances in the Study of Communication and Affect*, Vol. 3, *Attachment Behavior*. Plenum, New York.

Aronfreed J. (1968) *Conduct and Conscience*. Academic Press, New York.

Ausubel D.P. (1955) Relationships between shame and guilt in the socializing process. *Psychological Review* **62**, 378–390.

Ausubel D.P. & Sullivan E.V. (1970) *Theory and Problems of Child Development*. Grune & Stratton, New York.

Bandura A. (1977) *Social Learning Theory*. Lawrence Erlbaum, Hillsdale, New Jersey.

Barton S.J. (1981) Developing sharing: An analysis of modelling and other behaviour techniques. *Behaviour Modification* **5**, 396–398.

Berkowitz L. (1972) Social norms, feelings, and other factors affecting helping and altruism. In Berkowitz L. (ed.) *Advances in Experimental Social Psychology*, Vol. 6, pp. 63–108, Academic Press, New York.

Berndt T.J. (1977) The effect of reciprocity norms on moral judgment and causal attribution. *Child Development* **48**, 1322–1330.

Berndt T.J., Hawkins J.A. & Hoyle S.G. (1986) Changes in friendship during a school year: Effects on children's and adolescents' impressions of friendship and sharing with friends. *Child Development* **57**, 1284–1297.

Birch L.L. & Billman J. (1986) Preschool children's food sharing with friends and acquaintances. *Child Development* **57**, 387–395.

Blasi A. (1980) Bridging moral cognition and moral action: A critical review of the literature. *Psychological Bulletin* **88**, 1–45.

Boccia M. & Campos J. (1989) Maternal emotional signals, social referencing, and infants' reactions to strangers. In Eisenberg N. (ed.) *Empathy and Related Emotional Responses*. New Directions for Child Development, Vol. 44, pp. 25–49.

Borke H. (1971) Interpersonal perception of young children: Egocentrism or empathy? *Developmental Psychology* **5**, 263–269.

Bott H. (1934) *Personality Development in Young Children*. University of Toronto Press, Toronto.

Bowlby J. (1958) The nature of the child's tie to his mother. *International Journal of Psychoanalysis* **39**, 350–373.

Bowlby J. (1982) *Attachment and Loss*, Vol. 1, *Attachment*, 2nd edn. Hogarth Press, London.

Bronson W. (1985) Growth in the organization of behavior over the second year of life. *Developmental Psychology* **21**, 108–117.

Brownell C.A. & Corriger M.S. (1990) Changes in cooperation and self–other differentiation during the second year. *Child Development* **6**, 1164–1174.

Bryan J.H. & London P. (1970) Altruistic behavior by children. *Psychological Bulletin* **73**, 200–211.

Burns N. & Cavey L. (1957) Age differences in empathic ability among children. *Canadian Journal of Psychology* **11**, 227–230.

Burton R.V. (1976) Honesty and dishonesty. In Lickona T. (ed.) *Moral Development and Behavior*, pp. 173–197. Holt, Rinehart & Winston, New York.

Buss A.H. & Plomin R. (1975) *A Temperament Theory of Personality Development*. Wiley, New York.

Campbell D.T. (1983) The two distinct routes beyond kin selection to ultra sociality: Implications for the social sciences. In Bridgeman D. (ed.) *The Nature of Prosocial Development: Interdisciplinary Theories and Strategies*, pp. 11–41. Academic Press, New York.

Camras L.A. (1980) Children's understanding of facial expression used during conflict encounters. *Child Development* **51**, 879–885.

Camras L.A., Ribordy S., Hill J., Martino S., Spaccarelli S. & Stefani R. (1989) Recognition and posing of emotional expressions by abused children and their mothers. *Developmental Psychology* **24**(6), 776–781.

Caplan M. (1993) Inhibitory influences in development: The case of prosocial behavior. In Hay D.F. & Angold A. (eds) *Precursors and Causes in Development and Psychopathology*, pp. 169–198. Wiley, Chichester.

Caplan M. & Hay D.F. (1989) Preschoolers' responses to peers' distress and beliefs about bystander intervention. *Journal of Child Psychology and Psychiatry* **30**, 231–242.

Caplan M., Vespo J.E., Pedersen J. & Hay D.F. (1991) Conflict over resources in small groups of one- and two-year-olds. *Child Development* **62**, 1513–1524.

Caspi A., Lynam D., Moffitt T.E. & Silva P.A. (1993) Unravelling girls' delinquency: Biological, dispositional, and contextual contributions to adolescent misbehaviour. *Developmental Psychology* **29**, 19–30.

Chambers J.H. & Ascione F.R. (1987) The effects of prosocial and aggressive video games on children's donating and helping. *Journal of Genetic Psychology* **148**, 499–505.

Chandler M. (1973) Egocentrism and antisocial behavior: The assessment and training of social perspective-taking skills. *Developmental Psychology* **9**, 326–332.

Chandler M., Fritz A.S. & Hala S. (1989) Small-scale deceit: Deception as a marker of two-, three-, and four-year-olds' early theories of mind. *Child Development* **60**, 1263–1277.

Chandler M. & Moran T. (1990) Psychopathy and moral development: A comparative study of delinquent and nondelinquent youth. *Development and Psychopathology* **2**, 227–246.

Chapman M., Zahn-Waxler C., Iannotti R. & Cooperman G. (1987) Empathy and responsibility in the motivation of children's helping. *Developmental Psychology* **23**,

140−145.

Church J. (1966) (ed.) *Three Babies: Biographies of Cognitive Development*. Random House, New York.

Cohn J.F. & Tronick E.Z. (1988) Mother−infant face-to-face interaction: Influence is bidirectional and unrelated to periodic cycles in either partner's behavior. *Developmental Psychology* **24**, 386−392.

Colby A., Kohlberg L., Gibbs J. & Lieberman M. (1983) A longitudinal study of moral judgment. *Monographs of the Society for Research in Child Development* **48**, Serial No. 200.

Cummings E.M., Hollenbeck B., Iannotti R., Radke-Yarrow M. & Zahn-Waxler C. (1986) Early organization of altruism and aggression: Developmental patterns and individual difference. In Zahn-Waxler C., Cummings E.M. & Iannotti R. (eds) *Altruism and Aggression: Biological and Social Origins*, pp. 165−188. Cambridge University Press, Cambridge.

Cummings E.M., Zahn-Waxler C. & Radke-Yarrow M. (1981) Young children's responses to expressions of anger and affection by others in the family. *Child Development* **52**, 1274−1282.

Darwin C. (1872) *The Expression of the Emotions in Man and the Animals*. Murray, London.

Darwin C. (1877) A biographical sketch of an infant. *Mind* **2**, 285−294.

Dent C. & Rosenberg L. (1990) Visual and verbal metaphors: Developmental interactions. *Child Development* **61**, 983−994.

Deutsch M. (1949) A theory of cooperation and competition. *Human Relations* **2**, 129−152.

Dodge K. & Frame C.L. (1982) Social cognitive biases and deficits in aggressive boys. *Child Development* **53**, 629−635.

Dorval B. & Eckerman C.O. (1984) Developmental trends in the quality of conversation achieved by small groups of acquainted peers. *Monographs of the Society for Research in Child Development* **48**, Serial No. 206.

Dunn J. (1988) *The Beginnings of Social Understanding*. Harvard University Press, Cambridge, Massachusetts.

Dunn J., Kendrick C. & MacNamee R. (1981) The reaction of children to the birth of a sibling: Mothers' reports. *Journal of Child Psychology and Psychiatry* **22**, 1−18.

Dunn J. & Munn P. (1986) Siblings and the development of prosocial behaviour. *International Journal of Behavioural Development* **9**, 265−284.

Eckerman C.O., Davis C.C. & Didow S.M. (1989) Toddlers' emerging ways of achieving coordination with a peer. *Child Development* **60**, 440−453.

Eckerman C.O., Whatley J.L. & Kutz S.L. (1975) Growth of social play with peers during the second year of life. *Developmental Psychology* **11**, 42−49.

Edwards C.P. (1986) Another style of competence: The caregiving child. In Fogel A. & Melson G. (eds) *Origins of Nurturance*, pp. 95−121. Lawrence Erlbaum, Hillsdale, New Jersey.

Eisenberg N., Hertz-Lazarowitz R. & Fuchs J. (1990) Pro-social moral judgment in Israeli Kibbutz and city children: A longitudinal study. *Merrill-Palmer Quarterly* **36**, 273−285.

Eisenberg N., Lennon R. & Roth K. (1983) Prosocial development: A longitudinal study. *Developmental Psychology* **19**, 846−855.

Eisenberg N., Lundy T., Shell R. & Roth K. (1985) Children's justifications for their adult and peer-directed compliant (prosocial and nonprosocial) behaviors. *Developmental Psychology* **21**, 325−331.

Eisenberg-Berg N. & Lennon R. (1980) Altruism and the assessment of empathy in the preschool years. *Child Development* **51**, 552−557.

Emery R.E. (1988) *Marriage, Divorce, and Children's Adjustment*. Sage, Newbury Park, California.

Eron L.D. & Huesmann L.R. (1986) The role of television in the development of prosocial and antisocial behavior. In Olweus D., Block J. & Radke-Yarrow M. (eds) *Development of Antisocial and Prosocial Behavior: Research, Theories, and Issues*, pp. 285−314. Academic Press, London.

Ferguson T.J. & Rule B.G. (1988) Children's attributions of retaliatory aggression. *Child Development* **59**, 961−968.

Ferguson T.J., Stegge H. & Damhuis I. (1991) Children's understanding of guilt and shame. *Child Development* **62**, 827−839.

Feshbach N.D. & Roe K. (1968) Empathy in six- and seven-year-olds. *Child Development* **39**, 133−145.

Field T.M., Woodson R., Greenberg R. & Cohen D. (1982) Discrimination and imitation of facial expressions by neonates. *Science* **146**, 668−670.

Friedrich L.K. & Stein A.H. (1973) Aggressive and prosocial television programs and the natural behavior of preschool children. *Monographs of the Society for Research in Child Development* **38**, Serial No. 151.

Freud A. & Burlingham D. (1944) *Infants Without Families: The Case For and Against Residential Nurseries*. International University Press, New York.

Froming W.J., Allen L. & Underwood B. (1983) Age and generosity reconsidered: Cross-sectional and longitudinal evidence. *Child Development* **54**, 585−593.

Fuchs I., Eisenberg N., Hertz-Lazarowitz R. & Sharanany R. (1986) Kibbutz, Israeli city, and American children's moral reasoning about prosocial moral conflicts. *Merrill-Palmer Quarterly* **32**, 37−50.

Gerbner G. (1972) Violence in television drama: Trends and symbolic functions. In Comstock G.A. & Rubinstein E.A. (eds) *Television and Social Behavior*, Vol. 1, pp. 28−118. US Government Printing Office, Washington, DC.

Gewirtz J. (ed.) (1972) *Attachment and Dependency*. Winston, Washington, DC.

Gilligan C. (1977) In a different voice: Woman's conception of self and morality. *Harvard Educational Review* **47**, 481−517.

Gilligan J. (1976) Beyond morality: Psychoanalytic reflections on shame, guilt, and love. In Lickona T. (ed.) *Moral Development and Behaviour*, pp. 144−158. Holt,

Rinehart & Winston, New York.

Gordon F.R. & Flavell J.H. (1977) The development of intuition about cognitive cuing. *Child Development* **48**, 1027—1033.

Gouldner A.J. (1960) The norm of reciprocity: A preliminary statement. *American Sociological Review* **25**, 161—178.

Graham S., Doubleday C. & Guarino P.A. (1984) The development of relations between perceived controllability and the emotions of pity, anger, and guilt. *Child Development* **55**, 561—565.

Green E.H. (1933) Group play and quarreling among preschool children. *Child Development* **4**, 302—307.

Grych J.H. & Fincham F.D. (1990) Marital conflict and children's adjustment: A cognitive-contextual framework. *Psychological Bulletin* **108**, 267—290.

Gustafson G.E., Green J.A. & West M.J. (1979) The infant's changing role in mother—infant games: The growth of social skills. *Infant Behavior and Development* **2**, 301—308.

Haan N., Smith B. & Block J. (1968) Moral reasoning of young adults: Political—social behavior, family background, and personality correlates. *Journal of Personality and Social Psychology* **10**, 183—201.

Hapkiewicz W.G. (1979) Children's reactions to cartoon violence. *Journal of Clinical Child Psychology* **8**, 30—34.

Handlon B.J. & Gross P. (1959) The development of sharing behavior. *Journal of Abnormal and Social Psychology* **59**, 423—428.

Harris P.L. (1989) *Children and Emotion: Development of Psychological Understanding*. Basil Blackwell, Oxford.

Hartshorne H. & May M.A. (1930) *Studies in Deceit*. MacMillan, New York.

Hartup W.W., Laursen B., Stewart M.I. & Eastenson A. (1988) Conflict and the friendship relations of young children. *Child Development* **59**, 1590—1600.

Haviland J. & Lelwica M. (1987) The induced affect response: 10-week-old infants' responses to three emotional expressions. *Developmental Psychology* **23**, 97—104.

Hay D.F. (1979) Cooperative interactions and sharing between very young children and their parents. *Developmental Psychology* **15**, 647—653.

Hay D.F. (1984) Social conflict in early childhood. In Whitehurst G.J. (ed.) *Annals of Child Development*, Vol. 1, pp. 1—44. JAI Press, Greenwich, Connecticut.

Hay D.F., Caplan M., Castle J. & Stimson C.A. (1991) Does sharing become increasingly 'rational' in the second year of life? *Developmental Psychology* **27**, 987—993.

Hay D.F., Castle J., Stimson C.A. & Davies L. (in press) The social construction of character in toddlerhood. In Killen M. & Hart D. (eds) *Everyday Morality*. Cambridge University Press, Cambridge.

Hay D.F. & Murray P. (1982) Giving and requesting: Social facilitation of infants' offers to adults. *Infant Behavior and Development* **5**, 301—310.

Hay D.F., Murray P., Cecire S. & Nash A. (1985) Social learning of social behavior in early life. *Child Development* **56**, 43—57.

Hay D.F., Nash A. & Pedersen J. (1981) Response of six-month-olds to the distress of their peers. *Child Development* **52**, 1071—1075.

Hay D.F., Nash A. & Pedersen J. (1983) Interactions between six-month-old peers. *Child Development* **54**, 557—562.

Hay D.F. & Ross H.S. (1982) The social nature of early conflict. *Child Development* **53**, 105—113.

Hay D.F., Sharp D., Kumar C., Pawlby S. & Schmucker G. (1992a) *Maternal depression and intellectual development: The importance of timing and gender*. Presented at the Conference of the Developmental Section of the British Psychological Society, Edinburgh.

Hay D.F., Zahn-Waxler C., Cummings E.M. & Iannotti R. (1992b) Young children's views about conflict with peers: A comparison of the daughters and sons of depressed and well women. *Journal of Child Psychology and Psychiatry* **33**(4), 669—683.

Hoffman M.L. (1975) Developmental synthesis of affect and cognition and its implications for altruistic motivation. *Developmental Psychology* **11**, 607—622.

Hoffman M.L. (1976) Empathy, role taking, guilt, and development of altruistic motives. In Lickona T. (ed.) *Moral Development and Behavior*, pp. 124—143. Holt, Rinehart & Winston, New York.

Hoffman M.L. (1978) Empathy: Its development and prosocial implications. *Nebraska Symposium on Motivation* **25**, 169—217.

Hoffman M.L. & Levine L.E. (1976) Early sex differences in empathy. *Developmental Psychology* **12**(6), 557—558.

Holden G. (1983) Avoiding conflict: Mothers as tacticians in the supermarket. *Child Development* **54**, 233—240.

Howes C. (1988) Peer interaction of young children. *Monographs of the Society for Research in Child Development* **53**, Serial No. 217.

Howes C. & Olenick M. (1986) Family and child care influences on toddler's compliance. *Child Development* **57**, 202—216.

Hume D. (1957) *An Inquiry Concerning the Principles of Morals*. Bobbs-Merrill, New York.

Izard C.E., Huebner R.R., Risser D., McGinnes G.C. & Dougherty L.M. (1980) The young infant's ability to produce discrete emotion expressions. *Developmental Psychology* **16**, 132—140.

Jacobson J.L. & Wille D.E. (1986) The influence of attachment pattern on developmental changes in peer interaction from the toddler to the preschool period. *Child Development* **57**, 338—347.

Jones V. (1946) Character development in children: An objective approach. In Carmichael L. (ed.) *Manual of Child Psychology*, pp. 701—751. Wiley, New York.

Kagan J. (1981) *The Second Year*. Harvard University Press, Cambridge, Massachusetts.

Kagan J. (1989) *Unstable Ideas: Temperament. Cognition and Self.* Harvard University Press, Cambridge, Massachusetts.

Kant I. (1959) *Foundations of the Metaphysics of Morals.* Bobbs-Merrill, New York.

Karniol R. (1980) A conceptual analysis of immanent justice responses in children. *Child Development* 51, 118–130.

Klinnert M., Campos J., Sorce J., Emde R. & Svejda M. (1983) Emotions as behavioral regulators: Social referencing in infancy. In Plutchik R. & Kellerman H. (eds) *Emotions in Early Development*, pp. 63–65. Academic Press, New York.

Koestner R., Franz C. & Weinberger J. (1990) The family origins of empathic concern: A 26-year longitudinal study. *Journal of Personality and Social Psychology* 58, 709–716.

Kohlberg L. (1964) Development of moral character and moral ideology. In Hoffman M.L. & Hoffman L.W. (eds) *Review of Child Development Research*, Vol. 1, pp. 383–431. Russell Sage Foundation, New York.

Kuczynski L. & Kochanska G. (1990) Children's noncompliance from toddlerhood to age five. *Developmental Psychology* 26, 398–408.

Kurtines W. & Greif E.B. (1974) The development of moral thought: Review and evaluation of Kohlberg's approach. *Psychological Bulletin* 81, 453–470.

Latane B. & Darley J. (1970) *The Unresponsive Bystander: Why Doesn't He Help?* Appleton-Century-Crofts, New York.

Lewis H. (1971) *Shame and Guilt in Neuroses.* International University Press, New York.

Lewis M., Stanger C.S. & Sullivan M.W. (1989) Deception in three-year-olds. *Developmental Psychology* 25, 439–443.

Lickona T. (1976) Research on Piaget's theory of moral development. In Lickona T. (ed.) *Moral Development and Behavior*, pp. 219–240. Holt, Rinehart & Winston, New York.

Liu Y-C. & Hay D.F. (1986) *Young children's understanding of the costs of sharing.* Paper presented at the Annual Meeting of the American Psychological Association, Washington, DC.

Londerville S. & Main M. (1981) Security of attachment, compliance, and maternal training methods in the second year of life. *Developmental Psychology* 17, 289–299.

London P. (1970) The rescuers: Motivational hypotheses about Christians who saved Jews from the Nazis. In Macaulay J.R. & Berkowitz L. (eds) *Altruism and Helping Behavior*, pp. 241–250. Academic Press, New York.

Lorenz K. (1943) Die Angeborenen Formen Moglicher Erfahrung (Innate forms of possible experiences). *Zeitschrift für Tierpsychologie* 5, 235–409.

Luria A.R. (1961) *The Role of Speech in the Regulation of Normal and Abnormal Development.* Pergamon, London.

McGhee P (1976) Children's appreciation of humour: A test of the cognitive congruency principle. *Child Development* 47, 420–426.

Masten A.S. (1986) Humour and competence in school-aged children. *Child Development* 57, 461–473.

Matthews K.A., Batson C.D., Horn J. & Rosenman R.H. (1981) 'Principles in his nature which interest him in the fortunes of others . . .': The heritability of empathic concern for others. *Journal of Personality* 49, 237–247.

Maudsley H. (1897) *Responsibility in Mental Disease.* Appleton, New York.

Mazzoni G. (1992) *Two-years old spontaneous lies: A sign of children's theory of mind.* Poster presented at the Fifth European Conference on Developmental Psychology, Seville.

Meichenbaum D.H. & Goodman S. (1971) Training impulsive children to talk to themselves: A means of developing self-control. *Journal of Abnormal Psychology* 77, 115–126.

Messer D.J. & Vietze P.M. (1988) Does mutual influence occur during mother–infant social gaze? *Infant Behavior and Development* 11, 97–110.

Milgram S. (1974) *Obedience to Authority.* Harper & Row, New York.

Miller P.A. & Eisenberg N. (1988) The relation of empathy to aggressive and externalizing/antisocial behavior. *Psychological Bulletin* 103, 324–344.

Mills R.S.L. & Grusec J.E. (1989) Cognitive, affective and behavioral consequences of praising altruism. *Merrill-Palmer Quarterly* 35, 299–326.

Moffitt T. (1994) Adolescent-limited and life-course persistent antisocial behavior: A developmental taxonomy. *Psychological Review* 100, 674–701.

Moore B.S., Underwood B. & Rosenhan D.L. (1973) Affect and altruism. *Developmental Psychology* 8, 99–104.

Moss H. & Robson K. (1968) *The role of protest behavior in the development of mother–infant attachment.* Paper presented at the Annual Meeting of the American Psychological Association, San Francisco.

Murphy L.B. (1937) *Social Behavior and Child Personality: An Exploratory Study of Some Roots of Sympathy.* Columbia University Press, New York.

Murray J. (1973) Television and violence: Implications of the Surgeon General's research program. *American Psychologist* 28, 562–578.

Murray L. (1992) The impact of postnatal depression on infant development. *Journal of Child Psychology and Psychiatry* 33, 543–561.

Nash A. (1988) Ontogeny, phylogeny, and relationships. In Duck S. (ed.) *Handbook of Personal Relationships*, pp. 121–141. Wiley, Chichester.

Nash A. & Hay D.F. (1993) Relationships in infancy as precursors and causes of later relationships and psychopathology. In Hay D.F. & Angold A. (eds) *Precursors and Causes of Later Relationships and Psychopathology*, pp. 199–232. Wiley, Chichester.

Nathanson D.L. (1987) A timetable for shame. In Nathanson D.L. (ed.) *The Many Faces of Shame*, pp. 1–63. Guilford, New York.

Nisan M. (1987) Moral norms and social conventions: A cross-cultural comparison. *Developmental Psychology* **23**, 719–725.

Pearl R. (1985) Children's understanding of others' need for help: Effects of problem explicitness and type. *Child Development* **56**, 735–745.

Pelletier-Stiefel J., Pepler D., Crozier K., Stanhope L., Corter C. & Abramovitch R. (1986) Nurturance in the home: A longitudinal study of sibling interaction. In Foge A. & Melson G.F. (eds) *Origins of Nurturance*, pp. 3–24. Lawrence Erlbaum, Hillsdale, New Jersey.

Peterson L. (1980) Developmental changes in verbal and behavioral sensitivity to cues of social norms of altruism. *Child Development* **51**, 830–838.

Peterson L. & Reaven N. (1984) Limitations imposed by parents on children's altruism. *Merrill-Palmer Quarterly* **30**, 269–286.

Piaget J. (1972) *The Moral Judgement of the Child*. Routledge & Kegan Paul, London.

Power T.G., Hildebrandt K.A. & Fitzgerald H.E. (1982) Adults' responses to infants varying in facial expression and perceived attractiveness. *Infant Behavior and Development* **5**, 33–44.

Prentice N.M. & Fathman R.E. (1975) Joking riddles: A developmental index of children's humour. *Developmental Psychology* **11**, 210–216.

Putallaz M. & Sheppard B.H. (1990) Social status and children's orientations to limited resources. *Child Development* **61**, 2022–2027.

Radke-Yarrow M., Zahn-Waxler C. & Chapman M. (1983) Prosocial dispositions and behavior. In Hetherington E.M. (ed.) *Socialization, Personality and Social Development*, Vol. 4, *Mussen's Handbook of Child Psychology*, 4th edn, pp. 469–545. Wiley, New York.

Rheingold H.L. (1973) Independent behavior of the human infant. In Pick A.D. (ed.) *Minnesota Symposium on Child Psychology*, Vol. 7, pp. 178–203. University of Minneapolis Press, Minneapolis.

Rheingold H.L. (1982) Little children's participation in the work of adults, a nascent prosocial behavior. *Child Development* **53**, 114–125.

Rheingold H.L. & Emery G.N. (1986) The nurturant acts of very young children. In Olweus D., Block J. & Radke-Yarrow M. (eds) *The Development of Antisocial and Prosocial Behavior: Research, Theories, and Issues*, pp. 75–96. Academic Press, New York.

Rheingold H.L., Hay D.F. & West M.J. (1976) Sharing in the second year of life. *Child Development* **47**, 1148–1158.

Ross H.S. & Goldman B.D. (1977) Infants' sociability toward strangers. *Child Development* **48**, 638–642.

Ross H.S., Cheyne A. & Lollis S. (1988) Reciprocity in children's relationships. In Duck S. (ed.) *Handbook of Personal Relationships*, pp. 143–160. Wiley, Chichester.

Rousseau J-J. (1762/1979) *Emile or On Education* (translated by A. Bloom). Basic Books, New York.

Rubin K.H. & Schneider F.W. (1973) The relationship between moral judgment, egocentrism and altruistic behavior. *Child Development* **44**, 661–665.

Rushton J.P., Fulker D.W., Neale M.C., Nias D.K.B. & Eysenck H.J. (1986) Altruism and aggression: The heritability of individual differences. *Journal of Personality and Social Psychology* **50**, 1192–1198.

Schneider-Rosen K. & Wenz-Gross M. (1990) Patterns of compliance from eighteen to thirty months of age. *Child Development* **61**, 104–112.

Sears R.R., Maccoby E.E. & Levin H. (1957) *Patterns of Child Rearing*. Row, Peterson, Evanston, Illinois.

Sears R.R., Rau L. & Alpert R. (1965) *Identification and Child Rearing*. Stanford University Press, Stanford, California.

Shantz C.U. (1987) Conflicts between children. *Child Development* **58**, 283–305.

Sheather K. (1992) *Children's perceptions about social conflict: A developmental account*. Unpublished master's thesis, Institute of Education, University of London.

Sigman M.D. & Mundy P. (1993) Infant precursors of childhood intellectual and verbal abilities. In Hay D.F. & Angold A. (eds) *Precursors and Causes in Development and Psychopathology*, pp. 123–144. Wiley, Chichester.

Simner M.L. (1971) Newborn's response to the cry of another infant. *Developmental Psychology* **5**, 136–150.

Simpson E.L. (1974) Moral development research: A case of scientific cultural bias. *Human Development* **17**, 81–106.

Smetana J.G. (1981) Preschool children's conceptions of moral and social rules. *Child Development* **52**, 1333–1336.

Smetana J.G. (1985) Preschool children's conceptions of transgressions: Effects of varying moral and conventional domain-related attributes. *Developmental Psychology* **21**, 18–29.

Smetana J.G., Killen M. & Turiel E. (1991) Children's reasoning about interpersonal and moral conflicts. *Child Development* **62**, 629–644.

Snarey J.R., Reimer J. & Kohlberg L. (1985) Development of social–moral reasoning among kibbutz adolescents: A longitudinal cross-cultural study. *Developmental Psychology* **21**, 3–17.

Sprafkin J.H., Liebert R.M. & Poulos R.W. (1975) Effects of a prosocial televised example on children's helping. *Journal of Experimental Child Psychology* **20**, 119–126.

Stanhope L., Bell R.Q. & Parker-Cohen N.Y. (1987) Temperament and helping behaviour in preschool children. *Developmental Psychology* **23**(3), 347–353.

Staub E. (1978) *Positive Social Behavior and Morality*, Vol. 1, *Social and Personal Influences*. Academic Press, London.

Staub E. (1979) *Positive Social Behavior and Morality*, Vol. 2, *Socialization and Development*. Academic Press, London.

Stein A.H. & Friedrich L.K. (1972) Television content and young children's behavior. In Murray J.P., Rubenstein E.A. & Comstock G.A. (eds) *Television and Social Behavior*, Vol. 2: *Television and Social Learning*. US Government Printing Office, Washington, DC.

Stenberg C. & Campos J.J. (1983) The facial expression of anger in seven-month-old infants. *Child Development* **54**, 178–184.

Stern W. (1924) *The Psychology of Early Childhood up to the Sixth Year of Age*, 3rd edn. Holt, New York.

Steuer F.B., Applefield J.M. & Smith R. (1971) Televised aggression and the interpersonal aggression of preschool children. *Journal of Experimental Child Psychology* **11**, 442–447.

Stevenson J. (1992) Born nice, turned nasty: The origins of individual differences in sociability and prosocial and antisocial behavior.

Stewart R.B. & Marvin R.S. (1984) Sibling relations: The role of conceptual perspective-taking in the ontogeny of sibling caregiving. *Child Development* **55**, 1322–1332.

Sugarman S. (1987) *Piaget's Construction of the Child's Reality*. Cambridge University Press, Cambridge.

Sullivan E.V. (1970) Moral development. In Ausubel A.P. & Sullivan E.V. (eds) *Theory and Problems of Child Development*, pp. 461–502. Grune & Stratton, New York.

Tangney J.P. (1990) Assessing individual differences in proneness to shame and guilt: Development of the self-conscious affect and attribution inventory. *Journal of Personality and Social Psychology* **59**, 102–111.

Thoma S.J., Rest J.R. & Davison M.L. (1991) Describing and testing a moderator of the moral judgment and action rule. *Journal of Personality and Social Psychology* **61**, 659–669.

Thomas A., Chess S. & Birch H. (1968) *Temperament and Behavior Disorders in Children*. New York University Press, New York.

Thompson R.A. & Hoffman M. (1980) Empathy and the development of guilt in children. *Developmental Psychology* **16**, 155–156.

Thomson J.A.K. (1955) *The Ethics of Aristotle*. Penguin, London.

Tietjen A.M. (1986) Prosocial reasoning among children and adults in a Papua New Guinea society. *Developmental Psychology* **22**, 861–868.

Trivers R.L. (1971) The evolution of reciprocal altruism. *Quarterly Review of Biology* **46**, 35–57.

Underwood B., Froming W.J. & Moore B.S. (1977) Mood, attention, altruism: A search for moderating variables. *Developmental Psychology* **13**, 541–542.

Vaughan B.E., Kopp C.B. & Krakow J.B. (1984) The emergence and consolidation of self-control from eighteen to thirty months of age: Normative trends and individual differences. *Child Development* **55**, 990–1004.

Vuchinich S., Emery R.E. & Cassidy J. (1988) Family members as third parties in dyadic family conflict: Strategies, alliances, and outcomes. *Child Development* **59**, 1293–1302.

Vygotsky L. (1962) *Language and Thought*. MIT Press, Cambridge, Massachusetts.

Walker L.J. & Taylor J.H. (1991) Family interactions and the development of moral reasoning. *Child Development* **62**, 264–283.

Waters E., Hay D. & Richters J. (1986) Infant-parent attachment and the origins of prosocial and antisocial behavior. In Olweus D., Block J. & Radke-Yarrow M. (eds) *Development of Antisocial and Prosocial Behavior: Research, Theories, and Issues*, pp. 97–125. Academic Press, London.

Weiner B. (1985) An attributional theory of achievement motivation and emotion. *Psychological Review* **92**, 548–573.

Whiting B.B. (1983) The genesis of prosocial behavior. In Bridgeman D. (ed.) *The Nature of Prosocial Development: Interdisciplinary Theories and Strategies*, pp. 221–242. Academic Press, London.

Wilson C.C., Piazza C.C. & Nagle R.J. (1990) Investigation of the effect of consistent and inconsistent behavioral example upon children's emotional behaviors. *Journal of Genetic Psychology* **151**, 361–376.

Wimmer H., Gruber S. & Perner J. (1985) Moral intuition and the denotation and connotation of 'to lie'. *Developmental Psychology* **21**, 993–995.

Zahn-Waxler C., Cole P. & Barrett K.C. (1991) Guilt and empathy: Sex differences and implications for the development of depression. In Dodge K. & Garber J. (eds) *Emotion Regulation and Dysregulation*, pp. 243–272. Cambridge University Press, Cambridge.

Zahn-Waxler C., Kochanska G., Krupnick J. & McKnew D. (1990) Patterns of guilt in children of depressed and well mothers. *Developmental Psychology* **26**, 51–59.

Zahn-Waxler C., Radke-Yarrow M. & King R. (1979) Child-rearing and children's prosocial initiations toward victims of distress. *Child Development* **50**, 319–330.

Zahn-Waxler C., Robinson J. & Emde R. (1992) The development of empathy in twins. *Development Psychology* **28**, 1038–1047.

Zarbatany L., Hartmann D.P. & Gelfand D.M. (1985) Why does children's generosity increase with age: Susceptibility to experimenter influence or altruism? *Child Development* **56**, 746–756.

15: Developmental Perspective on Gender Differences and Similarities

ROBERT B. CAIRNS AND ALEXANDRA B. KROLL

On the whole ... girls have stood better than boys in measures of general intelligence. So far as I know, no one has drawn the conclusion that girls have greater native ability than boys. One is tempted to indulge in idle speculation as to whether this admirable restraint from hasty generalization would have been equally marked had the sex findings been reversed! (Wooley, 1914, p. 365)

A direct line of influence can be drawn between Helen Wooley's review, 'The psychology of sex' (1914) and Maccoby & Jacklin's (1974) volume *The Psychology of Sex Differences*. The early review demonstrated that sex-related differences could be systematically investigated by psychological methods; the later volume provided definitive structure for a modern field of scientific study. Thanks to Wooley and her intellectual heirs, the questions that gender differences and similarities pose for psychological theory and method can no longer be dismissed through 'flagrant personal bias' or confounded with 'sentimental rot' (Wooley, 1910, p. 340).

No brief chapter can do justice to the scholarship on sex-related differences in behaviour and cognition which is now available. To attempt to do so would compromise the quality of the science and the thoughtfulness of its practitioners. Besides, it is unnecessary. Expert reviews of specific areas have recently appeared that confirm, revise and extend the conclusions of the *Psychology of Sex Differences* (Maccoby & Jacklin, 1974). These reviews should be consulted directly, along with some of the key primary empirical reports.*

This chapter has a single goal, albeit an ambitious one: to illustrate how a dynamic view of development can clarify some unresolved issues that have recurred in the study of gender. This limited goal invites responsible selection in our coverage of ideas and findings. Accordingly, the first half of the chapter provides a theoretical overview of developmental science and some implications for the study of sex-related differences. It addresses, among other things, the dynamics of gender continuity and change, critical periods of gender identity and the periods of greatest similarity and difference. The second half is a review of research in selected areas; namely, cognition, social behaviours, mortality and morbidity, and sensorimotor performance. Unfortunately few empirical investigations of gender have been conducted within a systematic developmental framework (e.g. longitudinal research designs, developmentally sensitive measures, unbiased with respect to emergent gender and social differences). It is nonetheless informative to view recent studies of sex-related differences from the perspective provided by developmental science.

DEVELOPMENT AND GENDER

Developmental science refers to a new theoretical synthesis across disciplines that has evolved over the past two decades to guide research in behaviour and biology. The synthesis is a perspective on individual functioning that emphasizes the dynamic interplay among processes that operate across time frames, levels of analysis, and contexts (Cairns

---

* See, for example, Block, 1976, 1983; Frodi *et al.*, 1977; Berman, 1980; Jacklin, 1981; Denno, 1982; Hines, 1982; Taylor & Hall, 1982; Eisenberg & Lennon, 1983; Deaux, 1984; Caplan *et al.*, 1985; Thomas & French, 1985; Eagly & Steffen, 1986; Signorella & Jamison, 1986; Feingold, 1988; Hyde & Linn, 1988; Strickland, 1988; Hyde *et al.*, 1990a; Maccoby, 1990; Cohn, 1991; Lytton & Romney, 1991; Roberts, 1991.

et al., in press). On this view, development is not only about children. Development encompasses the entire manifold of the life-cycle, from conception to death, and into the next generation. Four emphases of the developmental perspective relevant for the study of sex-related differences are: (i) personal integration; (ii) time-relativity of sociobehavioural mechanisms; (iii) relevance and irrelevance of biology; and (iv) universality of developmental processes.

Personal integration

The natural unit for developmental study is the ontogeny of the person, not the ontogeny of variables. This means that the behavioural, emotional and cognitive characteristics of persons are integrated over development, and they should not be divorced in analysis. This 'holistic' proposition — although consistent with much of what has been learned about the correlated nature of behavioural adaptation — does not permit business as usual in the study of sex-related differences. Specifically, it implies that it would be hazardous to segment males and females into distributions of psychological or biological variables. Even if single characteristics of males and females can be reliably identified — such as verbal ability, mathematics proficiency, aggression, empathy — a problem remains to determine how they are integrated in adaptation. Persons adapt as integrated beings, regardless of how they may be categorized on economic, racial or sexual dimensions.

The holistic proposition is as much a methodological proposition as it is a theoretical one. It was proposed by Binet and Henri (1895) to solve the deadlock that had been encountered by the use of elementaristic tests of sensation, perception, and attention in order to construct mental tests. In contrast with the reductionistic assumption, Binet and Henri (1895) argued that the most efficient way to measure mental abilities in children would be to contrast them on meaningful tasks of everyday life. When this principle is applied to the study of gender similarities and differences, it does not mean that the hard-won gains of the field in the study of separate variables should be ignored. Rather, it indicates that the usual analyses are incomplete and possibly misleading if they fail to address the configuration of correlated characteristics and the inherent integration of the person.

Time, timing and gender development

Psychological processes may operate differentially across ontogeny. For example, the effects of gender social learning mechanisms that facilitate short-term adaptations may be overwhelmed by slower-acting maturational processes or cultural forces that function over the long term. Developmental considerations bring attention to the ways that these processes become coordinated and integrated.

Tanner (1962) distinguished the sexual monomorphism of childhood and the sexual dimorphism of adolescence. This biological shift is loosely correlated with a shift in social role and social expectations for the maturing girl or boy (Eagly, 1983; Magnusson, 1988). Moreover, sexual differentiation is not limited to a single phase of adolescent development; rather, there is a continuing interplay between biological and behavioural functions over the life-course. Beyond the initial sexual differentiation in embryogenesis and sexual dimorphism in adolescence, there is the onset of child-bearing and child-rearing in adulthood, and the cessation of reproductive capabilities in later maturity. There is, at each stage, a behavioural–biological coordination that may be anticipated in females by societal roles, social network norms and individual expectations. Although the biophysical changes in males are less abrupt, the social role, social network and individual expectations may be even more restrictive and constraining for boys and men. The several stages of biobehaviour differentiation are correlated with social roles and expectations, and together they can promote, or diminish, gender differences throughout the life-cycle.

All this is to say that organismic and contextual factors linked to gender differences may overwhelm the early social learning of childhood. If this is the case, it should not be surprising to find that carefully scripted similarities between males and females in attitudes and behaviours in preschool are not necessarily translated into gender similarities in the teenage years or later adulthood. Individual-difference continuity is not guaranteed in development because novelties arise from within and without (see Chapter 1). Taken together, emergent biological constraints and social role expectations can (i) revise or erode prior learning experiences; and (ii) create the conditions for new types of behaviour organization. At any developmental stage, these dual processes can serve to accentuate or diminish the differences between cultures, races or genders.

Developmental considerations can help identify why there is an early appearance of sex-related differences even in the absence of psychobiological or neurobiological support. In this regard, some gender differences of early childhood in behaviour may anticipate pubertal and adult differences in functioning. For instance, the robust sex-related differences in early childhood play and social preferences cannot be explained away in terms of psychobiological variables (e.g. morphology, coordination, hormonal status) because the similarities of young girls and young boys on these characteristics outweigh their differences (Tanner, 1962; Thomas & French, 1985). Play preferences and differential associations may be explained, however, in terms of the materials and opportunities that adults and peers provide them. Once the young child is in a relationship, a positive feedback process may be created so that the activities, settings and companions affect future choices, preferences and behaviours (Rheingold & Cook, 1975; Calder *et al.*, 1989; Maccoby, 1990).

Two other matters of developmental timing deserve mention; namely, the assumption of developmental primacy and the possible role of pubertal timing in the social development of girls. In brief, the primacy assumption is the view that early experience necessarily has higher priority than later experience in explaining behavioural development. This proposition is embedded in diverse theoretical models. It is sometimes erroneously identified as a fundamental proposition of the developmental perspective. There are good reasons to suspect that this proposition on the special status of early experience is sharply limited in its application to sex-related differences.

Animal behaviour research has helped clarify the limits of the primacy assumption for sexual development in vertebrates. For some species, experience in adulthood overrides early developmental exposure in determining sexual role. In this regard, coral reef fish constitute an interesting disconfirmation of the primacy hypothesis. Mature sexual

structure and function is determined in this species by social experience at maturity rather than biological factors in early ontogeny. When a male dies, leaves or is removed from the colony, a dominant adult female in the group undergoes sex transformation (Cairns, 1979; Shapiro, 1981; Gottlieb, 1991).

Yet coral reef fish are scarcely representative of sexual development in mammals. Sexual dimorphism — including the fine architecture of the brain as well as the form and function of gonadal structures — is significantly regulated in mammals by physiological events in embryogenesis, not by social experiences at maturity (Hines, 1982). In addition, the gonadoducts, once established in the prenatal period, stubbornly resist reorganization and change in mammals. Perhaps most important, sexual development is not a unitary thing. Some features of the sexual adaptation of humans, such as gonadal structure and function, resist the effects of variations in experience at puberty. Other aspects of sexual behaviour, such as preferred sexual activities and partners, may be strongly influenced in the pubertal years. Different features of sexuality call for different trajectories, and different formulations of the sensitive periods and bidirectionality (Cairns, 1991).

Consider individual differences in the timing of sexual–biophysical development at puberty.* In the 20-year longitudinal investigation of 1300 Swedish children, Stattin and Magnusson (1990; also Magnusson *et al.*, 1985) reported that girls who reached menarche very early (≤11 years of age) tended to show multiple signs of behavioural deviancy. Deviance at 13 years of age included alcohol consumption, more cheating in school, greater amounts of sexual activity and the adoption of antisocial norms among the early maturing girls. By age 15, most differences had diminished. But a follow-up in adulthood showed that some effects associated with early maturation still persisted. The very early maturing girls had married earlier, had

---

* This focus points to a curious gap in the theoretical and empirical literature. If the rate of sexual transition is deemed important for personality organization and behaviour, why has not parallel attention been given to other transitions, such as the early or late onset of menopause?

more children, and had less advanced education relative to average or late maturing girls.

Following a developmental model, Magnusson (1988) reasoned that the effects may be mediated by social interchanges that were provoked and supported by the early maturation. The girls affiliated more with older peers and adopted developmentally advanced behaviours and values. The upshot was that their sexual and social behaviours deviated, for a 2-year period, from age-appropriate standards. Support was obtained in the longitudinal data set for this maturation−affiliation−behaviour interpretation (Magnusson, 1988; Stattin & Magnusson, 1990). Consistent with the hypothesis, this effect was observed only among early maturing girls who had affiliated in early adolescence with older males who were out of school and working.

The broader point is that it is not merely a matter of the rate of onset of sexual maturity that accounts for the prediction of deviance in adolescence. On the contrary, a key mediational variable appears to be social affiliations that were promoted by the biological changes. When other girls reached a similar state of sexual maturity, there was no difference in female deviance as a function of rate of maturation. The behavioural differences had been eliminated, in part, by similarities in levels of sexual maturation that have been mediated by similarities in social interchange. Nor is it the case that early biological maturation is the only route that leads to differential association and deviance. It merely provides a biasing condition.

Essential features of these findings have been replicated in other settings and with other samples. For instance, Caspi and Moffitt (1993) found the same early maturation−deviance phenomenon in the longitudinal study of a sample of New Zealand girls. The effect was obtained, however, only if the girls were enrolled in a coeducational school. Presumably the opportunities for deviance by differential association were greater in the coeducational setting than in all-girl schools.

It is less clear how very early maturation is linked to deviance among girls in North American schools. Cairns and Cairns (1994) failed to find much support for the anticipated linkage of

early maturation → deviant social network → deviant behaviour

Why the partial failure to replicate across studies and across national boundaries? One problem is that there may be greater heterogeneity in American schools than either Sweden or New Zealand (in terms of race, socioeconomic status and living circumstances), and these factors could overwhelm the subtle effects of maturational rate. Such factors could account for the strong continuity between deviance in preadolescence and deviance in adolescence found among girls in American society (Cairns & Cairns, 1994). Even in USA samples, girls who mature early tend to hang around with other girls who have also matured very early (Cairns & Cairns, 1994). But this propensity for differential affiliation on the basis of maturational status is not necessarily translated into promiscuous sex and deviant behaviour.

Moreover, there are other psychobiological factors beyond menarcheal onset in the adolescence of American girls that can be highly relevant for the social adaptation and deviance. Consider, for example, physical attractiveness (see Chapter 4). Cairns and Cairns (1994) found in their longitudinal study of 695 persons from childhood to adulthood that physical attractiveness was an important antecedent of social and school success, particularly in girls. Girls judged to be unattractive by others were less popular in middle school, received lower grades, and, 5 years later, they were also more likely to drop out of school and become teenage mothers (Cairns & Cairns, 1994; see also Elder, 1974). There is an intriguing hint in some research that very early pubertal onset is marginally associated with unattractiveness in girls (Simmons & Blyth, 1987). It also appears that attractiveness is less important for adolescent males than females (Cairns & Cairns, 1994).

These findings on the relativity of the effects of psychobiological factors stimulate further questions on the relationship between psychobiological timing, physical attractiveness, the nature of social peer influences in early adolescence, and how these effects may be altered over time by forces from within and without. For example, it may be speculated that the emergence of anorexia as a major problem for adolescent females should be linked to the identification of feminine attractiveness with slenderness in the past two decades (Brumberg, 1988). If that is the case, the incidence of the disorder might be expected to decline if Western standards of female attractiveness swing back in the early twenty-first century to the buxom ideal of the mid-twentieth century.

The relativity of biology and behaviour

The concept of development implies a 'top—down' or holistic approach to behavioural study in that behaviour is considered to be a leading edge for biological organization and change. More broadly, it is expected that in normal development there should be a bidirectionality in function and structure at every stage of ontogeny. This perspective presupposes an intimate relation between behaviour and biology at every developmental stage. Gender development offers a special opportunity for the study of the behaviour—biology processes. Developmental markers of sexual onset (e.g. sexual dimorphism, menarche, pregnancy, menopause) promote investigation of the linkages between the onset of these biological landmarks and changes in gender behaviours and gender roles.*

Gender differences across species in behaviour and function are immediately linked to the evolutionary invention of sexual transmission as a means of reproduction (Hamilton, 1964; Cairns, 1979). Mammals must produce, in each generation, some individuals whose structures, behaviours, and

---

* In this chapter, *gender* refers to those psychological characteristics, behaviours, attitudes and beliefs believed to be differentially associated with females or males. *Sex* refers to the biosocial classification of the individual as female or male. Sex can be judged by the individuals themselves, by other persons, or by objective biological measures. Sexual classification of an individual by different sources are ordinarily convergent most of the time. But convergence is not inevitable, and the sex assigned to a person can change during the course of ontogeny (Money & Ehrhardt, 1972). On this score, the study of development has attracted special attention when the biological classification of sex is ambiguous or when it differs from self and social classification of gender. The usual state of affairs — where sex and gender development are convergent and consonant over ontogeny — may prove to be as fully complex as the curious occasions where there is divergence and dissonance. Both present significant puzzles for developmental science, and both provide opportunities for understanding how behaviour and biology are dynamically organized over time.

capabilities will permit sexual synchronization with another, sexually complementary, member of the species. In addition, mammals require individuals who are responsible for the survival and care of embryonic and neonatal organisms. If biological differences in structure and function were the dominant factors in mammalian gender development, it would follow that sex differences should be observed most strongly in behaviours that concern sexual reproduction, sexual dimorphism and infant care. Gender differences should arise at the point in ontogeny that these behaviour patterns emerge.

Two expectations follow. First, gender differences should not be static over the lifespan, but should wax and wane in relevance at the times in ontogeny that those functions are most relevant. Second, the biggest gender differences between males and females should be in those characteristics that are most closely linked to biological functions at the periods in ontogeny when those functions are activated. Hence the major gender differences between mammalian males and females should be observed at puberty and young adulthood, and they should involve characteristics that are linked to reproductive and care-taking functions.

But in human behaviour, biological influences rarely fix differences among individuals or across societies. One of the special features of behavioural adaptation is its joint regulation by biological constraints within the person and environmental constraints outside the person. Behaviour constitutes the interface between these two systems. In contrast with actions that are directly involved in sexual reproduction, gender behaviours are not likely to be fixed either by early experience or by genes. Even reproductive acts are highly plastic in human beings in terms of what gives rise to sexual arousal, what are preferred sexual objects, and what are desirable forms of sexual expression. The research task for systematic psychobiological studies of human development is to clarify how biological, contextual and cultural contributions collaborate and become balanced in ontogeny. In the case of gender, this balance seems to be dynamic and open to recalibration by virtue of temporal changes in the society and in the biosocial state of the individual. Understanding the interplay between such long-term and short-term processes is the stuff of a developmental analysis.

Universality of development

We have proposed elsewhere that a key for understanding gender differences lies in the solution of the problem of behavioural and social dispositions that develop in any child, whether male or female (Cairns, 1979). This assumption presupposes that developmental processes underlying behaviour are basic to human adaptation. Gender variations, somewhat like cultural variations, represent the fine-tuning of an enormously complex system. And it seems likely that both gender and cultural adaptations benefit from a modest organismic bias.

This leads to a counter intuitive proposition on parent—child effects. Basic psychological dimensions of human socialization may be too fundamental to be involved differentially for girls and boys. That is, the reason that few gender differences have been found in such socialization dimensions as social reciprocity, attachment, warmth and nurturance may mean these domains are basic for normal development in all human beings, both females and males.

Perhaps this is why there has been only a meagre harvest where studies have been conducted to identify sex-related differences in parental socialization. In an exhaustive review of the recent literature on socialization, Lytton and Romney (1991) concluded:

> The present meta-analysis has demonstrated a virtual absence of sex-distinctive parental socialization pressures, except in one area, at least as far as these have been captured by existing measures and reported in English-language publications. We realize that for many social scientists such findings are difficult to accept ... We believe that the finding of very few differences in parental treatment of boys and girls represents the best evidence we have on the topic at this time. (pp. 288—289)

This conclusion, although counter to broadly accepted theoretical models, does not stand alone. It is consistent with a reasonably large body of information that has been obtained over the past quarter century in this society and elsewhere (Sears *et al.*, 1957; Whiting & Edwards, 1973; Maccoby & Jacklin, 1974; Feldman & Nash, 1979; Eisenberg *et al.*, 1985; Lytton & Romney, 1991). There is only modest evidence to support the pervasive belief in behavioural science that parents are the primary shapers of their offspring's behaviour throughout childhood and adolescence, including gender behaviours. This is not to say that parents are without effect. On the contrary, Lytton and Romney (1991) reported that specific encouragement of sex-typed activities is the one area where there are differences in sex-related socialization in North American countries. In other Western countries, physical punishment occurs more often with boys than girls. All this is to say that differences in parental socialization are considerably more specific to sex role and sexual behaviour than has been commonly accepted.

It should be noted that these findings on socialization do not necessarily mean that gender differences are inherent. The problem may lie in a too narrow view of developmental influence rather than in the phenomena of development. In this regard, parental effects may be both direct (as in the socialization paradigm) or indirect (as agents who structure and mediate contextual influences). Indirect effects may be reflected in multiple ways, including the opportunities they provide for social and non-social engagement (e.g. the toys they buy), the attitudes they endorse and the schools they send their children to. But it may be inappropriate to assume that the parents have the sole or even primary responsibility for producing and maintaining gender differences. Beyond parents and familial factors, there are correlated factors in the child's life — from within and without — which lead to effective adaptation.

In this regard, peers and social networks seem to exercise powerful and continuing effects in gender role emergence and maintenance (Strayer & Noel, 1986; Cairns *et al.*, 1989a; Maccoby, 1990). Similarly, the choices of influence are themselves bidirectional, in that social agents invite participation as much as the individual seeks to join. That social invitation, as Magnusson (1988) has observed, may reflect very early maturation. 'Correlated constraints' occur because the characteristics of the individual, the family and the peers typically collaborate rather than compete. The concept of correlated constraints may also clarify why some simple 'turning points' can have a powerful effect on behaviour. For example, a single gift from an adolescent's parent — whether it be a violin, a rifle or a computer — can stimulate new interests and open new opportunities for affiliations and relationships. It also provides information about parental expectations and parental support, and can contribute to an extension or revision of the adolescent's concept of her or his gender role.

Finally, there are good reasons to focus upon gender development beyond the obvious need to clarify an important theoretical and social issue. Gender development constitutes a recurrent natural experiment in the linkages between biology and behaviour. In this regard, Susman and co-workers have conducted an elegant series of studies to identify how individual differences in endocrine status are linked to gender differences in aggressive and emotional behaviour (Susman *et al.*, 1985, 1987). Within-sex variations in gender behaviours and attitudes may, in addition, clarify the mechanisms by which these differences arise despite a common biological background.

GENDER COMPARISONS IN FOUR DOMAINS

Comparisons of gender similarity and difference cover virtually all aspects of human behaviours, attitudes and values. In the present overview, we have had to be selective. Our two-fold criterion has been: (i) the presumed importance of the phenomenon for gender identification and gender difference; and (ii) the extent to which longitudinal information is available on the emergence of the phenomenon. The domains selected are cognition and intelligence, social behaviours, morbidity and mortality, and sensorimotor abilities (see Chapter 17 for a discussion of sex differences in affective features; Earls, 1987 for sex differences in psychiatric disorders; and Rutter and Rutter, 1993 for mention of sex differences in a wide range of features across the lifespan).

Cognition, intelligence and ability

Are boys and men smarter than girls and women? Or do they merely think they are? Do ability differences favour females, and are girls and women too modest about their achievements? One of the more

controversial issues of gender and psychology concerns the possible linkages between intelligence and sex. Maccoby and Jacklin (1974) in their review of the literature concluded that there was a slight gender difference favouring girls in verbal ability and a somewhat larger difference favouring boys in quantitative and spatial cognitive abilities. These conclusions, because of their social implications, have formed the basis for one of the most carefully researched and hotly disputed areas of gender study.

Verbal ability

Maccoby and Jacklin (1974) cited 85 studies reporting verbal superiority in females. At least some follow-up work was consistent with that conclusion. For example, Denno (1982) and Halpern (1986) concluded that females have better verbal abilities than males and that a small superior performance in childhood grows throughout middle childhood before stabilizing in early adolescence. Systematic meta-analyses of this issue have yielded a different picture (Feingold, 1988; Hyde & Linn, 1988). Hyde and Linn (1988) compared the results of 165 studies and concluded that the slight female superiority was so insignificant that gender differences in verbal ability, if once common, no longer exist. In this regard, verbal ability, spatial ability and mathematics performance have seen recent declines in gender difference (Rosenthal & Rubin, 1982; Linn & Petersen, 1985; Signorella & Jamison, 1986; Roberts, 1991). In another careful meta-analysis, Feingold (1988) concluded that gender differences in verbal and mathematical achievement have diminished since 1960. The magnitude of gender differences in verbal cognitive abilities varied inversely with the year of the published study with more recent studies reporting smaller and smaller female advantages. Even when an effect was identified, it appeared to be modest and too small to be of practical importance. However, there is a sex difference in marked language delay, which is more frequent in boys. Similarly, although the sex difference in mean reading skills is very small, the proportion of boys with severe specific reading difficulties is much higher than that of girls (Rutter *et al.*, 1970).

If the data are now so uniform, why has the

myth of the verbal superiority of girls continued to persist? There are a couple of possible answers. One involves gender stereotypes and the belief systems in a society. In a cross-national investigation across three societies (Japanese, Chinese and American) Lummis and Stevenson (1990) found that the parents of girls and also boys believed that the girls were superior in verbal abilities. The children themselves shared that belief. There were, however, precious few differences in verbal achievement and/or verbal ability in any of the three societies.

The second possibility is provocative. Perhaps the common sense view that females have greater verbal skills is *not* a myth. The problem may be that the research has focused on cognitive skills rather than social skills. Differences may be present, but they cannot be identified by tests of verbal intelligence or verbal achievement (i.e. reading, vocabulary). In this regard, Maccoby and Jacklin (1974) observed that girls are advanced compared with boys on several developmental measures of verbal communication. Gender differences may lie in social functioning rather than cognitive functions. Language can be used to solve the multiple interpersonal problems of everyday life. In this regard, adolescent girls are more likely than boys to employ verbal strategies to produce and to resolve interpersonal conflicts (Austin *et al.*, 1987; Cairns *et al.*, 1989a).

Mathematics

In 1981, Anastasi noted that gender differences in computation do not appear until late elementary school. Similarly, Maccoby and Jacklin (1974) concluded that boys excel in mathematical ability and noted that these gender differences do not appear until 12–13 years of age. More recently, Halpern (1986) concluded that reliable differences favouring boys emerge between 13 and 16 years of age, particularly in complex problem-solving. In mathematical computations of less complexity, girls tend to show superior performance.

This finding of male mathematical superiority also has been challenged by meta-analyses over the past decade. Hyde *et al.* (1990a) examined 100 studies and concluded that in general population samples females outperformed males in some math-

ematical areas. For example, girls showed a slight superiority in computation during elementary school and middle school. Gender differences favouring males appeared in high school and increased in college, with larger differences being reported in highly selective samples of high achievers (Hyde *et al.*, 1990a).

Hyde *et al.* (1990b) has proposed that gender differences that favour males appear to be a function of the selectivity of the sample rather than a function of age. In this regard, Meece *et al.* (1982) noted that fewer females than males enrol in advanced high school and college mathematics courses. Accordingly there is a slight female superiority in mathematics in the general population but male superiority among college and graduate students. As in the case of verbal performance, recent studies of mathematical performance tend to show smaller gender differences than earlier studies.

The differences are not only relative to time, they are relative to place. The direction and magnitude of gender differences in mathematics has been explored in several cross-cultural analyses. Stevenson *et al.* (1985) examined individual differences in cognitive abilities across three cultures. Few significant sex differences were noted among 60 comparisons. Of special interest is the Hyde *et al.* (1990a) finding that there is no gender difference in mathematical performance for ethnic groups other than white Americans.

Despite these modest or null gender differences in cognitive performance, much effort has been expended in investigations that have been designed to explain the differences. Accordingly, some investigators have proposed that gender differences in mathematical achievement reflect sex typing and differential parental socialization (Maccoby & Jacklin, 1974; Block, 1976, 1983). This interpretation was challenged by Raymond and Benbow (1986) who reported that parental support for academic success did not vary as a function of the child's gender. It has also been assumed that girls view mathematics as a male domain and this view deters them from higher level maths courses and maths related careers. The results of a meta-analysis by Hyde *et al.* (1990b), however, indicated that males rather than females are likely to hold this stereotype of maths as male. More broadly, Meece *et al.* (1982) have argued that the differential effects of socialization are small and less likely to create differences than to solidify them (p. 328).

One of the findings in the study of verbal and mathematical performance calls for special comment. When gender differences are measured using grade point averages in mathematics in junior and senior high school, they virtually always favour girls. It has been broadly reported that girls outperform boys in all academic domains from grade school through university settings, despite their marginally poorer performances on standardized tests (Sabers *et al.*, 1987). At the university level, differences in grades do not exist or they favour girls (Benbow & Stanley, 1983; Kimball, 1989).

In summary, there have been few longitudinal studies designed to trace difference in cognitive performance over the lifespan. Cross-sectional work is nonetheless informative. The verbal superiority demonstrated by females in early childhood diminishes or disappears with age, time and place. Of special interest are the temporal changes. American females and males in the 1980s compared to their counterparts in the 1960s seemed to be virtually identical on measures of verbal and quantitative intelligence. Societal changes over this period — in opportunities, in education, in stereotypes — apparently have contributed to modify or cancel out gender differences in verbal and maths performance. There is one important exception. In assessments of advanced mathematics and in highly select samples, American males tend to show higher levels of performance than females (Benbow & Stanley, 1983; Feingold, 1988). The extent to which this residual difference at the upper end of the curve may be accounted for in terms of opportunities, motivation or aspiration remains to be determined.

Spatial skills

Maccoby and Jacklin (1974) concluded that males are superior to females in their ability to think about space and to use spatial concepts. This generalization has been left up in the air by many reviewers, and shot down by others. On the one hand, the meta-analysis of 172 studies by Linn and Petersen (1985) found effects that were small and, in most studies, the gender differences were not significant. The differences depended upon which subtype of spatial skill was explored. One

category, spatial perception, involves tasks such as identification of a horizontal water line in a tilted bottle. Where differences have been reported, they (i) favour males; and (ii) appear around age 7. Differences between males and females were larger for adults over 18 (Linn & Petersen, 1985). A second category of spatial ability — mental rotation — demonstrates significant male superiority as soon as the characteristic can be reliably measured (Maccoby & Jacklin, 1974; Block & Block, 1980). Linn and Petersen (1985) hypothesized that female slowness in answering mental rotation questions (30% slower than males) reflects caution rather than lack of ability. This is partially supported by Willis and Schaie (1988) who assessed spatial abilities in old age. Following training on mental rotation, there was no difference in spatial ability performance. Women made significantly greater gains as the result of training than men (Willis & Schaie, 1988).

Much of the controversy surrounding discussions of gender differences in spatial relations revolves around the nature of the differences, the magnitude of the differences, and the age at which the differences occur. Caplan *et al.* (1985) have catalogued several of the methodological shortcomings of the studies that have been conducted. Small sample size, lack of random sampling, inconsistency of findings and lack of consensus regarding definitions undermine much of the work. From their meta-analysis, they concluded that the magnitude of sex differences is quite modest, accounting for between 1 and 5% of the population variance depending on what is tested. Often samples were drawn from only students in white middle-class schools and from high ability populations. In addition, many studies relied on cross-sectional rather than longitudinal designs, thereby biasing comparisons across age spans (Denno, 1982; Caplan *et al.*, 1985). At least one team of reviewers indicated that 'the conclusion that males are superior is unwarranted' (Caplan *et al.*, 1985, p. 786).

That conclusion was immediately contested (Burnett, 1986; Eliot, 1986; Halpern, 1986; Hiscock, 1986; Sanders *et al.*, 1986). A significant number of researchers felt that the meta-analysis was misleading and the conclusion unwarranted. This points to one of the problems of the use of meta-analysis; namely, equal weight is given to superb and carefully conducted investigations, studies that are less meritorious, and investigations that are rather easy to conduct and, hence, multiplied in their influence. As Lytton and Romney (1991, p. 289) astutely observed, 'the reviewer cannot remedy the flaws and limitations of the primary literature, and if all the primary studies are weak, the meta-analysis will be built on sand'.

The empirical foundation for conclusions about development of sex differences in spatial abilities has recently become broadened. The year following the publication of the Caplan *et al.* (1985) meta-analysis, Johnson and Meade (1987) published a landmark investigation for the area. In this work, 1875 public school students (grades kindergarten through 12 and ages 6–18) were assessed with a battery of seven spatial ability tests. The findings indicated conclusively that there was a male advantage in spatial performance by age 10, and that the magnitude of the advantage remained constant through age 18. Even when possible problems in design are considered and taken into account (i.e. differential male school drop out beginning in grade 9; possible correlations with reading scores), the male superiority remains. Two additional points should be made. One is that there was considerably more variation within groups of males and females at all ages than between the sexes. Specifically, the average effect size was approximately 0.40 standard deviation units.

Second, Johnson and Meade (1987) did not explain why there may be spatial ability differences. On this count, it should be noted that a consistent and robust difference between males and females appears in their involvement with mechanical toys and trucks, from the first year onward (Rheingold & Cook, 1975). It may be proposed that this differential exposure, or correlated experiences over ontogeny, contributed to the small but reliable differences in spatial ability. Direct evidence for this speculation comes from the recent work of Serbin *et al.* (1990). These investigators found that 'access to stereotypic masculine toys and activities at home was, for both sexes, a predictor of children's visual-spatial ability' (Serbin *et al.*, 1990, p. 623).

Cognitive variability

It has long been argued that the major cognitive differences between sexes lie not in group means but in group variabilities. On the surface, this appears to be a provocative and potentially useful insight on psychometrics and the hazards of relying simply upon mean differences. But there is a theoretical assumption hidden in the proposal that goes beyond the measurement considerations and statistics. Shields (1975) noted that in the history of psychology, the variability hypothesis provided an argument for the essential inequality of females and males. As Shields (1975, pp. 744–745) put it, the assumption of greater male variability implies that '(a) genius ... is a peculiarly male trait; (b) men of genius naturally gravitate to positions of power and prestige (i.e. achieve eminence) by virtue of their talent; (c) an equally high ability level should not be expected of females; and (d) the education of women should, therefore, be consonant with their special talents and special place in society as wives and mothers. Such greater variability would be consistent with the assertion that males are more likely to be represented among the retarded as well as the gifted.

The variability hypothesis remains provocative. What appears to be a methodological psychometric proposal about ways to assess differences between males and females carries surplus theoretical baggage. Even if greater variability can be demonstrated (as it has been in several general population studies — see Rutter *et al.*, 1970), further direct analysis is required to clarify its implications and determine its causation. Is it due, for example, to inherent differences in cognitive ability? Or is it due to differences among men and women in the advanced educational opportunities or career pathways afforded by society? The variability hypothesis adds another point to methodological pitfalls and cautions listed by Jacklin (1981).

Social development

In contrast with cognitive functions where differences have been usually modest or negligible, certain social behaviour differences should be robust. When development is considered, social behaviour differences should emerge most strongly at those periods in ontogeny where the sexual–reproductive–social functions of males and females differ the most; namely, in adolescence and young adulthood.

Given the range of possible differences, our comments must necessarily be limited to three empirical generalizations; namely:

1 The most visible and reliable social behaviour differences associated with gender are those actions that involve aggression, violence and coercive behaviours. Moreover, the largest gender differences in aggressive behaviour should emerge in late childhood and adolescence and diminish in later maturity.

2 Gender differences in basic prosocial behaviours — including affection, popularity, dependency, empathy — may be observed, but they appear to be relatively modest and highly relative to context, age, setting and measurement operations (Berman, 1980). Again, the greatest differences should emerge in late childhood and adolescence and diminish in later maturity.

3 Social structures, including friendships and cliques, are a human phenomenon and transcend the categories of sex, race and social class. They provide, however, a vehicle for the development and support of sex-related behaviours and attitudes. This occurs because of the strong propensity for persons to affiliate in same-sex groups from childhood through adulthood.

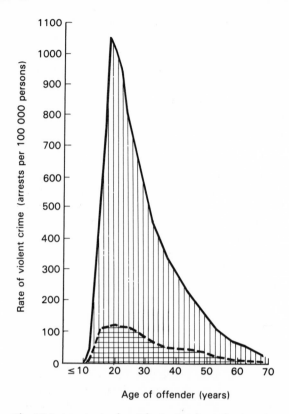

Fig. 15.1 Arrest rates for violent crime by males (——) and females (– – –) as a function of age, with rape excluded due to bias in statistical reporting (data from *Crime in the United States, 1982* and the US Census Report, 1980).

Aggression and violence

As in other arenas of gender comparison, there has been some debate in the psychological literature on whether men are more aggressive than women. On the one hand Frodi *et al.* (1977) have shown that adult females are often just as aggressive as adult males in social psychology experiments (see also Eagly & Steffen, 1986). On the other hand, most studies of children and adolescents show robust gender differences in aggressive behaviour (Feshbach, 1970; Olweus, 1979; Cairns *et al.*, 1989a). Moreover, if naturalistic measures of violence are employed, including assaults and homicides, both adolescent and adult males are considerably more likely than females to be the perpetrators and the victims (Cairns, 1979; Cairns & Cairns 1991b, 1994). This sex-related difference is found in such diverse statistics as arrests for violence (Fig. 15.1) and emergency department admissions (Cairns *et al.*, 1993) for traumatic injuries due to violence (see also Chapter 19). Indeed, the difference between males and females in serious acts of violence is enormous, typically five- to 10-fold.

Why the discrepancy in results? At least part of the explanation may be found in methodology. For example, some of the conditions of traditional social psychological experiments — hidden and non-reciprocated aggression, implicit authority to administer punishment — strip the research of some key sex-related constraints. Similarly, direct observations and judgments from others diminish the role of self-attributions and self-justifications. Hence a different picture is provided when self-constructions are permitted to play a major role in the results. For instance, when at-risk and violent adolescents provide global self-descriptions, the behaviour differences and sex-related differences diminish (Cairns & Cairns, 1994). In self-ratings, highly aggressive males, low aggressive males, highly aggressive females and low aggressive females describe themselves in a reasonably similar fashion.

More broadly, the measurement strategy employed — whether self-report, reports of others, or direct observation — is a major factor in determining the magnitude of the sex difference effect. Different developmental curves are required because they depend on which measures are adopted, which relationships are depicted, and which aggressive strategies are described in each measure. For example Cairns *et al.* (1989a) asked 695 children and adolescents to describe specific conflicts with peers, whether male or female. The results indicated that the conflicts that boys reported with other boys tended to involve physical aggression. This difference emerges at least by 10 years of age, and it persists through adolescence. Girls, on the other hand, rarely reported physical aggression in same-sex conflicts. Global self-ratings of aggression also yielded gender differences in this age range, but the mean differences were modest (Cairns *et al.*, 1989a; see also Barrett, 1979). In male—male conflicts, there is support for the developmental persistence of the aggression-begets-aggression norm, with the outcome that Ferguson and Rule (1980) describe as a 'brutality norm'. Judging from interview reports, there is a pervasive norm regarding the prohibition of physical assaults by boys towards girls, but not towards boys.

Observations and specific reports of conflict indicate, however, that direct confrontation continues to be the strategy of choice employed by adolescent boys in conflicts with other males. The stakes of confrontation become higher as boys grow older. This outcome follows because of (i) an age-related increase in the ability to produce serious injury; and (ii) the persistence of direct confrontation as a primary strategy when male—male conflicts arise. In the USA, the ownership and availability of firearms differs markedly between males and females (Sadowski *et al.*, 1989). In Sadowski *et al.*'s (1989) study of a representative sample of American teenagers, 49% of the adolescent males owned guns while only 4% of the females did so. The rate of serious injury in conflicts among males could increase when impulsive weapon use was coupled with the strategy of direct confrontation. This relationship should hold even if weapon use in conflicts is rare. One encounter in a lifetime can be a deadly conflict.

To be sure, adolescent firearm accessibility, ownership and injury may be a peculiarly American problem among industrialized nations (Fingerhut & Kleinman, 1990; Lee & Livingston, 1991; Lee *et al.*, 1991; Livingston & Lee, 1992). In this regard, recent studies of emergency departments in the UK show few instances of gunshot wounds (Hocking, 1989; Shepard *et al.*, 1990). For example, in a recent south east London study, 15% of the attacks involved knives, but these attacks accounted for 47% of the admissions and virtually all (90%) of the serious injuries due to violence (Hocking, 1989). This investigator observed that, 'The results support the view that it is becoming common for youths to be armed. Assault victims, particularly those with knife wounds, place a considerable burden on hospital resources' (p. 281). The difference between the USA and other industrialized nations appears to reflect the greater accessibility and ownership of firearms by youth in America.

It should be noted that all studies of emergency department populations — whether American or European — show significant gender difference in both the perpetrators and victims of injury. For example, a recent Los Angeles study found that (i) males were three times as likely as females to be admitted as trauma patients for serious injury; (ii) among trauma patients, males were twice as likely as females to be victims of violence; (iii) the primary mechanism of violence was gunshot wounds; and (iv) gunshot injuries had a higher incidence of death than knife injuries or motor vehicle injuries (Cairns *et al.*, 1993). These investigators also found males and females in the same age—ethnic category showed similar injury profiles, despite the over-representation of males in every age—ethnic class. This is to say, gunshot wounds were the most frequent mechanism of serious injury for African-American teenagers, regardless of their gender. Similarly, motor vehicle accidents were the leading cause of serious injury in both white males and females of this sample (Cairns *et al.*, 1993).

Across normative samples, aggressive expression in girls seems to follow a different development trajectory than in boys. Social manipulation and ostracism — as involved in alienation, rumours and social rejection — emerge as major properties of aggressive behaviour for girls in early adolescence (Feshbach & Sones, 1971; see also Cairns *et al.*, 1989b). Affiliation—romance—alienation themes

recur in conflicts among females in early adolescence. The strategy adopted seemed to be consonant with the form of perceived injury: alienation of
relationships leads to counteralienation. Rather
than report everyday offences of peers to adults as
they did in childhood, adolescent girls 'report' to
each other. In the early teenage years, boys persist
in their reliance upon direct confrontations and/or
physical aggression if the conflict cannot be otherwise ignored or avoided. Adolescent girls begin to
employ more advanced and less hazardous (to the
perpetrator) hostile strategies than boys. But it
would be incorrect to conclude that girls did not
retain the ability for direct aggressive confrontation.
Conflicts among girls can involve either direct confrontation or social manipulation (Cairns *et al.*,
1989a; Cairns & Cairns, 1991a).

Are girls and women becoming more violent in
our time? In a review of temporal changes in
aggressive expression among females, Schlossman
and Cairns (1993) concluded that the available data
are consistent with the hypothesis that there has
been a generational increase in the occurrence of
assaultive behaviours by adolescent girls outside
the home. In this regard, arrests for physical assault
have increased for girls from the 1950s to the
1980s. In the 1980s, physically aggressive behaviours that involve adolescent girls seem to be
becoming more frequent, more public and more
often adjudicated in the Los Angeles County Juvenile Courts than in previous decades in this century.
Schlossman and Cairns (1993) speculated that two
factors seem involved. First, male-typical confrontations appear to have become more acceptable for
female conflicts in the 1980s than in the 1950s.
Second, a shift in behavioural standards for girls
seems to have been correlated with — and perhaps
helped to provoke — counterresponses by the institutions of society (including schools and the courts).
The process may not be unlike the earlier response
of juvenile courts to female sexual misconduct,
whereby actions tolerated in adolescent males were
deemed unacceptable for adolescent females. The
phenomena and alternative explanations merit
vigorous exploration. Temporal changes in the
magnitude of sex-related differences in cognitive
measures appear to be paralleled by temporal
changes in the magnitude of sex differences in
social aggressive measures.

Prosocial behaviours

Girls are perceived to be more altruistic than boys
by their teachers and by their peers (Hartshorne &
May, 1929; Zarbatany *et al.*, 1985). Such perceptions
persist even though direct observations of the altruistic behaviours of boys and girls indicate there is
considerable variability across contexts and settings,
with modest gender differences. In an investigation
of the factors that contribute to ratings of altruism,
Zarbatany *et al.* (1985) found that boys were selected
more often for altruism when the tasks involved
masculine activity and girls were selected when the
tasks were feminine or neutral. (An example of
masculine activity would be 'get another kid's cat
out of a tree', a feminine activity would be 'talk to a
little kid who fell down and make the kid feel
better', and a neutral item would be 'share a crayon
with a kid who needed it'.) Such results are consistent with direct observations of altruistic behaviours
which suggest only modest differences in everyday
interchanges. What these data do not explain are
the pervasive gender differences in altruistic reputation that have been repeatedly found.

Similar measurement problems are found in self-
report measures of empathy as opposed to other,
non-self measures (i.e. behavioural, physiological).
As Jacklin (1981) observed, 'In general, males are
more defensive when filling out self-reports than
females . . . For example, boys do not disclose their
thoughts and personal feelings either to parents or
peers as much as do girls (Riverbark, 1971). Since
there is a sex-related difference in the willingness
and/or ability to be candid on self-report measures,
their use must be suspect in trying to establish sex-
related differences in personal attributes' (Jacklin,
1981, p. 269).

The literature seems to support Jacklin's (1981)
concern. Eisenberg and Lennon (1983, p. 100)
observed in their extensive review of the literature
on empathy that:

> In general, sex differences in empathy were a
> function of the methods used to assess
> empathy. There was a large sex difference
> favoring women when the measure of
> empathy was self-report scales; moderate
> differences (favoring females) were found for
> reflexive crying and self-report measures in
> laboratory situations; and no sex differences

were evident when the measure of empathy was either physiological or unobtrusive observations ... Moreover, few sex differences were found for children's affective role taking and decoding abilities.

These findings on the relativity of sex-related differences in empathy to method speak to a larger point; namely, the role of social categories and social construction in the report of gender differences. Taking the perspective of social psychology, Deaux (1984) argued that the categories of male and female are social constructions. Accordingly, research on sex-related differences should be concerned with variables that affect perceptions of gender and responses to the categories. In a review of the literature, Deaux (1984, p. 105) concluded 'Main effect differences of subject sex are found to be surprisingly small in most cases, and the status of androgyny is uncertain'. There are, however, consistencies across the lifespan and across cultures in the perceptions of what are distinguishing characteristics of males and females (Best *et al.*, 1977; Boldizar, 1991; Hyde *et al.*, 1991). Eagly and Crowley (1986) indicated that helping behaviours tend to be in accord with the expectations of the social role. They concluded, however, that 'sex differences in helping were extremely inconsistent across studies' (Eagly & Crowley, 1986, p. 283).*

Social structure and social organization

There have been few longitudinal studies of the structure of social groups and relationships, and even fewer studies of gender differences in these structures (cf. Bukowski *et al.*, 1993). To the extent that relevant data are available, they suggest that the gender similarities in the development of groups and friendships outweigh gender differences. The tendency is for female groups in childhood and adolescence to be marginally more cohesive and insulated than male groups (Eder, 1985; Cairns *et al.*, 1988a). Similarly, Benenson (1990) found that males and females did not differ in the number of best friends they reported, but that males did

have larger social networks than females. Such outcomes, though modest in magnitude, are consistent with the tendency for adolescent females to be more skilled in employing group processes to regulate and modulate social conflicts.

For the purposes of our present review, doubtless the most important finding from this literature — and possibly the most important finding on the origins of sex-related behaviour differences — is the ubiquitous tendency for males and females to affiliate in same-sex groups, from the preschool period to late adolescence (Cairns *et al.*, 1989b; Urberg & Kaplan, 1989; Maccoby, 1990). The effect is not limited to Western societies; it is as prominent in Taiwan and Hong Kong as it is in the USA, Iceland and Finland (Cairns *et al.*, 1987). The phenomenon of same-sex social affiliation has proved to be very robust, and it tends to overwhelm other demographic, behavioural and racial factors.

The propensity towards same-sex affiliations provides continuous direction, monitoring and day-to-day constraints for gender-related behaviours. These influences are ubiquitous and unconscious. In addition, the age grading of these groups ensures that the sex difference interchanges will dynamically shift with ontogeny and remain age appropriate. The negative conclusions of Lytton and Romney (1991) on parental socialization may have been hard to accept because they do not provide directions on what could be the effective factors. Peers and same-sex social networks provide the dynamic development mechanisms not found in studies of parental socialization.

Differences do not appear in the year-to-year stability of female and male groups. Nor are there reliable differences in the stability of female–female versus male–male friendships (Neckerman, 1992). Consistent with the above findings, studies of female leadership (among girls ranging from 8 to 15 years of age) demonstrate that the factors important for leadership in male groups are also important for leadership in female groups (Edwards, 1990). Similarly, Giordano *et al.* (1986) have shown that deviant female groups function like deviant male groups. To be sure, current investigations of group structure and process have only begun to scratch the surface. Despite world-wide changes in the roles and prerogatives of women, we still have only modest systematic information about how girls and

---

* It is beyond the limits of this chapter to discuss the current status of the gender classification of androgyny (see the valuable recent contributions of Taylor & Hall, 1982; Signorella & Jamison, 1986; Boldizar, 1991).

women function in social groups beyond the family. A better understanding of this issue seems as critical for society as for the science.

Morbidity, mortality and expendability

Gender is not usually seen in psychology and psychiatry as a life and death matter. Nonetheless, some of the largest gender differences in behaviour patterns are reflected in morbidity and mortality rates rather than in psychological and psychiatric variables (Strickland, 1988). In this regard, the recent National Center for Health Statistics (1989) volume on mortality suggests that males are at higher risk than females in virtually every behaviour-related area. As noted on p. 361, males are typically three times as likely as females to be admitted to emergency departments for non-fatal injuries, with the largest differences emerging in adolescence and early adulthood (Cairns *et al.*, 1993). These differences support three empirical generalizations. First, men are more at risk than women at virtually every stage in the life-course when behavioural factors are considered. Second, gender differences, though present at least from birth, emerge strongly at the onset of puberty. Third, gender differences are relative to race, circumstances and nature of the behavioural-linked mortality.

Consider first the proposition that males are at greater risk than females. When the mortality rates of males and females in the USA are considered across all age groups, males have consistently higher death rates than females (National Center for Health Statistics, 1989). The biggest gender differences appear in mortality linked to intentional and unintentional injury. This effect is shown clearly in the contrast between mortality rates for disease (Fig. 15.2) and for injury (Figs 15.3–15.5). In cardiovascular disease, men are consistently more vulnerable than women, with a modest difference in rate throughout the lifespan. By contrast, sex differences due to injury range from 2–1 to 8–1, depending upon age and the nature of the injury (accident, suicide, homicide).

Second, there is an interaction between sex, age and type of mortality (disease or injury). Cardiovascular disease and death rates due to malignant neoplasms show a sharp increases in old age, with a flat curve from infancy to maturity. In contrast,

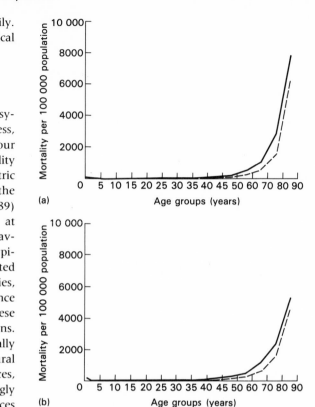

Fig. 15.2 Mortality rate by major cardiovascular disease as a function of sex, age and race (rates per 100 000 population in each sex–age–race category). Mortality rates from the National Center for Health Statistics (1989) (a) US whites; (b) African-Americans. ——, males; – – –, females.

morbidity and mortality rates in injuries show a sharp increase at puberty, with a subsequent levelling off and/or decrease.* It is noteworthy that pubertal onset is a period where there is accelerated and near-maximal differential between the sexes in mortality rate due to injury of all sorts: homicide, suicide and accidents. At adolescence, males are particularly vulnerable to death by injury. For example, there is a clear increase in morbidity and mortality in vehicular accidents among white males (Fig. 15.3) and an even greater increase in homicide

---

* In the case of suicide among white males, there are two points where a sharp increase may be observed: one at puberty and the other at the age of retirement.

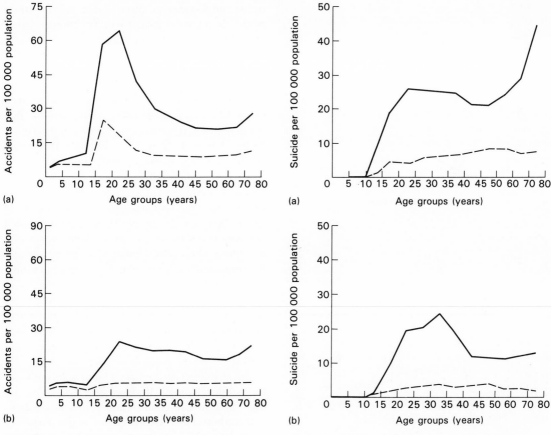

Fig. 15.3 Mortality rate by motor vehicle accidents as a function of sex, age and race (rates per 100 000 population in each sex–age–race category). Mortality rates from the National Center for Health Statistics (1989). (a) US whites; (b) African-Americans. ——, males; – – –, females.

Fig. 15.4 Mortality rate by suicide as a function of sex, age and race (rates per 100 000 population in each sex–age–race category). Mortality rates from the National Center for Health Statistics (1989). (a) US whites; (b) African-Americans. ——, males; – – –, females.

and violence-related injury among African-American males (Fig. 15.5). Suicide increases occur in both white and African-American males (except a delay in onset of suicide rates in black adolescents until 20–24 years of age). Specifically, the suicide rate is 19.6/100 000 for white males 15–19 years of age, while the comparable rate for African-American males is 9.7/100 000. This ethnic/race difference diminishes over the next 5 years, and the death rates are virtually the same in the 30–34 age group (Fig. 15.4).

Patterns of suicide morbidity — non-fatal injuries — reveal a somewhat different picture than

that shown by mortality rates. There are approximately 2.5–3 times as many suicides among males as among females. This ratio seems to hold across Western societies. For example, in Sweden in 1987, there were 16.9 suicides per 100 000 males in the 15–24 year age range, and 5.6 suicides per 100 000 females in the same age range (Statistical Abstract of Sweden, 1990). For attempted suicide, however, there are roughly two or three times as many attempts in females as in males. This ratio holds not only for general populations but for adolescents at high risk (Cairns *et al.*, 1988b). In this investigation, highly aggressive white females of 14–15 years of

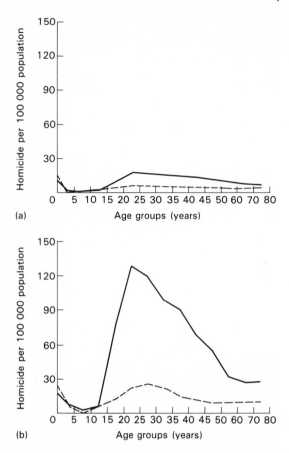

(a)

(b)

Fig. 15.5 Mortality rate by homicide as a function of sex, age and race (rates per 100 000 population in each sex—age—race category). Mortality rates from the National Center for Health Statistics (1991). (a) US whites; (b) African-Americans. ——, males; – – –, females.

males and females are more vulnerable than their white counterparts (Fig. 15.5). For motor vehicle accidents and suicide, the opposite holds.

These gender differences in mortality rates have stimulated a wide range of explanations, from evolutionary and neurobiological to developmental and sociocultural. For example, the apparent male expendability has been linked to the episodic role of males in reproduction and child-rearing (Wilson, 1975). It is a big leap, however, from theoretical speculations about evolutionary function to the concrete tragedies of living revealed in a longitudinal study. In this regard, studies of aggressive development indicate that adolescent males are more likely than females to persist in confrontational behaviours (Cairns *et al.*, 1989a). Moreover, males are more likely than females to own and use firearms. Such a combination of confrontational behavioural strategies and the availability of weapons can be deadly. Beyond whatever evolutionary biases that may exist, gender differences in interactional strategies related to morbidity and mortality are directly supported by the context and culture.

This is another area where longitudinal studies of normal development in males and females can be important. Among children and adolescents, behaviour rather than disease is the major factor in morbidity and mortality. Adolescent males are significantly more likely than females to appear as victims in emergency rooms. What underlies this young male vulnerability — or what buffers young females? At least one of the factors appears to be the heightened readiness of males to 'test the limits' (i.e. to take chances). This gender difference risk-taking appears in virtually all studies where appropriate comparisons are made between males and females. For example, Cairns and Cairns (1994) conducted a 12-year longitudinal study of 695 subjects. These investigators found that adolescent males who reported having been injured were judged to show higher levels of risk-taking than females in their cohort who reported similar injuries. Analyses of the injuries were also judged in whether carelessness played a role in the problem. Males were uniformly judged to be more careless than females, and less fearful in talking about the injuries. Group processes have been shown to contribute significantly to risk-taking behaviour, in-

age had an unusually high proportion of attempted suicide (39%), a rate that was about three times the rate observed in males (13.5%). A clue to this sex difference is that males are likely to employ more lethal means (e.g. firearms, hanging) than females (e.g. drug overdose).

The third empirical generalization concerns the relativity of sex differences in morbidity as a function of context, race and society. In both intentional and unintentional injury, there is great variability across sexes and races in the magnitude and type of gender difference. While males are more vulnerable than females in accidents, homicide and suicide, the nature of the sex difference is relative to ethnic/ racial background. For homicide, African-American cluding delinquency and crime (Giordano *et al.*, 1986).

The development of sexual dimorphism: biological and behavioural models

Tanner (1962) provides a thorough analysis of the mechanisms by which sex-related differences arise in biological development. Depending on the biological characteristic considered, sex differences (i) emerge in embryogenesis and are present at birth; (ii) develop continuously throughout the period of growth; or (iii) erupt full-blown or become sharply amplified at adolescence.

One obvious sex-related difference that emerges in embryogenesis involves the rudimentary structures of the reproductive system and external genitalia. In addition, boys are slightly larger at birth than girls (1–3% in length and about 4% in weight). Detailed analysis of the early development of limb growth indicates that the male arm is longer than the female, due to a sex difference in the development of the forearm. This difference is already established by 2 years of age, and possibly earlier.

Another picture of sex differences in biological development is provided by the analysis of skeletal and dental growth. These measures describe continuous and cumulative sex differences from birth to maturity. 'Skeletal age' is a measure of how advanced bones are in development as determined by X-ray appearances in the various stages of ossification and culminating in epiphyseal fusion. In terms of skeletal age, girls are 'more mature at birth, before it, and throughout the whole period of growth' (Tanner, 1962, p. 62). A similar pattern is observed in dental growth. Girls are more advanced in the eruption of every permanent tooth, from the first molars to the canines.* As Tanner (1962, p. 63) described skeletal age, 'At birth girls are ahead by a matter of weeks, at midgrowth by months, and at adolescence by the 2 years which separate the sexes in their growth spurts' (Tanner, 1962, p. 63).

The emergence of sexual dimorphism presents a

* Interestingly, there are no consistent sex differences in the eruption of deciduous teeth, and those that appear in humans suggest that males are more advanced than females (Tanner, 1962).

third picture of sex-related difference in development. Sexual dimorphism refers to the large sex differences at maturity in most mammalian species in body shape, size and tissue structure. Although there are detectable differences in human physique in infancy and childhood, the most striking sex differences in size and shape arise in adolescence. Some of the more precise measures of sexual dimorphism at different ages have been based on the amount of bone, muscle and fat in the calf. From early childhood, boys tend to have slightly more bone and muscle in the calf than girls. But the difference is small in childhood, and there is considerable overlap between boys and girls at age 7.5. Attempts to classify boys and girls solely on the basis of their calf X-rays would yield decisions that are only slightly more accurate than flipping a coin. In contrast, comparisons at 17 years of age permit accurate classification of men and women in 95% of the cases. Since the adolescent growth spurt in girls begins earlier than in boys, girls are temporarily larger in practically all respects for 2–3 years. The male growth spurt begins just when that of girls starts to taper off. Leg growth is one of the more rapidly changing skeletal dimensions and males have an extra 2 years to experience this acceleration. At the end of adolescence, boys weigh approximately 10% more and are 10% larger than girls (length of limbs, chest breadth, shoulder width).

In summary, studies of physical and physiological development provide at least three models for the growth of sex-related differences: (i) the development of primary reproductive systems and genitalia (where the differences appear in fetal development and are present at birth); (ii) skeletal and dental age (where there are continuous growth differences across childhood); and (iii) dimorphism in the development of gross size and shape (where the major differences emerge at adolescence). Which biological model is adopted has non-trivial implications for behavioural models of sex differences. On this count, some psychological models of sex differences in behaviour in psychology and psychiatry appear to have implicitly accepted the early differentiation model (e.g. classical psychoanalysis and classical behaviourism), while others have accepted the cumulative difference model (e.g. modern social learning theory). Less attention has been given in psychological analyses to the biological model of adolescent emergence which implies a sharp amplification of sex-related behavioural differences at adolescence.

One problem in linking biological and behaviour occurs because measures of sex difference in behavioural performance are less precise and objective than measures of biological growth. A possible exception would be the measurement of sensorimotor behaviour and athletic performance. Assessments in these domains provide useful information on which biological model best fits the data. For example, sex differences in measures of peak athletic performance seem to parallel sex differences in morphology during childhood and adolescence. The speed differentials between boys and girls in competitive swimming and track events appear to be roughly proportional to sex differences in size and strength. The performance differences are approximately 3–4% in childhood and preadolescence, and 10–12% at adolescence (Cairns, 1979). That a close relationship exists between sex difference morphology and sex differences in athletic performance should hardly be surprising, given the raw physical mechanics that contribute to performance differences in swimming and running.

But some athletic activities and most studies of play behaviours show continuous and cumulative differences between males and females. Throwing or catching objects accurately show markedly superior male performance (e.g. Thomas & French, 1985). These differences appear in preschool and persist across the lifespan, increasing in adolescence. Male superiority was significant even after partialling out prior experience and would seem to reflect the well-documented sex difference in forearm length and/or size. At least some reviewers have questioned whether the effects result primarily from sexual dimorphism and speculate that differences in throwing accuracy may in fact be due to some form of spatial function (Kimura, 1987).

Boys and girls differ markedly in terms of play patterns and play interests from early childhood onward (Maccoby & Jacklin, 1974). It has been suggested that such sex differences in the play and interests of young children may be the result of social anticipation of future role and biological differences rather than current morphological differences (Maccoby & Jacklin, 1974; Cairns, 1979).

The anticipation is not necessarily in the child so much as in the cumulative effects of the child's social ecology, including the dominant interests, values and activities of other persons of the same sex. In accord with this view, when preadolescent children are given common opportunities and encouragement in competitive sports, sex differences are trivial. In running and swimming, girls tend to be at least as competitive, achievement-oriented and skilled as boys.

More generally, it may be that sex differences in behaviour require domain-specific models of development, much as sex differences in physical/physiological characteristics require domain-specific models of growth. Accordingly, further study of sex-related differences in various behaviours could productively investigate which developmental model best fits the empirical data. Such research presupposes greater precision and objectivity in measuring the emergence and life-course of specific interests, self-identification, sexual preferences, physical activities and social interactions.

CONCLUSION

To our knowledge, no longitudinal study has yet been conducted to clarify the behavioural issues of gender role and gender typing over the life-course.* The non-developmental bias in research designs and conceptions of gender has been a serious handicap to understanding models of behavioural emergence and developmental course. Nonetheless, the information currently available indicates that certain key gender differences are not stable over the lifespan. Some of the largest differences — in mortality rates, social behaviour, sensorimotor capabilities and cognition — emerge at adolescence. There is, as well, evidence for the convergence in behaviour patterns and attitudes in later maturity (Cohn, 1991), although changes in gender role and gender behaviour that occur in later life have rarely been explored by developmentalists. Given the changing roles of women in Western cultures and societies world-wide, it seems important to obtain

---

* By contrast, longitudinal investigations have now revolutionized the modern understanding of aggressive, violent and criminal behaviour (Cairns & Cairns, 1991b).

up-to-date longitudinal information on the contemporary emergence and decay of gender differences.

A concluding comment is called for on the origins and support of sex-related differences in behaviour. The dominant assumption in contemporary models of personality development is that parental socialization is basic for establishing social behaviours, including sex differences in attitudes, concepts and behaviours. Exhaustive reviews of the available evidence have found only modest support for the parent-centric assumption (e.g. Lytton & Romney, 1991). One proposal of this chapter is that sex-related differences reflect the operation of correlated social and biological constraints, not merely parental actions. Consistent with this proposition is the finding that males and females in both Western and Asian societies tend to affiliate in same-sex groups. This phenomenon is observed across ontogeny, from the preschool period to early adulthood. The simplicity and ubiquity of this phenomenon may have blinded researchers to its powerful implications for social and sexual development.

REFERENCES

Anastasi A. (1981) Sex differences: Historical perspective and methodological implications. *Developmental Review* **1**, 187–206.

Austin A., Salehi M. & Leffler A. (1987) Gender and developmental differences in children's conversations. *Sex Roles* **16**, 497–510.

Barrett D.E. (1979) A naturalistic study of sex differences in children's aggression. *Merrill-Palmer Quarterly* **25**, 193–207.

Benbow C.P. & Stanley J.C. (1983) Sex differences in mathematical ability: More facts. *Science* **222**, 1029–1031.

Benenson J. (1990) Gender differences in social networks. *Journal of Early Adolescence* **10**, 472–495.

Berman P. (1980) Are women more responsive than men to the young? A review of developmental and situational variables. *Psychological Bulletin* **88**, 668–695.

Best D. & Williams J.E. (1977) Development of sex-trait stereotypes among young children in the United States, England, and Ireland. *Child Development* **48**, 1375–1384.

Binet A. & Henri V. (1895) La psychologie individuelle (Psychology of the individual). *L'Annee Psychologique* **2**, 411–465.

Block J. (1976) Issues, problems, and pitfalls in assessing sex differences: A critical review of *The Psychology of Sex Differences. Merrill-Palmer Quarterly* **22**, 283–308.

Block J. (1983) Differential premises arising from differen-

tial socialization of the sexes: Some conjectures. *Child Development* **54**, 1335–1354.

Block J.H. & Block J. (1980) The role of ego-control and ego-resiliency in the organization of behavior. In Collins W.A. (ed.) *Minnesota Symposium on Child Psychology*, Vol. 13, pp. 39–101. Lawrence Erlbaum, Hillsdale, New Jersey.

Boldizar J. (1991) Assessing sex typing and androgyny in children: The children's sex role inventory. *Developmental Psychology* **27**, 505–515.

Brumberg J.J. (1988) *Fasting Girls: The Emergence of Anorexia Nervosa as a Modern Disease*. Harvard University Press, Cambridge, Massachusetts.

Bukowski W.M., Newcomb A.F. & Hartup W.W. (eds) (1993) *The Company They Keep: Friendships in Childhood and Adolescence*. Cambridge University Press, Cambridge, Massachusetts.

Burnett S.A. (1986) Sex-related differences in spatial ability: Are they trivial? *American Psychologist* **40**, 1012–1014.

Cairns C.B., Neimeyer J., Neiman J. & Cairns R.B. Violence: A primary mechanism for serious injury among youth in Los Angeles. Unpublished ms.

Cairns R.B. (1979) *Social Development: The Origins and Plasticity of Social Interchanges*. W.H. Freeman, San Francisco, California.

Cairns R.B. (1991) Multiple metaphors for a singular idea. *Developmental Psychology* **27**, 23–26.

Cairns R.B. & Cairns B.D. (1991a) Social cognition and social networks: A developmental perspective. In Pepler D. & Rubin K. (eds) *The Development and Treatment of Childhood Aggression*, pp. 249–278. Lawrence Erlbaum, Hillsdale, New Jersey.

Cairns R.B. & Cairns B.D. (1991b) Sociogenesis of aggressive and antisocial behaviors. In McCord J. (ed.) *Facts, Frameworks, and Forecasts: Advances in Criminological Theory*, pp. 157–192. Transaction Press, New Jersey.

Cairns R.B. & Cairns B.D. (1994) *Lifelines and Risks: Pathways of Youth in our Time*. Harvester/Wheatsheaf, London.

Cairns R.B., Cairns B.D., Neckerman H.J., Gest S. & Gariépy J.-L. (1988a) Social networks and aggressive behavior: Peer support or peer rejection? *Developmental Psychology* **24**, 815–823.

Cairns R.B., Cairns B.D., Neckerman H.J., Ferguson L.L. & Gariépy J.-L. (1989a) Growth and aggression: I. Childhood to early adolescence. *Developmental Psychology* **25**, 320–330.

Cairns R.B., Elder Jr G.H., Costello E.J. & McGuire A. (in press) *Developmental Science*. Cambridge University Press, New York.

Cairns R.B., Gariépy J.-L. & Kindermann T. (1987) *Identifying social clusters in natural settings*. Unpublished ms, University of North Carolina, Chapel Hill.

Cairns R.B., Neckerman H.J. & Cairns C.B. (1989b) Social networks and the shadows of synchrony. In Adams

G.R., Gullota T.P. & Montemayor R. (eds) *Advances in Adolescent Development* pp. 275–305. Sage, Newbury Park, California.

Cairns R.B., Peterson G. & Neckerman H.J. (1988b) Suicidal behavior in aggressive adolescents. *Journal of Clinical Child Psychology* **17**, 298–309.

Caldera Y., Huston A. & O'Brien M. (1989) Social interactions and play patterns of parents and toddlers with feminine, masculine, and neutral toys. *Child Development* **60**, 70–76.

Caplan P.J., MacPherson G.M. & Tobin P. (1985) Do sex related differences in spatial abilities exist? *American Psychologist* **40**, 786–799.

Caspi A., Lynam D., Moffitt T. & Silva P. (1993) Unraveling girls' delinquency: Biological, dispositional and contextual contributions to adolescent misbehavior. *Developmental Psychology* **29**, 19–30.

Cohn L. (1991) Sex differences in the course of personality development: A meta-analysis. *Psychological Bulletin* **109**, 252–266.

Deaux K. (1984) From individual differences to social categories. *American Psychologist* **39**, 105–116.

Denno D. (1982) Sex differences in cognition: A review and critique of the longitudinal evidence. *Adolescence* **68**, 779–788.

Eagly A. (1983) Gender and social influence. *American Psychologist* **38**, 971–982.

Eagly A.H. & Crowley M. (1986) Gender and helping behavior: A meta-analytic review of the social psychological literature. *Psychological Bulletin* **100**, 283–308.

Eagly A. & Steffen V. (1986) Gender and aggressive behavior: A meta-analytic review of the social psychological literature. *Psychological Bulletin* **100**, 309–330.

Earls F. (1987) Sex differences in psychiatric disorders: Origins and developmental influences. *Psychiatric Developments* **1**, 1–23.

Eder D. (1985) The cycle of popularity: Interpersonal relations among female adolescents. *Sociology of Education* **58**, 154–165.

Edwards C.A. (1990) *Leadership, social networks, and personal attributes in school age girls*. Unpublished doctoral dissertation, University of North Carolina, Chapel Hill.

Eisenberg N. & Lennon R. (1983) Sex differences in empathy and related capacities. *Psychological Bulletin* **94**, 100–131.

Eisenberg N., Wolchik S., Hernandez R. & Pasternak J. (1985) Parental socialization of young children's play: A short term longitudinal study. *Child Development* **56**, 1506–1513.

Elder Jr G.H. (1974) *Children of the Great Depression: Social Change in Life Experience*. University of Chicago Press, Chicago.

Eliot J. (1986) Comment on Caplan, MacPherson, and Tobin. *American Psychologist* **40**, 1011.

Feingold A. (1988) Cognitive gender differences are disappearing. *American Psychologist* **44**, 95–103.

Feldman S. & Nash S. (1979) Changes in responsiveness to babies during adolescence. *Child Development* **50**, 942–949.

Ferguson T.J. & Rule B.G. (1980) Effects of inferential set, outcome severity, and basis of responsibility on children's evaluation of aggressive acts. *Developmental Psychology* **16**, 141–146.

Feshbach N. & Sones G. (1971) Sex differences in adolescent reactions toward newcomers. *Developmental Psychology* **4**, 381–386.

Feshbach S. (1970) Aggression. In Mussen P.H. (ed.) *Carmichael's Manual of Child Psychology*, Vol. 2, 3rd edn, pp. 159–259. Wiley, New York.

Fingerhut L.A. & Kleinman J.C. (1990) International and interstate comparisons of homicide among young males. *Journal of the American Medical Association* **263**, 3292–3295.

Frodi A., Macaulay J. & Thome P. (1977) Are women always less aggressive than men? A review of the experimental literature. *Psychological Bulletin* **84**, 634–660.

Giordano P.C., Cernkovich S.A. & Pugh M.D. (1986) Friendship and delinquency. *American Journal of Sociology* **91**, 1170–1201.

Gottlieb G. (1991) Experiential canalization of behavioral development: Theory. *Developmental Psychology* **27**, 4–13.

Halpern D.F. (1986) A different answer to the question, 'Do sex-related differences in spatial ability exist?' *American Psychologist* **40**, 1014–1015.

Hamilton W.D. (1964) The genetical evolution of social behavior. *Journal of Theoretical Biology* **7**, 1–52.

Hartshorne H. & May M.A. (1929) *Studies in the Nature of Character* Vol. 2, *Studies in Service and Self Control*. Macmillan, New York.

Hines M. (1982) Prenatal gonadal hormones and sex differences in human behavior. *Psychological Bulletin* **92**, 56–80.

Hiscock M. (1986) On sex differences in spatial abilities. *American Psychologist* **40**, 1011–1012.

Hocking M.A. (1989) Assaults in south east London. *Journal of the Royal Society of Medicine* **82**(5), 281–284.

Hyde J., Fennema E. & Lamon S. (1990a) Gender differences in mathematics performance: A meta-analysis. *Psychological Bulletin* **107**, 138–155.

Hyde J., Fennema E., Ryan M., Frost L. & Hoop C. (1990b) Gender comparisons of mathematics attitudes and affect. *Psychology of Women Quarterly* **14**, 299–324.

Hyde J., Krajnik S. & Skuldt K. (1991) Androgyny across the life span: A replication and longitudinal follow-up. *Developmental Psychology* **27**, 516–519.

Hyde J. & Linn M. (1988) Gender differences in verbal ability: A meta-analysis. *Psychological Bulletin* **104**, 53–69.

Jacklin C. (1981) Methodological issues in the study of sex related difference. *Developmental Review* **I**, 266–273.

Johnson E. & Meade A. (1987) Developmental patterns of

spatial ability: An early sex difference. *Child Development* **58**, 725–740.

Kimball M. (1989) A new perspective on women's math achievement. *Psychological Bulletin* **105**, 108–214.

Kimura D. (1987) Are men's and women's brains really different? *Canadian Psychology* **28**, 133–147.

Lee M.W. & Livingston M.M. (1991) Prevalence and accessibility of firearms among Louisiana students: Implications for firearm safety instruction. *Louisiana Association for Health, Physical Education, Recreation and Dance Journal* **53**, 20–21.

Lee R.K., Waxweiler R.J., Dobbins J.G. & Paschetag T. (1991) Incidence rates of firearm injuries in Galveston, Texas, 1979–1981. *American Journal of Epidemiology* **134**(5), 511–521.

Linn M. & Petersen A. (1985) Emergence and characterization of sex differences in spatial ability: A meta analysis. *Child Development* **56**, 1479–1498.

Livingston M.M. & Lee M.W. (1992) Attitudes toward firearms and reasons for firearm ownership among nonurban youth: Salience of sex and race. *Psychological Reports* **71**, 576–578.

Lummis M. & Stevenson H. (1990) Gender differences in beliefs and achievement: A cross-cultural study. *Developmental Psychology* **26**, 254–263.

Lytton H. & Romney D. (1991) Parents' differential socialization of boys and girls: A meta-analysis. *Psychological Bulletin* **109**, 267–296.

Maccoby E. (1988) Gender as a social category. *Developmental Psychology* **24**, 735–765.

Maccoby E. (1990) Gender and relationships — a developmental account. *American Psychologist* **46**, 513–520.

Maccoby E. & Jacklin C. (1974) *The Psychology of Sex Differences*. Stanford University Press, Stanford, California.

Magnusson D. (1988) Individual development from an interactional perspective. In Magnusson D. (ed) *Paths through Life: A Longitudinal Research Program*, Vol. 1. Lawrence Erlbaum, Hillsdale, New Jersey.

Magnusson D., Stattin H. & Allen V. (1985) Biological maturation and social development: A longitudinal study of some adjustment processes of mid-adolescence to adulthood. *Journal of Youth and Adolescence* **14**, 267–283.

Meece J.L., Eccles-Parsons J.E., Kaczala C.M., Goff S.B. & Futterman R. (1982) Sex differences in math achievement: Towards a model of academic choice. *Psychological Bulletin* **91**, 324–328.

National Center for Health Statistics (1989) *Vital and Health Statistics of the National Center for Health Statistics 1989*. US Printing Office, Washington, DC.

Neckerman H.J. (1992) *A longitudinal investigation of the stability and fluidity of social networks and peer relationships of children and adolescents*. Unpublished doctoral dissertation, University of North Carolina, Chapel Hill.

O'Brien M. & Huston A. (1985) Development of sex-typed play behavior in toddlers. *Developmental Psychology* **21**, 866–871.

Olweus D. (1979) Stability of aggressive reaction patterns in males: A review. *Psychological Bulletin* **86**, 852–875.

Raymond C.L. & Benbow C.P. (1986) Gender differences in mathematics: A function of parental support and student sex typing? *Developmental Psychology* **22**, 808–819.

Rheingold H. & Cook K.V. (1975) The contents of boys' and girls' rooms as an index of parental behavior. *Child Development* **46**, 459–463.

Riverbark W.H. (1971) Self disclosure among adolescents. *Psychological Reports* **28**, 35–42.

Roberts T. (1991) Gender and the influence of evaluations on self assessments in achievement settings. *Psychological Bulletin* **109**, 297–308.

Rosenthal R. & Rubin D. (1982) Further meta-analytic procedures for assessing cognitive gender differences. *Journal of Educational Psychology* **74**, 708–712.

Rutter M. & Rutter M. (1993) *Developing Minds: Challenge and Continuity Across the Lifespan*. Basic Books/Penguin, London.

Rutter M., Tizard J. & Whitmore K. (eds) (1970) *Education, Health and Behaviour*. Longman, London.

Sabers D., Cushing K. & Sabers D. (1987) Sex differences in reading and mathematics achievement for middle school students. *Journal of Early Adolescence* **7**, 117–129.

Sadowski L.S., Cairns R.B. & Earp J.A. (1989) Firearm ownership among nonurban adolescents. *American Journal of Diseases of Children* **143**, 1410–1413.

Sanders B., Cohen M.R. & Soares M.P. (1986) The sex difference in spatial ability: A rejoinder. *American Psychologist* **40**, 1015–1016.

Schlossman S. & Cairns R.B. (1993) Problem girls: Observations on past and present. In Elder Jr G.H., Parke R.D. & Modell J. (eds) *Children in Time and Place: Relations Between History and Developmental Psychology*. Cambridge University Press, New York.

Sears R.R., Maccoby E.E. & Levin H. (1957) *Patterns of Child Rearing*. Row-Peterson, New York.

Serbin L., Zelkowitz P., Doyle A. & Gold D. (1990) The socialization of sex differentiated skills and academic performance: A mediational model. *Sex Roles* **23**, 613–628.

Shapiro D.Y. (1981) Serial female sex changes after simultaneous removal of males from social groups of a coral reef fish. *Science* **209**, 1136–1137.

Shepard J.P., Robinson L. & Levers B.G. (1990) Roots of urban violence. *Injury* **21**(3), 139–141.

Shields S. (1975) Functionalism, darwinism, and the psychology of women. *American Psychologist* **30**, 739–754.

Signorella M. & Jamison W. (1986) Masculinity, femininity, androgyny and cognitive performance: A meta-analysis. *Psychological Bulletin* **100**, 207–228.

Simmons R.C. & Blyth D.A. (1987) *Moving into Adolescence; The Impact of Pubertal Change and School Context*. Aldine,

New York.

Stattin H. & Magnusson D. (1990) *Pubertal-Maturation in Female Development*. Lawrence Erlbaum, Hillsdale, New Jersey.

Statistical Abstracts (1990) *Statistical Abstracts*. The Swedish Census Bureau, Stockholm.

Stevenson H.W., Stigler J.W., Lee S.Y., Lucker G.W., Kitamura S. & Hsu C.C. (1985) Cognitive performance and academic achievement of Japanese, Chinese, and American children. *Child Development* **56**, 713–734.

Strayer F.F. & Noel J.M. (1986) The prosocial and antisocial functions of preschool aggression: An ethological study of triadic conflict among young children. In Zahn-Waxler C., Cummings E.M. & Iannotti R. (eds) *Altruism and Aggression: Biological and Social Origins*, pp. 107–131. Cambridge University Press, Cambridge.

Strickland B. (1988) Sex-related differences in health and illness. *Psychology of Women Quarterly* **12**, 381–399.

Susman E., Inoff-Germain G., Nottleman E., Loriaux L., Cutler G. & Chrousos G. (1987) Hormones, emotional dispositions and aggressive attributes in young adolescents. *Child Development* **58**, 1114–1134.

Susman E., Nottelmann E., Inoff-Germain G. *et al.* (1985) The relation of relative hormonal levels and physical development and social emotional behavior in young adolescents. *Journal of Youth and Adolescence* **14**, 245–262.

Tanner J.M. (1962) *Growth at Adolescence*. Blackwell Scientific Publications, Oxford.

Taylor M. & Hall J. (1982) Psychological androgyny: Theories, methods and conclusions. *Psychological Bulletin* **92**, 347–366.

Thomas J. & French K. (1985) Gender differences across age in motor performance: A meta-analysis. *Psychological Bulletin* **98**, 260–282.

Urberg K. & Kaplan M. (1989) An observational study of race, age, and sex heterogeneous interaction in preschoolers. *Journal of Applied Developmental Psychology* **10**, 299–311.

Whiting B.B. & Edwards C.P. (1973) A cross-cultural analysis of sex differences in the behavior of children three through eleven. *Journal of Social Psychology* **91**, 171–188.

Willis S. & Schaie K.W. (1988) Gender differences in spatial ability in old age: Longitudinal and intervention findings. *Sex Roles* **18**, 189–203.

Wilson E.O. (1975) *Sociobiology: A New Synthesis*. Harvard University Press, Cambridge, Massachusetts.

Wooley H. (1910) A review of the recent literature on the psychology of sex. *Psychological Bulletin* **7**, 335–342.

Wooley H. (1914) The psychology of sex. *Psychological Bulletin* **11**, 353–379.

Zarbatany L., Hartmann D., Gelfand D. & Vinciguerra P. (1985) Gender differences in altruistic reputation: Are they artifactual? *Developmental Psychology* **21**, 97–101.

16: Attachment:
Theory and Evidence

JAY BELSKY AND JUDE CASSIDY

INTRODUCTION

Attachment theory can be viewed, in large part, as a theory of personality development that arose from Bowlby's interest in the nature of human development. While still in medical training, Bowlby's observations at a school for maladjusted children convinced him that early family processes are influential in shaping development. Bowlby therefore viewed contemporary psychoanalytic theory (i.e. Freud) as inappropriately over-emphasizing the role of the individual's inner fantasies at the expense of actual environmental influences. This emphasis on the contribution of the internal world of the individual without considering the external environment was incompatible with Bowlby's biological training which had led him to seek to understand the interaction of the organism with the environment. Bowlby realized that undertaking this task with respect to human development would require a systematic knowledge of the effects of the family on the child.

To this end, there were many possible aspects of family experience that could be examined. Bowlby chose to examine the effects of major separation for two reasons. First, he was convinced that major separations and losses during childhood were particularly crucial. His own observations and those of others (Bender & Yarnell, 1941; Goldfarb, 1943) had revealed that the histories of severely disturbed children were characterized by a relatively high incidence of disruption in the child−mother relationship. Second, given the methodological limitations of the time, it was considerably easier to verify the existence of such a disruption than to establish the validity of assessments of other aspects of family experience. Members of Bowlby's research team therefore began a series of studies, the most productive of which was a prospective study of separation pioneered by James Robertson. These observations raised many questions: 'Why should a young child be so distressed by the loss of his mother? Why after her return home should he become so apprehensive lest he lose her again? What psychological processes account for his distress and for the phenomenon of detachment?' (Bowlby, 1989).

The need to explain these questions led Bowlby to realize that a new theory was required to understand the nature of a child's tie to his mother.* He was not satisfied with existing explanations which emphasized secondary drive processes. These suggested that because the mother satisfied the infant's primary need for nourishment, she became associated with feelings of satisfaction, and thereby came to be regarded positively by the infant. Interaction with her, according to Freud (e.g. 1910), thus came to be desired in its own right as a secondary, or acquired, drive. The insufficiency of this theory became further evident as a result of studies showing that motherless monkeys preferred contact with a soft cloth surrogate over an equally lifeless, wire-mesh substitute that provided milk through a bottle (Harlow & Harlow, 1965).

Finding himself thus dissatisfied with a variety of features of traditional analytic theory, Bowlby sought new understanding by exposing himself to ideas and colleagues from fields such as evolutionary biology, ethology, cognitive science and control systems theory (Bowlby, 1982). From this mix he crafted the original notion that as a result of evolutionary pressures the human infant evolved, in concert with a maternal care-giving system, to

---

* This chapter uses the convention of referring to the child as male and the parent as female.

develop an attachment relationship with his mother (or primary care-giving figure). In other words, and most significantly, the child's intense affective tie to his mother, which was dramatically revealed when the child was away from her, was not the result of some associational learning process, but rather was the direct consequence of a biologically based desire for proximity/contact with adults that arose as a direct result of natural selection.

This chapter reviews the basic tenets of attachment theory and surveys the research that it has stimulated, particularly that pertaining to individual differences in attachment security spawned by Mary Ainsworth's theoretical and methodological contributions (Ainsworth *et al.*, 1978). First, the nature of the child's tie to its mother (or primary attachment figure) is examined, and second the issue of individual differences from the perspective of theory, measurement and evidence is considered. The chapter ends with a section addressing some future directions for research and theory. Throughout all sections, questions and concerns are raised that have been directed towards the theory and research derived from it, hoping to illuminate both its strength and its limitations.

THE NATURE OF THE CHILD'S TIE TO THE MOTHER

Biological bases of attachment

The most fundamental aspect of attachment theory is its focus on the biological bases of attachment behaviour (Bowlby, 1973, 1980, 1982). Attachment behaviour is any behaviour that has the predictable outcome of increasing proximity of the child to the attachment figure (usually the mother). Some attachment behaviours (smiling, vocalizing) are signalling behaviours that indicate to the mother the child's interest in social interaction, and thus serve to bring her to the child for such interaction. Some (crying) are aversive, and bring the mother to the child to terminate them. Some (approaching, following) are active behaviours that move the child to the mother. Bowlby proposed that during the period when humans were evolving, the time he called 'the environment of evolutionary adaptedness', genetic selection favoured attachment behaviours because they increased the likelihood of child–mother proximity.

Many predictable outcomes beneficial to the child are thought to result from the child's proximity to the parent (Bowlby, 1982). These include feeding, learning about the environment and social interaction. All of these are important. But the predictable outcome of proximity thought to give survival advantage to the child is protection from predators. Infants who, in the environment of evolutionary adaptedness, were biologically predisposed to stay close to their mothers were less likely to be killed by predators. This is referred to as the 'biological function' of attachment behaviour. This is the most basic of predictable outcomes: without protection from predators, feeding is not necessary, and learning cannot take place. Because of this biological function of protection, infants are thought to be biologically predisposed particularly to seek the parent in times of distress.

Attachment behaviours are theorized to be organized into an attachment behavioural system in which the specific attachment behaviours may be less important than the internal organization of these behaviours. Bowlby (1982) borrowed the concept of the behavioural system from the ethologists to describe a species-specific system of behaviours which leads to certain predictable outcomes, at least one of which offers clear survival advantage to the individual. The concept of the behavioural system involves inherent motivation. There is no need to view attachment as the byproduct of any more fundamental process or 'drive'. This idea is supported by evidence that indicates that in contrast to secondary drive theories, attachment is not a result of associations with feeding (Schaffer & Emerson, 1964; Harlow & Harlow, 1965; Ainsworth, 1967). Bowlby's notion of the inherent motivation of the attachment system is compatible with Piaget's (1954) formulation of the inherent motivation of the child's interest in exploration.

Bowlby (1982) adopted a control system approach to attachment behaviour. Drawing on observations of ethologists who described instinctive behaviour in animals as serving to maintain them in a certain relation with the environment for long periods of time, Bowlby proposed that a control systems approach could also be applied to attachment behaviour. Bowlby described the workings of a thermostat as an example of a control system. When the room gets too cold, the thermostat activates the heater; when the desired temperature is reached, the thermostat turns off the heater. Bowlby described children as wanting to maintain a certain proximity to the mother. When a separation becomes too great in distance or time, the attachment system becomes activated, and when sufficient proximity has been achieved, it is terminated. Bowlby (1982; see also Bretherton, 1980) later described the attachment system as working slightly differently from a thermostat, being continually activated (with variations of relatively more or less activation) rather than ever being completely terminated.

The child's desired degree of proximity to the parent is thought to vary at different times and in different settings, and Bowlby (1982) was interested in understanding what leads to these relative increases and decreases in activation of the attachment system. He described three classes of causal factors: condition of the child (whether or not the child is sick, tired or in pain), condition of the environment (whether or not it contains threatening stimuli), and the location and behaviour of the mother (whether or not she is absent, moving away or rejecting). Interaction among the classes of causal factors can be quite complex; sometimes only one needs to be present, and at other times several are necessary. In relation to relative deactivation of attachment behaviour, Bowlby was clear that his approach has nothing in common with a model in which a behaviour stops when its energy supply is depleted. For Bowlby, attachment behaviour stops in the presence of a terminating stimulus. The nature of the stimulus that serves to terminate attachment behaviour differs according to the degree of activation of the attachment system. If the attachment system is intensely activated, contact with the parent may be necessary to terminate it. If it is moderately activated, the presence or soothing voice of the parent or even of a familiar substitute caregiver may be sufficient.

Interplay of the attachment system with other behavioural systems

The attachment behavioural system can only be fully understood in terms of its complex interplay with other biologically based behavioural systems. Bowlby highlighted several other behavioural systems in relation to young children, and two, the

fear and exploratory systems, will be discussed here. For Bowlby, the biological function of the fear system, like that of the attachment system, is protection. It is biologically adaptive for children to be frightened of certain stimuli. Bowlby (1973) described 'natural clues to danger', stimuli which are not inherently dangerous, but which increase the likelihood of danger. These include darkness, loud noises, aloneness and sudden, looming movements. Because the attachment and fear systems are intertwined so that a frightened infant increases his attachment behaviour, infants who find these stimuli frightening are thought to be more likely to seek protection and thus survive to pass on their genes. The presence (or absence) of the attachment figure is thought to play an important role in the activation of the infant's fear system such that an available and accessible attachment figure makes the infant much less susceptible to fear.

The exploratory behavioural system is also one which is thought to be closely linked to the attachment behavioural system. The complementary yet mutually inhibiting nature of the two systems is believed to have evolved to ensure that while the child is protected by maintaining proximity to attachment figures, he nonetheless gradually learns about the environment through exploration. The link between these two systems is best captured within the framework of an infant's use of an attachment figure as a 'secure base from which to explore', a concept first described by Ainsworth (1963) and central to attachment theory (Ainsworth *et al.*, 1978; Bowlby, 1982).

Noting the complementary activation and inhibition of these two behavioural systems, Ainsworth *et al.* (1971) referred to an 'attachment–exploration balance'. Most infants balance these two behavioural systems, responding flexibly to a specific situation after assessing both the environment's characteristics and the caregiver's availability. For instance, when the attachment system is activated (perhaps by separation from the attachment figure, illness, fatigue or by unfamiliar people and environments), infant exploration and play decline. Conversely, when the attachment system is not activated (e.g. when a healthy, well-rested infant is in a comfortable setting with an attachment figure nearby), exploration is enhanced. In terms of fostering exploration, Bowlby described as important not only the physical presence of an attachment figure, but also the infant's belief that the attachment figure will be available if needed. A converging body of empirical work, in which maternal physical or psychological presence was experimentally manipulated, provides support for the theoretically predicted associations between maternal availability and infant exploration (Ainsworth & Wittig, 1969; Rheingold, 1969; Carr *et al.*, 1975; Sorce & Emde, 1981).

Distinctions among attachment behaviour, the attachment behavioural system and an attachment bond

It is important to clarify the distinctions among attachment behaviour, the attachment behavioural system and an attachment bond (Ainsworth, 1973; Bowlby, 1982; Hinde, 1982a). Attachment behaviour is behaviour that promotes proximity to the attachment figure. The attachment behavioural system is the organization of a variety of attachment behaviours within the individual. An attachment bond refers to a tie, not between two people, but rather a tie which one individual has to another individual who is perceived as stronger and wiser (e.g. the bond of an infant to his mother). Attachment behaviour may or may not be present at any given time; it is situational. The attachment bond is considered to exist consistently over time, whether or not attachment behaviour is present. Furthermore, the presence of attachment behaviour does not necessarily indicate the existence of an attachment bond. The same behaviour can serve more than one behavioural system, and can have different meanings in different contexts or when directed to different people. For instance, just because a baby approaches an unfamiliar person does not mean he is attached to that individual; even though approach can be an attachment behaviour, it can also be an exploratory behaviour.*

---

* Distressed infants may seek comfort from a stranger (Rheingold, 1969; Ainsworth *et al.*, 1978; Bretherton, 1978) and approach in that context is considered attachment behaviour. Nonetheless, an enduring attachment bond of the infant to the individual cannot be assumed to exist, and it is thus possible for an infant to direct attachment behaviour to an individual to whom he is not attached.

In addition, as Bretherton (1980) has pointed out, the same behaviour, *even when directed to the same individual*, may serve different behavioural systems at different times. It would, for example, be a mistake to label as an attachment behaviour the child's approach to its mother in order to engage in peekaboo.

Beyond attachment: additional relationship components

The fact that not all behaviour directed to an attachment figure is attachment behaviour suggests that there are other components to the child–mother relationship beyond attachment. For Bowlby (1982), the attachment component is only one feature of a child's relationship with his mother: the component that deals with behaviour related to the child's protection and security in time of stress. In addition to serving as attachment figure, the mother may serve also as playmate, teacher or disciplinarian. These various roles are not incompatible, and it is possible that two or more may be filled by the same person. Thus, for example, a frightened child may direct attachment behaviour to his mother, and yet at other times interact with her in ways relatively unrelated to attachment (e.g. play). Clearly, there are many aspects of parental behaviour not related to attachment and which have important consequences for children's development (Maccoby & Martin, 1983).

The extent to which the various relationship components characterize child–mother relationships varies considerably both across and within cultures. For instance, as Bretherton (1985) has pointed out, among Mayan Indians in Mexico, mothers rarely serve as playmates for their infants, yet are quite available and responsive as caregivers (Brazelton, 1977). Within a particular culture, one mother might be a readily available attachment figure, yet stodgy and inept in the role of playmate, whereas another mother might be dazzling as a playmate yet consistently unavailable in times of trouble. Still another mother might be comfortable in interaction with her children only in her roles as teacher or coach when attention is focused on a task or skill, and be uncomfortable with attachment-related interactions. Relatively little is known about the connections among the various components of mother–child relationships, and it is unclear to what extent non-attachment components contribute to security. It is likely that the extent and nature of their contributions vary at different ages (Bretherton, 1980; Hinde, 1982a). Bowlby summarized his position on this issue as follows: 'A parent–child relationship is by no means exclusively that of attachment–caregiving. The only justification, therefore, for referring to the bond between a child and his mother in this way is that the shared dyadic programme given top priority is one of attachment–caregiver' (1982, p. 378).

Multiple attachment figures

Just as attachment is unlikely to be the sole component of any one relationship, so is any one relationship unlikely to be a child's only relationship containing an attachment component. According to Bowlby (1982), 'almost from the first, many children have more than one figure to whom they direct attachment behaviour' (p. 304). Indeed, empirical observations have revealed that the majority of children direct attachment behaviour towards more than one familiar attachment figure well before their first birthday (Schaffer & Emerson, 1964; Ainsworth, 1967). According to Bowlby (1982), determination of who will serve as attachment figures to an infant hinges on who spends time with the infant. In most cultures this means that the biological parents, the siblings, and in some cases the grandparents, are most likely to serve as attachment figures as well.

Although there is usually more than one attachment figure, the potential number of attachment figures is not limitless. Bretherton (1980) has described the infant as having a 'small hierarchy of major caregivers' which is in contrast to the larger group of individuals with whom the infant has other sorts of relationships (Weinraub et al., 1977). Although there is some preferential discrimination when choosing an individual for social interaction, it is considerably less than the discrimination when choosing an individual to provide comfort (Tracy et al., 1976).

Although most infants have multiple attachment figures, it is important not to assume that the infant treats all attachment figures as equivalent, or that they are interchangeable. Bowlby (1982) proposed

a strong tendency for infants to prefer a principal attachment figure, and to prefer her as a source of comfort and security if she is present (see also Ainsworth, 1964). However, in her absence the infant is likely to seek and derive comfort and security from other attachment figures as well. The principal figure is the one the infant consistently turns to first in times of stress. Consistent with this hierarchy notion are data from Lamb's (1976a, b) work with fathers and Kagan et al.'s (1978) work with child care providers showing that most infants prefer to seek comfort from their mothers when distressed rather than from these other individuals with whom they also have enduring relationships (see also Schaffer & Emerson, 1964; Ainsworth, 1967).*

Additional support for the hierarchy notion, and particularly the idea that not all attachment relationships are equally influential, comes from studies showing that when the child is securely attached to one individual and insecurely attached to another, children behave more competently when the secure relationship is with the mother rather than with the other attachment figure (Main & Weston, 1981; Belsky et al., 1984; Main et al., 1985; Easterbrooks & Goldberg, 1987; Howes et al., 1988). These same studies indicate, however, that the most well-functioning individuals have two secure relationships while the least competent children have none (of those studied).

Attachment across the lifespan

Bowlby (1982; see also Ainsworth, 1967) distinguished four phases in the development of

---

* Bowlby uses the term 'monotropy' to refer to the special role of a single mother figure to the infant. There has been some confusion over Bowlby's position on this issue. Lamb et al. (1985), for instance, mistakenly stated: 'Bowlby was firmly convinced that infants were initially capable of forming only one attachment bond' (p. 21), when, in fact, from Bowlby's earliest writings (1958, 1982) the role of multiple attachment figures was described. Indeed, Bowlby's position may have shifted somewhat over time (Rutter, 1979); it has at least been clarified. Current thinking emphasizes that infants have multiple attachment figures from early in life; that these are limited in number: and that all attachment figures are not treated equally. The mother figure is generally preferred in times of stress.

attachment in the human species. Three of these phases occur during the infant's first year of life. During the first phase, undiscriminating social responsiveness (birth to 2−3 months), the infant responds to nearly all social stimuli, not just a particular person. During the second phase, discriminating social responsiveness (2−3 to 7 months), not only does the baby begin to distinguish mother and other familiar people from strangers, with attachment behaviours being activated and terminated in response to specific others, but the infant shows a preference for a particular person (or persons). During the third phase, active initiation in seeking proximity and contact (7 months to 3 years), active attachment behaviours (e.g. approaching, following) increasingly emerge. Now that the infant can alter his behaviour as a function of the situation, continually choosing from a repertoire of attachment behaviours, 'goal-corrected' behaviour sequences become evident, and the infant can be said to be 'attached'.

Bowlby (1979) believed that attachment to parents remains important beyond infancy, and indeed throughout the lifespan. At approximately age 3, the child moves into the goal-corrected partnership, phase 4. During this phase, language, among other skills, enables the child to view the world from the mother's perspective and thus consider her plans and wishes in guiding his own behaviour. The term 'partnership' is used because the child can use his new knowledge of both his own and the mother's goals to negotiate a joint plan. Although throughout the school years a child's attachments to his parents continue to have a pervasive influence, increasingly they become less centrally important for the child, penetrating fewer aspects of his life than they did earlier (Hinde, 1976). Many people assume that the attachment of child to parent becomes steadily weaker in the course of development until it eventually disappears altogether, being supplanted by other more mature affectional bonds (Weiss, 1982). However, despite the fact that attachment behaviour directed to the parent becomes less frequent and less intense, there is no reason to believe that the attachment bond to parents altogether disappears, and it seems likely that adolescents and young adults rely on parents as attachment figures (Ainsworth, 1989). As Ainsworth (1989) has pointed out, there is little

research examining changes in behaviour that mediates attachment to parents as the child grows older, or examining the circumstances or ways in which attachment behaviour to parents later manifests itself. Similarly, there is no research evidence about the nature of the attachment of the adult child to parents. Some clinicians believe that the nature of the relationship never really changes — that it is always one of child to parent — whereas other clinicians feel that adult children and their parents can become close friends and interact as peers. Nonetheless, it seems likely that relationship roles may be healthily reversed when an adult child is called upon to provide care to an elderly or ill parent.

Most adult lives are characterized not only by attachments to parents but by additional attachment relationships as well. These typically include relationships with spouses, very close friends, siblings and other close kin. According to Bowlby (1979), it is a mistake to assume, as some psychoanalysts do, that the presence of attachment behaviour in adult life is pathological, regressive or reflects 'fixation'. It is viewed, in contrast, as a biologically based behaviour, and the adult's capacities to turn to a partner for care when needed (as well as to provide care to a partner) are considered signs of health (Bowlby, 1979).

There are both similarities and differences between attachments in childhood and attachments in adulthood. They are similar in that they are characterized by the same defining features: specificity of the attachment figure; duration of the bond over time; the wish for proximity, particularly in times of trouble; distress at involuntary separation; the seeking of security; and emotional significance (Weiss, 1982; Ainsworth, 1989). In both, the attachment component is likely to be only one of several components of the relationship. For instance, in addition to the attachment component within a marriage, there are sexual, care-giving, teaching and recreational components as well (Ainsworth, 1989, 1991). The notion of a secure base from which to explore also characterizes both: 'Evidence is accumulating that human beings of all ages are happiest and able to deploy their talents to best advantage ... with a secure base from which to operate' (Bowlby, 1979, p. 103). In addition, most adults, as do most infants, have more than one attachment figure. And finally, for adults as well as for children, not all important relationships are attachments (Ainsworth, 1989). On the other hand, attachments in adulthood are different from those in childhood in that the former typically involve a peer rather than a more powerful individual; are not nearly as powerful in overwhelming other behavioural systems: and often involve a person with whom a sexual relationship also exists (Weiss, 1982). In addition, adults tolerate distance from attachment figures for longer periods of time than can infants (Bowlby, 1989).

INDIVIDUAL DIFFERENCES: THEORY

Central to contemporary thinking about attachment is not only the notion that humans, like many other species, are biologically predisposed to develop attachments to other conspecifics, but that there exist noteworthy individual differences in the nature and quality of these attachment relationships. The current considerable interest in, and research on, the origins and consequences of variation in attachment derive in large part from the seminal theorizing and ground-breaking research of Ainsworth who developed a procedure for assessing individual differences (see below) and carried out the first work testing propositions regarding the origins of these differences. Interest in individual differences is also present in the work of Bowlby, evident in his work on the history of 44 juvenile thieves (1944), and in his notion of internal working models discussed in the first volume of his trilogy (1982), and much further developed in his 1973 volume.

Internal working models

Attachment theory differs importantly from psychoanalytic and object relations theories in terms of the emphasis it places upon the young child's real experience. In studying psychopathology, Freud, Klein and others stressed the fantasies and projections of their patients regarding their childhood experiences. Bowlby, in contrast, emphasized that the child's mental representations of his early relationships were based upon actual experiences which the child has with his caregiver and that it was these lived experiences which provided the

basis for his models of the workings, properties, characteristics and behaviour of attachment figures, of himself, of others and of the world more generally.

Central to Bowlby's theory of the working model of the self and of the attachment figure is the idea that, over time, there is an inextricable intertwining of the working model of the self and of the attachment figure. Thus, a child whose attachment needs are rebuffed not only comes to develop a model of the mother as rejecting, but of himself as unworthy of love and attention. Conversely, a child whose needs for contact and comfort are consistently met comes to represent the mother as available and caring and himself as loveable. It is a presumption of contemporary attachment theory that working models become so deeply ingrained that they influence feelings, thought and behaviour unconsciously and automatically. They do this, according to Bowlby, by directing the child's attention to particular actions and events in his world, by shaping what the child remembers and does not and, thereby, by guiding his behaviour towards others and, thus, theirs towards him.

Secure and insecure attachment

Ainsworth distinguished two general types of attachment relationships — secure and insecure. When a parent is experienced as usually available, responsive and accepting, a secure attachment develops. By serving as a secure base from which to explore, the parent fosters in the child the development of an internal working model of the parent as one on whom he can depend in times of trouble and of the self as one worthy of such care. Basic to the experience of a securely attached child is a fluid attachment—exploration balance (Ainsworth *et al.*, 1971). When the environment appears safe, is interesting and the mother is nearby, the exploration system is activated. But when danger looms or the mother's availability is compromised, the securely attached child readily seeks proximity to the mother (Main, 1990). Rather than being seen as incompatible with self-reliance, this secure attachment is considered to reflect developmentally appropriate dependency and is theorized to foster self-reliance and age-appropriate independence in the post-infancy years. In contrast, a premature attempt to push the very young child to independence by rebuffing attachment behaviour serves to further activate attachment behaviour and, in so doing, fosters an unwillingness to explore or an inability to do so confidently and competently (Ainsworth, 1984b).

When the attachment figure somehow fails to provide the child with a history of experiences that would foster a secure base, an insecure attachment develops. Insecurity itself can be promoted in a variety of ways. Consistent rejection, lack of availability and extreme forms of pathological parenting (e.g. maltreatment, parental mental illness) foster internal working models of others as unavailable and untrustworthy and complementary models of the self as unworthy of sensitive treatment. The actual strategies that insecure children develop in response to their rearing experiences are thought to involve manipulation of the balance between the attachment and exploratory systems such that either one or the other is emphasized.

In cases where a parent is minimally or inconsistently responsive, it is theorized that the infant develops an understandable strategy of emphasizing and exaggerating his attachment behaviour (e.g. crying, clinging, following) and increasing the bids for attention. This practice of displaying extremely dependent behaviour is seen to be a tactic that the infant uses to obtain the attention of an otherwise inattentive parent (Main & Solomon, 1986; see Cassidy & Berlin, in press for review). In cases where a parent is actively rejecting of the infant's attachment behaviour, the infant develops a strategy of ignoring cues that might activate the attachment system and defensively de-emphasizes his relation with the attachment figure (Bowlby, 1980; Main, 1981; Cassidy & Kobak, 1988). Complementing this tactic is that of emphasizing exploration which allows the infant to remain in proximity to the caregiver without engaging in either angry or clingy behaviour which could evoke still further rejection (Main, 1981).

Stability of attachment

Because of the nature of the internal working model, there is an almost implicit assumption built into attachment theory that individual differences in attachment security will remain stable over time.

After all, a fundamental idea pertaining to internal working models is that they are a conservative force with respect to developmental change, as they direct attention, memory and interpersonal experience to be consistent with prevailing expectations and understanding of the social and affective world. Even though Bowlby did theorize that working models were set largely in infancy and early childhood and thereafter were relatively resistant to change, he clearly acknowledged that under particular conditions they were susceptible to modification at older ages. This would suggest, therefore, that while stability of attachment is the norm, lawful discontinuity could be expected; that is, when circumstances change and affect the nature of the ongoing relationship between attachment figure and child, the security or insecurity of the relationship could also change.

It is interesting in light of such theory that even though the norm seems to be for measurements of attachment security in the early years to remain stable, especially in stable middle-class populations (Waters, 1978; Main & Weston, 1981; Owen *et al.*, 1984; Main *et al.*, 1985), some of the instability that has been chronicled in the research literature has been linked to changing family circumstances presumed to influence the nature of daily interactions between mother and child and, thus, the quality of the relationship (Egeland & Farber, 1984). To date, however, this assumption has not been tested directly, as no studies have chronicled short- or long-term changes in attachment security *per se* and linked them to interactions between mother and child that might mediate these changes. Erickson *et al.* (1985) did show, though, that some children judged insecurely attached to their mothers as toddlers looked more competent than age-mates with comparable insecure attachment histories and that the unexpected competencies of the former seemed to be mediated by differences in mother–child interactions which intervened between the initial assessment of attachment insecurity and the later measurement of socioemotional functioning. Lieberman *et al.* (1991) reported more recently another instance of what appears to be evidence of lawful discontinuity with respect to attachment security: relative to a control group of insecure 12 month olds who received no therapeutic intervention, those whose mothers had a full year of infant–parent psychotherapy were significantly more likely to look secure (or less insecure) in their attachments when remeasured a year later.

Consequences of attachment security/insecurity

As noted above, Bowlby's interest in attachment grew out of his observations of the dysfunctional development of children with multiple changes of a mother figure or a home (study of 44 thieves) or who grew up without a mother figure (institutionalized children). Thus, it is not surprising that a central tenet of contemporary attachment theory is that the security of the attachment bond will influence subsequent psychological and behavioural development. As Bowlby (1973, p. 322) noted, 'an unthinking confidence in the unfailing accessibility and support of attachment figures is the bedrock on which stable and self-reliant personality is built'. Of course, this notion that the quality of early relationships is important for later personality development was central to Freud's psychoanalytic theory as well.

Distinctive to attachment theory, though, is the notion of what it is that mediates the influence of early relationship experience upon later psychological development — the internal working model. On the basis of their experiences, individuals develop different representational models — that is, different beliefs about themselves, different expectations about others, and different sets of conscious and/or unconscious rules for organizing and accessing information about feelings, experiences, and ideas related to attachment — and these lead to particular kinds of interactions with new social partners and have long-lasting consequences for personality and close relationships. Whereas securely attached children are inclined to become self-confident adults who can effectively vary their behaviour to suit their situations, anxiously attached children are expected to be at risk for interpersonal difficulties, depression, compulsive self-reliance and problems pertaining to anxiety, anger and aggression. Although it is expected that children with anxious attachment histories will be at increased risk of low self-esteem, unhappiness and maladaptive responses in difficult to manage situations, insecurity in and of itself is not to be equated with psychopathology. Conversely, security is not to be equated with invulnerability to

stress, though it is expected to lay a foundation for the formation of other secure relationships, the seeking of support when needed, and the drawing of strength from support when available.

Special issues

Four fundamental theoretical issues regarding individual differences merit special attention: boundaries, mechanisms, processes and notions of adaptation.

Boundaries of attachment

There is no shortage of developmental phenomena to which attachment security has been linked, either longitudinally or concurrently. Developmental correlates of attachment security now include frustration tolerance, developmental quotient, interactions with peers, friends and siblings; relations with strange adults, teachers and parents; language competence, ego resilience, behaviour problems, exploration of a novel environment and play competence. Not unreasonably, one can wonder not merely if there is anything to which attachment security is not related, but what we mean by attachment security if it relates to all of these things. Is it merely a marker of general adjustment or a feature of a close relationship as experienced by the child, or are these one and the same (Sroufe, 1988)?

Reflection on a decade of research on the sequelae of early attachment security leads to the conclusion that Bowlby's and Ainsworth's theorizing has been the spring board for a broad continuum of implicit, if not explicit, theo*ries* of attachment. One end of the continuum is characterized by what might be regarded as a 'narrow' view of the attachment system and a theory that early attachment security should be related to a limited set of development phenomena, mostly having to do with interpersonal relations, especially close relationships, and perhaps developmental disorders that are relationship based. The 'broader' view of attachment seems to have involved the assimilation of Bowlby's and Ainsworth's ideas about security into earlier understanding of Erikson's (1950) views about basic trust and the foundation it lays for diverse aspects of development. Only such a reading of the evidence, it seems to us, explains why students of attachment theory came to relate things like sociability with strange adults and peers, and language and cognitive development more generally to early assessments of infant−mother attachment.

What has been particularly absent from research on both the antecedents and sequelae of attachment security are notions of discriminant validity. An important question is not simply what early attachment predicts and through what mechanisms, but what does it not predict — and why? In Fig. 16.1, three quite different models are depicted of the origins and consequences of attachment security that vary not only in what they would predict about interactional origins and developmental sequelae of attachment, but also in explanations

of why associations obtain. Model I is 'domain-specific' (i.e. narrow) in that only 'within-system' empirical relations are anticipated. Thus, maternal sensitivity to attachment signals forecasts attachment security, which itself predicts outcomes directly involving the attachment system (e.g. future security; close friendships; intimacy), whereas maternal sensitivity while playing with and teaching the child directly influence infant play and cognitive development, *respectively,* which themselves forecast directly related features of subsequent development.

Quite the opposite of the narrow, domain-specific model is the broad general model (III) that depicts

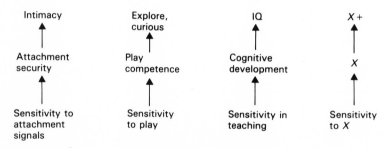

Model I: Domain specific

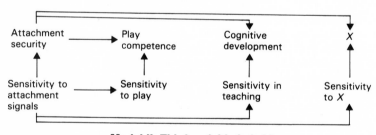

Model II: Third variable hybrid

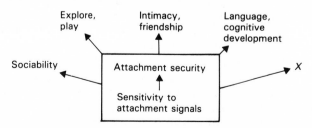

Model III: Domain general−foundational

Fig. 16.1 Alternative models of the origins and sequelae of attachment security: (I) domain specific; (II) third variable hybrid; and (III) domain-general — foundational. See text for further details.

attachment security as foundational to a variety of features of development. Thus, sensitivity to attachment signals promotes attachment security, which itself fosters development in a wide variety of domains (e.g. sociability, friendships, language, etc.).

Model II represents an attempt to explain model III findings in terms of model I and is thus something of a methodological hybrid. Basic to this model is the assumption that while attachment security functions narrowly (like model I), findings occur consistent with the broader model (III), but only as a function of 'third variable' processes. Specifically, what this model indicates is that attachment security is related to a variety of domains of development that would seem to lie outside the attachment system (e.g. sociability, language development), but only because the sensitivity which fosters attachment security is correlated with maternal sensitivity in other contexts of interaction (e.g. play, teaching) which themselves directly influence these other features of development. Note, then, that early attachment security comes to be related to later domains of development that do not appear to be directly attachment related because the features of early experience that foster security of attachment are also correlated with features of early experience that foster other aspects of development.

At present, there is no way of determining which of these models best accounts for the available data simply because the findings in the literature could be a function of any one of these models. While the breadth of correlates documented to date could reflect processes outlined in model III, they might also be a function of more domain-specific processes (model I) that masquerade as evidence of model III because of 'third variable' processes (model II). Needless to say, more research is required before these complexities can be teased apart and the derivative conundrums resolved.

Mechanisms of influence: the internal working model

Irrespective of whether one subscribes to a narrow or broad view of attachment and its influence upon development, one is left to ponder the mechanisms that explain the correlational evidence to be reviewed on the sequelae of attachment. Presuming for sake of argument that the findings to be con-

sidered reflect truly causal effects of early attachment security, the question to be asked, even if not fully answered, is 'why do these associations obtain?' Most answers to this question offered by students of attachment theory derive from Bowlby's thinking about 'internal working models'. Actual (as opposed to fantasized) experience in interaction with the mother, it is asserted, leads the child to develop expectations and understandings about how the interpersonal world, or perhaps more narrowly, the world of close relationships, operates. These ideas, impressions, understandings then lead the child selectively to attend to, encode and respond to particular experiences that are consistent with this world view — or to reinterpret as consistent events and experiences that are not — in a way that maintains and sustains that understanding of the interpersonal world. Thus, children who have been rejected or treated insensitively anticipate such treatment from others (or more narrowly, from others with whom they are in close relationships), respond principally to cues consistent with this view (which they selectively attend to) and, thereby, evoke treatment consistent with it. In contrast, a child who has experienced an accepting and responsive mothering figure anticipates and attends to quite different cues and experiences, responds selectively to them in a way that fosters their repetition and, in so doing, contributes to the creation of the more harmonious interpersonal world that he encounters (Bowlby, 1982; Bretherton, 1985; Main *et al.*, 1985).

Although there is some support for attachment-related differences in children's and adults' representations of attachment (Main *et al.*, 1985; Cassidy, 1988; Bretherton *et al.*, 1990), there is as yet little direct evidence that secure or insecure children differentially anticipate interpersonal events, selectively attend to different events, or differentially encode or transform (to be consistent with their internal working models) events and experiences (Main *et al.*, 1985). Therefore, the notion of internal working models as the causal process explaining the associations between attachment security and developmental sequelae remains a useful interpretive heuristic in need of empirical evaluation.

Until such work is carried out and demonstrates, in fact, that affective—cognitive processes do mediate linkages between attachment security and interpersonal functioning, many will assert, not unreasonably, that the construct of 'internal working model' has become a catch-all, *post-hoc* explanation (Hinde, 1989). Moreover, they will contend that the data might be more parsimoniously accounted for by stable temperamental proclivities or by the development of simple behavioural skills (that do not require complex notions about models and expectations).

Needless to say, understanding of causal processes has important implications for intervention. If it is skills that account for the cross-time associations that have been discerned, then it may simply be a matter of training children to engage in certain behaviours in order to reduce the developmental risks they may face. If, instead, the internal working model is the mechanism of influence, then interventions will be required to modify children's expectations and attentional proclivities. Depending upon whether one views the model as dependent upon experience in close relationships, it may or may not be possible to modify affective–cognitive processes with short-term and specifically targeted procedures. In any event, the point to be made is that the issue of causal processes is very important therapeutically.

Process of influence: the role of early experience

Like psychoanalytic theory before it, attachment theory is a theory of early experience. Even though contemporary attachment theorists and researchers are not adherents of a strong early experience, or critical period model of development, they are of the opinion that what happens early sets the stage for what happens later in development (via internal working model mechanisms). This is evident, as we shall see, in research designs that link attachment security in the first year or two of life to a broad array of developmental phenomena at later periods.

What remains unclear in all such research is not merely whether the postulated mechanism of influence (i.e. internal working model) is in fact responsible for across-time associations, but whether the linkage is a function of early experience or concurrent experiences that are correlated with earlier experiences (Lamb *et al.*, 1984, 1985). In

particular, if it is empirically demonstrated — as it has been — that young children with secure attachment histories are more ego resilient than are age-mates with insecure attachment histories, does this mean that it is *early* attachment history that causes later personality functioning? The alternative that attachment researchers have begun to address only recently is that it is the quality of the concurrent mother–child relationship, or some other feature of the concurrent environment that is correlated with early attachment, that is causally important. Thus, it remains possible that the 'influence' of early attachment in the research to be surveyed is only apparent, not real, and that it is continuity in the environment, rather than early experience/attachment that is causally influential.

In the context of this discussion two recent studies are particularly noteworthy, one dealing with attachment and the other not. In the attachment research, Renken *et al.* (1989) sought to determine whether early attachment history contributed to the prediction of later aggression once experiences subsequent to infancy were controlled. It was. In a study not directly concerned with attachment, Bradley *et al.* (1988) found that the very parameters of early maternal care that are considered central to the development of secure and insecure infant–mother attachments — acceptance and responsivity — predicted social functioning (i.e. considerateness) at age 10 even when these same features of maternal care at age 10 were statistically controlled. Both investigations, then, suggest that attachment or attachment-important features of early experience exert an influence on later development that can not be explained in terms of continuity in environment.

Adaptation

The fact that the evidence pertaining to the development of children judged securely and insecurely attached to their mothers as infants repeatedly indicates that the former look more socially skilled and better adjusted than the latter has resulted in some confusion about the notion that attachment is adaptive. When Bowlby discussed the evolutionary basis of attachment behaviour, he stressed the survival (i.e. adaptive) value of the infant maintaining proximity to his caregiver. Unfortunately, when attachment researchers have written about the functioning of secure and insecure children, frequently they have spoken in terms of the adaptive functioning of the former and the maladaptive functioning of the latter. By using the same terminology to discuss evolutionary−biological and psychological−mental health phenomena, it is not surprising that some have come to equate the mental health benefits of a secure attachment with evolutionary benefits. Indeed, Ainsworth (1979, p. 45) herself seemed to imply as much when she argued that 'securely attached' babies 'developed normally, i.e. along species-characteristic lines' (Hinde, 1982a, p. 69).

Yet, as Hinde (1982a; Hinde & Stevenson-Hinde, 1991) has made abundantly clear, and as Ainsworth (1984a) has acknowledged, levels of analysis need to be distinguished when terms like 'adaptation' are employed. Although it may be beneficial or adaptive in the mental health sense to develop a secure attachment, it is certainly mistaken to presume from an evolutionary or phylogenetic perspective that a secure attachment is better or more adaptive than an insecure attachment. As Hinde (1982a, pp. 71−72) has noted, 'there is no best mothering (or attachment) style, for different styles are better in different circumstances, and natural selection would act to favor individuals with a range of potential styles from which they select appropriately . . . mothers and babies will be programmed (by evolution) not simply to form one sort of relationship but a range of possible relationships according to circumstances . . . optimal mothering (and attachment) behaviour will differ according to the sex of the infant, its ordinal position in the family, the mother's social status, caregiving contributions from other family members, the state of physical resources, and so on . . . a mother−child relationship which produces successful adults in one situation may not do so in another.' In other words, while it may be the case that securely attached children develop, in contemporary Western society (or perhaps just in middle-class American society), more competently and are more likely to grow up into happy, mentally healthy adults in this ecology, it is completely inaccurate to infer from such evidence or otherwise to presume that, on the basis of natural selection theory, one attachment or mothering style is necessarily best.

INDIVIDUAL DIFFERENCES: METHODS OF ASSESSMENT

Initial efforts to assess attachment security focused upon infants and then young children. As attachment researchers have become more interested in the role of attachment across the lifespan, adult assessments have been developed.

Infant/early childhood assessment

The primary method used for assessing attachment security was developed by Ainsworth and Wittig (1969) for studying 12−18 month olds and is called the 'strange situation'. This procedure entails a series of structured observations of parent, child and an unfamiliar female in a laboratory playroom. The central events include two separations of parent from child (via parental leave taking), during one of which the child remains with the stranger and during the second the child is first alone and then briefly with the stranger prior to the return of the parent. It is the purpose of this 20-minute procedure to activate the attachment system by exposing the child to a series of progressive stressors: an unfamiliar place, an unfamiliar person, a parental separation and the experience of being alone.

The behaviour of the parent in the strange situation is purposefully controlled (via directions to her) and it is only the behaviour of the child that is used to make attachment classifications. Before describing the basis for these classifications, several points should be noted. First, it is the assumption of the classification system that what is being evaluated is the child's attachment to his mother and thus the security/insecurity of the relationship *as experienced by* the child. Thus, the strange situation does not provide an evaluation of the mother's bond to the baby nor of the relationship as an entity in and of itself. Further, the child's behaviour in the laboratory is presumed to reflect the quality of the attachment relationship as experienced by the child at the time of testing and thus, as already noted, is subject to change at later testings.

Infants classified as securely attached (pattern B) use the mother as a secure base from which to explore, reduce their exploration and may be distressed in her absence, but greet her positively on her return, and then return to exploration.

Secure infants classified into subcategories B1 and B2 are less distressed by separation than those subcategorized as B3 and B4, and greet the mother following separation by vocalizing, smiling or waving across a distance rather than by immediately seeking physical contact (Fig. 16.2). These secure patterns characterize 66% of infants in normative samples (Van Ijzendoorn & Kroonenberg, 1988).

Until recently, only two patterns of insecurity had been identified using the strange situation, each corresponding to one of the insecure patterns described above. Infants classified as insecure—avoidant (pattern A) explore with little reference to the mother, are minimally distressed by her departure and seem to ignore or avoid her on return. Infants classified as insecure—ambivalent/resistant (pattern C) fail to move away from the mother and explore minimally. These infants are highly distressed by separations and are difficult to settle on reunions. In normative samples this pattern characterizes 14% of babies, whereas the insecure—avoidant pattern is found about 20% of the time (Van Ijzendoorn & Kroonenberg, 1988).

As a result of recent research on clinical populations, a fourth pattern has been identified, known as insecure—disorganized (pattern D) (Main & Solomon, 1986). The development of this classification was precipitated by findings that a small number of cases could not be classified confidently into the other three categories; that in the three-classification system many children with known histories of abuse and neglect received classifications of B; and in some clinical samples infants were showing features of both avoidant and resistant

attachment (Van Ijzendoorn *et al.*, in press). The salient feature of infants classified as disorganized is that they appear to lack a coherent strategy for managing exploration and attachment. In addition, they engage in odd behaviours (e.g. repetitive rocking, covering face with hands, turning in circles) that are inexplicable except in the context of fear or confusion in the presence of the mother.

It must be noted that the boundaries of the D pattern are still being developed and that there are on-going attempts to ensure that this category does not become a miscellaneous classification for children not readily fitting into the other groups (Main & Solomon, 1990). Unlike the three original categories, this category has yet to be validated by home observation data, though there is increasing evidence that children placed in this group (or their parents) are likely to have experienced attachment-related trauma (Carlson *et al.*, 1989; Main & Hesse, 1990).

The strange situation has been subject to a variety of criticisms. Above all else, its artificiality and presumed ecological invalidity have been stressed by critics of the methodology. A point often not appreciated, however, is that the method, just like a cardiovascular stress test, is not intended to reflect the everyday experiences of a child, but rather is designed to stress the attachment system and thereby evoke attachment behaviour. It seems to us, then, that the critical issue is not its face validity, but whether differences discerned using it relate to external correlates (i.e. antecedents and sequelae) in ways that are consistent with theoretical expectations (i.e. construct validity).

Questions have also been raised about the cross-

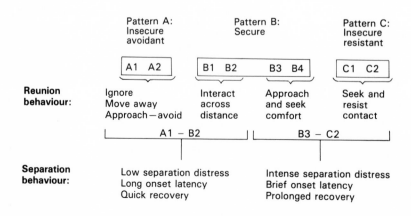

Fig. 16.2 Attachment classification system. See text for details.

cultural validity of the strange situation on the basis of studies showing that, relative to North American comparisons, a disproportionate number of infant—mother attachments are classified as insecure—avoidant in north Germany (Grossmann *et al.*, 1981) and insecure—resistant in Japan (Miyake *et al.*, 1985) and on Israeli kibbutzim (Sagi *et al.*, 1985). Although the Japanese data do seem to be a function of a methodological artefact, specifically, the fact that the strange situation is not experienced as a moderate stressor but rather an extreme one because infants in this culture are so rarely separated from their mothers, the German and Israeli data seem to reflect the theoretically expected effect of rearing regimen on attachment. After all, not only does there seem to be a 'premature' push towards avoidance-provoking independence in the first year of life in north German culture (Grossmann *et al.*, 1981), but Sagi *et al.* (1991) have shown recently that the elevated incidence of insecure—resistant attachments in Israel is restricted to kibbutzim in which children sleep in children's houses apart from their parents; noteworthy, too, is that it is not unusual for night waking and crying to be ignored or responded to only after much delay in such non-family sleeping arrangements.

Questions have also been raised about whether independent behaviour in the strange situation is mistakenly judged to be evidence of avoidance, especially in the case of infants who experience routine non-maternal care. Clarke-Stewart (1989), Thompson (1988) and others have argued that these children's daily separation experiences lead them to behave more independently in the strange situation because they are less stressed by the separations built into it and that it is such a methodological artefact that causes them to be (erroneously) classified as insecure—avoidant more frequently than children without early and extensive infant day care experience. Not only is it the case that a comprehensive review of relevant studies by Clarke-Stewart and Fein (1983) shows that infant day care experience is *not* related to less (or more) stress in the strange situation (as indexed by distress), but a recent study directly addressing this proposition found no support whatsoever for it (Belsky & Braungart, 1991).

All this is not to say that the strange situation is not without its limits. Coder agreement for classifi-

cations is typically greater than 90%, yet boundary issues remain. Even though the classificatory system has distinct advantages in certain ways (Ainsworth, 1989), there can be advantages to a continuous metric of security—insecurity as well (Waters & Deane, 1985). In addition, as with any measurement, two assessments surely provide more reliable data than one, yet repeated participation in the strange situation within a short time period is not likely to produce valid results (Ainsworth *et al.*, 1978). In order to address these and other issues, Waters and Deane (1985) developed an alternative assessment methodology known as the 'attachment Q sort'. This method, which has been used by mothers and observers (after hours of naturalistic home observations), involves sorting a list of 90—100 descriptive statements selected to capture behaviours central to the attachment, fear and exploratory systems (e.g. actively solicits comforting from adult when distressed, remains fearful of moving toys or animals, bouts of exploration and play away from the adult are brief) in terms of how well they characterize the behaviour of the child when observed in a familiar environment. The resulting distribution of items is then correlated with a 'criterion sort' based upon the averaged responses of a set of experts regarding how a proto-typically secure infant would behave. A major methodological contribution of this procedure is that it yields a continuous variable measure of attachment security. Although a number of studies document the validity of the measure when completed by trained personnel after several hours of careful observation (e.g. Vaughn & Waters, 1990) some have questioned the validity of the procedure when employed by mothers themselves because of the high correlation with socially desirable responses (Belsky & Rovine, 1990).

Recently, new procedures have been developed for assessing attachment quality in 3 and 4 year olds (Cassidy & Marvin, 1990) and 5—7 year olds (Main & Cassidy, 1988). Based on their reunion behaviour following laboratory separation from the parent, children are classified into one of four attachment groups. Although the discrete attachment behaviours of young children differ from those shown by infants, the underlying organization of these behaviours in young children is thought to be quite similar to that of infants. Age-appropriate manifestations of proximity seeking, contact maintaining, avoidance and resistance are organized into patterns of secure, avoidant and ambivalent attachment. In addition, some children (called insecure/disorganized−controlling) show disorganized behaviour similar to that seen in some infants (Main & Solomon, 1986) and/or they have taken control of the relationship. Although research validating these classifications with home observations of child−parent interactions has not yet been conducted, evidence of concurrent and predictive validity has emerged from studies indicating that security is associated with higher self-esteem (Cassidy, 1988), less fearfulness (Stevenson-Hinde & Shouldice, 1991), fewer behaviour problems in girls (Turner, 1991), and lower likelihood of clinical referral (DeMulder & Radke-Yarrow, 1991; Cicchetti & Barnett, 1992; Greenberg *et al.*, 1992) than is insecurity (see also Bretherton *et al.*, 1990; Shouldice & Stevenson-Hinde, 1991).

It must be noted that, for the present, all of these tools are research instruments, not clinical ones. After all, they were developed to study normal developmental processes, not to identify clinical cases. In fact, there is no evidence whatsoever that the strange situation or the Q sort are sufficiently precise to diagnose clinical problems or dictate professional intervention (Belsky & Nezworski, 1988).

Adult assessment

Two general approaches have been developed for assessing adolescent/adult internal working models of attachment. One approach involves a lengthy clinical interview, whereas the second was designed for use in survey research and is thus far less time consuming. The adult attachment interview (AAI) developed by Main and co-workers consists of 18 questions and is structured entirely around the topic of attachment, principally the individual's relationship to the mother and father during childhood (Main & Goldwyn, 1984, in press; George *et al.*, 1985;). Interviewees are instructed to describe their relationships with their parents and to provide specific biographical episodes to substantiate global evaluations. Subjects are asked directly about childhood experiences of rejection, being upset, ill and hurt as well as loss, abuse and separations. Subjects are also asked to offer explanations for the parent's

behaviour and to describe the current relationships with their parents and the influence they consider their childhood experiences exerted on their development. The interview is considered not so much to evoke the adult's actual, veridical experiences in childhood but, rather, their reconstructions of the meaning of early experiences. On the basis of this information obtained from the AAI, a specially trained evaluator rates the subject on a series of scales (e.g. role reversal, idealization, preoccupying anger, inability to recall) and then classifies the individual's 'state of mind' regarding attachment.

The secure−autonomous state of mind is reflected in an individual's inclination to value attachment relationships and regard attachment-related experiences as developmentally influential. In the course of the AAI, such persons appear self-reliant, objective and non-defensive. It is noteworthy that persons receiving this classification either convincingly describe a history of emotionally supportive relationship experiences or provide evidence that they have come to terms with a childhood lacking in them, thus permitting a balanced view of relationships.

Adults classified as insecure−dismissing have a tendency to deny negative experiences and emotions or to dismiss their developmental significance. These individuals can remember little and seem unable to re-evoke the feelings associated with the experiences they do recall. Often they offer an idealized picture of parent or parents but, in response to probes eliciting evidence to substantiate generalizations, may recall experiences quite inconsistent with their positive, global appraisals. Insecure−dismissing individuals present themselves as strong, independent people for whom closeness and attachment mean little. The defensive flavour of the detached pattern is reminiscent of the anxious−avoidant infant pattern.

Adults classified as insecure−preoccupied demonstrate a continuing involvement or preoccupation with their parents. They appear confused, incoherent and unobjective regarding relationships and their influences upon them. Anger over the past and present seems not to be resolved but, instead, to be a major organizing theme of their relationships with parents. These individuals seem caught up in their early relationships with little ability to move beyond them.

Perhaps the most intriguing work that has been done with this methodology is that showing a correspondence between maternal state of mind regarding attachment and infant strange situation classifications (autonomous−secure, dismissing−avoidant, preoccupied−resistant) (Grossmann *et al.*, 1988; Main & Goldwyn, 1994; van Ijzendoorn *et al.*, in press), even when AAIs are administered prior to the child's birth (Fonagy *et al.*, 1991). Noteworthy, too, are observational data suggesting that such associations are mediated by the quality of care that mothers provide, as mothers classified secure−autonomous have been observed to provide more sensitive care than mothers classified dismissing or preoccupied (Crowell & Feldman, 1988, 1991; Haft & Slade, 1989; Grossmann *et al.*, 1988).

In addition to Main's interview approach for assessing attachment in adults, far less expensive methods, derived from Main's work, have been developed by social psychologists studying romantic relationships. One assessment involves having respondents endorse one of three paragraphs characterizing their manner of relating to others (e.g. seek closeness versus maintain distance) which parallel strategies children use in the strange situation (Hazan & Shaver, 1987). Another involves subjects responding to a series of sentences taken from these paragraphs using a series of Likert-type scales (Collins & Read, 1990). While it is too soon to evaluate the soundness of these techniques, promising results pertaining to processes of dating and mating have been reported recently (Hazan & Shaver, 1987; Levy & Davis, 1988; Collins & Read, 1990).

It is noteworthy that all these adult assessments of attachment derive from ideas regarding individual differences developed on the basis of research on infants and young children. Given the fact that attachments in adulthood and in infancy are likely to be dramatically different, for example, proximity seeking being more important in infants and confiding more central to adults, it is reasonable to question whether this approach to assessment makes a great deal of sense. Reflection upon this issue highlights the need to distinguish between attachment behaviour and the underlying organization of the attachment system. Even though dramatic differences exist at the level of overt behaviour, organizational similarities can be discerned amongst children and adults. Common to both the strange situation and the AAI approaches to measurement is the notion, after all, that one can deny, limit or repress the expression of attachment feelings and behaviours (avoidance, dismissing), exaggerate them (resistance, preoccupation) or express them in an open and balanced way involving appropriate dependency and confidence in the partner (secure, autonomous).

INDIVIDUAL DIFFERENCES: EMPIRICAL EVIDENCE

Having considered some of the major theoretical and conceptual issues pertaining to attachment theory and research, a survey is now made of some of the empirical evidence that has been gathered by scientists studying attachment. The focus of this survey is exclusively upon individual differences in attachment security, assessed by means of the measurement tools described in the preceding section. The discussion is organized around the themes of the origins and sequelae of attachment security.

Origins of individual differences in attachment security

Central to Ainsworth's contribution to attachment theory is the notion that the quality of maternal care, particularly the mother's sensitive responsiveness, is the major determinant of variation in attachment security. In this section of the chapter research is considered pertaining to observed maternal behaviour, then research focused upon temperament as an alternative explanation of individual differences in attachment security. Then the evidence is considered from studies of clinical populations, before proceeding to summarize evidence pertaining to non-maternal care.

Maternal behaviour

Certainly consistent with Ainsworth's thesis that the nature of maternal care shapes the security of the infant−mother attachment bond is an abundance of correlational evidence showing that attachment security at age 12−18 months is related to ratings of sensitivity made in the first year in middle-class American (Ainsworth *et al.*, 1978) and German families (Grossmann *et al.*, 1985), as well as in economically disadvantaged, often single-parent ones (Egeland & Farber, 1984), and to frequency- and rate-based indices of responsiveness to distress (Crockenberg, 1981); moderate, appropriate stimulation (Belsky *et al.*, 1984), interactional synchrony (Isabella *et al.*, 1989; Isabella & Belsky, 1990), and warmth, involvement and responsiveness (Bates *et al.*, 1985). Noteworthy, too, is evidence that insecure−avoidant attachment is correlated with intrusive, excessively stimulating interactional styles of mothering, whereas insecure−resistant attachment is related to an unresponsive, underinvolved approach to caregiving (Belsky *et al.*, 1984; Smith & Pedersen, 1988; Isabella *et al.*, 1989; Lewis & Feiring, 1989; Malatesta *et al.*, 1989).

But perhaps the most important evidence concerning the influence of maternal care in the development of attachment security is to be found in a recent experimental manipulation of the caregiving behaviour of lower class Dutch mothers rearing babies who evinced especially high irritability on two separate neonatal evaluations (Van den Boom, 1990). Home-based intervention efforts to foster maternal sensitivity (operationalized as 'contingent, consistent and appropriate responses to both positive and negative infant signals') between 6 and 8 months resulted not only in a sizeable difference in the observed mothering of randomly assigned experimental and control mothers immediately after the intervention, but dramatically different percentages of 12 month olds classified as secure when seen in the strange situation — in favour of the experimental group (68% versus 28%, $n = 50$ in each group). The high rate of insecurity in the control group, approximating that found in abusive samples (see below), is likely to be a result of the synergistic effect of two risk conditions — economic adversity and infant irritability.

Temperament

Not only these data, but others from this same enquiry, would seem to argue against the claim which receives some correlational support in the literature that it is infant temperament that is the cause of 'insecurity' as measured in the strange situation (Chess & Thomas, 1982; Kagan, 1982). Contrary to the results of a meta-analysis of temperament−attachment studies which showed that neonatal irritability is weakly, though significantly linked to resistant behaviour and insecure−resistant classifications (Goldsmith & Alansky, 1987), Van den Boom (1990) found that the insecure infants in her control group, all with histories of neonatal irritability, were disproportionately classified as insecure−avoidant rather than insecure−resistant.

This is not to say that there is no temperament contribution to the development of attachment security or to strange situation classifications. Upon finding more early temperament correlates of an A1−B2 versus B3−C2 split of strange situation classifications than of an A versus B versus C (or secure versus insecure) split, Belsky and Rovine (1987) proposed that temperament might not so much determine whether a child is classified as secure or insecure, but rather the manner in which security (B1−B2 versus B3−B4) and insecurity (A versus C) are expressed. Thus, sensitive care to an irritable infant may result in a classification of secure and prone to distress (B3−B4) rather than insecure and prone to distress (C), whereas sensitive care to a non-irritable infant may result in a classification of B1−B2 rather than A. Yet to be clearly distinguished in the research literature, however, are the ways in which security-promoting (or insecurity-promoting) care to one type of infant (e.g. irritable) might differ from that to an infant with a distinctly different temperament.

However intriguing the correlational evidence linking quality of mothering to attachment security, and however impressive the results of Van den Boom's (1990) experimental manipulation of maternal behaviour to test Ainsworth's central theoretical proposition, it would be mistaken to conclude that maternal behaviour explains all the variance in attachment security. What remains unclear, in fact, in light of the modest magnitude of statistically significant correlational findings is whether their modesty is a function of limits of measurement (of mothering and of security) or of actual maternal influence. Additional correlational evidence from clinical samples continues, nevertheless, to point to the importance of both the mother and the care she provides.

Clinical samples

Consider, first, in this regard, the results of a recent analysis of almost 1000 cases obtained from eight studies of child maltreatment (Youngblade & Belsky, 1989). Not only were infants and toddlers with histories of parental maltreatment more than twice as likely as non-maltreated children drawn from similar socioeconomic circumstances to be classified as insecure (65 versus 31%), but there appeared to be some specificity between type of maltreatment and type of insecurity which mirrored results from so-called 'normal' samples: whereas abused children were disproportionately likely to develop insecure−avoidant attachments (recall intrusive−avoidance associations), neglected children were disproportionately likely to develop insecure−resistant attachments (recall unresponsiveness, underinvolved−resistance association). Also intriguing was the fact that maltreated children were more likely than controls to commingle patterns of avoidance and resistance and be classified as D.

The second set of data to consider highlighting the role of the mother in the development of attachment security comes from studies of maternal depression. Not only do insecurity rates among infants/toddlers whose mothers suffer from unipolar depression hover around 50% (Radke-Yarrow *et al.*, 1985; Teti *et al.*, 1991), but among mothers suffering from bipolar disorder (Radke-Yarrow *et al.*, 1985) or unipolar depression in the context of severe economic disadvantage (Lyons-Ruth, 1988) it is about 80%. What makes these data particularly notable is that depressed mothers are known to provide care that is often hostile and intrusive, as well as detached and unresponsive (Cohn *et al.*, 1986; Cohn & Tronick, 1988; for review, see Gelfand & Teti, 1990). Such evidence clearly suggests that the mother's psychological well-being may affect the care she provides her child and thus the development of attachment security. Notably consistent with such reasoning are Benn's (1986) data indicating that when an index of psychological well-being is controlled (in a non-clinical sample), pre-existing associations between quality of

maternal care and attachment security are substantially attenuated.

Non-maternal care

Because of the role that lengthy child−parent separations played in the original formulations of attachment theory, concern has been raised often about the consequences of more routine, short-term separations of the kind experienced on a daily basis by children cared for by someone other than a parent when the mother is employed. The initial work addressing this issue focused almost exclusively upon children being cared for in very high quality, university-based centres and generally failed to reveal any consistent association between day care and attachment insecurity (for reviews see Belsky & Steinberg, 1978; Rutter, 1981). To be noted, however, is that this first wave of attachment day care research used as an index of security the extent to which the child became upset upon separation from the parent, even though it was never clear conceptually whether greater or lesser distress should be considered a marker of security (or insecurity).

Recent compilations of the results of (many of the same) studies carried out in the USA of infants experiencing a variety of non-maternal care-giving arrangements (e.g. centres, family day care homes, nanny care) reveal a reliable association between more than 20 hours/week of such care in the first year of life and attachment insecurity. The actual strength of the association is open to question, with Belsky and Rovine (1988), Clarke-Stewart (1989) and Lamb *et al.* (1990) indicating, respectively, that the rate of infant−mother attachment insecurity were 65%, 24% and 83% higher amongst infants with more than 20 hours/week of non-parental care in their first year than for infants with less time (including none at all) in such care. Also noteworthy is that the only two investigations that focus upon attachment to father reveal that sons with more than 35 or more hours per week of such non-maternal care (in the USA) are more likely to develop insecure attachments to their fathers and thus two insecure attachments (one to mother and one to father) than are other boys (Chase-Lansdale & Owen, 1987; Belsky & Rovine, 1988).

A variety of explanations have been offered to

account for such findings. The fact that more than half of the children who experience early and extensive infant day care achieve secure classifications clearly indicates that separation *per se* is not the cause of these elevated rates of insecurity. The fact that the quality of child care in the USA is known to be limited; that toddlers are more likely to develop secure attachments to their caregivers when their caregivers are more sensitive, responsive and available to them (Howes *et al.*, 1988; Goosens & van Ijzendoorn, 1990); and that security of attachment to caregiver is itself related to more competent social functioning, especially in concert with secure attachment to mother (Howes *et al.*, 1988), would clearly seem to implicate the quality of non-maternal care which the child receives. Also to be considered is the quality of care that the child experiences at home when with his parents, especially since extensive time away from the parent may make it more difficult for the parent to provide the kind of care that fosters attachment security. Of course, the pressures that working parents experience when at home with the child may also make the provision of such care more difficult. In all likelihood, future work will reveal that the quality of care provided both by parent and by caregiver(s) will determine the security of the infant−parent attachment relationship.

What also remain unclear at present are the developmental implications of the elevated rates of insecurity observed in the case of children with early and extensive day care experience, at least as provided in the USA. This would seem to be especially so in light of evidence from the USA (Howes *et al.*, 1989), The Netherlands (van Ijzendoorn *et al.*, 1991) and Israel (Oppenheim *et al.*, 1988) showing in the case of children with such early day care experience, that it is security of attachment to caregiver, not to parent, which predicts future social functioning. Might it be that when children's non-parental care is initiated on a full-time or near full-time basis during the period when attachment bonds are first forming that the influence that parents might otherwise have exerted upon the child's future development is transferred to the alternative caregiver? Might this, in fact, explain why parents have been found repeatedly to report that their 3−8 year olds with early and extensive day care experience are less

compliant with their demands than children without such child care histories (for review see Belsky, 1990)?

Conclusion

The evidence reviewed provides repeated indication that the quality of care that mothers and day care workers provide, as well as mothers' own psychological well being, importantly influence the development of infant−caregiver attachment relationships in the opening years of life. Indeed, as severity of threats to maternal well-being and quality and quantity of such maternal care increase, so does the apparent risk of an insecure relationship developing. Recall that while the rate of insecurity hovers around 25−30% in low-risk samples, and increases to 40% (on average) when early and extensive non-maternal care is experienced, for children of clinically depressed mothers the rate of insecurity is approximately 50% − and higher still for manic−depressive mothers or depressed mothers who are severely economically disadvantaged − and 65% for children who are subjected to abuse and neglect. It seems safe to conclude, therefore, that as risks of inadequate and insufficient parenting accumulate (e.g. difficult temperament, maternal depression, marital conflict, poor quality maternal and non-maternal care), so does the likelihood of an insecure attachment (Belsky & Isabella, 1988).

Sequelae of attachment security

Central to attachment theory is the notion that early relationship experiences exert an important influence upon development. Having previously drawn attention to some of the weaknesses of the research that addresses this issue, it is now useful to summarize the evidence collected to date on the sequelae of attachment security, restricting the data to research on children's social development, including behaviour problems. Not only should comments made earlier regarding the boundaries of the attachment construct be kept in mind, as should issues of mechanism and process of influence, but attention also has to be called to the strength of the findings discerned. By no means are we dealing with a literature in which the statistically significant associations that have been discerned could be called overpowering or even strong. Modest, weak, yet consistent are frequently more appropriate adjectives. What remains unclear at present is whether such limits in the strength of the cross-time associations stem from limits in the measurement of attachment or the outcome to which it has been associated; from the fact that early attachments have only limited effects on later development; or from lawful processes of discontinuity that would attenuate predictions based on earlier attachment assessments.

Social development

In view of the fact that attachment theory is a theory about the characteristics, consequences and determinants of close relationships, it is surprising that efforts to conduct or even review research linking attachment history and social development have not attended to distinctions among the partners whose interactions with children are being studied. We deviate from this approach that essentially treats all social partners as equivalent and make distinctions between three classes of individuals — strangers, familiar others (class-mates, teachers) and persons with whom the child can be presumed to have a 'close' relationship (parent, sibling, friend). Fundamentally, we want to distinguish interactions with strangers that probably involve heritable tendencies concerning sociability (Plomin, 1986) from relationships with partners that probably involve processes of intimacy that we suspect to be far less heritable.

Interactions with unfamiliar children and adults. Whether one considers attachment-related research using unfamiliar children or adults as social partners, the conclusion to be drawn is the same: there is no consistent evidence that children with secure attachment histories are more sociable towards strangers than are age-mates with insecure histories. Although a number of studies present contemporaneous or longitudinal evidence indicating that secure children are more sociable (with adults: Main & Weston, 1981; Plunkett et al., 1988; with children: Pastor, 1981), other research repeatedly fails to replicate such findings (with adults: Lamb

et al., 1982; Frodi, 1983; Thompson & Lamb, 1984; with children: Jacobson & Wille, 1986).

Interactions with class-mates and teachers. More consistency is evident when interactions and relationships with more familiar individuals are the focus of enquiry. The only relevant investigation of teacher—child interactions indicates that pre-schoolers with secure attachment histories were less emotionally dependent upon their teachers than class-mates with insecure histories, but were more likely to call upon the teacher when the child faced a challenge which he could not manage alone (Sroufe et al., 1983). With respect to peer relations, a number of both contemporaneous and longitudinal correlational studies indicate that children with secure histories score higher on a variety of indices of peer relations during the preschool and elementary school years, including empathy towards peers (Sroufe, 1983); popularity with peers (Sroufe et al., 1983); (lack of) victimization by peers (Troy & Sroufe, 1987); inclusion in group activities (Grossmann et al., 1989); and social pretend and (less) conflict during play (Howes et al., 1990). Apparently, a foundation of a secure attachment history appears to be an asset that a child brings into the classroom (for further evidence, see Waters et al., 1979; Pierrehumbert et al., 1989; Strayer et al., 1989; Cohn, 1990).

Relations with parents, friends and siblings. As relations between child and social partner become closer or more intimate, the 'influence' of attachment security becomes more apparent. Consider first evidence pertaining to the mother—child relationship. Consistent with the notion that early security should foster a continuing positive orientation towards the parent, studies show that children with secure histories are more compliant to maternal directives and more cooperative and responsive in interacting with mother (Joffe, 1981; Londerville & Main, 1981; Main, 1983; Pierrehumbert et al., 1985). In all likelihood, such associations are mediated by continuity in the care-giving environment, as it has been shown repeatedly, too, that mothers of secure infants continue to be more sensitive and supportive as their children develop (Londerville & Main, 1981; Pierrehumbert et al., 1985; Bates et al., 1988; Bus & van Ijzendoorn, 1988).

Although the data base is by no means large, the 'effect' of attachment security is also evident in studies of close peer relationships. Best friend dyads of 4 year olds engage in more harmonious, less controlling and more responsive interaction when age-mates are both secure than when only one is secure (Park & Waters, 1989) and this might in part explain why, among 10 year olds, Grossmann *et al.* (1989) found that those with secure histories were more likely than those with insecure histories to report having one or a few good friends who were trustworthy and reliable. Also noteworthy in this context are Hodges and Tizard's (1989) finding that adolescents who spent their first few years in a residential nursery (due to family problems) that did not promote close, enduring relationships generally failed to develop confiding peer relationships.

When we turn attention to another close peer relationship, that between siblings, we find that older siblings with secure attachments to mother are not only more inclined to comfort a distressed younger sibling (Teti & Ablard, 1989), but also engage in less conflict with their younger sibling during joint play (Volling & Belsky, 1992). Importantly, this latter cross-age prediction obtains over a 4-year period even after contemporaneous and intervening measurements of parent–child relations are controlled.

In sum, there is repeated indication that security provides a foundation upon which subsequent harmonious relations with adults and peers are built. This seems to be true principally when the relationship under study is either a close relationship (with mother, friend or sibling), or when it involves a reasonably familiar social partner (teacher, class-mate) and is least likely to be valid when the child's partner is a strange child or adult. In thinking about the sequelae of attachment security, then, there seems to be a clear need to distinguish intimacy or intimacy-like relations from mere sociability.

Behaviour problems

The connection Bowlby (1945) drew between troublesome family experiences in early childhood and later 'affectionless psychopathy' in his retrospective study of 44 thieves, along with Tizard's subsequent, prospective study indicating that good quality institutional care in which close, enduring caregiver–child relationships were not encouraged was associated with attention seeking, restlessness, disobedience and unpopularity at age 8 (even when children were adopted into good homes after age 4), raised the prospect of a linkage between attachment insecurity and behaviour problems (Tizard & Tizard, 1971; Tizard & Rees, 1974; Tizard & Hodges, 1978). Certainly consistent with such thinking is evidence that children with insecure attachment histories, relative to those with secure attachments, are less compliant (e.g. Joffe, 1981), less able to control impulses (Easterbrooks & Goldberg, 1987), less able to tolerate frustration (Matas *et al.*, 1978) and experience more conflict and disharmony in relations with peers and parents (Maslin & Bates, 1982; Howes *et al.*, 1990).

As the field of developmental psychopathology developed (Cicchetti, 1984; Sroufe & Rutter, 1984), and as the attachment relationship has come to be conceptualized as a protective factor (if secure) or risk factor (if insecure) (Sroufe, 1988), increased attention has been paid to the attachment–behaviour problem linkage. Even though several investigations have discerned across-time associations between insecure attachment during the infant/toddler years and subsequent problematic behaviour (Lewis *et al.*, 1984; Erickson *et al.*, 1985; Renkin *et al.*, 1989), as well as contemporaneous relations (Turner, 1991), the evidence is by no means uniform (Bates *et al.*, 1985; Bates & Bayles, 1988; Fagot & Kavanaugh, 1990). What seems reasonably clear, though, is that attachment insecurity should not be equated with behaviour problems (Belsky & Nezworski, 1988); that whether or not behaviour problems develop is likely to be a function of other factors and processes that maintain or deflect developmental trajectories; and that additional research is required to determine if antecedent or contemporaneous attachment security plays a truly causal role or, instead, simply correlates with indices of developmental psychopathology via yet to be studied, third variable mechanisms.

Conclusion

There can be little doubt that indices of attachment security in infancy and early childhood (classifications and Q sorts) are related to a wide variety of developmental 'outcomes'. Even though the data do not by any means chronicle causal processes and are open to a variety of interpretations (effects of early attachment, temperament, continuity in environment), it should be abundantly clear that attachment theory and the measurement of individual differences in attachment security has generated a huge literature with many provocative findings. Many issues remain to be explored and these will be considered briefly in the next and closing section of this chapter.

CONCLUSION: FUTURE DIRECTIONS

It is our opinion that the most pressing agenda for attachment research is to respond to Hinde and Stevenson-Hinde's (1988) well-articulated plea to clarify, especially empirically, Bowlby's seminal notion of the internal working model. As was made clear earlier, this theoretical construct is so broad that, on the one hand, it seems to explain almost too much yet, on the other, it has been described in sufficient detail that it presents a clear direction for future research (e.g. Main *et al.*, 1985). In particular, the tendencies of individuals to selectively attend to, encode and recall interpersonal experiences needs to be studied, as does the influence of these hypothesized internal working model processes on relationship processes. Efforts also need to be undertaken to determine whether, as has been theorized, it is such processes which account for lawful discontinuity in development following what might be regarded as 'corrective emotional experiences'. Is it the case, for example, that changes in working model processes help account for why adults with risky child-rearing histories (e.g. maltreatment, institutionalization) who have experienced supportive close relationships (with friends, spouses, therapists) parent more competently than their counterparts with similar rearing histories who have not had the good fortune to experience such supportive close relationships (Quinton *et al.*, 1984; Egeland *et al.*, 1988)?

A question such as this draws attention to more general lifespan issues that also merit attention. To the extent that attachment processes shape relationship functioning, especially close, intimate relationships, one is forced to wonder about the degree of influence they exert on friendship formation and mate selection. Work by Kobak and Sceery (1988) indicates that a secure−autonomous state of mind is related to friendship processes among college students, whereas work by Davis and Kirkpatrick (1991) shows that heterosexual pairings among dating couples are by no means random from the standpoint of attachment categories (far more A−C and B−B pairings than A−A or C−C), but these studies only begin to scratch the surface. In particular, the fact that these studies rely upon contemporaneous assessments of attachment security leaves us uninformed about the role of early attachment history. In point of fact, a question of central importance that can only be addressed once children seen early in life are followed into adulthood concerns the relation between childhood evaluations of security and those obtained in adulthood.

One of the most pressing social policy issues among those studying the ageing process concerns the care that adult children provide their ageing parents. It is interesting to observe, as child developmentalists, that most work in this area seems totally to neglect the fact that these parent−child relationships have lengthy histories. As students of attachment theory we are led to wonder how the history of the attachment relationship affects the parent−child relationship when roles are reversed and adult children must become the caretakers or guardians of their elderly parents. Is it the case, for example, that a history of a secure relationship makes for both a readiness and an ability to provide sensitive care to an ageing parent, and for that parent to accept the role of dependent, whereas this is not so in the case of relationships characterized by insecure attachments?

This issue becomes complicated when we realize that the child establishes distinct relationships with each parent and thus that one relationship may have a history of insecurity whereas the other is marked by security. In such cases, how does the adult child behave towards his or her elderly parents? Of course, this issue of multiple relationships raises questions about the integration in the individual's internal working model of various relationship experiences. Whether we consider the internal working model of a child, adolescent or adult, it remains unclear how multiple attachments shape the individual's development. We need to think here in terms of multiple contemporaneous attachments (e.g. mother and father) as well as multiple attachments across the life course (to mother, to best friend, to mate).

A final issue amongst many that could be raised concerns the concordance of attachments to parent by siblings. Although evidence reviewed earlier indicates that maternal state of mind regarding attachment is systematically and reliably related to infant—mother attachment, even research documenting significant concordance across siblings in their attachments to their mothers (Ward *et al.*, 1988) reveals substantial inconsistency. Similarly, evidence from The Netherlands indicates that toddlers often vary in the security of their attachments to the very same caregiver in day care (Goosens & van Ijzendoorn, 1990). Such data clearly indicate that presumably stable features of the caregiver (e.g. state of mind regarding attachment, personality) are not the sole determinants of infant—adult attachment security, yet it remains unclear how to explain such 'inconsistent' relationships.

While space precludes us from raising more issues or discussing in depth even those just raised, it is clear that Bowlby's theory of attachment has spawned a very generative research paradigm. We suspect that as evidence accumulates, as it has over the past decade, showing that attachment relevant measurements relate to a host of antecedent factors and presumed sequelae in theoretically meaningful ways, efforts to apply attachment ideas to new domains of enquiry (e.g. romantic relationships, ageing processes) will grow while efforts to illuminate issues of process, mechanism and boundaries will themselves develop.

ACKNOWLEDGEMENT

Work on this chapter was supported by grants from the National Institute of Mental Health to the first author (RO1 MH45527) and to the second author (MH46572).

REFERENCES

Ainsworth M.D. (1963) The development of infant—mother interaction among the Ganda. In B. Foss (ed.) *Determinants of Infant Behavior*, Vol. 2, pp. 114—138. Wiley, New York.

Ainsworth M.D. (1964) Patterns of attachment behavior shown by the infant in interaction with his mother. *Merrill-Palmer Quarterly* 10, 51—58.

Ainsworth M.D. (1967) *Infancy in Uganda: Infant Care and the Growth of Attachment.* Johns Hopkins Press, Baltimore.

Ainsworth M.D. (1973) The development of infant—mother attachment. In Caldwell B.M. & Ricciuti H.N. (eds) *Review of Child Development Research*, Vol. 3, pp. 1—94. University of Chicago Press, Chicago.

Ainsworth M.D. (1979) Infant—mother attachment. *American Psychologist* 34, 932—937.

Ainsworth M.D. (1984a) *Adaptation and attachment.* Paper presented to the International Conference on Infant Studies, New York City, April.

Ainsworth M.D. (1984b) Attachment. In Endler N.S. & McV Hunt J. (eds) *Personality and the Behavioral Disorders*, Vol. 1, pp. 559—602. Wiley, New York.

Ainsworth M.D. (1989) Attachments beyond infancy. *American Psychologist* 44, 709—716.

Ainsworth M.D. (1991) Attachment and other affectional bonds across the life cycle. In Parkes C.M., Stevenson-Hinde J. & Morris P. (eds) *Attachment Across the Life Cycle*, pp. 33—51. Routledge, London.

Ainsworth M.D., Bell S.M. & Stayton D.J. (1971) Individual differences in strange situation behavior of one-year-olds. In Schaffer H.R. (ed.) *The Origins of Human Social Relations*, pp. 17—52. Academic Press, London.

Ainsworth M.D., Blehar M.C., Waters E. & Wall S. (1978) *Patterns of Attachment: A Psychological Study of the Strange Situation.* Lawrence Erlbaum, Hillsdale, New Jersey.

Ainsworth M.D. & Wittig B.A. (1969) Attachment and exploratory behavior of one-year-olds in a strange situation. In Foss B.M. (ed.) *Determinants of Infant Behavior*, Vol. 4, pp. 129—173. Methuen, London.

Bates J.E. & Bayles K. (1988) Attachment and the development of behavior problems. In Belsky J. & Nezworski T. (eds) *Clinical Implications of Attachment*, pp. 253—299. Lawrence Erlbaum, Hillsdale, New Jersey.

Bates J.E., Maslin C.A. & Frankel K.A. (1985) Attachment security, mother—child interaction, and temperament as predictors of behavior-problem ratings at age three years. In Bretherton I. & Waters E. (eds) Growing points in attachment theory and research. *Monographs of the Society for Research in Child Development* 50, Serial No. 209, 167—193.

Belsky J. (1990) Parental and nonparental care and children's socioemotional development: A decade in review. *Journal of Marriage and the Family* 52, 885—903.

Belsky J. & Braungart J. (1991) Are insecure—avoidant infants with extensive day care experience less stressed by and more independent in the strange situation? *Child Development* 62, 567—571.

Belsky J. & Isabella R. (1988) Maternal, infant, and social–contextual determinants of attachment security. In Belsky J. & Nezworski T. (eds) *Clinical Implications of Attachment*, pp. 41–94. Lawrence Erlbaum, Hillsdale, New Jersey.

Belsky J. & Nezworski T. (eds) (1988) *Clinical Implications of Attachment*. Lawrence Erlbaum, Hillsdale, New Jersey.

Belsky J. & Rovine M.J. (1987) Temperament and attachment security in the strange situation: An empirical rapprochement. *Child Development* **58**, 787–795.

Belsky J. & Rovine M.J. (1988) Nonmaternal care in the first year of life and the security of infant–parent attachment. *Child Development* **59**, 157–167.

Belsky J. & Rovine M.J. (1990) Q-sort security and first-year nonmaternal care. *New Directions for Child Development: Child Care and Maternal Employment* **49**, 7–22.

Belsky J., Rovine M. & Taylor D.G. (1984) The Pennsylvania Infant and Family Development Project, III: The origins of individual differences in infant–mother attachment: Maternal and infant contributions. *Child Development* **55**, 718–728.

Belsky J. & Steinberg L. (1978) The effects of day care: A critical review. *Child Development* **49**, 929–949.

Bender L. & Yarnell H. (1941) An observation nursery. *American Journal of Psychiatry* **97**, 1158–1174.

Benn R.K. (1986) Factors promoting secure attachment relationships between employed mothers and their sons. *Child Development* **57**, 1224–1231.

Bowlby J. (1944) Forty-four juvenile thieves: Their characters and home life. *International Journal of Psycho-Analysis* **25**, 19–52, 107–127.

Bowlby J. (1958) The nature of the child's tie to his mother. *International Journal of Psycho-Analysis* **39**, 350–373.

Bowlby J. (1973) *Attachment and Loss*, Vol. 2. *Separation: Anxiety and Anger*. Basic Books, New York.

Bowlby J. (1979) *The Making and Breaking of Affectional Bonds*. Tavistock, London.

Bowlby J. (1980) *Attachment and Loss*, Vol. 3, *Loss — Sadness and Depression*. Basic Books, New York.

Bowlby J. (1982) *Attachment and Loss*, Vol. 1, *Attachment*, 2nd edn. Basic Books, New York.

Bowlby J. (1989) Psychoanalysis as a natural science. In Sandler J. (ed.) *Dimensions of Psychoanalysis*, pp. 99–121. Karnac Books, London.

Bradley R., Caldwell B. & Rock S. (1988) Home environment and school performance: A ten-year follow-up and examination of three models of environmental action. *Child Development* **59**, 852–867.

Brazelton T.B. (1977) Implications of infant development among the Mayan Indians of Mexico. In Leiderman P.H., Tulkin S.R. & Rosenfeld Y.A. (eds) *Culture and Infancy*, pp. 151–187. Academic Press, New York.

Bretheton I. (1978) Making friends with one-year-olds: An experimental study of infant–stranger interaction. *Merrill-Palmer Quarterly* **24**, 29–51.

Bretherton I. (1980) Young children in stressful situation: The supporting role of attachment figures and unfamiliar caregivers. In Coelho G.V. & Ahmed P.I. (eds) *Uprooting and Development*, pp. 179–210. Plenum, New York.

Bretherton I. (1985) Attachment theory: Retrospect and prospect. In Bretherton I. & Waters E. (eds) Growing points of the attachment theory and research. *Monographs of the Society for Research in Child Development* **50**, Serial No. 209, 3–35.

Bretherton I., Ridgeway D. & Cassidy J. (1990) The role of internal working models in the attachment relationship: Theoretical, empirical, and developmental considerations. In Greenberg L.M., Cicchetti D. & Cummings E.M. (eds) *Attachment in the Preschool Years*, pp. 273–320. University of Chicago Press, Chicago.

Bus A.G. & Van Ijzendoorn M.H. (1988) Attachment and early reading: A longitudinal study. *Journal of Genetic Psychology* **149**, 199–210.

Carlson V., Cicchetti D., Barnett D. & Braunwald E. (1989) Finding order in disorganization: Lessons from research on maltreated infants' attachment to their caregivers. In Cicchetti D. & Carlson V. (eds) *Child Maltreatment: Theory and Research on the Causes and Consequences of Maltreatment*, pp. 494–528. Cambridge University Press, New York.

Carr S., Dabbs J. & Carr T. (1975) Mother–infant attachment: The importance of the mother's visual field. *Child Development* **46**, 331–338.

Cassidy J. (1988) Child–mother attachment and the self in six-year-olds. *Child Development* **59**, 121–134.

Cassidy J. & Berlin L.J. (in press) The insecure/ambivalent pattern of attachment: Theory and research. *Child Development*.

Cassidy J. & Kobak R.R. (1988) Ambivalence and its relation to other defensive processes. In Belsky J. & Nezworski T. (eds) *Clinical Implications of Attachment*, pp. 300–326. Lawrence Erlbaum, Hillsdale, New Jersey.

Cassidy J. & Marvin R.S. with the Attachment Working Group of the John D. and Catherine T. MacArthur Foundation Network on the Transition from Infancy to Early Childhood (1990) *Attachment organization in three- and four-year-olds: Guidelines for classification*. Unpublished ms, Pennsylvania State University, University Park.

Chase-Lansdale P.L. & Owen M.T. (1987) Maternal employment in a family context: Effects on infant–mother and infant–father attachments. *Child Development* **58**, 1505–1512.

Chess S. & Thomas A. (1982) Infant bonding: Mystique and reality. *American Journal of Orthopsychiatry* **52**, 213–222.

Cicchetti D. (1984) The emergence of developmental psychopathology. *Child Development* **55**, 1–7.

Cicchetti D. & Barnett D. (1992) Attachment organization in maltreated preschoolers. *Development and Psychopath-

ology **3**, 397–411.

Clarke-Stewart K. (1989) Infant day care: Maligned or malignant. *American Psychologist* **44**, 266–273.

Clarke-Stewart K.A. & Fein G.G. (1983) Early childhood programs. In Haith M.M. & Campos J.J. (eds) *Infancy and Developmental Psychobiology*, Vol. 2, *Mussen's Handbook of Child Psychology*, 4th edn, pp. 917–1000. Wiley, New York.

Cohn D. (1990) Mother–child attachment of six-year-olds and social competence at school. *Child Development* **61**, 152–162.

Cohn J., Matias R., Tronick E., Connell D. & Lyons-Ruth K. (1986) Face-to-face interactions of depressed mothers and their infants. *New Directions for Child Development* **34**, 31–43.

Cohn J. & Tronick E. (1989) Specificity in infants' response to mothers' affective behavior. *Journal of the American Academy of Child and Adolescent Psychiatry* **28**, 242–248.

Colin V. (1991) *Human Attachment: What We Know Now*. US Department of Health and Human Services, Washington, DC.

Collins N. & Read N. (1990) Adult attachment, working models, and relationship quality in dating couples. *Journal of Personality and Social Psychology* **58**, 644–663.

Crockenberg S.B. (1981) Infant irritability, mother responsiveness, and social support influences on the security of infant–mother attachment. *Child Development* **52**, 857–869.

Crowell J.A. & Feldman S.S. (1988) Mothers' internal models of relationships and children's behavioral and developmental status: A study of mother–child interaction. *Child Development* **59**, 1273–1285.

Crowell J.A. & Feldman S.S. (1991) Mothers' working models of attachment relationships and mother and child behavior during separation and reunion. *Developmental Psychology* **27**, 597–605.

Davis K. & Kirkpatrick L. (1991) *Attachment style, gender, and relationship stability: A longitudinal analysis*. Unpublished ms, University of South Carolina, Columbia.

DeMulder E.K. & Radke-Yarrow M. (1991) Attachment with affectively ill and well mothers: Concurrent behavioral correlates. *Development and Psychopathology* **3**, 227–242.

Easterbrooks M.A. & Goldberg W. (1987) *Consequences of early family attachment patterns for later social-personality development*. Paper presented at the biennial meetings of the Society for Research in Child Development, Baltimore, Maryland, April.

Egeland B. & Farber E.A. (1984) Infant–mother attachment: Factors related to its development and changes over time. *Child Development* **55**, 753–771.

Egeland B., Jacobvitz D. & Sroufe L. (1988) Breaking the cycle of abuse: Relationship predictors. *Child Development* **59**, 1080–1088.

Erickson M.F., Sroufe L.A. & Egeland B. (1985) The relationship between quality of attachment and behav-ior problems in preschool in a high-risk sample. In Bretherton I. & Waters E. (eds) Growing points in attachment theory and research. *Monographs of the Society for Research in Child Development* **50**, Serial No. 209, 147–166.

Erikson E. (1950) *Childhood and Society*. Norton, New York.

Eysenck H. (1980) Personality, marital satisfaction, and divorce. *Psychological Report* **47**, 1235–1238.

Fagot B. & Kavanaugh K. (1990) The prediction of anti-social behavior from avoidant attachment classification. *Child Development* **61**, 864–873.

Fonagy P., Steele H. & Steele M. (1991) Maternal representations of attachment during pregnancy predict the organization of infant–mother attachment at one year. *Child Development* **62**, 891–905.

Frodi A. (1983) Attachment behavior and sociability with strangers in premature and fullterm infants. *Infant Mental Health Journal* **4**, 14–22.

Gelfand D. & Teti D. (1990) The effects of maternal depression on children. *Clinical Psychology Review* **10**, 329–353.

George C., Kaplan N. & Main M. (1985) *Adult attachment interview*. Unpublished ms, Department of Psychology, University of California, Berkeley.

Goldberg W.A. & Easterbrooks M.A. (1984) The role of marital quality in toddler development. *Developmental Psychology* **20**, 504–514.

Goldfarb W. (1943) The effects of early institutional care on adolescent personality. *Journal of Experimental Education* **12**, 106–129.

Goldsmith H.H. & Alansky J.A. (1987) Maternal and infant temperamental predictors of attachment: A meta-analytic review. *Journal of Consulting and Clinical Psychology* **55**, 805–816.

Goosens F. & van Ijzendoorn M. (1990) Quality of infants' attachment to professional caregivers. *Child Development* **61**, 832–837.

Greenberg M., Speltz M.L., DeKlyen M. & Endniga M. (1992) Attachment security in preschoolers with and without externalizing behavior problems: A replication. *Developmental Psychopathology* **3**, 413–430.

Grossmann K., Fremer-Bombik E., Rudolph J. & Gross-mann K.E. (1988) Maternal attachment representations as related to patterns of infant–mother attachment and maternal care during the first years. In Hinde R. & Stevenson-Hinde J. (eds) *Relationships within Families*, pp. 241–262. Clarendon Press, Oxford.

Grossmann K., Grossmann K., Hubler F. & Wastner U. (1981) German children's behavior towards their mothers at 12 months and their fathers at 18 months in Ainsworth's Strange Situation. *International Journal of Behavioral Development* **4**, 157–182.

Grossmann K., Grossmann K.E., Spangler G., Suess G. & Unzner L. (1985) Maternal sensitivity and newborns' orientation responses as related to quality of attachment in northern Germany. In Bretherton I. & Waters E. (eds) Growing points in attachment theory and research. *Monographs of the Society for Research in Child Development* **50**, Serial No. 209, 233–257.

Grossmann K., Scheurer-Englisch H. & Stephen C. (1989). *Attachment research: Lasting effects and domains of validity.* Paper presented at the Tenth Biennial Meetings of the International Society for the Study of Behavioral Development, Jyvaskyla, Finland, July.

Haft W. & Slade A. (1989) Affect attunement and maternal attachment: A pilot study. *Infant Mental Health* **10**, 157–172.

Harlow H. & Harlow M. (1965) The affectional system. In Schrier A., Harlow H. & Stollnitz F. (eds) *Behavior of Nonhuman Primates*, Vol. 2, pp. 163–184. Academic Press, New York.

Hazan C. & Shaver P. (1987) Romantic love conceptualized as an attachment process. *Journal of Personality and Social Psychology* **52**, 511–524.

Hinde R.A. (1976) On describing relationships. *Journal of Child Psychology* **17**, 1–19.

Hinde R.A. (1982a) Attachment: Some conceptual and biological issues. In Murray Parkes C. & Stevenson-Hinde J. (eds) *The Place of Attachment in Human Behavior*, pp. 60–76. Basic Books, New York.

Hinde R.A. (1982b) *Ethology*, Oxford University Press, Oxford.

Hinde R.A. (1988) Continuities and discontinuities: Conceptual issues and methodological considerations. In Rutter M. (ed.) *Studies of Psychosocial Risk: The Power of Longitudinal Data*, pp. 95–122. Cambridge University Press, Cambridge.

Hinde R.A. & Stevenson-Hinde J. (eds) (1988) *Relationships within Families: Mutual Influences*. Oxford University Press, Oxford.

Hinde R.A. & Stevenson-Hinde J. (1991) Perspectives on attachment. In Parkes C.M., Stevenson-Hinde J. & Morris P. (eds) *Attachment Across the Life Cycle*, pp. 52–65. Routledge, London.

Hodges J. & Tizard B. (1989) Social and family relationships of ex-institutionalized adolescents. *Journal of Child Psychology and Psychiatry* **30**, 77–97.

Howes C., Galluzzo D., Hamilton C., Matheson C. & Rodning C. (1989) *Social relationships with adults and peers within child care and families.* Paper presented at the biennial meetings of the Society for Research in Child Development, Kansas City, Missouri, April.

Howes C., Rodning C., Galluzzo D.C. & Myers L. (1988) Attachment and child care: Relationships with mother and caregiver. *Early Childhood Research Quarterly* **3**, 403–416.

Howes C., Unger O. & Matheson C. (1990) *The collaborative construction of pretend: Social pretend play functions.* Paper presented at the International Conference on Infant Studies, Toronto, Canada, April.

Isabella R. & Belsky J. (1990) Interactional synchrony and the origins of infant–mother attachment: A replication study. *Child Development* **62**, 373–384.

Isabella R.A., Belsky J. & von Eye A. (1989) Origins of infant–mother attachment: An examination of interactional synchrony during the infant's first year. *Developmental Psychology* **25**, 12–21.

Jacobson J.L. & Wille D.E. (1986) The influence of attachment pattern on developmental changes in peer interaction from the toddler to the preschool period. *Child Development* **57**, 338–347.

Joffe L. (1981) *The quality of mother–infant attachment and its relationship to compliance with maternal commands and prohibitions.* Paper presented to the Society for Research in Child Development, Boston.

Kagan J. (1982) *Psychological Research on the Human Infant: An Evaluative Summary.* W.T. Grant Foundation, New York.

Kagan J., Kearsley R. & Zelazo P. (1978) *Infancy: Its Place in Human Development.* Harvard University Press, Cambridge, Massachusetts.

Kobak R.R. & Sceery A. (1988) Attachment in late adolescence: Working models, affect regulation, and representations of self and others. *Child Development* **59**, 135–146.

Lamb M.E. (1976a) Effects of stress and cohort on mother– and father–infant interaction. *Developmental Psychology* **12**, 435–443.

Lamb M.E. (1976b) Interactions between two-year-olds and their mothers and fathers. *Psychological Reports* **38**, 447–450.

Lamb M.E., Hwang C.P., Frodi A. & Frodi M. (1982) Security of mother– and father–infant attachment and its relation to sociability with strangers in traditional and non-traditional Swedish families. *Infant Behavior and Development* **5**, 355–367.

Lamb M.E., Sternberg K. & Prodromdis M. (1990) *Nonmaternal care and the security of infant–mother attachment: A reanalysis of the data.* Unpublished ms, National Institute of Child Health and Human Development, Bethesda, Maryland.

Lamb M.E., Thompson R.A., Gardner W.P., Charnov E.L. & Estes D. (1984) Security of infantile attachment as assessed in the 'strange situation': Its study and biological interpretation. *Behavioral and Brain Sciences* **7**, 127–172.

Lamb M.E., Thompson R.A., Gardner W.P. & Charnov E.L. (1985) *Infant–Mother Attachment.* Lawrence Erlbaum, Hillsdale, New Jersey.

Levy M. & Davis K. (1988) Lovestyle and attachment styles compared. *Journal of Social and Personal Relationships* **5**, 439–471.

Lewis M. & Feiring C. (1989) Infant, mother, and mother–infant interaction behavior and subsequent attachment. *Child Development* **60**, 831–837.

Lewis M., Feiring C., McGuffog C. & Jaskir J. (1984) Predicting psychopathology in six-year-olds from early social relations. *Child Development* **55**, 123–136.

Lieberman A.F., Weston D.R. & Pawl J.H. (1991) Preventive intervention and outcome with anxiously attached dyads. *Child Development* **62**, 199–209.

Loudersville S. & Main M. (1981) Security, compliance, and maternal training methods in the second year of life. *Developmental Psychology* **17**, 289–299.

Lyons-Ruth K. (1988) *Maternal depression and infant disturbance.* Paper presented at the International Conference on Infant Studies, Washington, DC, April.

Maccoby E.E. & Martin A. (1983) Socialization in the context of the family: Parent–child interaction. In Hetherington E.M. (ed.) *Socialization, Personality and Social Behavior*, Vol. 4, *Mussen's Handbook of Child Psychology*, 4th edn, pp. 1–102. Wiley, New York.

Main M. (1981) Avoidance in the service of attachment: A working paper. In Immelmann K., Barlow G., Main M. & Petrinovich L. (eds) *Behavioral Development: The Bielefeld Interdisciplinary Project*, pp. 651–693. Cambridge University Press, New York.

Main M. (1983) Exploration, play, and cognitive functioning related to infant–mother attachment. *Infant Behavior and Development* **6**, 167–174.

Main M. (1990) Cross-cultural studies of attachment organization: Recent studies, changing methodologies, and the concept of conditional strategies. *Human Development* **33**, 48–61.

Main M. & Cassidy J. (1988) Categories of response with the parent at age six: Predicted from infant attachment classifications and stable over a one month period. *Developmental Psychology* **24**, 415–426.

Main M. & Goldwyn R. (1984) Predicting rejection of her infant from mothers' representation of her own experience. *Child Abuse and Neglect* **8**, 203–217.

Main M. & Goldwyn R. (in press) Interview-based adult attachment classifications: Related to infant–mother and infant–father attachment. *Developmental Psychology.*

Main M. & Hesse E. (1990) Lack of mourning in adulthood and its relationship to infant disorganization: Some speculations regarding causal mechanisms. In Greenberg M., Cicchetti D. & Cummings M. (eds) *Attachment in the Preschool Years: Theory, Research, and Intervention*, pp. 161–182. University of Chicago Press, Chicago.

Main M., Kaplan N. & Cassidy J. (1985) Security in infancy, childhood, and adulthood: A move to the level of representation. In Bretherton I. & Waters E. (eds) Growing points in attachment theory and research. *Monographs of the Society for Research in Child Development* **50**, Serial No. 209, 66–104.

Main M. & Solomon J. (1986) Discovery of an insecure–disorganized/disoriented attachment pattern: Procedures, findings and implications for the classification of behavior. In Brazelton T.B. & Yogman M. (eds) *Affective Development in Infancy*, pp. 95–124. Ablex, Norwood, New Jersey.

Main M. & Solomon J. (1990) Procedures for identifying disorganized/disoriented infants in the Ainsworth Strange Situation. In Greenberg M., Cicchetti D. & Cummings M. (eds) *Attachment in the Preschool Years: Theory, Research, and Intervention*, pp. 121–160. University of Chicago Press, Chicago.

Main M. & Weston D. (1981) The quality of the toddler's relationship to mother and father: Related to conflict behavior and readiness to establish new relationships. *Child Development* **52**, 932–940.

Malatesta C.Z., Culver C., Tesman J. & Shepard B. (1989) The development of emotion expression during the first two years of life: Normative trends and patterns of individual difference. *Monographs of the Society for Research in Child Development* **54**, Serial No. 219.

Maslin C.A. & Bates J.E. (1982) *Anxious attachment as a predictor of disharmony in the mother–toddler relationship.* Paper presented to the International Conference on Infant Studies, Austin, Texas.

Matas L., Arend R.A. & Sroufe L.A. (1978) Continuity of adaptation in the second year: The relationship between quality of attachment and later competence. *Child Development* **49**, 547–556.

Miyake K., Chen S. & Campos J.J. (1985) Infant temperament, mother's mode of interaction, and attachment in Japan: An interim report. In Bretherton I. & Waters E. (eds) Growing points of attachment theory and research. *Monographs of the Society for Research in Child Development* **50**, Serial No. 209, 276–297.

Oppenheim D., Sagi A. & Lamb M. (1988) Infant–adult attachments on the kibbutz and their relation to socioemotional development four years later. *Developmental Psychology* **24**, 427–433.

Owen M.T., Easterbrooks M.A., Chase-Lansdale L. & Goldberg W.A. (1984) The relation between maternal employment status and the stability of attachments to mother and father. *Child Development* **55**, 1894–1901.

Park K. & Waters E. (1989) Security of attachment and preschool friendships. *Child Development* **60**, 1076–1081.

Pastor D.L. (1981) The quality of mother–infant attachment and its relationship to toddlers' initial sociability with peers. *Developmental Psychology* **17**, 326–335.

Piaget J. (1954) *The Construction of Reality in the Child.* Basic Books, New York.

Pierrehumbert B., Iannotti R.J. & Cummings M.E. (1985) Mother–infant attachment, development of social competencies and beliefs of self-responsibility. *Archives de Psychologie* **53**, 365–374.

Pierrehumbert B., Iannotti R.J., Cummings M.E. & Zahn-Waxler C. (1989) Social functioning with mother and peers at 2 and 5 years: The influence of attachment. *International Journal of Behavioral Development* **12**, 85–100.

Plomin R. (1986) *Development, Genetics, and Psychology.* Lawrence Erlbaum, Hillsdale, New Jersey.

Plunkett J.W., Klein T. & Meisels S.J. (1988) The relationship of preterm infant–mother to stranger sociability at

3 years. *Infant Behavior and Development* **11**, 83–96.

Quinton D., Rutter M. & Liddle C. (1984) Institutional rearing, parenting difficulties and marital support. *Psychological Medicine* **14**, 107–124.

Radke-Yarrow M., Cummings M.E., Kuczynski L. & Chapman M. (1985) Patterns of attachment in two- and three-year-olds in normal families and families with parental depression. *Child Development* **56**, 884–893.

Renkin B., Egeland B., Marvinney D., Sroufe L.A. & Manglesdorf S. (1989) Early childhood antecedents of aggression and passive withdrawal in early elementary school. *Journal of Personality* **57**, 257–282.

Rheingold H.L. (1969) The effect of a strange environment on the behavior of infants. In Foss B.M. (ed.) *Determinants of Infant Behavior*, Vol. 4, pp. 137–166. Methuen, London.

Rutter M. (1979) Maternal deprivation, 1972–1978: New findings, new concepts, new approaches. *Child Development* **50**, 283–305.

Rutter M. (1981) Socioemotional consequences of day care for preschool children. *American Journal of Orthopsychiatry* **51**, 4–28.

Sagi A., Aviezer O., Mayseless O. *et al.* (1991) *Development of infant–mother attachment in traditional and nontraditional kibbutzim.* Paper presented at the Biennial Meeting of the Society for Research in Child Development, Seattle, April.

Sagi A., Lamb M.E., Lewkowicz K.S., Shoham R., Dvir R. & Estes D. (1985) Security of infant–mother, father, metapelet attachments among kibbutz-reared Israeli children. In Bretherton I. & Waters E. (eds) Growing points of attachment theory and research. *Monographs of the Society for Research in Child Development* **50**, Serial No. 209, 167–193.

Schaffer H.R. & Emerson P.E. (1964) The development of social attachments in infancy. *Monographs of the Society for Research in Child Development* **29**(3), Serial No. 94.

Shouldice A. & Stevenson-Hinde J. (1991) Coping with security distress: The separation anxiety test and attachment classification at 4.5 years. *Journal of Child Psychology and Psychiatry* **33**, 331–348.

Smith P.B. & Pederson D.R. (1988) Maternal sensitivity and patterns of infant–mother attachment. *Child Development* **59**, 1097–1101.

Sorce J.F. & Emde R.M. (1981) Mother's presence is not enough: Effect of emotional availability on infant explorations. *Developmental Psychology* **17**, 737–745.

Sroufe L.A. (1983) Infant–caregiver attachment and patterns of adaptation in preschool: The roots of maladaptation and competence. In Perlmutter M. (ed.) *Minnesota Symposium in Child Psychology*, Vol. 16, pp. 41–81. Lawrence Erlbaum, Hillsdale, New Jersey.

Sroufe L.A. (1988) The role of infant–caregiver attachment in development. In Belsky J. & Nezworski T. (eds) *Clinical Implications of Attachment*, pp. 18–38. Lawrence Erlbaum, Hillsdale, New Jersey.

Sroufe L.A., Fox N.E. & Pancake V.R. (1983) Attachment and dependency in developmental perspective. *Child Development* **54**, 1615–1627.

Sroufe L.A. & Rutter M. (1984) The domain of developmental psychopathology. *Child Development* **55**, 17–29.

Stevenson-Hinde J. & Shouldice A. (1991) Fear and attachment in 2.5-year-olds. *British Journal of Developmental Psychology* **8**, 319–333.

Strayer F., Trudel M. & Jacques M. (1989) The influence of attachment and temperament on toddler social relations. In Strayer F. & Moss E. (eds) *The Development of Social and Representational Tactics During Early Childhood*, pp. 6–27. La Maison D'Ethologie De Montreal, Montreal.

Teti D. & Ablard K. (1989) Security of attachment and infant–sibling relationships. *Child Development* **60**, 1519–1528.

Teti D., Gelfand D., Messinger D. & Isabella R. (1991) *Security of infant attachment and maternal functioning among depressed and nondepressed mothers and infants.* Paper presented at the Biennial Meeting of the Society for Research in Child Development, Seattle, April.

Thompson R.A. (1988) The effects of infant day care through the prism of attachment theory: A critical appraisal. *Early Childhood Research Quarterly* **3**, 273–282.

Thompson R.A. & Lamb M.E. (1984) Infants, mothers, families, and strangers. In Lewis M. (ed.) *Beyond the Dyad*, pp. 195–222. Plenum, New York.

Tizard B. & Hodges J. (1978) The effect of early institutional rearing on the development of eight-year-old children. *Journal of Child Psychology and Psychiatry* **19**, 99–118.

Tizard B. & Rees J. (1974) A comparison of the effects of adoption, restoration to the natural mother, and continued institutionalization on the cognitive development of four-year-old children. *Child Development* **45**, 92–99.

Tizard J. & Tizard B. (1971) The social development of two-year-old children in residential nurseries. In Schaffer J. (ed.) *The Origins of Human Social Relations*, pp. 147–160. Academic Press, London.

Tracy L.R., Lamb M.E. & Ainsworth M.D.S. (1976) Infant approach as related to attachment. *Child Development* **47**, 571–578.

Troy M. & Sroufe L.A. (1987) Victimization of preschoolers: Role of attachment relationship history. *Journal of American Academy of Child and Adolescent Psychiatry* **26**, 166–172.

Turner P. (1991) Relations between attachment, gender and behavior problems with peers in preschool. *Child Development* **62**, 1475–1488.

Van den Boom D. (1990) Preventive intervention and the quality of mother–infant interaction and infant exploration in irritable infants. In Koops W., Soppe J., van der Linden P., Molenaar & Schroots J. (eds) *Develop-*

mental Psychology Behind the Dikes, pp. 249–270. Eburon, Amsterdam.

van Ijzendoorn M.H., Goldberg S., Kroonenberg P. & Frenkel O. (1993) The relative effects of maternal and child problems on the quality of attachment. *Child Development* **63**, 840–858.

van Ijzendoorn M.H. & Kroonenberg P.M. (1988) Cross-cultural patterns of attachment: A meta-analysis of the strange situation. *Child Development* **59**, 147–156.

Vaughn B. & Waters E. (1990) Attachment behavior at home and in the laboratory. *Child Development* **61**, 1965–1973.

Volling B. & Belsky J. (1992) The contribution of mother–child and father–child relationships to the quality of sibling relationships. *Child Development* **63**, 1209–1222.

Ward M.J., Vaughn B.E. & Robb M.D. (1988) Social-emotional adaptation and infant–mother attachment in siblings: Role of the mother in cross-sibling consistency. *Child Development* **59**, 643–651.

Waters E. (1978) The reliability and stability of individual differences in infant–mother attachment. *Child Development* **49**, 483–494.

Waters E. & Deane K.E. (1985) Defining and assessing individual differences in attachment relationships: Q-methodology and the organization of behavior in infancy and early childhood. In Bretherton I. & Waters E. (eds) Growing points of attachment theory and research. *Monographs of the Society for Research in Child Development* **50**, Serial No. 209, 41–65.

Waters E., Wippman J. & Sroufe L.A. (1979) Attachment, positive affect, and competence in the peer group: Two studies in construct validation. *Child Development* **50**, 821–829.

Weinraub M., Brooks J. & Lewis M. (1977) The social network: A reconsideration of the concept of attachment. *Human Development* **20**, 31–47.

Weiss R.S. (1982) Attachment in adult life. In Parkes C. & Stevenson-Hinde J. (eds) *The Place of Attachment in Human Behavior*, pp. 171–184. Basic Books, New York.

Youngblade L.M. & Belsky J. (1989) Child maltreatment, infant–parent attachment security, and dysfunctional peer relationships in toddlerhood. *Topics in Early Childhood Special Education* **9**, 1–15.

17: Emotional Development

TEDRA WALDEN AND JUDY GARBER

INTRODUCTION

Emotional expressions and emotional experience change in significant ways with age. For example, emotional expression becomes more graded, subtle and complex (Demos, 1986). Although most theorists agree that emotions change with development, specifying what aspects of emotions change and the way in which changes occur is a challenge for developmentalists. The task of a developmental analysis of emotion is to understand the development of both species-wide and individual differences and the impact of emotions on other areas of functioning. Thus, developmental issues include aspects of emotional functioning that are common among most individuals as well as aspects of emotional functioning that differ among individuals. This chapter presents evidence that a variety of influences impact emotional development. Some of these processes produce species-wide commonalities, whereas others contribute to the development of differences among individuals.

There are important theoretical debates among those who study emotional development regarding the identification of core components of emotions, and the separation and integration of the relative contributions of biological and environmental factors. Although these issues are discussed, they are not resolved in this chapter. An understanding of emotional development requires consideration of multiple processes and a variety of influences; therefore, this chapter describes contributions of a number of biological and environmental factors to the development of emotion, bypassing such difficult issues as defining emotion and distinguishing categories of emotion. Rather, we assert that many aspects of functioning are involved in emotional behaviour including eliciting events, sensory receptors and facial and bodily expressions; all are relevant to an understanding of an emotional response. Furthermore, emotion is viewed as a regulatory transaction between an individual and the environment and, as such, depends on one's appraisal or interpretation of environmental events.

A few components of emotion are widely acknowledged to be important. These include a set of neurophysiological, motoric/expressive, perceptual, cognitive and subjective/phenomenological responses. Physiological responses occur in both the central and autonomic nervous systems. The motor/expressive component includes vocalizations, facial activity, bodily posture and movement, and behavioural action. The phenomenological component involves subjective feeling states, cognitive appraisal and meaning. For any particular emotion there are complicated interactions among these components, with all contributing to emotional functioning. That is, emotion is a system comprised of several components, and changes in one aspect of the system will be associated with changes in other aspects (Averill, 1990).

This chapter first sketches the normal course and development of a few basic emotions, followed by discussions of the relation between emotions and psychopathology, and the development of emotion knowledge. Next, a set of processes that influence emotional development and individual differences in emotional functioning are described. Finally, we discuss how these processes contribute to emotion regulation and resulting adaptive and maladaptive emotional functioning across development.

DEVELOPMENT OF THE EXPRESSION AND EXPERIENCE OF EMOTIONS

Two questions are central regarding the development of emotional expression. (i) When do different emotional states first appear? (ii) What is the course of development once they emerge? There are two different perspectives with regard to the first question. According to discrete emotions theorists, there are a small number of biologically given fundamental emotions, each with a biological substrate governing its functioning (Plutchik, 1962; Tomkins, 1962; Ekman & Friesen, 1971; Izard, 1971). How many discrete emotional substrates exist is uncertain (e.g. some posit seven or eight basic emotions). Moreover, the capacity for expressive behaviours is presumably present at birth. Emotional states emerge in some predictable order and have an orderly time course (Izard & Malatesta, 1987).

Darwin (1872) suggested that there is an innate, universal basis for emotional expression and many fundamental facial expressions are present shortly after birth. This has been a challenge to demonstrate empirically, however. Parents have indicated on questionnaires that infants as young as 12 weeks old display at least 10 different emotional expressions (Johnson *et al.*, 1982). Studies also have shown that a few basic facial expressions (e.g. happiness and distress) can be reliable judged in young infants with greater than chance accuracy, although it is unclear whether infants simply display global expressions of positive and negative affect rather than discrete emotional expressions (Hiatt *et al.*, 1979; Izard *et al.*, 1980). Moreover, the universality of emotional expressions does not in itself establish their innateness (Harris, 1989).

In contrast to the discrete emotions position, the differentiation view asserts that the earliest emotions are relatively undifferentiated states of arousal characterized by positive or negative hedonic tone (Bridges, 1932; Emde *et al.*, 1976; Sroufe, 1979). Bridges (1932) observed that infants start with generalized excitement that differentiates into distress and delight. Further differentiation of emotional states presumably results from maturation of physiological and cognitive systems, as well as the interaction of the young organism with the social environment. Newborn emotional states are characterized along continua of arousal (quiet sleep to crying) and hedonic tone (pleasant versus unpleasant) rather than specific emotional states. Specific types of negative and positive affect become differentiated with increasing maturity and

social interaction (Brazelton *et al.*, 1974). Hedonic tone and arousal are the basic emotion dimensions along which more specific emotional states become differentiated (Emde *et al.*, 1976; Sroufe, 1979). These dimensions are similar to those identified in the literature on negative affectivity in adults (Watson & Tellegen, 1985).

The second major developmental issue concerns changes in emotional states once they emerge. That is, how do experience and expression of different emotions change with development? Emotional development represents a confluence of sociocultural, experiential, biological and cognitive developmental factors. This chapter tries to extract the most significant of these factors and illustrates the operation of each. A wide array of factors contribute in significant ways to emotional development; no single factor adequately explains the emotional life of an individual. Moreover, a different combination of factors may influence the development of different emotions. Thus, no one factor or set of factors explains all emotional development. Rather, a particular combination of biological, social and cognitive processes influence the development of different normal and abnormal emotional outcomes.

Below the early development of a few emotions that are particularly central for understanding psychopathology are highlighted, describing the ontogenesis of each emotion in terms of its initial emergence and subsequent development. Most investigations of infants' expressions have focused on the reliability with which adults can recognize and differentiate those expressions. Young infants' facial expressions generally are interpreted as reflecting their corresponding underlying states (Izard *et al.*, 1980), although the same expression can indicate more than one emotion. Until the third or fourth year of life young children are considered to have neither the capacity nor the motivation to hide or distort their emotional expressions. Thus, early emotional displays that fit adult categories of emotional expressions are often assumed to be accompanied by a corresponding state.

Happiness, smiling and laughter

Positive hedonic states are among the earliest emotions, and smiling is one of the infant's first emotional and social behaviours. Smiling and laughter typically reflect happiness, joy and pleasure, although this may not be so for the earliest smiles. Newborn infants show low-intensity 'endogenous smiles' that reflect internal changes in their physiological state, occur mainly during the middle phase of rapid eye movement (REM) sleep when cortical activity is low, and are correlated with spontaneous central nervous system discharge of subcortical origin (Sroufe & Waters, 1976). These smiles diminish over the first 3 months and may not necessarily correspond to positive emotional states (Wolff, 1963; Spitz *et al.*, 1970).

The earliest waking smiles occur at about $1-2$ weeks and are low-intensity responses to mild tactile and kinesthetic stimulation (Emde & Koenig, 1969). Larger magnitude, broader smiles occur following feeding (Wolff, 1963). During the early weeks, auditory stimulation, particularly a high-pitched voice or the mother's voice, is the most effective elicitor of these 'grins'. By about the fourth week more vigorous stimulation elicits broad smiles, and by week 5, visual stimulation (e.g. nodding heads, a masked face with a wagging tongue) begins to replace auditory stimulation as the main elicitor of smiles. Between 5 and 8 weeks smiling at stationary rather than dynamic faces increases (Shultz & Zigler, 1970) and cooing may co-occur with smiling.

Over the first year the number of stimuli capable of eliciting smiles increases as cognitive abilities increase, resulting in a rise in the frequency of smiling. Also during the first year, smiles become increasingly social. Because human stimuli elicit smiling more than other stimuli at this age, this smile has been labelled the 'social smile' (Lewis & Michalson, 1983). It is used to greet others and is performed preferentially to attachment figures. Across cultures, the social smile elicits approach from others, communicates well-being, promotes social interaction and the development of the caretaker–infant attachment (Ainsworth, 1967; Sroufe & Waters, 1976), elicits positive responses from others (Vine, 1973; Izard, 1977), and is central to the development of social reciprocity (Brazelton *et al.*, 1974). Smiling elicits positive emotions in adults, thereby binding them to the infant and serving both a survival and a social function (Lewis & Rosenblum, 1978).

By the third month, smiles may occur as a result of infants' own efforts to assimilate new stimuli into a familiar schema (Kagan, 1971; Zelazo & Komer, 1971; Sroufe & Waters, 1976). According to the tension-reduction model, smiling increasingly results from the infant's efforts to process stimulus content rather than from stimulation *per se* (Sroufe & Waters, 1976). Oster (1978) argued that there is a relation between frowning or brow-knitting and smiling during this time. Although the common pattern of frowning followed by smiling seems paradoxical (Stern, 1974; Emde *et al.*, 1976), Oster suggested that it represents the operation of perceptual, attentional, and cognitive processes involved in the infant's attempt to 'make sense of' an incongruous stimulus. When this is successful, the tension shown in the knit brow is released, and a smile follows.

Smiling has been associated with infants' growing sense of mastery and control over the environment. Watson (1972) reported that 8-week-old infants smiled more at mobiles activated by their head turns and leg kicks than at mobiles that moved independently. Kagan (1971) found that 2-year-old children smiled following the solution of difficult problems. Thus, smiling can occur in a non-social context and may reflect children's satisfaction with their growing mastery over the external world.

It is not clear whether smiling and laughing reflect the same processes (Sroufe & Waters, 1976). Laughter is a more extensive expression of positive affect and requires a more rapid build-up of tension than smiling (Rothbart, 1973; Cicchetti & Sroufe, 1978). Laughter can be observed to build from smiling and fade to smiling with continued stimulus presentations, particularly for incongruous events (Sroufe & Wunsch, 1972). Frequency of smiling, however, is not necessarily related to frequency of laughing during the first year (Washburn, 1929). Moreover, Sroufe *et al.* (1974) found that the potency of items that elicit smiling versus laughter was different and they concluded that not all smiles are small laughs.

There is considerable individual variability in the age at which laughter appears. Although laughter has been reported as young as 2 months of age (Wolff, 1963; Church, 1966), it is usually thought to onset at about 4 months (Sroufe & Wunsch, 1972; Sroufe & Waters, 1976). Similar to smiling, elicitors of laughter proceed from vigorous physical stimulation to provocative tactile and auditory stimuli to more subtle sociovisual events (Sroufe & Waters, 1976). By the end of the first year, infants laugh at things that provide cognitive incongruity (e.g. mother walking like a penguin), and in anticipation of another's behaviour (e.g. prior to their mothers kissing their stomachs). During the second year, laughing occurs during activities in which the infants themselves are active participants (e.g. when they cover their own faces).

Surprise

Startle expressions can be observed in neonates (Izard, 1971). Although startle and surprise may be related, they are not identical, as startle is thought to reflect perceptual/physiological processes and surprise cognitive/informational processes. Furthermore, surprise can be accompanied by varying degrees of startle. Surprised facial expressions occur as early as 4 months of age (Izard, 1971), often in response to vanishing objects and switched toys (Hiatt *et al.*, 1979). Surprise presumably results from a violated expectation. That is, surprise is a reaction to information that does not fit an individual's cognitive schema (Bock, 1980). The physiological correlate of surprise is the orienting response, a state of increased cortical readiness for perception and information processing. A lowering of threshold for sensory stimulation allows the individual to gather information about a new event quickly. The state is experienced as pleasant unless the increased arousal exceeds an optimum level (Bock, 1980).

The surprised expressions of infants are often found in blends with happiness, suggesting that the two emotions may co-occur (Hiatt *et al.*, 1979). Ekman and Friesen (1975) have argued that surprise is a reaction to a sudden and unanticipated event and lasts only a moment. Therefore, surprise often blends with the expression that follows it, resulting in mixed expressions. One might be surprised in pleasant, fearful, horrified or angry ways and each of these experiences may be accompanied by a different blend of expressions.

Children's ability to explain the conditions that produce surprise changes with age. Hadwin and Perner (1991) reported that 5-year-old, but not 3-year-old, children understood that someone expecting candy in a box will be surprised when the box is opened and the candy is not there. Similarly, Wellman and Banerjee (1991) found that 3-year-old children were less able than older children to articulate that the reason for surprise was a story character's mistaken expectation. Thus, although very young children show expressions of surprise, they are unable to explain that surprise results from the mismatch between a false expectation and reality.

Developmental changes in the nature of things children anticipate influence whether an event is experienced as surprising. For example, Keil (1979) found that children's causal intuitions were related to their ability to anticipate the outcomes of events involving removal of crucial support blocks from simple block structures. Whether children were surprised at the outcomes on certain impossible 'trick' trials was related to their knowledge of the physical laws involved. Older children, whose knowledge of physical laws was greater, were surprised at impossible events that younger children did not find surprising.

Distress, sadness and crying

Expressions of distress and sadness are common in infants (Emde *et al.*, 1965; Harmon *et al.*, 1982). Although facial expressions of distress have been identified in very young infants (Izard *et al.*, 1980), it is not clear whether types of distress can be distinguished (Sherman, 1927a, b). Field and Walden (1982) reported that 8-week-old infants displayed sad expressions in face-to-face play with mothers; the rate of sad expressions in 8-week-old infants was about twice that for 12-week-old infants.

One manifestation of distress and sadness is crying (Tomkins, 1963; Izard, 1977), although not all distress cries necessarily represent sadness, and not all crying is accompanied by tears (Penbharkkul & Karelitz, 1962). Crying in infancy has been reported in response to pain, hunger, frustration, pleasure, sudden loud noises, looming objects and the sound of another baby crying (Wasz-Hockert *et al.*, 1968; Wolff, 1969; Hruska & Yonis, 1972; Sagi &

Hoffman, 1976). Thus, crying represents a flexible response to a variety of aversive, and even some pleasurable, experiences.

Diary studies (Brazelton, 1962) and tapes of infant vocalizations (Revelsky & Black, 1972) have found that crying increases over the first 6 weeks of life and then decreases, and that crying is more frequent during the evening. Epidemiological studies of older children have shown that crying decreases with age, whereas moodiness increases during early adolescence (Shepherd *et al.*, 1971). Shepherd *et al.* reported that at age 6 approximately 18% of children cried 2 to 3 times per week, whereas by puberty the rate dropped to about 2%. When feelings of sadness rather than crying are measured, a different developmental picture emerges. In a general population survey, Rutter *et al.* (1970) reported that at 10−11 years old 13% of children showed depressed mood, whereas at ages 14 and 15 40% reported depressive feelings. Thus, whereas crying may decrease, expressions of sadness and depressed mood tend to increase with age.

Fear and anxiety

The developmental course of children's fears has been studied using behavioural observation of children's responses to potentially fear-provoking stimuli (Scarr & Salapatek, 1970), parent observations (Jersild & Holmes, 1935), parent interviews (Lapouse & Monk, 1959) and questionnaires (Miller *et al.*, 1972), and self-reports of children themselves (Bauer, 1976). These studies have shown that most children experience some fears and worries, particularly at certain ages.

The specific content of children's fears changes with age (Bauer, 1976). During the first few months of life infants show fearful responses to sudden, loud, unpredictable events and loss of support (Scarr & Salapatek, 1970). Wariness of heights co-occurs with skill in independent locomotion (Bertenthal *et al.*, 1984). Towards the end of the first year, infants show fear of strangers and novel objects, and begin to show distress at separation from their caretakers (Scarr & Salapatek, 1970). Anticipatory fear or wariness also becomes apparent during the second half of the first year, with wariness of strangers being common (Emde *et al.*, 1976).

Stranger anxiety commonly emerges at 8−9 months, peaks early in the second year, then gradually decreases by the end of the second year (Weinraub & Lewis, 1977). Stranger anxiety is seen in many cultures (Goldberg, 1972), although not all infants develop such anxiety to the same degree. A variety of contextual factors can alter infants' level of wariness and at times infants approach strangers and play with them (Bretherton & Ainsworth, 1974; Waters *et al.*, 1975). Generally infants react less fearfully to strangers if the mother is present, the setting is familiar, the stranger is a child, the stranger remains at a distance, the infant has had previous experience with unfamiliar people, and the infant has some control in the situation (Rheingold & Eckerman, 1973; Lewis & Brooks, 1974; Sroufe, 1977).

Separation anxiety emerges late in the first year and commonly peaks around 18 months. Individual variability in separation distress has been linked to patterns of attachment to the primary caregiver (Ainsworth *et al.*, 1978). Whereas secure babies show some distress at separation and relief during reunion, abused and/or insecurely attached infants are more likely to express fear or anger in the form of avoidance or resistance during separation and reunion (Ainsworth *et al.*, 1978; George & Main, 1979). Moreover, early maltreatment may hasten the development of fear. Gaensbauer and co-workers (Gaensbauer & Sands, 1979; Gaensbauer *et al.*, 1980) reported that maltreated infants as young as 3 or 4 months display fearful expressions when approached by a strange adult of the same gender as the abusive parent. This stranger anxiety appears earlier than typically is seen in normal infants (Malatesta *et al.*, 1989).

With increasing abilities to imagine and anticipate, toddlers report fears of the dark, animals, imaginary creatures and harm (Jersild & Holmes, 1935; Miller *et al.*, 1972). Whereas children in kindergarten and second-grade report fears of monsters, animals, thunder and storms, sixth-grade children report fearing natural disasters, bodily injury and poor school achievement. Adolescents report worries about injury and death, war, sexuality and social acceptance (Miller *et al.*, 1972; Bauer, 1976). Adults report fears of snakes, heights, injury or illness, and certain forms of transportation (Agras *et al.*, 1969). Some fears such as social anxiety, fear of failure, or fear of snakes are common across a wide age range and may persist within individuals (Campbell, 1986). Finally, certain fears, such as fear of sex and open spaces, tend to arise during adolescence and adulthood, and are often associated with other psychopathological symptoms (Barlow, 1988).

The rate of fears also varies with development. Most infants show some separation anxiety during the end of the first year. Number of fears peaks during preschool and decreases during elementary school (Jersild & Holmes, 1935; MacFarlane *et al.*, 1954) and adolescence (Ollendick *et al.*, 1989). Lapouse and Monk (1959) found that 43% of 6−12-year-old children reported seven or more fears. Typically, however, children's fears are not disabling or excessive and they generally decrease with age (Rutter *et al.*, 1970; Miller *et al.*, 1971).

Anger

According to mothers' reports, infants evidence anger during the early months of life (Johnson *et al.*, 1982). Detailed daily parent reports (Goodenough, 1931) and observations of mother−infant interactions (Main, 1981) indicate that displays of anger increase over the first year of life. Early observational studies were unable to find discrete angry facial or behavioural responses in children or adults, and judges only could identify anger when it was accompanied by information about instigating circumstances (Sherman, 1927a, b; Landis, 1929). Recent research, however, has found that angry facial expressions can be identified in infants even in the absence of contextual information (Ekman & Friesen, 1975; Izard, 1977). Others have reported difficulty detecting angry cries without situational cues (Muller *et al.*, 1974), although Wolff (1969) reportedly distinguished newborns' angry cries from other cries based on spectrographic analysis of cry sounds.

Physical restraint, pain and blocking of goal-directed behaviour (sucking during feeding), elicit anger in infants (Bell *et al.*, 1971; Stenberg & Campos, 1990). Stenberg and Campos (1990) found that physical restraint produced negative emotional expressions in 1-month-old infants, although no

patterns of specific facial expressions, such as anger, were observed. In 4−7-month-old babies, however, restraint produced angry expressions. Stenberg and Campos concluded that the capacity to express anger through coordinated facial expressions emerges around 4 months of age. These angry displays function as social signals that are at first directed to the immediate source of frustration (e.g. hands restraining them), but by 7 months are expressed to social agents such as the mother.

Berkowitz (1983, 1990) suggested that pain is an important elicitor of anger and aggression. He proposed that this anger occurs in the absence of cognitive mediation and can be observed at a very young age. In a longitudinal study of infants' emotional reactions, Izard *et al.* (1987) found a developmental trend in infants' expressions in response to the acute physical pain of medical inoculations. The proportion of pain expressions following inoculation decreased steadily with age. Replicating earlier work (Izard *et al.*, 1983), Izard *et al.* (1987) found a few angry expressions among 2-, 4- and 6-month-old infants but these expressions increased markedly between 7 and 19 months.

Goodenough (1931) reported a peak in frequency of angry outbursts during the second year. This period of the 'terrible twos', in which the child develops a sense of self and autonomy, is characterized by expressions of negativism, anger and temper tantrums that include hitting, biting and foot-stamping. Anger and frustration have been noted after the placement of a barrier between mothers and 1−2-year-old children (Jacklin *et al.*, 1973; Van Lieshout, 1975; Feiring & Lewis, 1979). Feiring and Lewis (1979) found that angry responses to the frustration of a barrier decreased as children became more competent at solving the problem. Thus, during the second year of life when children become more independent and try new things, they may be confronted with more frustrations and restrictions. As they become more competent at overcoming obstacles, frustration and anger may decrease.

Although the normative rates of anger responses change with development, there is intra-individual stability in the frequency of its expression. For example, avoidance of the parent in a reunion situation at 12 months has been related to attacking the mother, hitting and banging toys, and tantrums at 21 months (Main, 1981). Thus, although the mode of anger expression changes, the frequency of its expression shows some stability over the first 2 years of life (Lewis & Michalson, 1983).

Individual differences in children's level of anger also are marked. In over 40 hours of observation, Main (1981) found that the number of angry episodes ranged from 0 to 111 per infant. Characteristics of children as well as the socialization environment may contribute to individual variability in expression of anger. For example, Izard *et al.* (1987) found that infants who were slow to soothe showed proportionately more anger than fast soothers. Izard *et al.* suggested that slow soothers have a lower tolerance for pain; that is, they are less able to endure pain without overt negative affect. These infants, therefore, continue to express their distress and anger for a longer period of time.

Infants who express more anger in interactions with mothers late in the first year have been found to have mothers who are emotionally inexpressive and rigid, show aversion to physical contact with their infants, and are unresponsive to their infant's expressions of anger during the first 3 months of life (Ainsworth *et al.*, 1978; Main *et al.*, 1979). Early exposure to abuse and violence has been related to anger towards the mother during reunion (following separation), and verbal and non-verbal anger and aggression towards peers and caretakers during the preschool and early school years (George & Main, 1979; Dodge *et al.*, 1990). Thus, both intra-individual and interindividual factors contribute to variability in the expression of anger.

The rate, form and elicitors of anger vary with age. Shepherd *et al.* (1971) reported that tantrums decreased during the school years. Whereas 10% of 5-year-old boys had weekly tantrums, only 2% of 15-year-old boys had such outbursts. During the preschool years, angry outbursts are typically precipitated by conflicts with authority. Interpersonal conflict continues to be associated with anger with increasing age, although the content of the conflict changes with development. Whereas toddlers deal with issues around toileting and sharing toys, school-age children's conflicts with parents tend to centre around rules concerning such things as bedtime, homework and chores. Anger related to peer disputes increases during the elementary

school years (Dawe, 1934). During adolescence, the expression of anger becomes more subtle through sulking, sarcasm and withdrawal; the elicitors tend to involve conflicts with authorities concerning autonomy, individuation and peer issues, especially those involving heterosexual relationships (Montemayor, 1982; Steinberg & Silverberg, 1986).

Guilt and shame

Guilt involves both the feeling of remorse and the acknowledgement of responsibility for negative outcomes resulting from acts of either commission or omission (Hoffman, 1978). Shame is linked to hostility towards the self based on a perception of the self as deficient, unworthy or bad (Lewis, 1979). Guilt does not appear to have a distinct expressive component, although Izard (1977) suggests that the guilty face looks 'heavy'; shame has been associated with downcast eyes.

The cognitive skills that have been proposed as being necessary to experience guilt include recognition that others are separate entities, the ability to respond empathically to others' distress, awareness of having caused another's misfortune, the capacity for self-evaluation, and recognition that one has choice and control over one's behaviour (Hoffman, 1978, 1982a; Graham & Weiner, 1986). Frijda (1986) proposed that three appraisals are necessary to experience guilt, including evaluation of an act, evaluation of responsibility for the act, and a resulting negative evaluation of the self. During the second year of life, children acquire an appreciation of standards regarding prohibited behaviour, an awareness of the self and feeling states, and simple forms of perspective taking (Schulman & Kaplowitz, 1977; Kagan, 1982; Zahn-Waxler *et al.*, 1984). Kagan asserted that such cognitive skills are an inevitable consequence of maturation of the central nervous system and serve as the foundation for moral development and self-consciousness. These cognitive developments may be necessary prerequisites for the emergence of guilt and shame.

There is evidence that children's ability to express guilt increases with age (Chapman *et al.*, 1987; Zahn-Waxler *et al.*, 1990). Zahn-Waxler and co-workers (Zahn-Waxler & Radke-Yarrow, 1982; Zahn-Waxler & Kochanska, 1990) have argued that young children experience guilt but simply lack the 'cognitive structures and verbal skills to articulate these experiences in ways that can be measured'. Moreover, although young children are less capable of attributing feelings to actions in hypothetical contexts, they may experience guilt when they transgress in a real situation. When observations rather than interviews are used, children as young as 2 years show emotional distress and reparative behaviours after a wrongdoing; they also comfort others who show expressions of distress that they did not cause (Zahn-Waxler & Radke-Yarrow, 1982; Chapman *et al.*, 1987). These altruistic and reparative acts increase during the second year of life, although it is unclear whether these behaviours reflect actual feelings of guilt or simply an increasing sensitivity to and concern for the feelings of others.

Weiner (1985) suggested that guilt occurs when individuals take personal responsibility for negative outcomes over which they have control. Young children, however, more often have outcome-based rather than cause-linked emotions and may not consider their control over events. Therefore they may be less likely to experience guilt (Weiner *et al.*, 1980; Graham *et al.*, 1984; Thompson, 1987). Graham *et al.* (1984) found that young children did report guilt for any wrongdoing regardless of its controllability. Stipek and DeCotis (1988) did not find age differences in children's reports of guilt following a failure. However, 6-year-old children associated both controllable (effort) and uncontrollable (ability) failures with guilt, whereas older children reported guilt only for controllable outcomes.

Explanations for guilt also change with development (Thompson & Hoffman, 1980; Graham *et al.*, 1984). Thompson and Hoffman (1980) found that older children used internal justice principles and expressed concern for victims, whereas younger children focused on fear of detection and punishment. Nunner-Winkler and Sodian (1988) found that when evaluating a hypothetical moral violation, most 4-year-old children judged the wrongdoer to experience positive emotions, justifying this on the basis of the successful outcome achieved, whereas most 8 year olds attributed negative feelings, focusing on the moral value of the wrongdoer's action. Thus, there appear to be clear age trends in the development of guilt, although conclusions may vary depending on whether one assesses behavioural expressions of concern for others or cognitive understanding of guilt-producing circumstances.

Summary

Emotions such as fear, anger, surprise and happiness appear to be present very early in infancy, but more complex emotions such as guilt, shame, and embarrassment emerge later (Campos *et al.*, 1983; Izard, 1987). The elicitors, form of expression and frequency of various emotions change with development. For example, all children show some fears, although the specific content of these fears changes with age. The topography of the different emotions also changes with development. The same behaviour (e.g. crying) can have different meanings, and different behaviours can be manifestations of the same emotions at different points in development (e.g. anger can be expressed as biting during preschool and sarcasm during adolescence). Whereas the rate of expression of some emotions decreases with development (e.g. fears, crying, aggression), others increase (e.g. depression, guilt). Moreover, even though children may express various emotions, they may not be able to explain the conditions that produce these emotions until later in development. Changes in the expression and experience of emotions occur as a function of cognitive development, physical maturation and social experience.

Finally, there is important individual variability in emotional expressiveness with regard to intensity, duration, frequency, stability, age-appropriateness and regulation. The extent to which children are judged as expressing emotions within the normal range is a function of how they behave relative to their peers, and whether they show dysfunction in other important areas of their lives (e.g. academic, social) as a result of their emotions. Constitutional factors and idiosyncratic experiences contribute to the development of emotionality. Differences in threshold, characteristic responses to particular stimuli, tempo of intake, assimilation and coordination contribute to individual differences in emotional responding (Murphy, 1983).

EMOTIONS AND PSYCHOPATHOLOGY

When is emotional expression considered mal-adaptive? Several theorists have argued that emotions serve an evolutionary adaptive function for the species (Izard, 1977; Plutchik, 1980). At the individual level, however, emotions can become dysfunctional. A certain amount of emotion can be useful by helping to organize and motivate behaviour appropriate to the emotion-eliciting situation (Izard & Harris, 1994). However, emotions that become too intense, frequent or persistent can be disruptive. For example, a moderate amount of sadness can facilitate seeking social contact, whereas frequent and intense sadness can lead to social withdrawal or rejection. Appropriately expressed anger can motivate correction of injustice, whereas excessive anger may lead to aggression and serious interpersonal conflict.

Emotional dysfunction can be one among several symptoms of a psychopathological syndrome or it can be the fundamental feature that defines a disorder. For example, flat or grossly inappropriate affect is a symptom of schizophrenia. The expression of anger more frequently than that of most people of the same mental age is one of the 9 possible defining criteria for oppositional defiant disorder.

Autism is characterized by deviations in emotion recognition (i.e. marked lack of awareness of others' feelings) and emotional expression (i.e. absence of smiling during a social approach). Autistic children show deviant patterns of positive affect and smiling (Baron-Cohen, 1988; Mundy & Sigman, 1989) and more negative and incongruous blends of emotions (Yirmiya *et al.*, 1989). Delong (1978) reported that, according to parents' retrospective reports, only 18% of autistic children smiled socially. Volkmar (1987) observed that about 50% of autistic children smiled socially in infancy. Autistic children of 2—4 years show fewer displays of positive affect when interacting with adults than do matched developmentally delayed children (Snow *et al.*, 1986). Most autistic children also fail to show positive affect to their mirror reflections (Dawson & McKissick, 1984; Spiker & Ricks, 1984) compared to normal children who smile at their mirror images (Lewis & Brooks-Gunn, 1979). Hobson (1989) proposed that this deviant emotional responding may be a core deficit

in autism that is central to difficulties in social interactions.

Excesses or deficiencies in the expression or modulation of anger also are associated with mal-adaptation. Intense anger often accompanies displays of physical aggression that can produce injury to the self, others, or property. Moreover, inappropriate displays of anger can damage interpersonal relationships (Holt, 1970; Holmes & Horan, 1976), alter occupational functioning, and contribute to physical illness (Alexander & Flagg, 1965; Matthews, 1985).

Some forms of psychopathology involve deficiencies or excesses in guilt. Sociopaths appear to have an underdeveloped sense of guilt in which they either do not recognize their own wrongdoing or do not experience discomfort or remorse, and they often lack empathy towards others (Ellis, 1962). Paranoid states can result when individuals misinterpret events and project blame onto others for negative outcomes. Lewis (1971, 1979) has argued that unacceptable feelings of rage and fury are rendered inaccessible to consciousness by the development of guilt, resulting in obsessive thoughts. Lewis asserted that, in contrast, shame involves a perceived internal deficiency that results in hostility to the self and, ultimately, depression.

Two categories of psychopathological disorders are defined primarily with respect to deviations in emotions — mood and anxiety disorders. To diagnose major depressive disorder the *Diagnostic and Statistical Manual* (3rd edn revised) (DSM-III-R; American Psychiatric Association, 1987) indicates that an individual must manifest depressed mood or loss of·interest or pleasure, characterized as apathy, pervasive boredom or a feeling of emptiness. Similarly, the diagnosis of a manic episode requires abnormally and persistently elevated, expansive or irritable mood. The anxiety disorders include persistent fear or worry as a central defining symptom.

Mood disorders

Epidemiological studies indicate that there are age differences in the frequency of sadness and depression (Anderson *et al.*, 1987; Angold, 1988). However, this depends on whether sadness or depressive disorder is assessed, which index of depression is used, and gender. In a general population survey, Rutter *et al.* (1970) reported that among 10–11-year-old children 13% showed depressed mood, 17% failed to smile and 9% were preoccupied with depressive thoughts. Parents and teachers described about 10–12% of the children as feeling 'miserable'. When the same children were reassessed at 14–15 years, over 40% of the adolescents reported depressive feelings and about 8% reported suicidal thoughts. Parents and teachers were unaware of the adolescents' level of dysphoria (Rutter *et al.*, 1976).

Weiss and Garber (1992) reviewed studies of age differences in the core symptoms of depressive disorder and found no clear consensus as to which symptoms changed with age. Non-verbal expressions of sad affect are more common in younger children than adolescents and adults (Friedman *et al.*, 1983; Ryan *et al.*, 1987; Carlson & Kashani, 1988), whereas verbal expressions of sad mood either show no age trend or increase with age (Achenbach & Edelbrock, 1981; Garber, 1984; Carlson & Kashani, 1988). Several studies have found that anhedonia, hypersomnia, psychomotor agitation, fatigue, irritability and hopelessness are more common or more severe in adolescents (Friedman *et al.*, 1983; Garber, 1984; Ryan *et al.*, 1987).

Guilt has not been found to be a significant feature of depression in children (Kovacs & Paulauskas, 1984), but guilt is characteristic of depression during adolescence (Ushakov & Girich, 1971; McConville *et al.*, 1973; Garber, 1984). Nevertheless, depressed children as young as 7 or 8 are more likely than non-depressed children to explain negative events in internal, stable and global terms (Seligman *et al.*, 1984; Nolen-Hoeksema *et al.*, 1986). It is not clear, however, whether the instrument used to assess explanatory style indexes guilt and self-blame or rather negative expectations about the future and hopelessness. Depressogenic attributional style appears to be relatively stable during the middle school years (Nolen-Hoeksema *et al.*, 1986), and there is no relation between explanatory style and age during the early to middle adolescent years (Garber *et al.*, 1993).

Although it is rare to see depressive disorder in infants, transient periods of depressive symptoms

have been observed as young as 6 months and some extreme cases of infants have shown most of the full syndrome (Emde *et al.*, 1965; Harmon *et al.*, 1982). The rate of depressive disorder is low during preschool (Kashani & Ray, 1983), but increases from the pre- to postpubertal years (Rutter *et al.*, 1970; Kashani *et al.*, 1987; Rutter, 1991; Angold & Rutter, 1992). Rutter *et al.* (1970) found only three cases of depressive disorder at age 10 in a sample of over 2000 children, whereas by age 14–15 there were nine cases of 'pure' depressive disorder and 26 cases of mixed affective disorder. Whereas Anderson *et al.* (1987) found that at age 11 the prevalence of depression was 1.8%, Kashani *et al.* reported that between ages 14 and 16 the rate was 8%.

Studies of clinical samples have yielded similar results. Using chart notes to define depression, Pearce (1978) reported that depressive disorders were twice as common among postpubertal than prepubertal patients, although they were more frequent in boys before puberty and in girls after puberty. Rutter and co-workers (Angold & Rutter, 1992; Harrington *et al.*, 1990a) found an increase in depression during adolescence, particularly among girls. Angold and Rutter (1992) reported that after age 10, both boys and girls showed increasing rates of depression, although the rate of increase was faster in girls.

Suicide is extremely rare in early childhood and increases dramatically between 10 and 20 years old (Fowler *et al.*, 1986; Shaffer, 1986). Attempted suicide also is infrequent in childhood, increases during adolescence, and peaks in the late teenage years (Kreitman, 1977; Hawton, 1986). Hawton and Goldacre (1982) found that the peak age was 16 for girls and 18 for boys. Among psychiatric inpatients, 17% of preadolescents have attempted suicide as compared to almost 50% of adolescents (Carlson & Cantwell, 1982; Carlson *et al.*, 1987). Although attempted and completed suicide often are associated with depression (Taylor & Stansfeld, 1984; Brent *et al.*, 1986), they also occur in children with conduct or substance abuse disorders (Gould *et al.*, 1990).

Little is known about the developmental course of mania. Mania often emerges during late adolescence or the early twenties, although some cases are reported both after age 50 and prior to puberty

(Strober & Carlson, 1982; American Psychiatric Association, 1987; Varanka *et al.*, 1988). Reasons for the absence of good developmental information about mania include a difficulty distinguishing between attention deficit hyperactivity disorder and mania, and the recency of development of adequate methods for assessing symptoms of mania in children (Fristad *et al.*, 1992).

Anxiety disorders

Anxiety disorders are among the most common form of childhood psychopathology (Bernstein & Borchardt, 1991), with symptoms of overanxious disorder being particularly common (Bell-Dolan *et al.*, 1990). Rates of anxiety disorders vary with age, informant, and whether impairment in functioning is included among the criteria. Adolescents report more anxiety disorders than children, except separation anxiety disorder, which is more prevalent in prepubertal children (Anderson *et al.*, 1987; Kashani & Orvaschel, 1988, 1990). When separation anxiety and school refusal occur during early childhood they tend to have a better prognosis than when they first occur in adolescence (Rodriguez *et al.*, 1959).

Frances *et al.* (1987) found developmental differences in symptoms of separation anxiety. Young children (5–8 years) reported worries of harm to attachment figures, school refusal and nightmares; 9–12-year-old children reported distress about separation; and adolescents (13–16 years) reported school refusal and physical complaints. Adolescents with overanxious disorder reported more symptoms than did younger children, with worry or concern about past behaviour being especially common in adolescents (Strauss *et al.*, 1988; McGee *et al.*, 1990). Generalized anxiety shows no consistent age pattern during childhood and adolescence (Rutter & Garmezy, 1983).

Although mild fears are common among children and adolescents (Silverman & Nelles, 1990), phobias, which involve a persistent fear and avoidance behaviours that interfere with normal functioning, are less common (Anderson *et al.*, 1987; McGee *et al.*, 1990). Prevalence rates of simple phobias are 2.4% in children (Anderson *et al.*, 1987) and 3.6% in adolescents (McGee *et al.*, 1990). The focus of phobias varies with age, with younger children reporting more animal phobias and adolescents reporting more social phobias (e.g. eating or speaking in public; Marks & Gelder, 1966). Social phobias have been found in about 1% of older children and adolescents (Anderson *et al.*, 1987; McGee *et al.*, 1990).

Full panic disorders are rare prior to puberty, although panic attacks and other symptoms of panic have been noted in prepubertal children (Ballenger *et al.*, 1989; Last & Strauss, 1989). Panic disorders have been observed in adolescent psychiatric patients (Alessi *et al.*, 1987; Last & Strauss, 1989). The phenomenology of childhood panic attacks may be different from that of adolescents and adults. Nelles and Barlow (1988) suggested that children can experience the somatic symptoms of panic disorder, but they lack the cognitive ability to attribute these sensations to internal factors; rather, they tend to attribute their somatic distress to external events. As a result, they typically do not present with the criterion symptom of spontaneous panic attacks without an apparent external precipitant.

Symptoms such as those that define separation anxiety may be childhood precursors to adult agoraphobia and panic (Gittelman & Klein, 1984; Zitrin & Ross, 1988; Ayuso *et al.*, 1989). Alternatively, childhood and adult panic disorders could be qualitatively distinct disorders that result from different underlying processes such as exposure to trauma versus biological pathogenesis (Sheehan *et al.*, 1981; Thyer *et al.*, 1985). The longitudinal course of childhood anxiety disorders and the relation between childhood and adult anxiety disorders are important issues for further investigation.

Gender differences have been reported for some anxiety disorders. Separation anxiety, overanxious disorder, panic disorder (without agoraphobia) and generalized anxiety disorder occur about equally in boys and girls, though they are more common in females after adolescence (Frances *et al.*, 1987; Bowen *et al.*, 1990). Simple phobias, avoidant disorder, and agoraphobia are more common in girls, and social phobias are more common in boys (Costello, 1989; Links *et al.*, 1989).

The relation between depression and anxiety

Are depression and anxiety distinct constructs or

part of a more general construct of negative affectivity? The evidence is divided. Proponents of the view that depression and anxiety represent a common dimension note the high rate of comorbidity between anxiety and depressive disorders (Dobson, 1985; Brady & Kendall, 1992) and the high correlation between self-reported anxiety and depression in adults (Watson & Clark, 1984) and children (Wolfe *et al.*, 1987). Moreover, factor analytical studies of parents' behaviour checklists generally have yielded a common anxious–depressed dimension rather than two separate factors (Achenbach *et al.*, 1989).

Other evidence suggests that depression and anxiety can be differentiated if positive affectivity also is measured (Watson *et al.*, 1988). Watson *et al.* (1988) found that negative affectivity was broadly correlated with symptoms and diagnoses of both anxiety and depression, whereas low positive affectivity was correlated only with symptoms and diagnoses of depression. They concluded that low positive affectivity (i.e. lack of pleasure and engagement) is a distinctive feature of depression.

Blumberg and Izard (1986) found that profiles of emotions differed for children who were high on self-reported depression versus anxiety. Whereas sadness and inner-directed hostility were prominent for depression, fear was the key emotion in anxiety.

Depressed and anxious individuals also have been found to differ in family histories of depression and anxiety (Weissman *et al.*, 1984a). In addition, anxiety and depression in children have been found to be dissimilarly associated with other psychopathological constructs. For example, there is a tendency for children with conduct disorders to develop depression, but they rarely develop anxiety disorders (Rutter *et al.*, 1970; Harrington *et al.*, 1990b). Moreover, although self-reported anxiety and fear are correlated, the relation between depression and specific fears is not significant (except social evaluative fears, as assessed on the fear survey schedule for children; Ollendick & Yule, 1990). Finally, children who have only an anxiety disorder tend to be younger and to have less depressive symptomatology than children who have depression or both depression and anxiety (Hershberg *et al.*, 1982; Stavrakaki *et al.*, 1987). In addition, whereas the rate of depression increases

after puberty, there is no similar age trend for anxiety disorders (Rutter, 1991).

Thus, the relation between anxiety and depression is complex. Although they share some common symptoms and correlates, they also have several important differences. Studies are needed that examine the developmental course and outcome of these syndromes, and their relation to each and to other forms of psychopathology. For example, several authors have speculated that anxiety may precede the development to depression (Dobson, 1985; Brady & Kendall, 1992). In addition, further study of both common and distinct aetiological variables is needed. Although both anxiety and depression may share some biological or cognitive correlates, if they are truly distinct then each will be characterized by a specific combination of factors that uniquely predicts one syndrome and not the other (Garber & Hollon, 1991).

Continuity in emotional development

Two issues of continuity are relevant to emotional development and psychopathology. First, what is the relation between early emotional functioning and later adaptation? Prospective studies indicate that most children with emotional disorders grow up to be normal adults; about one-third of children with an emotional disorder continue to show emotional disturbance several years later (Robins, 1966; Kohlberg *et al.*, 1972). Fears are common during childhood and most appear to be mild and transient. Some phobias do persist, although these tend to be fears that are atypical for the developmental period and are accompanied by a more general pattern of maladaptation (Rutter, 1985). When emotional problems persist, they usually develop into a neurotic or depressive disorder during adulthood (Pritchard & Graham, 1966; Zeitlin, 1983). Similarly, if adults with a neurotic disorder had childhood problems, they usually involved emotional disturbance. For example, many adults with panic disorder and agoraphobia report childhood separation anxiety (Gittelman & Klein, 1984).

There is increasing evidence of the stability of depressive disorders from childhood to adulthood (Kovacs *et al.*, 1984; Harrington *et al.*, 1990a). Harrington *et al.* (1990a) found that individuals who had a depressive syndrome as children were more likely to have an affective disorder as adults than were persons with a history of non-depressed psychiatric problems. However, most depressed adults were not depressed as children (Weissman *et al.*, 1984b).

One relevant question is whether depression with earlier onset represents a more severe disorder with a stronger genetic basis. Early age of onset is associated with increased familial loading of depression (Weissman *et al.*, 1984b), and the affected relatives also have early age of onset (Weissman *et al.*, 1984b). On the other hand, Harrington *et al.* (1990a) found that individuals with postpubertal onset of depression had higher rates of depression in adulthood than did those with a prepubertal onset. Thus, the relation between age of onset of emotional disorders and later adaptation needs further study.

Overall, although most childhood emotional symptoms are transient, there is continuity between childhood and adult emotional disturbance. To address this issue adequately two research approaches are needed — prospective studies that follow children with emotional disorders into adulthood, and retrospective studies that examine the extent and type of psychopathology during the childhoods of adults with emotional disorders. Moreover, although emotional disorders generally show some continuity, it is less clear whether the specific emotional symptoms and disorders persist. Do children with dog phobias continue to have dog phobias or do they develop different phobias or even a different type of anxiety disorder during adulthood? Should we expect isomorphism in emotional symptoms or age-appropriate changes in the expression of the emotional disturbance? For example, are separation anxiety and agoraphobia age-appropriate manifestations of the same emotional disturbance? Finally, the prognosis of children with emotional symptoms depends in part on the extent and nature of other co-occurring symptoms and the degree of dysfunction associated with these symptoms.

The second continuity issue involves the relation between normal and abnormal expressions of emotion. For example, can depressive disorders be reduced simply to extreme sadness, or anxiety disorders to extreme anxiety? To answer this question,

parallels to two other constructs, intelligence and hypertension, are relevant (M. Rutter, personal communication). Intelligence functions as a continuous dimension, yet the processes underlying severe mental retardation differ from both mild mental retardation and normal intelligence. That is, in contrast to variations in intelligence within the normal range, severe forms of mental retardation (MR) are more strongly associated with biological causes such as single major gene disorder or detectable brain damage. Moreover, there tends to be genetic discontinuity between normal intelligence and severe retardation, but less so for mild MR.

Plomin and Rutter (Plomin, 1991; Plomin *et al.*, 1991; Rutter, 1991) have compared psychopathology to the model of MR in which severe forms of MR may be genetically distinct from normality, whereas mild retardation may represent the quantitative extreme of the normal distribution. They suggested that more common childhood emotional and conduct disorders may represent 'extremes of normality arising from a complex interplay of risk factors rather than genetically distinct diseases' (Rutter, 1991, p. 131), and that genetic influences result from many genes having small effects upon multiple broad behavioural tendencies rather than a single major gene producing a qualitatively distinct disorder (Plomin, 1991; Plomin *et al.*, 1991; see also Chapter 2). Thus, even though intelligence scores can be viewed as a single quantitative dimension, the underlying aetiology may involve different processes for extremely low scores.

Similarly, blood pressure can be thought of as a continuum extending from normality to malignant hypertension. Nevertheless, there is a sharp discontinuity between normal variations in blood pressure and malignant hypertension, which is associated with kidney pathology and mortality. Thus, severe disorders of intelligence and blood pressure may not simply represent extremes along these dimensions. Rather, their correlates suggest discontinuity regarding some severe forms of the disorders.

Does the same issue apply to emotional disorders? It is true that sadness and depression can be conceptualized along a single dimension, yet some depressive disorders may be more than simply extreme sadness. Although more evidence is needed, current genetic evidence (see section on heredity) suggests discontinuity in some mood disorders, such as bipolar disorder and severe recurrent unipolar depression. In contrast, less severe and possibly chronic forms of unipolar depression (e.g. dysthymia) may represent the extremes on the normal continuum of depressive symptomatology. However, some severe forms of depression may result from extreme levels of the same factors underlying normal variation in mood (e.g. cognitive vulnerability), whereas other forms of depression may result from aetiologically distinct processes (e.g. genetic vulnerability). Thus, the question of continuity between normal sadness and depressive disorder cannot be answered simply. It is likely that mood disorders are aetiologically heterogeneous and both dimensional and categorical approaches are appropriate for characterizing subtypes of emotional disorders.

THE DEVELOPMENT OF EMOTION KNOWLEDGE

As children develop, they become increasingly able to recognize emotional expressions of others and to identify circumstances that elicit emotions in themselves and others (Chandler, 1977; Saarni & Harris, 1989). This emotion knowledge can promote social interchanges that are important for survival and well-being. For example, recognition that another is experiencing emotional distress is necessary to offer sympathy or comfort. Recognition of another's anger can be an important cue to leave the situation and thereby promote one's own well-being.

Knowledge of the link between situations and emotions facilitates adaptive behaviour. To the extent that children understand the causes of emotions in themselves and others, they can anticipate and prepare for potentially emotion-provoking circumstances. This preparation includes redirecting and controlling their own emotional displays and responding strategically to expected emotions of others.

Recognition and discrimination of the emotion expressions of others

Discrete emotion theorists (Izard, 1971; Ekman, 1973) have argued that a few discrete emotional expressions are universally recognized as conveying particular emotional states. This expressive reper-toire is assumed to be part of a species-specific native endowment that influences infants' ability to recognize and discriminate the emotional expressions of others (Nelson, 1987). Thus, infants' early concepts of emotion are anchored to this biologically grounded signaling system of emotional expressions (Harris & Saarni, 1989).

To investigate infants' capacities to recognize and discriminate among different emotional expressions of others, investigators often use the fact that babies are selective in what they look at. Barerra and Maurer (1981) found that 3-month-old infants discriminated smiling from frowning faces posed by the mother or an unfamiliar female. LaBarbera et al. (1976) reported that 4- and 6-month-old infants looked longer at joy than angry or neutral expressions; there was no difference, however, in frequency of looking at angry versus neutral expressions. Young-Browne et al. (1977) used a habituation procedure and reported that 3-month-old infants discriminated surprise from happy expressions, but they did not discriminate happy from sad expressions or sadness from surprise. They also reported no differences in duration of looking at any of the three expressions. Nelson et al. (1979) found that 7-month-old infants discriminated photographs of happy and fearful expressions, and Nelson and Dolgin (1985) reported that infants generalized their discrimination of happiness and fear across different male and female faces.

Caron and co-workers (Caron et al., 1982, 1988) reported that infants as young as 5 months of age can discriminate expressions of sadness and happiness produced by different models conveying facial and vocal cues. Seven-month-old infants discriminated between happiness and anger and happiness and sadness, but only when vocal cues were present. Therefore, they concluded that young infants rely more on the voice than the face in distinguishing among expressions.

Walker (1982; Walker-Andrews, 1986) reported that 5- and 7-month-old infants recognized happy and sad facial expressions when they were paired with their appropriate sound tracks; 7-month-old infants also recognized angry expressions paired with the sound track. Furthermore, 7-month-old infants preferred happy facial expressions paired with happy vocal cues and sad expressions paired with sad vocal cues over inconsistent facial and vocal cues (Walker, 1982). This finding suggests that the infants detected inconsistent emotional cues conveyed in facial and vocal channels.

Anger, sadness and happiness are easily identifiable by 3- and 4-year-old children, even without sound (Walden & Field, 1982; Stifter & Fox, 1987). By the third or fourth year of life, children are capable of attending to facial and vocal cues to obtain emotional information and make inferences about another's happy, sad, angry or fearful emotional reactions in equivocal situations (Denham & Couchoud, 1990). Fear is one of the last of the primary emotions to be accurately identified (Michalson & Lewis, 1985; Denham & Couchoud, 1990).

Thus, humans can recognize and discriminate different emotional expressions at a very young age. However, the fact that young infants can discriminate among expressions does not mean that they understand the emotional states that these expressions convey (Nelson, 1987). The significance of emotional expressions as a reflection of a person's internal state takes time to learn (e.g. Stein & Trabasso, 1989), and the relation between expressed emotional behaviour and internal states may be discrepant (Lewis & Michalson, 1983). Moreover, children gradually acquire an understanding of emotions that do not have distinct emotional expressions. For example, children discriminate between feelings of pride and relief (Harris *et al.*, 1987), although there is no evidence that these emotions can be discriminated based on facial, postural or vocal cues.

Work on social referencing in ambiguous situations, however, suggests that infants do understand the meaning of some emotional expressions of others. By the end of the first year of life infants use their mothers' happy, fearful and disgusted expressions to regulate their behaviour towards events that supposedly elicited those reactions (Sorce *et al.*, 1985). Some have suggested that negative expressions have a particularly large impact on interpersonal regulation of behaviour because of their value in signaling aversive events (Lanzetta & Orr, 1980; Walden & Ogan, 1988).

Children as young as 2 years of age have been shown to be sensitive to level of 'background anger', that is, conflict between adults not involving the children themselves. Cummings *et al.* (1985)

reported that background anger was associated with heightened distress among children, an influence that became even more pronounced with repeated exposures to conflict. Witnessing conflict also increased aggression towards peers. This indicates that children are sensitive to emotions or conflict among others, even when it does not involve the child directly.

Children become increasingly adept at discriminating emotions as they develop language. Walden and Field (1982) reported that 3–5-year-old children were most accurate in discriminating happy and sad expressions, followed by surprise and anger; discrimination of all four expressions was above chance. Some children discriminated some expressions much better than others. Moreover, verbal labels increased the children's ability to discriminate expressions. When children demonstrated accurate understanding of verbal labels for emotional displays, their discrimination improved for all expressions. Thus, linguistic processes may play a role in the development of children's abilities to discriminate and categorize facial expressions.

Emotion labels for happy and sad are acquired early; by age 4 years children use such affect terms as happy, sad, angry and scared (Amen, 1941; Michalson & Lewis, 1985). Children produce verbal labels for emotional behaviours such as crying and laughing even earlier (Zahn-Waxler *et al.*, 1979). By the early school years, children's emotional lexicon has expanded to included concepts of pride, shame, guilt, embarassment, gratitude and other complex emotional states (Russell & Ridgeway, 1983; Schwartz & Trabasso, 1984).

With development, the expression and discrimination of emotions becomes more complex. In mature perceivers, a small set of facial expressions (a subset of the 'primary emotions') can be categorized with fairly high agreement (Izard, 1971), but most emotional expressions can be thought of as a collection of overlapping 'fuzzy sets' rather than a set of sharply defined categories (Russell & Bullock, 1986). When an expression more closely fits the prototypical exemplar of a set, it is more likely to be 'recognized' as being a member of the category than less prototypical exemplars.

'Blends' of more than a single expression also are possible. That is, some expressions may contain elements of two or more expressions. For example, when individuals display expressions that are not truly felt they are likely to blend aspects of the real and feigned expression; this has been called 'leakage'. That is, the expression contains incongruous elements that are not present in truly felt emotions. Adults can use these cues to detect deception in emotional displays (Ekman, 1985).

Deficits in the ability to recognize emotional expressions of others have been associated with lack of acceptance by peers (Walden & Field, 1990), MR (Adams & Markham, 1991), and with certain psychopathologies, such as autism (Hobson, 1986a, b). In normally developing preschool children, Walden and Field (1990) found that children who had lower ability to discriminate and categorize facial expressions of others' emotions were disliked by their preschool peers. As early problems in social relationships have been found to predict later social problems (Parker & Asher, 1987), it is likely that these children who are poor discriminators of others' emotions will be at increased risk for later social problems as well. Adams and Markham (1991) reported that middle school and high school children with MR performed more poorly than same-age peers without retardation in recognizing and labelling facial expressions of others. When retarded children were compared to those of similar mental ages, the differences were eliminated in the 7-year-old mental age group, but non-retarded persons still performed better than retarded persons with mental ages of about 10 years.

In a series of studies that examined the ability of autistic individuals to discriminate emotional expressions, Hobson (1986a, b) found that autistic children are deficient in recognizing expressions relative to mental age-matched retarded and non-retarded peers (although see Ozonoff et al., 1990; see also Chapter 13). Hobson (1986a) found that autistic elementary school aged children were impaired relative to peers in selecting facial expressions that matched bodily and vocal expressions of happiness, unhappiness, anger and fear in situations consistent with each emotion. Similarly, autistic individuals less accurately selected gestures that matched vocalizations and facial expressions of the same four emotional expressions in an emotion-eliciting situation (Hobson, 1986b). In contrast, autistic children have not been found to be deficient in tasks involving objects or meaningless social stimuli (Tantam et al., 1989). Hobson (1986b) concluded that autistic individuals are particularly deficient in recognizing emotions in others and in coordinating information from emotionally expressive faces, gestures and vocalizations.

In sum, these studies suggest that recognition of emotional expressions of others is an ability that develops early and improves with the development of language. Emotion recognition is important in predicting later social functioning, and deficits in emotion recognition may characterize certain clinical syndromes.

Knowledge about emotions and the emotion–situation link

By 2 or 3 years of age, children understand some links between situations and the emotions usually associated with them (Saarni & Harris, 1989). Borke (1971) presented 3-year-old children with stories describing common events such as a birthday party, losing a toy or being lost; she asked children to select a facial expression indicating how the actor would feel. Even in this somewhat demanding hypothetical task, children selected the happy face for appropriate situations. They were less accurate, but still above chance, at identifying sad situations; they performed no better than chance with anger-eliciting events, however. Denham (1986) also has reported that 2- and 3-year-old children could identify another's emotions in happy, sad, angry and fearful situations, although a great deal of individual variability was observed.

Trabasso et al. (1981) used a different strategy to assess children's emotion knowledge. Children were asked to provide a situation that might cause a particular emotion. Children between 3 and 4.5 years of age generated appropriate causes for the emotional responses of story characters who were described as feeling happy, sad, angry, scared, excited or surprised. The clearest distinction among the causes offered was between situations that elicited positive emotions and those that elicited negative emotions.

Bretherton and Beeghly (1982) interviewed mothers of 2.5-year-old children, who reported that words such as happy, sad, mad and scared were used by a majority of the children to refer to both themselves and other persons and that the context in which those terms were used indicated some degree of causal understanding. Bretherton and Beeghly concluded that, by 2−3 years of age, children begin to know and verbalize the links between certain behaviours and simple emotional states. Work by Dunn and co-workers (Dunn & Kendrick, 1982; Dunn & Munn, 1985; Dunn, 1988) in which children have been observed interacting with family members in naturalistic settings, is consistent with this conclusion. For example, Dunn and Kendrick (1982) described one toddler who took a sibling's comfort object in a deliberate attempt to upset the sibling; another toddler thrust a toy spider at the sibling to cause fear (Dunn & Munn, 1985).

Barden *et al.* (1980) interviewed kindergarten, third- and sixth-grade children about probable emotional responses to several affect-provoking situations. Children as young as 4 showed considerable consensus regarding expected emotional responses to a wide range of experiences (e.g. success, nurturance, dishonesty, punishment). There were age differences in children's expected emotional reactions to dishonesty, nurturance and failure. For example, younger children consistently reported that they would feel happy if they were not caught doing something wrong, whereas older children tended to report fear. Barden *et al.* suggested that this age difference could reflect children's developing moral reasoning (Hoffman, 1970).

Harris and co-workers (Harris *et al.*, 1981; Harris, 1985) have shown that children's concept of the causes of emotions changes between 6 and 11 years. Whereas 6-year-old children focus on the situation−response link, by 11 years old children recognize that mental processes also can engender emotional reactions. Harris and Olthof (1982) concluded that young children believe that there is a direct one-to-one link between situations and emotions, whereas older children recognize that the link is mediated by inner mental processes.

This has important clinical implications for cognitive psychotherapies. A fundamental assumption of cognitive therapy for the treatment of emotional disorders is that situations do not cause emotions, rather one's construal of situations produces emotions (Ellis, 1962; Beck *et al.*, 1979). If young children do not recognize the relation between mental processes and emotional reactions, it may be difficult to use this approach clinically.

Another important kind of emotion knowledge is the understanding that situations can elicit multiple emotions ('mixed feelings'). This ability is evidenced by preschool and early elementary school. For example, Gnepp (1983) showed young children pictures of children in emotion-eliciting situations in which the facial expression either matched or mismatched the situation. Children were asked to tell a story about the pictures. When the actors' facial expression did not match the situation depicted, even young children offered story elaborations that resolved the incongruence by describing the situations as having elements that elicit mixed emotional reactions.

Harter and co-workers (Harter & Buddin, 1987; Harter & Whitesell, 1989) outlined a sequence of accomplishments in the understanding of mixed feelings. Initially, children appear to be unable to recognize that two feelings can co-occur. Then, they acknowledge that two feelings can occur in temporal sequence but not simultaneously. Later, as children acquire the capacity simultaneously to consider two mental links between situations and emotions, they acknowledge that multiple feelings can occur at one moment.

According to Harter, the understanding of simultaneous emotions involves two factors: (i) positive/ negative valence of the emotions; and (ii) the number of targets of the emotion. For example, whereas 7-year-old children acknowledge that one can feel two negative emotions (e.g. sad and mad) towards a single target, children do not understand the experience of two opposite emotions towards two different targets until about 10 years old. Understanding that one can experience two opposite emotions towards the same target develops even later. Harter has suggested that clinicians can use children's level of understanding of simultaneous emotions across different areas of their lives as a barometer of potential adjustment problems. That is, difficulties in a particular domain of functioning (e.g. peer relationships) may preclude the development of age-appropriate emotional concepts in that domain (Harter & Whitesell, 1989).

Children's knowledge about how to alter emotional states in themselves and others also changes with age. Carlson *et al.* (1983) reported that 4–5-year-old children selected targets experiencing negative (as opposed to positive) emotions to have their emotions changed. McCoy and Masters (1985) reported that most children suggested appropriate strategies for altering emotions in the desired direction, but children between 5 and 12 years old suggested different types of strategies. Older children suggested more nurturance and social strategies, which presumably involved management of their own expressive behaviour, whereas younger children suggested more material strategies, such as giving a sad person candy.

Harris and Lipian (1989) reported that children's strategies for changing their own negative emotions changed with age. Whereas 6-year-old children suggested concrete distractions to remedy negative emotions (e.g. go play with a friend), 10-year-old children offered more mentalistic strategies involving psychological mechanisms that might ameliorate the negative emotion. Harris and Lipian also interviewed 8-year-old boys entering boarding school. Whereas only 25% of the boys believed that they could cheer themselves up simply by smiling, 77% believed that thinking about something else would help. This indicates that the boys' theory of emotion included beliefs that they could change emotional states by redirecting their thoughts even if the situation itself remained unchanged.

Finally, knowledge of the link between emotions and situations is relevant to the concept of emotion display rules. Ekman *et al.* (1972) proposed that socialized individuals develop emotion display rules, or social conventions about how one expresses particular feelings appropriately. The ability to conform to cultural display rules involves knowledge of the rules, ability to control overt expressions, and motivation to conform to expectations. Control over expressive behaviour may initially consist wholly of external constraints (e.g. by parents) that are overlaid on 'true' feelings, but presumably with development these rules become more internalized and may even become a part of our 'true' feelings. Saarni (1979) found that children's awareness of and reasoning about dissimulation of emotional expression increased between 6 and 10 years of age, and some situations consistently elicited more display rules than others. Thus, with

development children increasingly realize that external expressions need not echo internal experience.

Based on their history of socioemotional experiences young children learn to coordinate their emotional states and expressive behaviour; they also learn to produce overt emotional expressions that are discrepant from their experience. Saarni (1990) suggested that the earliest form of this discrepancy may be the exaggeration of emotional behaviour to gain another's attention, and this may occur as early as the second year of life. Children 3–4 years of age have been observed to cry after injuring themselves more often if they noticed someone looking at them than if they believed they were unnoticed (Blurton-Jones, 1967).

Another form of control over overt expressions involves minimization of emotional behaviours, or dampening the intensity of expressions. Saarni (1979) reported that elementary school children indicated that they would try to conceal their feelings of hurt/pain and fear to avoid embarrassment or ridicule from others. Older children cited many more occasions than younger children in which one should control one's overt emotional displays. Older children cited reasons such as status differences and degree of affiliation as factors that influence one's display of emotion.

In sum, knowledge of the link between situations and emotions develops with age and has implications for children's understanding of the simultaneous experience of multiple emotions, the development of strategies for regulation of emotions in oneself and others, and the use of emotion display rules. The later development of the understanding of the relation between mental processes and affect may limit the effectiveness of certain types of psychotherapy with young children.

The relation between cognition and emotion

Despite debate about the primacy of cognition versus emotion (Zajonc, 1980; Lazarus, 1981), there is little question that cognitions and emotions are interrelated. Although Zajonc (1980, 1984) argued that cognitions are not necessary to produce emotional states, he recognized that cognitive processes can and do activate emotions. Even Piaget

(1981), known best for his theory of cognitive development, acknowledged that affect and cognition are inseparable aspects of every sensorimotor or symbolic act (Piaget, 1981).

Several theorists have suggested that mature forms of emotional processing do not become possible until a sense of self emerges between 7 and 9 months of age (Sroufe, 1979; Lewis & Michalson, 1983; Harter, 1986). Sroufe (1979) recognized that infants are born with certain basic reactions (wariness–fear, rage–anger, pleasure–joy), but he asserted that emotional life becomes more complex through cognitive developmental accomplishments that allow children to organize emotions on the basis of meaning.

Campos and Barrett (Campos & Barrett, 1984; Campos *et al.*, 1989) argued that emotions are tied to specific eliciting conditions whose effects depend on particular cognitive competencies. For example, a crawling infant may fear a drop-off, but other fears (e.g. strangers) do not emerge until other cognitive abilities have developed (e.g. the ability to distinguish among people).

Level of cognitive functioning logically constrains emotional functions that require high levels of intellectual activity to perform (Cicchetti & Pogge-Hesse, 1981). As children mature cognitively, their ability to make complex attributions of causality increases and the capacity for self-reflection develops (Ruble & Rholes, 1981; Harter, 1983). Such development allows children to experience some feelings not possible without advanced cognitive capacities (e.g. guilt; hopelessness). Guilt and shame are emotions that have been said to require higher level cognitive functions that very young children do not possess and some individuals with mental retardation may never achieve (Zahn-Waxler & Kochanska, 1990). Cognitive development also can influence the experience of some emotions that might have been previously experienced. For example, infants' developing memory enables them to laugh not only in *response* to but in *anticipation* of the caregiver's return in 'peekaboo' (Sroufe & Wunsch, 1972).

Lazarus (1990, 1991) has proposed that cognitive appraisal is a central process in emotion, and that cognition and emotion are inseparable. He asserted that emotion is a response involving evaluative judgements about the personal meaning of an event. Primary appraisals focus on the relevance of an event for one's well-being; secondary appraisals focus on one's ability to cope with problematic events. Cognitive appraisals must reconcile an individual's goals and beliefs with environmental realities. Coping can alter either the actual situation or the appraisal of a situation, both of which affect subsequent emotions (Lazarus, 1991).

Lazarus and Folkman (1984) identified two types of coping responses — problem-focused coping emphasizes competent behaviours that deal with an event, and emotion-focused coping involves managing one's cognitions and emotions to change the interpretation or personal meaning of an event. Although Lazarus and Folkman (1984) proposed that these are two alternative ways to deal with an emotionally arousing event, it also is possible that both processes operate concurrently.

Cognitions can influence the type, duration and intensity of emotions experienced, and, conversely, emotional states can influence cognitive functioning. For example, according to the cognitive content-specificity hypothesis (Beck *et al.*, 1987; Smith & Lazarus, 1990) thoughts about danger and threat are associated with fear and anxiety, whereas cognitions about loss and failure characterize sadness and depression. The duration of depressive symptoms may be influenced by the extent to which individuals ruminate about causes and consequences of their symptoms instead of acting to distract themselves or alter the situation (Nolen-Hoeksema, 1991). Such ruminative thinking has been found to interfere with problem-solving behaviour (Carver *et al.*, 1989).

Positive emotional states can facilitate creativity and the retrieval of positively toned material in memory, whereas a sad emotional state either fails to facilitate recall of affectively congruent negative material or is less effective as a retrieval cue than positive affect (Isen, 1990). Isen proposed that positive affect increases perceptions of relatedness. For example, people experiencing positive affect tend to categorize a wider range of neutral stimuli or non-typical exemplars of a category together (Isen & Daubman, 1984), and they are more cognitively flexible; that is, they create more different groupings and sort stimuli into larger groupings (Isen, 1987). Positive affect may have a large and diffuse effect that is not affect-specific, whereas affect-specific content may be more characteristic of negative states such as sadness or anger. Isen (1990) proposed that positive affect is a general and diffuse phenomenon because it is organized diffusely in memory (Isen, 1990).

Language is an important and potent tool that allows individuals to understand emotions (Kopp, 1989). With the development of linguistic competence, children substantially increase their ability to communicate feelings to other persons, receive feedback about the appropriateness of their emotions, and obtain information about ways to manage emotional states.

Moreover, the development of language can be influenced by emotions. Bloom and Capatides (1987) reported that infants who spent more time in positive or negative affective states were delayed in acquiring early words as compared to infants who were more often neutral. They suggested that time spent in neutral affective states allows the reflective stance necessary for early word learning. Bloom (1990) proposed that emotions and early language are alternative modes of expression available to the young child, which become integrated with development.

Another important link in the emotion–cognition interface is empathy, a vicarious emotional response that is identical or very similar to that of another person (Eisenberg *et al.*, 1991). The mechanisms that produce empathic responding are not well-understood. Some believe that basic cross-modal equivalencies and affect attunement underlie empathy. For example, Sagi and Hoffman (1976) reported that infants in a neonatal nursery responded to cries of other infants by crying themselves. Others have hypothesized a more cognitive, perspective taking approach to the development of empathy (Feshbach, 1987). The capacity to take the perspective of another person has been proposed to be an important prerequisite or facilitator of empathic and sympathetic responding; the absence of perspective taking and empathy may be associated with psychopathology, such as conduct disorder (Hoffman, 1982; Feshbach, 1987).

Cognitive processes may be central to the development and maintenance of some psychopathology, such as depression, anxiety and aggression. Social information processing has been proposed as a mediator of aggressive behaviour

(Dodge *et al.*, 1986; Perry *et al.*, 1986). Differences in encoding of information, representation of information in thinking and memory, generation of potential responses to events, and anticipated success of these responses have been shown to contribute to differences in emotion and emotional behaviour such as aggression (Dodge & Crick, 1990) and depression (Quiggle *et al.*, 1992).

Cognitions are hypothesized to play a role in the aetiology of depression and anxiety (Beck, 1967; Abramson *et al.*, 1978; Beck & Emery, 1985). Beck proposed that depressed individuals have negative beliefs about the self, world and future. Individuals with this belief system tend to interpret aversive life events as confirming their negative self and world views, and therefore are likely to become depressed when faced with negative life circumstances. Abramson *et al.* (1978) proposed that individuals who tend to explain negative life events in terms of global, stable and internal causes are likely to become depressed when negative events occur. Abramson *et al.* (1989) suggested that hopelessness mediates this process. Data indicate that these negative cognitive styles exist during episodes of depression in both adults and children, although the persistence of these cognitive patterns between episodes, as well as their causal role in the development of mood disorders, is still the subject of debate (Barnett & Gotlib, 1988; Garber *et al.*, 1990).

Thus, whether emotions are considered a separate system from cognitions (Izard, 1977; Zajonc, 1980) or whether cognitions are a component of emotion (Dodge, 1989; Lazarus, 1991), they clearly are interrelated. Moreover, cognitive development and experience significantly increase the range of emotions children can experience as well as their ability to interpret, regulate and cope with these emotions.

PROCESSES OF EMOTIONAL DEVELOPMENT

Innate and biological processes

Primary emotions

A long philosophical and scientific tradition from Descartes to Darwin has claimed that a small set of emotions are 'primary' and common to all humans as part of our genetic and evolutionary endowment. More recently that position has been taken by Tomkins (1962), Ekman and Friesen (1971), Izard (1971) and Plutchik (1983), although there is no consensus as to exactly which emotions are considered to be primary. Plutchik (1980) asserted that the basic and earliest discrimination among emotions is between good (approach) and bad (avoid), with differentiation of these two dimensions occurring later developmentally. According to Plutchik (1983), the eight basic emotions (joy, sadness, acceptance, disgust, fear, anger, expectation and surprise) meet the following criteria. (i) They are applicable to the entire evolutionary scale; though their expression may vary across species, it does so in patterned ways that have at their core prototypical behaviours. (ii) A small core of basic emotions consisting of prototypes exists and all other emotions are mixed or derivative states. (iii) They are biologically adaptive, in that they involve key survival issues. (iv) Primary emotions are hypothetical constructs that can be conceptualized in terms of pairs of opposites. (v) Emotions vary in their similarity to each other and in their intensity or level of arousal. Emotions not considered primary are seen as blends or variations of intensity in primary emotions.

Izard (1971, 1977) identified a slightly different set of eight primary emotions (joy, interest, surprise, sadness, anger, disgust, contempt and fear), and argued that each is represented by a unique pattern of facial behaviour, which is an integral part of the experience of that emotion. He has presented cross-cultural evidence that the ability to recognize and experience the primary emotions is present in a variety of Western and non-Western literate and preliterate cultures. Although data support Izard's position, there remains considerable variability among raters of the emotions (for most emotions, no more than 50% were placed in the correct category). In later work, Izard *et al.* (1980) found that judges reliably identified a set of basic emotional expressions in 1–9-month-old infants. Thus, there is evidence that some discrete emotions are present early in life, but the relation of these primitive emotional expressions to mature emotional experience is still unclear.

Brain physiology

Physiologic systems play a significant part in regulating functions that contribute to an organism's emotional responses. Taking an evolutionary perspective, Ekman (1977, 1984) argued that each fundamental emotion is characterized not only by unique facial expressions, but also by unique patterns of physiological activity. There is some evidence that cerebral hemispheric asymmetry develops early in life and contributes to emotional functioning (Heller, 1990). For example, lateralized presentations of certain types of emotional information show a right-hemisphere advantage for discriminating among faces (Saxby & Bryden, 1985) and emotional vocal tone (Saxby & Bryden, 1984). Differential role of the hemispheres in experiencing positive or negative emotional states also has been investigated, with opposite patterns of frontal lobe activation for positive and negative emotion (Heller, 1990).

Tucker *et al.* (1990) suggested that the literature on brain lateralization indicates two different perspectives on cognition—emotion interactions. They noted that changes in hemispheric function are not simply emotional but involve changes in cognitive appraisal, as well. Thus, the emotional mechanisms of the two hemispheres may influence the regulation of cognitive appraisal processes. First, each hemisphere's cognitive functions may play a role in elaborating and regulating emotion. Second, each hemisphere's contribution may vary with different kinds of emotional arousal.

Tucker *et al.* (1990) further suggested that there are two qualitatively different neural control modes, a tonic activation system and a phasic arousal system, that represent neural mechanisms of habituation and sensitization, respectively. These two mechanisms are differentially engaged by stimuli of different intensities and they impose information-processing biases on ongoing neural operations. With low phasic arousal and high tonic activation an individual would sensitize to even moderate intensities of stimulation. With lower tonic activation and high phasic arousal, increasing intensity results in more positive hedonic tone. Differential activation of the two systems is thought to play a role in emotional experience and emotion-related cognitions. Tucker *et al.* (1990) concluded that 'there is no mechanism that alters the brain's activity in a simple quantitative fashion. Rather, there are multiple systems, each of which qualitatively modulates neural operations as it regulates the quantity of ongoing activity' (p. 148).

Fox (1991) has suggested that the development of emotion involves an initial appraisal of approach or withdrawal that results in motor programmes, including facial expressions, that promote approach and withdrawal responses. More complex emotions develop as a result of these initial appraisals and environmental interactions (Fox, 1991). Davidson *et al.* (1990) found support for the hypothesis that patterns of brain physiology during emotional experiences are emotion-specific. They reported electroencephalographic (EEG) data that, in the alpha power spectrum, disgust is associated with more activation in the right anterior temporal cortical region and happiness with more left-side activation. No differences were observed in the beta power spectrum or in the central and parietal regions.

Although the limbic system was once considered the centre of emotional activity (Papez, 1937; MacLean, 1952), there is little empirical support for this view (Durant, 1973; LeDoux, 1987). Current evidence suggests that the amygdala is a key structure in mediating emotional experience, particularly fear and anger (Aggleton & Mishkin, 1986; Kling, 1986). For example, amygdalectomy to relieve seizures significantly reduces emotionality (Kling, 1986). LeDoux (1987) found auditory fear conditioning through subcortical pathways that involved the transmission of sensory information from the thalamus to the neocortex, and then the hippocampus and amygdala. He suggested that the amygdala was the final gateway to hormonal release, autonomic changes and emotional behaviour.

The hypothalamus also has been considered important in the expression of emotion. For example, stimulation of the hypothalamus elicits aggressive behaviour in animals (Flynn, 1967). More recent evidence, however, indicates that the hypothalamus may be a relay station for sensory information rather than a central structure for neural processing of emotional behaviour (Bandler, 1982).

Jacobs and Nadel (1985) proposed a neurobio-logical theory that explained phobias in terms of stress-induced reactivation of learned responses established prior to maturity of the hippocampus. Noting that some phobic patients have difficulty recalling the origin of their fears, Jacobs and Nadel argued that early learning experiences have lasting effects but are difficult to remember because they occur before the hippocampus has matured sufficiently. Infants are capable of learning associations but not context learning, which the hippocampus mediates, and therefore they are unable to recall details of when and where the feared object was paired with the noxious stimulus. McNally (1989), however, challenged many of Jacob and Nadel's assumptions, particularly that clinical fears develop independently of environmental context. McNally argued that although the *external* stimulus context for panic attacks may vary greatly, the *internal* stimuli that trigger the attacks are clear and vary little.

Another physiological theory of emotional expression is the facial feedback hypothesis which states that facial expressions provide feedback to the expresser that influences emotional experience (Laird, 1984). Studies have shown that ongoing emotional experience can be amplified or attenuated in accord with subjects' voluntary control of their expressive behaviour (Izard, 1990). Critics of this theory, however, have argued that the average effect size for manipulated facial expression is small (Matsumoto, 1987), and it is difficult to discern whether or not subjects consciously or unconsciously infer the subjective feelings they 'should' be experiencing (Zajonc *et al.*, 1989).

Zajonc (Zajonc, 1985; Zajonc *et al.*, 1989) suggested a vascular theory of emotional efference that hypothesizes that facial muscle contractions affect venous blood flow to the cavernous sinus of the brain, which is an important structure in thermoregulation. Temperature changes in cerebral blood are thought to affect neurochemical processes such as those that mediate emotion. Zajonc *et al.* (1989) reported that directly controlling cerebral blood temperature by having subjects breathing cool or warm air produced expected pleasurable and aversive experiences, respectively. A limitation of this perspective is that although thermoregulation of cerebral blood and brain neurochemistry may produce changes in positivity and negativity of hedonic states, it does not easily account for more differentiated emotional experiences.

Another important link between physiology and emotions has been found with regard to the neurochemistry of mood disorders. Abnormalities of the catecholamine system may contribute to the pathogenesis of affective disorders, although both deficiencies and excesses in this system have been reported (Siever & Davis, 1985). Norepinephrine has been suggested to be involved in affective syndromes and in the function of antidepressant drug action. Three neurotransmitters, acetylcholine (Aston-Jones *et al.*, 1982) gamma-aminobutyric acid (Aston-Jones *et al.*, 1982), and serotonin (Kalus *et al.*, 1989), all have been implicated in the development of major depressive disorders. Rather than single transmitter effects, however, recent neurological evidence has emphasized complex interactions among neurotransmitter systems. Siever and Davis (1985) proposed a reformulation of the catecholamine hypotheses such that failure of regulation or buffering, rather than simply too much or too little activity, may best explain their role in affective disorders. Thus, a dysregulated neurotransmitter system may be highly variable, unstable, inappropriately responsive to stimulation, or lacking normal periodicities (Siever & Davis, 1985). Therapeutic effects of antidepressants may involve the regulation of homeostatic mechanisms of aminergic neurotransmitters.

Finally, children with Down's syndrome have been found to show delays in age-appropriate emotional responses and dampening of their expressions (Emde *et al.*, 1978). Neurochemical studies of persons with Down's syndrome suggest that they have dampened reactive systems that could result in attenuated emotion expressive behaviour and a deficiency in emotion communication (Cicchetti, 1990). Cicchetti (1990; Cicchetti & Sroufe, 1978) further suggested that children with Down's syndrome have abnormal catecholamine metabolism characterized by problems in the cholinergic and serotonergic systems and deficiencies in functioning of the sympathetic nervous system that result in deviation in their emotion system.

Hormones

Hormones can act on the brain to influence behaviour in terms of: (i) the organization of early brain development, which is usually permanent, such as the organizational effects of prenatal androgens on the embryonic brain and other structures and functions; and (ii) activation, which involves contemporaneous effects of peripheral and neural processes (Buchanan *et al.*, 1992). Hormonal effects on emotionality may be due to either tonic or episodic variations in concentrations of hormones. These effects are likely to involve, not simply main effects of hormones, but complex interactions between hormones and environmental contextual factors.

Moreover, there may be curvilinear as well as linear relations between hormone concentrations and emotion. For example, deLignieres and Vincens (1982) found that moderate levels of oestrogen were related to positive feelings, whereas both high and low levels of oestrogen were associated with behavioural manifestations of pathology (depression and aggression, respectively). In addition, the relation between hormones and emotions is bidirectional. Changes in hormones can affect behaviour, and shifts in social circumstances can influence hormonal levels as well (Maccoby & Jacklin, 1974). 'A testosterone level is not something that an individual "has" independently of experience ... a high testosterone level can be both a cause and a result of aggressive behaviour' (Maccoby & Jacklin, 1974, p. 246). Furthermore, the effects of hormones on mood and emotion represent the interaction of highly complex self-regulating systems, the nature of which are poorly understood (Bancroft, 1991).

Research on the relation between hormones and behaviour often has focused on the period of preadolescence and adolescence when changes in levels of circulating hormones are marked. The role of gonadal hormones in changing behavioural and affective states during puberty is controversial. Clearly, other psychosocial changes occur during this period that could account for changes during adolescence; these could act alone or in concert with hormonal effects. Rising levels of testosterone and oestrogen might be expected to have effects resulting from both absolute levels and adaptation to changing levels. Moreover, the relation between hormones and emotions during adolescence is not necessarily similar to the relation for adults. For example, adrenal androgens may be more influential early in adolescence (Susman *et al.*, 1991), whereas testosterone may be more critical during mid or late adolescence (Olweus *et al.*, 1988).

Bancroft (1991) has suggested that hormones interact among themselves and with social factors differently at different developmental periods. For example, during adolescence direct effects of androgens on some aggressive behaviours may be enhanced by the effects of testosterone on physical growth and sexuality. These effects are obscured, however, by social learning and other factors after adolescence. Exceptions to this learning process are considered to indicate poor adaptation in individuals 'whose continuing "androgen-driven" behavior is likely to lead them into criminal or otherwise antisocial behavior' (Bancroft, 1991, p. 275). This is an example of how deviations in normal emotional and behavioural functioning can occur in individuals who have not had adequate social learning experiences to accommodate the normal biological changes that occur during development.

The menstrual cycle and its accompanying cyclic fluctuations in hormone levels also has been associated with changes in mood and emotion, although the reasons for this and the strength and prevalence of the effect have been disputed (Bancroft, 1991). Perhaps the most dramatic example of this is 'premenstrual syndrome' (PMS), which is characterized by a cluster of cyclic physical (tenderness, bloating) and mood changes (increased or labile emotionality, irritability, tiredness and tension; Haskett *et al.*, 1980). Studies have shown a relation between premenstrual mood change and depressive illness in women (Endicott *et al.*, 1981; Mackenzie *et al.*, 1986). Whether the nature and severity of depressive symptoms that occur premenstrually are similar to those that occur during episodes of depressive disorder is unclear. A recent study reported that amongst women who did report premenstrual and menstrual mood changes, 35% had scores on the Beck depression inventory that were in the moderate range and 31% were in the severe range (Warner *et al.*, 1991). Thus, a fair number of PMS sufferers experienced a level of depressed mood and symptoms comparable to that seen in clinical depression. Similarly, the postpartum period is characterized by dramatic and rapid changes in hormonal levels, which may be linked to emotional effects such as labile affect or depression in many new mothers (O'Hara *et al.*, 1991).

Results of studies examining the relation between hormones and emotions in adolescents have been inconsistent. Susman, Nottelman and co-workers (Nottelman *et al.*, 1987; Susman *et al.*, 1987) reported that negative emotional tone was negatively correlated with the testosterone to oestradiol ratio, and testosterone–oestradiol binding globulin and androstenedione levels in males. Early maturation (measured by oestradiol levels and testosterone : oestradiol ratio), however, was associated with more negative affectivity in girls, but less negative affectivity in boys. Adrenal androgen levels were correlated with negative emotional tone in boys but not girls, whereas the opposite was true for follicle-stimulating hormone (FSH). Nottelman *et al.* (1990) concluded that it is important to examine more than one group of hormones and to explore hormone–behaviour relations in the context of other developmental markers such as age and pubertal status.

Moreover, factors other than hormones alone have been found to predict depression and aggression in children and adolescents. Brooks-Gunn and Warren (1989) reported that negative affect increased during times of rapid oestrogen rise in females during early adolescence, although social factors and the interaction between social factors and oestrogen changes both explained more of the variance in negative affect scores than hormonal status alone. Recent longitudinal studies have found that pre-existing depression was more strongly related to later depression than were hormone levels (Paikoff *et al.*, 1991; Susman *et al.*, 1991) and that depression is especially likely to increase during adolescence for children exhibiting prior evidence of disturbance (Achenbach & Edelbrock, 1981; Kovacs *et al.*, 1984). Similarly, higher testosterone is related to increased aggression, but the effect is stronger for normal boys in provocative situations and boys already prone to delinquency (Mattsson *et al.*, 1980). Testosterone levels are also more likely to distinguish aggressive from non-aggressive criminals than to differentiate criminals from non-criminals (Mattsson *et al.*, 1980; Rubin *et al.*, 1981).

Both testosterone and oestrogen have been linked

to increased activity and excitability and to greater response to stimulation (Wooley & Timiras, 1962; Beatty, 1979), which may create heightened positive and negative emotionality, depending on the nature of environmental stimulation. Abnormalities in gonadotrophin secretion (luteinizing hormone or LH, and FSH) and gonadotrophin-releasing hormones have been found in depressed patients (Tolis & Stefanis, 1983), and FSH levels and negative affect are positively related in normal males (Houser, 1979). Oestrogen levels also have been associated with mood changes during the menstrual cycle (Bardwick, 1976) and increases in oestradiol have been found to improve depressive symptoms in women with low oestrogen levels (Montgomery *et al.*, 1987).

During later adulthood, levels and cyclicity of oestrogens and progesterones drop in females and testosterone decreases in males. These changes are accompanied by a variety of other changes, including decreases in strength, muscle tone, speed and reaction time, increases in fatty tissue, increases in chronic illness, and social changes in family, work and recreation; all of these may contribute to changes in emotion. For example, a recent prospective study of menopausal women reported that although some vasomotor symptoms were more prevalent in peri- and postmenopausal women than in women who had not yet reached menopause, 51% of the variance in depressed mood during menopause was accounted for by past depression, cognitive and social factors (Hunter, 1990). Moreover, psychiatric symptoms are more likely to occur during menopause for women who have a history of psychiatric problems (Ballinger, 1975). It is possible that the reproductive hormones interact with life events to influence middle-aged women's physiological and psychological responses to stress (Saab *et al.*, 1989). In studies of more extreme affect, sociocultural factors have been found to be more important in the aetiology of mental illness in menopausal women than physiological changes (Ballinger, 1990).

Finally, stress also may interact with the hormone system, simultaneously activating the hypothalamic–pituitary–adrenal axis and suppressing the hypothalamic–pituitary–gonadal axis, and thereby influencing emotionality (Nottelman *et al.*, 1990). For example, depressed persons have been found to have increased levels of circulating cortisol (Sachar, 1967), a hormone typically associated with stress or challenge. Thus, hormone–behaviour relations may be mediated through affect and modified by environmental and personality factors.

Heritability

Although little is known about the heritability of particular emotional symptoms, there is considerable evidence that the predisposition to some forms of psychopathological disorders, such as bipolar affective disorder, schizophrenia, autism and criminality may be heritable (Vandenberg *et al.*, 1986; Folstein & Rutter, 1988; Gold *et al.*, 1988; see also Chapter 2). Depression appears to be a genetically heterogeneous disorder. Evidence from twin, adoption and family studies for the genetic transmission of bipolar affective disorders is relatively strong, whereas other mood disorders including dysthymia, depressive adjustment disorder and major depression without psychotic features appear to be considerably less influenced by genetic factors (Blehar *et al.*, 1988). Characteristics such as early age of onset, concomitant anxiety or alcoholism, recurrence of episodes, severe or psychotic symptomatology and suicidality may indicate a more heritable aetiology, whereas milder or chronic forms of depression such as dysthymia may be less heritable (Goldin & Gershon, 1988).

Anxiety disorders also are aetiologically heterogeneous. There is increasing evidence that panic disorder is highly familial (Cloninger *et al.*, 1981; Crowe *et al.*, 1983). For example, Crowe *et al.* found the risk of panic disorder to be 25% amongst first-degree relatives of patients with panic disorder versus 2% amongst relatives of controls. Torgersen (1983) also found evidence of heritability of panic disorder and agoraphobia — i.e. higher concordance for monozygotic (MZ) twins than dizygotic (DZ) twins — although he found no difference in the concordance between MZ and DZ twins with generalized anxiety disorder (GAD). Thus, the heritability of anxiety depends on the particular anxiety disorder studied.

Kendler *et al.* (1986, 1987) explored the aetiological role of genetic and environmental factors in symptoms of anxiety and depression among twins. They found evidence for genetic influences on predispositions for non-specific 'psychiatric distress' rather than specifically for symptoms of either anxiety or depression; the environment seemed to have more influence on the specific emotional symptoms expressed.

There is increasing evidence of genetic influences in autism from both family and twin studies (Folstein & Rutter, 1988; Smalley et al., 1988; Steffenberg et al., 1989). For example, in a Scandinavian twin study, Steffenberg et al. (1989) found a concordance of 91% for MZ versus 0% concordance for DZ twins for autism. Family studies have found that although there is some concordance among siblings for the full syndrome of autism, there is even greater concordance between autistic probands and their siblings with regard to cognitive and language dysfunction (August et al., 1981). Further genetic studies are needed to explore the extent to which there is concordance with regard to the social and emotional symptoms of autism.

Thus, there may be important interactions between biological and environmental contributions in the development of emotional disorders, suggesting that a 'vulnerability-stress' model may best describe their aetiology. Even within the Sprague–Dawley strain of rats, considered to be genetically homogeneous, there is considerable variability in indices of response to stress in an unfamiliar environment, with those showing greater stress-related behaviour having lower levels of dopamine and its metabolites in the corpus striatum (Pradhan et al., 1990). Because genetics explain only some of the variance in personality and emotional distress, attention is beginning to focus on why children in the same families differ from one another (Dunn & Plomin, 1990; Hoffman, 1991).

Temperament and individual differences

Individual differences in emotional propensities, or temperament, have been the focus of numerous empirical investigations (Thomas & Chess, 1977 identified 'easy', 'difficult' and 'slow to warm up' infants). Temperamental qualities that have been proposed to be fundamental include activity level, sociability, shyness, anger-proneness, pleasure,

emotionality, fussiness, interest/curiosity, persistence and adaptability (Buss & Plomin, 1975; Rothbart & Derryberry, 1981; see also Chapter 4). Temperament focuses more on stylistic aspects of behaviour (how a response is made) rather than content (what the response is).

Most models of temperament assume that infants begin life with a small number of broad inherited or congenital personality dispositions that contribute to individual differences in personality development. Supporting the influence of heritability on temperament are data reported by Buss and Plomin (1975) that correlations across four temperamental dimensions (emotionality, activity, sociability, impulsivity) were 0.66 for MZ twins as compared to 0.14 for same-sex DZ twins (mean age 55 months, range 1–9 years).

Basic temperamental predispositions are modifiable by the environment, and they influence the environment as well (Buss & Plomin, 1975). Initial broad temperamental tendencies differentiate as the child develops. Thus, temperament is expected to be identifiable early in life and under some circumstances is stable throughout life (i.e. given a stable environment). Belsky et al. (1991), however, found evidence of lawful discontinuity in positive and negative emotionality, two aspects of temperament, across the first year of life. They reported greater success in forecasting stability and change in negative than positive emotionality. Maternal personality, marital variables, and characteristics of the mother–child interaction predicted change from negative emotionality at 3 months of age to more positive emotionality at 9 months; comparable paternal factors predicted change from low negative emotionality to greater negative emotionality. Negative emotionality decreased and positive emotionality increased among infants whose parents were psychologically healthier and had more positive marriages, and when parent–child interactions were more complementary and harmonious and had higher levels of engagement. Thus, family antecedents predicted both continuity and discontinuity in negative emotionality.

Approach or avoidance of arousing or unfamiliar events is a temperamental quality that appears early in life, is moderately stable, and may be related to physiological characteristics that have been hypothesized to be partly under genetic control (Resnick *et al.*, 1986; Kagan & Snidman, 1991b). Kagan and Snidman (1991a) proposed that inhibited children have a low threshold of reactivity in the central nucleus of the amygdala and its projections to the hypothalamus, sympathetic chain and cardiovascular system. Infants' temperamental propensities interact with their social environment, such that these psychological characteristics are neither fixed by biology nor shaped entirely by the environment (Kagan & Snidman, 1991a).

Larsen and Diener (1987) proposed that affect intensity is a stable individual difference among children and adults. Affect intensity reflects differences in the typical intensity with which individuals experience emotions, both positive and negative. Intensity is distinct from variability in referring to the extremity of emotional experience, rather than the frequency of changes in affect. Larsen and Diener suggested that affect intensity reflects a homeostatic mechanism of arousal regulation. They suggested that it is similar to cyclothymia or mild forms of bipolar mood disorder, and they have reported that high affect intensity adults are at risk for developing bipolar affective disorder and cyclothymia (Diener *et al.*, 1985), and somatic disturbances (Derogatis *et al.*, 1974). However, affect intensity has not been found to be related to measures of psychological well-being (Diener, 1984; Larsen *et al.*, 1985).

Differences in affect intensity appear early in life and remain fairly stable across the lifespan (Buss & Plomin, 1975; Diener *et al.*, 1985). Cross-situational stability is high ($r = 0.79$ across work and recreation situations; Diener & Larsen, 1984). Larsen and Diener (1987) proposed that affect intensity is related to other temperamental dimensions of sociability, activity, arousability and emotionality. Affect intensity decreases with age, particularly from young adulthood to middle age, and females score higher on affect intensity than do males (Diener *et al.*, 1985). Cognitive operations differentiate high and low affect intensity individuals, with high-intensity individuals engaging in more personalizing/empathy, generalizing and selective abstraction, but only in response to affective stimuli and not neutral stimuli (Larsen *et al.*, 1987).

Finally, Olweus (1980) reported that a composite of boys' activity level and affect intensity (calm/hot-tempered) is a stable component of an aggressive personality pattern. Measured retrospectively, these indices of temperament in 5-year-old boys were significant predictors of the later development of an aggressive reaction pattern in adolescence (based on peer reports of unprovoked fighting and verbal aggression against peers and teachers). Early rearing conditions, however, also were found to contribute significantly to the development of aggressive behaviour and interacted with early temperament. Thus, there is some evidence of the stability of temperament and emotionality, but emotional development also is influenced by environmental factors and socialization processes.

The socialization of emotion

Several diverse theoretical perspectives from psychoanalytic theory to behaviourism suggest that psychopathological emotional patterns involve basically the same processes that characterize the socialization of healthy patterns of emotional adaptation. How do these normal processes go awry? Are the differences between normal and abnormal emotional functioning a matter of degree; that is, too much or too little socialization? Or does emotional dysfunction result from qualitatively different socialization experiences? Lewis and Saarni (1985) identified several important processes that contribute to the socialization of emotions including: classical conditioning, instrumental learning, identification, imitation, didactic teaching and social learning. These and other basic socialization processes are outlined here, describing how these processes contribute to emotional development and dysfunction.

Classical conditioning

Events often occur in a predictable fashion and this orderliness allows individuals to anticipate future outcomes; thus events that signal other events can come to produce reactions that they would not otherwise have produced. The typical conditioning paradigm involves presentation of a neutral stimulus prior to an unconditioned stimulus and response (unlearned, often reflexive). After repeated pairings, the neutral stimulus becomes linked with the unlearned sequence and acts as a signal for the sequence, producing emotional and behavioural effects due to the learned association.

In classical reward conditioning (e.g. Pavlov, 1927, 1928) a positive consequence follows the neutral stimuli that precede it, and in classical aversive conditioning (e.g. Watson & Rayner, 1920) an unpleasant event is associated with the stimuli that precede it. Any number of events that regularly precede the initial sequence may come to be associated with it. Generalization to similar stimuli can generate responses to sequences that have not occurred.

Although some learned responses are remarkably persistent, classical conditioning can be reversed with extinction or desensitization. Extinction involves the repeated presentation of the signal without the rewarding or aversive stimulus; thus, the association between the signals and its former consequence is weakened. Systematic desensitization involves extinction plus training or instruction to relax during the presentation of progressively more threatening stimuli (Wolpe, 1973).

Classical conditioning is hypothesized to account for negative (anxiety, fears, phobias, etc.) and positive emotions (love, humour, etc.) after only a small number of instances in which a signal is paired with an existing negative or positive response. Emotional responses also can occur as a byproduct of conditioning non-emotional stimuli; that is, emotional responses often are learned concurrently with non-emotional responses as complex constellations of responses are simultaneously produced.

In 1920, Watson and Rayner described conditioning of emotional responses in an 11-month-old infant (Little Albert). They paired the sight of a white rat with an aversive loud noise. Prior to conditioning, the infant displayed joy when he saw the rat, but after only two pairings of the rat and the noise the infant became wary of the animal. After five additional pairings, the sight of the rat alone produced crying and fleeing. There were no additional experiences with the rat and noise; however, 5 days later, the sight of the rat alone produced fearful, distressed behaviour in the infant, as did the sight of a white rabbit, a dog, a fur coat, a piece of white cotton wool and a variety of fuzzy, white stimuli to which the infant had apparently generalized his learned fear and distress. Directly con-

ditioned emotional responses, as well as those conditioned by transfer, persisted for over a month (the longest period tested). Other work has demonstrated classical conditioning in infants as young as 2 days of age (Blass *et al.*, 1984). Acquired taste aversions, which result from the pairing of a food with illness (Garcia & Koelling, 1966), demonstrate the operation of classical conditioning in the acquisition of another affect — disgust.

Although generalization can help to explain the pervasiveness of a learned fear, generalization tends to be selective. Attempts to replicate the conditioning procedure used with Little Albert, but using different objects such as curtains and wooden ducks, have failed to produce fear conditioning (Valentine, 1930; Rachman, 1990). The concept of 'prepared' classical conditioning has been used to explain the fact that classical conditioning is selective, positing that through evolution and adaptation we more easily notice and learn some associations than others (Seligman, 1970, 1971; Eysenck, 1979). In fact, many common phobias involve objects that were once actually dangerous to pretechnological man (De Silva *et al.*, 1977). Such stimuli can elicit fear with little or no conditioning at all. Seligman (1971) posited that phobias are instances of highly 'prepared' learning and 'such prepared learning is selective, highly resistant to extinction, probably noncognitive and can be acquired in one trial' (p. 451).

Conditioning theory does not adequately account for the acquisition of all fears and phobias, however. Rachman (1977) outlined the following limitations in the classical conditioning of fear. People fail to acquire fears of what might be expected to be a fear-provoking situation (e.g. air raids); attempts to condition fears in laboratory settings sometimes have been unsuccessful; there is little evidence to support the principle of equipotentiality — that all stimuli have an equal chance of becoming conditioned fear signals; all people are not equally vulnerable to developing fears under the same conditioning experiences; and phobic patients do not consistently recall exposure to a trauma that initiated their fear. Rachman further asserted that fears can be acquired in the absence of direct contact with the fear stimuli through vicarious exposure or transmission of information and instruction. Thus, classical conditioning may be useful in explaining fears of 'prepared' stimuli, whereas indirect methods such as instruction may more readily account for fear of non-prepared stimuli (e.g. social phobias).

Yule *et al.* (1990) studied adolescents' emotional reactions after their escape from a sinking cruise ship. Consistent with a conditioning perspective, they reported more fears of related situations such as deep water and travelling by boat than of unrelated stimuli (e.g. lizards). However, other stimuli related to the disaster (e.g. dark places, being in a crowd) showed no increment in fear, and other seemingly unrelated situations (e.g. having to talk to the class) did produce increments in associated fear. Thus, the study by Yule *et al.* provided limited support for the conditioning model.

Recent extensions of classical conditioning processes have emphasized indirect vicarious conditioning in which observers are empathically aroused by observation of another's expressed affective reactions to events, especially aversive events (Lanzetta & Orr, 1980). Lanzetta and Orr suggested that the fearful facial expression of another person serves as a valid signal for the occurrence of aversive events and as an excitatory stimulus because of its prior history of association with aversive outcomes. Thus, the expressive behaviour of others can play a critical role in emotional learning.

There also is evidence that fear conditioning can occur without the actual experience of trauma paired with a signal. Verbal threat of shock alone can produce fear, and social modelling (even without the threat of shock) also can produce fear to certain types of stimuli such as snakes or spiders (Bandura, 1969; Hygge & Ohman, 1978).

The main emotional disorders that classical conditioning has been used to explain are fears and phobias. Whereas so-called normal fears may result from the organism's survival response to threat in the environment, more extreme anxieties and phobias may result from the failure of a conditioned stimulus to be extinguished. That is, a phobic's response to the possibility of being around the feared object is to escape or avoid it, and thereby miss opportunities to learn that the feared negative outcome may not occur. In this way, the fear persists and may become associated with other dysfunctional behaviours such as evading occu-

pational or social opportunities in order to avoid the original feared stimulus or associated stimuli. Thus, some phobias may result from the process of classical conditioning. Conditioning alone, however, does not account for all fears and phobias, nor does it totally explain individual variation in fear responses. The combination of individual characteristics (e.g. inhibition), the particular nature of the stimulus, and the amount of exposure and conditioning to the stimulus all contribute to whether an individual develops a phobic response to a particular stimulus.

Instrumental learning

Instrumental learning involves voluntary behaviours that are followed by pleasant or aversive consequences. Organisms learn to repeat behaviours that have produced pleasant consequences and to avoid behaviours that have produced unpleasant consequences in the past. They also associate signals that precede pleasant or unpleasant events with those events, and the signals themselves can elicit emotional responses. Consequences that occur inconsistently, that is, less than 100% of the time, are actually more powerful in producing and sustaining behaviour change than perfectly consistent (predictable) consequences. By anticipating consequences and adjusting behaviour according to expected outcomes, individuals learn to control their own outcomes. Newborns and even fetuses have been shown to learn responses that produce pleasant or avoid unpleasant consequences (De Casper & Carstens, 1981). Thus, one normally learns positive emotional reactions to signals and behaviours that are associated with pleasant consequences and negative emotional reactions to signals accompanied by aversive consequences.

Parents influence their infants' emotions through selective reinforcement of the babies' expressions. Mothers report that they respond differently to infants' expressions of sadness, anger and pain (Huebner & Izard, 1988), and mothers respond differently to facial expressions of male and female infants (Malatesta & Haviland, 1982). These different maternal responses can influence the children's subsequent emotional expressions (Izard & Malatesta, 1987).

Learning that one has control over the occurrence

of a potentially aversive event can influence an individual's level of distress in response to that stimulus. For example, Gunnar (1980) reported that infants who controlled the onset of an aversive stimulus reacted with less negative emotion than infants who experienced the same stimulus in either a predictable or unpredictable fashion. The reduction of distress reactions under conditions of high control was observed in 12-month-old but not younger infants. She suggested that cognitive developmental changes might underlie changes in the effect of control late in the first year.

Child maltreatment may be one unpredictable aversive event that is associated with disruptions in normal emotional development (Aber & Cicchetti, 1984). Gaensbauer and co-workers (Gaensbauer & Sands, 1979; Gaensbauer *et al.*, 1980) found that abused children are deficient in positive emotion and high in negative emotional expression. Parent–child interactions involving an abusive parent were characterized by ambivalence, inconsistency and withdrawal. This may be partially the result of the children's difficulty in predicting and interpreting ambiguous parental emotional behaviours and expressions (Tronick, 1989).

Operant conditioning processes have been used to explain such maladaptive outcomes as depression (Lewinsohn, 1974) and aggression (Patterson, 1982). Lewinsohn's (1974) model asserted that depression results from a low rate of response contingent positive reinforcement. In support of this view, Lewinsohn and co-workers (Lewinsohn & Graf, 1973; Lewinsohn, 1975) found that depressed individuals reported engaging in fewer pleasant activities than non-depressed people. Lewinsohn proposed that increasing the rate of socially appropriate behaviour would increase the rate of positive reinforcement and thereby reduce depressed affect. Intervention programmes based on this view have yielded positive results (Lewinsohn *et al.*, 1968).

The original learned helplessness theory of depression (Seligman, 1975) focused on contingent and non-contingent relations between responses and outcomes. According to this model, depressed affect results when the probability of an outcome given a response is equal to the probability of the outcome given no response; that is, the organism lacks control. Organisms that are exposed to such

non-contingency develop symptoms of depression including sadness, lack of response initiation and a belief in their own helplessness (Seligman, 1975; Maier & Seligman, 1976). The learned helplessness model of depression has been revised twice and currently includes the cognitive constructs of attributions (Abramson *et al.*, 1978) and hopelessness (Abramson *et al.*, 1989). These newer perspectives emphasize the cognitive interpretations and meaning of negative events in terms of their causes and future consequences, more than the objective non-contingency between stimulus and response and the individual's actual degree of control.

Instrumental learning also may play an important role in the development and maintenance of aggressive behaviour (Patterson, 1982). Patterson and co-workers (Patterson & Cobb, 1971; Patterson, 1982) identified a coercive behaviour pattern that elicits, maintains and increases aggression in family members. The coercion process is described as follows: one person presents an aversive stimulus (e.g. yelling); a second person responds with an aversive stimulus (e.g. hitting). The aversive interchange may escalate in intensity until one person withdraws the aversive stimulus (e.g. stops yelling). The person who forces the other person to withdraw the aversive behaviour learns that highly aversive behaviour stops others' aversive behaviour. Thus, the aversive behaviour has been negatively reinforced by successfully reducing or eliminating an unpleasant stimulus, and it is likely to increase such behaviour in the future. This aversive and often aggressive behaviour is not necessarily accompanied by anger, although anger may accompany or result from the process.

Imitation. Imitation refers to a response, molecular or molar, that resembles previously observed behaviour and results from that demonstration (Parton, 1976). Recent research has shown that neonates can be induced to imitate a limited set of behaviours, most of them facial gestures such as smiling, mouth opening and tongue protrusion (Meltzoff & Moore, 1989).

Laboratory-reared monkeys were found to acquire a fear of snakes after observing other monkeys' reactions to one; the learned fear was strongest when the model was the monkey's mother (Mineka *et al.*, 1989). Vicarious transmission, however, tended to be more effective when the stimuli were snakes rather than flowers (Mineka, 1988). Mineka *et al.* (1989) concluded that observational learning is an important process in the development of fears and phobias, although this may be more true for a particular set of stimuli.

Work with mature individuals indicates that imitating facial expressions (e.g. smiling or frowning) may contribute to the actual experience of particular emotions through the process of facial feedback, in which facial expressions are thought to activate mental structures or functions that elicit emotional experiences (Laird, 1974; cf. Tourangeau & Ellsworth, 1979). Thus, individuals who are exposed to environments in which others display particular affective expressions may imitate those expressions in whole or in part and thus experience the associated emotions.

A concept that is related to, although different from, imitation is synchrony. In the proper context the perception of emotion in another's face, voice or gestures can elicit similar emotional states in observers (Stern, 1985; Haviland & Lelwica, 1987). This synchrony in emotions is thought to be based on a more general process of 'interactional synchrony' in which interpersonal behaviour becomes synchronized in time between individuals, with the synchrony being 'cross-modal' or not limited to the same perceptual/motor mode in which it was expressed (Condon & Sander, 1974; Bernieri *et al.*, 1988). Thus, the process is said to be non-imitative. When applied specifically to emotional responses, this synchrony has been called 'affect attunement' (Stern, 1985) or 'mutual regulation' (Tronick & Gianino, 1986). In becoming affectively attuned, the caregiver non-verbally reflects back to the infant how he or she is perceived, which is important in the socialization of emotion. Children also tend to reflect their caregiver's affect. For example, Haviland and Lelwica (1987) found that by 10 weeks of age infants showed facial expressions that were affectively similar to their mothers' happy or angry vocal expressions, although the infants did not demonstrate attunement to their mothers' sad expressions.

Lack of synchrony and negative affect are characteristic of the interactions between infants and their depressed mothers. Depressed mothers display more flat and negative affect, provide less stimu-lation, and respond less contingently to their infants (Field, 1984; Field *et al.*, 1988). Cohn and Tronick (1983) reported that 3-month-old infants responded to mothers' simulated displays of depressed affect with behaviour unlike their behaviour in unperturbed situations. Infants showed a pattern of brief smiling, followed by expressions of protest and wariness. This pattern of distressed behaviour persisted during periods in which the mother behaved normally. Field (1984) reported that infants of mothers with postpartum depression displayed less frequent positive facial expressions, more negative expressions, wariness, vocalizing and protest. The infants showed a similar aberrant interaction style even when interacting with non-depressed adults (Field *et al.*, 1988).

Activity and heart rate also have been found to be lower for infants with depressed mothers (Field, 1984). Field *et al.* (1988) reported that depressed mother−child dyads spent more time together in negative states, suggesting a contagion effect of negative mood and reciprocity of negative affect. Again, this process is distinct from imitation, although the mechanisms that produce the synchrony are still unknown. Lack of synchrony is thought to reflect a failure of mutual regulation in which the mother, because of her own emotional state, fails to respond to her child's communicative signals and does not provide the infant with appropriate regulatory help (Tronick & Gianino, 1986). The extent to which these early emotional reactions of infancy are related to sadness and depression later in life is not yet known and is an important issue for future research.

Finally, imitation may play a role in the social and emotional deficits found among autistic children. Autistic children consistently show marked delays in both vocal and gestural imitation, although they do imitate some movements of their bodies and objects (Dawson & Adams, 1984; Sigman & Ungerer, 1984). Dawson and Adams (1984) noted the relation between imitation and social responsiveness, and found that children who were more able to imitate exhibited more appropriate social behaviour. Rutter (1983) suggested that autistic children's deficits in imitation and social behaviour may reflect impaired ability to process stimuli that carry emotional or social meaning such as facial expressions and gestures. The absence of these abilities is a critical deficit that contributes to difficulties in autistic children's regulation of emotions and social interactions with others.

Identification

Identification is a process through which an organism incorporates the values, goals and behaviours of another and which can result in the copying of behaviour, including emotional behaviour (Lewis & Saarni, 1985). Identification is thought to develop out of attachment to other persons and to result in the development of attractiveness for another person or group; persons who are attractive to us are sometimes said to be objects of identification. For infants, attachment behaviours and early self–other differentiation are closely linked. For preschool children, social comparison processes develop as identification with caregivers wanes and self-identity becomes established.

A great deal of literature has described early attachment and specific social influence processes that are thought to result from identification (see Chapter 16). Attachment theory has been useful in explaining such diverse emotional responses as separation anxiety, mourning, defensive processes, fear of novelty, dependency, adult love, affection, openness and intimacy (e.g. Hinde, 1967). Bretherton (1985) suggested that attachment involves the construction of complementary 'internal working models' of attachment figures and the self that become integrated into the personality structure. She drew on Bowlby's (1982) steady state maintenance system model and conceptualizes attachment as an internal representation of the child's world. Through continual interactions with the world, the child develops expectations regarding what will happen. These become increasingly complex models of the world, self and others that are used in appraising and guiding behaviour and affect (Main et al., 1985). Thus, attachment becomes a form of self-regulation of affect and behaviour based on other-regulation (by the caregiver) and the mutually entraining system of attachment.

The attachment system does not become organized until the latter part of the first year of life, though it incorporates components that operate earlier (Bretherton, 1985; see also Chapter 16). Bretherton (1985) asserted that, once organized,

internal working models tend to operate outside conscious awareness and tend to be resistant to dramatic change.

Parent–child dyads are often characterized according to whether they demonstrate secure or insecure attachment (Main, 1973; Ainsworth, 1979). Attachment classification has been shown to relate to a variety of preschool social behaviours with peers such as leadership and sociability (Waters et al., 1979) and to a variety of emotional behaviours such as curiosity, enthusiasm, pleasure and other positive affect, anger and distress (Main, 1973; Matas et al., 1979). Recent work with adults, although based primarily on retrospective accounts, has suggested that conceptualization of early patterns of attachment is related to intimate relationships later in life including attachment, care-giving and sexuality (Shaver et al., 1988), social competence, ego-resiliency, hostility (Kobak & Sceery, 1988), and work orientation, work satisfaction and relationships with co-workers (Hazan & Shaver, 1990).

Cicchetti and Schneider-Rosen (1986) outlined an organizational approach to childhood depression that emphasized the importance of the attachment relationship and the continuing differentiation between self and other in the development of depression. Excessive dependence, which is predicted from type A insecure attachments (Sroufe, 1983), is considered to be a risk factor for depression (Bemporad & Wilson, 1978; Blatt et al., 1982). Ambivalent feelings towards attachment figures, which characterize type C insecure babies, also are considered to be important in the development of depression according to classic psychoanalytic theory (Abraham, 1960; Freud, 1968). Schneider-Rosen and Cicchetti (1984) reported a relation between the quality of attachment and the emergence of visual self-recognition, which is considered a precursor to the developing sense of self. Cicchetti and Schneider-Rosen (1986) suggested that securely attached children have a more secure sense of self, whereas insecurely attached children tend to lack clear differentiation between self and others. This less differentiated sense of self is associated with a deviation in the process of identification with the caretaker that can lead to the development of depression (Mahler, 1968; Kernberg, 1976).

Social referencing

Social referencing refers to the use of another's behaviour towards an event as a basis for the construction of one's own interpretation of the emotionally arousing event (Feinman, 1982; Campos, 1983). Social referencing occurs primarily in situations of uncertainty or ambiguity about how to interpret events or how to feel about them (Sorce *et al.*, 1985). Infants as young as 1 year of age regulate their behaviour and affect according to the affective displays of caregivers (Sorce *et al.*, 1985; Walden & Ogan, 1988). Thus, information may be sought and used as input in deciding how to interpret and respond to a novel or unusual event. This process represents the cognitive construction of the meaning of an event, rather than simply an imitative response or a directly conditioned response (Walden & Ogan, 1988). Adults have been observed to engage in social referencing too (Kerber & Coles, 1978), and this process may contribute to persuasion, attitude change and conformity. Information observed during social referencing may be genuine or feigned, and may be displayed either intentionally or unintentionally by the person being observed.

Most work on social referencing has focused on infants at 1 year of age, and some have suggested that perhaps this is one peak period for social referencing of others (Walden & Ogan, 1988). This peak may result from developments in both cognitive–social competencies and physical abilities. Social cognitive developments allow infants to appreciate and use social information regarding others' emotional reactions. New physical abilities, such as independent locomotion, take the infant farther from the safe proximity of the caregiver and offer opportunities for exploration, which include new and potentially dangerous situations (Bertenthal & Campos, 1990). If the infant is to maintain actual safety and a sense of security at greater distances from the caregiver, new forms of communication must be developed to compensate for the decrease in proximity and one form of communication is social referencing (Bertenthal & Campos, 1990). Thus, emotional and instrumental information from another's face, voice, gestures and verbal content all can be used to resolve ambiguity and to react to potentially dangerous situations.

Social referencing effects may be more powerful when negative rather than positive affect is displayed; this may result from the sociobiological importance of negative affective displays in signalling potentially life-threatening events (Lanzetta & Orr, 1980). For social referencing to be used successfully, the caregiver must be available to communicate with the infant and must be competent to send clear signals. The infant must be able to decode and use those signals appropriately. Although prior to locomotion infants are able to discriminate among emotional expressions, it is not until the end of the first year that infants seek out and use emotional cues from others as a guide to their own behaviour and affect (Walden & Ogan, 1988; Bertenthal & Campos, 1990). Thus, maternal availability and reliability and infants' seeking of information from caregivers contribute to infants' social learning of emotional and instrumental reactions to novel and/or ambiguous events.

Didactic teaching and therapy

The development of understanding of affect in oneself and others can be facilitated through educational interventions such as direct teaching and indirect exposure through various media (e.g. books, films, etc.). For example, teaching and therapy can be regarded as intentional efforts to provide information to another. These efforts are usually linguistically based and, therefore, require language. This limits the usefulness of this technique very early in life or with persons with limited verbal abilities (e.g. the severely mentally retarded).

Several curricula have been developed to teach affective skills. Few of these programmes, however, have been evaluated to determine their effectiveness in enhancing the understanding of affect. One common element in affective training programmes is a focus on empathy, an ability closely linked to young children's developing cognitive capacities. Generally children's affective experiences, sensitivity and understanding are seen as developing in concert with changes in their cognitive functions.

Feshbach and Cohen (1988) reported results from an experimental training programme designed to enhance affective understanding of others and perspective taking among 3–5-year-old children. Activities requiring children to identify emotions in photographs and videotapes, and role-playing games focusing on the identification of others' emotions comprised the three sessions of training. Effects of training on children's discrimination among happy, sad and angry facial expressions were identified immediately following the final training session but not 1 week later. Accurate descriptions of simple emotional situations were superior for the training group 1 week following training.

A less formal teaching technique, induction of emotional responses, has been observed in interactions between caregivers and children (Zahn-Waxler *et al.*, 1979). Induction involves appealing to empathic understanding of another's feelings or perspective and modification of behaviour based on that empathy. Eliciting guilt for transgressions and promoting reparation are common goals in using induction. Although induction need not involve emotionally toned communications, Zahn-Waxler *et al.* (1979) reported that about half of all maternal explanations about toddlers' misdeeds included affective overtones of moralizing and judging. Affectively laden but not neutral explanations were effective in eliciting reparations from the 15–20-month-old children, and unexplained verbal prohibitions and restraint deterred altruistic behaviour. Altruism often was accompanied by children's own expressions of emotion, particularly among children whose mothers gave many explanations.

The effectiveness of behavioural and cognitive–behavioural interventions suggests that people can and do learn important information about affect and affect regulation through didactic methods (Masters *et al.*, 1987). These therapeutic approaches were developed to help patients reduce and/or manage a range of emotional and behavioural disorders including anxiety (Beck & Emery, 1985), depression (Beck *et al.*, 1979), impulsivity (Kendall & Braswell, 1985), anger (Novaco, 1979), and pain (Turk *et al.*, 1983). Although specific techniques vary depending on the particular problem, all these therapies use didactic approaches to teach patients new affect and behavioural management skills. These skills include using self-statements to control emotions and behaviour, identifying one's thoughts and recognizing their role in the onset and maintenance of affect, assessing the accuracy of one's beliefs, and replacing dysfunctional beliefs with more accurate thoughts. In cognitive therapy for

depression, for example, therapists work collaboratively with patients to set up experiments that test the accuracy of their beliefs about a situation (Hollon & Beck, 1979). A central principle of this therapy is that verbal reassurance and persuasion may not be sufficient to change affect and behaviour. Rather, direct exposure and active participation in the acquisition of relevant information are more powerful strategies for change.

In cognitive–behavioural therapy, the therapist assists the patient in 'chunking' or breaking down large and often overwhelming tasks into smaller and more manageable parts. This approach is similar to scaffolding, a process in which an expert assists a novice in mastering new skills by breaking the tasks and required skills into small units and guiding performance to a higher level (Bruner, 1978; Heckhausen, 1987); this technique is thought particularly to enhance the performance of the novice learner. Scaffolding has been shown to facilitate language and task performance (Hodapp *et al.*, 1984; Heckhausen, 1987). Its efficacy in changing emotional responses has not been explicitly evaluated, however.

THE DEVELOPMENT OF ADAPTIVE AND MALADAPTIVE INDIVIDUAL DIFFERENCES IN EMOTIONAL FUNCTIONING

An infant is born with a set of biological potentials — a basic physiological and behavioural repertoire to notice and respond to some things preferentially over others. Some of these potentials are genetic and others congenital, the result of the prenatal environment or the birthing process. Some actions in the repertoire act to reduce or turn off stimulation, whereas other actions amplify or seek stimulation. These comprise basic positive, approach responses and negative, withdrawal responses that form the basis for a variety of emotional experiences. Immediately, the neonate's repertoire begins to transact with the environment. Characteristics of the neonate — such as the degree and intensity of reactivity to events, its ability to calm itself from highly excited states and to move smoothly through transitions from one state to another, the range of different behaviours in its repertoire, and even its physical appearance —

make some aspects of its environment more significant (e.g. the environment's level of reactivity, level of intensity, its tools to help manage state transitions, and so on). Furthermore, the newborn and the environment interact to facilitate or inhibit certain functions in each other.

These transactions involve functioning at all levels including genetic potential, anatomical and physiological functions, the behavioural repertoire, cognitive capacities and environmental circumstances and events that impinge upon the newborn even before its moment of birth. All these factors contribute to emotional development. To focus exclusively on any single aspect without consideration of the eliciting, inhibiting or permitting functions in other parts of the system is incompletely to understand the development of any emotional phenomenon. For example, a newborn's level of reactivity expresses itself in an environmental (caregiving) situation that responds to that reactivity; together the infant and the care-giving environment enter into the complex transaction that is development. At another level, gene-environment interactions and covariances (Scarr & McCartney, 1983) are operative in virtually every instance of behaviour. No gene develops its expression outside a particular environment and no environment exerts an influence that does not involve genetic factors; unique combinations of genetic and environmental conditions produce effects that could not be predicted from the operation of either factor alone.

Another example of the close interrelations among the subsystems are the changes produced in one subsystem by another. For example, learned responses that become classically conditioned may create changes in neurotransmitters presynaptically (Kandel, 1983) that partly (or wholly) store the effects of that memory, the memory 'engram' or stored trace of the experience. Characteristics of an individual and characteristics of the environment combine over time to produce individual differences that may be perfectly predictable if one completely understands their origin, even though those outcomes may not be widely shared among other members of the social group. Some innate factors and some environmental circumstances make the individual more or less vulnerable or resilient to stressors in another part of the system (Garmezy, 1974; Sameroff & Chandler, 1975).

Changes or development in one part of the system create changes in other parts of the system, even if only to accommodate to functioning the same way in a changing situation (Cairns, 1979). Disequilibrium among the components of the system is created inevitably as the system adapts to changes in any component (Piaget, 1952). The disequilibrium may be temporary, as the individual learns to adapt or cope with new circumstances, or the disequilibrium may be more enduring. At some point the duration of the disequilibrium, its intensity or its functioning under the wrong conditions becomes unusual and is considered to be maladaptive. Thompson (1990) enumerates several features of emotionality including intensity, the range and lability of expressions, the latency to onset and rise time to peak intensity of the emotion, and time to recovery to a pre-emotional baseline. Aberrations in any of these aspects of emotional reaction may deviate from the range or pattern considered normal and adaptive and thus may be considered to represent pathological development.

Emotions play an important role in social communication, personality, motivation, cognitive processing and the regulation of social interactions. Although emotions can disorganize and undermine healthy functioning, their capacity to organize healthy, adaptive behaviour also is significant (Thompson, 1990). Campos *et al.* (1989) recently proposed a working definition of emotion based on a consideration of the development of systems relevant to emotion and the many levels of operation of the components of the system:

> Emotions are processes of establishing, maintaining, or disrupting the relations between the person and the internal or external environment, when such relations are significant to the individual . . . This relational view renders emotion regulation central to emotion theory, because both the appreciation of the significance of events and the types of reactions that the organism makes to events are crucial phases of both the generation and the control of affect. (p. 395)

Thus, emotions are interpersonal and intrapersonal regulatory processes, with dual functions of maintaining or changing the individual's behaviour and signalling to others the impact of their interactions with the individual. Campos *et al.* (1989)

emphasized the importance of the motivational relevance of a person—event encounter, emotional communication among individuals and positive/negative hedonic value of many events and circumstances for the individual. These factors combine to form a situation in which the individual relates to the environment and emotion is the outcome (as well as a cause) of that particular relation (Smith & Lazarus, 1990). Emotions are behaviour regulators. Coregulation of the infant and the care-giving environment develop over time.

Emotional regulation is not the same as the regulation of emotional displays (as can occur when display rules regarding the intentional management of emotional expressions are used), although they are related. Emotional regulation refers to the underlying experience of emotional arousal, whether or not it is influenced by social factors determining emotional displays (Thompson, 1990).

Saarni (1990) has described 11 components of 'emotional competence', which refers to successful negotiation of social interactions in emotionally arousing situations. She proposed that the most successful or healthy emotional development allows individuals to respond emotionally, while strategically using their knowledge about emotions and relationships with others to get through a satisfying or successful social interaction. The 11 emotional competencies focus on social cognitive aspects of functioning, although those in no way preclude studying nor diminish the importance of understanding emotion at other levels described in this chapter.

Saarni (1990) focused on emotional behaviours that impact one important criterion of emotional functioning — whether an individual is liked by and/or likes other people and whether interpersonal interactions are successful. She included as important emotional skills the following: (i) accurate awareness of one's own emotional state (including multiple emotions that occur and understanding possible biases in one's own knowledge); (ii) ability to read others' emotions; (iii) ability to label verbally and discuss emotion; (iv) empathic involvement in others' emotions; (v) recognition of the possibility of incongruencies between an emotional expression and an inner state; (vi) knowledge of cultural display rules; (vii) understanding of unique personal information that

aids in interpreting another's behaviour; (viii) knowledge of the impact of one's own behaviour on others; (ix) ability to self-regulate negative emotions; (x) awareness of the contribution of genuine emotional expression to relationships; and (xi) self-satisfaction with one's own emotional experience and behaviour.

One can achieve emotional competence via different routes. Rarely would dysfunctional emotional development be expected to result from a single process or factor discussed in this chapter. Individual vulnerabilities combine with dysfunctional aspects of the care-giving environment to create maladaptive emotional patterns. Marshalling of intrapersonal and interpersonal strengths or resources is necessary to overcome intrapersonal and interpersonal vulnerabilities.

Furthermore, the internal and external processes underlying emotional development vary across different emotional outcomes. That is, the relative contribution of genes and environment, temperament and conditioning, physiology and modelling are not necessarily the same for depression, anxiety and aggression. Moreover, the particular cognitions and action tendencies associated with different emotions also vary.

Finally, features of emotions and their expression that may be adaptive within one context may be maladaptive in other contexts. This points to the importance of flexibility in functioning as an important feature of adaptive emotional development. Flexibility in both the experience and expression of emotion is necessary for successful adaptation in a variety of contexts usually encountered in normal living.

CONCLUSION: DIRECTIONS FOR FUTURE RESEARCH

The present chapter described the development of the experience, expression and recognition of several basic emotions and outlined the biological and socialization processes that may account for emotional development. Physiological and psychosocial processes are not mutually exclusive and act in concert in promoting development or change in any particular emotional skill or propensity. Furthermore, processes that account for the initial establishment of an emotional pattern need not be the same processes that are involved in the maintenance or change of that pattern (Cairns, 1979). Similarly, processes that change an emotional pattern are not necessarily those involved in the initial creation of that pattern.

Although emotions serve biologically adaptive and psychologically constructive functions such as social communication and goal achievement (Sroufe, 1979; Barrett & Campos, 1987; Izard & Malatesta, 1987), they also can become maladaptive. Moreover, there is important individual variability in the type and intensity of emotions experienced and expressed. The present chapter described processes that can contribute to variability in emotional displays. Several additional issues need to be addressed to account for individual differences and maladaptation in emotional development.

First, what is the relation between normal and abnormal emotional experiences? For example, are sadness and depressive syndrome, fears and phobias, anger and rage on a continuum of severity or are they qualitatively distinct states? This continuity issue has important implications regarding the underlying processes that cause these emotional states. If these emotions represent quantitative variations along a continuum, the same processes that produce the less severe emotional states probably also produce more extreme manifestations. If they are qualitatively distinct, they may have separate causes. It is likely that emotional disorders are aetiologically heterogeneous, as is sometimes argued to be the case for MR. Whereas some subtypes of emotional disorders represent extremes on the dimension, others are produced by distinctly different processes.

Second, what are the salient parameters that define 'emotional disturbance' or 'disorder'? What criteria indicate when the emotion has become maladaptive? Emotions can vary with regard to intensity, frequency of occurrence, latency of onset and latency to recovery (Thompson, 1990); that is, individuals vary regarding whether they become emotional at all, how intense the emotion becomes and how long it takes to recover. Whether an individual responds emotionally to a particular stimulus may be a function of an emotion threshold (Izard & Harris, in press). An individual who has a low threshold is more likely to react emotionally to a potential emotion-evoking circumstance than is one with a higher threshold. Some individuals may be predisposed to be more emotionally reactive than others. This could be the result of biological vulnerability (e.g. temperament, emotionality) or socialization (e.g. observing highly emotionally reactive models). In this case, maladaptation would be defined in terms of the frequency of emotional reactions.

A second type of maladaptation refers to the intensity of one's initial response to stimuli. For example, whereas most individuals might become mildly annoyed by being cut-off in traffic, a few may become outraged and dangerously aggressive. Whereas most people would be disappointed upon having an article rejected from a journal, others might become depressed and hopeless about their careers. In both cases, there are multiple reactions to the same situation. Cognitive theorists suggest that one's interpretation of a situation influences the type and degree of emotion experienced (Beck, 1967; Lazarus, 1991).

A third important kind of individual difference is regulation of emotions after they occur. Once in an emotional state, what self-regulatory processes promote return to emotional homeostasis, and what is the time course of the change? Emotion regulation involves neurophysiological, behavioural and cognitive management of arousal (Dodge & Garber, 1991). To what extent can the physiological system regulate arousal given no further stimulation, and what is the efficacy of the individual's behavioural and cognitive regulatory strategies for reducing distress?

Maladaptation occurs when a failure in one or more response systems creates a failure to regulate emotions. This can result from either a failure in existing systems (e.g. dysfunction of the vagal system; Porges, 1991) or the addition of new dysfunctional processes. For example, once sadness is activated, cognitive processes such as rumination or intrusive rehearsal of the originally distressing situation can exacerbate the emotional state rather than letting it dissipate with time. Such intrusive thinking can both intensify the initial emotional response and maintain the emotion so that it takes longer to return to the presadness level of emotion.

Finally, some individuals simply may be exposed to more potentially emotion-eliciting stimuli, even though there is nothing unusual or deviant about the individual's emotion threshold, sensitivity or regulation. We might expect that, for extreme levels of stress, anyone experiencing the same amount of aversive stimuli would have a similar emotional reaction. This might be the case for individuals who have had multiple or severe negative life events occur. However, even among individuals who have experienced intensely horrifying events (e.g. abuse, torture), there is variability in emotional and behavioural responses.

Thus, no single process accounts for the development of every emotion, nor does one process explain all forms of emotional maladaptation. We have outlined here biological, cognitive and social processes that contribute to normal and abnormal emotional outcomes across development. How these processes interact to result in particular emotions, whether the same processes explain both normal and abnormal emotionality, and how these processes change and influence emotions over the course of development are important issues for future study.

ACKNOWLEDGEMENT

Tedra Walden was supported by a grant from the National Science Foundation (BNS−9109634). Judy Garber was supported in part by a W.T. Grant Foundation Faculty Scholar Award (88−1214−88) and a First Award from the National Institute of Mental Health (R29-MH4545801A1) during completion of this chapter.

REFERENCES

Aber L. & Cicchetti D. (1984) Socioemotional development in maltreated children: An empirical and theoretical analysis. In Fitzgerald H., Lester B. & Yogman M. (eds) *Theory and Research in Behavioral Pediatrics*, Vol. 2, pp. 147−205. Plenum, New York.

Abraham K. (1960) Notes on the psychoanalytical investigation of manic−depressive insanity and allied conditions. In *Selected Papers on Psychoanalysis*, pp. 137−156. Basic Books, New York.

Abramson L.Y., Metalsky G. & Alloy L.B. (1989) Hopelessness depression: A theory-based subtype of depression. *Psychological Review* **96**, 358−372.

Abramson L.Y., Seligman M.E.P. & Teasdale J.D. (1978) Learned helplessness in humans: Critique and reformulation. *Journal of Abnormal Psychology* **87**, 49−74.

Achenbach T.M., Connors C.K., Quay H.C., Verhulst F.C. & Howell C.T. (1989) Replication of empirically derived syndromes as a basis for taxonomy of child/adolescent psychopathology. *Journal of Abnormal Child Psychology* **17**, 299−323.

Achenbach T.M. & Edelbrock C.S. (1981) Behavioral problems and competencies reported by parents of normal and disturbed children aged four through sixteen. *Monographs of the Society for Research in Child Development* **46**(1), Serial No. 188.

Adams K. & Markham R. (1991) Recognition of affective facial expressions by children and adolescents with and without mental retardation. *American Journal on Mental Retardation* **96**, 21−28.

Aggleton J.P. & Mishkin M. (1986) The amygdala in emotion. In Plutchik R. & Kellerman H. (eds) *Emotion: Theory, Research, and Experience*, Vol. 3, *Biological Foundations of Emotion*, pp. 281−299. Academic Press, New York.

Agras S., Sylvester D. & Oliveau D. (1969) The epidemiology of common fears and phobias. *Comprehensive Psychiatry* **10**, 151−156.

Ainsworth M.D.S. (1967) *Infancy in Uganda: Infant Care and the Growth of Love*. Johns Hopkins University Press, Baltimore.

Ainsworth M.D.S. (1979) Infant−mother attachment. *American Psychologist* **34**, 932−937.

Ainsworth M.D.S., Blehar M., Waters E. & Wall S. (1978) *Patterns of Attachment: A Psychological Study of the Strange Situation*. Lawrence Erlbaum, Hillsdale, New Jersey.

Alessi N.E., Robbins D.R. & Dilsaver S.C. (1987) Panic and depressive disorders among psychiatrically hospitalized adolescents. *Psychiatric Research* **20**, 275−283.

Alexander F. & Flagg G.W. (1965) The psychosomatic approach. In Wolman B.B. (ed.) *Handbook of Clinical Psychology*, pp. 805−947. McGraw-Hill, New York.

Amen E. (1941) Individual differences in apperceptive reaction: A study of the responses of preschool children to pictures. *Genetic Psychology Monographs* **23**, 319−385.

American Psychiatric Association (1987) *Diagnostic and Statistical Manual*, 3rd edn revised. American Psychiatric Association, Washington, DC.

Anderson J.C., Williams S., McGee R. & Silva P.A. (1987) DSM-III disorders in preadolescent children: Prevalence in a large sample from the general population. *Archives of General Psychiatry* **44**, 69−76.

Angold A. (1988) Childhood and adolescent depression: I. Epidemiological and aetiological aspects. *British Journal of Psychiatry* **152**, 601−617.

Angold A. & Rutter M. (1992) Effects of age and pubertal status on depression in a large clinical sample. *Development and Psychopathology* **4**, 5−28.

Aston-Jones G., Foote S.L. & Bloom F.E. (1982) How does ethanol disrupt sensory responses of brain noradrenergic neurones. *Nature* **296**, 857−860.

August G.J., Stewart M.A. & Tsai L. (1981) The incidence

of cognitive disabilities in the siblings of autistic children. *British Journal of Psychiatry* **138**, 416–422.

Averill J.R. (1990) Emotions in relation to systems of behavior. In Stein N., Leventhal B. & Trabasso T. (eds) *Psychological and Biological Approaches to Behavior*, pp. 385–404. Lawrence Erlbaum, Hillsdale, New Jersey.

Ayuso J.L., Alfonso S. & Rivera A. (1989) Childhood separation anxiety and panic disorder: A comparative study. *Progress in Neuropsychopharmacology and Biological Psychiatry* **13**, 665–671.

Ballenger J.C., Carek D.J., Steele J.J. & Cornish-McTighe D. (1989) Three cases of panic disorder with agoraphobia in children. *American Journal of Psychiatry* **146**, 922–924.

Ballinger C.B. (1975) Psychiatric morbidity and the menopause: Screening of a general population sample. *British Journal of Psychiatry* **3**, 344–346.

Ballinger C.B. (1990) Psychiatric aspects of the menopause. *British Journal of Psychiatry* **156**, 773–787.

Bancroft J. (1991) Reproductive hormones. In Rutter M. & Casaer P. (eds) *Biological Risk Factors for Psychosocial Disorders*, pp. 260–310. Cambridge University Press, Cambridge.

Bandler R.J. (1982) Neural control of aggressive behavior. *Trends in Neuroscience* **5**, 390–394.

Bandura A. (1969) *Principles of Behavior Modification*. Holt, Rinehart & Winston, New York.

Barden R.C., Zelko F.A., Duncan S.W. & Masters J.C. (1980) Children's consensual knowledge about the experiential determinants of emotion. *Journal of Personality and Social Psychology* **39**, 968–976.

Bardwick J.M. (1976) Psychological correlates of the menstrual cycle and oral contraceptive medication. In Sachar E.J. (ed.) *Hormones, Behavior and Psychopathology*, pp. 95–103.

Barerra M.E. & Maurer D. (1981) The perception of facial expressions by the three-month-old. *Child Development* **52**, 203–206.

Barlow D.H. (1988) *Anxiety and its Disorders: The Nature and Treatment of Anxiety and Panic*. Guilford Press, New York.

Barnett P.A. & Gotlib I.H. (1988) Psychosocial functioning and depression: distinguishing among antecedents, concomitants, and consequences. *Psychological Bulletin* **104**, 97–126.

Baron-Cohen S. (1988) Social and pragmatic deficits in autism: Cognitive or affective? *Journal of Autism and Developmental Disorders* **18**, 379–402.

Barrett K.C. & Campos J.J. (1987) Perspectives on emotional development II: A functionalist approach to emotions. In Osofsky J.D. (ed.) *Handbook of Infant Development*, 2nd edn, pp. 555–578. Wiley, New York.

Bauer D.H. (1976) An exploratory study of developmental changes in children's fears. *Journal of Child Psychology and Psychiatry* **17**, 69–74.

Beatty W.W. (1979) Gonadal hormones and sex differences in nonreproductive behaviors in rodents: Organizational and activational influences. *Hormones and Behavior* **12**, 112–163.

Beck A.T. (1967) *Depression: Clinical, Experimental, and Theoretical Aspects*. Harper & Row, New York.

Beck A.T., Brown G., Steer R.A., Eidelson J.Z. & Riskind J.H. (1987) Differentiating anxiety and depression utilizing the cognition checklist. *Journal of Abnormal Psychology* **96**, 179–183.

Beck A.T. & Emery G. (1985) *Anxiety Disorders and Phobias: A Cognitive Perspective*. Basic Books, New York.

Beck A.T., Rush A.J., Shaw B.F. & Emery G. (1979) *Cognitive Therapy for Depression: A Treatment Manual*. Guilford Press, New York.

Bell R.Q., Weller G.M. & Waldrop M.F. (1971) Newborn and preschooler: Organization of behavior and relations between periods. *Monographs of the Society for Research in Child Development* **36**(1–2), Serial No. 142.

Bell-Dolan D.J., Last C.G. & Strauss C.C. (1990) Symptoms of anxiety disorders in normal children. *Journal of the American Academy of Child and Adolescent Psychiatry* **29**, 528–533.

Belsky J., Fish M. & Isabella R. (1991) Continuity and discontinuity in infant negative and positive emotionality: Family antecedents and attachment consequences. *Developmental Psychology* **27**, 421–431.

Bemporad J. & Wilson A. (1978) A developmental approach to depression in childhood and adolescence. *Journal of the American Academy of Psychoanalysis* **6**, 325–352.

Berkowitz L. (1983) Aversively stimulated aggression: Some parallels and differences in research with animals and humans. *American Psychologist* **38**, 1135–1144.

Berkowitz L. (1990) On the formation and regulation of anger and aggression: A cognitive-neoassociationistic analysis. *American Psychologist* **45**, 494–503.

Bernieri F.K., Reznick S. & Rosenthal R. (1988) Synchrony, pseudosynchrony, and dissynchrony: Measuring the entrainment process in mother–infant interactions. *Journal of Personality and Social Psychology* **54**, 1–11.

Bernstein G.A. & Borchardt C.M. (1991) Anxiety disorders of childhood and adolescence: A critical review. *Journal of the American Academy of Child and Adolescent Psychiatry* **30**, 519–532.

Bertenthal B.I. & Campos J.J. (1990) A systems approach to the organizing effects of self-produced locomotion during infancy. In Rovee-Collier C. & Lipsett L. (eds) *Advances in Infancy Research*, Vol. 6, pp. 1–60. Ablex, Norwood, New Jersey.

Bertenthal B.I., Campos J.J. & Barrett K.C. (1984) Self-produced locomotion: An organizer of emotional, cognitive, and social development in infancy. In Emde R.N. & Harmon R.J. (eds) *Continuities and Discontinuities in Development*, pp. 175–210. Plenum, New York.

Blass E., Ganchrow J.R. & Steiner J. (1984) Classical

conditioning in newborn humans 2–48 hours of age. *Infant Behavior and Development* **7**, 223–235.

Blatt S.J., Quinlan D.M., Chevron E.S., McDonald C. & Zuroff D. (1982) Dependency and self-criticism: Psychological dimensions of depression. *Journal of Consulting and Clinical Psychology* **15**, 113–124.

Blehar M.C., Weissman M.M., Gershon E.S. & Hirschfeld R.M.A. (1988) Family and genetic studies of affective disorders. *Archives of General Psychiatry* **45**, 289–292.

Bloom L. (1990) Developments in expression: affect and speech. In Stein N., Leventhal B. & Trabasso T. (eds) *Psychological and Biological Approaches to Emotion*, pp. 215–245. Lawrence Erlbaum, Hillsdale, New Jersey.

Bloom L. & Capatides J. (1987) Expression of affect and the emergence of language. *Child Development* **58**, 1513–1522.

Blumberg S.H. & Izard C.E. (1986) Discriminating patterns of emotions in 10- and 11-year-old children's anxiety and depression. *Journal of Personality and Social Psychology* **49**, 194–202.

Blurton-Jones N.G. (1967) An ethological study of some aspects of social behavior of children in nursery school. In Morris D. (ed.) *Primate Ethology*, pp. 347–368. Weindenfeld & Nicholson, London.

Bock M. (1980) Cognitive and psychological aspects of surprise. *Psychologische-Rundschau* **31**, 248–260.

Borke H. (1971) Interpersonal perception of young children: Egocentrism or empathy? *Developmental Psychology* **5**, 263–269.

Bowen R.C., Offord D.R. & Boyle M.H. (1990) The prevalence of overanxious disorder and separation anxiety disorder: Results from the Ontario child health study. *Journal of the American Academy of Child and Adolescent Psychiatry* **29**, 753–758.

Bowlby J. (1982) *Attachment and Loss*, Vol. 1, *Attachment*. Basic Books, New York.

Brady E.U. & Kendall P.C. (1992) Comorbidity of anxiety and depression in children and adolescents. *Psychological Bulletin* **111**, 244–255.

Brazelton T.B. (1962) Crying in infancy. *Pediatrics* **29**, 579–588.

Brazelton T.B., Koslowski B. & Main M. (1974) The origins of reciprocity: The early mother–infant interaction. In Lewis M. & Rosenblum L. (eds) *The Effect of the Infant on its Caretaker*, pp. 49–76. Wiley, New York.

Brent D.A., Kala R., Edelbrock C., Costello A.J., Dulcan M.K. & Conover N. (1986) Psychopathology and its relationship to suicidal ideation in childhood and adolescence. *Journal of the American Academy of Child Psychiatry* **25**, 666–673.

Bretherton I. (1985) Attachment theory: Retrospect and prospect. In Bretherton I. & Waters E. (eds) Growing points of attachment theory and research. *Monographs of the Society for Research in Child Development* **50**, Serial No. 209, pp. 3–38.

Bretherton I. & Ainsworth M.D.A. (1974) Responses of 1-year-olds to a strange situation. In Lewis M. & Rosenblum L.A. (eds) *The Origins of Psychology*, Vol. 18, pp. 906–921. Wiley, New York.

Bretherton I. & Beeghly M. (1982) Talking about internal states: The acquisition of an explicit theory of mind. *Developmental Psychology* **18**, 906–921.

Bridges K. (1932) Emotional development in early infancy. *Child Development* **3**, 324–341.

Brooks-Gunn J. & Warren M.P. (1989) *How important are pubertal and social events for different problem behaviors and contexts?* Paper presented at the Society for Research on Child Development, Kansas City, Missouri.

Bruner J. (1978) How to do things with words. In Bruner J. & Garton A. (eds) *Human Growth and Development*, pp. 62–84. Oxford University Press, Oxford.

Buchanan C., Eccles J. & Becker J. (1992). Are adolescents the victims of raging hormones?: Evidence for activational effect of hormones on moods and behavior at adolescence. *Psychological Bulletin* **111**, 62–107.

Buss A. & Plomin R. (1975) *A Temperament Theory of Development*. Wiley, New York.

Cairns R. (1979) *Social Development: The Origins and Plasticity of Interchanges*. W.H. Freeman, San Francisco.

Campbell S.B. (1986) Developmental issues in childhood anxiety. In Gittelman R. (ed.) *Anxiety Disorders in Childhood*, pp. 24–57. Guilford Press, New York.

Campos J.J. (1983) The importance of affective communication in social referencing: A commentary on Feinman. *Merrill-Palmer Quarterly* **29**, 83–87.

Campos J.J. & Barrett K.C. (1984) Toward a new understanding of emotions and their development. In Izard C.E., Kagan J. & Zajonc R.B. (eds) *Emotions, Cognition, and Behavior*, pp. 229–263. Cambridge University Press, New York.

Campos J.J., Barrett K.C., Lamb M.E., Goldsmith H.H. & Stenberg C.R. (1983) Socioemotional development. In Campos J.J. & Haith M.H. (eds) *Infancy and Developmental Psychobiology*, Vol. 2, *Mussen's Handbook of Child Psychology*, 4th edn, pp. 783–915. Wiley, New York.

Campos J.J., Campos R.G. & Barrett K.C. (1989) Emergent themes in the study of emotional development and emotion regulation. *Developmental Psychology* **25**, 394–402.

Carlson G.A., Asarnow J.R. & Orbach I. (1987) Developmental aspects of suicidal behavior in children. *Journal of the American Academy of Child and Adolescent Psychiatry* **26**, 186–192.

Carlson G.A. & Cantwell D.P. (1982) Suicidal behavior and depression in children and adolescents. *Journal of the American Academy of Child Psychiatry* **21**, 361–368.

Carlson G.A. & Kashani J.H. (1988) Phenomenology of major depression from childhood through adulthood: Analyses of three studies. *American Journal of Psychiatry* **145**, 1222–1225.

Carlson M., Felleman E.S. & Masters J.C. (1983) Influence of children's emotional states on the recognition of emotion in peers and social motives to change another's emotional state. *Motivation and Emotion* **7**, 61−79.

Caron A.J., Caron R.F., & MacLean D.J. (1988) Infant discrimination of naturalistic emotional expressions: The role of face and voice. *Child Development* **59**, 604−616.

Caron R.F., Caron A.J. & Myers R.S. (1982) Abstraction of invariant face expressions in infancy. *Child Development* **53**, 1008−1015.

Carver C.S., Scheier M.F. & Weintraub J.K. (1989) Assessing coping strategies: A theoretically based approach. *Journal of Personality and Social Psychology* **56**, 267−283.

Chandler M.J. (1977) Social cognition: A selective review of current research. In Overton W.F. & Gallagher J.M. (eds) *Knowledge and Development*, Vol. 1, *Advances in Research and Theory*, pp. 93−147. Plenum, New York.

Chapman M., Zahn-Waxler C., Iannotti R. & Cooperman G. (1987) Empathy and responsibility in the motivation of children's helping. *Developmental Psychology* **23**, 140−145.

Church J. (ed.) (1966) *Three Babies: Biographies of Cognitive Development*. Random House, New York.

Cicchetti D. (1990) The organization and coherence of socioemotional, cognitive, and representational development: Illustrations through a developmental psychopathology perspective on Down syndrome and child maltreatment. In Thompson R. (ed.) *Nebraska Symposium on Motivation*, Vol. 36, pp. 259−366. University of Nebraska Press.

Cicchetti D. & Pogge-Hesse P. (1981) The relation between emotion and cognition in infant development. In Lamb M. & Sherrod L. (eds) *Infant Social Cognition*, pp. 205−272. Lawrence Erlbaum, Hillsdale, New Jersey.

Cicchetti D. & Schneider-Rosen K. (1986) An organizational approach to childhood depression. In Rutter M., Izard C.E. & Read P.B. (eds) *Depression in Young People: Clinical and Developmental Perspectives*, pp. 71−134. Guilford Press, New York.

Cicchetti D. & Sroufe L.A. (1978) An organizational view of affect: Illustration from the study of Down's syndrome infants. In Lewis M. & Rosenblum L. (eds) *The Development of Affect*, pp. 309−350. Plenum, New York.

Cloninger C.R., Martin R.L., Clayton P. & Guze S.B. (1981) Blind follow-up and family study of anxiety neurosis: Preliminary analysis of the St Louis 500. In Klein D.F. & Rabkin I. (eds) *Anxiety: New Research and Changing Concepts*, pp. 137−154. Raven, New York.

Cohn J. & Tronick E.Z. (1983) Three-month-old infants' reaction to simulated maternal depression. *Child Development* **54**, 185−193.

Condon W.S. & Sander L.W. (1974) Synchrony demonstrated between movements of the neonate and adult speech. *Child Development* **45**, 456−462.

Costello E.J. (1989) Child psychiatric disorders and their correlates: A primary care pediatric sample. *Journal of*

the American Academy of Child and Adolescent Psychiatry* **28**, 851−855.

Crowe R.R., Noyes R., Pauls D.L. & Slymen D. (1983) A family study of panic disorder. *Archives of General Psychiatry* **40**, 1065−1069.

Cummings E.M., Iannotti R.J. & Zahn-Waxler C. (1985) Influence of conflict between adults on the emotions and aggression of young children. *Developmental Psychology* **21**, 495−507.

Darwin C.R. (1872) *The Expression of Emotions in Man and Animals*. John Murray, London.

Davidson R., Ekman P., Saron C., Senulis J. & Friesen W. (1990) Approach−withdrawal and cerebral asymmetry: Emotional expression and brain physiology I. *Journal of Personality and Social Psychology* **58**, 330−341.

Dawe H.C. (1934) An analysis of two hundred quarrels of preschool children. *Child Development* **5**, 139−157.

Dawson G. & Adams A. (1984) Initiation and social responsiveness in autistic children. *Journal of Abnormal Child Psychology* **12**, 209−226.

Dawson G. & McKissick F.C. (1984) Self-recognition in autistic children. *Journal of Autism and Developmental Disorders* **14**, 383−394.

De Casper A.J. & Carstens A.A. (1981) Contingencies of stimulation: Effects on learning and emotion in neonates. *Infant Behavior and Development* **4** 19−35.

deLignieres B. & Vincens M. (1982) Differential effects of exogenous oestradiol and progesterone on mood in post-menopausal women: Individual dose/effect relationship. *Maturitas* **4**, 67−72.

DeLong G.R. (1978) A neuropsychologic interpretation of infantile autism. In Rutter M. & Schopler E. (eds) *Autism: A Reappraisal of Concepts and Treatment*, pp. 207−218. Plenum, New York.

Demos V. (1986) Crying in early infancy: An illustration of the motivational function of affect. In Brazelton T.B. & Yogman M. (eds) *Affect and Early Infancy*, pp. 39−73. Ablex, New York.

Denham S. (1986) Social cognition, prosocial behavior, and emotion in preschoolers: Contextual validation. *Child Development* **57**, 194−201.

Denham S. & Couchoud E.A. (1990) Young preschoolers' understanding of emotions. *Child Study Journal* **20**, 171−192.

Derogatis L.R., Lipman R.S., Rickels J., Uhlenhuth E.H. & Covi L. (1974) The Hopkins symptom checklist: A measure of primary symptom dimensions. In Pichot P. (ed.) *Psychological Measurements in Psychopharmacology: Modern Problems in Pharmacopsychiatry*, pp. 79−110. Karger, Basle.

De Silva P., Rachman S. & Seligman M.E.P. (1977) Prepared phobias and obsessions: Therapeutic outcome. *Behavior, Research and Therapy* **15**, 65−77.

Diener E. (1984) Subjective well-being. *Psychological Bulletin* **95**, 542−575.

Diener E. & Larsen R. (1984) Temporal stability and cross:

Situational consistency of affective, cognitive, and behavioral responses. *Journal of Personality and Social Psychology* **47**, 871–883.

Diener E., Sandvik E. & Larsen R. (1985) Age and sex effects for emotional intensity. *Developmental Psychology* **21**, 542–546.

Dobson K.S. (1985) The relationship between anxiety and depression. *Clinical Psychology Review* **5**, 307–324.

Dodge K.A. (1989) Coordinating responses to aversive stimuli: Introduction to a special section on the development of emotion regulation. *Developmental Psychology* **25**, 339–342.

Dodge K.A., Bates J.E. & Pettit G.S. (1990) Mechanisms in the cycle of violence. *Science* **250**, 1678–1683.

Dodge K.A. & Crick N. (1990) Social information-processing basis of aggressive behavior in children. *Personality and Social Psychology Bulletin* **16**, 8–22.

Dodge K.A. & Garber J. (1991) Domains of emotion regulation. In Garber J. & Dodge K.A. (eds) *The Development of Emotion Regulation and Dysregulation*, pp. 3–11. Cambridge University Press, New York.

Dodge K.A., Pettit G., McClaskey C. & Brown M. (1986) Social competence in children. *Monographs of the Society for Research in Child Development* **51**, Serial No. 213.

Dunn J. (1988) *The Beginnings of Social Understanding*. Basil Blackwell, Oxford.

Dunn J. & Kendrick C. (1982) *Siblings*. Cambridge University Press, Cambridge.

Dunn J. & Munn J. (1985) Becoming a family member: Family conflict and the development of social understanding in the first year. *Child Development* **50**, 306–318.

Dunn J. & Plomin R. (1990) *Separate Lives: Why Siblings are So Different*. Basic Books, New York.

Durant J.R. (1973) The science of sentiment: The problem of cerebral localization of emotion. In Bateson P.P.G. & Klopfer P.H. (eds) *Perspectives in Ethology*, Vol. 6, *Mechanisms*, pp. 1–30. Plenum, New York.

Eisenberg N., Fabes R., Schaller M. *et al.* (1991) Personality and socialization correlates of vicarious emotional responding. *Journal of Personality and Social Psychology* **61**, 459–470.

Ekman P. (1973) Cross-cultural studies of facial expression. In Ekman P. (ed.) *Darwin and Facial Expression*, pp. 169–222. Academic Press, New York.

Ekman P. (1977) Biological and cultural contributions to body and facial movements. In Blacking J. (ed.) *The Anthropology of the Body*, pp. 34–84. Academic Press, London.

Ekman P. (1984) Expression and the nature of emotion. In Scherer K.R. & Ekman P. (eds) *Approaches to Emotion*, pp. 319–344. Lawrence Erlbaum, Hillsdale, New Jersey.

Ekman P. (1985) *Telling Lies*. Berkley Books, New York.

Ekman P. & Friesen W.V. (1971) Constants across cultures in the face and emotion. *Journal of Personality and Social Psychology* **17**, 124–129.

Ekman P. & Friesen W.V. (1975) *Unmasking the Face*. Prentice-Hall, New Jersey.

Ekman P., Friesen W.V. & Ellsworth P. (1972) *Emotion in the Human Face*. Pergamon, New York.

Ellis A. (1962) *Reasons and Emotion in Psychotherapy*. Lyle Stuart, New York.

Emde R.N., Gaensbauer T.J. & Harmon R.J. (1976) Emotional expression in infancy: A biobehavioral study. *Psychological Issues Monograph Series* **10** (Monograph 37).

Emde R.N., Katz E. & Thorpe J. (1978) Emotional expression in infancy: II. Early deviations in Down's syndrome. In Lewis M. & Rosenblum L. (eds) *The Development of Affect*, pp. 125–148. Plenum, New York.

Emde R.N. & Koenig K.L. (1969) Neonatal smiling and rapid eye movement states. *Journal of the American Academy of Child Psychiatry* **8**, 57–67.

Emde R.N., Plak P.R. & Spitz R.A. (1965) Anaclitic depression in an infant raised in an institution. *Journal of the American Academy of Child Psychiatry* **4**, 545–553.

Endicott J., Halbreich U., Schacht S. & Nee J. (1981) Premenstrual changes and affective disorders. *Psychosomatic Medicine* **43**, 519–529.

Eysenck H.J. (1979) The conditioning model of neurosis. *Communication in Behavioral Biology* **2**, 155–199.

Feinman S. (1982) Social referencing in infancy. *Merrill-Palmer Quarterly* **29**, 83–87.

Feiring C. & Lewis M. (1979) Sex and age differences in young children's reactions to frustration: A further look at the Goldberg and Lewis subjects. *Child Development* **50**, 848–853.

Feshbach N.D. (1987) Parental empathy and child adjustment/maladjustment. In Eisenberg N. & Strayer J. (eds) *Empathy and its Development*, pp. 271–291. Cambridge University Press, Cambridge.

Feshbach N.D. & Cohen S. (1988) Training affect comprehension in young children: An experimental evaluation. *Journal of Applied Developmental Psychology* **9**, 201–210.

Field T. (1984) Early interactions between infants and their postpartum depressed mothers. *Infant Behavior and Development* **7**, 517–522.

Field T., Healy B., Goldstein S. & Guthertz M. (1988) Behavior-state matching and synchrony in mother–infant interactions of nondepressed versus depressed dyads. *Developmental Psychology* **26**, 7–14.

Field T. & Walden T. (1982) Perception and production of facial expression in infancy and early childhood. In Reese H.W. & Lipsitt L.P. (eds) *Advances in Child Development and Behavior*, pp. 169–211. Academic Press, New York.

Flynn J.P. (1967) The neural basis of aggression in cats. In Glass D.C. (ed.) *Neurophysiology of Emotion*, pp. 40–60. Rockefeller University Press/Russell Sage Foundation, New York.

Folstein S. & Rutter M. (1977) Infantile autism: A genetic study of 21 twin pairs. *Journal of Child Psychology and*

Psychiatry **18**, 297–321.

Folstein S. & Rutter M. (1988) Autism: Familial aggregation and genetic implications. *Journal of Autism and Developmental Disorders* **18**, 3–30.

Fowler R.C., Rich C.L. & Young D. (1986) San Diego suicide study: II. Substance abuse in young cases. *Archives of General Psychiatry* **43**, 962–965.

Fox N. (1991) If it's not left, it's right: Electroencephalograph asymmetry and the development of emotion. *American Psychologist* **46**, 863–872.

Frances G., Last C.G. & Strauss C.C. (1987) Expression of separation anxiety disorder: The roles of age and gender. *Child Psychiatry and Human Development* **18**, 82–89.

Freud S. (1968) Mourning and melancholia. In Strachey J. (ed.) *Standard Edition of the Complete Works of Sigmund Freud*, Vol. 14, pp. 239–260. Hogarth Press, London.

Friedman R.C., Hurt S.E., Clarkin J.F., Corn R. & Aronoff M. (1983) Symptoms of depression among adolescents and young adults. *Journal of Affective Disorders* **5**, 37–43.

Frijda N. (1986) *The Emotions*. Cambridge University Press, New York.

Fristad M.A., Weller E.B. & Weller R.A. (1992) The mania rating scale: Can it be used in children? A preliminary report. *Journal of the American Academy of Child and Adolescent Psychiatry* **31**, 252–257.

Gaensbauer T.J., Mrazek D. & Harmon R. (1980) Affective behavior patterns in abused and/or neglected infants. In Frude N. (ed.) *The Understanding and Prevention of Child Abuse: Psychological Approaches*, pp. 120–135. Concord Press, London.

Gaensbauer T.J. & Sands K. (1979) Distorted affective communications in abused/neglected infants and their potential impact on caretakers. *American Journal of Child Psychiatry* **18**, 236–250.

Garber J. (1984) The developmental progression of depression in female children. In Cicchetti D. & Schneider-Rosen K. (eds) *Childhood Depression, New Directions in Child Development*, pp. 29–58. Jossey-Bass, San Francisco.

Garber J. & Hollon S.D. (1991) What can specificity designs say about causality in psychopathology research? *Psychological Bulletin* **110**, 129–136.

Garber J., Quiggle N.L. & Shanley N. (1990) Cognition and depression in children and adolescents. In Ingram R.E. (ed.) *Contemporary Psychological Approaches to Depression: Theory, Research, and Treatment*. Plenum, New York.

Garber J., Weiss B. & Shanley N. (1993) Cognitions, depressive symptoms, and development in adolescents. *Journal of Abnormal Psychology* **102**, 47–57.

Garcia J. & Koelling R. (1966) Relation of cue to consequence in avoidance. *Psychonomic Science* **5**, 121–122.

Garmezy N. (1974) Children at risk: The search for the antecedents of schizophrenia: II. Ongoing research programs issues, and intervention. *Schizophrenia Bulletin*

9, 55–125.

George C. & Main M. (1979) Social interaction of young abused children: Approach, avoidance and aggression. *Child Development* **50**, 306–318.

Gittelman R. & Klein D.F. (1984) Relationship between separation anxiety and panic and agoraphobic disorders. *Psychopathology* **17** (Suppl. 1), 56–65.

Gnepp J. (1983) Children's social sensitivity: Inferring emotions from conflicting cues. *Developmental Psychology* **19**, 805–814.

Gold P.W., Goodwin F.K. & Chrousos G.P. (1988) Clinical and biochemical manifestations of depression: Relations to the neurobiology of stress. *New England Journal of Medicine* **319**, 348–413.

Goldberg S. (1972) Infant care and growth in urban Zambia. *Human Development* **15**, 77–89.

Goldin L.R. & Gershon E.S. (1988) The genetic epidemiology of major depressive illness. In Frances A.J. & Hales R.E. (eds) *Review of Psychiatry*, pp. 149–168. American Psychiatric Press, Washington, DC.

Goodenough F.L. (1931) *Anger in Young Children*. University of Minnesota Press, Minneapolis.

Gould M.S., Shaffer D. & Davies M. (1990) Truncated pathways from childhood to adulthood: Attrition in follow-up studies due to death. In Robins L.N. & Rutter M. (eds) *Straight and Devious Pathways from Childhood to Adulthood*, pp. 3–9. Cambridge University Press, Cambridge.

Graham S., Doubleday C. & Guarino P.A. (1984) The development of relations between perceived controllability and the emotions of pity, anger, and guilt. *Child Development* **55**, 561–565.

Graham S. & Weiner B. (1986) From an attributional theory of emotion to developmental psychology: A round-trip ticket? *Social Cognition* **4**, 152–179.

Gunnar M.R. (1980) Control, warning signals, and distress in infancy. *Developmental Psychology* **16**, 281–289.

Hadwin J. & Perner J. (1991) Pleased and surprised: Children's cognitive theory of emotion. *British Journal of Developmental Psychology* **9**, 215–234.

Harmon R.J., Wagonfeld S. & Emde R.N. (1982) Anaclitic depression: A follow-up from infancy to puberty. *Psychoanalytic Study of the Child* **37**, 67–94.

Harrington R., Fudge H., Rutter M., Pickles A. & Hill J. (1990a) Adult outcome of childhood and adolescent depression: I. Psychiatric status. *Archives of General Psychiatry* **47**, 465–473.

Harrington R., Fudge H., Rutter M., Pickles A. & Hill J. (1990b) Adult outcome of childhood and adolescent depression. II. Links with antisocial disorder. *Journal of the American Academy of Child and Adolescent Psychiatry* **30**, 434–439.

Harris P.L. (1985) What children know about the situations that provoke emotion. In Lewis M. & Saarni C. (eds) *The Socialization of Emotion*, pp. 161–185. Plenum, New York.

Harris P.L. (1989) *Children and Emotion: The Development of Psychological Understanding.* Basil Blackwell, Oxford.

Harris P.L. & Lipian M.S. (1989) Understanding emotion, and experiencing emotion. In Saarni C. & Harris P.L. (eds) *Children's Understanding of Emotion.* Cambridge University Press, Cambridge.

Harris P.L. & Olthof T. (1982) This child's concept of emotion. In Butterworth G. & Light P. (eds) *Social Cognition: Studies in the Development of Understanding,* pp. 188–209. University of Chicago Press, Chicago.

Harris P.L., Olthof T. & Meerum Terwogt M. (1981) Children's knowledge of emotion. *Journal of Child Psychology and Psychiatry* **22**, 247–261.

Harris P.L., Olthof T., Meerum Terwogt M. & Hartman C.E. (1987) Children's knowledge of the situations that provoke emotion. *International Journal of Behavioral Development* **10**, 319–344.

Harris P.L. & Saarni C. (1989) Children's understanding of emotion: An introduction. In Saarni C. & Harris P.L. (eds) *Children's Understanding of Emotion,* pp. 3–24. Cambridge University Press, Cambridge.

Harter S. (1983) Developmental perspectives on the self-system. In Hetherington E.M. (ed.) *Socialization, Personality, and Social Development,* Vol. 4, *Mussen's Handbook of Child Psychology,* 4th edn, pp. 275–385. Wiley, New York.

Harter S. (1986) Cognitive-developmental processes in the integration of concepts about emotions and the self. *Social Cognition* **4**, 119–151.

Harter S. & Buddin B.J. (1987) Children's understanding of the simultaneity of two emotions: A five-stage developmental acquisition sequence. *Developmental Psychology* **23**, 388–399.

Harter S. & Whitesell N.R. (1989) Developmental changes in children's understanding of single, multiple, and blended emotion concepts. In Saarni C. & Harris P.L. (eds) *Children's Understanding of Emotion,* pp. 81–116. Cambridge University Press, Cambridge.

Haskett R.F., Steiner M., Osmun J.N. & Carroll B.J. (1980) Severe premenstrual tension syndrome: Model for endogenous depression? *Biological Psychiatry* **15**, 121–139.

Haviland J.M. & Lelwica M. (1987) The induced affect response: 10-week-old infants' responses to three emotion expressions. *Developmental Psychology* **23**, 97–104.

Hawton K. (1986) *Suicide and Attempted Suicide Among Children and Adolescents.* Sage, Beverly Hills, California.

Hawton K. & Goldacre M. (1982) Hospital admissions for adverse effects of medicinal agents (mainly self-poisoning) among adolescents in the Oxford region. *British Journal of Psychiatry* **141**, 166–170.

Hazen C. & Shaver P. (1990) Love and work: An attachment — theoretical perspective. *Journal of Personality and Social Psychology* **59**, 270–280.

Heckhausen J. (1987) Balancing for weaknesses and challenging developmental potential: A longitudinal study of mother–infant dyads in apprenticeship interactions. *Developmental Psychology* **23**, 762–770.

Heller W. (1990) The neuropsychology of emotion: Developmental patterns and implications for psychopathology. In Stein N., Leventhal B. & Trabasso T. (eds) *Psychological and Biological Approaches to Emotion,* pp. 167–211. Lawrence Erlbaum, Hillsdale, New Jersey.

Hershberg S.G., Carlson G.A., Cantwell D.P. & Strober M. (1982) Anxiety and depressive disorders in psychiatrically disturbed children. *Journal of Clinical Psychiatry* **43**, 358–361.

Hiatt S.W., Campos J.T. & Emde R.N. (1979) Facial patterning and infant emotional expression: Happiness, surprise, and fear. *Child Development* **50**, 1020–1035.

Hinde R. (1976) On describing relationships. *Journal of Child Psychology and Psychiatry* **17**, 1–19.

Hobson R.P. (1986a) The autistic child's appraisal of expressions of emotion. *Journal of Child Psychiatry and Psychology* **27**, 321–342.

Hobson R.P. (1986b) The autistic child's appraisal of expressions of emotion: A further study. *Journal of Child Psychiatry and Psychology* **27**, 671–680.

Hobson R.P. (1989) Beyond cognition: A theory of autism. In Dawson G. (ed.) *Autism: Nature, Diagnosis, and Treatment,* pp. 22–48. Guilford Press, New York.

Hodapp R.M., Goldfield E.C. & Boyatzis C.J. (1984) The use and effectiveness of maternal scaffolding in mother–infant games. *Child Development* **55**, 772–781.

Hoffman L. (1991) The influence of the family environment on personality: Accounting for sibling differences. *Psychological Bulletin* **110**, 187–203.

Hoffman M.L. (1970) Moral development. In Mussen P.H. (ed.) *Handbook of Child Psychology,* Vol. 2, 3rd edn, pp. 497–548. Wiley, New York.

Hoffman M.L. (1978) Toward a theory of empathic arousal and development. In Lewis M. & Rosenblum L.A. (eds) *The Development of Affect,* pp. 227–256. Plenum, New York.

Hoffman M.L. (1982a) Development of prosocial motivation: Empathy and guilt. In Eisenberg N. (ed.) *The Development of Prosocial Behavior,* pp. 281–313. Academic Press, New York.

Hoffman M.L. (1982b) The measurement of empathy. In Izard C.E. (ed.) *Measuring Emotions in Infants and Children,* pp. 279–296. Cambridge University Press, Cambridge.

Hollon S.D. & Beck A.T. (1979) Cognitive therapy for depression. In Kendall P.C. & Hollon S.D. (eds) *Cognitive-Behavioral Intervention: Theory, Research, and Procedures,* pp. 153–203. Academic Press, New York.

Holmes D.P. & Horan J.J. (1976) Anger induction in assertion training. *Journal of Counselling Psychology* **23**, 108–111.

Holt R.R. (1970) On the interpersonal and intrapersonal consequences of expressing or not expressing anger.

Journal of Consulting and Clinical Psychology **35**, 8–12.

Houser B.B. (1979) An investigation of the correlation between hormone levels in males and mood, behavior, and physical discomfort. *Hormones and Behavior* **12**, 185–197.

Hruska K. & Yonis A. (1972) Developmental changes in cardiac responses to optical stimulus of impending collisions. *Psychophysiology* **9**, 272.

Huebner R.R. & Izard C.E. (1988) Mothers' responses to infants' facial expressions of sadness, anger, and physical distress. *Motivation and Emotion* **12**, 185–196.

Hunter M. (1990) Psychological and somatic experience of the menopause: A prospective study. *Psychosomatic Medicine* **52**, 357–367.

Hygge S. & Ohman A. (1978) Modeling processes in the acquisition of fears: Vicarious electrodermal conditioning to fear-relevant stimuli. *Journal of Personality and Social Psychology* **36**, 271–279.

Isen A.M. (1987) Positive affect, cognitive processes, and social behavior. In Berkowitz L. (ed.) *Advances in Experimental Social Psychology*, pp. 205–253. Academic Press, New York.

Isen A.M. (1990) The influence of positive and negative affect on cognitive organization: Some implications for development. In Stein N., Leventhal B. & Trabasso T. (eds) *Psychological and Biological Approaches to Emotion*, pp. 3–19. Lawrence Erlbaum, Hillsdale, New Jersey.

Isen A.M. & Daubman K.A. (1984) The influence of affect on cognition. *Journal of Personality and Social Psychology* **47**, 1206–1217.

Izard C.E. (1971) *The Face of Emotion*. Appleton-Century-Crofts, New York.

Izard C.E. (1977) *Human Emotions*. Plenum, New York.

Izard C.E. (1987) Infants' emotion expressions to acute pain: Developmental change and stability of individual differences. *Developmental Psychology* **23**, 105–113.

Izard C.E. (1990) Facial expression and the regulation of emotions. *Journal of Personality and Social Psychology* **58**, 487–498.

Izard C.E. & Harris P.L. (in press) Emotional development. In Cicchetti D. & Cohen D. (eds) *Handbook of Developmental Psychopathology*. Cambridge University Press, New York.

Izard C.E., Hembree E.A., Dougherty L.M. & Spizzirri C.L. (1983) Changes in facial expressions of 2- to 19-month-old infants following acute pain. *Developmental Psychology* **19**, 418–426.

Izard C.E., Hembree E.A. & Huebner R.R. (1987) Infants' emotion expressions to acute pain: Developmental change and stability of individual differences. *Developmental Psychology* **23**, 105–113.

Izard C.E., Huebner R.R., Risser D., McGinnes G. & Dougherty L. (1980) The young infant's ability to produce discrete emotion expression. *Developmental Psychology* **16**, 132–140.

Izard C.E. & Malatesta C.Z. (1987) Perspectives on emotional development I: Differential emotions theory of early emotional development. In Osofsky J.D. (ed.) *Handbook of Infant Development*, 2nd edn, pp. 494–554. Wiley, New York.

Jacklin C.N., Maccoby E.E., & Dick A.E. (1973) Barrier behavior and toy preference: Sex differences (and their absence) in the year-old child. *Child Development* **44**, 196–200.

Jacobs W.J. & Nadel L. (1985) Stress-induced recovery of fears and phobias. *Psychological Review* **92**, 512–531.

Jersild A.T. & Holmes F.B. (1935) *Children's Fears*. Teacher's College, New York.

Johnson W., Emde R.N., Pannabecker B., Stenberg C. & Davis M. (1982) Maternal perception of infant emotion from birth through 18 months. *Infant Behavior and Development* **5**, 313–322.

Kagan J. (1971) *Change and Continuity in Infancy*. Wiley, New York.

Kagan J. (1982) The emergence of self. *Journal of Child Psychology and Psychiatry* **23**, 363–382.

Kagan J. & Snidman N. (1991a) Infant predictors of inhibited and uninhibited profiles. *Psychological Science* **2**, 40–44.

Kagan J. & Snidman N. (1991b) Temperamental factors in human development. *American Psychologist* **46**, 856–862.

Kalus O., Asnis G.M. & van-Praag H.M. (1989) The role of serotonin in depression. Special issue: Depression. *Psychiatric Annals* **19**, 348–353.

Kandel E.R. (1983) From metapsychology to molecular biology: Explorations into the nature of anxiety. *American Journal of Psychiatry* **140**, 10, 1277, 1293.

Kashani J.H., Beck N.C., Hoeper E.W. *et al.* (1987) Psychiatric disorders in a community sample of adolescents. *American Journal of Psychiatry* **144**, 584–589.

Kashani J.H. & Orvaschel H. (1988) Anxiety disorders in mid-adolescence: A community sample. *American Journal of Psychiatry* **145**, 960–964.

Kashani J.H. & Orvaschel H. (1990) A community study of anxiety in children and adolescents. *American Journal of Psychiatry* **147**, 313–318.

Kashani J.H. & Ray J.S. (1983) Depressive related symptoms among preschool-age children. *Child Psychiatry and Human Development* **13**, 233–238.

Keil F. (1979) The development of the young child's ability to anticipate the outcomes of simple causal events. *Child Development* **50**, 455–462.

Kendall P.C. & Braswell L. (1985) *Cognitive-Behavioral Therapy with Impulsive Children*. Guilford Press, New York.

Kendler K.S., Heath A.C., Martin N.G. & Eaves L.J. (1986) Symptoms of anxiety and depression in a volunteer twin population. *Archives of General Psychiatry* **43**, 213–221.

Kendler K.S., Heath A.C., Martin N.G. & Eaves L.J. (1987). Symptoms of anxiety and symptoms of depression:

Same genes, different environment? *Archives of General Psychiatry* **44**, 451–457.

Kerber K.W. & Coles S.M.G. (1978) The role of perceived physiological activity in affective judgements. *Journal of Experimental Social Psychology* **14**, 419–433.

Kernberg O. (1976) *Object Relations Theory and Clinical Psychoanalysis*. Jason Aronson, New York.

Kling A.S. (1986) The anatomy of aggression and affiliation. In Plutchik R. & Kellerman H. (eds) *Emotion: Theory, Research, and Experience*, Vol. 3, *Biological Foundations of Emotion*, pp. 237–264. Academic Press, New York.

Kobak R.R. & Sceery A. (1988) Attachment in late adolescence: Working models, affect regulation, and perceptions of self and others. *Child Development* **59**, 135–146.

Kohlberg L., LaCross J. & Ricks D. (1972) The predictability of adult mental health from childhood behavior. In Wolman B.A. (ed.) *Manual of Child Psychopathology*, pp. 1217–1284. McGraw-Hill, New York.

Kopp C.B. (1989) Regulation of distress and negative emotions: A developmental view. *Developmental Psychology* **25**, 343–354.

Kovacs M., Feinberg T.L., Crouse-Novak M., Paulauskas S.L., Pollack M. & Finkelstein R. (1984) Depressive disorders in childhood: II. A longitudinal study of the risk for a subsequent major depression. *Archives of General Psychiatry* **41**, 643–649.

Kovacs M. & Paulauskas S.L. (1984) Developmental stage and the expression of depressive disorders in children: An empirical analysis. In Cicchetti D. & Schneider-Rosen K. (eds) *Childhood Depression. New Directions for Child Development*, No. 26, pp. 59–80. Jossey-Bass, San Francisco.

Kreitman N. (ed.) (1977) *Parasuicide*, Wiley, London.

LaBarbera J., Izard C., Vietze P. & Parisi S. (1976) Four- and six-month-old infants' visual responses to joy, anger, and neutral expressions. *Child Development* **47**, 535–538.

Laird J.D. (1974) Self-attribution of emotion: The effects of expressive behavior on the quality of emotional experience. *Journal of Personality and Social Psychology* **37**, 475–486.

Laird J.D. (1984) The real role of facial response in the experience of emotion: A reply to Tourangeau and Ellsworth, and others. *Journal of Personality and Social Psychology* **47**, 909–917.

Landis E. (1929) The interpretation of facial expression in emotion. *Journal of General Psychology* **2**, 59–72.

Lanzetta J. & Orr S. (1980) Influence of facial expressions on the classical conditioning of fear. *Journal of Personality and Social Psychology* **39**, 1081–1087.

Lapouse R. & Monk M.A. (1959) Fears and worries in a representative sample of children. *American Journal of Orthopsychiatry* **29**, 803–818.

Larsen R. & Diener E. (1987) Affect intensity as an individual differences characteristic: A review. *Journal of Research in Personality* **21**, 1–39.

Larsen R., Diener E. & Cropanzano R.S. (1987) Cognitive operations associated with individual differences in affect intensity. *Journal of Personality and Social Psychology* **53**, 767–774.

Larsen R., Diener E. & Emmons R. (1985) An evaluation of subjective well-being measures. *Social Indicators Research* **17**, 1–18.

Last C.G. & Strauss C.C. (1989) Obsessive-compulsive disorder in childhood. *Journal of Anxiety Disorders* **3**, 87–95.

Lazarus R.S. (1981) A cognitivist's reply to Zajonc on emotion and cognition. *American Psychologist* **36**, 222–223.

Lazarus R.S. (1990) Constructs of the mind in adaptation. In Stein N., Leventhal B. & Trabasso T. (eds) *Psychological and Biological Approaches to Emotion*, pp. 3–19. Lawrence Erlbaum, Hillsdale, New Jersey.

Lazarus R.S. (1991) *Emotion and Adaptation*. Oxford University Press, New York.

Lazarus R.S. & Folkman S. (1984) *Stress, Appraisal, and Coping*. Springer, New York.

LeDoux J.E. (1987) Emotion. In Plum F. (ed.) *Handbook of Physiology*, Vol. 5, *The Nervous System*, pp. 419–459. American Physiological Society, Washington, DC.

Lewinsohn P.M. (1974) A behavioral approach to depression. In Friedman R.J. & Katz M.M. (eds) *The Psychology of Depression: Contemporary Theory and Research*, pp. 157–178. Winston-Wiley, Washington, DC.

Lewinsohn P.M. (1975) Engagement in pleasant activities and depression level. *Journal of Abnormal Psychology* **84**, 718–721.

Lewinsohn P.M. & Graf M. (1973) Pleasant activities and depression. *Journal of Consulting and Clinical Psychology* **41**, 261–268.

Lewinsohn P.M., Weinstein M.S. & Shaw D. (1968) Depression: A clinical research approach. In Rubin R.D. & Franks C.M. (eds) *Advances in Behavior Therapy*, pp. 231–240. Academic Press, New York.

Lewis H.B. (1971) *Shame and Guilt in Neurosis*. International Universities Press, New York.

Lewis H.B. (1979) Guilt in obsession and paranoia. In Izard C. (ed.) *Emotions in Personality and Psychopathology*, pp. 369–396. Plenum, New York.

Lewis M. & Brooks J. (1974) Self, other and fear: infants' reactions to people. In Lewis M. & Rosenblum L.A. (eds) *The Origins of Fear*, pp. 195–228. Plenum, New York.

Lewis M. & Brooks-Gunn J. (1979) Self-knowledge and emotional development. In Lewis M. & Rosenblum L.A. (eds) *The Development of Affect*, pp. 205–226. Plenum, New York.

Lewis M. & Michalson L. (1983) *Children's Emotions and Moods: Developmental Theory and Measurement*. Plenum, New York.

Lewis M. & Rosenblum L.A. (1978) *The Development of Affect*. Plenum, New York.

Lewis M. & Saarni C. (1985) *The Socializations of Emotions*. Plenum, New York.

Links P.S., Boyer M.H. & Offord D.B. (1989) The prevalence of emotional disorder in children. *Journal of Nervous Mental Disorders* **177**, 85–91.

Maccoby E.E. & Jacklin C.N. (1974) *The Psychology of Sex Differences*. Stanford University Press, Palo Alto.

McConville B.J., Boag L.C. & Purohit A.P. (1973) Three types of childhood depression. *Canadian Psychiatric Association Journal* **18**, 133–138.

McCoy C.L. & Masters J.C. (1985) The development of children's strategies for the social control of emotion. *Child Development* **56**, 1214–1222.

MacFarlene J.W., Allen L. & Honzik M.R. (1954) *A Developmental Study of the Behavior Problems of Normal Children between 21 months and 14 years*. University of California Press, California.

McGee R., Feehan M., Williams S., Partridge F., Silva P.A. & Kelly J. (1990) DSM-III disorders in a large sample of adolescents. *Journal of the American Academy of Child and Adolescent Psychiatry* **29**, 611–619.

Mackenzie T.B., Wilcox K. & Baron H. (1986) Lifetime prevalence of psychiatric disorders in women with perimenstrual difficulties. *Journal of Affective Disorders* **10**, 15–19.

MacLean P.D. (1952) Some psychiatric implications of physiological studies on frontotemporal portion of limbic system (visceral brain). *Electroencephalography and Clinical Neurophysiology* **4**, 407–418.

McNally R.J. (1989) On 'stress-induced recovery of fears and phobias'. *Psychological Review* **96**, 180–181.

Mahler M. (1968) *On Human Symbiosis and the Vicissitudes of Individuation*, Vol. 1, *Infantile Psychosis*. International Universities Press, New York.

Maier S.F. & Seligman M.E.P. (1976) Learned helplessness: Theory and evidence. *Journal of Experimental Psychology, General* **105**, 3–46.

Main M. (1973) *Play, exploration, and competence as related to child–adult attachment*. Unpublished doctoral dissertation, John Hopkins University, Baltimore.

Main M. (1981) Abusive and rejecting infants. In Frude N. (ed.) *Psychological Approaches to Child Abuse*, pp. 19–38. Roman & Littlefield, New Jersey.

Main M., Kaplan N. & Cassidy J. (1985) Security in infancy, childhood, and adulthood: A move to the level of representation. In Bretherton I. & Waters E. (eds) *Growing points of attachment theory and research. Monographs of the Society for Research in Child Development* **50**, Serial No. 209, 66–104.

Main M., Tomasini L. & Tolan W. (1979) Differences among mothers of infants judged to differ in security. *Developmental Psychology* **15**, 472–473.

Malatesta C.Z., Culver C., Tesman J.R. & Shepard B. (1989) The development of emotion expression during the first two years of life: Normative trends and patterns of individual differences. *Monographs of the Society for Research in Child Development* **54**(1–2), Serial No. 219.

Malatesta C.Z. & Haviland J.M. (1982) Learning display rules: The socialization of emotion expression in infancy. *Child Development* **53**, 1001–1003.

Marks I.M. & Gelder M.G. (1966) Different ages of onset in varieties of phobia. *American Journal of Psychiatry* **123**, 218–221.

Masters J.C., Burish T.G., Hollon S.D. & Rimm D.C. (1987) *Behavior Therapy: Techniques and Empirical Findings*, Vol. 3. Harcourt Brace Jovanovich, San Diego.

Matas L., Arend R.A. & Sroufe L.A. (1979) Continuity of adaptation in the second year: The relationship between quality of attachment and later competence. *Child Development* **49**, 547–556.

Matsumoto D. (1987) The role of facial response in the experience of emotion: More methodological problems and a meta-analysis. *Journal of Personality and Social Psychology* **52**, 769–774.

Matthews K. (1985) Psychological perspectives on the Type A behavior pattern. *Psychological Bulletin* **91**, 293–323.

Mattsson A., Schalling D., Olweus D., Low H. & Svensson J. (1980) Plasma testosterone, aggressive behavior, and personality dimensions in young male delinquents. *Journal of the American Academy of Child Psychiatry* **19**, 476–490.

Meltzoff A. & Moore M.K. (1989) Imitation in newborn infants: Exploring the range of gesture imitated and the underlying mechanisms. *Developmental Psychology* **25**, 954–962.

Michalson L. & Lewis M. (1985) What do children know about emotions and when do they know it? In Lewis M. & Saarni C. (eds) *The Socialization of Emotions*, pp. 117–139. Plenum, New York.

Miller L., Barrett C.L., Hampe E. & Noble H. (1972) Factor structure of childhood fears. *Journal of Consulting and Clinical Psychology* **39**, 264–268.

Miller L., Hampe E., Barrett C.L. & Noble H. (1971) Children's deviant behavior within the general population. *Journal of Consulting and Clinical Psychology* **37**, 16–22.

Mineka S. (1988) A primate model of phobic fears. In Eysenck H. & Martin I. (eds) *Theoretical Foundations of Behavior Therapy*, pp. 81–111. Plenum, New York.

Mineka S., Davidson M., Cook M. & Keiri R. (1989) Observational conditioning of snake fear in rhesus monkeys. *Journal of Abnormal Psychology* **93**, 355–372.

Montemayor R. (1982) The relationship between parent–adolescent conflict and the amount of time adolescents spend alone and with parents and peers. *Child Development* **53**, 1512–1519.

Montgomery J.C., Brincat M., Tapp A. *et al.* (1987) Effect of oestrogen and testosterone implants on psychological disorders in the climacteric. *Lancet* **1**, 297–299.

Muller E., Hollien H. & Murry T. (1974) Perceptual responses to infant crying: Identification of cry types. *Journal of Child Language* **1**, 89–95.

Mundy P. & Sigman M. (1989) Specifying the nature of the social impairment in autism. In Dawson G. (ed.) *Autism: Nature, Diagnosis, and Treatment*, pp. 3–21. Guilford Press, New York.

Murphy L.B. (1983) Issues in the development of emotion in infancy. In Plutchik R. & Kellerman H. (eds) *Emotion: Theory, Research, and Experience*, Vol. 2, *Emotions and Early Development*, pp. 1–34. Academic Press, New York.

Nelles W.B. & Barlow D.H. (1988) Do children panic? *Clinical Psychology Review* **8**, 359–372.

Nelson C.A. (1987) The recognition of facial expression in the first two years of life: Mechanisms of development. *Child Development* **58**, 889–909.

Nelson C.A. & Dolgin K. (1985) The generalized discrimination of facial expressions by seven-month-old infants. *Child Development* **56**, 58–61.

Nelson C.A., Morse D.A. & Leavitt L.A. (1979) Recognition of facial expressions by seven-month-old infants. *Child Development* **50**, 1239–1242.

Nolen-Hoeksema S. (1991) Responses to depression and their effects on the duration of depressive episodes. *Journal of Abnormal Psychology* **100**, 569–582.

Nolen-Hoeksema S., Girgus J.S. & Seligman M.E.P. (1986) Learned helplessness in children: A longitudinal study of depression, achievement, and explanatory style. *Journal of Personality and Social Psychology* **51**, 435–442.

Nottelman E.D., Inoff-Germain G., Susman E.J. & Chrousos G.P. (1990) Hormones and behavior at puberty. In Bancroft J. & Reinisch J. (eds) *Adolescence and Puberty*, pp. 88–123. Oxford University Press, New York.

Nottelman E.D., Susman E.J., Dorn L.D. *et al.* (1987) Developmental processing in early adolescence: Relations among chronologic age, pubertal stage, height, weight, and serum levels of gonadotropins, sex steroids, and adrenal androgens. *Journal of Adolescent Health Care* **8**, 246–260.

Novaco R.W. (1979) The cognitive regulation of anger and stress. In Kendall P.C. & Hollon S.D. (eds) *Cognitive-Behavioral Interventions: Theory, Research, and Procedures*, pp. 241–285. Academic Press, New York.

Nunner-Winkler G. & Sodian B. (1988) Children's understanding of moral emotions. *Child Development* **59**, 1323–1338.

O'Hara M., Schlechte J., Lewis D. & Varner M. (1991) Controlled prospective study of postpartum mood disorders: Psychological, environmental, and hormonal variables. *Journal of Abnormal Psychology* **106**, 63–73.

Ollendick T.H., King N.J. & Frary R.B. (1989) Fears in children and adolescents: Reliability and generalizability across gender, age and nationality. *Behavior Research and Therapy* **27**, 19–26.

Ollendick T.H. & Yule W. (1990) Depression in British and American children and its relation to anxiety and fear. *Journal of Consulting and Clinical Psychology* **58**, 126–129.

Olweus D. (1980) Familial and temperamental determinants of aggressive behavior in adolescent boys: A causal analysis. *Developmental Psychology* **16**, 644–666.

Olweus D., Mattsson A., Schalling D. & Low H. (1988) Circulating testosterone levels and aggression in adolescent males: A causal analysis. *Psychosomatic Medicine* **50**, 261–272.

Oster H. (1978) Facial expression and affect development. In Lewis M. & Rosenblum L.A. (eds) *The Development of Affect*, pp. 43–76. Plenum, New York.

Ozonoff S., Pennington B.F. & Rogers S.J. (1990) Are there emotion perception deficits in young autistic children? *Journal of Child Psychology and Psychiatry* **31**, 343–361.

Paikoff R.L., Brooks-Gunn J. & Warren M.P. (1991) Predictive effects of hormonal change on affective expression in adolescent females over the course of one year. *Journal of Youth and Adolescence* **20**, 191–214.

Papez J.W. (1937) A proposed mechanism of emotion. *Archives of Neurology and Psychiatry* **38**, 725–743.

Parker R. & Asher S. (1987) Peer relations and later personality adjustment: Are low-accepted children at risk? *Psychological Bulletin* **102**, 357–389.

Parton D. (1976) Learning to imitate in infancy. *Child Development* **47**, 14–31.

Patterson G.R. (1982) *Coercive Family Processes*. Castilia Press, Eugene, Oregon.

Patterson G.R. & Cobb J.A. (1971) A dyadic analysis of 'aggressive behavior'. In Hill J.P. (ed.) *Minnesota Symposia on Child Psychology*, Vol. 5, pp. 72–129. University of Minnesota Press, Minneapolis.

Pavlov I.P. (1927) *Conditioned Reflexes: An Investigation of the Physiological Activity of the Cerebral Cortex*. Oxford University Press, London.

Pavlov I.P. (1928) *Lectures on Conditioned Reflexes*, Vol. 1. Lawrence & Wishart, London.

Pearce J.B. (1978) The recognition of depressive disorder in children. *Journal of the Royal Society of Medicine* **71**, 494–500.

Penbharkkul S. & Karelitz S. (1962) Lacrimation in the neonatal and early infancy period of premature and full-term infants. *Journal of Pediatrics* **61**, 859–863.

Perry D., Perry L. & Rasmussen P. (1986) Cognitive social learning mediators of aggression. *Child Development* **57**, 700–711.

Piaget J. (1952) *The Origins of Intelligence in Children*, 2nd edn. International Universities Press, New York.

Piaget J. (1981) *Intelligence and Affectivity: Their Relationship During Child Development*. Annual Reviews, Palo Alto.

Plomin R. (1991) Genetic risk and psychosocial disorders: Links between the normal and abnormal. In Rutter M. & Casaer P. (eds) *Biological Risk Factors for Psychosocial Disorders*, pp. 101–138. Cambridge University Press, Cambridge.

Plomin R., Rende R.D. & Rutter M. (1991). Quantitative genetics and developmental psychopathology. In Cicchetti D. & Toth S. (eds) *Rochester Symposium on Developmental Psychopathology*, Vol. 2, *Internalizing and Externalizing Expressions of Dysfunction*, pp. 155–202. Lawrence Erlbaum, Hillsdale, New Jersey.

Plutchik R. (1962) *The Emotions: Facts, Theories and a New Model*. Random House, New York.

Plutchik R. (1980) A general psychoevolutionary theory of emotion. In Plutchik R. & Kellerman H. (eds) *Emotion: Theory, Research, and Experience*, Vol. 1, *Theories of Emotion*, pp. 3–33. Academic Press, New York.

Plutchik R. (1983) Emotions in early development: A psychoevolutionary approach. In Plutchik R. & Kellerman H. (eds) *Emotion: Theory, Research, and Experience*, Vol. 2, *Emotions and Early Development* pp. 221–257. Academic Press, New York.

Porges S.W. (1991) Vagal tone: An automatic mediator of affect. In Garber J. & Dodge K.A. (eds) *The Development of Emotion Regulation and Dysregulation*, pp. 111–128. Cambridge University Press, New York.

Pradhan N., Arunasmitha S. & Udaya H. (1990) Behavioral and neurochemical differences in an inbred strain of rats. *Physiology and Behavior*, **47**, 705–708.

Pritchard M. & Graham P. (1966) An investigation of a group of patients who have attended both the child and adult departments of the same psychiatric hospital. *British Journal of Psychiatry* **112**, 603–612.

Quiggle N.L., Garber J., Panak W.R. & Dodge K.A. (1992) Social information processing in aggressive and depressed children. *Child Development* **63**, 1305–1320.

Rachman S. (1977) The conditioning theory of fear-acquisition: A critical examination. *Behavior Research and Therapy* **15**, 375–387.

Rachman S. (1990) *Fear and Courage*, 2nd edn. W.H. Freeman, New York.

Resnick J.S., Kagan J., Snidman N., Gersten M., Baak K. & Rosenberg A. (1986) Inhibited and uninhibited children: A follow-up study. *Child Development* **57**, 660–680.

Revelsky F. & Black R. (1972) Crying in infancy. *Journal of Genetic Psychology* **121**, 49–57.

Rheingold H. & Eckerman C. (1973) Fear of the stranger: A critical examination. In Rease H. (ed.) *Advances in Child Development and Behavior*, Vol. 8, pp. 186–222. Academic Press, New York.

Robins L. (1966) *Deviant Children Grown Up*. Williams & Wilkins, Baltimore.

Rodriguez A., Rodriguez M. & Eisenberg L. (1959) The outcome of school phobia: A follow-up study based on 41 cases. *American Journal of Psychiatry* **116**, 540–544.

Rothbart M.K. (1973) Laughter in young children. *Psychological Bulletin* **80**, 247–256.

Rothbart M.K. & Derryberry D. (1981) Development of individual differences in temperament. In Lamb M.E. & Brown A.L. (eds) *Advances in Developmental Psychology*, Vol. 1, pp. 37–86. Lawrence Erlbaum, Hillsdale, New Jersey.

Rubin R.T., Reinisch J.M. & Hasket R.F. (1981) Postnatal gonadal steroid effects on human behavior. *Science* **211**, 1318–1324.

Ruble D.N. & Rholes W.S. (1981) The development of children's perceptions and attributions about their social world. In Harvery J.H., Ickes W. & Kidd R.F. (eds) *New Directions in Attribution Research*, Vol. 3, pp. 3–36. Lawrence Erlbaum, Hillsdale, New Jersey.

Russell J.A. & Bullock M. (1986) Fuzzy concepts and the perception of emotion in facial expressions. *Social Cognition* **4**, 309–341.

Russell J.A. & Ridgeway D. (1983) Dimensions underlying children's emotion concepts. *Developmental Psychology* **19**, 795–804.

Rutter M. (1983) Continuities and discontinuities in socio-emotional development: Empirical and conceptual perspective. In Emde R. & Harmon R. (eds) *Continuities and Discontinuities in Development*, pp. 41–68. Plenum, New York.

Rutter M. (1985) Psychopathology and development: Links between childhood and adult life. In Rutter M. & Hersov L. (eds) *Child and Adolescent Psychiatry*, pp. 720–739. Blackwell Scientific Publications, Oxford.

Rutter M. (1991) Nature, nurture, and psychopathology: A new look at an old topic. *Development and Psychopathology* **3**, 125–136.

Rutter M. & Garmezy N. (1983) Developmental psychopathology. In Hetherinton E.M. (ed.) *Socialization, Personality, and Social Development*, Vol. 4, *Mussen's Handbook of Child Psychology*, 4th edn, pp. 775–911. Wiley, New York.

Rutter M., Graham P. & Chadwick O. (1976) Adolescent turmoil: Fact or fiction? *Journal of Child Psychology and Psychiatry* **17**, 35–56.

Rutter M., Tizard J. & Whitmore K. (1970) *Education, Health, and Behavior*. Longman, London.

Ryan N.D., Puig-Antich J., Ambrosini P. *et al.* (1987) The clinical picture of major depression in children and adolescents. *Archives of General Psychiatry* **44**, 854–861.

Saab P.G., Matthews K.A., Stoney C.M. & McDonald R.H. (1989) Premenopausal and postmenopausal women differ in their cardiovascular and neuroendocrine responses to behavioral stressors. *Psychophysiology* **26**, 270–280.

Saarni C. (1979) Children's understanding of display rules for expressive behavior. *Developmental Psychology* **15**, 424–429.

Saarni C. (1990) Emotional competence: How emotions and relationships become integrated. In Thompson R. (ed.) *Socioemotional Development. Nebraska Symposium on Motivation*, Vol. 36, pp. 115–181. University of Nebraska Press.

Saarni C. & Harris P.L. (1989) *Children's Understanding of Emotion*. Cambridge University Press, Cambridge.

Sachar E.J. (1967) Corticosteroids in depressive illness. *Archives of General Psychiatry* **17**, 544–567.

Sagi A. & Hoffman M.L. (1976) Empathic distress in newborn. *Developmental Psychology* **12**, 175–176.

Sameroff A. & Chandler M. (1975) Reproductive risk and the continuum of caretaking casualty. In Horowitz F.D. (ed.) *Review of Child Development Research*, Vol. 4, pp. 187–244. University of Chicago Press, Chicago.

Saxby L. & Bryden M.D. (1984) Left-ear superiority in children for processing auditory material. *Developmental Psychology* **20**, 72–80.

Saxby L. & Bryden M.D. (1985) Left-visual-field advantage in children for processing visual emotional stimuli. *Developmental Psychology* **21**, 253–261.

Scarr S. & McCartney K. (1983) How people make their own environments: A theory of genotype environment effects. *Child Development* **54**, 424–435.

Scarr S. & Salapatek P. (1970) Patterns of fear development during infancy. *Merrill-Palmer Quarterly* **16**, 54–60.

Schneider-Rosen K. & Cicchetti D. (1984) The relationship between affect and cognition in maltreated infants: Quality of attachment and the development of visual self-recognition. *Child Development* **54**, 648–658.

Schulman A.H. & Kaplowitz C. (1977) Mirror-image response during the first two years of life. *Developmental Psychology* **10**, 133–142.

Schwartz R.M. & Trabasso T. (1984) Children's understanding of emotions. In Izard C., Kagan J. & Zajonc R. (eds) *Emotions, Cognitions, and Behavior*, pp. 409–437. Cambridge University Press, New York.

Seligman M.E.P. (1970) On the generality of the laws of learning. *Psychological Review* **77**, 406–418.

Seligman M.E.P. (1971) Phobias and preparedness. *Behavior Therapy* **2**, 307–320.

Seligman M.E.P. (1975) *Helplessness.* W.H. Freeman, San Francisco.

Seligman M.E.P., Peterson C., Kaslow N.J., Tanenbaum R.L., Alloy L.B. & Abramson L.Y. (1984) Attributional style and depressive symptoms among children. *Journal of Abnormal Psychology* **93**, 235–238.

Schaffer D. (1986) Developmental factors in child and adolescent suicide. In Rutter M., Izard C.E. & Read P.B. (eds) *Depression in Young People: Developmental and Clinical Perspectives*, pp. 383–396. Guilford Press, New York.

Shaver P., Hazan C. & Bradshaw D. (1988) Love as attachment: The integration of three behavioral systems. In Stirnberg R. & Barnes M. (eds) *The Psychology of Love*, pp. 69–99. Yale University Press, Yale, Connecticut.

Sheehan D.V., Sheehan K.E. & Minichiello W.E. (1981) Age of onset of phobic disorders: A reevaluation. *Comprehensive Psychiatry* **22**, 544–553.

Shepherd M., Oppenheim B. & Mitchell S. (1971) *Childhood Behavior and Mental Health*. University of London Press, London.

Sherman M. (1927a) The differentiation of emotional responses in infants. I: Judgments of emotional responses from motion picture views and from actual observation. *Journal of Comparative Psychology* **7**, 265–284.

Sherman M. (1927b) The differentiation of emotional responses in infants. II: The ability of observers to judge the emotional characteristics of the crying of infants and of the voice of adults. *Journal of Comparative Psychology* **7**, 265–284.

Shultz T.R. & Zigler E. (1970) Emotional concomitants of visual mastery in infants: The effects of stimulus movement on smiling and vocalizing. *Journal of Experimental Child Psychology* **10**, 390–402.

Siever L.J. & Davis K.L. (1985) Overview: Toward a dysregulation hypothesis of depression. *American Journal of Psychiatry* **142**, 1017–1031.

Sigman M. & Ungerer J. (1984) Attachment behaviors in autistic children. *Journal of Autism and Developmental Disorders* **14**, 231–244.

Silverman W.K. & Nelles W.B. (1990) Simple phobia in childhood. In Hersen M. & Last C.G. (eds) *Handbook of Child and Adult Psychopathology: A Longitudinal Perspective*, pp. 183–196. Pergamon, New York.

Smalley S.L., Asarnow R.F. & Spence M.A. (1988) Autism and genetics. *Archives of General Psychiatry* **45**, 953–961.

Smith C.A. & Lazarus R. (1990) Emotion and adaptation. In Pervin L.A. (ed.) *Handbook on Personality: Theory and Research*, pp. 609–637. Guilford, New York.

Snow M., Hertzig M. & Shapiro T. (1986) *Affective expression in young autistic children*. Paper presented at the annual meeting of the American Academy of Child Psychiatry, Los Angeles.

Sorce J., Emde R., Campos J. & Klinnert M. (1985) Maternal emotional signaling: Its effect on the visual cliff behavior of 1-year-olds. *Developmental Psychology* **21**, 195–200.

Spiker D. & Ricks M. (1984) Visual self-recognition in autistic children: developmental relationships. *Child Development* **55**, 214–225.

Spitz R.A., Emde R.N. & Metcalf D.R. (1970) Further prototypes of ego formation: A working paper from a research project on early development. *Psychoanalytic Study of the Child* **25**, 417–441.

Sroufe L.A. (1977) Wariness and the study of infant development. *Child Development* **48**, 731–746.

Sroufe L.A. (1979) Socioemotional development. In Osofsky J. (ed.) *Handbook of Infant Development*, pp. 462–515. Wiley, New York.

Sroufe L.A. (1983) Infant–caregiver attachment and patterns of adaptation in preschool: The roots of maladaptation and competence. In Perlmutter M. (ed.) *Development and Policy Concerning Children With Special Needs*, pp. 41–83. Lawrence Erlbaum, Hillsdale, New Jersey.

Sroufe L.A. & Waters E. (1976) The ontogenesis of smiling

and laughter: A perspective on the organization of development in infancy. *Psychological Review* **83**, 173–189.

Sroufe L.A., Waters E. & Matas L. (1974) Contextual determinants of infant affective response. In Lewis M. & Rosenblum L. (eds) *The Origins of Fear*, pp. 49–72. Wiley, New York.

Sroufe L.A. & Wunsch J.P. (1972) The development of laughter in the first year of life. *Child Development* **43**, 1326–1344.

Stavrakaki C., Vargo B., Boodoosingh L. & Roberts N. (1987) The relationship between anxiety and depression in children: Rating scales and clinical variables. *Canadian Journal of Psychiatry* **32**, 433–439.

Steffenberg S., Gillberg C., Hellgren L. *et al.* (1989) A twin study of autism in Denmark, Finland, Iceland, Norway and Sweden. *Journal of Child Psychology and Psychiatry* **30**, 405–416.

Stein N.L. & Trabasso T. (1989) Children's understanding of changing emotional states. In Saarni C. & Harris P.L. (eds) *Children's Understanding of Emotion*, pp. 50–77. Cambridge University Press, Cambridge.

Steinberg L. & Silverberg S. (1986) The vicissitudes of autonomy in adolescence. *Child Development* **57**, 841–851.

Stenberg C.R. & Campos J.J. (1990) The development of anger expressions in infancy. In Stein N.L., Leventhal B. & Trabasso T. (eds) *Psychological and Biological Approaches to Emotion*, pp. 247–282. Lawrence Erlbaum, Hillsdale, New Jersey.

Stern D.N. (1974) The goal and structure of mother–infant play. *Journal of the American Academy of Child Psychiatry* **13**, 402–421.

Stern D.N. (1985) *The Interpersonal World of the Human Infant*. Basic Books, New York.

Stifter C. & Fox N. (1987) Preschool children's ability to identify and label emotions. *Journal of Nonverbal Behavior* **11**, 48–54.

Stipek D.J. & DeCotis K.M. (1988) Children's understanding of the implications of causal attributions for emotional experiences. *Child Development* **59**, 1601–1610.

Strauss C.C., Lease C.A., Last C.G. & Francis G. (1988) Overanxious disorder: An examination of developmental differences. *Journal of Abnormal Child Psychology* **16**, 433–443.

Strober M. & Carlson G.A. (1982) Bipolar illness in adolescents with major depression: Clinical, genetic, and psychopharmacological predictors in a 3–4 year prospective follow-up investigation. *Archives of General Psychiatry* **39**, 549–555.

Susman E.J., Dorn L.D. & Chrousos G.P. (1991) Negative affect and hormone levels in young adolescents: Concurrent and predictive perspectives. *Journal of Youth and Adolescence* **20**, 167–190.

Susman E.J., Nottelman E.D., Inoff-Germain G., Dorn L.D. & Chrousos G. (1987) Hormonal influences on aspects of psychological development during adolescence. *Journal of Adolescent Health Care* **8**, 492–504.

Tantam D., Monaghan L., Nicholson H. & Stirling J. (1989) Autistic children's ability to interpret faces: A research note. *Journal of Child Psychiatry and Psychology* **30**, 623–630.

Taylor E.A. & Stansfeld S.A. (1984) Children who poison themselves: I. A clinical comparison with psychiatric controls. *British Journal of Psychiatry* **143**, 127–132.

Thomas A. & Chess S. (1977) *Temperament and Development*. Bruner-Mazel, New York.

Thompson R.A. (1987) Development of children's inferences of the emotions of others. *Developmental Psychology* **23**, 124–131.

Thompson R.A. (1990) Emotion and self-regulation. In Thompson R. (ed.) *Socioemotional Development* pp. 367–467. University of Nebraska Press, Lincoln, Nebraska.

Thompson R.A. & Hoffman M. (1980) Empathy and the development of guilt in children. *Developmental Psychology* **16**, 155–156.

Thyer B.A., Parrish R.T., Curtis G.C., Nesse R.M. & Cameron O.G. (1985) Ages of onset of DSM-III anxiety disorders. *Comprehensive Psychiatry* **26**, 113–122.

Tolis G. & Stefanis C. (1983) Depression: Biological and neuroendocrine aspects. *Biomedicine and Pharmacotherapy* **37**, 316–322.

Tomkins S.S. (1962) *Affect, Imagery, and Consciousness*, Vol. 1, *The Positive Affects*. Springer, New York.

Tomkins S.S. (1963) *Affect, Imagery, and Consciousness* Vol. 2, *The Negative Affects*. Plenum, New York.

Torgersen S. (1983) Genetic factors in anxiety disorders. *Archives of General Psychiatry* **40**, 1085–1089.

Tourangeau R. & Ellsworth P. (1979) The role of facial response in the experience of emotion. *Journal of Personality and Social Psychology* **37**, 1519–1531.

Trabasso T., Stein N.L. & Johnson L. (1981) Children's knowledge of events: A causal analysis of story structure. In Bower G. (ed.) *Advances in Learning and Motivation*. Vol. 15. Academic Press, New York.

Tronick E.Z. (1989) Emotions and emotional communication in infants. *American Psychologist* **44**, 112–119.

Tronick E.Z. & Gianino A. (1986) The transmission of maternal disturbance to the infant. In Tronick E. & Field T. (eds) *Maternal Depression and Infant Disturbance*, pp. 5–12. Jossey-Bass, San Francisco.

Tucker D.M., Vannatta K. & Rothlind J. (1990) Arousal and activation systems and primitive adaptative controls on cognitive priming. In Stein N., Leventhal B. & Trabasso T. (eds) *Psychological and Biological Approaches to Behavior*, pp. 145–166. Lawrence Erlbaum, Hillsdale, New Jersey.

Turk D.C., Meichenbaum D. & Genest M. (1983) *Pain and Behavioral Medicine: A Cognitive-Behavioral Perspective*. Plenum, New York.

Ushakov G.K. & Girich Y.P. (1971) Special features of

psychogenic depression in children and adolescents. In Annell A.L. (ed.) *Depressive States in Childhood and Adolescence*, pp. 510–516. Almquist & Wiksell, Stockholm.

Valentine C.W. (1930) The innate bases of fear. *Journal of Genetic Psychology* **37**, 394–419.

Vandenberg S.G., Singer S.M. & Pauls D.L. (1986) *The Heredity of Behavior Disorder in Adults and Children*. Plenum, New York.

Van Lieshout C.F.M. (1975) Young children's reactions to barriers placed by their mothers. *Child Development* **46**, 879–886.

Varanka T.M., Weller R.A., Weller E.B. & Fristad M.A. (1988) Lithium treatment of manic episodes with psychotic features in prepubertal children. *American Journal of Psychiatry* **145**, 1557–1559.

Vine I. (1973) The role of facial signalling in early social development. In Von Cranach M. & Vine I. (eds) *Social Communication and Movement: Studies of Men and Chimpanzees*, pp. 195–299. Academic Press, London.

Volkmar F.R. (1987) Social development. In Cohen D.J., Donnellan A.M. & Paul R. (eds) *Handbook of Autism and Pervasive Developmental Disorders*, pp. 41–60. Wiley, New York.

Walden T. & Field T. (1982) Discrimination of facial expression by preschool children. *Child Development* **53**, 1312–1319.

Walden T. & Field T. (1990) Preschool children's social competence and the production and discrimination of affective expressions. *British Journal of Developmental Psychology* **8**, 65–76.

Walden T. & Ogan T. (1988) The development of social referencing. *Child Development* **59**, 1230–1240.

Walker A.S. (1982) Intermodal perception of expressive behavior by human infants. *Journal of Experimental Child Psychology* **33**, 514–535.

Walker-Andrews A.S. (1986) Intermodal perception of expressive behaviors: Relation of eye and voice? *Developmental Psychology* **22**, 373–377.

Warner P., Bancroft J., Dixson A. & Hampson M. (1991) The relationship between premenstrual mood change and depressive illness. *Journal of Affective Disorders* **23**, 9–23.

Washburn R.W. (1929) A study of the smiling and laughing of infants in the first year of life. *Genetic Psychology Monographs* **6**, 393–537.

Wasz-Hockert O., Lind J., Vuorenkoski V., Partanen T. & Valenne E. (1968) *The Infant Cry: A Spectrographic and Auditory Analysis*. Clinics in Developmental Medicine, No. 29. Heinemann/SIMP, London.

Waters E., Matas L. & Sroufe L.A. (1975) Infants' reactions to an approaching stranger: Description, validation and functional significance of wariness. *Child Development* **46**, 348–356.

Waters E., Wippman J. & Sroufe L.A. (1979) Attachment, positive affect, and competence in the peer group: Two studies in construct validation. *Child Development* **50**, 821–829.

Watson D. & Clark L.A. (1984) Negative affectivity: The disposition to experience aversive emotional states. *Psychological Bulletin* **96**, 465–490.

Watson D., Clark L.A. & Carey G. (1988) Positive and negative affectivity and their relation to anxiety and depressive disorders. *Journal of Abnormal Psychology* **97**, 219–235.

Watson D. & Tellegen A. (1985) Toward a consensual structure of mood. *Psychological Bulletin* **98**, 217–235.

Watson J.B. & Rayner R. (1920) Conditioned emotional reactions. *Journal of Experimental Psychology* **3**, 1–14.

Watson J.S. (1972) Smiling, cooing and 'the game'. *Merrill-Palmer Quarterly* **18**, 323–340.

Weiner B. (1985) An attributional theory of achievement motivation and emotion. *Psychological Review* **92**, 548–573.

Weiner B., Kun A. & Benesh-Weiner M. (1980) The development of mastery, emotions, and morality from an attributional perspective. In Collins W.A. (ed.) *Minnesota Symposium on Child Psychology*, Vol. 13, pp. 103–130. Lawrence Erlbaum, Hillsdale, New Jersey.

Weinraub M. & Lewis M. (1977) The determinants of children's responses to separation. *Monographs of the Society for Research in Child Development* **42**, Serial No. 172.

Weiss B. & Garber J. (1992) *Developmental Differences in Symptoms of Depression*. Unpublished ms.

Weissman M.M., Leckman J.F., Merikangas K.R., Gammon G.D. & Prusoff B.A. (1984a) Depression and anxiety disorders in parents and children. *Archives of General Psychiatry* **41**, 845–852.

Weissman M.M., Wickramaratne P., Merikangas K.R. *et al.* (1984b) Onset of major depression in early adulthood: Increased familial loading and specificity. *Archives of General Psychiatry* **41**, 1136–1143.

Wellman H.M. & Banerjee M. (1991) Mind and emotion: Children's understanding of the emotional consequences of beliefs and desires. *British Journal of Developmental Psychology* **9**, 191–214.

Wolfe V.V., Finch A.J., Saylor C.F., Blount R.L., Pallmeyer T.P. & Carek D.J. (1987) Negative affectivity in children: A multitrait-multimethod investigation. *Journal of Consulting and Clinical Psychology* **55**, 245–250.

Wolff P.H. (1963) Observations on the early development of smiling. In Foss B.M. (ed.) *Determinants of Infant Behavior*, Vol. 2, pp. 113–138. Methuen, London.

Wolff P.H. (1969) The natural history of crying and other vocalizations in early infancy. In Foss B.M. (ed.) *Determinants of Infant Behavior*, Vol. 4. Wiley, New York.

Wolpe P.H. (1973) *The Practice of Behavior Therapy*, 2nd edn, pp. 81–109. Pergamon, Oxford.

Wooley D.E. & Timiras P.S. (1962) The gonad–brain relationship: Effects of female sex hormones on electroshock convulsion in the rat. *Endocrinology* **70**, 196–209.

Yirmiya N., Kasari C., Sigman M. & Mundy P. (1989)

Facial expressions of affect in autistic, mentally retarded, and normal children. *Journal of Child Psychology and Psychiatry* **30**, 725–735.

Young-Browne G., Rosenfeld H. & Horowitz F.D. (1977) Infant discrimination of facial expressions. *Child Development* **48**, 555–562.

Yule W., Udwin O. & Murdoch K. (1990) The 'Jupiter' sinking: Effects on children's fears, depression and anxiety. *Journal of Child Psychology and Psychiatry* **31**, 1051–1061.

Zahn-Waxler C., Chapman M. & Cummings E.M. (1984) Cognitive and social development in infants and toddlers with a bipolar parent. *Child Psychiatry and Human Development* **15**, 75–85.

Zahn-Waxler C. & Kochanska G. (1990) The origins of guilt. In Thompson R. (ed.) *Socioemotional Development*. *Nebraska Symposium on Motivation*, Vol. 36, pp. 183–258. University of Nebraska Press, Lincoln.

Zahn-Waxler C., Kochanska G., Krupnick J. & McKnew D. (1990) Patterns of guilt in children of depressed and well mothers. *Developmental Psychology* **26**, 51–59.

Zahn-Waxler C. & Radke-Yarrow M. (1982) The development of altruism: Alternative research strategies. In Eisenberg N. (ed.) *The Development of Prosocial Behavior*, pp. 109–137. Academic Press, New York.

Zahn-Waxler C., Radke-Yarrow M. & King R.A. (1979) Child rearing and children's prosocial initiations toward victims of distress. *Child Development* **50**, 319–330.

Zajonc R.B. (1980) Feeling and thinking: Preferences need no inferences. *American Psychologist* **35**, 151–175.

Zajonc R.B. (1984) On the primacy of affect. *American Psychologist* **39**, 117–123.

Zajonc R.B. (1985) Emotion and facial efference: A theory reclaimed. *Science* **228**, 15–21.

Zajonc R.B., Murphy S.T. & Inglehart M. (1989) Feeling and facial efference: Implications of the vascular theory of emotion. *Psychological Review* **96**, 396–416.

Zeitlin H. (1983) *The natural history of psychiatric disorder in childhood*. MD thesis, University of London.

Zelazo P.R. & Komer M.J. (1971) Infant smiling to non-social stimuli and the recognition hypothesis. *Child Development* **42**, 1327–1339.

Zitrin C.M. & Ross D.C. (1988) Early separation anxiety and adult agoraphobia. *Journal of Nervous and Mental Disorders* **176**, 621–625.

18: Peer Relations

STEVEN R. ASHER, CYNTHIA A. ERDLEY AND SONDA W. GABRIEL

INTRODUCTION

As children develop, they become increasingly interactive, and their social exchanges with peers become more complex. Nevertheless, even very young children demonstrate socially directed behaviours towards their peers. During the first 6 months of life, babies exhibit social interest towards their peers, as shown through behaviours such as smiling, vocalizing and reaching towards peers (Field, 1979; Fogel, 1979). In a longitudinal study of infant–peer interaction, Vandell et al. (1980) observed social interactions of 6-, 9- and 12-month-old dyads. Although most of the infant–peer sequences were brief two-unit exchanges in which one child acted and the second child responded, children spent approximately half of their time together in such social interaction. Within these exchanges, vocalizations, smiles and touches were the most frequent social acts, and these acts increased with age. From 6 to 14 months, the rate per minute of peer-directed behaviours has also been observed to increase (Hay et al., 1982).

By 2 years of age, toddler–peer interactions are longer, more complex and more coordinated. They are characterized by more repetitive, predictable and contingent patterns. Cooperative play increases, as more turn-taking, imitative, complementary and reciprocal behaviour occurs (Eckerman & Stein, 1982; Howes, 1988). Moreover, toddler–peer communication becomes more effective. The use of actions, gestures and words to convey information becomes more frequent and varied and fosters interaction between toddlers (Ross et al., 1982). From the ages of 16–32 months, there is a marked increase with age in acts coordinated with those of a peer and imitations of a peer's nonverbal actions (Eckerman et al., 1989).

Interestingly, imitation appears to be a core behavioural strategy for achieving social coordination in peer interaction prior to reliance on verbal communication. Eckerman et al. (1989) observed that the use of words to direct a peer in a coordinated way increased with age, as did the frequency of game playing. However, as Rubin and Coplan (1992) note, although infants and toddlers make advances in their social interaction abilities, they still spend a majority of their time with peers either alone, near or watching others, not in coordinated, complex social exchanges. Also, there is considerable individual variability in children's social skills and sociability that is evident during infancy (Vandell et al., 1980) and that continues to exist throughout the toddler and preschool years (Howes, 1988).

During the preschool years (3–5 years of age), both pretend play and prosocial behaviour increase, and improving language abilities contribute to more verbal interchanges between peers (Howes, 1988). In addition, preschoolers have the ability to coordinate play with a wider range of peers (Howes, 1988). As children move through the elementary school years, improvements in their abilities to resolve interpersonal dilemmas, persuade others, engage in altruistic behaviour and participate in rule-governed games occur (see Rubin & Coplan, 1992 for a review).

In summary, children do show an interest in their peers from very early in life, but as their cognitive abilities improve, the potential for more complex, coordinated and sustained peer interaction increases. These advances lay the foundation for the complex social interactions that characterize peer relations throughout later childhood and into the adult years. These advances also lay the foundation for the development of close, dyadic peer relationships, i.e. friendships. By the end of the preschool years most children have at least one reciprocated friendship and many children have more than one (Hinde *et al.*, 1985; Howes, 1988).

This chapter focuses on the development of peer relations and social competence. As will be shown, research on peer relations provides valuable insights concerning individuals at developmental risk. Clinically oriented researchers have been attracted to the study of children's peer relations because they are an important barometer of children's overall adaptation. Children's adjustment with peers is influenced by a wide range of developmental problems. Children who are physically handicapped, chronically ill or have learning problems such as mental retardation, learning disabilities or attention deficit disorder have all been found to experience lower acceptance by the peer group. So too have children whose problems involve excessive antisocial behaviour or extreme patterns of submissiveness and withdrawal, or extremely low levels of prosocial skills. The peer system is also sensitive to stressful life circumstances or events that affect children, such as poverty, minority racial or ethnic status, unemployment, divorce and abuse or neglect by parents.

As research has progressed in this area, it has become evident that children's peer relations serve vital functions, have important short-term and long-term consequences, are linked to children's competence in coping with major social tasks, and can be facilitated by systematic interventions aimed at increasing social competence. We address each of these topics. The first section considers the wide range of functions served by peer relations, describing the ways in which friendships facilitate development and affect quality of life across the lifespan. Although much of this chapter is concerned with children and youth, the first section illustrates how the functions served in childhood also continue to operate throughout people's lives.

The varied functions of peer relations suggest that children who have peer relationship problems such as low acceptance by the peer group, lack of best friends or poor friendship quality, may be likely to suffer adverse consequences. Indeed, this seems to be the case. The second section examines various lines of enquiry that demonstrate how peer relationship problems affect children's concurrent

feelings of well-being, as well as their later life adjustment. This section also highlights how research on non-human primates has informed our understanding of the short-term and long-term significance of early peer relations.

The third section focuses on the role of social competence in promoting successful adaptation to the peer group. As will be seen, our view is that social competence is a complex phenomenon involving not only behavioural skills but also important social-cognitive processes and motivational dynamics. This section describes the ways in which behavioural, social-cognitive and motivational processes govern children's success in coping with major peer relationship tasks.

The final section takes up the important topic of intervention. The existing literature in this area gives reason for optimism about adults' abilities to help children who are having peer relationship problems. Social skills interventions have frequently been effective in improving children's social skills and their acceptance by the peer group. The intervention section focuses on several central issues or decisions faced by professionals seeking to assist children. These include decisions about the criteria to be used to select children for intervention, the specific skills or programme content to be taught, the choice of treatment methods, and the types of outcomes to be assessed.

Before progressing to the discussion of the functions of friendship and peer relations, explicit attention should be given to the issue of how the concept of a peer is defined. In Western societies, where most of the research has been done, peers are typically defined as those who are similar in age, and researchers interested in peer relations among children typically do their studies in schools (Corsaro, 1981; Ladd, 1983; Asher & Gabriel, 1993), camps (Hunt & Solomon, 1942; Wright *et al.*, 1986), or organized children's sports programmes such as soccer or baseball (e.g. Fine, 1987). In each of these settings children are likely to be grouped by age. The school, of course, represents this tendency at the extreme. In this setting children are grouped with others who are typically no more than one year apart in age. The importance of school as an institution shaping children's lives is pointed out by Edwards (1992; see also Chapter 6): 'School has truly revolutionized children's social lives by causing them to spend less and less time in the traditional socializing contexts of the child care-taking relationship and the multi-age playgroup' (p. 313).

Peer interaction in the neighbourhood is more likely to be multi-age; but research in neighbourhood contexts is far less frequent (for exceptions see Bryant, 1985; Goodwin, 1990). However, even in neighbourhoods, within Western societies, children's opportunities for cross-age peer interaction are often limited by the fewer number of children per household that characterizes the modern family (see Devereaux, 1976; Edwards, 1992 for discussions of how contextual factors affect the character of children's neighbourhood interactions).

In schools, peer interactions have become increasingly segregated by age. For example, in the USA there were about 200 000 one-room schools in 1915 (Allen & Devin-Sheehan, 1976). These are settings that promoted extensive cross-age interaction. Fifty years later there were only 2000 such schools remaining (Allen & Devin-Sheehan, 1976), and the number continues to decline.

It is also the case that not all contemporary societies function according to age-graded systems. Whiting and Edwards (1988) have pointed out that in non-Western societies children of many different ages may form peer play groups. Indeed, Konner (1975) has argued that for most primate species, including humans, care-taking of a younger individual by an older one, and interactions between siblings, half-siblings and cousins in a multi-age extended family play group are much more frequent and important than are interactions with similar-aged non-kin peers. Konner (1981) also reported that in modern-day hunter—gatherer societies where people live in small bands of families (e.g. the Kalahari !Kung San), there are not large numbers of same-aged children. Children in these societies tend to form multi-aged juvenile play groups, consisting of all the children available in the small community.

FUNCTIONS OF FRIENDSHIP AND PEER RELATIONS

Considerable attention has been given to the functions served by peer relationships, and especially by close friendships. Some of this work involves interviewing children and youth about their friendship expectations (e.g. Bigelow & La Gaipa, 1975; Bigelow, 1977; Selman, 1980), whereas other studies involve direct observations of children interacting with their friends (e.g. Fine, 1980; Gottman & Parkhurst, 1980). The interview studies generally indicate developmental differences in children's conception of the role of friendships. For example, preschool-aged children describe a friend mostly as a playmate and companion, whereas in middle childhood a friend is regarded as someone who helps and shares. In adolescence, individuals emphasize the intimacy and social support functions of friendship. It should be noted, however, that although new dimensions of friendship are described by older individuals, earlier dimensions are also described, suggesting there is a cumulative effect of development. Individuals who describe their expectations in terms of the more affect-related aspects of friendship also discuss the companionship and helping nature of friendship (Bigelow, 1977; Reisman & Shorr, 1978; Selman, 1980, 1981; Berndt & Perry, 1986).

Observational studies, by contrast, tend to document that, even in younger children's friendships, more internal, affective functions of friendship are operative. For example, when Gottman and Parkhurst (1980) had mothers tape record 3—5-year-old children's conversations with their best friends, numerous instances of intimacy, shared confidences and emotional support were recorded. It may be, therefore, that the evidence of developmental change from the friendship interviews research largely reflects the development of children's verbal abilities or their knowledge of normative, cultural expectations about friendship. Although young children may not verbalize the more internal, affective functions of friendship, these qualities are evident when observing friendship exchanges between young children.

This section examines the ways in which friendships function to provide companionship and stimulation, helping and sharing, social and emotional support, and intimacy throughout the lifespan. For earlier reviews with a focus on children's friendships, see Buhrmester and Furman (1986), Hartup and Sancilio (1986) and Asher and Parker (1989). It should be stressed that these functions are not unique to peer relationships. In fact, friends, parents, siblings, spouses and teachers serve many of these functions to some degree across the individual's lifespan. Nevertheless, different sources are associated with a different profile of provisions. For children, parents are the major source of affection, self-validation and instrumental aid, whereas friends are more often sought to provide companionship and intimacy. Moreover, with development, the intimacy and emotional support provisions become increasingly important characteristics of friendships (Furman & Buhrmester, 1985, 1992).

Companionship and stimulation

When individuals are with a friend, they generally have access to a partner who is willing to spend time with them and share in various activities. Throughout the lifespan, friends typically share similar interests (Larson *et al.*, 1986; Johnson, 1989). Friends spend a large amount of time with one another, especially as they enter adolescence. Adolescents report interacting with their best friend on a daily basis, and much of this interaction occurs at school. However, friends also maintain contact with one another outside of school for as much as 3 h a day (Crockett *et al.*, 1984). As individuals enter adolescence, they typically spend more time with their friends than with their family or by themselves (Fine, 1980).

The quantity of time spent with friends may be important, but the quality of that time is also a significant factor in contributing to the companionship and stimulation provided by friends. Children report being happy while they are with their friends (Csikszentmihalyi *et al.*, 1977). When children are in the company of friends rather than non-friends, the affective climate is more pleasing (Newcomb *et al.*, 1979; Foot *et al.*, 1980), and play is more coordinated, successful, non-stereotyped and extended (Gottman & Parkhurst, 1980; Roopnarine & Field, 1984). When children are with their friends instead of alone, their time is occupied with more physically active play and activities (Medrich *et al.*, 1982). Together, these findings suggest that time spent with friends is entertaining, exciting and satisfying.

The functions of companionship and stimulation continue to be important for individuals of all ages. Throughout adulthood, friends are chosen who are similar to each other in age, sex and social class, and interactions are likely to revolve around common experiences, interests and values. Friends are normally free to engage in leisure activities and pleasure (Larson *et al.*, 1986). Whereas the greatest amount of time with family members (including the spouse) is found to be spent in maintenance (e.g. housework) and passive leisure activities (e.g. television viewing and reading), time with friends is more likely to be used to socialize, to exchange news and to engage in more active pursuits such as hobbies, shopping, religious and cultural activities, and sports (Larson *et al.*, 1986; Roberto & Scott, 1987; Shea *et al.*, 1988).

Larson *et al.* (1986) found that older adults reported much more positive affect and higher arousal with friends than with family members. These findings held regardless of the respondent's marital status, health and socioeconomic status. Interestingly, it is not simply the nature of the activities that friends participate in that makes the interactions with friends more affectively positive. Larson *et al.* (1986) found that housework, eating, sports and hobbies were characterized by higher affect and arousal when done with friends versus family members. Interactions with friends may serve not only as sources of enjoyment but also as an important mechanism for social integration into the community and broader society, especially for older individuals who might become more socially isolated later in life because of retirement, declining health and potentially decreased mobility (Chown, 1981; Crohan & Antonucci, 1989).

Helping and sharing

Friends are sources of help to one another by offering various forms of guidance and assistance. One area in which friends may aid one another is in the learning and practice of various social skills that may not only benefit the friendship but also contribute to enhancing other social relationships (Sullivan, 1953; Youniss, 1980). In the company of friends, individuals can learn about social skills such as sharing, cooperating, taking turns and dealing with conflict. Fine (1981) asserted that friendships can also serve as a context for the emergence and elaboration of self-presentation and impression-management skills. Moreover, in the safety of friends, individuals can explore the boundaries of allowable behaviour without a severe loss of face. Furthermore, as Fine (1981) noted, for children and adolescents, friends are often sources of information regarding topics on which adults could not be very helpful (e.g. how 'really' to succeed in school, news on the latest fads).

When describing their actual friendships, children of all ages almost always mention sharing and helping as part of their friendship obligations (Reisman & Shorr, 1978; Sharabany *et al.*, 1981; Smoller & Youniss, 1982; Berndt, 1986). In addition, when compared to non-friends, friends are more likely to emphasize equity in the distribution of rewards and obligations (Newcomb *et al.*, 1979). Sex differences regarding children's references to instrumental aid, helping and sharing in friendships have been found in some studies, with girls being more likely to mention these friendship responsibilities (Sharabany *et al.*, 1981; Bukowski & Newcomb, 1985; Berndt *et al.*, 1986; Parker & Asher, 1993), although other studies have not documented these sex differences (Furman & Buhrmester, 1985; Berndt, 1986).

It is generally thought that the emphasis friends place on advice, sharing, helping and other forms of instrumental aid relative to the other functions of friendship peaks during middle childhood, when the emphasis turns increasingly to intimacy and mutual understanding (Bigelow & La Gaipa, 1975; Furman & Bierman, 1984). However, in a survey of young adults, aged 17–25 years, Richey and Richey (1980) found that these individuals expected to receive a great deal of material and psychological support from friends under a wide variety of circumstances. Moreover, during the early adult transition, friends are reported to be valuable sources of assistance, providing information about education, career choices and opposite sex relationships (Tokuno, 1986).

Studies of older adults' friendships have revealed a similar pattern of expectations regarding the receipt of guidance and assistance from friends. Forms of aid mentioned as being provided by friends include advice giving, shopping, household repairs, car care, transportation, help when ill and financial aid (Roberto & Scott, 1986a; Ingersoll-Dayton & Antonucci, 1988; Shea *et al.*, 1988; see Crohan & Antonucci, 1989 for a review). However, it appears that what is more important than the actual exchange is the knowledge that the friend would help if needed (Shea *et al.*, 1988; Jones & Vaughan, 1990). That is, friends seem to provide a sense of 'reliable alliance', defined by Weiss (1974) as the feeling of security and reduction in perceived vulnerability that results from the knowledge that one can count on a friend's continuing loyalty and availability.

As is the case for younger people, reciprocity appears to be an important feature of older adults' friendships. Older individuals in friendships that were perceived to be equitable reported less stress in their relationships (in areas such as overall relationship quality, helping behaviour and affective quality) than those involved in inequitable friendships (Roberto & Scott, 1986a, 1987; Rook, 1987). In addition, those who perceived themselves as 'overbenefited' in their friendships reported more distress in their friendships than did the 'underbenefited' respondents. Roberto and Scott (1986a) suggested that the overbenefited respondents' inability to reciprocate undermined their sense of independence and self-worth. In friendships in which equity is not expected (e.g. because the partner has poor health, low income, limited mobility, etc.), the underbenefited person does not feel distressed. Furthermore, giving support to a friend can be gratifying even though nothing tangible is received in return. Roberto and Scott (1986b) found that women are more likely than men not only to be involved in a variety of affective and instrumental exchanges but also to be in inequitable relationships. It is also interesting to note that friends typically provide more emotional and companionship support, whereas family members supply more instrumental support, illustrating the complementary functions of these various sources of social support (Rook, 1987). Finally, the nature of reciprocity in friendship varies depending on the length of the specific relationship. Shea *et al.* (1988) found that, in newer friendships, the participants seem relatively concerned that 'payback' would occur fairly quickly. However, in older, long-lasting friendships there was a more communal sense, and payback could occur over a longer period.

Social and emotional support

A third major function of friendship is the provision of social and emotional support. Although several researchers (e.g. Bigelow & La Gaipa, 1975; Selman, 1980) have suggested that this provision of friendship does not emerge until early adolescence, there are several examples from studies of younger children's friendships illustrating that young friends do indeed provide social support for one another. Friends are a source of self-validation and ego support, as well as emotional security. Unlike other kinds of social relationships, friendships are based on mutual choice. Being selected as a friend indicates to a person that he or she has desirable qualities and this helps in the development and maintenance of an image of the self as competent, attractive and worthwhile (Sullivan, 1953; Weiss, 1974; Wright, 1978; Duck, 1983; Furman & Buhrmester, 1985; Furman & Robbins, 1985; Reisman, 1985; Hartup & Sancilio, 1986; Crohan & Antonucci, 1989). Through friendships, individuals find the acceptance, support, and companionship that are vital to a sense of personal worth and emotional well-being (Roberto & Scott, 1986a; Lee & Ishii-Kuntz, 1987).

Friends may provide self-validation and ego support in both direct and indirect ways. Direct forms of validation include complimenting one another, expressing care and concern about each other's problems, and boasting to peers about a friend's accomplishments in the friend's presence (Asher & Parker, 1989). There are also indirect ways that such validation is provided. Duck (1983) has suggested that by listening, attending to one another's actions and asking for advice, friends convey to each other that they respect and value one another. Moreover, friendship is a relaxed, non-threatening context in which individuals can compare their own interests, attitudes and anxieties to those of someone whom they like and admire. Upon discovering that friends share in their attitudes and beliefs, individuals are more likely to view their beliefs as valid (Festinger, 1954).

Friends also create a feeling of status, as they elicit increased prestige, higher self-esteem and feelings of importance by making favourable evaluations of one another's personal qualities. In a survey of women, aged 14–80 years, Candy *et al.* (1981) found that friends are a particularly important source of status during adolescence and during older age (over 60 years). They proposed that adolescents may use friends in an egocentric way to gain status and increase self-esteem, whereas the older group may view friends as evidence that they are still worthwhile individuals despite their retirement and the decline of participation in the larger community. During adulthood, individuals may be more likely to derive status from career, civic and family roles, with friends being less important as providers of status (Shea *et al.*, 1988).

In addition to validating one's personal worth, friends are sources of emotional security, particularly in novel or threatening situations. Emotional security results from the kind of reassurance, or even enhanced confidence, that individuals experience through the presence of a best friend (Asher & Parker, 1989). Several studies with young children have demonstrated the comfort that a friend can provide. An early and widely cited, dramatic illustration of this function was reported in a case study by Freud and Dann (1951). Near the end of World War II, six 3-year-old orphaned children were taken from a German concentration camp, where they had lived from their first year of life, to a country house in England, where they stayed for 1 year. None of the children had had a stable caregiver in the adverse living conditions of the concentration camp, and they seemed to be the only constant companions and true attachment figures in one another's lives. Observations during their time at the country house demonstrated the emotional security that these young children provided for one another. The following is a description of the children shortly after they had arrived at the country house:

> The children's positive feelings were centered exclusively in their own group. It was evident that they cared greatly for each other and not at all for anybody or anything else. They had no other wish than to be together and became upset when they were separated from each other, even for short moments. No child would

consent to remain upstairs while the others were downstairs, or vice versa, and no child would be taken for a walk or on an errand without the others. If anything of the kind happened, the single child would constantly ask for the other children while the group would fret for the missing child. (p. 131)

Clearly this is a highly unusual situation that leads to far more extreme forms of peer attachment than would normally be found. The study indicates that young peers are capable of forming extremely close attachments especially when normal parental attachment figures are unavailable. The Freud and Dann study is important not because it demonstrates what is typical but because it demonstrates the degree to which peer attachment can fill a void under extraordinary circumstances.

Laboratory studies with children reared under more typical conditions also indicate that peers can provide security during stressful events. Schwarz (1972) sent 4-year-old children into a strange room containing novel but potentially interesting toys. Children entered this room either by themselves, with an unfamiliar peer or with a friend and were observed to determine how much they explored the environment or remained relatively immobilized and anxious. It was found that children explored the room the most and exhibited the most comfort when in the presence of a friend as opposed to when they were with an unfamiliar peer or alone. In a similar vein, Ispa (1981) observed even younger children, aged 1.5 and 3 years, in a strange room with either a familiar peer, an unfamiliar peer or alone. Children displayed the most comfort in the company of a familiar peer, the least comfort when alone, and an intermediate level of comfort when they were accompanied by an unfamiliar peer. Together, these findings suggest that even for very young children, peers, especially those with whom they are familiar, are a valuable source of comfort.

Friends and familiar peers may be particularly important during times of transition. Ladd and Price (1987) found that when children made the transition from preschool into kindergarten, it helped their adjustment if some of their classmates were previously known to them. Such children were found to like school better and make fewer visits to the school nurse and were less likely to be rejected by peers. The transition from elementary school into junior high school has also been found to be facilitated by the presence of friends (Berndt, 1989). Still later in life, friends have been found to act as a buffer to lessen the anxiety and tension produced by stressful events such as widowhood (Ferraro *et al.*, 1984; Crohan & Antonucci, 1989).

Intimacy

Friends also serve as sources of intimacy. Friendship generally involves some degree of intimate self-disclosure and confiding (Sullivan, 1953; Chown, 1981; Duck, 1983; Furman & Buhrmester, 1985; Hartup & Sancilio, 1986; Roberto & Scott, 1986a; Ingersoll-Dayton & Antonucci, 1988; Shea *et al.*, 1988; Jones & Vaughan, 1990). Psychologists frequently index the closeness of a particular friendship by the amount of reciprocal intimate self-disclosure that occurs, and when individuals are unwilling to share personal or private thoughts and feelings with one another, their friendship is not considered to be close (Sullivan, 1953; Mannarino, 1976; Serafica, 1982; Oden *et al.*, 1984). Moreover, it appears that among older adults the affective and personal domains make a more significant contribution to friendship well-being than do different aspects of social exchange, such as equity and reciprocity (Jones & Vaughan, 1990).

As children get older, they increasingly emphasize intimacy, self-disclosure and openness as important components of friendship. They convey these elements both when discussing their general beliefs about friendships (Bigelow & La Gaipa, 1975; Bigelow, 1977; Reisman & Shorr, 1978; Hunter & Youniss, 1982; Smoller & Youniss, 1982; Furman & Bierman, 1984) and when describing their actual friendships (Sharabany *et al.*, 1981; Crockett *et al.*, 1984; Berndt, 1986; Berndt & Perry, 1986). Compared to younger children, children over 8 years of age possess more intimate knowledge about their friends (Diaz & Berndt, 1982), describe their friends in a more integrated and extensive manner (Peevers & Secord, 1973) and view their friendships as more exclusive and individualized (Sharabany *et al.*, 1981; Smoller & Youniss, 1982).

Although young children do not report intimacy as a characteristic of their friendships, this does not mean that intimacy is not an important component of their relationships. By using an observational methodology, Gottman (Gottman & Parkhurst, 1980; Gottman, 1983) has shown that young children do participate in intimate, committed relationships with their peers. Gottman (1983) found that exploration of similarities and differences, self-disclosure and positive affective remarks occurred during the play of dyads of 3–9-year-old children, and such statements appeared important not only for building, but also for maintaining these children's friendships. Other researchers have also found that young children participate in intimate exchanges. For example, Reisman and Shorr (1978) reported that more than half of their 7–8-year-old subjects said they had talked about a problem with a friend. Ladd and Emerson (1984) found that as early as first grade (approximately 6–7 years old), close friends knew more about one another and were more aware of their similarities and differences than pairs of children who were not close friends. Thus, the evidence suggests that even young children's relationships with peers are characterized by intimacy.

Throughout the lifespan, females appear to be involved in more intimate friendships than males. Compared with males, females have been found to place greater emphasis on confiding and emotional support in their childhood friendships (Parker & Asher, 1993). This gender difference continues during adolescence and throughout the lifespan, into the retirement years (Wright, 1989). Although females are more intimate and self-disclosing in their same-sex friendships than are males (Reisman, 1990), interesting differences in the intimacy of cross-sex friendships occur across the lifespan. During adolescence, males report the same amount of disclosure to both males and females, whereas females report less intimacy with males than females. During early adulthood, males report higher levels of self-disclosure to females than to males, whereas females report similar levels to females and males (Reisman, 1990). Thus, both sexes become more confiding in their cross-sex relationships during young adulthood than they were during adolescence. Such cross-sex friendships occur more frequently among single young adults than any other age group (Wright, 1989). For both males and females, Reisman (1990) found a significant relation between reported self-disclosure and feelings of satisfaction with the friendship. It is not surprising, then, that Reisman found that females reported feeling significantly greater closeness and satisfaction with same-sex friends than did males.

It appears that gender differences in the intimacy of friendships during old age are consistent with, and may be an accentuation of, the patterns observed throughout adulthood (Wright, 1989). Cross-gender friendships amongst the elderly have been found to be relatively rare, perhaps because of demographic constraints and/or cultural norms. Older women are more likely than older men to have friends who are confidants, and their friendships are more apt to be close and intimate. Thus, older women would be more likely to continue to experience intimacy in their friendships than would men (Wright, 1989).

Given the important functions of peer relations described in this section, it seems plausible that individuals who have difficulties in their peer relationships would experience a variety of short-term and long-term negative consequences. The next section describes some of the more widely studied consequences.

CONSEQUENCES OF PEER RELATIONSHIP DIFFICULTIES

Most of the research on the consequences of early peer relationships has been conducted with humans. However, there is a smaller, yet nonetheless very significant, literature that points to the important role of peer relations in non-human primates. This section begins by discussing this literature, because it provides some fascinating insights into the possible consequences of peer relationship difficulties in the course of development.

Insights from the non-human primate literature

It is not possible experimentally to isolate human infants to investigate the long-term consequences that the deprivation of social contact would impose on the development of normal patterns of behaviour. However, there is an extensive literature examining the effects of social deprivation in non-human primates. Non-human primates, like humans, are highly social animals, and the typical early experience for most species of non-human primates includes growing up in a social group composed of related and unrelated animals of both genders and many different ages. Research using non-human primate models of human experience has contributed greatly to an increased understanding of many aspects of human psychological dysfunction, including depression (Rosenblum & Paully, 1987; Suomi, 1991), grief processes (McKinney, 1986; Laudenslager, 1988) and child abuse and neglect (Reite, 1987). The rhesus macaque (*Macaca mulatta*) and the chimpanzee (*Pan troglodytes*) are perhaps the most commonly used non-human primate species in social deprivation research. Experimental manipulations of early experience in non-human primates include rearing in social isolation, rearing only with the mother, rearing only with peers, separation from the mother, separation from peers and separation from both mother and peers.

In the non-human primate literature, the term social isolation is typically used to refer to conditions in which an animal is removed from its mother at birth and reared without opportunity for physical contact with another member of its own species. Social isolation of non-human primate infants for at least the first 6 months of life has been found to produce serious, long-term behavioural abnormalities, including the frequent performance of complex and idiosyncratic stereotypic behaviour, and very severe social, sexual, maternal and cognitive deficits (Davenport & Rogers, 1970; Harlow & Suomi, 1974; Davenport, 1979; see Mitchell, 1970 for an excellent review).

The importance of peers in the social development of non-human primates has been examined by rearing infants only with their mothers, thus depriving them of peer contact, and by rearing infants only with peers, without maternal contact. Although there appear to have been no direct comparisons of these two rearing manipulations focusing on behavioural outcomes, it is nevertheless interesting to compare the results across studies. To examine the effects of peer deprivation, infant rhesus macaques have been reared in individual cages with only their mothers as companions for the first few months of life (Alexander & Harlow, 1965; Alexander, 1966). When animals reared in

this condition (mother-only monkeys) were placed in groups with peers, they displayed deficits in play behaviour, were hyperaggressive and also showed a reluctance to make contact with their peers (Suomi, 1979). Repeated observations of the mother-only monkeys in many different situations over several years indicated that their social deficiencies, although not as profound as those reared in social isolation, were displayed well into adulthood (Mitchell, 1970).

Rearing infants only with peers, without contact with mothers, has resulted in somewhat different patterns of behaviour than those seen in mother-only rearing. In these experiments, infant rhesus macaques have been removed from their mothers shortly after birth, and housed with one or more infants as companions (Chamove, 1973). These 'together-together' monkeys (so-called because of their tendency to cling excessively to one another) typically do not develop normal play behaviour. In addition, such monkeys show elevated levels of anxiety, fearfulness and withdrawal, relative to mother- and peer-reared rhesus macaques (Chamove *et al.*, 1973; Higley & Suomi, 1989).

In sum, it appears that while both mother-only and peer-only monkeys show deficits in play behaviour, the peer-only monkeys become highly withdrawn and fearful, and are not particularly aggressive. This contrasts with the pattern shown by mother-only monkeys, who appear to exhibit high rates of aggressive behaviour along with a reluctance to make contact with other monkeys. (For interesting research on the co-occurrence of aggression and withdrawal in human children, see Ledingham, 1981.)

A different line of evidence regarding the importance of early experience focuses on the effects of separating a non-human primate infant from peers to whom it has become attached. This research, to be fully understood, should be prefaced with a brief discussion of the effects of maternal separation. Rhesus macaque infants who are separated from their mothers for 2 or 3 weeks exhibit the signs of anaclitic depression (Harlow & Suomi, 1974), a syndrome characterized by an initial period of agitation and protest followed by despair and depression. Even brief periods of maternal separation (e.g. 6 days) have been found to result in long-term effects on behaviour, with previously separated monkeys spending more time close to their mothers 2 years after separation (Hinde & McGinnis, 1977).

Interestingly, the effects of maternal separation appear to vary by species, in large part because in some species of non-human primates other members of the social group may fill the void left by the absent mother by providing what is referred to as allomaternal care. For example, Rosenblum and Kaufman (1968) and, more recently, Laudenslager *et al.* (1990) described very different behavioural reactions to maternal separation in pigtail (*Macaca nemestrina*) and bonnet (*Macaca radiata*) monkey infants. Bonnet macaque infants, who received allomaternal care from other females in the group during maternal separation, exhibited an agitation phase that did not progress to the depression characteristic of separated pigtail and rhesus macaque infants. These findings raise an interesting question. Is it the genetic composition of the different species that causes the different reactions to separation, or is it their differing social environments? Research by Kaufman and Stynes (1978) was designed to answer this question. Kaufman and Stynes raised a bonnet macaque infant in a group with its mother and other bonnet and pigtailed macaques, and then removed the infant's mother and other bonnet macaques from the group, leaving the infant with only pigtailed macaques. The pigtailed macaques did not provide allomaternal care for the bonnet macaque infant, resulting in a depressive reaction to separation in the infant.

Depressive behaviour can also be induced in non-human primates by means of separation from peers. Suomi *et al.* (1970) repeatedly separated peer-only reared rhesus monkeys from one another. Behaviour similar to that of monkey infants separated from their mothers was seen, i.e. a period of initial protest followed by despair (Suomi *et al.*, 1970). In addition, these monkeys showed severe maturational delays that persisted long after reunion with their peers. For example, at 9 months of age multiply separated peer-only reared monkeys had not developed normal patterns of play or other complex social behaviour, instead spending much of their time clinging to peers, a behavioural pattern more characteristic of 3-month-old infants (Harlow & Suomi, 1974). Chimpanzee infants reared without mothers, but with peers as companions, also show a strong separation reaction, including agitation, protest and withdrawn behaviour, when separated from these peers and placed in isolation (Snyder *et al.*, 1984).

The significance of peer contact for non-human primates is also illustrated by maternal separation studies showing that the presence of even unfamiliar peers can compensate for the loss of the mother, reducing the negative behavioural effects of separation. For example, Suomi *et al.* (1973) examined the effects of permanent maternal separation on rhesus macaque infants. Infants who were housed with a peer following maternal separation developed relatively normal patterns of behaviour, after an initial period of protest. In contrast, infants housed individually after separation exhibited chronic despair behaviour, and by 6 months of age these animals behaved like monkeys reared from birth in social isolation (Harlow & Suomi, 1974).

The 'nuclear family' separation studies conducted by Harlow (1971) also demonstrate the significant role of peer contact. Five-year-old (i.e. virtually adult) rhesus macaques, who had lived their entire lives as members of social groups composed of four mother–father pairs and their offspring, were separated from their familiar social groups and housed either with familiar peers, with familiar and unfamiliar peers or alone. Those animals who were housed alone developed severe depression after an extensive initial period of agitation, whereas those monkeys housed with peers, especially those with familiar peers, were relatively undisturbed by the separation.

Peers can also serve to rehabilitate non-human primates previously reared in social isolation. These rhesus monkeys, when gradually exposed to younger, socially competent infants and then housed in social groups with other isolates, are able, over time, to acquire some degree of social functioning and make a significant recovery (Novak & Harlow, 1975; Novak, 1979). Similar results have been obtained in efforts to rehabilitate former isolate chimpanzees. Chimpanzees who had undergone long-term social isolation beginning in infancy who are then placed, as adolescents or adults, in rehabilitation programmes with peers often are able to recover a significant degree of sociosexual functioning over time (Davenport & Rogers, 1970; Rogers, 1973; Pfeiffer & Koebner, 1978; Maple,

1980; Gabriel, 1986; Bloomsmith *et al.*, 1988).

The non-human primate studies reviewed in this section lead to two major conclusions. First, it appears that, just as removal from maternal contact can have serious deleterious effects, so too the removal of an individual from peers can substantially alter the course of normal development. Second, peers can serve to mitigate the effects of the traumatic experience of being separated from the mother and to rehabilitate non-human primates suffering from psychological disturbance as a result of prolonged social isolation.

Emotional consequences of peer relationship difficulties in childhood

In this section, attention is turned to the consequences of poor peer relationships in humans. It seems likely that these consequences would include increased feelings of loneliness, alienation and general dissatisfaction with one's social relationships. There is a large literature on loneliness in adulthood which points to the prevalence of loneliness in human society and indicates that individuals who are deficient in social relationships and lacking in social skills are indeed more lonely (Peplau & Perlman, 1982; Rook, 1988). Only recently, however, has a literature on loneliness in childhood emerged. Within the past decade several formal measures have been developed to assess loneliness in children (Asher *et al.*, 1984; Heinlein & Spinner, 1985; Marcoen & Brumagne, 1985), and it appears that feelings of loneliness can be reliably measured even in children as young as 5 and 6 years of age (Cassidy & Asher, 1992), apparently the youngest age group studied to date. Children in interview studies (Cassidy & Asher, 1992; Williams & Asher, 1992) demonstrate that they have a clear understanding of the meaning of loneliness (for young children loneliness means being alone and feeling sad), and children have a good understanding of the various kinds of life situations that can elicit feelings of loneliness. For example, Hayden *et al.* (1988) found several different kinds of eliciting factors, including loss of an important other, moving to an unfamiliar setting, temporary absence of an important other, conflict, rejection, broken loyalties, exclusion and being ignored.

There are several different lines of research that indicate a relation between loneliness and a child's adaptation in the peer group. Three different aspects of peer adaptation have been studied. One of these involves acceptance by peers. Acceptance refers to how well accepted or liked a child is by other members of the group. Acceptance can be operationalized by using rating-scale sociometric measures (Roistacher, 1974; Singleton & Asher, 1977) in which children rate (e.g. on a 1–5 scale) how much they like to play with, work with or be in a group with each of the other group members. It can also be operationalized by using a combination of positive nomination (e.g. 'Who do you like most?') and negative nomination (e.g. 'Who do you like least?') sociometric measures (Gronlund, 1959; Peery, 1979; Coie *et al.*, 1982; Newcomb & Bukowski, 1983). Studies with 5 and 6 year olds (Cassidy & Asher, 1992), 8–11 year olds (Asher *et al.*, 1984; Asher & Wheeler, 1985, Crick & Ladd, 1993), and 12–13-year-old students (Parkhurst & Asher, 1992) indicate that feelings of loneliness are more prevalent among children who are poorly accepted by their peers.

What are everyday interactions like for poorly accepted children that might cause them to feel lonely? First, there is evidence that poorly accepted children have more difficulty entering groups (Putallaz & Gottman, 1981), even when they employ entry strategies that are similar to those of their better accepted peers (Dodge *et al.*, 1983). Playground observations of low accepted children at school also indicate that such children are more likely to move frequently from one group to another and seem to be unable to sustain interactions with other children (Ladd, 1983). Low accepted children might also experience higher levels of overt rejection or even victimization. We have recently observed children at school using a wireless transmission methodology that allowed us to record both speech and non-verbal behaviour from a considerable distance (Asher & Gabriel, 1993). These observations document the wide variety of overt rejections that children experience in their day-to-day lives. These include being excluded, being denied access to information, resources or assistance, being targeted for aggression and receiving moral disapproval. Evidence from Perry *et al.* (1988) indicates that most victimized children are sociometrically rejected, and research by Olweus (1978) indicates that victimized children experience lower self-esteem. It seems plausible, then, that much of the loneliness that low accepted children experience could be due to overt rejection or even victimization.

A second and conceptually distinct aspect of peer adaptation involves best friendship. Friendship refers to the establishment of a particular dyadic relationship between two children that is characterized by strong mutual liking, a mutually expressed preference for one another and some shared history. Friendships can be assessed by using reciprocal sociometric friendship nominations as the key criterion for identification of friendship pairs. Recently, Parker and Asher (1993) found that friendship made an independent and additive contribution to children's feelings of well-being versus loneliness. Children who had a best friend were less lonely than children who lacked a best friend. This contribution of having a friend occurred at each level of acceptance. In other words, children who were low in acceptance benefitted from having a friend, as did children who were average or high in acceptance by their peers.

The quality of a child's best friendship is a third aspect of peer adaptation. Friendship quality refers to whether a friendship is characterized by dimensions such as companionship and recreation, emotional security and support, trust and loyalty, intimacy and the capacity to resolve interpersonal conflicts. Parker and Asher (1993), building on earlier efforts by Berndt (1984; Berndt & Perry, 1986), Bukowski *et al.* (1987) and others (e.g. Furman & Buhrmester, 1985; Hartup & Sancilio, 1986), operationalized friendship quality by giving children a questionnaire in which they reported on qualitative aspects of their best friendships. The questionnaire was individualized, so that the name of each child's best friend actually appeared in each of the questionnaire items (e.g. 'Jamie and I do special favours for each other'). Parker and Asher found that the qualities of a child's best friendship, that is, whether the friendship was characterized by supportiveness, guidance and assistance, validation, and so on predicted to feelings of loneliness versus well-being, and that the prediction was above and beyond the prediction that could be made based on simply knowing whether a child was accepted by peers.

The connection between peer relationship problems and loneliness fits with evidence about the link between peer adaptation and other types of psychological difficulties. There is evidence that peer acceptance relates to feelings of depression in children (Vosk *et al.*, 1982) and to feelings of anxiety (Hymel & Franke, 1985; Hymel *et al.*, 1985). Rubin *et al.* (1990) have recently speculated that peer relationship difficulties in childhood could be part of a pathway toward later serious 'internalizing' types of difficulties. These might include extreme withdrawal or depression in adulthood. Certainly the existing data on the links between peer relationship problems and loneliness, depression and anxiety tend to suggest that, for a certain proportion of children, peer relationship problems may be associated with these sorts of internalizing difficulties. One qualifying point is needed, however. There is evidence from recent studies that not all children who are rejected by their peers report elevated feelings of loneliness. Studies by Parkhurst and Asher (1992) and Williams and Asher (1987) indicate that when children who are rejected by their peers are subclassified according to their typical behavioural style, children who are submissive and rejected report higher levels of loneliness than do children who are aggressive and rejected. Whether the lower levels of loneliness amongst aggressive-rejected children result from defensive reporting processes or from the fact that some of these children form relationships with other aggressive youngsters (Cairns *et al.*, 1987), and are therefore not as isolated, is an issue that will need to be studied in future research. For now, it is important to stress that not all rejected children appear to be at risk for internalizing problems, and that indeed many of them tend instead to be on a pathway towards conduct disorder and later delinquency (Parker & Asher, 1987; Kupersmidt *et al.*, 1990; Rubin *et al.*, 1990).

Long-term consequences

Evidence regarding the long-term risks associated with peer relationship problems is a third and particularly compelling source of evidence concerning the consequences of peer relationship difficulties. Several decades ago, some studies were published that brought the attention of researchers to the possibility that low acceptance by peers in childhood could be predictive of later life adjustment problems. These long-term risk studies captured the attention of researchers, and served, as Kupersmidt *et al.* (1990) noted, as 'a potent stimulus for much of the current interest in children's peer relations' (p. 274). Three of the best-known studies of this period can be described to capture the extent and variety of the evidence that emerged.

One of these studies focused on the important topic of early school leaving. Gronlund and Holmlund (1958) administered positive nomination sociometric measures to over 1000 11-year-old students, following up a sample of 53 high accepted children and 49 low accepted children to compare their rates of dropping out of school. The high accepted children left school before graduation at a rate of 13%, compared to a drop-out rate for the low status children of 45%.

A second study focused on mental health outcomes. Cowen *et al.* (1973) examined a county psychiatric register to learn whether individuals who had taken part in an early detection mental health screening programme 11–13 years earlier had later received psychiatric services. Cowen *et al.* (1973) found that individuals with mental health problems had received significantly more negative nominations from peers in third grade on a peer assessment measure than individuals who did not appear in the psychiatric register. In fact, mental health problems were more strongly related to negative peer assessment scores than to teacher ratings, or to ratings of physical health, intellectual potential, academic performance, self-esteem and anxiety.

The third of these studies focused on the prediction of conduct disorder. Roff (1961) examined the child guidance clinical files of men in military service, and found that a much greater percentage of men who had disciplinary records of bad conduct or had received bad conduct discharges had had poor peer relationships as children, compared to men with good conduct records (56 and 26%, respectively).

Studies such as these have been guided by one of two implicit models (Parker & Asher, 1987). The first, a causal model, stems from the accumulating evidence described in the previous section that normative peer interaction serves many functions, and may play a very important role in the social,

cognitive and moral development of children. Because poorly accepted children are often excluded from peer interaction, they therefore are less likely to be able to engage in normal socialization experiences and garner the important benefits children derive from interacting with their peers. Eventually, poorly accepted children, because of long-term rejection and isolation from peers, would be expected to develop extreme and idiosyncratic modes of behaviour and cognition, and be more likely to succumb to stress, deviant influences and breakdown. Thus, poorly accepted children can be at risk for dropping out of school and criminality, and are more vulnerable to psychological instability.

The alternate, incidental model does not assume that peer relationship problems in childhood are responsible for later life difficulties. Rather, according to this model, disorders that will be seen to emerge fully in adulthood are present in an early form in childhood. Thus, an underlying disturbance (e.g. schizophrenia) leads to deviant behaviour in childhood, resulting in a negative influence on peer relationships. According to this model, early forms of disorder are responsible both for peer relationship problems in childhood and later maladaptive outcomes. In other words, according to the incidental model, poor peer relationships serve as a kind of 'lead indicator' of subsequent life difficulties. Parker and Asher (1987) suggest that what is needed is a more comprehensive model of the linkages between peer relationships and later maladjustment, one that allows for feedback between the causes of poor peer acceptance, the consequences of poor acceptance and the course of later maladjustment.

Regardless of the model that will best explain findings about long-term outcomes, it is important to know whether the three highly cited studies discussed above are representative of the larger body of studies addressing the links between peer adjustment and later outcomes. The more extensive literature has been recently reviewed by Parker and Asher (1987) and Kupersmidt *et al.* (1990). Several conclusions emerge from these reviews. The first conclusion concerns differences in predicted outcomes. The premise that at-risk children can be identified from peer relationship measures is strongest with regard to the outcome of dropping out of school. In numerous studies, children identified as low in peer acceptance dropped out at rates two, three and even eight times as high as other children. On average, about 25% of low accepted elementary school children left school before graduation, compared with about 8% of other children (Parker & Asher, 1987; Asher & Parker, 1989). Somewhat surprisingly, the weakest predictions have been in the area of psychopathology. This may be related to the fact that much of the research relating peer relationship problems to psychopathology has focused on very serious and low prevalence disorders such as schizophrenia (Parker & Asher, 1987; Kupersmidt *et al.*, 1990). The prediction of non-specified mental health problems in adolescence or adulthood (e.g. Cowen *et al.*'s 1973 evidence of contact with a mental health professional) appears to be somewhat more consistently successful than the prediction of schizophrenia (Kupersmidt *et al.*, 1990).

Second, the extent to which future negative outcomes (i.e. dropping out of school, criminality and psychopathology) can be accurately predicted for children varies as a function of the type of peer relationship index considered. The two indices of problematic peer relationships studied most successfully are peer acceptance and aggression, and it appears that acceptance and aggression show somewhat different relations to dropping out of school and criminality. Low peer acceptance is more predictive of later dropping out of school than criminality, whereas aggressiveness is more predictive of later criminality than dropping out of school (Parker & Asher, 1987).

A third conclusion from the risk literature is that, although peer relationship measures generally provide high overall predictive efficacy, they also make a significant number of errors of prediction. These predictive errors tend to follow a pattern characterized by few false negative errors and many false positive errors. In other words, although measures of peer relationship problems are fairly sensitive to those children who will eventually show problematic outcomes, they also tend to overselect children who are not actually at risk for serious later life difficulties. The extent to which one needs to be concerned about the degree and direction of prediction error depends on why children are being identified. If children are being selected to receive an intervention that may be stigmatizing, then researchers should avoid choosing children who are not actually in need of treatment. However, if the negative effects of labelling can be avoided and the intervention is one that may be helpful to many children, then over-selection is less of a concern.

THE ROLE OF SOCIAL COMPETENCE

Children vary considerably in the extent to which they gain acceptance from peers and form friendships with other children. The factors that contribute to children's success in the peer group are many, and it is important to appreciate that there are factors other than social competence that are influential. These include physical appearance, ethnicity, academic competence, athletic prowess and socioeconomic status. Nonetheless, children's social behaviour seems to be an especially important contributor to acceptance and friendship (see Rockhill & Asher, 1992 for recent evidence), and for this reason most of the research on peer acceptance and friendship has focused on the role of social competence in the origin and maintenance of children's status in the peer group (for recent reviews see Asher & Coie, 1990). This section provides a brief portrait of the behavioural characteristics of better accepted versus low-accepted children. Following this, we examine the kinds of thought processes and motivational dynamics that may give rise to behavioural variations and to differences in children's success with peers.

Social tasks and social behaviour

For children as for adults, peer relations pose a series of challenging tasks. Observations of social life suggest the existence of a large number of distinct types of social tasks. These include tasks such as initiating interaction or friendship, maintaining ongoing work or play relationships, persuasion, coping with winning or losing, responding to teasing and other forms of ambiguous provocation, managing conflict, defending the self, recruiting help or support, offering assistance and coping with rejection. Additional complexity is added by the fact that social life involves not only the pursuit of single goals but the coordination of multiple goals that may at times conflict with one another (Dodge *et al.*, 1989). For example, a child may be strongly orientated towards winning a game but at the same time be striving to maintain a positive relationship between himself or herself and the game opponent. Or, to provide another example, a child may want to get help with a problem but may not want to appear to be helpless or incompetent.

Everyday life is filled with such dilemmas and it appears that better accepted and low accepted children differ in how they respond to the social tasks they confront. In general, better accepted children are those who are more likely to engage in prosocial behaviour, be more cooperative in play, participate in social conversations, be active in interactions, be leaders and share more often (Coie & Kupersmidt, 1983; Dodge, 1983; Ladd, 1983). Better accepted children also have been found to engage in interactions of longer duration, have more affectively positive encounters and be less likely to terminate social interaction (Dodge, 1983). In a group entry situation, better accepted children have been observed to make more group-orientated statements, to attempt to determine the frame of reference common to the group members and then to establish themselves as sharing in this frame of reference (Putallaz & Gottman, 1981). Such behaviour is consequently apt to lead to acceptance and integration into the ongoing interaction. When better accepted children must deal with social conflicts, they are more likely to engage in constructive, prosocial solutions (Chung & Asher, 1992). They are also less apt to seek adult assistance (Asher & Renshaw, 1981; Chung & Asher, 1992), perhaps because, even for young children, seeking help from adults is not a predominant mode of resolving conflicts with peers (Hay, 1984). Moreover, when they encounter an ambiguous provocation by a peer, they are more apt to respond by asking the peer for clarification of the actions (Dodge *et al.*, 1984). When social failure is experienced, better accepted children are more likely to exhibit mastery oriented responses (Goetz & Dweck, 1980).

In contrast, low accepted children are more apt to participate in disruptive, aggressive, uncooperative and other non-normative behaviours, engage in solitary and inappropriate play, be more negative and exclude peers from play (Coie *et al.*, 1982;

Dodge *et al.*, 1982; Coie & Kupersmidt, 1983; Dodge, 1983). In group entry situations, low-accepted children are more likely to be disruptive, ask intrusive questions and call unnecessary attention to themselves (Putallaz & Gottman, 1981; Dodge *et al.*, 1983). When low-accepted children encounter social conflict, they are more likely to respond aggressively and escalate the conflict (Coie *et al.*, 1991). Moreover, when a peer performs an act of provocation with ambiguous motives, they are more apt to respond with aggression (Dodge, 1980; Dodge & Frame, 1982; Dodge *et al.*, 1984). When social failure is experienced, low accepted children are more likely to exhibit helpless responses, including withdrawal from the social encounter (Goetz & Dweck, 1980). Perhaps for all of these reasons, low accepted children are not only more likely to be alone, but also when they do interact, their interaction is more likely to be of shorter duration and with smaller groups, younger children or other low accepted children (Dodge, 1983; Ladd, 1983).

As these differences in the behaviour patterns of low and better accepted children have been identified, researchers have increasingly begun to focus on the social-cognitive processes that might underlie these behavioural differences and thus contribute to differences in peer acceptance. A variety of social-cognitive factors have been examined. It appears that children who vary in their level of peer acceptance show differences in their attributions of peers' intent, social goals and concerns, social strategy knowledge, social outcome expectations and attributions for social success and failure. The differences in these components of social information processing are associated with differences in children's behaviours in various kinds of social interactions. The next sections discuss these processes and examine how they operate when children face certain critical social tasks.

Attributions about the intentions of others

As children witness some action in their social world, the interpretations they make have important implications for their subsequent behaviour. Most studies concerning children's attributions about others' intentions have focused on a child's interpretations of a protagonist who performs with ambiguous intentions some potentially provoking act that has negative consequences for the child. An example of this can be seen on the playground when one child throws a ball that hits another child on the back. The child who is hit must interpret the protagonist's intentions and then decide how to respond. Another example of ambiguous provocation is teasing, where the recipient must infer whether the protagonist was being playful or intending harm (e.g. Eder, 1987).

Research on attributions of intentions has been pursued most extensively by Dodge and co-workers (e.g. Dodge, 1980; Dodge & Newman, 1981; Dodge & Frame, 1982). They have explored differences in the social perceptions of low-accepted, aggressive versus better accepted, non-aggressive boys. Dodge (1980) found that when compared to better accepted, non-aggressive boys, low accepted, aggressive boys were more likely to interpret a protagonist's behaviour in an ambiguous situation as having hostile intent. This same tendency to attribute hostile intentions to a protagonist was likewise documented in a group of aggressive emotionally disturbed boys (Nasby *et al.*, 1980).

In addition, the low-accepted, aggressive boys in Dodge's (1980) study were more likely to say that they would retaliate against the protagonist with an aggressive behavioural response; they expected to be the recipients of more aggression in the future; and they mistrusted the protagonist more. These findings led Dodge (1980) to propose a cyclical relation between attributions and aggressive behaviour. The cycle begins with an ambiguous action that low-accepted, aggressive children attribute to the peer's hostile intention. This attribution 'confirms' the children's general image of peers as hostile and may increase the likelihood that they will interpret future behaviours as hostile. Based on their hostile attribution, children will aggress against the peer, who will aggress back, further confirming for the low-accepted, aggressive children that others are acting with hostile intent towards them.

Interestingly, when examining other factors that have an influence on low-accepted, aggressive boys' tendency to attribute hostile intent, Dodge and Frame (1982) determined that these children believed that the protagonist had purposely caused the harm only when the negative actions or outcomes were directed at them and did not attribute hostility when another peer was the victim. This suggests that these children have a paranoid view of others rather than a cynical view, since they seemed to believe that peers were acting towards them with hostile intent, but peers were not generally viewed as acting towards other people with hostile intent. Thus, the aggressive behaviour of low-accepted, aggressive children appears to be related to the kinds of attributions they make about peers' intentions.

Although low-accepted, aggressive children exhibit systematic differences in attributing hostile intent depending on the victim (self versus peer), they continue to attribute hostility more than their better accepted, non-aggressive peers regardless of their feelings about the protagonist. Fitzgerald and Asher (1991) presented to children a set of hypothetical ambiguous provocation situations. In some situations the protagonist was a peer highly liked by the subject and in other situations the protagonist was a peer highly disliked by the subject. Despite the fact that children (both boys and girls were subjects in this study) attributed less hostility overall to highly liked peers, the greater tendency to attribute hostile intent still appeared in low-accepted, aggressive children, regardless of how well liked the protagonist was. Specifically, towards both highly liked and highly disliked peers, when compared to better accepted, non-aggressive children, low-accepted, aggressive children were more likely to infer negative intent and to report that they would respond aggressively to the protagonist. Thus, low-accepted, aggressive children seem to believe that others act towards them in hostile way, even when the protagonist is someone they report liking. Furthermore, they think the protagonist should be the recipient of harsh treatment.

Together, these findings suggest that low-accepted children, particularly those classified as aggressive, tend to believe that their peers intend to harm them. It is not surprising, then, that they are more likely than their better accepted peers to report that they would aggress in provoking situations (Dodge *et al.*, 1984). This antisocial behaviour is then apt to contribute to the maintenance of their low acceptance in the peer group.

Interpersonal goals

Differences in individuals' social goals may also help explain why people respond differently to the same social situation. Goals are defined as the intended outcome that the person is trying to achieve (Pervin, 1989). As Ford (1982) noted, social competence has often been described in terms of being able to achieve desired goals. However, this definition has overlooked the possibility that people may be pursuing maladaptive goals in their social interactions. It seems that the goals one chooses to pursue might help to account for individual differences in social competence (Renshaw & Asher, 1982; Taylor & Asher, 1984). However, this goal selection is probably largely an unconscious process, as people do not usually consciously think about their goals unless some kind of concern is aroused, uncertainty is involved, or unexpected circumstances arise (Parkhurst & Asher, 1985; Ladd & Crick, 1989). It has been proposed (Asher & Renshaw, 1981; Renshaw & Asher, 1982) that part of the social skill deficit of low-accepted children may be that they tend to define situations in terms of maladaptive goals that promote dysfunctional social behaviour. Because social situations are often ambiguous, the selection of social goals therefore may be a particularly important aspect of children's social problem-solving (Renshaw & Asher, 1982).

Several studies have demonstrated goal differences in low versus better accepted children. In one study, Renshaw and Asher (1983) found that low-accepted 8–11-year-old children were no more likely than their better accepted peers to suggest avoidance goals or hostile goals in response to hypothetical situations (e.g. entering a group). However, they proposed significantly fewer prosocial goals. Thus, the low-accepted children were not openly hostile in their social orientation but rather were somewhat less positive, friendly and outgoing in their goals for various social situations.

Recently, Wentzel (1991) assessed the goal patterns of children of various levels of acceptance by asking 11- and 12-year-old children how often they tried to pursue various outcomes. These included a set of prosocial goals (e.g. 'How often do you try to help other kids when they have a problem?') and a set of social interaction goals (e.g. 'How often do you try to be with other kids rather

than by yourself?'). Better accepted children reported trying to achieve social interaction and prosocial goals significantly more often than did the low-accepted children. These results suggest that better accepted children place higher priority on relationship-orientated goals, given that they appear to pursue such goals with greater frequency, whereas low-accepted children give relationship-orientated goals relatively lower priority.

Although many studies have focused on the pursuit of one goal versus another, as noted earlier in this section, it is more likely, particularly in social situations, that people must coordinate multiple goals. Consider, for example, the variety of goals potentially pursued by children in a game-playing context (Taylor & Asher, 1984). These include task mastery, winning, avoiding losing, self-protection, dominance, developing relationships and avoiding rejection. What people really seem to develop is a system of goals rather than isolated goals, and it is the system properties of goals that provide the basis for conflict as well as for simultaneous integrated satisfaction of a variety of goals (Pervin, 1982). In fact, it may be that social competence is best characterized as the ability to coordinate several goals in a manner most appropriate for the context (Dodge *et al.*, 1989).

Dodge *et al.* (1989) hypothesized that differences between highly competent and less competent children in social situations are less likely to be evident in the differential endorsement of single goals, and more apt to be found in how successfully children manage goal conflicts and integrate their various goals in a particular situation. Children typically hold a variety of goals for their social interactions, including to have fun, promote friendship, to acquire information, as well as possibly to dominate, win and avoid rejection. However, not all of these goals are pursued at the same time. Certain situations orient people towards the pursuit of particular goals (Argyle *et al.*, 1981; Kagan & Knight, 1981). For example, a child competing in a basketball tournament is probably more focused on performing well and winning than on developing friendships with the opposing team members. In contrast, a child who is playing a casual game with a group of neighbourhood friends is probably more concerned with having fun with peers than with achieving victories.

Although situations may seem to emphasize different goals, there are many occasions during which children must select from among a variety of potential goals. Under such circumstances, children are apt to show individual differences in their goal preferences. Within the social domain, three situations in which individual differences in goal priorities are quite likely to be observed are conflict situations, group entry attempts and ambiguous provocation situations. In such situations, children must coordinate a variety of goals that may often be incompatible. This goal coordination process has been considered in the literature from both the social information-processing perspective (Dodge, 1980; Dodge *et al.*, 1989) and the social problem-solving perspective (Shure & Spivack, 1972; Krasnor & Rubin, 1981; Rubin & Krasnor, 1986). Although sometimes this coordination may be smoothly pursued when the goals are facilitative of one another, difficulties are likely to emerge when goals come into conflict. At this point, children may have to decide which of several goals will rise to the top of the hierarchy and be pursued with the highest priority.

In conflict situations, the child frequently has to decide between the often incompatible goals of getting what one wants versus maintaining a relationship with the other person. Among the hypothetical situations that Renshaw and Asher (1983) presented to children, the greatest goal and strategy differences were observed as children described their responses to the conflict situation. A recent study by Chung and Asher (1992) focused exclusively on children's responses to conflict situations. The research was designed to learn about individual differences in children's goals and strategies and to learn about the relationship between goals and strategies. In this study, results indicated no differences in goals as a function of peer acceptance. However, several gender differences were found. Boys were more likely than girls to focus on the goal of maintaining control over the situation or their own decision-making. Girls tended to endorse the goal that focused on maintaining good relationships. Girls also were more concerned than boys with avoiding trouble. Chung and Asher (1992) also found clear linkages between children's goals and the strategies they proposed. For example, children who pursued the goal of maintaining personal control in the situation were more likely also to report that their mode of responding to conflict would involve unfriendly and coercive, as opposed to more prosocial and cooperative, types of strategies. In situations in which initiation of interaction must take place, the ultimate goal is gaining access into the ongoing activity. Here again, some children may become overwhelmed with the subgoal of self-protection or promoting the self, whereas others may focus more on other people and pursue the goal of smoothly easing their way into the group. Consequently, some children may protect themselves from overt rejection by simply hovering near the group, others may make self-orientated statements and barge into the group, and still others may adopt the frame of reference of the group as a means of helping themselves fit in (Putallaz & Wasserman, 1990). In fact, data from a study of the entry strategies of 5 and 7 year olds (Forbes *et al.*, 1982) suggested that for males, the goal of attaining positive status in the group took precedence over the goal of gaining acceptance by the group, as boys were observed more frequently than girls to make forceful opening moves as well as more face-saving moves in response to initial negative feedback. In contrast, girls were more likely to display a strategy that appeared to be more focused on gaining acceptance by the group, as they were more apt to exhibit group entry behaviours that were accommodating to others, particularly in response to negative feedback. These results are important because they demonstrate the possible existence of individual differences in goal pursuit when several goals are juxtaposed against one another.

A study by Erdley and Asher (1994) examined children's goals in ambiguous provocation situations. Three kinds of children were studied: (i) those who predominantly responded to ambiguous provocation with aggression; (ii) those who predominantly responded to ambiguous provocation by withdrawing; and (iii) those who predominantly responded to ambiguous provocation by giving problem-solving responses such as requesting clarification. When these children were individually interviewed about what they were trying to do in the situation, differences in their social goals were found. Specifically, compared to the problem-solving responders, aggressive responders were more likely to report pursuing the antisocial goals of getting back at the protagonist, making the protagonist feel bad, protecting the self and looking strong. Moreover, they were less apt to say that they would be trying to achieve the prosocial goals of getting along with the protagonist, working things out peacefully and taking care of the problem. The withdrawn responders, when compared to the problem-solving responders, were more likely to report that they would be trying to stay away from the protagonist. Thus, children's selection of varying social goals in response to the same kind of situation appears to contribute to differences in their behavioural choices with their peers.

Strategy knowledge

In order to accomplish a selected goal, individuals must have knowledge about what strategies might be effective in bringing about a desired outcome. It appears that better accepted children are able to produce not only a greater quantity of solutions but also a higher quality of solutions for various social situations (Rubin & Krasnor, 1986). It is assumed that having the flexibility to generate multiple solutions to social problems equips the child for better adaptation to an often complex and unpredictable social world (Spivack & Shure, 1974). Moreover, having a repertoire of higher quality strategies increases the likelihood that the child will enact prosocial behaviours that contribute to better acceptance by the peer group.

Several studies have found differences in the strategies produced by children of varying levels of acceptance. The typical methodology in these studies involves showing children a variety of hypothetical social situations and asking children what they would do in response to each situation. Ladd and Oden (1979) assessed the strategies of 8–10-year-old children who were presented with hypothetical situations in which a peer was depicted as in need of help. It was found that, in comparison to better accepted children, low accepted children were more likely to suggest strategies that were unique and often situationally inappropriate. In addition, Asher and Renshaw (1981) presented 5- and 6-year-old children of low- or better accepted status with nine hypothetical situations of three types: (i) initiating social relationships; (ii) maintaining social situations; and (iii) managing conflict.

When asked what the protagonist should do, the better accepted children were more apt to suggest strategies that were prosocial, resourceful and relationship-enhancing. On the other hand, low-accepted children were more likely to rely on adults or to suggest inappropriately negative and aggressive strategies.

Research on entry behaviours has also revealed differences between children of different levels of peer acceptance and has provided insights about the kinds of strategies that lead to successful group entry (Putallaz & Gottman, 1981; Putallaz, 1983; Dodge *et al.*, 1986). For example, Dodge *et al.* (1986) found that children who produced a larger number of non-aggressive versus aggressive strategies were rated as more successful and competent at joining groups of familiar peers, both in a laboratory task and in actual classroom and playground contexts. Thus, the quality of children's knowledge of how to enter into a group is related to their success at this task and also appears to be associated with their level of peer acceptance.

Differences in children's strategies for dealing with conflict situations have also been documented. For example, Richard and Dodge (1982) asked low- and better accepted children to generate multiple solutions to hypothetical situations involving conflict resolution. It was found that the better accepted children produced more solutions than the low-accepted children. Furthermore, although the first solutions the children produced were judged to be equal in quality, the subsequent solutions of the low-accepted children were evaluated as less effective, as they were more likely to be judged as aggressive, unique, inept, unsophisticated or vague. Likewise, Asarnow and Callan (1985) reported that, in response to hypothetical problems, low-accepted children generated fewer alternative solutions, proposed fewer assertive and mature solutions and produced more intense aggressive solutions than did better accepted children. Rabiner *et al.* (1990) found that in response to social dilemmas, low-accepted children generated fewer verbal assertion and more conflict-escalating responses than did better accepted children, even when they were given time to think about solutions. Chung and Asher (1992) found that low-accepted children were less likely to endorse prosocial strategies and were more likely to indicate that they would seek out adult intervention to help resolve the conflict. Overall, these results suggest that when low-accepted children confront a conflict, they are unable to generate as many effective strategies as do their better accepted peers, and thus their resulting behaviours are apt to be problematic for social relations.

Outcome expectations

Not only do children vary in their knowledge and pursuit of different social strategies, they also seem to have different expectations concerning what the outcomes of using particular strategies might be. Because social activity involves other people, the actor must take into account the effect of his or her behaviour on others (Ladd & Crick, 1989). Outcome expectations refer to how children expect peers and adults to react to particular strategies in social interactions. Crick and Ladd (1990) presented children with two hypothetical conflict situations, with six strategies associated with each situation. Children were asked to describe what the outcome would be if they had used a given strategy. Crick and Ladd found that when compared to their better accepted peers, low-accepted children more often focused on instrumental outcomes rather than relational outcomes. In other words, the low accepted children appeared to be more concerned with whether a strategy would result in the accomplishment of some instrumental goal, such as attaining compliance to a command, than with how the strategy might influence the relationship between the self and the peer, such as maintaining the friendship. According to Crick and Ladd, this finding raises the question of how aware low-accepted children are that aggressive behaviour has potentially negative consequences for a relationship. Additionally, low-accepted children's greater focus on instrumental outcomes may suggest that low-accepted children are more interested in pursuing an instrumental goal and will give this goal priority even at the expense of maintaining a relationship.

There is also evidence suggesting that children classified as aggressive expect the enactment of aggression to result in the achievement of tangible rewards and the reduction of aversive treatment by others (Perry *et al.*, 1986). Moreover, Boldizar *et al.* (1989) found that aggressive children were less worried by the possibility of causing suffering in their victim, were relatively unconcerned about the risk of retaliation and were more apt to minimize the importance of peer rejection that was likely to occur after the aggressive act. In other work comparing aggressive and non-aggressive children, Dodge *et al.* (1986) examined children's expectations regarding the consequences of using prosocial, aggressive and passive strategies in a group entry task as well as in an ambiguous provocation situation. Children did not differ in their endorsement of these strategies for the group entry situation. However, for the conflict situation, aggressive children were less likely than non-aggressive children to report that the prosocial response was a good way for the provoked child to respond. It seems, then, that relative to their non-aggressive peers, aggressive children are more likely to believe that aggressive behaviours will produce fairly positive outcomes. As suggested by Ladd and Crick (1989), it appears that children think about the outcome of their strategies in ways that are fairly consistent with the strategies they choose to enact in the peer group. In other words, children draw upon strategies that they think will result in favourable consequences.

Attributions for success and failure

In addition to evaluating the impact of their behaviour on others, individuals often make assessments about their own social successes and failures. People encounter frequent challenges in their social lives, including the possibility that their efforts with others will be met with rejection. Certainly, failed attempts in social encounters are a very real part of everyday life for children. In a sample of nursery school children, Corsaro (1981) observed that 54% of all initial group entry attempts were met with rejection. In their research with 7 and 8 year olds, Putallaz and Gottman (1981) reported that, even for children who were well accepted by their peers, 27% of their attempts to join a game in which two peers were engaged were rejected and 11% were ignored. Even more striking was that amongst low-accepted children, 43% of their entry attempts were rejected, whereas 26% of their attempts were ignored. Therefore, children must learn to deal with social failure on a fairly regular basis.

Children's perceptions of the causes underlying their social successes and failures seem to influence their motivation to change their behaviour in the face of social failure, their persistence in social situations, their strategy enactment and their feelings about their social experiences (Goetz & Dweck, 1980; Hymel *et al.*, 1985; Sobol & Earn, 1985; Ladd & Crick, 1989). In one of the earliest studies to document individual differences in children's attributional styles, Ames *et al.* (1977) compared the locus of control attributions for positive and negative interpersonal outcomes given by low- and better accepted 9–11-year-old children. They found that low-accepted children were more likely to attribute causes of positive outcomes externally, whereas causes of negative outcomes were attributed internally. The better accepted children demonstrated an opposite pattern, taking credit for social successes and absolving themselves from blame for failures. Likewise, Sobol and Earn (1985) reported that better accepted children took more credit for social success and tended to externalize social failure.

In a study that explored the link between children's attributions and coping styles in a socially challenging situation, Goetz and Dweck (1980) found that interpersonal coping problems could occur regardless of children's acceptance level but were associated with different attributional styles, specifically, children's beliefs about the reasons for social rejection. In this study children were initially presented with hypothetical situations involving social failure and were asked why the failures might occur (for example, 'Suppose you move to a new neighbourhood. A girl/boy you meet doesn't like you very much. Why would this happen to you?'). Some children stressed personal social incompetence, whereas others emphasized external factors like the negative characteristics of the rejector, his or her bad mood or a misunderstanding. Several weeks later the children were put in an actual social situation that involved the possibility of personal social rejection. Specifically, children tried out for a pen pal club by communicating a getting-to-know-you letter to a 'peer evaluator' who was a 'representative' of the club. The evaluator initially expressed uncertainty about admitting the child to the club, but allowed the

child to compose a second letter, after which the child was always accepted.

Children were classified into groups on the basis of their attributions on the hypothetical situations interview. Those who blamed their own personal social incompetence for rejection showed a more helpless response pattern to the initial failure on the pen pal attempt, whereas those who attributed rejection to other factors displayed a more mastery oriented pattern. Interestingly, as has been found in research in the academic achievement domain (see Dweck & Leggett, 1988 for a review), the two groups initially showed no differences in their skill at the task, since their first letters were of equal length and quality. However, following rejection, clear differences between the groups emerged, just as they had in the achievement research. The helpless children exhibited disrupted performance in the second letter, as some withdrew from the situation or just repeated the first letter. These helpless children were less likely to try new strategies and instead tended to repeat ineffective strategies or to abandon effective strategies entirely. In contrast, the mastery oriented children were more likely to give new information or try new strategies in their second letter.

Consistent with other research (Ames *et al.*, 1977; Sobol & Earn, 1985), Goetz and Dweck (1980) did find differences in the attributional styles of low- and better accepted children. Low-accepted children were more apt to attribute hypothetical social failures to their incompetence and to exhibit helpless responses to the failure experience. However, it is interesting to note that those children who showed a more helpless response to rejection were also more likely, across acceptance levels, to have made attributions of personal incompetence. Thus, attributional style seems to be a stronger mediator of reactions to rejection than is acceptance level. Goetz and Dweck suggested that there are apt to be some better accepted children who probably have not had many failure experiences. Nevertheless, these better accepted children are vulnerable to the inevitable social rejections that individuals are likely to encounter at some time. Despite good social skills, their attributional style may lead them to view a salient social rejection experience as insurmountable, resulting in a helpless pattern of response. If children exhibit a helpless attributional style regarding social failure, this may contribute to negative self-evaluations and a disengagement from social encounters. Repeated instances of such help-less, avoidant behaviours may consequently have a negative impact on evaluations made by the peer group.

SOCIAL RELATIONSHIP SKILLS INTERVENTIONS

Interest in social skills training with children having peer relationship problems has been stimulated by evidence concerning the functions of peer relations, research on the negative consequences of peer relationship problems, and the accumulating evidence that processes involving social competence play an important role in adaptation to the peer group. Most social skills training research with children has been conducted within the past two decades (see Wanlass & Prinz, 1982; Ladd & Mize, 1983; Asher, 1985; Ladd & Asher, 1985; Coie & Koeppl, 1990 for reviews), and several different paradigms have evolved. These paradigms vary in the procedures used to select children for social skills training, in the particular instructional content emphasized, in the methods of intervention employed, and in the outcomes that are assessed. This section describes research related to these four features of social skills research.

Criteria used to select children

A frequently employed approach to selecting children for intervention has been to observe children's behaviour or obtain behavioural assess-ments from children's teachers, peers or parents, and then to intervene with those children judged to be deviant in some aspect of their behaviour. One variant of this approach is to use low rates of interaction with peers as a selection criterion. How-ever, the evidence suggests that children's rate of peer interaction, without regard to the quality of their interaction, is not related to measures of either concurrent or long-term social adjustment (see Asher *et al.*, 1981 for a review). Other more meaningful dimensions of children's behaviour to use for selecting children for intervention efforts are aggressive behaviour, withdrawn behaviour or deficits in prosocial skills. Interventions aimed at

specific problems such as these, all of which are known to be related to peer relationship difficulties, are better founded than those which simply attempt to change children's rate of interaction without regard to the quality of interaction.

Another means of selecting children for social skills training has been to identify children based on low sociometric status in the peer group (e.g. Gottman *et al.*, 1976; Oden & Asher, 1977; Ladd, 1981). It is important, however, to distinguish between children who lack friends and are highly disliked by many of their peers (sociometrically rejected or low accepted children), and those who, although they lack friends, are fairly well liked by their peers (sociometrically neglected children). This latter group appears not to be at as high a risk for concurrent or long-term adjustment problems. For example, although these children are behav-iourally distinct in certain respects (see Mounts & Asher, 1992 for a recent review), they do not report levels of loneliness that are significantly different from those of average children (Asher & Wheeler, 1985; Crick & Ladd, 1993), nor are they likely to remain sociometrically neglected over time or across contexts (Coie & Dodge, 1983; Coie & Kupersmidt, 1983; Newcomb & Bukowski, 1984). For these reasons, research on social skills training has been focused on low-accepted or rejected children rather than sociometrically neglected children.

A somewhat distinct domain of children's peer relationships is that of children's friendships and friendship quality. Neither 'friendlessness', nor deficiencies in the qualities of children's friendships, have been generally used as selection criteria in social skills training research. These are omissions that warrant attention. As discussed in the earlier section on the emotional consequences of peer relationship difficulties, even well accepted children who lack friends are more lonely than well accepted children who have a friend. Furthermore, the qualities of children's friendships make a further contribution to children's feeling of well-being versus loneliness (Parker & Asher, 1993b). Both a general lack of friends and the lack of positive features in certain children's friendships could be used to select children for social skill training (Furman & Robbins, 1985).

Children might also be selected for intervention based on their own self-reports of loneliness and social dissatisfaction, or, even more directly, by inviting children to indicate explicitly their desire for assistance with peer relationship problems. Neither loneliness nor self-referral has been used as selection criteria in existing social skills intervention research with children. Recent evidence from Asher *et al.* (1991) suggests, however, that inviting children to self-refer for help would identify a large number of interested children. These investigators conducted three studies with 8–12-year-old children. In the first study, after children completed a number of questionnaires assessing their friendships and feelings of loneliness at school, they were told:

> We just asked about some of your thoughts and feelings about things at school. Some questions might have been about things that bother you. Some questions might have been about things you want to change. If you want to, you can talk to the school social worker about these things. This will only happen if you want to. If you would like to talk to the school social worker, please check this box.

In the second and third studies, a question was asked that made reference to a friendship expert rather than a specific school professional. Here children were told:

> Some kids are kind of worried about how they are getting along with other kids. These children are having some problems making friends or keeping friends. Imagine that there was a person in the school whose job was to help children learn how to make friends and get along better with other kids. This person's job would be to help children change how well they get along with other kids. Now imagine that all the kids in the school had a chance to get help from this person. Would you like to get help if this person really worked at the school?

Results from these three studies indicated that the second version of the self-referral question elicited much higher rates of self-referral and that in each study low-accepted children were about three times more likely than better accepted children to self-refer. In the third study, low-accepted children were subclassified as either aggressive or withdrawn based on peer reports of behavioural style. Results for self-referral indicated

that a significantly higher proportion of the withdrawn subgroup expressed interest in receiving help. Interestingly, the proportion of aggressive–rejected children self-referring differed little from average children. These findings are noteworthy in light of evidence that children who are referred by adult professionals for behavioural intervention in school are far more likely to be aggressive or conduct disordered than to exhibit internalizing sorts of problems (Rutter *et al.*, 1975). Given that many withdrawn or rejected children express interest in receiving help, there may be a special window of opportunity for intervening with these children.

Content of social skills interventions

In much of the intervention research with poorly accepted children, children have been taught prosocial skills thought to promote positive social interactions and peer acceptance (Gottman *et al.*, 1976; Oden & Asher, 1977; Gresham & Nagle, 1980; Ladd, 1981; Mize & Ladd, 1990). For example, Oden and Asher (1977) brought pairs of children together to play a game but first taught the child who was the focus of the intervention concepts related to cooperation, participation, communication and being supportive. Ladd (1981) trained 8-year-old children in three somewhat more specific skills: asking questions, leading peers and offering supportive statements. In both of these studies, relative to a control group of untrained children, children who received social skills training made gains in sociometric status that were apparent both at the end of the intervention and at follow-up. In Oden and Asher's (1977) study, children who received training went from approximately 1.5 standard deviations below the mean in acceptance to close to the mean at follow-up assessment 1 year later.

Although an emphasis on teaching positive, prosocial skills seems to provide good results for many children, not all children exhibit gains in sociometric status following intervention. Asher and Renshaw (1981) estimated that about 50–60% of the children made substantial improvements in peer acceptance as a result of intervention. More recently, Coie and Koeppl (1990) have argued that some children who do not experience gains in peer acceptance from prosocial skills training may need interventions targeted to more specific problems, especially aggressive or disruptive behaviour. Coie and Koeppl suggest that although many aggressive or disruptive children need training in prosocial skills, such children also require additional and more explicit help specifically aimed at reducing the frequency of their aversive behaviour in order to become better accepted by their peers. Coie *et al.* (1991b) have recently described various approaches to modifying aggression, including behaviour management strategies and instruction in anger control.

Mode of treatment

There have been three primary modes of treatment used in previous social skills training with children: (i) modelling, in which children observe peers demonstrating specific social behaviours (e.g. O'Connor 1969); (ii) contingency management, in which the social environment is altered so that children experience rewards for engaging in particular behaviours (e.g. Allen *et al.*, 1964); and (iii) coaching, in which children are trained in particular concepts or skills and given opportunities for rehearsal along with postrehearsal feedback (e.g. Oden & Asher, 1977; Ladd, 1981). Of these methods, interventions using coaching techniques have generally resulted in more long-term gains in peer acceptance than have interventions using modelling or shaping techniques (see Ladd & Mize, 1983).

Another aspect of the mode of treatment issue is whether the intervention is done (individually or in small groups) with children identified as having problems or with larger groups of unselected children, such as an entire classroom. To illustrate the latter approach, Elias *et al.* (1986) implemented a preventive social problem-solving programme in all of the fifth-grade classrooms in four elementary schools (children were approximately 10 years of age). The programme, which included 20 lessons aimed at developing students' social problem-solving skills, was carried out by the classroom teachers. Elias *et al.* (1986) compared the later adjustment to middle school of children who had received no training, a half-year of training and a full school year of training, and found that 1 year of training was significantly related to reductions in

the severity of a variety of middle school stressors. In another study, Hepler and Rose (1988) taught a classroom of fifth graders several social skills: initiating and maintaining a conversation with peers, joining an ongoing activity and including others in activities. When compared with fifth graders in a classroom that was not included in the social skills training, the students receiving the intervention improved in sociometric status and on a role play test, and five low status children in the classroom showed significant improvement on a negative peer nomination measure. Interventions such as these, applied to everyone in a class, could prevent problems that may occur with regard to labelling and stigmatization of children when only a few children from each classroom are selected for intervention.

An issue that has been relatively neglected in the literature on social skills training thus far concerns the developmental level of the children receiving instruction (see Furman, 1980 for an extended discussion of this issue). Certainly the mode, as well as the content, of instruction may need to be adapted for children of different age levels. Concepts may need to be simplified for younger children, and using dolls, puppets or other props (Chittenden, 1942; Mize & Ladd, 1990) may also improve young children's understanding of concepts and may help make the experience more enjoyable. A related issue is that of the timing of intervention. Most of the intervention research thus far has been conducted with children in middle childhood. As children grow older, it may become more difficult to change longer standing patterns of behaviour and cognition, both in the children who receive the intervention, and in their peer groups (for a discussion of the potential effects of reputational biases see Hymel *et al.*, 1990).

Outcome assessment

The issue of which outcomes to assess is closely tied to the goals of an intervention effort. Typically, researchers and clinicians have had two broad goals and two related indicators of effectiveness in those goals. One general goal has been to promote behavioural change and the other general goal has been to increase children's peer acceptance. These are, of course, related goals, but as the literature documents, it is possible to obtain behavioural change without finding gains in peer acceptance (La Greca & Santagrossi, 1980; Bierman & Furman, 1984), and it is possible to find gains in acceptance and not be able to document behavioural changes (e.g. Oden & Asher, 1977). It is important, therefore, as work proceeds in this area, to continue to assess both behavioural changes and relationship outcomes.

With regard to relationship outcomes, there is the need to attend not only to changes in overall peer acceptance, but also to growth in the child's ability to form best friendships and friendships of high quality. Our recommendation is that rating scale measures be used to assess changes in acceptance because these measures have excellent demonstrated reliability that results from a child being rated by each of the other group members (see Asher & Hymel, 1981). To assess best friendship, we recommend that reciprocal friendship nominations be the measure of choice, given their high degree of face validity (see Bukowski & Hoza, 1989; Parker & Asher, 1993 for recent discussions of friendship assessment). Finally, there now exist highly reliable ways to assess the specific qualities of a best friendship (e.g. Parker & Asher, 1993), and this opens up the possibility of learning whether intervention not only helps children gain peer acceptance and friends, but also helps children improve the quality of their best friendships.

Finally, intervention assessments could be broadened to learn not just whether children change on behavioural or relationship outcomes, but what psychological processes account for the change. The earlier section on social competence examined the role of attributions, interpersonal goals, strategy knowledge and outcome expectations. The relevance of these processes to children's successful adaptation to the peer system is becoming better understood, but there is a lag in attention to these factors in the intervention literature. We need to know whether intervention affects these processes and whether changes in them are associated with changes in behavioural and relationship outcomes. It is possible not only to document changes in outcome, but also to learn what sorts of processes account for observed changes (Bierman, 1986). We hope this chapter provides promising leads for researchers and clinicians interested in focusing on competence-related processes, as well as competence-related outcomes in the peer domain.

REFERENCES

Alexander B.K. (1966) *The effects of early peer-deprivation on juvenile behavior of rhesus monkeys*. Unpublished doctoral dissertation, University of Wisconsin, Madison.

Alexander B.K. & Harlow H.F. (1965) Social behavior of juvenile rhesus monkeys subjected to different rearing conditions during the first six months of life. *Zoologische Jahrbucher Physiologie* **60**, 167–174.

Allen E., Hart B., Buell J., Harris F. & Wolfe M. (1964) Effects of social reinforcement on isolate behavior of a nursery school child. *Child Development* **35**, 511–518.

Allen V.L. & Devin-Sheehan L. (1976) *The One-Room School: A Social Psychological Analysis*. Working Paper No. 161, Wisconsin Research and Development Center for Cognitive Learning, Madison.

Ames R., Ames C. & Garrison W. (1977) Children's causal ascriptions for positive and negative interpersonal outcomes. *Psychological Reports* **41**, 595–602.

Argyle M., Furnham A. & Graham J.A. (1981) *Social Situations*. Cambridge University Press, Cambridge.

Asarnow J.R. & Callan J.W. (1985) Boys with peer adjustment problems: Social cognitive processes. *Journal of Consulting and Clinical Psychology* **53**, 80–87.

Asher S.R. (1985) An evolving paradigm in social skill training research with children. In Schneider B.H., Rubin K.H. & Ledingham J.E. (eds) *Children's Peer Relations: Issues in Assessment and Intervention*, pp. 157–171. Springer, New York.

Asher S.R. & Coie J.D. (eds) (1990) *Peer Rejection in Childhood*. Cambridge University Press, New York.

Asher S.R. & Gabriel S.W. (1993) Using a wireless transmission system to observe conversation and social interaction on the playground. In Hart C.H. (ed.) *Children on Playgrounds: Research Perspectives and Applications*, pp. 184–209. State University of New York Press, Albany, New York.

Asher S.R. & Hymel S. (1981) Children's social competence in peer relations: Sociometric and behavioral assessment. In Wine J.D. & Smye M.D. (eds) *Social Competence*, pp. 122–157. Guilford Press, New York.

Asher S.R., Hymel S. & Renshaw P.D. (1984) Loneliness in children. *Child Development* **55**, 1456–1464.

Asher S.R., Markell R.A. & Hymel S. (1981) Identifying children at risk in peer relations: A critique of the rate of interaction approach to assessment. *Child Development* **52**, 1239–1245.

Asher S.R. & Parker J.G. (1989) The significance of peer relationship problems in childhood. In Schneider B.H., Attili G., Nadel J. & Weissberg R.P. (eds) *Social Competence in Developmental Perspective*, pp. 5–23. Kluwer, Amsterdam.

Asher, S.R. & Renshaw P.D. (1981) Children without friends: Social knowledge and social skills. In Asher S.R. & Gottman J.M. (eds) *The Development of Children's Friendships*, pp. 273–296. Cambridge University Press, New York.

Asher S.R. & Wheeler V.A. (1985) Children's loneliness: A comparison of rejected and neglected peer status. *Journal of Consulting and Clinical Psychology* **53**, 500–505.

Asher S.R., Zelis K.M., Parker J.G. & Bruene C.M. (1991) Self-referral for peer relationship problems of aggressive and withdrawn low-accepted children. In Parkhurst J.T. & Rabiner D.L. (Chairs) *The Behavioral Characteristics and the Subjective Experiences of Aggressive and Withdrawn/ Submissive Rejected Children*. Symposium conducted at the Biennial Meeting of the Society for Research in Child Development, Seattle, April.

Berndt T.J. (1984) Sociometric, social-cognitive, and behavioral measures for the study of friendship and popularity. In Field T., Roopnarine J.L. & Segal M. (eds) *Friendships in Normal and Handicapped Children*, pp. 31–52. Ablex, Norwood, New Jersey.

Berndt T.J. (1986) Children's comments about their friendships. In Perlmutter M. (ed.) *Cognitive Perspectives on Children's Social and Behavioral Development: Minnesota Symposia on Child Psychology*, Vol. 18, pp. 189–212. Lawrence Erlbaum, Hillsdale, New Jersey.

Berndt T.J. (1989) Obtaining support from friends in childhood and adolescence. In Belle D. (ed.) *Children's Social Networks and Social Supports*, pp. 308–331. Wiley, New York.

Berndt T.J., Hawkins J.A. & Hoyle S.G. (1986) Changes in friendship during a school year: Effects on children's and adolescents' impressions of friendship and sharing with friends. *Child Development* **57**, 1284–1297.

Berndt T.J. & Perry T.B. (1986) Children's perceptions of friendships as supportive relationships. *Developmental Psychology* **22**, 640–648.

Bierman K.L. (1986) Process of change during social skills training with preadolescents and its relation to treatment outcome. *Child Development* **57**, 230–240.

Bierman K.L. & Furman W. (1984) The effects of social skills training and peer involvement on the social adjustment of preadolescents. *Child Development* **55**, 151–162.

Bigelow B.J. (1977) Children's friendship expectations: A cognitive-developmental study. *Child Development* **48**, 246–253.

Bigelow B.J. & La Gaipa J.J. (1975) Children's written descriptions of friendships: A multidimensional study. *Developmental Psychology* **11**, 857–858.

Bloomsmith M.A., Alford P.L. & Maple T.L. (1988) Successful feeding enrichment for captive chimpanzees. *American Journal of Primatology* **16**, 155–164.

Boldizar J.P., Perry D.G. & Perry L.C. (1989) Outcome values and aggression. *Child Development* **60**, 571–579.

Bryant B.K. (1985) The neighborhood walk: Sources of support in middle childhood. *Monographs of the Society for Research in Child Development* **50**(3), Serial No. 210.

Buhrmester D. & Furman W. (1986) The changing function of friends in childhood: A neoSullivanian perspective. In Derlaga V. & Winstead B. (eds) *Friendship and Social Interaction*, pp. 41–62. Springer, New York.

Bukowski W.M. & Hoza B. (1989) Popularity and friendship: Issues in theory, measurement, and outcome. In Berndt T.J. & Ladd G.W. (eds) *Peer Relationships in Child Development*, pp. 15–45. Wiley, New York.

Bukowski W.M., Hoza B. & Newcomb A.F. (1987) *Friendship, popularity, and the 'self' during adolescence*. Unpublished ms, University of Maine, Orono.

Bukowski W.M. & Newcomb A.F. (1985) *Friendship conceptions among early adolescents: A longitudinal study of stability and change*. Unpublished ms, University of Maine, Orono.

Cairns R.B., Cairns B.D., Neckerman H.J., Gest S. & Gariepy J.L. (1987) *Peer networks and aggressive behavior: Social support or social rejection?* Report from the Carolina Longitudinal Study, University of North Carolina, Chapel Hill.

Candy S., Troll L. & Levy S. (1981) Developmental explorations of friendship functions in women. *Psychology of Women Quarterly* **5**, 456–472.

Cassidy J. & Asher S.R. (1992) Loneliness and peer relations in young children. *Child Development* **63**, 350–365.

Chamove A.S. (1973) Rearing infant rhesus together. *Behaviour* **47**, 48–66.

Chamove A.S., Rosenblum L.A. & Harlow H.F. (1973) Monkeys (*Macaca mulatta*) raised only with peers. A pilot study. *Animal Behavior* **21**, 316–325.

Chittenden C.E. (1942) An experimental study in measuring and modifying assertive behavior in young children. *Monographs of the Society for Research in Child Development* **7**(1), Serial No. 31.

Chown S. (1981) Friendship in old age. In Duck S.W. & Gilmour R. (eds) *Personal Relationships*, Vol. 2, *Developing Personal Relationships*, pp. 231–276. Academic Press, New York.

Chung T. & Asher S.R. (1992) *Children's strategies and goals in resolving conflicts with peers*. Paper presented at the Annual Meeting of the American Psychological Association, Washington, DC, August.

Coie J.D. & Dodge K.A. (1983) Continuities and changes in children's social status: A five year longitudinal study. *Merrill-Palmer Quarterly* **29**, 261–281.

Coie J.D., Dodge K.A. & Coppotelli H. (1982) Dimensions and types of social status: A cross-age perspective. *Developmental Psychology* **18**, 557–570.

Coie J.D., Dodge K.A., Terry R. & Wright V. (1991a) The role of aggression in peer relations: An analysis of aggression episodes in boys' play groups. *Child Development* **62**, 812–826.

Coie J.D. & Koeppl G.H. (1990) Adapting intervention to the problems of aggressive and disruptive rejected children. In Asher S.R. & Coie J.D. (eds) *Peer Rejection in Childhood*, pp. 309–337. Cambridge University Press, New York.

Coie J.D. & Kupersmidt J.B. (1983) A behavioral analysis of emerging social status in boys' groups. *Child Development* **54**, 1400–1416.

Coie J.D., Underwood M. & Lochman J.E. (1991b)

Programmatic intervention with aggressive children in the school setting. In Pepler D.J. & Rubin K.H. (eds) *The Development and Treatment of Childhood Aggression*, pp. 389–410. Lawrence Erlbaum, Hillsdale, New Jersey.

Corsaro W.A. (1981) Friendship in the nursery school: Social organization in a peer environment. In Asher S.R. & Gottman J.M. (eds) *The Development of Children's Friendships*, pp. 207–241. Cambridge University Press, Hillsdale, New Jersey.

Cowen E.L., Pederson A., Babigian H., Izzo L.D. & Trost M.A. (1973) Long-term followup of early detected vulnerable children. *Journal of Consulting and Clinical Psychology* **41**, 438–446.

Crick N.R. & Ladd G.W. (1990) Children's perceptions of the outcomes of social strategies: Do the ends justify being mean? *Developmental Psychology* **26**, 612–620.

Crick N.R. & Ladd G.W. (1993) Children's perceptions of their peer experiences: Attributions, social anxiety, and social avoidance. *Developmental Psychology* **29**, 244–254.

Crockett L., Losoff M. & Petersen A.C. (1984) Perceptions of the peer groups and friendship in early adolescence. *Journal of Early Adolescence* **4**, 155–181.

Crohan S.E. & Antonucci T.C. (1989) Friends as a source of social support in old age. In Adams R.G. & Blieszner R. (eds) *Older Adult Friendship: Structure and Process*, pp. 129–146. Sage, Newbury Park, California.

Csikszentmihalyi M., Larson R. & Prescott S. (1977) The ecology of adolescent activity and experience. *Journal of Youth and Adolescence* **6**, 281–294.

Davenport R.K. (1979) Some behavioral disturbances of great apes in captivity. In Hamburg D.A. & McCown E.R. (eds) *The Great Apes*, pp. 341–357. Benjamin/Cummings, Menlo Park, California.

Davenport R.K. & Rogers C.M. (1970) Differential rearing of the chimpanzee. A project survey. In Bourne G.H. (ed.) *The Chimpanzee*, Vol. 3, pp. 337–360. University Park Press, Baltimore.

Devereaux E.C. (1976) Backyard versus little league baseball: The impoverishment of children's games. In Landers D.M. (ed.) *Social Problems in Athletics*, pp. 37–56. University of Illinois Press, Urbana.

Diaz R.M. & Berndt T.J. (1982) Children's knowledge of a best friend: Fact or fancy? *Developmental Psychology* **18**, 787–794.

Dodge K.A. (1980) Social cognition and children's aggressive behavior. *Child Development* **51**, 162–170.

Dodge K.A. (1983) Behavioral antecedents of peer social status. *Child Development* **54**, 1386–1399.

Dodge K.A., Asher S.R. & Parkhurst J.T. (1989) Social life as a goal coordination task. In Ames C. & Ames R. (eds) *Research on Motivation in Education*, Vol. 3, pp. 107–135. Academic Press, San Diego, California.

Dodge, K.A., Coie J.D. & Brakke N.D. (1982) Behavioral patterns of socially rejected and neglected preadolescents: The roles of social approach and aggression. *Journal of Abnormal Child Psychology* **10**, 389–409.

Dodge K.A. & Frame C.L. (1982) Social cognitive biases and deficits in aggressive boys. *Child Development* **53**, 620–635.

Dodge K.A., Murphy R.R. & Buchsbaum K. (1984) The assessment of intention-cue detection skills in children: Implications for developmental psychopathology. *Child Development* **55**, 163–173.

Dodge K.A. & Newman J.P. (1981) Biased decision-making processing in aggressive boys. *Journal of Abnormal Psychology* **90**, 375–379.

Dodge K.A., Pettit G.S., McClaskey C.L. & Brown M.M. (1986) Social competence in children. *Monographs of the Society for Research in Child Development* **51**(2), Serial No. 213.

Dodge K.A., Schlundt D.G., Schocken I. & Delugach J.D. (1983) Social competence and children's social status: The role of peer group entry strategies. *Merrill-Palmer Quarterly* **29**, 309–336.

Duck S. (1983) *Friends for Life: The Psychology of Close Relationships*. St Martin's Press, New York.

Dweck C.S. & Leggett E.L. (1988) A social-cognitive approach to motivation and personality. *Psychological Review* **95**, 256–273.

Eckerman C.O., Davis C.C. & Didow S.M. (1989) Toddlers' emerging ways of achieving social coordinations with a peer. *Child Development* **60**, 440–453.

Eckerman C.O. & Stein M.R. (1982) The toddler's emerging interactive skills. In Rubin K.H. & Ross H.S. (eds) *Peer Relationships and Social Skills in Childhood*, pp. 41–71. Springer, New York.

Eder D. (1987) *The role of teasing in adolescent peer group culture*. Paper presented at the Conference on Ethnographic Approaches to Children's Worlds and Peer Cultures, Trondheim, Norway, June.

Edwards C.P. (1992) Cross-cultural perspectives on family–peer relations. In Parke R.D. & Ladd G.W. (eds) *Family–Peer Relationships: Modes of Linkage*, pp. 285–316. Lawrence Erlbaum, Hillsdale, New Jersey.

Elias M.J., Gara M., Ubriaco M., Rothbaum P.A., Clabby J.F. & Schuyler T. (1986) Impact of a preventive social problem solving intervention on children's coping with middle-school stressors. *American Journal of Community Psychology* **14**, 259–275.

Erdley C.A. & Asher S.R. (1994) *Children's social goals and self-efficacy perceptions as influences on their responses to ambiguous provocation*. Unpublished ms, University of Maine, Orono.

Ferraro K.F., Mutran E. & Barresi C.M. (1984) Widowhood, health, and friendship support later in life. *Journal of Health and Social Behavior* **25**, 245–259.

Festinger L. (1954) A theory of social comparison processes. *Human Relations* **7**, 117–140.

Field T. (1979) Infant behaviors directed towards peers and adults in the presence and absence of mother. *Infant Behavior and Development* **2**, 47–54.

Fine G.A. (1980) The natural history of preadolescent

male friendship groups. In Foot H.C., Chapman A.J. & Smith J.R. (eds) *Friendship and Social Relations in Children*, pp. 293–320. Wiley, New York.

Fine G.A. (1981) Friends, impression management, and preadolescent behavior. In Asher S.R. & Gottman J.M. (eds) *The Development of Children's Friendships*, pp. 29–52. Cambridge University Press, New York.

Fine G.A. (1987) *With the Boys: Little League Baseball and Preadolescent Culture*. University of Chicago Press, Chicago.

Fitzgerald P.D. & Asher S.R. (1987) *Aggressive-rejected children's attributional biases about liked and disliked peers*. Paper presented at the Annual Meeting of the American Psychological Association, New York, August.

Fogel A. (1979) Peer- vs. mother-directed behavior in 1- to 3-month-old infants. *Infant Behavior and Development* 2, 215–226.

Foot H.C., Chapman A.J. & Smith J.R. (1980) Patterns of interaction in children's friendships. In Foot H.C., Chapman A.J. & Smith J.R. (eds) *Friendship and Social Relations in Children*, pp. 267–287. Wiley, New York.

Forbes D.L., Katz M.M., Paul B. & Lubin D. (1982) Children's plans for joining play: An analysis of structure and function. *New Directions for Child Development* 18, 61–79.

Ford M.E. (1982) Social cognition and social competence in adolescence. *Developmental Psychology* 18, 323–340.

Freud A. & Dann S. (1951) An experiment in group upbringing. *Psychoanalytic Study of the Child* 6, 127–168.

Furman W. (1980) Promoting social development: Developmental implications for treatment. In Lahey B.B. & Kazdin A.E. (eds) *Advances in Clinical Child Psychology*, Vol. 3, pp. 1–40. Plenum, New York.

Furman W. & Bierman K.L. (1984) Children's conceptions of friendship: A multimethod study of developmental changes. *Developmental Psychology* 20, 925–931.

Furman W. & Buhrmester D. (1985) Children's perceptions of the personal relationships in their social networks. *Developmental Psychology* 21, 1016–1024.

Furman W. & Buhrmester D. (1992) Age and sex differences in perceptions of networks of personal relationships. *Child Development* 63, 103–115.

Furman W. & Robbins P. (1985) What's the point?: Selection of treatment objectives. In Schneider B., Rubin K.H. & Ledingham J.E. (eds) *Children's Peer Relations: Issues in Assessment and Intervention*, pp. 41–54. Springer, New York.

Gabriel S.W. (1986) *Differential early experience and behavior in adult male chimpanzees*. Unpublished doctoral dissertation, University of Texas, Austin.

Goetz T.S. & Dweck C.S. (1980) Learned helplessness in social situations. *Journal of Personality and Social Psychology* 39, 246–255.

Goodwin M.H. (1990) *He-Said-She-Said: Talk as Social Organization Among Black Children*. Indiana University Press, Bloomington, Indiana.

Gottman J.M. (1983) How children become friends. *Monographs of the Society for Research in Child Development* 48(3), Serial No. 201.

Gottman J.M., Gonso J. & Schuler P. (1976) Teaching social skills to isolated children. *Journal of Abnormal Child Psychology* 4, 179–197.

Gottman J.M. & Parkhurst J.T. (1980) A developmental theory of friendship and acquaintanceship processes. In Collins W.A. (ed.) *Minnesota Symposia on Child Psychology*, Vol. 13, pp. 197–253. Lawrence Erlbaum, Hillsdale, New Jersey.

Gresham F.F. & Nagle R.J. (1980) Social skills training with children: Responsiveness to modeling and coaching as a function of peer orientation. *Journal of Consulting and Clinical Psychology* 18, 718–729.

Gronlund N.E. (1959) *Sociometry in the Classroom*. Harper, New York.

Gronlund N.E. & Holmlund W.S. (1958) The value of elementary school sociometric status scores for predicting pupils' adjustment in high school. *Educational Administration Supervision* 44, 225–260.

Harlow H.F. & Suomi S.J. (1974) Induced depression in monkeys. *Behavioral Biology* 12, 273–296.

Harlow M.K. (1971) Nuclear family apparatus. *Behavior Research Methods and Instrumentation* 3, 301–304.

Hartup W.W. & Sancilio M.F. (1986) Children's friendships. In Schopler E. & Mesibov G.B. (eds) *Social Behavior in Autism*, pp. 61–80. Plenum, New York.

Hay D.F. (1984) Social conflict in early childhood. In Whitehurst G. (ed.) *Annals of Child Development*, Vol. 1, pp. 1–44. JAI Press, Greenwich, Connecticut.

Hay D.R., Pedersen J. & Nash A. (1982) Dyadic interaction in the first year of life. In Rubin K.H. & Ross H.S. (eds) *Peer Relationships and Social Skills in Childhood*, pp. 11–39. Springer, New York.

Hayden L., Tarulli D. & Hymel S. (1988) *Children talk about loneliness*. Paper presented at the Biennial Meeting of the University of Waterloo Conference on Child Development, Waterloo, Ontario, May.

Heinlein L. & Spinner B. (1985) *Measuring emotional loneliness in children*. Paper presented at the Biennial Meeting of the Society for Research in Child Development, Toronto, April.

Hepler J.B. & Rose S.D. (1988) Evaluation of a multi-component group approach for improving the social skills of elementary school children. *Journal of Social Service Research* 11, 1–18.

Higley J.D. & Suomi S.J. (1989) Temperamental reactivity in non-human primates. In Kohnstamm G.A., Bates J.E. & Rothbart M.K. (eds) *Temperament in Childhood*, pp. 153–167, Wiley, New York.

Hinde R.A. & McGinnis L. (1977) Some factors influencing the effects of temporary mother–infant separation: Some experiments with rhesus monkeys. *Psychological Medicine* 7, 197–212.

Hinde R.A., Titmus G., Easton D. & Tamplin A. (1985)

Incidence of 'friendship' and behavior toward strong associates versus nonassociates in preschoolers. *Child Development* **56**, 234–245.

Howes C. (1988) Peer interaction of young children. *Monographs of the Society for Research in Child Development* **53**, Serial No. 217.

Hunt J. McV & Solomon R.L. (1942) The stability and some correlates of group-status in a summer-camp group of young boys. *American Journal of Psychology* **55**, 33–45.

Hunter F.T. & Youniss J. (1982) Changes in functions of three relations during adolescence. *Developmental Psychology* **18**, 806–811.

Hymel S. & Franke S. (1985) Children's peer relations: Assessing self-perceptions. In Schneider B.H., Rubin K.H. & Ledingham J.E. (eds) *Children's Peer Relations: Issues in Assessment and Intervention*, pp. 75–92. Springer, New York.

Hymel S., Franke S. & Freigang R. (1985) Peer relationships and their dysfunction: Considering the child's perspective. *Journal of Social and Clinical Psychology* **3**, 405–415.

Hymel S., Wagner E. & Butler L.J. (1990) Reputational bias: View from the peer group. In Asher S.R. & Coie J.D. (eds) *Peer Rejection in Childhood*, pp. 156–186. Cambridge University Press, New York.

Ingersoll-Dayton B. & Antonucci T.C. (1988) Reciprocal and nonreciprocal social support: Contrasting sides of intimate relationships. *Journal of Gerontology* **43**, 565–573.

Ispa J. (1981) Peer support among Soviet day care toddlers. *International Journal of Behavioral Development* **4**, 255–269.

Johnson M.A. (1989) Variables associated with friendship in an adult population. *Journal of Social Psychology* **129**, 379–390.

Jones D.C. & Vaughan K. (1990) Close friendships among senior adults. *Psychology and Aging* **5**, 451–457.

Kagan S. & Knight G.P. (1981) Social motives among Anglo-American and Mexican-American children: Experimental and projective measures. *Journal of Research in Personality* **15**, 93–106.

Kaufman I.C. & Stynes A.J. (1978) Depression can be induced in a bonnet macaque infant. *Psychosomatic Medicine* **40**, 71–75.

Konner M. (1975) Relations among infants and juveniles in comparative perspective. In Lewis M. & Rosenblum L.A. (eds) *Friendship and Peer Relations*, pp. 99–129. Wiley, New York.

Konner M. (1981) Evolution of human behavior development. In Munroe R.H., Munroe R.L. & Whiting B.B. (eds) *Handbook of Cross-cultural Human Development*, pp. 3–51. Garland STPM Press, New York.

Krasnor L.R. & Rubin K.H. (1981) The assessment of social problem-solving skills in young children. In Merluzzi T., Glass C. & Genest M. (eds) *Cognitive Assess-ment*, pp. 452–476. Guilford Press, New York.

Kupersmidt J.B., Coie J.D. & Dodge K.A. (1990) The role of poor peer relationships in the development of disorder. In Asher S.R. & Coie J.D. (eds) *Peer Rejection in Childhood*, pp. 274–305. Cambridge University Press, New York.

Ladd G.W. (1981) Effectiveness of a social learning method for enhancing children's social interaction and peer acceptance. *Child Development* **52**, 171–178.

Ladd G.W. (1983) Social networks of popular, average, and rejected children in school settings. *Merrill-Palmer Quarterly* **29**, 283–307.

Ladd G.W. & Asher S.R. (1985) Social skill training and children's peer relations. In L'Abate L. & Milan M. (eds) *Handbook of Social Skills Training*, pp. 219–244. Wiley, New York.

Ladd G.W. & Crick N.R. (1989) Probing the psychological environment: Children's cognitions, perceptions, and feelings in the peer culture. In Maehr M.L. & Ames C. (eds) *Advances in Motivation and Achievement: Motivation Enhancing Environments*, pp. 1–44. JAI Press, Greenwich, Connecticut.

Ladd G.W. & Emerson E.S. (1984) Shared knowledge in children's friendships. *Developmental Psychology* **20**, 932–940.

Ladd G.W. & Mize J. (1983) A cognitive-social learning model of social skill training. *Psychological Review* **90**, 127–157.

Ladd G.W. & Oden S. (1979) The relationship between peer acceptance and children's ideas about helpfulness. *Child Development* **50**, 402–408.

Ladd G.W. & Price J.M. (1987) Predicting children's social and school adjustment following the transition from preschool to kindergarten. *Child Development* **58**, 1168–1189.

La Greca A.M. & Santogrossi D. (1980) Social skills training with elementary school students: A behavioral group approach. *Journal of Consulting and Clinical Psychology* **48**, 220–227.

Larson R., Mannell R. & Zuzanek J. (1986) Daily well-being of older adults with friends and family. *Psychology and Aging* **1**, 117–126.

Laudenslager M.L. (1988) The psychobiology of loss: Lessons from humans and nonhuman primates. *Journal of Social Issues* **44**, 19–36.

Laudenslager M.L., Held P.E., Boccia M.L., Reite M.L. & Cohen J.J. (1990) Behavioral and immunological consequences of brief mother-infant separation: A species comparison. *Developmental Psychobiology* **23**, 247–264.

Ledingham J.E. (1981) Developmental patterns of aggressive and withdrawn behavior in childhood: A possible method for identifying preschizophrenics. *Journal of Abnormal Child Psychology* **9**, 1–22.

Lee G.R. & Ishii-Kuntz M. (1987) Social interaction, loneliness, and emotional well-being among the elderly.

Research on Aging **9**, 459–482.

McKinney W.T. (1986) Primate separation studies: Relevance to bereavement. *Psychiatric Annals* **16**, 281–287.

Mannarino A.P. (1976) Friendship patterns and altruistic behavior in preadolescent males. *Developmental Psychology* **12**, 555–556.

Maple T.F. (1980) *Chimpanzee reproduction, rearing, and rehabilitation in captivity.* Report presented to the Ad Hoc Task Force, National Chimpanzee Breeding Program, Georgia Institute of Technology Publications, Atlanta.

Marcoen A. & Brumagne M. (1985) Loneliness among children and young adolescents. *Developmental Psychology* **21**, 1025–1031.

Medrich E.A., Roizen J., Rubin V. & Buckley S. (1982) *The Serious Business of Growing Up: A Study of Children's Lives Outside of School.* University of California Press, Berkeley.

Mitchell G. (1970) Abnormal behavior in primates. In Rosenblum L.A. (ed.) *Primate Behavior: Developments in Field and Laboratory Research*, pp. 195–249. Academic Press, New York.

Mize J. & Ladd G.W. (1990) A cognitive-social learning approach to social skill training with low-status preschool children. *Developmental Psychology* **26**, 388–397.

Mounts N.S. & Asher S.R. (1992) *Are sociometrically neglected children behaviorally distinct from average status children?* Unpublished ms, University of Illinois, Urbana-Champaign.

Nasby W., Hayden B. & DePaulo B.M. (1980) Attributional bias among aggressive boys to interpret unambiguous social stimuli as displays of hostility. *Journal of Abnormal Psychology* **89**, 459–468.

Newcomb A.F., Brady J.E. & Hartup W.W. (1979) Friendship and incentive condition as determinants of children's task-oriented social behavior. *Child Development* **50**, 878–888.

Newcomb A.F. & Bukowski W.M. (1983) Social impact and social preference is determinants of children's peer group status. *Developmental Psychology* **19**, 856–867.

Newcomb A.F. & Bukowski W.M. (1984) A longitudinal study of the utility of social preference and social impact classification schemes. *Child Development* **55**, 1424–1447.

Novak M.A. (1979) Social recovery of monkeys isolated for the first year of life: II. Longterm assessment. *Developmental Psychology* **15**, 50–61.

Novak M.A. & Harlow H.F. (1975) Social recovery of monkeys isolated for the first year of life: I. Rehabilitation and therapy. *Developmental Psychology* **11**, 453–465.

O'Connor R.D. (1969) Modification of social withdrawal through symbolic modeling. *Journal of Applied Behavior Analysis* **2**, 15–22.

Oden S. & Asher S.R. (1977) Coaching children in social skills for friendship making. *Child Development* **48**, 495–506.

Oden S., Herzberger S.E., Mangione P.L. & Wheeler V.A. (1984) Children's peer relationships: An examination of social processes. In Masters J.C. & Yarkin-Levin K. (eds) *Boundary Areas in Social and Developmental Psychology*, pp. 131–160. Academic Press, New York.

Olweus D. (1978) *Aggression in the Schools: Bullies and Whipping Boys.* Hemisphere, Washington, DC.

Parker J.G. & Asher S.R. (1987) Peer relations and later personal adjustment: Are low-accepted children at risk? *Psychological Bulletin* **102**, 357–389.

Parker J.G. & Asher S.R. (1993) Friendship and friendship quality in middle childhood: Links with group acceptance and feelings of loneliness and social dissatisfaction. *Developmental Psychology* **29**.

Parkhurst J.T. & Asher, S.R. (1985) Goals and concerns: Implications for the study of children's competence. In Lahey B.B. & Kazdin A.E. (eds) *Advances in Clinical Child Psychology*, Vol. 8, pp. 199–228. Plenum, New York.

Parkhurst J.T. & Asher S.R. (1992) Peer rejection in middle school: Subgroup differences in behavior, loneliness, and interpersonal concerns. *Developmental Psychology* **28**, 231–241.

Peery J.C. (1979) Popular, amiable, isolated, rejected: A reconceptualization of sociometric status in preschool children. *Child Development* **50**, 1231–1234.

Peevers B.H. & Secord P.F. (1973) Developmental changes in attribution of descriptive concepts to persons. *Journal of Personality and Social Psychology* **27**, 120–128.

Peplau L.A. & Perlman D. (1982) *Loneliness: A Sourcebook of Current Theory, Research, and Therapy.* Wiley, New York.

Perry D.G., Kusel S.J. & Perry L.L. (1988) Victims of peer rejection. *Developmental Psychology* **24**, 807–814.

Perry D.G., Perry L.C. & Rasmussen P.R. (1986) Aggressive children believe that aggression is easy to perform and leads to rewards. *Child Development* **57**, 700–711.

Pervin L.A. (1989) Goal concepts in personality and social psychology: A historical perspective. In Pervin L.A. (ed.) *Goal Concepts in Personality and Social Psychology*, pp. 1–17. Lawrence Erlbaum, Hillsdale, New Jersey.

Pfeiffer A.J. & Koebner A.J. (1978) The resocialization of single-caged chimpanzees and the establishment of an island colony. *Journal of Medical Primatology* **7**, 70–81.

Putallaz M.C. (1983) Predicting children's sociometric status from their behavior. *Child Development* **54**, 1417–1426.

Putallaz M. & Gottman J.M. (1981) An interactional model of children's entry into peer groups. *Child Development* **52**, 986–994.

Putallaz M. & Wasserman A. (1990) Children's entry behavior. In Asher S.R. & Coie J.D. (eds) *Peer Rejection in Childhood*, pp. 60–89. Cambridge University Press, New York.

Rabiner D.L., Lenhart L. & Lochman J.E. (1990) Automatic vs. reflective social problem solving in relation to children's sociometric status. *Developmental Psychology* **26**, 1010–1016.

Reisman J.M. (1985) Friendship and its implications for mental health or social competence. *Journal of Early Adolescence* **5**, 383–391.

Reisman J.M. (1990) Intimacy in same-sex friendships. *Sex Roles* **23**, 65–82.

Reisman J.M. & Shorr S. (1978) Friendship claims and expectations among children and adults. *Child Development* **49**, 913–916.

Reite M.L. (1987) Infant abuse and neglect: Lessons from the primate laboratory. *Child Abuse and Neglect* **11**, 347–355.

Renshaw P.D. & Asher S.R. (1982) Social competence and peer status: The distinction between goals and strategies. In Rubin K.H. & Ross H.S. (eds) *Peer Relationships and Social Skills in Childhood*, pp. 375–395. Springer, New York.

Renshaw P.D. & Asher S.R. (1983) Children's goals and strategies for social interaction. *Merrill-Palmer Quarterly* **29**, 553–574.

Richard B.A. & Dodge K.A. (1982) Social maladjustment and problem solving in school-aged children. *Journal of Consulting and Clinical Psychology* **50**, 226–233.

Richey M.H. & Richey H.W. (1980) The significance of best-friend relationships in adolescence. *Psychology in the Schools* **17**, 535–540.

Roberto K.A. & Scott J.P. (1986a) Equity considerations in the friendships of older adults. *Journal of Gerontology* **41**, 241–247.

Roberto K.A. & Scott J.P. (1986b) Friendships of older men and women: Exchange patterns and satisfaction. *Psychology and Aging* **1**, 103–109.

Roberto K.A. & Scott J.P. (1987) Friendships in late life: A rural–urban comparison. *Lifestyles* **8**, 16–26.

Rockhill C.M. & Asher S.R. (1992) *Peer assessment of the behavioral characteristics of poorly accepted boys and girls.* Paper presented at the meeting of the American Educational Research Association, San Francisco, April.

Roff M. (1961) Childhood social interactions and young adult bad conduct. *Journal of Abnormal and Social Psychology* **63**, 333–337.

Rogers C.M. (1973) Implications of a primate early rearing experiment for the concept of culture. In Montagna W. (ed.) *Symposium of the IVth International Congress of Primatology*, Vol. 1, pp. 185–191. Karger, Basel.

Roistacher R.C. (1974) A microeconomic model of sociometric choice. *Sociometry* **37**, 219–238.

Rook K.S. (1987) Reciprocity of social exchange and social satisfaction among older women. *Journal of Personality and Social Psychology* **52**, 145–154.

Rook K.S. (1988) Toward a more differentiated view of loneliness. In Duck S.W. (ed.) *Handbook of Personal Relationships*, pp. 571–589. Wiley, New York.

Roopnarine J.L. & Field T.M. (1984) Play interactions of friends and acquaintances in nursery school. In Field T., Roopnarine J.L. & Segal M. (eds) *Friendships in Normal and Handicapped Children*, pp. 89–98. Ablex, Norwood, New Jersey.

Rosenblum L.A. & Kaufman I.C. (1968) Variations in infant development and response to maternal loss in monkeys. *American Journal of Orthopsychiatry* **38**, 418–426.

Rosenblum L.A. & Paully G.S. (1987) Primate models of separation-induced depression. *Psychiatric Clinics of North America* **10**, 437–447.

Ross H.S., Lollis S.P. & Elliott C. (1982) Toddler-peer communication. In Rubin K.H. & Ross J.S. (eds) *Peer Relationships and Social Skills in Childhood*, pp. 73–98. Springer, New York.

Rubin K.H. & Coplan R.J. (1992) Peer relationships in childhood. In Bornstein M. & Lamb M. (eds) *Developmental Psychology: An Advanced Textbook*, pp. 519–578. Lawrence Erlbaum, Hillsdale, New Jersey.

Rubin K.H. & Krasnor L.R. (1986) Social-cognitive and social behavioral perspectives on problem solving. In Perlmutter M. (ed.) *The Minnesota Symposia on Child Psychology*, Vol. 18, pp. 1–68. Lawrence Erlbaum, Hillsdale, New Jersey.

Rubin K.H., LeMare L.J. & Lollis S. (1990) Social withdrawal in childhood: Developmental pathways to peer rejection. In Asher S.R. & Coie J.D. (eds) *Peer Rejection in Childhood*, pp. 217–249. Cambridge University Press, New York.

Rutter M., Cox A., Tupling C., Berger M. & Yule W. (1975) Attainment and adjustment in two geographical areas: I. The prevalence of psychiatric disorder. *British Journal of Psychiatry* **126**, 493–509.

Schwarz J.C. (1972) Effects of peer familiarity on the behavior of preschoolers in a novel situation. *Journal of Personality and Social Psychology* **24**, 276–284.

Selman R.L. (1980) *The Growth of Interpersonal Understanding: Developmental and Clinical Analyses.* Academic Press, New York.

Selman R.L. (1981) The child as a friendship philosopher. In Asher S.R. & Gottman J.M. (eds) *The Development of Children's Friendships*, pp. 242–272. Cambridge University Press, New York.

Serafica F.C. (1982) Conceptions of friendship and interaction between friends: An organismic-developmental perspective. In Serafica F. (ed.) *Social-Cognitive Development in Context*, pp. 100–132. Guilford Press, New York.

Sharabany R., Gershoni R. & Hoffman J.E. (1981) Girlfriend, boyfriend: Age and sex differences in intimate friendship. *Developmental Psychology* **17**, 800–808.

Shea L., Thompson L. & Blieszner R. (1988) Resources in older adults' old and new friendships. *Journal of Social and Personal Relationships* **5**, 83–96.

Shure M.B. & Spivak G. (1972) Means-ends thinking, adjustment, and social class among elementary-school-aged children. *Journal of Consulting and Clinical Psychology* **38**, 348–353.

Singleton L.C. & Asher S.R. (1977) Peer preferences and social interaction among third-grade children in an integrated school district. *Journal of Educational Psychology* **69**, 330–336.

Smoller J. & Youniss J. (1982) Social development through friendship. In Rubin K.H. & Ross H.S. (eds) *Peer Relationships and Social Skills in Childhood*, pp. 277–298. Springer, New York.

Snyder D.S., Graham C.E., Bowen J.A. & Reite M. (1984) Peer separation in infant chimpanzees: A pilot study. *Primates* **25**, 78–88.

Sobol M.P. & Earn B.M. (1985) Assessment of children's attributions for social experiences: Implications for social skills training. In Schneider B.H., Rubin K.H. & Ledingham J.E. (eds) *Children's Peer Relations: Issues in Assessment and Intervention*, pp. 93–110. Springer, New York.

Spivack G. & Shure M.B. (1974) *The Problem Solving Approach to Adjustment*. Jossey-Bass, Washington, DC.

Sullivan H.S. (1953) *The Interpersonal Theory of Psychiatry*. Norton, New York.

Suomi S.J. (1979) Peers, play, and primary prevention in primates. In Kent M.W. & Rolf J.E. (eds) *Primary Prevention of Psychopathology*, Vol. 3, pp. 127–149. University Press of New England, Hanover, New Hampshire.

Suomi S.J. (1991) Adolescent depression and depressive symptoms: Insights from longitudinal studies with rhesus monkeys. *Journal of Youth and Adolescence* **20**, 273–287.

Suomi S.J., Collins M. & Harlow H.F. (1973) Effect of permanent separation from mother on infant monkeys. *Developmental Psychology* **9**, 376–384.

Suomi S.J., Harlow H.F. & Domek C.J. (1970) Effect of repetitive infant–infant separation of young monkeys. *Journal of Abnormal Psychology* **76**, 161–172.

Taylor A.R. & Asher S.R. (1984) Children's goals and social competence: Individual differences in a game-playing context. In Field T., Roopnarine J.L. & Segal M. (eds) *Friendships in Normal and Handicapped Children*, pp. 53–77. Ablex, Norwood, New Jersey.

Tokuno K.A. (1986) The early adult transition and friendships: Mechanisms of support. *Adolescence* **21**, 593–606.

Vandell D.L., Wilson K.S. & Buchanan N.R. (1980) Peer interaction in the first year of life: An examination of its structure, content, and sensitivity to toys. *Child Development* **51**, 481–488.

Vosk B., Forehand R., Parker J.B. & Rickard K. (1982) A multimethod comparison of popular and unpopular children. *Developmental Psychology* **18**, 571–575.

Wanlass R.L. & Prinz R.J. (1982) Methodological issues in conceptualizing and treating social isolation. *Psychological Bulletin* **92**, 39–55.

Weiss R.S. (1974) The provisions of social relationships. In Rubin Z. (ed.) *Doing Unto Others*, pp. 17–26. Prentice-Hall, Englewood Cliffs, New Jersey.

Wentzel K.R. (1991) Social and academic goals at school: Motivation and achievement in context. In Maehr M. & Pintrich P.R. (eds) *Advances in Motivation and Achievement*, Vol. 7, pp. 185–212. JAI Press, Greenwich, Connecticut.

Whiting B.B. & Edwards C.P. (1988) *Children of Different Worlds: The Formation of Social Behavior*. Harvard University Press, Cambridge, Massachusetts.

Williams G.A. & Asher S.R. (1987) *Peer- and self-perceptions of peer rejected children: Issues in classification and subgrouping*. Paper presented at the biennial meeting of the Society for Research in Child Development, Baltimore, April.

Williams G.A. & Asher S.R. (1992) Assessment of loneliness at school among children with mild mental retardation. *American Journal of Mental Retardation* **96**, 373–385.

Wright J.C., Giammarino M. & Parad H.W. (1986) Social status in small groups: Individual-group similarity and the social 'misfit'. *Journal of Personality and Social Psychology* **50**, 523–536.

Wright P.H. (1978) Toward a theory of friendship based on a conception of self. *Human Communication Research* **4**, 196–207.

Wright P.H. (1989) Gender differences in adults' same- and cross-gender friendships. In Adams R.G. & Blieszner R. (eds) *Older Adult Friendship: Structure and Process*, pp. 197–221. Sage, Newbury Park, California.

Youniss J. (1980) *Parents and Peers in Social Development: A Sullivan–Piaget Perspective*. University of Chicago Press, Chicago.

19: Developmental Approaches to Aggression and Conduct Problems

ROLF LOEBER AND DALE F. HAY

OBJECTIVES

The aim of this chapter is to apply a developmental perspective to the study of aggression and other types of antisocial behaviour. The phenomena under investigation range from the infant's earliest conflicts with parents to the diagnostic categories of oppositional disorder and conduct disorder, as described in DSM-III, DSM-III-R, ICD-9 or ICD-10 diagnoses (American Psychiatric Association, 1980, 1987; World Health Organization, 1992). The phenomena under discussion also extend to delinquency, defined here as those acts for which youngsters can be prosecuted in court. We are seeking pathways from oppositional behaviours in early childhood to later conduct problems, delinquency in adolescence and adult criminality.

In attempting to apply a general developmental perspective to this topic, one must grapple with three critical aspects of the phenomena in question:

1 There is considerable evidence for stability in problematic behaviour from childhood to adulthood, yet
2 there is a wide diversity and change with age in attitudes and behaviours subsumed under the rubric of aggression, and
3 there is a range of variation within normal populations, so that many children and adults show some or all of these attitudes and behaviours some of the time.

Let us consider each of these issues in some detail.

Long-term stability of disruptive behaviour

Several longitudinal studies have shown that early disruptive behaviours are predictive of similar behaviours later or more serious behaviours over time (Loeber & Stouthamer-Loeber, 1987). For example, the review by Olweus (1979) of aggression studies documented considerable continuity over time, with disattenuated correlations (i.e. coefficients corrected for measurement error) averaging 0.60 over an interval of 10 years. Remarkably, his review included several studies in which aggression was first measured during the preschool period (Kohn & Rosman, 1972).

Evidence for continuity is not limited to overt aggression. For example, predictions based on early lying have similarly shown a reasonably high utility in forecasting later delinquency (Mitchell & Rosa, 1981). Theft, drug use and truancy in middle childhood are also predictive of later delinquency (Loeber & Dishion, 1983; Loeber & Stouthamer-Loeber, 1987), as are more general indices of problematic behaviours such as 'troublesome behaviour' (West & Farrington, 1973, 1977) and referral for antisocial behaviour (Robins, 1966). Nonetheless, the picture shown in these studies is often one of heterotypic rather than homotypic continuity; this bears on the second issue, the very great diversity of antisocial activities.

The heterogeneity of disruptive behaviour

One of the most perplexing aspects of children's disruptive behaviour is its changing quality. Children may switch from shoplifting to vandalism, from truancy to substance use, and from bullying to violence. Does this changeable appearance really reflect unpredictable behaviour? Or is it possible to discern an orderly structure to these behaviours?

Does any problem behaviour correlate equally well with all other problem behaviours, or are there sets of behaviours that are more likely to be intercorrelated than other sets? Reviews of factor analytic studies of parents' or teachers' ratings of school-aged children (Quay, 1986; Loeber *et al.*, 1991) show that two main factors are usually extracted. One factor can be categorized as an oppositional/defiant factor, characterized by confrontational, aggressive behaviours, whereas the other factor shares features with more covert symptoms of conduct disorder such as theft and vandalism. In contrast, factor analyses of ratings of preschoolers often have resulted in a single 'externalizing factor', mostly consisting of oppositional/defiant behaviours (McDermott, 1983; Achenbach *et al.*, 1987). This can partly be explained by the fact that the more covert conduct problems might emerge somewhat later in childhood; this chapter returns to this question.

If most factor analytic studies of older children show two factors, does this mean that the two factors represent a single behavioural dimension, or can several different dimensions of problematical behaviours be distinguished? Here we define behavioural dimensions as concepts that link together discretely different behaviours. Loeber and Schmaling (1985) calculated how often particular problem behaviours loaded on the same factor. Multidimensional scaling allowed the plotting of the distance between the behaviours, reflecting the probability of how often the behaviours did indeed load on the same factor. Thus, a larger distance reflected a lower probability, whereas a closer distance implied a higher probability of the two behaviours being placed on the same factor.

Loeber and Schmaling (1985) found that a single dimension could best account for the pattern of factor loadings, which consisted of overt (or confrontational) problem behaviours on one pole and covert (or concealing) problem behaviours on the other pole. Recently, Frick *et al.* (1993), using the same meta-analytic technique, expanded on this approach and included more recent studies. Figure 19.1 shows the results on 23 401 youth, which largely paralleled the findings reported by Loeber and Schmaling (1985). Frick *et al.* (1993) extracted two dimensions: one showing a clustering of overt problem behaviour on one pole and covert problem behaviour on the other pole. The second dimension consisted of a continuum from destructive to non-destructive problem behaviours.

The two general dimensions of problem behaviour, however, provide little information at the individual level of analysis. The results of the Frick *et al.* (1993) analyses suggest, but do not prove, that there may be different individuals in each quadrant of Fig. 19.1. That is, quadrant D may represent individuals who are oppositional, quadrant B those who are aggressive, and quadrant A those who wantonly destroy property, and so on. Furthermore, in that the results of the meta-analysis are concurrent rather than longitudinal, they raise two basic developmental questions. First, do these different quadrants represent a sequence in development from less to more serious behaviours, and is there only one such sequence to be discerned (e.g. from quadrant D to B and to A)? Second, do disruptive youngsters develop in such a way that they substitute different sets of problem behaviours for each other over time, or do they tend to retain behaviours characteristic of earlier phases of development? To address these questions, longitudinal data are obviously required.

Continuities between normal and pathological forms of disruptive behaviour

One of the most important stumbling blocks for any investigator who wishes to measure continuities in antisocial behaviour across the lifespan is the fact that several of the behaviours in Fig. 19.1 are statistically normative at particular points in the life-course. Thus, most toddlers show some form of oppositional behaviour in the form of temper tantrums or disobedience. Furthermore, the majority of adolescents occasionally engage in at least mild forms of disruptive behaviour or criminal activities (DiLalla & Gottesman, 1989; Moffitt, 1993). In view of these age trends, the most meaningful individual differences may exist as a behavioural pattern over the life-course, not at the level of traits measured at any particular point in the life-course. For example, DiLalla and Gottesman (1989) hypothesized that three different sorts of individuals need to be distinguished: '(i) continuous antisocials — youths who are delinquent and then criminal as adults; (ii) transitory delinquents — youths who are delinquent but not criminal; and (iii) late bloomers — adults who are criminal but not delinquent' (p. 339). Somewhat

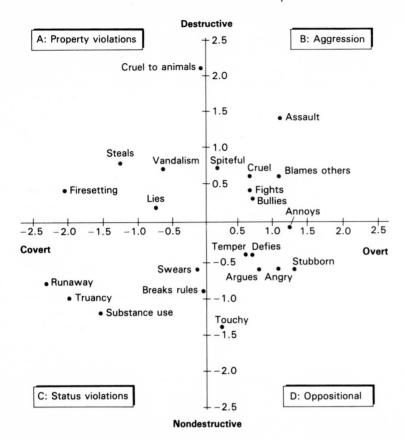

Fig. 19.1 Results of the meta-analysis of factor analyses of disruptive child behaviour (from Lahey *et al.*, 1990; © retained by B.B. Lahey).

analogously, Moffitt (1993) argued for a basic distinction between 'life-course persistent' and 'adolescent onset' antisocial behaviour, the former deriving from basic neurodevelopmental impairments that manifest themselves in difficult temperament and anxious attachment relationships as early as infancy and the latter provoked by a disparity between biological age and cultural expectations. These proposals remind us that, in any developmental analysis, it is important to chart marked changes in the developmental functions of the phenomenon of interest as well as examining the stability of individual differences (Appelbaum & McCall, 1983). However, it is often useful to examine the content and function of behaviours in addition to their life-course.

The suggestion that it will be more useful to base a taxonomy of antisocial behaviour on developmental pattern rather than particular features at a given age is in many ways the ontogenetic ana-

logue to current thinking by biological taxonomists (Wiley, 1981). In the last decade or so they shifted from an emphasis on numerical analyses of morphological features (the biological equivalent of research diagnostic criteria) to one that focuses on evolutionary history and relatedness to a common ancestor. In Moffitt's scheme, the 'common ancestor' in individual development might be a basic neurodevelopmental impairment. However, her observations raise real problems for prediction and intervention. For example, if most toddlers are oppositional and most adolescents somewhat delinquent, are there any quantitative or qualitative markers at either age to identify those individuals most at risk to go on to the next stage of the process? Moreover, not all disruptive youngsters show clear symptoms of neurodevelopmental impairment.

Not only are several of the behaviours shown in Fig. 19.1 displayed by the majority of individuals at particular ages; they are also seen by other members of society to be justifiable under particular circumstances at any age. Thus, for example, in legal decision-making, we distinguish between planned violence, unplanned violence and violence used to defend oneself. Similarly, young children state that retaliatory aggression is more acceptable than aggression that is unprovoked (Ferguson & Rule, 1988). Many respondents to Kohlberg's (1964) famous moral dilemmas have concluded that, yes, it is acceptable for Heinz to steal the drug needed for medical treatment (see Chapter 14). Thus, any developmental analysis of antisocial behaviour needs not only to chart the rise and fall of particular behavioural tendencies over the life-course, but also the extent to which those tendencies come to be regulated in accordance with the expectations of particular social groups, be those the family circle, mainstream society at large or particular delinquent groups and criminal subcultures. Hence one must examine the cognitive and affective dimensions of aggression and other delinquent or criminal activities, as well as the particular acts themselves.

With these three general considerations in mind, a chronological account is sketched of the developmental course of aggression from infancy to adulthood. We consider the nature of individual differences reported within each period of development and then examine continuities and discontinuities across periods of life, as well as the forces within individuals and their societies that either promote conduct problems and criminality or protect children against such outcomes. This section begins with an examination of the normal rise of social conflict in the first 2 years of life.

THE EMERGENCE OF OPPOSITIONAL BEHAVIOUR IN INFANCY

General developmental trends

Both opposition to parents and aggression with siblings and peers emerge in the first 2 years of human life. Both phenomena seem rooted in the basic maturational progressions of the species. Many mammalian infants undergo a prolonged period of dependency on their mothers, after which they are weaned and enjoined to seek and eat food somewhat more independently. Trivers (1974) out-lined some reasons why conflict between parents and offspring is a natural outcome of the transition to independence: it is in the parent's biological interest to limit investment in a single offspring or litter, turning attention to the next-born, whereas it is in the young organism's interest to get as much attention from the parent as possible. In this perspective, conflict between parent and toddler would be expected, and might be particularly fraught around the time of the birth of a younger sibling (for example, see Dunn, 1988). Moreover, it would not be surprising that, the more positive the relationship between the mother and first-born, the more intense the reactions to the birth of the sibling (Dunn *et al.*, 1981).

The prediction that there will be increased conflict between mother and child in the toddler period is also made by other theorists; for example, within a psychoanalytic framework, Mahler (1968) stressed the importance of separation from the mother and individuation of the child within the same developmental period. Within this perspective, a number of investigators have examined the emergence of oppositional behaviour in the second year of life, including temper tantrums and deliberate acts of disobedience (Escalona, 1968; Wenar, 1972). It has been argued that conflict with family members at this point in development supplies toddlers with important socializing experiences, so that the children gain a new understanding of themselves and their relations with other persons (Dunn, 1988). As this process occurs, conflict with parents would be expected to decline.

As infants grow older, they evince more interest in their possessions and in exerting control over their activities; thus conflict with peers also would be expected to increase in frequency over the first 2 years of life. 6 month olds appear to be not all that bothered by peers' designs on their possessions or invasions of their personal space (Maudry & Nekula, 1939; Hay *et al.*, 1983); in contrast, 12 month olds react by protesting, resisting or retaliating against such activities, and they engage in conflict with peers about as often as 24 month olds do (Caplan *et al.*, 1991). Thus, it seems likely that conflict between peers emerges somewhere around 9 months of age, when infants are beginning to grasp the concepts of cause and effect and the permanence of objects. Clear anger expressions also begin to be shown around this time, in the second half of the first year (Goodenough, 1931; Stenberg *et al.*, 1983; for a review see Chapter 17).

Changes in the capacity for conflict over the second year of life are more qualitative than quantitative; 24 month olds are more likely than 12 month olds to use speech in conflict situations and to attempt to resolve their disputes through pro-social means (Caplan *et al.*, 1991). Thus, in general, in both the family circle and the peer domain, one would expect to see oppositional behaviour rise and fall over the first 3 or 4 years of life. The population prevalence of oppositional behaviours should decrease between the ages of 3 and 6, as children acquire new strategies and tactics for dealing with conflict, and become more reconciled to their own independence. Certainly, simple struggles for the possession of objects decline in frequency over the preschool period (Hay, 1984). Furthermore, the expectation of a decline in oppositional behaviours is supported by the available epidemiological findings (summarized in Loeber *et al.*, 1991). In fact, the epidemiological data show that most oppositional symptoms continue to decrease beyond the age of 6 suggesting that the 'outgrowing' of these behaviours may take place over a longer period of time. These studies were based on different age cohorts, and so longitudinal analyses are needed to clarify whether some oppositional behaviours emerge again after the preschool period.

Individual differences

Given the normative nature of conflict in infancy, do any systematic differences amongst individuals become manifest at such an early age? Are there any qualitative features of conflicts that distinguish some children from other toddlers? We believe that it is important to look at the *intensity*, the *reactivity* and the *pervasiveness* of infants' activities in conflict with others.

Intensity

With respect to the first of these features, certain toddlers are more likely to commit acts of intense aggression than others are. For example, Brownlee and Bakeman (1981) observed the peer interactions

of 1–3-year-old boys in preschool classes. After a period of pilot observations, they distinguished three different ways in which one boy might hit another: (i) an 'open hit', which they defined as 'a low-intensity hit or swipe to the torso or limbs, usually with an open hand'; (ii) 'an object hit', defined as 'a low-intensity hit or swipe with an object (e.g. a stuffed animal) delivered to any part of the body'; and (iii) a 'hard hit', defined as 'any high-intensity hit or any hit to the head, usually with a lightly clenched fist' (Brownlee & Bakeman, 1981, p. 1076). Hard hits occurred very infrequently; Brownlee and Bakeman do not comment on individual differences in this regard, but the rates suggest that they are delivered by a small proportion of boys. Furthermore, hard hits, as opposed to less intense ones, systematically lead to prolonged, negative interaction, especially amongst 2 year olds.

It seems likely that the tendency to hit hard might be a characteristic of individual children that becomes consolidated into a more general aggressive stance with associated peer difficulties. More systematic analysis of the form of early oppositional behaviours is required, particularly with respect to the prevalence and stability of personally directed violence as opposed to actions used to gain or defend toys; conflict over toys is known to decline over the first 5 years of life (Hay, 1984), but the developmental course of physical violence over the same years is less well known. This distinction raises the issue, however, of the social circumstances in which opposition is displayed.

Reactivity

A second dimension of interest is the extent to which toddlers use aggression proactively or reactively — to initiate conflict or to defend themselves in response to the initiations of others. The theoretical distinction between hostile and instrumental aggression (Hartup, 1974) is one that children themselves uphold; 5-year-old children are less likely to condemn aggression in defence of an object than personally directed aggression, and they are less likely to blame the retaliator than the initiator in a conflict (Ferguson & Rule, 1988; Hay *et al.*, 1992). Thus, it seems possible that most young children will tug on objects they are trying to defend and push their opponents' hands away, but not all will typically initiate conflict and not all will use aggression proactively rather than reactively. Those who use aggression proactively may be of special interest in terms of prediction to later problems. It would be of interest to determine whether such children are also likely to hit hard and to show personally directed violence rather than mere attempts to seize possession of toys.

It might also be possible that children who continue in the fray for long periods of time, rather than yielding to or compromising with their peers, are of special interest in terms of later problems. However, the extent to which very young children continue to aggress rather than yield to their peers seems to be more a function of the immediate social setting than of enduring individual characteristics. For example, amongst unacquainted toddlers, the tendency to initiate conflict was a stable characteristic of individuals that transferred across peer partners, but the tendency to yield to the peer depended upon the partner with whom a focal child was paired (Hay & Ross, 1982). In groups of young children, the frequency of yielding to particular peers becomes stable over time, leading to 'dominance structures' that regulate the incidence of conflict in the group, at least amongst boys (Strayer, 1980).

Pervasive 'oppositional states' in infancy: difficult temperament and insecure attachment

Another important dimension of difference amongst individual infants and toddlers is the extent to which conflict as opposed to ease and harmony is a pervasive feature of their interactions with others, so that, more often than other infants, they are in an 'oppositional state' *vis-à-vis* the social world. Two such 'oppositional states' have been studied in detail — 'difficult' temperament and insecure attachment relationships.

Early in infancy, some infants enter into a state of opposition to their parents' ministrations; they are difficult to soothe, irregular in their habits and sometimes highly reactive to stimulation of various sorts (Thomas *et al.*, 1968). Dimensions along which infants vary include intensity of the children's behaviour (Garrison *et al.*, 1984), lack of adaptability (Graham *et al.*, 1973; Earls, 1987), and high

rates of negative emotion (Himmelfarb *et al.*, 1985; Hinde *et al.*, 1985). This cluster of qualities, often subsumed under the label of 'difficult temperament' (for a review see Chapter 4), is associated with higher rates of mother–child conflict (Lee & Bates, 1985).

Another important phenomenon that can be described as a form of 'oppositional state' in infancy is the condition of insecure attachment (see Chapter 16). Insecure attachment relationships are inherently conflictual, in that there is an incompatibility of responsiveness between parent and child. Lack of a harmonious relationship between child and caregiver may take different forms, as attempts to distinguish avoidant, ambivalent and disorganized attachment patterns have shown (see Chapter 16). Insecure attachment is associated with and presumed to derive from insensitive or unresponsive mothering in earlier infancy (Isabella, 1993); factors such as depression that interfere with mothers' abilities to interact with their infants lead to an elevated rate of insecure attachments (DeMulder & Radke-Yarrow, 1991).

Attachment theorists have been at pains to emphasize the fact that attachment is an interpersonal phenomenon that is more than simply the child's own individual temperament; in support of this claim, they noted that security with one parent is a very weak predictor of security with the other parent (Main & Weston, 1981). Nonetheless, longitudinal analyses have shown that attachment classifications are predicted by certain items on the Brazelton neonatal examination (Waters *et al.*, 1980), and some theorists have placed greater emphasis on the contribution of infant temperament to the quality of the parent–child relationship (Dunn, 1993b). It seems likely that there is a synergistic effect of difficult temperament and insensitive care-giving so that some babies paired with some caregivers are especially likely to be in a state of opposition during most of infancy, culminating in the development of an insecure attachment; for example, both infant temperament and the sensitivity of care influence infants' behavioural and physiological reactions to separation (Gunnar *et al.*, 1992).

In general, then, if one were attempting to identify important dimensions of differences amongst infants in the realm of aggression and conflict, it would seem useful to note the early occurrence of general interpersonal difficulties manifested by a difficult temperament and insecure attachment relationships, plus tendencies to use intense aggression in conflict with peers without provocation. We may now ask whether, in attempting to find such toddlers at risk for later problems, we should use a simple screening question, namely, noting whether the toddler in question is a girl or a boy.

AGGRESSION IN THE PRESCHOOL YEARS: THE EMERGENCE AND CONSOLIDATION OF GENDER DIFFERENCES

After the capacity for aggression emerges in infancy, it gradually becomes more the province of males than of females. Gender differences emerge and consolidate in the preschool years. However, an analysis of differences between males and females throughout childhood are hampered by the failure of investigators to pay much attention to girls' behaviour in conflict with family members and peers. All too often results based on studies of aggression and conduct problems in boys are assumed to be applicable to girls as well. The study of disruptive behaviour in girls has been hampered by the lower base rates of many problem behaviours, as compared with boys, the generally lower level of seriousness of disruptive behaviour, and the lower research priority given by funding agencies. To redress the balance, Zoccolillo (1993) has argued that diagnostic criteria should be changed so that girls need a lower threshold to be labelled as having conduct disorder (but see Zahn-Waxler, 1993 for a rebuttal to this suggestion).

There is overwhelming evidence that, in general, the prevalence of disruptive behaviour is lower in girls than in boys. It is not completely clear, however, that this difference is present from the outset. Studies of infants and toddlers show few if any gender differences; for example, in a study of 21-month-old children tested with same-sex peers, the only sex difference of the many tested was the observation that girls seemed to deliberate more over their moves in conflict; thus their conflicts were slower in pace (Hay & Ross, 1982). A short-term longitudinal study of children between 18 and 36 months of age, observed in their own homes with their most familiar peers, revealed no sex differences in mothers' reports of aggression nor in the actual alacrity with which children become embroiled in conflict with mothers and peers (Hay *et al.*, in press).

A search for early gender differences in overt, non-instrumental aggression is limited by the fact that most laboratory studies have yielded relatively few instances of forceful acts. One experimental study of 1- and 2-year-old peers, however, indicated that groups containing two girls and a boy were more likely to use personal force than groups containing two boys and a girl; the overall frequency of conflict was also greater in the groups with a preponderance of girls (Caplan *et al.*, 1991). Further inspection of the data indicated that this difference was not due to a basic difference between girls and boys at the individual level of analysis; at that level, no reliable gender differences emerged. Rather, it appeared that girls and boys behaved somewhat differently when they were the minority versus the majority members of their peer groups. When girls were in the majority, they were more likely to show designs on their peers' possessions; when boys were in the minority, they were more likely to protest their peers' actions. These two factors together appeared to contribute to a more volatile situation in groups dominated by girls: girls were more likely to take toys from their peers and boys were more likely to object to this.

The latter finding suggests that interest in peers' possessions, rather than aggression *per se*, may be a critical precursor to later gender differences in aggression. When tested in same-sex pairs, even 6-month-old boys are reliably more likely than 6-month-old girls to touch toys that their peers are holding, though the boys are not reliably more likely to touch toys in general (Hay *et al.*, 1983). Amongst 6-month-olds, this tendency does not lead to a greater frequency of conflict in male dyads, because infants at that age, males and females alike, tend not to rise to the challenge and defend their own objects; on about three-quarters of the occasions, the original holder of an object ends up with it still, without overt signs of protest or resistance.

By the time children are in naturally occurring preschool groups, however, there is evidence of gender differences in the frequency of conflict and the incidence of forceful acts (Smith & Green, 1975). In mixed-sex groups, girls tend to withdraw from situations where they need to compete for resources; furthermore, in same-sex groups, competition for limited resources is handled in different ways in girls' and boys' groups (Charlesworth & LaFrenière, 1982; Charlesworth & Dzur, 1987). The speed with which children tend to outgrow their tendency towards oppositional behaviour over the preschool years appears to differ between the sexes, with girls probably outgrowing these tendencies at a higher rate and at an earlier age than boys do (Richman *et al.*, 1985).

Maccoby (1986) has argued that, over the course of the preschool years and into middle childhood, peer society becomes increasingly differentiated on the basis of sex; male and female peer groups then take on lives of their own, shaping individual children's behaviour in accordance with the norms of the group. Maccoby noted several distinctive features of boys' as opposed to girls' groups. Boys tend to play in public places, in larger groups, in a rougher fashion; there is more fighting in boys' groups, and more dominance issues arise. In contrast, girls' groups show a greater concern with and adherence to turn-taking rules and more intensive, as opposed to extensive, friendship patterns. Maccoby argued strongly that these features of group life potentiate initial differences between the sexes: 'sex differences in children's characteristics in early childhood may contribute somewhat both to the segregation of the sexes in middle childhood and to the characteristics of the groups that are formed by male and female children, but once the groups are formed, they develop their own dynamics that are powerful in shaping the children's prosocial and antisocial behaviour' (p. 281). In this manner, aggression and competition become part of what boys do together, whereas it is a much less prominent feature of girls' activities.

One reason for self-segregation of the sexes is, of course, the overlapping but distinct distributions of interests held by the two sexes. It seems likely that girls and boys are interested in and pay attention to different aspects of the physical and social world; their tendencies to attend to some things rather than others then open up further opportunities for differentiating experiences. For example, boys (and

adult males) seem more likely than girls (and adult women) to pay close attention to televised material; boys look longer and are less easily distracted whilst looking at television than girls are (Anderson *et al.*, 1987). This differential level of interest in television then might increase the effect television has on children's aggression (for a review see Eron & Huesmann, 1986). It seems, for example, that extensive exposure to intense programming, even that without explicit aggressive content, stimulates aggression in young children (Singer & Singer, 1981); to the extent that boys are more 'plugged into' such programming than girls are, differences between the sexes may be exaggerated.

Most studies of gender differences in preschoolers' aggression have focused on either naturally occurring or experimentally contrived groups of peers. A somewhat different picture is revealed when children are studied at home, with their siblings. Again, girls and boys seem to behave differently in different social contexts; mixed-sex sibling pairs are more likely to aggress against each other than are same-sex pairs (e.g. Pepler *et al.*, 1981). This stands in contrast to peer dyads, where there is more aggression in same-sex male pairs than in mixed-sex pairs (Smith & Green, 1975).

Sibling conflict provides many opportunities for young children to hone their capacity for argument and their problem-solving skills (Dunn, 1988); in childhood and early adolescence female and male sibling pairs report approximately equal amounts of conflict (Dunn, 1993a). In addition to normative conflict amongst siblings, the sibling relationship has also been characterized as a training ground for aggression at problematic levels (Patterson, 1986). We now turn to ways in which parents, siblings and peers contribute to the maintenance and intensification of problematic aggressive behaviour, most often amongst boys, over the transition from early to middle childhood.

SOCIALIZATION EXPERIENCES THAT PROMOTE AGGRESSION IN CHILDHOOD: COERCIVE PROCESSES AND SELF-FULFILLING PROPHECIES

The transition from early to middle childhood is a time when most children show aggression less often, but some children become very troublesome indeed. Once a child has entered onto an aggressive trajectory, perhaps due to individual temperamental characteristics or as a reaction to difficult attachment relationships, other dimensions of the social world appear to conspire to exacerbate the problem. At this point in the child's development, the picture appears to be one of a failure of socialization and a carrying forward of unsuccessful social strategies into new situations, partly as a result of self-fulfilling prophecies.

Family relationships

Caregivers often end up in a struggle with disruptive children, not only for control in the immediate situation, but also in their overall attempts to socialize the child. The failure of socialization of disruptive children is shown by the persistence of patterns of highly oppositional and defiant behaviour at ages when other children have outgrown such behaviours. Thus there are two components to this breakdown of the socialization process: (i) the disruptive behaviour of the child; and (ii) parents' inappropriate child-rearing practices which either directly fuel the disruptive behaviour or which, although seemingly appropriate, do not lead to the desired effect of curtailing the problem behaviour. Patterson (1982) characterized the behavioural outcome of this process for the child as 'arrested socialization', but it can equally well be characterized as 'inadequate socialization'.

In children who are so adversely affected by inadequate socialization practices, oppositional and defiant behaviours occur at levels characteristic of younger children. Moreover, the retention of oppositional behaviour into the childhood years is often accompanied by a delay in the development of prosocial skills such as problem-solving, regulation of emotional arousal, and the maintenance of intimate relationships (see Chapter 14). This developmental delay on two fronts is particularly difficult for parents. The more a child displays disruptive behaviour in response to the parent's normal child-rearing practices, the less likely is the parent to persist in such practices. It is often much easier for the parent to give in or to complete a required task themselves than to compel, coax or exhort the child to do what is required. The struggles between the disruptive child and the care-giver often wear down the caregiver over time, making it less likely that appropriate socialization methods will be used by the parents; they may resort to coercive methods that only exacerbate the problematic behaviour (Patterson, 1980).

It is important to note that, faced with constant disruptive behaviour and non-compliance, parents may begin to avoid interacting with their children and fail to have many positive experiences. For example, mothers of disruptive children are less likely to initiate interactions with their children than other mothers; when they do interact with their children, these mothers are less likely to express positive affect and more likely to express negative affect than other mothers (Pettit & Bates, 1989; Gardner, 1992). Clinical observations of the parents of aggressive children find little evidence of the parents' interest in and affection for their children (Minde, 1992). In such families, it is the problem child who has the responsibility for initiating most interactions, positive as well as negative (Pettit & Bates, 1989).

Patterson (1986) suggested that, once the socialization process has begun to be less than adequate, sibling relationships contribute to further problems:

> A disruption in family-management (discipline) practices creates a situation in which the mother and the problem child become more frequently involved in (extended) coercive exchanges. Presumably, during these exchanges both the mother and the problem child are at risk to escalate the amplitude of their coercive behaviours. This was thought to define the basic or first step in training for fighting. The children 'win' enough of these interchanges to be in a position to effectively control the family through pain. As part of this control, they now are permitted to more frequently attack their siblings. Only the problem child is permitted to be out-of-control in interacting with the parents; but in these families, all children are permitted to be out-of-control in interacting with each other. (Patterson, 1986, p. 258).

Patterson added that, in families where management of conflict is poor, siblings are more likely than not to spend a great deal of unsupervised time together.

This parental toleration or encouragement of

sibling conflict in certain families is accompanied by an elevation of rates of aggression in all the siblings; although only that child who is labelled as the problem child shows high rates of aggression with the mother, all the siblings show higher than usual rates of aggression with each other (Patterson, 1986). Presumably, then, in such an atmosphere, each child in the family is exposed to many instances of expressed anger, an experience that is thought to provoke aggression (Cummings, 1987).

Peer relationships

Coercive processes within the family circle are but one dimension of the socialization experiences during middle childhood that promote and escalate aggression in certain children. Peer influences are also of considerable importance (see Chapter 18).

For many children, the transition from interactions with siblings to interactions with peers outside the home occurs already in the early childhood years, in such settings as nursery schools or day care centres. As new settings and peers present themselves to children, the consistency of disruptive behaviour across settings and playmates becomes more of an issue. Some children are disruptive at home, but not with peers; others are aggressive outside the home, but relatively well behaved with their parents. When early problem behaviours are observed in more than one setting, the continuity of the problem behaviour tends to be higher than when the early problem behaviour is present in one setting only. Furthermore, conduct problems that transcend settings appear to have different correlates from ones that are relatively restricted to one relationship or setting. For example, in a study of 191 child psychiatric patients, boys were evaluated with respect to specific conduct symptoms by a psychiatrist blind to the clinical diagnosis and family history of each boy (Hamdan-Allen *et al.*, 1989). On the basis of specific diagnostic criteria, boys who showed pervasive conduct problems across settings could be compared and contrasted with those boys who showed conduct problems at home or at school but not in both arenas. There were no differences between these groups in the rates of physical illness, developmental disorders, illegitimacy, adoption, placement in care or sibship status. The two groups did differ however in important ways. The boys

who showed pervasive problems had an earlier onset of such problems and were more likely to show associated hyperactivity. The pervasive problems were also associated with lower socioeconomic status, alcohol and substance abuse in the mothers and antisocial behaviour in the fathers. The authors unfortunately did not go on to examine whether situational problems shown at home versus school have different correlates, but the possibility remains that they do.

The peer group thus appears to be a setting that effectively encourages the consolidation of aggression and other conduct problems, at least for children who have already stepped forward on that trajectory. Two different processes are often taking place: (i) initial rejection by normal peers, and (ii) subsequent selection of deviant peers. What appears to happen over the course of childhood is that aggressive children tend to aggress more and more as a function of rejection by their normal, non-aggressive peers. Thus, in this way, normal classmates assist in the socialization of aggression, and aggressive children are often friendless. By the time of adolescence, however, aggressive youngsters are not necessarily without friends (Cairns *et al.*, 1988) and their aggressive tendencies are encouraged further by other delinquent peers. This section now examines each of these processes in turn.

Peer rejection and the emergence of self-fulfilling prophecies

In the preschool and early school years, when children first come together in same-age groups, particular friendships form and children acquire a certain status in the group; some children characteristically are rejected by their peers (see Chapter 18). Rejection by peers is especially likely to be attributed by the peers to aggression on the part of the rejected child (Parker & Asher, 1987; Pope *et al.*, 1989). Rejection can already be evident as early as 6 years of age and is predictive of later negative outcomes (Tremblay *et al.*, 1988).

Some investigators (Dodge *et al.*, 1986) have speculated that aggression in the peer group, which seems to lead inexorably to peer rejection, is associated with social cognitive deficits and biases; children who aggress tend to misattribute other children's acts as aggressive and fail to find other ways of resolving social problems (see Chapter 18). Dodge and co-workers (Dodge *et al.*, 1986, 1990) have examined children's responses to various hypothetical situations portrayed in cartoon videos, such as an attempt to join in play with children who have already been playing together, or having one's building bricks knocked over by another child. They have examined several steps in children's processing of the information presented in such vignettes — recalling what happened, making an accurate inference about peers' intentions, generating possible solutions to the dilemmas and evaluating the likely outcomes of pursuing one sort of tactic rather than another.

Both deficiencies in generating responses to dilemmas and biased attribution are linked to children's own aggressive behaviour with peers. For example, in a community sample of 5-year-old children, those who were judged to be aggressive by their teachers and peers tended to generate fewer non-aggressive solutions to such dilemmas and to evaluate aggression more positively; furthermore, children who were actually observed aggressing against their peers on the playground showed a marked tendency to assume that peers' intentions were hostile (Dodge *et al.*, 1990).

The social cognitive perspective acknowledges the fact that children's dealings with peers are not conflict-free; even friends quarrel regularly (Green, 1933; Hartup *et al.*, 1988). However, with age, children acquire diverse strategies for resolving conflict (Selman, 1980), and even very young children occasionally try to resolve their disputes by sharing or other positive gestures (Sackin & Thelen, 1984; Caplan *et al.*, 1991). When interviewed about simulated disputes between two glove puppets, 4- and 5-year-old children offer a variety of solutions; the extent to which the solutions they propose are aggressive is associated with their own observed tendencies to engage in sustained conflict with familiar peers (Hay *et al.*, 1992; Sheather, 1992). It seems likely that during the preschool years there is a general shift in young children's abilities to understand the intentions of others and to react to social dilemmas in non-aggressive ways, related to the general changes in children's understanding of other people's intentions and beliefs that take place around the time of the fourth birthday (see Chapter 13). Against this background of normative improvements in social cognitive abilities, individual differences in these skills stand in relief.

Children's deficiencies at social problem-solving are themselves linked to family adversity and psychopathology in the parents (Beardslee *et al.*, 1987; Pettit *et al.*, 1988; Downey & Walker, 1989) and in particular to the experience of physical abuse and harsh discipline (Dodge *et al.*, 1990; Weiss *et al.*, 1992). Dodge and co-workers have provided convincing evidence that social cognitive deficiencies and biases actually mediate the link between maltreatment by parents and children's own aggression (Dodge *et al.*, 1990; though somewhat weaker links were found in a second cohort reported in Weiss *et al.*, 1992). Thus it seems possible that problems in socialization, such as those described by Patterson and co-workers, translate into a child's approach to social life that makes peer relations especially difficult; thus peer rejection becomes yet another potentiating factor in the trajectory towards conduct problems.

However, the links between family experiences, social problem-solving deficits, and poor outcomes are not completely clear. In some cases, social problem-solving skills seem to represent a compensatory influence in the presence of family adversity (Downey & Walker, 1989), but in other circumstances acute social problem-solving ability may be more of a risk than a protective factor; for adolescent girls, high levels of social problem-solving are associated with similarly high levels of psychological disturbance (Beardslee *et al.*, 1987). Furthermore, in the middle childhood years, social cognitive deficiencies and biases are not shown only by aggressive children; children who report themselves to be depressed (i.e. showing an elevated score on the Childhood Depression Inventory) also are more likely than other children to assume peers' intentions are hostile (Quiggle *et al.*, 1992). Finally, treatment procedures may improve social cognitive abilities but fail to reduce overt aggression (Minde, 1992).

Sorting out which components of social cognitive abilities are linked to difficulties with peers is itself a complex task (see Chapter 18). It does seem clear, however, that children who are aggressive tend to be rejected, tend to be seen as being likely to aggress in a given situation, even when behaving neutrally, and tend to see the actions of others as similarly aggressive; these factors work together to create a restricted peer environment, which cannot help but limit opportunities for positive socialization.

Selection of deviant peers

In adolescence, and probably even earlier, disruptive youngsters select like-minded deviant youth as playmates and co-offenders. Although the evidence is by no means clear, it seems possible that aggressive children's first opportunities for positive affiliation with others comes in the context of associations with other delinquent peers. In later childhood and adolescence, peer influences are usually seen as promoting rather than discouraging conduct problems and delinquent acts. The negative effects of these influences on decreasing prosocial behaviour and increasing antisocial behaviour are well known (Quinton *et al.*, 1993). What is much less studied is the socializing role that peers can play in shaping alternatives to antisocial behaviour (Feldman *et al.*, 1984).

It is important to realize that most disruptive youngsters in adolescence are no longer friendless (Cairns *et al.*, 1988), although their friendship networks are perhaps less stable than those of other youngsters. Furthermore, delinquent acts are frequently committed with other companions present; no particular category of delinquent act is likely to be a solitary activity, in contrast to other types of acts. Hence even temporary friendships and alliances in the adolescent period serve as a mechanism to indoctrinate non-aggressive youngsters into disruptive behaviour.

Moffitt (1993) has argued that a form of social mimicry is taking place in the adolescent years, with many youngsters who had never shown problems before imitating the activities of their delinquent peers. She noted that the more delinquent peers may appear to less daring adolescents as more mature and independent, less tied to family prohibitions and values, and therefore particularly attractive at a time when most youngsters are struggling to create identities for themselves independent of their families and childhood achievements. Hence a great number of youngsters who become delinquent for the first time in adolescence, and desist thereafter, do so in the context of such influential peer relationships. Thus both aggressive and non-aggressive adolescents select deviant peers.

Socialization in the neighbourhood and at school

It would be too simplistic to state that disruptive child behaviour is the sum of all socialization practices. Children's socialization occurs in a variety of environments or contexts, such as neighbourhoods and schools (see Chapters 6 and 7). These contexts may vary in important ways and, as a result, may profoundly affect children's adjustment. In some neighbourhoods, law breaking is so common as to be normative; often these neighbourhoods are also economically deprived (Shaw & McKay, 1969). In areas such as these, one of the major ways of socially advancing oneself, getting respect from others, and obtaining money is to partake in the rackets, drug dealing or extortion that prevail in these areas.

Likewise, schools form an important context for the development of disruptive behaviours. School entry itself has been considered to be a life event that might provoke behavioural problems; however, those children showing behavioural problems in the first term of school typically had shown such problems already before entering school (Davies, 1992). However, several dimensions of children's experiences in school may exacerbate pre-existing problems. Adverse teaching techniques may affect multiple students and aid uncontrolled behaviour in classrooms. Unruliness outside of the classrooms, in corridors, playgrounds, or in the vicinity of the school, may contribute to patterns of victimization of schoolchildren. Some of the victims may eventually join the ranks of the aggressors. There are large differences amongst schools in the level of pupils' misbehaviour present (Rutter *et al.*, 1980). On the other hand, clear attempts by schools and national policies to reduce the level of bullying can control such behaviour (Olweus, 1991).

Consideration of these broader influences on children's behaviour is a reminder that, in the middle childhood and adolescence years, conduct problems multiply and diversify. Diagnosable conduct disorder includes more than overt aggression. Thus it is useful to return to the issue of heterogeneity of disruptive behaviour, and to reconsider information about gender differences, as they manifest themselves in later childhood and adolescence. Furthermore, in discussing the nature and correlates of conduct problems in childhood, we need to take up the issue of the comorbidity of children's psychopathological symptoms.

THE DEVELOPMENT AND DIVERSIFICATION OF CONDUCT PROBLEMS IN LATER CHILDHOOD AND PREADOLESCENCE

This section considers the emergence of diverse conduct problems of clinical concern. Here we are not considering aggression along a normal continuum, but rather are focusing on sets of symptoms as defined in psychiatric diagnostic instruments. In contrast to early occurring oppositional behaviours, most conduct problems, as defined by DSM-III or IDC-10, can be considered deviant at any age. This assertion applies both to milder sorts of acts that occur at high frequencies, such as frequent stealing or frequent acts of vandalism, but also to single, serious acts such as rape. Unlike oppositional behaviours, conduct problems tend to *increase* in prevalence from childhood to adolescence (Loeber *et al.*, 1991). A less serious set of conduct problems may start as early as the primary school period (e.g. theft and truancy), whereas the more serious conduct problems typically emerge from middle adolescence onwards (e.g. breaking and entering, robbery and rape). Some conduct problems consist of the youngster adopting adult behaviours — drinking, driving, going to adult cinemas — at a premature age; the onset of these behaviours usually takes place in early adolescence.

There are orderly sequences in the emergence of different sorts of conduct problems in childhood. In the Pittsburgh Youth Study (Loeber *et al.*, 1993b) (Fig. 19.2), the availability of six subsequent half-yearly assessments made it possible to expand the retrospective data for each boy so as to include a further prospective tracing of the sequence of onset of different problem behaviours over the next 2 years.

The median ages of onset for the oldest sample (thus, based on retrospective and prospective data) show that stubborn behaviour tended to occur earliest (median age 9, with a wide range of onset: the 25th percentile at age 3 and the 75th percentile at age 13). This was followed by minor covert acts such as lying and shoplifting, with a median age of 10, closely followed by defiance (i.e. doing things in one's own way, refusing to do things, disobedience) with a median age of onset of 11, while aggressive behaviours (i.e. bullying, annoying others) followed at age 12. Property damage (i.e. vandalism and firesetting) tended to emerge by age 12 as well. More serious delinquent acts, such as physical fighting and violence, came last and had a median age of 13. Also at that age, authority avoidance (i.e. truancy, running away, and staying out late at night) emerged.

It should be kept in mind that many youngsters in this sample had not yet gone through the full risk period. This implies that the median ages of onset are restricted and are likely to change as a result of the emergence of youngsters who experience the onset of problem behaviour later.

Gender differences in later childhood and adolescence

At this point, we must return to the issue of gender differences. Having discussed aggression in early childhood as an increasingly masculine activity, gender differences are considered with respect to the diversification of conduct problems manifested in later childhood and adolescence.

As a rule, the age of onset of conduct problems is later for girls than for boys (Robins, 1966, 1986; Guze, 1976). However, Robins's findings from the Epidemiological Catchment Area surveys suggest that girls begin to lie and steal at slightly earlier ages on average than boys do (Robins, 1986), but this needs to be verified by studies using shorter retrospective reports. Furthermore, data from a community sample in St Louis, Missouri, suggested that conduct problems are organized in similar ways for girls and for boys; separate factor analyses on the problems shown by girls as opposed to boys found very similar, though not identical, factor structures (Robins, 1986). Three virtually identical factors were: (i) precocious sex, substance abuse and fighting; (ii) school behaviour problems including discipline, expulsion, truancy and underachievement; and (iii) arrest and running away. Only

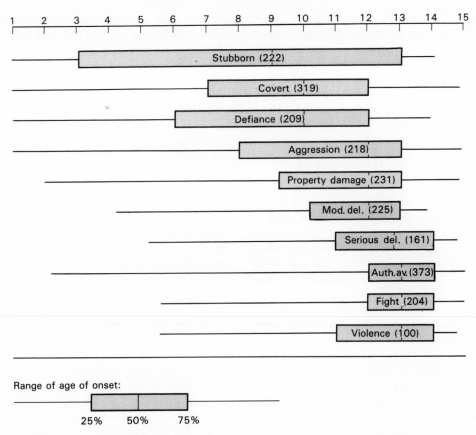

Fig. 19.2 Sequence of age of onset of disruptive child behaviour (oldest sample in the Pittsburgh Youth Study) (from Loeber *et al.*, 1993b); *n* is given in parentheses.

the more covert activities of vandalism, lying and stealing had different correlates for the two sexes.

Although the gender gap has narrowed in recent years, boys still show conduct problems at higher levels than girls do (Farrington, 1987). This statement is of course qualified by the fact that diagnostic criteria for conduct problems might be seen to be biased against women (Zoccolillo, 1993). However, assuming that it is indeed appropriate to apply the same diagnostic criteria to men and women alike and conceptually problematical to think about making the criteria gender-specific (Zahn-Waxler, 1993), does the lower prevalence suggest that girls' problems are less likely to be entrenched and stable over time?

Several studies have demonstrated that stability coefficients for aggression are often as high for girls

as for boys (Olweus, 1981; Cairns *et al.*, 1989a; Verhulst *et al.*, 1990). Both the prevalence and the stability of girls' problematic behaviours may be estimated differently, depending on whether the girls are reporting on their own behaviour or other informants are making reports about them; gender differences are less marked in self-reports (Cairns *et al.*, 1989). For girls the association between early and later aggression and other problem behaviours tends to be somewhat weaker than it does for boys (Kellam *et al.*, 1980; Stattin & Magnusson, 1989; Cummings *et al.*, 1990; however, for exceptions with respect to continuities in female aggression see Olweus, 1981; Cairns *et al.*, 1989a; Verhulst *et al.*, 1990).

There has long been interest in the proposition that girls aggress in more verbal, covert ways (Muste

& Sharpe, 1947; Robins, 1986). However, differences between the sexes in rates of verbal aggression do not always favour girls (Muste & Sharpe, 1947; Cummings *et al.*, 1989). Where girls and boys seem to differ is not simply in the age at onset of conduct problems, but in the nature of the other problems that girls and boys with conduct disorder have.

CONTINUITIES AND DISCONTINUITIES ACROSS THE LIFESPAN

So far a general model has been set forth for the development of aggression and conduct problems with a high rate of oppositional behaviours in infancy and early childhood, an emerging gender differentiation in early childhood, and the emergence of problematic levels of aggression and other forms of conduct problems as a response to various socialization pressures in middle childhood. It is now important to examine the issue of the prediction of individual differences from one time period to the next, in the light of the argument set forth. Thus, this section reviews the evidence for continuities from early oppositional behaviours to later criminality, violence and other poor psychological outcomes, whilst at the same time examining the striking developmental trends after childhood that produce discontinuities in individual development: the rise of conduct problems to high levels in adolescence and the apparent desistance from such activities in adulthood.

Continuities from early opposition to conduct problems

Given the high frequency of oppositional behaviours in toddlerhood and early childhood, to what extent are early disruptive behaviours relevant for the study of later conduct problems and criminality? From one perspective, early disruptive behaviour might be seen as a temporary phenomenon, a tendency that most children outgrow, and which, as a consequence, would have little prognostic utility in forecasting later problems. Alternatively, these early behaviours might be seen as stepping stones towards more serious behaviours. Within the latter perspective, one can picture an escalation towards more serious defiant or aggressive acts, or

one can think of a differentiation of problems into such qualitatively different activities as truancy or theft.

In addressing the question of continuities from infancy to preschool, investigators are limited by current diagnostic practices. A large proportion of disruptive behaviour during the preschool period of concern to adult caregivers consists of physical aggression, especially in boys (Tremblay *et al.*, 1991). We have speculated that toddlers who are at special risk for continuing problems may not only show high rates of physical aggression, but their aggression would be more intense, more proactive and less likely to be an instrumental means of securing access to favoured resources. It remains to be seen, however, to what extent aggression is implicated independently of a high level of hyperactivity or attentional problems. Thus, accurate measurement of the form and features of early aggression and accompanying behaviours and cognitive functions is critical.

Current diagnostic classifications of oppositional disorder (American Psychiatric Association, 1980, 1987; World Health Organization, 1992), however, are limited in that they do not focus on early physical aggression; physical aggression is categorized under conduct disorder. There is an urgent need to define empirically which characteristics of disruptive behaviour in the preschool period best predict later maladjustment. A survey of mental health professionals in the USA (Setterberg *et al.*, 1989) shows that the majority of respondents (65.4%) use different diagnostic criteria for preschoolers compared with older children, although there are no generally accepted criteria for disruptive behaviour in the preschool period.

Perhaps because of these somewhat confusing diagnostic issues, studies of the predictive utility of oppositional symptoms, as defined in DSM-III-R or ICD-10, have been scarce. Loeber *et al.* (1993a) followed up a sample of clinic referred boys over a period of 3 years and found that about a third of the boys diagnosed with oppositional defiant disorder did develop conduct disorder later. When the diagnosis of oppositional defiant disorder was qualified so as to include lying (currently a conduct disorder symptom) and to exclude swearing (developmentally more appropriate as a conduct disorder symptom), about half of the oppositional defiant disorder boys without conduct disorder incurred a diagnosis of conduct disorder in the next 3 years. The results illustrate that in a proportion of cases oppositional behaviours will spill over into conduct problems. It should be kept in mind, however, that follow-up results for a non-clinic sample, using the same criteria, are bound to be less strong.

Somewhat stronger evidence of prediction from preschool to later childhood is found when the diagnosis of oppositional defiant disorder is not used, but rather predictions are made on the basis of ratings of behavioural problems, including aggression (Richman *et al.*, 1985; Campbell & Ewing, 1990). For example, in discriminant analyses of the Dunedin birth cohort in New Zealand, five preschool variables, including parents' ratings of behavioural problems on the Rutter child scales, successfully classified 70% of the cases showing antisocial disorders at age 11 and 55% of the delinquency cases at age 15 (White *et al.*, 1990).

Given these links from the preschool period to later childhood, is any prediction possible on the basis of infants' behaviour? Some clues may be found in the literature on the two 'oppositional states' discussed above, difficult temperament and insecure attachment. The findings on prediction from difficult temperament are mixed (see Chapter 4); yet we have found only one study that failed to find any link between difficult temperament and later behavioural problems (Renken *et al.*, 1989).

Insecure attachment has similarly been held to predict later behavioural problems (see Chapter 16). There is also considerable evidence that separation from parents in childhood places children at risk for later conduct problems and adult maladjustment below the threshold of actual disorder (Zoccolillo *et al.*, 1992). Indeed, for girls residing in inner city London, the risk of conduct disorder is almost negligible without disrupted family circumstances (Quinton *et al.*, 1993). However, covariation of separation with other variables needs to be taken into account in tracing such links. It seems likely that children from homes with features that predict later aggression and conduct (low socioeconomic status, parents with convictions, violent family interactions) are quite likely to be separated from their parents in infancy, with consequent disruption of the attachment system. In such circumstances, the quality of substitute care may be especially important; for example, in a clinical sample of aggressive preschoolers contrasted with non-aggressive children from equally violent, disrupted homes, Minde (1992) found that both groups had been about equally likely to undergo separation from their parents, but the aggressive preschoolers had been more likely to be placed in foster care, whereas the others had been more likely to be cared for by relatives. The impact of parental absence may also depend on other dimensions of the family background; for example, father absence is predictive of criminality in upper income families, but protects against criminality in lower income households (Farrington, 1993). Thus, disordered attachment relationships resulting from separation may indeed be seen as manifestations of 'oppositional states' in infancy, but must be interpreted in terms of the larger family context. Moreover, the proportion of false negative and false positive errors in prediction from either difficult temperament or attachment security is not known.

Predictions from childhood conduct problems to crime and antisocial personality

There are three ways to examine the predictive utility of conduct problems. First, one can ask to what extent certain types of conduct problems predict later ones or antisocial personality in adulthood. A second question concerns the existence of developmental pathways in disruptive behaviour. A third question concerns the extent to which highly antisocial individuals in adulthood had displayed conduct problems earlier in life. The latter question addresses the degree to which early problems are a 'necessary' condition for the serious problems to emerge later.

Several reviews have indicated that theft, aggression, drug use and truancy are predictive of later delinquency (Loeber & Dishion, 1983; Loeber & Stouthamer-Loeber, 1987). Aside from individual behaviours, however, it is useful to examine which patterns of behaviour are most predictive. Patterns of importance include the timing, sequencing and covariation of disruptive behaviour.

Timing

The age of onset of conduct problems, as defined in the diagnostic instruments, is an important indicator of the continuity and exacerbation of such problems, at least in males (Robins, 1966; Loeber, 1982; Tolan, 1987; Farrington *et al.*, 1990a). Earlier onset associated with more serious problems later (Farrington *et al.*, 1990a; Loeber *et al.*, 1992). For girls, the link between early onset and continuity of problems is not as clear (Fleming *et al.*, 1982). Indeed, there is some evidence that later onset in girls, associated with higher intelligence, is more associated with continuity over time (Von Knorring *et al.*, 1987).

Sequencing

The general developmental sequence shown in Fig. 19.2 does not indicate the proportion of youth whose problematic behaviour unfolds along that sequence. To look at this, it is necessary to examine individuals' development, and establish whether individuals go through a single pathway of deviant development, or whether one can discern different pathways. In the Pittsburgh Youth Study, although boys' first problematic behaviours started at different ages, the sequence of different problems displayed, with some minor variations, was often similar. Loeber *et al.* (1993b) identified three conceptually distinct pathways (Fig. 19.3). The first and earliest pathway consists of authority conflict: this sequence starts with stubborn behaviour, can be followed by defiance (refusal, disobedience), and later by authority avoidance (e.g. truancy and running away from home). The second pathway consists of an escalation in covert acts, which tend to start with minor covert behaviours (lying, shoplifting), then are followed by property damage (vandalism, firesetting) and more serious forms of delinquency somewhat later. Finally, a third pathway, the overt pathway, consists of an escalation in the severity

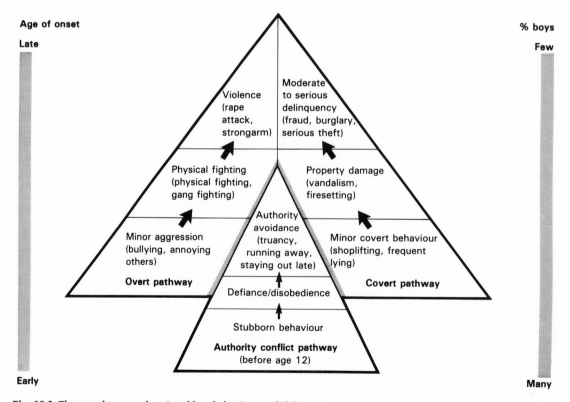

Fig. 19.3 Three pathways to boys' problem behaviour and delinquency.

of aggression. It starts with minor aggression (annoying others, bullying), is followed by physical fighting (including gang fighting), and then by violence (attacking someone, strong-arming, rape).

Most boys with disruptive behaviours fitted one or more of the pathways. The combination of certain pathways was particularly associated with high rates of offending. Those boys in the dual overt and authority conflict pathways had the lowest rate of offending, while those in the other dual pathways (overt and covert pathways, and covert and authority conflict pathways) and in the triple pathways (overt, covert and authority conflict pathways) had the highest rates of offending. The results were replicated across the two samples and across the different outcomes of the rate of self-reported delinquency and the rate of referral to the juvenile court (Loeber *et al.*, 1993b).

To what extent are certain predictors 'necessary' conditions for later deviant outcomes? This question is of importance since it helps to define individuals' pathways over time. When a necessary condition is identified, it is likely that a single pathway leads to the later outcome. In the case of arrest for a violent act by age 21, Farrington (1978) found that seven out of 10 violent offenders had been rated as highly aggressive between the ages of 12 and 14. Similarly Magnusson *et al.* (1983) found that nine out of 10 violent offenders by age 26 had been rated as highly aggressive by ages 10–13. This indicates that probably there is a main pathway towards adult violence, at least for males, with only a small proportion of individuals travelling alternative routes. Whether the alternative pathways are devoid of earlier aggression at other ages remains to be seen. It should be recognized, however, that some violence in adulthood appears to spring from other causes, including such biological influences as head trauma and tumours. Such influences can change behaviour at any age: when girls experience head injuries, they show behavioural problems that are more like those typically shown by boys (Goodman, 1993).

Several other patterns of conduct problems in childhood can enhance long-term prediction, in particular, their frequency, variety and occurrence across multiple settings (Loeber, 1982). The higher the initial frequency or variety of the conduct problems in early life, the more likely the behaviour will continue over time or be exacerbated. Also, when early problem behaviours are observed in more than one setting, such as both the home and the school, the continuity of the problems tends to be higher than when they are observed in one setting only.

Covariation and comorbidity

Finally, patterns of comorbidity with other disorders and covariation with other sets of problems aid prediction. The risk of comorbid or coexisting conditions is pronounced for disruptive youngsters. Examples of conditions that are comorbid with conduct problems are substance abuse, depression and somatization problems (Caron & Rutter, 1991; Loeber & Keenan, in press). A developmental model of comorbid risk appears appropriate in that such risk tends to unfold over time with some comorbid conditions emerging early and others later. For example, the comorbid risk of depression or substance abuse tends to occur from late childhood onwards and rarely occurs earlier, whereas the comorbid risk of learning disability can be recognized in the primary school period.

Are these conditions activated by pre-existing conduct problems or do the comorbid conditions activate conduct problems? The investigation of the causes of comorbid risk is still in its infancy (Caron & Rutter, 1991; Loeber & Keenan, in press). One possibility is that comorbid and focal conditions are associated with identical antecedent conditions, suggesting a common origin. Alternatively, comorbid conditions may emerge as a result of antecedent risk factors that are not associated with the focal condition. Developing our knowledge of these indices is essential for clinical practice in order to recognize which disruptive youngsters are at risk for the development of comorbid conditions later. Given that not all disruptive youngsters develop one or more comorbid conditions, the study of comorbidities also can help to differentiate subgroups within all disruptive youngsters for whom the aetiology of disorder is different (Magnusson & Bergman, 1991).

A comorbid condition of particular interest, especially in the early and middle childhood years, is hyperactivity and attentional problems (see Chapter 8). The presence of hyperactivity (and presumably the impulsive behaviours often associated with it) increases the risk for the *onset* of conduct problems or their persistence over time (Schachar *et al.*, 1981; Farrington *et al.*, 1990b). The presence of hyperactivity is also related to the age at onset of conduct problems and their eventual severity. For example, Loeber *et al.* (1992) found that in a referred sample of boys, those referred to a clinic at an early age had a higher hyperactivity score than boys referred at later ages, and on average experienced the onset of problem behaviours 2 years earlier than those referred at a later age. Thus, the early onset boys were more likely to be comorbid for hyperactivity and to travel up a deviant pathway at a *faster* pace. Furthermore, boys' pervasive conduct problems, as opposed to those that manifest themselves either at home or at school but not in both settings, are more likely to show both an earlier onset and an association with hyperactivity (Hamdan-Allen *et al.*, 1989).

The picture regarding comorbidity is somewhat more complicated for girls. For example, the prevalence of hyperactivity in girls is much lower than in boys; fewer girls tend to show hyperactivity, substance use, and precocious sexual behaviour (Horn *et al.*, 1989; James & Taylor, 1990). Do these findings also imply that disruptive girls have fewer of such other behaviours than disruptive boys? Studies show that the patterns of comorbidity often are vastly different for girls (reviewed in Loeber & Keenan, in press). In general, although the prevalence of disruptive behaviour in girls is lower than that in boys, the risk of comorbid conditions developing is substantially higher for girls than for boys (this fact is known as the gender paradox of comorbidities). It appears that girls with conduct problems may grow up to show more varied deviant outcomes, including somatizing and internalizing disorders (Robins, 1986) and their adult problems may be more pervasive than those of males (Zoccolillo *et al.*, 1992). Thus, although early disruptive behaviour in girls tends to be less ominous for later problems, once established, it tends to spread to other disorders as well. Why this is so remains to be investigated.

Comorbidity with hyperactivity increases long-term prediction (Schachar *et al.*, 1981; Farrington *et al.*, 1990b). Indeed, Magnusson has argued that,

in order to predict individuals' pathways into criminality, it is important to abandon the psychologist's traditional emphasis on the construct of aggression and instead adopt a more person-oriented approach (Magnusson & Bergman, 1988, 1991). In Magnusson's longitudinal sample of Swedish youth, when cluster analysis was used to identify individuals with different sets of problems, it became clear that no cluster was characterized by aggression in isolation from other problems; furthermore, only severe (as opposed to moderate) aggression in childhood, accompanied by motor restlessness and academic problems, predicted criminal records in adulthood. Less severe problems across a number of domains also predicted maladjustment in adulthood. Aggression on its own, however, did not predict adult criminality.

The cessation of conduct problems from adolescence to adulthood

Developmental theories must take into account discontinuities as well as continuities over time (see Chapter 1). Adolescence seems to be a peak time at which many individuals are defiant and commit delinquent acts (Moffitt, 1993); somewhat thereafter, after the age of 18, however, many people desist and most forms of delinquency decline in frequency. This decrease continues through the third decade of life (Blumstein *et al.*, 1986; Farrington *et al.*, 1986b).

Just as there are developmental sequences in the onset of problem behaviours, there are probably developmental sequences in their cessation. Le Blanc and Frechette (1989) examined the median age of termination of various offence types in a follow-up of a sample to age 25. They found, for example, that the median age of termination of vandalism was 13.3 years; that for petty theft was age 17; that for fraud age 21. In general, the age of desistance was earlier for minor crimes and later for more serious forms of delinquency. Across behaviours, however, those crimes that have an early onset tend to remit earlier, whereas those crimes with a later onset tend to cease later. It is unclear to what extent desistance in one behaviour is associated with desistance in other behaviours, and to what extent different individuals are represented in developmental sequences in desistance. Inevitably, however, the data are curtailed because the subjects by the age of 25 had not yet reached the maximum age of desistance.

Desistance should not be perceived as an all-or-nothing process. Le Blanc and Frechette (1989) distinguished between deceleration, de-escalation, reaching a ceiling, and specialization. Deceleration concerns a decrease in the frequency of problem behaviour prior to its cessation, while de-escalation involves a decrease in the seriousness level of the problematic acts. Reaching a ceiling refers to individuals' staying below a certain seriousness level without further escalating to more serious acts. Finally, specialization occurs when individuals contract their repertoire of deviant acts. Obviously, the four processes may coincide somewhat. The reason for distinguishing them here is to alert the reader to the fact that different forms of desistance may take place as intermediate stages towards full cessation.

One of the pernicious features of conduct problems is that youngsters often appear to desist for some time, but in fact go through a period of temporary desistance prior to relapsing into their old ways. Baicker-McKee (1990), in her reanalysis of the Cambridge Study in Delinquent Development, found that some boys after a period of disruptive behaviour paused for several years, only to relapse later. This finding underscores the persistence of some elements of disruptive behaviour even in the absence of overt manifestations. It is also possible that deviant behaviour amongst males in particular becomes increasingly covert, so that men with a history of criminality stop committing crimes in public but continue to abuse their spouses and children in private (Moffitt, 1993).

TOWARDS GENERAL MODELS OF DEVELOPMENT

The foregoing discussion has shown that there is substantial continuity over time in the general tendency to display disruptive behaviour, but there are also points in the lifespan when disruptive actions are more or less common in the population. There is also considerable diversification of antisocial activities over the life-course. Developmental pathways towards criminality and personality problems in adulthood seem gender-specific, and so it is not completely clear whether a general theory can explain the life-course of disruptive behaviour for females and males alike.

This final section moves beyond traditional models, which have tended to focus either on factors within the aggressive child or in the socializing environment, evaluating possibilities for reciprocal models of influence, in which vulnerable children are set forth on one trajectory or another in different families and communities (for similar models in other areas of development, see Chapters 1 and 10).

Vulnerabilities within the child

The clear continuities in aggression and conduct problems over time suggest that there may in fact be some inborn vulnerability factors that place individual children at risk for such factors; these may be manifested as basic neurodevelopmental impairments that appear early in development and are bound up with the construct of difficult temperament (Moffitt, 1993). However, the available genetic evidence is not completely clear. Studies on adults using an adoption or twin design have provided evidence for genetic influences on antisocial behaviour (Rutter & Giller, 1983). Concordance between monozygotic twins is slightly higher than that for dizygotic twins; however, there is considerable resemblance between siblings in general (Patterson, 1986), thus suggesting the importance of shared environmental effects as well as genetically based differences between individuals. Nonetheless, at the level of the phenotype, there has been much concern to identify factors within the child that promote aggression and other problematic behaviours.

It has already been noted that certain temperamental features of individual infants place them in an 'oppositional state' in the first year of life, which may contribute to the development of insecure attachment relationships. Similarly, two features of individuals in later childhood and adolescence — impulsivity and risk-taking — may constrain individuals' opportunities for socialization, or may make it likely that they are exposed to situations that provoke crime and likely to join in with the activities of delinquent peers.

On average, disruptive youngsters take more risks than other youngsters. Risk-taking does not have to be antisocial, but, amongst those with a habitual antisocial mode of interaction, risk-taking tends to increase the probability of victimizing others. Different degrees of risk-taking and anxiety may influence the outcome of disruptive behaviours, although the mechanisms by which these conditions interact remain to be clarifed (McBurnett *et al.*, 1991; Russo *et al.*, 1991). Youngsters who show a high degree of risk-taking may have relatively low levels of anxiety, whereas relatively anxious youngsters may be less likely to engage in risky behaviour, including forbidden acts.

Risk-taking and impulsive behaviours are correlated, but whereas some risk-taking can be done in a calculated and planned manner, impulsive behaviours, by definition, refer more to poor self-regulation (see Chapter 8). Examples of manifestations of poor self-regulation and impulsivity are easily elicited aggression and the spur-of-the-moment theft. Impulsivity as a construct has intuitive appeal, but its measurement is often problematic (Milich & Kramer, 1984). Typically, impulsive behaviours measured in different ways are poorly correlated. The measurement of impulsive behaviours through computer tasks is an important addition to more conventional ratings or self-reports. For example, White *et al.* (1991) found that the lifetime severity of delinquency was linearly related to boys' performance on an index of impulsivity consisting of the child's performance on computer tasks measuring delay of gratification, complemented by parents' reports of undercontrolled behaviour, independently observed restlessness, and teachers' and self-reports of impulsivity.

Impulsivity is of course a feature of hyperactivity, and it is important to disentangle the associations between conduct problems, hyperactivity and an impulsive approach to situations. There is some evidence that impulsivity might derive from hyperactivity, rather than conduct disorder *per se*. For example, an experimental study of hyperactive and conduct-disordered girls, with and without the other condition, indicated that hyperactive children were less able to delay their responding; there was no main effect of conduct problems, nor an interaction of conduct problems with hyperactivity (Sonuga-Barke *et al.*, 1992b). If it is possible that a certain level of impulsivity leads children into dangerous, crime-provoking situations, this is a developmental pathway that may be limited to those with associated hyperactivity; the possibility deserves further investigation.

To what extent ordinary levels of anxiety facilitate ordinary learning from experience is not clear. It is often assumed that differences between youngsters in learning from experience are stable individual traits, but as yet there is little evidence to confirm this. It is not impossible that youngsters' failure to modify their behaviour in the face of punishment is more likely to occur when physical punishment by parents is common and erratic. Non-contingent physical punishment elicits aggression, rather than serving as a contingent response to children's actions, and contingency learning would be impaired. It is also possible that failure to learn from adverse experiences may be associated with a child's basic impulsivity; for example, hyperactive children's desire to avoid delay interferes with their attention to various aspects of learning tasks (Sonuga-Barke *et al.*, 1992a, b).

Less is known about risk-taking and impulsivity in girls. We should note, however, that a protective factor against adult maladjustment in women is reflective planning of one's life, which might be seen as the opposite of impulsivity (Quinton *et al.*, 1993). In Quinton's sample, few conduct disordered girls show any planning for their educational or vocational futures; only if their families or non-deviant peers do some planning for them are they protected.

Individual differences amongst youngsters in their tendency to show conduct problems and impulsivity have been linked to individual differences in biological measures (Klintberg, 1993). The evidence has recently been reviewed by Lahey *et al.* (in press), who concentrated on distinctions between undersocialized (aggressive) and non-aggressive conduct-disordered children. The non-aggressive youngsters were more likely to show higher levels of reactive skin conductance, resting heart rate, cortisol, peripheral noradrenaline and blood serotonin. Based on a variety of studies, they argued that these differences reflected differences in central nervous system functioning, which are expressed as variations along the dimensions of aggression and anxiety. It is probable, but yet unproven, that the aggressive, non-anxious group would have an earlier onset of conduct problems; anxiety might inhibit the non-aggressive group until peer encouragement begins to take its effects.

It would be too simplistic to state that any or all of these factors within individuals are sufficient to explain variations in the age of onset and degree of children's escalation in disruptive behaviour. There is substantial evidence that these individual factors are moulded over time by contextual aspects of children's lives (Farrington, 1993).

Protective factors in the social environment

It has already been noted that the effects of parents, siblings, peers, schools and neighbourhoods in the initial development of aggression and other conduct problems are important. One way to characterize the continuities in individuals who pursue disruptive behaviour throughout life is to say that they remain in conflict with others in many situations they enter. However, examination of social influences on the development of and desistance from disruptive behaviour is incomplete without consideration of factors working against disruptive behaviour. One of these in young adulthood seems to be relationships with non-deviant companions, and especially a marital relationship with a non-deviant spouse. It appears, however, that earlier experiences may make it less likely that girls in particular will be able to form relationships with non-deviant men (Rutter *et al.*, 1990; Quinton *et al.*, 1993). This is partly a function of the higher base rate of deviance in the male sex and partly the product of a series of events leading to assortative pairing; girls with conduct disorder who spend their teenage years without a stable family life and who spend time with deviant peers are more likely to pair with deviant men, particularly if they also experience early pregnancy. It also seems likely that selection of deviant, not to say dangerous, men, and entering into sexual relationships without contraception, may be a mode of impulsivity and risk-taking that is particularly feminine. Thus characteristics of the individual may constrain the possibilities for protection from the environment.

Even for men, marriage to a non-deviant spouse will not necessarily be long-lasting and protective; for many, marriage may be yet another form of 'oppositional state'. Antisocial individuals have a higher rate of marital problems than do other persons (Robins, 1966). Analyses of the Berkeley and Oakland Growth Studies have shown that those boys who showed temper tantrums in late childhood were more likely than other boys to experience divorce as adults (Caspi, 1987). Thus marriage to a non-deviant spouse may be an important socializing influence in adulthood but one difficult to achieve for individuals with a long history of disruptive behaviour. These findings suggest the continuities found throughout the lifespan may reflect long-standing reciprocity between a vulnerable individual and an unresponsive or deviant environment.

Reciprocity between individual and environment and the emergence of social handicaps

The foregoing account of the development of aggression and other conduct problems suggests that vulnerable children fail to profit from and indeed disrupt normal socializing experiences. Disruptive behaviour appears to create a socializing environment in which it is difficult to learn pro-social alternatives. There is ample evidence to suggest that individuals' actions play an important role in shaping their future environments (Scarr & McCartney, 1983; Scarr, 1992), and disruptive behaviour is no exception to this pattern. Youngsters who are oppositional produce negative reactions in others, to which the youngster reacts by escalating his or her level of aggression. Over time the youngster may learn that escalation to more serious forms of aggression 'works' to suppress the disciplinary reactions of parents and teachers (Patterson, 1982). However, this process seriously interferes with the functions of the parent–child relationship. Furthermore, parents in this sort of situation may begin to feel powerless with their children; mothers who feel powerless find children's unresponsive behaviour difficult (Bugental & Shennum, 1984). Thus, even when the disruptive child is not being disruptive, but merely passive or unresponsive, his or her behaviour may be seen to be difficult or provocative, and the situation may rapidly escalate to conflict once again.

As disruptive individuals move along the life-course, their behaviour seems to lead to predictable, handicapping consequences. They may experience reading problems, academic failure and, in those countries where such an educational practice is used, retention in grade (Ledingham *et al.*, 1984; Maughan *et al.*, 1985; Brown & Borden, 1986; McGee *et al.*, 1994), although it is not clear whether this consequence is due to the disruptive behaviour or to associated conditions such as hyperactivity and reading problems (Olweus, 1983; Barkley *et al.*, 1990). Placement in special classes may reduce the likelihood of social adjustment years later, even when the effects of academic ability and negative classroom adjustment are controlled for (Spivack & Marcus, 1989). Disruptive youngsters may be expelled from more than one school (Barkley *et al.*, 1990; Kupersmidt *et al.*, 1990), with consequent disruption of education and lessening of job opportunities. Aggression is associated with dropping out from school (Cairns *et al.*, 1989a). Perhaps partly because of their failure to obtain academic qualifications, delinquents are more likely to go through long periods of unemployment than are non-delinquents, and unemployment can further activate delinquency. The rate of offending tends to be higher during periods of unemployment than during periods of employment (Farrington *et al.*, 1986a). Moreover, delinquent men compared to non-delinquent men also tend to earn less, at least in legal ways (Farrington, 1989).

To the extent that substance abuse is a feature of disruptive behaviour, other handicapping conditions may arise. Impairments resulting from substance abuse may already emerge during adolescence and often become evident during early adulthood. Long-term substance use may affect learning and cognitive functions (Baumrind & Moselle, 1985; Block *et al.*, 1990). Also, increased uninhibited or impulsive behaviour caused by intoxication or the secondary effects of substance abuse may further increase the risk of antisocial behaviour.

As noted earlier, disruptive individuals are also handicapped by their failure to establish supportive family relationships. Such individuals may leave their families of origin and begin their own families at young ages; aggressive males and females not only begin sexual intercourse early, but are at risk of becoming parents at an early age (Cairns *et al.*, 1989b). They are more likely to divorce and to

neglect or abuse their own children (Robins, 1966). Child abuse is more likely to occur when the parent is very young, so the transition to early parenthood may mediate continuities in antisocial behaviour from one generation to the next. It has been suggested that early puberty and consequently earlier sexual activity is itself a response to adverse family experiences such as those that generally promote disruptive behaviour (Belsky *et al.*, 1991; but see also Moffitt *et al.*, 1992).

The ways in which disruptive behaviours and their comorbidities produce social handicaps are likely to vary tremendously from child to child. The presence of certain protective factors may buffer the negative impact of particular handicaps. The present discussion, however, serves to illustrate some ways in which disruptive activities along with comorbid conditions and associated handicaps yield a network of interlocking influences over time.

The complexity of these reciprocal relations between children and their environments, as well as the heterotypic continuity of disruptive activities over time, may be one reason why interventions targeted to preventing particular disruptive actions, crimes or delinquent activities may often fail. Sometimes mere maintenance of aggressive behaviour at pre-existing levels and preventing escalation is seen as a positive treatment outcome (Minde, 1992). On the other hand, it appears that interventions such as Head Start, designed to promote cognitive development in inner-city children, have incidentally decreased the occurrence of delinquent acts when those children reached adolescence (Zigler *et al.*, 1992). Zigler and his colleagues argued that Head Start-type interventions, in addition to providing cognitive stimulation, gave low-income parents a great deal of support from the society as a whole in rearing their children. In other words, vulnerable children were provided with socializing experiences other than those their stressed parents could provide, and the parents' own socialization techniques were therefore enhanced and supported.

This finding, if replicated, demonstrates the importance of a lifespan longitudinal approach to the origins of delinquency and crime, such as has been set out in this chapter. To be effective, intervention programmes must be directed to the early stages of the development of disruptive behaviour, when vulnerable children might be provided with the sort of social experiences that can remediate, not aggravate, their disruptive activities. Better theoretical understanding of the nature of the vulnerabilities that emerge in infancy and childhood, as well as empirical knowledge about how those vulnerabilities translate into disruptive behaviour of different sorts over the life-course, could better target such interventions in the future.

REFERENCES

Achenbach T.M., Edelbrock C.S. & Howell C.T. (1987) Empirically based assessment of the behavioral/emotional problems of 2- and 3-year-old children. *Journal of Abnormal Child Psychology* **15**, 629–650.

American Psychiatric Association (1980) *Diagnostic and Statistical Manual of Mental Disorders*, 3rd edn. APA, Washington, DC.

American Psychiatric Association (1987) *Diagnostic and Statistical Manual of Mental Disorders*, 3rd edn, revised. APA, Washington, DC.

Anderson D.R., Choi H.P. & Lorch E.P. (1987) Attentional inertia reduces distractibility during young children's TV viewing. *Child Development* **58**, 798–806.

Appelbaum M. & McCall R. (1983) Design and analysis in developmental psychology. In Kessen W. (ed.) *History, Theory, and Methods*, Vol. 1, *Mussen's Handbook of Child Psychology*, 4th edn, pp. 415–476. Wiley, New York.

Baicker-McKee C. (1990) *Saints, sinners, and prodigal sons: An investigation of continuities and discontinuities in antisocial development.* Unpublished doctoral dissertation, University of Virginia, Charlottesville.

Barkley R.A., Fischer M., Edelbrock C.S. & Smallish L. (1990) The adolescent outcomes of hyperactive children diagnosed by research criteria: An 8-year prospective follow up study. *Journal of the American Academy of Child and Adolescent Psychiatry* **29**, 546–557.

Baumrind D. & Moselle K.A. (1985) A developmental perspective on adolescent drug abuse. In Brook J.S., Lettieri D.J., Brook D.W. & Stimmel B. (eds) *Alcohol and Substance Use in Adolescence*, pp. 41–68. Haworth Press, New York.

Beardslee W.R., Schultz L.H. & Selman R.L. (1987) Level of social-cognitive development, adaptive functioning and DSM-III diagnoses in adolescent offspring of parents with affective disorders: Implications of the development of the capacity for mutuality. *Developmental Psychology* **23**, 807–815.

Belsky J., Steinberg L. & Draper P. (1991) Childhood experience, interpersonal development, and reproductive strategy: An evolutionary theory of socialization. *Child Development* **62**, 647–650.

Block R.I., Farnham S., Braverman K., Noyes R. & Ghoneim M.M. (1990) Long-term marijuana use and subsequent effects on learning and cognitive functions related to school achievement: Preliminary study. In Spencer J.W. & Boren J.J. (eds) *Residual Effects of Abused Drugs on Behavior*, pp. 96–111. National Institute on Drug Abuse Research Monograph No. 101. Rockville, Maryland.

Blumstein A., Cohen J., Roth J.A. & Visher C.A. (eds) (1986) *Criminal Careers and 'Career Criminals'.* National Academy of Sciences, Washington, DC.

Brown R.T. & Borden K.A. (1986) Hyperactivity at adolescence: Some misconceptions and new directions. *Journal of Clinical Child Psychology* **15**, 194–209.

Brownlee J.R. & Bakeman R. (1981) Hitting in toddler peer interaction. *Child Development* **52**, 1076–1079.

Bugental D.B. & Shennum W.A. (1984) Difficult children as elicitors and targets of adult and communication patterns: An attributional-behavioural transactional analysis. *Monographs of the Society for Research in Child Development* **48**(1), Serial No. 205.

Cairns R.B., Cairns B.D. & Neckerman H.J. (1989a) Early school dropout: Configurations and determinants. *Child Development* **60**, 1437–1452.

Cairns R.B., Cairns B.D., Neckerman H.J., Gest S.D. & Gariepy J-L. (1988b) Social networks and aggressive behavior: Peer support or peer rejection? *Developmental Psychology* **24**, 815–823.

Cairns R.B., Cairns B.D., Neckerman H.J., Gariepy J-L. & Ferguson L.L. (1989b) Growth and aggression: I. Childhood to early adolescence. *Developmental Psychology* **25**, 320–330.

Campbell S.B. & Ewing L.J. (1990) Follow-up of hard-to-manage preschoolers: Adjustment at age 9 and predictors of continuing symptoms. *Journal of Child Psychology and Psychiatry* **31**, 871–889.

Caplan M., Vespo J.E., Pedersen J. & Hay D. F. (1991) Conflict over resources in small groups of one- and two-year-olds. *Child Development* **62**, 1513–1524.

Caron C. & Rutter M. (1991) Comorbidity in child psychopathology: Concepts, issues and research strategies. *Journal of Child Psychology and Psychiatry* **32**, 1063–1080.

Caspi A. (1987) Personality in the life course. *Journal of Personality and Social Psychology* **53**, 1203–1213.

Caspi A., Elder G.H. & Bem D.J. (1988) Moving away from the world: Life course patterns of shy children. *Developmental Psychology* **24**, 824–831.

Charlesworth W.R. & Dzur C. (1987) Gender comparisons of preschoolers' behavior and resource utilization in group problem solving. *Child Development* **58**, 191–200.

Charlesworth W.R. & LaFreniere P.J. (1982) Dominance, friendship, and resource utilization in preschool children's groups. *Ethology and Sociobiology* **4**, 175–186.

Cummings E.M., Iannotti R.J. & Zahn-Waxler C. (1989) Aggression between peers in early childhood: Individual continuity and developmental change. *Child Development*

60, 887−895.

Davies L. (1992) *Children's negotiation of the life event of starting school*. Paper presented at the European Conference on Developmental Psychology, Seville.

DeMulder E. & Radke-Yarrow M. (1991) Attachment with affectively ill and well mothers: Concurrent behavioral correlates. *Development and Psychopathology* **3**, 227−242.

DiLalla L.F. & Gottesman I. (1989) Heterogeneity of causes for delinquency and criminality: Life span perspectives. *Development and Psychopathology*. **1**, 339−349.

Dodge K.A., Bates J.E. & Pettit G.S. (1990) Mechanisms in the cycle of violence. *Science* **250**, 1678−1683.

Dodge K.A., Pettit G.S., McClaskey C.L. & Brown M.M. (1986) Social competence in children. *Monographs of the Society for Research in Child Development* **51**, Serial No. 213.

Downey G. & Walker E. (1989) Social cognition and adjustment in children at risk for psychopathology. *Developmental Psychology* **25**, 835−845.

Dunn J. (1988) *The Beginnings of Social Understanding*. Harvard University Press, Cambridge, Massachusetts.

Dunn J. (1993a) *From preschool to adolescence: A ten-year follow-up of siblings in Cambridge*. Presentation to the Centre for Family Research, Cambridge, Massachusetts.

Dunn J. (1993b) *Young Children's Close Relationships: Beyond Attachment*. Harvard University Press, Cambridge, Massachusetts.

Dunn J., Kendrick C. & MacNamee R. (1981) The reaction of children to the birth of a sibling: Mothers' reports. *Journal of Child Psychology and Psychiatry* **22**, 1−18.

Earls F. (1987) Sex differences in psychiatric disorders: Origins and developmental influences. *Psychiatric Developments* **5**, 1−24.

Eron L.D. & Huesmann L.R. (1986) The role of television in the development of prosocial and antisocial behavior. In Olweus D., Block J. & Radke-Yarrow M. (eds) *Development of Antisocial and Prosocial Behavior: Research, Theories, and Issues*, pp. 285−314. Academic Press, New York.

Escalona S. (1968) *The Roots of Individuality: Normal Patterns of Development in Infancy*. Aldine, Chicago.

Farrington D.P. (1978) The family background of aggressive youths. In Hersov L.A., Berger M. & Shaffer D. (eds) *Aggression and Antisocial Behaviour in Childhood and Adolescence*, pp. 73−93. Pergamon, Oxford.

Farrington D.P. (1987) Epidemiology. In Quay H.C. (ed.) *Handbook of Juvenile Delinquency*, pp. 33−61. Wiley, New York.

Farrington D.P. (1989) Later adult life outcomes of offenders and nonoffenders. In Brambring M., Losel F. & Skowronek H. (eds) *Children at Risk: Assessment, Longitudinal Research and Intervention*, pp. 220−244. de Gruyter, New York.

Farrington D.P. (1993) Interactions between individual and contextual factors in the development of offending.

In Silbereisen R. & Todt E. (eds) *Adolescence in Context*, pp. 366−389. Springer, New York.

Farrington D.P., Gallagher L., Morley L., St Ledger R. & West D.J. (1986a) Unemployment, school leaving, and crime. *British Journal of Criminology* **26**, 335−356.

Farrington D.P., Loeber R., Elliott D.S. *et al.* (1990a) Advancing knowledge about the onset of delinquency and crime. In Lahey B.B. & Kazdin A.E. (eds) *Advances in Clinical Child Psychology*, Vol. 13, pp. 282−342. Plenum, New York.

Farrington D.P., Loeber R. & Van Kammen W.B. (1990b) Long term criminal outcomes of hyperactivity-impulsivity-attention deficit and conduct problems in childhood. In Robins L.N. & Rutter M. (eds) *Straight and Devious Pathways from Childhood to Adulthood*, pp. 62−81. Cambridge University Press, New York.

Farrington D.P., Ohlin L.E. & Wilson J.Q. (1986b) *Understanding and Controlling Crime: Toward a New Research Strategy*. Springer, New York.

Feldman R.A., Caplinger T.E. & Wodarski J.S. (1984) *The St Louis Conundrum*. Prentice-Hall, Englewood Cliffs, New Jersey.

Ferguson T.J. & Rule B.G. (1988) Children's attributions of retaliatory aggression. *Child Development* **59**, 961−968.

Fleming J.P., Kellam S.G. & Brown C.H. (1982) Early predictors of age at first use of alcohol, marijuana, and cigarettes. *Drug and Alcohol Dependence* **9**, 285−303.

Frick P.J., Lahey B.B., Loeber R., Tannenbaum L., Van Horn Y. & Christ M.A.G. (1993) Oppositional defiant disorder and conduct disorder: I. Meta-analytic review of factor analyses. *Clinical Psychology Review* **13**, 319−340.

Garrison W., Earls F. & Kindlon D. (1984) Temperament characteristics in the third year of life and behavioral adjustment at school entry. *Journal of Clinical Child Psychology* **13**, 298−303.

Gardner F. (1992) *The quality of joint interactions between mothers and their preschool children with behaviour problems*. Presented at the BPS Developmental Section Conference, Edinburgh.

Goodenough F. (1931) *Anger in Young Children*. University of Minnesota Press, Minneapolis.

Goodman R. (1993) Brain abnormalities and psychological development. In Hay D.F. & Angold A. (eds) *Precursors and Causes in Development and Psychopathology*, pp. 51−85. Wiley, Chichester.

Graham P., Rutter M. & George S. (1973) Temperamental characteristics as predictors of behavior disorders in children. *American Journal of Orthopsychiatry* **43**, 328−339.

Green E.H. (1933) Group play and quarreling among preschool children. *Child Development* **4**, 302−307.

Gunnar M.R., Larson M.C., Herstgaard L., Harris M.L. & Brodersen L. (1992) The stressfulness of separation among nine-month-old infants: Effect of social context variables and infant temperament. *Child Development* **63**, 290–303.

Guze S.B. (1976) *Criminality and Psychiatric Disorders*. Oxford University Press, Oxford.

Hamdan-Allen G., Stewart M.A. & Beeghly J.H. (1989) Subgrouping conduct disorder by psychiatric family history. *Journal of Child Psychology and Psychiatry* **30**, 889–897.

Hartup W.W. (1974) Aggression in childhood: Developmental perspectives. *American Psychologist* **29**, 336–341.

Hartup W.W., Laursen B., Steward M.I. & Eastenson A. (1988) Conflict and the friendship relations of young children. *Child Development* **59**, 1590–1600.

Hay D.F. (1984) Social conflict in early childhood. In Whitehurst G.J. (ed.) *Annals of Child Development*, Vol. 1, pp. 1–44. JAI Press, Greenwich, Connecticut.

Hay D.F., Nash A. & Pedersen J. (1983) Interactions between six-month-old peers. *Child Development* **54**, 557–562.

Hay D.F. & Ross H.S. (1982) The social nature of early conflict. *Child Development* **53**, 105–113.

Hay D.F., Stimson C.A., Castle J. & Davies L. (in press) The construction of character in toddlerhood. In M. Killen & D. Hart (eds) *Morality in Every Day Life*. Cambridge University Press, Cambridge.

Hay D.F., Zahn-Waxler C., Cummings E.M. & Iannotti R. (1992) Young children's views about conflict with peers: A comparison of the daughters and sons of depressed and well women. *Journal of Child Psychology and Psychiatry* **33**, 669–683.

Himmelfarb S., Hock E. & Wenar C. (1984) Infant temperament and noncompliant behavior at four years: A longitudinal study. *Genetic, Social, and General Monographs* **111**, 7–21.

Hinde R.A., Stevenson-Hinde J. & Tamplin A.M. (1985) Characteristics of 3 to 4-year-olds assessed at home and their interactions at preschool. *Developmental Psychology* **21**, 130–140.

Horn W., Wagner A.E. & Ialongo N. (1989) Sex differences in school-aged children with pervasive attention deficit hyperactivity disorder. *Journal of Abnormal Child Psychology* **17**, 109–125.

Isabella R.A. (1993) Origins of attachment: Maternal interactive behavior across the first year. *Child Development* **64**, 605–621.

James A. & Taylor E. (1990) Sex differences in the hyperkinetic syndrome of childhood. *Journal of Child Psychology and Psychiatry* **31**, 437–446.

Kellam S., Ensminger M.E. & Simon M.B. (1980) Mental health in first grade and teenage drug, alcohol and cigarette use. *Drug and Alcohol Dependency* **5**, 273–304.

Klintberg B.A. (1993) *The psychopathic personality in a longitudinal perspective*. Paper presented at the Berzelivs Symposium XXVI, Linköping, Sweden.

Kohlberg L. (1964) Development of moral character and moral ideology. In Hoffman M.L. & Hoffman L.W. (eds) *Review of Child Development Research*, Vol. 1, pp. 383–431. Russell Sage Foundation, New York.

Kohn M. & Rosman B.L. (1972) A social competence scale and symptom checklist for the preschool child: Factor dimensions, their cross-instrument generality, and longitudinal persistence. *Developmental Psychology* **6**, 430–444.

Kupersmidt J.B., Coie J.D. & Dodge K.A. (1990) The role of poor peer relationships in the development of disorder. In Asher S.R. & Coie J.D. (eds) *Peer Rejection in Childhood*, pp. 274–305. Cambridge University Press, Cambridge.

Lahey B.B., McBurnett K., Loeber R. & Hart E.L. (in press) Psychobiology of conduct disorder. In Sholevar G.P. (ed.) *Conduct Disorders in Children and Adolescents: Assessments and Interventions*. American Psychiatric Press, Washington, DC.

Le Blanc M. & Frechette M. (1989) *Male Offending from Latency to Adulthood*. Springer, New York.

Ledingham J., Schwartzman A.E. & Serbin L.A. (1984) Current adjustment and family functioning of children behaviorally at risk for adult schizophrenia. *New Directions for Child Development* **24**, 99–112.

Lee C. & Bates J.E. (1985) Mother–child interaction at age two years and perceived difficult temperament. *Child Development* **56**, 1314–1325.

Lewis M., Feiring C., McGuffog C. & Jaskir J. (1984) Predicting psychopathology in 6-year-olds from early social relations. *Child Development* **55**, 123–136.

Loeber R. (1982) The stability of antisocial and delinquent child behavior: A review. *Child Development* **53**, 1431–1446.

Loeber R. & Dishion T.J. (1983) Early predictors of male delinquency: A review. *Psychological Bulletin* **94**, 68–99.

Loeber R., Green S.M., Lahey B.B., Christ M.A.G. & Frick P.J. (1992) Developmental sequences in the age of onset of disruptive child behaviors. *Journal of Child and Family Studies* **1**, 21–41.

Loeber R. & Keenan K. (in press) The interaction between conduct disorder and its comorbid conditions: Effects of age and gender. *Clinical Psychology Review*.

Loeber R., Keenan K., Green S.M., Lahey B.B. & Thomas C. (1993a) Evidence for developmentally based diagnoses of oppositional defiant disorder and conduct disorder. *Journal of Abnormal Child Psychology* **21**, 377–410.

Loeber R., Lahey B.B. & Thomas C. (1991) Diagnostic conundrum of oppositional defiant disorder and conduct disorder. *Journal of Abnormal Psychology* **100**, 379–390.

Loeber R. & Schmaling K.B. (1985) Empirical evidence for overt and covert patterns of antisocial conduct problems: A meta-analysis. *Journal of Abnormal Child Psychology* **13**, 337–352.

Loeber R. & Stouthamer-Loeber M. (1986) Family factors as correlates and predictors of juvenile conduct problems and delinquency. In Morris N. & Tonry M. (eds) *Crime and Justice*, Vol. 7, pp. 29−149. University of Chicago Press, Chicago.

Loeber R. & Stouthamer-Loeber M. (1987) Prediction. In Quay H.C. (ed.) *Handbook of Juvenile Delinquency*, pp. 325−382. Wiley, New York.

Loeber R., Wung P., Keenan K., Giroux B., Stouthamer-Loeber M., Van Kammen W.B. & Maughan B. (1993b) Developmental pathways in disruptive child behavior. *Development and Psychopathology* **5**, 103−133.

McBurnett K., Lahey B.B., Frick P.J. *et al.* (1991) Anxiety, inhibition, and conduct disorder in children: II. Relation to salivary cortisol. *Journal of the American Academy of Child and Adolescent Psychiatry* **30**, 192−196.

Maccoby E.E. (1986) Social groupings in childhood: Their relationship to prosocial and antisocial behavior in boys and girls. In Olweus D., Block J. & Radke-Yarrow M. (eds) *Development of Antisocial and Prosocial Behavior: Research, Theories, and Issues*, pp. 263−284. Academic Press, New York.

Maccoby E.E. & Jacklin C.M. (1974) *The Psychology of Sex Differences*. Stanford University Press, Stanford, California.

McDermott P.A. (1983) A syndrome typology for analyzing school children's disturbed social behavior. *School Psychology Review* **12**, 250−259.

McGee R., Share D., Moffitt T.E., Williams S. & Silva P.A. (1988) Reading disability, behavior problems and juvenile delinquency. In Saklofski D. & Eysenck S. (eds) *Individual Differences in Children and Adolescents: International Research Perspectives*, pp. 158−172. Hodder & Stoughton, New York.

Magnusson D. & Bergman L.R. (1988) Individual and variable-based approaches to longitudinal research on early risk factors. In Rutter M. (ed.) *Studies of Psychosocial Risk: The Power of Longitudinal Data*, pp. 45−61. Cambridge University Press, New York.

Magnusson D. & Bergman L.R. (1991) A pattern approach to the study of pathways from childhood to adulthood. In Robins L. & Rutter M. (eds) *Straight and Devious Pathways from Childhood to Adulthood*, pp. 101−115. Cambridge University Press, Cambridge.

Magnusson D., Stattin H. & Duner A. (1983) Aggression and criminality in a longitudinal perspective. In Van Dusen K.T. & Mednick S.A. (eds) *Antecedents of Aggression and Antisocial Behavior*, pp. 272−302. Kluwer-Nijhoff, Boston, Massachusetts.

Mahler M. (1968) *On Human Symbiosis and the Vicissitudes of Individuation*. International Universities Press, New York.

Main M. & Weston D.R. (1981) Security of attachment to mother and father: Related to conflict behavior and the readiness to form new relationships. *Child Development* **52**, 932−940.

Maudry M. & Nekula M. (1939) Social relations between children of the same age during the first two years of life. *Journal of Genetics Psychology* **54**, 193−215.

Maughan B., Gray G. & Rutter M. (1985) Reading retardation and antisocial behaviour: A follow-up into employment. *Journal of Child Psychology and Psychiatry and Allied Disciplines* **26**, 741−758.

Milich R. & Kramer J. (1984) Reflections on impulsivity: An empirical investigation of impulsivity as a construct. *Advances in Learning and Behavioral Disabilities* **3**, 57−94.

Minde K. (1992) Aggression in preschoolers: In relation to socialization. *Journal of the American Academy of Child and Adolescent Psychiatry* **31**, 853−862.

Mitchell S. & Rosa P. (1981) Boyhood behavior problems as precursors of criminality: A fifteen year follow-up study. *Journal of Child Psychology and Psychiatry* **22**, 19−33.

Moffitt T.E. (1993) Life course persistent and adolescent limited aggression. *Psychological Review* **100**, 674−701.

Moffitt T.E., Caspi A., Belsky J. & Silva P.A. (1992) Childhood experience and the onset of menarche: A test of a sociobiological model. *Child Development* **63**, 47−58.

Muste M.J. & Sharpe D.I. (1947) Some influential factors on the determination of aggressive behavior in preschool children. *Child Development* **51**, 823−829.

Olweus D. (1979) Stability of aggressive reaction patterns in males. A review. *Psychological Bulletin* **86**, 852−857.

Olweus D. (1981) Continuity in aggressive and withdrawn, inhibited behavior patterns. *Psychiatry and Social Science* **1**, 141−159.

Olweus D. (1983) Low school achievement and aggressive behavior in adolescent boys. In Magnusson D. & Allen V. (eds) *Human Development: An Interactional Perspective*, pp. 353−365. Academic Press, New York.

Olweus D. (1991) Bully/victim problems among school children: basic facts and effects of a school-based intervention program. In Pepler D.J. & Rubin K.H. (eds) *The Development and Treatment of Childhood Aggression*, pp. 411−448. Lawrence Erlbaum, Hillsdale, New Jersey.

Parker J.G. & Asher S.R. (1987) Peer relations and later personal adjustment: Are low accepted children at risk? *Psychological Bulletin* **102**, 357−389.

Patterson G.R. (1980) Mothers: The unacknowledged victims. *Monographs of the Society for Research in Child Development* **45**, Serial No. 186.

Patterson G.R. (1982) *Coercive Family Interactions*. Castalia Press, Eugene, Oregon.

Patterson G.R. (1986) The contribution of siblings to training for fighting: A microsocial analysis. in Olweus D., Block J. & Radke-Yarrow M. (eds) *Development of Antisocial and Prosocial Behavior: Research, Theories, and Issues*, pp. 235−261. Academic Press, New York.

Pepler D.J., Abramovitch R. & Corter C. (1981) Sibling interaction in the home: A longitudinal study. *Child Development* **52**, 1344−1347.

Pettit G. & Bates J.E. (1989) Family interaction patterns and children's behavior problems from infancy to 4 years. *Developmental Psychology* **25**, 413–420.

Pettit G.S., Dodge K. & Brown M.M. (1988) Early family experience, social problem solving patterns, and children's social competence. *Child Development* **59**, 107–120.

Pope A.W., Bierman K.L. & Mumma G.H. (1989) Relations between hyperactive and aggressive behaviors and peer relations at three elementary grade levels. *Journal of Abnormal Child Psychology* **17**, 253–267.

Quay H.C. (1986) Conduct disorders. In Quay H.C. & Werry J.S. (eds) *Psychopathological Disorders in Childhood*, 3rd edn, pp. 35–72. Wiley, New York.

Quiggle N.L., Garber J., Panak W.F. & Dodge K.A. (1992) Social information processing in aggressive and depressed children. *Child Development* **63**, 1305–1320.

Quinton D., Pickles A., Maughan B. & Rutter M. (1993) Partners, peers, and pathways: Assortative pairing and continuities in conduct disorder. *Development and Psychopathology* **5**, 609–783.

Renken R., Egeland B., Marvinney D., Mangelsdorf S. & Sroufe L.A. (1989) Early childhood antecedents of aggression and passive-withdrawal in early elementary school. *Journal of Personality* **57**, 257–281.

Richman N., Stevenson J. & Graham P. (1985) Sex differences in outcome of pre-school behaviour problems. In Nicol A.R. (ed.) *Longitudinal Studies in Child Psychology and Psychiatry*, 75–89. Wiley, New York.

Robins L.N. (1966) *Deviant Children Grown Up: A Sociological and Psychiatric Study of Sociopathic Personality*. Williams & Wilkins, Baltimore.

Robins L.N. (1986) The consequences of conduct disorder in girls. In Olweus D., Block J. & Radke-Yarrow M. (eds) *Development of Antisocial and Prosocial Behavior: Research, Theories, and Issues*, pp. 385–414. Academic Press, New York.

Russo M.F., Lahey B.B., Christ M.A.G. *et al.* (1991) Preliminary development of a sensation seeking scale for children. *Personality and Individual Differences* **12**, 399–405.

Rutter M. & Giller H. (1983) *Juvenile Delinquency: Trends and Perspectives*. Penguin, Harmondsworth.

Rutter M., Maughan B., Mortimore P. & Ouston J. (1980) *Fifteen Thousand Hours: Secondary Schools and their Effects on Children*. Open Books, London.

Rutter M., Quinton D. & Hill J. (1990) Adult oucome of institution-reared children. In Robins L. & Rutter M. (eds) *Straight and Devious Pathways from Childhood to Adulthood*, pp. 135–157. Cambridge University Press, Cambridge.

Sackin S. & Thelen E. (1984) An ethological study of peaceful associative outcomes to conflict in preschool children. *Child Development* **55**, 1098–1102.

Scarr S. (1992) Developmental theories for the 1990s: Development and individual differences. *Child Development* **63**, 1–19.

Scarr S. & McCartney K. (1983) How people make their own environments: A theory of genotype→ environment effects. *Child Development* **54**, 424–435.

Schachar R., Rutter M. & Smith A. (1981) The characteristics of situationally and pervasively hyperactive children: Implications for syndrome definition. *Journal of Child Psychology and Psychiatry* **22**, 375–392.

Schachar R. & Wachsmuth R. (1990) Oppositional disorder in children: A validation study comparing conduct disorder, oppositional disorder, and normal control children. *Journal of Child Psychology and Psychiatry* **31**, 1089–1102.

Selman R. (1980) *The Growth of Interpersonal Understanding: Developmental and Clinical Analyses*. Academic Press, New York.

Setterberg S., Campbell M., Carlson G. *et al.* (1989) *The DSM-IV Child Psychiatry Workgroup Survey: Results and Implications*. Unpublished ms, College of Physicians and Surgeons of Columbia University, New York.

Shaw C.R. & McKay H. (1963) Are broken homes a causative factor in juvenile delinquency? *Social Forces* **10**, 514–524.

Shaw C.R. & McKay H. (1969) *Juvenile Delinquency and Urban Areas*, revised edn. University of Chicago Press, Chicago, Illinois.

Sheather K. (1992) *Children's perceptions about social conflict: A developmental account*. Unpublished master's thesis, University of London.

Singer J.L. & Singer D.G. (1981) *Television, Imagination, and Aggression: A Study of Preschoolers' Play*. Lawrence Erlbaum, Hillsdale, New Jersey.

Smith P.K. & Green M. (1975) Aggressive behavior in English nurseries and play groups: Sex differences and responsiveness of adults. *Child Development* **46**, 211–214.

Sonuga-Barke E.J.S., Taylor E. & Heptinstall E. (1992a) Hyperactivity and delay aversion. II. The effect of self versus externally imposed stimulus presentation periods on memory. *Journal of Child Psychology and Psychiatry* **33**, 399–409.

Sonuga-Barke E.J.S., Taylor E., Sembi S. & Smith J. (1992b) Hyperactivity and delay aversion: I. The effect of delay on choice. *Journal of Child Psychology and Psychiatry* **33**, 387–398.

Spivack G. & Marcus J. (1989) *Long-term Effects of Retention in Grade and Special Class Placement among Inner City School Children*. Hahnemann University, Philadelphia, Pennsylvania.

Stattin H. & Magnusson D. (1989) The role of early aggressive behavior in the frequency, seriousness and types of later crimes. *Journal of Consulting and Clinical Psychology* **57**, 710–718.

Stenberg C.R., Campos J.J. & Emde R.N. (1983) The facial expression of anger in seven-month-old infants. *Child Development* **54**, 178–184.

Strayer F.F. (1980) Social ecology of the preschool peer group. In Collins W.A. (ed.) *Minnesota Symposium on Child Psychology*, Vol. 13. *Development of Cognition, Affect, and Social Relations*, pp. 165—196. Lawrence Erlbaum, Hillsdale, New Jersey.

Szegal B. (1985) Stages in the development of aggressive behavior in early childhood. *Aggressive Behavior* **11**, 315—322.

Thomas A., Chess S. & Birch H. (1968) *Temperament and Behavior Disorders in Children*. New York University Press, New York.

Tolan P.H. (1987) Implications of age of onset for delinquency. *Journal of Abnormal Child Psychology* **15**, 47—65.

Tremblay R.E., Le Blanc M. & Schwartzman A.E. (1988) The predictive power of first-grade peer and teacher ratings of behavior and personality at adolescence. *Journal of Abnormal Child Psychology* **16**, 571—584.

Tremblay R.E., Loeber R., Gagnon C., Charlebois P., Larivee S. & Le Blanc M. (1991) Disruptive boys with stable and unstable high fighting behavior patterns during junior elementary school. *Journal of Abnormal Child Psychology* **19**, 285—300.

Trivers R.L. (1974) Parental—offspring conflict. *American Zoologist* **46**, 35—57.

Verhulst F.C., Koot H.M. & Berden G.F.M.G. (1990) Four-year follow-up of an epidemiological sample. *Journal of the American Academy of Child and Adolescent Psychiatry* **29**, 440—448.

Von Knorring A., Anderson O. & Magnusson D. (1987) Psychiatric care and course of psychiatric disorders from childhood to early adulthood in a representative sample. *Journal of Child Psychology* **28**, 329—341.

Walker J.L., Lahey B.B., Russo M.F. *et al.* (1991) Anxiety, inhibition, and conduct disorder in children: I. Relations to social impairment and sensation seeking. *Journal of the American Academy of Child and Adolescent Psychiatry* **30**, 187—191.

Waters E., Vaughan B. & Egeland B. (1980) Individual differences in infant-mother attachment: Antecedents in neonatal behavior in an urban economically disadvantaged sample. *Child Development* **51**, 208—216.

Webster-Stratton C. & Eyberg S.M. (1982) Child temperament: Relationship with child behavior problems and parent—child interactions. *Journal of Clinical Child Psychology* **11**, 123—129.

Weiss B., Dodge K.A., Bates J.E. & Pettit G.S. (1992) Some consequences of early harsh discipline: Child aggression and a maladaptive social information processing style. *Child Development* **63**, 1321—1335.

Wenar C. (1972) Executive competence and spontaneous social behavior in one year olds. *Child Development* **43**, 56—260.

West D.J. & Farrington D.P. (1973) *Who Becomes Delinquent?* Heinemann Educational, London.

West D.J. & Farrington D.P. (1977) *The Delinquent Way of Life*. Heinemann Educational, London.

White J.L., Moffitt T.E., Caspi A. & Stouthamer-Loeber M. (1991) *Measuring impulsivity and its relationship to delinquency*. Unpublished ms, University of Wisconsin, Madison, Wisconsin.

White J.L., Moffitt T.E., Earls F., Robins L. & Silva P.A. (1990) How early can we tell? Predictors of childhood conduct disorder and adolescent delinquency. *Criminology* **28**, 507—533.

Wiley E.O. (1981) *Phylogenetics: The Theory and Practice of Phylogenetic Systematics*. Wiley, New York.

World Health Organization (1992) *Mental, Behavioural and Developmental Disorders, Clinical Descriptions and Diagnostic Guidelines*. World Health Organization, Geneva.

Zahn-Waxler C. (1993) Warriors and worriers: Gender and psychopathology. *Development and Psychopathology* **5**, 79—89.

Zigler E., Taussig C. & Black K. (1992) Early childhood intervention: A promising preventative for juvenile delinquency. *American Psychologist* **47**, 997—1006.

Zoccolillo M. (1993) Gender and the development of conduct disorder. *Development and Psychopathology* **5**, 65—78.

Zoccolillo M., Pickles A., Quinton D. & Rutter M. (1992) The outcome of childhood conduct disorder: Implications for defining adult personality disorder. *Psychological Medicine* **22**, 971—986.

20: Sleeping and Feeding Across the Lifespan

DIETER WOLKE

INTRODUCTION

Feeding and sleeping are necessary biological functions across the lifespan which, if not accomplished successfully, lead to a range of problems for individuals and their caretakers (Erman, 1987a; Lugaresi & Montagna, 1990; Wolke & Skuse, 1992). The study of developmental changes in sleeping and feeding provides a general understanding of the integrative functions of biological and social systems. In infancy, the accomplishment of predictable and controlled patterns of sleeping and feeding are the first indicators of self-regulation and competence in the infant (Sander, 1987). In contrast, pervasive, systematic and generally irreversible changes in sleeping and to a lesser extent in eating represent a normal part of the ageing process (Webb, 1989). A focus on developmental periods of integration and disintegration of functions in infancy, childhood, adolescence and old age provides insights into what can be considered 'normal' eating or sleeping (Anders et al., 1980). The epidemiological evidence of widespread sleeping and feeding problems will be examined against the background of what is known about normal variations in development and dynamic sequences of organization of sleep and feeding behaviour. This knowledge should provide clues to the aetiology and treatment of sleeping and eating disturbances throughout the lifespan.

SLEEPING

Sleep is a complex amalgam of physiological and behavioural processes, which can be measured by interviews and questionnaires (Welstein et al., 1983; Mullington et al., 1987), sleep diaries or logs (Richman, 1985; Kales & Kales, 1987), direct observation, using motility monitors (Thoman & Glazier, 1987; Sadeh et al., 1991), or video-somnography (Hobson et al., 1978; Anders & Keener, 1985). Questions have been raised about the reliability, validity and practicality of each of these methods (Webb, 1989). The distinction between different types of sleep has been made possible by the recording of various physiological functions, including cortical and muscular activity in sound-attenuated and temperature and humidity-controlled sleep laboratories. These rigorously controlled conditions provide highly objective measures of sleep during a whole night (Bixler & Vela-Bueno, 1987; Sassin, 1990). However, 'first night' phenomena such as decreased rapid eye movement (REM) and active sleep in the strange laboratory environment have been noted (Agnew et al., 1966). Moreover, the placement of electrodes is stressful and often unacceptable for valid recording in infants and young children (Anders & Sostek, 1976), thus limiting possibilities for ecologically valid developmental analyses.

Despite these limitations, as a result of the physiological measurement of sleep, it is now generally accepted that sleep consists of two distinct states. REM sleep (or paradoxical sleep) is typified by spontaneous binocular rapid eye movements under closed lids, suppressed resting activity, high rates of brain activity, enhanced brain metabolism and irregular respiration and heart rate. It is accompanied by vivid hallucinatory imagery and dreaming in humans. In contrast, non-REM (NREM) sleep, further subdivisible into four stages (see below), is typified by no eye movements, resting muscle tonus, regular heart rate and respiration, and reduced brain metabolism.

The different patterns of electrical activity in the brain (electroencephalography or EEG), eyeballs (electro-oculogram or EOG) and muscles (electro-myogram or EMG) are shown in Fig. 20.1. Although the precise neural mechanisms are unknown, it is evident that the transitions from sleep to wakefulness and between the two states of sleep require a series of brain stem and diencephalic structures (Moore, 1990). Recent attention has focused on the upper brain stem reticular formation, including the locus ceruleus and the midbrain raphe. Hobson and Steriade (1986) have proposed that NREM sleep is generated by a distributed noradrenergic network centred in the dorsal raphe nucleus, peribracheal region and locus ceruleus. In contrast, REM sleep is assumed to be controlled by a cholinergic system within pontine and medullar or bulbar reticular formation (Roffwarg et al., 1966). In Hobson and Steriade's (1986) model, the REM—NREM cycle is controlled by two sets of inhibitory and excitatory brain stem generators. The basic transition between sleep and wakefulness is thought to be regulated by the suprachiasmatic nucleus of the hypothalamus although the precise pathways and mechanisms are not known (Czeisler & Jewett, 1990).

The function of sleep

Two major theories, homeostatic recovery and evolutionary adaptation theories, have been advanced to account for the human need to sleep. The recovery theories state that the awake state, and the activity associated with it, causes an internal condition that is incompatible with the continuation of wakefulness; sleep leads to recovery of the awake state (Webb, 1981). Recovery theories are homeostatic models, with body cells assumed to be exhausted during the waking hours and 'restored' during sleep. Support for the recovery theory would be the finding that body cells, including neurones, accumulate substances that are related to an increasing urge to fall asleep. Already in 1913, one such substance, 'hypnotoxine', was identified by Henri Pieron (Knapp, 1989), who demonstrated the effect

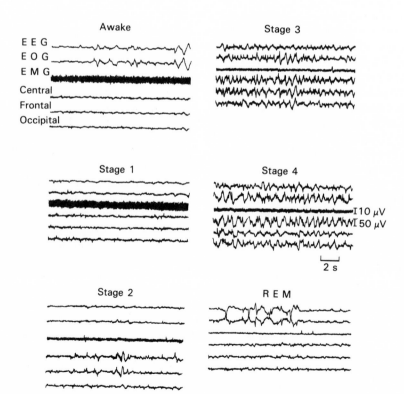

Fig. 20.1 Stages and states of sleep. Awake: low amplitude and fast frequency activity, with a relatively high amplitude electroencephalogram (EEG). Stage 1: low amplitude, fast (mixed) EEG pattern. Stage 2: low amplitude, mixed-frequency EEG pattern with large amounts of theta waves (4—7.5 Hz) and intermittent sleep spindles (brief bursts of 11.5—15 Hz waves) and K complexes (sharp biphasic waves followed by a high voltage low waves). Stage 3: slow (< 2 Hz) high amplitude waves. Stage 4: slow waves, often difficult to distinguish from stage 3. Rapid eye movement (REM) sleep described in text (redrawn from Kales et al., 1990).

by injecting liquor from sleep-deprived rats into well-rested rats to induce sleep (Borbely, 1986). Similar substances such as the peptide 'factor S' or the 'delta sleep-inducing peptide' have been proposed in recent years (Adam & Oswald, 1983), but the evidence is still not convincing.

Proponents of evolutionary theories argue that those species that sleep have gained an evolutionary advantage with respect to energy conservation, security during light or dark times, depending on visual requirements, and so forth (Meddis, 1977). Chronobiological approaches can also be considered adaptive theories, as they try to elucidate how different endogenous rhythms are paced (Czeisler & Jewett, 1990) and how these depend on external conditions. Chronobiologists suggest that the urge to sleep and the intensity of sleep are controlled by an internal pacemaker (the suprachiasmatic nucleus of the hypothalamus) while recovery theorists postulate that the sleep urge and sleep intensity are functions of the amount of prior wakefulness (Bixler & Vela-Bueno, 1987). Borbely (1982) integrated both postulates into a two-process model, demonstrating that sleep-deprived individuals recovered quickly when the recovery sleep occurred at a normal sleeping time, but only partially recovered if it coincided with normal waking time; if the latter, recovery was only completed at the time of the next normal sleep cycle.

There are a number of phenomena that cannot be readily explained by the above theories (Horne, 1988; Knapp, 1989). REM and NREM sleep should be considered separately (Erman, 1987a). Roffwarg *et al.* (1966) proposed an ontogenetic hypothesis that REM sleep, which is seen in high concentration (50%) of sleep time in the newborn and which diminishes as a percentage of total sleep during early childhood, plays an important role in the structural maturation and differentiation of key sensory and motor areas and is an early driving force in the development of the central nervous system (CNS). There are also suggestions that REM sleep is involved in cognitive processes (Erman, 1987a), including the consolidation of newly learned material (Pearlman, 1981). In contrast, Crick and Mitchison (1983) suggested that REM sleep may function to 'unlearn' irrelevant or incongruous data, and that we may 'dream to forget'. From an evolutionary viewpoint, REM sleep may also have

survival advantage under natural conditions by periodically decreasing individuals' threshold of arousal (Lenard, 1970).

Less evidence has been accumulated regarding the role of NREM sleep. The assumption that REM sleep and dreaming are synonymous (Roffwarg *et al.*, 1966) is no longer tenable (Antrobus, 1983). However, while REM dreams are vivid, and often bizarre and hallucinatory in nature, NREM dream reports are usually more like stories involving real people. NREM sleep, and in particular slow-wave delta-wave sleep, is considered to have a protective function against pathological ageing and neuro-psychiatric disorders (Kupfer & Reynolds, 1989).

Horne (1988) has proposed an integrative approach in which the organization of the two sleep states in tandem is important. The first two or three sleep cycles that contain large amounts of slow-wave delta-wave sleep and the associated REM sleep seem essential for CNS restitution. As the night progresses, however, sleep can be reduced or extended according to need, energy conservation, circadian factors and mood changes. Sleep reduction studies show that sleep losses are not fully made up subsequently; habitually short sleepers have similar amounts of slow-wave delta-wave sleep, and the first two or three cycles of habitually short sleepers' sleep is identical to that of long sleepers (Erman, 1987a; Horne, 1988).

Normative changes in sleep phenomenology

Total sleep duration

An approximation of the changes in total amounts of mean sleeping time across the lifespan is given in Fig. 20.2. Total day and night-time sleep decreases rapidly during the first 3 years of life (from about 65 to 45–50% of a 24-hour period), with a more gradual decrease until adolescence (Roffwarg *et al.*, 1966; Anders & Keener, 1985). During puberty, total amount of sleep decreases more rapidly and settles to adult levels (Prinz *et al.*, 1990b). In contrast to commonly held beliefs, the total amount of sleep does not reduce dramatically in the over 60 year olds, though there may be a small increase in total daily sleep time (Pressman & Fry, 1988; Webb, 1989). Newer studies point to subgroups of elderly

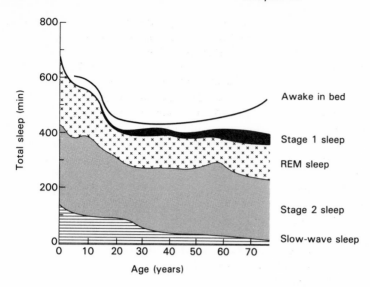

Fig. 20.2 Nocturnal sleep in humans from birth to old age. A characteristic pattern of declining total sleep and slow-wave sleep (stage 3 and 4) and increased time awake in bed (indicated by top line) is evident with increasing age (reprinted from Prinz *et al.*, 1990b).

persons who sleep longer than 9 or less than 5 hours a day (Webb, 1989).

There is great variation amongst individuals in total sleep time, in particular during infancy and early childhood (Klackenberg, 1968) and in old age, although estimates of total sleep time vary according to the measurement method. Furthermore, the stability of total sleep time is relatively low in the first 12 months of life (Bamford *et al.*, 1990). Sex differences in total sleep duration have been noted in the preschool years, with girls sleeping slightly longer, and in old age, when women have more prolonged night-time waking (Basler *et al.*, 1980; Webb, 1989).

Changes with age in sleep patterns

Circadian rhythms emerge by 2–6 weeks of age, with a 12-hour periodicity superimposed already at 6 weeks and a further 8-hour periodicity at 26 and 52 weeks (Bamford *et al.*, 1990; Hurry *et al.*, 1992; Fig. 20.3). This suggests not only a circadian but also ultradian (wake–sleep cycles during a 24-hour period) periodicity at an early age (Minors & Waterhouse, 1981). Sleep onset in young infants is predominantly through active REM sleep (Mamone *et al.*, 1990).

Starting in the first 4 weeks of life there is a shift towards an increase of sleep during the night and a reduction of sleep during the day (Anders & Keener,

1985), with a change in the day:night sleep ratio from around 0.93 at 1 week to 0.15–0.21 at 1 year of age (Parmelee *et al.*, 1964; Klackenberg, 1968). Sustained waking periods increase from about 128 min at 6 weeks to 210 min at 6 months of age, located mainly in the late afternoon (Coons & Guilleminault, 1982). At 6 months virtually all infants have two or three naps during the day, with only about 50% of infants having more than one nap a day at 1 year. By 2 years, most infants only have one nap, usually in the afternoon (Basler *et al.*, 1980). There are cultural differences in how long infants maintain a daytime nap. In Sweden most infants shed their daytime sleep completely between 2 and 3 years of age (Klackenberg, 1971). In contrast, Swiss mothers have expectations that children should sleep during the day until school age and enforce daytime naps more strictly, with the result that Swiss children give up their naps between 3 and 5 years of age (Basler *et al.*, 1980).

Active–quiet sleep cycles are about 50–65 min in duration in infancy (Anders & Keener, 1985), with the ultradian REM–NREM sleep cycle duration increasing during childhood, reaching a 90–100-min periodicity by adolescence (Ferber, 1990). While only active versus quiet sleep can be distinguished in the first 3 months of life, a differentiation into quiet sleep EEG stages 1, 2 and 3–4 appears successively between 3 and 9 months, indicating significant CNS maturation (Coons &

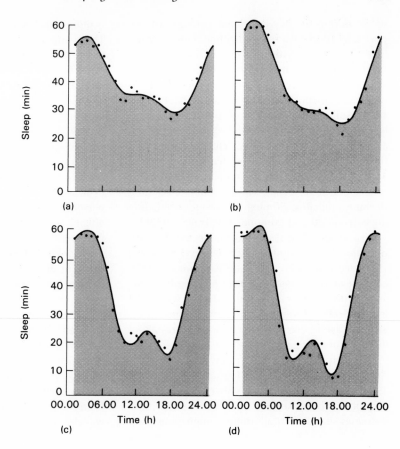

Fig. 20.3 Sleep distribution over 24 hours (h) in the first year of life (redrawn from Bamford *et al.*, 1990): (a) 6 weeks; (b) 13 weeks; (c) 26 weeks; and (d) 52 weeks.

Guilleminault, 1982). The pattern of NREM sleep being predominant in the first third of the night and REM sleep being more prolonged in the early morning hours, which is characteristic of older children and adults, starts appearing as early as 4–6 months of age (Coons & Guilleminault, 1982).

Although the total amount of sleep reduces in the preschool years, the amount of night-time sleep does not change over the first 5 years, during which time children sleep between 11 and 12.5 hours at night (Basler *et al.*, 1980). Individual differences in total night-time sleep are moderately stable, with significant prediction into middle childhood being possible from about 1–2 years onwards (Klackenberg, 1971). Although the amount of night-time sleep does not change, its patterning does, with the longest sleep period increasing from 233 min at 2 weeks to 371 min at 8 weeks with a further increase of 30–60 min at 1 year (Anders & Keener,

1985). Even by 8 weeks of life, most of the long sleep periods occur between midnight and 5 a.m. (Anders & Keener, 1985). Infants with many wakeful periods are more likely to remain so over the next 9–12 months (Snow *et al.*, 1980; Bamford *et al.*, 1990). There is a marked reduction of REM sleep over childhood, decreasing from around 40–50% of sleep time in the newborn to 15–20% in adulthood. Sex differences have been noted with boys having a higher percentage of active sleep as toddlers than girls (Sadeh *et al.*, 1991).

A decrease of 1 hour of night-time sleep is noted at the time school starts (Klackenberg, 1971), with further gradual changes until adolescence (Webb & Agnew, 1975). Adolescents sleep about an hour less than preadolescents on school nights, but not on the weekend (Anders *et al.*, 1978). Daytime sleepiness is low and not a problem for preadolescent children, but increases in the tendency to feel sleepy during the day are noted amongst 14—18 year olds; 10 to 35% report daytime naps, a strong urge to sleep or daytime drowsiness (Anders *et al.*, 1980; Simonds & Parraga, 1982a, b; Lugaresi *et al.*, 1983). Furthermore, adolescents are less likely to wake spontaneously in the morning (Anders *et al.*, 1980). Summer camp studies of children's and adolescents' sleep patterns have demonstrated an association with physiological changes; increased sleepiness in the day was associated with stages 3 to 5 of Tanner's (1962) classification of pubertal status (Carskadon *et al.*, 1980). The tendency to daytime sleepiness remains, although less pronounced, during early adulthood (Simonds & Parraga, 1982b).

On average, adults sleep 7—8.5 hours a night, with no major changes until the fifth decade (Kales *et al.*, 1990; see Fig. 20.2). There are variations in total amount of sleep associated with job requirements and features such as shift work, frequent travel and jet lag (Scott & Ladou, 1990) and with pregnancy, as well as in accordance with the care-taking demands of young infants.

Although there are still reviews claiming that sleep decreases with advancing age (Kales *et al.*, 1990), studies that compare self-reports and polygraphic analyses suggest that total sleep time decreases slightly if at all, though night-time sleep is more interrupted (Webb, 1989; Haponik, 1990). The changes in sleep behaviour in the elderly, relative to young adults, are summarized in Table 20.1. These include increased demand for sleep, especially after about 80 years of age, changes in the modulation of circadian tendencies, more frequent early morning awakenings and increased tendency to nap (Webb, 1989; Prinz *et al.*, 1990a, b). All these changes point to an increasingly destabilized circadian system, replaced by a polyphasic distribution of wake and sleep periods, rather like that in infancy (Von Oefele & Rüther, 1989). Although older persons spend more time resting in bed, their sleep efficiency is reduced (Von Oefele & Rüther, 1989; Haponik, 1990).

A major reduction in the percentage of time spent in deep sleep starts around mid-life. In old age, the reduction of slow-wave sleep is explained by the near elimination of stage 4 sleep (Von Oefele & Rüther, 1989). A comparison of sleep patterns of children, adults and the elderly is shown in Fig. 20.4. While REM sleep and the REM—NREM sleep periodicity remain constant across ages, a shedding of stage 4 sleep and disorganization of sleep in the elderly occurs. The elderly are more easily aroused from sleep, and thus there is increased night-time wakefulness and an increased fragmentation of sleep

Table 20.1 Subjective and objective changes of sleep in the elderly

	Subjective reports	Objective monitoring
Total time in bed	Increased	Increased
Total sleep time	Decreased	Variable (usually decreased)
Night-time sleep	Decreased, more disturbed	Decreased, more disturbed
Sleep latency	Increased	Variable (usually increased)
Wakefulness after sleep onset	Increased	Increased
Early morning final awakenings	Increased	Increased
Daytime naps	Increased	Variable
Sleep efficiency*	Decreased	Decreased

* Sleep efficiency is the quotient between total (net) sleeping time and resting time (time in bed).

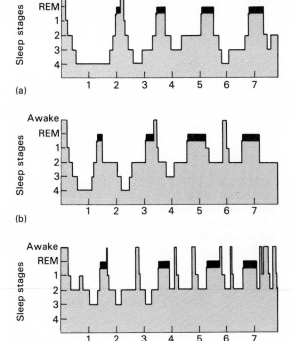

Fig. 20.4 Normal sleep cycles across age groups: (a) children; (b) young adults; and (c) the elderly. At intervals of approximately 90 minutes, rapid eye movement (REM) sleep (darkened area) occurs cyclically throughout the night in all age groups. The amount of REM sleep decreases only slightly in the elderly, whereas stage 4 sleep decreases dramatically with age, so that little, if any, is present in the elderly. Also, in the elderly, there are frequent awakenings and a considerable increase in wake time after sleep onset (redrawn from Bixler & Vela-Bueno, 1987). h, hours.

(Prinz *et al.*, 1990b). There are associated changes in other physiological parameters, including reduced respiration amplitude, increased noradrenalin secretion, reduced growth hormone secretion, reduced amplitude of urine secretion (therefore an increased tendency to urinate at night), reduced metabolism for certain products such as alcohol, and reduction of body temperature (Von Oefele & Rüther, 1989).

A summary of the major changes in sleep—wake patterns across the lifespan is presented in Table 20.2.

Sleep disturbances and disorders

Sleep disturbances, in particular the inability to sustain sleep adequately, have been recognized as disorders since early writings on medicine (Thorpy, 1990a). Sleep problems may be divided into four major categories: (i) insomnias (disorders in initiating and maintaining sleep); (ii) parasomnias (disorders associated with partial arousal such as night terrors, sleep-walking, talking in sleep); (iii) hypersomnias (disorders of excessive somnolence); and (iv) disorders of the sleep—wake cycle (e.g. chronic delayed sleep phase syndrome or transient changes due to shift work or jet lag) (Thorpy, 1990a; Horne, 1992).

Disturbances in infancy and toddlerhood (0–3 years)

Infants are not born with the ability to sleep through the night but rather wake up at irregular intervals, anywhere between 20 min and 6 hours (Bamford *et al.*, 1990). The early establishment of ultradian REM—NREM cycles is mostly under biological control and care-taking manoeuvres, such as rocking, stroking, feeding, car rides, etc., can contribute to the infant's own internal control (Wolke, 1993b). Problems of settling the infant at night and night-time waking are thus normal in the first 6 months of life (Anders & Keener, 1985; Wolke, 1993a). Most infants sleep through the night (i.e. do not cry between midnight and 5 a.m.) by 3–6 months of age, but 10% of infants are still not sleeping through the night by 12 months (Moore & Ucko, 1957).

In contrast, the major temporal organization and structural diurnal and circadian organization of sleep and wake periods in children older than 6 months is basically the same as the adult's (Ferber, 1990), with the exception of the persistence of daytime naps. However, at least through the toddler years, parents must help their children get to sleep. Infants and toddlers do not get themselves ready for bed, choose their bedtime, read or watch television to feel sleepy, or change their nappies at night. The development of new cognitive abilities such as the understanding of other's intentions (Trevarthen, 1987) contribute to a new sense of self-determination, which may manifest itself in temper tantrums (Ounsted & Simons, 1978). It is thus interesting that a recurrence of night-waking has

Table 20.2 Sleep—wake pattern changes across the lifespan (physiology)

	Infant	Adult	Elderly
Sleep onset states	REM sleep onset	NREM sleep onset	NREM sleep onset
Sleep state proportions REM—NREM (%)	40/60	20−25/75−80	15−20/80−85
Percentage of stage 4 sleep of total sleep	Stage 3/4 discrimination — not established (children: 20−25%)	15−20%	1−5%
Periodicity of sleep states	50−65 min REM—NREM cycle	90−100 min REM—NREM cycle	80−100 min REM—NREM cycle
Temporal organization of sleep during night sleep	REM—NREM cycles equally distributed through night; predominance of NREM sleep in first third of night from 6 months	NREM stages 3−4 predominant first third of night; REM state predominant in last third of night	See adult
Development of EEG pattern	Newborn: 1 NREM sleep stage. Emergence of sleep spindles: 4−8 weeks. K complex: 6−24 months. Delta activity 4−6 months	4 NREM stages	Near loss of NREM stage 4
Awakenings during the night	Infants: frequent (5−7 times). Children: low (0−2 times) and short	Low (0−2 times)	High (0−10 times) and long

EEG, electroencephalogram; NREM, non-rapid eye movement; REM, rapid eye movement.

been observed in the later part of the first year for infants who had slept through the night in early infancy (Anders & Keener, 1985; Ferber, 1987; St James-Roberts & Halil, 1991). Furthermore, parents have expectations that children of a certain age should sleep through the night (Johnson, 1991). These factors in combination determine the perception, development and maintenance of sleep disturbances in toddlerhood. Sleep problems in toddlers are special because of the inherent need for parental control of sleep and thus they demand different methods of evaluation and treatment than those occurring at later ages (Wolke, 1993a).

The major problems for toddlers are behavioural insomnias. Night-waking is relatively common, with 15−35% of toddlers awaking most nights at least once, according to parental reports (Lozoff & Zuckerman, 1988). Between 20 and 38% of parents consider night-waking (and/or night-time settling)

a mild or serious problem disrupting the family and the parents' night-time rest (Johnson, 1991). Most concerned are those parents of toddlers who wake more than twice, about 6−10% of the population (Largo & Hunziker, 1984).

Variability in prevalence estimates is partly due to variable definitions of night-waking, ranging from waking between 10 p.m. and 6 a.m. (Bernal, 1973) to between 12 p.m. and 5 a.m. (Moore & Ucko, 1957). Anders *et al.* (1983) showed that all infants wake at night but a significant number soothe themselves and begin sleeping without waking their parents.

Problems in settling to sleep (resistance at bedtime, prolonged bedtime routines, repeated 'curtain calls', etc.) increase during the second year to a peak level at about 3−5 years of age (Klackenberg, 1971; Beltramini & Hertzig, 1983). Between 25 and 50% of parents report that their toddler resists going to bed. Around 8–15% are reported to take longer than 1 hour to fall asleep once put to bed or to scream for prolonged periods (Basler *et al.*, 1980; Ferber, 1985). Children who have a hard time settling down to sleep are also likely to wake up in the night (van Tassel, 1985).

Discrepancies in the findings regarding the stability of sleeping problems over the preschool years can be explained on methodological grounds. Those studies looking at whole populations, using non-clinical definitions of night-waking, have found no significant stability over age (Garrison & Earls, 1985). In contrast, studies that use clinical definitions (at least four consecutive nights or more are disturbed and wakings occur frequently during the night) report significant continuities from 6 months onwards (Jenkins *et al.*, 1984; Wolke *et al.*, in press). Most recently, in a national sample of more than 13 000 children, Pollock (1992) reported that infants with sleeping difficulties in the first 6 months of life were about three times more likely than other children to have sleep problems at 5 years and two times more likely at 10 years, even allowing for a whole variety of confounding factors.

A number of factors predict night-waking problems in young children, including prenatal and perinatal influences (Blurton-Jones *et al.*, 1978), temperament (van Tassel, 1985), prolonged breast-feeding and late introduction of solid foods (Elias *et al.*, 1986), night-feeding (Ferber, 1987), sleeping in the parental bed (van Tassel, 1985), the use of pacifiers (Johnson, 1991), as well as family factors such as maternal depression, stressful life events or the birth of a sibling (Richman, 1981; Dunn & Kendrick, 1982; van Tassel, 1985; Zuckerman *et al.*, 1987). The direction of causation is unclear; some of the factors associated with night-waking may be measuring a similar temperamental variable (Wolke, 1990), or may be partly the result of night-waking problems and the parents' associated sleep deprivation (Valman, 1981). For example, up to 90% of night-wakers sleep at least part of the night in the parental bed (Richman, 1981; Wolke *et al.*, in press), which is often a strategy to calm the crying toddler quickly (Klackenberg, 1971). Johnson (1991) showed that, although parents believe taking the child to their bed is effective in settling him or her, few parents like having the child in bed with them. Furthermore, this practice is correlated with

other child-rearing techniques: parents who take their toddler into bed tend to have less firm and clear bedtime and night-time rules (Lozoff *et al.*, 1984).

Background factors such as socioeconomic status, education or maternal employment status are generally unrelated to young children's sleeping problems (Lozoff & Zuckerman, 1988); however, a predominance of night-waking problems in boys has been noted (Basler *et al.*, 1980). There are also some suggestions of an association with ethnicity, with West Indian-born families reporting more sleeping problems (Earls & Richman, 1980; Zuckerman *et al.*, 1987). However, the sleeping problems may have been associated with other factors distinguishing the West Indian-born and British-born comparison groups: for example, the fact that West Indian mothers were more likely to work night shifts. General cultural practices regarding sleep and bedtime are relevant: sleep problems are less prevalent in countries such as Switzerland where strict bedtime rules are enforced (Basler *et al.*, 1980).

Sleeping problems in the first 18 months of life are circumscribed and not usually related to other behavioural problems (Zuckerman *et al.*, 1987). Nevertheless, toddlers with persistent sleeping problems also tend to show other behavioural problems at 3 or even 5–10 years of age (Zuckerman *et al.*, 1987; Pollock, 1992).

Prepubertal children (4–12 years)

Frequent waking in the night (more than three nights per week) is still found in about 10–15% of children 4–6 years of age (Basler *et al.*, 1980; Wolke *et al.*, in press). Parental concern is reduced, since most preschool children are cheerful on waking, they merely have to go to the toilet often, and the parents have got used to them sleeping part or the whole night in the parental bed. Only a minority of the children are upset or frightened (Klackenberg, 1971; Wolke, 1993a). The night-time disturbances in preschool and school-aged children leading to increased concern in parents are the parasomnias, including night terrors, sleep-walking and enuresis (Anders, 1982). Parasomnias have often been viewed as curiosities, but, since polysomnographic study of these conditions has been used more intensively, they are now known to represent a variety of specific, diagnosable and treatable developmental disturbances (Strunz, 1991).

A distinction may be made between primary sleep parasomnias and secondary ones associated with organic morbidity (Mahowald & Ettinger, 1990). The primary parasomnias consist of disturbances of the sleep–wake cycling mechanism between NREM, REM and waking states (Anders, 1982; Mahowald & Rosen, 1990). For some individuals, at certain points in development, the various physiological state markers become dissociated, or oscillate rapidly, resulting in unusual and often dramatic behaviours (Mahowald & Ettinger, 1990). NREM parasomnias, disorders of arousal, include sleep-walking (somnambulism) and the so-called night or sleep terror (*pavor nocturnus*) (Broughton, 1968), which occur most typically during the first third of the night's sleep, most often in the first 3 hours after sleep onset (Thorpy, 1990b). Normally, a child reaches the deepest NREM sleep within 15 min. After about an hour, a transition takes place to REM sleep, a lighter stage of NREM sleep, or a brief awakening; at this point, partial arousal takes place (Fig. 20.5), and the child may get 'caught' between deep sleep and full arousal, in a state characterized by a high arousal threshold, mental confusion and disorientation, increased autonomic behaviour and a lack of clear mental imagery or dreams (Anders *et al.*, 1980).

Sleep-walking is characterized by an abrupt onset of motor activity, with the child getting up and walking about the house in a disoriented way, with eyes open but glassy (Mahowald & Rosen, 1990). Occasionally, sleep-walking children will engage in inappropriate activities such as urinating on the floor, and sleep-walking adults may be violent (Oswald & Evans, 1985). Sleep-walking is most frequent in school children with an onset between 4 and 6 years of age and a peak prevalence between 7 and 12 years of age; most have 'outgrown' sleep-walking by 15 years of age (Klackenberg, 1982). The high prevalence of sleep-walking with childhood onset and resolution by puberty suggests the involvement of CNS maturation (Anders, 1982). The fact that sleep-walking can be induced by standing a person up during slow-wave sleep is further evidence that it is not the result of mentation prior to sleep-walking (Mahowald & Ettinger, 1990). It occurs more frequently after sleep deprivation, illness, unusual daytime stresses or in response to medications (Anders, 1982; McMenamy & Katz, 1989; Thorpy, 1990b). Sleep-walking that persists into adulthood is most frequently associated with psychiatric disturbance, in particular personality disorders (Kales *et al.*, 1987).

The sleep terror is the most dramatic form of

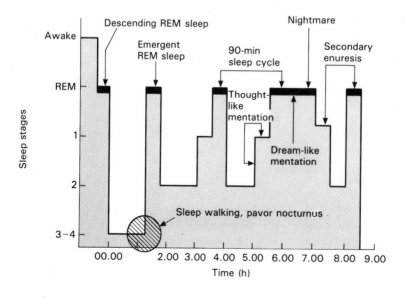

Fig. 20.5 Association of parasomnias with sleep stages. The arousal disorders *pavor nocturnus* and sleep-walking tend to occur in the first non-rapid eye movement (NREM) sleep period. Typical nightmares tend to occur in the later portion of sleep (Redrawn with slight changes from Anders *et al.*, 1980). h, hours.

arousal disorder, starting often with a loud, piercing scream, followed by motor activity such as sitting or jumping up and accompanied by autonomic activity such as tachycardia, tachypnoea, profuse sweating and dilated pupils (Thorpy, 1990b; Strunz, 1991). Episodes are usually short, lasting up to 15 min, and it is rare to have more than one episode a night; the sleeper is usually unaware of the episode. Night terrors are associated with sleep-walking and talking in sleep.

The prevalence rates range from 1 to 7% in children between 2 and 15 years, with a peak prevalence somewhere between the ages of 3 and 7 years (DiMario & Emery, 1987; Klackenberg, 1987). DiMario and Emery (1987) reported that sleep terrors that begin before 3.5 years of age have a higher peak frequency, averaging one episode per week. Usually night terrors persist for about 4 years, but children from families with a history of sleep-walking had longer durations. Fifty per cent stopped by age 8, while 36% continued into adolescence. The adult prevalence is estimated to be less than 1% and is usually associated with psychopathology (Thorpy, 1990b).

A third type of arousal disorder, confusal arousal, also occurs in the first third of the night during arousal from deep sleep, but does not encompass sleep-walking or high autonomic arousal; it may be a less dramatic form of night terrors and has been described as sleep drunkenness or sleep inertia (Thorpy, 1990b). The onset is usually before 5 years of age, with a prevalence of approximately 3−5% (Mahowald & Ettinger, 1990; Thorpy, 1990b).

The arousal disorders are all associated with the transition from deep sleep; in contrast, nightmares are associated with REM sleep. Conventional nightmares are frightening dreams, often accompanied by moderate autonomic activity and sometimes including images of demons or evil spirits (Mahowald & Ettinger, 1990). The arousal due to the frightening mentation wakes the child, who usually fully recalls the dream (Mahowald & Schenck, 1990). Nightmares usually occur in the second half of the night, often in the morning hours (Erman, 1987b). Features differentiating nightmares from night terrors are shown in Table 20.3.

Nightmares are common in childhood, with parents reporting around 50−70% of children

Table 20.3 Differential diagnostic features of sleep terrors and nightmares

	Sleep terror	Nightmare
Prevalence	Uncommon	Common
Behaviour during episodes	Intense vocalizations, fear, high autonomic activity, motor activity	Less intense; fear, vocalizations, motor activity, autonomic activity
Onset time during night	Within first third of night	Second half of night
Sleep state/stage	NREM stage 3 and 4	REM sleep
Mentation	Little	Vivid, elaborate
Memory of event	Amnesia	Vivid recall
Ability to arouse	Low	High
Level of consciousness when awoken	Very confused	Oriented
Potential for injury	High, likely	Low, unlikely
Violent behaviour	Common in older children, adults	Uncommon
Family history	Yes, often	Uncommon

NREM, non-rapid eye movement; REM, rapid eye movement.

having experienced at least one in the last year; around 14−30% of children are reported to have more frequent nightmares (Fisher & Wilson, 1987). The prevalence of nightmares decreases steadily from a peak between 4 and 10 years, with low rates in adolescence (Simonds & Parraga, 1982b; Yang *et al.*, 1987). However, 80% of adults report that they have had a nightmare recently. Childhood nightmares are not usually associated with psychopathology but rather with current stressful experiences (Cirignotta *et al.*, 1983; Ferber, 1985). Family history may be important (Cashman & McCann, 1988). The continued presence of repetitive dream anxiety attacks in adolescence and adulthood usually suggests significant psychopathology, in particular anxiety disorders (Erman, 1987b).

Other sorts of parasomnias can occur in various stages of sleep. These include bruxism (teeth-grinding), which is reported to occur in about 10−22% of children (Simonds & Parraga, 1982a); sleep-talking, which is very frequent in the general population throughout the lifespan (Mahowald & Rosen, 1990); rhythmic movement disorders, including head-banging, which show the greatest prevalence within the first 12 months of life and reduce to 5% by 5 years of age (Klackenberg, 1971); and nocturnal enuresis, which is relatively common in 5 year olds (around 13−15%) and reduces steadily through the school years to about 1−2% of adolescents who wet their beds occasionally (Feehan *et al.*, 1990). Primary enuresis accounts for about 90% of cases and is generally characterized by a genetic predisposition coupled with maturational features of bladder control. In contrast, secondary enuresis is usually the result of psychological or medical factors (Scharf *et al.*, 1987). Nocturnal enuresis is associated with other parasomnias such as night terrors and sleep-walking (Simonds & Parraga, 1982a, b), but is not usually related to psychopathology (Scharf *et al.*, 1987).

Adolescence

The available data suggest that about 10−15% of adolescents complain about frequent night-time insomnia, with a further 38% reporting occasional insomnia (Price *et al.*, 1978; White *et al.*, 1980). Complaints about early morning awakenings are rare (Price *et al.*, 1978). Adolescent insomnias are related to a variety of factors such as the increased number of other medical complaints and psychological symptoms, particularly tension, worrying and depression. Social habits and academic demands may lead to changing bedtimes and irregular sleep−wake schedules in adolescence.

As noted earlier, there is a marked tendency for increased daytime sleepiness occurring during puberty (Anders *et al.*, 1980). Daytime somnolence is relatively frequent in adolescence, but, if prolonged and persistent, is likely to be associated with various psychiatric disorders such as depression (Dinges, 1989). For a small minority of adolescents, excessive daytime somnolence is the first sign of the development of the severe, rare sleeping disorders narcolepsy and hypersomnia (Parkes, 1985; Broughton, 1990). Narcolepsy, characterized by excessive daytime sleepiness and several irresistible sleep attacks each day, is a distinct neurological disorder related to dysfunctional brain stem sleep−wake mechanisms, best explained by a multifactorial inheritance model with environmental factors such as emotional stress and excessive social demands playing an additional role (Manfredi *et al.*, 1987; Honda & Matsuki, 1990). The short arm of chromosome 6 has been implicated in the genetic expression of narcolepsy occurring around puberty (Anders *et al.*, 1980; Honda & Matsuki, 1990). In contrast, hypersomnia is a disorder of excessive daytime or night-time sleep, with recurrent, lengthy periods of excessive sleepiness. Common complaints are difficulties with waking up in the morning, sleep drunkenness, and confusion upon awakening; onset is usually during puberty, and the disorder is chronic and lifelong (Manfredi *et al.*, 1987; Reynolds, 1987).

Adulthood

The prevalence rates of some sleep disturbances that start appearing in childhood such as the parasomnias reduce in adulthood. In contrast, insomnias remain the most frequent complaint (Kales & Kales, 1987). Transient insomnia is mostly related to undesirable, stressful life events, including interpersonal and occupational losses or changes. For about 15−20%, with higher prevalence amongst women and the higher social classes (Kales & Kales, 1982), the distress caused by insomnias is large enough to ask for a physician's help, which usually takes the form of repeat prescriptions of hypnotics. For example, 14 million prescriptions for benzodiazepines were written in Britain in 1989 (Horne, 1992). Those seeking help have usually experienced the disorder for more than 5 years (Kales & Kales, 1984) and often have other psychiatric problems such as depression, anxiety disorder or hypochondriasis (Buysse & Reynolds, 1990; Gillin & Byerley, 1990). Other disorders have insomnia as a symptom, including obsessive−compulsive disorder, schizophrenia, mania or borderline personality disorder (Reynolds, 1987), and about 10−15% of patients with chronic insomnia have an underlying problem of alcohol or substance abuse (Gillin & Byerley, 1990). Thus insomnia is a symptom of various psychiatric disturbances or is likely to be caused by the same pathological conditions as the psychiatric disturbance (comorbidity).

Many chronic insomniacs sleep as much as other adults do on average (Buysse & Reynolds, 1990), but feel drained and fatigued during the day (Horne, 1992). Various studies have shown that insomniacs are more inaccurate than other individuals in their perception of sleep, reporting lighter sleep though no differences in auditory waking threshold could be detected (Mendelson *et al.*, 1986). While most insomniacs report having been awake when aroused from stage 2 sleep, only the minority of healthy sleepers do so (Borkovec *et al.*, 1981). Insomniacs often have a better knowledge about good sleep routines than healthy subjects do, and often patients with the worst sleep problems have the best sleep routines (Lacks & Rotert, 1986). The associated psychiatric problems often contribute to continued insomnia, in that worrying at bedtime, fearing sleeplessness and so on are incompatible with sleep (Buysse & Reynolds, 1990). Furthermore, external factors such as occupational demands can also provoke insomnia; shift-workers whose work schedules change frequently from day to night shifts show insomnia and chronic sleep deprivation (Gillin & Byerley, 1990; Scott & Ladou, 1990). In summary, in adulthood, more than in childhood, insomnia is associated with psychiatric disturbance and with environmental and social stresses.

The elderly

Elderly individuals are more likely than younger ones to complain about insomnia, excessive daytime sleepiness, or a shifting of the major sleep period to an earlier time of the night (Haponik, 1990; Vitiello & Prinz, 1990). Up to 45% of the elderly report sleep problems (Thornby *et al.*, 1977; Miles & Dement, 1980). More older women than men report sleep problems (Lugaresi *et al.*, 1983; Ancoli-Israel, 1989), although age-related changes in sleep patterns start about 10 years earlier for men than for women (Ancoli-Israel, 1989; Von Oefele & Rüther, 1989; Webb, 1982). The prescriptions for sedative hypnotic agents are 66% higher in the over 60 year olds than in the 40−59 year olds, with older women about 1.7 times more likely to receive a prescription than older men (Prinz *et al.*, 1990b). Sleep problems are more prevalent in elderly patients in nursing homes (Ancoli-Israel, 1989), due to the higher incidence of neurodegenerative disorders and associated sleep disturbances such as night wanderings, delirium and nocturnal incontinence, which often lead to admission to institutions. The general trend of disintegration of sleep functioning, major changes in social life and the more frequent occurrence of major distressing life events, such as loss of family members, make it difficult to determine whether these sleep complaints in elderly nursing home residents represent a normal ageing phenomenon or are specific sleep disorders (Dement *et al.*, 1984).

As noted earlier, insomnia in the elderly most often takes the form of early morning awakenings, followed by disrupted sleep and difficulties in settling to sleep. Although about 15% of elderly individuals sleep less than 5 hours a night (McGhee & Russell, 1962), there is also a tendency for a higher incidence of persons over 75 years of age sleeping more than 9 hours a night (Lugaresi *et al.*, 1983). Short as well as long sleepers have a significantly increased risk for morbidity and mortality (Kripke *et al.*, 1979). Up to 60% of men and up to 40% of women over 60 years of age are habitual snorers (Lugaresi *et al.*, 1983). Habitual snoring is related to obesity and is more frequent in individuals with hypertension, angina pectoris, ischaemic heart disease, stroke or cerebral infarction (Ancoli-Israel, 1989); it is rarely associated with insomnia for the sleeper, though it provokes insomnia in partners who may then move out of the shared bedroom. Sleep apnoeas (where breathing ceases for 10 seconds or longer) occur in most individuals occasionally during sleep. Frequent occurrence (20 or more times a night) leads to multiple episodes of reduced blood oxygen saturation, brief awakenings, excessive daytime sleepiness and impaired daytime functioning and again is more frequent in older men (Guilleminault & Dement, 1988; Haponik, 1990; Prinz *et al.*, 1990a). Untreated sleep apnoea syndrome can compromise cardiac function and lead to death (Ancoli-Israel, 1989). Overall, the characteristic changes in normal sleep patterns in the elderly, including frequent awakenings and increased need for daytime naps, may to a great part be explained by the high prevalence of nocturnal respiratory dysfunction.

Organic illness and its pharmacological treatment, more prevalent in the elderly, often lead to sleep impairment as a secondary symptom. Furthermore, Alzheimer's disease and other disorders such as vascular (multi-infarct) dementia, Parkinson's disease and alcohol-related encephalopathy are other common causes of sleep disturbance (Vitello & Prinz, 1990). Socioeconomic and emotional changes such as retirement, death of the partner and other friends and relatives, and no scheduled daily activities also have detrimental effects on the daily sleep–wake schedule for the elderly (Reynolds *et al.*, 1989). Little activity and exercise during the day are associated with little urge to sleep at night (Prinz *et al.*, 1990b). Furthermore, the elderly may stick to a schedule of drinking coffee, tea or alcoholic drinks at inappropriate times. Due to metabolic changes with age in the breakdown of alcohol, its intake may lead to better sleep in the evening but earlier awakenings in the morning (Buysse & Reynolds, 1990).

Major developmental principles governing sleep

Viewed from a developmental perspective, the following general principles can be deduced:
1 The occurrence of certain sleep problems (e.g. night-wakings, bedtime problems, parasomnias or excessive sleepiness) are 'normal' phenomena occurring in most or a significant minority of individuals at certain times during the lifespan.
2 The onset of sleep problems at an age deviating from the normative peak onset time, after physio-

logical reorganization has taken place in the vast majority of individuals, is usually associated with other psychological or psychiatric disturbances or organic syndromes. Similarly, the persistence of sleep phenomena beyond the period of normal occurrence in most individuals showing the behaviour (e.g. the parasomnias) suggests more general psychiatric disturbances, family problems, poor sleep hygiene, or organic or drug-related disturbances.
3 At times of rapid development and maturational change, interindividual differences in the speed of the internal reorganization to external demands need to be considered. At these times it is more difficult to decide whether certain sleep problems represent a delayed (or, in the case of the elderly, accelerated) adaptation or deterioration, or a clinically significant disorder. Functioning in other developmental domains needs to be taken into account to derive a clinical judgement. It thus becomes of interest to examine some parallel changes over the lifespan in another basic biological function, eating.

FEEDING AND EATING

Feeding refers to a complex of interactions that take place between parent and young child, who depends almost entirely on the caretaker for nourishment (Satter, 1990). In contrast, in older children and adults the intake of nutrients — eating — is much more under the control of the individual. However, what nutrients are taken and what eating habits are established remain greatly dependent on caretakers, peers and cultural values. Eating problems may arise at any time in the lifespan, and, although they often differ in origin and symptomatology at different ages, there are some commonalities across age. Three general types of problems may occur at any age: (i) highly restricted diet; (ii) insufficient food intake to maintain an optimal body weight; and (iii) excessive food intake leading to obesity. There are also other problems that are specific to certain ages or certain individuals at a given age, such as colic or pica in infancy and bulimia nervosa in the adolescent and adult. We now examine the normative trends in feeding and eating and different sorts of problems arising at different ages.

Normative trends in eating patterns

Infancy

Feeding is a prerequisite for growth of the infant. During the first 6 months of life, the child's rate of weight gain is greater than it will ever be again until puberty (Tanner, 1989). In this early phase, CNS maturation proceeds at a rate never achieved again (Smart, 1991; see also Chapter 3). The energy cost of that growth is exceptionally high, constituting 30% of normal energy intake at 1−2 months and falling to about 3% by 9−12 months. The infant's weight typically doubles in 4−6 months and has tripled by 1 year of age (Widdowson, 1981).

At the same time, effective feeding is an essential opportunity for socialization, and is often considered a major influence on other sorts of interactions and subsequent preferences and aversions (Lipsitt *et al.*, 1985). The social and psychological importance of feeding is evident from the amount of time infants and parents engage in feeding activities and their variety, as well as the effects that feeding problems have on the parent−infant relationship. In the early weeks of life, a third to half of waking time is spent feeding, and only a little of the remaining time is spent in direct social contact with the caretaker (Bunton *et al.*, 1987). Feeding thus represents the major opportunity for parent−infant interaction; pauses in feeding for burping, nappy changes, and so on, provide an important time for social interaction (Lipsitt *et al.*, 1985). It is thus not surprising that studies of early mother−infant interaction have most frequently focused on feeding (Wolke, 1991c), although the ethological attachment theorists were at pains to disentangle attachment behaviour from feeding (Bowlby, 1969). One must ask how much the infant's eating skills, the caretaker's feeding skill, the infant's feelings of hunger, and so on, contribute to more general interaction patterns and the maternal sensitivity presumed to contribute to secure attachments (see Chapter 16). Until recently, observational studies of mothers and infants in a feeding situation have rarely differentiated the actual process of transferring food into the child from more general parameters such as eye contact, vocalizations, sensitivity, and so on. Lack of attention to feeding issues

per se may well be a pitfall when studying infants at risk for later problems (Wolke *et al.*, 1990c; Dahl & Sundelin, 1992), and may also explain findings that are contradictory to attachment theory: for example, the early feeding interactions of mothers and preterm infants are less reciprocal than those of other mother−infant pairs, probably because preterms have more frequent oral−motor problems, are more difficult to feed and more irritable, but there are no differences between preterms and fullterms in attachment security at 12 months (Frodi & Thompson, 1985; Wolke, 1991b, c).

The graduation from liquid to coarsely chopped food is an intricate process regulated by brain structures and physiology involved in the development of oral−motor control, adaptive motor skills, taste perception and sensory regulation of feeding, hunger, appetite and food preferences (Wyrwicka, 1987), in interaction with gastric physiological regulation (Nicolaidis & Even, 1989), the provision of differently textured foods, their attractiveness, as well as the caregiver's behaviour and the social and cultural context (Birch, 1987; Wright, 1987). Thus, the success of early feeding depends critically on (i) species-specific constitutional factors; (ii) environmental conditions that are favourable towards capitalizing upon the reflexes and oral skills the infant is normally born with; and (iii) age-appropriate shifts in psychobiological control and self-regulation of food-getting and ingestive behaviours (Lipsitt *et al.*, 1985). The development of different oral−motor skills, the introduction of different textures and types of food, and the development of feeding-related adaptive skills at different ages is summarized in Table 20.4. Roughly four important 'stages' can be distinguished in the first 2 years: (i) the exclusive breast- or bottle-feeding of milk; (ii) the introduction of non-milk solids; (iii) the final weaning from the breast or bottle; and (iv) the acquisition of self-feeding skills and table manners.

Breast- or bottle-feeding. Newborns' sucking behaviour is largely a matter of taste — newborns prefer sweet tastes (Lipsitt *et al.*, 1985). The preference for sweet tastes makes evolutionary sense, as sweet nutrients usually contain the most calories; breast milk, for example, is relatively sweet and low in sodium (Harris *et al.*, 1990). Patterns of breastfeeding vary widely between different societies, in

Table 20.4 Developmental sequence of oral–motor and self-feeding skills and common feeding difficulties

Approximate age	Food types/textures	Oral skills	Adaptive/social skills	Positioning	Difficulties
0–12 weeks	Liquid breast or bottle-feeding	*Reflexes:* Rooting lip closure/opening lateral tongue movements; mouth opening; biting; Babkin; gag reflex *Functional:* Rhythmic; sucking or sucking swallow pattern (burst-pause pattern); ? nutritive (1 suck/swallow) vs. non-nutritive (2 sucks/swallows – comforting); loses some liquid during sucking at corner of mouth – rarely drools (minimal saliva production)	Begins hand to mouth; increasing control of behavioural state and alertness; responsiveness, smile; day and night rhythm shift starts	Supine with the head slightly elevated; or prone; or at an angle of less than 45° or side-lying (e.g. next to caretaker)	Nipple problems: too little milk (perceived), poor suck, spitting up
12–20 weeks	May begin cereals or strained (soft)/pureed foods (semi-solids)	*Reflexes* As above *Functional:* Suckling/suck pattern as food approaches or touches lips; upper lip does not assist food removal – primitive suckle/swallow response – intermittent gagging or choking occurs; prechewing movements present (i.e. moving bolus from lateral to centre, brief rhythmic, symmetrical, bilateral depressions –	Begins mouthing objects; begins reaching purposefully; begins anticipatory mouth opening for nipple; prolonged alertness and face to face play (primary) intersubjectivity – self/other distinction; conditioned reactions (e.g. happiness)	Semi-solids fed in a supported semi-sitting position reclining at an angle of 45–90°	Not interested, choking, refusal, spits out lumps

Age	Foods	Oral-motor (Reflexes/Functional)	Development/skills	Position	Problems
		solids then ejected); decrease in loss of milk from corners of mouth; increase in strength of sucking			
20–28 weeks (6 months)	Strained/pureed foods: mashed in cracker/rusks; teething biscuits introduced	*Reflexes:* As above — generally more subtle involving fewer movements. *Functional:* Chewing pattern with lip closure ('munching'); starts swallowing higher textured foods, jaw more stabilized; moves lips in eating	Recognizes spoon, opens and positions mouth for spoon insertion; transfers objects; drops objects; readiness to hold digestive biscuits etc.; consolidation self/other distinction	Approximating 90° sitting position, external support (side, back, e.g. pillow) in high chair/baby chair	Excessive drooling, refusal
28–32 weeks (7 months)	Junior foods: mashed, cooked, canned; introduction of liquids from cup	*Reflexes:* Very subtle — ? rooting, babkin disappearing. *Functional:* Centring, processing and swallowing get established; lips remove food from spoon (upper lip)	Begins finger feeding; holding two objects and bangs together	90° sitting position — some lateral support needed	Asserts himself; may want to finger feed (see above)
8–10 months	Junior mashed foods, minced fine table food, finger foods (crackers)	Closes mouth on cup rim; bites on objects; holds crackers between gums and breaks off (? phasic bite pattern — munching); still problems: suck/swallow/breathe when drinking from cup; moves food with tongue; food from centre to side mount — blows 'raspberries'	Finger feeds crackers/rusks; accepts 1 sip at a time from cup; holds a bottle; emerging specific emotions expressed (separation anxiety, love, attachment); secondary intersubjectivity (understands others' motivations and 'willingly' coordinates or obstructs)	Sitting infant/high chair, no additional side support	Refuses lumps, behaviour problems

Continued on p. 534

Table 20.4 continued

Approximate age	Food types/textures	Oral skills	Adaptive/social skills	Positioning	Difficulties
10–12 months	Mashed to coarsely chopped table foods; finely chopped meats/ dried fruits	Controlled sustained bite on biscuit, uses an intermittently elevated tongue when swallowing; no/little loss of food during swallowing – moves tongue from side to side; licks food from lower lip; rotary chewing beginning; when drinking from cup, swallowing follows sucking with no pause – some choking may occur if too fast flowing liquid from cup	Finger feeds small pieces, begins to grasp spoon and stir and lift food with spoon; accepts 4–5 continuous sips; strives for autonomy and control; picks up small objects; starts coordinated placing of objects on table	Sitting in high/infant chair	Refuses lumps; tantrums; wants to self-feed; very messy

| 12–18 months | Coarsely chopped foods, raw fruits and vegetables | Rotary chewing; licks all of lower lip with tongue; little loss of food or saliva during chewing; decreased drooling; spits foods | Grasps spoon; attempts to take to mouth (starts messy self-feeding); drinks from beaker independently and cup with assistance; decrease in mouthing objects; scribbles with crayon; emerging words and basic comprehension of commands; starting to drink from straw; development of guilt, embarrassment; consolidation of attachment and at same time increasing struggle for autonomy | Infant/high chair; clip-on chair on table; seating on infant table in chair with side and back rest; feet reaching floor | Faddiness; power struggles |
| 18–24 months | Regular table foods; some chopped fine meats | Mature rotary chewing; controlled sustained biting (grades jaw opening to bite foods of different thickness) | Self-feeding (still messy); drinks from cup and places on table; weaning off bottle completely; unscrews lids; turns pages in book; sustained attention | Infant chair/own table/booster seat (i.e. with the adults at table) | As above; wants to use knife and fork |

particular developed and developing countries and within societies according to social class and rural versus urban setting (Department of Health and Social Security, 1980; World Health Organization, 1981). Hospital practices as well as maternal perceptions of infant satiety, lack of milk supply or excessive crying also affect breastfeeding (Wright *et al.*, 1983; Loughlin *et al.*, 1985). Two opposite trends are apparent in the patterns of breastfeeding in Western societies during this century. A downward trend from approximately 70% of mothers beginning breastfeeding in 1910 to a low of just 24–28% doing so in the early 1970s was found in national surveys (Hendershot, 1984). Until the middle of this century, breastfeeding was more frequent in the lower social classes. This trend was reversed in the 1970s, with around 50–67% of women in the UK and the USA attempting to breastfeed (Department of Health and Social Security, 1980; Martin & White, 1988). Nowadays breastfeeding is less frequent and continued for shorter periods in the lower social classes (Martin & White, 1988). Although the incidence of breastfeeding has remained stable since the mid-1970s through the mid-1980s, new US surveys indicate a second downward trend in the late 1980s, with fewer mothers beginning to breastfeed and continuing for shorter periods (Ryan *et al.*, 1991).

There is now little doubt that 'there is no better nutrition for healthy infants' than breastfeeding (Department of Health and Social Security, 1988). Breast milk has distinct advantages over proprietary cow's milk preparations because of its nutritional value, the adaptation of milk consistency according to infant need and its protection against minor infections (Leventhal *et al.*, 1986; Department of Health and Social Security, 1988). It has also been shown that breastfeeding infants show less physiological arousal and better physiological integrity than bottle-fed infants during feeding (DiPietro *et al.*, 1987). Breastfeeding is associated with increased maternal contact and less need for the mother to exert control over the infant (Wright, 1989). Findings about the long-term consequences of breastfeeding are contradictory (Taylor & Wadsworth, 1984; Fergusson *et al.*, 1987), the studies either not being fine grained enough or failing adequately to control for confounding variables. It can, however, be stated that bottle-feeding does not have distinct long-term disadvantages for the child's psychological development.

4–8 months: the introduction of solids. The transition from an exclusive milk or formula diet to an omnivorous one takes place at a time of rapid growth and may be risky (Birch, 1990), and so there has been a long-standing controversy about when solid foods should first be introduced. Advice is based on weight or age criteria (Spock, 1968; Leach, 1986); ages vary from 3 (Leach, 1986) to 7 (Illingworth & Lister, 1964) months. Despite these varying recommendations, parents now tend to introduce solids at an older age than was common in the 1960s and 1970s (Department of Health and Social Security, 1988). Large variations in the age at which solids are introduced are found between various countries (Underwood & Hofvander, 1982; Hitchcock *et al.*, 1986). In Western cultures, infant sex, growth patterns and behavioural changes are major influences on parents' decisions to introduce solid food, overriding subcultural differences; boys are given solids sooner and relevant behavioural cues include demands for more frequent feeding and crying after feeds as well as night-waking, which are interpreted as signs that the infant is not satisfied by milk alone (Harris, 1988).

One must ask what the consequences are of experiences such as introducing solid food too early or too late, the exposure to a variety of tastes and the social and affective setting of feeding to the development of appetite, food acceptance patterns, food preferences, and the instrumental use of eating in childhood and even later (Beauchamp & Cowart, 1986). The young infant is endowed with a well-regulated control system for nutritional needs. For example, Drewett *et al.* (1989) showed that milk intake is reduced proportionally to the nutritional provision from solids. Evidence for a self-regulating mechanism of *ad libitum* food intake comes also from recent work by Lucas *et al.*, (1992a), who found that 50% of preterm infants, who are often small for date and show poor growth during hospitalization (Brothwood *et al.*, 1988), consumed more than the upper recommended limits for energy intake during the first 16 weeks after the discharge home; 35% did so for protein intake as well. It appears that preterm infants, if physically intact, use high volume intakes on a body weight basis to achieve the often necessary catch-up growth. Davis (1928), in her classic experiment at Mount Sinai Hospital in Cleveland, studied three weaned infants who were allowed to choose and compose their own diets freely from a whole range of foods, including vegetables, fruit, meat and milk products, orange juice, and so on. The infants' intake was observed meticulously, and the results of the study were clear-cut: all three infants chose a diet that was optimal for promoting growth and satiety.

Current limited evidence suggests that negative consequences occur when the infants' biological predisposition for self-regulation of food intake is not supported or is interfered with by their experiences. The basic oral–motor movement patterns for solid feeding are dependent on maturation but the acceptance of lumpy food and the associated mouth opening, lip movements, munching and swallowing patterns appear to involve practice and experience with such food (Evans-Morris, 1977; Mathisen *et al.*, 1989). It has been suggested that if the child does not experience solid food until 9 months of age, it will be excessively difficult to introduce lumpy foods later and will lead in some cases to growth failure (Illingworth & Lister, 1964; Skuse *et al.*, 1992).

Taste preferences also depend on experience: salt tastes are better accepted if the infant has been exposed to them more frequently, by being introduced to solids rather than being maintained on low sodium breast milk (Harris & Booth, 1987). Evidence from research with adults and non-human primates underlines the importance of variety of tastes for food acceptance and satiety. A person will eat more food when given a variety of foods than when only a single food is available (Rolls *et al.*, 1981). In primates who are offered a single food (e.g. banana), no firing of neurones in the lateral hypothalamus was observed but renewed firing occurred when a new food (e.g. raisins) was offered (Rolls, 1982). These observations are in line with longitudinal, naturalistic observations of mothers who master the introduction of solids without great problems by exposing their infants to a large variety of tastes and textures early in the weaning process (Lipsitt *et al.*, 1985). The limited information about selective food refusers underscores the fact that early associations with the social interaction and the food provided are important determinants of food acceptance patterns in infancy and beyond (Birch, 1990; Dahl & Sundelin, 1992; Harris & Booth, 1992; Wolke & Skuse, 1992). Diet and feeding in early infancy may have long-lasting effects on the nutritional programming, health and achievement in humans (Lucas, 1991).

9–24 months: newly emerging feeding skills and mealtime manners. As noted earlier, with respect to bedtime struggles and night-waking, the period between 6 and 12 months represents an important bio-behavioural shift with infants acquiring greater mobility, adaptive skills and understanding of their own and other people's intentions (Trevarthen, 1988; Bakeman *et al.*, 1990). Important changes in the mother–child feeding relationship occur at this time (see Table 20.4), but, surprisingly, these changes have hardly been studied longitudinally in normal infants. One exception is Negayama's (1991) monthly videotaping of the feeding relationship between 4 and 19 months in Japanese mothers and infants. Infants started to feed themselves with their hands at 9 months and with utensils from 13 months onwards. At about the same time they started to turn their faces away or push food away when it was offered by their mothers, and the mothers' own empathic behaviour during feeding declined with power struggles becoming more common. Although rejecting food offered by the mother, the infants began playfully to offer their mother food, and the mothers began to show vicarious behaviour such as opening their mouths when the infants transferred food to their own mouths. Overall, this is an example of how changes in the infant's motoric and social competence drive important changes in the parent–infant system.

Mealtimes constitute a prime situation for conflicts between toddlers and parents, but are also a great opportunity to acquire acceptable behaviour patterns and to learn to appreciate different tastes and textures of food (Birch, 1987). Thus toddlers' attempts to feed themselves are part of a normal developmental process, and in some cases where parents are unable to adapt to these interactional changes and the messiness of self-feeding, growth failure results (Chatoor, 1989; Satter, 1990).

Trends in children's eating

Major individual differences in eating patterns begin in infancy and consolidate in childhood. Detailed data on older children's eating habits have recently been published by the Expert Panel on Blood Cholesterol Levels in Children and Adolescents (1992) for the USA. Although eating practices vary considerably in modern Western societies and social classes, the findings from the USA illustrate trends likely to be taking place in the Western world as a whole. In the USA, snacking is common, with children aged 1–5 years obtaining 10–22% of total calories from snacks and those 6–11 years 18%. Changes in family demographics, such as an increasing number of single-parent families, dual-income families and older first-time parents, and the associated decreased time spent on preparing food at home, have contributed to the rapidly increasing trend for children to eat more meals and snacks away from home than did previous generations. In the USA, $1 of every $3 spent on food is spent away from home. In the Anglo-Saxon countries where schooling involves afternoon tutoring (which is much rarer, for example, in Germany), school is the most common but by no means the only place where children eat away from home. Visits by children under 6 years of age to both fast-food and table-service restaurants increased by 36% between 1982 and 1986 in the USA. The restaurant foods most popular with preschool and school children are soft drinks, closely followed by french-fried potatoes, hamburgers, pizzas, fried chicken and ice cream (Expert Panel on Blood Cholesterol Levels in Children and Adolescents, 1992), all of which are high in saturated fatty acids, total fat, cholesterol and calories. Overall, the social setting for eating is changing with children's mealtimes being less regular, more frequently taken standing or in front of the television, and either alone or with same-aged peers (Dietz & Gortmaker, 1985). The eating of 'unhealthy' foods becomes associated with peer activities, an association likely to contribute to the maintenance of the same eating habits in a significant minority of children beyond the childhood years (Kemm, 1987).

There is, however, also a notable converse trend in Western societies. A small but sizeable minority of often middle- and upper-class adults adopt veg-

etarian diets for health benefits, philosophical or, occasionally, economic reasons (Hanning & Zlotkin, 1985). A well-managed and varied vegetarian diet can meet the nutritional needs of the schoolchild. However, vegetarian diets that are sufficient for adults are often insufficient, in particular in energy terms, for the young child. For example Dwyer *et al.* (1983) and Robson (1977) reported on significant relative growth retardation in vegetarian as compared to non-vegetarian children, in particular at the time the children were weaned to an exclusive vegetarian diet (12–36 months of age). The more extreme the dietary habits, the more growth-retarded were the children. Vitamin D deficiency rickets has also recently reappeared in vegetarian children (Hanning & Zlotkin, 1985).

There is also an increasing use of vitamin and mineral supplements, which are not needed by healthy individuals consuming balanced meals (Truswell, 1990). Despite this fact, about one-third to one-half of the Canadian population take vitamin supplements, 24% of them children (Hanning & Zlotkin, 1985). There are many, mostly unfounded or controversial, claims that vitamin supplements prevent colds, help cope with stress, increase energy levels and promote cognitive development (Truswell, 1990; Benton & Cook, 1991; *Psychologist*, 1992). Problems with vitamin ingestion can arise and are more frequently reported in recent years in paediatric practice when parents hand out megadose amounts: excessive intakes of fat-soluble as well as water-soluble vitamins may be toxic and interfere with the actions of other vitamins or drugs (Hanning & Zlotkin, 1985).

Acquisition of adult eating patterns: changes during puberty

Important changes in eating patterns occur predominantly at or around puberty. Restraint eating and dieting is already prevalent, though much more so for girls than boys, in the early teenage years. Wardle and Beales (1986), in their survey of 12–18-year-old school children in Britain, found that the majority of girls regarded themselves as too large. Davies and Furnham (1986) reported that about half of 12–18-year-old girls wished to lose weight, and, whereas less than 4% were actually overweight, more than 40% considered themselves so. The desire to lose weight was highest amongst 14 year olds. Not surprisingly, then, although children usually eat breakfast, the number who skip breakfast increases throughout the teenage years, again mainly amongst girls (Expert Panel on Blood Cholesterol Levels in Children and Adolescents, 1992). A recent report suggests that weight concern may start, in a minority of girls, as early as 9 years of age (Hill, 1991).

The studies of changes with age in eating patterns do not provide answers to the crucial question of whether social and cultural factors are responsible for the changes in eating patterns or whether hormonal changes, physical maturation and associated physiological changes are important contributors to the rise in restraint eating. Weight gain occurs in both sexes during puberty, but, whereas increase in muscle tissue accounts for most of the male weight spurt, weight gain in females is due to a greater extent to the proliferation of adipose tissue, an oestrogen-dependent phenomenon (Tanner, 1989). Females progress from the childhood baseline of 8% body fat to 22% by the end of puberty. Furthermore, in girls the pelvic inlet widens and the hips broaden while few changes in the waist are found (Hammer *et al.*, 1991), contributing to the appearance of increasing lower body fatness which is viewed negatively by most girls (Johnson-Sabine *et al.*, 1988).

Cultural and subcultural factors are seen to be responsible for the rise of dieting, and an important role has been ascribed to the publications of mortality rates and insurance risks by life insurance companies in the USA, which, based often on quite spurious findings, raise the distinction between actual, normal and ideal weights (Pudel & Westenhöfer, 1991). Furthermore, the mass media and advertising are assumed to be a major factor in promoting the idea that slim women are more attractive, achieving and successful (Russell, 1992). Garner *et al.* (1980) analysed the average weight of the centrefold models of *Playboy* magazine and of the contestants for the 'Miss America' competition between 1959 and 1979. They found that the average weight of the models had reduced by around 10% over the 20 year period, whereas the actual weight of American women had increased during the same period by about the same amount (Garner *et al.*, 1980). Furthermore, they remarked that the

Playboy models were still relatively voluminous compared to the typical model in fashion magazines, which tend to be purchased by women rather than men (a phenomenon referred to as the '*Vogue–Playboy* dichotomy', Bennett & Gurin, 1982).

Restraint eating and dieting has become such a widespread and common part of the adolescent and adult life in Western societies that some speak of 'collective dieting behaviour' or 'diet mania' (Pudel & Westenhöfer, 1991). For example, roughly 10% of women and 3–4% of men in Germany have dieted more than 15 times in their life or are regular dieters (Iglo-Forum, 1991) and up to 29% of women do so in the USA (Fairburn & Beglin, 1990). Twenty-six per cent of Germans weigh themselves weekly and another 37% weigh themselves a few times a month (Deutsche Gesellschaft für Ernährung, 1980). Between 34 and 77% of German women exercise to reduce weight. Weight control, slimness and associated physical attractiveness, particularly for women, seems to be an important source of self-perceived psychological well-being as well as self-control (Yates, 1989).

Eating and ageing

The current recommended daily allowance is around 7560 kJ (1800 kcal) for the active elderly woman and about 10 080 kJ (2400 kcal) for an elderly man (Olsen-Noll & Bosworth, 1989). A recent review on the nutritional status of the elderly in the USA (Morley & Silver, 1988) provides shocking reading. Nutritional surveys showed that 16% of Caucasians and 18% of blacks older than 60 consumed less than 4200 J (1000 cal) per day. For those whose incomes fell below the poverty level, these percentages rose to 27 and 36%, respectively. Malnutrition in the elderly is most prevalent in nursing homes, with up to 50% of residents showing some degree of malnutrition (Asplund *et al.*, 1981).

Current evidence suggests that malnutrition in old age is due to accumulating factors (Table 20.5). Reduced activity and lowered basal oxygen consumption and metabolic rate can only partly explain lower caloric intake. There is furthermore the normal concomitant of ageing, the decrease in the chemical senses. The gustatory papillae (taste buds) begin to atrophy in women in the early forties and in men in the fifties. Young adults have around 250

Table 20.5 Causes of malnutrition/anorexia in the elderly

Normal ageing effects on appetite and satiety control
Decreased demand
  lowered metabolic rate
  reduced activity

Decreased hedonic qualities
  taste
  smell
  vision

Decreased feeding drive
  neurotransmitters, e.g. endogenous opioids

Increased activity of satiety factors
  cholecystokinin

Social factors
Poverty
Social isolation (e.g. no socialization at mealtimes)

Psychological factors
Bereavement
Dementia
Depression
Alcohol abuse
Inadequate knowledge of healthy diet

Physical factors
Immobility
Inability to feed oneself
Poor oral hygiene and dentition
Ill-fitting dentures

Diseases
Very frequent: infections, gastrointestinal problems, pain syndromes
Increased: from hormonal imbalances to cancer
Drug side-effects on eating

taste buds while older adults have less than 100 (Morley & Silver, 1988). Similarly, a decrease in olfaction and odour detection of food has been reported with age (Schiffman, 1977). Furthermore, most drugs that are particularly frequently prescribed for elderly persons affect taste perception and appetite adversely (Olsen-Noll & Bosworth, 1989). The neurotransmitter regulation of eating, in particular supports for the drive to eat and signal satiety, also change in old age, possibly leading to sooner experienced satiety (Leibowitz, 1988).

Physical factors contributing to reduced caloric intake include immobility problems with self-feedings, poor dentition, ill-fitting dentures, and so on (Olson-Noll & Bosworth, 1989). Psychological factors such as loss of a spouse and social isolation also interfere with eating habits. Furthermore, elderly persons may often not be aware of what constitutes a good diet. In one study, although 83% rated their intake as good or excellent, only 60% were rated as eating well during controlled observations (Brown, 1976). In sum, the normal processes of physical ageing are insufficient to account for the degree of malnutrition found in the elderly. Additional psychological factors as well as social isolation, poverty, illness and a lack of care by others are major contributors.

Feeding and eating problems

Feeding problems in infancy and toddlerhood

Transitory and persistent feeding difficulties. Apart from sleeping problems, problems in feeding are the most frequent reason why parents of young children seek advice (Troutman *et al.*, 1991); however, current diagnostic criteria are inadequate (Luiselli, 1989). The problems that occur in early childhood include: (i) food refusal; (ii) lack of appetite for any foods or most foods; (iii) self-feeding deficits; (iv) extremely slow feeding; (v) mealtime behavioural problems; and (vi) rumination disorder and vomiting. Two further conditions — infantile colic with excessive crying and non-organic failure to thrive (NOFT) with growth failure — are often considered feeding problems, although multiple symptoms apart from feeding difficulties are defining criteria.

The overall incidence of feeding problems as reported by mothers of infants and preschool children in community surveys is around 20–30% (Jenkins *et al.*, 1980; Luiselli, 1989). The problems include lack of appetite, selective food refusal, problems in introducing solids and mealtime behaviour problems; the rate of problems is even higher if issues about breast- and bottle-feeding and infantile colic are added.

Problems with breastfeeding, including both maternal complaints (sore or cracked nipples, engorgement, mastitis) and infant's difficulties in feeding, are reported by about one in three mothers after leaving the hospital (Wolke & Skuse, 1992). Fewer bottle-feeding mothers, about one in five, report problems, which are mainly vomiting, diarrhoea, constipation or crying (Forsyth *et al.*, 1985a; Martin & White, 1988). Regardless of type of feeding method, excessive crying or 'colic' is amongst the most common concerns brought to the attention of community physicians in the first 3 months (Forsyth *et al.*, 1985b), with the reported prevalence ranging from 7 to 29%, depending on criteria varying from evening crying to excessive crying after most feeds (Forsyth *et al.*, 1985a; St James-Roberts & Halil, 1991; Wolke, 1993a). The definition set by Wessel *et al.* (1954), 'paroxysms of irritability, fussing, or crying lasting for a total of more than three hours a day and occurring on more than three days in any one week' is most commonly used. There are conflicting opinions on whether colic represents the upper range of the spectrum of crying in healthy infants (St James-Roberts & Halil, 1991), is a distinct clinical syndrome (Illingworth, 1985) or simply is a set of behaviours that exceed the parents' tolerance (Wolke & St James-Roberts, 1987).

Some investigators report colic to be more frequent in breastfed infants (Rubin & Prendergast, 1984), while others have found no association with type of feeding (Forsyth *et al.*, 1985a, b). In approximately 10–15% of colicky infants, cows' milk allergy may be involved (Forsyth, 1989; Sampson, 1989). Overall, normal developmental changes in crying during the first 3 months of life, coupled with individual characteristics of infants and parents, appear to contribute to the incidence of and recovery from colic (Wolke, 1993a, b).

Severe, persistent feeding difficulties such as total food refusal, vomiting or rumination, or extreme colicky crying, are found in about 1–2% of infants (Dahl & Sundelin, 1986a, b; Lindberg *et al.*, in press). Rumination (where previously ingested food is voluntarily regurgitated and partially reswallowed) and pica (repeated eating of non-nutritive substances) are very rare, often self-limiting and more prevalent in mentally retarded or socially and emotionally deprived children (Minde & Minde, 1986). Refusal to eat is the most prevalent of the persistent problems, and in only 14% of food refusers some form of physical disorder is found to be contributing to the problem (Dahl & Sundelin, 1987a; Skuse & Wolke, 1992; Lindberg *et al.*, in press). Food refusal persists into early childhood, with 36% of infants who were found to refuse food in the first year still often having severe feeding problems at 2 years (Dahl & Sundelin, 1987a, b); at 4 years of age minor to severe feeding difficulties were found in 71% of early food refusers, with behaviour problems, in particular hyperactivity, a further adverse sequelae (Dahl & Sundelin, 1992). Chronic food refusal seen in the outpatient setting is mostly due to a maladaptive feeding relationship with the caretaker (Harris & Booth, 1992; Wolke & Skuse, 1992).

Failure to thrive (FTT). FTT has been described under many different names, including maternal deprivation syndrome (Field, 1987), reactive attachment disorder (Minde & Minde, 1986), anorexia nervosa of infancy (Chatoor, 1989) or hospitalism syndrome (Spitz, 1945), and has been defined using clinical and behavioural criteria (Drotar, 1990), although there is now growing consensus that it should be defined on growth parameters alone (Bithony & Dubowitz, 1985). However, definitions referring to weight for age, height for age, weight for height or indices of the velocity of growth lead to quite diverse prevalence estimates (*Lancet*, 1990a). We have proposed that a minimum criterion should be weight below the third centile for population standards that has persisted for more than 3 months (Wolke *et al.*, 1990a).

The onset of FTT is usually in the first year of life and has to be distinguished from nutritional or psychosocial dwarfism, which usually begins after the second year and is most frequently associated with major family disruption (Oates, 1984; Skuse, 1989). A recent community survey in Britain, the largest of its kind, found a prevalence of FTT of 3.4% in full term, appropriate for gestational age 1 year olds (Skuse *et al.*, 1992). About 2.9% of children on community child abuse registers are included with FTT as primary diagnosis (Creighton, 1985).

Long-term prognosis for infants who fail to thrive is poor, with 22–60% achieving no long-term catch-up growth (Wolke, 1991a) and FTT children as a group having cognitive abilities 1–1.5 standard deviations below population or control group means (Fig. 20.6). Around 20–40% are mildly to moderately mentally handicapped (IQ < 70), and FTT infants are much more likely than their age-mates to be seriously delayed in reading (Oates *et al.*, 1985) and to fail in school (Glaser *et al.*, 1968). About 28–50% show other behavioural problems in middle to later childhood (Oates *et al.*, 1985)

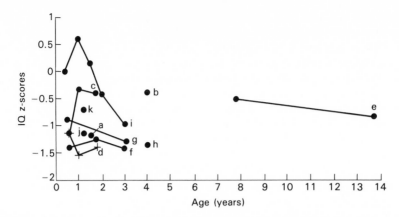

Fig. 20.6 Standardized DQ/IQ scores of non-organic failure to thrive (NOFT) children (11 studies) (z-scores computed according to test norms or according to mean and standard deviation of the normal growing control group when available). Data from: (a) Fitch *et al*. (1975, 1976); (b) Mitchell *et al*. (1980); (c) Field (1984), MDI (Mental Development Index); (d) Field (1984), PDI (Psychomotor Development Index); (e) Oates *et al*. (1984, 1985); (f) Singer & Fagan (1984); (g) Singer (1986, 1987); (h) Dowdney *et al*., (1987); (i) Drotar & Sturm (1988); (j) Wolke *et al*. (1990a); (k) Skuse *et al*. (1994).

with eating problems persisting in many children (Heptinstall *et al*., 1987).

Two questions have often been confounded in the literature, namely (i) which factors might explain the occurrence of growth failure? and (ii) are these the same factors that lead to the poor outcomes for FTT children or are the attributes of FTT itself responsible for the poor outcomes? Traditionally, FTT has been thought of as either due to organic factors or to an insufficient nurturing environment that leads to reactive attachment disorder and poor growth despite adequate food intake (Spitz, 1945; Field, 1987). The latter is referred to as NOFT. Often the distinction has been drawn on the basis of improved weight gain during hospitalization (Ellerstein & Ostrov, 1985), with those showing weight gain with adequate caloric intake considered NOFT cases. However, newer studies show that this criterion is based on false assumptions; for example, in one study FTT infants with treatable organic diseases were seven times more likely to show improved growth than were NOFT infants (Kristiansson & Fällström, 1987). More recently it has been proposed that many organic diseases, including congenital heart failure and cerebral palsy, only in interaction with poor feeding and nutritional provision, lead to FTT (Menon & Poskitt, 1985; *Lancet*, 1990b), and should be considered mixed cases. Although organic illness is

implicated in roughly 20–40% of infants in hospital samples (Frank & Zeisel, 1988), organic FTT is rarely found in the community; in the largest community survey, it accounted for only 6% of the cases (Skuse *et al*., 1992). This indicates the biases in clinical samples and underscores the fact that growth faltering in most infants is due to non-organic reasons. Most concerning, however, is that more than 80% of cases, associated with non-organic factors, in that community survey remained undetected by the community health services.

Spitz (1951) first systematically described the effect of the 'loss of affective input' in a penal institution and nursing home in the first 2 years of life, with infants who experienced prolonged maternal deprivation showing a characteristic pattern of indiscriminate seeking of social contacts, later total social withdrawal, loss of appetite, weight loss and intellectual and social developmental regression. He labelled this clinical picture 'anaclitic depression'. His observations had a major impact on the psychological and psychiatric focus in research on NOFT. Subsequently, a whole range of socio-economic and proximal environmental factors, as well as maternal characteristics, have been suggested to contribute to growth failure, including poverty and poor parental education (McJunkin *et al*., 1987) and less responsive, under- or overstimulating mother–infant interaction (Drotar *et al*., 1990).

Others have described an overrepresentation of mothers with psychiatric problems and low intelligence (Hess *et al.*, 1977; Singer *et al.*, 1990).

The empirical evidence indicates that emotional deprivation *per se* is not the major cause of non-organic FTT; for example, observations of mother–infant interaction are often based on samples of referred infants, which are likely to include a preponderance of infants from families with dysfunctional relationships (Skuse *et al.*, 1992) and where the observations of interaction are assessed after diagnosis of the infant. Thus the inadequate interactions between infant and mother are as likely to be the consequence of persistent feeding problems and parental anxiety about getting food into the infant as to be the cause of NOFT. Furthermore, where attachment has been assessed in clinic samples using the Ainsworth 'strange situation' procedure (see Chapter 16), there is indeed a substantial proportion (around 50%) of NOFT infants who are insecurely attached, but half show secure attachment (Brinich *et al.*, 1989). When the insecure and secure NOFT infants were contrasted 2.5 years later, the insecure infants showed no poorer growth and indeed showed a trend for greater catch-up growth (Brinich *et al.*, 1989). Thus attachment difficulties are neither necessary nor sufficient for non-organic FTT to occur.

In the only reported community study where NOFT and adequately growing control children and families were matched on socioeconomic indices, no differences in social interaction patterns were found in either feeding or play situations or in an abbreviated separation–reunion procedure; nor were there any differences in the psychiatric morbidity or IQ scores of the mothers (Wolke *et al.*, 1990c; Skuse *et al.*, 1992, 1994). Only in a small minority of NOFT cases (7%) was there sufficient evidence of neglect or abuse to justify the infant's placement on the at risk register.

Rather than deriving primarily from organic disease or deficient social environments, FTT provides a good illustration of the ways in which characteristics of individual infants interact with environmental features to create developmental problems. It is now widely accepted that the primary biological insult in all non-organic and most organic cases of FTT is malnutrition because the infant is not offered, refuses or cannot take in nutrition sufficient for growth (Field, 1984; Skuse, 1985). Although there are no overall differences in mother–infant interactions, FTT infants are taking in substantially fewer calories (a reduction of 25%) during their meals (Wolke *et al.*, 1990c). There is evidence that NOFT infants receive inadequate nourishment for quite heterogeneous reasons, including those who are neglected, without regular, sufficient or organized meals (Heptinstall *et al.*, 1987), and those who receive insufficient diets because of prolonged exclusive breastfeeding or errors in the preparation of bottle-feeds (Schmitt & Mauro, 1989; Reilly *et al.*, 1994), maternal eating disorder (Smith *et al.*, 1972; Van Wezel-Meijler & Wit, 1989) religious or cultural reasons (Pugliese *et al.*, 1987). Furthermore, infants may be malnourished partly because of their own subtle oral–motor problems, making the intake of higher textured and denser food difficult (Mathisen *et al.*, 1989), are insufficiently demanding (Habbick & Gerrard, 1984), or are difficult to feed or food refusers (Dahl & Sundelin, 1986a, b; Harris & Booth, 1992).

In early infancy, temperamental features, in particular the amount of crying during day and night, can powerfully affect nutritional provision. Carey (1985) showed that infants rated as temperamentally more difficult showed a higher velocity of growth between 6 and 12 months than did easy, less demanding infants. Indeed, Masai infants in Africa who were assessed as temperamentally more difficult were more likely to have survived a subsequent drought (De Vries, 1984): 'The babies who yelled the most probably got the most food and survived' (Carey, 1986, p. 161). In our own studies, both NOFT and control infants who slept through the night earlier showed a lower relative velocity of growth during the first 6 months; however, mothers of NOFT infants were much more likely *not* to wake their infants for a feed than were control mothers. Thus individual infant characteristics, in interaction with maternal care-taking strategies, lead to the missing of feeds and most likely lower caloric intake. Often factors such as disorganized mealtimes, oral–motor problems, parental provision of nutritionally inadequate diets, and so on, occur in conjunction.

In our own studies, large differences in the incidence of NOFT in different ethnic groups living within the same community were found: while 3–5% of white UK, Chinese Asian, Carribean and mixed race infants suffered NOFT, some 15% of Indian Asian and none of the African infants all residing in the same London health region did so (Skuse *et al.*, 1992). This finding can be interpreted to reflect genotypic differences in growth patterns between ethnic groups, differential socioeconomic factors and cultural differences in eating patterns and food intake. Within the Indian Asian community, both the late introduction of solids of low caloric density (Underwood & Hofvander, 1982), as well as the frequent social isolation of the mothers (Fenton *et al.*, 1989), are likely contributors to the high rates of FTT. Cultural groups also differ in terms of preferred body shapes for infants as well as adults. The concern amongst many adults regarding their own shape and weight described above also influences maternal behaviour. Wolke *et al.* (1990b), using drawings of infants varied in adiposity, found that mothers of NOFT infants preferred leaner infants than did matched control mothers, with larger mothers preferring leaner infants. These mothers often commented that, if they could not control their own intake, they could do so with their infants, a type of vicarious dieting. The Gerber Foods survey of 2000 mothers in the USA similarly showed that 57% worried about their babies becoming fat, and nearly 75% said that information about the desirability of reducing fat in adult diets led them to believe that it was desirable to reduce fat and calories in babies' diets (Birch, 1990). In fact, given that babies typically triple their weight in the first year, calories and fat are essential during this period. In sum, cultural, parental, and infant characteristics, most likely in interaction, lead to a resetting of the internal nutrient demand of NOFT infants and provide them with different oral–motor experiences (i.e. provision of low-textured foods). Little appetite and interest in food leads to further caloric deprivation, with important health implications, such as recurrent infections and anaemia, which in turn are associated with lower exploratory behaviour and motivation (Frank & Zeisel, 1988). Thus, although enhanced environmental stimulation can partly compensate for the early effects of undernutrition on brain development (Lozoff, 1989; Grantham-McGregor *et al.*, 1991), these infants may be less likely to take advantage of environmental opportunities. Infants with rapid growth failure in the first 6 months of life, in contrast with those with major growth failure later in the first year, are at particular risk for cognitive impairment, with low maternal cognitive stimu-

lation making an additional cumulative, rather than interactive, contribution to poor outcome (Skuse *et al.*, 1994). Generally, hospitalization has only short-term effects and does not prevent the occurrence of later problems (Fryer, 1988; Skuse *et al.*, 1992). However, when detected early, the adverse developmental effects are potentially avoidable (Skuse *et al.*, 1994). For example, Lucas *et al.* (1990, 1992b) found that preterm infants fed a specially adapted and enriched milk formula or breast milk via tube showed not only accelerated growth but also superior cognitive development in the first few years of life, relative to preterm infants fed normal milk formulations.

Eating problems in childhood

In contrast to concern with infant and toddler difficulties in obtaining adequate nutrition, a common problem reported by parents of older children is obesity, which appears to be on the increase, affecting 5–19% of children (Epstein *et al.*, 1985). Obese children are likely to become obese adults, with the associated risk for cardiovascular disease (Kannel & Cupples, 1989), and also may experience peer rejection (Deutsche Gesellschaft für Ernährung, 1984), which has its own negative consequences for development (see Chapter 18). The risk of adult obesity increases with the child's age; 70% of obese 10–13-year-olds go on to be obese adults (Epstein *et al.*, 1985). Children of two obese parents are more likely to be obese than those of normal weight parents, a pattern reported independent of ethnicity (Gallaher *et al.*, 1991). Birth weight has been found consistently to predict later overweight (Seidman *et al.*, 1991), although a recent prospective study of infants born to obese and non-obese mothers found no initial differences in birth weight; rather, the weight but not height trajectories of the two groups of infants started to diverge from 6 months of age onwards (Rummler & Woit, 1992).

There is evidence from adoption and twin studies that a tendency for obesity is hereditary (Sorensen *et al.*, 1989; Stunkard, 1989). However, the intra-uterine environment also seems important: infants of Pima Indian mothers who were diabetic during pregnancy were much more likely to become obese later than were their siblings who were born before the full manifestation of their mothers' diabetes (Byers, 1992). Obesity is also associated with difficult temperament (Carey *et al.*, 1988), earlier giving up of breastfeeding (Kramer *et al.*, 1985), and overfeeding in infancy (Mogan, 1986). Whether obese children have a clearly delineated eating disorder, including false perception of meal sizes, poor regulation of satiety and aberrant eating patterns (Kissileff, 1989) is still far from clear.

Eating problems in adolescents and adults

The overall increase in restraint eating in adolescence and adulthood has been already noted. Anorexia and bulimia are the predominant eating disorders emerging at this point in development, both featuring disturbed eating patterns that reflect underlying fears of weight gain (Herzog & Bradburn, 1992). While the syndrome of anorexia nervosa has been described as an eating disorder since the mid-nineteenth century (Yates, 1989), the first articles describing bulimia nervosa appeared in the 1970s (Russell, 1979). There is a steep rise in the prevalence of these eating disorders during or after puberty (Herzog & Copeland, 1985; Lask & Bryant-Waugh, 1992), and female adolescents are particularly at risk.

Anorexia nervosa is a syndrome characterized by extreme weight loss (more than 15% of previous body weight) or failure to gain weight, body-image disturbance, and an intense fear of becoming obese (American Psychiatric Association, 1987), with grave psychological and physical consequences (Herzog & Copeland, 1985). More than one-third of cases have recurrent affective illness and the suicide rate can be up to 2−5%; the mortality rate, excluding suicide, can be as high as 9% in severe cases. Overall, the morbidity and mortality rates in anorexia nervosa are among the highest recorded for psychiatric disorders. Most surveys establish the prevalence at 0.5−1% amongst adolescent girls (Herzog & Bradburn, 1992), with rates from the higher social classes notably increased (Russell, 1992).

Some suggest a bimodal age of onset at 13−14 or 17−18 years (Herzog & Copeland, 1985). Anorexia nervosa has also been reported to occur prior to puberty (Russell, 1992), which is of theoretical interest, as it has been argued that the disorder represents a maladaptive biological response to the growth changes of puberty (Crisp, 1980). Early

onset cases tend to come predominantly from intact, highly achieving families with well-functioning parental relationships (Pugliese *et al.*, 1983; Gowers *et al.*, 1991; Sandberg *et al.*, 1991). The high achievement orientation of the families, their concerns about diet and healthy eating, as well as the high number of boys affected, point to family preoccupations about food and weight rather than to biological factors. The key diagnostic signs of prepubertal anorexia are the failure to gain weight, followed by actual weight loss with a variety of other symptoms often present (e.g. vomiting, abdominal pain, depression, food avoidance, etc.). However, most paediatricians (*c.* 75%) and nearly all primary care physicians (98%) do not include anorexia nervosa in their differential diagnosis when confronted with cases of severe weight loss, abdominal pain and vomiting in children (Bryant-Waugh *et al.*, 1992). Prepubertal anorexia often disrupts the pubertal process, leading to significant stunting of growth (Russell, 1992). Early onset anorexia nervosa is not characteristically accompanied by other psychiatric disturbance, but psychiatric problems such as depression and compulsive states are observed in 30−40% of postpubertal patients (Steinhausen & Glanville, 1983). Whether this association is the result of similar endocrinological mechanisms (Rutter, 1991; Russell, 1992), the occurrence of negative self-evaluations and cognitive sets, or the increased expression of genetic factors (Holland *et al.*, 1988; Rutter *et al.*, 1990) is unknown. Largo (1993) reported that adolescents studied in the Zurich Longitudinal Growth Study who experienced weight loss in puberty had shown large fluctuations in weight gain throughout childhood. It appears that these children lacked a clear set-point and boundaries for physiological regulation of food intake and growth, from early childhood onwards.

Bulimia nervosa is an eating disorder with three core features: (i) recurrent episodes of overeating, called 'binges'; (ii) various forms of behaviour designed to control shape and weight, including extreme dieting, excessive exercising, self-induced vomiting and the taking of laxatives or diuretics; and (iii) extreme concerns about shape and weight (Fairburn & Beglin, 1990). The peak onset has been reported to be between 17 and 25 years of age (Herzog & Copeland, 1985), although new evidence suggests that it often has its onset earlier during mid to late puberty (Killen *et al.*, 1992). The prevalence rate according to DSM-III-R criteria is around 3% by self-report and 1% by standardized interviews (Fairburn & Beglin, 1990). The condition is six to 10 times more prevalent in females than in males (Herzog & Bradburn, 1992), and is more prevalent in the higher socioeconomic groups, non-whites, athletes and the performing arts (Rowley, 1987; Fairburn & Beglin, 1990; Herzog & Bradburn, 1992). Some clinical studies of patients have found high rates of affective disorders (24–88%), in particular depression, while others have reported no significant relationships (Fairburn & Beglin, 1990; Herzog & Bradburn, 1992). Some have argued that the distinction between anorexia nervosa and bulimia is not clear-cut, but rather that symptoms of both disorders wax and wane over time in some individuals (Yates, 1989). However, although the overlap may be considerable in some cases, bulimic individuals, unlike anorexic patients, are often indistinguishable from same-aged peers on weight, and are usually aware that their eating behaviour is deviant and are embarrassed and ashamed by it, practising bingeing and purging in secrecy (Herzog & Copeland, 1985).

Given the normative trends for dieting in the adolescent and adult years, it is not clear whether non-anorexic bulimia is an illness or simply an interesting constellation of symptoms that is best understood as women's response to the cultural emphasis on body weight and shape (Beumont, 1988). Certainly there is little argument that normal dieting precedes bulimia (Herman & Polivy, 1988a, b). Viewed this way, bulimia may constitute one extreme on a continuum of behaviours, attitudes and self-control cognitions present in most women (Thompson *et al.*, 1987), likely to occur at a vulnerable time of weight increase and social change, i.e. puberty.

Eating problems in the elderly

The incidence of malnutrition in the elderly population has already been noted; this is often referred to as anorexia of the elderly (Olsen-Noll & Bosworth, 1989). Further specific problems with eating are associated with senile dementia; the incidence of malnutrition in demented or multi-infarct patients has been reported to be around 50%. Demented patients often have weight loss because of indiffer-

ence, memory loss and impairment of judgement (Morley & Silver, 1988). Furthermore, their motoric problems and oral apraxia call for the help of others in eating, so that, as in infancy, the interactional aspects of feeding again become important. However, there may be insufficient time spent on assistance with eating in nursing homes; one study reported that only 18 min a day were spent on feeding in nursing homes, as opposed to 99 min if the patients were kept at home (Hu *et al.*, 1986).

THE INTERRELATIONSHIPS AMONGST SLEEPING, FEEDING AND OTHER DOMAINS OF FUNCTIONING

In the foregoing review, the development of sleeping and eating behaviour and problems has been discussed separately, to deal with the complexity of these simple psychobiological functions which we all engage in daily. However, some important developmental principles can be identified in both domains: (i) the development of self-regulation in infancy; (ii) the parallel effects of changes in puberty on psychological functioning of adolescents; and (iii) the understanding of biological influences on functioning when comparing CNS integration in infancy and disintegration in old age.

Crying, sleeping, temperament and cognition in infancy

Between 2 and 4 months of age, a major biobehavioural shift takes place (Wolff, 1987), when infants become able to maintain active wakefulness (Coons & Guilleminault, 1982). The increased sleep–wake organization permits a shift in information-processing from inner-directed programmes to more externally derived organizations, in particular the increase of attentional skills. The ability to habituate to stimuli stabilizes after 9 weeks of age (Bornstein & Sigman, 1986) and a significant negative correlation between active sleep, as measured by polygraphic recordings, and both recovery and habituation is detectable (Mamone *et al.*, 1990). In other words, infants with less mature active sleep show poorer information processing.

Coons and Guilleminault (1982) also provided evidence that a precursor of circadian organization is the placing of the longest period of wakefulness in the late afternoon or evening, which is followed by the longest period of sleeping. Interestingly, there is a universal, culture-independent increase in crying between 4 and 8 weeks of age, with most crying occurring during the late afternoon and evening (Barr, 1990; Wolke, 1993b). Integrating the findings from sleeping, feeding and cognitive research, the phenomenon of colic, which is often identified from evening crying, appears to be a normal precursor or correlate of major developmental reorganizations and regulation of information processing (Wolke, 1992). Notable also is the fact that, at 3–4 months of age, when more differentiated sleep patterns become established, the infant is more prepared for the introduction of semi-solid food. Viewed within such a developmental framework, parental interventions are 'optimal' when they facilitate the chain of reorganizations of biological functioning by providing external support appropriate to the stage of CNS reorganization (Wolke, 1993a, b). Prospective longitudinal designs that examine crying, sleeping, feeding and temperament in the same sample of infants are required. Furthermore, in almost all known cross-sectional and longitudinal studies, age is seen as an obstacle rather than a facilitator. Infants need to be compared according to maturational stage (as inferred from their peak time of crying, placement of their waking time in the evening, acquired circadian rhythms, etc.), not simply according to chronological age.

Sleeping, eating and affective regulation in adolescence

Eating and sleeping both undergo major changes in adolescence. Many more girls than boys show a rise in eating problems and in depression (Rutter, 1991), while information about gender differences in sleeping problems in adolescence is lacking. Both daytime sleepiness and eating problems show an increase with successive stages of puberty, with a particular increase around stage 3 or 4 of Tanner's criteria (Carskadon *et al.*, 1980; Killen *et al.*, 1992). Similar data relating pubertal stage to depressed mood have not been reported so far. Considering that eating and sleep problems are important symptoms of depression and that increased concern with diet and weight is associated with negative self-concepts, it would not be surprising if the rise in depression is closely related to the rise of these other problems, either because one set of problems is a precursor to another or because they are all different expressions of biological changes and social adaptation in different adolescents. However, persistent eating and sleeping problems in adults are associated with a high prevalence of depressive disorder. Again, prospective, longitudinal studies of all three sets of symptoms in the same samples are required, and pubertal stage rather than chronological age appears to be the crucial variable (Magnusson *et al.*, 1986; Belsky *et al.*, 1991).

Sleeping and feeding in early childhood and old age

Infancy and early childhood are periods of rapid organization of the CNS and the acquisition of behavioural control. In old age, there is an increased disintegration of the CNS, with the described shedding of slow-wave sleep, increased night-waking and daytime napping. There are also changes in taste perception and appetite regulation. There are of course many more differences than parallels between CNS organization in early childhood and its disintegration in old age. The cognitive and social competence of the elderly is obviously much higher than that of children, and any arising problems are compensated for by cognitive as well as motor strategies. Older people have acquired wisdom and can draw on many years of experience (see Chapter 22).

Nevertheless, it may be possible to learn more about the influences of CNS integration on eating, sleeping and other domains of functioning when comparing children and elderly adults at similar levels of functioning, i.e. showing similar sleep patterns and feeding dependency. For example, what are the influences of sleep stage differentiation and attentional regulation in both age groups? How necessary are the different sleep stages for recovery of which bodily functions, in both age groups? These are some of the questions that may or may not be answerable when children and the elderly are matched according to stages of physiological maturation or disintegration.

The foregoing review points to intriguing principles of normative development and insufficiently studied biological and social factors that contribute to both sleeping and eating disorders at times of major psychobiological transitions.

ACKNOWLEDGEMENT

I would like to thank Dale Hay and Michael Rutter for their patient and thoughtful editing of this chapter. The author was supported by grant JUG 14 of the Federal Government of Germany, Ministry of Research and Technology.

REFERENCES

Adam K. & Oswald I. (1983) Protein synthesis, bodily renewal and the sleep–wake cycle. *Clinical Science* **65**, 561–567.

Agnew Jr H.W., Webb W.B. & Williams R.L. (1966) The first night effect: An EEG study of sleep. *Psychophysiology* **2**, 263–266.

American Psychiatric Association (1987) *Diagnostic and Statistical Manual of Mental Disorders*, 3rd edn revised. American Psychiatric Association, Washington, DC.

Ancoli-Israel S. (1989) Epidemiology of sleep disorders. *Sleep Disorders in the Elderly* **5**(2), 347–362.

Anders T.F. (1982) Neurophysiological studies of sleep in infants and children. *Journal of Child Psychology and Psychiatry* **23**, 75–83.

Anders T.F., Carskadon M.A. & Dement W.C. (1980) Sleep and sleepiness in children and adolescents. *Pediatric Clinics of North America* **27**, 29–43.

Anders T.F., Carskadon M.A., Dement W.C. & Harvey K. (1978) Sleep habits of children and the identification of pathologically sleepy children. *Child Psychiatry and Human Development* **9**, 56–63.

Anders T.F. & Keener M.A. (1985) Developmental course of nighttime sleep–wake patterns in full-term and premature infants during the first year of life. I. *Sleep* **8**(3), 173–192.

Anders T.F., Keener M.A., Bowe T.R. & Shoaff B.A. (1983) A longitudinal study of nighttime sleep–wake patterns in infants from birth to one year. In Call J.D., Galenson E. & Tyson R.L. (eds) *Frontiers of Infant Psychiatry*, pp. 150–166. Basic Books, New York.

Anders T.F. & Sostek A. (1976) The use of time-lapse videorecording of sleep–wake behaviors in human infants. *Psychophysiology* **13**, 155–158.

Antrobus J. (1983) REM and NREM sleep reports: Comparison of word frequencies by cognitive classes. *Psychophysiology* **20**, 562–568.

Asplund K., Normark M. & Pettersson V. (1981) Nutritional assessment of psychogeriatric patients. *Age and Ageing* **10**, 87–94.

Bakeman R., Adamson L.B., Konner M. & Barr R.G. (1990) !Kung infancy: The social context of object exploration. *Child Development* **61**, 794–809.

Bamford F.N., Bannister R.P., Benjamin C.M., Hillier V.F., Ward B.S. & Moore W.M.O. (1990) Sleep in the first year of life. *Developmental Medicine and Child Neurology* **32**, 718–724.

Barr R.G. (1990) The normal crying curve: What do we really know? (Annotation). *Developmental Medicine and Child Neurology* **32**, 356–362.

Basler K., Largo R.H. & Molinari L. (1980) Die Entwicklung des Schlafverhaltens in den ersten fünf Lebensjahren (The development of sleeping behaviour in the first five years of life). *Helvetica Paediatrica Acta* **35**, 211–223.

Beauchamp G.K. & Cowart B.J. (1986) Congenital and experiential factors in the development of human flavor preferences. *Appetite* **6**, 357–372.

Belsky J., Steinberg L. & Draper P. (1991) Childhood experiences, interpersonal development, and reproductive strategy: An evolutionary theory of socialization. *Child Development* **62**, 647–670.

Beltramini A.U. & Hertzig M.E. (1983) Sleep and bedtime behavior in preschool-aged children. *Pediatrics* **71**(2), 153–158.

Bennett W. & Gurin J. (1982) *The Dieter's Dilemma. Why Diets are Obsolete — The New Setpoint Theory of Weight Control*. Basic Books, New York.

Benton D. & Cook R. (1991) Vitamin and mineral supplements improve the intelligence scores and concentration of six-year-old children. *Personality and Individual Differences* **12**, 1151–1158.

Bernal J. (1973) Night waking in infants during the first 14 months. *Developmental Medicine and Child Neurology* **14**, 362–372.

Beumont P.J.V. (1988) Bulimia: Is it an illness entity? *International Journal of Eating Disorders* **7**, 167–176.

Birch L.L. (1990) Development of food acceptance patterns. *Developmental Psychology* **26**, 515–519.

Birch L.L. (1987) The acquisition of food acceptance patterns in children. In Boakes R.A., Popplewell D.A. & Burton M.J. (eds) *Eating Habits: Food, Physiology and Learned Behaviour*, pp. 107–130. Wiley, New York.

Bithony W.G. & Dubowitz A. (1985) Organic concomitants of nonorganic failure to thrive: Implications for research. In Drotar D. (ed.) *New Directions in Failure to Thrive: Implications for Research, and Practice*, pp. 47–68. Plenum, London.

Bixler E.O. & Vela-Bueno A. (1987) Normal sleep: Patterns and mechanisms. *Seminars in Neurology* **7**(3), 227–235.

Blurton-Jones N., Rosetti Ferreira M.C., Farquar Brown M. & McDonald L. (1978) The association between perinatal factors and later night waking. *Developmental Medicine and Child Neurology* **20**, 427–434.

Borbely A.A. (1982) A two process model of sleep regulation. *Human Neurobiology* **1**, 195–204.

Borbely A.A. (1986) Endogenous sleep substances and sleep regulation. *Journal of Neural Transmission* **21**(Suppl.), 243–254.

Borkovec T.D., Lane T.W. & van Oot P.H. (1981) Phenomenology of sleep among insomniacs and good sleepers: Wakefulness experience when cortically asleep. *Journal of Abnormal Psychology* **90**, 607−609.

Bornstein M. & Sigman M.D. (1986) Continuity in mental development from infancy. *Child Development* **57**, 251−274.

Bowlby J. (1969) *Attachment*. Basic Books, New York.

Brinich E.B., Drotar D.D. & Brinich P.M. (1989) Die Bedeutung der Bindungssicherheit vom Kind zur Mutter für die psychische und physische Entwicklung von gedeihschwåchen Kindern (The relevance of infant–mother attachment security for the psychological and physical development of failure to thrive children). *Praxis der Kinderpsychologie und Kinderpsychiatrie* **38**, 70−77.

Brothwood M., Wolke D., Gamsu H. & Cooper D. (1988) Mortality, morbidity, growth and development of babies weighing 501−1000 g and 1001−1500 g at birth. *Acta Paediatrica Scandinavica* **77**, 10−18.

Broughton R.J. (1968) Sleep disorders: Disorders of arousal? *Science* **159**, 1070−1076.

Broughton R.J. (1990) Narcolepsy. In Thorpy M.J. (ed.) *Handbook of Sleep Disorders*, pp. 197−216. Marcel Dekker, New York.

Brown E.L. (1976) Factors influencing food choices and intake. *Geriatrics* **31**(9), 89−92.

Bryant-Waugh R.J., Lask B.D., Shafran R.L. & Fosson A.R. (1992) Do doctors recognise eating disorders in children? *Archives of Disease in Childhood* **67**, 103−105.

Bunton J., Bisset E. & Harvey D. (1987) The social experience of newborn babies in hospital. In Harvey D. (ed.) *Parent−Infant Relationships*, Vol. 4, *Perinatal Practice*, pp. 131−141. Wiley, New York.

Buysse D.J. & Reynolds III C.F. (1990) Insomnia. In Thorpy M.J. (ed.) *Handbook of Sleep Disorders*, pp. 373−434. Marcel Dekker, New York.

Byers T. (1992) The epidemic of obesity in American Indians. *American Journal of Diseases of Children* **146**, 285−286.

Carey W.B. (1985) Temperament and increased weight gain. *Developmental and Behavioral Pediatrics* **6**, 128−131.

Carey W.B. (1986) Early weight gains and other correlates of temperament. In Kohnstamm G.A. (ed.) *Temperament Discussed: Temperament and Development in Infancy and Childhood*, pp. 159−164. Swets & Zeitlinger, Lisse.

Carey W.B., Hegvik R.L. & McDevitt S.C. (1988) Temperamental factors associated with rapid weight gain and obesity in middle childhood. *Developmental and Behavioral Pediatrics* **9**, 194−198.

Carskadon M.A., Harvey K., Duke P., Anders T.F., Litt, I.F. & Dement W.C. (1980) Pubertal changes in daytime sleepiness. *Sleep* **2**, 453−460.

Cashman M.A. & McCann B.S. (1988) Behavioral approaches to sleep/wake disorders in children and adolescents. In Hersen M., Eisler R.M. & Miller P.M. (eds) *Progress in Behavior Modification*, pp. 215−282. Sage, London.

Chatoor I. (1989) Infantile anorexia nervosa: A develop-

mental disorder of separation and individuation. *Journal of the American Academy of Psychoanalysis* **17**, 43−64.

Cirignotta F., Zucconi M., Mondini S., Lenzi P.L. & Lugaresi E. (1983) Enuresis, sleepwalking, and nightmares: An epidemiological survey in the republic of San Marino. In Guilleminault C. & Lugaresi E. (eds) *Sleep/Wake Disorders: Natural History, Epidemiology, and Long-term Evolution*, pp. 237−241. Raven, New York.

Coons S. & Guilleminault C. (1982) Development of sleep−wake patterns and non-rapid eye movement sleep stages during the first six months of life in normal infants. *Pediatrics* **69**, 793−798.

Creighton S.J. (1985) An epidemiological study of abused children and their families in the United Kingdom between 1977 and 1982. *Child Abuse and Neglect* **9**, 441−448.

Crick F. & Mitchison G. (1983). The function of dream sleep. *Nature* **304**, 111−114.

Crisp A.H. (1980) *Anorexia Nervosa: Let Me Be*. Academic Press, London.

Czeisler C.A. & Jewett M.E. (1990) Human circadian physiology: Interaction of the behavioral rest−activity cycle with the output of the endogenous circadian pacemaker. In Thorpy M.J. (ed.) *Handbook of Sleep Disorders*, pp. 117−137. Marcel Dekker, New York.

Dahl M. & Sundelin C (1986a) Early feeding problems in an affluent society: ii. Determinants. *Acta Paediatrica Scandinavica* **75**, 380−387.

Dahl M. & Sundelin C. (1986b) Early feeding problems in an affluent society: iv. Categories and clinical signs. *Acta Paediatrica Scandinavica* **75**, 370−379.

Dahl M. & Sundelin C. (1987a) Early feeding problems in an affluent society: iii. Follow-up at 2 years: natural courses, health, behaviour and development. *Acta Paediatrica Scandinavica* **76**, 872−880.

Dahl M. & Sundelin C. (1987b) Early feeding problems in an affluent society: iv. Impact on growth up to 2 years of age. *Acta Paediatrica Scandinavica* **76**, 881−888,

Dahl M. & Sundelin C. (1992) Feeding problems in an affluent society. Follow-up at four years of age in children with early refusal to eat. *Acta Paediatrica Scandinavica* **81**, 575−579.

Davies E. & Furnham A. (1986) The dieting and body shape concerns of adolescent females. *Journal of Child Psychology and Psychiatry* **27**, 417−428.

Davis C.M. (1928) Self selection of diet by newly weaned infants. *American Journal of Diseases of Children* **36**, 651−679.

Dement W.C., Seidel W. & Carskadon M. (1984) Issues in the diagnosis and treatment of insomnia. In Hindmarch I., Ott H. & Roth R. (eds) *Sleep: Benzodiazepines and Performance, Psychopharmacology Supplementum I*, pp. 11−43. Springer, Berlin.

Department of Health and Social Security (1980) *Present Day Practice in Infant Feeding*. HMSO, London.

Department of Health and Social Security (1988) *Present*

Day Practice in Infant Feeding: Third Report. HMSO, London.

Deutsche Gesellschaft für Ernährung (German Association for Nutrition) (1980) *Ernährungsbericht 1980* (Nutrition Report 1980). Druckerei Henrich, Frankfurt.

Deutsche Gesellschaft für Ernährung (German Association for Nutrition) (1984) *Ernährungsbericht 1984* (Nutrition Report 1984). Druckerei Henrich, Frankfurt.

De Vries M.W. (1984) Temperament and infant mortality among the Masai of East Africa. *American Journal of Psychiatry* **141**, 1189–1194.

Dietz W.H. & Gortmaker S.L. (1985) Do we fatten our children at the television set? Obesity and television viewing in children and adolescents. *Pediatrics* **75**, 807–812.

DiMario F.J. & Emery E.S. (1987) The natural history of night terrors. *Clinical Pediatrics* **26**(10), 505–511.

Dinges D.F. (1989) The nature of sleepiness: Causes, contexts and consequences. In Stunkard A.J. & Baum A. (eds) *Eating, Sleeping and Sex*, pp. 147–179. Lawrence Erlbaum, Hillsdale, New Jersey.

DiPietro J.A., Larson S.K. & Porges S.W. (1987) Behavioural and heart rate pattern differences between breast- and bottlefed neonates. *Developmental Psychology* **23**, 467–474.

Drewett R.F., Woolridge M.W., Jackson D.A. *et al.* (1989) Relationships between nursing patterns, supplementary food intake and breast-milk intake in a rural Thai population. *Early Human Development* **20**, 13–23.

Drotar D. (1990) Sampling issues in research with non-organic failure-to-thrive children. *Journal of Pediatric Psychology* **15**(2), 255–273.

Drotar D., Eckerle D., Satola J., Pallotta J. & Wyatt B. (1990) Maternal interactional behavior with nonorganic failure to thrive infants: A case comparison study. *Child Abuse and Neglect* **14**, 41–51.

Dunn J. & Kendrick C. (1982) *Sibling Love, Envy and Understanding.* Penguin, London.

Dwyer J.F., Andrew E.M., Berkey C. *et al.* (1983). Growth in 'new' vegetarian preschool children using the Jenss-Bayley curve fitting technique. *American Journal of Clinical Nutrition* **37**, 815–827.

Earls F. & Richman N. (1980) The prevalence of behavior problems in three-year-old children of West Indian-born parents. *Journal of Child Psychology and Psychiatry* **21**, 99–106.

Elias M.F., Nicolson N.A., Bora C. & Johnston J. (1986) Sleep/wake patterns of breast-fed infants in the first 2 years of life. *Pediatrics* **7**, 322–329.

Ellerstein N.S. & Ostrov B.E. (1985) Growth patterns in children hospitalized because of caloric-deprivation failure to thrive. *American Journal of Diseases of Children* **139**, 164–166.

Epstein L.H., Wing R.R. & Valoski A. (1985) Child obesity. *Pediatric Clinics of North America* **32**, 363–380.

Erman M.K. (1987a) Insomnia. *Psychiatric Clinics of North*

America **10**(4), 526–539.

Erman M.K. (1987b) The nightmare. *Psychiatric Clinics of North America* **10**(4), 667–674.

Evans-Morris S. (1977) Oral-motor development: Normal and abnormal. In Wilson J.M. (ed.) *Oral Motor Function and Dysfunction in Children*, pp. 114–128. University of North Carolina, Chapel Hill.

Expert Panel on Blood Cholesterol Levels in Children and Adolescents (1992) Characteristics of eating patterns of children and adolescents. *Pediatrics* **89**, 540–544.

Fairburn C.G. & Beglin S.J. (1990) Studies of the epidemiology of bulimia nervosa. *American Journal of Psychiatry* **147**(4), 401–408.

Feehan M., McGee R., Stanton W. & Silva P. (1990) A 6 year follow-up of childhood enuresis: Prevalence in adolescence and consequences for mental health. *Journal of Pediatrics and Child Health* **26**, 75–79.

Fenton T.R., Bhat R., Davies A. & West R. (1989) Maternal insecurity and failure to thrive in Asian children. *Archives of Disease in Childhood* **64**, 369–372.

Ferber R. (1985) Sleep, sleeplessness, and sleep disruptions in infants and young children. *Annals of Clinical Research* **17**, 227–234.

Ferber R. (1987) Sleeplessness, night awakening, and night crying in the infant and toddler. *Pediatrics in Review* **9**(3), 69–82.

Ferber R. (1990) Childhood Insomnia. In Thorpy M.J. (ed.) *Handbook of Sleep Disorders*, pp. 435–456. Marcel Dekker, New York.

Fergusson D.M., Horwood L.J. & Shannon F.T. (1987) Breastfeeding and subsequent social adjustment in six- to eight-year-old children. *Journal of Child Psychology and Psychiatry* **28**(3), 378–386.

Field T. (1984) Follow-up developmental status of infants hospitalized for nonorganic failure to thrive. *Journal of Paediatric Psychology* **9**, 241–256.

Field T. (1987) Affective and interactive disturbances in infants. In Osofsky J.D. (ed.) *Handbook of Infant Development*, 2nd edn, pp. 972–1105. Wiley, New York.

Fisher B.E. & Wilson A.E. (1987) Selected sleep disturbances in school children reported by parents: Prevalence, interrelationships, behavioral correlates and parental attributions. *Perceptual and Motor Skills* **64**, 1147–1157.

Forsyth B.W.C. (1989) Colic and the effect of changing milk formulas: A double-blind, multiple-crossover study. *Journal of Pediatrics* **115**, 521–526.

Forsyth B.W.C., Leventhal J.M. & McCarthy P.L. (1985a) Mothers' perceptions of problems of feeding and crying behaviors. *American Journal of Diseases of Children* **139**, 269–272.

Forsyth B.W.C., McCarthy P.L. & Leventhal J.M. (1985b) Problems of early infancy, formula changes, and mothers' beliefs about their infants. *Journal of Pediatrics* **106**(6), 1012–1017.

Frank D.A. & Zeisel S.H. (1988) Failure to thrive. *Pediatric*

Clinics of North America **35**, 1187–1205.

Frodi A. & Thompson R. (1985) Infants' affective responses in the strange situation: Effects of prematurity and of quality of attachment. *Child Development* **56**, 1280–1290.

Fryer G.E. (1988) The efficacy of hospitalization of non-organic failure-to-thrive children: A metaanalysis. *Child Abuse and Neglect* **12**, 373–381.

Gallaher M.M., Hauck F.R., Yang-Oshida M. & Serdula M.K. (1991) Obesity among Mescalero preschool children. *American Journal of Diseases of Children* **145**, 1262–1265.

Garner D.M., Garfinkel P.E., Schwartz D. & Thompson M. (1980) Cultural expectations of thinness in women. *Psychological Reports* **47**, 483–491.

Garner D.M., Rockert W., Olmsted M.P., Johnson C. & Coscina D.V. (1985) Psychoeducational principles in the treatment of bulimia and anorexia nervosa. In Garner D.M. & Garfinkel P.E. (eds) *Handbook of Psychotherapy for Anorexia Nervosa and Bulimia*, pp. 513–572. Guilford Press, New York.

Garrison W. & Earls F. (1985) Change and continuity in behaviour problems from the preschool period through school entry: an analysis of mothers' reports. In Stevenson J. (ed.) *Recent Research in Developmental Psychopathology*, pp. 51–65. Pergamon, Oxford.

Gillin J.C. & Byerley W.F. (1990) The diagnosis and management of insomnia. *New England Journal of Medicine* **322**(4), 239–248.

Glaser H.H., Heagarty M.C., Bullard D.M. & Pivchik B.A. (1968) Physical and psychological development of children with early failure to thrive. *Journal of Pediatrics* **73**, 690–698.

Gowers S.G., Crisp A.H., Joughin N. & Bhat A. (1991) Premenarcheal anorexia nervosa. *Journal of Child Psychology and Psychiatry* **32**, 515–524.

Grantham-McGregor S.M., Powell C.A., Walker S.P. & Himes J.H. (1991) Nutritional supplementation, psychosocial stimulation, and mental development of stunted children: The Jamaican Study. *Lancet* **338**, 1–5.

Guilleminault C. & Dement W.C. (1988) Sleep apnoea syndromes and related sleep disorders. In Williams R.L., Karacan I. & Moore C.A. (eds) *Sleep Disorders: Diagnosis and Treatment*, 2nd edn, pp. 47–71. Wiley, New York.

Habbick B.F. & Gerrard J.W. (1984) Failure to thrive in the contented breast-fed baby. *Canadian Medical Association Journal* **131**, 765–768.

Hammer L.D., Wilson D.M., Litt I.F. *et al.* (1991) Impact of pubertal development on body fat distribution among white, Hispanic, and Asian female adolescents. *Journal of Pediatrics* **118**, 975–980.

Hanning R.M. & Zlotkin S.H. (1985) Unconventional eating practices and their health implications. *Pediatric Clinics of North America* **32**, 429–446.

Haponik E.F. (1990) Disordered sleep in the elderly. In Huzzard W.R., Andres R., Bierman E.L. & Blass J.P.

(eds) *Principles of Geriatric Medicine and Gerontology*, 2nd edn, pp. 1109–1112. McGraw-Hill, London.

Harris G. (1988) Determinants of the introduction of solid food. *Journal of Reproductive and Infant Psychology* **6**, 241–249.

Harris G. & Booth D.A. (1987) Infant's preference for salt in food: Its dependence upon recent dietary experience. *Journal of Reproductive and Infant Psychology* **5**, 97–104.

Harris G. & Booth I.W. (1992) The nature and management of eating problems in preschool children. In Cooper P.J. & Stein A. (eds) *Feeding Problems and Eating Disorders in Children and Adolescents*, pp. 61–84. Harwood Academic Publishers, New York.

Harris G., Thomas A. & Booth D.A. (1990) Development of salt taste in infancy. *Developmental Psychology* **26**(4), 534–538.

Healey E.S., Kales A., Monroe L.J., Bixler E.O., Chamberlin K. & Soldatos C.R. (1981) Onset of insomnia: Role of life-stress events. *Psychosomnia Medicine* **43**(5), 439–451.

Hendershot G.E. (1984) Trends in breastfeeding. *Pediatrics* **74**(Suppl.), 591–602.

Heptinstall E., Puckering C., Skuse D., Downdey L. & Zur-Szpiro L. (1987) Nutrition and mealtime behaviour in families of growth retarded children. *Human Nutrition: Applied Nutrition* **41**, 390–402.

Herman C.P. & Polivy J. (1988a) Restraint and excess in dieters and bulimics. In Pirke K.M., Vandereycken W. & Ploog D. (eds) *The Psychobiology of Bulimia Nervosa*, pp. 33–41. Springer, Berlin.

Herman C.P. & Polivy J. (1988b) Studies of eating in normal dieters. In Walsh T. (ed.) *Eating Behavior in Eating Disorders*, pp. 95–112. American Psychiatric Press, Washington, DC.

Herzog D. & Bradburn I. (1992) The nature of anorexia nervosa and bulimia nervosa in adolescents. In Cooper P.J. & Stein A. (eds) *Feeding Problems and Eating Disorders in Children and Adolescents*, pp. 123–138. Harwood Academic Publishers, New York.

Herzog D.B. & Copeland P.M. (1985) Eating disorders. *New England Journal of Medicine* **313**, 295–303.

Hess A.K., Hess K.A. & Hard H.E. (1977) Intellective characteristics of mothers of failure-to-thrive-syndrome children. *Child: Care, Health and Development* **3**, 377–387.

Hill A.J. (1991) Fear and loathing of obesity: The rise of dieting in childhood. *International Journal of Obesity* **15**(Suppl. 1), 90.

Hitchcock N.E., Gracey N., Gilmour A.I. & Owles E.N. (1986) Nutrition and growth in infancy and early childhood. In Falkner F., Kretchmer N. & Rossi E. (eds) *Monographs in Paediatrics* **19**. Karger, Basel.

Hobson J.A., Spagna T. & Malenka R. (1978) Ethology of sleep studied with time-lapse photography: Postural immobility and sleep-cycle phase in humans. *Science* **201**, 1251–1253.

Hobson J.A. & Steriade M. (1986) Neuronal basis of

behavioral state control. In Mountcastle V.B. (ed.) *Handbook of Physiology: The Nervous System*, Vol. 4, pp. 701–723. American Physiological Society, Bethesda, Maryland.

Holland A., Sicotte N. & Treasure J. (1988) Anorexia nervosa — Evidence for a genetic basis. *Journal of Psychosomatic Research* **32**, 561–571.

Honda Y. & Matsuki K. (1990) Genetic aspects of narcolepsy. In Thorpy M.J. (ed.) *Handbook of Sleep Disorders*, pp. 217–234. Marcel Dekker, New York.

Horne J. (1988) *Why We Sleep. The Functions of Sleep in Humans and Other Mammals*. Oxford University Press, Oxford.

Horne J. (1992) Insomnia. *Psychologist* **5**, 216–218.

Hu T., Huang L. & Cartwright W.S. (1986) Evaluation of the costs of caring for the senile demented elderly: A pilot study. *Gerontologist* **26**, 158–163.

Hurry J., Bowyer J. & St James-Roberts I. (1992) *The development of infant crying and its relationship to sleep-waking organisation*. 4th International Workshop on Infant Cry Research, Institute for Social Paediatrics, Munich, July.

Iglo (1991) *Iglo-Forum-Studie '91 'Genussvoll essen — bewusst ernähren'* (Iglo-Forum study 1991. 'Tasteful eating-deliberate eating'). Hamburg.

Illingworth R.S. (1985) Infantile colic revisited. *Archives of Disease in Childhood* **60**, 981–985.

Illingworth R.S. & Lister J. (1964) The critical or sensitive period, with special reference to certain feeding problems in infants and children. *Journal of Pediatrics* **65**, 839–848.

Jenkins S., Bax M. & Hart H. (1980) Behaviour problems in pre-school children. *Journal of Child Psychology and Psychiatry* **21**, 5–17.

Jenkins S., Owen C., Bax M. & Hart H. (1984) Continuities of common behaviour problems in preschool children. *Journal of Child Psychology and Psychiatry* **25**, 75–89.

Johnson C.M. (1991) Infant and toddler sleep: A telephone survey of parents in one community. *Developmental and Behavioral Pediatrics* **12**(2), 108–114.

Johnson-Sabine E., Wood K., Patton G., Mann A. & Wakeling A. (1988) Abnormal eating attitudes in London schoolgirls — A prospective epidemiological study: Factors associated with abnormal response on screening questionnaires. *Psychological Medicine* **18**, 615–622.

Kales A. & Kales J.D. (1982) Rest and sleep. In Taylor, R.B., Ureda J.R. & Denham J.W. (eds) *Health Promotion: Principles and Clinical Applications*, pp. 307–337. Appleton-Century-Crofts, Norwalk, Connecticut.

Kales A. & Kales J.D. (1984) *Evaluation and Treatment of Insomnia*. Oxford University Press, New York.

Kales A. & Kales J.D. (1987) Evaluation and diagnosis of sleep disorders patients. *Seminars in Neurology* **7**(3), 243–249.

Kales A., Vela-Bueno A. & Kales J.D. (1987) Sleep disorders: Sleep apnea and narcolepsy. *Annals of Internal Medicine* **106**, 434–443.

Kales J.D., Carvell M. & Kales A. (1990) Sleep and sleep disorders. In Cassel C.K., Riesenberg D.E., Sorensen L.B. & Walch J.R. (eds) *Geriatric Medicine*, pp. 562–578. Springer, London.

Kannel W.B. & Cupples L.A. (1989) Cardiovascular and noncardiovascular consequences of obesity. In Stunkard A.J. & Baum A. (eds) *Eating, Sleeping and Sex*, pp. 109–129. Lawrence Erlbaum, Hillsdale, New Jersey.

Kemm J.R. (1987) Eating patterns in childhood and adult health. *Nutrition and Health* **4**, 205–215.

Killen J.D., Hayward C., Litt I. *et al.* (1992) Is puberty a risk factor for eating disorders? *American Journal of Diseases of Children* **146**, 323–325.

Kissileff H.R. (1989) Is there an eating disorder in the obese? *Annals of the New York Academy of Sciences* **575**, 410–419.

Klackenberg G. (1968) The development of children in a Swedish urban community. A prospective longitudinal study: I. The sleep behaviour of children up to three years of age. *Acta Paediatrica Scandinavica* **187**(Suppl.), 105–121.

Klackenberg G. (1971) A prospective longitudinal study of children: Data on psychic health and development up to 8 years of age. *Acta Pediatrica Scandinavica* **224**(Suppl.), 74–82.

Klackenberg G. (1982) Somnambulism in childhood — Prevalence, course and behavior correlates. A prospective longitudinal study (6–16 years). *Acta Paediatrica Scandinavica* **71**, 495–499.

Klackenberg G. (1987) Incidence of parasomnias in children in a general population. In Guilleminault C. (ed.) *Sleep and its Disorders in Children*, pp. 99–113. Raven, New York.

Knapp R. (1989) *Schlafstörungen* (Disturbed sleep). Kohlhammer, Stuttgart.

Kramer M.S., Barr R.G., Leduc D.G., Boisjoly C. & Pless I.B. (1985) Infant determinants of childhood weight and adiposity. *Journal of Pediatrics* **107**, 104–107.

Kripke D.F., Simons R.N., Garfinkel L. & Hammond E.C. (1979) Short and long sleep and sleeping pills. Is increased mortality associated? *Archives of General Psychiatry* **36**, 103–116.

Kristiansson B. & Fällström S.P. (1987) Growth at the age of 4 years subsequent to early failure to thrive. *Child Abuse and Neglect* **11**, 35–40.

Kupfer D.J. & Reynolds C.F. (1989) Slow-wave sleep as a 'protective' factor. In Stunkard A.J. & Baum A. (eds) *Eating, Sleeping and Sex*, pp. 131–145. Lawrence Erlbaum, Hillsdale, New Jersey.

Lacks P. & Rotert M. (1986) Knowledge and practice of sleep hygiene techniques in insomniacs and good sleepers. *Behavioral Research Therapy* **24**, 365–368.

Lancet (1990a) Failure to thrive revisited (editorial). *Lancet* **335**, 662–663.

Lancet (1990b) Growth and nutrition in children with cerebral palsy (editorial). *Lancet* **335**, 1253–1254.

Largo R.H. (1993) Catch-up growth during adolescence. *Hormone Research* **39**(Suppl. 3), 41–48.

Largo R.H. & Hunziker U.A. (1984) A developmental approach to the management of children with sleep disturbances in the first three years of life. *European Journal of Pediatrics* **142**, 170–173.

Lask B. & Bryant-Waugh R. (1992) Early-onset anorexia nervosa and related eating disorders. *Journal of Child Psychology and Psychiatry* **33**, 281–300.

Leach P. (1986) *Baby and Child*. Dorling Kindersley, London.

Leibowitz S.F. (1988) Brain neurotransmitters and drug effects on food intake and appetite: Implications for eating disorders. In Walsh T. (ed.) *Eating Behavior in Eating Disorders*, pp. 19–36. American Psychiatric Press, Washington, DC.

Lenard H.G. (1970) Sleep studies in infancy. *Acta Paediatrica Scandinavia* **59**, 572–581.

Leventhal J.M., Shapiro E.D., Aten C.B., Berg A.T. & Egerter S.A. (1986) Does breast-feeding protect against infections in infants less than 3 months of age? *Pediatrics* **78**(5), 896–903.

Lindberg L., Bohlin G. & Hagekull B. (in press) Early feeding problems in a normal population.

Lipsitt L.P., Crook C. & Booth C.A. (1985) The transitional infant: behavioral development and feeding. *American Journal of Clinical Nutrition* **41**, 485–496.

Loughlin H.H., Clapp-Channing N.E., Gehlbach S.H., Pollard J.C. & McCutchen T. (1985) Early termination of breast-feeding: Identifying those at risk. *Pediatrics* **75**(3), 508–513.

Lozoff B. (1989) Nutrition and behavior. *American Psychologist* **44**, 231–236.

Lozoff B., Wolf A.W. & Davis N.S. (1984) Cosleeping in urban families with young children in the United States. *Pediatrics* **72**, 171–182.

Lozoff B. & Zuckerman B. (1988) Sleep problems in children. *Pediatric Review* **10**, 19–24.

Lucas A. (1991) Programming by early nutrition in man. In Bock G.R. & Whelau J. (eds) *The Childhood Environment and Adult Disease*, pp. 39–55. Ciba Foundation Symposium No. 156. Wiley, Chichester.

Lucas A., King F. & Bishop N.B. (1992a) Postdischarge formula consumption in infants born preterm. *Archives of Disease in Childhood* **67**, 691–692.

Lucas A., Morley R., Cole T.J. *et al.* (1990) Early diet in preterm babies and developmental status at 18 months. *Lancet* **335**, 1477–1481.

Lucas A., Morley R., Cole T.J., Lister G. & Leeson-Payne C. (1992b) Breast milk and subsequent intelligence quotient in children born preterm. *Lancet* **339**, 261–264.

Lugaresi E., Cirignotta F., Zucconi M., Mondini S., Lenzi P. & Coccagna G. (1983) Good and poor sleepers: An epidemiological survey of the San Marino population. In Guilleminault C. & Lugaresi E. (eds) *Sleep/Wake Disorders: Natural History, Epidemiology, and Long-term Evolution*, pp. 1–12. Raven, New York.

Lugaresi E. & Montagna P. (1990) Fatal familial insomnia. In Thorpy M.J. (ed.) *Handbook of Sleep Disorders*, pp. 479–492. Marcel Dekker, New York.

Luiselli J.K. (1989) Behavioral assessment and treatment of pediatric feeding disorders in developmental disabilities. In Hersen M., Eisler R.M. & Miller P. (eds) *Progress in Behavior Modification*, pp. 91–129. Sage, London.

McGhee A. & Russell S.M. (1962) The subjective assessment of normal sleep patterns. *Journal of Mental Science* **108**, 642–654.

McJunkin J.E., Bithoney W.G. & McCormick M.C. (1987) Errors in formula concentration in an outpatient population. *Journal of Pediatrics* **111**, 848–850.

McMenamy C. & Katz R.C. (1989) Brief parent-assisted treatment for children's nighttime fears. *Developmental and Behavioral Pediatrics* **10**, 145–148.

Magnusson D., Statin H. & Allen V. (1986) Differential maturation among girls and its relation to social adjustment in a longitudinal perspective. In Baltes P., Featherman D. & Lerner R. (eds) *Lifespan Development and Behavior*, Vol. 7, pp. 74–101. Lawrence Erlbaum, Hillsdale, New Jersey.

Mahowald M.W. & Ettinger M.G. (1990) Things that go bump in the night: The parasomnias revisited. *Journal of Clinical Neurophysiology* **7**, 119–143.

Mahowald M.W. & Rosen G.M. (1990) Parasomnias in children. *Pediatrician* **17**, 21–31.

Mahowald M.W. & Schenck C.H. (1990) REM-sleep behavior disorder. In Thorpy M.J. (ed.) *Handbook of Sleep Disorders*, pp. 567–594. Marcel Dekker, New York.

Mamone P., Braibanti P. & Bertini M. (1990) *Sleep development and habituation processes in human infants*. Unpublished ms, University of Rome 'La Sapienza'.

Manfredi R.L., Brennan R.W. & Cadieux R.J. (1987) Disorders of excessive sleepiness: narcolepsy and hypersomnia. *Seminars in Neurology* **7**(3), 250–258.

Martin J. & White A. (1988) *Infant Feeding*. HMSO, London.

Mathisen B., Skuse D., Wolke D. & Reilly S. (1989) Oral-motor dysfunction and failure to thrive among inner-city infants. *Developmental Medicine and Child Neurology* **31**, 293–302.

Meddis R. (1977) *The Sleep Instinct*. Routledge & Kegan Paul, London.

Mendelson W.B., James S.P., Garnett D., Sack D.A. & Rosenthal N.A. (1986) A psychophysiologic study of insomnia. *Psychiatry Research* **19**, 267–284.

Menon G. & Poskitt E.M.E. (1985) Why does congenital heart disease cause failure to thrive? *Archives of Disease in Childhood* **60**, 1134–1139.

Miles L. & Dement W.C. (1980) Sleep and aging. *Sleep* **3**,

119−220.

Minde K. & Minde R. (1986) *Infant Psychiatry. An Introductory Textbook*. Sage, London.

Minors D.S. & Waterhouse J.M. (1981) Development of circadian rhythms in infancy. In Davies J.A. & Dobbing J. (eds) *Scientific Foundations of Paediatrics*, 2nd edn, pp. 980−997. Heinemann, London.

Mogan J (1986) Parental weight and its relation to infant feeding patterns and infant obesity. *International Journal of Nursery Studies* **23**, 255−264.

Moore R.Y. (1990) The circadian timing system and the organization of sleep−wake behavior. In Thorpy M.J. (ed.) *Handbook of Sleep Disorders*, pp. 103−115. Marcel Dekker, New York.

Moore T. & Ucko L.E. (1957) Night waking in early infancy. *Archives of Disease in Childhood* **32**, 333−342.

Morley J.E. & Silver A.J. (1988) Anorexia in the elderly. *Neurobiology of Aging* **9**, 9−16.

Mullington J., Spielman A. Wells R. & Purcell S. (1987) Subjective estimation of nocturnal sleep length and stability of sleep patterns: A 42 night sleep log study. *Sleep Results* **16**, 342.

Negayama K.N. (1991) *Changes in patterns of infant feeding in Japan*. Presentation at the eleventh conference of the ISSBD, Minneapolis, July.

Nicolaidis S. & Even P. (1989) Metabolic rate and feeding behavior. *Annals of the New York Academy of Sciences* **575**, 86−105.

Oates R.K. (1984) Similarities and differences between nonorganic failure to thrive and deprivation dwarfism. *Child Abuse and Neglect* **8**, 439−445.

Oates R.K., Peacock A. & Forrest D. (1985) Long-term effects of nonorganic failure to thrive. *Pediatrics* **75**, 36−40.

Olsen-Noll C.G. & Bosworth M.F. (1989) Anorexia and weight loss in the elderly. *Postgraduate Medicine* **85**(3), 140−144.

Oswald I. & Evans J. (1985) On serious violence during sleep-walking. *British Journal of Psychiatry* **147**, 688−691.

Ounsted M.K. & Simons C.D. (1978) The first-born child: Toddlers' problems. *Developmental Medicine of Child Neurology* **20**, 710−719.

Parkes J.D. (1985) *Sleep and its Disorders*. W.B. Saunders, London.

Parmelee Jr A.H., Wenner W.A. & Schulz M.A. (1964) Infant sleep patterns: From birth to 16 weeks of age. *Journal of Pediatrics* **65**, 576−582.

Pearlman C. (1981) Rat models of the adaptive function of REM sleep. In Fishbein W. (ed.) *Sleep, Dreams and Memory*, pp. 37−45. Spectrum, New York.

Pollock J.I. (1992) Predictors and longterm associations of reported sleeping difficulties in infancy. *Journal of Reproductive and Infant Psychology* **10**, 151−168.

Pressman M.R. & Fry J.M. (1988) What is normal sleep in the elderly? *Clinics in Geriatric Medicine* **4**(1), 71−81.

Price V.A., Coates T.J., Thoresen C.E. & Grinstead O.A. (1978) Prevalence and correlates of poor sleep among adolescents. *American Journal of Diseases of Children* **132**, 583−586.

Prinz P.N., Poceta J.S. & Vitiello M.V. (1990a) Sleep in the dementing disorders. In Boller F. & Grafmann J. (eds) *Handbook of Neuropsychology*, Vol. 4, pp. 335−347. Elsevier, Amsterdam.

Prinz P.N., Vitiello M.V., Raskind M.A. & Thorpy M.J. (1990b) Geriatrics: Sleep disorders and aging. *New England Journal of Medicine* **32**(8), 520−526.

Psychologist (1992) Special issue on IQ and nutrition. *Psychologist* **5**(September).

Pudel V. & Westenhöfer J. (1991) *Ernährungspsychologie* (Psychology of Nutrition). Hogrefe, Göttingen.

Pugliese M.T., Lifshitz F., Grad G., Fort P. & Marks-Katz M. (1983) Fear of obesity. *New England Journal of Medicine* **309**, 513−518.

Pugliese M.T., Weyman-Daum M., Moses N. & Lifshitz F. (1987) Parental health beliefs as a cause of nonorganic failure to thrive. *Pediatrics* **80**, 175−182.

Reilly S., Skuse D. & Wolke D. (1994) Nutritional intakes of failure to thrive infants. (Submitted)

Reynolds C.F. (1987) Sleep and affective disorders: A mini-review. *Psychiatric Clinics of North America* **10**, 583−591.

Reynolds C.F., Hoch C.C. & Monk T.H. (1989) Sleep and chronobiologic disturbances in late life. In Busse E.W. & Blazer D.G. (eds) *Geriatric Psychiatry*, pp. 475−488. American Psychiatric Press, Washington, DC.

Richman N. (1981) Sleep problems in young children. *Archives of Disease in Childhood* **56**, 491−493.

Richman N. (1985) A double-blind drug trial of treatment in young children with waking problems. *Journal of Child Psychology and Psychiatry* **26**, 591−598.

Robson J.R.K. (1977) Food faddism. *Pediatric Clinics of North America* **24**, 189−201.

Roffwarg H.P., Muzio J.N. & Dement W.C. (1966) Ontogenetic development of the human sleep-dream cycle. *Science* **152**, 604−619.

Rolls B.J., Rolls E.T., Rowe E.A. & Sweeney K. (1981) Sensory specific satiety in man. *Physiological Behaviour* **27**, 137−142.

Rolls E.T. (1982) Feeding and reward. In Hoebel B. & Novin D. (eds) *Neural Basis of Feeding and Reward*, p. 323. Haer Institute, Maine.

Rowley S. (1987) Psychological effects of intensive training in young athletes. *Journal of Child Psychology and Psychiatry* **28**, 371−378.

Rubin S.P. & Prendergast M. (1984) Infantile colic: Incidence and treatment in a Norfolk community. *Child: Care, Health and Development* **10**, 219−226.

Rummler S. & Woit I. (1992) Zur postnatalen Entwicklung von Kindern adipöser Mütter (The postnatal development of children of obese mothers. *Deutsche Hebammen Zeitschrift* **44**, 218−222.

Russell G.F.M. (1979) Bulimia nervosa: An ominous variant of anorexia nervosa. *Psychological Medicine* **9**, 429–448.

Russell G.F.M. (1992) Anorexia nervosa of early onset and its impact on puberty. In Cooper P.J. & Stein A. (eds) *Feeding Problems and Eating Disorders in Children and Adolescents*, pp. 85–111. Harwood Academic Publishers, New York.

Rutter M. (1991) Age changes in depressive disorders: Some developmental considerations. In Garber J. & Dodge K. (eds) *The Development of Emotion and Dysregulation*, pp. 273–300. Cambridge University Press, New York.

Rutter M., MacDonald H., Le Conteur A., Harrington R., Bolton P. & Bailey A. (1990) Genetic factors in child psychiatric disorders — II. Empirical findings. *Journal of Child Psychology and Psychiatry* **31**, 39–83.

Ryan A.S., Rush D., Krieger F.W. & Lewandowski G.E. (1991) Recent declines in breast-feeding in the United States, 1984 through 1989. *Pediatrics* **88**, 719–727.

Sadeh A., Lavie P., Scher A., Tirosh E. & Epstein R. (1991) Actigraphic home-monitoring of sleep-disturbed and control infants and young children: a new method for pediatric assessment of sleep–wake patterns. *Pediatrics* **87**, 494–499.

St James-Roberts I. & Halil T. (1991) Infant crying patterns in the first year: Normal community and clinical findings. *Journal of Child Psychology and Psychiatry* **32**(6), 951–968.

Sampson H.A. (1989) Infantile colic and food allergy: Fact or fiction? *Journal of Pediatrics* **115**, 583–584.

Sandberg D.E., Smith M.M., Fornari V., Goldstein M. & Lifshitz F. (1991) Nutritional dwarfing: Is it a consequence of disturbed psychosocial functioning? *Pediatrics* **88**(5), 926–933.

Sander L.W. (1987) Awareness of inner-experience: A systems perspective on self-regulation process in early development. *Child Abuse and Neglect* **11**, 339–346.

Sassin J.F. (1990) Prologue: The development of sleep disorders medicine. In Thorpy M.J. (ed.) *Handbook of Sleep Disorders*, pp. 1–9. Marcel Dekker, New York.

Satter E. (1990) The feeding relationship: Problems and interventions. *Journal of Pediatrics* **117**, 181–189.

Scharf M.B., Pravda M.F., Jennings S.W., Kauffman R. & Ringel J. (1987) Childhood enuresis: A comprehensive treatment program. *Psychiatric Clinics of North America* **10**, 655–666.

Schiffman S. (1977) Food recognition by the elderly. *Journal of Gerontology* **32**, 586–592.

Schmitt B.D. & Mauro R.D. (1989) Nonorganic failure to thrive: An outpatient approach. *Child Abuse and Neglect* **13**, 235–248.

Scott A.J. & Ladou J. (1990) Shiftwork: Effects on sleep and health with recommendations for medical surveillance and screening. *Occupational Medicine: State of the Art Reviews* **5**, 273–299.

Seidman D.S., Laor A., Gale R., Stevenson D.K. & Danon Y.L. (1991) A longitudinal study of birth weight and being overweight in late adolescence. *American Journal of Diseases of Children* **145**, 782–785.

Simonds J.F. & Parraga H. (1982a) The parasomnias: Prevalence and relationships to each other and to positive family histories. *Hillside Journal of Clinical Psychiatry* **4**, 25–38.

Simonds J.F. & Parraga H. (1982b) Prevalence of sleep disorders and sleep behaviors in children and adolescents. *Journal of the American Academy of Child Psychiatry* **21**(4), 383–388.

Singer S.T., Song L.-Y., Hill B.P. & Jaffe A.C. (1990) Stress and depression in mothers of failure-to-thrive children. *Journal of Pediatric Psychology* **15**, 711–720.

Skuse D. (1985) Non-organic failure to thrive: A reappraisal. *Archives of Disease in Childhood* **60**, 173–178.

Skuse D. (1989) Emotional abuse and delay in growth. *British Medical Journal* **299**, 113–115.

Skuse D., Pickles A., Wolke D. & Reilly S. (1994) Postnatal growth and mental development: evidence for a 'sensitive period'. *Journal of Child Psychology and Psychiatry* **35**, 521–545.

Skuse D. & Wolke D. (1992) The nature and consequences of feeding problems in infants. In Cooper P. & Stein A. (eds) *The Nature and Management of Feeding Problems and Eating Disorders in Young People*, pp. 1–25. Harwood Academic Publishers, New York.

Skuse D., Wolke D. & Reilly S. (1992) Failure to thrive. Clinical and developmental aspects. In Remschmidt H. & Schmidt M. (eds) *Child and Youth Psychiatry. European Perspectives*, Vol. III, *Developmental Psychopathology*, pp. 46–71. Hogrefe & Huber, Göttingen.

Smart J.L. (1991) Critical periods in brain development. In Bock R. & Whelan J. (eds) *The Childhood Environment and Adult Disease*, pp. 109–123. Ciba Foundation Symposium No. 156. Wiley, Chichester.

Smith S.M. & Hanson R. (1972) Failure to thrive and anorexia nervosa. *Postgraduate Medical Journal* **48**, 382–384.

Snow M.E., Jacklin C.N. & Maccoby E.E. (1980) Crying episodes and sleep–wakefulness transitions in the first 26 months of life. *Infant Behavior and Development* **3**, 387–394.

Sorensen T.I.A., Price R.A., Stankard A.J. & Schulsinger F. (1989) Genetics of obesity in adult adoptees and their biological siblings. *British Medical Journal* **298**, 87–90.

Spitz R.A. (1945) Hospitalism: An inquiry into the genesis of psychiatric condition in early childhood. *Psychoanalytic Study of the Child* **1**, 53–74.

Spitz R.A. (1951) The psychogenic diseases in infancy: An attempt at their etiologic classification. *Psychoanalytic Study of the Child* **6**, 255–275.

Spock B. (1968) *Baby and Child Care*, 3rd edn. New English Library, Boston.

Steinhausen H.C. & Glanville K. (1983) Follow-up studies

of anorexia nervosa: a review of research findings. *Psychological Medicine* **13**, 239–249.

Strunz F. (1991) Die Alpträume der Kinder — Ursachen, Vorbeugung, Heilung (The nightmares of children — Causes, prevention and treatment). *Fortschritte der Neurologie und Psychiatrie* **59**, 117–133.

Stunkard A.J. (1989) Perspectives on human obesity. In Stunkard A.J. & Baum A. (eds) *Eating, Sleeping and Sex*, pp. 9–30. Lawrence Erlbaum, Hillsdale, New Jersey.

Tanner J.M. (1962) *Growth at Adolescence*, 2nd edn. Blackwell Scientific Publications, Oxford.

Tanner J.M. (1989) *Foetus into Man: Physical Growth from Conception to Maturity*, 2nd edn. Castlemead Publications, Ware.

Taylor B. & Wadsworth J. (1984) Breastfeeding and child development at five years. *Developmental Medicine and Child Neurology* **26**, 73–80.

Thoman E.B. & Glazier R.C. (1987) Computer scoring of motility patterns for states of sleep and wakefulness: Human infants. *Sleep* **10**, 122–129.

Thompson D.A., Berg K.M. & Shatford L.A. (1987) The heterogeneity of bulimic symptomatology. *International Journal of Eating Disorders* **6**, 215–234.

Thornby J., Karacan I., Searle R., Salis P.J., Ware C. & Williams R.L. (1977) Subjective reports of sleep disturbance in a Houston metropolitan health survey. *Sleep Research* **6**, 180.

Thorpy M.J. (1990a) Classification and nomenclature of the sleep disorders. In Thorpy M.J. (ed.) *Handbook of Sleep Disorders*, pp. 155–178. Marcel Dekker, New York.

Thorpy M.J. (1990b) Disorders of arousal. In Thorpy M.J. (ed.) *Handbook of Sleep Disorders*, pp. 531–550. Marcel Dekker, New York.

Trevarthen C. (1987) Sharing makes sense: intersubjectivity and the making of an infant's meaning. In Steele R. & Threadgold T. (eds) *Language Topics Essays in Honor of Michael Halliday*, pp. 177–199. John Benjamins, Philadelphia.

Trevarthen C. (1988) Universal co-operative motives: How infants begin to know the language and culture of their parents. In Jahoda G. & Lewis I.M. (eds) *Acquiring Culture: Cross Cultural Studies in Child Development*, pp. 37–90. Croom Helm, London.

Troutman J.L., Wright J.A. & Shifrin D.L. (1991) Pediatric telephone advice: Seattle hotline experience. *Pediatrics* **88**(4), 814–816.

Truswell S. (1990) Who should take vitamin supplements? Healthy people eating a healthy diet do not need them. *British Medical Journal* **301**, 135–136.

Underwood B.A. & Hofvander Y. (1982) Appropriate timing for complementary feeding of the breast-fed infant — A review. *Acta Paediatrica Scandinavica* **294**(Suppl.), 1–32.

Valman H.B. (1981) Sleep problems. *British Medical Journal* **283**, 422–423.

Van Tassel E.B. (1985) The relative influence of child and

environmental characteristics on sleep disturbances in the first and second years of life. *Journal of Developmental and Behavioral Pediatrics* **6**, 81–87.

Van Wezel-Meijler K.Y. & Wit J.M. (1989) The offspring of mothers with anorexia nervosa: A high-risk group for undernutrition and stunting? *European Journal of Pediatrics* **149**, 130–135.

Vitiello M.V. & Prinz P.N. (1990) Sleep and sleep disorders in normal aging. In Thorpy M.J. (ed.) *Handbook of Sleep Disorders*, pp. 139–151. Marcel Dekker, New York.

Von Oefele K. & Rüther E. (1989) Schlafverhalten und Schlafstörungen (Sleeping behaviour and sleep disorders). In Platt D. (ed.) *Neurologie, Psychiatrie*, Vol. 5, pp. 356–372. Fischer Verlag, Stuttgart.

Wardle J. & Beales S. (1986) Restraint, body image and food attitudes in children from 12 to 18 years. *Appetite* **7**, 209–217.

Webb W.B. (1981) Patterns of sleep in healthy 50–60 year-old males and females. *Research Communications in Psychology, Psychiatry and Behavior* **6**, 133.

Webb W.B. (1982) The measurement and characteristics of sleep in older persons. *Neurobiology of Aging* **3**, 299–308.

Webb W.B. (1989) Age-related changes in sleep. *Clinics in Geriatric Medicine* **5**(2), 275–287.

Webb W.B. & Agnew H. (1975) Are we chronically sleep deprived? *Bulletin of the Psychonomic Society* **6**, 47–48.

Welstein L., Dement W.C., Redington D., Guilleminault C. & Mitler M. (1983) Insomnia in the San Francisco Bay area: A telephone survey. In Guilleminault C. & Lugaresi E. (eds) *Sleep/Wake Disorders: Natural History, Epidemiology, and Long-term Evolution*, pp. 73–85. Raven, New York.

Wessel M.A., Cobb J.C., Jackson E.B., Harris G.S. & Detwiler A.C. (1954) Paroxysmal fussing in infancy, sometimes called 'colic'. *Pediatrics* **14**, 421–434.

White L., Hahn P.M. & Mitler M.M. (1980) Sleep questionnaire in adolescents (abstract). *Sleep Research* **9**, 108.

Widdowson E.M. (1981) Nutrition. In Davis J.A. & Dobbing J. (eds) *Scientific Foundations of Paediatrics*, 2nd edn, pp. 41–53. Heinemann Medical Books, London.

Wolff P.H. (1987) *The Development of Behavioural States and the Expression of Emotions in Early Infancy*. University of Chicago Press, London.

Wolke D. (1990) Schwierige Säuglinge: Wirklichkeit oder Einbildung? (Difficult infants: Fact or fantasy?) In Pachler M.J. & Strassburg H.M. (eds) *Der Unruhige Säugling*, pp. 70–88. Hansischer Buchverlag, Hamburg.

Wolke D. (1991a) *Non-organic failure to thrive children*. Paper presented at the 11th Biennial Meeting of the ISSBD, Minneapolis, July.

Wolke D. (1991b) Psycho-biologische Aspekte der Pflege von Frühgeborenen (Psychobiological aspects of the care of preterm infants). *Deutsche Krankenpflege-Zeitschrift* **44**, 478–483.

Wolke D. (1991c) Supporting the development of low-birthweight infants (annotation). *Journal of Child Psychology and Psychiatry* **32**, 723–741.

Wolke D. (1992) *Sleeping, waking, crying and temperament. What are the links?* Presentation at the 4th International Cry Workshop, Institute for Social Paediatrics, Munich, July.

Wolke D. (1993a) Die Entwicklung und Behandlung von Schlafproblemen und exzessivem Schreien im Vorschulalter (The development and treatment of sleeping problems and excessive crying in preschool children). In Petermann F. (ed.) *Verhaltenstherapie für Kinder. Therapieforschung für die Praxis*, Vol. 13, pp. 145–199. Gerhard Röttger Verlag, München.

Wolke D., Meyer R., Ohrt B., Riegel K. (in press) The incidence of sleeping problems in preterm and fullterm infants discharged from neonatal intensive care: An epidemiological longitudinal study. *Journal of Child Psychology and Psychiatry*.

Wolke D. & St James-Roberts I. (1987) Multi-method measurement of the early parent-infant system with easy and difficult newborns. In Rauh H. & Steinhausen H.C. (eds) *Psychobiology and Early Development*, pp. 49–70. North-Holland, Oxford.

Wolke D. & Skuse D. (1992) The management of infant feeding problems. In Cooper P. & Stein A. (eds) *Feeding Problems and Eating Disorders in Children and Adolescents*, pp. 29–32. Harwood Academic Publishers, New York.

Wolke D., Skuse D. & Mathisen B. (1990a) Behavioral style in failure to thrive infants — A preliminary communication. *Journal of Pediatric Psychology* **15**, 237–254.

Wolke D., Skuse D. & Reilly S. (1990b) *Maternal perceptions of infant body schematas and infant growth.* Plenary presentation at the 62nd Annual Meeting of the British Paediatric Association, Warwick, April.

Wolke D., Skuse D., Reilly S. & Sumner M. (1990c) *Socioemotional development, diet and feeding behaviour of non-organic failure to thrive infants: a whole population survey.* Paper presented at the Fourth European Conference on Developmental Psychology, Stirling, September.

World Health Organization (1981) *Contemporary Patterns of Breast-feeding.* Report on the WHO Collaborative Study on Breast-Feeding, Geneva.

Wright P. (1987) Hunger, satiety and feeding behaviour in early infancy. In Boakes R.A., Popplewell D.O. & Burton M.J. (eds) *Eating Habits, Food, Physiology and Learned Behaviour*, pp. 75–105. Wiley, London.

Wright P. (1989) Feeding experiences in early infancy. In Shepherd R. (ed.) *Handbook of the Psychophysiology of Human Eating*, pp. 157–178. Wiley, Chichester.

Wright P., McLeod H.A. & Cooper M.J. (1983) Waking at night: The effect of early feeding experiences. *Child Care Health Development* **9**, 309–319.

Wyrwicka W. (1987) *Brain and Feeding Behavior.* Charles C. Thomas, Springfield.

Yang L., Zuo C. & Eaton L.F. (1987) Sleep problems of normal Chinese adolescents. *Journal of Child Psychology and Psychiatry* **28**, 167–172.

Yates A. (1989) Current perspectives on the eating disorders: I. History, psychological and biological aspects. *Journal of the American Academy of Child and Adolescent Psychiatry* **28**(6), 813–828.

Zuckerman B., Stevenson J. & Bailey V. (1987) Sleep problems in early childhood: Continuities, predictive factors, and behavioral correlates. *Pediatrics* **80**, 664–671.

21: Psychosexual Development Across the Lifespan

ROBERTA L. PAIKOFF AND JEANNE BROOKS-GUNN

INTRODUCTION

Individuals are confronted with a number of developmental challenges throughout the life-course that are psychosexual in nature. While the term psychosexual is perhaps overly inclusive, we prefer it to the term sexuality, in order to emphasize the fact that sexual development is more than just sexual behaviour. This chapter identifies seven psychosexual issues, three of which focus on an individual's identity and four of which are concerned with an individual's actual behaviour. Identities and behaviours are related, as the former in part guide the latter. Both are influenced by a series of biological, self-system, sociocognitive, sociorelational and cultural processes. Here, the three identity and four behavioural psychosexual issues are reviewed, *vis-à-vis* their content over the lifespan. Then, the processes underlying their development are considered, with the normative processes and the non-normative processes discussed separately.

PSYCHOSEXUAL DEVELOPMENTAL ISSUES

As mentioned above, seven important issues have been identified that underlie psychosexual development. Three represent different aspects of identity, here labelled gender, sex role and sexual identity. Gender identity refers to an individual's biological sex or sex of rearing. One is born male or female, or, in cases where one's sex is unclear, one is labelled male or female and reared accordingly. An individual's sex role identity, however, is a separate aspect of his or her total self-identity. The sex roles of the culture to which a child belongs form a basis for his or her own developing sex role identity, as do the socialization practices to which

he or she is exposed and the personal beliefs and attitudes he or she has acquired along the way.

Gender identity and sex role identity differ from each other in the same way that 'male' differs from 'masculine', or 'female' from 'feminine'. One set of terms, 'male' and 'female', refers to an individual's sex; the other set, 'masculine' and 'feminine', refers to an individual's sex role. A boy, having a male gender identity, does not necessarily have a masculine sex role identity; he can be either 'masculine', 'feminine' or 'androgenous' (a combination of both). He can grow up to be a steam fitter, a hairdresser or a postal clerk. A woman, having a female gender identity, does not necessarily have a feminine sex role identity; she too can have either a masculine, feminine or androgenous sex role, and she too can be a steam fitter, a hairdresser or a postal clerk.

Sex role identity is not the same as sexual identity either. Sexual identity typically refers to preferences for sexual relationships with men, with women, with both or with neither. Sexual identity is usually established in late childhood or adolescence, when sexual activity begins, and is not necessarily linked to sex role identity. Women who exhibit many so-called masculine characteristics do not necessarily have homosexual preferences just as men who exhibit many so-called feminine characteristics do not necessarily have homosexual preferences (Brooks-Gunn & Matthews, 1979).

The last four issues are more behaviourally oriented, and include body image, sex role behaviour, sexual behaviour and fertility management. Development of body image involves both feelings about body attractiveness and behavioural aspects of comfort and carriage of the body. Sex role behaviour is defined by the degree to which an individual adopts behaviours that are culturally considered to be stereotypically masculine or feminine. Sexual behaviour, however, refers to behavioural expressions of sexual arousal, while fertility management involves adopting behaviours aimed at meeting fertility-related goals (e.g. optimizing the chances of either getting pregnant or avoiding pregnancy). In the 1990s, fertility management may be related to disease avoidance as well.

A parallel between identities and behaviours exists; gender identity and body image are associated, as are sex role identity and sex role behaviour and sexual identity and sexual behaviour/fertility management. However, no direct one-to-one correspondence between identities and behaviours exists. For example, individuals with same-sex and opposite-sex sexual identities may engage in some of the same sexual behaviours.

It is important to consider how these psychosexual issues are influenced by life phase. Figure 21.1 presents the developmental progression of psychosexual issues by age period. Issues of gender and sex role identity are important from infancy on through the lifespan, while the issue of sexual identity is expected to arise in late childhood or early adolescence. Body image, sex role and sexual behaviour also are important issues from infancy on, while fertility management becomes an issue at puberty, when reproductive maturity is attained.

Gender identity

Infants are able to distinguish between genders via facial representations around 6−9 months of age (Fagan & Singer, 1979; Lewis & Brooks-Gunn, 1979; Fagan & Shepherd, 1982), though they do not appear to prefer faces of one gender over the other. The particular cues used by infants to distinguish male from female faces are not known (Maccoby, 1988).

By the second year of life, children have a sense of gender identity (e.g. a basic acknowledgement of their own particular gender label, 'girl' or 'boy'; Brooks-Gunn & Lewis, 1979). Within the next couple of years, children increase in their ability to distinguish and label the gender of others correctly as well, and to recognize and identify children of the same gender as themselves (Thompson, 1975; Maccoby, 1988). By the beginning of the school years (age 5 or so), most children will have not only achieved gender identity but gender constancy (an understanding that one's gender is a permanent state, and cannot be changed by clothing or activity changes).

Body image

Concerns with body image begin in infancy and the toddler years. While little is known about the particular body image issues of these early years, exploration of the body is normal and healthy at this time. How early body exploration is reacted to by others, and ways that others' reactions to the infant's body are linked to subsequent body image, are not clear.

By the preschool years, individualized body images are clearly emerging. Young children are already able to categorize themselves as fat, skinny or 'normal' (Lerner & Schroeder, 1971), as well as

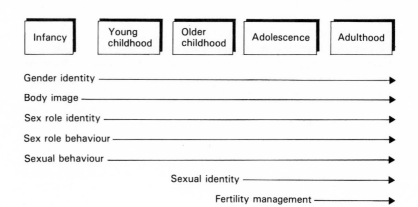

Fig. 21.1 Psychosexual issues across the lifespan.

on dimensions of physical attractiveness (Langlois & Stephan, 1981; Harter, 1983; Hartup, 1983, 1989). Given Western cultural biases emphasizing the positive aspects of thinness and prettiness, categorization of the self as heavy (and thus physically unappealing) may influence subequent definitions of the body as sexually attractive. In many non-Western cultures, however, heaviness is actually viewed as attractive and desirable. Indeed, the degree to which thinness is valued varies by both ethnicity and by socioeconomic status within the USA as well as across cultures (Dornbusch *et al*, 1984; Silber, 1986; see also Dolan, 1991 for a review with regard to eating disorders).

During the ages of 6–10 body image issues continue to revolve around concerns with weight and physical attractiveness. Social cognitive changes that heighten the child's ability to use social comparison information for self-evaluation (see Ruble, 1987; Brooks-Gunn & Paikoff, 1992) may make such issues even more difficult for relatively heavy or unattractive children, as they begin to evaluate themselves in terms of other's physical appearance (as well as in terms of the labels used by others in self-descriptions*).

At adolescence, biological and social changes occur which promote heightened concern on the part of young adolescents and those around them regarding their body. As they progress through the changes of puberty, young adolescents must adapt both to a new appearance and to different treatment by others (Brooks-Gunn, 1984; Brooks-Gunn & Warren, 1988; Hill, 1988; Paikoff & Brooks-Gunn, 1991). The asynchrony of change in boys (often resulting in 'gawky' stages) and the body fat changes in girls (resulting in weight gain and differential distribution of body fat) may be particularly difficult to cope with, in terms of changes in body image.

While adult body changes are rarely as dramatic as adolescent ones, changes related to ageing and loss of reproductive abilities may provoke body image concerns, especially for menopausal women

(Baruch & Brooks-Gunn, 1984; Parlee, 1984; Paikoff *et al.*, 1991; Matthews, 1992).[†] For men, changes related to ageing can be difficult as well; however, no single defining feature occurs to mirror the experience of women (see Vaillant, 1977 for a discussion of psychosexual issues of adult and ageing men).

Sex role identity

Knowledge regarding gender is accompanied by a series of explicit and tacit cultural beliefs and assumptions regarding gender appropriate activities, interests and appearance. Sex role stereotyping begins at birth (Fagot, 1974; Brooks-Gunn & Matthews, 1979; Bem, 1981). The degree to which such stereotypes are consciously recognized by toddlerhood is not known; soon thereafter, however, sex role stereotypes become an important component of the peer culture (Bem, 1981).

Most children retain these specific sex role stereotypes about appropriate activities, usually received via parental or greater cultural (e.g. media, peer play) influences. Young children are likely to have fairly rigid perceptions of sex role appropriate behaviour, and may enforce these beliefs in their interactions with peers (Kohlberg, 1969). While such beliefs may dissipate during middle and later childhood, they often reappear with the onset of adolescence (Hill & Lynch, 1983).

Sex role behaviour

Sex role behaviour refers to the ways in which stereotypes with regard to sex role identity are translated into social behaviour. Differences in the play behaviour of boys and girls have been noted as early as the preschool years (Maccoby & Jacklin, 1974; Ruble & Ruble, 1982; Zaslow & Hayes, 1986; Jacklin, 1989; Maccoby, 1990), evidenced by toy preferences, activity levels and physical aggression (Ruble & Ruble, 1982; Maccoby, 1988). Much of the current research in this area focuses on understanding the mechanisms that may account for

---

* Anecdotal evidence from a private girls' school in Manhattan suggests that eating behaviour problems often arise when young girls hear their peers discussing weight problems and engage in self-comparison evaluation processes (e.g. 'I didn't think I was fat until she said she was fat — I figured if she was fat then I must be, since I'm heavier than she is').

† We do not discuss the literature on physiological and psychological effects of menopause in detail (see Haspels & Musaph, 1977; Greene, 1984; Parlee, 1984; Matthews *et al.*, 1990; Matthews, 1992, for reviews).

these behaviours (Jacklin, 1989). Particular emphasis has been paid to biological predispositions (Maccoby & Jacklin, 1974; Jacklin, 1989), socialization factors (Ruble & Ruble, 1982) and to cognitive developmental mechanisms such as gender schema (Jacklin, 1989; Levy & Carter, 1989).

More recent empirical work on sex role behaviour has focused on children's behaviour in the classroom and on same-peer groupings, given concerns about the differential patterns of achievement by gender, as well as the implications of behaviour in same-sex peer groups for later sexual intimacy. In the classroom, gender differences in behaviour have been documented, with girls evaluating themselves more negatively than boys in a study of classroom observation (Frey & Ruble, 1987). In addition, girls have been found more likely to attribute academic success to luck and failure to ability; the reverse is true for boys (Dweck *et al.*, 1980). The ways in which these behavioural and attributional differences in the classroom are linked to actual achievement patterns, or to peer group interaction, are not clear.

Another frequently studied aspect of sex-role behaviour from preschool through middle school has been the phenomenon of gender segregation in free play groups (Thorne, 1986; Thorne & Luria, 1986; Maccoby, 1988). Children tend to spend more time in same-sex than mixed-sex groupings, with increases in the ratio of same-sex to mixed-sex play occurring from nursery school to elementary school ages, and relatively consistent findings across culture (Edwards & Whiting, 1988), regardless of adult influence (Maccoby, 1988). By late childhood, while same-sex groupings remain primary, cross-group fraternization, teasing and romantic initiations begin to occur (Thorne & Luria, 1986).

In same-sex play groups of all ages, gender-specific patterns of activity can readily be described, and mirror those of preschool play described above. While boy and girl groups may engage in the same overall levels of activity, boys are more likely to engage in rough-and-tumble play, while girls' activities are likely to be less physical. Similarly, while boys and girls may attempt to influence one another equally frequently, girls are more likely to make indirect, 'polite' suggestions, with boys more likely to assert direct demands (Savin-Williams,

1987; Maccoby, 1988). In the middle childhood years and at the beginning of adolescence, girls are likely to congregate in smaller, less clearly structured groups than boys, and to focus on shared expressions of ideas or feelings, with boys focusing more directly on shared activities (Thorne & Luria, 1986; Savin-Williams, 1987).

When mixed-sex groupings occur prior to adolescence, they often result in diminished activity and influence for girls (largely affirming girls' relatively negative stereotypes for these cross-sex interactions, Maccoby, 1988). Young adolescents experience the intensification of sex role identification and stereotypes (Hill & Lynch, 1983); at the same time, peer group activities may begin to shift towards a more mixed sex, group dating nature (Dunphy, 1963; Katchadourian, 1990). Sex role behaviour may be as rigidly enforced in mixed-sex as in same-sex groupings; however, very little is known about the descriptive properties of these cross-sex interactions.

Given that same-sex grouping preferences occur early and are seen across cultures and individuals, what are the developmental bases for this phenomenon? It has been suggested that while socialization models may be particularly useful in considering the development of sex role identity (Maccoby, 1988; Jacklin, 1989), biological gender cues, as well as the understanding of gender labels and gender schemas, may have important implications for sex role behaviour and same-sex social groupings in children and young adolescents (Maccoby, 1988; Jacklin, 1989). While research has not examined the implications of same-sex groupings and behaviours conducted within these groups for development of later intimate relationships, Maccoby (1990) has suggested that the modes of achieving intimacy may differ for boys and girls (see also Gilligan, 1982). In particular, the emphasis on competition and dominance in male peer groups may translate to an enjoyment of debate and argument in young men, while the emphasis on reciprocity of influence in female peer groups may translate to enjoyment of shared influence and acknowledgement of feelings. Maccoby (1990) has hypothesized that these differences may make mixed-sex intimacy a challenge for both men and women; however, she suspected that the adaptation process is more difficult for women than for men.

Sexual identity

Issues of sexual identity often arise at the end of childhood and beginning of adolescence.* Many homosexual adults report retrospectively that they felt 'different' from other children early on in development, and that they could first give a name to this difference at the end of childhood or the beginning of adolescence, when they initially experienced feelings of sexual attraction to members of the same, rather than the other, sex; however, no prospective data on the development of sexual identity in normative samples exist (Boxer *et al.*, 1989; Savin-Williams, 1990). At the same time, many children may engage in sex play with a same-sex peer, without implications for later sexual identity. Such sex play is simply considered part of the maturational process, an expression of the child's curiosity about the genitals and their function.

Sexual behaviour

Sexual arousal occurs as early as infancy, with infant males experiencing erections. Societies (and parents) differ in their responses to infant erections and genital exploration — some encourage such behaviours, some ignore them and others discourage them. Whether these early experiences and others' responses to them are predictive of later sexual behaviour is not known.

Exploration of one's own body continues during childhood. Sex play with young peers often occurs as well. Such behaviour is generally considered well within the bounds of normal sexual development (assuming it is voluntary and of mutual interest to children involved — see Cicchetti & Carlson, 1989 for a review of the substantial literature on child physical and sexual abuse). Societies and parents differ in the messages given to children when they are seen exploring themselves or playing with other children. Again, the implications of these early messages for later sexual behaviour have not been systematically examined.

Traditionally, psychoanalysts have considered the later childhood years as a time of 'latency' *vis-à-vis* sexual behavioural concerns, but this view is not supported by empirical evidence (Rutter, 1971). Despite the above-mentioned tendency for almost exclusively same-sex peer interaction during these years, sexual behaviour continues. Self-exploration continues and sex play with others, if it occurs, is likely to be actively discouraged at these times.

In the USA, dating behaviour often arises at the end of childhood and prior to the onset of puberty (Westney *et al.*, 1983). Dependent upon the neighbourhood and peer culture, such dating behaviour may be relatively normative and may take place in the context of group activities or parties, or in actual dating situations. In other cultures, the concept of dating is less relevant due to either increased permissiveness and decreased parental control (Stattin & Magnusson, 1990) or increased restrictiveness with regard to other sex contact (Ford & Beach, 1951).

Increases in hormonal levels alter sexual arousal in both boys and girls, resulting in heightened desire for sexual intimacy (Udry, 1988; Paikoff & Brooks-Gunn 1990a, b; Brooks-Gunn & Paikoff, 1993). These hormonal changes are also responsible for puberty, the end result of which is a reproductively mature individual.

If dating has not begun prior to adolescence, it is likely to begin during these years (in the USA and similar cultures). Again, issues of social comparison and self-evaluation are likely to be involved in adolescents' feelings about themselves as sexual beings, due to either early, on-time or late onset of dating behaviour, relative to one's peers. Particular ages at which dating behaviour onset is normative are likely to vary by social context as well as by pubertal maturity level (Gargiulo *et al.*, 1987; Simmons & Blyth, 1987).

Due to hormonal links, sexual arousal changes with age. Sexual potency (or achievement of orgasm) is a concern for older adults, as the physical and physiological changes of ageing result in lower hormone levels and associated body changes.

Fertility management and health issues

The issue of fertility management first arises during adolescence, when individuals become reproductively mature. Due to the potentially negative

---

* Homosexual and bisexual behaviour is defined in a similar fashion to the DSM-III and DSM-III-R. Dissatisfaction with sexual identity is indicative of low sexual well-being while actual sexual identity is not.

consequences of unprotected sexual activity (sexually transmitted diseases as well as unplanned pregnancies), adolescents must cope with heightened sexual arousal in constructive ways in order to minimize risk of illness or unintended pregnancy. For many adolescents, this will result in continued self-exploration or masturbation; for others, in sexually intimate behaviours other than sexual intercourse. For those adolescents who do engage in sexual intercourse, safe sex practices are necessary to ensure fertility management and sexual well-being through the teenage years (Brooks-Gunn & Furstenberg, 1989; Brooks-Gunn & Paikoff, 1993). Dependent upon individual fertility goals and sexual preference, fertility management continues to be important throughout the premenopausal adult years.

PROCESSES UNDERLYING PSYCHOSEXUAL DEVELOPMENT

Our brief discussion of psychosexual tasks underscores the fact that their content and salience are altered over time. These changes are due to the influence of biological, self-system, sociocognitive, sociorelational and cultural processes (Fig. 21.2). In this section, each of these processes is discussed, both in terms of normative and non-normative paths for psychosexual development.

Biological processes

Levels of the sex-linked hormones define sexual differentiation in the prenatal and pubertal period. Short- and long-term consequences of these processes exist.

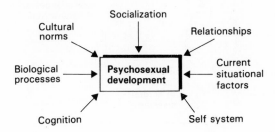

Fig. 21.2 Factors influencing psychosexual development (interrelationships between factors are assumed).

Normative biological processes

Prenatal period. Five events predominate in the complex biological sequence leading to sex differentiation in the early months after conception. The first and major event involves the fertilization of the ovum by the sperm. The newly conceived organism is normally differentiated as either a male (XY) or a female (XX). Research has confirmed that gender is controlled by a gene on the Y chromosome in mammals (Griffiths, 1991); methods for sex identification and cloning have been applied successfully to human cells (Nagai *et al.*, 1991; Nakahori *et al.*, 1991). Occasional chromosomal abnormalities (e.g. Turner syndrome (XO), Klinefelter syndrome (XXY), etc.) do occur, but are rare (these chromosomal risk factors are discussed in the following section). The second event centres upon the formation of the gonads, or sex glands. During the periods of the ovum and of the embryo, development proceeds similarly for both males and females. Settling into the uterine area, the newly formed organism grows and develops a basic structure that includes arm and leg buds, a primitive heart, some structures that are precursors of the brain and spinal cord, and a ridge of tissue out of which will grow the main internal organs of urination and reproduction. The beginnings of the gonads are discernible as two different structures, a situation that Money and Athanasion (1973) have described as 'bipotential' since one has the potential of becoming the male gonad and the other the female gonad. After 6 weeks or so of prenatal existence, shortly after the beginning of the fetal period, the gonadal structure of the male differentiates, resulting in the formation of the testes and the disappearance of the female structure: if the organism is female, the gonadal structure does not differentiate until the twelfth week, when it is transformed into ovaries, with the male structure disappearing. By the sixth month of gestation, both the male and female gonads have entirely formed. The male testes, whose task is the secretion of male hormones, begin to function prenatally, producing and releasing the male hormone androgen; but the female gonads, or ovaries, do not release any of the female hormones until later (Forest & Cathiard, 1978).

The third and fourth events involve the development of the internal and external genitalia in males and in females (Fig. 21.3). The presence of the male hormone androgen promotes the development of a male internal structure (vas deferens and prostate) and male external genitalia (the penis). The absence of this hormone leads to the development of a female internal structure (uterus and vagina) and female external genitalia (the clitoris).

The fifth event has to do with the birth of a boy or a girl and the spontaneous responses of parents, friends, relatives and medical personnel to the sex of the child. Technological advances such as amniocentesis may even allow parents and relatives to

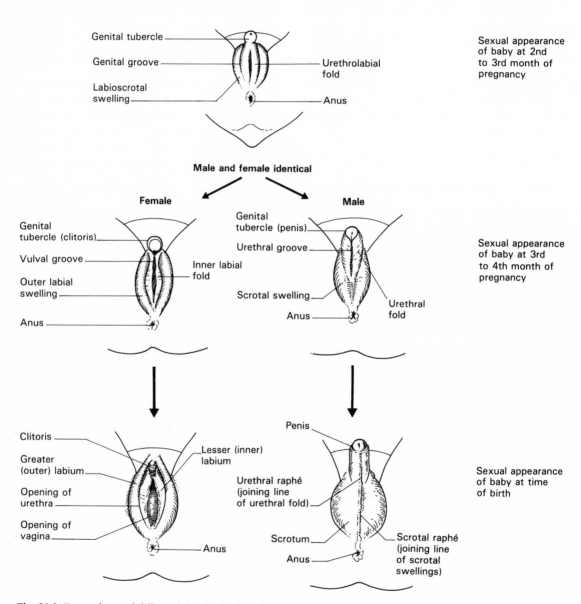

Fig. 21.3 External genital differentiation in the human fetus (from Money & Ehrhardt, 1972).

be aware of the gender of the child prior to birth.

Since little socialization has occurred in the first few weeks of life, investigators are willing to assume that behavioural differences among male and female neonates are, in all likelihood, biologically determined. This assumption only holds for the neonatal period (the first few weeks of an infant's life), since after this time enough socialization has occurred to render a demonstration of purely biological effects, rather than an interaction between the two, much more tenuous. For example, mothers are more likely to reinforce their 3-month-old daughters' babbling by vocalizing back, whereas they are more likely to touch their 3-month-old sons when they babble, even though 3-month-old male and female infants babble for equal amounts of time (Lewis, 1972). These differential responses probably contribute to sex differences in vocalization seen in toddlerhood.

During infancy (and especially the first 6 months of life), males are more biologically vulnerable than females (Waldron, 1983, 1985). They are more often spontaneously aborted and more likely to die of birth trauma, birth injuries and infectious diseases (Garai & Scheinfeld, 1968). They are also slightly larger and heavier at birth, which may account for the higher incidence of birth injury. Males are also likely to experience longer labour, even in non-problematic deliveries, which has been linked to later difficulties (Jacklin, 1989). Several biological explanations for the greater vulnerability of males have been offered, including a genetic susceptibility to infectious diseases, since susceptibility may be conferred in part by a gene carried on the X chromosome, of which the male has only one (Waldron, 1983). The higher mortality rate of males is partially offset by the higher incidence of males conceived and born (between 120 to 150 boys are conceived for every 100 girls).

Females tend to be 1–6 weeks more mature skeletally than males at birth although there seem to be no differences in areas of physical development such as the maturation of the parts of the brain that control vision and audition. Girl infants may exhibit less crying and more sleeping than boy infants in the first 3 months of life (Moss, 1967).

However, in most aspects, male and female neonates are remarkably similar. Studies of sight, smell, taste and audition yield no sex differences. Female neonates *may* be more sensitive to touch (as measured by brushing the newborn on the mouth or directing a jet of air towards the baby's abdomen), although not all researchers have found these differences (Bell *et al.*, 1971; Maccoby & Jacklin, 1974). In observational work with infants and toddlers, boys received more spontaneous positive touch (e.g. holding, hugging, care-giving) from adults than did girls; early touch experiences have been found to promote infant growth (Harding *et al.*, 1992).

One of the most intriguing questions in the field of early sex differences involves the possible effects of prenatal hormones on later behaviour. In part, these research questions arise from literature on non-human animals regarding hormonal effects upon sexual differentiation of the brain (Stewart & Cygan, 1980), resulting in differential activity and aggression levels (Beatty, 1979; Meaney *et al.*, 1985). Gonadal hormones circulate in the body, starting prenatally and continuing throughout life. Both males and females produce androgens, oestrogens and progesterones, with the levels varying across age, across the menstrual cycle for women, and even diurnally. The adrenal glands produce small amounts of hormones throughout the life-cycle, the reproductive organs produce the largest amounts, starting around the time of puberty, and the placenta of a developing fetus in a pregnant woman also produces oestrogens and progesterones (Money & Ehrhardt, 1972).

Typically, during the fetal period, boys have a greater amount of androgen circulating than do girls; the presence of androgen results in the development of the sexual characteristics of males. At birth, male babies have a higher level of circulating testosterone (one of the androgens) than do girls, as measured by collecting blood from the placental cord (Maccoby *et al.*, 1979). No differences in oestrogen levels have been found at birth. Sex differences in levels of progesterones in child blood level have been reported. Birth order and spacing may account for these differences (as later-born children, especially those born close together, have lower progesterone levels; Maccoby *et al.*, 1979).

Two types of studies examine prenatal or birth hormonal levels and behaviour. The first is the assessment of hormonal levels via analysis of umbilical cord blood. Using 24-h maternal diaries for children's mood during the first 26 months of life, progesterone, oestrogen and androstenedione were found to be positively associated with happy/excited moods and negatively associated with calm/quiet moods in boys only (Marcus *et al.*, 1985). These effects were small. Prenatal androgens were negatively associated with spatial ability in girls but not in boys at age 6 (Jacklin *et al.*, 1988). Androgen levels in child blood are associated with activity level in toddlers, although the size of the associations is small here as well.

A second set of studies directly examine hormonal levels via blood, urine or saliva samples from children after birth. Work in this area, however, has focused primarily on the adrenocortical system rather than on adrenal androgens, oestrogens or other hormones (*cf.* Gunnar *et al.*, 1989, 1992).

Pubertal period. Biological factors also play a major role in the development of reproductive maturity during the pubertal period, as well as in the level of sexual desire and arousal from this period through adulthood. The endocrinological and physical changes of puberty have been extensively studied and thus are relatively easy to describe. The underlying mechanisms responsible for these changes, however, are not as well understood (Katchadourian, 1977; Grumbach & Sizonenko, 1986). Two endocrinological processes, adrenarche and gonadarche, increase sex steroid secretion in the prepubertal and pubertal periods. Adrenarche involves production of androgens by the adrenal gland while gonadarche involves reactivation of the hypothalamic − pituitary − gonadotropin − gonadal system that had been quiescent since the fetal period and first few months of life. Gonadarche follows adrenarche after approximately 2 years, and the two are controlled by different mechanisms and operate independently of one another (Brooks-Gunn & Reiter, 1990, p. 21).

The hypothalamic–pituitary–gonadal axis goes through a period of sex steroid activity during the first few months after birth. The dynamics and functions of this activity are not clear. After the infancy period, the system is suppressed to a low level of activity for almost a decade and is reactivated at the middle of childhood (Kaplan *et al.*, 1976). When the gonads' dampening effect upon the hypothalamic−pituitary axis is released in middle childhood, increases in the amplitudes and frequency of pulses of luteinizing hormone-releasing hormones (LHRH) as well as in the responsiveness of gonadotropins to LHRH occur. Secretion of follicle-stimulating hormone (FSH) and luteinizing hormone (LH) also increases, with nocturnal rises in the secretion of both these hormones in a pulsatile fashion. Increased responsiveness of the gonads to the pulses of LH and FSH and increases in the secretion of gonadal hormones occur as well (Goy & McEwen, 1980; Grumbach & Sizonenko, 1986).

These hormonal changes are responsible for the many physical changes of puberty resulting in a reproductively mature individual. The pubertal growth spurt in girls begins approximately 6−12 months before breast budding, at a mean age of 9.6 years. Typically, breast budding is the first secondary sex characteristic to appear in girls' puberty, at approximately 10.5 years. The time between breast budding and adult breast configuration is similar for girls who mature at younger and older ages (approximately 4.5 years). Appearance of pubic hair follows shortly thereafter, though pubic hair development occurs prior to breast buds in approximately 20% of girls. The first menses occurs approximately 2 years after breast buds appear (average age−12.5). Menarche follows peak height velocity, the age at which the most rapid growth occurs. Peak height velocity occurs before pubic hair development in about one-quarter of girls and in the initial stage of, or before, breast development in one-quarter of girls. Much variation exists in the sequencing of events involving breast and pubic hair growth and genital maturation (Evelyth & Tanner, 1976; Fig. 21.4).

The initial sign of sexual development for boys is the onset of testicular growth, which occurs on average at 11−11.5 years. On average, it takes approximately 3 years for boys to pass from the first signs of genital growth to adult male genitalia, but a duration of 4.7 years is still within the normal range. The mean age of boys' initiation of the pubertal height spurt is approximately 11.7 years, shortly after evidence of gonadal maturation. Peak height velocity for boys averages at between 13 and 14 years. Spermarche (the onset of the release of spermatozoa) occurs between 12 and 14 years of age, together with an early stage of pubic hair growth and within an extremely wide variation of

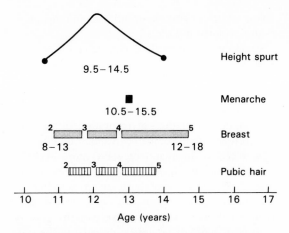

Fig. 21.4 The developmental course of four pubertal processes for girls. The numbers in bold refer to Tanner's pubertal stages (from Tanner, 1962).

testicular volume. Peak height velocity and maximum levels of testosterone production follow initial spermarche (Evelyth & Tanner, 1976; Fig. 21.5).

Hormone–behaviour links during the pubertal life phase have only recently begun to be studied (see Paikoff & Brooks-Gunn, 1990b; Buchanan *et al.*, 1992 for reviews). Levels of circulating androgens have been associated with sexual arousal in boys and girls, and with sexual behaviour in boys

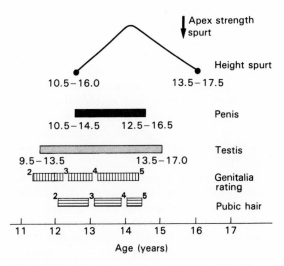

Fig. 21.5 The developmental course of five pubertal processes for boys. The numbers in bold refer to Tanner's pubertal stages (from Tanner, 1962).

(Udry, 1988). These effects are found even when controlling for pubertal stage, which has social stimulus value for the pubescent youth and others (Brooks-Gunn, 1989). Timing of puberty is associated with sexual behaviour; whether these effects are independent of hormonal level is not known (Brooks-Gunn, 1988). Hormonal levels seem to be associated with aggressive behaviour and depressive feelings (Paikoff & Brooks-Gunn, 1990b), which may also mediate sexual expression in adolescence and adulthood.

Non-normative biological processes

Chromosomal abnormalities and hormonal abnormalities result in non-normative biological maturation, which in turn may influence aspects of psychosexual development.

Chromosomal abnormalities. Sex chromosome abnormalities can be diagnosed in newborns if not prenatally (Ross, 1990). Several different types of chromosomal abnormalities exist, and have been described (e.g. Turner syndrome (XO); Klinefelter syndrome (XXY, XYY and XXX). These abnormalities have been linked to deficits in cognitive functioning, specifically to learning disorders (Bender *et al.*, 1990).

Chromosomal abnormalities have not been reliably associated with gender identity disorders (Ehrhardt *et al.*, 1970; Nielsen & Sillesen, 1981; Berch & McCauley, 1990; Evans *et al.*, 1991). However, lowered sexual drive has been associated with both Turner syndrome (Garron & Vander Stoep, 1969) and with Klinefelter syndrome (Money & Pollitt, 1964; Becker, 1972). In addition, individuals with Turner syndrome, Klinefelter syndrome and XYY karyotypes may experience less satisfying sexual relationships and more discomfort with intimate relationships than other individuals (Berch & McCauley, 1990). In a recent study, adult women with Turner syndrome exhibited less mental disorder and comparable psychiatric symptoms to both constitutional short stature and sibling controls. Turner syndrome women, however, were behind controls in their achievement of adult social functioning milestones (such as intimate relationships; Downey *et al.*, 1989). Similar findings have not been reported for XXX females. These reported associations may be due to biological factors, to socialization, or to individuals' awareness of the particular chromosomal disorder. That these findings are not similar across all chromosomal abnormalities suggests some important biological basis for these differences.*

Hormonal abnormalities. Hormonal abnormalities have been studied with regard to hormonal dysfunction in the fetal and pubertal periods. Individuals have been studied from childhood through adolescence (Bancroft, 1991).

Hormonally disordered individuals such as those with congenital adrenal hyperplasia (CAH) typically do not have difficulties with gender identity or sex role identity (Ehrhardt *et al.*, 1968; Baker & Ehrhardt, 1974; Meyer-Bahlburg *et al.*, 1985b, Berenbaum, 1990). Girls who have been exposed to excess amounts of androgens in early development, however, are likely to exhibit tomboyish behaviour, as well as more male stereotypic behaviour. When this hormonal condition is left untreated during childhood and puberty, these women also may report more homosexual or bisexual fantasies (Bancroft, 1991). Similar findings are reported for those children with 5-alpha-reductase deficiency, which results in androgen insensitivity in the fetal period. Children are sometimes classified as female at birth as the phallus looks like a clitoris and the testes are in the inguinal canals or labioscrotal folds (Peterson *et al.*, 1977). At puberty, with the increase in testosterone, the phallus and scrotum grow. In a study of almost 40 individuals in the Dominican Republic, 18 individuals were raised as girls but 17 changed to a male gender identity during or shortly after puberty. All but one adopted a male sex role (Imperato-McGinley *et al.*, 1979). The majority of individuals with hormonal disorders are heterosexual in orientation. Little is known about sexual satisfaction or intimacy in individuals with hormonal disorders.

Children whose mothers were given hormones with progesterone properties during pregnancy to prevent spontaneous abortions or premature births have lower levels of activity and aggression than children whose mothers were not. For example, sons of diabetic mothers given oestrogens and progesterones, when compared to sons of diabetics who received no treatment, were more likely to exhibit somewhat less aggression at age 6 (Yalom *et al.*, 1973). More recently, a study controlling for pregnancy complications (as well as for age) reported decreased activity levels in the play of both boys and girls prenatally exposed to the synthetic oestrogen diethylstilboestrol (DES) (Meyer-Bahlburg *et al.*, 1988). Prenatal exposure to DES also has been linked to lower levels of orientation to parenting, of sexual desire, enjoyment and excitability, as well to more difficulties in intimate and other social relationships in adult women (Meyer-Bahlburg *et al.*, 1985b; Ehrhardt *et al.*, 1987, 1989).

Difficulties with the hormonal regulation system may either speed up or delay the pubertal processes. Both precocious and excessively delayed puberty may have consequences for the individual (Meyer-Bahlburg *et al.*, 1985a; Brooks-Gunn, 1988). Clinical concerns with patients exhibiting delayed puberty focus on reassuring individuals of normality. Clinical concerns in precocious puberty revolve around coping with reproductive maturity at an early age (August, 1990). In addition to these clinical concerns, however, the process of precocious puberty may be 'slowed down' via LHRH therapies (Pescovitz *et al.*, 1986; Rappaport *et al.*, 1987). Technological advances, such as cerebral computed tomography and abdominal sonography improve the chances for early and accurate diagnosis and treatment of idiopathic precocious puberty (Ortner *et al.*, 1987).

In summary, then, evidence from both chromosomal and hormonal disorders in children suggests that, while lowered levels of sexual well-being are possible, they are likely to involve childhood activity level, adult sexual satisfaction, or particular modes of sexual intimacy and fantasy, rather than child or adolescent gender or sex role identity issues.

---

* In addition to the problem of distinguishing biological from social causation in these association, Berch and McCauley (1990) point to many methodological difficulties in understanding links between chromosomal and hormonal abnormalities and social or psychological functioning. Among the key methodological concerns are small sample sizes, bias in sample selection (e.g. via mental health or penal institutions), control groups and use of raters who are not blind to diagnostic category in behavioural assessments.

Self-system processes

Normative processes

The self begins to be constructed during the infant years. Conscious self-recognition and self-definition appear in the toddler years (Lewis & Brooks-Gunn, 1979; Harter, 1983). As mentioned above, the concept of gender becomes a relevant label for the child as early as the second year of life (Brooks-Gunn & Lewis, 1979; Harter, 1983). Gender constancy (or belief in the consistency of one's own gender over time), also becomes established during the childhood years.

Very little is known about changes in gender-based or other self-constructions due to the onset of dating or sexual relationships. The changes of puberty have been linked to changes in self-image, particularly in girls (Faust, 1960, 1983; Brooks-Gunn, 1984, 1988; Simmons & Blyth, 1987; Brooks-Gunn & Warren, 1988). Menarche has been associated with increases in social maturity, peer prestige and self-esteem (Grief & Ulman, 1982; Simmons *et al.*, 1983). Onset of breast development is associated with better peer relationships, leadership and a more positive body image (Brooks-Gunn, 1984; Brooks-Gunn & Warren, 1988). Reasons for these alterations have not been systematically examined. These findings are probably due in part, however, to the social stimulus value of pubertal change. Because breast growth is a normative event signalling the onset of maturity, this exhibition of 'adulthood' may confer enhanced status to young adolescents. Comparisons with others, though probably covert, are common; fifth- to seventh-grade girls can easily categorize classmates regarding stage of pubertal development (Brooks-Gunn *et al.*, 1986). If onset of puberty is valued by the peer group and the physical comparisons girls make are akin to processes discussed in literature on social comparisons (Ruble, 1983, 1987), pubertal girls may initiate more frequent and positive contacts with others, as well as more peer interaction. Such influences on the self may be associated indirectly with onset of dating as well, since more pubertally mature girls are likely to begin dating at an earlier age (Magnusson *et al.*, 1985). In addition, the experience and timing of dating may have different meanings for and

impacts upon self-definition dependent upon context (Gargiulo *et al.*, 1987; Simmons & Blyth, 1987).

In addition to these pubertal status effects, the literature has examined effects of pubertal timing (Brooks-Gunn, 1988; Crockett & Petersen, 1993). Very early maturation has been linked to depressive affect (Rierdan & Koff, 1991), more intense parent–child conflict (Hill, 1988; Paikoff & Brooks-Gunn, 1991) and increases in problem behaviour (Stattin & Magnusson, 1990) in girls; findings for boys are less clear.

Non-normative processes

Non-normative self-system processes include disorders of gender identity as well as dissatisfaction with gender or with sexual identity (see Zucker & Green, 1992 for a review). Problems with gender identity are most likely to arise during the toddler or preschool years — once the notions of gender identity and constancy have been achieved, these issues are likely to transform into issues of dissatisfaction with gender.

Using a sample of boys referred for extreme disorders of sex role and gender identity (e.g. cross-gender dressing and play patterns, stating a preference or wish to be of the other sex) as well as a control sample, Green (1987) reported that a far greater percentage of his 'sissy boys' were likely to engage later in homosexual activity and/or transvestism than were the boys in his 'normal' sample (Green, 1987). As Boxer and Cohler (1989) have noted, this study has methodological limitations, due to the initial restrictiveness of the sample (clinical referrals for extreme gender-disordered behaviour at relatively early ages) and the inherent difficulties of obtaining appropriate controls. However, the findings do suggest that this extreme subtype of the population is at increased likelihood of later homosexuality, though the mechanisms for this link are not clear. Although Green's (1987) research suggests a developmental trajectory of early gender disorder to later homosexuality in males, alternative pathways may exist as well. It is also possible that gender disordered behaviour and homosexuality are linked via a prior mechanism (such as genetic predisposition, see Bailey & Pillard, 1991). Little work has examined similar developmental trajectories in the development of female same-sex preferences (Zucker & Green, 1992).

Gender dissatisfaction may now be resolved through surgical procedures. Given the relatively recent availability of these procedure and the small numbers of adults who participate in them, little is known about the long-term effects of sex change surgery from a physical or a psychological perspective.

For the most part, dissatisfaction with sexual identity is considered equivalent to ego dystonic homosexuality. Ego dystonic homosexuality is distinguished from ego syntonic homosexuality on the basis of self-acceptance. From a clinical perspective, only ego dystonic homosexuality is considered a disorder (see discussion in DSM-III and DSM-III-R). In most cases, ego dystonic homosexuals represent individuals whose biological sexual identity is almost exclusively homosexual (assuming that those ego dystonic homosexuals who are more fluid in sexual identity are likely to opt for heterosexual lifestyles). In such cases, it is generally recommended that treatment revolve around self-acceptance of sexual identity rather than changing it.

Sociocognitive processes

Normative processes

Certain conceptual abilities are regarded as necessary, but not sufficient, for achieving gender, sex role and sexual identity (Kohlberg, 1966; Stangor & Ruble, 1987; Levy & Carter, 1989). In particular, the attainment of gender constancy appears to increase sensitivity to gender-related information, as well as motivation to adopt behaviours appropriate to sex role and to enforce sex role stereotypes (Carter & McCloskey, 1983; Stangor & Ruble, 1987; Taylor & Carter, 1987; Levy & Carter, 1989). Although children within a 'normal' IQ range universally achieve gender constancy by the end of the preschool years, all children do not become equally attuned to issues of gender with regard to sex role identity, nor do all children become equally sextyped in their behaviour. Thus, gender constancy may be necessary, but not sufficient, for sex role identity and sex role behaviour. Comparable processes may exist with regard to understanding the constancy of sexual identity and the implications

for self-definition with regard to sexual identity; however, little empirical research has examined the sociocognitive bases of sexual identity (Boxer & Cohler, 1989).

In addition to these direct links between sociocognitive abilities, sexual identity and sexual behaviour, aspects of the quality of thought, or the conceptual abilities for understanding social relationships and social problem-solving, may be important to consider. The degree to which substantial changes in the quality of thinking occur from early childhood through adolescence remains an issue of controversy (Inhelder & Piaget, 1958; Linn, 1983; Kuhn *et al.*, 1988; Keating, 1990; Lapsley, 1990). However, studies have suggested that adolescents, relative to children, tend to be more relativistic rather than absolutistic in their thoughts, to be more systematic in their thinking as well as in their incorporation of abstractions into their thinking and may be more likely to consider future consequences in decision-making and problem-solving (Lewis, 1981; Gouze *et al.*, 1986; Keating, 1990). Such changes in thought may impact upon children's and adolescents' understanding of intimate relationships and of the biological processes of conception, as well as upon more straightforward cognitive skills such as problem-solving, decision-making and perception of risk. Discussion of these sociocognitive factors with regard to the transition from childhood to adolescence is presented elsewhere (Brooks-Gunn & Paikoff, 1992; Paikoff & Brooks-Gunn, in press).

Non-normative processes

Very few investigators have been able to document associations between sociocognitive abilities and psychosexual issues, particularly those that are behaviourally oriented (see Gfellner, 1986; Paikoff, 1990; Brooks-Gunn & Paikoff, 1993 for reviews). Several interesting hypotheses remain untested — for example, does the increasing ability to solve problems systematically, and to incorporate relativistic approaches, enable mid to late adolescents to be more flexible with regard to sex role behaviour, and more tolerant of violations of sex traditional behaviour in others?

The degree to which the interplay between

knowledge and conceptual abilities influences behaviour is of relevance as well. Certainly accurate understanding of the process of conception and ways in which pregnancy and sexually transmitted diseases may be prevented is a necessary condition for adopting practices of safe sex. Developmental studies of children's knowledge of the process of conception suggest that children are able to represent the process of conception relatively accurately by age 10 or 11 (though youth in the USA tend to lag a year or two behind other Western countries, Bernstein & Cowan, 1975; Goldman & Goldman, 1982). Few investigators, however, have examined children's knowledge about pregnancy and sexually transmitted disease prevention, though this may change as education about the human immunodeficiency virus (HIV) and the acquired immune deficiency syndrome (AIDS) becomes an increasing concern (Brooks-Gunn & Furstenberg, 1990). In studies of teenagers' beliefs regarding pregnancy prevention, many investigators have suggested that teenage perceptions of pregnancy prevention are often inaccurate; however, since most studies have asked teenagers to cite retrospective reasons for their own pregnancies, it is not clear whether these misperceptions are representative of adolescent thinking, or are better considered as *post hoc* rationalizations for an individual experience.

Intellectual abilities are likely to play a role in the speed, rather than the sequence, of psychosexual development. For example, the development of gender, sex role and sexual identity is likely to occur later in mentally retarded children and adolescents than in those of normal cognitive ability (Morganstern, 1973; Edmonson, 1988). Pubertal development is sometimes delayed among the mentally retarded, resulting in later onset of sexual behaviour as well. While severely and profoundly retarded persons are likely to engage in masturbatory sexual behaviour to the exclusion of intercourse behaviour, moderately and mildly retarded persons are likely to seek the company of others for sexual behaviour (Edmonson, 1988).

In addition to basic dimensions of knowledge and understanding, other high level sociocognitive processes, such as self-insight, consideration of future consequences and problem-solving or decision-making skills, may be associated with more plan-

ning for sexual activity. Few studies have investigated this possibility, however, and those that have do not suggest strong effects of considering future consequences upon contraceptive use (Paikoff, 1990).

Sociorelational processes

Normative processes

Given that many aspects of psychosexual development involve intimate relationships with others, developing social skills and intimacy is important in all life phases. Much has been written about the importance of infant−parent and infant−caregiver attachment for the development of later autonomous and social behaviour (Bowlby, 1969; Sroufe & Waters, 1977; Sroufe, 1979; Sroufe *et al.*, 1990). In general, investigators agree that dimensions of warmth and responsiveness are key in early care-giving interactions. Investigators differ, however, in beliefs regarding the relative roles of infants and adults in contributing to these characterizations (Belsky, 1981; Sroufe, 1983; Belsky *et al.*, 1984; Mangelsdorf *et al.*, 1990; see also Chapter 16).

In addition to these early influences, the development of social relationships during the childhood and adolescent years sets the stage for later intimate relationships of adulthood. During childhood, same-sex friendships become of central importance (Hartup, 1983, 1989; Berndt, 1986; Savin-Williams & Berndt, 1990). Within the context of these same-sex close relationships or chumships, children are presented with opportunities to develop behavioural patterns of interaction which differ from those of adult−child relationships. In particular, dimensions of power and dominance in decision-making tend to be more equitably distributed in such relationships (although hierarchical dominance structures may continue to exist, Savin-Williams, 1987), and discussions may be more directly focused on developmentally relevant topics, including sharing of feelings regarding school and social events. Children may feel able to take more liberties in expressing themselves in peer contexts and may use these opportunities to build bonds based on shared experiences, interests or events.

As children progress through childhood, friendships become increasingly based on psychological or abstract similarities, rather than on concrete factors such as proximity (Hartup, 1983; Berndt, 1986). At the same time, opposite-sex relationships and dating situations may emerge (Dunphy, 1963; Westney *et al.*, 1983), and children with same-sex preferences often become aware of their desires (Green, 1987; Boxer & Cohler, 1989; Boxer *et al.*, 1989; Savin-Williams, 1990).

Very little information exists regarding the development of opposite-sex dating behaviour. While information about the progression of particular dating behaviours (Westney *et al.*, 1983; Simmons & Blyth, 1987; Udry, 1988) and age at first intercourse exists (Hofferth & Hayes, 1987; Sonenstein *et al.*, 1989), little is known about the progress and structure of opposite- or same-sex dating relationships *per se*. We do not know how youth feel about their first sexual experiences, with whom they share and from whom they withhold information, or how they decide to have sex the first time (although most recall not having planned for it). Information is non-existent on the conversations between boys and girls that lead to intercourse or negotiations regarding the use of contraception. Few investigators have attempted to test whether same-sex friendships in late childhood and early adolescence have any bearing on dating relationships, or whether early dating relationships are associated with the quality of later intimate relationships.

Much of the research conducted on the development of social relationships is based on the earlier noted assumptions that these relationships form the basis from which sexual identity and sexual behaviour develop; however, very little work has systematically examined the processes by which this is accomplished. In the past, research in this area focused on ways in which early social relationships might impact upon later sexual identity with particular emphasis on ways that family experiences might impact upon homosexual lifestyles (Green, 1987; Boxer & Cohler, 1989). Research is moving away from a 'solitary influence' model of sexual identity development, and towards a more multifaceted exploration of particular family or other social relationship factors in determining the degree to which heterosexual or homosexual identity will be manifest, as well as adopting a more lifespan perspective (Boxer & Cohler, 1989). The

degree to which early social relationships have implications for patterns of sexual behaviour and fertility management has not been explicitly examined.

Non-normative processes

Potential consequences of insecure (avoidant or resistant) attachment patterns in the first years of life have been implicated as precursors to later intimacy problems (Bowlby, 1969; Ainsworth, 1973; Sroufe, 1979). Insecure infant attachment relationships that have resulted in peer isolation or behavioural problems are likely to manifest themselves in an inability to form or maintain satisfying intimate relationships during adolescence (see Chapter 16).

Relationships with peers provide an arena of potential vulnerability for children and adolescents (see Chapter 18). In particular, problems of aggressive and of isolated children may be predictive of later social difficulties in achieving and maintaining friendships and intimate relationships. While studies have not yet linked problems in peer relationships to later psychosexual development, considerable consistency in both aggression and in isolation or social withdrawal is found through childhood and adolescence (Huesmann *et al.*, 1984; Kandel & Davies, 1986; Cairns *et al.*, 1989; Baydar *et al.*, 1991). Even when sexually intimate relationships are formed and maintained, these relationships may be characterized by maladaptive interactions (involving either extreme aggression or extreme detachment).

Thus, difficulties with social relationships have potential implications for sexual identity and for sexual behaviour. In addition to the normative issues of sexual identity mentioned above, problems in establishing social relationships could result in adoption of either an asexual identity or in an asocial sexual identity (e.g. reliance on self, rather than others, to meet sexual desires). In addition, lack of intimacy may translate into sexual behaviour involving multiple partners and no contraceptive use, placing the individual at risk for sexually transmitted disease and unplanned pregnancy (Brooks-Gunn & Furstenberg, 1989, 1990). Belsky *et al.* (1991) have suggested that insecure attachments in infancy and early childhood may heighten the chances of adopting reproductive strategies involving multiple partners and resulting in many children from these temporary bonds; however, empirical evidence directly bearing on this research question is not currently available. In addition, these theoretical conjectures have been called into question due to concerns over gender specificity (Maccoby, 1991) as well as with regard to the biological mechanism which might drive such an association (Hooper, 1991).

Non-normative sociorelational processes may increase the chances of sexual abuse or non-voluntary intercourse. For example, Moore *et al.* (1989) found the chances of experiencing non-voluntary sexual activity were increased if girls in a national sample lived apart from their parents, were raised in poverty and/or had parents who used alcohol or illegal substances.

In some cases, problems in intimate relationships result in difficulties with physical aspects of sexual activity (e.g. inability to achieve orgasm in both sexes, inability to achieve erection in males). When no physiological cause exists for these problems, they are considered instances of psychogenic impotence. While case studies of such problems in males abound, very few comparable studies of female inability for orgasm exist. In addition, few studies have gone beyond the case study approach to these issues. In one such study, self-administered drug treatments that enhanced male erection increased both partners' sexual satisfaction (Althof *et al.*, 1987).

Cultural processes

Normative processes

Very little psychological research on cultural contributions to psychosexual development has been conducted. Important ethnographic and anthropological work, however, has focused on how messages regarding sexuality are communicated to members of a society, as well as the implications of studying sexuality for understanding a broad range of social organizational concepts. Particularly important for our purposes is the message a society sends to its young regarding sexual behaviour.

The majority of cultures are relatively similar with regard to issues of gender identity. However, cultural differences do exist with regard to processes of sex role and sexual identity. Such differences are largely manifest through the meaning attached to particular behaviours. For example, cultures vary in the degree to which sex role identity is rigidly and narrowly defined (Mead, 1928). In addition, the degree to which sexual behaviour defines sexual identity (e.g. whether a single homosexual experience or heterosexual experience is definitive of sexual identity) varies across culture as well.

Cultural differences in sex role and sexual identity may result in sexual behaviour differences. In particular, the importance of fertility management is influenced by cultural beliefs regarding sex role and sexuality. A landmark study regarding cultural influences on sexual behaviour was conducted by Ford and Beach (1951), who examined approximately 100 cultures. They reported that the majority of world cultures examined could be categorized into three basic groups, defined by their attitudes towards sexual development: (i) restrictive societies, where premarital sexual behaviour and sexual exploration (and often contact between sexes) are restricted; clear prohibitions exist for such activities; punishment for violation of such rules is public (and often violent), carrying a long-term social stigma along with it; (ii) semi-restrictive societies, where cultural prohibitions regarding premarital sexual behaviour exist but are not enforced; rather, the consequences of such activities (e.g. pregnancy, sexually transmitted diseases) are considered problematic and are punished; and (iii) permissive societies, where premarital sex, homosexual behaviour and various forms of sexual exploration are not prohibited, but rather on some level are encouraged via opportunities for viewing such activities at a relatively early age, participating in such activities, and, in some cases, providing easy access to contraceptives or medical services.

By general consensus, most Western countries (with the possible exception of Scandinavian countries) are classified as semi-restrictive. The mixed messages that occur in such cultures may be more detrimental to psychosexual development than those of either restrictive or permissive societies.

Western societal messages about youthful sexual behaviour are mixed at best. Fine (1988) has identified four sexual discourses to which the adolescent is exposed. Sexual behaviour is equated with: (i) a lack of individual morality; (ii) desire; (iii) victimization; and (iv) danger.

The discourse of morality colours most discussions of sexual behaviour. While premarital sex is a fact of current Western societal experience, teenagers are still told not to have sex. What youth see across the wider age spectrum is adults of all ages engaging in sex outside the confines of marriage. Even within their own age cohort, youth find the societal message at odds with reality. Over the past 25 years, youth have been having sex at earlier and earlier ages. The most recent estimates of female sexual behaviour in the USA come from the 1988 National Survey of Family Survey Growth-Cycle IV (Centers for Disease Control, 1991). By age 15, over one-quarter of unmarried girls were sexually experienced; by age 17, the percentage was almost one-half; and by age 19, three-quarters of girls have had sex. The percentages for black and white girls differed by less than four percentage points at each of these ages, suggesting that previous large ethnic differences have all but disappeared (Brooks-Gunn & Furstenberg, 1989). However, societal beliefs have not kept pace with actual behavioural practices, and opprobrium about teenage sexual behaviour still exists.

Because sexual prohibitions are couched in moralistic terms, youth are in a quandary. If sexual intercourse prior to marriage is not acceptable, then planning for it is unacceptable as well. Youth are told to act responsibly and to avoid sex. We believe that the contradiction between the increasing numbers of sexually active girls (especially those aged 17 and younger) and the moral prohibitions against sexual behaviour fuel many of the institutional, familial, and individual responses to teenage contraceptive use in the USA. This may, in fact, be an underlying reason for our apparent failure to assist teenagers in responsible contraceptive use, which is reflected in rates of teenage pregnancy higher than most Western European countries (rates of teenage sexuality are essentially the same in the USA and Western Europe, Jones *et al.*, 1988).

The discourse of desire also provides mixed messages to youth. It is downplayed for girls while seen as part and parcel of the male experience. Girls' desires are almost never discussed, only the consequences of their sexual behaviour (e.g. unplanned pregnancy). By pretending that female desire does not exist, girls are given few strategies for incorporating it into their lives or for planning on how to handle it. Contrast this situation with that of males, for whom desire is a given. Males may even be socialized to accept demonstration of their potency as more important than acting responsibly. In one study, for example, mother–daughter communication about contraceptive use and sexuality was associated with later age at first intercourse, as was mother–son communication. However, father–son discussions were linked to earlier sexual activity in boys (Kahn *et al.*, 1984), perhaps because their discussions centred on desire.

The discourses of victimization and danger are linked to male desire. Females, in being portrayed as having little desire and having to face the practical and moral consequences of sexual behaviour, are characterized as victims. Girls must protect themselves against the desires of men outside of marriage (it is estimated that as many as one-quarter of today's adolescent girls have had sex against their will; Moore *et al.*, 1989). Given that many societal controls to protect girls seem no longer to be in place (chaperonage, after school parental supervision, community sanctions encouraging marriage when a pregnancy occurs, sex not being glorified in the media) and that the majority of teenagers are having sex, girls are seen as victims of male sexual desire. Even in cases without direct physical coercion, such a situation sets up males and females as antagonists — males as the perpetrators and females as victims. How sexual behaviour is negotiated in such a situation is not clear. However, it suggests that males and females probably use very different strategies, and that direct negotiation is rare (Brooks-Gunn & Furstenberg, 1990). Both danger and desire coexist for girls (Fine, 1988, p. 36). How do they manage the two, and do so without sacrificing male relationships?

The difficulties in sexual negotiations between boys and girls were aptly summarized by Simon and Gagnon (1969). While the percentage of youth having sexual intercourse is much higher today than 20 years ago, the difficulty in balancing sexual pleasure and intimacy remains:

Dating and courtship may well be considered

processes in which each sex trains the other in what each wants and expects. What data (are) available suggest that this exchange system does not always work very smoothly. Thus, normally, it is not uncommon to find that the boy becomes emotionally involved with his partner and therefore lets up trying to seduce her, at the same time that the girl comes to feel that the boy's affection is genuine and therefore sexual intimacy is more permissible. (Simon & Gagnon, 1969, p. 15)

The discourse of victimization also is played out when a pregnancy occurs. Most teenage births occur outside the context of marriage — currently 90% of births to black teenagers and over 50% of births to white youth in the USA. Furthermore, the incidence of child support and paternal involvement following a teenage birth is very low — lower today than it was 20 years ago, even in non-marital situations (Furstenberg *et al.*, 1990). These mixed messages about youthful sexual behaviour, as exemplified by the sexual discourses of morality, desire, victimization and danger, have probably impeded discussions about health in the sexual domain. Instead, the negative consequences of sexual behaviour are emphasized, rather than the positive conditions that are associated with the delay of sexual activity and the practice of responsible sexual behaviour (Brooks-Gunn & Paikoff, 1993, p. 187).

In addition to these macrolevel cultural influences, subgroup cultural differences may be operating as well. Few studies have attempted to examine ethnic and class diversity with regard to sexual behaviour, even though subgroup differences probably exist in perceptions of appropriate sexual standards as well as in the role of familial versus societal authority in enforcing rules or prohibitions (Spencer & Dornbusch, 1990). In addition to subgroup cultural beliefs, an understanding of the current social practices within neighbourhood communities is essential in order to understand the opportunities individuals have to engage in sexual behaviour (Brooks-Gunn *et al.*, 1991).

Non-normative processes

Particular cultural processes defining non-normative development are, of course, specific to and reflective of cultural prohibitions regarding certain sexual practices or feelings (with the exception that almost universal prohibitions exist against paedophiles or incest perpetrators). With regard to gender identity, for example, the work of Imperato-McGinley *et al.* (1979) reported cultural acceptance of changes in gender identity and sex role behaviour around the pubertal period. Changes in gender and sex role identity are probably less accepted in the USA as evidenced by social controversies over gender dissatisfaction and surgical amelioration.

As mentioned above, defining features of sexual identity vary across culture. While homosexuality is universal across culture and historical era, acceptance of homosexuality does vary substantially. Cultural processes in this regard can involve learning to cope with and accept one's sexual identity and behaviour in an unfriendly environment. For example, the social pressures burdening homosexuals (Remafedi, 1987; Boxer & Cohler, 1989; Herdt, 1989; Savin-Williams, 1990) can involve problems with regard to individual acceptance of one's own sexual identity, the more public behavioural acts of dating, disclosure of sexual identity to significant others and to the community at large. At each step, the homosexual adolescent or adult faces the possibility of rejection, hostility and violence, as well as of discrimination. The stresses of either facing such societal problems or keeping sexual identity hidden over the long term may pose general mental and physical health risks (Remafedi, 1987; Herdt, 1989; Savin-Williams, 1990).

The normative nature of sexual behaviour and fertility management varies across culture as well, as evidenced by differences in prevalence of particular sexual acts as well as in contraceptive use. In addition, normative behaviour may vary within culture as a function of gender or age. For example, in the USA teenage sexual intercourse involves a cultural norm violation. Teenagers who feel guilty or ashamed of their sexual feelings and behaviour may be at heightened risk of problems with fertility management, due to lack of planning and resultant non-use of contraceptives (Brooks-Gunn & Furstenberg, 1989, 1990).

CONCLUSION

This chapter provides a rather broad overview of the psychosexual issues to be mastered across the lifespan. Several general conclusions may be drawn *vis-à-vis* future research directions. First, research must focus on the interplay between biological factors, self-beliefs and the sociocultural messages transmitted to and received by individuals. At the same time, behavioural studies must move beyond these cultural beliefs. For example, studies of teenage pregnancy and motherhood abound, yet few studies have examined the development of dating and sexual intimacy during the teenage years.

Second, links between particular processes and psychosexual issues need to be studied longitudinally, in order to examine the interplay among the developmental processes noted in Fig. 21.2 within a particular life phase. For example, the interplay between gender identity, hormonal dysfunction and sociocultural influence could be examined over time. Prenatal hormonal exposure may lay the groundwork for early childhood experience and gender identity. At puberty, an increase in hormonal levels may influence sexual behaviour and fertility management as well. How might these hormonal changes be mediated by prior social experience and by cognitive level?

In the case of CAH, girls may experience increased activity level and more tomboyish behaviour due to prenatal androgen exposure, and such activity and behaviour may influence the nature of the young girls' social relationships. Hormonal and physiological changes may exacerbate this more masculinized behaviour, if girls are not responsive to or not exposed to hormone therapy by puberty and consequently develop fewer signs of feminine secondary sexual characteristics. These effects may in turn influence social relationships in girls who do not fit stereotypes for ideal female bodies. Finally, all of these factors are likely to be mediated by the girls' cognitive ability, and by the cultural norms and beliefs regarding sex role behaviour and body change. The literature in this area needs to move beyond simple associative findings into positing and testing more complex models of influence.

Third, differences in gender representation within specific psychosexual issues are startling. For example, the research literature on teenage sexual behaviour focuses predominantly on females while the literature on sexual identity focuses almost exclusively on males. These cleavages reflect societal concerns: pregnant girls and sissy boys are seen as problems while teenage fathers and tomboys are not. A more impartial emphasis on psychosexual issues with regard to both genders is necessary; such research should incorporate the substantial literature on gender differences in sex role behaviours and social interaction as these differences may help to explain similarities and differences in other areas of psychosexual development.

It is likely that there are multiple pathways to normative psychosexual development; indeed we have specified how such pathways may vary as a function of factors as diverse as biological status and cultural membership. To advance the study of psychosexual development, it will be necessary to articulate and specify particular pathways of development, as well as to specify antecedents and developmental trajectories (Jessor & Jessor, 1977; Powers *et al.*, 1989; Hauser & Bowlds, 1990). For example, particular pathways could be identified with regard to onset of sexual intercourse with separate pathways for each of the following factors: age at which intercourse first occurs; length of relationship prior to intercourse; use or non-use of contraception; and voluntary or non-voluntary nature of intercourse, etc. Examination of these more complex pathways from a lifespan perspective will enable researchers to pinpoint particular cases in which early onset of sexual intercourse may be relatively more or less optimal. Knowledge of the developmental antecedents to relatively adaptive or maladaptive pathways of psychosexual development is central to scientific understanding as well as to therapeutic intervention and public policy advances.

ACKNOWLEDGEMENT

This chapter was prepared with the generous and welcome support of the National Institutes of Health (NICHD) and the W.T. Grant Foundation. The assistance of Rosemary Diebler, Linda Immordino and Ninfa Sarabia in manuscript preparation is gratefully acknowledged.

REFERENCES

Ainsworth M. (1973) The development of infant–mother attachment. In Caldwell B. & Ricciuti H. (eds) *Review of Child Development Research*, Vol. 3, pp. 1–94. University of Chicago Press, Chicago.

Althof S.E., Turner L.A., Levine S.B. *et al.* (1987) Intracavernosal injection in the treatment of impotence: A prospective study of sexual, psychological, and marital functioning. *Journal of Sex and Marital Therapy* **13**(3), 155–167.

August G.P. (1990) Disorders of the sex hormones: A medical overview. In Holmes C.S. (ed.) *Psychoneuroendocrinology: Brain, Behavior, and Hormonal Interactions*, pp. 184–192. Springer, New York.

Bailey J.M. & Pillard R.C. (1991) A genetic study of male sexual orientation. *Archives of General Psychiatry* **48**, 1089–1096.

Baker S.W. & Ehrhardt A.A. (1974) Prenatal androgen, intelligence, and cognitive sex differences. In Friedman R.C., Richart R.M. & Vande Weile R.L. (eds) *Sex Differences in Behavior*. Wiley, New York.

Bancroft J. (1991) Reproductive hormones. In Rutter M. & Casaer P. (eds) *Biological Risk Factors for Psychosocial Disorders*, pp. 260–310. Published for the European Network on Longitudinal Studies on Individual Development (ENLS), European Science Foundation. Cambridge University Press, Cambridge.

Baruch G. & Brooks-Gunn J. (eds) (1984) *Women in Midlife*. Plenum, New York.

Baydar N., Brooks-Gunn J. & Warren M.P. (1991) *Changes of depressive symptoms in adolescent girls over four years: The effects of pubertal maturation and life events*. Unpublished ms, Educational Testing Service, Princeton, New Jersey.

Beatty W.W. (1979) Gonadal hormones and sex differences in non-reproductive behaviors in rodents: Organizational and activational influences. *Hormones and Behavior* **12**, 112–163.

Becker K.L. (1972) Clinical and therapeutic experiences with Klinefelter Syndrome. *Fertility and Sterility* **23**, 568–578.

Bell R.Q., Weller G.M. & Waldrop M.F. (1971) Newborn and preschooler: Organization of behavior and relations between periods. *Monographs of the Society for Research in Child Development* **36**, Series No. 142.

Belsky J. (1981) Early human experience: A family perspective. *Developmental Psychology* **17**, 3–23.

Belsky J., Rovine M. & Taylor D.G. (1984) The Pennsylvania Infant and Family Development Project, III: The origins of individual differences in infant–mother attachment: Maternal and infant contributions. *Child Development* **55**, 706–717.

Belsky J., Steinberg L. & Draper P. (1991) Childhood experience, interpersonal development, and reproductive strategy: An evolutionary theory of socialization. *Child Development* **62**, 647–670.

Bem S.L. (1981) Gender schema theory: A cognitive account of sex typing. *Psychological Review* **88**(4), 354–364.

Bender B.G., Puck M.H., Salbenblatt J.A. & Robinson A. (1990) Cognitive development of children with sex chromosome abnormalities. In Holmes C.S. (ed.) *Psychoneuroendocrinology: Brain, Behavior, and Hormonal Interactions*, pp. 138–163. Springer, New York.

Berch D.B. & McCauley E. (1990) Psychosocial functioning of individuals with sex chromosome abnormalities. In Holmes C.S. (ed.) *Psychoneuroendocrinology: Brain, Behavior, and Hormonal Interactions*, pp. 164–183. Springer, New York.

Berenbaum S.A. (1990) Congenital adrenal hyperplasia: Intellectual and psychosexual functioning. In Holmes C.S. (ed.) *Psychoneuroendocrinology: Brain, Behavior, and Hormonal Interactions*, pp. 227–260. Springer, New York.

Berndt T.J. (1986) Children's comments about their friendships. In Perlmutter M. (ed.) *Cognitive Perspectives on Children's Social and Behavioral Development*, pp. 189–212. Lawrence Erlbaum, Hillsdale, New Jersey.

Bernstein A.C. & Cowan P.A. (1975) Children's concepts of how people get babies. *Child Development* **46**, 77–91.

Bowlby J. (1969) *Attachment and Loss*, Vol. I, *Attachment*. Basic Books, New York.

Boxer A.M. & Cohler B.J. (1989) The life course of gay and lesbian youth: An immodest proposal for the study of lives. *Journal of Homosexuality* **17**(3/4), 315–355.

Boxer A.M., Cook J.A. & Herdt G. (1989) *First homosexual and heterosexual experiences reported by gay and lesbian youth in an urban community*. Paper presented at the Annual Meetings of the American Sociological Association, San Francisco, California, August.

Brooks-Gunn J. (1984) The psychological significance of different pubertal events to young girls. *Journal of Early Adolescence* **4**(4), 315–327.

Brooks-Gunn J. (1988) Antecedents and consequences of variations in girls' maturational timing. *Journal of Adolescent Health Care* **9**(5), 365–373.

Brooks-Gunn J. (1989) Pubertal processes and the early adolescent transition. In Damon W. (ed.) *Child Development Today and Tomorrow*, pp. 155–176. Jossey-Bass, San Francisco, California.

Brooks-Gunn J., Duncan G.J., Kato P. & Sealand N. (1991) *Do neighborhoods influence child and adolescent behavior?* Paper presented at the Society for Research in Child Development Meetings, Seattle, Wisconsin, April.

Brooks-Gunn J. & Furstenberg Jr F.F. (1989) Adolescent sexual behavior. *American Psychologist* **44**(2), 249–257.

Brooks-Gunn J. & Furstenberg Jr F.F. (1990) Coming of age in the era of AIDS: Sexual and contraceptive decisions. *Milbank Quarterly* **68**, 59–84.

Brooks-Gunn J. & Lewis M. (1979) 'Why mama and papa?': The development of social labels. *Child Development* **50**, 1203–1206.

Brooks-Gunn J. & Matthews W. (1979) *He and She: How Children Develop Their Sex-Role Identity*. Prentice-Hall, Englewood Cliffs, New Jersey.

Brooks-Gunn J. & Paikoff R.L. (1992) Changes in self feelings during the transition towards adolescence. In McGurk H. (ed.) *Childhood Social Development: Contemporary Perspectives*, pp. 63–97. Routledge, London.

Brooks-Gunn J. & Paikoff R.L. (1993) 'Sex is a gamble, kissing is a game': Adolescent sexuality, contraception, and pregnancy. In Millstein S.P., Petersen A.C. & Nightingale E. (eds) *Promotion of Health Behavior in Adolescence*, pp. 180–208. Oxford University Press, New York.

Brooks-Gunn J. & Reiter E.O. (1990) The role of pubertal processes in the early adolescent transition. In Feldman S. & Elliott G. (eds) *At the Threshold: The Developing Adolescent*, pp. 16–53. Harvard University Press, Cambridge, Massachusetts.

Brooks-Gunn J. & Warren M.P. (1988) The psychological significance of secondary sexual characteristics in 9- to 11-year-old girls. *Child Development* **59**, 161–169.

Brooks-Gunn J., Warren M.P., Samelson M. & Fox R. (1986) Physical similarity of and disclosure of menarcheal status to friends: Effects of age and pubertal status. *Journal of Early Adolescence* **6**(1), 3–14.

Buchanan C.M., Eccles J.S. & Becker J.B. (1992) Are adolescents the victims of raging hormones?: Evidence for activational effects of hormones on moods and behavior at adolescence. *Psychological Bulletin* **111**(1), 62–107.

Cairns R.B., Cairns B.D., Neckerman H.J., Ferguson L.L. & Gariepy J.L. (1989) Growth and aggression: 1. Childhood to early adolescence. *Developmental Psychology* **25**(2), 320–330.

Carter D.B. & McCloskey L.A. (1983) Peers and the maintenance of sex-typed behavior: The development of children's conceptions of cross gender behavior in their peers. *Social Cognition* **2**(4), 294–314.

Centers for Disease Control (1991) *Morbidity and Mortality Weekly Report*, Vol. 39, Nos 51–52. US Department of Health and Human Services, Washington, DC.

Cicchetti D. & Carlson V. (eds) (1989) *Child Maltreatment: Theory and Research on the Causes and Consequences of Child Abuse and Neglect*. Cambridge University Press, New York.

Crockett L.J. & Petersen A.C. (1993) Adolescent development: Health risks and opportunities for health promotion. In Millstein S.P., Petersen A.C. & Nightingale E. (eds) *Promotion of Health Behavior in Adolescence* , pp. 13–37. Oxford University Press, New York.

Dolan B. (1991) Cross cultural aspects of anorexia and bulimia: A review. *International Journal of Eating Disorders* **10**(1), 67–78.

Dornbusch S.M., Carlsmith J.M., Duncan P.D. *et al.* (1984) Sexual maturation, social class, and the desire to be thin among adolescent females. *Developmental and Behavioral Pediatrics* **5**, 308–314.

Downey J., Ehrhardt A.A., Gruen R., Bell J.J. & Morishima A. (1989) Psychopathology and social functioning in women with Turner syndrome. *Journal of Nervous and Mental Disorders* **177**(4), 191–201.

Dunphy D.C. (1963) The social structure of urban adolescent peer groups. *Sociometry* **XXVI**, 230–246.

Dweck C.S., Goetz T.E. & Strauss N.L. (1980) Sex differences in learned helplessness: IV. An experimental and naturalistic study of failure generalization and its mediators. *Journal of Personality and Social Psychology* **38**(3), 441–452.

Edmonson B. (1988) Disability and sexual adjustment. In Van Hasselt V.B., Strain P.S. & Hersen M. (eds) *Handbook of Developmental and Physical Disabilities*, pp. 91–106. Pergamon, New York.

Edwards C.P. & Whiting B.B. (1988) *Children of Different Worlds*. Harvard University Press, Cambridge, Massachusetts.

Ehrhardt A.A., Epstein R. & Money J. (1968) Fetal androgens and female gender identity in the early treated adrenogenital syndrome. *Johns Hopkins Medical Journal* **122**, 160–167.

Ehrhardt A.A., Feldman J.F., Rosen L.R. *et al.* (1987) Psychopathology in prenatally DES-exposed females: Current and lifetime adjustment. *Psychosomatic Medicine* **49**(2), 183–196.

Ehrhardt A.A., Greenberg N. & Money J. (1970) Female gender identity and absence of fetal hormones: Turner's syndrome. *Johns Hopkins Medical Journal* **126**, 234–248.

Ehrhardt A.A., Meyer-Bahlberg H.F., Rosen L.R. *et al.* (1989) The development of gender-related behavior in females following prenatal exposure to diethylstilbestrol (DES). *Hormones and Behavior* **23**(4), 526–541.

Evans J.A., Hamerton J.L. & Robinson A. (1991) *Children and Young Adults with Sex Chromosome Aneuploidy*. Wiley-Liss, New York.

Evelyth P.B. & Tanner J.M. (1976) *Worldwide Variation in Human Growth*. Cambridge University Press, London.

Fagan J.F. & Shepherd P.A. (1982) Theoretical issues in the early development of visual perception. In Lewis M. & Taft L. (eds) *Developmental Disabilities: Theory, Assessment, and Intervention*, pp. 9–34. S.P. Medical and Scientific Books, New York.

Fagan J.F. & Singer L.T. (1979) The role of single feature differences in infant recognition of faces. *Infant Behavior and Development* **2**, 39–45.

Fagot B.I. (1974) Sex differences in toddler's behavior and parental reaction. *Developmental Psychology* **10**, 554–558.

Faust M.S. (1960) Developmental maturity as a determinant in prestige of adolescent girls. *Child Development* **31**, 173–186.

Faust M.S. (1983) Alternative constructions of adolescent growth. In Brooks-Gunn J. & Petersen A.C. (eds) *Girls at Puberty: Biological and Psychosocial Perspectives*, pp. 105–125. Plenum, New York.

Fine M. (1988) Sexuality, schooling, and adolescent females: The missing discourse of desire. *Harvard Educational Review* **58**(1), 29–53.

Ford C. & Beach F. (1951) *Patterns of Sexual Behavior.* Harper & Row, New York.

Forest M.G. & Cathiard A.M. (1978) Ontogenic study of plasma 17-α hydroxyprogesterone in the human, I: Postnatal period: Evidence for a transient ovarian activity in infancy. *Pediatric Research* **12**, 6–11.

Frey K.S. & Ruble D.N. (1987) What children say about classroom performance: Sex and grade differences in perceived competence. *Child Development* **58**(4), 1066–1078.

Furstenberg Jr F.F., Levine J.A. & Brooks-Gunn J. (1990) The daughters of teenage mothers: Patterns of early childbearing in two generations. *Family Planning Perspectives* **22**(2), 54–61.

Garai J.E. & Scheinfeld P. (1968) Sex differences in mental and behavioral traits. *Genetic Psychology Monographs* **77**, 169–299.

Gargiulo J., Attie I., Brooks-Gunn J. & Warren M.P. (1987) Girls' dating behavior as a function of social context and maturation. *Developmental Psychology* **23**(5), 730–737.

Garron D.C. & Vander Stoep L.R. (1969) Personality and intelligence in Turner syndrome. *Archives of General Psychiatry* **21**, 339–346.

Gfellner B. (1986) Concepts of sexual behavior: Construction and validation of a developmental model. *Journal of Adolescent Research* **1**(3), 327–347.

Gilligan C. (1982) *In a Different Voice: Psychological Theory and Women's Development.* Harvard University Press, Cambridge, Massachusetts.

Goldman R.J. & Goldman J.D. (1982) How children perceive the origin of babies and the roles of mothers and fathers in procreation: A cross-national study. *Child Development* **53**, 491–504.

Gouze K.R., Strauss D. & Keating D.P. (1986) *Adolescents' conceptions of stress and coping.* Paper presented at the Biennial Meeting of the Society for Research on Adolescence, Madison, Wisconsin.

Goy R.W. & McEwen B.S. (1980) *Sexual Differentiation of the Brain.* MIT Press, Cambridge, Massachusetts.

Green R. (1987) *The 'Sissy' Boy syndrome and the Development of Homosexuality.* Yale University Press, New Haven, Connecticut.

Greene J.G. (1984) *The Social and Psychological Origins of the Climacteric Syndrome.* Gower Press, Aldershot.

Grief E.B. & Ulman K.J. (1982) The psychological impact of menarche on early adolescent females: A review of the literature. *Child Development* **53**, 1413–1430.

Griffiths R. (1991) The isolation of conserved DNA sequences related to the human sex-determining region Y gene from the lesser black-backed gull (*Larus fuscus*). *Proceedings of the Royal Society — London Series B: Biological Sciences* **22**(244), (1310): 123B.

Grumbach M.M. & Sizonenko P.C. (1986) *Control of the Onset of Puberty,* Vol. II. Academic Press, New York.

Gunnar M.R., Larson M.C., Hertsgaard L., Harris M.L. & Brodersen L. (1992) The stressfulness of separation among nine-month-old infants: Effects of social context variables and infant temperament. *Child Development* **63**, 290–303.

Gunnar M.R., Mangelsdorf S., Larson M. & Hertsgaard L. (1989) Attachment, temperament, and adrenocortical activity in infancy: A study of psychoendocrine regulation. *Developmental Psychology* **25**, 355–363.

Harding J., Soliday B., Field T., Lasko D., Gonzales N. & Valdeon C. (1992) *Touching in infant, toddler, and preschool nurseries.* Unpublished ms, University of Miami Medical School.

Harter S. (1983) Developmental perspectives on the self-system. In Hetherington E.M. (ed.) *Handbook of Child Psychology,* Vol. 4, *Socialization, Personality, and Social Development,* pp. 275–385. Wiley, New York.

Hartup W.W. (1983) Peer relations. In Hetherington E.M. (ed.) *Handbook of Child Psychology,* Vol. IV, *Socialization, Personality, and Social Development,* pp. 103–196. Wiley, New York.

Hartup W.W. (1989) Social relationships and their developmental significance. *American Psychologist* **44**(2), 120–126.

Haspels A.A. & Musaph H. (1979) *Psychosomatics in Peri-Menopause.* University Park Press, Baltimore, Maryland.

Hauser S.T. & Bowlds M.K. (1990) Stress, coping and adaptation within adolescence: Diversity and resilience. In Feldman S.S. & Elliott G.R. (eds) *At the Threshold: The Developing Adolescent,* pp. 388–413. Harvard University Press, Cambridge, Massachusetts.

Herdt G. (1989) Introduction: Gay and lesbian youth, emergent identities, and cultural scenes at home and abroad. *Journal of Homosexuality* **17**, 1–42.

Hill J.P. (1988) Adapting to menarche: Familial control and conflict. In Gunnar M.R. & Collins W.A. (eds) *Development During the Transition to Adolescence,* Vol. 21, pp. 43–77. Lawrence Erlbaum, Hillsdale, New Jersey.

Hill J.P. & Lynch M.E. (1983) The intensification of gender-related role expectations during early adolescence. In Brooks-Gunn J. & Petersen A.C. (eds) *Girls at Puberty: Biological and Psychosocial Perspectives,* pp. 201–228. Plenum, New York.

Hofferth S.L. & Hayes C.D. (1987) *Risking the Future: Adolescent Sexuality, Pregnancy, and Childbearing,* Vol. II. National Academy of Sciences Press, Washington, DC.

Hooper C. (1991) The birds, the bees, and human sexual strategies. *Journal of National Institute of Health Research* **3**, 54–60.

Huesmann L.R., Eron L.D., Lefkowitz M.M. & Walder L.O. (1984) Stability of aggression over time and generations. *Developmental Psychology* **20**(6), 1120–1134.

Imperato-McGinley J., Peterson R.E., Gautier T. & Sturla

E. (1979) Androgens and the evolution of male-gender identity among male pseudohermaphrodites with 5 alpha-reductase deficiency. *New England Journal of Medicine* **300**(22), 1233–1237.

Inhelder B. & Piaget J. (1958) *The Growth of Logical Thinking from Childhood to Adolescence*. Basic Books, New York.

Jacklin C.N. (1989) Female and male: Issues of gender. *American Psychologist* **44**, 127–133.

Jacklin C.N., Wilcox K.T. & Maccoby E.E. (1988) Neonatal sex-steroid hormones and cognitive abilities at six years. *Developmental Psychobiology* **21**(6), 567–574.

Jessor R. & Jessor S.L. (1977) *Problem Behavior and Psychosocial Development*. Academic Press, New York.

Jones E., Forrest J., Goldman N., Henshaw S.K., Silverman J. & Torres A. (1988) Unintended pregnancy, contraceptive practice and family planning services in developed countries. *Family Planning Perspectives* **20**(2), 53–67.

Kahn J., Smith K. & Roberts E. (1984) *Familial Communication and Adolescent Sexual Behavior*. Final report to the Office of Adolescent Pregnancy Programs. American Institute for Research, Cambridge, Massachusetts.

Kandel D.B. & Davies M. (1986) Adult sequelae of adolescent depressive symptoms. *Archives of General Psychiatry* **43**, 225–262.

Kaplan S.L., Grumbach M.M. & Aubert M.L. (1976) The ontogenesis of pituitary hormones and hypothalamic factors in the human fetus: Maturation of the central nervous system regulation of anterior pituitary function. *Recent Progress in Hormone Research* **32**, 161–243.

Katchadourian H. (1977) *The Biology of Adolescence*. W.H. Freeman, San Francisco, California.

Katchadourian H. (1990) Sexuality. In Feldman S.S. & Elliott G.R. (eds) *At the Threshold: The Developing Adolescent*, pp. 330–351. Harvard University Press, Cambridge, Massachusetts.

Keating D.P. (1990) Adolescent thinking. In Feldman S.S. & Elliott G.R. (eds) *At the Threshold: The Developing Adolescent*, pp. 54–90. Harvard University Press, Cambridge, Massachusetts.

Kohlberg L. (1966) A cognitive-developmental analysis of children's sex-role concepts and attitudes. In Maccoby E.E. (ed.) *The Development of Sex Differences*, pp. 82–173. Stanford University Press, Stanford, California.

Kohlberg L. (1969) Stage and sequence: The cognitive-developmental approach to socialization. In Goslin D.A. (ed.) *Handbook of Socialization Theory and Research*, pp. 347–480. Rand-McNally, Chicago, Illinois.

Kuhn D., Amsel E. & O'Loughlin M. (1988) *The Development of Scientific Thinking Skills*. Academic Press, San Diego, California.

Langlois J.H. & Stephan C.W. (1981) Beauty and the beast: The role of physical attractiveness in the development of peer relations and social behavior. In Brehm S.S., Kassin S.M. & Gibbons F.X. (eds) *Developmental Social Psychology: Theory and Research*, pp. 152–168. Oxford University Press, New York.

Lapsley D.K. (1990) Continuity and discontinuity in adolescent social cognitive development. In Montemayor R., Adams G.R. & Gullotta T.P. (eds) *Advances in Adolescent Development*, Vol. 2, *From Childhood to Adolescence: A Transitional Period?*, pp. 183–204. Sage, Newbury Park, California.

Lerner R.M. & Schroeder C. (1971) Physique identification, preference, and aversion in kindergarten children. *Developmental Psychology* **5**, 578.

Levy G.D. & Carter D.B. (1989) Gender schema, gender constancy and gender-role knowledge: The roles of cognitive factors in preschoolers' gender-role stereotype attributions. *Developmental Psychology* **25**(3), 444–449.

Lewis C. (1981) How adolescents approach decisions: Change over grades seven to twelve and policy implications. *Child Development* **52**(2), 538–544.

Lewis M. (1972) Parents and children: Sex-role development. *School Review* **80**(92), 229–240.

Lewis M. & Brooks-Gunn J. (1979) *Social Cognition and the Acquisition of Self*. Plenum, New York.

Linn M.C. (1983) Content, context, and process in reasoning during adolescence: Selecting a model. *Journal of Early Adolescence* **3**, 63–82.

Maccoby E.E. (1988) Gender as a social category. *Developmental Psychology* **24**(6), 755–765.

Maccoby E.E. (1990) Gender and relationships: A developmental account. *American Psychologist* **45**(4), 513–520.

Maccoby E.E. (1991) Different reproductive strategies in males and females. *Child Development* **62**, 676–682.

Maccoby E.E., Doering C.H., Jacklin C.N. & Kraemer H. (1979) Concentrations of sex hormones in umbilical-cord blood: Their relation to sex and birth order of infants. *Child Development* **50**, 602–612.

Maccoby E.E. & Jacklin C.N. (1974) *The Psychology of Sex Differences*. Stanford University Press, Stanford, California.

Magnusson D., Stattin H. & Allen V.L. (1985) Biological maturation and social development: A longitudinal study of some adjustment processes from mid-adolescence to adulthood. *Journal of Youth and Adolescence* **14**(4), 267–283.

Mangelsdorf S., Gunnar M., Kestenbaum R., Lang S. & Andreas D. (1990) Infant proneness-to-distress temperament, maternal personality, and mother–infant attachment: Associations and goodness of fit. *Child Development* **61**(3), 820–831.

Marcus J., Maccoby E.E., Jacklin C.N. & Doering C.H. (1985) Individual differences in mood in early childhood: Their relation to gender and neonatal sex steroids. *Developmental Psychobiology* **18**, 327–340.

Matthews K.A. (1992) Myths and realities: The menopause. *Psychosomatic Medicine* **54**(1), 1–9.

Matthews K.A., Bromberger J. & Egeland G. (1990)

Behavioral antecedents and consequences of the menopause. In Korenman S.G. (ed.) *The Menopause*, pp. 1–15. Serono Symposia, Norwell, Massachusetts.

Mead M. (1928) *Coming of Age in Samoa*. William Morrow, New York.

Meaney M.J., Stewart J. & Beatty W.W. (1985) Sex differences in social play: The socialization of sex roles. *Advances in the Study of Behavior* **15**, 1–58.

Meyer-Bahlburg H.F., Ehrhardt A.A., Bell J.J. *et al.* (1985a) Idiopathic precocious puberty in girls' psychosexual development and psychosocial development. *Journal of Youth and Adolescence* **14**(4), 339–353.

Meyer-Bahlburg H.F., Ehrhardt A.A., Feldman J.F., Rosen L.R., Veridiano N.P. & Zimmerman I. (1985b) Sexual activity level and sexual functioning in women prenatally exposed to diethylstilbestrol. *Psychosomatic Medicine* **47**(6), 497–511.

Meyer-Bahlburg H.F., Feldman J.F., Cohen P. & Ehrhardt A.A. (1988) Perinatal factors in the development of gender related play behavior: Sex hormones versus pregnancy complications. *Psychiatry* **51**(3), 260–261.

Money J. & Athanasion R. (1973) Eve first, or Adam? *Contemporary Psychology* **18**, 593–594.

Money J. & Ehrhardt A.A. (1972) *Man and Woman, Boy and Girl*. Johns Hopkins University Press, Baltimore, Maryland.

Money J. & Pollitt E. (1964) Cytogenetic and psychosexual ambiguity: Klinefelter's syndrome and transvestism compared. *Archives of General Psychiatry* **11**, 589–595.

Moore K.A., Nord C.W. & Peterson J.L. (1989) Nonvoluntary sexual activity among adolescents. *Family Planning Perspectives* **21**(3), 110–114.

Morganstern M. (1973) The psychosexual development of the retarded. In de la Cruz F.F. & LaVeck G.D. (eds) *Human Sexuality and the Mentally Retarded*, pp. 15–28. Brunner/Mazel, New York.

Moss H. (1967) Sex, age, and state as determinants of mother–infant interaction. *Merrill-Palmer Quarterly* **13**, 19–36.

Nagai K., Yanagisawa I. & Hayashi K. (1991) The cloning of size heterogeneous, Y specific repetitive DNAs and their clinical application. *Molecular and Cellular Biochemistry* **16**(100), 71–78.

Nakahori Y., Hamano K., Iwaya M. & Nakagome Y. (1991) Sex identification by polymerase chain reaction using X-Y homologous primer. *American Journal of Medical Genetics* **39**(4), 472–473.

Nielsen J. & Sillesen I. (1981) Turner's syndrome in 115 Danish girls born between 1955 and 1966. *Acta Jutlandica LIV, Medicine Series ZZ*, Arhus.

Ortner A., Glatzl J. & Karpellus E. (1987) Clinical and endocrinologic study of precocious puberty in girls. *Archives of Gynecological Research* **240**(2), 81–93.

Paikoff R.L. (1990) Attitudes toward consequences of pregnancy in young women attending a family planning clinic. *Journal of Adolescent Research* **5**(4), 467–484.

Paikoff R.L. & Brooks-Gunn J. (1990a) Associations between pubertal hormones and behavioral and affective expression. In Holmes C.S. (ed.) *Psychoneuroendocrinology: Brain, Behavior, and Hormonal Interactions*, pp. 205–226. Springer, New York.

Paikoff R.L. & Brooks-Gunn J. (1990b) Physiological processes: What role do they play during the transition to adolescence? In Montemayor R., Adams G. & Gullotta T. (eds) *Advances in Adolescent Development*, Vol. 2, *The Transition from Childhood to Adolescence*, pp. 63–81. Sage, Newbury Park, California.

Paikoff R.L. & Brooks-Gunn J. (1991) Do parent–child relationships change during puberty? *Psychological Bulletin* **110**, 47–66.

Paikoff R.L. & Brooks-Gunn J. (in press) Taking fewer chances: Teenage pregnancy prevention programs. *American Psychologist*.

Paikoff R.L., Brooks-Gunn J. & Carlton-Ford S. (1991) Effect of reproductive status changes upon family functioning and well-being of mothers and daughters. *Journal of Early Adolescence* **11**(2), 201–220.

Parlee M.B. (1984) Reproductive issues, including menopause. In Baruch G. & Brooks-Gunn J. (eds) *Women in Midlife*, pp. 303–314. Plenum, New York.

Pescovitz O.H., Comite F., Hench K. *et al.* (1986) The National Institute of Health experience with precocious puberty: Diagnostic sub-groups and response to short-term luteinizing hormone releasing hormone analogue therapy. *Journal of Pediatrics* **108**(1), 47–54.

Peterson R.E., Imperato-McGinley J., Gautier T. & Sturla E. (1977) Male pseudohermaphrodism due to steroid 5 alpha-reductase deficiency. *American Journal of Medicine* **62**, 170–191.

Powers S.I., Hauser S.T. & Kilner L.A. (1989) Adolescent mental health. *American Psychologist* **44**(2), 200–208.

Rappaport R., Fontoura M. & Brauner R. (1987) Treatment of central precocious puberty with an LHRH agonist (Buserelin): Effect on growth and bone maturation after three years of treatment. *Hormone Research* **28**(24), 149–154.

Remafedi G. (1987) Homosexual youth: A challenge to contemporary society. *Journal of the American Medical Association* **258**(2), 222–225.

Rierdan J. & Koff E. (1991) Depressive symptomatology among very early maturing girls. *Journal of Youth and Adolescence* **20**(4), 415–425.

Ross J.L. (1990) Disorders of the sex chromosomes: Medical overview. In Holmes C.S. (ed.) *Psychoneuroendocrinology: Brain, Behavior, and Hormonal Interactions*, pp. 127–137. Springer, New York.

Ruble D.N. (1983) The development of social-comparison processes and their role in achievement-related self-socialization. In Higgins E.T., Ruble D.N. & Hartup W.W. (eds) *Social Cognition and Social Development*, pp. 134–157. Cambridge University Press, New York.

Ruble D.N. (1987) The acquisition of self-knowledge: A self-socialization perspective. In Eisenberg N. (ed.) *Contemporary Topics in Developmental Psychology*, pp. 243–270. Wiley, New York.

Ruble D.N. & Ruble T.L. (1982) Sex-role stereotypes. In Miller A.G. (ed.) *In the Eye of the Beholder: Contemporary Issues in Stereotyping*, pp. 188–252. Holt, Rinehart & Winston, New York.

Rutter M. (1971) Normal psychosexual development. *Journal of Child Psychology and Psychiatry* **11**, 259–283.

Savin-Williams R.C. (1987) *Adolescence: An Ethological Perspective*. Springer, New York.

Savin-Williams R.C. (1990) *Gay and Lesbian Youth: Expressions of Identity*. Hemisphere Publishing Corporation, Washington, DC.

Savin-Williams R.C. & Berndt T.J. (1990) Friendships and peer relations. In Feldman S. & Elliott G. (eds) *At the Threshold: The Developing Adolescent*, pp. 277–307. Harvard University Press, Cambridge, Massachusetts.

Silber T.J. (1986) Anorexia nervosa in blacks and hispanics. *International Journal of Eating Disorders* **51**, 121–128.

Simon W. & Gagnon J. (1969) On psychosexual development. In Goslin D. (ed.) *Handbook of Socialization Theory and Research*, pp. 733–752. Rand-McNally, Chicago, Illinois.

Simmons R.G. & Blyth D.A. (1987) *Moving into Adolescence: The Impact of Pubertal Change and School Context*. Aldine De Gruyter, New York.

Simmons R.G., Blyth D.A. & McKinney K.L. (1983) The social and psychological effects of puberty on white females. In Brooks-Gunn J. & Petersen A.C. (eds) *Girls at Puberty: Biological and Psychosocial Perspectives*, pp. 229–272. Plenum, New York.

Sonentstein F.L., Pleck J.H. & Ku L.C. (1989) Sexual activity, condom use and AIDS awareness among adolescent males. *Family Planning Perspectives* **21**(4), 152–158.

Spencer M.B. & Dornbusch S.M. (1990) Challenges in studying minority youth. In Feldman S.S. & Elliott G.R. (eds) *At the Threshold: The Developing Adolescent*, pp. 123–146. Harvard University Press, Cambridge, Massachusetts.

Sroufe L.A. (1979) The coherence of individual development: Early care, attachment and subsequent developmental issues. *American Psychologist* **34**(10), 834–841.

Sroufe L.A. (1983) Infant caregiver attachment and patterns of adaptation in pre-school: The roots of maladaptation and competence. In Perlmutter M. (ed.) *Minnesota Symposium on Child Psychology*, Vol. 16, pp. 41–83. Lawrence Erlbaum, Hillsdale, New Jersey.

Sroufe L.A., Egeland B. & Kreutzer T. (1990) The fate of early experience following developmental change: Longitudinal approaches to individual adaptation in childhood. *Child Development* **61**(5), 1363–1372.

Sroufe L.A. & Waters E. (1977) Attachment as an organizational construct. *Child Development* **48**, 1184–1199.

Stangor C. & Ruble D.N. (1987) Development of gender role knowledge and gender constancy. *New Directions for Child Development* **38**, 5–22.

Stattin H. & Magnusson D. (1990) *Pubertal Maturation in Female Development*. Lawrence Erlbaum, Hillsdale, New Jersey.

Stewart J. & Cygan D. (1980) Ovarian hormones act early in development to feminize adult open-field behavior in the rat. *Hormones and Behavior* **14**, 20–32.

Tanner J.M. (1962) *Growth at Adolescence*. Blackwell Scientific Publications, Oxford.

Taylor R.D. & Carter D.B. (1987) The association between children's gender understanding, sex-role knowledge, and sex-role preferences. *Child Study Journal* **17**(3), 185–196.

Thomson S.K. (1975) Gender labels and early sex-role development. *Child Development* **46**, 339–347.

Thorne B. (1986) Girls and boys together . . . but mostly apart: Gender arrangements in elementary schools. In Hartup W.W. & Rubin Z. (eds) *Relationships and Development*, pp. 167–184. Lawrence Erlbaum, Hillsdale, New Jersey.

Thorne B. & Luria Z. (1986) Sexuality and gender in children's daily worlds. *Social Problems* **33**(3), 176–190.

Udry J.R. (1988) Biological predispositions and social control in adolescent sexual behavior. *American Sociological Review* **53**, 709–722.

Vaillant G.E. (1977) *Adaptation to Life: How the Best and Brightest Came of Age*. Little, Brown & Co., Boston, Massachusetts.

Waldron I. (1983) Sex differences in human mortality: The role of genetic factors. *Social Science Medicine* **17**(6), 321–333.

Waldron I. (1985) What do we know about causes of sex differences in mortality? A review of the literature. *Population Bulletin of the United Nations* **18**, 59–76.

Westney O.E., Jenkins R.R. & Benjamin C.M. (1983) Sociosexual development of pre-adolescents. In Brooks-Gunn J. & Petersen A.C. (eds) *Girls at Puberty: Biological and Psychosocial Perspectives*, pp. 273–300. Plenum, New York.

Yalom I.D., Green R. & Fisk N. (1973) Prenatal exposure to female hormones: Effect on psychosexual development in boys. *Archives of General Psychiatry* **28**(4), 554–561.

Zaslow M.J. & Hayes C.D. (1986) Sex differences in children's response to psychosocial stress: toward a cross-context analysis. In Lamb M.E., Brown A. & Rogoff B. (eds) *Advances in Developmental Psychology*, Vol. 4, pp. 285–337. Lawrence Erlbaum, Hillsdale, New Jersey.

Zucker K.J. & Green R. (1992) Psychosexual disorders in children and adolescents. *Journal of Child Psychology and Psychiatry* **33**(1), 107–151.

22: Psychological Ageing in Lifespan Perspective

MARGIE E. LACHMAN AND PAUL B. BALTES

INTRODUCTION

In contrast to the static view of old age portrayed in traditional gerontological approaches, a lifespan view conveys the dynamic and developmental nature of ageing. To treat old age merely as a period at the end of life is to miss the process of ageing, the variety of pathways and the multitude of outcomes. A lifespan perspective allows one to see the diversity of ageing across individuals and time periods and to understand old age as the outcome of life history as well as cultural and historical contexts (Featherman, 1983; Baltes, 1987; Riley, 1987).

The goal of this chapter is to illuminate the nature of psychological ageing using a lifespan perspective. This approach embodies four major themes. First, there is much heterogeneity in the nature and course of ageing. Second, ageing is characterized by both gains and losses. This multidirectional nature of ageing is best understood using a multidimensional conception of functioning, enabling the depiction of diverse life course trajectories. A third theme is the modifiability and plasticity of ageing processes. Many people assume that changes in later life are inevitable and irreversible. In fact, there is evidence that — despite a reduced range of plasticity — declines can be modulated and functioning in some areas can be enhanced to earlier levels. Indeed there is the possibility of promoting continued growth in some psychological realms in later life through intervention programmes. A fourth theme touches on the psychological mechanisms of successful ageing, specifically the processes of selective optimization with compensation and self-management strategies. Along with the rapid growth in the proportion of elderly adults and increasing longevity, there has been an increasing focus among scientists and policy makers on maintaining the quality of life and promoting 'successful ageing'. In discussing these four themes, findings are used primarily from two substantive areas, cognition and personality, to illustrate the fruitfulness of a lifespan approach to ageing.

HETEROGENEITY OF AGEING

Interindividual variability

A central assumption since gerontology emerged as a field of study had been the expectation of a high degree of similarity between persons who have reached old age (Cowdry, 1939; Birren, 1959). In general, it was assumed that the determinants of ageing were such a powerful and common force that older persons would manifest much communality. The assumption of homogeneity may derive from the belief that development in later life is similar to that in childhood, where there is some degree of 'universality' and a fair amount of regularity in the nature and course of development. As to old age, however, the scientific evidence, especially that from long-term longitudinal studies, did not corroborate this expectation (Schaie, 1979; Lehr & Thomae, 1987; Maddox, 1987; Nesselroade, 1989; Dannefer & Nelson, 1992). For example, there is little empirical evidence in support of an invariant sequence of stages during adulthood as proposed by some theorists (Erikson, 1963; Vaillant, 1977; Levinson, 1986).

A number of longitudinal analyses have demonstrated the long-term continuity of behaviour (Caspi et al., 1987; Costa & McCrae, 1992). However, the patterns are variable. Individual differences in childhood experiences are played out years later in adulthood. Elder and Liker (1982) found that girls in the middle class whose families had experienced significant financial loss during the Depression had higher mastery and coped better with stress in old age than those in the working class and those in the middle class who had few financial difficulties in childhood. Childhood personality also seems to show consistency over time. Caspi *et al.* (1987) found that undercontrolled children, characterized by temper tantrums and aggressive behaviours, had difficulties in adulthood. The ill-tempered children had lower educational attainment, more unstable employment patterns, and were more likely to divorce than other children when they reached middle age.

There is much evidence of diversity in the nature of development in later life (Maddox, 1987; Institute of Medicine, 1991). It is particularly noteworthy that the substantial interindividual variability observed applies not only to behavioural functioning but to biomedical indicators as well (Costa & Andres, 1986; Rowe & Kahn, 1987; Dannefer & Nelson, 1992).

In the psychological realm, interindividual variability is clearly demonstrated for the case of intellectual ageing. Using cohort-sequential and longitudinal designs, Schaie (1988) demonstrated that persons who, for example, traverse the age range from 60 to 80 years exhibit quite distinct patterns of change. Although many show stability or decreases in level of performance, some demonstrate an increase (Fig. 22.1). In the light of these findings, it is certainly inappropriate to speak of a general and universal ageing loss in intelligence.

The spectrum of interindividual variability is sup-plemented with intraperson variability in the direction of change. Not only between persons but also within people, some aspects of functioning improve (e.g. crystallized intelligence) while others decline (e.g. fluid intelligence) or remain stable over time. Moreover, the directionality of change on the same dimension may vary between individuals. Some people may increase functioning in a particular area, but others may show decrements or stability.

Group differences among the elderly

The important distinction that Neugarten (1974) made in the 1970s between the young-old and old-old has become even more critical as the old-old group has become the fastest growing segment of the populations in many Western nations. Much of what is known about ageing is based on the study of the 'young-old' (Neugarten, 1974), covering the age range of approximately 60–75. There are tremendous differences between the young-old and old-old (Institute of Medicine, 1991). This heterogeneity within the elderly group is not only tied to age because to a large extent individual differences are not age-related at all, but the result of a complex set of genetic, psychosocial and experiential factors. There are many examples of 75 year olds who function at a higher level than some 65 year olds. In the first wave of the Berlin Ageing Study, for instance, which is based on a representative sample of 70–100 year olds, an 87-year-old woman was the top performer in an extensive battery of cognitive tests (Lindenberger, 1990).

There is also great diversity in the experience of ageing across gender, ethnic and other subgroups. Starting with very basic demographic facts, it becomes apparent how the nature of ageing can be so vastly different. For example, it is well known that the life expectancy of women is higher than that of men. Today in the USA, at birth men can expect to live to 71.4 and women to 78.3. Such demographic facts have important implications for daily life. Whereas 77.7% of men over 65 years of age are married, only 41.5% of women in this age group are. The result is that a larger proportion of women live alone or in institutions than do men. Although only 5% of Americans over age 65 live in institutions such as nursing homes, 75% of those who do are female.

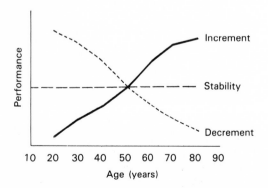

Fig. 22.1 Interindividual differences and intraindividual variability in lifespan trajectories.

Normal versus pathological ageing

Another way to highlight the significance of diversity in human ageing is the focus on optimal versus normal versus pathological ageing. These distinctions are not easily drawn (Rowe & Kahn, 1987; Fries, 1989; Manton, 1989; Gerok & Brandtstadter, 1992), but they are heuristically useful. Normal ageing refers to growing old without a manifest illness, whether physical or mental. Up to age 70 or 80, this is a fairly frequent process. Optimal ageing implies ageing under the best personal and environmental conditions. Understanding the conditions for optimal ageing is the primary research motivation for many gerontologists. Finally, pathological ageing refers to a process of ageing where there is clear evidence for physical or mental pathology.

Using the area of memory functioning it is possible to illustrate the differing views on the nature of human ageing that can result from a consideration of the difference between optimal, normal and pathological ageing. Memory in the optimal sense would continue to function at levels comparable to early ages, perhaps through use of mnemonics. Normal ageing would be associated with some memory loss, most often in working memory, without major implications for everyday functioning. In contrast, pathological ageing would be characterized by serious organic impairments in memory due to senile dementia of the Alzheimer type.

This distinction leads to two possible scenarios. The first, an optimistic vision of the future of old age, foresees healthy ageing and a general state of well-being of future elderly cohorts. In gerontology, this scenario has been proffered and defended primarily by the medical researcher Fries (1989, 1990). He derives this view from two main assumptions. The first assumption is that there is a definite biological maximum to the human lifespan. On average, this genetically fixed limit to length of life is estimated by Fries to be close to 90 years with a standard deviation of some 5–10 years. Death is expected to occur whenever individuals have reached their maximum lifespan.

Fries' second basic assumption is that the time course of many illnesses can be slowed down to such a degree that they would not be manifest before the genetically fixed lifespan was completed. According to Fries, such a deceleration of pathological processes is a real possibility because twentieth century medical research had demonstrated that chronic diseases, the major component of pathological ageing, are subject to much deceleration or even prevention.

The second vision of the future of an ageing society stands in sharp contrast with Fries' model and focuses on pathological ageing. Increased longevity would not be associated with more health and vitality but with increased sickness. The primary reasons for this prediction are the so-called ageing diseases, that is, diseases whose incidence rates increase in old age. The most widely discussed exemplar is senile dementia of the Alzheimer type, which currently has no cure. The incidence probability of this disease correlates highly with age. The incidence rate in the Western world is estimated to be about 5% by age 70, 15% by age 80 and 30% by age 90 (Häfner, 1986; Sorensen *et al.*, 1986; Evans *et al.*, 1989). It is assumed that as more and more people reach an advanced age, more and more people would be afflicted.

Current research evidence does not permit a decision on which of the two scenarios is more likely to be true. If anything, the evidence suggests that both arguments have some validity and that both types of processes are operative. What is critical in the present context, however, is the importance of the distinction between normal and pathological ageing. For the most part, it is the process of pathological ageing that alters the quality of human ageing. The majority of older persons, at least up to age 75 or so, are fairly healthy. The focus of the present chapter, therefore, is on the 'normal' course of ageing; that is, the gains and losses that typically accompany growing old in industrialized countries.

MULTIDIMENSIONALITY AND MULTIDIRECTIONALITY

Psychological ageing not only varies across individuals; it also varies within individuals and across domains of functioning, with some dimensions increasing, others decreasing, and some remaining stable (see Fig. 22.1). It is important to take a multidimensional approach when conceptualizing and operationalizing variables to maximize sensitivity to the differential patterns of change.

Intellectual ageing

The importance of taking a multidimensional approach to the assessment of psychological functioning is dramatically illustrated in the field of intellectual ageing. The conclusion reached from studies using unidimensional (omnibus) assessments of intelligence such as IQ is not very informative, and perhaps misleading, as such intelligence scores are a composite of rather diverse categories of functioning (Horn, 1970). In contrast, when intelligence was separated into subcomponents, such as 'fluid' and 'crystallized' abilities (Horn, 1970; Cattell, 1971; Baltes *et al.*, 1984), it became apparent that different aspects of intelligence showed differential trajectories of age change. These differential patterns were obscured when subtests were summed to create one general intelligence score.

A robust pattern of intellectual ageing has emerged in the literature. Those skills that are dependent on knowledge and experience show maintenance and stability into the seventh and eighth decade of life, whereas those that involve speed of information processing, basic memory functioning and complex reasoning skills show declines with ageing (Baltes *et al.*, 1984; Salthouse, 1991). Baltes and co-workers have contrasted the fluid 'mechanics' of intelligence (comparable to the neurophysiological architecture of the brain) with the crystallized and knowledge-based 'pragmatics' of intelligence which are comparable to aspects of knowledge-based software. In accord with Cattell (1971) and Horn (1970, 1982), the expectation is that there is a loss with ageing in the mechanics of the mind, but that pragmatic knowledge is an important modulator that can enrich the mind in important new ways, including the compensation of ageing losses in the cognitive mechanics (Baltes, 1987; Kliegl & Baltes, 1987; Staudinger *et al.*, 1989; Baltes & Smith, 1990).

In keeping with the heterogeneity theme, the magnitude and timing of these changes vary widely. In fact, there is some evidence that the majority of older adults do not experience major decrements in

functioning until their seventies (Schaie, 1990). However, around age 80 or so, there is a cumulative hazard, with more and more of the cognitive abilities involved in more and more individuals.

What declines?

What accounts for declines in intelligence, memory and other cognitive functions? There are a number of viable hypotheses, but there is no conclusive evidence in support of any one. One of the most prominent hypotheses is the speed hypothesis (Salthouse, 1987, 1991). Given that most intelligence tests are timed, if older adults suffer from peripheral or central slowing, this could account for age differences in performance. In fact, when intelligence tests are given under untimed conditions, performance does improve (Hofland *et al.*, 1981). Moreover, in efforts to analyse the contributing role of speed factors (Hertzog *et al.*, 1990), it was demonstrated that controlling for a measure of speed eliminates a major share of the observed age decline (Mayr *et al.*, 1991).

Another viable hypothesis is that age differences reflect the relative disuse of cognitive functions by the elderly (Salthouse, 1987). Because older adults do not regularly participate in environments that demand the use of complex cognitive or speeded functions their performance may have deteriorated, similar to the atrophy of unused muscles. Indeed, when older adults practise cognitive tasks, their performance improves significantly (Baltes & Lindenberger, 1988; Lachman, 1991). However, because the age differences are typically not eliminated after practice and younger adults improve as much when trained, disuse has not gained a great deal of support as an explanatory factor.

What is the application of these findings for everyday functioning? It does suggest that older adults will be slower and less efficient at solving complex problems, especially if the problems are novel. However, tasks that require knowledge and experience will find the older adult in a comparatively better situation. In this context, education and health function as added protective factors.

What improves with age? — wisdom

There is evidence that in some areas, such as professional expertise (Charness, 1985; Ericsson, 1990; Featherman *et al.*, 1990) and wisdom (Clayton & Birren, 1980; Holliday & Chandler, 1986; Baltes & Smith, 1990; Dittman-Kohli & Baltes, 1990; Smith & Baltes, 1990; Sternberg, 1990), older adults can exhibit advances in select domains of knowledge and problem-solving. For many, scientists and lay-persons alike, wisdom is inherently not a subject for empirical, scientific analysis. Despite a legitimate concern for the possible shortcomings of empirical methodology, Baltes and co-workers have joined the growing number of scholars in various fields ranging from history (Assmann, 1991) to philosophy (Kekes, 1983; Oelmüller, 1989) and psychology (Sternberg, 1990), who have begun to tackle this task.

The conceptual approach of the Berlin group to the study of wisdom is developed from three lines of research: (i) lifespan developmental psychology (Sorensen *et al.*, 1986; Baltes, 1987); (ii) the study of expert systems (Chi *et al.*, 1982; Glaser, 1984; Hoyer, 1985; Ericsson, 1990); and (iii) efforts to identify positive aspects of cognitive ageing (Labouvie-Vief, 1977, 1982; Dixon & Baltes, 1986; Commons *et al.*, 1989; Staudinger *et al.*, 1989;

Perlmutter, 1990). The Berlin model of the facets of wisdom is shown in Fig. 22.2.

By integrating perspectives offered by each of these lines of scholarship, the content domain of wisdom is specified as an 'expertise in the fundamental pragmatics of life permitting exceptional insight and judgment involving complex and uncertain matters of the human condition'. The body of knowledge associated with wisdom entails, for example, insight into the core conditions of life and the course of life, including its plasticity, limitations and essential vulnerability. It also involves knowledge about differing pathways of life development, frequent patterns of conflict, and the embeddedness of lifespan development in the process of generational and historical flow. Furthermore, the body of wisdom-associated knowledge contains information concerning the structure, dynamics and weighting of life goals, their likely sequencing, and the meaning of life.

In the next step and as shown in Fig. 22.2, the Berlin group has specified a set of five criteria: (i) expertise in pragmatics of life; (ii) interpretive and evaluative knowledge; (iii) contextual richness; (iv) consideration of uncertainty and relativism; and

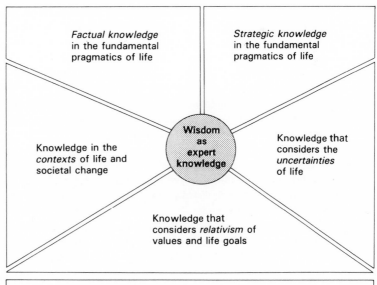

Fig. 22.2 The Berlin model of wisdom as an expertise in the fundamental pragmatics of life.

(v) good judgement and advice giving. They are postulated to define the nature of a body of knowledge about the fundamental pragmatics of life that is necessary to qualify as an expert. Together, these criteria can be used to evaluate the quantity and quality of the targeted knowledge domain.

The main methodological strategy in the investigation of wisdom has been to ask people to respond to difficult life problems by thinking aloud about the problems (after they have practised the method of thinking aloud; see Ericsson & Simon, 1984) and to record their answers. For example, one dilemma involves a 60-year-old widow who recently opened her own business. After hearing that her son, who lives out of town, was just left alone to care for his two small children, she must decide whether to give up her business and move to help her son (Baltes & Smith, 1990). Subsequently, the answers are transcribed and evaluated for the degree to which the five criteria are represented. Responses are judged to reflect wisdom only if the entire family of five criteria are represented at a level considered to be superior.

In several studies, adults of differing ages and professional backgrounds were studied (Baltes & Smith, 1990; Smith & Baltes, 1990). The research participants were asked to think aloud about various problems of life planning and life review. First, unlike what is often found with traditional measures of intellectual functioning, there was no evidence for lower performance of older adults. Second, there was definite evidence that growing old, if it is combined with relevant professional experience, could result in comparatively higher levels of performance. For example, in some tasks a large share of the highest scores was achieved by older practising clinical psychologists. Such findings are in clear contrast to work on the fluid 'mechanics' of the mind, such as research on primary memory, where no older adults are found in the top region of the performance distribution (Kliegl *et al.*, 1989; Baltes & Kliegl, 1992).

This emerging research on wisdom has demonstrated that certain facets of wisdom are measurable and that wisdom-related knowledge may be a part of the latent cognitive potential occasionally attributed to the ageing mind. Old age in itself, of course, does not guarantee wisdom. But it seems possible in principle that growing old — when embedded in a facilitative social context and not impaired by a brain-related illness — provides the opportunity for growth in select bodies of knowledge, such as professional expertise and wisdom.

Personality and ageing

In the psychometric personality field, multidimensional conceptions have long been the dominant view. Starting with early views of temperament (e.g. the Roman physician Galen's idea of the sanguine, melancholic, choleric and phlegmatic types) (Liebert & Spiegler, 1990), personality has been conceptualized in terms of types or traits. Cattell (1965), for example, presented a view of personality with 16 primary dimensions (e.g. tough-minded, suspicious).

The most prominent view of personality today is that there are five major dimensions, known as the 'big five', that account for much of the variation in individual differences (see Chapter 4). The dimensions are known as neuroticism (stability), extraversion, openness to experience (intellectual flexibility), agreeableness and conscientiousness. As with intelligence, there is evidence that some dimensions are more stable than others. It appears that older adults become more extraverted and less open to experience, but show little change on other dimensions (McCrae & Costa, 1990; Costa & McCrae, 1992). These findings are consistent with findings from the Kansas City studies regarding a shift from active to passive mastery and an introspective orientation in later life (Neugarten, 1968).

Some researchers emphasize primarily the stability of personality (McCrae & Costa, 1990). Those who are extraverted at early ages continue to be more extraverted relative to others in later life, even if average levels of extraversion decrease in later life.

However, it is also possible that the amount of stability obtained in such research is an overestimation. When people respond on self-report questionnaires, they are likely to use different and age-adjusted levels of comparison; that is, at 30 years of age one's assessment is based on comparisons with other 30 year olds, and a 70 year old may compare herself implicitly with other 70 year olds.

The stability view of personality, therefore, is currently undergoing a major re-examination.

Sense of control

Control has been identified as a central dimension for well-being and continued adaptivity in later life (Rodin *et al.*, 1985; Baltes & Baltes, 1986; Rowe & Kahn, 1987). Along with social support, the sense of control is among the best psychosocial predictors of good psychological and physical functioning, including morbidity and mortality (Rowe & Kahn, 1987).

In a review of age differences in locus of control, Lachman (1986) found that most studies had used unidimensional conceptions of control. The results were mixed, with some finding increases in external control, others finding decreases in external control and others finding no differences in control between age groups. In recent work using multidimensional conceptions of control, with separate internal and external control dimensions, as well as domain-specific assessments, the findings have been more consistent.

What happens to control beliefs over the adult lifespan?

One would expect that perceived control would wane because, in fact, the frequency of uncontrollable events does increase with ageing (e.g. mandatory retirement, increasing probability of being touched by illness or death). The evidence suggests that changes in control beliefs are specialized, in that they occur in some domains and not in others. With age there appears to be an increase in external beliefs in control, but the sense of internal control does not decline. Thus, older adults are more likely to believe that external factors are operating to affect outcomes in their life. At the same time, however, they do not lose a sense of their own personal efficacy. This balance seems to be maintained well into later life (Lachman, 1986).

The sense of control varies across dimensions and domains. Levenson (1981) has offered a three-dimensional conception, including internal factors, chance and powerful others as sources of control. We have examined changes in the sense of control in the intellectual, health, interpersonal and political domains.

Our assessment of control in the domain of intellectual/cognitive functioning is the Personality in Intellectual Contexts Inventory (PIC; Lachman *et al.*, 1982; Lachman, 1986), which assesses perceived control over problem-solving and memory tasks. For example, respondents indicate their agreement with statements such as: 'I know if I keep using my memory I will never lose it', 'There's nothing I can do to preserve my mental clarity', and 'I would have to ask a salesperson to figure out how much I'd save with a 20% discount'.

The age patterns are remarkably consistent across studies. The means for general and intellectual control from one study of 200 adults randomly drawn from four town registers in suburban Boston are presented in Fig. 22.3 (Lachman, 1991). There were no significant age differences for the general control scales on the internal and powerful others scales, but there was an age difference on the general chance scale, with the two older groups more externally orientated than the young and middle-aged groups.

There were significant age differences on all three dimensions for intellectual control: the older groups had lower internal beliefs and higher chance and powerful others beliefs than the young. Note that a loss of control in Fig. 22.3 is indicated by decreases in the internal dimension (a) and increases in the external dimensions (b and c). For internal intellectual control beliefs, the significant decrease occurred for the oldest group (over 75). In contrast, for the external intellectual dimensions, the significant changes (i.e. increases) were earlier, from the middle-aged to the 60–75-year-old group. It is important to note that the differences remained significant when health (number of reported illnesses) and education were partialled out using analysis of covariance.

Comparable age differences have been found for the health domain. Older adults believed they were less in control of their health than the younger adults. There was, however, no indication that control beliefs decline in all domains. No age differences have been found for control beliefs in the interpersonal and political domains (Paulus & Christie, 1981).

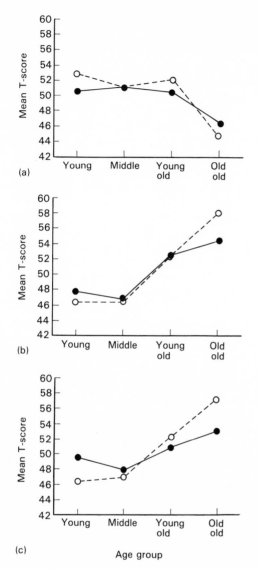

Dixon, 1987; Grover & Hertzog, 1991). A similar developmental pattern was found in a recent 5-year longitudinal study with older adults (Lachman & Leff, 1989). Over the 5-year period, adults over the age of 65 showed a decline in their sense of control over memory and other cognitive processes as well as in perceived control over health. In contrast, their beliefs about general control did not decline.

Control beliefs and cognitive performance

What are the implications of these control beliefs for performance? There is evidence that those with stronger external control beliefs show poorer performance than those who are more internally oriented (Lachman *et al.*, 1982; Grover & Hertzog, 1991). Also, maladaptive attributions have been associated with poorer performance. In one study, the elderly adults who did not take credit for memory success (that is, they made pessimistic, external, unstable and specific attributions) showed significant decrements in their performance over two trials (Lachman *et al.*, 1987).

A goal for future research is to explore the mechanisms that link control beliefs and performance (Cavanaugh, 1989). One possible mechanism is that the belief that one has low efficacy and little control over an outcome may curtail effort. Berry (1987) found that older adults with low self-efficacy for a memory task spent less time studying for the task than those with high efficacy. The better older adults believed their memories to be, the more time they devoted to processing memory tasks, and higher processing effort subsequently produced better memory performance (Berry, 1987). As Bandura (1989) suggested, people who view memory as a cognitive skill that they can improve are likely to exert the effort needed to memorize effectively. 'Those who regard memory as an inherent capacity that declines with biological aging have little reason to try to exercise control over their memory functioning' (Bandura, 1989, p. 733).

Control beliefs and health

Another important question concerns the role of control beliefs in health promotion. On the basis of

Fig. 22.3 Age group differences in general (●) and intellectual (○) control beliefs about dimensions of (a) internal; (b) chance; and (c) powerful others control (Lachman, 1991).

The pattern of cross-sectional results shows that older adults feel their cognitive efficacy and competence is declining, that there is little that can be done about it, and that they need to depend on others for problem-solving and remembering things (Cornelius & Caspi, 1986; Hultsch, Hertzog &

experimental interventions, longitudinal studies and surveys there is evidence that control beliefs play a role in health (Rodin *et al.*, 1985; Peterson, Seligman & Vaillant, 1988; Abeles, 1991; Rodin & Timko, 1992). Beliefs may affect health through physiological mechanisms such as the immunological or neuroendocrine systems (Rodin & Timko, 1992). Another potential class of mediators of the relationship between control and health are cognitive factors, which may bias a person's awareness or reporting of symptoms. Also, behavioural factors, i.e. whether or not a person takes action to prevent disease and promote health, may serve as mediators (Rakowski, 1986).

We investigated the mediating role of a healthy lifestyle in a sample of 150 middle-aged and older adults (Ziff *et al.*, 1991). Control beliefs were found to be significantly correlated with both subjective and objective assessments of health. Those with higher mastery and internal control beliefs were healthier and those with higher external beliefs were less healthy. Health-promoting behaviours (e.g. exercise, regulation of diet) were positively correlated with mastery and negatively correlated with chance. A healthy lifestyle was correlated with only one of the health variables, the subjective health rating. Those who engaged in more good health practices reported they were in better health.

The behavioural mediation hypothesis was supported for the subjective health variable. Those who believed less in chance were more likely to participate in a healthy lifestyle, and were more likely to perceive themselves as being healthier. Those who did not believe fate or chance played much of a role in their lives were more likely to take actions to influence their health, and in turn, were more likely to feel good about their health, relative to that of their peers.

The lack of a relationship between a healthy lifestyle and current actual health status (number or seriousness of health problems) was not completely surprising. The benefits from changes in personal behaviour are likely to be cumulative and are rarely seen in the short run. Longitudinal data (Rutter, 1988) will be necessary to examine the long-term impact of a healthy lifestyle. The results support the notion that a healthy lifestyle makes people 'feel good', perhaps because it reflects a willingness to improve oneself or take control over one's life. Another interpretation is that it is health that affects control beliefs and health-promoting behaviour. Those who experience health problems may begin to feel that they have less control over their lives than they used to and they may not be as able to engage in health-promoting behaviours, such as exercise.

MODIFIABILITY

The theme of modifiability has two facets in the field of ageing. A first is the need to counteract the prevailing stereotype of old age as a state of frailty. Some of the evidence has been discussed for losses in various areas of psychological functioning in later life. One of the pervasive myths about ageing, however, is that such decrements are irreversible. The assumption is that declines are the result of 'the' ageing process and that they can not be modified. On the contrary, there is evidence that effective interventions can be implemented to remediate or enhance functioning in later life (Baltes, 1988; Carstensen, 1988; Riley & Riley, 1989).

The second theme is, as in many other areas of health research and policy, the consideration of different forms of intervention, including prevention. Interventions typically take the form of remedial treatment to 'fix what is already broken'. From a lifespan perspective it is also desirable to implement interventions for prevention, enhancement or optimization purposes (Fries, 1989). The design and timing of such interventions may be based on predictions about the anticipated direction and course of development, thereby making it possible to intervene in advance to stop the deteriorative processes or even to make ageing better than it exists under current medical and cultural conditions. The goal of intervention from a lifespan perspective is not just to avoid decline but to promote growth.

The period of old age is a relatively recent phenomenon. It is likely that older people have much developmental reserve capacity, which can be used to create better states of ageing. As intuitively true as it may seem, convincing empirical support for this has come only recently from intervention-oriented psychological research (Riley & Riley, 1989), although the call for such work was already evident in the 1970s (Baltes, 1973; Labouvie-Vief, 1977).

Cognitive training interventions

Research on the effects of cognitive training has demonstrated the ability of older persons to profit from practice and to engage in new learning (Denney, 1984; Willis, 1987; Baltes & Lindenberger, 1988; Perlmutter, 1988; Lachman *et al.*, 1992).

The main result from the study of cognitive reserve capacities in old age is clear and consistent. In the area of psychometric intelligence, it has been repeatedly demonstrated that most older adults (excluding those who have a brain-related disease such as Alzheimer's disease) are able to raise their level of performance following relatively simple programmes of cognitive training to that displayed by younger adults without training (see also Schaie & Willis, 1986; Willis, 1987). Even when older adults practise without explicit training in relevant problem-solving skills, they are successful in increasing their level of performance (Baltes *et al.*, 1989; Hayslip, 1989).

Similar and perhaps even more striking results have been obtained in another area, that is, memory functioning. Older adults taught new mnemonic techniques (such as the method of loci) can increase their recall for digits and words to a level that is clearly outside the usual range of adult perform-ance, such as recalling 25–30 words in correct position after a single (albeit slow) presentation (Kliegl *et al.*, 1989).

In this and related work, older adults have been trained to use a mnemonic technique called the method of loci (Bower, 1970; Yesavage & Rose, 1984; Kliegl *et al.*, 1989; Weaver & Lachman, 1992). In the method of loci, items on a list are visually associated with a route of familiar locations. The familiar locations serve as retrieval cues for the items on the list.

In one research paradigm used by Baltes and Kliegl, subjects continue to practise the method of loci for many sessions until they approximate the highest level of performance possible for them. It is important to recognize that such research is not only the study of a specific memory technique. Rather, the technique is useful for the study of mental imaging and associative ability which are not only key components of the method of loci but also fundamental constituents of many other cogni-tive activities.

This kind of intensive cognitive intervention identifies two characteristics of the ageing mind. On the one hand, the ageing mind holds more plasticity than is generally expected. At the same time, at limits of functioning, there are definite losses. The results show that by using the method of loci most elderly persons can perform outside the usual range of performance when recalling lists of words and digits (Kliegl & Baltes, 1987; Kliegl *et al.*, 1989; Baltes & Kliegl, 1992). On the other hand, when these training gains are compared with train-ing gains of young adults, older adults even after extensive training are not able to reach the level of performance that young adults can reach after very few sessions of training. Plasticity and age-associated limits to plasticity coexist. This finding is shown in Fig. 22.4.

In the study summarized in Fig. 22.4, healthy and well-educated young and older adults partici-pated in a 38-session training study, the length of the lists of words to be remembered in correct order was 30 words (Baltes & Kliegl, 1992). Note first that older adults were able to acquire the method of loci and recall on average about twice as many words as before training. Young adults, however, did better. In fact, the magnitude and robustness of the ageing loss in use of the method of loci is dramatic. Even after extensive training, older adults did not reach the same level of performance displayed by young adults after a few training sessions. Furthermore, as shown in the right panel of Fig. 22.4, none of the older adults performed at or above the average level of young adults. Not shown in the figure is another effect, that of speed. On average, older adults need about four to five times as long to produce the required mental images than young adults and they make more mistakes. Taken together, these findings suggest — despite substan-tial plasticity — a rather substantial ageing-related loss in at least some of the mental functions used in the memory task under consideration.

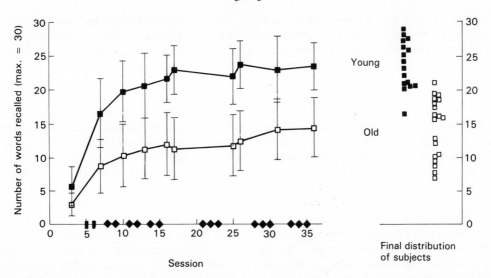

Fig. 22.4 Mean number of words recalled by young (■) and older (□) adults after instruction (▮) or practice (◆) in testing-the-limits research (Baltes & Kliegl, 1990).

Differential cognitive plasticity and clinical assessment

Research on the limits of cognitive efficacy (testing the limits) enriches past cognitive training work on age differences in developmental reserve capacity in the following manner: ageing losses of the mind seem to be clearly evident, especially when we approach the upper limits of the 'fluid' cognitive mechanics. In the case of mnemonic strategies involving processes of mental imagination and associative ability, these ageing losses are of such magnitude and robustness that practically none of the older persons could function at the same level as most young adults. Nevertheless, the degree of modifiability (plasticity) for older adults is quite large. The level of performance achieved after training is substantially better than prior levels.

Recently, there has been an effort to utilize the testing the limits paradigm for the purpose of clinical assessment. One of the main challenges in ageing research is the early and premorbid identification of Alzheimer's dementia. M. Baltes and co-workers predicted that persons in the early states of this illness may be different from other older persons in that their 'cognitive plasticity' would show early signs of loss. This prediction was supported in research with the kind of cognitive training pro-

grammes of fluid intelligence described above (M. Baltes *et al.*, 1992). Whereas the 'normal' old adult benefits from such training, the subgroup identified as at risk for Alzheimer's dementia (based on a standardized psychiatric interview) showed no evidence for training gains, although their baseline performance was not different from the no-risk group.

Such findings are encouraging and point to the potential of plasticity oriented assessment strategies. It is the deviation from standards of normality, that is that most if not all 'healthy' older persons have cognitive reserves (plasticity) to benefit from training, which makes the absence of training gains a significant finding. It will be interesting to see whether the notions of 'differential' plasticity or 'testing of limits' become salient in other domains of ageing research as well.

Diagnosis and treatment of depression in later life

Although Alzheimer's disease is receiving a great deal of attention, depression is of equal significance. In fact, according to some psychologists, depression is the number one mental health concern in later life (Newmann, 1989; Gatz & Hurwicz, 1990; Kessler *et al.*, 1992). And the highest suicide rate, one possible consequence of depression, is found among men over the age of 65 (Cohen, 1990). Not only is depression the most common mental health problem among the elderly, there is also evidence that the incidence of depression is highest in old age relative to other points in the lifespan. This conclusion, however, is not shared by medical epidemiological researchers (Hafner, 1992) who do not report an ageing-correlated increase in clinical depression. In future research, more attention needs to be paid to the question of symptoms which, when assessed with screening scales, show a U-shaped function, with the highest levels in those over age 70 (Kessler *et al.*, 1992).

An important goal for diagnosis and treatment in later life is to separate organic from non-organic problems, or the untreatable from the treatable. Symptoms are often attributed to the ageing process with the assumption they are untreatable. There are many factors that can mask or complicate symptoms in later life. Many older adults take multiple prescription and over-the-counter medications and the proper dosages as well as the interaction effects are not well known. A presenting problem of memory loss could be due to medication effects, depression, hearing impairment or cardiovascular disease, as well as senile dementia such as Alzheimer's disease.

As in other age groups, a large share of ageing-related problems may indeed be treatable with pharmacological, nutritional or psychosocial interventions. Cognitive behaviour therapy is one promising psychotherapeutic intervention for depression and other psychological problems among the elderly (Carstensen, 1988; Smyer *et al.*, 1990). One of the key techniques used in cognitive behavior therapy is cognitive restructuring of maladaptive beliefs. This technique has been successfully applied to the area of memory with older adults (Elliott & Lachman, 1989).

Cognitive restructuring of memory self-conceptions

It has been shown that older adults can successfully learn mnemonic techniques such as method of loci and imagery for names and faces (Zarit *et al.*, 1981; Poon, 1984; West, 1985; Yesavage, 1985; Baltes &

Lindenberger, 1988). On the one hand, this work has shown us the reserve capacity and plasticity of functioning in later life. On the other hand, it has shown us something about the limits of the ageing mind. In addition to the implications for clinical assessment outlined above (see also Albert, 1988), what are other practical implications of this intervention work in an area such as memory, which serves as a prototype of the negative aspects of the ageing mind?

One area involves the restructuring of negative beliefs about the ageing process (Elliott & Lachman, 1989; Lachman, 1991). Even though the older adult can learn mnemonic strategies, there is evidence that mnemonic strategies are rarely used after the training is completed (Poon, 1985; Anschutz *et al.*, 1987; Scogin & Bienias, 1988). Training effects show limited maintenance and generalizability. In fact, when the focus is on practical relevance, there has been a great deal of criticism of these mnemonic techniques because they have only limited utility for a small subset of tasks and few memory researchers endorse the use of such formal mnemonics for the purpose of intervention (Park *et al.*, 1990).

It is possible that strategy training is relatively ineffective because of the beliefs that the participants hold about memory ageing (Elliott & Lachman, 1989; Lachman *et al.*, 1992), i.e. that memory loss is inevitable and irreversible. Training may be more effective if it focuses on retraining efficacy and control beliefs about memory in addition to memory-enhancing strategies (Rodin *et al.*, 1987; Cavanaugh & Green, 1990). A growing body of research has demonstrated that good cognitive performance requires not only the requisite skills but also self-conceptions and efficacy beliefs that foster effective use of one's skills (Sternberg & Kolligian, 1990).

Those who believe memory problems are caused by ageing, and assume nothing can be done about it, will be unlikely to try remedial strategies or to engage in the extra effort required to compensate for memory problems in later life. Although some memory changes are related to ageing, cognitive intervention work suggests that there may be more reserve capacity with the possibility for remediation and compensation. It is important for older adults to understand that they *can* do something to improve their memories, by using effort or new strategies.

Lachman *et al.* (1992) hypothesized that motivation and performance would be strongly influenced by beliefs about memory functioning. On the one hand, age-associated maladaptive beliefs about memory are rooted in a 'shrinking entity' conception (Elliott & Lachman, 1989). From this perspective, the process of ageing is seen as leading to memory deficits that are inevitable and uncontrollable. Memory problems are attributed to lost capacity, and effort is seen as futile. This view sets the stage for decreases in efficacy expectations and a sense of hopelessness and helplessness (see also Langer, 1989).

In contrast, a sense of control over memory functioning is at the heart of an adaptive view of memory (Elliott & Lachman, 1989; Cavanaugh & Green, 1990). From this perspective, memory is seen as a body of skills that can be developed and maintained with effort. A view of memory as a body of acquirable skills may predispose people to persist in developing strategies to cope with memory problems and to make adaptive attributions in the face of difficulties. These tendencies may protect people against decreases in efficacy expectations and actually enhance them, by fostering effective problem-solving.

We developed a cognitive restructuring intervention (Elliott & Lachman, 1989; Lachman *et al.*, 1992) to educate people about these two conceptions of memory and to promote the adaptive view. This intervention involved modelling how people approach tasks from the two perspectives and discussing these perspectives, with a focus on how to implement the positive view through self-instructional training.

There were three main components to this intervention: (i) education about adaptive and maladaptive conceptions of memory; (ii) promotion of an adaptive conception of memory; and (iii) self-instructional training to implement a view of memory as controllable. The effectiveness of this intervention was examined alone and in combination with a memory training condition.

In the memory training condition, participants were asked to generate their own strategies for remembering materials to be learned. This approach was adopted because of the poor track record of mnemonic techniques in past research and for theoretical reasons. Self-generation of strategies was used also because it was consistent with the goal of increasing perceptions of personal control over memory. When people devise their own solutions to problems, rather than adopting those created by others, they are more likely to develop a sense of efficacy and mastery (Bandura, 1989; Cavanaugh & Green, 1990). There is evidence from several studies that those in self-guided practice conditions, without instruction, improved as much as training groups who were taught specific strategies, suggesting that older adults can find their own effective strategies if the skills are already in their repertoire (Blackburn *et al.*, 1988; Baltes *et al.*, 1989; Kotler-Cope & Camp, 1990; Willis, 1990; Weaver & Lachman, 1992).

The goal of this research was to examine the effectiveness of the cognitive restructuring and strategy training in improving perceptions of memory ability and control. The results show that through the use of a cognitive behavioural intervention, older adults' beliefs about memory controllability were improved. The cognitive restructuring was most effective when it was combined with the self-generated memory strategy training. Older adults in the combined condition developed more favourable beliefs about their ability to improve, the contribution of effort to memory performance and the inevitability of memory loss. Thus, the combined group increased their sense of control, in terms of viewing memory functioning as controllable through their own efforts. The results suggest that performance feedback and/or experience with memory tasks, alone, were not sufficient to change control beliefs. Elderly adults appear to need some direct intervention focused on beliefs, such as developing awareness of the potential for improvement.

Such research emphasizes the interface between cognitive intervention, personality and context. For cognitive interventions with the elderly to have practical implications, they need to enlist factors of personality (such as efficacy beliefs) and to be coordinated with the contexts of everyday life.

PROMOTING SUCCESSFUL AGEING

This chapter concludes with some observations on successful ageing. This topic has attracted much recent attention, perhaps because of the success of intervention work and the counterintuitive juxtaposition of old age with success. This juxtaposition is stimulating because it challenges the negative stereotype of ageing and conveys the potential for lifelong growth and development (Ryff, 1989; Baltes & Baltes, 1990).

Gains and losses: a changing balance

The most general definition of successful ageing (Fries, 1990) defines it as a maximization of desirable events (such as longevity or life satisfaction) with minimization of negative events (such as physical morbidity or loss in mental vitality). Although this is likely to be true for all periods of the lifespan, ageing is characterized by a shifting ratio in gains and losses towards a less positive balance (Baltes, 1987). In other words, the intensity and frequency of losses become more and more prominent in advanced age. The primary reasons lie in the facts that old age brings with it a higher likelihood for pathology and a definite reduction in the scope and range of adaptive or reserve capacity. For example, older adults solve problems at a slower pace than younger adults, possibly due to changes in the central nervous system (Salthouse, 1991). In addition, ageing is typically accompanied by decreases in sensory functioning including vision, hearing, smell, taste and touch (Fozard, 1990) and declines in muscle strength (Spirduso & MacRae, 1990).

Do older adults recognize on a subjective level this 'objective' fact of a reduced capacity in old age? In a recent study, Heckhausen *et al.* (1989) showed that this indeed is the case and that subjective expectations about the adult life course entail a shifting balance between gains and losses towards a less positive ratio. In this study, adults of different ages were asked about changes in a large number of psychological attributes (such as healthy, intelligent, dominant) that they expected to occur between the ages of 20 and 90, and the degree of desirability of the changes. A gain was defined as an expected increase with age in a desirable attribute; for example, the expectation of an increase in wisdom with age. A loss was defined as an age-related increase in an undesirable attribute, such as the expectation that rigidity increases with age.

Figure 22.5 shows the overall outcome of the Heckhausen *et al.* (1989) research. In general, people of all adult ages expect more positive changes (gains) than negative changes (losses). But, the balance shifts towards a less positive ratio with increasing age, reaching a negative value (more losses than gains) after age 80. Yet, even in their eighties, people have some expectations about positive changes, such as an increase in wisdom.

Undesirable changes (losses) were also evaluated as being less subject to personal control than the expected positive changes (gains) (Heckhausen & Baltes, 1991). In other words, the research participants believed that ageing is associated with changes that are less desirable *and* less controllable. Also noteworthy is that these expectations are rather similar for all subjects studied. There are few individual differences by age or gender.

Similar expectations guide beliefs about memory in old age. One of the most pervasive beliefs about loss in later life revolves around memory. If you ask people over the age of 40 what changes they associate with growing older, they are quite likely to say that memory declines. Another common belief is that memory deficits are uncontrollable and irreversible. Based on extensive research, it is clear that loss of memory in later life occurs in varying degrees across persons and dimensions of memory, and most likely has multiple causes (Poon, 1985; Baddeley, 1986; Hultsch & Dixon, 1990). Moreover, as described above, there is good evidence that

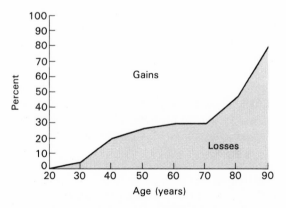

Fig. 22.5 The balance between expected gains (increase in desirable attributes) and expected losses (increase in undesirable attributes) becomes less positive with increasing age (Heckhausen *et al.*, 1989).

memory (e.g. for names or items on lists) to some degree is modifiable (Yesavage, 1985; Hultsch & Dixon, 1990).

Indeed, one of the most common complaints among middle-aged and older adults is that their memory is not as good as it used to be. Cutler and Grams (1988) recently reported that in a national probability sample of 14 783 people aged 55 and older, 74% reported they had some difficulty in remembering things during the past year. Aldwin (1990), using a stress inventory developed specifically for older adult populations, examined the incidence of events and life changes in three samples of community-residing adults ranging in age from 40 to 80. She found that, of all the events listed, deterioration of memory was the most frequently checked for all three samples, with 79, 43 and 50% of the respondents reporting that they had experienced some deterioration of memory during the last year. These surveys make it clear that large percentages of middle-aged and older adults believe that they have some problems with their memory.

As further evidence, Gatz and co-workers (cf. Gatz & Pearson, 1988) have shown that about 45–50% of both young and elderly adults overestimate the incidence of Alzheimer's disease. (The overall rate of Alzheimer's disease for those over 65 is about 10%, but the rate increases dramatically with age; Evans *et al.*, 1989.)

How can ageing be 'successful' in the face of these concerns about loss of memory and shifting ratio of gains and losses towards a less positive balance? One approach focuses on changing the environment to meet the challenges of ageing (Skinner & Vaughan, 1983; Lawton, 1989; Baltes *et al.*, 1991; Kruse, 1992). For example, one can compensate for visual impairments by reading printed material with larger type. There are also prosthetic devices (e.g. hearing aids) that can be utilized to adapt to ageing-related losses. Large interventions can be expected from technological advances in housing and community design. Another approach involves self-management strategies that focus on shifting the way one sees oneself and the world (Baltes & Baltes, 1990). In the face of declines, one can change one's goals and aspirations or find substitutes (Brim, 1988, 1992).

Selective optimization with compensation

One such management strategy involving personal and environmental factors and processes is the model of 'selective optimization with compensation', which Baltes and others have attempted to formulate over the last decade (Baltes & Baltes, 1980, 1990; Baltes, 1988; Perlmutter, 1988, 1990; Featherman *et al.*, 1990). This model of good or successful ageing is based on the interplay among three components: selection, optimization and compensation.

The model is illustrated first by a real-life example from a television interview with the 80-year-old pianist Artur Rubinstein. When asked how he succeeded in remaining such an admired concert pianist, Rubinstein mentioned three factors. First, Rubinstein offered observations that indicated that he mastered the weaknesses of old age by reducing the scope of his repertoire and playing fewer pieces (an example of selection). Second, he spent more time at practice than earlier in his life (an example of optimization). And third, he used special 'tricks', such as slowing down his play before fast segments, thereby creating the impression of faster play than was objectively true (an example of compensation).

Figure 22.6 illustrates this dynamic interplay between selection, optimization and compensation. The first component, selection, is based on the argument that a reduced capacity reserve and the age-associated increase in losses and illness-related morbidity mandates a reduction of certain activities. The second component, optimization, is derived from the argument that it is possible to maintain high levels of functioning in some areas, by practice and the acquisition of new bodies of knowledge and technology. For example, there is evidence that exercise and physical activity are beneficial for a wide range of mental and physical functions and declines in bone density and muscle strength and mass are smaller for active adults (Spirduso & MacRae, 1990). The third component, compensation, becomes relevant when life tasks require a level of capacity beyond the current level of performance potential. We experience such needs for compensation especially in situations with high mental or physical demands, such as when having to think and memorize new material very fast, or

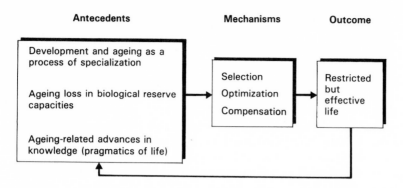

Fig. 22.6 A model of successful ageing: selective optimization with compensation (Baltes & Baltes, 1990).

having to react very quickly when driving a car, climbing a mountain or having to run fast. In addition, the occurrence of illness makes the need for compensation most salient, and physical illnesses are more likely to happen in old age than at earlier periods of the lifespan.

The process of compensation can be illustrated further in the area of cognitive functioning. A loss in the maximum range of cognitive mechanics does not necessarily result in a reduction of intellectual performance. Not all cognitive products require maximum levels of potential, and in addition there is the fact that knowledge, what we term cognitive pragmatics (Baltes *et al.*, 1984; Dixon & Baltes, 1986; Staudinger *et al.*, 1989), is a powerful modulator of the activities of the mind. Knowledge and pragmatics are often more important than cognitive mechanics. Factual and procedural knowledge (Brown, 1982; Glaser, 1984; Klix, 1984; Mandl & Spada, 1988) not only can enrich the mind but also might compensate for deficits in cognitive mechanics.

Research by Salthouse (1984) is an exemplary case to illustrate the significance of knowledge-based, pragmatic strategies in compensating for losses in cognitive mechanics. Salthouse investigated how older typists are able to produce high levels of performance, even though we expect their psychomotor and reaction skills to exhibit losses.

According to Salthouse (1984, 1987), effective typing is governed by two main components. The first component is the psychomotor reaction time necessary to translate the recognition of a given letter into a stroke on the keyboard. The second component is the amount of text previewed by the typist. When studying older expert typists, Salthouse was able to show that they have slower reaction times than comparable young adult typists of comparable typing skill, but that they can use anticipatory reading as a compensatory technique. By doing so, older typists can type as fast as younger ones. In other words, older expert typists appear to use a knowledge-based pragmatic (that is, anticipatory reading) to compensate for a deficit in the speed of psychomotor mechanics (actually, the specific evidence of Salthouse's work is that older typists are more affected than younger typists by shortening the length of text to be previewed).

The process of optimization through selection and compensation is considered a general, prototypical process of effective planning for and management of old age (Baltes & Baltes, 1990). Its phenotypic manifestation, however, will vary widely between individuals. Thus, although all ageing persons are likely to engage in some form of selection, optimization and compensation, the specific phenotypic form of mastery will vary depending on individual life histories and patterns of interests, values, health, skills and resources. Finally, we should not forget the fact of the resilient self in old age. Most people are quite effective at maintaining selfhood by making adaptive attributions, changing the substantive focus of the self and levels of aspiration and goal structures, as well as partners selected for social comparison (Brandstadter & Baltes-Gotz, 1990; Brim, 1992). Therefore, despite much individual variation in the nature of one's life circumstances with their particular set of constraints and opportunities, most people should be able to experience successful ageing.

Self-management

The previous model of successful ageing as a process of selective optimization with compensation suggested that a major part of ageing well is based on internal, subjective processes of self-management. Despite the objective and subjective losses in capacity reserve and the negatively changing balance between gains and losses, older adults on the average do not show a reduction in various indicators related to the self, such as self-esteem or a sense of personal control (Baltes & Baltes, 1986; Lachman, 1986; Brim, 1992) or happiness and well-being (Ryff, 1989).

Are there psychological principles that can account for this counterintuitive finding that objective losses and subjective experiences of such losses should not result in a weakening of older adults' sense of self-esteem and personal control? People are highly effective in construction and reconstruction with the remarkable power to reorganize and readjust in response to rather differing life circumstances (Greenwald, 1980; Filipp & Klauer, 1986; Markus & Nurius, 1986; Brim, 1988; 1992; Baltes & Baltes, 1990, Brandstädter, 1990; Schulz *et al.*, 1991).

Positive selves

A first important avenue towards maintaining a positive sense of self is the principle of many 'possible selves' (Markus & Nurius, 1986; Ryff, 1991; Cross & Markus, 1991). Our self involves more than one self; it is a system of selves. Thus most humans have rather differing expectations of who they are, who they were, who they would like to be, who else they could be and who they would not want to be at all. The existence of such possible selves provides one effective mechanism of adjustment to differing life circumstances. If one kind of self is challenged — for example, being a tennis player by a specific injury — another self, such as being a sports writer, can take its place or unfold.

Changing goals

A second important strategy of self-management is a change in goals and level of aspirations (Brim, 1988, 1992; Baltes & Baltes, 1990; Brandstädter &

Baltes-Götz, 1990; Brandstädter & Renner, 1990). If it is not possible to achieve certain goals, one can alter one's level of aspiration and structure of goals, or new goals can be considered. It is also possible to modify the time span in which these goals are to be reached, for example, by moving goals back and forth in one's lifetime perspective. In fact, Brandstädter and co-workers have demonstrated that during adulthood people seem to get better at using this principle. That is, older adults seem to become more flexible in accommodating their life goals to new circumstances. Older adults seem to become adept at using 'secondary' means of control, that is finding ways to change themselves to adapt to the situations that seem uncontrollable (Schulz *et al.*, 1991).

Social comparisons

The third principle of self-management involves the process of social comparison and the possibility of finding new points of comparison when circumstances have changed (Festinger, 1954; Suls & Miller, 1977; Wills, 1981; Wood, 1989; Baltes & Baltes, 1990). New reference groups are often available, permitting a reorganization of one's standards and values. For instance, if we have lost a significant other, there are usually others who have experienced the same or worse. People who suffer from cancer increasingly compare themselves to others who have also had cancer. As we grow old, others grow old. Because some are in worse circumstances, they permit us to make downward comparisons (Taylor & Lobel, 1989; Wood, 1989). As a result, the experience of ageing and old age can be seen in a new light, and a positive sense of the self can be maintained.

Social comparisons can have profound effects on one's identity. The majority of older adults have a subjective age identity that is 10–15 years younger than their actual age (Montepare & Lachman, 1985). Those with th youngest age identities tend to be the healthiest and most satisfied with their lives. This implies that healthy older adults compare themselves to those who are much younger (an upward comparison), perhaps because they see their own functioning to be better than what they perceive is typical of their age-mates (a downward comparison). Similarly, based on the model of selective optimization with compensation, one would expect that older adults will use upward comparisons for those domains of functioning which they have chosen for selection and downward comparisons for those that become of less personal significance.

Adaptive attributions

Another mechanism for managing losses is to maintain an optimistic viewpoint. It is considered optimistic if undesirable events are attributed to external and/or unstable sources (Abramson *et al.*, 1978). When older adults experience losses and failures, the causes are often assumed to be recurrent (Blank, 1982; Rodin *et al.*, 1985; Lachman & McArthur, 1986; Lachman, 1990). For example, older adults are more likely than younger adults to blame forgetting on poor memory rather than on unstable factors such as lack of effort (Blank, 1982; Lachman & McArthur, 1986; Weaver & Lachman, 1990). Such maladaptive attributions can have far-reaching consequences (Bandura, 1989). These consequences may include increased dependency on others, avoidance of memory challenges, seeking unnecessary medical attention, reliance on medication, depression, anxiety, reduced effort and decreased motivation to use one's memory (Elliot & Lachman, 1989).

There is evidence that adaptive attributions can be taught, with positive consequences for cognitive performance and health (Rodin, 1983). Such attributions emphasize personal responsibility for both successes and failures, with the added feature that the causes of failures are often amenable to change and not necessarily recurrent or pervasive.

CONCLUSION

This chapter identifies four key themes from a lifespan perspective and uses them to exemplify some of the latest theory and research on ageing. Ageing is characterized by (i) heterogeneity and variability; (ii) multidimensionality and multidirectionality; (iii) continued plasticity despite a reduction in capacity reserves; and (iv) the possibility for successful resolution in spite of the shifting balance of losses relative to gains. Successful ageing involves processes of selection, optimization and

compensation, along with self-management strategies such as adopting alternative self-conceptions, reappraising goals and standards, adjusting priorities and aspirations, selecting appropriate social comparisons and making adaptive attributions.

As to selfhood, individuals have remarkable resilience and adaptive capacity for reorganization and maintaining integrity. It seems possible for most older persons to continue to use this dynamic and adaptive feature of the self as a kind of protective shield against the adversities associated with becoming old. Although with ageing, the individual does become increasingly vulnerable to chronic conditions (e.g. Alzheimer's disease), age alone should not imply disability. There is tremendous diversity in the ageing experience — and there is a high degree of overlap in the distributions of capacity and performance for early and late adulthood. Older adults may be at greater risk than younger adults for decrements in psychological and physical functioning, but there is greater potential for prevention, remediation, and compensation of losses associated with ageing than is commonly assumed.

ACKNOWLEDGEMENTS

Preparation of this chapter was supported in part by The John D. and Catherine T. MacArthur Foundation Research Network on Successful Midlife Development. In addition, research reported in this chapter was made possible by grants AG06038 and AG07790 from the National Institute on Aging.

REFERENCES

Abeles R.P. (1991) Sense of control, quality of life, and frail older people. In Birren J.E., Deutchman D.E., Lubben J. & Rowe J. (eds) *The Concept and Measurement of Quality of Life in the Later Years*, pp. 297–314. Academic Press, New York.

Abramson L.Y., Seligman M.E.P. & Teasdale J.D. (1978) Learned helplessness in humans: Critique and reformulation. *Journal of Abnormal Psychology* **87**, 49–74.

Albert M.S. (1988) Cognitive function. In Albert M.S. & Moss M. (eds) *Geriatric Neuropsychology*, pp. 33–35. Guilford Press, New York.

Aldwin C. (1990) The elder's life stress inventory: egocentric and non-egocentric stress. In Stephens M.A.P., Hobfoll S.E., Crowther J.H. & Tennenbaum D.L. (eds) *Stress and Coping in Late Life Families*, pp. 49–69.

Hemisphere, New York.

Anschutz L., Camp C.J., Markley R.P. & Kramer J.J. (1987) Remembering mnemonics: A three-year follow-up on the effects of mnemonics training in elderly adults. *Experimental Aging Research* **13**, 141–143.

Assmann A. (1991) (ed.) *Weisheit Archeologie der Kommunikation*. (Wisdom. Archaeology of Communication). Fink Verlag, Munich.

Baddeley A.D. (1986) *Working Memory*. Oxford University Press, Oxford.

Baltes M.M. (1988) The etiology and maintenance of dependency in the elderly: Three phases of operant research. *Behavior Therapy* **19**, 301–319.

Baltes M.M. & Baltes P.B. (eds) (1986) *The Psychology of Control and Aging*. Lawrence Erlbaum, Hillsdale, New Jersey.

Baltes M.M., Kuhl K.-P. & Sowarka D. (1992) Testing for limits of cognitive reserve capacity: A promising strategy for early diagnosis of dementia? *Journal of Gerontology: Psychological Sciences* **47**, 165–167.

Baltes M.M., Wahl H.W. & Reichert M. (1991) Successful aging in institutions? In Schaie K.W. (ed.) *Annual Review of Gerontology and Geriatrics*, Vol. 11, pp. 311–337. Springer, New York.

Baltes P.B. (1973) Strategies for psychological intervention in old age. *Gerontologist* **13**, 4–6.

Baltes P.B. (1987) Theoretical propositions of life-span developmental psychology: On the dynamics between growth and decline. *Developmental Psychology* **23**, 611–626.

Baltes P.B. & Baltes M.M. (1980) Plasticity and variability in psychological aging: Methodological and theoretical issues. In Gurski G.E. (ed.) *Determining the Effects of Aging on the Central Nervous System*, pp. 41–66. Schering, Berlin.

Baltes P.B. & Baltes M.M. (1990) Psychological perspectives on successful aging: The model of selective optimization with compensation. In Baltes P.B. & Baltes M.M. (eds) *Successful Aging: Perspective from the Behavioral Sciences*, pp. 1–34. Cambridge University Press, New York.

Baltes P.B., Dittman-Kohli F. & Dixon R.A. (1984) New perspectives on the development of intelligence in adulthood: Toward a dual-process conception and a model of selective optimization with compensation. In Baltes P.B. & Brim Jr O.G. (eds) *Life-span Development and Behavior*, Vol. 6, pp. 33–76. Academic Press, New York.

Baltes P.B. & Kliegl R. (1992) Further testing of limits of cognitive plasticity: Negative age differences in a memory skill are robust. *Developmental Psychology* **28**, 121–125.

Baltes P.B. & Lindenberger U. (1988) On the range of cognitive plasticity in old age as a function of experience: 15 years of intervention research. *Behavior Therapy* **19**, 283–300.

Baltes P.B., Sowarka D. & Kliegl R. (1989) Cognitive training research on fluid intelligence in old age: What can older adults achieve by themselves? *Psychology and Aging* **4**, 217–221.

Baltes P.B. & Smith J. (1990) The psychology of wisdom and its ontogenesis. In Sternberg R.J. (ed.) *Wisdom: Its Nature, Origins, and Development*, pp. 87–120. Cambridge University Press, New York.

Bandura A. (1989) Regulation of cognitive processes through perceived self-efficacy. *Developmental Psychology* **25**, 729–735.

Berry J.M. (1987) *A self-efficacy model of memory performance*. Paper presented at the meeting of the American Psychological Association, New York, September.

Birren J.E. (1959) Principles of research on aging. In Birren J.E. (ed.) *Handbook of Aging and the Individual: Psychological and Biological Aspects*, pp. 3–42. University of Chicago Press, Chicago, Illinois.

Blackburn J.A., Papalia-Finlay D., Foyce B.F. & Serlin R.C. (1988) Modifiability of figural relations performance among elderly individuals. *Journal of Gerontology: Psychological Sciences* **43**, 87–89.

Blank T.O. (1982) *A Social Psychology of Developing Adults*. Wiley, New York.

Bower G.H. (1970) Analysis of a mnemonic device. *American Scientist* **58**, 496–510.

Brandstädter J. (1990) Development as a personal and social construction. In Gergen K. & Semin G. (ed.) *Everyday Understanding: Social and Scientific Implications*, pp. 83–107. Sage, London.

Brandstädter J. & Baltes-Götz B. (1990) Personal control over development and quality of life perspective in adulthood. In Baltes P.B. & Baltes M.M. (eds) *Successful Aging: Perspectives from the Behavioral Sciences*, pp. 197–224. Cambridge University Press, New York.

Brandstädter J. & Renner G. (1990) Tenacious goal pursuit and flexible goal adjustment: Explication and age-related analysis of assimilative and accommodative models of coping. *Psychology and Aging* **5**, 58–67.

Brim Jr O.G. (1988) Losing and winning: The nature of ambition in everyday life. *Psychology Today* **9**, 48–52.

Brim G. (1992) *Ambition: How We Manage Success and Failure Throughout our Lives*. Basic Books, New York.

Brown A.L. (1982) Learning and development: The problem of compatibility, access, and induction. *Human Development* **25**, 89–115.

Carstensen L.L. (1988) The emerging field of behavior gerontology. *Behavior Therapy* **19**, 259–281.

Caspi A., Elder Jr G.H. & Bem D.J. (1987) Moving against the world: Life-course patterns of explosive children. *Developmental Psychology* **22**, 303–308.

Cattell R.B. (1965) *The Scientific Analysis of Personality*. Penguin, Baltimore.

Cattell R.B. (1971) *Abilities: Their Structure, Growth, and Action*. Houghton Mifflin, Boston.

Cavanaugh J.C. (1989) The importance of awareness in memory aging. In Poon L.W., Rubin D.C. & Wilson B.A.

(eds) *Everyday Cognition in Adulthood and Late Life*, pp. 416–436. Cambridge University Press, New York.

Cavanaugh J.C. & Green E.E. (1990) I believe, therefore I can: Self-efficacy beliefs in memory aging. In Lovelace E.A. (ed.) *Aging and Cognition: Mental Processes, Self-awareness, and Interventions*, pp. 189–230. Elsevier, Amsterdam.

Charness N. (ed.) (1985) *Aging and Human Performance*. Wiley, Chichester.

Chi M.T.H., Glaser R. & Rees E. (1982) Expertise in problem-solving. In Sternberg R.J. (ed.) *Advances in the Psychology of Human Intelligence*, Vol. 7, pp. 7–76. Lawrence Erlbaum, Hillsdale, New Jersey.

Clayton V. & Birren J.W. (1980) The development of wisdom across the life span: A reexamination of an ancient topic. In Baltes P.B. & Brim Jr O.G. (Eds) *Life-span Development and Behavior*, Vol. 3, pp. 103–135. Academic Press, New York.

Cohen G.D. (1990) Psychopathology and mental health in the mature and elderly adult. In Birren J.E. & Schaie K.W. (eds) *Handbook of the Psychology of Aging*, 3rd edn, pp. 359–374. Academic Press, San Diego.

Commons M.L., Sinnott J.D., Richards F.A. & Armon C. (eds) (1989) *Adult Development: Comparisons and Applications of Developmental Models*. Praeger, New York.

Cornelius S.W. & Caspi A. (1986) Self-perceptions of intellectual control and aging. *Educational Gerontology* **12**, 345–357.

Costa Jr P.T. & Andres R. (1986) Patterns of age change. In Rossman I. (ed.) *Clinical Geriatrics*, pp. 23–30. Lippincott, New York.

Costa Jr P.T. & McCrae R. (1992) Trait psychology comes of age. In Sonderegger T.B. (ed.) *Nebraska Symposium on Motivation: Psychology and Aging*, pp. 169–204. University of Nebraska Press, Lincoln.

Cowdry E.V. (ed.) (1939) *Problems of Aging: Biological and Medical Aspects*. Williams & Wilkins, Baltimore.

Cross S. & Markus H. (1991) Possible selves across the life span. *Human Development* **34**, 230–255.

Cutler S.J. & Grams A.E. (1988) Correlates of self-reported everyday memory problems. *Journal of Gerontology* **43**, 582–590.

Dannefer D. & Nelson E.A. (1992) Aged heterogeneity: Fact or fiction? The fate of diversity in gerontological research. *Gerontologist* **32**, 17–23.

Denney N.W. (1984) A model of cognitive development across the life span. *Developmental Review* **4**, 171–191.

Dittmann-Kohli F. & Baltes P.B. (1990) Toward a neo-functionalist conception of adult intellectual development: Wisdom as a prototypical case of intellectual growth. In Alexander C. & Langer E. (eds) *Beyond Formal Operations: Alternative Endpoints to Human Development*, pp. 54–78. Oxford University Press, New York.

Dixon R.A. & Baltes P.B. (1986) Toward life-span research on the functions and pragmatics of intelligence. In Sternberg R.J. & Wagner R.K. (eds) *Practical Intelligence:*

Nature and Origins of Competence in the Everyday World, pp. 203–235. Cambridge University Press, New York.

Elder Jr G.H. & Liker J.K. (1982) Hard times in women's lives: Historical influences across forty years. *American Journal of Sociology* **88**, 241–269.

Elliott E. & Lachman M.E. (1989) Enhancing memory by modifying control beliefs, attributions, and performance goals in the elderly. In Fry P.S. (ed.) *Psychology of Helplessness and Control and Attributions of Helplessness and Control in the Aged*, pp. 339–367. North-Holland, Amsterdam.

Ericsson K.A. (1990) Peak performance and age: An examination of peak performance in sports. In Baltes P.B. & Baltes M.M. (eds) *Successful Aging: Perspectives from the Behavioral Sciences*, pp. 164–196. Cambridge University Press, New York.

Ericsson K.A. & Simon H.A. (1984) *Protocol Analysis: Verbal Reports as Data*. MIT Press, Cambridge, Massachusetts.

Erikson E.H. (1963) *Childhood and Society*, 2nd edn. Norton, New York.

Evans D.A., Funkenstein H., Albert M.S. *et al.* (1989) Prevalence of Alzheimer's disease in a community population of older persons — higher than previously reported. *Journal of the American Medical Association* **262**, 2551–2556.

Featherman D.L. (1983) Life-span perspective in social science research. In Baltes P.B. & Brim Jr O.G. (eds) *Life-span Development and Behavior*, Vol. 5, pp. 1–57. Academic Press, New York.

Featherman D.L., Smith J. & Peterson J.G. (1990) Successful aging in a 'post-retired' society. In Baltes P.B. & Baltes M.M. (eds) *Successful Aging: Perspectives from the Behavioral Sciences*, pp. 50–93. Cambridge University Press, New York.

Festinger L. (1954) A theory of social comparison processes. *Human Relations* **7**, 117–140.

Filipp S.-H. & Klauer T. (1986) Conceptions of self over the life span: Reflections on the dialectics of change. In Baltes M.M. & Baltes P.B. (eds) *The Psychology of Control and Aging*, pp. 167–205. Lawrence Erlbaum, Hillsdale, New Jersey.

Fozard J.L. (1990) Vision and hearing in aging. In Birren J.E. & Schaie K.W. (eds) *Handbook of the Psychology of Aging*, 3rd edn, pp. 150–171. Academic Press, San Diego.

Fries J.F. (1989) *Aging Well*. Addison-Wesley, Reading, Massachusetts.

Fries J.F. (1990) Medical perspectives upon successful aging. In Baltes P.B. & Baltes M.M. (eds) *Successful Aging: Perspectives from the Behavioral Sciences*, pp. 35–49. Cambridge University Press, New York.

Gatz M. & Hurwicz M. (1990) Are old people more depressed? Cross-sectional data on Center for Epidemiological Studies Depression Scale factors. *Psychology and Aging* **5**, 284–290.

Gatz M. & Pearson C.G. (1988) Ageism revisited and the

provision of psychological services. *American Psychologist* **43**, 184—188.

Gerok W. & Brandstadter J. (1992) Normales, krankhaftes und optimales Altern; Variations und Modifikationsspielraume (Normal, pathological and optimal aging: Ranges of variation and modification). In Baltes P.B. & Mittelstrab J. (eds) *Zukunft des Alterns und Gesellschaftliche Entwicklung*, Vol. 5, pp. 356—385. de Gruyter, Berlin.

Glaser R. (1984) Education and thinking. *American Psychologist* **39**, 93—104.

Greenwald A.G. (1980) The totalitarian ego: Fabrication and revision of personal history. *American Psychologist* **35**, 603—618.

Grover D.R. & Hertzog C. (1991) Relationships between intellectual control beliefs and psychometric intelligence in adulthood. *Journal of Gerontology: Psychological Sciences* **46**, 109—115.

Häfner H. (1986) *Psychologische Gesundheit im Alter (Psychological Health in Old Age)*. G. Fischer, Stuttgart.

Häfner H. (1992) Psychitrie des hoheren Lebensalters (Psychiatry of old age). In Baltes P.B. & Mittelstrab J. (eds) *Zukunft des Alterns und Gesellschaftliche Entwicklung*, Vol. 5, pp. 151—179. de Gruyter, Berlin.

Hayslip Jr B. (1989) Alternative mechanisms for improvement in fluid ability performance among older adults. *Psychology and Aging* **4**, 122—124.

Heckhausen J. & Baltes P.B. (1991) Perceived controllability of expected psychological change across adulthood and old age. *Journal of Gerontology: Psychological Sciences* **46**, 165—173.

Heckhausen J., Dixon R.A. & Baltes P.B. (1989) Gains and losses in development throughout adulthood as perceived by different adult age groups. *Developmental Psychology* **25**, 109—121.

Hertzog C., Dixon R.A. & Hultsch D.F. (1990) Relationships between metamemory, memory predictions, and memory task performance in adults. *Psychology and Aging* **5**, 215—227.

Hofland B.F., Willis S.L. & Baltes P.B. (1981) Fluid intelligence performance in the elderly: Intraindividual variability and conditions of assessment. *Journal of Educational Psychology* **73**, 573—586.

Holliday S.G. & Chandler M.J. (1986) Wisdom: Explorations in adult competence. In Meacham J.A. (ed.) *Contributions to Human Development*, Vol. 17, pp. 1—96. Karger, Basel.

Horn J.L. (1970) Organization of data on life-span development of human abilities. In Goulet L.R. & Baltes P.B. (eds) *Life-span Developmental Psychology: Research and Theory*, pp. 423—466. Academic Press, New York.

Horn J.L. (1982) The theory of fluid and crystallized intelligence in relation to concepts of cognitive psychology and aging in adulthood. In Craik F.I.M. & Trehub S.E. (eds) *Aging and Cognitive Processes*, pp. 847—870. Plenum, New York.

Hoyer W.J. (1985) Aging and the development of expert cognition. In Schlechter T.M. & Toglia M.P. (eds) *New Directions in Cognitive Science*, pp. 69—87. Ablex, Norwood, New Jersey.

Hultsch D.F. & Dixon R.A. (1990) Learning and memory and aging. In Birren, J.E. & Schaie K.W. (eds) *Handbook of the Psychology of Aging*, 3rd edn, pp. 258—274. Academic Press, San Diego.

Hultsch D.F., Hertzog C. & Dixon R.A. (1987) Age differences in metamemory: Resolving the inconsistencies. *Canadian Journal of Psychology* **41**, 193—208.

Institute of Medicine (1991) *Extending Life, Enhancing Life*. IOM, Washington, DC.

Kekes J. (1983) Wisdom. *American Philosophical Quarterly* **20**, 277—286.

Kessler R.C., Foster C., Webster P.S. & House J.S. (1992) The relationship between age and depressive symptoms in two national surveys. *Psychology and Aging* **7**, 119—126.

Kliegl R. & Baltes P.B. (1987) Theory-guided analysis of development and aging mechanisms through testing-the-limits and research on expertise. In Schooler C. & Schaie K.W. (eds) *Cognitive Functioning and Social Structure Over the Life Course*, pp. 95—119. Ablex, Norwood, New Jersey.

Kliegl R., Smith J. & Baltes P.B. (1989) Testing-the-limits and the study of adult age differences in cognitive plasticity of a mnemonic skill. *Developmental Psychology* **25**, 247—256.

Klix F. (1984) *Gedachtnis, Wissen, Wissensnutzung (Memory, Knowledge, and Utilization of Knowledge)*. Deutscher Verlag der Wissenschaften, Berlin.

Kotler-Cope S. & Camp C. (1990) Memory interventions in aging populations. In Lovelance E.A. (ed.) *Aging and Cognition: Mental Processes, Self-awareness and Interventions*, pp. 231—261. North-Holland, Amsterdam.

Kruse A. (1992) Altersfreundliche Umwelten: Der Beitrag der Technik (Age-friendly environments: The contribution of technology). In Baltes P.B. & Mittelstrass J. (eds) *Zukunft des Alters und Gesellschaftliche Entwicklung*, pp. 668—694. de Gruyter, Berlin.

Labouvie-Vief G. (1977) Adult cognitive development: In search of alternative interpretations. *Merrill-Palmer Quarterly* **23**, 227—263.

Labouvie-Vief G. (1981) Proactive and reactive aspects of constructivism: Growth and aging in life-span perspective. In Lerner R.M. & Busch-Rossnagel N.A. (eds) *Individuals as Producers of their Development*, pp. 197—230. Academic Press, New York.

Labouvie-Vief G. (1982) Dynamic development and mature autonomy: A theoretical prologue. *Human Development* **25**, 161—191.

Lachman M.E. (1986) Locus of control in aging research: A case for multidimensional and domain-specific assessment. *Psychology and Aging* **1**, 34—40.

Lachman M.E. (1990) When bad things happen to older people: Age differences in attributional style. *Psychology and Aging* **5**, 607−609.

Lachman M.E. (1991) Personal control over memory aging: Developmental and intervention perspectives. *Journal of Social Issues* **47**, 159−175.

Lachman M.E., Baltes, P.B., Nesselroade J.R. & Willis S.L. (1982) Examination of personality−ability relationships in the elderly: The role of the contextual (interface) assessment mode. *Journal of Research in Personality* **16**, 485−501.

Lachman M.E. & Leff R. (1989) Beliefs about intellectual efficacy and control in the elderly: A five-year longitudinal study. *Developmental Psychology* **25**, 722−728.

Lachman M.E. & McArthur L.Z. (1986) Adulthood age differences in causal attributions for cognitive, physical, and social performance. *Psychology and Aging* **1**, 127−132.

Lachman M.E., Steinberg E.S. & Trotter S.D. (1987). The effects of control beliefs and attributions on memory self-assessment and performance. *Psychology and Aging* **2**, 266−271.

Lachman M.E., Weaver S.L., Bandura M., Elliott E. & Lewkowicz C. (1992) Enhancing memory performance and control beliefs in elderly adults. *Journal of Gerontology: Psychological Sciences* **47**, 293−299.

Langer E.J. (1989) *Mindfulness*. Addison-Wesley, Reading, Massachusetts.

Lawton M.P. (1989) Behavior-relevant ecological factors. In Schaie K.W. & Schooler C. (eds) *Social Structure and Aging*, pp. 57−78. Lawrence Erlbaum, Hillsdale, New Jersey.

Lehr U. & Thomae H. (eds) (1987) *Formen Seelischen Alterns (Patterns of Psychological Aging)*. Enke, Stuttgart.

Levenson H. (1981) Differentiating among internality, powerful others, and chance. In Lefcourt H.M. (ed.) *Research with the Locus of Control Construct: Assessment Methods*, Vol. 1, pp. 15−63. Academic Press, New York.

Levinson D.J. (1986) A conception of adult development. *American Psychologist* **41**, 3−13.

Liebert R.M. & Spiegler M.D. (1990) *Personality: Strategies and Issues*, 6th edn. Brooks/Cole, Belmont, California.

Lindenberger U. (1990) *The effects of professional expertise and cognitive aging on skilled memory performance*. Doctoral dissertation, Free University of Berlin, Berlin.

McCrae R.R. & Costa Jr P.T. (1990) *Personality in adulthood*. Guilford Press, New York.

Maddox G.L. (1987) Aging differently. *Gerontologist* **27**, 557−564.

Mandl H. & Spada H. (eds) (1988) *Wissenspsychologie (The Psychology of Knowledge)*. Psychologie Verlags Union, Munchen-Weinheim.

Manton K.G. (1989) Life-style risk factors. *Annals of the Academy of Political and Social Sciences* **503**, 72−88.

Markus H. & Nurius P. (1986) Possible selves. *American Psychologist* **41**, 954−969.

Mayr U., Lindenberger U. & Kliegl R. (1991) *Cognitive slowing as a causal factor of intellectual development in old*

age. Paper presented at the 44th Meeting of the Gerontological Society of America, San Francisco.

Montepare J. & Lachman M.E. (1989) 'You're only as old as you feel'. Self-perceptions of age, fears of aging, and life satisfaction from adolescence to old age. *Psychology and Aging* **4**, 73−78.

Nesselroade J.R. (1989) Adult personality development: Issues in addressing constancy and change. In Rabin A.I., Zucker R.A., Emmons R.A., & Frank S. (eds) *Studying Persons and Lives*, pp. 41−85. Springer, New York.

Neugarten B.L. (1968) *Middle Aging and Aging*. University of Chicago Press, Chicago.

Neugarten B.L. (1974) Age groups in American society and the rise of the young-old. *Annals of the American Academy of Political and Social Science* September, 187−198.

Newmann J.P. (1989) Aging and depression. *Psychology and Aging* **4**, 150−165.

Oelmüller W. (1989) *Philosophie und Weisheit (Philosophy and Wisdom)*. Schoningh, Paderborn.

Park D.C., Smith A.D. & Cavanaugh J.C. (1990) Meta-memories of memory researchers. *Memory and Cognition* **18**, 321−327.

Paulhus D. & Christie R. (1981) Spheres of control: An interactionist approach to assessment of perceived control. In Lefcourt H.M. (ed.) *Research with the Locus of Control Construct: Assessment Methods*, Vol. 1, pp. 161−188. Academic Press, New York.

Perlmutter M. (1988) Cognitive potential throughout life. In Birren J.E. & Bengtson V.L. (eds) *Emergent Theories of Aging*, pp. 247−268. Springer, New York.

Perlmutter M. (ed.) (1990) *Late Life Potential*. Gerontological Society of America, Washington, DC.

Peterson C., Seligman M.E.P. & Vaillant G.E. (1988) Pessimistic explanatory style is a risk factor for physical illness: A thirty-five-year longitudinal study. *Journal of Personality and Social Psychology* **55**, 23−27.

Poon L.W. (1984) Memory training for older adults. In Abrams J.P. & Crooks V.J. (eds) *Geriatric Mental Health*, pp. 136−150. Grune & Stratton, New York.

Poon L.W. (1985) Difference in human memory with aging: Nature, causes and clinical implications. In Birren J. & Schaie K. (eds) *Handbook of the Psychology of Aging*, 2nd edn, pp. 427−462. Van Nostrand & Reinhold, New York.

Rakowski W. (1986) Personal health practices, health status, and expected control over future health. *Journal of Community Health* **11**, 189−203.

Riley M.W. (1987) On the significance of age in sociology. *American Sociological Review* **52**, 1−14.

Riley M.W. & Riley Jr J.W. (eds) (1989) The quality of aging: Strategies for interventions. *Annals of the American Academy of Political and Social Sciences*, **503**.

Rodin J. (1983) Behavioral medicine: Beneficial effects of self-control training in aging. *International Review of*

Applied Psychology **32**, 153–181.

Rodin J., Cashman C. & Desiderato L. (1987) Intervention and aging: Enrichment and prevention. In Riley M.W., Matarazzo J.D. & Baum A. (eds) *Perspectives in Behavioral Medicine: The Aging Dimension*, pp. 149–172. Lawrence Erlbaum, Hillsdale, New Jersey.

Rodin J. & Timko C. (1992) Sense of control, aging, and health. In Ory M.G., Abeles R.P. & Lipman P.D. (eds) *Aging, Health, and Behavior*, pp. 174–206. Sage, Newbury Park, California.

Rodin J., Timko C. & Harris S. (1985) The construct of control: Biological and psychosocial correlates. In Eisdorfer C., Lawton M.P. & Maddox G.L. (eds) *Annual Review of Gerontology and Geriatrics*, pp. 3–55. Springer, New York.

Rowe J.W. & Kahn R.L. (1987) Human aging: Usual and successful. *Science* **237**, 143–149.

Rutter M. (ed.) (1988) *Studies of Psychological Risk Factors: The Power of Longitudinal Data*. Cambridge University Press, New York.

Ryff C.D. (1989) In the eye of the beholder: Views of psychological well-being among middle-aged and older adults. *Psychology and Aging* **4**, 195–210.

Ryff C.D. (1991) Possible selves in adulthood and old age: A tale of shifting horizons. *Psychology and Aging* **6**, 286–295.

Salthouse T.A. (1984) Effects of age and skill in typing. *Journal of Experimental Psychology: General* **113**, 345–371.

Salthouse T.A. (1987) The role of experience in cognitive aging. In Schaie K.W. & Eisdorfer C. (eds) *Annual Review of Gerontology and Geriatrics*, pp. 135–158. Springer, New York.

Salthouse T.A. (1991) *Theoretical Perspectives on Cognitive Aging*. Lawrence Erlbaum, Hillsdale, New Jersey.

Schaie K.W. (1979) The primary mental abilities in adulthood: An exploration in the development of psychometric intelligence. In Baltes P.B. & Brim Jr O.G. (eds) *Life-span Development and Behavior*, Vol. 3, pp. 67–115. Academic Press, New York.

Schaie K.W. (1988) Variability in cognitive function in the elderly: Implications for societal participation. In Woodhead A.D., Bender M.A. & Leonard R.C. (eds) *Phenotypic Variation in Populations*, pp. 191–211. Plenum, New York.

Schaie K.W. (1990) The optimization of cognitive functioning in old age: Predictions based on cohort-sequential and longitudinal data. In Baltes P.B. & Baltes M.M. (eds) *Successful Aging: Perspectives from the Behavioral Sciences*, pp. 99–117. Cambridge University Press, New York.

Schaie K.W. & Willis S.L. (1986) Can decline in adult intellectual functioning be reversed? *Developmental Psychology* **2**, 223–232.

Schulz R. (1980) Aging and control. In Garber J. & Seligman M.P. (eds) *Human Helplessness: Theory and Applications*, pp. 261–277. Academic Press, New York.

Schulz R., Heckhausen J. & Locher J.L. (1991). Adult development, control, and adaptive functioning. *Journal of Social Issues* **47**, 177–196.

Scogin F. & Bienias J.L. (1988) A three-year follow-up of older adult participants in a memory-skills training program. *Psychology and Aging* **3**, 334–337.

Skinner B.F. & Vaughan M.E. (1983) *Enjoy Old Age: A Program of Self-management*. Norton, New York.

Smith J. & Baltes P.B. (1990) A study of wisdom-related knowledge: Age/cohort differences in responses to life planning problems. *Developmental Psychology* **26**, 494–505.

Smyer M.A., Zarit S.H. & Qualls S.H. (1990) Psychological intervention with the aging individual. In Birren J.E. & Schaie K.W. (eds) *Handbook of the Psychology of Aging*, 3rd edn, pp. 375–404. Academic Press, San Diego.

Sorensen A.B., Weinert F. & Sherrod L. (eds) (1986) *Human Development and the Life Course*. Lawrence Erlbaum, Hillsdale, New Jersey.

Spirduso W.W. & MacRae P.G. (1990) Motor performance and aging. In Birren J.E. & Schaie K.W. (eds) *Handbook of the Psychology of Aging*, 3rd edn, pp. 184–200. Academic Press, San Diego.

Staudinger U.M., Cornelius S.W. & Baltes P.B. (1989) The aging of intelligence: Potential and limits. *Annals of the American Academy of Political and Social Sciences* **503**, 43–59.

Sternberg R.J. (ed.) (1990) *Wisdom: Its Nature, Origins, and Development*. Cambridge University Press, New York.

Sternberg R.J. & Kolligian Jr J. (eds) (1990) *Competence Considered*. Yale University Press, New Haven, Connecticut.

Suls J.M. & Miller R.L. (eds) (1977) *Social Comparison Processes: Theoretical and Empirical Perspectives*. Hemisphere, Washington, DC.

Taylor S.E. & Lobel M. (1989). Social comparison activity under threat: Downward evaluation and upward contacts. *Psychological Bulletin* **96**, 569–575.

Vaillant G.E. (1977) *Adaptation to Life*. Little, Brown & Co., Waltham, Massachussetts.

Weaver S.L. & Lachman M.E. (1990). *When memory fails: Adulthood age differences in attributions for memory*. Paper presented at the Meeting of the American Psychological Association, Boston, Massachusetts, August.

Weaver S.L. & Lachman M.E. (1992). *Enhancing memory and self-efficacy: What works and for whom?* Unpublished ms, Brandeis University, Waltham, Massachusetts.

West R.L. (1985) *Memory Fitness over 40*. Triad Publishing, Gainesville, Florida.

Willis S.L. (1987) Cognitive training and everyday competence. In Schaie K.W. (ed.) *Annual Review of Gerontology and Geriatrics*, Vol. 7, pp. 159–188. Springer, New York.

Willis S.L. (1990) Current issues in cognitive training research. In Lovelace E.A. (ed.) *Aging and Cognition: Mental Processes, Self-awareness and Interventions*, pp. 263–280. North-Holland, Amsterdam.

Wills T.A. (1981) Downward comparison principles in social psychology. *Psychological Bulletin* **90**, 245–271.

Wood J.V. (1989) Theory and research concerning social comparisons of personal attributes. *Psychological Bulletin* **106**, 231–248.

Yesavage J.A. (1985) Nonpharmacologic treatments for memory losses with normal aging. *American Journal of Psychiatry* **142**, 600–605.

Yesavage J.A. & Rose T.L. (1984) Semantic elaboration and the method of loci: A new trip for older learners. *Experimental Aging Research* **10**, 155–159.

Zarit S.H., Cole K.D. & Guider R.L. (1981) Memory training strategies and subjective complaints of memory in the aged. *Gerontologist* **21**, 158–164.

Ziff M., Lachman M.E. & Lewkowicz C. (1991). *Lifestyle not luck: Perceived control, healthy lifestyle, and health.* Paper presented at the Meeting of the American Psychological Association, San Francisco, California, August.

Index